SPECIAL FEATURES

Welcome to South India & Kerala

Like a giant wedge plunging into the ocean, South India is the subcontinent's steamy heartland – a lush contrast to the peaks and plains up north.

A Fabulous Heritage

Wherever you go in the south you'll be bumping into the magnificent relics of the splendid civilisations that have inhabited this land over two millennia – the amazing rock-cut shrines carved out by Buddhists, Hindus and Jains at Ajanta and Ellora; the palaces, tombs, forts and mosques of Muslim dynasties on the Deccan; Tamil Nadu's inspired Pallava sculptures and towering Chola temples; the magical ruins of the Vijayanagar capital at Hampi...and a whole lot more. It's a diverse cultural treasure trove with few parallels.

Luscious Landscapes

Thousands of kilometres of coastline frame fertile plains and rolling hills in South India – a constantly changing landscape kept glisteningly green by the double-barrelled monsoon. The palm-strung strands and inland waterways of the west give way to spice gardens, tea plantations, tropical forests and cool hill-station retreats in the Western Ghats. The drier Deccan 'plateau' is far from flat, being crossed by numerous craggy ranges and often spattered with dramatic, fort-topped outcrops. And across the region, preserved wild forests shelter wildlife from elephants and tigers to monkeys and sloth bears.

Delicious Dining

South India's glorious culinary variety and melange of dining options beckon hungry travellers. Some of India's most famous and traditional staples hail from here: large *idlis* (fermented rice cakes) and papery dosas (savoury crêpes) are the backbone of South Indian fare. Mouth-watering Mumbai (Bombay) is India's top destination for gastronomic indulgence, be it vibrant street food or diverse haute cuisine; Goa's spicy, Portuguese-influenced fare is inventive fiery fusion at its finest; and Kerala's coconut-laced seafood is the stuff of legend – resulting in a deliciously rewarding culinary journey for visitors.

Sophisticated Cities

The south's vibrant cities are the pulse of a country that is fast-forwarding through the 21st century while also at times seemingly stuck in the Middle Ages. From in-yer-face Mumbai and increasingly sophisticated Chennai (Madras) to historic Hyderabad, IT capital Bengaluru (Bangalore) and quaint, colonial-era Kochi (Cochin) and Puducherry (Pondicherry), southern cities are great for browsing teeming markets and colourful boutiques, soaking up culture and indulging in India's trendier side. Think fashionable cafes and coffee houses, imaginative gourmet restaurants and a blitzkrieg of hipsterised microbreweries and cocktail bars.

Why I Love South India & Kerala

By Kevin Raub, Writer

Forgetting the first time I landed in Mumbai on the tail end of a late '90s monsoon is a hopeless endeavour. Never had I encountered such thunderstorms, an absolute onslaught of Armageddon proportions. But once the clouds cleared over the gateway to South India, one of the world's most cinematic cities sprung to life, a kaleidoscopic potpourri of colour and chaos, a high-spirited melange of mayhem and masala. Be it Mumbai's gastronomic feats, Goa's sun-drenched sands, Tamil Nadu's heaving temple towns or Kerala's lazy backwaters, the South Indian see-saw of shock and awe never lets you forget.

For more about our writers, see p544.

Above: Gliding through Kerala's backwaters (p286)

South India & Kerala

Mumbai
India's cosmopolitan capital
of cool (p42)

Ajanta
Fantastic ancient
rock-cut shrines (p95)

Goa
Warm waters,
golden beaches (p117)

Kerala
Lazy boats along palm-fringed
backwaters (p255)

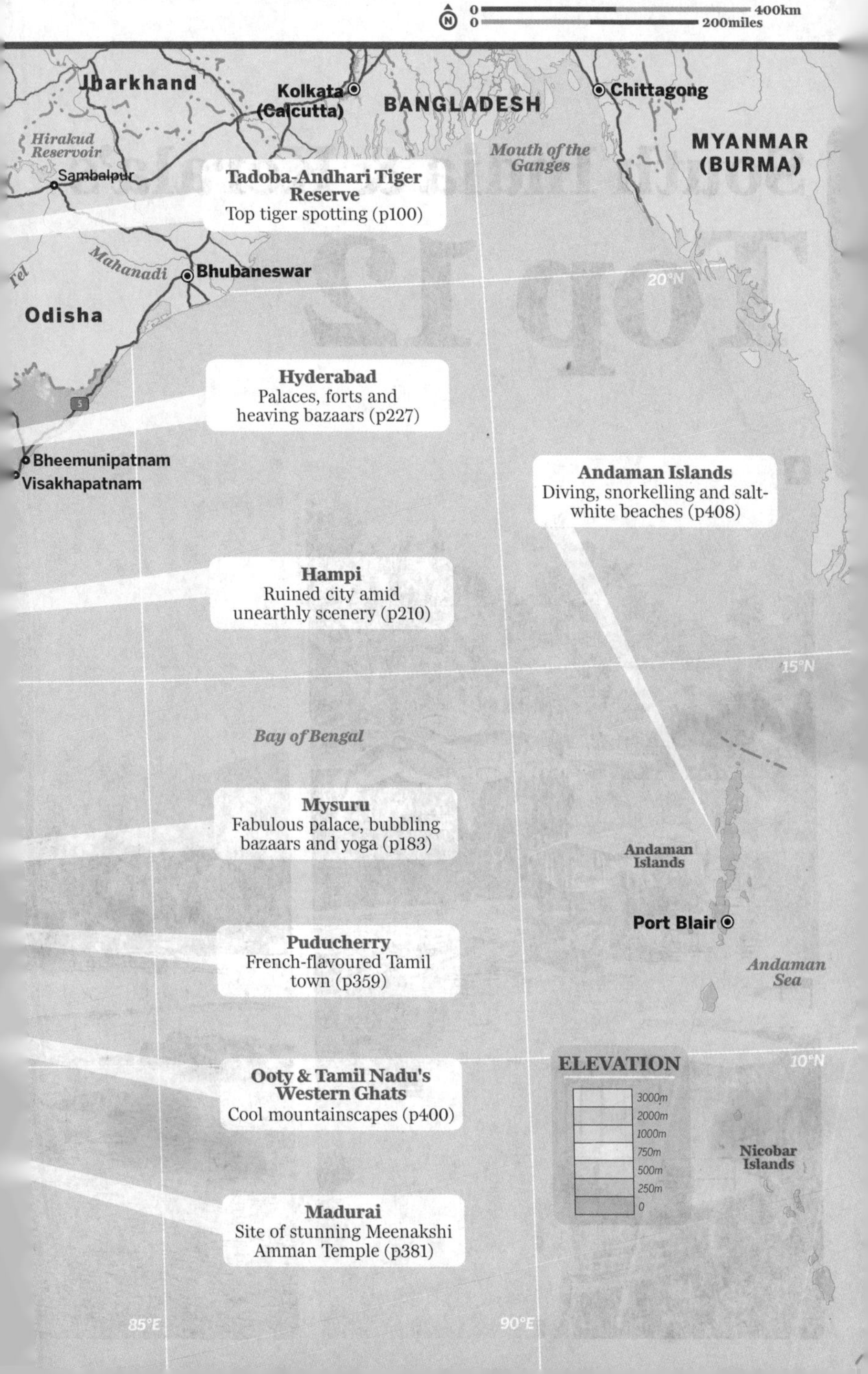

Jharkhand

Kolkata (Calcutta)

BANGLADESH

Chittagong

Hirakud Reservoir

Sambalpur

Tadoba-Andhari Tiger Reserve
Top tiger spotting (p100)

Mouth of the Ganges

MYANMAR (BURMA)

Mahanadi • **Bhubaneswar**

Tel

20°N

Odisha

Hyderabad
Palaces, forts and heaving bazaars (p227)

Andaman Islands
Diving, snorkelling and salt-white beaches (p408)

• **Bheemunipatnam**
Visakhapatnam

Hampi
Ruined city amid unearthly scenery (p210)

15°N

Bay of Bengal

Mysuru
Fabulous palace, bubbling bazaars and yoga (p183)

Andaman Islands

Puducherry
French-flavoured Tamil town (p359)

Port Blair ◉

Andaman Sea

Ooty & Tamil Nadu's Western Ghats
Cool mountainscapes (p400)

10°N

ELEVATION

	3000m
	2000m
	1000m
	750m
	500m
	250m
	0

Nicobar Islands

Madurai
Site of stunning Meenakshi Amman Temple (p381)

85°E

90°E

South India & Kerala's
Top 12

ALEXANDRA LANDE / GETTY IMAGES ©

Kerala's Beautiful Backwaters

1 It's not every day you come across a place as sublime as Kerala's backwaters (p266): 900km of interconnected rivers, lakes and glassy lagoons lined with lush tropical flora. And if you do, it's unlikely there will be a way to experience it that's quite as serene and intimate as a few days on a teak-and-palm-thatch houseboat. Float along the water – as the sun sinks behind whispering palms, while nibbling on seafood so fresh it's almost wriggling – and forget about life on land for a while.

Go Goa

2 Silken sand, gently crashing waves, thick coconut groves, hot-pink sunsets...yes, if there's one place that effortlessly fulfils every beach paradise cliché, it's Goa (p117). With few exceptions Goa's beaches are a riot of activity, with a constant cavalcade of roaming sarong vendors, stacks of ramshackle beachside eateries and countless oiled bodies slowly baking on row after row of sun lounges. Goa is also known for its inland spice plantations and lovely heritage buildings, most notably its handsome Portuguese-era cathedrals. Palolem (p154)

2

PROGSO.KZ / SHUTTERSTOCK ©

Astounding Ancient Caves

3 The 2nd-century-BC Buddhist monks who created the Ajanta caves (p165) certainly had an eye for the dramatic. The 30 rock-cut forest shrines and monasteries punctuate a horseshoe-shaped cliff, and originally had staircases leading down to the river. Along an escarpment at Ellora, Hindus, Jains and Buddhists spent five centuries carving out another 34 elaborate cave shrines and monasteries – plus Kailasa Temple, the world's biggest monolithic structure. Ellora Caves (p92)

Enigmatic Hampi

4 Today's surreal boulderscape of Hampi (p210) was once the glorious Vijayanagar, capital of a powerful Hindu empire. Still glorious in ruin, its temples and royal structures combine with the terrain in mystical ways: giant rocks balance on skinny pedestals near an ancient elephant garage and temples tuck into crevices between boulders. Watching the sunset cast a rosy glow over the extraordinary landscape, you might just forget what planet you're on. Hanuman Temple (p217)

ALEXANDER MAZURKEVICH / SHUTTERSTOCK ©

EDUARD KYSLYNSKYY / SHUTTERSTOCK ©

Puducherry Savoir Faire

5 In this former French colony, mango-yellow houses line cobbled rues, imposing cathedrals are adorned with architectural frou-frou, and the croissants are the real deal. But Puducherry (Pondicherry; p359) is also a classic Indian town – with all the history and hubbub that go along with that – and a popular retreat town, too, with the Sri Aurobindo Ashram at its heart. Turns out that yoga, *pain au chocolat*, exquisite heritage hotels, Hindu deities and colonial-era architecture make for a *très* atmospheric mix. Sri Aurobindo Ashram (p360)

Mumbai's Architectural Gems

6 Mumbai (Bombay; p42) has long embraced its global influences and made them it's own. The result is a heady architectural melange of buildings with a raft of design influences. Art deco and modern towers lend the city its cool, but it's the eclectic Victorian-era structures – Indo-Saracenic, Venetian Gothic and other old flourishes – that have made Mumbai the flamboyant beauty it is. All those slender spires, curvaceous arches and puffy onion domes are apt embellishments for this movie-star city. Chhatrapati Shivaji Terminus (p47)

Out in the Wild

7 Getting out into the wild jungles, bush and hills of South India is always a thrilling experience, and dozens of parks and protected areas await. Tadoba-Andhari Tiger Reserve (p100) has some of India's best tiger-spotting chances (while Mudumalai Tiger Reserve boasts one of the country's highest tiger population densities), and Nagarhole National Park and Wayanad Wildlife Sanctuary are top wild elephant territory. In almost any park you can expect to see a range of deer, antelope and primates, and plenty of birds; and the landscapes themselves are always stunning.

CAMBUFF / SHUTTERSTOCK ©

Majestic Mysuru

8 Welcome to Mysuru (Mysore; p183) – a city whose name describes the spot where a brave goddess conquered a ferocious demon. Apart from taking in its formidable history and flamboyant palaces, it's a place for a leisurely wander through ancient bazaars filled with intoxicating aromas of sandalwood and fresh flowers. Mysuru is also an international yoga centre and is known for its energetic festivals. Dussehra, celebrating the triumph of good over evil, is one of the most spectacular occasions, with merry street parades and the dazzling illumination of the enormous maharaja's palace.

Historic Hyderabad

9 If you're a history buff, you'll get your fill in Hyderabad (p227). The city has a great story and oodles of historic attractions, including massive Golconda Fort; the graceful Charminar mosque-cum-monument, and magnificent tombs and palaces. But it's also a city of buzzing bazaars (fabrics, scented oils, billions of bangles...) and a feast for the tummy. Acclaimed for its traditional Mughal-style spicy kebabs and biryani (steamed rice with meat or vegetables), Hyderabadi fare gets a hearty round of applause for its inventive preparations. Golconda Fort (p231)

Ooty & Tamil Nadu's Western Ghats

10 The palm-fringed beaches, pancake-flat plains and temple-tastic cities are all well and good, but it gets hot down there! India's princes and British colonials long retreated to cool mountain towns such as Ooty (Udhagamandalam; p401), Kodai, Coonoor (p398) and Kotagiri to escape the relentless lowland heat. Today, the hill stations still have plenty of crisp air, shady forests, mountain hikes, sprawling tea plantations and echoes-of-the-Raj charm. Experience India's chilled-out side. Tea plantation, Coonoor

Madurai's Meenakshi Amman Temple

11 Madurai's joyful Meenakshi Amman Temple (p381) is surrounded by 12 lofty *gopurams* (gateway towers) encrusted with thousands of Technicolor deities, demons and heroes – it's rightly considered the high point of South India's spectacular temple architecture. Dedicated to Sundareswarar (a form of Shiva) and his consort, Meenakshi, the complex is a feast of pillars, sculptures, friezes and bright murals. Try to be there for the incense-clouded evening processions.

Andaman Island Eden

12 If lazing on magical beaches is your thing, look no further than the Andaman Islands (p408). This deliciously lush slice of paradise has managed to retain a pristine beauty. The inhabitants are a friendly mix of South and Southeast Asian settlers as well as a handful of reclusive tribal groups. The islands are blessed with divine aquamarine waters that lap sugar-white shores, with a number offering some excellent snorkelling and diving opportunities. So what are you waiting for? Paradise beckons! Havelock Island (p417)

11

12

Need to Know

For more information, see Survival Guide (p489)

Currency
Indian rupees (₹)

Languages
Hindi, English and regional languages.

Visas
Many nationalities obtain 30-day visas through India's e-tourist visa scheme (eTV). For longer trips, most people get a six-month tourist visa, valid from the date of issue.

Money
ATMs widely available; credit/debit cards are accepted in midrange hotels, shops and restaurants, but much of India remains a cash-based economy.

Mobile Phones
Roaming connections are excellent in urban areas, poor in the countryside and hills. Local prepaid SIMs are widely available; the paperwork is fairly straightforward but you'll have to wait 24 hours for activation.

Time
Indian Standard Time (GMT/UTC plus 5½ hours).

When to Go

Mumbai
GO Nov–Feb

Hyderabad
GO Nov–Mar

Panaji
GO Nov–Mar

Chennai
GO Dec–Apr

Thiruvananthapuram
GO Nov–Mar

Desert, dry climate
Tropical climate, rain year-round
Tropical climate, wet & dry seasons
Warm to hot summers, mild winters

High Season
(Dec–Mar)

➡ Pleasant weather – warm days, reasonably cool nights.

➡ Peak tourists. Peak prices.

➡ December and January bring chilly nights further north.

➡ Temperatures climb steadily from February.

Shoulder
(Jul–Nov)

➡ Monsoon rain-showers persist through to September.

➡ The eastern coast and southern Kerala see heavy rain and sometimes cyclones from October to early December.

Low Season
(Apr–Jun)

➡ April is hot; May and June are scorching. Competitive hotel prices.

➡ From June, the monsoon sweeps from south to north, bringing draining humidity.

➡ Beat the heat (but not the crowds) in the cool hills.

Useful Websites

Incredible India (www. incredibleindia.org) Official India tourism site.

Lonely Planet (www.lonely planet.com/india) Destination information, hotel bookings, traveller forum and more.

Templenet (www.templenet. com) Temple talk.

Rediff News (www.rediff.com/ news) Portal for India-wide news.

The Alternative (www.thealter native.in) A green and socially conscious take on travel and Indian life.

Important Numbers

As of 2017, a single number for emergencies – 112 – will be operative across India, though the following will continue to work until 2018.

Country code	📞91
International access code	📞00
Ambulance	📞102
Police	📞100
Fire	📞101

Exchange Rates

Australia	A$1	₹49
Canada	C$1	₹48
Euro zone	€1	₹73
Japan	¥100	₹59
New Zealand	NZ$1	₹46
UK	UK£1	₹83
US	US$1	₹64

For current exchange rates see www.xe.com.

Daily Costs
Budget:
Less than ₹2500

➡ Double room in a budget hotel: ₹700–1200

➡ All-you-can-eat thali (plate meal): ₹80–300

➡ Transport: ₹200–600

Midrange:
₹2500–7500

➡ Double hotel room: ₹1500–4000

➡ Meal in midrange restaurant: ₹300–1000

➡ Admission to historic sights and museums: ₹200–800

Top End:
More than ₹7500

➡ Deluxe hotel room: ₹5500–20,000

➡ Meal in superior restaurant: ₹1000–4000

➡ First-class train travel: ₹750–2000

➡ Renting a car and driver: per day ₹2000–3000

Opening Hours

Some outdoor-centric spots may close or alter their hours during the monsoon months (June to September).

Banks 10am to 4pm Monday to Friday, to 1pm Saturday

Restaurants 8am or 9am to 10pm or 11pm (some midrange and top-end restaurants may not open till lunchtime; some restaurants close between 3pm and 7pm, and others in metro cities may stay open until 1.30am)

Bars noon to midnight (as late as 1.30am in Mumbai)

Shops 10am or 11am to 8pm or 9pm (some close Sunday)

Markets 7am to 8pm, but very variable

Arriving in South India

Chhatrapati Shivaji International Airport, Mumbai (p76) Prepaid taxis cost ₹680/820 (non-AC/AC) to Colaba and Fort; ₹400/480 to Bandra. Suburban trains to Fort (₹10) run from Andheri train station, a ₹90 autorickshaw ride from the airport.

Kempegowda International Airport, Bengaluru (p181) Metered AC taxis from the airport to the city centre cost between ₹750 and ₹1000, including the airport toll charge of ₹120. Airconditioned Vayu Vajra buses run very regularly between the airport and destinations around the city; fares start at ₹180.

Chennai International Airport (p343) Prepaid taxis cost ₹550/600 (non-AC/AC) to Egmore, and ₹450/500 to T Nagar. Suburban trains to central Chennai (₹10) run from Tirusulam station, 10 minutes' walk from the terminal. The partly opened Chennai Metro Rail rapid transit system connects with the main bus station; sections linking with central Chennai aren't due for completion until 2018.

Getting Around

Air Most larger cities have flights to other Indian cities with a variety of airlines.

Train Railways criss-cross almost every part of the country, with frequent services on most routes.

Bus Buses go everywhere, at similar speed to trains. Some routes are served 24 hours but others may have just one or two buses a day.

Car & Driver The most convenient option for multistop trips or trips to out-of-the-way places.

For much more on **getting around**, see p508

What's New

Backpacker Hostels

Real-deal backpacker hostels – dorms, wi-fi, kitchens, common rooms, lockers – are soaring in number across South India. Goa hosts the liveliest collection, but you'll find hostels in Kerala, Mumbai (Bombay), Bengaluru (Bangalore), Mysuru (Mysore) and Tamil Nadu too.

Southern Surf

South India's surf scene is booming. Hit the waves with surf schools in Kovalam and Varkala in Kerala; Agonda, Aswem and Arambol in Goa; Kovalam and Puducherry (Pondicherry) in Tamil Nadu; and Little Andaman in the Andaman Islands. Kitesurfing, SUP (stand up paddle boarding) and other water sports are also popular.

Mumbai Craft Beer

Kiss Kingfisher goodbye: the craft-beer revolution has begun in Mumbai! Following the 2013 launch of Mumbai's original microbrewery, Barking Deer, a string of craft-brew boozers has sprung into the spotlight. (p70)

Metro Mania

Bengaluru's brand-new Namma Metro (p182) has sped up travel, while the much-awaited Metro Rail (p345) in Chennai (Madras) partly launched in late 2016. Hyderabad Metro Rail (p243) is *scheduled* to kick off in late 2017 or 2018.

Nasik Wine Tasting, Maharashtra

As Indian wine continues its upswing among oenophiles, Nasik's peaceful, serene vineyards (p86) are looking juicer by the minute. Beyond by Sula (p84) is a slick new winery hotel in the thick of it.

Royal Opera House, Mumbai

Following a six-year revamp and two decades out of action, India's only still-standing opera house was relaunched in 2016 in full British-era splendour. The Indo-European baroque beauty (commissioned by George V) will host plays, musical performances and film festivals. (p72)

Cool Divers, Kovalam, Kerala

As well as regular PADI diving, this new, up-to-the-minute Kovalam dive outfit provides nifty underwater scooters with oxygen supplied to helmets. (p271)

Kovalam (Covelong), Tamil Nadu

Fronting the Bay of Bengal between Chennai and Mamallapuram (Mahabalipuram), pocket-sized fishing village Kovalam has morphed into a mellow beachside travellers' hang-out, with surfing, yoga, kayaking and more. (p347)

Baga Snow Park, Goa

This giant fridge in Baga is crammed with snow, ice sculptures, igloos and a snow slide. Great fun for kids – and an extreme new way to escape the tropical heat. (p133)

Avalanche Valley, Tamil Nadu

Travellers tiring of hill-station crowds in Ooty (Udhagamandalam) can escape to quieter, wilder tracts of the Nilgiris amid the protected Avalanche Valley, filled with *shola* (virgin forest), now accessible only by official 'ecotours'. (p404)

For more recommendations and reviews, see lonelyplanet.com/india/south-india

If You Like...

Forts & Palaces

South India's history is a uniquely colourful tapestry of wrangling dynasties interwoven with influxes of seafaring traders and conquerors. Their legacy lives on in a remarkable collection of palaces and forts.

Mysuru Palace A spectacular royal confection of rare artworks, stained glass, mosaics and beautifully carved wood. (p184)

Daulatabad Fort A magnificent Maharashtrian hilltop fortress constructed by Yadava kings through the 12th century. (p91)

Janjira A remarkably preserved island fortress built off the Konkan Coast in 1571. (p101)

Hyderabad Golconda Fort complements the opulent palaces and ethereal royal tombs of the city of pearls. (p231)

Bidar Fort So weathered and peaceful, it's shocking this marvellous complex once commanded a powerful sultanate. (p223)

Beaches

South India has the country's most breathtaking stretches of coastline.

Kerala Varkala (p275), backed by dramatic cliffs, and palm-shaded and more deserted Thottada are absolute visions (p320).

Goa Despite crowds, Goa's beaches still shine: Cola (p152), Agonda (p153), Palolem (p154) and Mandrem are among the prettiest (p145).

Mumbai (Bombay) Hit Chowpatty beach for local snacks, people-watching and hot-pink sunsets. (p53)

Andaman Islands Pristine tropical beaches far away from everything on Havelock (p417), Neil (421) and Little Andaman islands (p425).

Grand Temples & Ancient Ruins

Nowhere does grand temples like the subcontinent. From Tamil Nadu's psychedelic Hindu towers to the faded splendour of the Buddhist caves of Ajanta and Ellora, the range is as vast as it is sublime.

Meenakshi Amman Temple Fantastical structure in Tamil Nadu that soars skyward in riotous rainbows of sculpted deities. (p381)

Ajanta Unesco-listed cluster of magnificent rock-cut temples, revered for their spiritual significance and architectural prowess. (p95)

Ellora Five centuries of extraordinary rock-cut temples chiselled by generations of Buddhist, Hindu and Jain monks. (p92)

Hampi Mighty Vijayanagar's rosy-hued temples and crumbling palaces are strewn among otherworldly looking boulders and hills. (p210)

Mamallapuram (Mahabalipuram) Medieval relief carvings, sculpted by Pallava artisans, and rock-cut temples dot this easygoing seaside town. (p347)

Bazaars & Markets

Megamalls may be popping up like monsoon frogs in the cities, but the traditional outdoor bazaars – with their tangled lanes lined by shops selling everything from freshly ground spices to kitchen utensils and colourful saris – can't be beat.

Goa Anjuna and Baga flea markets mesmerise; bazaars at Margao and Panaji (Panjim) make for atmospheric wandering. (p140)

Mumbai Wonderful old markets are conveniently theme-dedicated: Mangaldas (fabric), Zaveri (jewellery), Crawford (food) and Chor (antiques). (p74)

Mysuru (Mysore) Iconic 125-year-old Devaraja Market is filled with about 125 million flowers, fruits and spices. (p184)

Hyderabad Historic Charminararea bazaars hawk everything from pearls and bangles to livestock. (p240)

Meditation & Yoga

The art of well-being has long been ardently cultivated in the south. Numerous courses and treatments strive to heal mind, body and spirit, with meditation and yoga especially abundant.

Mysuru Home of ashtanga yoga; one of India's most popular places to practise and get certified. (p190)

Goa Yoga, meditation and other spiritual-health pursuits are taught and practised chiefly between October and April. (p141)

Vipassana International Academy This centre at Igatpuri, Maharashtra, conducts intensive meditation courses in the Theravada Buddhist tradition. (p87)

Sri Aurobindo Ashram This Puducherry (Pondicherry) ashram, founded by the renowned Sri Aurobindo, seeks to synthesise yoga and modern science. (p360)

Krishnamacharya Yoga Mandiram Well-known and highly regarded yoga courses, yoga therapy and intensive teacher training in Chennai (Madras). (p333)

City Sophistication

It's true that most Indians live in villages, but India's cities have vibrant arts scenes, terrific multicuisine restaurants and oodles of style.

Mumbai (Bombay) Fashion, film, art, dining, nightlife and a backdrop of fanciful architecture and scenic water views. (p42)

Hyderabad The architecture of extraordinarily wealthy bygone dynasties sits just across town from a refined restaurant, nightlife and arts scene. (p227)

Bengaluru (Bangalore) Progressive and modern IT industry nucleus and superb for drinking, dining and shopping. (p169)

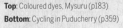

Top: Coloured dyes, Mysuru (p183)
Bottom: Cycling in Puducherry (p359)

Nasik Surrounded by gorgeous vineyards, India's wine-country capital lures juice-loving city sophisticates. (p82)

Puducherry (Pondicherry) Lively coastal town known for its quaintly faded French flavour, boho boutiques and arty cafes. (p359)

Chennai (Madras) Long-standing urban hub which now counts sophisticated layers of luxury hotels, contemporary eateries, boutiques and nightspots. (p327)

Pune Progressive Pune relishes in its juxtapositional relationship between cutting-edge capitalism and age-old spirituality. (p107)

Nature

South India offers plenty of opportunities to search for wild things in wild places.

Wayanad Wildlife Sanctuary Remote, beautiful, unspoiled Keralan sanctuary with good chances of spotting wild elephants. (p317)

Nagarhole National Park Little-visited park good for elephant sightings and – if you're lucky! – a tiger or two. (p196)

Tadoba-Andhari Tiger Reserve Top Indian tiger territory, plus gaurs (bison), chital deer, nilgai antelope, sloth bears and leopards. (p100)

Periyar Wildlife Sanctuary Keralan sanctuary with gaurs, sambar deer, around 1000 elephants and a few tigers. (p290)

Hill Stations

The colonial-era tradition of heading for the cool, green elevations of the Western Ghats, when the plains get just too hot, is alive and

well among honeymooners, families and pretty much everyone else.

Ooty (Udhagamandalam) The 'Queen of Hill Stations' combines Indian bustle with green parks and Raj-era bungalows. (p401)

Kodaikanal A smaller, quirkier, more scenic alternative to Ooty, centred on a pretty lake. (p391)

Matheran A scenic and car-free weekend retreat for Mumbai-kars, reached on foot or by horseback. (p105)

Munnar A beautiful out-of-town resort base for trekking through emerald-green South Indian tea plantations. (p294)

Traveller Enclaves

Sometimes you just want to chill with fellow travellers: swap travel tales, read, take afternoon naps, play cards or drink beer...

Hampi The stunning beauty of Hampi's landscape and architecture sucks everyone in for a while. (p210)

Arambol Goa is one big traveller enclave, but Palolem and cheaper Arambol are its current epicentres. (p146)

Gokarna Cosy, beautiful and relaxed beaches that are part of a scared village in Karnataka. (p207)

Mamallapuram Cheap accommodation, exquisite ancient architecture and a booming surf scene on Tamil Nadu's coast. (p347)

Colaba Mumbai's boisterous melange of street stalls, classic watering holes, budget accommodation and bucket list tourist sights. (p45)

Water Sports

Diving, snorkelling and surfing all are growing rapidly along South Indian coasts.

Andaman Islands World-class diving and snorkelling in coral- and marine-life-rich, crystal-clear waters – 1370km from mainland India. (p408)

Malvan India's little diving destination that could: caves, coral, marine life and a top-class scuba school. (p103)

Tamil Nadu Surf's up in Kovalam, Mamallapuram and Puducherry. (p324)

Aswem Beach A Goa surf favourite with beginners for its modest 1m to 2m waves. (p145)

Lakshadweep Pristine lagoons and unspoiled coral reefs 300km off Kerala have wonderful diving and snorkelling. (p323)

Boat Trips

Seeing South India from the water offers a whole new angle on its attractions.

Alappuzha (Alleppey) Houseboat drifting from Kerala's backwater hub is one of the region's most cinematic experiences. (p282)

Kollam (Quilon) Observe village life on three-hour punted canoe rides through networks of canals around Munroe Island. (p280)

Goa Dolphin- and croc-spotting tours on the Mandovi River. (p131)

Andaman Islands See mangroves, rainforest and reefs at coral-rich Mahatma Gandhi Marine National Park. (p416)

Malvan Take a trip along Maharashtra's little-known but beautiful Karli River backwaters. (p103)

Month by Month

January

Postmonsoon cool lingers, although it never gets truly cool in the most southerly states. Pleasant weather and several festivals make it a popular time to travel (book ahead!).

✨ Free India

Republic Day commemorates the founding of the Republic of India on 26 January 1950.

✨ Kite Festival

Sankranti, the Hindu festival marking the sun's passage into Capricorn and the end of the harvest, is celebrated with mass kite-flying in Maharashtra, Telangana and Andhra Pradesh (among other states).

✨ Pongal Festival

In Tamil Nadu the Pongal festival marks the end of the harvest season. Families prepare pots of *pongal* (a mixture of rice, sugar, dhal and milk), symbolic of prosperity and abundance, then feed them to decorated cows. (p326)

✨ Celebrating Saraswati

On Vasant Panchami, the 'fifth day of spring', Hindus dress in yellow and place books, instruments and other educational objects in front of idols of Saraswati, the goddess of learning, to receive her blessing. May fall in February.

February

The weather is comfortable in most areas, with summer heat starting to percolate in the south. It's still peak travel season.

☆ SulaFest

In Maharashtra, Nasik's biggest party is three wine-fuelled days at Sula Vineyards, which has become one of India's best boutique music festivals. (p84)

✨ Shivaratri

This day of Hindu fasting recalls the *tandava* (cosmic victory dance) of Lord Shiva. Temple processions are followed by the chanting of mantras and anointing of linga (phallic images of Shiva). Can also fall in March.

✨ Carnival in Goa

The four-day party kicking off Lent is particularly big in Goa, especially in Panaji (Panjim). Sabado Gordo (Fat Saturday) starts it off with elaborate parades, and the revelry continues with street parties, concerts and general merry-making. Can also fall in March. (p119)

March

The last month of the travel season, March is full-on hot in most of India.

✨ Holi

Mumbaikars and other southerners embrace this mostly northern festival, an ecstatic Hindu celebration at the beginning of spring (February or March, according to the lunar calendar), by throwing coloured water and *gulal* (powder) at everyone and everything.

Rama's Birthday

During Ramanavami, which lasts anywhere from one to nine days, Hindus celebrate Rama's birth with processions, music, fasting and feasting, enactments of scenes from the Ramayana, and ceremonial weddings of Rama and Sita idols.

April

The hot has well and truly arrived in South India, and with the rise in temperature also comes a rise in competitive travel deals and a drop in tourist traffic.

Mahavir's Birthday

In April or late March, Mahavir Jayanti commemorates the birth of Jainism's 24th and most important *tirthankar* (teacher and enlightened being). Temples are decorated and visited, Mahavir statues are given ritual baths, processions are held and offerings are given to the poor.

May

In most of the country it's hot. Really hot. Which makes it high season in Ooty (Udhagamandalam), Kodaikanal (Kodai) and the south's other hill stations. Festivals slow down as humidity builds up in anticipation of the rain.

Ramadan (Ramazan)

Thirty days of dawn-to-dusk fasting mark the ninth month of the Islamic calendar. Ramadan begins around 16 May 2018 and 6 May 2019.

June

The monsoon begins in most areas, and where it doesn't you've got premonsoon extreme heat, so June's not a popular travel month in South India.

Eid al-Fitr

Muslims celebrate the end of Ramadan with three days of festivities. Prayers, shopping and gift-giving may all be part of the celebrations. Around 15 June 2018 and 5 June 2019.

July

It's really raining almost everywhere, with many remote roads being washed out. Consider doing a rainy-season meditation retreat, an ancient Indian tradition.

August

It's still high monsoon season: wet, wet, wet. Some folks swear by visiting tropical areas like Kerala or Goa at this time of year: the jungles are lush, bright green and glistening in the rain.

Snake Festival

Naag Panchami, particularly vibrant in Pune and Kolhapur, Maharashtra, is dedicated to Ananta, the serpent upon whose coils Vishnu rested between universes. Women fast at home, while serpents are venerated as totems warding off evils. Dates: 15 August 2018 and 5 August 2019.

Independence Day

This public holiday, on 15 August, marks the anniversary of India's independence from Britain in 1947. Celebrations include flag-hoisting ceremonies, parades and patriotic cultural programs.

Nehru Trophy Boat Race

On the second Saturday of August, this fiercely contested regatta sees 40m-long Chundan Vallams (snake boats) go head-to-head, powered by up to 100 rowers each, on Punnamada Lake near Alappuzha (Alleppey, Kerala). Quite a spectacle. (p283)

Parsi New Year

Parsis celebrate Pateti, the Zoroastrian new year, especially in Mumbai (Bombay). Houses are cleaned and decorated with flowers and *rangoli,* the family dresses up and eats special fish dishes and sweets, and offerings are made at the Fire Temple.

Eid al-Adha

Muslims commemorate Ibrahim's readiness to sacrifice his son to God by slaughtering a goat or sheep and sharing it with family, the community and the poor. Around 20 August 2018 and 10 August 2019.

September

The rain begins to ease up somewhat, but with temperatures still relatively high throughout southern India the moisture-filled air can create a fatiguing steam-bath-like environment.

✦ Krishna's Birthday

Janmastami celebrations range from fasting to *puja* (prayers) and offering sweets, to drawing elaborate *rangoli* (rice-paste designs) outside homes. Held around 3 September 2018 and 23 August 2019.

✦ Onam

Kerala's biggest cultural celebration, a 10-day Hindu soirée glorifying the golden age of mythical King Mahabali, is celebrated at the beginning of the first month of the Malayalam Calendar (August or September). (p257)

✦ Ganesh's Birthday

Hindus celebrate Ganesh Chaturthi, the birth of the elephant-headed god, by displaying decorative statues of him on many streets then parading them around town before ceremonially depositing them in rivers, lakes, reservoirs or the sea. Particularly riotous in Mumbai. Dates: 13 September 2018 and 2 September 2019. (p45)

October

The southeast coast (and southern Kerala) can still be rainy, but this is when India starts to get its travel mojo on.

✦ Gandhi's Birthday

The national holiday of Gandhi Jayanti (2 October) is a solemn celebration of

Top: Dussehra festival celebrations (p185), Mysuru
Bottom: Diwali, festival of lights

Mohandas Gandhi's birth, with prayer meetings at his cremation site in Delhi, and no alcohol on sale countrywide.

✸ Navratri

The Hindu 'Festival of Nine Nights' leading up to Dussehra celebrates the goddess Durga in all her incarnations. Festivities, in September or October, are particularly vibrant in Maharashtra.

✸ Dussehra

Colourful Dussehra celebrates the victory of the Hindu god Rama over the demon-king Ravana and the triumph of good over evil. Dussehra is big in Mysuru (Mysore), which hosts one of India's grandest parades. Falls around 19 October 2018 and 8 October 2019. (p185)

✸ Muharram

Shiite Muslims commemorate the martyrdom of Prophet Mohammed's grandson Imam Hussain, an event during this Islamic month of grieving and remembrance known as Ashura. The 10th day brings beautiful processions, especially in Hyderabad. Dates: 10 September 2018 and 30 August 2019.

✸ Diwali

In the lunar month of Kartika, Hindus celebrate Diwali for five days, giving gifts, lighting fireworks, drawing colourful *rangoli* and burning butter and oil lamps (or hanging lanterns) to lead Lord Rama home from exile. Dates: 19 Octo-

ber 2017, 7 November 2018 and 27 October 2019.

November

The northeast monsoon is sweeping Tamil Nadu and Kerala, but it's a good time to be anywhere low altitude, as the temperatures are generally pleasant.

✸ Guru Nanak's Birthday

Nanak Jayanti, birthday of Guru Nanak, founder of Sikhism, is celebrated with prayer, *kirtan* (devotional singing) and processions for three days. Around 4 November 2017, 23 November 2018 and 12 November 2019.

☆ Movie Mania

The International Film Festival of India (www.iffi.nic.in), the country's biggest movie jamboree, attracts Bollywood's finest to Panaji, Goa, for premieres, parties and screenings. (p126)

✸ The Prophet's Birthday

The Islamic festival of Eid-Milad-un-Nabi celebrates the birth of the Prophet Mohammed with prayers and processions. Around 30 November 2017, 21 November 2018 and 10 November 2019. May also fall in December.

December

December is peak tourist season for a reason: the

weather is lovely, the humidity is lower than usual, the mood is festive and the beach is simply sublime.

✸ Karthikai Deepam

Celebrating Shiva's restoration of light to the world, this festival is especially massive at Tiruvannamalai, where Shiva appeared atop Mt Arunachala as a lingam of fire. Throngs of pilgrims converge on the town for the full-moon night (2 December 2017, 23 November 2018 and 10 December 2019). (p357)

✸ Christmas Day

Christians celebrate the birth of Jesus Christ on 25 December. The festivities are especially big in Goa and Kerala, with musical events, elaborate decorations and special Masses, while Mumbai's Catholic neighbourhoods become festivals of lights.

Itineraries

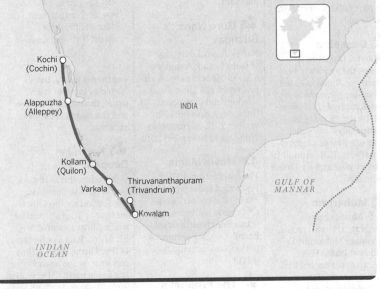

 2 WEEKS **Classic Kerala**

With its coconut-palm-fringed beaches and lazy backwater boat rides, Kerala can justly claim to be India's most laid-back state. But there's plenty of colour and fun to spice up your tropical idyll – elephant festivals and snake-boat races, Kathakali dance-dramas, quaint colonial-era quarters and a famously flavoursome cuisine.

Spend a day visiting the zoological gardens and museums in the capital, **Thiruvananthapuram**, aka Trivandrum, before making the half-hour hop to the beach resort of **Kovalam**. Then shift down another gear at **Varkala**, a holy town with a dizzying clifftop guesthouse-and-restaurant enclave, where you can chill out with some yoga or surfing. Continue north to **Kollam** (Quilon) and take the tourist cruise along the canals to Alappuzha (Alleppey) with an overnight stop at the Matha Amrithanandamayi Mission, the pink ashram of 'The Hugging Mother'. Reaching **Alleppey**, you're at houseboat central. Scout for a houseboat or canoe operator and discover what the sublime backwaters are all about. Continuing north by train to **Kochi** (Cochin), take the short ferry ride to the old colonial outpost of Fort Cochin. Aromatic seafood barbecues, wonderfully warm homestays, colonial-era mansions, Kathakali shows and the intriguing Jewish quarter at Mattancherry make this a fascinating place to while away a few days.

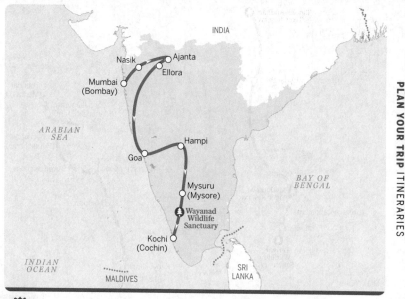

4 WEEKS Goa, Caves & Cities

City lights, historic sites, beachy bliss, jungle adventure and a touch of colonial-era quaintness – this trip will give you the flavour of all that's best about the south.

Begin in cosmopolitan **Mumbai** (Bombay), Bollywood's beating heart and home to some of the nation's best spots to shop, eat and drink. Take a sunset stroll along Marine Dr, a curvaceous oceanside promenade dubbed the 'Queen's Necklace' because of its sparkling night lights, finishing with *bhelpuri* (fried rounds of dough with rice, lentils and chutney) and a neck massage on Chowpatty beach. Catch a ferry to Elephanta Island from Mumbai's historic Gateway of India to explore its stunning rock-cut temples and the triple-faced sculpture of Lord Shiva.

Next, make your way to the dazzling vineyards of Indian wine country around **Nasik**, sipping on award-winning juice at Grover Zampa or Sula Vineyards, an outside-the-box Indian experience. Continue northeast to explore the ancient cave art at **Ajanta** and **Ellora**, situated within 150km of each other near Aurangabad. The incredible frescoed Buddhist caves of Ajanta are clustered along a horseshoe-shaped gorge, while the rock-cut caves of Ellora – containing a mix of Hindu, Jain and Buddhist shrines – are set on a 2km escarpment. Next stop: the tropical beach haven of **Goa** for some soul-reviving sandcastle therapy. Wander through a lush spice plantation, visit Portuguese-era cathedrals at Old Goa, shop at Anjuna's colourful flea market and take your pick from dozens of fabulous beach spots, before travelling east to the traveller hot spot of **Hampi** in neighbouring Karnataka. Ramble around Hampi's enigmatic boulder-strewn landscape and imagine what life here was like when it was a centre of the mighty Vijayanagar empire. Make the long trip down to **Mysuru** (Mysore) to explore the Maharaja's Palace, one of India's grandest royal buildings, and shop for silk and sandalwood in its colourful markets. From Mysuru it's an exciting bus ride across the Western Ghats into Kerala and the **Wayanad Wildlife Sanctuary**, a pristine forest and jungle reserve and one of the best places in the south to spot wild elephants. Finally, take the hair-raising road down to the coast and make your way to **Kochi**, Kerala's intriguing colonial-era city, where a blend of Portuguese, Dutch and English history combines with wonderful homestays and a buzzing traveller scene.

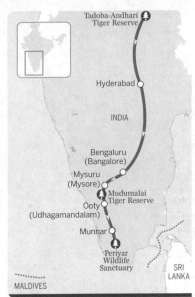

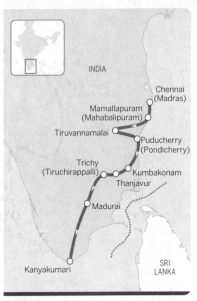

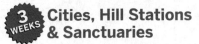

3 WEEKS — Cities, Hill Stations & Sanctuaries

An offbeat trip through the contrasting cities, wildlife parks and hill stations of the Deccan and Western Ghats will give you a true taste of the fascinating variety of inland South India.

Start with a venture to the little-visited but fantastic **Tadoba-Andhari Tiger Reserve**, offering some of India's best prospects for sighting wild tigers, then journey south to the wonderful old princely capital **Hyderabad**. Continue south to India's 21st-century IT capital, **Bengaluru** (Bangalore), and glimpse a royal past at its whimsical Bangalore Palace. Next stop: the royal city of **Mysuru** (Mysore). Gawp at the Maharaja's Palace, an ubergrand complex topped with rhubarb-red and chalky-white domes. Head south to **Mudumalai Tiger Reserve**, where you can spot wild elephants and take a safari through pristine jungle, and on to the cool hill town of **Ooty** (Udhagamandalam). Take the toy train down to Coimbatore, then cross into Kerala and the emerald-green, tea-covered hills of **Munnar**. Finish with some jungle trekking and more chances of a tiger sighting at pretty **Periyar Wildlife Sanctuary**.

12 DAYS — Sacred Tamil Nadu

A journey through Tamil Nadu is a trip into South India's spiritual soul.

Delve into the rich history of **Chennai** (Madras) with a wander around the Government Museum before visiting the ancient Kapaleeshwarar and Parthasarathy Temples. Travel south to beachside **Mamallapuram** (Mahabalipuram) and its superb rock-cut shrines carved under the ancient Pallava dynasty. Move inland to **Tiruvannamalai**, where the Arunachaleshwar Temple is one of India's largest sacred complexes. Trade in temples for flamboyant churches and cathedrals in the quaint old French seaside colony of **Puducherry** (Pondicherry) before heading back inland to the stunning Unesco World Heritage–listed medieval temples around **Kumbakonam** and **Thanjavur**. Continue to **Trichy** (Tiruchirappalli), home to the spectacular Rock Fort Temple and the Sri Ranganathaswamy Temple. Then head south to **Madurai** and the incredible Meenakshi Amman Temple, widely reckoned the pinnacle of South Indian temple architecture. Wind down at **Kanyakumari**, the southern tip of India, with its temple to the virgin sea goddess Kumari.

Plan Your Trip
Booking Trains

In India, riding the rails has a romance all of its own. The Indian rail network snakes almost all over the country, almost all the time, and trains have seats to suit every size of wallet. However, booking can be a hassle – booking online is usually best.

Booking Online

Bookings currently open 120 days before departure (this is subject to change) for long-distance trains, sometimes less for short-haul trips. Seats fill up quickly – reserve at least a week ahead where possible, though shorter journeys are usually easier to obtain.

Express and mail trains form the main-stay of Indian rail travel. Not all classes are available on every train, but most long-distance services have general (2nd-class) compartments with unreserved seating and more comfortable reserved compart-ments, usually with the option of sleeper berths for overnight journeys. Sleeper trains offer the chance to travel huge distances for not much more than the price of a midrange hotel room.

Shatabdi express trains are same-day services with seating only; Rajdhani express trains are long-distance overnight services between Delhi and state capitals with a choice of 1AC, 2AC, 3AC and 2nd class. More expensive sleeper categories provide bedding. In all classes, a padlock and a length of chain are useful for securing your luggage to baggage racks.

These websites are useful for online international bookings.

Cleartrip (www.cleartrip.com) A reliable private agency and the easiest way to book; accepts in-ternational MasterCard and Visa credit cards. Can only book direct journeys. If booking from outside India before you have a local mobile number, a work-around is to enter a random number, and use email only to communicate.

Train Classes
Air-Conditioned 1st Class (1AC)
The most expensive class, with two- or four-berth compartments with locking doors and meals included.

Air-Conditioned 2-Tier (2AC)
Two-tier berths arranged in groups of four and two in an open-plan carriage. Bunks convert to seats by day and there are curtains, offering some privacy.

Air-Conditioned 3-Tier (3AC)
Three-tier berths arranged in groups of six in an open-plan carriage with no curtains; popular with Indian families.

AC Executive Chair (ECC)
Comfortable, reclining chairs and plenty of space; usually on Shatabdi express trains.

AC Chair (CC)
Similar to the Executive Chair carriage but with less-fancy seating.

Sleeper Class (sl)
Open-plan carriages with three-tier bunks and no AC; the open windows afford great views.

Unreserved/reserved 2nd Class (II/SS or 2S)
Wooden or plastic seats and a lot of people – but cheap!

RAILWAY RAZZLE DAZZLE

You can live like a maharaja on one of India's luxury train tours, with accommodation on board, tours, admission fees and meals included in the ticket price.

Palace on Wheels (www.palaceonwheels.net) Eight- to 10-day luxury tours of Rajasthan, departing from Delhi. Trains run on fixed dates from September to April; the fare per person for seven nights starts at US$6500/4890/4325 (in a single/double/triple cabin). Try to book 10 months in advance.

Royal Rajasthan on Wheels (www.royalrajasthanonwheels.co.in) Runs lavish one-week trips from October to March, starting and finishing in Delhi. The fare per person per night starts from US$875/625 for single/twin occupancy in deluxe suites.

Deccan Odyssey (www.deccan-odyssey-india.com) Seven nights covering the main tourist spots of Maharashtra and Goa. Fares per person start at US$5810/4190 (Indian tourists ₹371,900/268,360) for single/double occupancy. There are also several other shorter luxurious trips on offer.

Golden Chariot (www.goldenchariottrain.com) Seven-night tours seeing the south in sumptuous style from October to March, starting in Bengaluru (Bangalore). Fares per person start at single/double US$5530/4130 (Indian tourists ₹182,000/154,000).

Mahaparinirvan Express (aka Buddhist Circuit Special; www.railtourismindia.com) Running September to March to Buddhist sites over eight days, starting in Delhi, with overnight stays in hotels. Rates start from US$1155/945 per person in 1st class/AC 2 Tier class.The trip includes Nepal (the visa fee is not included in the price).

IRCTC (www.irctc.co.in) Government site offering bookings for regular trains and luxury tourist trains; Mastercard and Visa are accepted.

Make My Trip (www.makemytrip.com) Reputable private agency; accepts international cards. Again, you'll need an Indian mobile number. You'll then need to create an IRCTC User ID: choose a User ID (username), put in your name, birth date and address. For the 'Pincode' (postcode) '123456' will work. For the State choose 'Other'.

Yatra (www.yatra.com) Books flights and trains; accepts international cards.

Reservations

You must make a reservation for all chair-car, executive chair-car, sleeper, 1AC, 2AC and 3AC carriages. No reservations are required for general (2nd-class) compartments. Book well ahead for overnight journeys or travel during holidays and festivals. Waiting until the day of travel to book is not recommended.

Train Passes

IndRail passes permit unlimited rail travel for a fixed period, ranging from half a day to 90 days, but offers limited savings and you must still make reservations. Sample prices are US$19/43/95 (sleeper/2AC, 3AC & chair car/1AC) for 24 hours. The easiest way to book these is through the IndRail pass agency in your home country – click on the Passenger Info/Tourist Information link on www.indianrailways.gov.in/railwayboard for further details.

Plan Your Trip

Yoga, Spas & Spiritual Pursuits

Birthplace of at least three religions, India offers a profound spiritual journey for those so inclined. Even sceptical travellers can enjoy spas, ayurvedic centres and yoga schools.

Ayurveda

Ayurveda – ancient Indian herbal medicine – aims to restore balance in the body.

Goa

Shanti Ayurvedic Massage Centre, Mandrem (p146) Massages and facials.

Karnataka

Arya Ayurvedic Panchakarma Centre, Gokarna (p209) Beachside ayurveda.

Ayurvedagram, Bengaluru (p174) In a garden setting.

Soukya, Bengaluru (p174) Ayurveda and yoga.

Indus Valley Ayurvedic Centre, Mysuru (p185) Therapies from ancient scriptures.

Swaasthya Ayurveda Retreat Village, Coorg (p198) Retreats and therapies.

SwaSwara, Gokarna (p208) Therapies and artistic pursuits.

Kerala

Ayur Dara, Kochi (p302) Treatments of one to three weeks.

Dr Franklin's Panchakarma Institute, Chowara (p274) South of Kovalam.

Eden Garden, Varkala (p277) Treatments and packages.

What to Choose

Ashrams

India has hundreds of ashrams – places of communal living established around the philosophies of a guru (spiritual guide or teacher).

Ayurveda

Ayurveda is the ancient science of Indian herbal medicine and holistic healing, based on natural plant extracts, massage and therapies for body and mind.

Meditation

Many centres in Buddhist areas offer training in *vipassana* (mindfulness meditation) and Buddhist philosophy; many require vows of silence and abstinence from tobacco, alcohol and sex.

Spa Treatments

India's spas offer an enticing mix of international therapies and local ayurveda-based techniques.

Yoga

Yoga's roots lie firmly in India; you'll find hundreds of schools to suit all levels.

Santhigiri Ayurveda Centre, Kollam (p280)
Seven- to 21-day packages and day treatments;
also at Periyar (p291).

Shree Krishna Ayurveda Panchkarma Centre, Alleppey (p283) Multinight packages.

Mumbai

Yogacara (p57) Ayurveda and massage.

Tamil Nadu

Sita, Puducherry (p362) Ayurveda and yoga.

Yoga

You can practise yoga everywhere, from
beach resorts and mountain retreats to
serious-study schools. In 2014, at India's
initiative, the UN declared 21 June to be
International Yoga Day.

Andaman Islands

Flying Elephant, Havelock Island (p420) Yoga
and meditation in tropical surroundings.

Goa

Bamboo Yoga Retreat, Patnem (p158) Beachside
yoga.

Himalaya Yoga Valley, Mandrem (p146) Popular
training school.

Himalayan Iyengar Yoga Centre, Arambol (p146)
Reputable courses.

Swan Yoga Retreat, Assagao (p141) Retreat in a
soothing jungle location.

Karnataka

Mysuru (Mysore) was the birthplace of
ashtanga yoga; there are centres across
Karnataka (p190).

IndeaYoga, Mysuru (p190) Hatha and ashtanga.

Namaste Yoga Farm, Gorkarna (p209) Leafy-
setting yoga.

Yoga Bharata, Mysuru (p190) Ashtanga and
hatha.

Kerala

Thiruvananthapuram (Trivandrum), Varkala and Kochi (Cochin) are popular for yoga.

Sivananda Yoga Vedanta Dhanwantari Ashram
(p262) Renowned for extended hatha yoga
courses; 30km from Trivandrum.

Maharashtra

Kaivalyadhama Yoga Hospital, Lonavla (p106)
Yogic healing.

**Ramamani Iyengar Memorial Yoga Institute,
Pune** (p111) Advanced courses.

Mumbai

Yoga Institute (p59) Daily and longer-term
programs.

Yoga House (p58) Hatha yoga in a homey
setting.

Yogacara (p57) More hatha.

Tamil Nadu

**International Centre for Yoga Education
& Research, Puducherry** (p362) Introductory
courses and advanced training.

Krishnamacharya Yoga Mandiram, Chennai
(p333) Yoga courses, therapy and training.

Sivananda Vedanta Yoga Centre, Madurai
(p383) Drop-in yoga and rigorous courses.

Meditation

Whether for introduction or advanced
study, there are South India–wide courses
and retreats.

Maharashtra

Vipassana International Academy, Igatpuri
(p87) Renowned 10-day *vipassana* courses.

Mumbai

Global Pagoda, Gorai Island (p56) *Vipassana*
courses from one to 10 days.

Telangana & Andhra Pradesh

Numerous Burmese-style *vipassana*
courses.

Dhamma Nagajjuna, Nagarjuna Sagar (p248)

Dhamma Vijaya, near Eluru (p248)

**Vipassana International Meditation Centre,
Hyderabad** (p234)

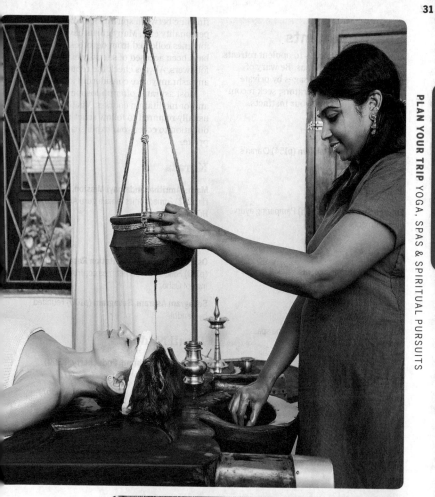

Top: An ayurvedic treatment (p279)

Bottom: Warrior yoga pose

NINA LISHCHUK / SHUTTERSTOCK ©

Spa Treatments

From solo practitioners to opulent retreats, South India is full of spas. Be wary of dodgy one-on-one massages by private (often unqualified) operators; seek recommendations and trust your instincts.

Goa

Hummingbird Spa, Palolem (p154) Ciaran's beachside spa.

Karnataka

Emerge Spa, Mysuru (p185) Pampering ayurvedic treatments.

Kerala

Neeleshwar Hermitage, near Bekal (p322) Beachside ecoresort.

Mumbai

Palms Spa (p59) Renowned Colaba spa.

Tamil Nadu

Hyatt Regency, Chennai (p337) Glitzy hotel spa.

Ashrams

Many ashrams ('places of striving') are headed by charismatic gurus. Some tread a fine line between spiritual community and personality cult. Many gurus have amassed fortunes collected from devotees; others have been accused of sexually exploiting followers. Always check the reputation of any ashram you're considering joining.

Most ashrams offer philosophy, yoga and/or meditation courses. Visitors are usually required to follow strict rules. A donation to cover your expenses is appropriate.

Kerala

Matha Amrithanandamayi Mission, Amrithapuri (p282) Famed for its female guru Amma, 'The Hugging Mother'.

Maharashtra

Osho International Meditation Resort, Pune (p110) Follows the sometimes controversial teachings of Osho.

Sevagram Ashram, Sevagram (p100) Founded by Gandhi.

Tamil Nadu

Sri Aurobindo Ashram, Puducherry (p360) Founded by Sri Aurobindo.

Sri Ramana Ashram, Tiruvannamalai (p357) Established by Sri Ramana Maharshi.

Plan Your Trip

Volunteering

For all India's beauty, rich culture and history, poverty and hardship are unavoidable facts of life. Many travellers feel motivated to help, and charities and aid organisations across the country welcome committed volunteers. Here's a guide to help you start making a difference.

Aid Programs in South India

India faces considerable challenges and there are numerous opportunities for volunteers. It may be possible to find a placement after you arrive, but charities and nongovernment organisations (NGOs) almost always prefer volunteers who have applied in advance and been approved for the kind of work involved (which may require a specific visa or background checks). **Responsible Volunteering** (www.responsiblevolunteering.co.uk) is a useful resource.

As well as international organisations, local charities and NGOs often have opportunities, though it can be harder to assess that these organisations are doing. For listings of local agencies, check **NGOs India** (www.ngosindia.com) or contact the Delhi-based **Concern India Foundation** (☎011-64598584; www.concernindiafoundation.org; A-52 Amar Colony, Lajpat Nagar IV; Ⓜ Lajpat Nagar).

Note that Lonely Planet does not endorse any organisation that we do not work with directly, so it is essential that you do your own thorough research to assess the standards and suitability of a project before agreeing to volunteer with an organisation.

How to Volunteer

Choosing an Organisation

Consider how your skills will benefit the people you are trying to help, and choose an organisation that can specifically benefit from your abilities.

Time Required

Think realistically about how much time you can devote to a project. You're more likely to be of help if you commit for at least a month; experts recommend at least a three-month commitment.

Money

Giving your time for free is only part of the story; most organisations expect volunteers to cover their own accommodation, food and transport.

Working Nine to Five

Make sure you understand what you are signing up for; many organisations expect volunteers to work full time, five days a week.

Transparency

Ensure that the organisation you choose is reputable and transparent about how it spends its money. Where possible, get feedback from former volunteers.

Community

Many volunteer projects work to provide health care and education to villages.

Karnataka

Kishkinda Trust, Hampi (p217) Volunteers assist with sustainable community development.

Working with Children

Ethical organisations which provide support for disadvantaged children should require background checks to be undertaken.

Goa

Mango Tree Goa, Mapusa (p130) One- to three-month placements for teaching assistants to help disadvantaged children.

El Shaddai, Assagao (p141) Helping impoverished and homeless children; one-month minimum.

Environment & Conservation

Andaman Islands

ANET, Wandoor (p416) Assist with activities from field projects to general maintenance.

Reef Watch Marine Conservation, Lacadives (p416) Marine conservation nonprofit organisation accepting volunteers for anything from beach clean-ups to fish surveys.

Karnataka

Rainforest Retreat, Kodagu (p198) A spice-plantation hideaway with openings for volunteers.

Tamil Nadu

Keystone Foundation, Kotagiri (p400) Occasional opportunities to help improve environmental conditions, working with indigenous communities.

Working with Animals

There are plentiful options for animal lovers.

Goa

Animal Rescue Centre, Chapolim (p151) Animal welfare group that also has volunteer opportunities.

Goa Animal Welfare Trust, Curchorem (☑0832-2653677; www.gawt.org; Old Police Station, Curchorem; ⊙9am-5.30pm Mon-Sat, 10am-1pm & 2.30-5.30pm Sun) GAWT operates a stray-animal shelter near Margao.

International Animal Rescue, Assagao (p140) Well-established animal-rescue operation with short-term volunteering opportunities.

Tamil Nadu

Arunachala Animal Sanctuary, Tiruvannamalai (p358) Short- and long-term volunteer openings at a 200-animal dog- and cat-rescue operation.

Madras Crocodile Bank, Vadanemmeli (p346) A reptile conservation centre with placements for volunteers (minimum two weeks).

Telangana

Blue Cross of Hyderabad (p234) A shelter with over 1300 animals; volunteers help care for animals or work in the office; minimum 20 hours.

Heritage & Restoration

Opportunities for those with architecture and building skills.

Tamil Nadu

ArCHeS, Kothamangalam (p380) Aims to preserve the architectural and cultural heritage of Chettinadu; openings for historians, geographers and architects.

Plan Your Trip

Travel with Children

Fascinating and thrilling: India can be every bit as exciting for children as it is for their wide-eyed parents. The scents, sights and sounds of India will inspire and challenge young enquiring minds, and, with careful preparation and vigilance, a lifetime of vivid memories can be sown.

South India for Kids

In many respects, travel with children in India can be a delight, and warm welcomes are frequent. Locals will thrill at taking photographs beside your bouncing baby, and there's an endless stream of family-friendly activities and sights to keep kids busy. But, while all this is fabulous for outgoing children, it may prove tiring, or even disconcerting, for younger kids and those with more retiring dispositions.

As a parent on the road in India, the key is to stay alert to your children's needs and remain firm in fulfilling them, even if you feel you may offend a well-meaning local by doing so. The attention children will inevitably receive is almost always good-natured; kids are the centre of life in many Indian households, and your own will be treated just the same. Hotels will almost always provide an extra bed or two, and restaurants a familiar meal.

Best Regions for Kids

Goa

Palm-fringed, salt-white beaches and inexpensive local food make Goa an ideal choice for family holidays. If you're looking to stay for a while, you'll find apartments and homey guesthouses to suit all budgets.

Karnataka & Bengaluru

Hampi's magical World Heritage–listed ruins bewitch travellers of all ages, there's beach bliss at Gokarna, and who wouldn't get excited about searching for wild elephants and hoping to glimpse a tiger or leopard in Bandipur and Nagarhole National Parks?

Kerala

Canoe and houseboat adventures, surf beaches, Arabian Sea sunsets, snake-boat races, wildlife-spotting and elephant festivals. From the Ghats down to the coast, Kerala offers family-friendly action and relaxation in equal measure.

WHAT TO PACK

You can get some of these items in many parts of India, but prices are often at a premium and brands may not be those you recognise.

➡ For babies or toddlers: disposable or washable nappies, nappy rash cream (calendula cream works well against heat rash too), extra bottles, a good stock of wet wipes, infant formula and canned, bottled or rehydratable food.

➡ A fold-up baby bed or the lightest possible travel cot you can find (some companies make pop-up tent-style beds), as hotel cots may prove precarious.

➡ Don't take a pushchair/stroller, as this will be impractical to use and pavements are often scarce. For smaller kids, a much better option is a backpack, so they're lifted up and out of the daunting throng.

➡ A few less-precious toys that won't be mourned if lost or damaged.

➡ A swimming jacket, life jacket or water wings for the sea or pool.

➡ Good sturdy footwear.

➡ Audiobooks or tablets loaded with games, films and music for long journeys – and headphones!

➡ Child-friendly insect repellent, hats and sun lotion: essential.

Children's Highlights

Best Natural Encounters

Elephants
Kids will love spotting wild elephants on jeep safaris in Wayanad (p317), Kerala; Bandipur (p194) and Nagarhole (p196), Karnataka; and Mudumalai (p406), Tamil Nadu.

Dolphins, Goa
Splash out on a dolphin-spotting boat trip from almost any Goan beach to see them cavorting in the waves.

Hill Station Monkeys, Matheran (p105) Climb into Maharashtra's hills for close encounters with cheeky monkeys.

Tigers, Tadoba-Andhari Tiger Reserve (p100)
Look for tigers on outstanding wildlife-sighting jeep safaris in this little-visited Maharashtra reserve.

Funnest Forms of Transport

Autorickshaw, anywhere
Hurtle at top speed in these child-scale vehicles.

Hand-pulled rickshaw, Matheran (p105) Kids can roam this monkey-patrolled Maharashtra hill station on horseback or in traditional hand-pulled rickshaws.

Houseboat, Alappuzha (p282)
Hop on a houseboat to luxuriously cruise Kerala's beautiful backwaters. If you hit town on the second Saturday in August, take the kids to see the spectacular Nehru Trophy Boat Race (p283).

Nilgiri Mountain Railway, Ooty (p406)
Roll through the gorgeous Nilgiris on Tamil Nadu's super-scenic Unesco-listed 'toy' train.

Best Beaches

Do take care when swimming at South India's beaches: there can be strong undertows.

Palolem, Goa (p154)
Hole up in a palm-thatched seafront hut and watch your kids cavort at Palolem's beautiful beach, featuring Goa's safest waters.

Arambol, Goa (p146)
Popular with backpackers, long-stayers and families for wide-ranging accommodation, safe swimming, water sports and surfing.

Havelock Island, Andaman Islands (p417)
Splash about in the shallows at languid Havelock Island, where, for older kids, there's spectacular diving.

Gokarna, Karnataka (p207)
Low-key family fun on pristine golden sands at Kudle and Om Beaches.

Planning

Before You Go

➡ Look at climate charts: choose your dates to avoid the extremes of temperature that may put younger children at risk.

➡ Visit your doctor well in advance to discuss vaccinations, health advisories and other heath-related issues involving your children.

➡ For more tips on travel in India, and first-hand accounts of travels in the country, pick up Lonely Planet's *Travel with Children* and visit the Thorn Tree travel forum at lonelyplanet.com.

Eating

➡ You may have to work hard to find something to satisfy sensitive childhood palates, but if you're travelling in South India's more family-friendly regions, such as Goa, Kerala or the big cities (where there are plenty of familiar Continental dishes), you'll find it easier to feed your brood.

➡ Portable snacks such as bananas, samosas, *puri* (puffy dough pockets) and packaged biscuits are easily available.

➡ Adventurous eaters and vegetarian children will delight in paneer (unfermented cheese) dishes, simple dhals (mild lentil curries), creamy kormas, buttered naans (tandoori breads), *parathas* (flaky breads), pilaus (rice dishes) and Tibetan *momos* (steamed or fried dumplings).

➡ Few children, no matter how culinarily unadventurous, can resist the finger-food fun of a vast South Indian dosa (paper-thin savoury crêpe).

Accommodation

➡ India offers such an array of accommodation – from beach huts to heritage boutiques to five-star fantasies – that you're bound to find something to suit the whole family.

➡ Swish upmarket hotels are almost always child-friendly, but so are many upper midrange hotels, whose staff can usually rustle up extra mattresses. Some places won't mind cramming several children into a regular-sized double room along with their parents; there are often interconnecting rooms for families too.

➡ The very best five-stars come equipped with children's pools, games rooms, kids clubs and babysitting services. An occasional night with a warm bubble bath, room service, macaroni cheese and the Disney Channel will revive even the most disgruntled young traveller's spirits.

On the Road

➡ Travel in India, be it by taxi, local bus, train or air, can be arduous for the whole family. Concepts such as clean public toilets, changing rooms, safe playgrounds etc are rare in much of the country. Public transport is often extremely overcrowded. Plan fun, easy days to follow longer bus or train rides.

➡ Pack plenty of diversions. Tablet computers stocked with movies make invaluable travel companions, as do audiobooks and the good old-fashioned storybooks, cheap toys and games available widely across India.

➡ If you're hiring a car and driver (a sensible, flexible option) and you require safety capsules, child restraints or booster seats, you'll need to make this absolutely clear to the hiring company as early as possible. Don't expect to find these items readily available. And finally, never be afraid to tell your driver to slow down, stop checking their phone and drive responsibly.

Health

➡ The availability of decent health care varies widely in India.

➡ Talk to your doctor about where you will be travelling to get advice on vaccinations and what to include in your first-aid kit.

➡ Access to health care is significantly better in traveller-frequented parts of India, where it's almost always easy to track down a doctor at short notice. Most hotels can recommend reliable doctors.

➡ Prescriptions are quickly and cheaply filled over the counter at numerous pharmacies, which often congregate near hospitals.

➡ Diarrhoea can be very serious in young children. Seek medical help if persistent or accompanied by fever; rehydration is essential, so pack rehydration sachets or similar.

➡ Heat rash and skin complaints such as impetigo, insect bites and stings can be treated with a well-equipped first-aid kit.

➡ Keep kids away from stray animals and try to ensure they understand the dangers of rabies; rabies vaccinations are worth considering.

Regions at a Glance

South India is made up of a wonderfully diverse patchwork of states. The vernaculars are varied, the customs are distinctive, there's a variety of culinary choices and the topography is spectacularly manifold. A mind-shaking mix of state-of-the-art and timeless tradition, the south rewards you with an invigorating, all-out sensory assault, regardless of your chosen destination.

For travellers, South India's remarkable diversity is most often apparent in its extraordinary wealth of architecture, wildlife, landscapes, festivals, handicrafts, cuisine and performing arts. And then there's spirituality – the heart, indeed, of the entire nation – which faithfully beats all the way from the jagged peaks of the snowy Himalaya to the lush, steamy jungles of the southern plains.

Mumbai (Bombay)

Architecture
Cuisine
Nightlife

Colonial-Era Relics

The British left striking colonial-era architecture in Mumbai, highlighted by Unesco-listed Chhatrapati Shivaji Terminus, the High Court and the University of Mumbai.

Culture & Cuisines

Mumbai's collision of cultures makes it a haven for foodies. A kaleidoscope of flavour from all over India vies for taste-bud attention with cuisines imported from the world over. Yum.

Bollywood & Booze

As India's financial powerhouse and home to the world's most prolific film industry, Mumbai parties hard! The subcontinent's wildest bars, hottest clubs and exclusive Bollywood bashes showcase a tipsier, more liberal side.

p42

Maharashtra

Caves
Beaches
Wine

Rock-Carved Temples

The Unesco World Heritage Sites of Ajanta and Ellora house the most exquisite collection of cave paintings and rock sculptures dating back to India's golden ages – and are miraculous feats of architecture and engineering to boot.

Sun-Toasted Konkan Sands

Strung out along Maharashtra's Konkan Coast are some of the most secluded and beautiful beaches, custom-made for romantics, adventurers, loners and philosophers alike.

Nasik's Vineyards

Nasik, the *grand cru* of India's up-and-coming wine industry, proudly flaunts a few world-class drops in the many excellent (and gorgeous!) vineyards in the surrounding countryside.

p80

Goa

Beaches
Food
Architecture

Golden Goan Shores

Goa's stunning beachscapes are so beautiful that they're practically a cliché, but even the most hardcore travellers can't resist them. Many are backed by shady palm-tree groves.

Fresh Fiery Seafood

Goa has fresh, fresh seafood and a long tradition of preparing it in brilliant ways. Sometimes it's the random shack on the beach that does it best.

Old-World Portuguese Relics

Portuguese colonialism's most attractive legacy may be its pretty buildings. Mansions in Chandor, houses in Panaji, Old Goa's grand religious structures, and little homes and churches across the state are pure eye candy.

p117

Karnataka & Bengaluru

Temples
National Parks
Cuisine

Diverse Shrines

From the Hoysala beauties at Belur, Halebid and Somnathpur to the electric Virupaksha Temple in Hampi, Karnataka is strewn with fantastic temples that overwhelm you with their ambience and ritual finery.

Biosphere & Bengals

The Nilgiri Biosphere Reserve boasts some of the most pristine forests in India, and there's abundant wildlife to be sighted in national parks such as Bandipur and Nagarhole.

Masalas & Craft Brews

Start off with the delectable Udupi vegetarian thali, then move on to some fiery Mangalorean seafood, and finally wash it all down with fresh ale in beer-town Bengaluru (Bangalore).

p167

Telangana & Andhra Pradesh

Religious Sites
Food
Beaches

Soulful Sites

Hindus flock to the Venkateshwara Temple at Tirumala. There are ancient ruins of once flourishing Buddhist centres across the state, while Hyderabad has grand Islamic architecture.

Biryani Bonanza

Biryani is a local obsession, the taste of which will leave you salivating. Meanwhile, *hyderabadi haleem* (a thick meat, lentil and wheat stew) has been patented so that it can't be served unless it meets strict quality standards.

Beaching with Locals

Visakhapatnam has a sweeping stretch of sandy coastline. Tourism is geared towards the domestic market, bringing a unique and festive atmosphere.

p225

Kerala

Backwaters
Food
Wildlife

Tranquil Inland Waterways

Kerala's backwaters are vast lakes and long canals that spread inland like tendrils. One of India's most relaxing and beautiful experiences is to stay overnight on a houseboat or take a canoe trip.

Coconut-Laced Spice Bounty

Delicious, delicate cuisine flavoured with coconut and myriad spices – Kerala's table is born of a melting pot of influences and remarkable geography that has earned it the nickname 'Land of Spices'.

Jungle Safaris

Kerala has a concentration of national parks inland where, amid lush mountainous landscapes, you can spot wild elephants, tigers, lions, numerous birds and other wildlife.

p255

Tamil Nadu & Chennai

Temples
Hill Stations
Heritage Hotels

Towers & Pavilions

The astounding architecture, rituals and festivals of Tamil Nadu's Hindu temples draw pilgrims from around the country.

Colonial-Era Hilltop Refuges

The hill stations of the Western Ghats offer cool weather, the chance to hike to gorgeous mountain vistas, bustling festival seasons, and cosy colonial-era guesthouses.

Dignified Digs

Restored spots to lay your head include romantic heritage houses in Puducherry's (Pondicherry's) French Quarter, palace hotels in the hill stations and Chettiar mansions in the south.

p324

Andaman Islands

Diving & Snorkelling
Beaches
Tribal Groups

Corals & Clear Waters

Apart from terrific snorkelling possibilities, this prime diving destination offers easy ocean dips for first-timers as well as more challenging drift dives for veterans.

White Sands

This is a superb place to sink your toes in soft white sand and splash in warm aquamarine waters.

Timeless Societies

The Andamans are home to an extraordinary mix of tribal groups with some still literally living in the Stone Age. Most reside on outlying islands, which tourists are prohibited from visiting, but elsewhere you'll encounter a vibrant array of South and Southeast Asian settlers.

p408

On the Road

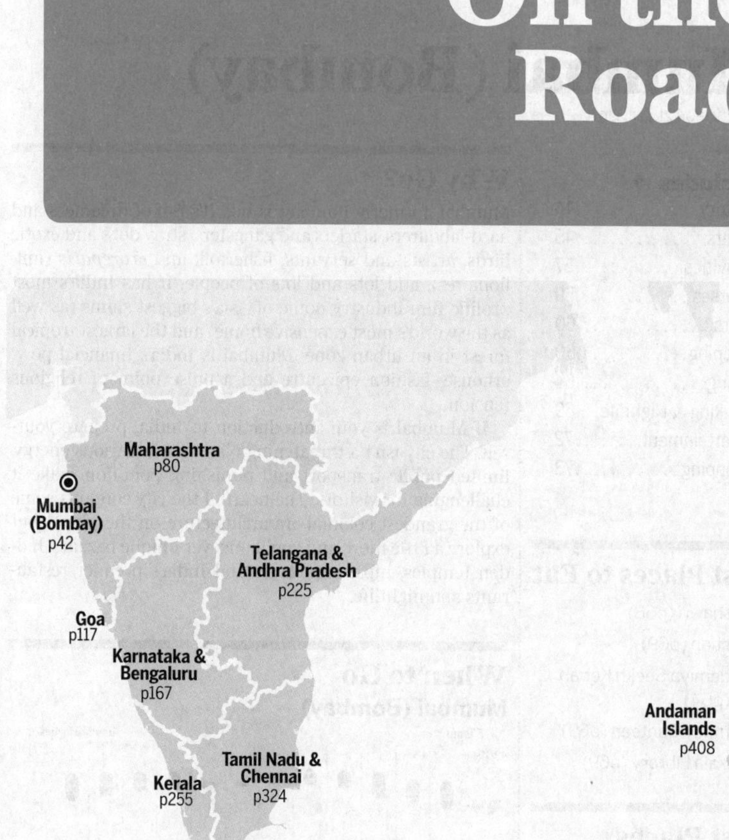

Maharashtra
p80

Mumbai
(Bombay)
p42

Goa
p117

Karnataka &
Bengaluru
p167

Telangana &
Andhra Pradesh
p225

Kerala
p255

Tamil Nadu &
Chennai
p324

Andaman
Islands
p408

Mumbai (Bombay)

022 / POP 21.1 MILLION

Best Places to Eat

➡ Peshawri (p68)

➡ Bastian (p69)

➡ Bademiya Seekh Kebab Stall (p64)

➡ Bombay Canteen (p69)

➡ Masala Library (p69)

Best Places to Sleep

➡ Taj Mahal Palace, Mumbai (p62)

➡ Abode Bombay (p62)

➡ Residency Hotel (p62)

➡ Sea Shore Hotel (p60)

➡ Juhu Residency (p63)

Why Go?

Mumbai, formerly Bombay, is big. It's full of dreamers and hard-labourers, starlets and gangsters, stray dogs and exotic birds, artists and servants, fisherfolk and *crorepatis* (millionaires), and lots and lots of people. It has India's most prolific film industry, some of Asia's biggest slums (as well as the world's most expensive home) and the largest tropical forest in an urban zone. Mumbai is India's financial powerhouse, fashion epicentre and a pulse point of religious tension.

If Mumbai is your introduction to India, prepare yourself. The city isn't a threatening place but its furious energy, limited public transport and punishing pollution make it challenging for visitors. The heart of the city contains some of the grandest colonial-era architecture on the planet but explore a little more and you'll uncover unique bazaars, hidden temples, hipster enclaves and India's premier restaurants and nightlife.

When to Go
Mumbai (Bombay)

Dec & Jan The very best, least sticky weather.

Aug & Sep Mumbai goes Ganesh-crazy during its most exciting festival, Ganesh Chaturthi.

Oct–Apr There's very little rain, post-monsoon; the best time of year for festivals.

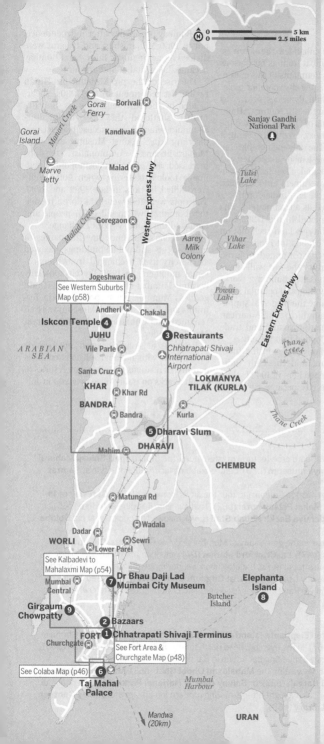

Mumbai (Bombay) Highlights

1 Chhatrapati Shivaji Terminus (p47) Marvelling at Mumbai's colonial-era architecture, including this monumental train station.

2 Bazaars (p74) Investigating the labyrinthine lanes and stalls in the ancient bazaar district.

3 Restaurants (p68) Dining like a maharaja at one of India's best restaurants, such as Peshawri.

4 Iskcon Temple (p56) Feeling the love with the Krishna crowd at this unique temple.

5 Dharavi Slum (p52) Taking a tour through of Asia's largest shantytown.

6 Taj Mahal Palace, Mumbai (p62) Sleeping at one of the world's most iconic hotels, or having a drink at its bar, Mumbai's first.

7 Dr Bhau Daji Lad Mumbai City Museum (p52) Ogling this museum's gorgeous Renaissance revival interiors.

8 Elephanta Island (p57) Beholding the commanding triple-headed Shiva on this island.

9 Girgaum Chowpatty (p53) Catching the sea breeze among playing kids, big balloons and a hot-pink sunset.

History

Koli fisherfolk have inhabited the seven islands that form Mumbai from as far back as the 2nd century BC. Remnants of this culture remain huddled along the city shoreline today. A succession of Hindu dynasties held sway over the islands from the 6th century AD until the Muslim Sultans of Gujarat annexed the area in the 14th century, eventually ceding it to Portugal in 1534. The only memorable contribution the Portuguese made to the area was christening it Bom Bahai. They handed control to the English government in 1665, which leased the islands to the East India Company.

Bombay flourished as a trading port. The city's fort was completed in the 1720s, and a century later ambitious land reclamation projects joined the islands into today's single landmass. The city continued to grow, and in the 19th century the fort walls were dismantled and massive building works transformed the city in grand colonial style. When Bombay became the principal supplier of cotton to Britain during the American Civil War, the population soared and trade boomed as money flooded into the city.

Bombay was a major player in the Independence movement, and the Quit India campaign was launched here in 1942 by Mahatma Gandhi. The city became capital of the Bombay presidency after Independence, but in 1960 Maharashtra and Gujarat were divided along linguistic lines – and Bombay became the capital of Maharashtra.

The rise of the pro-Marathi, pro-Hindu regionalist movement in the 1980s, spearheaded by the Shiv Sena (literally 'Shivaji's Army'), shattered the city's multicultural mould when it was accused of actively discriminating against Muslims and non-Maharashtrians. Communalist tensions increased, and the city's cosmopolitan self-image took a battering when 900 people were killed in riots in late 1992 and 1993. The riots were followed by a dozen retaliatory bombings which killed 257 people and damaged the Bombay Stock Exchange.

Shiv Sena's influence saw the names of many streets and public buildings – as well as the city itself – changed from their colonial monikers. In 1996 the city officially became Mumbai (derived from the Hindu goddess Mumba). The airport, Victoria Terminus and Prince of Wales Museum were all renamed after Chhatrapati Shivaji, the great Maratha leader.

Religious tensions deepened and became intertwined with national religious conflicts and India's relations with Pakistan. A series of bomb attacks on trains killed over 200 in July

MUMBAI IN ...

Two Days

Begin at one of Mumbai's architectural masterpieces, the **Chhatrapati Shivaji Maharaj Vastu Sangrahalaya museum** (p50), before grabbing lunch Gujarati-style at **Samrat** (p66).

In the afternoon head to Colaba and tour the city's iconic sights, the **Gateway of India** (p46) and **Taj Mahal Palace hotel** (p62). That evening, fine dine at **Indigo** (p65) or chow down at **Bademiya Seekh Kebab Stall** (p64), followed by cocktails at hip **Colaba Social** (p69).

The next day, take in the grandaddy of Mumbai's colonial-era giants, **Chhatrapati Shivaji Terminus** (p47); and **Crawford Market** (p74) and its maze of bazaars, hidden temples and unique street life. Kill the afternoon wandering the tiny lanes of **Khotachiwadi** (p57), followed by beach *bhelpuri* at **Girgaum Chowpatty** (p53). Need a drink? Hip nightlife hub Lower Parel beckons for dinner and craft beers at **White Owl** (p70) or **Woodside Inn** (p70).

Four Days

Sail to Unesco-listed **Elephanta Island** (p57), returning for lunch in artsy Kala Ghoda at **Burma Burma** (p67). In the evening, head north for exquisite seafood at **Bastian** (p69), followed by seriously happening bar action in Bandra.

Spend your last day visiting the **Mahalaxmi Dhobi Ghat** (p53), **Mahalaxmi Temple** (p53) and **Haji Ali Dargah** (p53); or **Sanjay Gandhi National Park** (p51) for a peaceful walk in the woods. Call it a night after exploring modern Indian fare at **Bombay Canteen** (p69) or **Masala Library** (p69).

TOP FESTIVALS IN MUMBAI

Mumbai Sanskruti (www.asiaticsociety.org.in; ☉ Jan) This free, two-day celebration of Hindustani classical music is held on the steps of the gorgeous Asiatic Society Library in the Fort area.

Kala Ghoda Festival (www.kalaghodaassociation.com; ☉ Feb) Getting bigger and more sophisticated each year, this two-week-long art fest held in Kala Ghoda and the Fort area sees tons of performances and exhibitions.

Elephanta Festival (www.maharashtratourism.gov.in; ☉ Feb/Mar) This classical music and dance festival takes place on the waterfront Apollo Bunder at the Gateway of India.

Nariyal Poornima (☉ Aug) This Koli celebration in Colaba marks the start of the fishing season and the retreat of monsoon winds.

Ganesh Chaturthi (www.ganeshchaturthi.com; ☉ Aug/Sep) Mumbai gets totally swept up by this 10- to 12-day celebration of the Hindu god Ganesh. On the festival's first, third, fifth, seventh and 11th days, families and communities take their Ganesh statues to the seashore at Chowpatty and Juhu beaches and auspiciously submerge them.

Mumbai Film Festival (MFF; www.mumbaifilmfestival.com; ☉ Oct) New films from the subcontinent and beyond are screened at the weeklong MFF at cinemas across Mumbai.

2006. Then, in November 2008, a coordinated series of devastating attacks (by Pakistani gunmen) targeted landmark buildings across the city, as the Taj Mahal Palace hotel burned, passengers were gunned down inside the Chhatrapati Shivaji railway station and 10 killed inside the Leopold Cafe backpacker haunt.

In late 2012, when the Sena's charismatic founder Bal Thackeray died (500,000 attended his funeral), the Shiv Sena mission begin to falter, and in the 2014 assembly elections, President Modi's BJP became the largest party in Mumbai.

Mumbaikars are a resilient bunch. Increased security is very much part of everyday life today and the city's status as the engine room of the Indian economy remains unchallenged. However, Mumbai politicians certainly have their work cut out, with the megacity's feeble public transport, gridlocked streets, pollution and housing crisis all in desperate need of attention.

☉ Sights

Mumbai is an island connected by bridges to the mainland. The city's commercial and cultural centre is at the southern, claw-shaped end of the island known as South Mumbai. The southernmost peninsula is Colaba, traditionally the travellers' nerve centre, with many of the major attractions.

Directly north of Colaba is the busy commercial area known as Fort, where the British fort once stood. This part of the city is bordered on the west by a series of interconnected grassy areas known as maidans (pronounced may-*dahns*).

Continuing north you enter 'the suburbs', which contain the airport and many of Mumbai's best restaurants, shops and nightspots. The upmarket districts of Bandra, Juhu and Lower Parel are key areas (the bohemians and hippies that used to claim Bandra have now moved further north to Andheri West and Vesova).

☉ Colaba

Along the city's southernmost peninsula, Colaba is a bustling district packed with elegant art deco and colonial-era mansions, budget-to-midrange lodgings, bars and restaurants, street stalls and a fisherman's quarter. Colaba Causeway (Shahid Bhagat Singh Marg) dissects the district.

If you're here in August, look out for the Koli festival Nariyal Poornima, which is big in Colaba.

★ **Taj Mahal Palace, Mumbai**   LANDMARK
(Map p46; https://taj.tajhotels.com; Apollo Bunder) Mumbai's most famous landmark, this stunning hotel is a fairy-tale blend of Islamic and Renaissance styles, and India's second-most photographed monument. It was built in 1903 by the Parsi industrialist JN Tata, supposedly after he was refused entry to nearby European hotels on account of being 'a native'. Dozens were killed inside the hotel when it was targeted during the 2008 terrorist attacks, and images of its burning facade were

Colaba

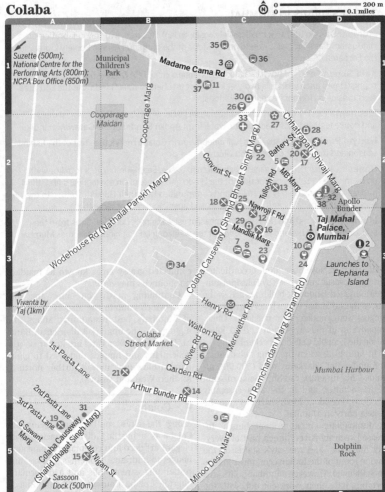

beamed worldwide. The fully restored hotel reopened on Independence Day 2010.

Much more than an iconic building, the Taj's history is intrinsically linked with the nation: it was the first hotel in India to employ women, the first to have electricity (and fans), and it also housed freedom-fighters (for no charge) during the struggle for independence.

Today the Taj fronts the harbour and Gateway of India, but it was originally designed to face the city (the entrance has been changed).

Gateway of India   MONUMENT

(Map p46) This bold basalt arch of colonial triumph faces out to Mumbai Harbour from the tip of Apollo Bunder. Incorporating Islamic styles of 16th-century Gujarat, it was built to commemorate the 1911 royal visit of King George V, but wasn't completed until 1924. Ironically, the British builders of the gateway used it just 24 years later to parade the last British regiment as India marched towards independence.

These days, the gateway is a favourite gathering spot for locals and a top place for people-watching. Giant-balloon sellers, photographers, vendors making *bhelpuri* (puffed rice tossed with fried rounds of dough, lentils, onions, herbs and chutneys) and touts rub shoulders with locals and

Colaba

tourists, creating all the hubbub of a bazaar. In February/March they are joined by classical dancers and musicians who perform during the Elephanta Festival (p45).

Boats depart from the gateway's wharves for Elephanta Island.

Sassoon Dock   WATERFRONT
Sassoon Dock is a scene of intense and pungent activity at dawn (around 5am) when colourfully clad Koli fisherfolk sort the catch unloaded from fishing boats at the quay. The fish drying in the sun are *bombil,* used in the dish Bombay duck. Photography at the dock is prohibited.

◎ Fort Area & Churchgate

Lined up in a row and vying for your attention with aristocratic pomp, many of Mumbai's majestic Victorian buildings pose on the edge of **Oval Maidan**. This land, and the **Cross** and **Azad Maidans** immediately to the north, was on the oceanfront in those days, and this series of grandiose structures faced west directly to the Arabian Sea.

Kala Ghoda, or 'Black Horse', is a hip, atmospheric sub-neighbourhood of Fort just north of Colaba. It contains many of Mumbai's museums, galleries and design boutiques alongside a wealth of colonial-era buildings and some of the city's best restaurants and cafes.

**★Chhatrapati
Shivaji Terminus**   HISTORIC BUILDING
(Victoria Terminus; Map p48) Imposing, exuberant and overflowing with people, this monumental train station is the city's most extravagant Gothic building and an aphorism for colonial-era India. It's a meringue of Victorian, Hindu and Islamic styles whipped into an imposing Daliesque structure of buttresses, domes, turrets, spires and stained glass.

Some of the architectural detail is incredible, with dog-faced gargoyles adorning the magnificent central tower and peacock-filled windows above the central courtyard. Designed by Frederick Stevens, it was completed in 1887, 34 years after the first train in India left this site.

Officially renamed Chhatrapati Shivaji Terminus (CST) in 1998, it's still better known locally as VT. Sadly, its interior is far less impressive, with ugly modern additions

48

Fort Area & Churchgate

MUMBAI (BOMBAY)

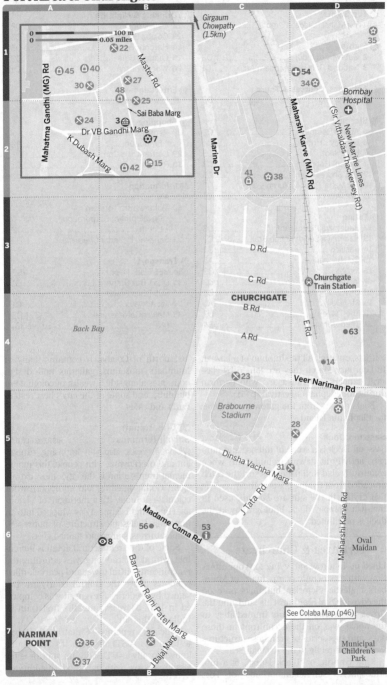

Girgaum Chowpatty (1.5km)

Bombay Hospital

New Marine Lines (Sir Vithaldas Thackersey Rd)

Marine Dr

Mahatma Gandhi (MG) Rd

Master Rd

Sai Baba Marg

Dr VB Gandhi Marg

K Dubash Marg

Maharshi Karve (MK) Rd

D Rd

C Rd

Churchgate Train Station

CHURCHGATE

B Rd

A Rd

E Rd

Veer Nariman Rd

Brabourne Stadium

Back Bay

Dinsha Vachha Marg

J Tata Rd

Madame Cama Rd

Barrister Rajni Patel Marg

Maharshi Karve Rd

Oval Maidan

NARIMAN POINT

J Bajaj Marg

Municipal Children's Park

See Colaba Map (p46)

0 — 100 m
0 — 0.05 miles

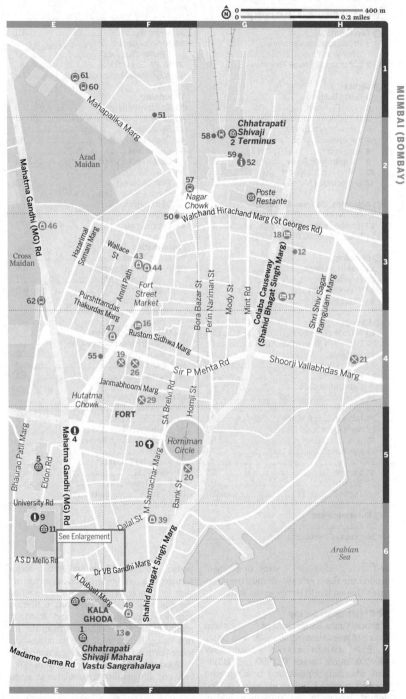

0 400 m
0 0.2 miles

Mahapalika Marg

61
60

51

58 Chhatrapati Shivaji 2 Terminus
59 52

Mahatma Gandhi (MG) Rd

Azad Maidan

57
Nagar Chowk

Poste Restante

46

50 Walchand Hirachand Marg (St Georges Rd)

Cross Maidan

18
12

Wallace St

43
44

Fort Street Market

Bora Bazar St
Perin Nariman St
Mody St
Mint Rd

Colaba Causeway (Shahid Bhagat Singh Marg)

17

Shri Shiv Sagar Ramgulam Marg

62

Purshttamdas Thakurdas Marg

47
16
Rustom Sidhwa Marg

55
19
26

Sir P Mehta Rd

Shoorji Vallabhdas Marg

21

Janmabhoomi Marg

29

SA Brelvi Rd
Homji St

Hutatma Chowk

FORT

4

10
Horniman Circle

Bhaurao Patil Marg

5
Eldon Rd

University Rd

9
11

See Enlargement

A S D Mello Rd

Dalal St
39

M Samachar Marg
Bank St

20

Shahid Bhagat Singh Marg

Arabian Sea

Dr VB Gandhi Marg

K Dubash Marg

6
KALA GHODA

49

Madame Cama Rd

1
13

Chhatrapati Shivaji Maharaj Vastu Sangrahalaya

Fort Area & Churchgate

and a neglected air – stray dogs roam around the ticket offices – despite the structure's Unesco World Heritage Site status.

★ **Chhatrapati Shivaji Maharaj Vastu Sangrahalaya**   MUSEUM
(Prince of Wales Museum; Map p48; www.csmvs. in; 159-161 Mahatma Gandhi Rd; Indian/foreigner ₹70/500, mobile/camera ₹50/100; ⊘10.15am-6pm) Mumbai's biggest and best museum displays a mix of India-wide exhibits. The domed behemoth, an intriguing hodge-

podge of Islamic, Hindu and British architecture, is a flamboyant Indo-Saracenic design by George Wittet (who also designed the Gateway of India). Its vast collection includes impressive Hindu and Buddhist sculpture, terracotta figurines from the Indus Valley, Indian miniature paintings and some particularly vicious-looking weaponry.

Good information is provided in English, and audioguides are available in seven languages. Five of the galleries are air-conditioned, offering a welcome relief from

SANJAY GHANDI NATIONAL PARK

Within 1½ hours of Mumbai's teeming metropolis is 104 sq km of protected tropical forest at Sanjay Gandhi National Park (☑ 022-28868686; https://sgnp.maharashtra.gov. in; Borivali; adult/child ₹44/23, vehicle ₹105, safari admission ₹50; ⊙7.30am-6pm Tue-Sun, last entry 4pm). Bright flora, birds, butterflies and leopards replace pollution and concrete, surrounded by forested hills on the city's northern edge. Urban development exists on the park's fringes, but the heart of the park is very peaceful.

The easiest way to take a walk in the woods is by going with Bombay Natural History Society (p57) – many of the park's highlights require advanced permission, which BNHS takes care of for you. You might see Shilonda waterfall, Vihar and Tulsi lakes or even the park's highest point, Jambol Mal. Kanheri Caves (Indian/foreigner ₹15/200; ⊙9am-5pm), a set of 109 dwellings and monastic structures for Buddhist monks 6km inside the park, is the most intriguing option. From the 1st century BC, the caves were developed over 1000 years as part of a sprawling monastic university complex. Avoid the zoo-like lion and tiger 'safari' as the animals are in cages and enclosures. October to April is the best time to see birds, and August to November to see butterflies. At time of research a huge restoration project – a new lakeside promenade, tourist huts, mangrove walkway, taxidermy gallery, nature trails and nature interpretation centres – had been approved.

An information centre with a small exhibition on the park's wildlife is inside the park's main northern entrance. The nearest station is Borivali, served by trains on the Western Railway line from Churchgate station (₹15 to ₹140, 30 minutes, frequent).

---

the summer heat. For a quick historical overview of Mumbai, the new 20-minute Mumbai Experience (Indian/foreigner ₹40/50) is shown in English five times per day. There's a fine cafeteria at the entrance and the museum shop is also excellent.

High Court
HISTORIC BUILDING
(Map p48; Eldon Rd; ⊙10.45am-2pm & 2.45-5pm Mon-Fri) A hive of daily activity, packed with judges, barristers and other cogs in the Indian justice system, the High Court is an elegant 1848 neo-Gothic building. The design was inspired by a German castle and was obviously intended to dispel any doubts about the authority of the justice dispensed inside.

Keneseth Eliyahoo Synagogue
SYNAGOGUE
(Map p48; Dr VB Gandhi Marg, Kala Ghoda; camera/video ₹100/500; ⊙11am-5pm Sun-Thu) Built in 1884, this unmistakable sky-blue synagogue still functions and is tenderly maintained by the city's dwindling Jewish community. It's protected by very heavy security, but the caretaker is welcoming (and will point out a photo of Madonna, who dropped by in 2008). Bring a copy of your passport.

Marine Drive
WATERFRONT
(Map p48; Netaji Subhashchandra Bose Rd) Built on reclaimed land in 1920, Marine Dr arcs along the shore of the Arabian Sea from Nariman Point past Girgaum Chowpatty and continues to the foot of Malabar Hill. Lined

with flaking art deco apartments, it's one of Mumbai's most popular promenades and sunset-watching spots. Its twinkling nighttime lights have earned it the nickname 'the Queen's Necklace'.

University of Mumbai
HISTORIC BUILDING
(Bombay University; Map p48; Bhaurao Patil Marg) Looking like a 15th-century French-Gothic mansion plopped incongruously among Mumbai's palm trees, this structure was designed by Gilbert Scott of London's St Pancras train station fame. There's an exquisite University Library and Convocation Hall, as well as the 84m-high Rajabai Clock Tower (Map p48), decorated with detailed carvings. Since the 2008 terror attacks there's no public access to the grounds, but it's still well worth admiring from the street.

Jehangir Art Gallery
GALLERY
(Map p48; www.jehangirartgallery.com; 161B Mahatma Gandhi Rd, Kala Ghoda; ⊙11am-7pm) FREE Renovated in recent years, this excellent gallery hosts exhibitions of all types of visual arts by Mumbaikar, national and international artists.

National Gallery of Modern Art
MUSEUM
(NGMA; Map p46; www.ngmaindia.gov.in; Mahatma Gandhi Rd; Indian/foreigner ₹20/500; ⊙11am-6pm Tue-Sun) Well-curated shows of Indian and international artists in a bright and spacious five-floor exhibition space.

DAG Modern
GALLERY

(Map p48; www.dagmodern.com; 58 Dr VB Gandhi Marg, Kala Ghoda; ⊙11am-7pm Mon-Sat) **FREE** This gallery is spread over four floors of a beautifully restored cream-coloured colonial-era structure. With well-curated exhibitions it showcases important modern Indian art from its extensive collection.

St Thomas' Cathedral
CHURCH

(Map p48; Veer Nariman Rd; ⊙7am-6pm) This charming cathedral, begun in 1672 and finished in 1718, is the oldest British-era building standing in Mumbai and the city's first Anglican church: it was once the eastern gateway of the East India Company's fort (the 'Churchgate'). The cathedral is a marriage of Byzantine and colonial-era architecture, and its airy interior is full of grandiose colonial memorials.

◉ Kalbadevi to Mahalaxmi

★ Dr Bhau Daji Lad Mumbai City Museum
MUSEUM

(Map p54; www.bdlmuseum.org; Dr Babasaheb Ambedkar Rd; Indian/foreigner ₹10/100; ⊙10am-6pm Thu-Tue) This gorgeous museum, built in Renaissance revival style in 1872 as the Victoria & Albert Museum, contains 3500-plus objects centring on Mumbai's history – photography, maps, textiles, books, manuscripts,

---

DHARAVI SLUM

Mumbaikars were ambivalent about the stereotypes in 2008's *Slumdog Millionaire*, but slums are very much a part of – some would say the foundation of – Mumbai city life. An astonishing 60% of Mumbai's population lives in slums, and one of the city's largest slums is Dharavi, originally inhabited by fisherfolk when the area was still creeks, swamps and islands. It became attractive to migrant workers from South Mumbai and beyond when the swamp began to fill in due to natural and artificial causes. It now incorporates 2.2 sq km of land sandwiched between Mumbai's two major railway lines, and is home to perhaps as many as a million people.

While it may look a bit shambolic from the outside, the maze of dusty alleys and sewer-lined streets of this city-within-a-city is actually a collection of abutting settlements. Some parts of Dharavi have mixed populations, but in other parts inhabitants from different regions of India, and with different trades, have set up homes and tiny factories. Potters from Saurashtra (Gujarat) live in one area, Muslim tanners in another; embroidery workers from Uttar Pradesh work alongside metalsmiths; while other workers recycle plastics as women dry pappadams in the searing sun. Some of these thriving industries, as many as 20,000 in all, export their wares, and the annual turnover of business from Dharavi is thought to exceed US$700 million.

Up close, life in the slums is fascinating to witness. Residents pay rent, most houses have kitchens and electricity, and building materials range from flimsy corrugated-iron shacks to permanent multistorey concrete structures. Perhaps the biggest issue facing Dharavi residents is sanitation, as water supply is irregular – every household has a 200L drum for water storage. Very few dwellings have a private toilet or bathroom, so some neighbourhoods have constructed their own (to which every resident must contribute financially) while other residents are forced to use run-down public facilities.

Many families have been here for generations, and education achievements are higher than in many rural areas: around 15% of children complete a higher education and find white-collar jobs. Many choose to stay, though, in the neighbourhood they grew up in.

Slum tourism is a polarising subject, so you'll have to decide for yourself. If you opt to visit, the award-winning Reality Tours & Travel (p60) has an illuminating tour (from ₹850), and puts 80% of profits back into Dharavi social programs. They can also now arrange a meal with a local family for further insight.

Some tourists opt to visit on their own, which is OK as well – just don't take photos. Take the train from Churchgate station to Mahim, exit on the west side and cross the bridge into Dharavi.

To learn more about Mumbai's slums, check out Katherine Boo's 2012 book *Behind the Beautiful Forevers*, about life in Annawadi, a slum near the airport, and *Rediscovering Dharavi*, Kalpana Sharma's sensitive and engrossing history of Dharavi's people, culture and industry.

MUMBAI FOR CHILDREN

Kidzania (www.kidzania.in; 3rd fl, R City, LBS Marg, Ghatkopar West; child/adult Tue-Fri ₹950/500, Sat & Sun ₹1200/550; ⏱10am-9pm Tue-Sun) is Mumbai's latest attraction, an educational activity centre where kids can learn all about flying, fire-fighting and policing, and get stuck into lots of arts and crafts. It's on the outskirts on the city, 10km northeast of the Bandra Kurla Complex.

Little tykes with energy to burn will love the Gorai Island amusement parks, **Esselworld** (www.esselworld.in; adult/child ₹949/699; ⏱10.30am-6.30pm) and **Water Kingdom** (www.waterkingdom.in; adult/child ₹999/699; ⏱10am-7pm). Both have lots of rides, slides and shade. Combined tickets are adult/child ₹1299/899.

The free **Hanging Gardens**, in Malabar Hill, have animal topiaries, swings and coconut-wallahs. **Kamala Nehru Park**, across the street, has a two-storey 'boot house'. Bombay Natural History Society (p57) conducts nature trips for kids.

Bidriware, lacquerware, weaponry and exquisite pottery. The landmark building was renovated in 2008, with its Minton tile floors, gilded ceiling mouldings, ornate columns, chandeliers and staircases all gloriously restored.

Haji Ali Dargah   MOSQUE
(Map p54; www.hajialidargah.in; off V Desai Chowk) Floating like a sacred mirage off the coast, this Indo-Islamic shrine located on an offshore inlet is a striking sight. Built in the 19th century, it contains the tomb of the Muslim saint Pir Haji Ali Shah Bukhari. Legend has it that Haji Ali died while on a pilgrimage to Mecca and his casket miraculously floated back to this spot.

It's only possible to visit the shrine at low tide, via a long causeway (check tide times locally). Thousands of pilgrims, especially on Thursday and Friday (when there may be *qawwali;* devotional singing), cross it daily, many donating to beggars who line the way. Sadly, parts of the shrine are in a poor state, damaged by storms and the saline air, though a renovation plan exists. It's visited by people of all faiths.

Mahalaxmi Dhobi Ghat   GHAT
(Map p54; Dr E Moses Rd; ⏱4.30am-dusk) This 140-year-old dhobi ghat (place where clothes are washed) is Mumbai's biggest human-powered washing machine: every day hundreds of people beat the dirt out of thousands of kilograms of soiled Mumbai clothes and linen in 1026 open-air troughs. The best view is from the bridge across the railway tracks near Mahalaxmi train station.

Babu Amichand Panalal
Adishwarji Jain Temple   JAIN TEMPLE
(Walkeshwar Marg, Malabar Hill; ⏱5am-9pm) This temple is renowned among Jains for its beauty – given how beautiful Jain temples are, that's

saying a lot. Check out the paintings and especially the ecstatically colourful zodiac dome ceiling. It's a small, actively used temple; visitors should be sensitive and dress modestly.

Girgaum Chowpatty   BEACH
(Map p54) This city beach is a favourite evening spot for courting couples, families, political rallies and anyone out to enjoy what passes for fresh air. Evening *bhelpuri* at the throng of stalls at the beach's southern end is an essential part of the Mumbai experience. Forget about taking a dip: the water's toxic.

Mahalaxmi Temple   HINDU TEMPLE
(Map p54; off V Desai Chowk) It's only fitting that in money-mad Mumbai one of the busiest and most colourful temples is dedicated to Mahalaxmi, the goddess of wealth. Perched on a headland, it is the focus for Mumbai's Navratri (Festival of Nine Nights) celebrations in September/October.

Malabar Hill   AREA
(around BG Kher Marg) Mumbai's most exclusive neighbourhood, at the northern end of Back Bay, surprisingly contains one of Mumbai's most sacred oases. Concealed between apartment blocks is **Banganga Tank**, an enclave of serene temples, bathing pilgrims, meandering, traffic-free streets and picturesque old *dharamsalas* (pilgrims' rest houses). According to Hindu legend, Lord Ram created this tank by piercing the earth with his arrow.

For some of the best views of Chowpatty, about 600m east, and the graceful arc of Marine Dr, visit **Kamala Nehru Park**.

Mani Bhavan   MUSEUM
(Map p54; www.gandhi-manibhavan.org; 19 Laburnum Rd, Gamdevi; donations appreciated; ⏱9.30am-5.30pm) As poignant as it is tiny, this museum is in the building where

MUMBAI (BOMBAY)

Kalbadevi to Mahalaxmi

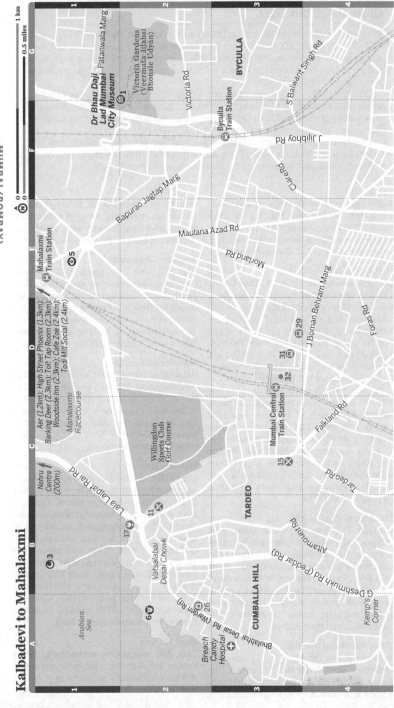

0 ─── 1 km
0 ─── 0.5 miles

Dr Bhau Daji Lad Mumbai City Museum 1

Patanwala Marg

Victoria Gardens (Veermata Jijabai Bhonsle Udyan)

Victoria Rd

BYCULLA

Byculla Train Station

S Balwant Singh Rd

J Jijibhoy Rd

Clare Rd

Bapurao Jagtap Marg

Maulana Azad Rd

Morland Rd

J Boman Behram Marg

Foras Rd

Mahalaxmi Train Station 5

Aer (1.2km); High Street Phoenix (1.3km); Barking Deer (2.3km); Toit Tap Room (2.3km); Woodside Inn (2.3km); Cafe Zoe (2.4km); Totfi Mill Social (2.4km)

Mahalaxmi Racecourse

29

31

32

Mumbai Central Train Station

Falkland Rd

Willingdon Sports Club Golf Course

Nehru Centre (200m)

Lala Lajpat Rai Rd

11

15

Tardeo Rd

TARDEO

17

Vatsalabai Desai Chowk

Altamount Rd

G Deshmukh Rd (Peddar Rd)

3

Arabian Sea

6

Bhulabhai Desai Rd (Warden Rd)

26

CUMBALLA HILL

Breach Candy Hospital

Kemp's Corner

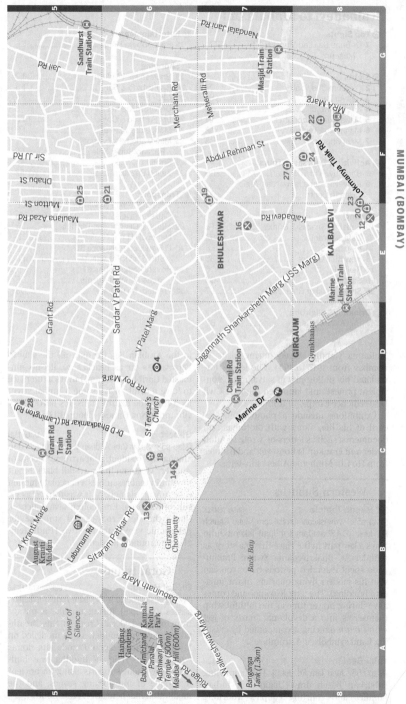

MUMBAI (BOMBAY)

Kalbadevi to Mahalaxmi

Mahatma Gandhi stayed during visits to Bombay from 1917 to 1934. The leader formulated his philosophy of satyagraha (nonviolent protest) and launched the 1932 Civil Disobedience campaign from here.

Exhibitions include a photographic record of his life, along with dioramas and documents, such as letters he wrote to Adolf Hitler and Franklin D Roosevelt and tributes from Ho Chi Minh and Albert Einstein.

◎ Western Suburbs

★Iskcon Temple   HINDU TEMPLE
(Map p58; www.iskconmumbai.com; Juhu Church Rd, Juhu; ⊙4.30am-1pm & 4-9pm) Iskcon Juhu plays a key part in the Hare Krishna story, as founder AC Bhaktivedanta Swami Prabhupada spent extended periods here (you can visit his modest living quarters in the adjacent building). The temple compound comes alive during prayer time as the faithful whip themselves into a devotional frenzy of joy, with *kirtan* dancing accompanied by crashing hand symbols and drumbeats.

Juhu Beach   BEACH
(Map p58; Juhu Tara Rd, Juhu) This sprawling suburban beach draws legions of Indian families and courting couples frolicking in the Arabian Sea for 6km all the way to Versova. As far as beaches go, it's no sun-toasted Caribbean dream, but it's a fun place to have a drink or try some Mumbai street food from the nearby stalls. It's particularly vibrant during Ganesh Chaturthi (p45).

Gilbert Hill   MOUNTAIN
(Map p58; Sagar City, Andheri West) Smack dab among the residential apartment blocks of Andheri West sits this 61m-tall black basalt mountain that resembles a chocolate molten cake (unsurprisingly, as it was formed as result of Mesozoic Era molten lava squeeze). Climb the steep rock-carved staircase for panoramic views and the two Hindu temples set around a garden.

◎ Gorai Island

Global Pagoda   BUDDHIST TEMPLE
(www.globalpagoda.org; ⊙9am-7pm, meditation classes 10am-6pm) Rising up like a mirage from polluted Gorai Creek is this breathtaking, golden 96m-high stupa modelled on Myanmar's Shwedagon Pagoda. Its dome, which houses relics of Buddha, was built entirely without supports using an ancient technique of interlocking stones, and the meditation hall beneath it seats 8000.

KHOTACHIWADI

The storied *wadi* (hamlet) of **Khotachiwadi** (Map p54), a heritage village nearly 180 years old, is clinging onto Mumbai life as it was before high-rises. A Christian enclave of elegant two-storey Portuguese-style wooden mansions, it's 500m northeast of Girgaum Chowpatty, lying amid Mumbai's predominantly Hindu and Muslim neighbourhoods. The winding lanes allow a wonderful glimpse into a quiet(ish) life away from noisier Mumbai.

It's not large, but you can spend a while wandering the alleyways and admiring the old homes and, around Christmas, their decorations. You can also plan an East Indian feast in advance at the home of celebrated fashion designer, Khotachiwadi activist and amateur chef James Ferreira (www.jamesferreira.co.in).

To find Khotachiwadi, head for St Teresa's Church, on the corner of Jagannath Shankarsheth Marg (JSS Marg) and Rajarammohan Roy Marg (RR Rd/Charni Rd), then head directly opposite the church on JSS Marg and duck down the third lane on your left (look for the Khotachiwadi wall stencil map that says 'Khotachiwadi Imaginaries').

There's a museum dedicated to the life of the Buddha and his teaching. Twenty-minute meditation classes are held daily; an on-site meditation centre also offers 10-day courses. To get here, take a train from Churchgate to Borivali (exit the station at the 'West' side), then take bus 294 (₹5) or an autorickshaw (₹40) to the ferry landing, where Esselworld ferries (return ₹50) depart every 30 minutes. The last ferry to the pagoda is at 5.30pm.

⊙ Elephant Island

★**Elephanta Island** HINDU TEMPLE
(Gharapuri; Indian/foreigner ₹30/500; ⊙caves 9am-5pm Tue-Sun) Northeast of the Gateway of India in Mumbai Harbour, the rock-cut temples on Gharapuri, better known as Elephanta Island, are a Unesco World Heritage Site. Created between AD 450 and 750, the labyrinth of cave temples represent some of India's most impressive temple carving.

The main Shiva-dedicated temple is an intriguing latticework of courtyards, halls, pillars and shrines; its magnum opus is a 6m-tall statue of Sadhashiva, depicting a three-faced Shiva as the destroyer, creator and preserver of the universe, his eyes closed in eternal contemplation.

It was the Portuguese who dubbed the island Elephanta because of a large stone elephant near the shore (this collapsed in 1814 and was moved by the British to Mumbai's Jijamata Udyan). There's a small museum on-site, with informative pictorial panels on the origin of the caves.

Pushy, expensive guides are available – but you don't really need one as Pramod Chandra's *A Guide to the Elephanta Caves,* widely for sale, is more than sufficient.

Launches (Map p46; economy/deluxe ₹145/180) head to Gharapuri from the Gateway of India every half-hour from 9am to 3.30pm. Buy tickets at the booths lining Apollo Bunder. The voyage takes about an hour.

The ferries dock at the end of a concrete pier, from where you can walk or take the miniature train (₹10) to the stairway (admission ₹10) leading up to the caves. It's lined with souvenir stalls and patrolled by pesky monkeys. Wear good shoes.

🏃 Activities

Mumbai has surprisingly good butterfly- and birdwatching opportunities. Sanjay Gandhi National Park (p51) is popular for woodland birds, while the mangroves of Godrej (13km east of Bandra) are rich in waders. The **Bombay Natural History Society** (BNHS; Map p48; ☑022-22821811; www.bnhs.org; Hornbill House, Shahid Bhagat Singh Marg; ⊙9am-5.30pm Mon-Fri) runs excellent trips every weekend. The mudflats viewable from the Sewri Jetty (p59) also receive thousands of migratory pink flamingos from November to March.

Outbound Adventure OUTDOORS
(☑9820195115; www.outboundadventure.com) Runs one-day rafting trips on the Ulhas River from July to early September (₹2300 per person). After a good rain, rapids can get up to Grade III+, though the rafting is calmer. Also organises guided nature walks, birdwatching, camping (from ₹2000 per person per day) and canoeing trips in the Western Ghats.

Yogacara YOGA, MASSAGE
(Map p58; ☑022-26511464; www.yogacara.in; 1st fl, SBI Bldg, 18A New Kant Wadi Rd, Bandra West; ⊙yoga per class/week ₹650/1600) Classic ha-

Western Suburbs

N
0 ____ 2 km
0 ____ 1 mile

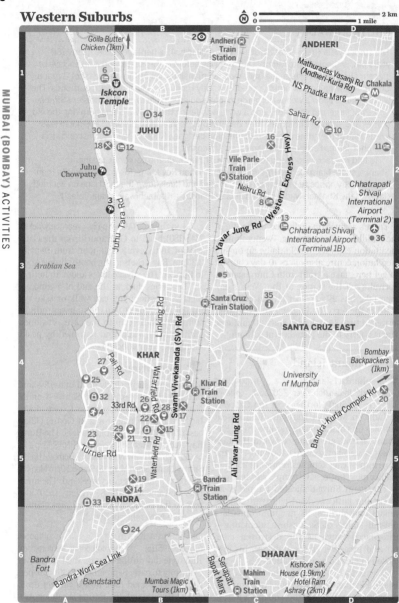

Goila Butter Chicken (1km)

Andheri Train Station

ANDHERI

Mathuradas Vasanji Rd (Andheri-Kurla Rd) Chakala

NS Phadke Marg

Sahar Rd

Iskcon Temple

JUHU

Vile Parle Train Station

Nehru Rd

Chhatrapati Shivaji International Airport (Terminal 2)

Juhu Chowpatty

Juhu Tara Rd

Chhatrapati Shivaji International Airport (Terminal 1B)

Arabian Sea

Ali Yavar Jung Rd (Western Express Hwy)

Linking Rd

Santa Cruz Train Station

SANTA CRUZ EAST

KHAR

Swami Vivekanada (SV) Rd

Waterfield Rd

Pali Rd

Khar Rd Train Station

University of Mumbai

Bombay Backpackers (1km)

Bandra-Kurla Complex Rd

33rd Rd

Turner Rd

Bandra Train Station

Ali Yavar Jung Rd

BANDRA

Bandra Fort

Bandra-Worli Sea Link

Bandstand

Mumbai Magic Tours (1km)

Senapati Bapat Marg

Mahim Train Station

DHARAVI

Kishore Silk House (1.9km); Hotel Ram Ashray (2km)

tha and iyengar yoga institute, with excellent massages (from ₹1850 per hour) and treatments; the Abhyangam rejuvenating massage is recommended. Ayurvedic cooking, meditation and Chakra healing classes are also offered sporadically.

Yoga House YOGA
(Map p58; ☏022-65545001; www.yogahouse.in; Nargis Villa/Water Bungalow Sherly Rajan Rd, Bandra West; class ₹700; ⊙8am-9.30pm Tue-Sun) A variety of yoga traditions are taught at this homey, traditional-style yoga centre. There's

Western Suburbs

also a charming cafe (p68) on the 3rd floor of the bright-green colonial-style bungalow.

Sewri Jetty   BIRDWATCHING
(Sewri) This jetty about 5km east of Lower Parel is an ideal place for gawking at thousands of migratory pink flamingos that come from as far away as Siberia between November and March. The birds descend on the surrounding mudflats to forage for sustenance. The best time to visit is between 6am and 10am.

Enquire at Bombay Natural History Society (p57) for trips here. Or come on your own by taking a taxi from Sewri station on the Harbour Railway line from CST.

Palms Spa   SPA
(Map p46; ☑ 022-66349898; www.thepalms spaindia.com; Dhanraj Mahal, Chhatrapati Shivaji Marg, Colaba; 1hr massage from ₹3200; ⏱10am-10pm) Indulge in a rub, scrub or tub at this renowned Colaba spa. The exfoliating lemongrass and green-tea scrub is ₹2500.

🎓 Courses

⭐ **Yoga Institute**   YOGA, HEALTH & WELLBEING
(Map p58; ☑ 022-26122185; www.theyogainsti tute.org; Shri Yogendra Marg, Prabhat Colony, Santa Cruz East; per 1st/2nd month ₹700/500) At its peaceful leafy campus, the respected Yoga Institute has daily classes as well as weekend and weeklong programs, and longer residential courses including teacher training (with the seven-day course a prerequisite).

⭐ **Bharatiya Vidya Bhavan**   LANGUAGE, MUSIC
(Map p54; ☑ 022-23631261; www.bhavans.info; 2nd fl, cnr KM Munshi Marg & Ramabai Rd, Girgaum; language per hr ₹500, music per month ₹900; ⏱4-8pm) Excellent private Hindi, Marathi, Gujarati and Sanskrit language classes. Contact Professor Ghosh (a Grammy Award–winning composer and musician) for lessons in tabla, vocals, sitar or classical dance.

Kaivalyadhama Ishwardas Yogic Health Centre   HEALTH & WELLBEING
(Map p54; ☑ 022-22818417; www.yogcenter.com; 43 Netaji Subhash Rd, Marine Dr; ⏱6am-7pm

Mon-Sat) Several daily yoga classes as well as workshops; fees include a ₹1000 monthly membership fee and a ₹700 admission fee. A four-month teaching certification course is ₹20,000.

☞ Tours

Fiona Fernandez' *Ten Heritage Walks of Mumbai* (₹395) has walking tours of the city, with fascinating historical background. The Government of India tourist office can provide a list of approved multilingual guides; official prices are ₹1368/1734 per half/full day for up to five people.

★ Reality Tours & Travel   TOURS
(Map p48; ☑9820822253; www.realitytours andtravel.com; 1/26 Unique Business Service Centre, Akber House, Nowroji Fardonji Rd; most tours ₹750-1700; ☺8am-9pm) 🍃 Compelling tours of the Dharavi slum, with 80% of post-tax profits going to the agency's own NGO, Reality Gives (www.realitygives.org). Street food, market, bicycle and Night Mumbai tours are also excellent.

New offerings further afield include socially responsible multiday tours of South India, the Golden Triangle and Rajasthan, including community visits.

Bombay Heritage Walks   WALKING
(☑9821887321, www.bombayheritagewalks.com; per 2hr tour (up to 5 people) from ₹3750) Started by two enthusiastic architects and operating with a slew of colleagues and art historians, BHW has terrific tours of heritage neighbourhoods.

Mumbai Magic Tours   TOURS
(☑9867707414; www.mumbaimagic.com; 5 Bhaskar Mansion, Sitladevi Temple Rd; 2hr tour per 2/4 people from ₹1750/1500; ☺10am-5pm Mon-Fri, to 2pm Sat) Designed by the authors of the fabulous blog Mumbai Magic (www. mumbai-magic.blogspot.com), these city tours focus on Mumbai's quirks, culture, community, food, bazaars, festivals, Jewish heritage and more.

MTDC/Nilambari Bus Tours   BUS
(MTDC; ☑020-22845678; www.maharashtratour ism.gov.in; 1hr tour lower/upper deck ₹60/180; ☺7pm & 8.15pm Sat & Sun) Nilambari in partnership with Maharashtra Tourism runs open-deck bus tours of illuminated heritage buildings on weekends. Buses depart from and can be booked at both the MTDC booth (p76) and the MTDC office (p76). Cash only.

🛏 Sleeping

Mumbai has the most expensive accommodation in India and you'll never quite feel like you're getting your money's worth.

Colaba is compact, has the liveliest tourist scene and many budget and midrange options. The neighbouring Fort area is convenient for the main train stations and is a dining and shopping epicentre. Most top-end places are along Marine Dr and in the western suburbs.

No matter where you stay, always book ahead.

🛏 Colaba

★ Sea Shore Hotel   GUESTHOUSE $
(Map p46; ☑022-22874237; 4th fl, 1-49 Kamal Mansion, Arthur Bunder Rd; s/d without bathroom ₹700/1100; 🖭) This place is really making an effort, with small but immaculately clean and inviting rooms, all with flat-screen TVs, set off a railway-carriage-style corridor. Half the rooms even have harbour views (the others don't have a window). The modish communal bathrooms are well scrubbed and have a little gleam and sparkle. Wi-fi in the reception and *some* rooms.

Bentley's Hotel   HOTEL $
(Map p46; ☑022-22841474; www.bentleyshotel. com; 17 Oliver Rd; r incl breakfast ₹2350-3150; ❄🖭) A welcoming Parsi-owned place in the heart of Colaba that travellers either love or hate depending on which of the five apartment buildings they end up in. First choice are the spacious, colonial-style rooms in the main building (snag 31 or 39 for generous balconies); avoid Henry Rd and JA Allana Marg. Air-conditioning is ₹350 extra. Cash only.

★ YWCA   GUESTHOUSE $$
(Map p46; ☑022-22025053; www.ywcaic.info; 18 Madame Cama Rd; s/d/tr with AC incl breakfast & dinner ₹2450/3720/5560; ❄@🖭) Efficiently managed, and within walking distance of all the sights in Colaba and Fort, the YMCA is a good deal and justifiably popular. The spacious, well-maintained rooms boast desks and wardrobes and multi-chanelled TVs (wi-fi is best from the lobby). Tariffs include a buffet breakfast, dinner and a daily newspaper. In addition to the room rates there's a one-time ₹50 membership fee.

Hotel Moti   GUESTHOUSE $$
(Map p46; ☑9920518228; hotelmotiinterna tional@yahoo.co.in; 10 Best Marg; d/tr with fan

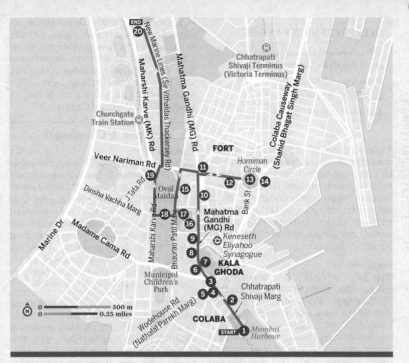

🏃 City Walk
Architectural Mumbai

START GATEWAY OF INDIA
END LIBERTY CINEMA
LENGTH 3.5KM; 1¼ HOURS

Mumbai's defining feature is its distinctive mix of colonial-era and art deco architecture. Starting from the ❶ **Gateway of India** (p46), walk up Chhatrapati Shivaji Marg past the art deco residential-commercial complex ❷ **Dhunraj Mahal**, towards ❸ **Regal Circle**. Walk the circle for views of the surrounding buildings – including the art deco ❹ **Regal Cinema** (p72) and the ❺ **Majestic Hotel**, now the Sahakari Bhandar cooperative store. Continue up Mahatma Gandhi (MG) Rd, past the beautifully restored facade of the ❻ **National Gallery of Modern Art** (p51). Opposite is the landmark ❼ **Chhatrapati Shivaji Maharaj Vastu Sangrahalaya** (p50), built in glorious Indo-Saracenic style. Back across the road is the 'Romanesque Transitional' ❽ **Elphinstone College** and the ❾ **David Sassoon Library & Reading Room**, where members escape the afternoon heat lazing on planters' chairs on the upper balcony.

Continue north to admire the vertical art deco stylings of the ❿ **New India Assurance Company Building**. On an island ahead lies ⓫ **Flora Fountain**, depicting the Roman goddess of flowers. Turn east down Veer Nariman Rd, walking towards ⓬ **St Thomas' Cathedral** (p52). Ahead lies the stately ⓭ **Horniman Circle**, an arcaded ring of buildings laid out in the 1860s around a beautifully kept botanical garden. It's overlooked from the east by the neoclassical ⓮ **Town Hall**, home to the Asiatic Society library. Backtrack to Flora Fountain, turning south onto Bhaurao Patil Marg to see the august ⓯ **High Court** (p51) and the ornate ⓰ **University of Mumbai** (p51). Unfortunately, the university's 84m-high ⓱ **Rajabai Clock Tower** (p51) is off-limits for visitors, but is best observed from within the ⓲ **Oval Maidan**. Turn around to compare the colonial edifices with the row of art deco beauties lining Maharshi Karve (MK) Rd – most notably the wedding cake tower of the ⓳ **Eros cinema** (p72).

Wrap things up by heading 1km north to the ⓴ **Liberty Cinema** (p72), a dazzling, 1200-capacity single-screen art deco gem.

₹3000/4000, with AC ₹3500/4500; 🅰🛜) A gracefully crumbling, colonial-era building on prime Colaba real estate, where owner Raj is a consummate host. Rooms are simply furnished (many have period charm, like ornate stucco ceilings), with LED satellite TVs and new, thicker-than-average mattresses, and are *just* adequately maintained. A rooftop garden is planned.

Regent Hotel
HOTEL $$

(Map p46; ☎022-22021518; www.regenthotel colaba.in; 8 Best Marg; r with AC incl breakfast from ₹5360; 🅰🖥🛜) A dependable choice where staff go the extra mile to help out guests. Located just off Colaba's main drag, it has big, well-furnished rooms with good-quality mattresses and modern marble-floored bathrooms. Falconry art and Gulf state flags hint at its most popular clientele.

⭐ Taj Mahal Palace, Mumbai
HERITAGE HOTEL $$$

(Map p46; ☎022-66653366; https://taj.tajhotels. com; Apollo Bunder; s/d tower from ₹16,000/17,500, palace from ₹21,000/22,500; 🅰🖥🛜🏊) The grande dame of Mumbai is one of the world's most iconic hotels and has hosted a roster of presidents and royalty. Sweeping arches, staircases and domes, and a glorious garden and pool ensure an unforgettable stay. Rooms in the adjacent tower lack the period details of the palace itself, but many have spectacular, full-frontal Gateway of India views.

With a myriad of excellent in-house eating and drinking options, plus spa and leisure facilities, it can be a wrench to leave the hotel premises. There's even a new (small but discernibly curated) art gallery. Heritage walks for guests at 5pm daily provide illuminating context about the hotel's role in the city's history.

⭐ Abode Bombay
BOUTIQUE HOTEL $$$

(Map p46; ☎8080234066; www.abodeboutique hotels.com; 1st fl, Lansdowne House, MB Marg; r with AC incl breakfast ₹4760-16,000; 🅰🛜) A terrific 20-room boutique hotel, stylishly designed

with colonial-style and art deco furniture, reclaimed teak flooring and original artwork; the luxury rooms have glorious free-standing bath tubs. Staff are very switched on to travellers' needs, and breakfast is excellent, with fresh juice and delicious local and international choices. A little tricky to find, it's located behind the Regal Cinema.

🛏 Fort Area & Churchgate

Traveller's Inn
HOTEL $

(Map p48; ☎022-22644685; www.hoteltravellers inn.co; 26 Adi Marzban Path; dm with/without AC incl breakfast ₹800/600, d without AC ₹1800, d with AC incl breakfast ₹2300; 🅰🖥🛜) On a quiet, tree-lined street, this small hotel is a very sound choice with clean, if tiny, rooms with cable TV and king-sized beds that represent good value. The two dorms are cramped (and the non-AC one Hades-hot in summer) but are a steal for Mumbai. The location's excellent, staff are helpful and there's free wi-fi.

Hotel Lawrence
GUESTHOUSE $

(Map p48; ☎022-22843618; 3rd fl, ITTS House, 33 Sai Baba Marg, Kala Ghoda; s/d/tr without bathroom ₹900/1000/1800) Run by kindly folk, this venerable place has been hosting shoestring travellers for years. Rooms are certainly basic but kept pretty tidy, as are the communal bathrooms. It boasts an excellent Kala Ghoda location, on a quiet little lane accessed by a ramshackle old lift. No breakfast or wi-fi.

⭐ Residency Hotel
HOTEL $$

(Map p48; ☎022-22625525; www.residency hotel.com; 26 Rustom Sidhwa Marg; s/d with AC incl breakfast from ₹4640/5120; 🅰🖥🛜) The Residency is the kind of dependable place where you can breathe a sigh of relief after a long journey and be certain you'll be looked after well. It's fine value too, with contemporary rooms, some boasting mood lighting, mini-bars, flat-screens and hip en suite bathrooms. Best of all, staff are friendly, polite and understand the nuance of unforced hospitality.

Its Fort location is also excellent. The best-run midranger in Mumbai.

Welcome Hotel
HOTEL $$

(Map p48; ☎022-66314488; www.welcome hotel.co.in; 257 Shahid Bhagat Singh Marg; s/d incl breakfast from ₹3330/3870, without bathroom from ₹1900/2080; 🅰🛜) Service is a little hit and miss and the hallways are dark but the simple rooms here are spacious and comfortable, and shared bathrooms are well kept. Top-floor executive rooms are more boutique than midrange.

Western & Northern Suburbs

Backpacker Panda   HOSTEL $

(Map p58; ☑022-28367141; www.backpacker panda.com; Shaheed Bhagat Singh Society, Andheri East; dm with AC ₹900-950; ❄️🛜) Mumbai's first vaguely hostel-like backpackers features a rather makeshift lobby (improvised palette-supported lounges, for example) but the six- and eight-bed dorms are cool, clean and climate-controlled (though cramped). There's a tiny kitchen and outdoor patio and it sits next to Chakala Metro (which connects with the main train line at Andheri), 10 minutes by taxi from both of Mumbai's airports.

Bombay Backpackers   HOSTEL $

(☑9096162246; 1 Uttam Jeevan, LBS Rd, Kurla West; dm ₹1000; ❄️🛜) In an oddly east (but lively) location at Mumbai's BKC business district, this artsy backpackers is another welcome newcomer to a previously nonexistent scene. Sturdy six- and eight-bed teak-like dorm beds in some cases come triple-stacked, and there's a colourful kitchen. It's just a few minutes' walk from Kurla Junction and a five-minute rickshaw ride to Bandra.

★Juhu Residency   BOUTIQUE HOTEL $$

(Map p58; ☑022-67834949; www.juhuresidency. com; 148B Juhu Tara Rd, Juhu; s/d with AC incl breakfast from ₹6250; ❄️@🛜) The aroma of sweet lemongrass greets you in the lobby at this excellent boutique hotel with an inviting atmosphere (and a fine location, five minutes' walk from Juhu beach). The chocolate-and-coffee colour scheme in the modish rooms works well, each room boasting marble floors, dark woods, artful bedspreads and flat-screen TVs. There are three restaurants – good ones – for just 18 rooms.

To top it all off, free airport pick-ups are included.

Iskcon   GUESTHOUSE $$

(Map p58; ☑022-26206860; www.iskconmum bai.com/guest-house; Juhu Church Rd, Juhu; r from ₹3000, with AC ₹4000; ❄️🛜) An intriguing place to stay inside Juhu's lively Iskcon complex. Though the hotel building is a slightly soulless concrete block, some rooms enjoy vistas over the Hare Krishna temple compound. Spartan decor is offset by the odd decorative flourish such as Gujarati *sankheda* (lacquered country wood) furniture, and staff are very welcoming.

Anand Hotel   HOTEL $$

(Map p58; ☑022-26203372; anandhote@yahoo. co.in; Gandhigram Rd, Juhu; s/d with AC from ₹2620/4170; ❄️🛜) Yes, the decor's in 50 shades of beige but the Anand's rooms are comfortable, spacious and represent decent value, considering the prime location on a quiet street next to Juhu beach. The excellent in-house Dakshinayan restaurant (p68) scores highly for authentic, inexpensive meals too. It's a particularly good deal for solo travellers.

Hotel Columbus   HOTEL $$

(Map p58; ☑022-42144343; www.hotelcolumbus.in; 344 Nanda Patkar Rd, Vile Parle East; s/d with AC incl breakfast from ₹4170/4700; ❄️@🛜) Rooms at the best midrange option in the domestic airport area aren't new – they're a little scuffed up – but are very homey. Staff are helpful and willing to solve issues. Just 900m away is the local's secret seafooder Gajelee (Map p58; ☑022-26166470; www.gajalee.com; Kadamgiri Complex, Hanuman Rd, Vile Parle East; mains ₹275-875; ⏱11.30am-3.30pm & 7-11.30pm).

★ITC Maratha   HOTEL $$$

(Map p58; ☑022-28303030; www.itchotels.in; Sahar Rd, Andheri East; s/d incl breakfast from ₹21,450/23,240; ❄️@🛜🖼) The five-star hotel with the most luxurious local character – from the Muhammed Ali Rd–inspired *jharokas* (lattice windows) around the atrium to the Maratha-influenced Resident's Bar (a guest-only level overlooking public areas), the details are extraordinary. The rooms, awash in lush colour schemes, exude Indian opulence. Peshawri (p68), Mumbai's most memorable Northwest Frontier restaurant, is located here.

★Taj Santacruz   BOUTIQUE HOTEL $$$

(Map p58; ☑022-62115211; https://taj.tajhotels. com/en-in/taj-santacruz-mumbai; Chhatrapati Shivaji International Airport (Domestic Terminal); s/d from ₹14,500/16,500; ❄️@🛜) Forget the 3500 hand-blown chandelier bulbs or the 75-species aquarium in the lobby of this recently opened hotel connected to the domestic airport terminal – at the lap-of-luxury Taj Santacruz it's all about the gorgeous Tree of Life art installation forged from 4000 pieces of broken glass (a Rajasthani technique) in the Tiqri bar and restaurant.

The standard rooms, decked out in soothing yellow, fuchsia and orange, are the city's largest at nearly 54 sq metres (some have direct runway views). If you cannot stay here, visit on a layover for a massage at Jiva Spa (from ₹4600) or a cocktail.

THE PARSIS

Mumbai is home to the world's largest surviving community of Parsis, people of the ancient Zoroastrian faith, who fled Iran in the 10th century to escape religious persecution by the new Muslim rulers of Persia. 'Parsi' literally means Perisan. Zoroastrians believe in a single deity, Ahura Mazda, who is worshipped at *agiaries* (fire temples) across Mumbai, which non-Parsis are forbidden to enter. Parsi funeral rites are unique: the dead are laid out on open-air platforms to be picked over by vultures. The most renowned of these, the Tower of Silence, is located below the Hanging Gardens in Malabar Hill, yet screened by trees and hidden from public view.

The Mumbai Parsi community is extremely influential and successful, with a 98.6% literacy rate (the highest in the city). Famous Parsis include the Tata family (India's foremost industrialists), author Rohinton Mistry and Freddie Mercury. The best way for travellers to dig into the culture is by visiting one of the city's Parsi cafes. These atmospheric time capsules of a bygone era are a dying breed, but several sail on, including the excellent Brittania restaurant, Kyaani and Co (Map p54; Ratan Heights, Dr DB Rd; snacks ₹15-120; ⊙7am-8.30pm Mon-Sat, to 6pm Sun) and tourist hotbed Cafe Mondegar.

Hotel Regal Enclave HOTEL $$$

(Map p58; ☎022-67261111; www.regalenclave.com; 4th Rd, Khar West; r with AC incl breakfast from ₹7740; ❋ 🖵) Hotel Regal Enclave enjoys a stellar location in an exceedingly leafy part of Khar, right near the station (some rooms have railway views) and close to all of Bandra's best eating, drinking and shopping. Rooms are spacious and comfortable – save the tight bathrooms – with pleasant if unoriginal decor. Rates include airport pick-up.

Hotel Suba International BOUTIQUE HOTEL $$$

(Map p58; ☎022-67076707; www.hotelsuba international.com; Sahar Rd, Andheri East; s/d with AC incl breakfast from ₹7600/8700; ❋ 🖵) A 72-room 'boutique business' hotel that's very close to the international airport (free transfers included) and boasts rooms with stylish touches, iPads and a wee bit of chipped paint.

🍴 Eating

Flavours from all over India collide with international trends and taste buds in Mumbai. Colaba has most of the cheap tourist haunts, while Fort and Churchgate are more upscale, a trend that continues in Mahalaxmi and the western suburbs, where you'll find Mumbai's most international and expensive restaurants.

Subscribe to Brown Paper Bag (http://brownpaperbag.in/mumbai) for daily news on the latest and hottest dining destinations.

🍴 Colaba

★Bademiya Seekh Kebab Stall MUGHLAI, FAST FOOD $

(Map p46; www.bademiya.com; Tulloch Rd; light meals ₹110-220; ⊙5pm-4am) These side-by-side, outrageously popular late-night street stalls (split between veg and nonveg) are in Bademiya's original location, where they remain a key Colaba hang-out for their trademark buzz and bustle and delicious meat-heavy menu. Expect spicy, fresh-grilled kebabs and tikka rolls hot off the grill. They also have sit-down restaurants in Colaba (Map p46; 19A Ram Mention, Nawroji Furdunji St; meals ₹150-290; ⊙1pm-2am) and Fort (Map p48; ☎022-22655657; Botawala Bldg, Horniman Circle; mains ₹190-410; ⊙11.30am-1.30am).

Olympia MUGHLAI $

(Map p46; Rahim Mansion, 1 Shahid Bhagat Singh Marg; meals ₹80-140; ⊙7am-11.45pm) This old-school Mughlai cheapie does a recommended *masala kheema* (spicy minced meat; ₹50) for breakfast – scoop it up with some roti. A simple place renowned for its pocket-friendly meat dishes; the *seekh* kebab (₹160) and chicken butter fry masala (₹90) are also great.

Theobroma CAFE $$

(Map p46; www.theobroma.in; 24 Cusrow Baug, Shahid Bhagat Singh Marg; confections ₹60-190, light meals ₹180-200; ⊙7am-11pm) Perfectly executed cakes, tarts and brownies go well with the coffee at this staple Mumbai patisserie. The pastries change regularly; if you're lucky, you'll find popular decadence like the chocolate opium pastry, but it's all great. For brunch have the *akoori* – Parsi-style scrambled eggs – with green mango. The Bandra branch (Map p58; 33rd Rd, near Linking Rd, Bandra West; confections ₹60-190; ⊙8am-midnight) is big and airy, though with a smaller menu.

★ Indigo FUSION, CONTINENTAL $$$
(Map p46; ☑022-66368980; www.foodindigo.com; 4 Mandlik Marg; mains ₹885-2185; ☉noon-3pm & 7-11.45pm; ☎) This incredibly classy Colaba institution is a colonial-era property converted into a temple of fine dining. It serves inventive, expensive European and Asian cuisine and offers a long wine list, sleek ambience and a gorgeous rooftop deck. Favourites include creamed pumpkin and sage ravioli and maple orange-glazed duck breast – if you can pass on mac and cheese lasagne, that is!

Reserve ahead.

Indigo Delicatessen CAFE $$$
(Map p46; www.indigodeli.com; Pheroze Bldg, Chhatrapati Shivaji Marg; sandwiches/mains from ₹625/645; ☉8.30am-midnight; ☎) A bustling and fashionable cafe-restaurant with cool tunes and massive wooden tables. The menu includes all-day breakfasts (₹399 to ₹725) and straightforward international classics like pork ribs, thin-crust pizza and inventive sandwiches. It's always busy so service can get stretched.

Table FUSION $$$
(Map p46; ☑022-22825000; www.thetable.in; Kalapesi Trust Bldg, Apollo Bunder Marg; small plates ₹405-1075, mains ₹825-1375; ☉noon-4pm & 7pm-1am, tea 4.30-6.30pm; ☎) San Francisco chef Alex Sanchez is all the rage in Colaba, where his market-fresh, globally inspired fusion menu changes daily and does everything in its power to satisfy your cravings for a curry-free evening out. There's a lot to love: a crunchy kale salad with Iranian dates and toasted pistachios, zucchini spaghetti with almonds and Parmesan and house-made black truffle taglierini.

Basilico MEDITERRANEAN $$$
(Map p46; ☑022-66345670; www.cafebasilico.com; Sentinel House, Arthur Bunder Rd; mains ₹320-950; ☉9am-12.30am; ☎) Euro-style Basilico does decadent sweets and especially creative fare when it comes to vegans and vegetarians. There are exquisite salads (from ₹320) like quinoa, organic avocado and papaya, and numerous other interesting options like veg Moroccan tagines. It draws a top-end Indian crowd. If you can walk past that crunchy chocolate cake without biting, you're better than us.

The Bandra **branch** (Map p58; St John Rd, Pali Naka, Bandra West; mains ₹320-950; ☉9am-midnight; ☎) has outdoor seating.

Self-Catering

Colaba Market MARKET $
(Map p46; Lala Nigam St; ☉7am-11pm) A colourful and atmospheric fresh fruit and vegetables street market.

Star Daily SUPERMARKET $
(Map p46; www.starbazaarindia.com; Sanghvi House, 3rd Pasta Lane, Colaba; ☉10am-9.30pm) This new Tata/Tesco initiative is easily Colaba's best supermarket for self-caterers. It's an air-con, Western-style affair with all your daily needs, including fresh produce.

✕ Fort Area & Churchgate

K Rustom SWEETS $
(Map p48; 87 Stadium House, Veer Nariman Rd, Churchgate; desserts ₹30-80; ☉9.30am-11pm Mon-Sat, 3-11pm Sun) K Rustom has nothing but a few metal freezers, but the ice-cream sandwiches (pick from 48 flavours) here have been pleasing Mumbaikar palettes since 1953.

STREET EATS

Mumbai's street cuisine is vaster than many Western culinary traditions. Stalls tend to get started in late afternoon, when chai complements much of the fried deliciousness; items are ₹10 to ₹80.

Most street food is vegetarian. Chowpatty Beach is a great place to try Mumbai's famous *bhelpuri* (puffed rice tossed with fried rounds of dough, lentils, onions, herbs and chutneys). Stalls offering samosas, *pav bhaji* (spiced vegetables and bread), *vada pav* (deep-fried spiced lentil-ball sandwich), *bhurji pav* (scrambled eggs and bread) and *dabeli* (a mixture of potatoes, spices, peanuts and pomegranate, also on bread) are spread through the city.

For a meaty meal, Mohammed Ali and Merchant Rds in Kalbadevi are famous for kebabs. In Colaba, Bademiya Seekh Kebab Stall is a late-night Mumbai rite of passage, renowned for its chicken tikka rolls.

The office workers' district on the north side of Kala Ghoda is another good hunting ground for street snacks.

Badshah Snacks & Drinks INDIAN $

(Map p54; 52/156 Umrigar Bldg, Lokmanya Tilak Marg; snacks & drinks ₹55-240; ⏱7am-12.30am) Opposite Crawford Market, Badshah has been serving snacks, fruit juices and its famous *falooda* (rose-flavoured drink made with milk, cream, nuts and vermicelli), *kulfi falooda* (with ice cream) and *kesar pista falooda* (with saffron and pistachios) to hungry bargain-hunters for more than 100 years.

★ La Folie CAFE $$

(Map p48; www.lafolie.in; 16 Commerce House, Kala Ghoda; cakes ₹260; ⏱noon-11pm) Chocoholics and cake fetishistas look no further – this minuscule Kala Ghoda place will seduce and hook you. Owner Sanjana Patel spent seven years in France studying the art (addiction?) of pastry- and chocolate-making, which was obviously time well spent. Try the delectable Madagascar cake (chocolate with raspberry mousse) or the Infinite Caramel (salted caramel and hazelnut) with a latte (₹150).

★ Samrat GUJARATI $$

(Map p48; www.prashantcaterers.com; Prem Ct, J Tata Rd; thali lunch/dinner ₹330/415; ⏱noon-11pm; ▣) Samrat has an à la carte menu but most rightly opt for the famous Gujarati thali – a cavalcade of taste and texture, sweetness and spice that includes four curries, three chutneys, curd, rotis and other bits and pieces. Samrat is air-conditioned and beer is available.

A Taste of Kerala KERALAN $$

(Map p48; Prospect Chambers Annex, Pitha St, Fort; mains ₹96-250, thali from ₹170; ⏱9am-midnight) An inexpensive Keralan eatery with lots of coconut and southern goodness on the menu; try one of the epic thalis (served on a banana leaf) or the seafood specials like prawn pepper masala. Don't skip the *payasam* (rice pudding with jaggery and coconut milk) for dessert. Staff are very welcoming, and there's an air-conditioned dining room.

Brittania PARSI $$

(Map p48; Wakefield House, Ballard Estate; mains ₹250-900; ⏱noon-4pm Mon-Sat) This Parsi institution is the domain of 95-year-old Boman Kohinoor, who will warm your heart with his stories (and he still takes the orders!). The signature dishes are the *dhansak* (meat with curried lentils and rice) and the berry *pulao* – spiced and boneless mutton or chicken, veg or egg, buried in basmati rice and tart barberries imported from Iran. Cash only.

Oye Kake NORTH INDIAN $$

(Map p48; 13C Cawasji Patel Rd; mains ₹209-289; ⏱11am-4pm & 7-11pm) An intimate all-veg Punjabi place where the daily thali (₹219) is wildly popular with local office workers and renowned for its authenticity. Signature dishes include the paneer tikka masala, *sarson da saag* (mustard leaf curry; seasonal from December to February) and *parathas* (flaky flatbread); lassis are excellent too. Prepare to wait for a table.

Pantry CAFE $$

(Map p48; www.thepantry.in; ground fl, Yashwanth Chambers, Military Square Lane, B Bharucha Marg, Kala Ghoda; breakfast/meals from ₹195/275; ⏱8.30am-11pm; 🛜) 🍴 Pantry is a bakery-cafe that offers a choice of fine pies and organic breads, soups and sandwiches (the gourmet cheese toastie is exceptional) plus delicious mains. Cold-brew coffee, too. Breakfasts are legendary: try the scrambled eggs with tomato, gruyère and local ham, or some organic-flour waffles with fruit. The elegantly restored historic building channels a Martha Stewart vibe.

Shree Thakkar Bhojnalaya INDIAN $$

(Map p54; 31 Dadisheth Agyari Lane, Marine Lines; thali ₹500; ⏱11.30am-3pm & 7-10.30pm Mon-Sat, 11.30am-3.30pm Sun) With a cult following and festive lavender tables to boot, this thali mainstay, one of the oldest in the city, puts on the full-court flavour press with their never-ending Gujarati/Rajasthani set meals, full of *farsans* (bite-size snacks) and scrumptious veg curries. The air-con environs are a welcome retreat from the busy congestion below. They've been at it since 1945.

Suzette FRENCH $$

(Map p48; www.suzette.in; Atlanta Bldg, Vinayak K Shah Marg, Nariman Point; meals ₹300-450; ⏱9am-11pm Mon-Sat; 🛜) 🍴 Relaxed Parisian-style place steeped where possible in organically sourced ingredients. Delectable crêpes, croques, salads, juices and soothing lounge music attract flocks of foreigners in need of a curry recess. On the crêpe front, sweet tooths should try the organic jaggery; for a savoury flavour, order a croque feta (with tomato, mozzarella, creamed spinach and feta).

The **Bandra branch** (Map p58; St John St, Pali Naka, Bandra West; mains ₹220-560; ⏱9am-11pm) 🍴 has outdoor seating and is open daily.

Kala Ghoda Café CAFE $$

(Map p48; www.kgcafe.in; 10 Ropewalk Lane, Kala Ghoda; mains ₹170-530; ⏱8.30am-11.45pm Mon-Fri, from 8am Sat & Sun; 🛜) 🍴 Once tiny, this

DABBA-WALLAHS

A small miracle of logistics, Mumbai's 5000 *dabba-wallahs* (literally 'food container person'; also called tiffin-wallahs) work tirelessly to deliver hot lunches to office workers throughout the city (and to the poor later on in the evenings, a 2015 initiative).

Lunch boxes are picked up each day from restaurants and homes and carried on heads, bicycles and trains to a centralised sorting station. A sophisticated system of numbers and colours (many wallahs don't read) identifies the destination of each lunch. More than 200,000 meals are delivered – always on time, come (monsoon) rain or (searing) shine.

This system has been used for over a century and there's only about one mistake per six million deliveries. (In a 2002 analysis, *Forbes Magazine* found that the *dabba-wallahs* had a six-sigma, or 99.999999%, reliability rating.) The system was also the subject of a Harvard Business School study in 2010.

Look for these master messengers mid-morning at Churchgate and CST stations.

boho cafe was expanded in 2016 with the addition of a vintage Mumbai backroom, and now turns away fewer of its artsy and creative fanbase. It serves organic coffee and tea, sandwiches, salads and breakfasts, and there's usually some interesting art or photography on the walls.

★ Burma Burma
BURMESE $$$

(Map p48; ☏022-40036600; www.burmaburma.in; Oak Lane, off Mahatma Gandhi Rd; meals ₹330-500; ⊘noon-2.45pm & 7-11pm; 🖘) A sleek, stylish restaurant that marries contemporary design with a few traditional artefacts (prayer wheels line one wall), providing a beautiful setting for the cuisine of Myanmar (Burma). The menu is well priced, intricate and ambitious, with inventive salads (the pickled tea leaf is extraordinary), curries and soups: *Oh No Khow Suey* is a glorious coconut-enriched noodle broth. No alcohol.

★ Khyber
MUGHLAI, INDIAN $$$

(Map p48; ☏022-40396666; www.khyberrestaurant.com; 145 Mahatma Gandhi Rd; mains ₹510-1100; ⊘12.30-4pm & 7.30-11.30pm) The much-acclaimed Khyber has a Northwest Frontier–themed design that incorporates murals depicting turbaned Mughal royalty, lots of exposed brickwork and oil lanterns – just the sort of place an Afghan warlord might feel at home. The meat-centric menu features gloriously tender kebabs, rich curries and lots of tandoori favourites roasted in the Khyber's famous red masala sauce.

Mahesh Lunch Home
SEAFOOD $$$

(Map p48; ☏022-22023965; www.maheshlunchhome.com; 8B Cowasji Patel St, Fort; mains ₹230-640; ⊘11.30am-4pm & 6-11pm) A great place to try Mangalorean or Chinese-style seafood in Mumbai. It's renowned for its ladyfish, pom-

fret, lobster, crab (try it with butter garlic pepper sauce) and anything else out of the sea.

There's also a bigger Juhu **branch** (Map p58; ☏022-66955554; Juhu Tara Rd; mains ₹350-975; ⊘12-3.30pm & 7pm-12.30am; 🖘) with an extended menu.

Trishna
SEAFOOD $$$

(Map p48; ☏022-22703214; www.trishna.co.in; Ropewalk Lane, Kala Ghoda; mains ₹400-1800; ⊘noon-3.30pm & 6.15pm-midnight Mon-Sat, noon-3.30pm & 7pm-midnight Sun) Behind a modest entrance on a quiet Kala Ghoda lane is this often-lauded, intimate South Indian seafood restaurant. It's not a trendy place – the decor is old school, the seating a little cramped and the menu perhaps too long – but the cooking is superb. Witness the Hyderabadi fish tikka, jumbo prawns with green pepper sauce and the outstanding crab dishes.

Mamagoto
ASIAN $$$

(Map p48; ☏022-61054586; www.mamagoto.in; 5 Surya Mahal, B Bharucha Marg, Kala Ghoda; mains ₹529-799; ⊘noon-11.30pm; 🖘) Mamagoto means 'play with food' in Japanese and this zany hot spot is certainly fun, with a relaxed vibe, cool tunes and kooky decor (think pop and propaganda art). The menu really delivers, with punchy Pan-Asian flavours: the authentic Malay-style Penang curry is terrific and the fiery Bangkok bowl packs a wallop of spice.

There's also a branch in **Bandra** (Map p58; ☏022-61054585; Gezebo House, 133 Hill Rd, Bandra West; mains ₹529-799; ⊘noon-11.30pm; 🖘).

Self-Catering

Nature's Basket
SUPERMARKET $

(Map p48; www.naturesbasket.co.in; 27 Khetan Bhavan, 198 Jamshedi Tata Rd, Churchgate; ⊘8am-10pm) An eco-leaning well-to-do supermarket chain with fresh produce, a deli counter, loads of international items as well as a sizeable organic section.

Kalbadevi to Mahalaxmi

Sardar   STREET FOOD $

(Map p54; 166A Tardeo Rd Junction, Tulsiwadi; pav bhaji from ₹125; ☺11am-2am) If you're spooked about Indian street food, try one of the city's most beloved street staples, *pav bhaji,* at this Mumbai institution. The curried veg mishmash is cooked to death on a series of scalding *tawas* (hotplates) and served with a butter floater the size of a Bollywood ego. Get in line; the entire restaurant turns over at once.

New Kulfi Centre   ICE CREAM $

(Map p54; 556 Marina Mansion, Sukh Sagar, Sardar V Patel Rd, Girgaon; kulfi per 100g ₹40-90; ☺9.30am-1am) Serves 36 flavours of the best *kulfi* (Indian firm-textured ice cream) you'll have anywhere. Killer flavours include pistachio, *malai* (cream) and mango.

Cafe Noorani   NORTH INDIAN $$

(Map p54; www.cafenoorani.com; Tardeo Rd, Haji Ali Circle; mains ₹140-450; ☺8am-11.30pm) Inexpensive, old-school eatery that's a requisite stop before or after visiting Haji Ali Dargah (p53). Mughlai and Punjabi staples dominate, with kebabs chargrilled to perfection and great biryanis; try the chicken tikka biryani (₹300).

Western Suburbs

North Mumbai is home to the city's trendiest dining, centred on Bandra West and Juhu.

Hotel Ram Ashraya   SOUTH INDIAN $

(Bhandarkar Rd, King's Circle, Matunga East; light meals ₹40-75; ☺5am-9.30pm) In the Tamil enclave of King's Circle, 80-year-old Ram Ashraya is beloved by southern families for its spectacular dosas, *idli* (spongy, round, fermented rice cake) and *uttapa* (pancake with toppings). Filter coffee is strong and flavoursome. The menu (no English) changes daily. It's just outside Matunga Rd train station's east exit.

★Dakshinayan   SOUTH INDIAN $$

(Map p58; Anand Hotel, Gandhigram Rd, Juhu; mains ₹130-250; ☺11am-11pm Mon-Sat, from 8am Sun) With *rangoli* on the walls, servers in lungis and sari-clad women lunching (*chappals* – sandals – off under the table), Dakshinayan channels Tamil Nadu. There are delicately textured dosas, *idli* and *uttapam*, village-fresh chutneys and perhaps the best *rasam* (toma-

to soup with spices and tamarind) in Mumbai. Finish off with a South Indian filter coffee, served in a stainless-steel set.

Kitchen Garden by Suzette   CAFE $$

(Map p58; www.suzette.in; 9 Gasper Enclave, St John St, Bandra West; light meals ₹190-550; ☺9am-11pm; ☎) ∥ From the same French trio that brought us Suzette comes this new, superb organic cafe, a haven of health and homesick-remedying salads, sandwiches, cold-press juices and coffee sourced from local cooperatives and organic farms around Maharashtra and worldwide. The burrata, made by an American-Indian Hare Krishna in Gujarat, is outstanding, but then again so is everything.

★Yoga House   CAFE $$

(Map p58; www.yogahouse.in; Nargis Villa/Water Bungalow Sherly Rajan Rd, Bandra West; light meals ₹140-390; ☺8am-9.30pm; ☎) This haven of pastel shades, scatter cushions and greenery in the bungalow of Yoga House (p58) is the perfect little retreat from Mumbai's mean streets. The menu is very creative and healthy – much of it vegan, raw and all of it wholesome. Signature items include its famous salads (₹215 to ₹370), 10-grain toasts (₹130), soups and gussied-up hash browns (with spinach, mozzarella and peppers).

Goila Butter Chicken   INDIAN $$

(☎8080809102; www.goilabutterchicken.com; 26 Sai Kanwal Complex, JP Rd, Andheri West; mains ₹275-335; ☺noon-3pm & 6pm-midnight) Don't miss this takeaway/delivery-only gourmet stand dedicated to celebrity chef Saransh Goila's take on one of India's most iconic dishes: butter chicken. Goila, who won Indian TV's *Food Food Maha Challenge,* gets the gravy just right – a perfect marriage of tang and spice – and whips it up various ways (traditional, with paneer, in biryani or rolls). Delivers to airport-area hotels.

Raaj Bhog   GUJARATI $$

(Map p58; 3rd Rd, Cosmos Commercial Center, Khar West; meals ₹180-300; ☺11am-3.30pm & 7-11pm) Modestly priced restaurants are not easy to find in this part of town, so this friendly Gujarati place by Khar train station is a welcome addition. The (unlimited) deluxe thali costs ₹330 and is filling and varied; hilarious staff will talk your ears off.

★Peshawri   NORTH INDIAN $$$

(Map p58; ☎022-28303030; www.itchotels.in; ITC Maratha, Sahar Rd, Andheri East; mains ₹1600-3000; ☺12.45-2.45pm & 7-11.45pm) Make this Northwest Frontier restaurant, outside the international airport, your first or last stop in Mumbai. It's a carbon-copy of Delhi's famous Bukhara (p89), with the same menu and decor. Folks flock here for the buttery *dhal bukhara* (a 24-hour simmered black dhal; ₹800), but its kebabs are sublime: try the *Murgh Malai* (tandoori-grilled chicken marinated in cream cheese, malt vinegar, green chilli and coriander).

Despite the five-star surrounds (and prices) you're encouraged to eat with your hands and the seating is low.

★Bastian   SEAFOOD $$$
(Map p58; www.facebook.com/BastianSeafood; B/1, New Kamal Bldg, Linking Rd, Bandra West; mains for 2 ₹700-2600; ⏰7pm-12.45am Tue-Sun; ☎) All the praise bestowed upon this trendy seafood restaurant is indisputably warranted. Chinese-Canadian chef Boo Kwang Kim and his culinary sidekick, American-Korean Kelvin Cheung, have forged an East-meets-West gastronomic dream. Go with the market-fresh side menu: choose your catch (prawns, fish, mud crab or lobster) then pick from an insanely difficult list of impossibly tasty Pan-Asian sauces.

Don't miss the stir-fried lotus root, either.

★Bombay Canteen   INDIAN $$$
(☎022-49666666; www.thebombaycanteen.com; Process House, Kamala Mills, SB Rd, Lower Parel; small plates ₹175-450, mains ₹300-975; ⏰noon-1am; ☎) Bombay Canteen is Mumbai's hottest restaurant, courtesy of former New York chef and Top Chef Masters winner Floyd Cardoz and executive chef Thomas Zacharias, who spent time at New York's three-Michelin-star Le Bernardin. India-wide regional dishes and traditional flavours dominate – Kejriwa toast, Goan pulled-pork vindaloo tacos, smoked mutton guijiya curry – each dish an explosion of texture and flavour.

Excellent cocktails (₹350 to ₹900) like Incredible India (vodka, basil, ginger, pineapple juice and orange juice) are perfect for jump-starting a night out in Lower Parel. Reservations are essential (7.30pm/8pm and 10pm/10.30pm seatings only). Don't miss the comment card – it's a riot.

★Masala Library   MODERN INDIAN $$$
(Map p58; ☎022-66424142; www.masalalibrary.co.in; ground fl, First International Financial Centre, G Block, Bandra East; mains ₹500-900, tasting menu ₹2300-2500, with wine ₹3800-4000; ⏰noon-2.15pm & 7-11pm) Daring and imaginative Masala Library dangles the contemporary Indian carrot to foodies and gastronauts,

challenging them to rethink their notions of subcontinent cuisine. The tasting menus are an exotic culinary journey – think pan-tossed mushrooms with black pepper, dill crust and truffle haze; kashmiri chilli duck, *jalebi* caviar and a betel-leaf candy floss to finish.

🍷 Drinking & Nightlife

🍸 Colaba

★Colaba Social   BAR
(Map p46; www.socialoffline.in; ground fl, Glen Rose Bldg, BK Boman Behram Marg, Apollo Bunder; ⏰9am-1.30am; ☎) Colaba is the best of the locations of the hip Social chain, which combines a restaurant/bar with a collaborative work space. The happening bar nails the cocktails (₹295 to ₹450) – the Acharroska is the perfect East-meets-West marriage of Indian pungency and Brazilian sweet. The food (mains ₹160 to ₹360) spans everything from fish and chips and *poutine* (French fries and cheese curds topped with gravy) to Punjabi and Mangalorean (with great Parsi dishes for breakfast).

There are also Social locations in Lower Parel – **Todi Mill** (242 Mathuradas Mill Compound; ⏰9am-1am; ☎) – and **Khar** (Map p58; Rohan Plaza, 5th Rd, Ram Krishna Nagar; mains ₹160-360; ⏰9am-1am; ☎).

★Harbour Bar   BAR
(Map p46; Taj Mahal Palace, Apollo Bunder; ⏰11am-11.45pm) With unmatched views of the Gateway of India and harbour, this timeless bar inside the Taj Mahal Palace is an essential visit. Drinks aren't uberexpensive (from ₹450/670/900 for a beer/wine/cocktail) given the surrounds and the fact that they come with very generous portions of nibbles (including jumbo cashews).

Woodside Inn   PUB
(Map p46; www.facebook.com/WoodsideInn; Indian Mercantile Mansion, Wodehouse Rd; ⏰11am-1am Mon-Fri, from 10am Sat & Sun; ☎) As close as you'll get to a London pub in Mumbai, this cosy place has a gregarious vibe and serves Gateway and Independence craft beers on draught (pints from ₹295). There's comfort food (mains ₹425 to ₹895) and a great two-for-one happy hour (4pm to 8pm daily).

Cafe Mondegar   PUB
(Map p46; Metro House, 5A Shahid Bhagat Singh Marg; ⏰7.30am-12.30am Sun-Wed, to 1am Thu-Sat) Iranian-founded 'Mondy's' has been drawing a heady mix of foreigners and locals since

DON'T MISS

CRAFT BREW BOMBAY

Few visitors to India would argue that an ice-cold Kingfisher in a dingy, smoke-filled bar isn't a quintessential Indian experience, but craft-beer connoisseurs might also add that India's ubiquitous native lager gets old pretty quick. And then there's those distinctly disgusting YouTube videos of oily, urine-coloured *something* being drained out from beer bottles before drinking (it's usually glycerine, widely used in Indian beers as a preservative). Cheers? Not really.

While certainly late to the craft-brew boozefest, Mumbai has finally embraced hop-heavy IPAs, roasty, chocolatey porters and refreshing saisons, thanks to the city's very own craft-beer wallah, American expat Greg Kroitzsh. Kroitzsh opened Mumbai's first microbrewery, **Barking Deer** (www.barkingdeer.in; Mathuradas Mill Compound, Senapati Bapat Marg, Lower Parel; ⏲ noon-1.30am; 🕾), in 2013, and the taps began flowing in Mumbai as they already had been for some time in craftier Indian cities like Pune, Bangalore and Gurgaon.

Fancy a pint? In Andheri West, **Independence Brewing Company** (www.independencebrewco.com; Boolani Estate Owners Premises Co-Op, New Link Rd, Andheri West; ⏲ 1pm-1.15am; 🕾) and **Brewbot** (www.brewbot.in; Morya Landmark 1, off New Link Rd, Andheri West; ⏲ 4pm-1am Mon-Fri, noon-1am Sat; 🕾) are worth the journey north, as is the excellent **Doolally Taproom** (Map p58; www.facebook.com/godoolallybandra; Shop 5/6, Geleki, ONGC Colony, Bandra West; ⏲ 7am-1am; 🕾) in Bandra. In Lower Parel are Barking Deer, **White Owl** (www.whiteowl.in; One Indiabulls Center, Tower 2 Lobby, Senapati Bapat Marg, Lower Parel; ⏲ noon-1am), **Toit Tap Room** (www.toit.in; Zeba Centre, Mathuradas Mill Compound, Senapati Bapat Marg, Lower Parel; ⏲ noon-1.30am) and, to get a sampling of nearly all of them, the new, 25-tap **Woodside Inn** (www.facebook.com/WoodsideInn; Mathuradas Mills Compound, NM Joshi Marg, Lower Parel; ⏲ 11am-1am Mon-Fri, from 10am Sat & Sun) – all are within walking distance of each other. It's only a matter of time before taps start flowing in Fort and Colaba as well. Ubiquitous draught-only craft beer includes Gateway Brewing Company and Bira 91 ('Bira' meaning 'Bro' in Punjabi, '91' for the country code!).

The city's signature brew has quickly become Belgian Wit – citrusy and refreshing, it's a perfect accompaniment for hot and humid Mumbai. *Jai ho!*

1871. It's first and foremost a rowdy bar serving ice-cold mugs of Kingfisher (₹220), but don't discount it for its wide range of American, English and Parsi breakfast choices (₹130 to ₹350).

Leopold Cafe BAR
(Map p46; www.leopoldcafe.com; cnr Colaba Causeway & Nawroji F Rd; ⏲ 7.30am-midnight) Love it or hate it, most tourists end up at this clichéd Mumbai travellers' institution at one time or another. Around since 1871, Leopold's has wobbly ceiling fans, crap service and a rambunctious atmosphere conducive to swapping tales with strangers. There's also food and a cheesy DJ upstairs on weekend nights.

🍷 Kalbadevi to Mahalaxmi

Haji Ali Juice Centre JUICE BAR
(Map p54; Lala Lajpat Rai Rd, Haji Ali Circle; ⏲ 5am-1.30am) Serves fresh juices and milkshakes (₹80 to ₹380), mighty fine *falooda* and fruit salads. Strategically placed at the entrance to Haji Ali mosque, it's a great place to cool

off after a visit. Try the Triveni, a gorgeous trifecta of mango, strawberry and kiwi (₹280).

🍷 Western Suburbs

★ One Street Over COCKTAIL BAR
(Map p58; Navarang Bldg, 35th Rd, off Linking Rd, Khar West; ⏲ 7pm-1am Tue-Sun; 🕾) With an emphasis on Prohibition-era craft mixology, this shotgun-style cocktail bar (cocktails ₹500 to ₹850), housed where high-class orgies once went down, is currently Khar's drinkery of desire. DJs spin hip-hop to a beautiful and trendy crowd, who are content to gaggle away at the long and sociable central share table over drinks and internationally inspired tapas.

★ Aer LOUNGE
(www.fourseasons.com/mumbai; Four Seasons Hotel, 34th fl, 114 Dr E Moses Rd, Worli; ⏲ 5.30pm-midnight; 🕾) Boasting astounding sea, sunset and city views, Aer is Mumbai's premier sky bar. Drink prices are steep (cocktails ₹1000 to ₹1500),

but that's kind of the point. DJs spin house and lounge tunes nightly, including over groovy happy hour sundowner specials, concocted by some of Mumbai's best mixologists.

Monkey Bar BAR

(Map p58; Summerville, cnr 14th & 33rd Rd, Linking Rd, Bandra West; ⊙6pm-1am Mon-Fri, from noon Sat & Sun; 🕿) Successful ventures in Delhi and Bangalore led this chill gastropub to Bandra, where scenesters gather on the excellent patio – particularly great when it's pouring rain a metre or so away. Cheekily named cocktails (ask a local to get in on the joke; ₹320 to ₹650) and Gateway Brewing craft beer on tap ensure a fun and festive mood over DJ-spun hip-hop/Latin hits.

Masala Bar COCKTAIL BAR

(Map p58; www.masalabar.co.in; 1st fl, Gagangiri Apt, Carter Rd, Bandra West; ⊙12.30-4pm & 5pm-1am) Take unorthodox ingredients like thyme foam, mudfig purée, orange-skin oil and sattu fizz, then shake, stir, cook or otherwise manipulate them along with alcohol using things like vacuum-sealing machines, rotovaps, siphons, centrifuges and sous-vide machines, and you have an idea of what to expect from the innovative molecular cocktails at this new Bandra hot spot overlooking the beach on Carter Rd. Signature cocktails are ₹550.

Toto's Garage BAR

(Map p58; ☑022-26005494; 30th Rd, Bandra West; ⊙6pm-1am) A highly sociable, down-to-earth local dive done up in a car-mechanic theme, where you can go in your dirty clothes, drink draught beer (₹200 a glass) and listen to classic rock. Check out the up-ended VW Beetle above the bar. It's always busy and has a good mix of guys and gals.

Olive Bar & Kitchen BAR

(Map p58; ☑022-26058228; www.olivebarand kitchen.com; 14 Union Park, Khar West; ⊙8pm-1am daily, plus 12.30-3.30pm Sat & Sun; 🕿) A perennial watering hole of choice for Bandra's filmi elite and aspiring starlets, Olive is a Mediterranean-style bar-restaurant whose white-washed walls, candle-lit terraces and rooms

QUEER MUMBAI

Homosexuality remains illegal in India, so Mumbai's LGBTQ scene is still quite underground, especially for women, but it's gaining momentum. No dedicated LGBTQ bars/clubs have opened yet, but gay-friendly 'safe house' venues often host private gay parties (announced on Gay Bombay).

Humsafar Trust (Map p58; ☑022-26673800; www.humsafar.org; 3rd fl, Manthan Plaza Nehru Rd, Vakola, Santa Cruz East) Runs tons of programs and workshops; one of its support groups organises the weekly gathering 'Friday Workshop' and another, Umang, organises monthly events (called 'Chill Outs'), workshops and runs a helpline (☑99300-95856). It's also closely connected to the erratically published but pioneering magazine Bombay Dost (www.bombaydost.co.in).

Gaylaxy (www.gaylaxymag.com) India's best gay e-zine; well worth consulting and has lots of Mumbai content.

Gay Bombay (www.gaybombay.org) A great place to start, with event listings including meet-ups in Bandra, GB-hosted bar and film nights (including somewhat regular gay Saturday nights at Liquid Lounge in Girgaum Chowpatty), plus hiking trips, picnics and other queer-community info.

Kashish Mumbai International Queer Film Festival (www.mumbaiqueerfest.com) Excellent annual event in May, with a mix of Indian and foreign films; in 2016 182 films from 54 countries were featured.

LABIA (Lesbian & Bisexuals in Action; www.labiacollective.org) Lesbian and bi support group based in Mumbai; provides a counselling service for women.

Queer Azaadi Mumbai (www.queerazaadi.wordpress.com) Organises Mumbai's Pride Parade (www.mumbaipride.in), which is usually held in early February.

Queer Ink (www.queer-ink.com) Online publisher with excellent books, DVDs and merchandise. Also hosts a monthly arts event with speakers, workshops, poetry, comedy, music and a marketplace.

Salvation Star A Facebook community organising and promoting gay events and parties.

evoke Ibiza and Mykonos. It's the perfect setting for inspired Greek and Italian food (mains ₹600 to ₹1500) and vibing DJ sounds. Thursdays and weekends are packed.

Bad Cafe
CAFE

(Map p58; www.thebadcafe.com; 22G Kapadia House, New Kantwadi Rd, Bandra West; ⊙9am-11pm; 🛜) 🍽 Thoroughly hidden down a quiet lane off Perry Cross Rd, this is the caffeinated stomping grounds of the Bandra cool and creative set. Co-owner and coffee fiend Amit Dhanani sources organic, 80% Arabica beans from South India, which are turned into espressos, ristretto, cortados, flat whites and the like by old-school trained baristas. Porch-swing seating and globally inspired tapas (₹250 to ₹520) encourage lingering.

Cafe Zoe
BAR

(www.cafezoe.in; Mathurdas Mills Compound, NM Joshi Marg, Lower Parel; ⊙7.30am-1.30am) This cafe/bar is not merely another unassuming hipster enclave hidden away in the redeveloped cotton mill at Mathurdas Mills Compound. Exposed brick and railing dominate the bi-level space that's long on atmosphere and serves strong, fruit-forward cocktails (₹470 to ₹600) like black grape caipiroskas and watermelon martinis. Old black-and-white photos of its former life dot the walls.

☆ Entertainment

Mumbai has an exciting live-music scene, some terrific theatres, an emerging network of comedy clubs and, of course, cinemas and sporting action.

Consult **Time Out Mumbai** (www.time out.com/mumbai) and **Insider** (https://in sider.in) for events and/or live-music listings. Unfortunately, Hindi films aren't shown with English subtitles. You can book movies, theatre and sporting events online with **Book My Show** (https://in.bookmyshow.com).

Royal Opera House
OPERA

(Map p54; ☑022-23690511; Mama Parmanand Rd; ⊙box office 11am-6pm) India's only surviving opera house reopened to suitably dramatic fanfare with a 2016 performance by Mumbai-born British soprano Rozario, after a meticulous six-year restoration project that saw the regal address returned to full British-rule glory. Architect Abha Narain Lambah combed through old photographs of gilded ceilings, stained-glass windows and a baroque Indo-European foyer to restore the three-level auditorium.

Liberty Cinema
CINEMA, LIVE MUSIC

(Map p48; ☑022-22084521; www.thelibertycine ma.com; 41/42 New Marine Lines, Fort) The stunning art deco Liberty was once the queen of Hindi film – think red-carpet openings with Dev Anand. It fell on hard times in recent years, but is on the rebound and now hosts private events and more. It's near the Bombay Hospital.

National Centre for the Performing Arts
THEATRE, LIVE MUSIC

(NCPA; Map p48; www.ncpamumbai.com; Marine Dr & Sri V Saha Rd, Nariman Point; tickets ₹150-7500) This vast cultural centre is the hub of Mumbai's highbrow music, theatre and dance scene. In any given week, it might host experimental plays, poetry readings, photography exhibitions, a jazz band from Chicago or Indian classical music. Many performances are free. The **box office** (Map p48; ☑022-66223724; www.ncpamumbai.com; Marine Dr & Sri V Saha Rd, Nariman Point; ⊙9am-7pm) is at the end of NCPA Marg.

Regal Cinema
CINEMA

(Map p46; ☑022-22021017; www.regalcinema.in; Shahid Bhagat Singh Marg, Regal Circle, Apollo Bunder; tickets ₹100-200) A faded art deco masterpiece that's good for Hollywood blockbusters.

Wankhede Stadium
SPECTATOR SPORT

(Mumbai Cricket Association; Map p48; ☑022-22795500; www.mumbaicricket.com; D Rd, Churchgate; ⊙ticket office 9am-6pm) Test matches and one-day internationals are played a few times a year here in season (October to April). Contact the Cricket Association for ticket information; for a test match you'll probably have to pay for the full five days.

Prithvi Theatre
THEATRE

(Map p58; ☑022-26149546; www.prithvitheatre. org; Juhu Church Rd, Juhu; tickets ₹175-500) A Juhu institution that's a great place to see both Hindi- and English-language theatre or an arthouse film, with the **Prithvi Cafe** (Map p58; light meals ₹35-150; ⊙10am-10.45pm) for drinks. Its excellent theatre festival in November showcases contemporary Indian theatre and includes international productions.

Eros
CINEMA

(Map p48; www.eroscinema.co.in; Maharshi Karve Rd, Churchgate; tickets ₹130-180) To experience Bollywood blockbusters in situ, the Eros cinema is the place.

BOLLYWOOD DREAMS

Mumbai is the glittering epicentre of India's gargantuan Hindi-language film industry. The Lumière brothers screened the first film ever shown in India at the Watson Hotel in Mumbai in 1896, and beginning with the 1913 silent epic *Raja Harishchandra* (with an all-male cast, some in drag) and the first talkie, *Lama Ara* (1931), Bollywood now churns out more than 1000 films a year – doubling Hollywood's output, and not surprising considering it has a captive audience of one-sixth of the world's population.

Every part of India has its regional film industry, but Bollywood continues to entrance the nation with its escapist formula in which all-singing, all-dancing lovers fight and conquer the forces keeping them apart. These days, Hollywood-inspired thrillers and action extravaganzas vie for moviegoers' attention alongside the more family-oriented saccharine formulas.

Bollywood stars can attain near godlike status in India and star-spotting is a favourite pastime in Mumbai's posher establishments. You can also see the stars' homes as well as a film/TV studio with **Bollywood Tours** (Map p48; ☑9820255202; www.bollywood-tours.in; 8 Lucky House, Goa St, Fort; per person 4/8hr tour ₹8000/10,000), but you're not guaranteed to see a dance number and you may spend much of it in traffic.

Extra! Extra!

Studios sometimes want Westerners as extras to add a whiff of international flair (or provocative dress, which locals often won't wear) to a film. If you're game, just hang around Colaba (especially the Salvation Army hostel) where studio scouts, recruiting for the following day's shooting, will find you.

A day's work, which can be up to 16 hours, pays around ₹500 (more for speaking roles). You'll get lunch, snacks and (usually) transport. The day can be long and hot with loads of standing around the set; not everyone has a positive experience.

Complaints range from lack of food and water to dangerous situations and intimidation when extras don't comply with the director's orders. Others describe the behind-the-scenes peek as a fascinating experience. Before agreeing to anything, always ask for the scout's identification and go with your gut feeling.

Metro Big   CINEMA
(Map p48; ☑022-39894040; www.bigcinemas.com; Mahatma Gandhi Rd, New Marine Lines, Fort; tickets ₹150-800) This grande dame of Bombay talkies has been renovated into a multiplex cinema.

🔒 Shopping

Mumbai is India's great marketplace, with some of the best shopping in the country. Spend a day at the markets north of CST for the classic Mumbai shopping experience. Booksellers set up daily on the sidewalks along the main thoroughfare between Colaba and Fort. Snap up a bargain backpacking wardrobe at **Fashion Street** (Map p48; Mahatma Gandhi Rd). Kemp's Corner and Kala Ghoda have good shops for designer threads.

🔒 Colaba

Cottonworld Corp   CLOTHING
(Map p46; www.cottonworld.net; Mandlik Marg, Colaba; ☺10.30am-8pm Mon-Sat, noon-8pm Sun) A great shop for stylish Indian-Western-hybrid goods made from cotton, linen and natural materials. Think Indian Gap, but cooler.

Phillips   ANTIQUES
(Map p46; www.phillipsantiques.com; Wodehouse Rd, Colaba; ☺10am-7pm Mon-Sat) Art deco and colonial-era furniture, wooden ceremonial masks, silver, Victorian glass, plus high-quality reproductions of old photos, maps and paintings.

Bungalow 8   FASHION & ACCESSORIES
(Map p48; www.bungaloweight.com; North Stand, E & F Block, Wankhede Stadium, D Rd, Churchgate; ☺10.30am-7.30pm) Original, high-end, artisanal clothing, jewellery, home decor and other objects of beauty under the bleachers of the cricket stadium. Enter via Gate 2 from Vinoo Mankad Rd.

Central Cottage Industries Emporium   ARTS & CRAFTS
(Map p46; www.cottageemporium.in; Chhatrapati Shivaji Marg, Apollo Bunder; ☺10am-7pm Mon-Sat, to 6pm Sun) Fair-trade-like souvenirs including pashminas.

WORTH A TRIP

BAZAAR DISTRICT

Mumbai's main market district is one of Asia's most fascinating, an incredibly dense combination of humanity and commerce that's a total assault on the senses. If you've just got off a plane from the West, or a taxi from Bandra – hold on tight. This working-class district stretches north of Crawford Market up as far as Chor Bazaar, a 2.5km walk away. Such are the crowds (and narrowness of the lanes), you'll need to allow yourself two to three hours to explore it thoroughly.

You can buy just about anything here, but as the stores and stalls are very much geared to local tastes, most of the fun is simply taking in the street life and investigating the souk-like lanes rather than buying souvenirs. The markets merge into each other in an amoeba-like mass, but there are some key landmarks so you can orientate yourself.

Crawford Market (Mahatma Phule Market; Map p54; cnr DN & Lokmanya Tilak Rds; 10.30am-9pm) Crawford Market is the largest in Mumbai, and contains the last whiff of British Bombay before the tumult of the central bazaars begins. Bas-reliefs by Rudyard Kipling's father, Lockwood Kipling, adorn the Norman Gothic exterior. Fruit and vegetables, meat and fish are mainly traded, but it's also an excellent place to stock up on spices.

If you're here during alphonso mango season (May to June) be sure to indulge.

Mangaldas Market (Map p54) Mangaldas Market, traditionally home to traders from Gujarat, is a mini-town, complete with lanes of fabrics. Even if you're not the type to have your clothes tailored, drop by DD Dupattawala (Map p54; 022-22019719; Shop 217, 4th Lane; 11am-8pm Mon-Sat) for pretty scarves and dupattas at fixed prices. Zaveri Bazaar (Map p54) for jewellery and Bhuleshwar Market (Map p54; cnr Sheikh Memon St & M Devi Marg; 10am-9pm) for fruit and veg are just north of here.

Just a few metres further along Sheikh Memon St from Bhuleshwar are a Jain pigeon feeding station, a flower market and a religious market.

Chor Bazaar (Map p54; Mutton St, Kumbharwada) Chor Bazaar is known for antiques, though nowadays much of them are reproductions. The main area of activity is Mutton St, where shops specialise in these 'antiques' and miscellaneous junk. Dhabu St, to the east, is lined with fine leather goods.

🏠 Fort Area & Churchgate

⭐ **Contemporary Arts & Crafts** HOMEWARES (Map p48; www.cac.co.in; 210 Dr Dadabhai Naoroji Rd, Fort; 10.30am-7.30pm) Modish, high-quality takes on traditional crafts: these are not your usual handmade souvenirs.

⭐ **Sabyasachi** CLOTHING (Map p48; www.sabyasachi.com; Ador House, 6 K Dubash Marg, Fort; 11am-7pm Mon-Sat) It's worth popping in to see the space itself, a gorgeous, cavernous, rose-oil-scented stunner chock-full of owner and designer Sabyasachi Mukherjee's collection of chandeliers, antiques, ceramics, paintings and carpets. As far as retail goes it's unlike anything you have ever seen.

Chimanlals ARTS & CRAFTS (Map p48; www.chimanlals.com; Wallace St, Fort; 9.30am-6pm Mon-Fri, to 5pm Sat) The beautiful traditional printed papers here will make you start writing letters.

Fabindia CLOTHING, HOMEWARES (Map p48; www.fabindia.com; Jeroo Bldg, 137 Mahatma Gandhi Rd, Kala Ghoda; 10am-9pm) Ethically sourced cotton and silk fashions and homewares in everybody's favourite modern-meets-traditional Indian shop.

Nicobar HOMEWARES, CLOTHING (Map p48; www.nicobar.com; 10 Ropewalk Lane, Kala Ghoda; 11am-8pm) This new and excellent high-end boutique from the same folks who brought us Good Earth is a great spot to pick up carefully curated homewares, travel totes and select Indian hipsterware.

Bombay Shirt Company CLOTHING (Map p48; 022-40043455; www.bombay shirts.com; ground fl, 3 Sassoon Bldg, Kala Ghoda; 10.30am-9pm) A trendy, bespoke shirt tailor for men and women. You can customise everything (collars, buttons, cuffs and twill tapes), the results are stunning and the prices a fraction of those back home (unless home is Vietnam). Shirts (from ₹2000) take two weeks, and they will deliver or ship internationally. They're also in Bandra (Map p58; ☑ 022-26056125; ground fl, Kamal Vishrantee Kutir, 24th Rd; ◷ 10.30am-9pm).

Bombay Paperie ARTS & CRAFTS
(Map p48; ☑ 022-66358171; www.bombaypaperie. com; 63 Bombay Samachar Marg, Fort; ◷ 10.30am-6pm Mon-Sat) Championing a dying art, this fascinating shop sells handmade, cotton-based paper crafted into charming cards, sculptures and lampshades.

Chetana Book Centre BOOKS
(Map p48; www.chetana.com; K Dubash Marg, Kala Ghoda; ◷ 10.30am-7.30pm Mon-Sat) This great spirituality bookstore has lots of books on Hinduism, and the attached restaurant does excellent Gujarati and Rajasthani thalis (₹459 to ₹595).

Khadi & Village
Industries Emporium CLOTHING
(Khadi Bhavan; Map p48; 286 Dr Dadabhai Naoroji Rd, Fort; ◷ 10.30am-6.30pm Mon-Sat) A dusty, 1940s time warp full of traditional Indian clothing, silk, *khadi* (homespun cloth) and shoes, plus very popular Khadi natural soaps and shampoos.

🏠 Kalbadevi to Mahalaxmi

LM Furtado & Co MUSIC
(Map p54; ☑ 022-22013163; www.furtadosonline. com; 540-544 Kalbadevi Rd, Kalbadevi; ◷ 10.30am-8pm Mon-Sat) The best place in Mumbai for musical instruments – sitars, tablas, accordions and local and imported guitars. Another branch under the same Furtados umbrella (but with a slightly different name) is BX Furtado & Sons (Map p54; ◷ 10.30am-8pm Mon-Sat), located on Lokmanya Tilak Rd.

Shrujan ARTS & CRAFTS
(Map p58; ☑ 022-26183104; www.shrujan.org; Hatkesh Society, 6th North South Rd, JVPD Scheme; ◷ 10am-7.30pm Mon-Sat) Nonprofit Shrujan aims to help women from 114 villages in Kutch, Gujarat, earn a livelihood while preserving their spectacular embroidery traditions – the intricate embroidery work sold here makes great gifts. Shrujan also has a branch in Breach Candy (Map p54; ☑ 022-23521693; ground fl, Krishnabad Bldg, 43 Bhulabhai Desai Marg; ◷ 10am-7.30pm Mon-Sat) 🖉.

Mini Market/Bollywood
Bazaar/Super Sale ANTIQUES, SOUVENIRS
(Map p54; ☑ 9820032923; 33/31 Mutton St; ◷ 11am-8pm Sat-Thu) Sells vintage Bollywood posters and other movie ephemera.

🏠 Western Suburbs

★ Kulture Shop DESIGN
(Map p58; www.kultureshop.in; 241 Hill Rd, Bandra West; ◷ 11am-8pm) Behold Bandra's – and Mumbai's – coolest shop, featuring exclusive graphic art and illustrations sourced from a global army of Indian artists. You'll find thought-provoking and conceptually daring T-shirts, art prints, coffee mugs, notebooks, stationery and other cutting-edge objets d'art.

It's co-owned by well-known American-Indian street artist Jas Charanjiva, her urban culture and design enthusiast husband, and their curator friend.

Indian Hippy ART
(Map p58; ☑ 8080822022; www.hippy.in; 17C Sherly Rajan Rd, Bandra West, off Carter Rd; ◷ by appointment) Indian Hippy will put your name in lights, with custom-designed vintage Bollywood posters hand-painted on canvas by the original studio artists (a dying breed since the advent of digital illustrating). Bring (or email) a photo and your imagination (or let them guide you). Also sells LP clocks, vintage film posters and all manner of (frankly bizarre) Bollywood-themed products. Portraits cost ₹7500 to ₹15,000. Ships worldwide.

Kishore Silk House CLOTHING, HANDICRAFTS
(Dedhia Estate 5/353, Bhandarkar Rd, Matunga East; ◷ 10am-8.30pm Tue-Sun) Handwoven saris (from ₹300) and dhotis (from ₹250) from Tamil Nadu and Kerala.

High Street Phoenix MALL
(www.highstreetphoenix.com; 462 Senapati Bapat Marg, Lower Parel; ◷ 11am-11pm) High Street Phoenix, one of India's first and largest shopping malls, and its mall-within-a-mall, the luxury-oriented Palladium, is an indoor/outdoor retail orgy that hosts top shops, great restaurants, fun bars and clubs, a 20-lane bowling alley and an IMAX cineplex. It's also where you go when you want a horn-free few hours.

ℹ Information

EMERGENCY
As of 2017, a single number for emergencies (112) will be in operation across India, though the following will continue to work until 2018.

AMBULANCE	☑ 102 (public) or 1298 (private)
POLICE	☑ 100
FIRE	☑ 101

MUMBAI (BOMBAY) INFORMATION

INTERNET ACCESS

While cyber cafes are increasingly scarce, all but the simplest hotels, restaurants, cafes and bars now have wi-fi. Commercial establishments generally require a connection via social media accounts or via a mobile phone number, to which a unique one-time password is sent.

MEDIA

Newspapers The *Hindustan Times* is the best paper; its *Ht Café* insert has a good what's-on guide.

Websites *Time Out Mumbai* (www.timeout. com/mumbai) no longer publishes a Mumbai magazine but its website is worth consulting.

MEDICAL SERVICES

Bombay Hospital (Map p48; ☑ 022-22067676; www.bombayhospital.com; 12 New Marine Lines) A private hospital with the latest medical technology and equipment.

Breach Candy Hospital (Map p54; ☑ 022-23672888, emergency 022-23667890; www. breachcandyhospital.org; 60 Bhulabhai Desai Marg, Breach Candy) The best hospital in Mumbai, if not India. It's 2km northwest of Girgaum Chowpatty.

Royal Chemists (Map p48; www.royal chemists.com; 89A Queen's Chambers, Maharshi Karve Rd, Marine Lines; ⊙ 8.30am-8.30pm Mon-Sat) Delivers also.

Sahakari Bhandar Chemist (Map p46; cnr Colaba Causeway & Wodehouse Rd, Colaba; ⊙10am-8.30pm) Handy Colaba pharmacy.

MONEY

ATMs are everywhere, and foreign-exchange offices are also plentiful.

Thomas Cook has a branch in the Fort area with foreign exchange.

POST

Main Post Office (Map p48; www.indiapost. gov.in; Walchand Hirachand Marg; ⊙9am-8pm Mon-Sat, to 4pm Sun) The main post office is an imposing building beside CST. Poste restante (Map p48; Walchand Hirachand Marg; ⊙10am-3pm Mon-Sat) is at the 'Delivery Department'. Opposite the post office are parcel-wallahs who will stitch up your parcel for between ₹50 and ₹200 (find them under the banyan tree).

TELEPHONE

Call ☑197 for directory assistance.

TOURIST INFORMATION

Indiatourism (Government of India Tourist Office; Map p48; ☑ 022-22074333; www. incredibleindia.com; Western Railways Reservation Complex, 123 Maharshi Karve Rd; ⊙ 8.30am-6pm Mon-Fri, to 2pm Sat) Provides information for the entire country, as well as

contacts for Mumbai guides and homestays. Oddly, branches at the airports had been shut at the time of research.

Maharashtra Tourism Development Corporation Head Office (MTDC; Map p48; ☑ 022-22845678; www.maharashtratourism. gov.in; Madame Cama Rd, Nariman Point; ⊙10am-5.30pm) The MTDC's head office has helpful staff and lots of pamphlets and information on Maharashtra and bookings for MTDC hotels. This is also the only MTDC office of note that accepts credit cards. There are additional booths at Apollo Bunder (MTDC; Map p46; ☑ 022-22841877; ⊙ 9am-4pm Tue-Sun) and Chhatrapati Shivaji Terminus (MTDC; Map p48; ☑ 022-22622859; ⊙10am-5pm Mon-Sat), but airport booths were closed at the time of research.

TRAVEL AGENCIES

Akbar Travels (Map p46; ☑ 022-22823434; www.akbartravels.com; 30 Alipur Trust Bldg, Shahid Bhagat Singh Marg, Colaba; ⊙10am-7pm Mon-Fri, to 6pm Sat) Extremely helpful and can book long-distance car/drivers and buses with advance notice. Also has good exchange rates. There's another branch in Fort (Map p48; ☑ 022-22633434; www.akbar travels.com; 167/169 Dr Dadabhai Naoroji Rd, Fort; ⊙10am-7pm Mon-Fri, to 6pm Sat).

Thomas Cook (Map p48; ☑ 022-61603333; www.thomascook.in; 324 Dr Dadabhai Naoroji Rd, Fort; ⊙ 9.30am-6pm Mon-Sat) Flight and hotel bookings, plus foreign exchange.

VISAS

Foreigners' Regional Registration Office (FRRO; Map p48; ☑ 022-22621169; www.boi. gov.in; Annexe Bldg No 2, CID, Badaruddin Tyabji Marg, near Special Branch; ⊙ 9.30am-1pm Mon-Fri) Tourist and transit visas can no longer be extended except in emergency situations; check the latest online.

⊙ Getting There & Away

AIR

Mumbai's **Chhatrapati Shivaji International Airport** (Map p58; ☑ 022-66851010; www. csia.in), about 30km from the city centre, was recently modernised to the tune of US$2 billion. Now handling all international arrivals is the impressive, remodelled international Terminal 2 (T2), which includes India's largest public art program (a skylighted, 3.2km multistorey Art Wall along moving walkways, boasting over 5000 pieces of art from every corner of India).

Domestic flights operate out of both the new T2 and the older Terminal 1B (T1B), also known locally as Santa Cruz Airport, 5km away. An inter-terminal fixed-rate taxi service (₹230 from T1B to T2, ₹245 from T2 to T1B) operates between the terminals. Both terminals have ATMs and foreign-exchange counters, and T2 also houses a luxurious transit hotel.

Air India (Map p48; ☑ 022-27580777, airport 022-28318666; www.airindia.com; Air India Bldg, cnr Marine Dr & Madame Cama Rd, Nariman Point; ⊙ 9.15am-6pm Mon-Fri, 9.15am-1pm & 2-6pm Sat), **Jet Airways** (Map p46; ☑ 022-39893333; www.jetairways.com; B1, Amarchand Mansion, Madam Cama Rd, Colaba; ⊙ 9.30am-6pm Mon-Sat) and **Vistara** (Map p58; ☑ 0186-1089999; www.airvistara.com) operate out of T2, while **GoAir** (Map p58; ☑ 022-26156113; www.goair.in), **IndiGo** (Map p58; ☑ call centre 099-10383838; www.goindigo.in) and **SpiceJet** (Map p58; ☑ airport 0987-1803333; www.spicejet.com) operate out of T1B – be sure to check ahead for any changes on the ground. Travel agencies and the airlines' websites are usually best for booking flights.

There are also normally MTDC tourist information booths at both terminals but these had been removed at the time of research due to the airport renovations, with no planned time frame for their return.

BUS

Numerous private operators and state governments run long-distance buses to and from Mumbai.

Long-distance government-run buses depart from the **Mumbai Central bus terminal** (Map p54; ☑ enquiries 022-23024075; Jehangir Boman Behram Marg, RBI Staff Colony) right by Mumbai Central train station. They're cheaper and more frequent than private services, but standards are usually lower. The website of the **Maharashtra State Road Transport Corporation** (MSRTC; ☑ 022-23023900; www.msrtc.gov.in) theoretically has schedules and is supposed to permit online booking, though in practice it's next to useless.

Private buses are usually more comfortable and simpler to book (if a bit more costly). Most depart from Dr Anadrao Nair Rd near Mumbai Central train station, but some buses to southern destinations depart from Carnac Bunder near Crawford Market or Dadar TT Circle (free transport is usually provided to both by ticketing agents). Check departure times and prices with **Citizen Travels** (Map p54; ☑ 022-23459695; www.citizenbus.com; G Block, Sitaram Bldg, Palton Rd) or **National NTT/CTC** (Map p54; ☑ 022-23074854, 022-23015652; Dr Anadrao Nair Rd; ⊙ 6.20am-11.30pm). Fares to popular destinations (like Goa) are up to 75% higher during holiday periods.

Private buses to Goa are more convenient; these vary in price from as little as ₹450 (a bad choice) to ₹1000. Many leave from way out in the suburbs, but **Naik Bus** (Map p48; ☑ 022-23676840; www.naibus.com; ⊙ 6pm, 7pm, 8.30pm & 9pm), **Paolo Travel** (Map p48; ☑ 022-26433023; www.paolotravels.com; ⊙ 5.30pm & 8pm) and government-run **Kadamba Transport** (Map p48; ☑ 9969561146; www.goakadamba.com; ⊙ 6pm) are convenient for the centre, leaving from in front of Azad Maidan. The trip takes 14 hours.

Private long-distance bus stands and ticket agents are on **Palton Road** (Map p54; Palton Rd) and **Dr Anadrao Nair Road** (Map p54; Dr Anadrao Nair Rd, RBI Colony).

TRAIN

Three train systems operate out of Mumbai, but the most important services for travellers are Central Railways and Western Railways. Tickets for either system can be bought from any station that has computerised ticketing.

Central Railways (Map p48; ☑ 139; www.cr.indianrailways.gov.in), handling services to the east, south, plus a few trains to the north, operates from CST (also known as 'VT'). Foreign-tourist-quota tickets and Indrail passes

MAJOR LONG-DISTANCE BUS ROUTES

DESTINATION	PRIVATE NON-AC/AC SLEEPER (₹)	GOVERNMENT NON-AC (₹)	DURATION (HR)
Ahmedabad	300-1500/700-1500	N/A	7-12
Aurangabad	500-700/500-1300	600 (two daily)	9-11
Hyderabad	800-5000 (all AC)	N/A	16
Mahabaleshwar*	500-900 (all AC)	400 (five daily)	7-8
Murud	N/A	200 (10 daily)	8-10
Nasik	200-300/500-600	290 (half-hourly, 6am-11.15pm)	13-16
Panaji (Panjim)	600-750/700-3000	N/A	14-16
Pune*	508-730/425-2800	250 (half-hourly, 6.45am-12.30am)	3-5
Udaipur	200-812/1000-2500	N/A	14-17

* Leaves from Dadar TT Circle.

can be bought at Counter 52 on the 1st floor of the **reservation centre** (Map p48; ⊘ 8am-8pm Mon-Sat, to 2pm Sun). There is a prepaid taxi scheme near the MTDC tourist information booth (₹160 to Colaba, ₹360 to Bandra, ₹430 to the domestic terminal and ₹500 to the international terminal).

Some Central Railways trains depart from Dadar (D), a few stations north of CST, or Lokmanya Tilak (LTT), 16km north of CST.

Western Railways (Map p54; ☑ 139; www. wr.indianrailways.gov.in) has services to the north from Mumbai Central train station, usually called Bombay Central (BCT). The **reservation office** (Map p48; ⊘ 8am-8pm Mon-Sat, to 2pm Sun), opposite Churchgate station, has foreign-tourist-quota tickets.

ℹ Getting Around

M-Indicator (http://m-indicator.soft112.com) is an invaluable app for Mumbai public transit – from train schedules to rickshaw fares it covers the whole shebang.

TO/FROM THE AIRPORTS
Terminal 2

Prepaid Taxi Set-fare taxis cost ₹680/820 (non-AC/AC; including one piece of luggage) to Colaba and Fort and ₹400/480 to Bandra. The journey to Colaba takes about an hour at night (via the Sea Link) and 1½ to two hours during the day.

Autorickshaw Although available, they only go as far south as Bandra – walk out of the terminal and follow the signs. Prices are ₹18 per kilometre (a traffic warden *should* keep them honest).

Train If you arrive during the day (but not during 'rush hour' – 6am to 11am) and are not weighed down with luggage, consider the train: take an autorickshaw to Andheri train station and then the Churchgate or CST train (₹10, 45 minutes).

Taxi The trip from South Mumbai to the international airport in an AC taxi should cost from ₹650 to ₹800, plus the ₹60 toll if you take the time-saving Sea Link Bridge. Allow two hours for the trip if you travel between 4pm and 8pm. From Colaba, an UberGo is around ₹385 off-peak.

Terminal 1B

Taxi There's a prepaid taxi counter in the arrivals hall. A non-AC/AC taxi costs ₹560/683 to Colaba or Fort and ₹283/340 to Bandra (a bit more at night).

Autorickshaw Alternatively, if it's not rush hour, catch an autorickshaw (between ₹22 and ₹27) to Vile Parle station, where you can get a train to Churchgate (₹10, 45 minutes).

MAJOR TRAINS FROM MUMBAI

DESTINATION	TRAIN NO & NAME	SAMPLE FARE (₹)	DURATION (HR)	DEPARTURE
Agra	12137 Punjab Mail	613/1596/2281/3856 (A)	22	7.40pm CST
Ahmedabad	12901 Gujarat Mail	348/876/1206/1996 (A)	9	10pm BCT
	12009 Shatabdi Exp	860/1701 (E)	7	6.25am BCT
Aurangabad	11401 Nandigram Exp	268/691/961/1571 (A)	7	4.35pm CST
	17617 Tapovan Exp	173/571 (C)	7	6.15am CST
Bengaluru	11301 Udyan Exp	533/1416/2031/3421 (A)	24	8.05am CST
Chennai	12163 Chennai Exp	603/1561/2226/3766 (A)	23½	8.30pm CST
Delhi	12951 Mumbai Rajdhani	1856/2641/4481 (D)	16	5pm BCT
Hyderabad	12701 Hussainsagar Exp	458/1191/1671/2781 (A)	14½	9.50pm CST
Indore	12961 Avantika Exp	473/1226/1721/2866 (A)	14	7.10pm BCT
Jaipur	12955 Bct Jp Sf Exp	568/1481/2106/3546 (A)	18	6.50pm BCT
Kochi	16345 Netravati Exp	648/1711/2481 (B)	25½	11.40am LTT
Madgaon (Goa)	10103 Mandovi Exp	423/1131/1601/2661 (A)	12	7.10am CST
	12133 Mangalore Exp	453/1176/1646 (B)	9	10pm CST
	11085 Mao Doubledecker	906 (F)	12	5.33am Wed, Fri & Sun LTT
Pune	11301 Udyan Exp	173/556/761/1226 (A)	3½	8.05am CST

Station abbreviations: CST (Chhatrapati Shivaji Terminus); BCT (Mumbai Central); LTT (Lokmanya Tilak)

Fares: (A) sleeper/3AC/2AC/1AC; (B) sleeper/3AC/2AC; (C) second class/CC; (D) 3AC/2AC/1AC; (E) CC/Exec CC; (F) CC

BOAT

PNP (Map p46; ☏ 022-22885220) and **Maldar Catamarans** (Map p46; ☏ 022-22829695) run regular ferries to Mandwa (one way ₹125 to ₹165), useful for access to Murud-Janjira and other parts of the Konkan Coast, avoiding the long bus trip out of Mumbai. Buy tickets at their Taj Gateway Plaza offices.

BUS

Few travellers bother with city buses but **BEST** (Map p46; www.bestundertaking.com) has a useful search facility for hardcore shoestringers and masochists – you'll also need to read the buses' Devanagari numerals and beware of pickpockets. Fares start at ₹8.

BEST bus stands are on the **east** (Map p46) and **west** (Map p46) sides of Mahatma Gandhi Rd and at CST.

CAR & MOTORCYCLE

Cars with drivers can be hired for moderate rates. Air-conditioned cars start at ₹1550/1800 for half-/full-day rental with an 80km limit. For long-distance treks out of Mumbai, prices vary by type of car and service but expect to pay between ₹13 (non-AC) to ₹15 (AC) per kilometre. **Clear Car Rental** (☏ 8888855220; www.clearcarrental. com) is a handy online car-booking service.

Allibhai Premji Tyrewalla (Map p54; ☏ 022-23099417, 022-23099313; www.premjis.com; 205/20 Dr D Bhadkamkar (Lamington) Rd; ⊙10am-7pm Mon-Sat) sells new and used motorcycles with a guaranteed buy-back option. Long-term rental schemes (two months or more) start at around ₹35,000, with a buy-back price of around 60% after three months.

METRO

Line 1 of Mumbai's **metro** (www.mumbaimetro one.com) opened in 2014, the first of a long-phase project expected to finish by 2020. It connects 12 stations in the far northern suburbs to Ghatkopar Station in the east, mostly well away from anywhere of interest to visitors save the growing nightlife hubs of Andheri West and Versova, accessed by DN Nagar and Versova stations, respectively. However, Line 1 of the monorail was scheduled to be extended south as far as Jacob Circle (5km north of Chhatrapati Shivaji Terminus) by early 2017 (after missing deadlines in 2010, 2011 and 2016), bringing it past nightlife hub Lower Parel.

Single fares are based on distance and cost between ₹10 and ₹45, with monthly Trip Passes (₹725 to ₹950) also available. Access to stations is by escalator, carriages are air-conditioned, and there are seats reserved for women and the disabled.

Line 3 (a 33.5km, 27-station underground line connecting Cuffe Pde south of Colaba, all the main railway terminals, Bandra and the airport) is the next line to be constructed. It's been approved and contracted but won't open until at least 2020.

TAXI & AUTORICKSHAW

Mumbai's black-and-yellow taxis are very inexpensive and the most convenient way to get around southern Mumbai; drivers *almost* always use the meter without prompting. The minimum fare is ₹22 (for up to 1.5km); a 5km trip costs about ₹80. **Meru Cabs** (☏ 022-44224422; www.merucabs. com) is a reliable call-ahead taxi service.

Game-changing taxi apps in play include **Uber** (www.ubercom) and **Ola** (www.olacabs.com); the latter is good for booking autorickshaws as well – no more rickshaw-wallah price gouging!

Autorickshaws are the name of the game north of Bandra. The minimum fare is ₹18, up to 1.5km; a 3km trip is about ₹36 during daylight hours.

Both taxis and autorickshaws tack 50% onto the fare between midnight and 5am.

Tip: Mumbaikars tend to navigate by landmarks, not street names (especially new names), so have some details before heading out.

TRAIN

Mumbai's suburban train network is one of the world's busiest; forget travelling during rush hours. Trains run from 4am to 1am and there are two main lines of most interest to travellers:

Western Line The most useful; operates out of Churchgate north to Charni Rd (for Girgaum Chowpatty), Mumbai Central, Mahalaxmi (for the Dhobi Ghat), Bandra, Vile Parle (for the domestic airport), Andheri (for the international airport) and Borivali (for Sanjay Gandhi National Park), among others. Make sure you don't catch an express train when you need a slow train – the screens dictate this by an 'S' (Slow) or 'F' (Fast) under 'Mode'.

Central Line Runs from CST to Byculla (for Veermata Jijabai Bhonsle Udyan, formerly Victoria Gardens), Dadar and as far as Neral (for Matheran).

From Churchgate, 2nd-/1st-class fares are ₹5/50 to Mumbai Central, ₹10/55 to Vile Parle, and ₹15/75 to Borivali. 'Tourist tickets' permit unlimited travel in 2nd/1st class for one (₹75/275), three (₹115/440) or five (₹135/515) days.

To avoid the queues, buy a rechargeable **SmartCard** (₹100, ₹52 of which is retained in credit), good for use on either train line, then print out your tickets at the numerous automatic ticket vending machines (ATVMs) before boarding (place your card on the reader, touch the zone of your station, pick the specific station, choose the amount of tickets, choose 'Buy Ticket' and then 'Print').

Watch your valuables, and gals, stick to the ladies-only carriages except late at night, when it's more important to avoid empty cars.

Maharashtra

Best Places to Eat

➜ Malaka Spice (p112)

➜ Sadhana (p85)

➜ Bhoj (p90)

➜ Green Leaf (p90)

➜ Kinara Dhaba Village (p107)

Best Places to Sleep

➜ Beyond by Sula (p84)

➜ Verandah in the Forest (p105)

➜ Tiger Trails Jungle Lodge (p100)

➜ Hotel Sunderban (p111)

➜ Hotel Plaza (p98)

Why Go?

India's third-largest and second-most populous state, Maharashtra is an expansive canvas showcasing many of India's iconic attractions. There are palm-fringed beaches; lofty, cool-green mountains; Unesco World Heritage Sites; and bustling cosmopolitan cities. In the far east of the state are some of the nation's most impressive national parks, including Tadoba-Andhari Tiger Reserve.

Inland lie the extraordinary cave temples of Ellora and Ajanta, undoubtedly Maharashtra's greatest monuments, hewn by hand from solid rock. Matheran, a colonial-era hill station served by a toy train, has a certain allure, while pilgrims and inquisitive souls are drawn to cosmopolitan Pune, a city famous for its 'sex guru' and alternative spiritualism. Westwards, the romantic Konkan Coast, fringing the Arabian Sea, is lined with spectacular, crumbling forts and sandy beaches; some of the best are around pretty Malvan resort, which is fast becoming one of India's premier diving centres.

When to Go
Nasik

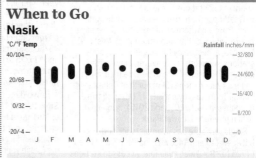

Jan It's party time at Nasik's wineries, marked by grape harvesting and crushing galas.

Sep The frenzied, energetic Ganesh Chaturthi celebrations reach fever pitch.

Dec Clear skies, mild temperatures; the secluded beaches of Murud, Ganpatipule and Tarkali are lovely.

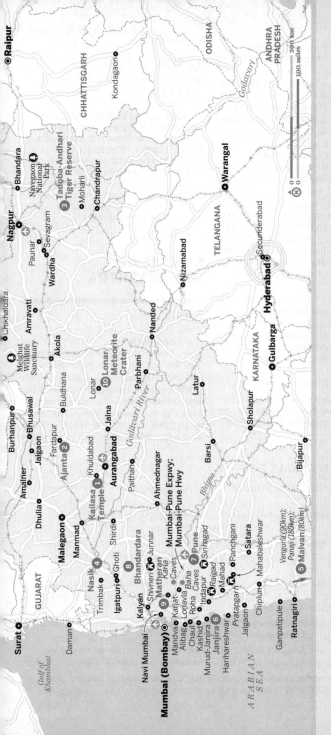

Maharashtra Highlights

1 Kailasa Temple (p92)
Being amazed by the beauty in the Ellora temple complex.

2 Ajanta (p95) Wandering through ancient cave galleries and admiring Buddhist art.

3 Tadoba-Andhari Tiger Reserve (p100) Searching for big cats inside the reserve.

4 Nasik (p82) Sipping on a Chenin Blanc or Cab-Shiraz in this gorgeous wine country.

5 Malvan (p103) Diving or snorkelling in the big blue off this picturesque seaside town.

6 Janjira (p101) Pondering the might of a lost civilisation at a colossal fort.

7 Pune (p107) Delving into spiritualism and Indian cuisine in this progressive centre.

8 Bhandardara (p85) Riding out a monsoon tucked away amid mountain scenery.

9 Matheran (p105) Exploring the spectacular hill station viewpoints.

10 Lonar Meteorite Crater (p91) Contemplating Mother Nature at a primordial crater.

History

Maharashtra was given its political and ethnic identity by Maratha leader Chhatrapati Shivaji (1627–80), who lorded over the Deccan plateau and much of western India from his stronghold at Raigad. Still highly respected today, Shivaji is credited for instilling a strong, independent spirit among the region's people, as well as establishing Maharashtra as a dominant player in the power relations of medieval India.

From the early 18th century, the state was under the administration of a succession of ministers called the Peshwas, who ruled until 1819, ceding thereafter to the British. After Independence in 1947, western Maharashtra and Gujarat were joined to form Bombay state. But it was back to the future in 1960, when modern Maharashtra was formed with the exclusion of Gujarati-speaking areas and with Mumbai (Bombay) as its capital.

Since then the state has forged ahead to become one of the nation's most prosperous, with India's largest industrial sector, mainly thanks to agriculture, coal-based thermal energy, nuclear electricity and technology parks and software exports.

ⓘ Getting There

Mumbai is Maharashtra's main transport hub, though Pune, Aurangabad and Nagpur also have busy airports. Jalgaon station is an important gateway for Ajanta.

Goa airport is handily placed for the far southern resort of Malvan.

ⓘ Getting Around

Because the state is so large, internal flights (eg Pune to Nagpur) will really speed up your explorations.

The **Maharashtra State Road Transport Corporation** (MSRTC; www.msrtc.gov.in) runs a comprehensive bus network spanning all major towns and many remote places. Private operators also have comfortable Volvo and Mercedes Benz services between major cities.

Renting a car and driver to explore the Konkan coastline is a good option as public transport is poor on this stretch: allow four or five days to travel between Mumbai and Goa.

NORTHERN MAHARASHTRA

Nasik

☎ 0253 / POP 1.57 MILLION / ELEV 565M

Located on the banks of the holy Godavari River, Nasik (or Nashik) gets its name from the episode in the Ramayana where Lakshmana, Rama's brother, hacked off the *nasika* (nose) of Ravana's sister. Today this large provincial city's old quarter has some intriguing wooden architecture, interesting temples that reference the Hindu epic and some huge bathing ghats. The city is notice-

---

TOP STATE FESTIVALS

Naag Panchami (⊙ Jul/Aug) A traditional snake-worshipping festival held in Pune and Kolhapur.

Ganesh Chaturthi (⊙ Aug/Sep) Celebrated with fervour all across Maharashtra; Pune goes particularly hysterical in honour of the elephant-headed deity.

Dussehra (⊙ Sep & Oct) A Hindu festival, but it also marks the Buddhist celebration of the anniversary of the famous humanist and Dalit leader BR Ambedkar's conversion to Buddhism.

Ellora Ajanta Aurangabad Festival (⊙ Oct/Nov) Aurangabad's cultural festival brings together the best classical and folk performers from across the region while promoting a number of artistic traditions and handicrafts on the side.

Kalidas Festival (⊙ Nov) Commemorates the literary genius of legendary poet Kalidas through spirited music, dance and theatre in Nagpur.

Sawai Gandharva Sangeet Mahotsav (⊙ Dec) An extravaganza of unforgettable performances in Pune by some of the heftiest names in Indian classical music.

SulaFest (www.sulafest.com; Sula Vineyards, Gat 36/2, Govardhan Village, off Gangapur-Savargaon Rd; tickets ₹1700-4700; ⊙ Feb) Nasik's biggest party and one of India's best boutique music festivals.

Nasik

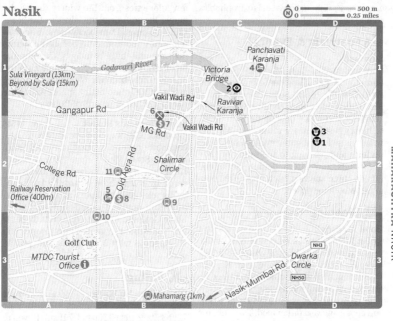

ably cleaner, better maintained and greener than many Indian cities of its size.

As Indian wine continues its coming of age, Nasik's growth potential as a wine tourism destination is wide open. India's best wines are produced locally and an afternoon touring the gorgeous vineyards (p86) in the countryside surrounding the city is a great reason to point your nose in Nasik's direction.

Every 12 years Nasik plays host to the grand **Kumbh Mela**, the largest religious gathering on Earth (the last one was in 2015, the next one in 2027).

◉ Sights

Ramkund   GHAT
This bathing ghat in the heart of Nasik's old quarter sees hundreds of Hindu pilgrims arriving daily to bathe, pray and – because the waters provide *moksha* (liberation of the soul) – to immerse the ashes of departed friends and family. There's an adjacent market that adds to the alluring and fascinating scene.

Kala Rama Temple   HINDU TEMPLE
(⊙6am-10pm) The city's holiest shrine dates back to 1794 and contains unusual blackstone representations of Rama, Sita and

Nasik

Lakshmana. Legend has it that it occupies the site where Lakshmana sliced off Surpanakha's nose.

Sita Gumpha   HINDU TEMPLE
(⊙6am-9.30pm) Sita is said to have hidden in this cave-like temple while being assailed by the evil Ravana. You'll have to stoop and shuffle your way into the cave as the

entrance is very narrow – claustrophobics should keep on walking.

✤ Festivals & Events

SulaFest
WINE

(www.sulafest.com; Sula Vineyards, Gat 36/2, Govardhan Village, off Gangapur-Savargaon Rd; tickets ₹1700-4700; ☺Feb) Sula Vineyard's Sula-Fest, which takes place the first weekend of February, is Nasik's biggest party and one of India's best boutique music festivals. The winery is swarmed with revellers, hyped up on juice and partying to the sound of 120+ live bands and internationally acclaimed DJs on three stages. Check https://in.book-myshow.com for tickets.

🛏 Sleeping

Hotel Abhishek
HOTEL $

(☎0253-2514201; www.hotelabhishek.com; Panchavati Karanja; s/d from ₹425/560, with AC ₹875/980; ❄🌐) Found just off the Panchavati Karanja roundabout, this great-value budget place offers clean if ageing rooms, 'gourmet by a German company' hot showers (6am to 10am) and appetising vegetarian food. The economy rooms are in way too good a shape to be going this cheap. The hands-on owner is tuned into foreign-traveller needs and is around most days.

Hotel Samrat
HOTEL $

(☎0253-2306100; www.hotelsamratnasik.com; Old Agra Rd; s/d from ₹950/1330, with AC ₹1640/1960; ❄🌐) Its veg restaurant has fallen out of favour as a local hot spot, but Samrat's hotel still offers superb value, with comfortable rooms, some of which have large windows and pine furniture. Located right next to the bus stand, with a private bus agent at its doorstep, it's a sensible choice. Wi-fi is speedy but their system is maddening.

★ Beyond by Sula
RESORT $$$

(☎7875555725; www.sulawines.com; Gangavarhe; r week/weekend incl breakfast ₹7870/9680, Sky Villa from ₹32,670; ❄🌐🏊) Sula Vineyard's brand-new seven-room flagship resort sits a few kilometres from the winery (hence the name: Beyond) near the edges of the beautiful Gangapur Dam backwaters. Ubercontemporary rooms feature polished concrete flooring and huge windows framing the picturesque setting, which culminates in the massive three-bedroom Sky Villa, a modern, architecturally fascinating space evoking the modernist luxury resorts of Patagonia.

Soma Vineyards Resort
RESORT $$$

(☎7028066016; www.somavinevillage.com; Gat 1, Gangavarhe; d/ste incl breakfast from ₹6000/9650; ❄🌐🏊) Soma Vine Village's luxury resort, 17km west of Nasik, sits by a lake and is bordered by rolling hills. Roam the landscape by bicycle, laze the hours away at the spa or grab a bottle of award-winning Chenin Blanc Gold and tuck into one of its 32 beautifully designed, contemporary rooms and villas, some with lush plants and private pools.

🍴 Eating

Divtya Budhlya Wada
MAHARASHTRIAN $$

(Anadwali, Gangapur Rd; mains ₹130-340, thalis ₹210-350; ☺11am-3.30pm & 7-11pm) If you're looking for a spicy kick in the gut, this local hot spot is the place to come for authentic Maharashtrian food that'll make your nose run. Under an atmospheric, lantern-lit bamboo canopy, locals devour the special mutton thali (which could be more generous) and rustic à la carte countryside dishes bone-in, grease, fat and all. Tasty stuff.

It's located 5km northwest of the centre – order an Uber for ₹85 or so. Signed in Marati only.

Dhaba
INDIAN $$

(Hotel Panchavati, 430 Vakil Wadi Rd; thali ₹260; ☺11.30am-3pm & 7-10.30pm) This wildly popular restaurant known as Panchavati around town (but actually called Dhaba) will take your tastebuds on a roller coaster of flavour via its Gujarati thalis spruced up with local touches like mini *bakri* (bread made with sorghum) and served with bullet-train efficiency. Great *dhal tadka* (dhal flavoured with tempered ghee and spices), too. It's inside Hotel Panchavati.

❶ Information

MTDC Tourist Office (☎0253-2570059; www.maharashtratourism.gov.in; T/1, Golf Club, Old Agra Rd, Matoshree Nagar; ☺10am-6pm) About 1km south of the Old Central bus stand; helpful staff.

EATING PRICE RANGES

The following price ranges refer to the price of a main course.

$ below ₹150

$$ ₹150 to ₹300

$$$ above ₹300

MISAL PAV!

Nasik's undeniable breakfast of champions is *misal pav*, an unusual Maharashtrian dish prepared locally with bean sprouts and pulses, topped with a *potato-chiwda* (flattened puffed rice) mixture, *gathiya sev* (crunchy chickpea flour noodles), onions, lemon and coriander and served with a buttered bun – a cornucopia of flavour and texture born in Kolhapur but religiously adopted by Nashikkars.

Opinions are heated, but **Sadhana** (www.facebook.com/sadhanarestaurant.misal; Hardev Bagh, Motiwala College Rd, Barden Phata; meals ₹80; ☺8am-3pm), 8km west of the city centre (a ₹110 or so Uber ride), is consistently awarded the best in town. Chefs at this rustic institution light up a 560L wood-fired cauldron at 5am every morning, three hours ahead of a breakfast rush that will see bow-tied waiters dance among the jam-packed, straw-topped tables and cot seating within minutes of opening.

So how do you eat it? Fill your bowl with small torn bits of bread, throw a wallop of onions and coriander in the mix and a squeeze of fresh lemon, drizzle a bit of *tari* (a heavily spiced oil mix) to taste (careful now!) and pour a healthy portion of *rassa*, a soupy red masala-laced liquid, over the whole thing until it's all floating in favourful goodness. Dig in with a spoon. Finish things off with *gulachi jalebi* (*jalebi* are orange-coloured coils of deep-fried batter made with jaggery rather than refined sugar) and its absolutely excellent chai. You're welcome!

❶ Getting There

BUS

The **New Central Bus Stand** (☏ 0253-2309308) has services to Aurangabad (from ₹237, 4½ hours, hourly 6am to 3am), Mumbai (₹275, four hours, hourly) and Pune (non-AC/AC ₹350/650, 4½ hours, hourly). Nasik's **Old Central Bus Stand** (CBS; ☏ 0253-2309310) has buses to Trimbak (₹33, 45 minutes, hourly 5am to 11pm) and Igatpuri (₹57, one hour, hourly 10.30am to 11pm). South of town, the Mahamarg Bus Stand has services to Mumbai (non-AC ₹250, 4½ hours, hourly), Shirdi (non-AC ₹108, 2½ hours, hourly 6am to 10.30pm) and Ghoti (non-AC ₹45, 1¾ hours, hourly).

Private buses head to Ahmedabad (non-AC/AC sleeper from ₹600/1000, 12 hours), Mumbai (from ₹250/450, four hours), Pune (from ₹300/450, six hours) and Nagpur (AC sleeper f₹1000, 12 hours). There is a handy private bus agent outside Hotel Samrat.

Most private buses depart from Dwarka Circle and most Mumbai-bound buses terminate at Dadar TT Circle in Mumbai.

TRAIN

The Nasik Rd train station is 8km southeast of the town centre, but a useful **railway reservation office** (1st fl, Palika Bazaar, Sharanpur Rd; ☺8am-8pm Mon-Sat, to 2pm Sun) is 500m west of the Old Central Bus Stand. There are around 15 daily trains to Mumbai so you won't have to wait long; these include the daily Pushpak Express (1st/2AC/sleeper ₹1301/806/203, 4½ hours, 3.15pm). Connections to Aurangabad are not good, with only four daily departures; try the Tapovan Express (2nd class/chair ₹118/391, 3½ hours, 9.50am). An autorickshaw to the station costs about ₹150.

Around Nasik

Bhandardara

The picturesque village of Bhandardara is nestled deep in the folds of the Sahyadris, about 70km from Nasik. A little-visited place surrounded by craggy mountains, it is one of Maharashtra's best escapes from the bustle of urban India. The lush mountain scenery, especially during the monsoon, is extraordinary.

Most of Bhandardara's habitation is thrown around **Arthur Lake**, a horse-shoe-shaped reservoir fed by the waters of the Pravara River, which counts as one of India's largest. The lake is barraged on one side by the imposing Wilson Dam, a colonial-era structure dating back to 1910. Hikers should consider a hike to the summit of **Mt Kalsubai**, which at 1646m was once used as an observation point by the Marathas. Alternatively, you could hike to the ruins of the **Ratangad Fort**, another of Shivaji's erstwhile strongholds; or to several Bollywood-preferred waterfalls like **Randha Falls** or **Umbrella Falls**. Guided highlight tours run ₹600.

The charming **Anandvan Resort** (☏ 02424-257320; www.anandvanresorts.com; Ghatghar Rd,

GRAPES OF NASIK

From wimpy raisins to full-bodied wines, the grapes of Nasik have come a long way. The surrounding region had been producing table grapes since ancient times; however, it was only in the early 1990s that a couple of entrepreneurs realised that Nasik, with its fertile soils and temperate climate, boasted good conditions for wine cultivation. In 1997 industry pioneer **Sula Vineyards** fearlessly invested in a crop of Sauvignon Blanc and Chenin Blanc and the first batch of domestic wines hit the shelves in 2000. Nasik hasn't looked back.

'Over the last 10 years, quality and wine consistency have been ramped up, as has investment (both by mergers/takeovers and via foreign investment and know-how)', says international wine consultant, writer and sommelier Harshal Danger-Shah. 'The results are in the glass: Indian wine is tasting fresher and more enjoyable than ever before.'

These days the wine list in most of Nasik's wineries has stretched to include Shiraz, Merlot, Cabernet, Semillon and Zinfandel as well as a few sparkling wines; and bars and restaurants in India's bigger cities have finally got hip to domestic wines. Even the pairings have evolved: ever tried a nice Indian Chenin Blanc alongside Keralan seafood? Or an Indian Chardonnay with butter chicken?

It's well-worth sampling these drops firsthand by visiting one of the region's beautiful estates. Oenophiles should enlist **Wine Friend** (☏9822439051; www.winefriend.in), the only experienced guide doing wine speciality tours around Nasik's vineyards (₹6000 plus tasting fees). If you're just looking for a designated driver, cars can be hired from ₹2400. Try the friendly and English-speaking Sanil at **SCK Rent-A-Car** (☏8888080525; scktravels2015@gmail.com) for a horn-free ride.

Sula Vineyards (☏9970090010; www.sulawines.com; Gat 36/2, Govardhan Village, off Gangapur-Savargaon Rd; ⊙11am-11pm), located 15km west of Nasik, offers a professional tour (around 45 minutes) of its impressive estate and high-tech facilities. This is rounded off with a wine-tasting session (four/six wines ₹150/250) that features its best drops, including at least one from its top-end Rasa line. The cafe here has commanding views of the countryside.

York Winery (☏0253-2230701; www.yorkwinery.com; Gat 15/2, Gangavarhe Village, Gangapur-Savargaon Rd; ⊙noon-10pm, tours 12.30-6pm) A further kilometre from Sula Vineyards, family-owned York Winery offers tours and wine-tasting sessions (five/seven wines ₹150/250) in a top-floor room that has scenic views of the lake and surrounding hills. Four reds, including its flagship barrel-aged Cab Shiraz, three whites, a Rosé and a sparkling are produced. There's a large garden where Western snacks (olives, cheeses) are offered.

Soma Vine Village (☏7028066016; www.somavinevillage.com; Gat 1, Gangavarhe; ⊙11.30am-6.30pm) One of Nasik's newest wineries, Soma Vine Village, 17km west of the city centre on the same road as Sula and York, offers 45-minute tours that end in a sampling plucked from its 11-wine portfolio (five/seven wines ₹250/350), including its award-winning Chenin Blanc Gold and its new Rosé dessert wine, both excellent.

Chandon (☏9561065030; www.chandon.co.in; Gat 652/653, Taluka-Dindori Village; ⊙9am-6pm) Nasik's newest winery is a world-class facility on meticulously manicured grounds that easily rank as Nasik's most peaceful and beautiful. Tastings (₹500), by appointment only, feature India's leading sparkling wines, Chandon Brut (Chenin Blanc/Chardonnay/Pinot Noir) and Brut Rosé (Shiraz/Pinot Noir). Sip your bubbly in the upscale contemporary lounge, wine gallery or on the tremendously picturesque terrace. It's 26km north of Nasik.

Grover Zampa (☏02553-204379; www.groverzampa.in; Gat 967/1026, Village Sanjegaon, Tallgatpuri; ⊙10am-5.30pm, tours 10.30am, 2.30pm & 4pm) It first produced juice with imported French vines at its Karnataka estate in 1992. Today, it's India's oldest surviving winery and easily its most lauded (74 international awards between 2014 and 2016 alone). Tours and tastings at its Nasik estate, 53km southwest of the city, take place in its cinematic cave (five/seven wines ₹500/650). The Soirée Brut Rosé and the top-end Chêne Grand Réserve Tempranillo-Shiraz are fantastic. If you come out this way, do dine at nearby **Malaka Spice** (www.malakaspice.com; Vallonné Vineyard, Gat 504, Kavnai Shiver; mains ₹285-535; ⊙11.30am-11.30pm), Nasik's best and most scenic wine country restaurant.

Village Shendi; s/d from ₹5450/5950; ❋ 🛜), a hilltop hotel with a choice of comfy cottages and villas overlooking Arthur Lake, allows you to sleep in style.

Bhandardara can be accessed by taking a local bus from Nasik's **Mahamarg bus stand** to Ghoti (₹64, one hour), from where shared jeeps carry on the remaining kilometres to Bhandardara (₹40, 45 minutes). A taxi from Nasik can also drop you at your resort for about ₹2000.

Igatpuri

Vipassana International Academy
MEDITATION
(📋 02553-244076; www.giri.dhamma.org; Dhamma Giri, Igatpuri; donations accepted; ⊙ visitors centre 9.30am-5.30pm) Located about 44km south of Nasik, Igatpuri is home to the headquarters of the world's largest *vipassana* meditation institution, the Vipassana International Academy. Ten-day residential courses (advance bookings compulsory) are held throughout the year, though teachers warn that it requires rigorous discipline. Basic accommodation, food and meditation instruction are provided free of charge, but donations upon completion are accepted. Visitors can watch a 20-minute intro video or take part in a 10-minute mini Anapana meditation session.

This strict form of meditation was first taught by Gautama Buddha in the 6th century BC and was reintroduced to India by teacher SN Goenka in the 1960s.

Buses (₹57, one hour, hourly 10.30am to 11pm) and shared taxis (per person ₹500) for Igatpuri depart from Nasik's Old Bus Stand. Numerous daily trains call at Igatpuri from Nasik Rd station and Mumbai's CST.

Trimbak

Trimbakeshwar Temple
HINDU TEMPLE
(entrance ₹200, to avoid queue ₹200; ⊙ 6am-10pm) The moody Trimbakeshwar Temple stands in the centre of Trimbak, 33km west of Nasik. It's one of India's most sacred temples, containing a highly venerated *jyoti linga,* one of the 12 most important shrines to Shiva. Although the sign says only Hindus are allowed in, it's outdated and non-Hindus are welcome to enter (expect mere seconds in the inner sanctum as security corrals the crowd through). Mobile phones are prohibited.

Nearby, the waters of the Godavari River flow into the Gangadwar bathing tank, where all are welcome to wash away their sins.

Trimbak is a quick day trip from Nasik so most folks don't spend the night. But there are loads of guesthouses and resorts, many of which have panoramic views of the striking Bhahmagiri mountain range. The road leading to the temple is chock-full of snack stalls and restaurants if you fancy a bite.

Buses for Trimbak depart Nasik's Old Bus Stand hourly 5am to 11pm (₹33, 45 minutes). The last bus back to Nasik departs at 10.30pm

Aurangabad

📋 0240 / POP 1.28 MILLION / ELEV 515M

Aurangabad laid low through most of the tumultuous history of medieval India and only hit the spotlight when the last Mughal emperor, Aurangzeb, made the city his capital from 1653 to 1707. With the emperor's death came the city's rapid decline, but the brief period of glory saw the building of some fascinating monuments, including Bibi-qa-Maqbara, a Taj Mahal replica, and these continue to draw a steady trickle of visitors. Alongside other historic relics, such as a group of ancient Buddhist caves, these Mughal relics make Aurangabad a good choice for a weekend excursion from Mumbai. But the real reason for traipsing here is because the town is an excellent base for exploring the World Heritage Sites of Ellora and Ajanta.

Silk fabrics were once Aurangabad's chief revenue generator and the town is still known across the world for its hand-woven Himroo and Paithani saris.

⊙ Sights

★ Bibi-qa-Maqbara
MONUMENT
(Indian/foreigner ₹15/200; ⊙ 6am-8pm) Built by Aurangzeb's son Azam Khan in 1679 as a mausoleum for his mother Rabia-ud-Daurani, Bibi-qa-Maqbara is widely known as the poor man's Taj. With its four minarets flanking a central onion-domed mausoleum, the white structure certainly does bear a striking resemblance to Agra's Taj Mahal.

Aurangabad Caves
CAVE
(Indian/foreigner ₹15/200; ⊙ 6am-6pm) Architecturally speaking, the Aurangabad Caves aren't a patch on Ellora or Ajanta, but they do shed light on early Buddhist architecture and make for a quiet and peaceful outing. Carved out of the hillside in the 6th or 7th century AD, the 10 caves, comprising two

Aurangabad

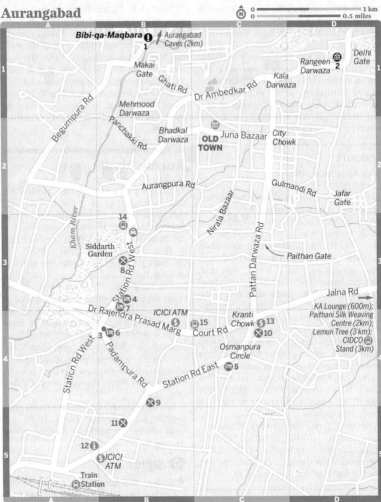

MAHARASHTRA AURANGABAD

groups 1km apart (retain your ticket for entry into both sets), are all Buddhist.

**Shrimat Chatrapati
Shivaji Museum** MUSEUM
(Dr Ambedkar Rd; ₹5; ⊙10.30am-6.30pm Fri-Wed)
This simple museum is dedicated to the life of the Maratha hero Shivaji. Its collection includes a 500-year-old chain-mail suit and a copy of the Quran, handwritten by Aurangzeb.

👉 Tours

MSRTC (🕿0240-2242164; www.msrtc.gov.
in; Central Bus Stand, Station Rd West) operates

daily Volvo AC bus tours to the Ajanta (₹682) and Ellora (₹265) Caves. Be aware that these are mass-market tours popular with domestic tourists and designed to cover as much ground as possible in a short period of time. Prices are transport only – they do not cover a guide or admission fees. The Ellora tour also includes all the other major Aurangabad sites along with Daulatabad Fort, which is a lot to swallow in a day. Though tours technically start at the Central Bus Stand (p91), you can hop on at the second stop at MTDC Holiday Resort (Station Rd East) at

Aurangabad

7.30am (Ajanta) and 8.30am (Ellora), which is also the best spot for information.

Ashoka Tours & Travels SIGHTSEEING
(☏ 9890340816, 0240-2359102; www.touristaurangabad.com; Hotel Panchavati, Station Rd West; ⊙ 7am-8pm) The stand-out Aurangabad agency, with excellent city and regional tours and decent car hire at fair rates. Prices for an air-con car with up to four people are ₹1450 for Ellora and ₹2450 for Ajanta. Run by Ashok T Kadam, a knowledgeable former autorickshaw driver.

🛏 Sleeping

★ Hotel Panchavati HOTEL $
(☏ 0240-2328755; www.hotelpanchavati.com; Station Rd West; s/d ₹1000/1130, r with AC ₹1250; ❄ @ �̂) A traveller-oriented budget hotel in town, the Panchavati is run by ever-helpful, switched-on management who understand travellers' needs. Rooms are compact but thoughtfully appointed, with crown moulding, comfortable beds (with paisley-style bedspreads) and thick bath towels. There are two decent restaurants and a 'bar' (read:

drinking room) and it's a great place to hook up with fellow intrepid nomads.

Hotel Raviraj HOTEL $
(☏ 0240-2352124; www.hotelraviraj.in; Rajendra Prasad Marg; r with AC from ₹1690; ❄ �̂) The standard rooms at this pleasant midrange option masquerading as a budget hotel are easily Aurangabad's best deal. Spacious, comfy linens, flat-screen TVs, good bathrooms (with motion-sensor lighting) and (weak) wi-fi. The pricier executives are basically the same, with more polished furniture. Tack on a friendly staff, a leafy foyer, restaurant/bar and beer-friendly 1st-floor terrace and it's tough to beat.

Hotel Gurjas HOTEL $
(☏ 0240-2323841; www.hotelgurjas.com; Osmanpura Circle, Station Rd East; s/d ₹1026/1139, with AC ₹1250/1370; ❄ �̂) The former Hotel Oberoi was manhandled by the well-known, five-star luxury chain into changing its name. Voila! Hotel Gurjas was born. Owned by the same people behind Hotel Panchavati, this means good service and helpful staff. The spacious rooms are modern with flat-screen TVs, comfy beds, desks and attractive, newly renovated bathrooms.

Call for a free pick-up from the train or bus stations.

Hotel Green Olive HOTEL $$
(☏ 0240-2329490; www.hotelgreenolive.com; 13/3 Bhagya Nagar, CBS Rd; s/d from ₹3570/4760; ❄ �̂) Cramped bathrooms aside, this boutique-ish business hotel offers stylish, well-equipped and -maintained rooms. The friendly staff here looks after guests commendably and can organise transport and tours; there's a good bar and restaurant on the premises.

★ Lemon Tree HOTEL $$$
(☏ 0240-6603030; www.lemontreehotels.com; R7/2 Chikalthana, Airport Rd; s/d incl breakfast from ₹7790/9350; ❄ @ �̂ ≋) The Lemon Tree offers elegance and class, looking more like a billionaire's luxury whitewashed Mediterranean villa than an Indian hotel. It's well designed too: all rooms face inwards, overlooking perhaps the best pool in the Decca plateau – all 50m of it. The artsy standard rooms, though not large, are brightened by vivid tropical tones offset against snow-white walls.

🍴 Eating

Kailash INDIAN $
(Station Rd East; mains ₹50-150; ⊙ 8am-11pm; ❄) This bustling pure-veg restaurant looks and

MAHARASHTRA AURANGABAD

feels vaguely like an half-hearted Indian take on an American diner, with big portions of food in familial surrounds. There's lots of Punjabi and South Indian food, as well as rice and noodle dishes, and an extensive list of *pav bhaji* options, a Mumbai street-food staple. It's rightfully popular.

★ Bhoj INDIAN $$
(Station Rd West; thali ₹210; ⊘ 11am-3pm & 7-11pm) Rightly famous for its delicious, unlimited Rajasthani and Gujarati thalis, Bhoj is a wonderful place to refuel and relax after a hard day on the road (or rail). It's on the 1st floor of a somewhat scruffy little shopping arcade, but the decor, ambience, service and presentation are all first rate. Best thali in Maharashtra!

Green Leaf INDIAN $$
(www.greenleafpureveg.com; Shop 6-9, Fame Tapadiya Multiplex, Town Centre; mains ₹140-280; ⊘ noon-11pm; ☏) Aurangabad's favourite modern vegetarian is loved for delectable pure-veg dishes that really pop with flavour (try the veg handi or paneer Hyderabadi) and come with spice level indicators (one chilli pepper equals medium!). Teal-panted servers gracefully navigate the clean, contemporary surrounds. So clean, in fact, the kitchen is open for all to see. It's 400m from CIDCO Bus Stand.

Swad Restaurant INDIAN $$
(Station Rd East, Kanchan Chamber; thali ₹200) Though prices are similar, always-packed Swad is the simpler, more local and slightly greasier counterpart to some of our other favourite spots in town. Waiters clad in bright Rajasthani-style turbans sling spicy *sabzi* (vegetables), dhal and other Gujarati-Rajasthani thali delights – an endless flavour train under the benevolent gaze of patron saint swami Yogiraj Hanstirth.

Tandoor NORTH INDIAN $$
(Station Rd East, Shyam Chambers; mains ₹150-380; ⊘ 11am-11pm) Offers fine tandoori dishes, flavoursome North Indian veg and nonveg options and an extensive beer list (for Aurangabad) in a weirdly Pharaonic atmosphere. Try the wonderful sizzler kebabs. A few Chinese dishes are also on offer, but patrons clearly prefer the dishes coming out of... well... the tandoor.

🍷 Drinking & Nightlife

KA Lounge BAR
(Satya Dharam Complex, Akashwari Cir, Jalna Rd; cocktails from ₹320; ⊘ noon-11pm Mon-Fri, to 1am Sat & Sun; ☏) Aurangabad's one and only trendy cocktail bar is brand-spanking new and caters to the city's upwardly hip who plop down on cosy lounge seating amid exposed brick walls and groove to DJ-spun hip-hop, jazz and house on Saturday and Sunday. Try the basil and green chilli mojito for a cool burn.

🛍 Shopping

Himroo material is a traditional Aurangabad speciality made from cotton, silk and metallic threads. Most of today's Himroo shawls and saris are produced using power looms, but some showrooms still stock hand-loomed cloth.

Himroo saris start at around ₹2000 for a cotton and silk blend. Paithani saris, which are of superior quality, range from ₹8000 to ₹150,000 – but some of them take more than a year to make. If you're buying, make sure you get authentic Himroo, not 'Aurangabad silk'.

Paithani Silk Weaving Centre TEXTILES
(www.paithanisilk.com; 54, P-1, Town Center, Lokmat Nagar; ⊘ 9.30am-9pm) One of the best places to come and watch weavers at work is the Paithani Silk Weaving Centre where you'll find good-quality products for sale. It's about 6km east of Kranti Chowk (behind the Air India office), so take a taxi.

ⓘ Information

Indiatourism (Government of India Tourism; ☏ 0240-2364999; www.incredibleindia. org; MTDC Holiday Resort, Station Rd East; ⊘ 9.30am-6pm Mon-Fri) India-wide information is available at India's national tourist board office in Aurangabad.

MTDC Office (☏ 0240-2343169; www.maharashtratourism.gov.in; MTDC Holiday Resort, Station Rd East; ⊘ 10am-1pm & 1.30-5.30pm Mon-Sat) Quite helpful and has a stock of brochures.

Post Office (www.indiapost.gov.in; Juna Bazaar; ⊘ 10am-6pm Mon-Sat)

ⓘ Getting There & Away

AIR
Aurangabad Airport (Chikkalthana Airport) is 10km east of town. Daily direct flights go to Delhi and Mumbai with both **Air India** (☏ 0240-2483392; www.airindia.in; Airliens House, Town Centre, Jalna Rd; ⊘ 10am-1pm & 2-5pm Mon-Sat) and **Jet Airways** (☏ 0240-2441392; www.jetairways.com; 4, Santsheel, Vidyanagar 7 Hills, Jalna Rd) and to Hyderabad with **Trujet**

(☎ 0240-2471818; www.trujet.com; Aurang-abad Airport).

BUS

Buses leave about every half-hour from the **MS-RTC/Central Bus Stand** (☎ 0240-2242164; Station Rd West) to Pune (non-AC/AC ₹341/661, 5½ hours, 5am to 11.30pm) and Nasik (non-AC ₹214, 4½ hours, 6am to 12.15pm). Private bus agents are clustered on Dr Rajendra Prasad Marg and Court Rd; a few sit closer to the bus stand. Deluxe overnight bus destinations include Mumbai (AC sleeper ₹774 to ₹1400, 7½ to 9½ hours), Ahmedabad (AC/non-AC sleeper from ₹800/500, 13 to 15 hours) and Nagpur (AC sleeper ₹660 to ₹1100, non-AC ₹800, 8½ to 10 hours).

Ordinary buses head to Ellora from the MSRTC bus stand every half-hour (AC/non-AC ₹251/32, 30 minutes, 5am to 12.30am) and Jalgaon (non-AC ₹177, four hours, 5am to 8pm) via Fardapur (₹120, three hours), which is the drop-off point for Ajanta.

From the **CIDCO Bus Stand** (☎ 0240-2240149; Airport Rd), by the Lemon Tree hotel junction, six ordinary buses leave direct for the Lonar meteorite crater (₹180, 4½ hours, 5am, 6am, 8am, 10am, 12.30pm and 1pm).

TRAIN

Aurangabad's **train station** (Station Rd East) is not on a main line, but it has four daily direct trains to/from Mumbai. The Tapovan Express (2nd class/chair ₹173/571, 7½ hours) departs Aurangabad at 2.35pm. The Janshatabdi Express (2nd class/chair ₹223/686, 6½ hours) departs Aurangabad at 6am. For Hyderabad, trains include the Ajanta Express (sleeper/2AC ₹233/1226, 10 hours, 10.45pm). To reach northern or eastern India, take a bus to Jalgaon and board a train there.

❶ Getting Around

Autorickshaws are common here and are bookable (along with taxis) with Ola Cabs (www.olacabs.com). The taxi stand is next to the MSRTC/Central Bus Stand; shared 4WDs also depart from here for Ellora and Daulatabad but are usually very packed. Renting a car and driver is a much better option.

You can hire a car and driver through **Ashoka Tours & Travels** (p89): a return trip to Ellora is ₹1250/1450 in a car/AC car, to Ajanta it's ₹2250/2450.

Around Aurangabad

Daulatabad

This one's straight out of a Tolkien fantasy. A most beguiling structure, the 12th-century

WORTH A TRIP

LONAR METEORITE CRATER

If you like offbeat adventures, travel to Lonar to explore a prehistoric natural wonder. About 50,000 years ago, a meteorite slammed into the earth here, leaving behind a massive crater 2km across and 170m deep (it's said to be the world's third largest). In scientific jargon, it's the only hypervelocity natural-impact crater in basaltic rock in the world. In lay terms, it's as tranquil and relaxing a spot as you could hope to find, with a shallow green lake at its base and wilderness all around, including aquatic birds. The lake water is supposedly alkaline and excellent for the skin. Scientists think the meteorite is still embedded about 600m below the southeastern rim of the crater.

The crater's edge is home to several Hindu temples as well as wildlife, including langurs, peacocks, deer and numerous birds.

There are regular buses between Lonar and the CIDCO bus stand in Aurangabad (₹180, 4½ hours, 5am, 6am, 8am, 10am, 12.30pm and 1pm).

hilltop fortress of **Daulatabad** (Indian/foreigner ₹15/200; ☉ 6am-6pm) is located about 15km north of Aurangabad, en route to Ellora. Now in ruins, the citadel was originally conceived as an impregnable fort by the Yadava kings. Its most infamous high point came in 1328, when it was named Daulatabad (City of Fortune) by eccentric Delhi sultan Mohammed Tughlaq and made the capital – he even marched the entire population of Delhi 1100km south to populate it. Ironically, Daulatabad – despite being better positioned strategically than Delhi – soon proved untenable as a capital due to an acute water crisis, and Tughlaq forced the weary inhabitants all the way back to Delhi, which had by then been reduced to a ghost town.

Daulatabad's central bastion sits atop a 200m-high craggy outcrop known as Devagiri (Hill of the Gods), surrounded by a 5km **fort** (Indian/foreigner ₹15/200; ☉ 6am-6pm). The climb to the summit takes about an hour, and leads past an ingenious series of defences, including multiple doorways designed with odd angles and spike-studded doors to prevent elephant charges. A tower of victory, known as the Chand Minar (Tower of the Moon), built in 1435, soars 60m above the ground to the right; it's closed to visitors. Higher up, you can walk into the Chini Mahal, where Abul Hasan Tana Shah, king of Golconda, was held captive for 12 years before his death in 1699. Nearby, there's a 6m cannon, cast from five different metals and engraved with Aurangzeb's name.

Part of the ascent goes through a pitch-black, bat-infested, water-seeping, spiralling tunnel. Guides (₹500) are available near the ticket counter to show you around, and their torch-bearing assistants will lead you through the dark passageway for a small tip. On the way down you'll be left to your own devices, so carry a torch.

As the fort is in ruins (with crumbling staircases and sheer drops) and involves a steep ascent, the elderly, children and those suffering from vertigo or claustrophobia will find it a tough challenge. Allow 2½ hours to explore the structure, and bring water.

Ellora

📋 02437

Give a man a hammer and chisel and he'll create art for posterity. Come to the Unesco World Heritage Site **Ellora cave temples** (Indian/foreigner ₹30/500; ⊘ 6am-6pm Wed-Mon), located 30km from Aurangabad, and you'll know exactly what we mean. The epitome of ancient Indian rock-cut architecture, these caves were chipped out laboriously over five centuries by generations of Buddhist, Hindu and Jain monks. Monasteries, chapels, temples – the caves served every purpose and they were stylishly embellished with a profusion of remarkably detailed sculptures.

Undoubtedly Ellora's shining moment is the awesome Kailasa Temple (Cave 16), the world's largest monolithic sculpture, hewn top to bottom against a rocky slope by 7000 labourers over a period of 150 years. Dedicated to Lord Shiva, it is clearly among the best that ancient Indian architecture has to offer.

○ Sights

Ellora has 34 caves in all: 12 Buddhist (AD 600–800), 17 Hindu (AD 600–900) and five Jain (AD 800–1000) – though the exact time scales of these caves' construction is the subject of academic debate.

Unlike the caves at Ajanta, which are carved into a sheer rock face, the Ellora caves line a 2km-long escarpment, the gentle slope of which allowed architects to build elaborate courtyards in front of the shrines and render them with sculptures of a surreal quality.

The established academic theory is that Ellora represents the renaissance of Hinduism under the Chalukya and Rashtrakuta dynasties, the subsequent decline of Indian Buddhism and a brief resurgence of Jainism under official patronage. However, due to the absence of inscriptional evidence, it's been impossible to accurately date most of Ellora's monuments - some scholars argue that some Hindu temples predate those in the Buddhist group. What is certain is that their coexistence at one site indicates a lengthy period of religious tolerance.

Official guides can be hired at the ticket office in front of the Kailasa Temple for ₹1370 (up to five people). Guides have an extensive knowledge of cave architecture so are worth the investment. If your tight itinerary forces you to choose between Ellora or Ajanta, Ellora wins hands down in terms of architecture (though Ajanta's setting is more beautiful and more of a pleasure to explore).

Ellora is very popular with domestic tourists; if you can visit on a weekday, it's far less crowded.

★ Kailasa Temple   HINDU TEMPLE

One of India's greatest monuments, this astonishing temple, carved from solid rock, was built by King Krishna I in AD 760 to represent Mt Kailasa (Kailash), Shiva's Himalayan abode. To say that the assignment was daring would be an understatement. Three huge trenches were bored into the sheer cliff face, a process that entailed removing 200,000 tonnes of rock by hammer and chisel, before the temple could begin to take shape and its remarkable sculptural decoration could be added.

Covering twice the area of the Parthenon in Athens and being half as high again, Kailasa is an engineering marvel that was executed straight from the head with zero margin for error. Modern draughtsmen might have a lesson or two to learn here.

The temple houses several intricately carved panels, depicting scenes from the Ramayana, the Mahabharata and the adventures of Krishna. Also worth admiring are the immense monolithic pillars that stand in the courtyard, flanking the entrance on both sides, and the southeastern gallery that has 10 giant and fabulous panels depicting the different avatars (incarnations of a deity) of Lord Vishnu.

After you're done with the main enclosure, bypass the hordes of snack-munching day trippers to explore the temple's many dank, bat urine–soaked corners with their numerous forgotten carvings. Afterwards, hike up an overgrown foot trail (or bypass the scaffolding to walk up sturdier rock) to the south of the complex that takes you to the top perimeter of the 'cave', from where you can get a bird's-eye view of the entire temple complex.

Buddhist Caves
CAVE

Calm and contemplation infuse the 12 Buddhist caves, which stretch to the south of Kailasa. All are Buddhist *viharas* (monasteries) used for study and worship, but these multistoreyed structures also included cooking, living and sleeping areas. The one exception is Cave 10, which is a *chaitya* (assembly hall). While the earliest caves are simple, Caves 11 and 12 are more ambitious; both comprise three storeys and are on par with the more impressive Hindu temples.

Cave 1, the simplest *vihara,* may have been a granary. **Cave 2** is notable for its ornate pillars and the imposing seated Buddha that faces the setting sun. **Cave 3** and **Cave 4** are unfinished and not well preserved.

Cave 5 is the largest *vihara* in this group at 18m wide and 36m long; the rows of stone benches hint that it may once have been an assembly hall.

Cave 6 is an ornate *vihara* with wonderful images of Tara, consort of the Bodhisattva Avalokitesvara, and of the Buddhist goddess of learning, Mahamayuri, looking remarkably similar to Saraswati, her Hindu equivalent. **Cave 7** is an unadorned hall. **Cave 8** is the first cave in which the sanctum is detached from the rear wall. **Cave 9**, located above Cave 8, is notable for its wonderfully carved fascia.

Cave 10 is the only *chaitya* in the Buddhist group and one of the finest in India. Its ceiling features ribs carved into the stonework; the grooves were once fitted with wooden panels. The balcony and upper gallery offer a closer view of the ceiling and a frieze depicting amorous couples. A decorative window gently illuminates an enormous figure of the teaching Buddha.

Cave 11, the Do Thal (Two Storey) Cave, is entered through its third basement level, not discovered until 1876. Like Cave 12, it

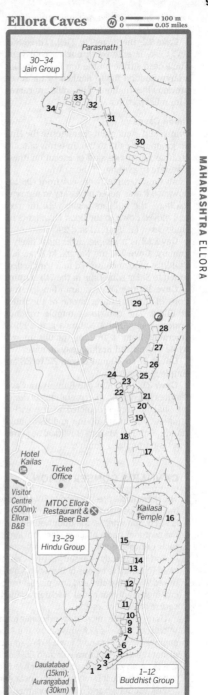

Ellora Caves

MAHARASHTRA ELLORA

possibly owes its size to competition with Hindu caves of the same period.

Cave 12, the huge Tin Thal (Three Storey) Cave, is entered through a courtyard. The locked shrine on the top floor contains a large Buddha figure flanked by his seven previous incarnations. The walls are carved with relief pictures.

Hindu Caves   CAVE

Drama and excitement characterise the Hindu group (Caves 13 to 29). In terms of scale, creative vision and skill of execution, these caves are in a league of their own.

All these temples were cut from the top down, so it was never necessary to use scaffolding – the builders began with the roof and moved down to the floor. Highlights include caves 14, 15, 16, 21 and 29.

Cave 13 is a simple cave, most likely a granary. Cave 14, the Ravana-ki-Khai, is a Buddhist *vihara* converted to a temple dedicated to Shiva sometime in the 7th century.

Cave 15, the Das Avatara (Ten Incarnations of Vishnu) Cave, is one of the finest at Ellora. The two-storey temple contains a mesmerising Shiva Nataraja and a Shiva emerging from a *lingam* (phallic image) while Vishnu and Brahma pay homage.

Caves 17 to 20 and Caves 22 to 28 are simple monasteries.

Cave 21, known as the Ramesvara Cave, features interesting interpretations of familiar Shaivite scenes depicted in the earlier temples. The figure of the goddess Ganga standing on her Makara (mythical sea creature) is particularly notable.

The large Cave 29, the Dumar Lena, is thought to be a transitional model between the simpler hollowed-out caves and the fully developed temples exemplified by the Kailasa. It has views over a nearby waterfall, though the path was inaccessible at time of writing. It's best reached via the MSRTC bus.

Jain Caves   CAVE

The five Jain caves, the last created at Ellora, may lack the ambitious size of the best Hindu temples, but they are exceptionally detailed, with some remarkable paintings and carvings.

The caves are 1km north of the last Hindu temple (Cave 29) at the end of the bitumen road; there is a MSRTC bus departing from in front of Kailasa Temple that runs back and forth (₹21 return).

Cave 30, the Chhota Kailasa (Little Kailasa), is a poor imitation of the great Kailasa Temple and stands by itself some distance from the other Jain temples. It's reached via the unmarked stairway between Caves 31 and 32.

In contrast, Cave 32, the Indra Sabha (Assembly Hall of Indra), is the finest of the Jain temples. Its ground-floor plan is similar to that of the Kailasa, but the upstairs area is as ornate and richly decorated as the downstairs is plain. There are images of the Jain *tirthankars* (great teachers) Parasnath and Gomateshvara, the latter surrounded by wildlife. Inside the shrine is a seated figure of Mahavira, the last *tirthankar* and founder of the Jain religion.

CANNABIS CONSERVATION

The remarkable preservation of Ellora's caves and paintings could be attributed to many things, but perhaps none more surprising than a healthy dose of hemp. While the jury is still out on whether the Buddhist, Hindu and Jain monks that called Ellora home over the centuries had a proclivity for smoking cannabis, archaeologists are sure they knew a thing or two about its preservation effects.

An 11-year study released in 2016 revealed that hemp, a variety of the *Cannabis sativa* plant (believed to be one of the world's oldest domesticated crops), has been discovered mixed in with the clay and lime plaster used at Ellora and is credited with being the secret ingredient that has slowed degradation at the Unesco World Heritage Site over the course of 1500 years.

Using electron microscopes, Fourier transforms, infra-red spectroscopy and stereomicroscopic studies, chemists from the Archaeological Survey of India found that samples from Ellora contained 10% *Cannabis sativa*, which resulted in reduced levels of insect activity at Ellora – around 25% of the paintings at Ajanta have been destroyed, where hemp was not used. In addition to Ellora, hemp was also implemented by the Yadavas, who built Daulatabad Fort near Aurangabad in the 12th century.

Talk about high and mighty monuments!

Cave **31** is really an extension of Cave **32**. Cave **33**, the Jagannath Sabha, is similar in plan to Cave **32** and has some well-preserved sculptures. The final temple, the small **Cave 34**, also has interesting sculptures. On the hilltop over the Jain temples, a 5m-high image of Parasnath looks down on Ellora.

🛏 Sleeping & Eating

Ellora B&B
GUESTHOUSE **$**

(📞 9960589867; ellorabedandbreakfast@gmail.com; Ellora Village; s/d incl breakfast from ₹500/800) For a bit of rustic cultural immersion, good-hearted man about town Sadeek and his uncle Rafiq have four simple rooms in their village home, 2km from the caves (and the crowds). The three best rooms open out onto a breezy terrace with farmland and mountain views and feature renovated en suite bathrooms with sit-down flush toilets and 24-hour hot water.

Grandma cooks up *poha* (flattened rice with spices), *upma* (semolina cooked with onions, spices, chilli peppers and coconut) and *aloo paratha* (potato-filled flatbread) for breakfast. Fancy it ain't, but the hospitality makes up for it.

Hotel Kailas
HOTEL **$$**

(📞 02437-244446; www.hotelkailas.com; r with/without AC ₹3570/2500; 🕸 🛜) The sole decent hotel near the site, with attractive air-con stone cottages set in leafy grounds. The restaurant (mains ₹90 to ₹280) is excellent, with a menu chalked up on a blackboard that includes sandwiches, breakfasts, curries and tandoori favourites. Sold in increments of three hours for ₹100, wi-fi, however, is ridiculous.

ℹ Information

Ellora Visitor Centre (🕒 9am-5pm Wed-Mon) Ellora's impressive visitor centre, 750m west of the site, is worth dropping by to put the caves in historical context. It features modern displays and information panels, a 15-minute video presentation and two galleries: one on the Kailasa Temple (with a diorama of the temple) and the other dedicated to the site itself.

ℹ Getting There & Away

Note that the temples are closed on Tuesday. Buses depart Aurangabad every half-hour (AC/non-AC ₹251/32, 30 minutes, 5am to 12.30am); the last bus departs from Ellora at 9pm. Share 4WDs are also an option, but get packed; they leave when full and stop outside the bus stand in Aurangabad (₹30). A full-day tour to Ellora, with stops en route, costs ₹1450 in an air-con car; try **Ashoka Tours & Travels** (p89). Autorickshaws ask for ₹800.

Ajanta
🎧 02438

Superbly set in a remote river valley 105km northeast of Aurangabad, the remarkable cave temples of Ajanta are this region's second World Heritage Site. Much older than Ellora, these secluded caves date from around the 2nd century BC to the 6th century AD and were among the earliest monastic institutions to be constructed in the country. Ironically, it was Ellora's rise that brought about Ajanta's downfall and historians believe the site was abandoned once the focus shifted to Ellora.

As the Deccan forest claimed and shielded the caves, with roots and shoots choking the sculptures, Ajanta remained deserted for about a millennium, until 1819 when a British hunting party led by officer John Smith stumbled upon it purely by chance.

◉ Sights

One of the primary reasons to visit Ajanta is to admire its renowned 'frescoes', actually temperas, which adorn many of the caves' interiors. With few other examples from ancient times matching their artistic excellence and fine execution, these paintings are of unfathomable heritage value.

Despite their age, the paintings in most caves remain finely preserved and many attribute this to their relative isolation from humanity for centuries. However, it would be a tad optimistic to say that decay hasn't set in.

It's believed that the natural pigments for these paintings were mixed with animal glue and vegetable gum to bind them to the dry surface. Many caves have small, crater-like holes in their floors, which acted as palettes during paint jobs.

Most buses ferrying tour groups don't arrive until noon. To avoid the crowds stay locally in Fardapur or make an early start from Aurangabad.

★ Ajanta Caves
CAVE

(Indian/foreigner ₹30/500, video ₹25, authorised guide ₹1370; 🕒 9am-5.30pm Tue-Sun) Ajanta's caves line a steep face of a horseshoe-shaped gorge bordering the Waghore River. Five of the caves are *chaityas* while others are *viharas*. Caves 8, 9, 10, 12, 13 and part of 15 are

Ajanta Caves

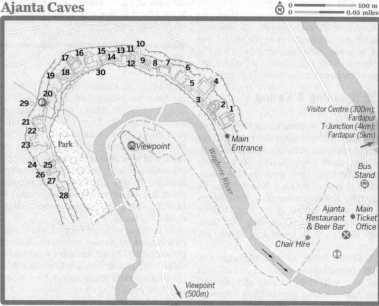

early Buddhist caves, while the others date from around the 5th century AD (Mahayana period). In the austere early Buddhist school, the Buddha was never represented directly but always alluded to by a symbol such as the footprint or wheel of law.

During busy periods, viewers are allotted 15 minutes within the caves, which have to be entered barefoot (socks/shoe covers allowed; flip-flops will make your life a lot easier). Caves 3, 5, 8, 22, 28, 29 and 30 remain either closed or inaccessible.

Cave 1
CAVE

Cave 1, a Mahayana *vihara,* was one of the last to be excavated and is the most beautifully decorated. This is where you'll find a rendition of the *Bodhisattva Padmapani,* the most famous and iconic of the Ajanta artworks. A verandah in front leads to a large congregation hall housing sculptures and narrative murals known for their splendid perspective and elaborate detailing of dress, daily life and facial expressions.

The colours in the paintings were created from local minerals, with the exception of the vibrant blue made from Central Asian lapis lazuli. Look up to the ceiling to see the carving of four deer sharing a common head.

Cave 2
CAVE

Cave 2 is a late Mahayana *vihara* with deliriously ornamented columns and capitals and some fine paintings. The ceiling is decorated with geometric and floral patterns. The murals depict scenes from the Jataka tales, including Buddha's mother's dream of a six-tusked elephant, which heralded his conception.

Cave 4
CAVE

Cave 4 is the largest *vihara* at Ajanta and is supported by 28 pillars. Although never completed, the cave has some impressive sculptures, such as the four statues surrounding a huge central Buddha. There are also scenes of people fleeing from the 'eight great dangers' to the protection of Avalokitesvara.

Cave 6
CAVE

Cave 6 is the only two-storey *vihara* at Ajanta, but parts of the lower storey have collapsed. Inside is a seated Buddha figure and an intricately carved door to the shrine. Upstairs the hall is surrounded by cells with fine paintings on the doorways.

Cave 7
CAVE

Cave 7 has an atypical design, with porches before the verandah leading directly to the four cells and the elaborately sculptured shrine.

Cave 9 CAVE

Cave 9 is one of the earliest *chaityas* at Ajanta. Although it dates from the early Buddhist period, the two figures flanking the entrance door were probably later Mahayana additions. Columns run down both sides of the cave and around the 3m-high dagoba (pagoda) at the far end.

Cave 10 CAVE

Cave 10 is thought to be the oldest cave (200 BC) and was the first one to be spotted by the British hunting party. Similar in design to Cave 9, it is the largest *chaitya*. The facade has collapsed and the paintings inside have been damaged, in some cases by graffiti dating from soon after their rediscovery. One of the pillars to the right bears the engraved name of Smith, who left his mark here for posterity.

Cave 16 CAVE

Cave 16, a *vihara,* contains some of Ajanta's finest paintings and is thought to have been the original entrance to the entire complex. The best known of these paintings is of the 'dying princess', Sundari, wife of the Buddha's half-brother Nanda, who is said to have fainted at the news her husband was renouncing the material life (and her) in order to become a monk.

Carved figures appear to support the ceiling and there's a statue of the Buddha seated on a lion throne teaching the Noble Eightfold Path.

Cave 17 CAVE

With carved dwarfs supporting the pillars, cave 17 has Ajanta's best-preserved and most varied paintings. Famous images include a princess applying make-up, a seductive prince using the old trick of plying his lover with wine and the Buddha returning home from his enlightenment to beg from his wife and astonished son.

A detailed panel tells of Prince Simhala's expedition to Sri Lanka: with 500 companions he is shipwrecked on an island where ogresses appear as enchanting women, only to seize and devour their victims. Simhala escapes on a flying horse and returns to conquer the island.

Cave 19 CAVE

Cave 19, a magnificent *chaitya,* has a remarkably detailed facade; its dominant

AJANTA PHOTOGRAPHY ETIQUETTE

Flash photography is strictly prohibited within the caves, due to its adverse effect on the natural dyes used in the paintings. Authorities have installed rows of tiny pigment-friendly lights, which cast a faint glow within the caves, as additional lighting is required for glimpsing minute details, but you'll have to rely on long exposures for photographs.

feature is an impressive horseshoe-shaped window. Two fine, standing Buddha figures flank the entrance. Inside is a three-tiered dagoba with a figure of the Buddha on the front. Outside the cave, to the west, sits a striking image of the Naga king with seven cobra hoods around his head. His wife, hooded by a single cobra, sits by his side.

Cave 26 CAVE

A largely ruined *chaitya,* cave 26 is now dramatically lit and contains some fine sculptures that shouldn't be missed. On the left wall is a huge figure of the reclining Buddha, lying back in preparation for nirvana. Other scenes include a lengthy depiction of the Buddha's temptation by Maya.

Viewpoints

Two lookouts offer picture-perfect views of the whole horseshoe-shaped gorge. The first is a short walk beyond the river, crossed via a bridge below Cave 8. A further 40-minute uphill walk (not to be attempted during the monsoons) leads to the lookout from where the British party first spotted the caves.

🛏 Sleeping

Padmapani Park HOTEL $

(☑ 0240-244280; www.hotelpadmapaniparkajanta. com; Jalgaon-Aurangabad Hwy, Fardapur; s/d ₹800/1000, with AC ₹1500; ❀ 🛜) It's definitely not going to thrill you, but this is one of the better run-down options in Fardapur, mainly due to the friendly, English-speaking manager, wi-fi in the reception/restaurant and the free rides they will give you to the Ajanta Visitor Centre.

MTDC Ajanta Tourist Resort HOTEL $$

(☑ 02438-244230; www.maharashtratourism.gov. in; Aurangabad-Jalgaon Rd, Fardapur; d with/ without AC ₹1900/2260; ❀) This government hotel is pricey but the best option at Ajanta, set amid lawns in a peaceful location off the main road in Fardapur, 5km from the caves. Air-con rooms, in apple green structures, are spacious; non-AC rooms are less interesting but fine. There's a bar, garden and restaurant with veg thalis (₹160 to ₹225) and cold beer (₹175).

✕ Eating

Hotel Radhe Krishna   DHABA $
(Aurangabad-Jalgaon Hwy, Fardapur; mains ₹90-160, thalis from ₹180; ⊘24hr) The best of Fardapur's streetside dhabas (casual eatery serving basic meals), this excellent spot is fresh, cheap and satisfying. The famous cook, Babu, and his team (Sunil on the chapati!) get a big kick out of foreigners dropping in, and just watching these guys whip up various curries, fries and thalis is pure entertainment.

ℹ Information

Ajanta Visitor Centre (⊘9am-5.30pm Tue-Sun) This new, state-of-the-art facility is one of India's very best, with highly impressive replicas of four caves (Nos 1, 2, 16 and 17) in real scale, audioguides available in many languages, excellent painting and sculpture galleries detailing the story of Buddhism in India, an audiovisual arena and a large cafe.

ℹ Getting There & Away

Buses from Aurangabad or Jalgaon will drop you at the Fardapur T-junction (where the highway meets the road to the caves), 4km from the site. From here, after paying an 'amenities' fee (₹10), walk to the departure point for the buses (with/without AC ₹22/16), which zoom up to the caves. Buses return half-hourly to the T-junction; the last bus is at 5pm. Note that the caves are closed on Monday.

All MSRTC (www.msrtc.gov.in) buses passing through Fardapur stop at the T-junction. After the caves close you can board buses to either Aurangabad or Jalgaon outside the MTDC Holiday Resort in Fardapur, 1km down the main road towards Jalgaon. Taxis are available in Fardapur; ₹1500/2500 should get you to Jalgaon/Aurangabad.

Jalgaon

☏ 0257 / POP 468,300 / ELEV 208M

Apart from being a handy base for exploring Ajanta 60km away, the industrial city of Jalgaon is really nothing more than a convenient transit town. It has rail connections to all major cities across India.

🛏 Sleeping & Eating

★Hotel Plaza   HOTEL $
(☏9370027354, 0257-2227354; hotelplaza_jal@yahoo.com; Station Rd; dm ₹300, s/d from ₹650/950, r with AC incl breakfast ₹1300-1650; ❄@⊛) This extremely well-managed and well-presented hotel is only a short hop from the station. Rooms vary in size and layout, but with whitewashed walls, a minimalist feel and bathrooms cleaner than a Jain temple, it's modestly boutique and brilliant value. Everything from the hospitality to the bed linens exceeds expectations.

Hotel Arya   INDIAN $
(Navi Peth; mains ₹50-110; ⊘11am-10.30pm) Delicious vegetarian food, particularly Punjabi cuisine, though a few Chinese and South Indian dishes are also offered. It's a short walk south along Station Rd, left at MG Rd and left at the clock tower. You may have to queue for a table at lunchtime.

ℹ Information

There is a State Bank of India ATM at the station and an Axis Bank ATM just off to the left when exiting; otherwise, you'll find ATMs spread out along Nehru Rd, which runs along the top of Station Rd.

Internet cafes can be found along Nehru Rd.

ℹ Getting There & Around

Jalgaon's train station and bus stand are about 2km apart (₹30 by autorickshaw).

Several express trains connecting Mumbai (sleeper/2AC ₹313/1076, eight hours), Delhi (₹558/2051, 18 hours), Ahmedabad (₹373/1316, 14 hours) and Varanasi (₹518/1981, 20 hours) stop at Jalgaon train station. Nine daily trains head for Nagpur (₹313/1076, seven to nine hours).

Buses to Fardapur T-junction (₹71, 1½ hours), for access to Ajanta, depart hourly from the bus stand between 6am and 9pm, continuing to Aurangabad (₹177, four hours).

Private bus companies on Station Rd offer services to Mumbai (₹500 to ₹1400, 9½ hours) and Nagpur (₹750, nine hours).

Nagpur

☏ 0712 / POP 2.43 MILLION / ELEV 305M

Way off the main tourist routes, the isolated city of Nagpur holds the distinction of being the dead geographical centre of India. It lacks must-see sights but is an important gateway to several reserves and parks including Tadoba-Andhari Tiger Reserve and

Pench National Park. It's also close to the temples of Ramtek and the ashrams of Sevagram. Summer is the best time to taste the city's famous oranges.

🛏 Sleeping

Hotel Blue Moon
HOTEL $
(📞 0712-2726061; www.hotelbluemoon.org; Central Ave; s/d from ₹720/960, with AC ₹1350/1600; ❄🔊) Large, plain rooms that don't win any awards for imagination but are among the better budget options in this pricey city. It's one of the closest hotels to the train station. Management is helpful and friendly, which eases the blow of those sickly marble bathtubs and poor man's stained glass.

Legend Inn
HOTEL $$
(📞 0712-6658666; www.thelegendinn.com; 15 Modern Society, Wardha Rd; s/d from ₹4180/4840; ❄@🔊) On the main highway for the Tadoba-Andhari Tiger Reserve, this is an efficiently run hotel, owned by an Indian mountaineering legend, with well-appointed rooms, a good restaurant, smoky bar and smiley staff (which might make up for the low water pressure). Free pick-ups from the airport, 1km away, are included.

Peanut Hotel
HOTEL $$
(📞 0712-3250320; www.peanuthotels.com; Bharti House, 43 Kachipura Garden, New Ramdaspeth; s/d incl breakfast from ₹2500/3200; ❄🔊) Located on a leafy residential street, this hotel's modern, whitewashed rooms are spruced up with orange throws and are kept spick and span. It's 2km southeast of the train station and the best overall value in town.

🍴 Eating

Krishnum
SOUTH INDIAN $
(www.krishnum.com; Central Ave; mains ₹60-160; ⊙8am-10pm) This popular place dishes out South Indian snacks and generous Punjabi thalis, as well as freshly squeezed fruit juices. There are branches in other parts of town.

★ Breakfast Story
CAFE $$
(www.facebook.com/thebreakfastorynagpur; Sai Sagar Apt, Hingna Rd; mains ₹100-300; ⊙8am-2.30pm & 3.30-7pm Mon-Tue & Thu-Sat, 8am-3pm Sun; 🔊) This stylish all-day breakfast-only hot spot in a residential building 7km southwest of the centre is worth a diversion. English, American and Belgian breakfast combos, sandwiches, pancakes and waffles, along with daily chalkboard specials, are served up on artsy wooden tables covered in comics. Cassette tapes, newspapers and other pop art line the walls, completing the cosy, hipster atmosphere.

ℹ Information

Numerous ATMs line Central Ave.

MTDC (📞 0712-2533325; www.maharashtratourism.gov.in; West High Court Rd, Civil Lines; ⊙10am-6pm) Staff here can help with getting to national parks near Nagpur. There is also an airport counter (📞 9405143376; www.maharashtratourism.gov.in; Arrivals Hall, Dr Babasaheb Ambedkar International Airport; ⊙7am-7pm Mon-Sat).

ℹ Getting There & Around

AIR
Dr Babasaheb Ambedkar International Airport (📞 0712-2807501) is 8km southwest of the centre. Domestic airlines, including Air India, IndiGo, Jet Airways and GoAir, fly direct to Delhi, Mumbai, Kolkata, Ahmedabad, Bengaluru, Chennai and Pune. Internationally, Qatar and Air Arabia fly to Doha and Sharjah, respectively.

BUS
The main **MSRTC/Ganesh Peth Bus Stand** (📞 0712-2726221) is 2km south of the train station. Ordinary buses head for Aurangabad (₹750 to ₹1200, six daily), Pune (₹1100, 1pm, 4pm, 5pm and 6.30pm), Ramtek (₹50, 1½ hours, every 30 minutes 6.15am to 9.30pm) and Wardha (₹45, three hours, every 10 minutes 6am to 10pm).

Government buses to Madhya Pradesh leave from the **MP Bus Stand** (📞 0712-2533695), 350m south of the train station. Destinations include Khawasa (for access to Pench Tiger Reserve; ₹90, every 30 minutes, 6am to 1.30am) and Jabalpur (from ₹270, 2.30pm and 11pm).

Private buses leave from the Bhole Petrol Pump, 3km southwest of the train station. **Sanjay Travels** (📞 0712-2550701; www.sanjaytravels.com; near Bhole Petrol Pump) books air-con seaters and sleepers with the best companies, such as Purple (www.prasannapurple.com), to Mumbai (₹1400, 4.45pm), Pune (₹900 to ₹1100, 3pm and 10pm), Aurangabad (₹750, hourly, 3pm to 10pm), Jalgaon (₹700, 5pm, 7pm, 9pm and 10pm) and Hyderabad (₹750 to ₹1000, 9pm and 10.30pm). For Jabalpur, **Nandan Bus** (📞 7620941415; www.nandanbus.com; Gitanjali Cinema Sq) goes daily at 2.30pm and 11pm (₹450 to ₹500) from Central Ave.

TRAIN
From Mumbai's CST, the Duronto Express runs daily to Nagpur (sleeper/2AC ₹523/1946,

WORTH A TRIP

TADOBA-ANDHARI TIGER RESERVE

The seldom-visited **Tadoba-Andhari Tiger Reserve** (⊙ 6am-10am & 3-6pm with seasonal variations), 150km south of Nagpur, is one of the best places to see tigers in India. Seeing fewer visitors than most other Indian forest reserves – it gets around 60% less visitors than neighbouring parks in Madhya Pradesh – this is a place where you can get up close to wildlife without having to jostle past truckloads of shutter-happy tourists. Rather than restrict access to certain zones of the park like other tiger parks in India, Tadoba-Andhari opted to limit the number of gypsy safaris per day instead (48) but give them free rein throughout the park. The results are excellent for wildlife-sighting opportunities. The park also remains open throughout the year, unlike many in India.

You'll find comfortable, well-furnished rooms and cottage at the **MTDC Resort** (☑ 9579314261; Moharli Gate; r with/without AC from ₹2380/1900; ❄), but the true treat in these parts is **Tiger Trails Jungle Lodge** (☑ 0712-6541327; www.tigertrails.in; Khutwanda Gate; s/d incl all meals ₹9500/19,500; ❄ 🎱 ❄) ✿, where Passionate enthusiasts have run this conservation-minded lodge deeply entrenched in studying Tadoba tigers for two decades. It's located in the wildlife-rich buffer zone and has its own private park gate. Accommodation is spacious and divided between rooms nearer to forest or watering holes – there's also the option of overnighting under the stars in a 6m-high observation tower. Save room for the absolutely excellent tribal-style Maharashtra thalis!

Most folks reach the park by private vehicle. That said, to reach Khutwanda Gate on public transport, catch a Chandrapur-bound bus from Nagpur to Warora (₹120, three hours), where you can catch a second bus for the last 42km to Khutwanda Gate (₹57, 1½ hours). For Moharli, stay on the bus to Chandrapur (₹175, four hours) and catch a second bus on to Moharli (₹29, one hour).

10 hours, 8.15pm). From Nagpur it departs at 8.40pm and arrives at 7.55am the following morning. Heading north to Kolkata is the Gitanjali Express (sleeper/2AC ₹563/2076, 17½ hours, 7.05pm). Several expresses bound for Delhi and Mumbai stop at Jalgaon (sleeper/2AC ₹313/1076, eight hours) for Ajanta caves.

Around Nagpur

Ramtek

About 40km northeast of Nagpur, Ramtek is believed to be the place where Lord Rama, of the epic Ramayana, spent some time during his exile with his wife, Sita, and brother Lakshmana. The place is marked by a cluster of 10 or so ancient temples (⊙ 6am-9pm), which sit atop the Hill of Rama and have their own population of resident langur monkeys.

Ramtek is beginning to fancy itself as a burgeoning adventure sports destination. MTDC was building an adventure sports training centre and hotel at the time of research and Khindsi Lake is indeed a beautiful spot for kayaking, paragliding or hot-air ballooning.

Mansar, 7km west of Ramtek, is an important archaeological site believed to be the 5th-century remains of Pravarapura, the capital ruled by the Vakataka King Pravarasena II.

Buses run half-hourly between Ramtek and the MSRTC bus stand in Nagpur (₹50, 1½ hours). The last bus to Nagpur is at 9.30pm.

Sevagram

☑ 07152

About 85km from Nagpur, Sevagram (Village of Service) was chosen by Mahatma Gandhi as his base during the Indian Independence Movement. Throughout the freedom struggle, the village played host to several nationalist leaders, who regularly come to visit the Mahatma at his **Sevagram Ashram** (☑ 07152-284754; www.gandhiashramsevagram.org; ⊙ 6am-5.30pm). The overseers of this peaceful ashram, which is built on 40 hectares of farmland, have carefully restored the original huts where Gandhi lived and worked and which now house some of his personal effects. There is a **small museum** (Sevagram Ashram; ⊙ 10am-6pm) as well.

Very basic lodging is available at **Rustam Bhavan** (☑ 07152-284754; nayeetaleem.75@gmail.com; r per person ₹150) and **Yatri Nivas**

(☎ 7276160260; sevagram_ashram@yahoo.in; r without AC ₹200-300), across the road from the entry gate; advance booking is recommended. Simple organic meals are available at the atmospheric **Prakrutik Ahar Kendra** (Sevagram Ashram; meals ₹120-150; ⏰ 11.30am-6pm) 🌿.

Sevagram can be reached by taking a bus from Nagpur to Wardha (₹85, three hours), where you'll need to switch to a Sevagram-bound bus (₹12, 10 minutes), which drops you at Medical Sq, 1km from the ashram; or catch a shared autorickshaw (₹20).

SOUTHERN MAHARASHTRA

Konkan Coast

A little-developed shoreline running south from Mumbai all the way to Goa, this picturesque strip of coast is peppered with picture-postcard beaches, fishing villages and magnificent ruined forts. Travelling through this tropical backwater can be sheer bliss, whether you're off to dabble in the sands with Mumbaikars in Ganpatipule, visit the stunning Janjira Fort at Murud-Janjira or head into the blue at Malvan, the last beach town of significance before the sands give way to Goa.

Murud-Janjira

☎ 02144 / POP 13,100

The sleepy fishing hamlet of Murud-Janjira – 165km from Mumbai – should be on any itinerary of the Konkan Coast. The relaxed pace of life, fresh seafood, stupendous offshore Janjira fort (and the chance to feel the warm surf rush past your feet) make the trip here well worthwhile.

Murud-Janjira's beach is fun for a run or game of cricket with locals and it comes alive with street stalls and beach tomfoolery nightly. Alternatively, you could peer through the gates of the off-limits Ahmedganj Palace, estate of the Siddi Nawab of Murud, or scramble around the decaying mosque and tombs on the south side of town.

👁 Sights

⭐ **Janjira**   FORT

(⏰ 7am-dusk) **FREE** The commanding, brooding fortress of Janjira, built on an island 500m offshore, is the most magnificent of the string of forts that line the Konkan coastline. This citadel was completed in 1571 by the Siddis, descendants of slaves from the Horn of Africa, and was the capital of a princely state.

Over the centuries Siddi alignment with Mughals provoked conflict with local kings, including Shivaji and his son Sambhaji, who attempted to scale the walls and tunnel to it, respectively. However, no outsider (including British, French and Portuguese colonists) ever made it past the fort's 12m-high granite walls which, when seen during high tide, seem to rise straight from the sea. Unconquered through history, the fort is finally falling to forces of nature as its mighty walls slowly crumble and wilderness reclaims its innards.

Still, there's a lot to see today, including the remarkable close-fitting stonework that's protected the citadel against centuries of attack by storms, colonists and gunpowder. You approach the fort via a brooding grey-stone gateway and can then explore its ramparts (complete with giant cannons) and 19 bastions, large parts of which are intact. Its inner keep, palaces and mosque are in ruins, though the fort's huge twin reservoirs remain. As many of the surviving walls and structures are in poor shape, tread carefully while you explore the site, which is unfortunately littered with trash.

The only way to reach Janjira is by boat (₹61 return, 20 minutes) from Rajpuri port. Boats depart with a minimum 20 people from 7am to noon and 2pm to 5.30pm on weekdays and 7am to 5.30pm on weekends, and allow you 45 minutes to explore the fort. To get to Rajpuri from Murud-Janjira, take an autorickshaw (₹150) or hire a bicycle.

🛏 Sleeping & Eating

Sea Shore Resort   GUESTHOUSE $

(☎ 9209240603; www.seashoreresortmurud.com; Darbar Rd; r with/without AC ₹2000/1500; ❄ 🛜) The advantage at this dead-simple guesthouse is a palm-fringed sea-view room with a small balcony and wi-fi for ₹2000 or less. The beach-facing garden is a bit ramshackle, but there are a few hammocks. Faisal, the friendly man about the place, speaks some English.

Devakinandan Lodge   GUESTHOUSE $

(☎ 9273457057; Darbar Rd; r with/without AC ₹2000/1500; ❄) This sparkling little green-and-red guesthouse has clean, basic rooms with TV and attached bathrooms with hot water. The family owners are friendly but speak very little English.

Sea Shell Resort
HOTEL $$

(📞02144-274306; www.seashellmurud.com; Darbar Rd; r with/without AC from ₹2500/2000; ❇ ❄) Set back from the beachside road, this cheery place has glistening, spacious and breezy sea-facing rooms with hot-water bathrooms (rain-style showers, thick bath towels) that look far better than the facade would indicate. There's a tiny pool as well.

Hotel Vinayak
INDIAN $$

(Darbar Rd; mains ₹120-400; ⊘7am-10pm) Its sea-facing terrace is the perfect place to tuck into a delicious and fiery Konkani thali (₹120 to ₹300), with fish curry, *tawa* (hotplate) fish fry, *sol kadhi* (pink-coloured, slightly sour digestive made from coconut milk and kokum fruit) and more. Fresh fish, prawn dishes and good breakfasts are also available.

🛈 Getting There & Around

Ferries and catamarans (₹125 to ₹165) from the Gateway of India in Mumbai cruise to Mandva pier between 6am and 7pm. The ticket includes a free shuttle bus to Alibag (30 minutes). Rickety local buses from Alibag head down the coast to Murud-Janjira (₹70, two hours, every 30 minutes). Alternatively, 10 buses depart Mumbai Central bus stand between 6am and 1am and take almost six hours to reach Murud-Janjira (non-AC ₹200). Four buses a day continue on to Pune (₹215, seven hours, 7.30am, 2pm, 3pm and 4pm).

The nearest railhead is at Roha, two hours away and poorly connected.

Bicycles (per hour/day ₹150/250) and cars (₹15 per kilometre) can be hired at the **Golden Swan Beach Resort** (📞9225591131; www.goldenswan.com; Darbar Rd).

Around Murud-Janjira
RAIGAD FORT

Alone on a high and remote hilltop, 24km off Hwy 66, the enthralling **Raigad Fort** (Indian/foreigner ₹15/200; ⊘8am-5.30pm) served as Shivaji's capital from 1648 until his death in 1680. The fort was later sacked by the British and some colonial structures added, but monuments such as the royal court, plinths of royal chambers, the main marketplace and Shivaji's tomb still remain – it's worth an excursion.

You can hike a crazy 1475 steps to the top, but for a more 'levitating' experience, take the vertigo-inducing **ropeway** (www.raigadropeway.com; return ₹250; ⊘8am-7pm) – actually a cable car – which climbs up the cliff and offers a bird's-eye view of the deep gorges below. Be warned this is a very popular attraction with domestic tourists and you may have to wait up to an hour for a ride during holiday times. Guides (₹500) are available within the fort complex. **Sarja Restaurant** (snacks ₹35-80; ⊘8am-7pm), adjoining the ropeway's base terminal, is a basic place for lunch or snacks.

Autorickshaws shuttle up to the ropeway from the town of Mahad on Hwy 66 (look out for the 'Raigad Ropeway' sign) for ₹700 return including wait time. Mahad is 158km south of Mumbai and 88km from Murud-Janjira. The Mahad–Raigad road is paved and in good condition. Car and drivers charge ₹15 per kilometre for a day trip here from Murud-Janjira. There are buses every two to three hours from Mahad to Mahabaleshwar (₹70, two hours).

Ganpatipule
📞02357

The tiny beach resort of Ganpatipule has been luring a steady stream of beach lovers over the years with its warm waters and wonderful stretches of sand. Located about 375km from Mumbai, it's a village that snoozes through much of the year, except during holidays such as Diwali or Ganesh Chaturthi. These are times when hordes of boisterous tourists turn up to visit the seaside **Swayambhu Temple** (⊘6am-9pm), which houses a monolithic Ganesh (painted a bright orange). For more solitude, the beaches just south of the main beach (such as Neware Beach) are both more spectacular than Ganpatipule and less crowded – have an autorickshaw take you there.

To reach Ganpatipule, you'll pass through the transport hub of Ratnagiri, home to the crumbling **Thibaw Palace** (Thibaw Palace Rd; ⊘10am-5.30pm Tue-Sun) FREE, where the last Burmese king, Thibaw, was interned by the British.

🛌 Sleeping & Eating

Grand Konkan Resort
GUESTHOUSE $

(📞02357-235291; www.atithilodgeganpatipule.com; r with/without AC ₹1800/1500) A tad ambitiously named, but this family-run guesthouse behind the simple and cheaper Atithi Lodge (same owners) offers quite nice rooms with a wee bit of character (curtains, wood-

ALL ABOARD THE KONKAN RAILWAY

One in a long list of storied Indian train rides, the Konkan Railway hugs the southwest Indian coast along a 738km journey between Maharashtra, Goa and Karnataka. The line, which has hosted passenger trains since 1998, is considered the biggest and most expansive infrastructure project the country has undertaken (and completed) since independence. So much so, the very idea was dismissed outright in the early 20th century by the British, who deemed the whole adventure an impossible task of construction and engineering, leaving it to the locals to finish the job over the course of several decades (10 of whom lost their lives in the disaster-plagued process).

Today, the ridiculously scenic route, chock-full of picturesque paddy fields, rolling green hills, craggy mountaintops, storybook sea views and numerous tunnels, waterfalls, viaducts and jungly landscapes, is made possible by 92 tunnels and 2000 bridges, including Panval Viaduct, India's highest (and Asia's third) viaduct at 64m tall.

Most travellers enjoy the Konkan ride on the Mandovi Express from Mumbai to Goa, but train enthusiasts can take in the whole shebang on the Mangalore Express, a 14-hour journey from Mumbai to Mangalore.

framed art) just five minutes' walk from the beach. Hardwood flooring and shelving give off a rustic forest lodge feel. Brothers Jayesh and Rajesh speak English and are more than helpful.

MTDC Resort HOTEL $$
(☏ 02357-235248; www.mararashtratourism.gov.in; d with/without AC from ₹2740/2380; ❉ 🛜) Spread over prime beachfront, this huge operation is something of a holiday camp for Mumbaikar families. Its concrete rooms and cottages would benefit from a little updating, but all boast magnificent full-frontal ocean views. It also packs in a decent restaurant that serves cold beer.

Bhau Joshi Bhojnalay INDIAN $
(mains ₹55-125; ⊙11.30am-3pm & 7.30-10.30pm) It's not the easiest place to eat (no English sign, nearly no English spoken and no napkins, so bring some baby wipes!), but the delicious Maharashtrian food in this clean, orderly restaurant inland from the beach makes up for the struggles. Try the fantastic *baingan masala* (eggplant curry; ₹90). Jain and Punjabi dishes also on offer.

Hotel Naivedya INDIAN $
(mains ₹80-170, thali ₹85; ⊙10am-7pm) A simple local's joint in the village serving up a wonderful daily veg thali with a kick (₹85) and the most refreshing *sol kadhi* we had on the coast.

ℹ️ Information

There are several ATMs in Ganpatipule, including one about 400m inland from the MTDC Resort.

ℹ️ Getting There & Around

Ganpatipule has limited transport links. Ratnagiri, 40km to the south, is the nearest major town. Hourly buses (₹33, 1½ hours) connect the two places; autorickshaws cost ₹400.

Two government buses per day leave Ganpatipule for Pune (₹350, five hours, 6.45am and 7.30pm). For Mumbai and Kolhapur (or more timely government departures in general), head back to Ratnagiri (₹33, 1¼ hours, every 30 minutes 7am to 8pm).

There are private buses to Mumbai (Volvo non-AC seater/AC sleeper ₹700/1000, 10 hours, 7pm) and Pune (Volvo AC sleeper ₹800, nine hours, 7pm).

Ratnagiri train station is on the Konkan Railway line. From Ratnagiri, the Mandovi Express goes daily to Mumbai (2nd class/sleeper/2AC ₹188/293/1061, 7½ hours, 2.05pm). The return train heading for Goa (₹163/248/896, 5½ hours) is at 1.15pm. From Ratnagiri's old bus stand, buses leave for Goa (semideluxe ₹270, six hours) and Kolhapur (₹160, four hours).

Malvan
☏ 02365

A government tourism promo promotes the emerging Malvan region as comparable to Tahiti, which is a tad ambitious, but it does boast near-white sands, sparkling seas and jungle-fringed backwaters. Offshore there are coral reefs, sea caves and vibrant marine life – diving is becoming a huge draw with the opening of a new world-class diving school.

Malvan town is one of the prettiest on the Konkan Coast. It's a mellow, bike-friendly place with a good stock of old wooden buildings, a busy little harbour and bazaar and a slow, tropical pace of life. Stretching directly south of the centre is lovely Tarkali beach, home to many hotels and guesthouses.

◉ Sights & Activities

There are several dive shops operating in Malvan that allow unqualified diving; if you want to dive, stick with a registered operator. The Malvan Marine Sanctuary is the region's top scuba draw with its 67-nautical-mile reef often hailed as India's Great Barrier Reef.

The southern end of Tarkali beach is bordered by the broad, beautiful Karli River. Several boat operators (you'll find them moored on the northern bank) offer multistop boat trips along this backwater to Seagull Island, Golden Rock, Dolphin Point and cove beaches and/or Vengurla Rock lighthouse. Trips range from ₹1200 to ₹3500 per boat for up to 10 people.

Sindhudurg Fort   FORT
Built by Shivaji and dating from 1664, this monstrous fort lies on an offshore island and can be reached by frequent ferries (adult/child ₹70/40, 8am to 5.30pm) from Malvan's harbour. It's not as impressive as Janjira up the coast, and today lies mostly in ruins, but it remains a powerful presence. You can explore its ramparts and the coastal views are impressive. Boat operators allow you one hour on the island.

Tarkali Beach   BEACH
A golden arc south of Malvan, this crescent-shaped sandy beach is a vision of tropical India, fringed by coconut palms and casuarina trees, plus the odd cow. At dusk (between October and February) fishermen work together to haul in huge, kilometre-long nets that are packed with sardines. A rickshaw here from Malvan town is ₹150.

★ IISDA   DIVING
(Indian Institute of Scuba Diving & Aquasports; ✆02365-248790; www.maharashtratourism.gov. in; Tarkali Beach; per dive ₹3700, PADI Open Water course ₹22,000; ⊗7am-7pm) This state-of-the-art PADI diving centre, an initiative of Maharashtra Tourism, is India's finest, run by marine biologist and all-round diving pro Dr Sarang Kulkarni. It offers professional instruction, a 20m-long and 8m-deep pool for training, air-conditioned classrooms and comfortable sleeping quarters for students. IISDA is also a marine conservation centre and there's even a restaurant, bar and tennis court.

Located 7km south of Malvan.

🛏 Sleeping & Eating

Vicky's Guest House   GUESTHOUSE $
(✆9823423046; www.malvanvickysguesthouse. com; near Heravi Batti, Dandi Beach; r with/without AC from ₹1500/1000; ❄️ 🛜) Down a quiet residential lane surrounded by lush palms 400m from Dandi Beach and steps form Malvan town, cool and mellow Vicky has five purpose-built rooms that don't look like much on arrival but are actually spacious, well-equipped and extremely comfortable for the price. Vicky himself is super helpful

MALVAN MARINE SANCTUARY

The shoreline around Malvan is incredibly diverse, with rich wetlands, sandy and rocky beaches, mangroves and backwaters. But underwater it's arguably even more compelling, with coral patches and caves that shelter abundant marine life and extensive forests of *sargassum* seaweed that acts as a nursery for juvenile fish. Rocky offshore islands attract schools of snapper and large grouper, butterfly fish, yellow-striped fusiliers, manta and sting rays and lobster. Pods of dolphins are regularly seen between October to May and the world's largest fish, the whale shark, even puts in an appearance every now and then.

Presently only a small section is protected as the Malvan Marine Sanctuary, which encompasses the Sindhudurg Fort; yet such is its rich diversity that marine biologists, including the director of the Indian Institute of Scuba Diving & Aquasports (IISDA), Dr Sarang Kulkarni, feel it's essential that the boundaries are extended. The reef extends for 67 nautical miles offshore and has been described as India's Great Barrier Reef. A submerged plateau, the Angria Bank, is 40km long and 20km wide, with healthy coral and an abundance of sealife: nurse sharks are seen on almost every dive. IISDA has big plans in the works to operate day trips and live-aboard excursions to Angria.

and hospitable as is the downright gracious family.

⭐ **Chaitanya** MALVANI **$$**
(502 Dr Vallabh Marg; mains ₹150-325; ⊘11am-11pm) On Malvan's main drag, this great, family-run place specialises in Konkan cuisine including *bangda tikhale* (fish in thick coconut sauce), prawns *malvani* and very flavoursome crab *masala;* portions won't thrill you, but it's first-rate seafood. Its vegetarian dishes are also excellent. It's always packed with locals and has an air-con section.

Athithi Bamboo MALVANI **$$**
(Church St, Chival; thalis ₹80-325; ⊘noon-4pm & 8-10.30pm) On the north side of the harbour, this large casual place offers excellent Malvani thalis and lots of fresh fish. There's no sign or menu in English and you sit under a tin roof (so it gets very hot during the day), but the seafood is surf-fresh and the cooking Konkan-authentic.

ℹ️ Getting There & Away

The closest train station is Kudal, 38km away. Frequent buses (₹38, one hour) cover the route from **Malvan Bus Stand** (✆ 02365-252034; Shri Babi Hadkar Marg) or an autorickshaw is about ₹500. Malvan has ordinary buses to Kolhapur (non-AC from ₹189, five hours), Mumbai (₹562, 12 hours, 8am), Panaji (non-AC from ₹102, four hours, 6.45am, 7.45am, 2.30pm and 3.15pm) and Ratnagiri (non-AC from ₹190, five hours, 6am, 7.45am and 11.15am). Slightly quicker to Goa are the blue-and-white Kadamba Goan government buses (₹135, 3½ hours, 7.45am, 2.30pm and 3pm) to Mapusa and Panaji.

There are private bus agents on Dr Vallabh Marg selling more comfortable seats on Volvo buses to Mumbai and Pune, but these depart 33km inland from Malvan in Kasal and transport is not provided.

Malvan is only 80km from northern Goa; private drivers charge ₹2000 (non-AC) to ₹2500 (AC) for the two-hour trip.

Matheran

✆ 02148 / POP 5750 / ELEV 803M

Matheran, literally 'Jungle Above', is a tiny patch of peace and quiet capping a craggy Sahyadri summit within spitting distance of Mumbai's heat and grime. Endowed with shady forests criss-crossed with foot trails and breathtaking lookouts, it still retains an elegance and colonial-era ambience, though creeping commercialism and illegal construction are marring its appeal (it could do without the Ferris wheel and wax museum, for example).

In the past, getting to Matheran was really half the fun. While speedier options were available by road, nothing beat arriving in town on the narrow-gauge toy train that chugged up to the heart of the settlement, but derailment woes caused the suspension of the train in 2016, with no planned timetable for getting it moving again.

Motor vehicles are banned within Matheran, making it an ideal place to give your ears and lungs a rest and your feet some exercise.

◉ Sights & Activities

You can walk along shady forest paths to most of Matheran's viewpoints in a matter of hours; it's a place well suited to stress-free ambling. To catch the sunrise, head to **Panorama Point**, while **Porcupine Point** (also known as Sunset Point) is the most popular (read: packed) as the sun drops. **Louisa Point** and **Little Chouk Point** also have stunning views of the Sahyadris.

If you're here on a weekend or public holiday you might want to avoid the most crowded section around **Echo Point**, **Charlotte Lake** and **Honeymoon Point**, which get rammed with day trippers.

You can reach the valley below One Tree Hill down the path known as **Shivaji's Ladder**, supposedly trod upon by the Maratha leader himself.

🛏️ Sleeping & Eating

Hope Hall Hotel HOTEL **$**
(✆ 8149621803; www.hopehallmatheran.com; MG Rd; d Mon-Fri ₹1200, Sat & Sun ₹1500) Run by a very hospitable family, this long-running place has been hosting happy travellers for years; the house dates back to 1875. Spacious rooms with high ceilings and arty touches are in two blocks at the rear of the leafy garden. Good breakfasts and drinks are available.

⭐ **Verandah in the Forest** HERITAGE HOTEL **$$$**
(✆ 02148-230296; www.neemranahotels.com; Barr House; d incl breakfast Sun-Thu from ₹4760, Sat & Sun from ₹5950; 🖧) This deliciously preserved 150-year-old bungalow exudes undiluted nostalgia, with quaintly luxurious rooms. Reminisce about bygone times in the company of ornate candelabras, oriental rugs, antique teak furniture, Victorian canvases and

grandfather clocks. The verandah has a lovely aspect over Matheran's wooded hillsides.

The in-house restaurant offers a terrific four-course Continental dinner (₹700; guests only for dinner, lunch is open to the public).

Shabbir Bhai　　　　　　　INDIAN $
(Merry Rd; mains ₹100-210; ⊙ 9am-10.30pm) Known locally as the 'Byrianiwala', this funky joint has a full North Indian menu, but it's all about the spicy biryanis: spiced steamed rice with chicken, mutton and veg. To find it, take the footpath uphill beside the Jama Masjid on MG Rd and follow your nose.

ⓘ Information

Entry to Matheran costs ₹50 (₹25 for children), which you pay at the Dasturi car park.

ⓘ Getting There & Away

TAXI

Shared taxis (₹70) run from just outside Neral train station to Matheran's Dasturi car park (30 minutes). Horses (₹350 to all hotels except Verandah in the Forest, which is ₹550) and hand-pulled rickshaws (₹700) wait here to whisk you (relatively speaking) to Matheran's main bazaar. The horse-wallahs are unionised and their prices are officially posted, but do not agree on a price until you have seen the board, which is located 50m *after* the Matheran ticket counter (hotel fares bottom-right in smaller font than the rest of the board). You can also walk this stretch in a little under an hour (around 3.5km uphill) and your luggage can be hauled for around ₹250.

TRAIN

Matheran's toy train was suspended in 2016 after two derailments. It normally chugs between Matheran and Neral Junction six times daily.

From Mumbai's CST station there are two daily express trains to Neral Junction at 7am and 8.40am (2nd class/chair car ₹93/326, 1½ hours), but they cannot be booked online as Neral and Mumbai are considered the same metropolitan area by IRCTC. You must book a further destination (Lonavla, for example) and then hop down at Neral. Alternatively, numerous local trains ply the route from Mumbai CST and Dadar.

Other expresses from Mumbai stop at Karjat, down the line from Neral, from where you can backtrack on a local train or catch a bus to Matheran (₹31, 30 minutes, four times daily 5.45am, 11am, 1.30pm and 4.15pm). From Pune there are numerous daily departures to Karjat. Note: trains from Pune don't stop at Neral Junction.

ⓘ Getting Around

Apart from hand-pulled rickshaws and horses, walking is the only other transport option in Matheran. Horse-wallahs will hustle you constantly for rides (about ₹400 per hour).

Lonavla

🔲 02114 / POP 57,400 / ELEV 625M

Lonavla is a raucous resort town about 106km southeast of Mumbai. Its main drag consists almost exclusively of garishly lit shops flogging *chikki,* the rock-hard, brittle sweet made in the area, and you get fun-for-the-whole-family kind of stuff like wax museums, go-carts and India's largest water park. But there are some pleasant side streets, serene residential areas and destination yoga places along with the pastoral surrounding countryside that means you can choose your own path here.

The main reason you'd want to come here is to visit the nearby Karla and Bhaja Caves which, after those at Ellora and Ajanta, are the best in Maharashtra.

Hotels, restaurants and the main road to the caves lie north of the train station. Most of the Lonavla township and its markets are located south of the station.

🏃 Activities

Kaivalyadhama Yoga Hospital　　　YOGA
(🔲 8551092986, 02114-273039; www.kdham.com; 40-day course incl full board US$1000) This progressive yoga centre is located in neatly kept grounds about 2km from Lonavla, en route to the Karla and Bhaja Caves. Founded in 1924 by Swami Kuvalayananda, it combines yoga courses with naturopathic therapies. Courses cover full board, yoga classes, programs and lectures.

Nirvana Adventures　　　PARAGLIDING
(🔲 022-26053724; www.flynirvana.com) Mumbai-based Nirvana Adventures offers paragliding courses (two-day learner course ₹12,000 per person including full board) and short tandem flights (from ₹2500) in a charming rural setting near the town of Kamshet, 25km from Lonavla.

🛏 Sleeping & Eating

★ Ferreira Resort　　　HOTEL $
(🔲 02114-272689; http://ferreiraresortlonavala.blogspot.co.uk; DT Shahani Rd; r Mon-Thu ₹1300, Fri-Sun ₹1800-2100, with AC Mon-Thu ₹1500, Fri-Sun ₹2000-2500; ❄ 🛜) It's certainly not

a resort, but it is something of a rarity in Lonavla: a well-priced, family-run place in a quiet residential location that's close to the train station. Ten of the 15 clean but worn air-con rooms have a balcony and there's a little garden as well as room service.

Hotel Rama Krishna   SOUTH INDIAN, PUNJABI **$$**
(Mumbai Pune Rd; mains ₹40-420; ⊙7am-11.45pm) It seems everyone in town – along with passing motorcycle road warriors – gathers on this restaurant's pleasant terrace at breakfast, where great South Indian staples (generously portioned dosas etc) are the way to go. As the day wears on, diners pack in for spicy Punjabi dishes and there's plenty of cold beer to go around.

★**Kinara**
Dhaba Village   NORTH INDIAN, CHINESE **$$$**
(www.thekinaravillage.com; Vaksai Naka, Old Mumbai Pune Hwy; mains ₹280-560; ⊙11am-11.30pm; ▣) A bit of a *dhaba* Disneyland, but therein lies the fun. About 5km east of Lonavla nearer Karla and Bhaja Caves is this fun-for-all restaurant/entertainment venue. Dine under traditional *shamiana* huts amid obnoxious festival lighting, camel and donkey rides, *jalebi* (deep-fried batter dunked in sugar syrup) carts, fish pedicure pools and live *ghazal* (Urdu love songs) music nightly (7pm).

🛈 Getting There & Away

Lonavla is serviced by MSRTC buses departing from the bus stand to Dadar in Mumbai (from ₹150, two hours) and Pune (from ₹100, two hours). From Lonavla, **Neeta Bus** (📞8652222640; www.neetabus.in; 57/2/2/A Valvan Dam, Old Mumbai Pune Hwy) offers luxury air-con buses to Pune (₹250, hourly 8am to 11pm) and Mumbai (₹400, hourly 7am to 11pm) from its fancy station 3km northeast of the train station. It stops at Sion Station (for access to Churchgate) then heads north through the suburbs, stopping in Vila Parle for the domestic airport and on to Borivali.

All express trains from Mumbai's CST to Pune stop at Lonavla (2nd class ₹98 to ₹123, chair ₹326 to ₹371, 2½ to three hours).

Karla & Bhaja Caves

While they pale in comparison to Ajanta or Ellora, the Karla and Bhaja rock-cut caves, which date from around the 2nd century BC, are among the better examples of Buddhist cave architecture in India. They are also low on commercial tourism, making them ideal places for a quiet excursion. Karla has the most impressive single cave, but Bhaja is a quieter site to explore.

⊙ Sights

Karla Caves   CAVE
(Indian/foreigner ₹15/200, video ₹25; ⊙9am-5pm) Karla Cave, the largest early *chaitya* in India, is reached by a 20-minute climb from a minibazaar at the base of a hill. Completed in 80 BC, the *chaitya* is around 40m long and 15m high and sports a vaulted interior and intricately executed sculptures of Buddha, human and animal figures.

Excluding Ellora's Kailasa Temple, this is probably the most impressive cave temple in the state. A semicircular 'sun window' filters light in towards a dagoba or stupa (the cave's representation of the Buddha), protected by a carved wooden umbrella, the only remaining example of its kind. The cave's roof also retains ancient teak buttresses. The 37 pillars forming the aisles are topped by kneeling elephants. The carved elephant heads on the sides of the vestibule once had ivory tusks.

There's a **Hindu temple** in front of the cave, thronged by pilgrims whose presence adds colour to the scene.

Bhaja Caves   CAVE
(Indian/foreigner ₹15/200, video ₹25; ⊙8.30am-5.30pm) On the other side of the expressway from Karla Caves in a lush setting 3km off the main road, Bhaja Caves is the greener and quieter of the region's caves. Thought to date from around 200 BC, 10 of the 18 caves here are *viharas*, while Cave 12 is an open *chaitya* containing a simple dagoba.

🛈 Getting There & Around

Karla is 11km east of Lonavla, and Bhaja 9km. Both can be visited on a local bus to the access point, from where it's about a 6km return walk on each side to the two sites – but that would be exhausting and hot. Autorickshaws charge between ₹800 and ₹1000 (depending on the day of the week) from Lonavla for the tour, including waiting time.

Pune

📍020 / POP 5.14 MILLION / ELEV 535M
A thriving, vibrant metropolis, Pune is a centre of academia and business that epitomises 'New India' with its baffling mix of capitalism and spiritualism (ancient and modern). It's also globally famous, or notorious, for an ashram, the Osho International

(margin) MAHARASHTRA KARLA & BHAJA CAVES

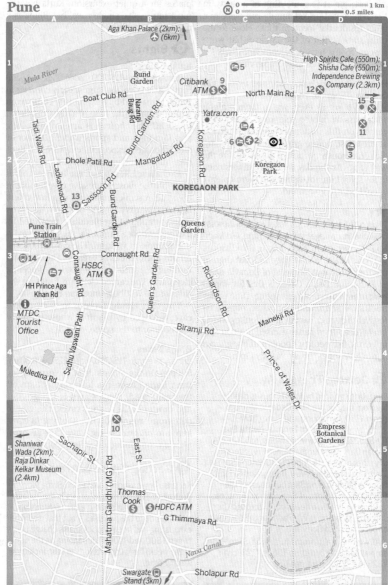

Meditation Resort (p110), founded by the late guru Bhagwan Shree Rajneesh.

Pune was initially given pride of place by Shivaji and the ruling Peshwas, who made it their capital. The British took the city in 1817 and, thanks to its cool and dry climate, soon made it the Bombay Presidency's monsoon capital. Globalisation knocked on Pune's doors in the 1990s, following which it went in for an image overhaul. However, some colonial-era charm was retained in a few old buildings and residential areas, bringing

Pune

about a pleasant coexistence of the old and new, which (despite the pollution and hectic traffic) makes Pune a worthwhile place to explore.

◎ Sights

★ Raja Dinkar Kelkar Museum   MUSEUM
(www.rajakelkarmuseum.com; Kamal Kunj, Natu Baug, 1377-78, Shukrawar Peth; Indian/foreigner ₹50/200, mobile/camera ₹100/500; ☺10am-5.30pm) An oddball of a museum that's one of Pune's true delights, housing only a fraction of the 20,000-odd objects of Indian daily life painstakingly collected by Dinkar Kelkar (who died in 1990). The quirky pan-Indian collection includes hundreds of hookah pipes, writing instruments, lamps, textiles, toys, entire doors and windows, kitchen utensils, furniture, puppets, ivory playing cards and betel-nut cutters.

And there's an amazing gallery of musical instruments, including peacock sitars!

Joshi's Museum of Miniature Railway   MUSEUM
(www.minirailways.com; 17/1 B/2 GA Kulkarni Rd, Kothrud; ₹90; ☺9.30am-5.30pm Mon-Fri, 9.30am-4pm & 5-8pm Sat, 5-8pm Sun) Inside the small Soudamini Instruments factory in eastern Pune is what is claimed to be India's only miniature city, the lifelong obsession of model train enthusiast Bhau Joshi. In short, it's one of the world's great model train layouts, a detailed, fully functional and passionate display of mechanical and engineering wow.

It's the stuff of boyhood dreams (and many adults, frankly). It features 65 signals, 26 points, fences, lamp posts and flyovers, a swimming pool, circus fairground (with roller coaster), drive-in theatre and dual-carriageway with moving vehicles among

other bells and whistles, all controlled by a panel boasting 5km of wiring.

Aga Khan Palace   PALACE
(Pune Nagar Rd, Kalyani Nagar; Indian/foreiger ₹15/200, video ₹25; ☺9am-5.30pm) The grand Aga Khan Palace is set in a peaceful wooded 6.5-hectare plot northeast of the centre. Built in 1892 by Sultan Aga Khan III, this graceful building was where Mahatma Gandhi and other prominent nationalist leaders were interned by the British following Gandhi's Quit India campaign in 1942.

The main palace now houses the **Gandhi National Memorial** where you can peek into the room where the Mahatma used to stay. Photos and paintings exhibit moments in his extraordinary life. Both Kasturba Gandhi, the Mahatma's wife, and Mahadeobhai Desai, his secretary for 35 years, died here in confinement. You'll find their shrines (containing their ashes) in a quiet garden to the rear.

Osho Teerth Gardens   GARDENS
(www.osho.com; DH Dhunjibhoy Rd, Koregaon Park; ☺6-9am & 3-6pm) The 5-hectare Osho Teerth Gardens are a verdant escape from urban living with giant bamboo, jogging trails, a gurgling brook and smooching couples. You don't have to be an Osho member, they're accessible to all.

Shaniwar Wada   FORT
(Shivaji Rd; Indian/foreigner ₹15/200, sound-and-light show ₹50/100; ☺9am-5.30pm) The remains of this fortressed palace of the Peshwa rulers are located in the old part of the city. Built in 1732, Shaniwar Wada was destroyed by a fire in 1828, but the massive walls and ramparts remain, as does a mighty fortified gateway.

🏃 Activities

Osho International
Meditation Resort
MEDITATION

(📞 020-66019999; www.osho.com; 17 Koregaon Park) Indelibly linked with Pune's identity, this iconic ashram-resort, located in a leafy, upscale northern suburb, has been drawing thousands of *sanyasins* (seekers) since the death of Osho in 1990. With its swimming pool, sauna and spa, 'zennis' and boutique guesthouse, it is, to some, the ultimate place to indulge in some luxe meditation.

Alternatively, detractors point fingers at the blatant commercialisation and high cost and accuse it of marketing a warped version of the mystic East to rich, gullible Westerners.

To make up your own mind you'll have to cough up the (steep) registration and daily meditation fees. Tours of the facilities are no longer permitted – the only way to access Osho is to pay an initial ₹1560, which covers registration (passport required) and a mandatory on-the-spot HIV test (sterile needles used). You'll also need two robes (one maroon and one white, ₹1000 per robe) and will have to attend a welcome session (daily at 9.30am). Note that the rules and regulations are very strict, even pedantic: swimmers are only allowed to wear, and have to pay for, Osho maroon swimwear (₹400 to ₹700) and there are mandatory (Osho maroon) clothes for the gym. Indian nationals are also lectured about behaviour (eg not hassling Western women) in special etiquette classes – female security is taken extremely seriously.

Once you've got all this out of the way, you can then pay for a meditation pass (₹870/1790 per day Indian/foreigner, with discounts for longer stays). Oh, that's apart from the fee to enter the Basho Spa (where the pool, Jacuzzi, gym, saunas and tennis courts are all located), which will be a further ₹290. Cash only for day trippers.

The main centre for meditation and the nightly white-robed spiritual dance is in the Osho Auditorium (no coughing or sneezing, please). The Osho Chuang Tzu, where the guru's ashes are kept, is also open for meditation. The commune's 'Multiversity' runs a plethora of courses in meditation and other esoteric techniques.

In the evenings, as well as meditation sessions, there's a 'nightlife' program, with parties, cinema, theatre and 'creativity nights'.

Photography is not permitted anywhere in the resort. The Welcome Center is open daily from 9am to 12.30pm and 2pm to 3.30pm.

OSHO GURU OF SEX

Ever tried mixing spirituality with primal instincts and garnishing with oodles of expensive trinkets? Well, Bhagwan Shree Rajneesh (1931–90) certainly did. Osho, as he preferred to be called, was one of India's most flamboyant 'export gurus' to market the mystic East to the world and undoubtedly the most controversial.

Initially based in Pune, he followed no particular religion or philosophy and outraged many across the world with his advocacy of sex as a path to enlightenment. A darling of the international media, he quickly earned himself the epithet 'sex guru'. In 1981, Rajneesh took his curious blend of Californian pop psychology and Indian mysticism to the USA, where he set up an agricultural commune in Oregon. There, his ashram's notoriety, as well as its fleet of (material and thus valueless!) Rolls Royces grew, until raging local opposition following a bizarre, infamous food poisoning incident (designed to manipulate local elections) moved the authorities to charge Osho with immigration fraud. He was fined US$400,000 and deported.

An epic journey then began, during which Osho and his followers, in their search for a new base, were either deported from or denied entry into 21 countries. By 1987, he was back at his Pune ashram, where thousands of foreigners soon flocked for his nightly discourses and meditation sessions.

They still come from across the globe. Such is the demand for the resort's facilities that prices are continually on the rise, with luxury being redefined every day. Interestingly, despite Osho's discourse on how nobody should be poor, no money generated by the resort goes into helping the disadvantaged.

In recent years the Osho institute has embraced the digital age, with its online iOsho portal offering iMeditate programs, Osho radio and Osho library; subscriptions are required.

Ramamani Iyengar Memorial Yoga Institute   YOGA

(☏ 020-25656134; www.bksiyengar.com; 1107 B/1 Hare Krishna Mandir Rd, Model Colony) To attend classes at this famous institute, 7km northwest of the train station, you need to have been practising yoga for at least eight years.

🛌 Sleeping

Pune's main accommodation hubs are around the train station (where budget places proliferate) and leafy Koregaon Park, where you'll find good midrange options. Many upmarket places are on the road to the airport, 6km or so from the centre.

Hotel Surya Villa   HOTEL $

(☏ 020-26124501; www.hotelsuryavilla.com; 294/2 German Bakery Lane, Koregaon Park; r with/without AC from ₹2380/1690; ❄ 🛜) The Surya's functional, tiled rooms are well-kept and generously proportioned and, though a little spartan, they do have bathrooms with hot water, wi-fi and cable TV. It enjoys a good location on a quiet street in Koregaon Park, close to popular cafes.

Samrat Hotel   HOTEL $$

(☏ 020-26137964; www.thesamrathotel.com; 17 Wilson Garden; s/d from ₹1700/2100, with AC from ₹2100/2600; ❄ 🛜) It's not quite as grand as its fancy reception area would indicate, but with a central location just a few steps from the train station and spacious, well-maintained rooms, the 49-room Samrat represents good value. The staff is courteous and eager to please. Complimentary airport pick-up (not drop-off!) and breakfast.

Hotel Lotus   HOTEL $$

(☏ 020-26139701; www.hotelsuryavilla.com; Lane 5, Koregaon Park; s/d ₹1930/2260, with AC ₹2260/2860; ❄ 🛜) Hotel Lotus is good value for the quiet, Koregaon Park location and though the rooms are not that spacious, they are light and airy, and all but four have balconies. There's no restaurant, but they offer room service and there are plenty of good eating options close by.

★ Hotel Sunderban   HOTEL $$$

(☏ 020-26124949; www.tghotels.com; 19 Koregaon Park; s/d without bathroom ₹1100/1430, incl breakfast from ₹4760/5950; ❄ 🛜) Set around a manicured lawn right next to the Osho resort, this renovated art deco bungalow effortlessly combines colonial-era class with boutique appeal. Deluxe rooms in the main building sport antique furniture, while even the cheapest

options are beautifully presented and spacious (though lack a private bathroom). The best-value rooms are the lawn-facing studios.

There is a yoga centre, spa and two restaurants on the premises, including highly regarded Dario's (p112).

Osho Meditation Resort Guesthouse   GUESTHOUSE $$$

(☏ 020-66019900; www.osho.com; Koregaon Park; s/d ₹6020/6620; ❄ 🛜) This uberchic, 60-room place will only allow you in if you come to meditate at the Osho International Meditation Resort. The rooms and common spaces are an elegant exercise in modern minimalist aesthetics with several ultraluxe features – including Biotique amenities and purified fresh air supplied in all rooms!

🍴 Eating

Juice World   CAFE $

(2436/B East St, Camp; snacks ₹40-200, juices ₹65-300; ⏰ 11am-11.30pm) Delicious fresh fruit juices and shakes. This casual cafe with outdoor seating serves wholesome snacks such as *pav bhaji* (spiced vegetables and bread). On a hot day it's impossible to walk past its fruit displays and not drop in for a drink. Try the seasonal *kabuli amar* (pomegranate).

Arthur's Theme   EUROPEAN $$

(☏ 020-26152710; www.arthurstheme.com; 2, Vrindavan Apts, Lane No 6, Koregaon Park; mains ₹280-990; ⏰ 11.30am-11.30pm; 🛜) This eclectic European bistro has rave reviews seeping from its pores. Indeed the food, a lengthy list that includes rarely seen proteins like turkey and duck in addition to extensive choices of veg, fish, chicken and buffalo, presents a tantalising opportunity for a sophisticated curry-free evening. Most dishes fall in the ₹300 to ₹400 range, so the price is right.

German Bakery   BAKERY $$

(North Main Rd, Koregaon Park; cakes ₹100-140, mains ₹90-380; ⏰ 7am-11pm; 🛜) A Pune institution famous for its traveller-geared grub, including omelettes, cooked breakfasts, Greek salads, cappuccinos and lots of sweet treats (try the mango cheesecake). Located on a very busy traffic-plagued corner. A fatal terrorist attack took place here in 2010 – a painful memory in this peace-loving city.

Prem's   MULTICUISINE $$

(www.facebook.com/PremsResto.Pune; North Main Rd, Koregaon Park; mains ₹60-550; ⏰ 8am-12.15am; 🛜) In a quiet, tree-canopied courtyard, Prem's is perfect for a lazy, beery

TRANSIT HUB: MAHABALESHWAR

Once a summer capital under the British, today the best thing about the hill station of Mahabaleshwar (1327m) is the jaw-dropping mountain scenery on the road to get here. It's an overdeveloped mess, tainted by an ugly building boom and traffic chaos as tourists attempt a mad dash to tick off its viewpoints and falls. There's no compelling reason to visit – it's basically one big bustling bazaar surrounded by resorts and views – though the town can be used as a base to visit the impressive **Pratapgad Fort** (p115) or Kass Plateau of Flowers, both nearby.

Forget about coming during the monsoon when the whole town virtually shuts down (and an unbelievable 6m of rain falls). If you have an hour or so to kill between buses, budget-friendly **Nature Care Spa** (☑ 7066327423; Hotel Shreyas, opposite ST Bus Stand; massages from ₹1899; ⊙ 8am-8pm), across the street from the bus stand at Hotel Shreyas, hits the spot in a place like Mahabaleshwar. And don't miss **Grapevine** (☑ 02168-261100; Masjid Rd; mains ₹160-700; ⊙ 9.30am-3pm & 5-10pm) – its gourmet Parsi cuisine and Maharashtran wine are a godsend in Mahabaleshwar.

From Mahabaleshwar bus stand, state buses leave regularly for Pune (non-AC ₹180, four hours, hourly 7.30am to 6.30pm), Kolhapur (non-AC ₹265, 5½ hours, hourly from 8am) and Satara (non-AC ₹57, two hours, hourly 6am to 7pm). Seven daily buses head to Mumbai Central between 9am and 9.30pm (non-AC ₹400, seven hours) and one ordinary bus to Goa (non-AC ₹423, 12 hours, 8am).

RB Travels, located on a corner between an alley shortcut to Masjid Rd and the bazaar (across from Meghdoot restaurant), books luxury coaches to Goa (non-AC seater/Volvo AC sleeper ₹850/1800, 12 hours). You will depart from the bazaar in a car at 7.30pm to Surur Phata junction, 42km away, to wait for the bus on the way from Pune. Transport to Mumbai (Volvo AC seater/sleeper ₹500/600, six hours, noon and 9pm) and Pune (Volvo AC seater ₹375, 3½ hours, 11.30am) is available as well.

For the Pratapgad Fort, a state bus (₹130 return, one hour, 9.15am) does a daily round-trip, with a waiting time of around one hour; taxi drivers charge a fixed ₹1000 return.

---

daytime drinking session on the breezy patio, with some decent local craft beers to try,. perhaps with one of its famous sizzlers. The morning after? Well, Prem's is the logical choice again, with the city's best breakfast selection: eggs Benedict with smoked salmon (₹160), pancakes and detox shots.

Its sister bar next door, Swig, is its wilder counterpart, quite a happy hour hot spot.

★ **Malaka Spice**   ASIAN $$$
(www.malakaspice.com; Lane 5, North Main Rd, Koregaon Park; mains ₹305-780; ⊙ 11.30am-midnight; ❀ 🛜) Maharashtra's shining culinary moment is a fury of Southeast Asian fantasticness; trying to choose one dish among the delectable stir-fries, noodles and curries – all strong on seafood, vegetarian options, chicken, duck and mutton – is futile. Dine alfresco under colourful tree lights and relish the spicy and intricate flavour cavalcade from star chefs reared on a Slow Food, stay-local philosophy.

Many of their ingredients come from their own farm as well. Reserve ahead and starve yourself all day in preparation!

Dario's   ITALIAN $$$
(www.darios.in; Hotel Sunderban, 19 Koregaon Park; mains ₹480-610, pizza ₹260-680; ⊙ 8am-11.30pm) At the rear of Hotel Sunderban, this Italian-run veg paradise is one of Pune's most elegant dining experiences, providing you plant yourself on the gorgeous and intimate courtyard for an alfresco meal. Homemade pastas, very good pizzas and fine salads (try the Bosco; ₹480), including wholewheat, vegan and gluten-free options, fill the extensive menu of delectable homesick remedies.

🍷 Drinking & Nightlife

★ **Independence
Brewing Company**   CRAFT BEER
(☑ 020-66448308; www.independencebrewco. com; Zero One, 79/1, Pingle Vasti, Mundhwa Rd, Mundhwa; pints from ₹300) Reserve a table in the outstanding beer garden at this industrially hip craft brewery – Pune's finest – and you'll swear you're in California. The seven taps change often – Four Grain saison, Method to Madness IPA and the chocolate-bomb Ixcacao porter are standouts – and the funky-flavoured, Indian-Asian bar

grub means it's very easy to settle in for the night.

High Spirits Cafe BAR
(www.dahigh.com; 35A/1, North Main Rd, Mundhwa; cocktails ₹300-575; ☺8-11.45pm) Pune's most happening evenings take place in this artistically inclined bar with a ramshackle, good-time outdoor patio. Every night something cool is on, such as comedy Wednesdays, disco Saturdays and an unskippable Sunday barbecue (1.30pm to 4.30pm). The crowd, stretching from starving artists to wayward soul-searchers to 40-something trendsetters, goes bananas. No cover!

☆ Entertainment

★**Shisha Cafe** JAZZ
(☑020-26880050; www.facebook.com/shisha-jazzcafe; ABC Farms, Mundhwa; Thu ₹250) It's a magical atmosphere anytime, but live jazz Thursday nights at alfresco Shisha are a Pune institution. Snuggle up on Irani-an-style lounges downstairs or reserve a seat at a marble table under hanging Arabian carpets in the elevated main stage area. It's inside a nightlife enclave in Mundhwa called ABC Farms.

🛍 Shopping

Fabindia CLOTHING
(www.fabindia.com; Sakar 10, Sassoon Rd; ☺10.30am-8.30pm) Sells Indian saris, silks and cottons, as well as linen shirts for men, and diverse accessories including bags and jewellery.

ℹ Information

For exchange services, there is a Thomas Cook branch on General Thimmaya Rd. There are dozens of ATMs spread through the city and at the train station.
Citibank ATM (Tulsidas Apartment, N Main Rd)
HDFC ATM (East St)
HSBC ATM (Bund Garden Rd)

You'll find several internet cafes along Pune's main thoroughfares. Wi-fi is common in trendier bars and restaurants and most hotels.
Main Post Office (www.indiapost.gov.in; Sadhu Vaswani Path; ☺10am-6pm Mon-Sat)
MTDC Tourist Office (☑020-26128169; www.maharashtratourism.gov.in; I Block, Central Bldg, Dr Annie Besant Rd; ☺10am-6pm Mon-Sat, to 5pm Sun, closed 2nd & 4th Sat) Buried in a government complex south of the train station.
Thomas Cook (☑020-66007903; www.thomascook.in; Thackers House, 2418 General Thimmaya Rd; ☺9.30am-6pm Mon-Sat) Cashes travellers cheques and exchanges foreign currency.
Yatra.com (☑020-65007605; www.yatra.com; Koregaon Park Rd; ☺10am-7pm Mon-Sat) The city office of the reputed internet ticketing company.

ℹ Getting There & Away

AIR
A flashy new international airport is planned but infighting over the exact location was stalling the project at time of writing. Until then, airlines fly daily from **Pune International Airport** (PNQ; New Airport Rd, Mhada Colony, Lohgaon) to Mumbai, Delhi, Jaipur, Bengaluru (Bangalore), Nagpur, Goa, and Chennai, among others.

BUS
Pune has three bus stands. Buses leave the **Pune train station stand** (☑020-26126218) for Belgaum (₹700, seven hours, 11pm), Goa (₹600 to ₹1000, 10 hours, 6.30pm and 7.30pm), Kolhapur (₹400, six hours, hourly 5.30am to 11.30pm), Lonavla (₹62, hourly), Mahabaleshwar (₹230, four hours, hourly 5.30am to 5.30pm) and Mumbai's Dadar TT Circle station (₹266 to ₹531, four hours, every 15 minutes).

From the **Shivaji Nagar bus stand** (☑020-24431240; Shivajinagar Railway Station Rd), air-con buses go to Aurangabad (from ₹661, five to six hours, hourly 6am to 11.30pm), Nasik (from ₹611, every 20 minutes, 6am to 12.30am) and Mumbai (₹650, frequent). Non-AC buses also go

MAJOR TRAINS FROM PUNE

DESTINATION	TRAIN NO & NAME	FARE (₹)	DURATION (HR)	DEPARTURE
Bengaluru	11301 Udyan Express	460/1785	21	11.45am
Chennai	12163 Chennai Express	525/1980	19½	12.10am
Delhi	11077 Jhelum Express	625/2435	27½	5.20pm
Hyderabad	17031 Hyderabad Express	340/1310	13½	4.35pm
Mumbai CST	12124 Deccan Queen	115/395	3½	7.15am

Express fares are sleeper/2AC; Deccan Queen fares are 2nd class/AC chair.

to Mahabaleshwar (₹230, four hours, 6.15am, 8.30am and 9.30am).

Ticket agents selling private long-distance bus tickets are across the street from Shivaji Nagar station – try **Sana Travels** (☑ 8888808984; 2, Sita Park, Shivajinagar). Destinations (all AC sleepers) include Bengaluru (₹1050, 14 hours, hourly 1pm to 10pm), Hyderabad (₹500, 10 hours, hourly 7pm to 1am), Goa (₹1000, 10 hours, 7pm and 10pm), Mangalore (₹1500, 14 hours, 6pm and 10pm) and Nagpur (₹800, 14 hours, hourly 4am to 10pm). Buses for Bengaluru and Mangalore as well as Sinhagad leave from the **Swargate bus stand** (☑ 020-24441591; Satara Rd).

TAXI

Shared taxis (up to four passengers) link Pune with Mumbai airport around the clock. They leave from the **taxi stand** (☑ 020-26121090) in front of Pune train station (per seat ₹400 to ₹475, 2½ hours). To rent a car and driver try **Simran Travels** (☑ 020-26153222; www.mumbaiairportcab.com; 1st fl, Madhuban Bldg, Lane No 5, Koregaon Park; ☑ 24hr).

TRAIN

Pune train station (sometimes called Pune Junction) is in the heart of the city on HH Prince Aga Khan Rd. There are very regular, roughly hourly services to Mumbai and good links to cities including Delhi, Chennai and Hyderabad.

ⓘ Getting Around

The modern airport is 8km northeast of the city. From Koregaon Park an autorickshaw costs about ₹150 and a taxi around ₹200, but an UberGo at nonsurge pricing is only around ₹115. Autorickshaws can be found everywhere; a trip from the train station to Koregaon Park costs about ₹50 (more at night).

Around Pune

Sinhagad

The ruined **Sinhagad** (Lion Fort; ☑ dawn-dusk) **FREE**, about 24km southwest of Pune, was wrested by Maratha leader Shivaji from the Bijapur kings in 1670. In the epic battle (where he lost his son Sambhaji), Shivaji is said to have used monitor lizards yoked with ropes to scale the fort's craggy walls. Today, it's in a poor state, but worth visiting for the sweeping views and opportunity to hike in the hills. Bus 50 runs frequently to Donje (Golewadi) village from Swargate (₹30, 45 minutes), from where it's a 4km hike if you want to walk or catch a shared 4WD (₹50)

that can cart you 10km to the base of the summit.

Shivneri

Situated 90km northwest of Pune, above the village of Junnar, **Shivneri Fort** (☑ dawn-dusk) **FREE** holds the distinction of being the birthplace of Shivaji. Within the ramparts of this ruined fort are the old royal stables, a mosque dating back to the Mughal era and several rock-cut reservoirs. The most important structure is Shivkunj, the pavilion in which Shivaji was born.

About 8km from Shivneri, on the other side of Junnar, is an interesting group of Hinayana Buddhist caves called **Lenyadri** (Indian/foreigner ₹15/200; ☑ 8am-6pm). Of the 27 caves, cave 7 is the most impressive and, interestingly, houses an image of the Hindu god Ganesh.

Views from both monuments are spectacular.

There are seven or so buses per day (₹88, two hours) connecting Pune's Shivaji Nagar terminus with Junnar (a day cab from Pune will cost about ₹2625). From Junnar's bus stand, a return rickshaw including one hour's wait time runs ₹200 to Shivneri and ₹300 to Lenyadri.

Kolhapur

☑ 0231 / POP 561,300 / ELEV 550M

A little-visited city, Kolhapur is the perfect place to get intimate with the flamboyant side of India. Only a few hours from Goa, this historic settlement boasts an intensely fascinating temple complex. In August Kolhapur is at its vibrant best when Naag Panchami (p82), a snake-worshipping festival, is held in tandem with one at Pune. Gastronomes take note: the town is also the birthplace of the famed, spicy Kolhapuri cuisine, especially chicken and mutton dishes.

◉ Sights

The atmospheric old town quarter around the Mahalaxmi Temple and Old Palace has a huge (traffic-free) plaza and is accessed by a monumental gateway.

★ **Shree Chhatrapati Shahu Museum** MUSEUM
(Indian/foreigner ₹25/80; ☑ 9.15am-5.30pm) 'Bizarre' takes on a whole new meaning at this 'new' palace, an Indo-Saracenic behemoth designed by British architect 'Mad' Charles

Mant for the Kolhapur kings in 1884. The madcap museum is a maze of countless trophies from the kings' trigger-happy jungle safaris, including walking sticks made from leopard vertebrae and ashtrays fashioned out of tiger skulls and rhino feet. The armoury houses enough weapons to stage a minicoup. The horror-house effect is brought full circle by the taxidermy section.

Don't miss the highly ornate Durbar Hall, where the rulers held court sessions, and dotted around the palace you'll find dozens of portraits of the portly maharajas to admire. Photography is prohibited inside.

It's located about 2.5km north of the train station. A rickshaw from the train station/ bus stand will cost ₹35/50.

★ **Mahalaxmi Temple** HINDU TEMPLE
(⊙3am-11pm) One of Maharastra's most important and vibrant places of worship, the Mahalaxmi Temple is dedicated to Amba Bai (Mother Goddess). The temple's origins date back to AD 10, but much of the present structure is from the 18th century. It draws an unceasing tide of humanity, as pilgrims press to enter the holy inner sanctuary and bands of musicians and worshippers chant devotions. Non-Hindus are welcome and it's a fantastic place for people-watching.

Motibag Thalim TRAINING CENTRE
(⊙4am-4pm) Kolhapur is famed for the calibre of its Kushti wrestlers and at the Motibag Thalim you can watch young athletes train in an earthen pit. The *akhara* (training ground) is reached through a low doorway and passage to the left of the entrance to Bhavani Mandap (ask for directions). You are free to walk in and watch, as long as you don't mind the sight of sweaty, seminaked men and the stench of urine emanating from the loos.

🛌 Sleeping & Eating

Hotel K Tree HOTEL $$
(☎0231-2526990; www.hotelktree.com; 517E, Plot 65, Shivaji Park; s/d incl breakfast from ₹3330/3700; ❄🖥) With high service standards and 26 very inviting modish rooms, this newer hotel is fine value and wildy popular with Indians for its 15-item buffet breakfast. It's a toss up between the clandestine bathrooms in deluxe rooms or elevated Asian-style beds in executive rooms.

Hotel Pavillion HOTEL $$
(☎0231-2652751; www.hotelpavillion.co.in; 392E Assembly Rd, Shaupuri; s/d incl breakfast ₹1850/2080,

DON'T MISS
PRATAPGAD FORT

Pratapgad Fort (⊙9am-dusk) FREE, built by Shivaji in 1656 (and still owned by his descendants), straddles a high mountain ridge 24km northwest of the town of Mahabaleshwar. In 1659, Shivaji agreed to meet Bijapuri General Afzal Khan here in an attempt to end a stalemate. Despite a no-arms agreement, Shivaji, upon greeting Khan, disembowelled his enemy with a set of iron *baghnakh* (tiger's claws). Khan's tomb (out of bounds) marks the site of this painful encounter at the base of the fort. Pratapgad is reached by a 500-step climb that affords brilliant views.

From the bus stand in Mahabaleshwar, a state bus tour (₹165 return, one hour, 9.30am) does a daily shuttle to the fort, with a waiting time of around one hour. Taxi drivers in Mahabaleshwar charge a fixed ₹1000 for the return trip, including one hour's waiting time.

with AC from ₹2260/2500; ❄@) Located at the far end of a leafy park-cum-office-area, this hotel guarantees a peaceful stay, occasionally uninspired bathrooms aside. Its large, well-equipped rooms are perhaps a little dated, but many have windows that open out to delightful views of seasonal blossoms. Book room 101 to catch the lobby-only wi-fi signal in-room.

Chorage Misal INDIAN $
(Mahadwar Rd, near Gujri Corners; mains ₹40; ⊙8.30am-8pm) Near Mahalaxmi Temple, this hole-in-the-wall *misal* (spicy curry made from moth bean sprouts) joint has been at it since 1963 and is the spiciest of the city's classic joints. Rajesh is the third generation behind the recipe and acts as a one-man show. There's no English sign. It's directly to the right of the beautiful Jain temple with the Coca-Cola signage.

★ **Dehaati** INDIAN $$
(Ayodha Park, Old Pune-Bangalore Hwy, Nimbalkar Colony; thalis ₹230-320; ⊙12.30-3.30pm & 7.30-10.30pm) The city's Kolhapuri thali specialist. Meals come in a variety of mutton variations as well as chicken and veg. The vibrant curries, the spiced-up dhal, the rich *aakkha masoor* (Kolhapuri-style whole lentil curry), the intricate *tambda rassa* (spicy red mutton curry), the perfectly flaky chapatis – it's all delicious.

Little Italy
ITALIAN $$

(☑ 0231-2537133; www.littleitaly.in; 517 A2 Shivaji Park; pizza ₹225-445, pasta ₹215-365; ⊙ 11.30am-10pm) If you've been clocking up some hard yards on India's roads, this authentic, professionally run restaurant is just the place to sustain you for the next trip. All the flavours are to savour, with a delicious, veg-only menu of antipasti, thin-crust pizzas (from a wood-fired oven), al dente pasta and a great Indian-heavy wine list (by the glass available).

Don't pass on the desserts, particularly the panna cotta.

ℹ Information

ICICI Bank ATM Located next to Mahalaxmi Temple.

MTDC Tourist Office (☑ 0231-2652935; www.maharashtratourism.gov.in; 254B Udyog Bhavan, Assembly Rd; ⊙ 10am-5.30pm Mon-Sat) Located behind the Collector's Office near Hotel Pavillion. At the time of research, it had opened a far more convenient booth (☑ 0231-2652935; www.maharashtratourism.gov.in) near Mahalaxmi Mandir on a trial basis.

State Bank of India ATM Handy ATM across the street from Hotel Pavillion.

ℹ Getting There & Around

BUS

From the **Kolhapur bus stand** (☑ 0231-2650620; Benadikar Path, Shahupur), services head regularly to Pune (non-AC from ₹396, five hours, hourly 5am to 11pm), Ratnagiri (ordinary/semideluxe ₹177/199, 4½ hours, every 30 minutes 5am to 1am), five ordinary-only buses to Malvan (₹201, five hours, 5.15am, 6.5am, noon, 1.30pm and 5pm) and 12 daily buses to Mumbai (ordinary/semideluxe ₹480/600, 10 hours). There is a reservation counter for all buses.

The best private bus agents gather at the Royal Plaza building at Dabholkar Corner, 300m north of the bus stand. **Paulo Travels** (☑ 0231-6681812; www.paulotravels.com; B/22, Royal Plaza, Dhabolkar Corner) heads to Goa (Volvo AC seater/sleeper from ₹500/600, eight hours, 9am, noon, 2am, 3am, 4am, 5am and 6am). **Neeta Travels** (☑ 0231-3290061; www.neeta-bus.in; B/16, Royal Plaza, Dabholkar Corner) is a good bet for overnight air-con services heading to Mumbai (Volvo AC sleeper from ₹850, nine hours, 5pm, 9.45pm and 10.45pm) and Pune (Volvo AC seater from ₹350, five hours, 7am, 9am, 4pm, 5pm, 8pm and 11.30pm).

TRAIN

The train station, known as Chattrapati Shahu Maharaj Terminus, is 10 minutes' walk west of the bus stand. Three daily expresses, including the 10.50pm Sahyadri Express, go to Mumbai (sleeper/2AC ₹338/1241, 13 hours, 10.50pm) via Pune (₹243/876, eight hours). The Rani Chennama Express makes the long voyage to Bengaluru (₹433/1636, 17½ hours, 2.05pm). There are no direct trains to Goa.

Goa

Best Beaches

➡ Palolem (p154)
➡ Mandrem (p145)
➡ Cola & Khancola (p152)
➡ Anjuna (p137)
➡ Arambol (p146)

Best Places to Sleep

➡ Panjim Inn (p124)
➡ Red Door Hostel (p137)
➡ Mandala (p146)
➡ Indian Kitchen (p135)
➡ Ciaran's (p154)

Why Go?

Pint-sized Goa is much more than beaches and trance parties. A kaleidoscopic blend of Indian and Portuguese cultures, sweetened with sun, sea, sand, seafood and spirituality, there's nowhere in India quite like it.

The central region (practically beach-free) is Goa's historic and cultural heart, home to capital Panaji, Old Goa's glorious churches, inland islands, bird sanctuaries, spice plantations and the wild Western Ghats.

North Goa is the Goa you've heard all about: busy beaches, upbeat nightlife, Goan trance, great food, hippie markets and yoga retreats. Calangute and Baga are the epicentre. Anjuna (with its famous Wednesday market) and Vagator still exude some hippie cool and party vibe. Laid-back Morjim, Aswem and Mandrem are burgeoning family-friendly beach resorts. Northern, budget-loving Arambol hosts paragliding.

South Goa is the state's more serene half, with cleaner, whiter, quieter beaches ranging from village-feel Benaulim to beach-hut bliss at Palolem, Patnem and Agonda.

When to Go

Goa (Panaji)

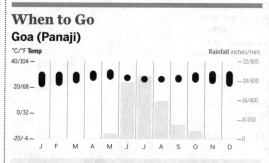

Sep–Nov Some shacks up, but prices are lower and crowds fewer; humid weather post-monsoon.

Nov–Mar Wonderful weather; yoga, festivals in full swing; peak prices and crowds mid-Dec to early Jan.

Mar–Apr Carnival and Easter celebrations as the season winds down.

Goa Highlights

1 Panaji (p121)
Exploring the historic Latin Quarter, shopping and eating well in India's most laid-back state capital.

2 Assagao (p140)
Dropping in to a yoga class at Assagao, Anjuna, Arambol or Mandrem.

3 Anjuna Flea Market (p140)
Haggling for a bargain at this touristy but fun Wednesday market.

4 Old Goa (p127)
Standing in silence in the extraordinary churches and cathedrals of Old Goa.

5 Cola Beach (p152) Trekking down to secluded Cola, one of Goa's prettiest beaches.

6 Mandrem (p145)
Sleeping in style and stretching out with a good book at this peaceful beach.

7 Palolem (p154)
Checking into a beach hut on beautiful Palolem Beach, where you can kayak, learn to cook and relax.

8 Chandor (p150)
Marvelling at colonial mansions and *palácio* in this village near Margao.

9 Agonda (p153)
Booking into a luxurious beachfront hut and learning to surf.

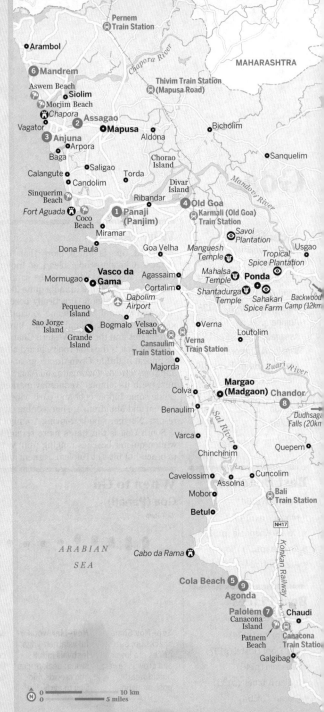

History

A 100,000-year look back through the history of Goa offers a keen insight into some of the region's most mysterious and alluring archaeological and historic remains, and into the Goan psyche itself.

Goa went through a dizzying array of rulers from Ashoka's Mauryan empire in the 3rd century BC to the long-ruling Kadambas from the 3rd century AD. Subsequent conflict saw rival sultanates fighting the Hindu Vijayanagar empire for control, before the Adil Shahs of Bijapur created the capital we now call Old Goa in the 15th century.

The Portuguese arrived in 1510 and steadily extended their power from their grand capital at Old Goa out into the provinces, zealously converting the locals to Christianity. Their 400-year reign came to an end in 1961, after a three-day siege by the Indian Army, but the Portuguese legacy lives on in the state's colonial-era mansions, its cuisine, churches and even in its language.

🏃 Activities

Yoga & Alternative Therapies

Every imaginable form of yoga, meditation, reiki, ayurvedic massage and other spiritually orientated health regime is practised, taught and relished in Goa. The best time is mid-November to early April, when all outfits or retreats are open and courses are in full swing. A handful of classes operate year-round.

Palolem, Agonda and Patnem in the south, and Arambol, Mandrem, Anjuna and Assagao in the north, are particularly great places for yoga classes and courses.

Ayurvedic treatments can be found in most beach villages. Ask around for personal recommendations and ensure that massages are conducted by a female if you're a woman and a male if you're a man. The spas at Goa's five-star hotels offer a superluxurious alternative.

Wildlife-Watching

Goa's hinterland is great for spotting wildlife, from the blazing kingfishers that fleck the coastal strip's luminescent paddy fields, to the water buffalo that wander home come sunset. Goa's wildlife sanctuaries host hard-to-spot wonders such as gaurs (Indian bison), porcupines, wild boar and the occasional pangolin (scaly anteater) or leopard. A loud rustle in the leaves overhead often signals the arrival of mischievous langur monkeys. Taking a riverine trip inland, you might spot crocodiles, otters, and yet more birdlife.

John's Boat Tours (p131) in Candolim runs dolphin- and crocodile-spotting trips.

Water Sports

Most water-sports outfits run on a seasonal, itinerant basis; it's enough to turn up at a beach and look around for a shack offering your chosen activity. Calangute and Colva are the busiest water-sports beaches. Activities include jet skiing, parasailing, wake-boarding, kayaking, surfing and kitesurfing. Paragliding (p146) is popular at Arambol. The best places for kayaking are Palolem's calm bay or Goa's numerous rivers and estuaries. Surfing outfits include Vaayu Waterman's Village (p145) in Aswem, Surf Wala (p147) in Arambol and Aloha Surf School (p153) in Agonda.

TOP STATE FESTIVALS

Feast of the Three Kings (Chandor & Reis Magos; ⊘6 Jan) Boys re-enact the story of the three kings bearing gifts for Christ.

Shigmotsav of Holi (Shigmo; statewide; ⊘Feb/Mar) Goa's version of the Hindu festival Holi sees coloured powders thrown about and parades in most towns.

Sabado Gordo (Panaji; ⊘Feb/Mar) A procession of floats and street parties on the Saturday before Lent.

Carnival (statewide; ⊘Mar) A four-day festival kicking off Lent; the party's particularly jubilant in Panaji.

Fama de Menino Jesus (Colva; ⊘2nd Mon in Oct) Statue of the baby Jesus is paraded through the streets of Colva.

Feast of St Francis Xavier (Panaji, Old Goa; ⊘3 Dec) A 10-day celebration of Goa's patron saint.

Feast of Our Lady of the Immaculate Conception (Margao, Panaji; ⊘8 Dec) Fairs and concerts around Panaji's famous church.

Although Goa is not an internationally renowned diving destination, its waters are India's third-best diving spot (after the Andaman and Lakshadweep Islands). Dive season runs from late October to April. Recommended Professional Association of Dive Instructors (PADI) accredited operations in Goa include Barracuda Diving (p133) in Baga, Dive Goa (p131) in Candolim, Goa Aquatics (p133) in Calangute and **Goa Diving** (☑ 9049442647; www.goadiving.com; courses from ₹11,000, 1-/2-tank dive ₹3000/5000) in Bogmalo.

ⓘ Information

The **Goa Tourism Development Corporation** (www.goa-tourism.com) provides maps and information, operates hotels throughout the state and runs a host of tours.

ⓘ Getting There & Away

AIR

Goa's airport, **Dabolim** (Goa International Airport; ☑ 0832-2540806), is served directly by domestic flights, a handful of international flights from the Middle East, and seasonal package-holiday charters (mostly from Russia, Europe and the UK).

GOA

SLEEPING PRICE RANGES

The following price ranges refer to a double room with bathroom:

$ below ₹1200

$$ ₹1200–₹5000

$$$ above ₹5000

Accommodation prices in Goa can vary considerably depending on the season and demand. The high season runs from November to late February, but prices climb even higher during the crowded Christmas and New Year period (around 22 December to 3 January). Mid-season is October and March to April, and low season is the monsoon (May to September). These dates can vary a little depending on the monsoon and the granting of shack licences, which are renewed every couple of years.

All accommodation rates listed are for the high season – but not for the peak Christmas period, when you'll almost certainly have to book in advance. Always call ahead for rates and ask about discounts.

Unless you're on a charter, you'll generally have to fly into a major city such as Mumbai or Delhi and change to a domestic flight with Jet Airways, Air India, SpiceJet or IndiGo.

BUS

Private and state-run long-distance buses run to/from Goa daily; in many cases you simply turn up at the bus station and jump on the next available bus. State-run and private companies offer 'ordinary', 'deluxe' 'superfast' and VIP services. Most comfortable are Volvo buses, with reclining seating and air-conditioning. Note that travel into and out of Mumbai by road is interminably slow; the train is faster and more comfortable.

Buses for Mumbai and other cities depart from Panaji, Margao and Mapusa between 5.30pm and 8.30pm daily; there are dozens of operators and departures, but fares are standard to/from anywhere in Goa. **Kadamba** (www.goakadamba.com), the state government bus company, serves the state and neighbouring regions. For booking private buses, try www.redbus.in.

TRAIN

The 760km-long **Konkan Railway** (www.konkan railway.com), completed in 1998, is the main train line running through the state, connecting Goa with Mumbai to the north and Mangalore to the south.

The biggest station in Goa is Margao's Madgaon station (p149), and many trains also pass through Karmali station near Old Goa, 12km from Panaji. Smaller stations on the line include Pernem for Arambol, Thivim for Mapusa and the northern beaches, and Canacona for Palolem.

ⓘ Getting Around

TO/FROM THE AIRPORT

From Dabolim Airport, prepaid taxis to central Panaji or Margao charge ₹870 (₹920 for AC). Alternatively, if you don't have much luggage, catch a bus from the main road to Vasco da Gama, then a bus direct from Vasco to Panaji (₹30, 45 minutes).

BUS

Goa's extensive network of buses shuttle to and from almost every tiny town and village; the main hubs are Panaji, Margao and Mapusa. Travelling between north and south Goa you'll generally need to change at Margao, Panaji or both. Fares range from ₹5 to ₹40.

CAR & MOTORCYCLE

It's easy in Goa to organise a private car with driver (or simply a taxi) for long-distance day trips. Expect to pay from ₹2000 for a full day (usually eight hours and 80km). Self-drive hire cars start from ₹900 to ₹1200 per day for a small Maruti to upwards of ₹2000 for a large

4WD, excluding fuel and usually with a per kilo-metre limit. Your best bet for rentals is online at sites such as www.goa2u.com.

You'll rarely go far on a Goan road without seeing a local or tourist whizzing by on a scooter or motorbike, and renting one is a breeze. You'll likely pay from ₹200 to ₹400 per day for a scooter, ₹400 to ₹500 for a smaller Yamaha motorbike, and ₹450 to ₹600 for a Royal Enfield Bullet. Prices can drop considerably if you're renting for more than a few days or if it's an off-peak period – bargain if there are lots of machines around.

Goan roads can be treacherous, filled with human, bovine, canine, feline, mechanical and avian obstacles, as well as potholes and hairpin bends. Take it slowly, be on the lookout for 'speed breakers', try not to drive at night (country lanes are poorly lit), and don't attempt a north–south day trip on a 50cc bike.

TAXI & AUTORICKSHAW

Taxis are widely available for town-hopping, but the local union cartel means prices are high, especially at night and more so around expensive hotels. A full day's sightseeing, depending on the distance, is likely to be around ₹1500 to ₹2000. Agree on a price beforehand.

A new initiative by Goa Tourism is the **Women's Taxi Service** (☑0832-2437437), with female drivers, phone-only bookings and only women, couples or families accepted as passengers. The vehicles are fitted with accurate meters and GPS monitoring, and the drivers are trained in first aid and self-defence. Fares can even be paid with a credit card.

Autorickshaws are about a third cheaper than taxis and generally better for short trips; count on ₹50 minimum for a short journey and ₹100 for a slightly longer one. Negotiate the fare before you jump in.

Motorcycle taxis, known as 'pilots', are also a licensed form of taxi in Goa, identified by a yellow front mudguard. They're only really common around major taxi stands and beach resorts, and cost half the price of a taxi.

PANAJI & CENTRAL GOA

Panaji (Panjim)
☑0832 / POP 115,000
One of India's most relaxed state capitals, Panaji (Panjim) crowds around the peninsula overlooking the broad Mandovi River, where cruise boats and floating casinos ply the waters, and advertising signs cast neon reflections in the night.

OFF THE BEATEN TRACK

DUDHSAGAR FALLS

Goa's most impressive **waterfall** splashes 603m down on the eastern border with Karnataka, in the far southeastern corner of the Bhagwan Mahavir Wildlife Sanctuary. The falls are best visited as soon after monsoon as possible (October is perfect), when water levels are highest.

Get here via Colem village, 7km south of Molem, by car or by the scenic 8.15am local train from Margao (return train times vary seasonally). From Colem, pick up a shared jeep (₹500 per person for six people) for the bumpy remaining 45-minute journey. An easier option is a taxi or a full-day Goa Tourism 'Dudhsagar Special' tour (₹1200), starting at 9am from Calangute, Mapusa, Panaji or Miramar on Wednesday and Sunday, and returning at 6pm. Private travel agents also offer tours.

A glorious whitewashed church lords over the animated city centre, a broad leafy boulevard skirts around the river, and grand colonial-era buildings rub shoulders with arty boutiques, old-school bookshops, state-of-the-art malls and backstreet bars.

But it's the tangle of narrow streets in the old Latin Quarter that really steal the show. Nowhere is the Portuguese influence felt more strongly than here, where the late afternoon sun lights up yellow houses with purple doors, and around each corner you'll find restored ochre-coloured mansions with terracotta-tiled roofs, wrought-iron balconies and arched oyster-shell windows.

A day or two in Panaji really is an essential part of the Goan experience.

Sights & Activities

Some of Panaji's great pleasures are leisurely strolls through the sleepy Portuguese-era districts of **Fontainhas and Sao Tomé** and **Altinho**. Riverside **Campal Gardens**, west of the centre, and **Miramar Beach**, 4km southwest of the city, are also popular spots.

★**Church of Our Lady of the Immaculate Conception** CHURCH
(cnr Emilio Gracia & Jose Falcao Rds; ☺10am-12.30pm & 3-5.30pm Mon-Sat, 11am-12.30pm & 3.30-5pm Sun, English Mass 8am daily) Panaji's spiritual, as well as geographical, centre is this elevated, pearly white church, built in

Panaji (Panjim)

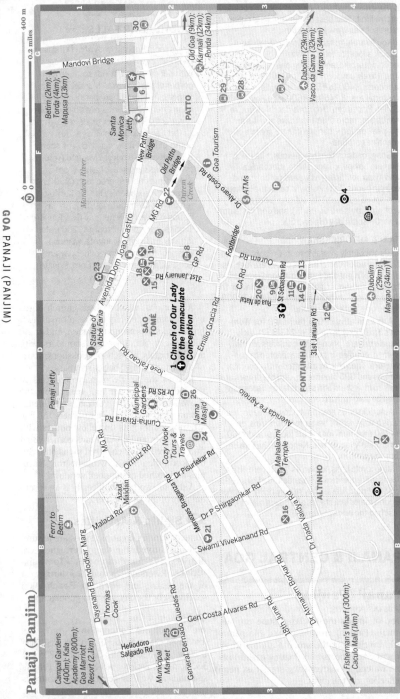

Panaji (Panjim)

1619 over an older, smaller 1540 chapel, and stacked like a fancy white wedding cake. When Panaji was little more than a sleepy fishing village, this church was the first port of call for sailors from Lisbon, who would give thanks for a safe crossing, before continuing to Ela (Old Goa) further east up the river. The church is beautifully illuminated at night.

Goa State Museum   MUSEUM
(☑ 0832-2438006; www.goamuseum.gov.in; EDC Complex, Patto; ⊙ 9.30am-5.30pm Mon-Sat) **FREE** This spacious museum east of town houses an eclectic, if not extensive, collection of items tracing aspects of Goan history. As well as some beautiful Hindu and Jain sculptures and bronzes, there are nice examples of Portuguese-era furniture, coins, an intricately carved chariot and a pair of quirky antique rotary lottery machines.

Goa State Central Library   LIBRARY
(Sanskruti Bhavan, Patto; ⊙ 9am-7.30pm Mon-Fri, 9.30am-5.45pm Sat & Sun) **FREE** Panaji's ultra-modern new state library, near the state museum, has six floors of reading material, a bookshop and gallery. The 2nd floor features a children's book section and internet browsing (free, but technically only for academic research). The 4th floor has Goan

history books and the 6th a large collection of Portuguese books.

⊙ Tours

Organised boat cruises are a popular way to see the Mandovi River.

Paradise Cruises   CRUISE
(☑ 0832-2437960; http://paradisecruises.in; Tourist Boat Jetty; per person ₹300; ⊙ cruises 5.30pm & 7pm) This private operator runs two evening 'party' cruises on the Mandovi River aboard its triple-decker boat. There's a bar on board and usually a cultural or dance show on the upper deck.

Mandovi River Cruises   CRUISE
(sunset cruise ₹300, dinner cruise ₹650, backwater cruise ₹900; ⊙ sunset cruise 6pm, sundown cruise 7.15pm, dinner cruise 8.45pm Wed & Sat, backwater cruise 9.30am-4pm Tue & Fri) Goa Tourism operates a range of entertaining hour-long cruises along the Mandovi River aboard the *Santa Monica* or *Shantadurga*. All include a live band and usually performances of Goan folk songs and dances. There are also twice-weekly, two-hour dinner cruises and backwater cruises, which takes you down the Mandovi to Old Goa, a spice plantation and then heads back past Divar and Chorao

ⓘ WARNING: DRUGS

Acid, ecstasy, cocaine, charas (hashish), marijuana and most other forms of drugs are illegal in India (though still readily available in Goa), and purchasing or carrying drugs is fraught with danger. Goa's Fort Aguada jail houses a number of prisoners, including some foreigners, serving drug-related sentences. Being caught in possession of even a small quantity of illegal substances can mean a 10-year stretch.

Islands. All cruises depart from the Santa Monica Jetty next to the Mandovi Bridge.

🌟 Festivals & Events

Carnival   RELIGIOUS
(statewide; ⊙ Mar) A four-day festival kicking off Lent; Panaji's party is particularly jubilant.

**Feast of Our Lady of
the Immaculate Conception**   RELIGIOUS
(Margao, Panaji; ⊙ 8 Dec) Fairs and concerts are held, as is a beautiful church service at Panaji's Church of Our Lady of the Immaculate Conception.

🛏 Sleeping

Panaji has its fair share of accommodation for all budgets. In the middle range are some of Goa's better boutique heritage hotels and guesthouses, mostly in the Fontainhas area.

★ Old Quarter Hostel   HOSTEL $
(☑ 0832-6517606; www.thehostelcrowd.com; 31st Jan Rd, Fontainhas; dm ₹550-600, d with AC ₹1600-2000; ❋ 🛜) In an old Portuguese house in historic Fontainhas, this flamboyant hostel offers slick four-bed dorms with lockers as well as private doubles in a separate building, along with the Urban Cafe, arty murals, good wi-fi and bikes for hire. Noon checkout.

A Pousada Guest House   GUESTHOUSE $
(☑ 9850998213, 0832-2422618; sabrinateles@yahoo.com; Luis de Menezes Rd; s/d from ₹800/1050, d with AC ₹1575; ❋ 🛜) The five rooms in this bright-yellow place are simple but clean and come with comfy spring-mattress beds and TV. Owner Sabrina is friendly and no-nonsense, and it's one of Panaji's better budget guesthouses.

Afonso Guesthouse   GUESTHOUSE $$
(☑ 9764300165, 0832-2222359; www.afonsoguesthouse.com; St Sebastian Rd; d ₹2900-3250;

❋🛜) Run by the friendly Jeanette, this pretty Portuguese townhouse offers spacious, well-kept rooms with timber ceilings. The little rooftop terrace makes for sunny breakfasting (not included) with Fontainhas views. It's a simple, serene stay in the heart of the most atmospheric part of town. Checkout is 9am and bookings are accepted online but not by phone.

La Maison   BOUTIQUE HOTEL $$
(☑ 0832-2235555; www.lamaisongoa.com; 31st January Rd; r incl breakfast ₹4700-5300; ❋🛜) Another boutique heritage hotel in Fontainhas, La Maison is historic on the outside but thoroughly modern and swanky within. The eight rooms are deceptively simple and homely but five-star comfortable with soft beds, cloud-like pillows, writing desks and flat-screen TVs. Breakfast is included and attached is the European fusion **Desbue** restaurant.

Caravela Homestay   BOUTIQUE HOTEL $$
(☑ 0832-2237448; www.caravela.in; 27 31st January Rd; s/d incl breakfast from ₹2000/2500, ste ₹4000; ❋🛜) In a beautiful Sao Tome heritage building, Caravela has 10 minimalist but comfortable rooms with extra touches such as minibar and toiletries. Across the lane is the cafe where breakfast is served.

★ Panjim Inn   HERITAGE HOTEL $$$
(☑ 9823025748, 0832-2226523; www.panjiminn.com; 31st January Rd; s ₹5100-8000, d ₹5750-9200; ❋🛜) One of the original heritage hotels in Fontainhas, the Panjim Inn has been a long-standing favourite for its character and charm, friendly owners and helpful staff. This beautiful 19th-century mansion has 12 charismatic rooms in the original house, along with newer rooms with modern touches to complement four-poster beds, colonial furniture and artworks. There's also a day spa and rooftop jacuzzi.

Goa Marriott Resort   HOTEL $$$
(☑ 0832-2463333; www.marriott.com; Miramar Beach; d ₹11,700-17,000; ❋🛜🏊) Miramar's plush Goa Marriott Resort is the best in the area. It's expertly choreographed, with the five-star treatment beginning in the lobby and extending right up to the rooms-with-a-view. The 24-hour Waterfront Terrace & Bar is a great place for a sundowner overlooking the pool, while its Simply Grills restaurant is a favourite with well-heeled Panjimites.

Panjim Pousada   GUESTHOUSE $$$
(☑ 0832-2226523; www.panjiminn.com; 31st January Rd; s ₹5100-8000, d ₹5750-9200; ❋🛜) In an

old Hindu mansion, the nine divine, colonial fantasy rooms at Panjim Pousada are set off by a stunning central courtyard, with antique furnishings and lovely art on the walls. Various doorways and spiral staircases lead to the rooms; those on the upper level are the best.

✖ Eating

A stroll down 18th June or 31st January Rds will turn up a number of cheap but tasty canteen-style options, as will a quick circuit of the Municipal Gardens. The Latin Quarter has a developing foodie scene, where you can dine on traditional Goan specialities or Western comfort food.

Anandashram   INDIAN, GOAN $
(31st January Rd; thalis ₹90-140, mains ₹100-350; ⊙noon-3.30pm & 7.30-10.30pm Mon-Sat, noon-3pm Sun) This little place is renowned locally for seafood, serving up simple but tasty fish curries, as well as veg and nonveg thalis for lunch and dinner.

Vihar Restaurant   INDIAN $
(MG Rd; veg thali ₹100-150; ⊙7-9am, 11am-3pm & 7.30-10.30pm) A vast menu of 'pure veg' food, great big thalis, South Indian dosas and a plethora of fresh juices make this clean, simple canteen a popular place for locals and visitors. One of the few places in this area that's still busy late into the evening.

★Viva Panjim   GOAN $$
(☑0832-2422405; 31st January Rd; mains ₹130-220; ⊙11.30am-3.30pm & 7-11pm Mon-Sat, 7-11pm Sun) Well known to tourists, this little side-street eatery, in an old Portuguese house and with a few tables out on the laneway, still delivers tasty Goan classics at reasonable prices. There's a whole page devoted to pork dishes, along with tasty *xacuti* (a spicy chicken or meat dish cooked in red coconut sauce) and *cafreal* (a marinated chicken dish) style meals, seafood such as kingfish vindaloo and crab *xec xec,* and desserts such as *bebinca* (richly layered Goan dessert made from egg yolk and coconut).

★Cafe Bodega   CAFE $$
(☑0832-2421315; Altinho; mains ₹140-340; ⊙10am-7pm Mon-Sat, 10am-4pm Sun; 🛜) It's well worth a trip up to Altinho Hill to visit this serene cafe-gallery in a lavender-and-white Portuguese mansion in the grounds of Sunaparanta Centre for the Arts. Enjoy good coffee, juices and fresh-baked cakes around the inner courtyard or lunch on super pizzas and sandwiches.

Verandah   GOAN $$
(☑0832-2226523; 31st January Rd; mains ₹180-420; ⊙11am-11pm) The breezy 1st-floor restaurant at Panjim Inn is indeed on the balcony, with just a handful of finely carved tables, Fontainhas street views and snappy service. Goan cuisine is the speciality, but there's also a range of Indian and continental dishes and local wines.

Fisherman's Wharf   SEAFOOD $$
(☑8888493333; http://thefishermanswharf.in; Dr Braganza Pereira Rd; mains ₹220-450; ⊙noon-11pm) The successful formula from its long-running restaurant down in Mobor has been transplanted in the capital with fresh seafood, North Indian tandoor, kebabs and Goan specialities. The atmosphere on the open-side restaurant is relaxed but upmarket.

★Black Sheep Bistro   EUROPEAN $$$
(☑0832-2222901; www.blacksheepbistro.in; Swami Vivekanand Rd; tapas ₹190-280, mains ₹320-650; ⊙noon-4pm & 7-10.45pm) Among the best of Panaji's burgeoning boutique restaurants, Black Sheep's impressive pale-yellow facade gives way to a sexy dark-wood bar and loungy dining room. The tapas dishes are light, fresh and expertly prepared in keeping with their farm-to-table philosophy. Salads, pasta, seafood and dishes like lamb osso bucco grace the menu, while an internationally trained sommelier matches food to wine.

★Hotel Venite   GOAN $$$
(31st January Rd; mains ₹340-460; ⊙9am-10.30pm) With its cute rickety balcony tables overhanging the cobbled street, Venite has long been among the most atmospheric of Panaji's Goan restaurants. The menu is traditional, with spicy sausages, fish curry

---

GOAN CUISINE

Goan cuisine is a tantalising fusion of Portuguese and South Indian flavours. Goans tend to be hearty meat and fish eaters, and fresh seafood is a staple: the quintessential Goan lunch of 'fish-curry-rice' is fried mackerel steeped in coconut, tamarind and chilli sauce. Traditional dishes include vindaloo (a fiery dish in a marinade of vinegar and garlic), *xacuti* (a spicy chicken or meat dish cooked in red coconut sauce) and *cafreal* (dry-fried chicken marinated in a green masala paste and sprinkled with toddy vinegar). For dessert try the layered *bebinca* cake.

GOA PANAJI (PANJIM)

BACKWOODS CAMP

In a forest near Bhagwan Mahavir Wildlife Sanctuary, in far east Goa, rustic **Backwoods Camp** (☎9822139859; www.backwoodsgoa.com; Matkan, Tambdi Surla; 2-/3-day stay per person ₹8500/12,000; 🛜) is a magical, serene spot. The area is one of Goa's richest birding spots, with everything from Ceylon frogmouths and Asian fairy bluebirds to puff-throated babblers and Indian pittas putting in regular appearances. Accommodation is in tents on raised forest platforms, bungalows or farmhouse rooms; rates include meals and birdwatching guides.

rice, pepper steak and *bebinca,* but Venite is popular with tourists and prices are consequently inflated. Drop in for a beer or shot of *feni* (Goan spirit) before deciding.

🍷 Drinking & Nightlife

Panaji's local drinking scene is in the town's tiny, tucked-away bars, mostly equipped with rudimentary plastic tables, a fridge, a few stools and an almost-exclusively male clientele. More upscale bars can be found in high-end hotels, along with a few English-style pubs.

Cafe Mojo   BAR

(www.cafemojo.in; Menezes Braganza Rd; ⊙10am-4am Mon-Thu, to 6am Fri-Sun) The decor is cosy English pub, the clientele young and up for a party, and the novelty is the e-beer system. Each table has its own beer tap and LCD screen: you buy a card (₹500), swipe it at your table and start pouring – it automatically deducts what you drink (you can use the card for spirits, cocktails or food too).

Riverfront & Down the Road   BAR

(cnr MG & Ourem Rds; ⊙11am-1am) The balcony of this restaurant-bar overlooking the creek and Old Patto Bridge makes for a cosy beer or cocktail spot with carved barrels for furniture. The ground-floor bar (from 6pm) is the only real nightspot on the Old Quarter side of town, with occasional live music.

⭐ Entertainment

Panaji's most visible form of entertainment are the casino boats anchored out in the Mandovi River, but the city is also home to

India's biggest **international film festival** (www.iffi.nic.in; ⊙Nov) and the cultural offerings of the excellent Kala Academy.

Kala Academy   CULTURAL CENTRE

(☎0832-2420452; http://kalaacademygoa.org; Dayanand Bandodkar Marg) On the west side of the city, in Campal, is Goa's premier cultural centre, which features a program of dance, theatre, music and art exhibitions throughout the year. Many shows are in Konkani, but there are occasional English-language productions. The website has an up-to-date calendar of events.

Deltin Royale   CASINO

(☎8698599999; www.deltingroup.com/deltin-royale; Noah's Ark, RND Jetty, Dayanand Bandodkar Marg; weekday/weekend ₹3000/4000, premium package ₹4500/5500; ⊙24hr, entertainment 9pm-1am) Goa's biggest and best luxury floating casino, Deltin Royal has 123 tables, the Vegas Restaurant, a Whisky Bar and a creche. Entry includes gaming chips worth ₹2000/3000 weekday/weekend and to the full value of your ticket with the premium package. Unlimited food and drinks included.

🛍 Shopping

Caculo Mall   MALL

(☎0832-2222068; http://caculomall.in; 16 Shanta, St Inez; ⊙10am-9pm) Goa's biggest mall is four levels of air-conditioned family shopping heaven with brand-name stores, food court, kids' toys and arcade games.

Municipal Market   MARKET

(Heljogordo Salgado Rd; ⊙from 7.30am) This atmospheric place, where narrow streets have been converted into covered markets, makes for a nice wander, offering fresh produce, clothing stalls and some tiny, enticing eateries. The fish market is a particularly interesting strip of activity.

Singbal's Book House   BOOKS

(Church Sq; ⊙9.30am-1pm & 3.30-7.30pm Mon-Sat) On the corner opposite Panaji's main church, Singbal's has an excellent selection of international magazines and newspapers, and lots of books on Goa and travel.

Khadi India   ARTS & CRAFTS

(Dr Atmaram Borkar Rd; ⊙9am-1pm & 3-7pm) 🍃 Goa's only outpost of the government's Khadi & Village Industries Commission has a fine range of hand-woven cottons, oils, soaps, spices and other handmade products that come straight from (and directly benefit) regional villages.

Marcou Artifacts ARTS & CRAFTS
(☑0832-2220204; www.marcouartifacts.com; 31st January Rd; ☺9am-8pm) This small Fontainhas shop showcases one-off painted tiles, fish figurines and hand-crafted Portuguese and Goan ceramics at reasonable prices. Also has showrooms at Caculo Mall, Hotel Delmon and Margao's market.

ℹ Information

Goa Medical College Hospital (☑0832-2458700; www.gmc.goa.gov.in; Bambolim; ☺24hr) This 1000-bed hospital is 9km south of Panaji on NH17 in Bambolim.

Goa Tourism (GTDC; ☑0832-2437132; www.goa-tourism.com; Paryatan Bhavan, Dr Alvaro Costa Rd; ☺9.30am-5.45pm Mon-Fri) Better known as Goa Tourism, the GTDC office is in the large Paryatan Bhavan building across the Ourem Creek and near the bus stand. However, it's more marketing office than tourist office and is of little use to casual visitors, unless you want to book one of GTDC's host of tours.

Government of India Tourist Office (☑0832-2223412; www.incredibleindia.com; Communidade Bldg, Church Sq; ☺9.30am-1.30pm & 2.30-6pm Mon-Fri, 10am-1pm Sat) The staff at this central tourist office can be helpful, especially for information outside Goa. This office is planning a move to the same building as Goa Tourism in Patto.

Main Post Office (MG Rd; ☺9.30am-5.30pm Mon-Sat) Offers swift parcel services and Western Union money transfers.

ℹ Getting There & Away

BUS

All local buses depart from Panaji's **Kadamba bus stand** (☑interstate 0832-2438035, local 0832-2438034; www.goakadamba.com; ☺reservations 8am-8pm), with frequent local services every few minutes (to no apparent timetable); major destinations are Mapusa (₹30, 30 minutes) in the north, Margao (₹30, 45 minutes) to the south and Ponda (₹20, one hour) to the east. Most bus services run from 6am to 10pm.

For South Goa's beaches, take an express bus to Margao and change there; to get to beaches north of Baga, head to Mapusa and change there. There are direct buses to Candolim (₹20, 20 minutes), Calangute (₹25, 25 minutes) and Baga (₹30, 30 minutes).

State-run long distance services also depart from the Kadamba bus stand, but private operators offer similar prices and greater choice in type of bus and departure times. Many private operators have booths outside the entrance to the bus stand, but most private interstate services depart from the interstate bus stand across the highway next to the New Patto Bridge.

Paulo Travels (☑0832-2438531; www.paulo-bus.com; G1, Kardozo Bldg)

TRAIN

The closest train station to Panaji is Karmali (Old Goa), 12km east near Old Goa. A number of long-distance services stop here, including services to and from Mumbai. Many trains coming from Margao also stop here (but check in advance). Panaji's **Konkan Railway Reservation Office** (☑0832-2712940; www.konkanrailway.com; ☺8am-8pm Mon-Sat) is on the 1st floor of the Kadamba bus stand (*not* at the train station).

ℹ Getting Around

A taxi from Panaji to Dabolim Airport costs ₹900 and takes 45 minutes, but allow an hour for traffic. From the airport, prepaid taxis charge ₹870 (₹920 for AC).

It's easy enough to get around central Panaji and Fontainhas on foot. Taxis and autorickshaws charge extortionately for short trips. A return taxi to Old Goa costs ₹400; an autorickshaw should charge ₹300. Lots of taxis hang around at the Municipal Gardens. Autorickshaws and motorcycle taxis can be found in front of the post office, on 18th June Rd, and just south of the church.

Local buses run to Miramar (₹4, 10 minutes), Dona Paula (₹6, 15 minutes) and Old Goa (₹10, 20 minutes).

Taking the rusty but free passenger/vehicle **ferry** (☺every 20min 6am-10pm) across the Mandovi River to the fishing village of Betim makes a fun shortcut en route to the northern beaches. It departs the jetty on Dayanand Bandodkar Marg.

Old Goa

☑0832

From the 16th to the 18th centuries, when Old Goa's population exceeded that of Lisbon or London, Goa's former capital was considered the 'Rome of the East'. You can still sense that grandeur as you wander what's left of the city, with its towering churches and cathedrals and majestic convents. Its rise under the Portuguese, from 1510, was meteoric, but cholera and malaria outbreaks

ℹ **EMERGENCIES**

Dialling ☑112 will connect you to the police, fire brigade or medical services.

GOA OLD GOA

forced the abandonment of the city in the 1600s. In 1843 the capital was officially shifted to Panaji. Some of the most imposing churches and cathedrals are still in use and are remarkably well preserved, while other historical buildings have become museums or simply ruins. It's a fascinating day trip, but it can get crowded: consider visiting on a weekday morning.

◉ Sights

Remember to cover your shoulders and legs when entering the churches and cathedral.

★ Basilica of Bom Jesus   CHURCH
(⊙ 7.30am-6.30pm) Famous throughout the Roman Catholic world, the imposing Basilica of Bom Jesus contains the tomb and mortal remains of St Francis Xavier, the so-called Apostle of the Indies. St Francis Xavier's missionary voyages throughout the East became legendary. His 'incorrupt' body is in the mausoleum to the right, in a glass-sided coffin amid a shower of gilt stars. Freelance guides at the entrance will show you around for ₹100.

★ Sé Cathedral   CATHEDRAL
(⊙ 9am-6pm; Mass 7am & 6pm Mon-Sat, 7.15am, 10am & 4pm Sun) At over 76m long and 55m wide, the cavernous Sé Cathedral is the largest church in Asia. Building commenced in 1562, on the orders of King Dom Sebastiao of Portugal, and the finishing touches were finally made some 90 years later. The exterior is notable for its plain style, in the Tuscan tradition. Also of note is its rather lopsided look resulting from the loss of one of its bell towers, which collapsed in 1776 after being struck by lightning.

Church of St Francis of Assisi   CHURCH
(⊙ 9am-5pm) West of the Sé Cathedral, the Church of St Francis of Assisi is no longer in use for worship, and consequently exudes a more mournful air than its neighbours.

Archaeological Museum   MUSEUM
(adult/child ₹10/free; ⊙ 9am-5pm) The archaeological museum houses some lovely fragments of sculpture from Hindu temple sites in Goa, and some Sati stones, which once marked the spot where a Hindu widow com-

Old Goa

Old Goa

◉ Top Sights
1 Basilica of Bom Jesus B2
2 Sé Cathedral C1

◉ Sights
3 Adil Shah Palace Gateway C1
   Archaeological Museum .... (see 5)
4 Chapel of St Anthony A2
5 Chapel of St Catherine B1
6 Church & Convent of St Cajetan C1

7 Church & Convent of St Monica B2
8 Church of Our Lady of the Mount D2
9 Church of Our Lady of the
   Rosary A2
10 Church of St Francis Xavier D2
11 Convent & Church of St John B2
12 Monastery of St Augustine A2
13 Museum of Christian Art A2
14 Sisters' Convent B2
15 Viceroy's Arch C1

SPICE UP YOUR LIFE

The Ponda region, southeast of Panaji, is the centre of commercial spice farms in Goa and several have opened their doors as tourist operations, offering guided plantation tours, buffet thali-style lunches and, in some cases, cultural shows.

These farms typically produce spices such as vanilla, pepper, cardamom, nutmeg, chilli and turmeric, along with crops such as cashew, betel nut, coconut, pineapple and papaya. To reach them you'll need your own transport or a taxi.

Savoi Plantation (☑ 0832-2340272, 9423888899; http://savoiplantations.com; adult/child ₹700/350; ⊗ 9am-4.30pm) This 200-year-old plantation, 12km north of Ponda, is the least touristy in the region (and elephant-free). Knowledgeable guides will walk you through the 40-hectare plantation. Local crafts are also for sale and there are a couple of cottages for overnight stays.

Pascoal Spice Farm (☑ 0832-2344268; farm tour & lunch ₹400; ⊗ 9am-4.30pm) About 7km east of Ponda, Pascoal offers bamboo river-rafting and cultural shows, along with farm tours and lunch.

Tropical Spice Plantation (☑ 0832-2340329; www.tropicalspiceplantation.com; Keri; tour incl lunch ₹400; ⊗ 9am-4pm) Accessed via a bamboo bridge, around 5km north of Ponda, this is one of the most popular farms with tour groups, so is often busy. An entertaining 45-minute tour of the spice plantation is followed by a banana-leaf buffet lunch.

mitted suicide by flinging herself onto her husband's funeral pyre.

Church & Convent of St Cajetan CHURCH
(⊗ 8am-6pm) Modelled on the original design of St Peter's in Rome, this impressive church was built by Italian friars of the Order of Theatines, sent here by Pope Urban VIII to preach Christianity in the kingdom of Golconda (near Hyderabad). The friars, however, were refused entry to Golconda, so settled instead at Old Goa in 1640. The construction of the church began in 1655, and although it's perhaps less interesting than the other churches, it's still a beautiful building and the only domed church remaining in Goa.

Museum of Christian Art MUSEUM
(www.museumofchristianart.com; ₹50, camera ₹100; ⊗ 9.30am-4.30pm Mon-Sat) This museum, in a beautifully restored space within the 1627 Convent of St Monica, contains a collection of statues, paintings and sculptures. Interestingly, many of the works of Goan Christian art made during the Portuguese era, including some of those on display here, were produced by local Hindu artists.

Other Sights

There are plenty of other monuments in Old Goa to explore, including the Viceroy's Arch, Adil Shah Palace Gateway, the Chapel of St Anthony, the Chapel of St Catherine, the **Church & Convent of St Monica** (⊗ 8am-5pm), the Convent & Church of St John, the

Sisters' Convent, the **Church of Our Lady of the Rosary** (⊗ 8am-5pm), the Monastery of St Augustine, and 2km east of the centre, the Church of Our Lady of the Mount.

🛈 Getting There & Away

There are frequent buses to Old Goa (₹10, 25 minutes) from the Kadamba bus stand in Panaji to Old Goa's bus stand. Buses to Panaji or Ponda from Old Goa leave when full (around every 10 minutes) from either the main roundabout or the bus stop/ATM just beside the Tourist Inn restaurant.

NORTH GOA

Mapusa

☑ 0832 / POP 40,500

Mapusa (pronounced 'Mapsa') is the largest town in northern Goa, and is most often visited for its busy Friday **market** (⊗ 8am-6.30pm Mon-Sat), which attracts scores of buyers and sellers from neighbouring towns and villages. It's a good place to pick up the usual range of embroidered bed sheets and the like, at prices far lower than in the beach resorts.

Many travellers pass through Mapusa anyway as it's the major transport hub for northern Goa buses. Most amenities are arranged around the Municipal Gardens, just north of the Kadamba bus station and main market site.

🏃 Activities

Mango Tree Goa VOLUNTEERING
(📞 9881261886; www.mangotreegoa.org; The Mango House, near Vrundavan Hospital, Karaswada) Offers one- to three-month placements for volunteers providing teaching support for disadvantaged children around Mapusa.

🛏 Sleeping

With the northern beaches so close and most long-distance buses departing in the late afternoon or early evening, it's hard to think of a good reason to stay in Mapusa, but there are a few options if you do.

Hotel Satyaheera HOTEL $$
(📞 0832-2262949; www.hotelsatyaheeragoa.com; d without/with AC from ₹1950/2300; ❄) Next to the little Maruti temple in the town centre, this is Mapusa's best central hotel, which isn't saying much. Rooms are comfortable enough and **Ruchira** (mains ₹90-190; ⊙11am-11pm), the roof garden restaurant, is a decent place to eat.

🍴 Eating & Drinking

Hotel Vrundavan INDIAN $
(thalis from ₹80; ⊙7am-10pm Wed-Mon) This all-veg place bordering the Municipal Gardens is a great place for a hot chai, *pav bhaji* (bread with curried vegetables) or a quick breakfast.

Pub PUB
(mains from ₹100; ⊙11am-4pm & 6.30-11pm Mon-Sat) Don't be put off by the dingy entrance or stairwell: once you're upstairs, this breezy place opposite the market is great for watching the milling crowds over a cold beer or *feni*. Eclectic daily specials make it a good spot for lunch.

🛍 Shopping

Other India Bookstore BOOKS
(📞 0832-2263306; www.otherindiabookstore.com; Mapusa Clinic Rd; ⊙9am-5pm Mon-Fri, to 1pm Sat) This friendly and rewarding little bookshop, at the end of an improbable, dingy corridor, specialises in books about Goa and India with a focus on spirituality, environment, politics and travel. It's signposted near the Mapusa Clinic, a few hundred metres up the hill from the Municipal Gardens.

ℹ Getting There & Away

BUS
If you're coming to Goa by bus from Mumbai, Mapusa's **Kadamba bus stand** (📞 0832-2232161) is the jumping-off point for the northern beaches. Local bus services run every few minutes. For buses to the southern beaches, take one of the frequent buses to Panaji, then Margao, and change there.

Local services include:
Anjuna ₹15, 20 minutes
Arambol ₹30, one hour

GREEN GOA

Goa's environment has suffered from an onslaught of tourism over the last 40 years, but also from the effects of logging, mining and local customs (rare turtle eggs have traditionally been considered a delicacy). Construction proceeds regardless of what the local infrastructure or ecosystem can sustain, while plastic bottles pile up in vast mountains. There are, however, a few easy ways to minimise your impact on Goa's environment.

Take your own bag when shopping and refill water bottles with filtered water wherever possible. Rent a bicycle instead of a scooter, for short trips at least; bicycle rentals are declining as a result of our scooter infatuation and the bikes are poor quality, but they'll bounce back if the demand is there. Goa Tourism now employs cleaners to comb the beaches each morning picking up litter, but all travellers should do their part by disposing of cigarette butts and any litter in bins.

Turtles are protected by the **Forest Department** (www.forest.goa.gov.in), which operates information huts on beaches such as Agonda, Galgibag and Morjim, where turtles arrive to lay eggs. Also doing good work over many years is the **Goa Foundation** (📞 0832-2256479; www.goafoundation.org; St Britto's Apartments, G-8 Feira Alta), the state's main environmental pressure group based in Mapusa. It has spearheaded a number of conservation projects since its inauguration in 1986, including pressure to stop illegal mining, and its website is a great place to learn more about Goan environmental issues. The group's excellent *Fish Curry & Rice*, a sourcebook on Goa's environment and lifestyle, is sold at Mapusa's Other India Bookstore. The Foundation occasionally runs volunteer projects.

Calangute ₹12, 20 minutes
Candolim ₹15, 35 minutes
Panaji ₹30, 30 minutes
Thivim ₹15, 20 minutes

Long-distance services are run by both government and private bus companies. Private operators have booking offices outside the bus stand (opposite the Municipal Gardens). Most long-distance buses depart in the late afternoon or evening. Sample fares include:

Bengaluru ₹900, with AC ₹1200; 13-14 hours
Hampi sleeper ₹1000; 9½ hours
Mumbai ₹850, with AC ₹900; 12-15 hours
Pune ₹700, with AC ₹900, 11-13 hours

TAXI

There's a prepaid taxi stand in the town square with a signboard of fixed prices. Cabs to Anjuna or Calangute cost ₹280; Candolim ₹350; Panaji ₹350; Arambol ₹600; and Margao ₹1100. An autorickshaw to Anjuna or Calangute should cost ₹200.

TRAIN

Thivim, about 12km northeast of town, is the nearest train station on the Konkan Railway. Local buses to Mapusa meet trains (₹15); an autorickshaw to or from Thivim station costs around ₹200.

Candolim

📞 0832 / POP 8600

Candolim's long and languid beach, which curves to join smaller Sinquerim Beach to the south, is largely the preserve of charter tourists from the UK, Russia and, increasingly, elsewhere in India. It's fringed with an unabating line of beach shacks, all offering sunbeds and shade in exchange for your custom.

In all it's an upmarket, happy holiday strip, but independent travellers may find it a little soulless. The post office, supermarkets, travel agents, pharmacies and plenty of banks with ATMs are all located on the main Fort Aguada Rd, running parallel to the beach.

◎ Sights & Activities

Fort Aguada FORT
(◷8.30am-5.30pm) FREE Standing on the headland overlooking the mouth of the Mandovi River, Fort Aguada occupies a magnificent and successful position, confirmed by the fact it was never taken by force. A highly popular spot to watch the sunset, with uninterrupted views both north and south, the fort was built in 1612, following

the increasing threat to Goa's Portuguese overlords by the Dutch, among others.

John's Boat Tours TOURS
(📞0832-6520190, 9822182814; www.johnboat tours.com; Fort Aguada Rd; ◷9am-9pm) A respected and well-organised Candolim-based operator offering a wide variety of boat and jeep excursions, as well as overnight houseboat cruises (₹6000 per person including meals). Choose from dolphin-watching cruises (₹1000) or the renowned 'Crocodile Dundee' river trip (₹1200), to catch a glimpse of the Mandovi's mugger crocodile.

Sinquerim Dolphin Trips BOATING
(per person ₹300; ◷8.30am-5.30pm) The boatmen on the Nerul River below Fort Aguada have banded together, so trips are fixed price. A one-hour dolphin-spotting and sightseeing trip costs ₹300 per person with a minimum of 10 passengers. Trips pass Nerul (Coco) Beach, Fort Aguada Jail, the fort and 'Jimmy Millionaire's House'.

Dive Goa DIVING
(📞9325030110; www.divegoa.com; Fort Aguada Rd) Based next to SinQ Beach Club, this established scuba-diving outfit offers PADI and SSI courses, and boat dives to Netrani Island, Grande Island and more.

🛏 Sleeping

★**Bougainvillea Guest House** GUESTHOUSE $$
(📞0832-2479842, 9822151969; www.bougainvillea goa.com; Sinquerim; r incl breakfast ₹3000-4000, penthouse ₹6000; ❄🛜) A lush, plant-filled garden leads the way to this gorgeous family-run guesthouse, located off Fort Aguada Rd. The eight light-filled suite rooms are spacious and spotless, with fridge, flat-screen TV and either balcony or private sit-out; the top-floor penthouse has its own rooftop terrace. This is the kind of place guests come back to year after year. Book ahead.

D'Hibiscus BOUTIQUE HOTEL $$
(www.dehibiscus.com; 83 Sinquerim; d ₹3300, penthouse ₹4950; ❄🛜) Huge modern rooms with balconies are the draw at this newly renovated Portuguese home off Sinquerim beach. The top-floor penthouse rooms, with jacuzzi, big-screen TV and balcony sunbeds, are worth a splurge.

D'Mello's Sea View Home HOTEL $$
(📞0832-2489650; www.dmellos.com; Monteiro's Rd, Escrivao Vaddo; d ₹1200-1800; ❄@🛜)

D'Mello's has grown up from small beginnings, but is still family-run and occupies four buildings around a lovely garden. The front building has the sea-view rooms so check out a few, but all are clean and well-maintained. Add ₹500 if you want aircon. Wi-fi is available in the central area.

★**Marbella Guest House**   BOUTIQUE HOTEL **$$$**
(☑0832-2479551, 9822100811; www.marbellagoa.com; Sinquerim; r ₹3600-6000, ste ₹5400-7000; ❋ ➔) This beautiful Portuguese villa, filled with antiques and enveloped in a peaceful courtyard garden, is a romantic and sophisticated old-world remnant. Rooms are individually themed, including Moghul, Rajasthani and Bouganvillea. The penthouse suite is a dream of polished tiles, four-poster bed with separate living room, dining room and terrace. The kitchen serves up some imaginative dishes. No kids under 12.

✖ Eating

Candolim has a high concentration of international restaurants and seafront beach shacks serving world cuisine and fresh seafood. Much of the best on offer is along Fort Aguada Rd, though if you take the side streets towards the beach you'll find a few gems, along with local joints serving a cheap, tasty breakfast *pav bhaji* or lunchtime thali.

Viva Goa!   GOAN **$**
(Fort Aguada Rd; mains ₹90-200; ❋11am-midnight) This inexpensive, locals-oriented little place, also popular with in-the-know tourists, serves fresh fish and Goan seafood specialities such as a spicy mussel fry. Check the market price of seafood before ordering.

★**Café Chocolatti**   CAFE **$$**
(409A Fort Aguada Rd; sweets ₹50-200, mains ₹250-420; ❋9am-7pm Mon-Sat; ➔) The lovely garden tearoom at Café Chocolatti may be on the main Fort Aguada Rd, but it's a divine and peaceful retreat where chocolate brownies, waffles and banoffee pie with a strong cup of coffee or organic green tea taste like heaven. Also has a great range of salads, paninis, crepes and quiches for lunch. Take away a bag of chocolate truffles, homemade by the in-house chocolatier.

Moroccan Shisha & Grill   MOROCCAN **$$**
(☑8600544442; Calangute-Candolim Rd; mains ₹200-500, sheesha ₹600; ❋11am-2am) Relax on cushions amid wafts of fragrant sheesha smoke at this Arabian-style cafe. Naturally there's strong coffee, mint tea and North Af-

rican dishes such as shish kebab and chicken tagine.

Stone House   STEAKHOUSE **$$**
(Fort Aguada Rd; mains ₹200-800; ❋11am-3pm & 7pm-midnight) Surf 'n' turf's the thing at this venerable old Candolim venue, inhabiting a stone house and its leafy front courtyard, with the improbable-sounding 'Swedish Lobster' topping the list, along with some Goan dishes. It's also a popular blues bar with live music most nights of the week in season.

★**Bomra's**   BURMESE **$$$**
(☑9767591056; www.bomras.com; 247 Fort Aguada Rd; mains ₹470-580; ❋noon-2pm & 7-11pm) Wonderfully unusual food is on offer at this sleek little place serving interesting modern Burmese cuisine with a fusion twist. Aromatic curries include straw mushroom, lychee, water-chestnut, spinach and coconut curry, and duck curry with sweet tamarind and groundnut shoot. Decor is palm-thatch style huts in a lovely courtyard garden.

Tuscany Gardens   ITALIAN **$$$**
(☑0832-6454026; www.tuscanygardens.in; Fort Aguada Rd; mains ₹300-465; ❋1-11pm) You can easily be transported to Tuscany at Candolim's cosy, romantic Italian restaurant with check tablecloths and imported wine. Perfect antipasti, pasta, pizza and risotto are the order of the day; try the seafood pizza or buffalo mozzarella salad.

☕ Drinking & Nightlife

LPK Waterfront   CLUB
(couples ₹1500; ❋9.30pm-4am) The initials stand for Love, Peace and Karma: the whimsical, sculpted waterfront LPK across the Nerul River from Candolim is the biggest club in the area, attracting party-goers from all over with huge indoor and outdoor dance areas.

Bob's Inn   BAR
(Fort Aguada Rd; ❋noon-4pm & 7pm-midnight) The African wall hangings, palm-thatch, communal tables and terracotta sculptures are a nice backdrop to the *rava* (semolina) fried mussels, but this Candolim institution is really just a great place to drop in for a drink.

🛍 Shopping

Broadway Book Centre   BOOKS
(☑0832-6519777; www.booksingoa.com; Fort Aguada Rd; ❋10am-8pm) With four stores in Goa, Broadway is the state's biggest book-

store chain, and a publisher, so you should be able to find what you're looking for here. Staff here are friendly and helpful.

❶ Getting There & Away

Buses run about every 10 minutes to and from Panaji (₹15, 35 minutes), and stop at the central bus stop near John's Boat Tours. Some continue south to the Fort Aguada bus stop at the bottom of Fort Aguada Rd, then head back to Panaji along the Mandovi River road, via the villages of Verem and Betim.

Frequent buses also run from Candolim to Calangute (₹8, 15 minutes) and can be flagged down on Fort Aguada Rd.

Calangute & Baga

❷ 0832 / POP 16,000

For many visitors, particularly cashed-up young Indian tourists from Bangalore and Mumbai plus Europeans on package holidays, this is Goa's party strip, where the raves and hippies have made way for modern thumping nightclubs and wall-to-wall drinking. The Calangute market area and the main Baga road can get very busy but everything you could ask for – from a Thai massage to a tattoo – is in close proximity and the beach is lined with an excellent selection of restaurant shacks with sunbeds, wi-fi and attentive service.

Stretching between the blurred lines of Candolim and Baga, Calangute is centred on the busy market road leading to the beachfront. To the north, Baga beach consists of jostling shacks, peppered with water sports, and late-night clubs along infamous Tito's Lane.

◉ Sights

Museum of Goa ARTS CENTRE
(❷ 07722089666; www.museumofgoa.com; 79, Pilerne Industrial Estate, Calangute; Indian/foreigner ₹100/300; ⊙ 10am-6pm) Not so much a museum as a repository for art, MOG features artworks, exhibitions, workshops, courses, sitar concerts and an excellent cafe. It's the brainchild of well-known local artist and sculptor Subodh Kerkar, with the philosophy of making art accessible to all.

☆ Activities

Yoga classes pop up around Calangute and Baga each season. You don't have to go far to find beach water sports along the Calangute–Baga strip.

Two local scuba-diving operators are recommended: **Goa Aquatics** (❷ 9822685025;

www.goaaquatics.com; 136/1 Gaura Vaddo, Calangute; dive trip from ₹5000, dive course ₹22,000) and **Barracuda Diving** (❷ 9822182402, 0832-2279409; www.barracudadiving.com; Sun Village Resort, Baga; dive trip/course from ₹5000/17,000).

Baga Snow Park SNOW SPORTS
(❷ 9595420781; http://snowparkgoa.com; Tito's Lane 2; ₹495; ⊙ 11am-8pm; ⊕) This giant fridge is a mini wonderland of snowmen, igloos, slides and ice sculptures. You get kitted out with parka, pants and gloves (included) – it's very cold! Good for kids.

GTDC Tours TOURS
(Goa Tourism Development Corporation; ❷ 0832-2276024; ⊙ www.goa-tourism.com) Goa Tourism's tours can be booked online or at the GTDC Calangute Residency hotel beside the beach. The full-day North Goa tour (₹300, 9.30am to 6pm daily) departs from Calangute or Mapusa and takes in the Mandovi estuary, Candolim, Calangute, Anjuna and inland to Mayem Lake.

⏨ Sleeping

Quite a few places remain open year-round, though it's not a particularly budget-friendly destination, except in the off-season.

⏨ Calangute

★ **Ospy's Shelter** GUESTHOUSE $
(❷ 7798100981, 0832-2279505; ospeys.shelter@gmail.com; d ₹800-1000) Tucked away between the beach and St Anthony's Chapel, in a quiet, lush little area full of palms and sandy paths, Ospey's is a traveller favourite and only a two-minute walk from the beach. Spotless upstairs rooms have fridges and balconies and the whole place has a cosy family feel. Take the road directly west of the chapel – but it's tough to find, so call ahead.

Johnny's Hotel HOTEL $
(❷ 0832-2277458; www.johnnyshotel.com; s ₹500-600, d ₹800-900, with AC ₹1200-1400; ❄ ☋) The 15 simple rooms at this backpacker-popular place make for a sociable stay, with a downstairs restaurant-bar and regular yoga and reiki classes. A range of apartments and houses are available for longer stays. It's down a lane lined with unremarkable midrange hotels and is just a short walk to the beach.

Zostel HOSTEL $
(❷ 917726864942; www.zostel.com; Calangute; dm ₹450-550, d ₹1800; ❄ ☋) Zostel brings budget dorm beds to package-tour central

GOA CALANGUTE & BAGA

Calangute & Baga

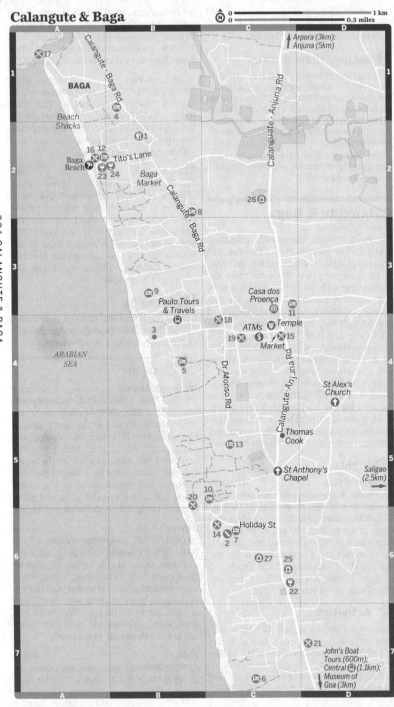

0 _____ 1 km
0 _____ 0.5 miles

Arpora (3km);
Anjuna (5km)

17

BAGA

Calangute - Baga Rd

Beach
Shacks

4

1

16 12

Baga
Beach

23 24

Tito's Lane

Baga
Market

Calangute - Anjuna Rd

8

Calangute - Baga Rd

26

9

Paulo Tours
& Travels

ARABIAN
SEA

3

Casa dos
Proença

11

18

ATMs

19

Temple

15

Market

Dr Afonso Rd

5

Calangute - Anjuna Rd

St Alex's
Church

13

Thomas
Cook

St Anthony's
Chapel

Saligao
(2.5km)

10

20

14

2 7

Holiday St

27

25

22

21

John's Boat
Tours (600m);
Central (1.1km);
Museum of
Goa (3km)

6

Calangute & Baga

with four- to 12-bed dorms, some with air-con, all in a whitewashed two-storey house set back from the main road. Facilities include a kitchen, free wi-fi, common room and lockers. There's just one double room.

Coco Banana GUESTHOUSE $
(☑9960803790; d ₹1200, with AC ₹1500; ❋🛜) Among the palms south of the main entrance to Calangute Beach, colourful Coco Banana has been providing a soothing retreat for travellers for many years. Run by the friendly Walter, rooms are spacious and spotless and the vibe mellow. For families or groups, ask about the self-contained apartments at nearby Casa Leyla.

Hotel Seagull HOTEL $$
(☑0832-2179969; http://seagullgoa.com; Holiday St; d from ₹2800; ❋🛜☒) Bright, friendly and welcoming, the Seagull's rooms, set in a cheerful blue-and-white house in south Calangute, are light and airy with air-con, and

a small pool out back. Downstairs is the fine Blue Mariposa bar-restaurant, serving Goan, Indian and continental dishes.

★Pousada Tauma BOUTIQUE HOTEL $$$
(☑0832-2279061; www.pousada-tauma.com; ste incl meals US$360-530; ❋🛜☒) If you're looking for luxury with your ayurvedic regime, this gorgeous little boutique hotel in busy Calangute is appropriately shielded from the outside world. Spacious, nicely furnished suites are set around a super fountain-fed pool. Rates include all meals at the romantic little open-air Copper Bowl restaurant, though ayurvedic treatments in the private centre are extra.

Baga

★Indian Kitchen GUESTHOUSE $
(☑0832-2277555, 9822149615; www.indiankitchen-goa.com; s/d/chalet ₹770/880/1500; ❋@🛜☒) If a colourful budget stay is what you're after, look no further than this family-run guesthouse, which offers a range of rooms from basic to more spacious, comfy apartments and wooden chalets by the pool. There's a neat central courtyard and a sparkling-clean pool. Each room has its own terrace or sit-out. Add ₹600 for air-con.

★Alidia Beach Cottages GUESTHOUSE $$
(☑9822876867, 0832-2279014; Calangute-Baga Rd, Saunta Waddo; d ₹2000, with AC from ₹3300; ❋🛜☒) Set back behind a whitewashed chapel off busy Baga Rd, this convivial but quiet place has beautifully kept Mediterranean-style rooms orbiting a gorgeous pool. The cheaper non-AC rooms at the back are not as good, but all are in good condition, staff are eager to please, and there's a path leading directly to Baga Beach.

Resort Fiesta BOUTIQUE HOTEL $$$
(☑9822104512; http://fiestagoa.com; Tito's Lane, Baga; d & ste incl breakfast ₹5000-8000; ❋@🛜☒) Large, light-filled rooms are the signature at this beautifully designed boutique resort behind the beachfront restaurant of the same name. The labour of love by owner Yellow Mehta is stylishly appointed with a lovely garden and pool, large verandahs and modern touches like TV, minibar and dual wash basins.

Eating

The beach shacks are an obvious go-to, but there are some interesting gems along the 'Strip' and excellent upmarket offerings on the north side of the Baga River.

Calangute

Plantain Leaf   INDIAN $
(☑ 0832-2279860; veg thali ₹120, mains ₹110-250; ⊙ 11am-5pm & 7-11.45pm) In the heart of Calangute's busy market area, 1st-floor Plantain Leaf has consistently been the area's best pure veg restaurant for many years, with classic South Indian banana leaf thalis and dosas, along with more North Indian flavours. Most dishes sneak in to the budget category.

Cafe Sussegado Souza   GOAN $$
(☑ 09850141007; Calangute-Anjuna Rd; mains ₹160-300; ⊙ noon-11pm) In a little yellow Portuguese house just south of the Calangute market area, Cafe Sussegado is the place to come for Goan food such as fish curry rice, chicken *xacuti* and pork *sorpotel* (a vinegary stew made from liver, heart and kidneys), with a shot of *feni* to follow. Authentic, busy and good atmosphere.

Infantaria   ITALIAN $$
(Calangute-Baga Rd; pastries ₹50-200, mains ₹140-580; ⊙ 7.30am-midnight) Once Calangute's best bakery, Infantaria is now a popular Italian-cum-Indian fondue-meets-curry restaurant. The bakery roots are still there, though, with homemade cakes, croissants, little flaky pastries and real coffee. Get in early for breakfast before the good stuff runs out. Regular live music in season.

★ A Reverie   INTERNATIONAL $$$
(☑ 8380095732; www.areverie.com; Holiday St; mains ₹475-700; ⊙ 7pm-late) A gorgeous lounge bar, all armchairs, cool jazz and whimsical outdoor space, this is the place to spoil yourself, with the likes of Serrano ham, grilled asparagus, French wines and Italian cheeses. A Reverie likes to style itself as 'fun dining' and doesn't take itself too seriously.

Pousada by the Beach   SEAFOOD, GOAN $$$
(Holiday St; mains ₹550-710; ⊙ 11am-7pm) This permanent beachfront restaurant is simple in appearance but the lunch-only menu is bona fide fine dining – the chef also oversees Pousada Tauma's upmarket Copper Bowl. The menu is kept uncluttered with just a handful of expertly prepared Goan and seafood specialities.

Baga

★ Go With the Flow   INTERNATIONAL $$$
(☑ 7507771556; www.gowiththeflowgoa.com; Baga River Rd; mains ₹200-650; ⊙ noon-10.30pm) Stepping into the fantasy neon-lit garden of illuminated white-wicker furniture is wow factor enough, but the food is equally out of this world. With a global menu leaning towards European and Asian flavours, this remains one of Baga's best dining experiences. Try some of the small bites (ask about a tasting plate) or go straight for the signature pork belly or prawn laksa.

★ Fiesta   ITALIAN $$$
(☑ 0832-2279894; www.fiestagoa.in; Tito's Lane; mains ₹350-950; ⊙ 7pm-late) Long-running Fiesta has undergone a classy makeover: a rustic beachfront bar with all-day dining, and fine dining by candlelight around the pool in the evening. Overseen by style queen Yellow Mehta, it's an intimate and sophisticated Mediterranean-style dining experience that starts with homemade pizza and pasta and extends to French-influenced seafood dishes and tiramisu.

🍷 Drinking & Nightlife

Baga's boisterous club scene, centred on Tito's Lane, has long been well known among the tourist crowd looking for a good time. Some find the scene here a little sleazy and the bar staff indifferent. Solo women are welcomed into clubs (usually free) but should exercise care and take taxis to and from venues.

Café Mambo   CLUB
(☑ 7507333003; www.cafemambogoa.com; Tito's Lane, Baga; cover charge couples ₹800; ⊙ 6pm-3am) Part of the Tito's empire, Mambo is one of Baga's most happening clubs with

---

SATURDAY NIGHT MARKETS

There are two well-established evening markets, **Saturday Night Market** (www.snmgoa.com; ⊙ from 6pm Sat late Nov-Mar) in Arpora and **Mackie's** (⊙ from 6pm Sat Dec-Apr) in Baga, that make an interesting evening alternative to the Anjuna flea market.

The attractions here are as much about food stalls and entertainment as shopping, but there's a big range of so-so stalls, flashing jewellery, laser pointers and other novelties that would be difficult to sell during daylight hours.

Both start up in late November and are occasionally known to be cancelled at short notice, so check locally or with taxi drivers.

an indoor/outdoor beachfront location and nightly DJs pumping out house, hip hop and Latino tunes. Couples or women only.

Tito's　CLUB
(📞9822765002; www.titosgroup.com; Tito's Lane, Baga; cover charge couples/women/stags from ₹8000/free/2000; ⏱8pm-3am) The long-running titan of Goa's clubbing scene, Tito's has done its best to clean up the locals-leering-at-Western-women image of yester-year. It's generally couples or ladies only – solo men (stags) might get in at an inflated rate, depending on the mood of door staff.

🛍 Shopping

Literati Bookshop & Cafe　BOOKS
(📞0832-2277740; www.literati-goa.com; Calangute; ⏱10am-6.30pm Mon-Sat) A refreshingly different bookstore, in the owners' South Calangute home, and a very pleasant Italian-style garden cafe. Come for a fine espresso or pizza and browse the range of books by Goan and Indian authors as well as anti-quarian literature. Check the website for readings and other events.

Karma Collection　GIFTS & SOUVENIRS
(www.karmacollectiongoa.com; Calangute-Arpora Rd, Calangute; ⏱9.30am-10.30pm) Beautiful home furnishings, textiles, ornaments, bags and other enticing stuff – some of it an-tique – has been sourced from across India, Pakistan and Afghanistan and gathered at Karma Collection, which makes for a mouth-watering browse. Fixed prices mean there's no need to bargain, though it's not cheap.

❶ Getting There & Around

Frequent buses go to Panaji (₹15, 45 minutes) and Mapusa (₹12, 30 minutes) from both the Calangute and Baga bus stands.

A taxi from Calangute or Baga to Panaji costs around ₹450 and takes about half an hour. A prepaid taxi from the airport to Calangute costs ₹1150.

A local bus runs between the Calangute and Baga stands every few minutes (₹5); catch it anywhere along the way, though when traffic is bad it might be quicker to walk.

Taxis between Calangute and northern Baga Beach charge an extortionate ₹100.

Anjuna
📞0832 / POP 9640
Good old Anjuna has been a stalwart of the hippie scene since the 1960s and still drags out the sarongs and sandalwood each Wednesday (in season) for its famous flea market. Though it continues to pull in droves of backpackers, midrange and domestic tourists are increasingly making their way here for a dose of hippie-chic. An-juna is continuing to evolve, with a heady beach party scene and a flowering of new restaurants and bars.

The village itself is a bit ragged around the edges and is spread out over a wide area. Do as most do: hire a scooter or motorbike and explore the back lanes and southern beach area and you'll find a place that suits. Anjuna will grow on you.

◎ Sights & Activities

Anjuna's charismatic, narrow **beach** runs for almost 2km from the rocky, low-slung cliffs at the northern village area right down beyond the flea market in the south. In sea-son there are water sports here, including jet skis (₹400), banana boats (₹1000 for four people) and parasailing (₹700).

Lots of yoga, ayurveda and other alterna-tive therapies and regimes are on offer in season (p141); look out for noticeboards at popular cafes such as Artjuna (p139).

🥢 Courses

Mukti Kitchen　COOKING
(📞0800-7359170; www.muktikitchen.com; An-juna-Baga Rd, Arpora; veg/nonveg/Goan class ₹1500/2000/2500; ⏱11am-2pm & 5-8pm) Mukti shares her cooking skills twice daily at these recommended classes on the Anjuna Rd in Arpora. Courses include around five dishes which can be tailored – veg or nonveg, Goan, Indian or ayurvedic. Minimum four people, maximum six; book one day ahead.

🛏 Sleeping

Dozens of basic rooms are strung along An-juna's northern clifftop, while pricier plac-es front the main beach. Plenty of small, family-run guesthouses are also tucked back from the main beach strip, offering nicer double rooms for a similar price; look out for signs announcing 'rooms to let' or 'house to let'.

Red Door Hostel　HOSTEL $
(📞0832-2274423; reddoorhostels@gmail.com; dm without/with AC ₹550/660, d without/with AC ₹1900/2200; ❄🎧) Red Door is a welcoming backpacker place close to Anjuna's central crossroads with clean four- and six-bed

Anjuna

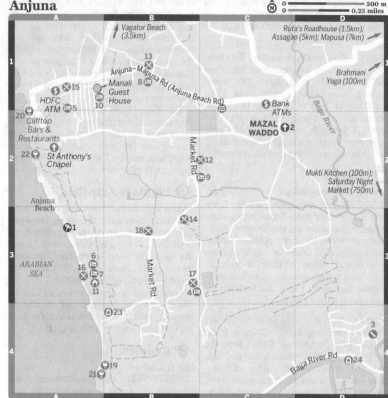

GOA ANJUNA

dorms plus a few private rooms. Facilities include lockers, free wi-fi, a garden, good communal areas – including a well-equipped kitchen – and a sociable cafe-bar. There's a laid-back vibe and resident pet dogs.

Prison Hostel HOSTEL **$**
(☏ 0832-2273745; www.thehostelcrowd.com; 940 Market Rd; dm ₹400, with AC ₹500, d ₹1500; ✳ ☏) This quirky backpacker hostel on Anjuna's Market Rd is themed like a jail with bars on the windows, B&W decor and, strangely, an old bus for a cafe. Clean four- to 10-bed dorms have individual lockers and bed-lights, there's a good kitchen, and breakfast and wi-fi are included.

Florinda's GUESTHOUSE **$**
(☏ 9890216520; s/d ₹500/800, with AC ₹1500; ✳ ☏) One of the better budget places near the beach, Florinda's has clean rooms, with 24-hour hot water, window screens and

mosquito nets, set around a pretty garden. The few air-con rooms fill up fast.

Paradise GUESTHOUSE **$**
(☏ 9922541714; janet_965@hotmail.com; Anjuna-Mapusa Rd; d ₹1000, with AC ₹1500-2000; ✳ @ ☏) This friendly place is fronted by an old Portuguese home and offers neat, clean rooms with well-decorated options in the newer annexe. The better rooms have TVs, fridges and hammocks on the balcony. Friendly owner Janet and family also run the pharmacy, general store, restaurant, internet cafe, Connexions travel agency and money exchange!

Palms N Tides COTTAGE **$$**
(☏ 9988882021; www.palmsntides.com; d ₹3800-4300) The dome-shaped cottages here are some of the roomiest and best-designed on the beachfront. Set in a garden they feature huge beds and bathrooms, and air-con to justify the price. It's behind Elephant Art Cafe.

Anjuna

GOA ANJUNA

Sea Horse   HUT $$
(☎ 9764465078; www.vistapraiaanjuna.com; ⊙ hut
without/with AC ₹2000/3000; ❋ 🤖) A line-up
of timber cabins behind the beach restaurant of the same name, Sea Horse has a good
location. The huts are small and get a little
hot – go for the air-con rooms if it's humid.
Staff are friendly and accommodating. The
same owners have a pricier beachfront set-
up called Vista Praia Anjuna.

Banyan Soul   BOUTIQUE HOTEL $$
(☎ 9820707283; www.thebanyansoul.com; d
₹2500; ❋ 🤖) A slinky 12-room option,
tucked down the lane off Market Rd, and
lovingly conceived and run by Sumit, a
young Mumbai escapee. Rooms are chic and
well equipped with AC and TV, and there's
a lovely library and shady seating area beneath a banyan tree.

Casa Anjuna   HERITAGE HOTEL $$$
(☎ 0832-2274123; www.casaboutiquehotels.com;
D'Mello Vaddo 66; d incl breakfast from ₹9850;
❋ 🤖 ⚄) This heritage hotel is enclosed in
lovely plant-filled gardens around an inviting pool, managing to shield itself from
the hype of central Anjuna. All rooms have
antique furnishings and period touches; like
many upmarket places it's better value out
of season, when rates halve.

✗ Eating

Café Diogo   CAFE $
(Market Rd; snacks ₹80-160; ⊙ 8.30am-3pm) Excellent fruit salads are sliced and diced at
Café Diogo, a small family-run cafe on the
way down to the market. The generous avoca-

do, cheese and mushroom toasted sandwiches and the range of lassis are also worth a try.

★ Artjuna Cafe   CAFE $$
(☎ 0832-2274794; www.artjuna.com; Market Rd;
mains ₹130-350; ⊙ 8am-10.30pm; 🤖) Artjuna
is right up there with our favourite cafes in
Anjuna. Along with all-day breakfast, outstanding espresso coffee, salads, sandwiches and Middle Eastern surprises like baba
ganoush, tahini and falafel, this sweet garden cafe has an excellent craft and lifestyle
shop, yoga classes and a useful noticeboard.
Great meeting place.

★ Burger Factory   BURGERS $$
(Anjuna-Mapusa Rd; burgers ₹300-450;
⊙ 11.30am-3.30pm & 6.30-10.30pm Thu-Tue)
There's no mistaking what's on offer at this
little alfresco diner/kitchen. The straightforward menu of burgers isn't cheap, but they
are interesting and expertly crafted. Choose
between beef or chicken burgers and toppings such as cheddar or beetroot and aioli.

Goa's Ark   MIDDLE EASTERN $$
(Market Rd; mains ₹150-670, meze from ₹50;
⊙ 10am-11pm; 🤖 ♿) Set in a lovely garden,
Goa's Ark is a Middle Eastern–style restaurant with meze, barbecued meat and falafel.
It's also a petting zoo with farmyard animals, birds and a kids' playground.

Elephant Art Cafe   BEACH CAFE $$
(mains ₹190-370; ⊙ 8am-10pm; 🤖) A standout
among the restaurants lining the beach, Elephant Art Cafe does a great range of tapas,
sandwiches, fish and chips and speciality
breakfasts.

DON'T MISS

ANJUNA FLEA MARKET

Anjuna's weekly Wednesday **flea market** (🕙8am-late Wed, Nov-Apr) is as much part of the Goan experience as a day on the beach. More than three decades ago, it was conceived and created by hippies smoking jumbo joints, convening to compare experiences on the heady Indian circuit. Nowadays things are far more mainstream and the merchandise comes from all over India: sculptures and jewellery courtesy of the Tibetan and Kashmiri traders; colourful Gujarati tribal women selling T-shirts; richly colourful saris, bags and bedspreads from Rajasthan; sacks of spices from Kerala; and the hard-to-miss tribal girls from Karnataka pleading passers-by to 'come look in my shop'.

For a rest from the shopping there are chai stalls and a couple of restaurant-bars with live music. **Cafe Looda** has a fabulous sunset beachfront location and live music from 5pm. The best time to visit is early (from 8am) or late afternoon (around 4pm till close just after sunset).

German Bakery　MULTICUISINE **$$**
(www.german-bakery.in; bread & pastries ₹20-160, mains ₹160-470; 🕙8.30am-11pm; 🛜) Leafy and adorned with prayer flags, occasional live music and garden lights, German Bakery is a long-standing favourite for hearty and healthy breakfasts, fresh-baked bread and organic food, but the menu also runs to pasta, burgers and pricey seafood. Has healthy juices (think wheatgrass) and espresso coffee.

Dhum Biryani & Kebabs　INDIAN **$$**
(Anjuna-Mapusa Rd; mains ₹180-350; 🕙9am-1am) Loved by visitors and locals alike, Dhum Biryani serves up consistently good kebabs as well as plates of biryani (steamed rice with meat or vegetables) and other usual suspects.

🍷 Drinking & Nightlife

Anjuna vies with Vagator as the trance party capital of Goa and the southern end of the beach has several nightclubs that are the most happening places in North Goa when the night is right. Market day is always fun, with live music at one or both of the two bars there.

Curlies　BAR
(www.curliesgoa.com; 🕙9am-3am) Holding sway at South Anjuna Beach, Curlies mixes laid-back beach-bar vibe with sophisticated nightspot – the party nights here are notorious and loud. There's a rooftop lounge bar and an enclosed late-night dance club. Thursday and Saturday are big nights, as are full moon nights.

Purple Martini　COCKTAIL BAR
(☎9823772890; Sunset Point; 🕙9pm-midnight) The clifftop sunset views, blue-and-white colour scheme and swanky bar at this beautifully situated restaurant-bar could easily transport you to Santorini. Come for a sundowner cocktail and check out the menu of Greek kebabs and Mediterranean salads.

ℹ Getting There & Away

Buses to Mapusa (₹15, 30 minutes) depart every half-hour or so from the main bus stand at the end of the Anjuna–Mapusa Rd near the beach; some buses coming from Mapusa continue on to Vagator and Chapora.

A couple of direct daily buses head south to Calangute; otherwise, take a bus to Mapusa and change there.

Plenty of motorcycle taxis and autorickshaws gather at the main crossroads and you can also easily hire scooters and motorcycles here from ₹250 to ₹400 – most Anjuna-based travellers get around on two wheels.

Assagao

On the road between Mapusa and Anjuna or Vagator, Assagao is one of North Goa's prettiest villages, with almost traffic-free country roads passing old Portuguese mansions and whitewashed churches. The area is inspiring enough to be home to several of North Goa's best yoga retreats.

🏃 Activities

International Animal Rescue　VOLUNTEERING
(Animal Tracks; ☎0832-2268272; www.internationalanimalrescuegoa.org.in; Madungo Vaddo; 🕙9am-4pm) The well-established International Animal Rescue collects and cares for stray dogs, cats and other four-legged animals in distress, carrying out sterilisations and vaccinations. Volunteers are welcome to help with dog walking and playing with puppies

and kittens, but must have evidence of rabies vaccination.

El Shaddai VOLUNTEERING
(📞 0832-6513286, 0832-2461068; www.child rescue.net; El Shaddai House, Socol Vaddo) El Shaddai is a British-founded charity that aids impoverished and homeless children throughout Goa. Volunteers able to commit to more than four weeks' work with El Shaddai can apply through the website. There's a rigorous vetting process, so start well in advance.

🕮 Courses

Spicy Mama's COOKING
(📞 9623348958; www.spicymamasgoa.com; 138/3 Bairo Alto; 1-day course veg/nonveg ₹2000/3000, 3-day ₹5000/7000, 5-day ₹10,000/12,000) For cooking enthusiasts, Spicy Mama's specialises in spicy North Indian cuisine, from butter chicken to *aloo gobi* (cauliflower and potato curry) and *palak paneer* (cheese in a puréed spinach gravy), prepared at the country home of Suchi. The standard one-day course is four hours; book online for in-depth multiday masterclasses.

🛏 Sleeping

Hopping Frog HOSTEL $
(📞 8007669996; www.hoppingfrog.in; dm/d ₹400/1500; 🛜) This new hostel in leafy Assagao is a fun backpacker alternative to the beach. The four dorms are clean, and open out to a very cool garden space. The loungy cafe-bar is very sociable and there are bikes available for cruising Assagao's back lanes.

🍴 Eating

★ Villa Blanche Bistro CAFE $$
(www.villablanche-goa.com; 283 Badem Church Rd; breakfast ₹90-200, mains ₹320-480; ⏰ 9am-11pm Mon-Sat, 10am-4pm Sun, Oct-Apr) This lovely, chilled garden cafe in the back lanes of Assagao is run by a German-Swiss couple. Salads, sandwiches, filled bagels and cakes are specialities, but you'll also find Thai curry and German sausages. For an indulgent breakfast or brunch try the waffles and pancakes.

Ruta's Roadhouse INTERNATIONAL $$
(📞 8380025757; www.rutas.in; Mapusa Rd; breakfast ₹300, small/big plates ₹200/300; ⏰ 8.30am-6.30pm) Ruta's has found a new home in an old Portuguese house in Assagao, serving up excellent set breakfasts and global culinary offerings from jambalaya to spicy laksa.

ℹ Getting There & Away
Local buses between Mapusa and Anjuna (about 15 minutes from each) or Siolim pass through Assagao, but the village is best explored on a rented scooter or by taxi from your beach resort.

Vagator & Chapora
📞 0832
Dramatic red stone cliffs, thick palm groves and a crumbling 17th-century Portuguese fort give Vagator and its diminutive village neighbour Chapora one of the prettiest settings on the North Goan coast. Once known for their wild trance parties and heady, hippie lifestyles, things have slowed down

GOA VAGATOR & CHAPORA

NORTH GOA YOGA RETREATS

The Anjuna/Vagator/Assagao area has a number of yoga retreats where you can immerse yourself in courses, classes and a Zen vibe during the October-March season.

Purple Valley Yoga Retreat (📞 0832-2268363; www.yogagoa.com; 142 Bairo Alto; dm/s 1 week from £690/820, 2 weeks £1100/1350) Popular yoga resort in Assagao offering one- and two-week residential and nonresidential courses in Ashtanga yoga.

Swan Yoga Retreat (📞 8007360677, 0832-2268024; www.swan-yoga-goa.com; drop-in classes ₹350, 1 week from ₹23,300) In a peaceful jungle corner of Assagao, Swan Retreat is a very Zen yoga experience. Daily drop-in classes are available, or minimum week-long yoga retreats start every Saturday.

Yoga Magic (📞 0832-6523796; www.yogamagic.net; Mapusa-Chapora Rd, Anjuna; lodge s/d ₹6750/9000, ste ₹9000/12,000) 🍃 Solar lighting, vegetable farming and compost toilets are just some of the worthy initiatives practised in this luxurious yoga resort. The lodge features dramatic Rajasthani tents under a thatched shelter.

Brahmani Yoga (📞 9545620578; www.brahmaniyoga.com; Tito's White House, Aguada-Siolim Rd; class ₹700, 10-class pass ₹5000; ⏰ classes 9.30am) Drop-in classes at Tito's White House.

Vagator & Chapora

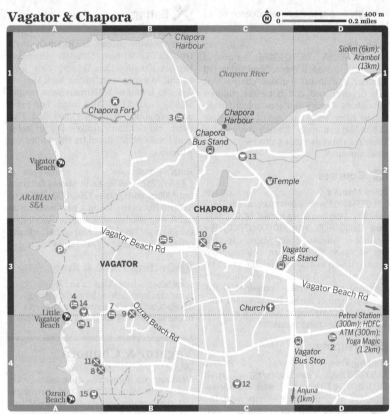

Vagator & Chapora

🛏 Sleeping
1	Alcove Resort	A4
2	Bean Me Up	D4
3	Casa de Olga	B1
4	Casa Vagator	A3
5	Dreams Hostel	B3
6	Jungle Hostel	C3
7	Pappi Chulo	B3

🍴 Eating
8	Antares	A4
	Bean Me Up	(see 2)

9	Bluebird	B3
10	Mango Tree Bar & Cafe	C3
11	Thalassa	A4

🍷 Drinking & Nightlife
12	Hilltop	C4
13	Jai Ganesh Fruit Juice Centre	C2
14	Nine Bar	A3
15	Waters Beach Lounge	A4

considerably these days and upmarket restaurants are more the style, though Vagator has some of Goa's best clubs. Chapora – reminiscent of the Mos Eisley Cantina from *Star Wars* – remains a favourite for hippies and long-staying smokers, with the smell of charas (resin of the marijuana plant) clinging heavily to the light sea breeze.

🛏 Sleeping

Budget accommodation, much of it in private rooms, ranges along Ozran Beach Rd and Vagator Beach Rd; you'll see lots of signs for 'rooms to let' on the side roads in simple private homes and guest houses, from ₹400 to ₹600 per double.

Head down the road to the harbour at Chapora and you'll find lots of rooms – and whole homes – for rent.

Vagator

★ Jungle Hostel
HOSTEL $

(📞 0832-2273006; www.thehostelcrowd.com; Vagator Beach Rd; dm without/with AC ₹500/600, s/d ₹1000/1500; ✳@🌐) One of the original backpacker hotels in North Goa, Jungle brought the dorm experience and an international vibe to Vagator and has expanded to three properties. The six-bed dorms are clean and bright and things like lockers, wi-fi, breakfast, a communal kitchen and travel advice are free.

Enterprise Guest House
GUESTHOUSE $

(📞 7769095356; www.beanmeup.in; 1639/2 Deulvaddo; d incl breakfast without/with bathroom ₹1100/1400; 🌐) Set around a leafy, parachute-silky courtyard that's home to Vagator's best vegan restaurant Bean Me Up, rooms at the Enterprise Guest House look simple but are themed with individual exotic decor, earthy shades, mosquito nets and shared verandahs. The mellow yoga-friendly vibe matches the clientele and the included breakfast is decadent.

Pappi Chulo
HOSTEL $

(📞 9075135343; pappichulohostel@gmail.com; Ozran Beach Rd; dm without/with AC ₹400/500) Unashamedly Vagator's party hostel, Pappi's has a bar in the garden, movie nights and an international vibe of travellers just hanging out. Themed dorms have lockers and bunk beds.

Dreams Hostel
HOSTEL $

(📞 9920651760; dreamshostel.com; off Vagator Beach Rd; dm ₹500) With a philosophy of 'art, music, wellness', former backpacker and DJ Ravi has established a great little creative space for like-minded travellers with a spacious garden, three clean dorms and chilled common areas.

Alcove Resort
HOTEL $$

(📞 0832-2274491; www.alcovegoa.com; Little Vagator Beach; d ₹4500-8500; ✳@🌐) The location overlooking Little Vagator Beach is hard to beat at this price. Attractively furnished rooms, slightly larger cottages, and four suites surrounding a decent central pool, restaurant and bar, make this a good place for those who want a touch of affordable luxury.

Casa Vagator
HOTEL $$$

(📞 0832-2416738; www.casaboutiquehotels.com; d incl breakfast from ₹11,200; ✳@🌐) A successfully rendered outfit in the deluxe Casa boutique mould, this is one of Vagator's most stylish accommodation options, with gorgeous rooms offering equally gorgeous views out to the wide blue horizon. A bit close to techno-heavy Nine Bar.

Chapora

Casa de Olga
GUESTHOUSE $

(📞 0832-2274355, 9822157145; eadsouza@yahoo.co.in; r ₹700-1200, without bathroom from ₹400) This welcoming family-run homestay, set around a nice garden on the way to Chapora harbour, offers spotless rooms of varying sizes in a three-storey building. The best are the brand-new top-floor rooms with swanky bathrooms, TV and balcony.

✖ Eating

Vagator has a handful of outstanding dining spots along its clifftop, along with the usual range of much-of-a-muchness shacks down on the beach.

The dining scene at tiny Chapora isn't as evolved as Vagator, but that's what the people who hang out there like about it. With a couple of popular juice joints and a handful of nondescript restaurants, Chapora stays cool while the fine dining is elsewhere.

★ Bean Me Up
VEGAN $$

(www.beanmeup.in; 1639/2 Deulvaddo; mains ₹180-380; ⊙8am-11pm; 🌐) Bean Me Up is vegan, but even nonveg travellers will be blown away by the taste, variety and filling plates on offer in this relaxed garden restaurant. The extensive menu includes vegan pizzas, ice creams, housemade tofu curry and innovative salads. Ingredients are as diverse as coconut, cashew milk and cashew cheese, quinoa, tempeh and lentil dhal.

Bluebird
GOAN $$

(www.bluebirdgoa.com; Ozran Beach Rd; mains ₹250-480; ⊙8.30am-11pm) Bluebird specialises in Goan cuisine, with genuine vindaloos, chicken *cafreal* (marinated in a sauce of chillies, garlic and ginger), fish curry rice and Goan sausages among the temptations, as well as some delicately spiced seafood dishes. Dine in the lovely open garden cafe.

Mango Tree Bar & Cafe
MULTICUISINE $$

(Vagator Beach Rd; mains ₹130-430; ⊙24hr) With loud reggae, crappy service, dark-wood furniture, a sometimes rambunctious bar scene, ancient expats leaning over the bar, draught beer and an overall great vibe, the Mango Tree is a classic Vagator meeting place. It's open late (24 hours if it's busy enough) with a menu from Goan to European, pizza and Mexican.

★ Thalassa   GREEK $$$

(☑ 9850033537; www.thalassagoa.com; mains ₹300-750; ⏲ 4pm-midnight) Authentic and awesomely good Greek food is served alfresco on a breezy clifftop terrace. Kebabs, souvlaki and thoughtful seafood dishes are the speciality, but this is also a great bar and fills up late in the evening when you might see some Greek dancing and plate smashing. Come early, order a jug of sangria and enjoy the sunset.

Antares   MODERN AUSTRALIAN $$$

(☑ 7350011528; www.antaresgoa.com; Ozran Beach Rd; mains ₹200-1400; ⏲ 11.30am-midnight) The latest addition to Vagator's clifftop dining scene, Antares is known as the project of Australian Masterchef contestant Sarah Todd. The atmosphere is beachfront chic and the food Modern Australian meets Indian, with some Goan dishes such as crab *xacuti*.

▼ Drinking & Nightlife

Waters Beach Lounge   CLUB

(☑ 9767200012; ⏲ from 6pm Thu-Sun) Terracing down the hillside on the Vagator cliffs, this deluxe restaurant, bar and club is best known for its party nights, with open-air dance floors overlooking the Arabian Sea and a soundproof room for late at night. Top DJs come to play.

Nine Bar   BAR

(⏲ 5pm-4am) Once the hallowed epicentre of Goa's trance scene, the open-air Nine Bar

terrace, on the clifftop overlooking Little Vagator Beach, has now moved into a soundproof indoor space so the parties can still go all night. Look out for flyers and local advice to see when the big party nights are on.

Jai Ganesh Fruit Juice Centre   CAFE

(juices ₹50-80; ⏲ 8.30am-midnight) Thanks to its corner location, with views up and down Chapora's main street, this may be the most popular juice bar in Goa. It's a prime meeting spot and, once parked, most people are reluctant to give up their seat.

Hilltop   CLUB

(⏲ sunset-late) Hilltop is a long-serving Vagator trance and party venue that's deserted by day but comes alive from sunset. Its edge-of-town neon-lit coconut grove location allows it, on occasion, to bypass noise regulations to host concerts, parties and international DJs. Sunday sessions (5pm to 10pm) are legendary.

ⓘ Getting There & Away

Fairly frequent buses run to both Chapora and Vagator from Mapusa (₹15, 30 minutes) throughout the day, many via Anjuna. Practically anyone with legs will rent you a scooter/motorcycle from ₹250/400 per day.

Vagator has North Goa's most popular petrol station.

Morjim

☑ 0832

Morjim Beach was once very low-key (almost deserted) and its southern end is still protected due to the presence of rare olive ridley marine turtles, which lay their annual clutches of eggs between November and February. These days Morjim is popular with Russian tourists and there's a bit of an in-season clubbing

---

WHERE'S THE PARTY?

Though Goa was long legendary among Western visitors for its all-night, open-air hippie trance parties, a central government 'noise pollution' ban on loud music in open spaces between 10pm and 6am largely curtailed its often notorious, drug-laden party scene. Of course, the parties quickly moved inside and the big trance and dance clubs still go all night in season.

The trance party scene is going strong in Anjuna at Curlies (p140); in Vagator at Hilltop, Nine Bar and Waters; in Aswem/Morjim at Club M; and in Palolem at Leopard Valley (p157), which runs silent discos (p156). In Baga, the clubs on Tito's Lane are as wild as ever.

Over the busy Christmas–New Year period the authorities tend to turn a blind eye to parties so you might find some of the old-school variety happening. Taxi drivers will know. Online check out www.goa-freaks.com or www.whatsupgoa.com.

scene, but the southern beach is more black sand than golden due to river run-off.

🛏 Sleeping

★**Wanderers Hostel**   HOSTEL $

(📞9619235302; www.wanderershostel.com; dm ₹500, shared tent ₹300, luxury tent d ₹1700-2000; ❋🛜🏊) About five minutes' walk back from Morjim Beach, Wanderers is a real find for budget travellers. The main building, decorated with original travellers murals, has spotless air-con dorms with lockers, bed lights and wi-fi, full kitchen, cosy communal areas and a pool table. In the garden next door is a tent village with swimming pool and yoga retreat centre and outdoor cinema.

Goan Café & Resort   RESORT $$

(📞0832-2244390; www.goancafe.com; apt & cottage from ₹1800, with AC ₹2200, treehouse without/with bathroom from ₹1200/1700; ❋🛜) Fronting Morjim Beach, this excellent family-run resort has a fine array of beachfront stilted 'treehouse' huts and more solid rooms (some with AC) at the back. The Friends Corner restaurant is good.

ℹ Getting There & Away

Occasional local buses run between Siolim and Morjim village (₹8, 15 minutes), but most travellers taxi to their chosen accommodation, then either hire a scooter/motorbike or use taxis from there.

Aswem

📞0832

Aswem Beach is growing busier each year, but it's still overshadowed by Mandrem to the north. Beach-hut accommodation and beach-shack restaurants spring up each season on its very broad stretch of clean, white sand (with few hawkers). The main Morjim-Mandrem road is set some way back from the sands.

🏃 Activities

★**Vaayu Waterman's Village**   SURFING

(📞9850050403; http://vaayuoceanadventures.in; surfboard hire per hr ₹500, lessons ₹2500) Goa's premier surf shop is also an activity and art centre where you can arrange lessons and hire equipment for surfing, kiteboarding, stand up paddleboarding, kayaking and wakeboarding. A highlight is the full-day SUP tour to Paradise Lagoon in Maharashtra. The enthusiastic young owners also run an art gallery, cafe and funky accommoda-

tion (📞9850050403; http://vaayuoceanadventures.in; hut ₹2250-4000, d without/with AC ₹3500; ❋🛜) across the road from Aswem Beach.

🛏 Sleeping & Eating

You can still find basic beach huts and rooms back from the beach for ₹1000 (less out of high season).

Yab Yum   HUT $$$

(📞0832-6510392; www.yabyumresorts.com; hut/cottage from ₹8500/9700; ❋🛜) 🍴 This top-notch choice has unusual, stylish, dome-shaped huts – some look like giant hairy coconuts – made of a combination of all-natural local materials, including mud, stone and mango wood, as well as more traditional AC cottages. A host of yoga and massage options are available, and it's set in one of the most secluded beachfront jungle gardens you'll find in Goa.

Marbela Beach Resort   TENTED CAMP $$$

(📞0832-6450599, 9158881180; www.marbelabeach.com; tent/villa/ste ₹8000/9000/20,000; ❋🛜) The luxury tents and 'Spanish-style' villas at this slick resort are pricey but fitted out like five-star hotel rooms. Even if you don't stay here, the beachfront cabanas are a divine spot for a drink and for the resort's thumping **Club M** (📞0832-6450599; www.marbelabeach.com; Marbela Beach Resort; 🕐Fri-Sun) parties, till late from Friday to Sunday.

La Plage   MEDITERRANEAN $$

(📞9822121712; Aswem Beach; mains ₹200-450; 🕐9am-10pm Nov-Apr) Renowned in these parts, La Plage takes beach shack to the next level with its inspired gourmet French-Mediterranean food. Along with excellent salads, seafood and fabulous desserts (try the chocolate thali), La Plage stocks great wines. It's usually open from late November to April.

ℹ Getting There & Away

Buses run between Siolim and Aswem, but it's easier to get a taxi to your accommodation, then use a scooter/motorbike or taxis.

Mandrem

Mellow Mandrem has developed in recent years from an in-the-know bolt-hole for those seeking respite from the relentless traveller scene of Arambol and Anjuna to a fairly mainstream but still very lovely beach hangout. There's plenty of yoga, meditation and ayurveda on offer here, plus good dining and space to lay down with a good book. Many believe there's no better place in North Goa.

◎ Sights & Activities

Shanti Ayurvedic
Massage Centre
AYURVEDA

(📱 8806205264; 1/1½hr massage from ₹1000/1500; ⊙ 9am-8pm) Ayurvedic massage is provided here by the delightful Shanti. Try the rejuvenating 75-minute massage and facial package, or go for an unusual 'Poulti' massage, using a poultice-like cloth bundle containing 12 herbal powders. You'll find her place on the right-hand side as you head down the beach road.

Himalaya Yoga Valley
YOGA

(📱 9960657852; www.yogagoaindia.com; Mandrem Beach) The winter home of a popular Dharamsala outfit, HYV specialises in hatha and ashtanga residential teacher-training courses, but also has daily drop-in classes (₹2000 for five).

🛏 Sleeping & Eating

★ Dunes Holiday Village
HUT $

(📱 0832-2247219; www.dunesgoa.com; r & hut ₹1000-1200; @ 🛜) The pretty huts here are peppered around a palm-filled lane leading to the beach; at night, lamps light up the place like a palm-tree dreamland. Huts range from basic to more sturdy 'treehouses' (huts on stilts). It's a friendly, good-value place with a decent beach restaurant, massage, yoga classes and a marked absence of trance.

★ Mandala
RESORT $$

(📱 9158266093; www.themandalagoa.com; r & hut ₹1600-5500; ❄ 🛜) Mandala is a very peaceful and beautifully designed eco-village with a range of huts and a couple of quirky air-con rooms in the 'Art House'. Pride of place goes to the barn-sized two-storey villas inspired by the design of a Keralan houseboat. The location, overlooking the tidal lagoon, is serene, with a large garden, daily yoga sessions and an organic restaurant.

Elsewhere
COTTAGE $$$

(www.aseascape.com; tent ₹9000, beachhouse ₹14,400-29,000; @ 🛜) The exact location of this heavenly place, on some 500m of beachfront, is a closely guarded secret. Choose from four beautiful beachfront houses, intriguingly named the Piggery, Bakery, Priest's House and Captain's House, or from three luxury tents, and revel in the solitude that comes with a hefty price tag and a 60m walk across a bamboo bridge.

Bed Rock
MULTICUISINE $$

(mains ₹130-370; ⊙ 8am-11pm; 🛜) Bed Rock is a welcome change from the beach shacks with a reliable menu of Indian and continental faves (pizza, pasta etc) and a cosy chill-out lounge upstairs.

ℹ Getting There & Away

Buses run between Siolim and Mandrem village (₹10, 20 minutes) hourly, but it's hard work trying to get anywhere in a hurry on public transport. Most travellers taxi to their chosen accommodation, then either hire a scooter/motorbike or use taxis from there.

Arambol (Harmal)

📱 0832 / POP 5320

Arambol (also known as Harmal) is the most northerly of Goa's developed beach resorts and is still considered the beach of choice for many long-staying budget-minded travellers in the north.

Arambol first emerged in the 1960s as a mellow paradise for long-haired long-stayers escaping the scene at Calangute. Today things are still cheap and cheerful, with budget accommodation in little huts clinging to the cliffsides, though the main beach is now an uninterrupted string of beach shacks, many with beach-hut operations stacked behind.

The main beach is gently curved and safe for swimming but often crowded – head south towards Mandrem for a quieter beach scene. A short walk around the northern headland brings you to little Kalacha Beach, another popular place thanks to the 'Sweetwater Lake' back from the beach. The headland above here is the best place in Goa for paragliding.

🏃 Activities

Arambol Paragliding
PARAGLIDING

(10min flight ₹2000; ⊙ noon-6pm) The headland above Kalacha Beach (Sweetwater Lake) is an ideal launching point for paragliding. There are a number of independent operators: ask around at the shack restaurants on the beach, arrange a pilot, then make the short hike to the top of the headland. Most flights are around 10 minutes, but if conditions are right you can stay up longer.

Himalayan Iyengar Yoga Centre
YOGA

(www.hiyogacentre.com; Madhlo Vaddo; 5-day yoga course ₹4000; ⊙ 9am-6pm Tue-Sun Nov-Mar) Arambol's reputable Himalayan Iyengar

Yoga Centre, which runs five-day courses in hatha yoga from mid-November to mid-March, is the winter centre of the Iyengar yoga school in Dharamkot, near Dharamsala in north India. First-time students must take the introductory five-day course, and can then continue with more advanced five-day courses at a reduced rate.

Surf Wala
SURFING

(☑ 9011993147; www.surfwala.com; Surf Club, Arambol Beach; 1½hr lesson from ₹2500, 3-/5-day course ₹6500/11,000) If you're a beginner looking to get up on a board, join the international team of surfers based on the beach just north of Arambol's Surf Club. Prices include board hire, wax and rashie. Check the website for instructor contact details – between them they speak English, Russian, Hindi, Konkani and Japanese! Board-only rental is ₹500.

🛏 Sleeping

Accommodation in Arambol has expanded from the basic huts along the clifftop walk and the guesthouses back in the village to a mini-Palolem of beach huts behind the shacks along the main beach. Enter at the 'Glastonbury St' entrance and walk north to find plenty of places clinging to the headland between here and Kalacha Beach, or enter at the south end and ask at any of the beach shacks.

★ Happy Panda
HOSTEL $

(☑ 9619741681; www.happypanda.in; dm ₹300; 🛜) Traveller-painted murals cover the walls in this very chilled backpacker place near the main village. Young owners have worked hard making the three dorms, neon common area, bar and garden into a well-equipped and welcoming budget place to crash. Bikes for hire.

Chilli's
HOTEL $

(☑ 9921882424; d ₹600, apt with AC ₹1200; ❄🛜) Near the beach entrance on Glastonbury St, this friendly canary-yellow place is one of Arambol's better nonbeachfront bargains. There are 10 decent, no-frills rooms, all with attached bathroom, fan and a hot-water shower. The top-floor apartment with AC and TV is good value. Owner Derek hires out motorbikes and scooters.

Pitruchaya Cottages
COTTAGES $

(☑ 9404454596; r ₹800) The sea-facing timber cottages here are among the best on the cliffs, with attached bathrooms, fans and verandahs.

Lotus Sutra
RESORT $$

(☑ 9146096940; www.lotussutragoa.com; s ₹1420, d with AC ₹2130-3320, cottages ₹6500-7100; ❄🛜) The fanciest place on Arambol's beachfront has a series of bright rooms in a quirky two-storey building and cute individual timber cottages facing a garden-lawn setting. The restaurant-bar features live music.

Surf Club
GUESTHOUSE $$

(www.facebook.com/surfclubgoa; d ₹1650-2300; 🛜) In a quiet space at the end of a lane, on the southern end of Arambol Beach, the Surf Club is one of those cool little hang-outs that offer a bit of everything: simple but clean rooms, yoga and a fun bar with live music.

🍴 Eating & Drinking

Arambol certainly hasn't escaped the beach shack invasion, and you'll find about two dozen of them wall to wall along the main beach in season, complete with sunbeds and beach umbrellas.The northern cliff walk has a string of budget restaurants with good views, and the road down to the beach also has some interesting dining options. In the upper village, chai shops and small local joints will whip up a chai for ₹5 and a thali for ₹80.

★ Shimon
MIDDLE EASTERN $

(☑ 9011113576; Glastonbury St; meals ₹120-200; ⊙9am-11pm; 🛜) Just back from the beach, and understandably popular with Israeli backpackers, Shimon is the place to fill up on exceptional falafel or *sabich* (crisp slices of eggplant stuffed into pita bread along with boiled egg, boiled potato and salad). The East-meets-Middle-East thali (₹450) comprises a little bit of almost everything on the menu.

Dylan's Toasted & Roasted
CAFE $

(☑ 9604780316; www.dylanscoffee.com; coffee & desserts from ₹70; ⊙9am-11pm Nov-Apr; 🛜) The Goa (winter) incarnation of a Manali institution, Dylan's is a fine place for an espresso, chocolate chip cookies and old-school dessert. It's a nice hang-out, just back from the southern beach entrance, with occasional live music and open-mic nights.

Fellini
ITALIAN $$

(☑ 9881461224; Glastonbury St; mains ₹200-380; ⊙from 6.30pm) On the left-hand side just before the beach, this unsignposted but long-standing Italian joint is perfect if you're craving a carbonara or calzone. More than 40 wood-fired, thin-crust pizza varieties are on the menu, but save space for a very decent rendition of tiramisu.

Double Dutch
MULTICUISINE $$

(mains ₹120-400, steaks ₹420-470; ⊙7am-10pm) In a peaceful garden set back from the main road to the Glastonbury St beach entrance, Double Dutch has long been popular for its steaks, salads, Thai and Indonesian dishes, and famous apple pies. It's a relaxed meeting place with secondhand books, newspapers and a useful noticeboard for current Arambolic affairs.

ℹ Information

The closest ATM is on the main highway in Arambol's village, about 1.5km back from the beach. If it's not working there's another about 3km north in Paliyem or about the same distance south in Mandrem.

ℹ Getting There & Away

Frequent buses to/from Mapusa (₹30, one hour) stop on the main road at the 'backside' (as locals say) of Arambol village. From here, it's a 1.5km trek down through the village to the main beach drag; an autorickshaw or taxi charges at least ₹50.

Plenty of places in the village hire scooters and motorbikes (per day scooter/motorbike ₹250/350).

A taxi to Mapusa or Anjuna should cost ₹600. If you're heading north to Mumbai, travel agents can book bus tickets and you can board at a stop on the highway in the main village.

SOUTH GOA

Margao

📞0832 / POP 94,400

Margao (also known as Madgaon) is the capital of South Goa, a busy – at times traffic-clogged – market town of a manageable size for getting things done. As the major transport hub of the south, lots of travellers pass through Margao's train station or Kadamba bus stand; fewer choose to stay here, but it's a useful place for shopping, catching a local sporting event or simply enjoying the busy energy of big-city India in small-town form.

Margao's compact town centre ranges around the oblong Municipal Gardens, with shops, restaurants, ATMs and the covered market all within easy reach. To the north of

town is the old Portuguese-influenced Largo de Igreja district; about 1km north further is the main (Kadamba) bus station, and 1.5km southeast of the Municipal Garden is Margao's train station.

◉ Sights

The city's **Largo de Igreja** district features a number of traditional old Portuguese mansions; the most famous is the grand 1790 **Sat Burnzam Ghor** (Seven Gabled House). It's also home to the whitewashed **Church of the Holy Spirit**, built in 1565 on the site of an important Hindu temple.

At the southern end of the Municipal Gardens, on the west side of the canary-yellow **Secretariat Building**, the prim **Municipal Library** (Abade Faria Rd; ⊙8am-8pm Mon-Fri, 9am-noon & 4-7pm Sat & Sun) houses good books about Goa.

🛏 Sleeping

Nanutel Margao HOTEL $$
(📞0832-6722222; www.nanuhotels.in; Padre Miranda Rd; s/d incl breakfast ₹3800/4500, ste ₹5000-5500; ❄️🛜🏊) Margao's best business-class hotel by some margin, Nanutel is modern and slick with a lovely pool, good restaurant, bar and coffee shop, and clean air-con rooms. The location, between the Municipal Gardens and Largo de Igreja district, is convenient for everything.

Om Shiv Hotel HOTEL $$
(📞0832-2710294; www.omshivhotel.com; Cine Lata Rd; d ₹3000-4250, ste ₹5400; ❄️@🛜) In a bright-yellow building tucked away behind the Bank of India, Om Shiv does a decent line in fading 'executive' rooms, all of which have air-con and balcony. The suites have good views, there's a gym and the 7th-floor **Rockon Pub**.

🍴 Eating

Café Tato INDIAN $
(Valaulikar Rd; thalis ₹90; ⊙7am-10pm Mon-Sat) A favourite local lunch spot: tasty vegetarian fare in a bustling backstreet canteen, and delicious all-you-can-eat thalis.

Swad INDIAN $
(New Market; ₹60-110; ⊙7.30am-8pm; ❄️) Some of Margao's best veg food is dished up at the family-friendly, lunch-break favourite Swad, across from Lotus Inn. The thalis, South Indian tiffins and other mains are all reliably tasty.

★ **Longhuino's**   GOAN, MULTICUISINE **$$**
(Luis Miranda Rd; mains ₹110-250; ⊙ 8.30am-
10pm) A local institution since 1950, quaint
old Longhuino's serves up tasty Indian,
Goan and Chinese dishes, popular with lo-
cals and tourists alike. Go for a Goan dish
like *ambot tik* (a slightly sour but fiery curry
dish), and leave room for the retro desserts
like rum balls and tiramisu. Service is as lan-
guid as the whirring ceiling fans but it's a
great place to watch the world go by over a
coffee or beer.

Martin's   INTERNATIONAL **$$**
(mains ₹290-500; ⊙ 11am-3.30pm & 7-11pm) It's a
welcome feeling to step off Margao's hot and
busy street into the cool and classy interior
of Martin's. There's just 10 tables, attentive
service and an eclectic menu of tapas starters, pan-Indian dishes and stone-cooked
steaks. Just off the north end of the Municipal Gardens.

🛍 Shopping

Golden Heart Emporium   BOOKS
(Confidant House, Abade Faria Rd; ⊙ 10am-1.30pm
& 4-7pm Mon-Sat) One of Goa's best bookshops,
Golden Heart is crammed from floor to ceiling with fiction, nonfiction, children's books,
and illustrated volumes on the state's food,
architecture and history. It also stocks otherwise hard-to-get titles by local Goan authors.
It's down a little lane off Abade Faria Rd.

MMC New Market   MARKET
(⊙ 8.30am-9pm Mon-Sat) Margao's crowded,
covered canopy of colourful stalls is a fun
but busy place to wander around, sniffing
spices, sampling soaps and browsing the
household merchandise.

ℹ Information

There are plenty of banks offering currency
exchange and 24-hour ATMs ranged around the
Municipal Gardens.

ℹ Getting There & Around

BUS
Local and long-distance buses use the Kadamba
bus stand, 2km north of the Municipal Gardens.
Buses to Palolem (₹30, one hour), Colva (₹15, 20
minutes), Benaulim (₹15, 20 minutes) and Betul
(₹20, 40 minutes) stop both at the Kadamba bus
stand and at informal bus stops on the east and
west sides of the Municipal Gardens. For Panaji
(₹30), take any local bus to the Kadamba bus
stand and change to a frequent express bus.

Daily AC state-run buses go to Mumbai (₹700,
16 hours), Pune (₹660, 13 hours) and Bengaluru
(₹650, 13 hours). Non-AC buses are about
one-third cheaper. Private long-distance buses
depart from the stand opposite Kadamba. You'll
find booking offices all over town; **Paulo Travels**
(☑ 0832-2702405; www.paulobus.com; Padre
Miranda Rd) is among the best.

TAXI & AUTORICKSHAW
Taxis are plentiful around the Municipal Gardens
and Kadamba bus stand, and are a quick and
comfortable way to reach any of Goa's beaches,
including Palolem (₹1150), Calangute (₹1355),
Anjuna (₹1500) and Arambol (₹1900). Prepaid
taxi stands are at the train station and main bus
stand.

For Colva and Benaulim, autorickshaws will
happily do the trip for around ₹120.

TRAIN
Margao's well-organised train station (Madgaon
on train timetables), 2km south of town, serves
the Konkan Railway and local South Central
Railways routes, and is the main hub for trains

GOA MARGAO

MAJOR TRAINS FROM MARGAO (MAGDAON)

DESTINATION	TRAIN NO & NAME	FARE (₹)	DURATION (HR)	DEPARTURES
Bengaluru	02779 Vasco da Gama-SBC Link (D)	390/1025	15	3.50pm
Chennai (Madras); via Yesvantpur	17312 Vasco da Gama-Chennai Express (C)	475/1285/1865	21	3.20pm Thu
Delhi	12431 Rajdhani Express (A)	2765/3800	14½	10.10am
Ernakulam (Kochi)	12618 Lakshadweep Express (C)	445/1175/1665	14½	7.20pm
Mangalore	12133 Mangalore Express (C)	290/745/1035	5½	7.10am
Mumbai (Bombay)	10112 Konkan Kanya Express (C)	390/1065/1535	12	6pm
Pune	12779 Goa Express (C)	335/935/1325	12	3.50pm

Fares: (A) 3AC/2AC, (B) 2S/CC, (C) sleeper/3AC/2AC, (D) sleeper/3AC

WORTH A TRIP

HAMPI

The surreal ruins of the Vijayanagar empire at Hampi (p896), in Karnataka, are a popular detour or overnight trip from Goa. Hampi can be reached by train from Margao to Hospet on the VSG Howrah Express which departs at 7.10am Tuesday, Thursday, Friday and Saturday (sleeper/3AC/2AC ₹235/620/885, eight hours). More convenient are the overnight sleeper buses direct to Hampi from Margao and Panaji operated by Paulo Travels (₹800 to ₹1500, 10 to 11 hours, two to three daily).

from Mumbai to Goa and south to Kochi and beyond. Its **reservation hall** (☑ 0832-2712790; Train Station; ☺ 8am-2pm & 2.15-8pm Mon-Sat, 8am-2pm Sun) is on the 1st floor; there's a foreign-tourist quota counter upstairs.

Outside the station you'll find a prepaid taxi stand. Taxis or autorickshaws to/from the town centre cost around ₹80.

Chandor

The small village Chandor, about 15km east of Margao, is an important stop for its collection of once-grand Portuguese mansions, exemplified by the wonderful Braganza House. It's a photogenic place, with fading but still grand facades and gables – many topped with typically Portuguese carved wooden roosters – and the looming white Nossa Senhora de Belem church.

Between the late 6th and mid-11th centuries Chandor was better known as Chandrapur, the most spectacular city on the Konkan coast. This was the grand seat of the ill-fated Kadamba dynasty until 1054, when the rulers moved to a new, broad-harboured site at Govepuri, at modern-day Goa Velha. When Govepuri was levelled by the Muslims in 1312, the Kadambas briefly moved their seat of power back to Chandrapur, though it was not long before Chandrapur itself was sacked in 1327, and then its glory days were finally, definitively, over.

⊙ Sights

Braganza House   HISTORIC BUILDING
Braganza House, built in the 17th century and stretching along one whole side of Chandor's village square, is the biggest Portuguese mansion of its kind in Goa and the best example of what Goa's scores of once-grand and glorious mansions have today become. Granted the land by the King of Portugal, the Braganza family built this oversized house, which was later divided into the east and west wings when it was inherited by two sisters from the family.

Fernandes House   HISTORIC BUILDING
(☑ 0832-2784245; donation ₹200; ☺ 9am-6pm)
A kilometre east past the church, and open to the public, is the Fernandes House, whose original building dates back more than 500 years, while the Portuguese section was tacked on by the Fernandes family in 1821. The secret basement hideaway, full of gun holes and with an escape tunnel to the river, was used by the family to flee attackers. Admission includes a guided tour.

❶ Getting There & Away

Local buses run infrequently from Margao to Chandor (₹10, 30 minutes) but the best way to get here is with your own transport. A taxi from Margao should cost ₹400 round trip, including waiting time.

Colva

☑ 0832 / POP 10,200
Once a sleepy fishing village, and in the '60s a hang-out for hippies escaping the scene up at Anjuna, Colva is still the main town-resort along this stretch of coast, but these days it has lost any semblance of beach paradise. Travel a little way north or south, though, and you'll find some of the peace missing in central Colva.

🏃 Activities

Colva's beach entrance throngs with watersports operators keen to sell you **parasailing** (₹1000), **jet skiing** (15 minutes single/double ₹400/600) and **dolphin-watching trips** (per person around ₹330). Rates are fixed, but ensure that life jackets are supplied.

🛏 Sleeping

Sam's Guesthouse   HOTEL $
(☑ 0832-2788753; r ₹650; 🛜) Away from the fray, north of Colva's main drag on the road running parallel to the beach, Sam's is a big, cheerful place with friendly owners and spacious rooms that are a steal at this price. Rooms are around a pleasant garden courtyard and there's a good restaurant and whacky 'cosy cave'. Wi-fi in the restaurant only.

La Ben
HOTEL **$**

(☎0832-2788040; www.laben.net; Colva Beach Rd; r without/with AC ₹1100/1400; ❄️🛜) Neat, clean and not entirely devoid of atmosphere. If you're not desperately seeking anything with character, La Ben has decent, good-value rooms and has been around for ages. A great addition is the adjacent **Garden Restaurant** (mains ₹100-320; ⏱7-10am & 6-11pm; 🛜).

★ Skylark Resort
HOTEL **$$**

(☎0832-2788052; www.skylarkresortgoa.com; d with AC ₹3350-4500, f ₹5000; ❄️🛜🏊) A serious step up from the budget places, Skylark's clean, fresh rooms are graced with bits and pieces of locally made teak furniture and block-print bedspreads, while the lovely pool makes a pleasant place to lounge. The best (and more expensive) rooms are those facing the pool.

✖️ Eating & Drinking

Sagar Kinara
INDIAN **$**

(Colva Beach Rd; mains ₹70-190; ⏱7am-10.30pm) A pure-veg restaurant upstairs (nonveg is separate, downstairs) with tastes to please even committed carnivores, this place is clean, efficient and offers cheap and delicious North and South Indian cuisine all day.

★ Leda Lounge & Restaurant
BAR

(⏱7.30am-midnight) Part sports bar, part music venue, part cocktail bar, Leda is Colva's best nightspot by a long shot. There's live music from Thursday to Sunday, fancy drinks (Mojitos, Long Island iced teas) and good food at lunch and dinner.

ℹ️ Information

Colva has plenty of banks and ATMs, as well as the odd internet cafe and travel agent, strung along Colva Beach Rd.

ℹ️ Getting There & Away

Buses from Colva to Margao run roughly every 15 minutes (₹15, 20 minutes) from 7.30am to about 7pm, departing from the parking area at the end of the beach road. A taxi to Margao is ₹300.

Benaulim
☎0832

A long stretch of largely empty sand peppered with a few beach shacks and water-sports enthusiasts, the beaches of Benaulim and nearby Sernabatim are much quieter than Colva, partly because the village is a good kilometre back from the beach and linked by several laneways. Out of season there's a somewhat desolate feel, but the lack of traffic or serious beachfront development is an obvious attraction.

Most accommodation, eating options, grocery shops and pharmacies are concentrated along the Vasvaddo Beach Rd near the Maria Hall intersection.

◉ Sights

★ Goa Chitra
MUSEUM

(☎0832-6570877; www.goachitra.com; St John the Baptist Rd, Mondo Vaddo; ₹300; ⏱9am-6pm Tue-Sun) Artist and restorer Victor Hugo Gomes first noticed the slow extinction of traditional objects – from farming tools to kitchen

GOA BENAULIM

IT'S A DOG'S LIFE

South Goa has two animal welfare shelters that welcome volunteers or visitors to help walk or play with rescued stray dogs.

The **Goa Animal Welfare Trust** (☎9763681525, 0832-2653677; www.gawt.org; Curchorem; ⏱9am-5.30pm Mon-Sat, 10am-1pm & 2.30-5pm), in the small inland town of Curchorem, works hard at providing veterinary help for sick animals, shelter for puppies and kittens, sterilisation programs for street dogs and low-cost veterinary care (including anti-rabies injections) for Goan pets. Volunteers are welcome, even just for a few hours on a single visit, to walk or play with the dogs. Items such as your old newspapers can be used for lining kennel floors, as can old sheets, towels and anything else you might not be taking home.

You can make contact with the shelter at the **Goa Animal Welfare Trust Shop** (☎0832-2653677; ⏱9.30am-1pm & 4-7pm Mon-Sat) in Colva, a charity shop selling souvenirs and secondhand books.

At Chapolim, a few kilometres northeast of Palolem Beach, the small **Animal Rescue Centre** (☎0832-2644171; Chapolim; ⏱10am-1pm & 2.30-5pm Mon-Sat) also takes in sick, injured or stray animals. Volunteers welcome. Look out for the sign on the road to Chaudi; it's about 2km north near the Chapolim dam.

COLA BEACH

Cola Beach is one of those hidden gems of the south coast – a relatively hard-to-reach crescent of sand enclosed by forested cliffs and with a gorgeous emerald lagoon stretching back from the beach.

It has been discovered of course and in November and April several hut and tent villages set up here, but it's still a beautiful place and popular with day trippers from Agonda and Palolem.

Further north around the headland is an even more remote beach known as **Khancola Beach**, or Kakolem, with one small resort reached via a steep set of jungly steps from the clifftop above.

utensils to altarpieces – as a child in Benaulim. He created this ethnographic museum from the more than 4000 cast-off objects that he collected from across the state over 20 years. Admission is via a one-hour guided tour, held on the hour. Goa Chitra is 3km east of Maria Hall – ask locally for directions.

San Thome Museum MUSEUM
(☎9822363917; www.goamuseum.com; Colva Rd; ₹200; ⊙9am-6pm) This quirky new museum, dubbed 'Back in Time', has three floors of carefully presented technology through the ages, from old cameras and typewriters to gramophones, clocks and projectors. Highlights include a Scheidmier grand piano, Raleigh bicycle and an anchor cast from the same pattern as the *Titanic*.

🛏 Sleeping

Lots of budget rooms for rent can be found along the roads towards Benaulim and Sernabatim Beach; the big five-stars are further south. The best of the budget beachfront accommodation is at Sernabatim Beach, a few hundred metres north of Benaulim.

D'Souza Guest House GUESTHOUSE $
(☎0832-2770583; d ₹600) With just three rooms, this traditional blue-painted house in the back lanes is run by a local Goan family and comes with bundles of homely atmosphere and a lovely garden. It's often full so book ahead.

Anthy's Guesthouse GUESTHOUSE $
(☎0832-2771680; anthysguesthouse@rediffmail.com; Sernabatim Beach; d ₹1500, with AC ₹1800; ❄🌐) One of a handful of places lining Serna-

batim Beach, Anthy's is a favourite with travellers for its good restaurant, book exchange and well-kept chalet-style rooms, which stretch back from the beach, surrounded by a garden. Ayurvedic massage is available.

★ Blue Corner HUT $$
(☎9850455770; www.bluecornergoa.com; huts ₹1200; 🌐) Behind the beach shack restaurant a short walk north of the main beach entrance, this group of sturdy palm-thatch cocohuts – not so common around here – are the best in Benaulim, with fan and verandah. The restaurant gets good reviews from guests.

Taj Exotica HOTEL $$$
(☎0832-6683333; www.tajhotels.com; d ₹17,000-28,000; ❄@🌐) Bollywood stars and sheiks are known to stay at the Taj Exotica, one of Goa's plushest resorts. Set in 23 hectares of tropical gardens 2km south of Benaulim, it has all the spas, restaurants and pools that you would expect. Most travellers will be content to visit its swish restaurants, including the Goan cuisine of Allegria and the beachfront Lobster Shack.

🍴 Eating & Drinking

Cafe Malibu INDIAN $
(mains ₹110-200; ⊙8am-11pm) This unpretentious little family-run cafe offers a nice dining experience in its roadside garden setting on a back lane a short walk back from the beach. It does a good job of Goan specialities as well as Indian and continental dishes.

Pedro's Bar & Restaurant MULTICUISINE $$
(Vasvaddo Beach Rd; mains ₹120-360; ⊙7am-midnight; 🌐) Set amid a large, shady garden on the beachfront and popular with local and international travellers, Pedro's offers standard Indian, Chinese and Italian dishes, as well as Goan choices and 'sizzlers'.

Club Zoya CLUB
(☎9822661388; www.clubzoya.com; ⊙from 8pm) The party scene has hit sleepy little Benaulim in the form of barn-sized Club Zoya, with international DJs, big light shows and a cocktail bar featuring speciality flavoured and infused vodka drinks. Something is on most nights here in season but check the website for upcoming events and DJs.

ⓘ Transport

Buses from Margao to Benaulim are frequent (₹15, 15 minutes). Buses stop at the Maria Hall crossroads, or at the junctions to Sernabatim or Taj Exotica (ask to be let off). From Maria Hall, autorickshaws cost ₹60 for the five-minute ride to the sea.

Agonda

☑ 0832 / POP 3800

Travellers have been drifting to Agonda for years and seasonal hut villages – some very luxurious – now occupy almost all available beachfront space, but it's still more low-key than Palolem and a good choice if you're after some beachy relaxation. The coast road between Betul and Palolem passes through Agonda village, while the main traveller centre is a single lane running parallel behind the beach.

◎ Sights & Activities

Agonda Beach is a fine 2km stretch of white sand framed between two forested headlands. The surf can be fierce and swimming is not as safe as at Palolem, but lifeguards are on patrol. Olive ridley marine turtles nest (and are protected) at the northern end in winter.

South of Agonda are pretty **Honeymoon Beach** and then **Butterfly Beach** (from ₹1700), both accessible on foot or by boat (but there are no facilities).

Lots of local and foreigner-run yoga, meditation and ayurveda courses and classes set up in season. Local boats can take you on dolphin-spotting trips.

Aloha Surf School   SURFING
(☑ 7507582933; 1hr/2hr/full day board rental ₹300/500/1500, lesson from ₹1500; ◷ 8am-6pm) The first surf school in Goa's deep south, Aloha is run by a passionate local crew. Learn to surf on Agonda's gentle waves or hire a board.

🛌 Sleeping

Agonda has gone seriously upmarket in its beach-hut operations in recent years, with the best beachfront resorts offering air-con, TV and giant open-sky bathrooms and all with a restaurant and bar, usually beach-facing. As with any seasonal accommodation, standards and ownership can change.

Back from the beach on the parallel road are a few cheaper guesthouses and rooms to let.

Fatima Guesthouse   GUESTHOUSE $
(☑ 0832-2647477; www.fatimasguesthouse.com; d ₹1000-1500, with AC ₹1500-2500; ❄ 🛜) An

ever-popular budget guesthouse set back from the beach, with clean rooms, a good restaurant and obliging staff. Rooftop yoga classes in season.

★**Agonda White Sand**   HUT $$
(☑ 9823548277; www.agondawhitesand.com; Agonda Beach; hut from ₹4200-5200; 🛜) Beautifully designed and constructed cottages with open-air bathrooms and spring mattresses surround a central bar and restaurant at this stylish beachfront place.

Chattai   HUT $$
(☑ 9423812287; www.chattai.co.in; hut ₹2100) Overlooking the north end of the beach, Chattai offers lovely, airy huts on the sands, and popular yoga classes under its secluded Yoga Dome.

H2O Agonda   HUT $$$
(☑ 9423836994; www.h2oagonda.com; d incl breakfast ₹4500-6500; ❄ 🛜) With its purple and mauve muslin curtains and Arabian nights ambience, H2O is among the most impressive of Agonda's luxury cottage setups. From the hotel-style reception, walk through a leafy garden to the spacious cottages with air-con and enormous open-air bathrooms. The more expensive sea-facing cottages with king-size beds may be worth paying extra for.

🍴 Eating

★**Blue Planet Cafe**   VEGAN $$
(☑ 0832-2647448; mains ₹110-250; ◷ 9.30am-3pm & 6.30-9pm) With a soul-food and healthy vibe and a small, mostly vegan menu, Blue Planet is a welcoming detox from the beach scene. The menu offers salads, smoothies and innovative veg dishes. It's in an off-track jungle location about 2km from Agonda village (follow the signs off the main Agonda–Palolem road).

Kopi Desa   EUROPEAN $$
(☑ 7767831487; mains ₹120-450; ◷ 8am-11pm) The name translates from Indonesian as 'coffee village' but this new expat restaurant and cocktail bar is making waves with its imaginative Euro-centric menu and live music.

❶ Getting There & Away

Scooters and motorbikes can be rented from places on the beach road for around ₹300/400. Autorickshaws depart from the main T-junction near Agonda's church to Palolem (₹250) and Patnem (₹300). Taxis are around ₹50 more.

Local buses run from Chaudi sporadically throughout the day (₹12), but ask for Agonda Beach, otherwise you'll be let off in the village about 1km away.

Palolem

📞 0832 / POP 12,440

Palolem is undoubtedly one of Goa's most postcard-perfect beaches: a gentle curve of palm-fringed sand facing a calm bay. But in season the beachfront is transformed into a toytown of colourful and increasingly sophisticated timber and bamboo huts fronted by palm-thatch restaurants. It's still a great place to be and is popular with backpackers, long-stayers and families. The protected bay is one of the safest swimming spots in Goa and you can comfortably kayak and paddleboard for hours here.

Away from the beach you can learn to cook, drop in to yoga classes or hire a motorbike and cruise to surrounding beaches, waterfalls and wildlife parks.

🏃 Activities

Palolem offers no shortage of yoga, reiki and meditation classes in season. Locations and teachers tend to change seasonally – ask around locally to see whose hands-on healing powers are hot this season.

Palolem's calm waters are perfect for kayaking and stand-up paddleboarding. Kayaks are available for hire for around ₹150 per hour, paddleboards for ₹500. Mountain bikes (₹100 per day) can be hired from Seema Bike Hire (Ourem Rd).

Local fishermen will take you on dolphin-spotting and fishing expeditions on their outrigger boats. They charge a minimum of ₹1200, or ₹1600 for four or more people, for a one-hour trip. They also do trips to nearby Butterfly and Honeymoon Beaches, or Agonda and Cola Beaches.

⭐ Goa Jungle Adventure   OUTDOORS
(📞 9850485641; www.goajungle.com; trekking & canyoning trips ₹2090-3990; ⏰ Oct-May) This adventure company, run by experienced French guide Manu, will take you out for thrilling trekking and canyoning trips in the Netravali area at the base of the Western Ghats, where you can climb, jump and abseil into remote waterfilled plunges. Trips run from a half-day to several days, and extended rafting trips into Karnataka are also sometimes offered.

🌿 Courses

Rahul's Cooking Class   COOKING
(📞 07875990647;   www.rahulcookingclass.com;
Palolem Beach Rd; per person ₹1500; ⏰ 11am-2pm & 6-9pm) Rahul's is one of the original cooking schools, with three-hour morning and afternoon classes each day. Prepare five dishes including chapati and coconut curry. Minimum two people; book at least one day in advance.

Masala Kitchen   COOKING
(per person ₹1000) Well-established cooking classes; enquire at the Butterfly Book Shop (p157) and book a day in advance.

🛏 Sleeping

Most of Palolem's accommodation is of the seasonal beach-hut variety, though there are plenty of old-fashioned guesthouses or family homes with rooms to rent back from the beach. It's still possible to find a basic palm-thatch hut or plywood cottage somewhere near the beach for as little as ₹800, but many of the huts these days are more thoughtfully designed – the very best have air-con, flat-screen TV and sea-facing balcony.

Travellers Blues Bus   HOSTEL $
(📞 9665510281;   Ourem Rd;   dm ₹300-500, d ₹2000-2500; ❄🛜) There's a blue-and-white Kombi parked in the open-air bar and travellers handing around a guitar. The atmosphere is chilled at TBB, an excellent new hostel just off the beach. Spotless four- to 10-bed dorms (no bunks), private rooms and seasonal huts are all good value.

Sevas   HUT $
(📞 9422065437;   www.sevaspalolemgoa.com;   d hut ₹800, family cottage ₹1800; @🛜) Hidden in the jungle on the Colomb Bay side of Palolem, Sevas has a range of simple palm-thatch huts with open-air bathrooms and larger family huts and rooms set in a lovely shaded garden area.

⭐ Ciaran's   HUT $$
(📞 0832-2643477;   www.ciarans.com;   hut incl breakfast ₹3000-3500, r with AC ₹4500; ❄🛜) 🍃 Ciaran's has some of the most impressive huts on the beachfront. Affable owner John has worked hard over the years to maintain a high standard and his beautifully designed cottages around a plant-filled garden and pond are top-notch. There's a popular multi-cuisine restaurant, tapas restaurant and quality massage and spa centre (1hr massage from ₹1900).

Palolem

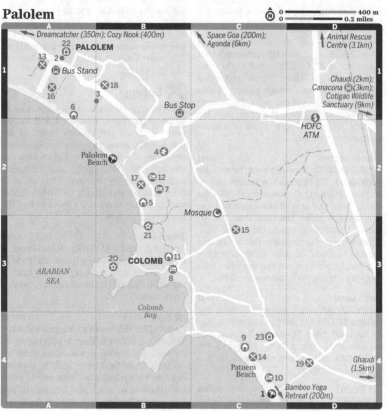

GOA PALOLEM

Palolem

★ **Cozy Nook**   HUT $$
(☎ 9822584760, 0832-2643550; www.cozynook
goa.com; hut ₹2500-3500) Long-running Cozy
Nook, at the northern end of the beach,
has some well-designed cottages including
two-storey pads, upstairs chill-out deck,

more pedestrian rooms and a funky bar. Yoga and kayak rental.

Kate's Cottages GUESTHOUSE **$$**
(☑ 9822165261; www.katescottagesgoa.com; Ourem Rd; d ₹3000-5000; ❄ 🕿) The two stunning rooms above Fern's restaurant are beautifully designed with heavy timber finishes, huge four-poster beds, TV, modern bathrooms and views to the ocean from the balcony. There are also a couple of cheaper ground-floor cottages.

Dreamcatcher HUT **$$**
(☑ 0832-2644873; www.dreamcatcher.in; hut ₹2200-6600; 🕿) Perhaps the largest hut resort in Palolem, Dreamcatcher's 60-plus sturdy huts are nevertheless secluded, set in a coconut grove just back from the far northern end of the beach. One of the highlights here is the riverside restaurant and cocktail bar, and the wide range of holistic treatments, massage and yoga on offer, with drop-in yoga and reiki courses available.

La La Land RESORT **$$**
(☑ 7066129588; http://lalaland.in; Colomb Bay; cottages ₹4000-7200; ❄ 🕿) On Colomb Bay, La La Land takes Keralan-style cottages to another level with a range of quirky but stylish huts and A-frame chalets all set in a beautiful garden.

Art Resort HUT **$$$**
(☑ 9665982344; www.art-resort-goa.com; Ourem Rd; hut ₹6000-9500; ❄ 🕿) The nicely de-

---

SILENT DISCO

Neatly sidestepping Goa's statewide ban on loud music in open spaces after 10pm, Palolem's 'silent parties' are the way to dance the night away without upsetting the neighbours.

Turn up around 10pm, don your headphones with a choice of two or three channels featuring Goan and international DJs playing trance, house, hip hop, electro and funk, and then party the night away in inner bliss but outer silence. At the time of research there were two headphone parties in Palolem:

Silent Noise (www.silentnoise.in; On the Rocks; cover charge ₹600; ⊙ 9pm-4am Sat Nov-Apr)

Neptune Point (www.neptunepoint.com; Neptune's Point, Colomb Bay; cover charge ₹600; ⊙ 9.30am-4am Sat Nov-Apr)

---

signed beach-facing cottages around an excellent beachfront restaurant have a Bedouin camp feel with screened sit-outs and modern artworks sprinkled throughout. The resort hosts art exhibitions and has regular live music.

🍴 Eating

Palolem's beach doesn't have the sort of beach shack restaurants you'll find further north – there's not enough room on the beach – but in season every hut operation lining the beach perimeter has its own restaurant, often with tables and umbrellas plonked down on the sand. They all serve fresh seafood and largely indistinguishable menus, so just check out a few and find the ambience that suits.

Shiv Sai INDIAN **$**
(thalis ₹90, mains ₹100-200; ⊙ 9am-11pm) A thoroughly local lunch joint on the parallel beach road, Shiv Sai serves tasty thalis of the vegie, fish and Gujarati kinds, as well as Goan dishes.

★ Space Goa CAFE **$$**
(☑ 80063283333; www.thespacegoa.com; mains ₹150-280; ⊙ 8.30am-5.30pm; 🕿) On the Agonda road, Space Goa combines an excellent organic whole-food cafe with a gourmet deli, craft shop and a wellness centre offering meditation, ayurvedic treatments and Zen cosmic healing. The food is fresh and delicious, with fabulous salads, paninis and meze, and the desserts – such as chocolate beetroot cake – are divine. Drop-in morning yoga classes are ₹500.

★ Magic Italy ITALIAN **$$**
(☑ 8805767705; Palolem Beach Rd; mains ₹260-480; ⊙ 5pm-midnight) On the main beach road, Magic Italy has been around for a while and the quality of its pizza and pasta remains high, with imported Italian ingredients like ham, salami, cheese and olive oil, imaginative wood-fired pizzas and homemade pasta. Sit at tables, or Arabian-style on floor cushions. The atmosphere is busy but chilled.

Café Inn CAFE **$$**
(☑ 7507322799; Palolem Beach Rd; mains ₹100-450; ⊙ 8am-11pm; 🕿) If you're craving a cappuccino or a rum-infused slushie, semi-open-air Café Inn, which grinds its own blend of beans to perfection, is one of Palolem's favourite hang-outs – and it's not even on the beach. Breakfasts are filling, and

DAY-TRIPPING DOWN SOUTH

Goa's far south is tailor-made for day-tripping. Hire a motorbike or charter a taxi and try these road trips from Palolem, Patnem or Agonda.

Tanshikar Spice Farm (☑ 0832-2608358, 9421184114; www.tanshikarspicefarm.com; Netravali; tour incl lunch ₹500; ☺10am-4pm) About 35km inland from Palolem via forest and farms is this excellent spice plantation, along with jungle treks to waterfalls and the enigmatic 'bubble lake'.

Talpona & Galgibag These two near-deserted beach gems are scenically framed (naturally) by the Talpona and Galgibag Rivers. Olive ridley turtles nest on Galgibag and there are a couple of excellent shack restaurants and huts. The winding country drive here is half the fun.

Polem Beach Goa's most southerly beach, 25km south of Palolem, has just one set of beach huts and a real castaway feel. A trip here should be combined with the detour to Talpona and Galgibag.

GOA PATNEM

comfort-food burgers and panini sandwiches hit the spot.

★ **Ourem 88**   FUSION $$$
(☑ 8698827679; mains ₹540-750; ☺6-10pm Tue-Sun) British-run Ourem 88 is a gastro sensation with just a handful of tables and a small but masterful menu. Try baked brie, tender calamari stuffed with Goan sausage, braised lamb shank or fluffy soufflé. Worth a splurge.

🍷 Drinking & Nightlife

Leopard Valley   CLUB
(www.leopardvalley.com; Palolem-Agonda Rd; entry from ₹600; ☺9pm-4am Fri) South Goa's biggest outdoor dance club is a sight (and sound) to behold, with 3D laser light shows, pyrotechnics and state-of-the-art sound systems blasting local and international DJs on Friday nights. It's in an isolated but easily reached location between Palolem and Agonda.

🛍 Shopping

Butterfly Book Shop   BOOKS
(☑ 9341738801; ☺10am-1pm & 3-8pm) The best of several good bookshops in town, this cosy place stocks best sellers, classics, and a good range of books on yoga, meditation and spirituality. This is also the contact for yoga classes and cooking courses (p154).

ℹ Getting There & Around

Frequent buses run to nearby Chaudi (₹7) from the **bus stop** on the corner of the road down to the beach. Hourly buses to Margao (₹40, one hour) depart from the same place, though these

usually go via Chaudi anyway. From Chaudi you can pick up regular buses to Margao, from where you can change for Panaji, or south to Polem Beach and Karwar in Karnataka.

The closest train station is Canacona, 2km from Palolem's beach entrance.

An autorickshaw from Palolem to Patnem should cost ₹100, or ₹150 to Chaudi. A taxi to Dabolim Airport is around ₹1500.

Scooters and motorbikes can be hired on the main road leading to the beach from around ₹300.

Patnem
☑ 0832

Smaller and less crowded than neighbouring Palolem, pretty Patnem makes a much quieter and more family-friendly alternative. The waters aren't as calm and protected as Palolem's, but relaxed **Patnem Beach** is patrolled by lifeguards and safe for paddling. It's easy enough to walk around the northern headland to Colomb Bay and on to Palolem.

🛏 Sleeping

Long-stayers will revel in Patnem's choice of village homes and apartments available for rent from ₹10,000 to ₹40,000 per month. There are a dozen or so beach-hut operations lining the sands; many change annually, so walk along to find your perfect spot.

Micky's   HUT $
(☑ 9850484884; www.mickyhuts.com; Patnem Beach; d ₹800-1000; 🛜) Micky's is an old-timer at the north end of Patnem Beach with a range of simple budget huts (some without

attached bath) and rooms. It's run by a friendly family and open for most of the year. There's a cruisy beachfront bar and cafe.

Papaya's   COTTAGE $$

(📞 9923079447; www.papayasgoa.com; hut ₹2000-3000, with AC ₹5000; 🌀🛜) Solid huts constructed with natural materials head back into the palm grove from Papaya's popular restaurant, which does great versions of all the beachfront classics. Each hut is lovingly built, with lots of wood, four-poster beds and floating muslin.

Bamboo Yoga Retreat   HUT $$$

(📞 9637567730; www.bamboo-yoga-retreat.com; s/d from ₹6500/10,000; 🛜) This laid-back yoga retreat, exclusive to guests, has a wonderful open-sided *shala* facing the ocean at the southern end of Patnem Beach, and three more *shalas* among the village of comfortable timber and thatched huts. Yoga holiday rates include brunch, meditation and two daily yoga classes, but there are also training courses and ayurvedic treatments.

✖ Eating

Karma Cafe & Bakery   CAFE $

(📞 9764504253; Patnem Rd, Colomb; baked goods from ₹60; ⊙ 7.30am-6pm; 🛜) Pull up a cushion at this chilled cafe and bakery opposite the Colomb road and delve into a superb range of fresh baked breads, yak cheese croissants and pastries as well as coffee and smoothies.

★ Jaali Cafe   CAFE $$

(📞 8007712248; small plates ₹150-250; ⊙ 9am-6pm Tue-Sun, dinner Thu-Sat) The menu at this lovely garden cafe is something special with a delicious range of tapas-style Middle Eastern and Mediterranean plates – choose two or three dishes each and share. Sunday brunch is a popular event with local expats. There's also an excellent **boutique** (⊙ 9.30am-6.30pm) and a highly regarded massage therapist on-hand.

Home   INTERNATIONAL $$

(📞 0832-2643916; www.homeispatnem.com; Patnem Beach; mains ₹120-300; ⊙ 8am-10pm; 🛜) Standing out from the beach shacks like a beacon, this bright white, relaxed vegetarian restaurant serves up good breakfasts, pastas, risotto and salads. A highlight here is the dessert menu – awesome chocolate brownies, apple tart and cheesecake. Home also rents out eight nicely decorated, light rooms (from ₹1800).

Zest Patnem   CAFE $$

(📞 8806607919; mains ₹190-320; ⊙ 8am-8pm; 🛜🍴) Bowls of pad Thai, plates of meze or sushi and Mexican dishes, all freshly prepared, make Zest a popular hang-out. With similar cafes in Palolem and Agonda, they're certainly doing something right among the beach-loving, health-conscious crowd.

❶ Getting There & Away

The main entrance to Patnem Beach is reached from the country lane running south from Palolem, then turning right at the Hotel Sea View. Alternatively, walk about 20 minutes along the path from Palolem via Colomb Bay, or catch a bus heading south (₹5). An autorickshaw charges around ₹100 from Palolem.

DMYTRO GILUTUKHA / SHUTTERSTOCK ©

Ancient & Historic Sites

South India has a remarkable assortment of monuments and ruins that testify to the splendour of the many varied cultures that have paraded across its broad canvas. From serene places of worship to remnants of grandiose empires, the opportunities to marvel at the genius of long-gone civilisations are manifold here. Temples all over the region are awash with colourful South Indian life, while wondrous hilltop forts and opulent palaces recall the lofty aspirations of long-gone leaders.

Contents
➡ Hindu Sacred Sites
➡ Forts
➡ Caves
➡ Palaces & Tombs

Above Vittala Temple, Hampi (p210)

Hindu Sacred Sites

South India is home to some of the most spectacular devotional architecture in this Hindu-majority country: soaring *gopurams* (gateway towers), exquisite *mandapas* (pavilions) and some of the most intricately chiselled deity sculptures you'll ever see.

Madurai

Madurai's Meenakshi Amman Temple (p381), abode of the triple-breasted goddess Meenakshi, is generally considered the pinnacle of classic South Indian temple architecture. This Tamil Nadu temple, with its 12 sky-reaching *gopurams*, predominantly dates from the 17th century, but its origins reach back 2000 years to when Madurai, one of India's most ancient cities, was a Pandyan capital.

Hampi

Now a sleepy Karnataka hamlet, from 1336 to 1565 Hampi was the thriving centre of the mighty Vijayanagar empire. Its World Heritage–listed ruins are strewn amid boulders of all shapes and sizes, the result of hundreds of millions of years of volcanic activity and erosion. Especially fine examples of temple art can be seen at the 15th-century Virupaksha Temple (p210) and 16th-century Vittala Temple (p210).

1. Five Rathas, Mamallapuram (p347)
2. Virupaksha Temple, Hampi (p210)
3. Meenakshi Amman Temple (p381), Madurai

Mamallapuram

The exquisite sculptures dotted around the seaside Tamil Nadu town of Mamallapuram (Mahabalipuram) were carved by artisans of the Pallava dynasty in the 7th and 8th centuries. They range from the beautifully sculpted free-standing Shore Temple (p347) to the Five Rathas (p347) – temples carved from the living rock, including several wonderful animal figures – and the giant Arjuna's Penance (p349) relief carving, exploding with episodes of Hindu myth.

Thanjavur

The multitiered *vimana* (tower) soaring above the Brihadishwara Temple (p372) in Tamil Nadu's Thanjavur (Tanjore) is the ultimate expression of the power and creativity of the medieval Chola dynasty. This 11th-century temple, still very much a living place of worship, is adorned with glorious graceful sculptures of Hindu deities and elaborately carved *gopurams*.

Forts

Battleground of many a rival empire in centuries gone by, South India is dotted with fantastical forts that have survived the vagaries of time – many of them sprawled across strategic hilltops and wrapped within sturdy walls protecting a treasure trove of monuments.

Golconda Fort

Hyderabad's 16th-century Qutb Shahs transformed the preexisting Golconda Fort (p231), on a 120m-high granite hill, into a fortified city with two rings of ramparts, one 11km in circumference. Mughal ruler Aurangzeb had to resort to bribing a defending general to conquer the fort in 1687, after a fruit-less year-long siege. Golconda is a feast of crenellated walls, cannon-mounted bastions and imposing gates studded with iron spikes to repel raiding war elephants.

Daulatabad Fort

The central bastion of Maharashtra's crumbling Daulatabad Fort is reached by an hour's climb via spiralling tunnels, multiple doorways and spiked gates. Eccentric Delhi sultan Mohammed Tughlaq marched the entire population of Delhi 1100km here in 1328 to make Daulatabad his capital – but his dream was swiftly cut short when Daulatabad proved strategically unviable as a capital.

Bidar Fort

South India's now-neglected largest fort (p223) was once the bustling capital of much of the region. Although mostly in a state of deteriorating disrepair, this Karnataka fortress still retains noteworthy remnants of its glory days, including the Rangin Mahal (Painted Palace) and Sixteen-Pillared Mosque.

Janjira

The brooding fortress of Janjira (p101) looms sheer out of the sea 500m off the Konkan Coast. Built in the 16th century by descendants of African slaves, Janjira was never conquered by enemies. Only nature is succeeding in reclaiming the now-abandoned fort.

Gingee Fort

A spectacular example of South Indian fort architecture, Tamil Nadu's abandoned Gingee Fort (p359) encompasses three hilltop citadels within a 6km perimeter of sheer cliffs and chunky walls. It was built mostly by the Vijayanagars in the 16th century, before being taken over by the Marathas, Mughals, French and British.

KAY MAERITZ / GETTY IMAGES ©

1. Golconda Fort (p231), Hyderabad
2. Daulatabad Fort (p91), Aurangabad
3. Bidar Fort (p223), Bidar

KEREN SU / GETTY IMAGES ©

SAURABH / GETTY IMAGES ©

1. Ellora Caves (p92) **2.** Kailasa Temple, (p92) Ellora
3. Tempera paintings, Ajanta Caves (p95) **4.** Ajanta Caves (p95)

ALEXANDER MAZURKEVICH / SHUTTERSTOCK ©

Buddhist, Hindu & Jain Caves

Maharashtra's World Heritage–listed caves of Ajanta and Ellora are just the most spectacular of the many cave or rock-cut shrines from the times before South India started building free-standing stone structures.

Ajanta

The 30 Buddhist caves of Ajanta (p95), with origins in the 2nd century BC, are clustered along a horseshoe-shaped gorge above the Waghore River. One of their most renowned features is the natural-dye tempera paintings (similar to frescoes) decorating many of the caves' interiors. Some of these murals are even coloured with crushed semiprecious stones such as lapis lazuli. Don't miss Cave 1, with particularly superb artwork including a wonderful rendition of Buddhism's Bodhisattva Padmapani, or Cave 16, whose especially fine paintings include the famous 'dying' (actually fainting) princess.

Ellora

The Ellora Cave Temples (p92) – a collection of Hindu, Jain and Buddhist shrines constructed between AD 600 and 1000 – are situated on a 2km-long escarpment. There are 34 in all: 17 Hindu, 12 Buddhist and five Jain. Most famed is Cave 16, the Kailasa Temple in honour of the Hindu god Shiva, which is the world's biggest monolithic sculpture and was skilfully carved into the cliff face by thousands of labourers over 150 years.

Guntupalli

One of more than 100 ancient Buddhist sites in rural Andhra Pradesh, the 2nd-century-BC monastery at Guntupalli (p247) sits high on a hilltop overlooking an expanse of forest and rice fields. Monks' dwellings line the cliffside, with lovely arched stone facades sculpted to look like wood.

Golgumbaz (p221), Vijapura (Bija

Palaces & Tombs

The rulers of South India's bygone kingdoms and sultanates not only proclaimed their pomp by building ridiculously opulent palaces, but many of them were also buried in splendid tombs – some of which rank among the region's most exquisite architecture.

Southern Palaces

First prize among South India's flamboyant royal residences goes to fabulous Mysuru Palace (p186, but Mysuru's (Mysore's) rival princely state of Hyder -abad puts up a stern challenge with the shimmering, chandelier-laden Chowmahalla Palace (p228) and the hilltop Falaknuma Palace (p235), a splendiferous neoclassical construction now reincarnated as an ultraluxurious hotel.

Vijapura's Tombs

Vijapura (Bijapur) ruled one of the five Deccan sultanates that dominated the plateau lands in the 16th and 17th centuries. Its delicately graceful Ibrahim Rouza (p222) is a sort of southern Taj Mahal, in that it was built by a sultan as a mausoleum for his wife and its minarets are said to have inspired those of the Taj itself. Vijapura's massive Golgumbaz (p221), another royal mausoleum, boasts what is said to be the world's second-largest dome (with incredible acoustics).

Qutb Shahi Tombs

The final resting place of the builders of Golconda Fort and their kin, the 21 magnificent domed Qutb Shahi Tombs (p233) stand within sight of the fort on the edge of Hyderabad. The domes are mounted on cubical bases with beautiful colonnades and delicate stucco ornamentation.

Karnataka & Bengaluru

Best Places to Eat

➜ Karavalli (p177)

➜ Mavalli Tiffin Rooms (p177)

➜ Vinayaka Mylari (p191)

➜ Lalith Bar & Restaurant (p203)

➜ Fatty Bao (p177)

Best Places to Sleep

➜ Uramma Cottage (p217)

➜ Electric Cats B&B (p175)

➜ Dhole's Den (p195)

➜ Honey Valley Estate (p199)

Why Go?

A stunning introduction to southern India, Karnataka is a prosperous, compelling state loaded with a winning blend of urban cool, glittering palaces, national parks, ancient ruins, beaches, yoga centres and legendary hang-outs.

At its nerve centre is the capital Bengaluru (Bangalore), a progressive city famous for its craft beer and restaurant scene. Heading out of town you'll encounter the evergreen rolling hills of Kodagu, dotted with spice and coffee plantations, the regal splendour of Mysuru (Mysore), and jungles teeming with monkeys, tigers and Asia's biggest population of elephants.

If that all sounds too mainstream, head to the counter-cultural enclave of tranquil Hampi with hammocks, psychedelic sunsets and boulder-strewn ruins. Or the blissful, virtually untouched coastline around Gokarna, blessed with beautiful coves and empty sands. Or leave the tourist trail behind entirely, and take a journey to the evocative Islamic ruins of northern Karnataka.

When to Go
Bengaluru

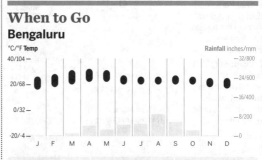

| **Mar–May** The best season to watch tigers and elephants in Karnataka's pristine national parks. | **Oct** Mysuru's Dussehra (Dasara) carnival brings night-long celebrations and a jumbo parade. | **Dec & Jan** The coolest time to explore Hampi and the northern forts, palaces, caves and temples. |

Karnataka & Bengaluru Highlights

1 Hampi (p210) Soaking up the surreal landscapes, sociable travellers' scene and epic ruins in this magical, evocative destination.

2 Gokarna (p207) Searching for the perfect cove beach in this low-key coastal hideaway, then touring its atmospheric temples.

3 Bengaluru (p169) Sampling craft beers, dining out in style and enjoying the museums and sights of this cosmopolitan city.

4 Kodagu (p197) Savouring aromatic coffee and hiking trails in these temperate, evergreen highlands.

5 Mysuru Palace (p184) Getting bowled over by one of India's most grandiose structures and touring its glittering halls.

6 Nagarhole National Park (p196) Spying on lazy tuskers in the forests bordering serene Kabini Lake.

7 Vijapura (p221) Strolling in the peaceful manicured grounds of exquisite 16th-century Islamic monuments.

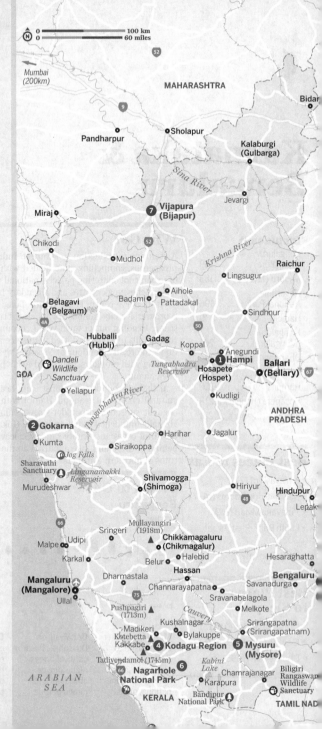

History

A rambling playing field of religions, cultures and kingdoms, the Karnataka region has been ruled by a string of charismatic rulers through history. India's first great emperor, Chandragupta Maurya, made the Karnataka area his retreat when he embraced Jainism at Sravanabelagola in the 3rd century BC. From the 6th to the 14th centuries, the land was under a series of dynasties such as the Chalukyas, Cholas, Gangas and Hoysalas, who left a lasting mark in the form of stunning cave shrines and temples across the state.

In 1327 Mohammed Tughlaq's army sacked Halebid. In 1347 Hasan Gangu, a Persian general in Tughlaq's army, led a rebellion to establish the Bahmani kingdom, which was later subdivided into five Deccan sultanates. Meanwhile, the Hindu kingdom of Vijayanagar, with its capital in Hampi, rose to prominence. Having peaked in the early 1550s, it fell in 1565 to a combined effort of the sultanates.

In subsequent years the Hindu Wodeyars of Mysuru grew in stature and extended their rule over a large part of southern India. They remained largely unchallenged until 1761, when Hyder Ali (one of their generals) deposed them. Backed by the French, Hyder Ali and his son Tipu Sultan set up capital in Srirangapatna and consolidated their rule. However, in 1799 the British defeated Tipu Sultan and reinstated the Wodeyars. Historically, this battle consolidated British territorial expansion in southern India.

Mysuru remained under the Wodeyars until Independence – post-1947, the reigning maharaja became the first governor. The state boundaries were redrawn along linguistic lines in 1956 and the extended Kannada-speaking state of Mysore was born. It was renamed Karnataka in 1972, with Bangalore (now Bengaluru) as the capital.

SOUTHERN KARNATAKA

Bengaluru (Bangalore)

♪ 080 / POP 11.5 MILLION / ELEV 920M

Cosmopolitan Bengaluru (formerly Bangalore) is one of India's most progressive and developed cities, blessed with a benevolent climate and a burgeoning drinking, dining and shopping scene. Yes, its creature comforts are a godsend to the weary traveller who has done the hard yards and it's a great city for mixing with locals in craft beer joints or quirky independent cafes. Though there are no world-class sights, you'll find lovely parks and striking Victorian-era architecture.

The past decade has seen a mad surge of development, coupled with traffic congestion

TOP STATE FESTIVALS

Udupi Paryaya (☉ Jan/Feb) Held even-numbered years, with a procession and ritual marking the handover of swamis at Udupi's Krishna Temple in January.

Classical Dance Festival (☉ Jan/Feb) Some of India's best classical dance performances take place in Pattadakal.

Vijaya Utsav (p210) A three-day extravaganza of culture, heritage and the arts in Hampi.

Tibetan New Year (☉ Jan/Feb) Lamas in Tibetan refugee settlements in Bylakuppe take shifts leading nonstop prayers that span the weeklong celebrations.

Vairamudi Festival (☉ Mar/Apr) Lord Vishnu is adorned with jewels at Cheluvanarayana Temple in Melkote, including a diamond-studded crown belonging to Mysore's former maharajas, attracting 400,000 pilgrims.

Ganesh Chaturthi (☉ Sep) Families march their Ganesh idols to the sea in Gokarna at sunset in September.

Dussehra (p185) Mysuru Palace is lit up in the evenings and a vibrant procession hits town to the delight of thousands.

Lakshadeepotsava (p204) Thousands and thousands of lamps light up the Jain pilgrimage town of Dharmasthala in November, offering spectacular photo ops.

Huthri (Nov/Dec) The Kodava community in Madikeri celebrates the start of the harvesting season with ceremony, music, traditional dances and much feasting for a week.

Bengaluru (Bangalore)

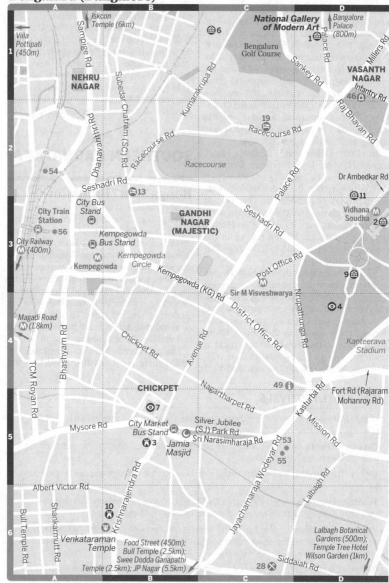

KARNATAKA & BENGALURU BENGALURU (BANGALORE)

and rising pollution levels. But the central district (dating back to the British Raj years) remains little changed, and the landmark corporate HQs and business parks of the city's booming IT industry are mostly in the outer suburbs.

History

Literally meaning 'Town of Boiled Beans', Bengaluru supposedly derived its name from an ancient incident involving an old village woman who served cooked pulses to a lost and hungry Hoysala king. Kempegowda, a

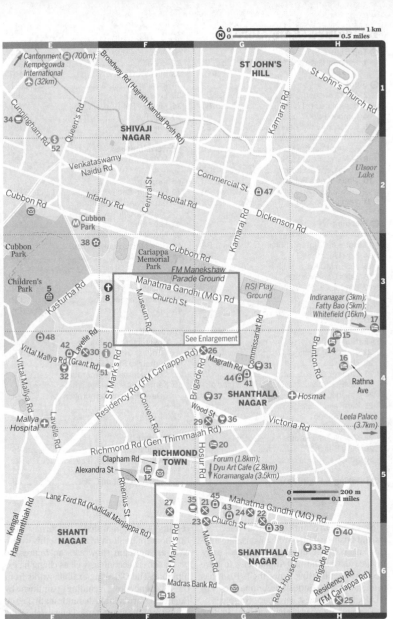

feudal lord, was the first person to mark out Bengaluru's extents by building a mud fort in 1537. The town remained obscure until 1759, when it was gifted to Hyder Ali.

The British arrived in 1809 and made it their regional administrative base in 1831, renaming it Bangalore. During the Raj era the city played host to many a British officer, including Winston Churchill, who enjoyed life here during his greener years and famously left a debt (still on the books) of ₹13 at the Bangalore Club.

Bengaluru (Bangalore)

KARNATAKA & BENGALURU BENGALURU (BANGALORE)

Now home to countless software, electronics and business-outsourcing firms, Bengaluru's knack for technology developed early. In 1905 it was the first Indian city to have electric street lighting. Since the 1940s it has been home to Hindustan Aeronautics Ltd (HAL), India's largest aerospace company.

The city's name was changed back to Bengaluru in November 2006, though few care to use it in practice.

◎ Sights

★**National Gallery of Modern Art** GALLERY
(NGMA; ☎ 080-22342338; www.ngmaindia.gov.in/ngma_bangaluru.asp; 49 Palace Rd; Indian/foreigner ₹20/500; ⊙10am-5pm Tue-Sun) Housed in a

century-year-old mansion – the former vacation home of the Raja of Mysuru – this world-class art museum showcases an impressive permanent collection as well as changing exhibitions. The Old Wing exhibits works from pre-Independence, including paintings by Raja Ravi Varma and Abanindranath Tagore (founder of the avant-garde Bengal School art movement). Interconnected by a walk bridge, the sleek New Wing focuses on contemporary post-Independence works by artists including Sudhir Patwardhan and Vivan Sundaram.

Karnataka Chitrakala Parishath GALLERY
(www.karnatakachitrakalaparishath.com; Kumarakrupa Rd; ₹50; ⊙10am-7.30pm Mon-Sat) A superb gallery with a wide range of Indian and

international contemporary art, as well as permanent displays of Mysuru-style paintings and folk and tribal art from across Asia. A section is devoted to the works of Russian master Nicholas Roerich, known for his vivid paintings of the Himalaya, and the Pan Indian Panorama collection, which includes progressive art from SG Vasudev and Yusuf Arakkal.

★ **Cubbon Park**   GARDENS
(www.horticulture.kar.nic.in/cubbon.htm; Kasturba Rd; Ⓜ Cubbon Park) In the heart of Bengaluru's business district is Cubbon Park, a well-maintained 120-hectare garden where Bengaluru's residents converge to steal a moment from the rat race that rages outside. The gardens encompass the red-painted Gothic-style **State Central Library**. Unfortunately, Cubbon is not completely closed to traffic, except on Sundays when there are concerts, fun runs, yoga and even a small farmers market.

Other wonderful colonial architecture around the park includes the colossal neo-Dravidian-style **Vidhana Soudha** (Dr Ambedkar Rd; Ⓜ Vidhana Soudha), built in 1954 and which serves as the legislative chambers of state government, and neoclassical **Attara Kacheri** (High Court) built in 1864 and housing the High Court. The latter two are closed to the public.

Government Museum   MUSEUM
(Kasturba Rd; ₹4; ⊘10am-5pm Tue-Sun, closed every 2nd Sat; Ⓜ Cubbon Park) In a beautiful red colonial-era building dating from 1877, you'll find a dusty, neglected collection of ancient stone carvings and artefacts excavated from Halebid, Hampi and Attriampakham. Your ticket also gets you into the **Venkatappa Art Gallery** (Kasturba Rd; ⊘10am-5pm Tue-Sun; Ⓜ Cubbon Park) FREE next door, where you can see works and personal memorabilia of K Venkatappa (1887–1962), court painter to the Wodeyars (the former maharajas of the state).

St Mark's Cathedral   CHURCH
(www.saintmarks.in; MG Rd; Ⓜ MG Rd) Atmospheric cathedral built in 1812 with a distinct domed roof based on St Paul's Cathedral. Check out the entrance's ornate carvings. There are four services on Sundays.

Lalbagh Botanical Gardens   GARDENS
(www.horticulture.kar.nic.in/lalbagh.htm; Lalbagh Rd; ₹10; ⊘6am-7pm) Spread over 96 hectares of landscaped terrain, the expansive Lalbagh Botanical Gardens were laid out in 1760 by the famous ruler Hyder Ali. As well as amazing centuries-old trees it claims to have the world's most diverse species of

plants. Try to visit in the early morning for the bird chorus. You can take a guided tour with Bangalore Walks (p174).

Krishnarajendra Market   MARKET
(City Market; Silver Jubilee Park Rd; ⊘6am-10pm) For a taste of traditional urban India, dive into the bustling Krishnarajendra Market and the dense grid of commercial streets that surround it. Weave your way around this lively colourful market past fresh produce, piles of vibrant dyes, spices and copperware. The colourful **flower market** in the centre is the highlight.

Bangalore Fort   FORT
(KR Rd) This ruined 1761 fort is a peaceful escape from the chaotic city surrounds, with its manicured lawn and stone pink walls. The fort remained in use until its destruction by the British in 1791, and today the gate and bastions are the only structures remaining. There's a small dungeon here, and Ganesh temple with its Mooshak (ratlike creature) statue.

Bangalore Palace   PALACE
(Palace Rd; Indian/foreigner ₹230/460, mobile/camera/video ₹285/685/1485; ⊘10.30am-5.30pm) The private residence of the Wodeyars, erstwhile maharajas of the state, Bangalore Palace preserves a slice of bygone royal splendour. Still the residence of the current maharaja, an audio guide provides a detailed explanation of the building, and you can marvel at the lavish interiors and galleries featuring hunting memorabilia, family photos and a collection of nude portraits.

Tipu Sultan's Palace   PALACE
(Albert Victor Rd; Indian/foreigner ₹15/200, video ₹25; ⊘8.30am-5.30pm) The elegant Indo-Islamic summer residence of the ruler Tipu Sultan is notable for its teak pillars and ornamental frescoes.

Bull Temple   HINDU TEMPLE
(Basavanagudi; Bull Temple Rd, Basavanagudi; ⊘7am-8.30pm; 🚲) FREE Built by Kempegowda in the 16th-century Dravidian style, the Bull Temple contains a huge stone monolith of Nandi (Shiva's bull), which is always embellished with lavish flower garlands. This is one of Bengaluru's most atmospheric temples and is located about 1km south of Tipu Sultan's Palace.

Iskcon Temple   HINDU TEMPLE
(www.iskconbangalore.org; Chord Rd, Hare Krishna Hill; ⊘7.15am-1pm & 4.15-8.20pm Mon-Fri,

7.15am-8.30pm Sat & Sun; Ⓜ Mahalakshmi) Built by the International Society of Krishna Consciousness (Iskcon), also referred to as the Hare Krishnas, this impressive hilltop temple, inaugurated in 1997, is lavishly decorated in a mix of ultra-contemporary and traditional styles. There are many food stalls here so bring an appetite, and concerts and lectures are regularly held. It's around 8km northwest from the centre of town.

HAL Aerospace Museum
& Heritage Centre   MUSEUM
(www.hal-india.com; Airport-Varthur Rd; ₹50, camera/video ₹50/75; ⊙ 9am-5pm Tue-Sun) For a peek into India's aeronautical history, visit this wonderful museum past the old airport, where you can see some of the indigenous aircraft models designed by HAL. Interesting exhibits include a MIG-21, home-grown models such as the Marut and Kiran, and a vintage Canberra bomber.

🏃 Activities

Equilibrium   CLIMBING
(☑ 8861684444; www.equilibrium.co.in; 3rd fl, 546 CMH Rd, Indiranagar; from ₹150; ⊙ 6am-11pm) India's first climbing centre is more indoor bouldering, which will suit those en route to Hampi, a world-renowned climbing destination. It also arranges weekend climbing excursions.

Soukya   YOGA
(☑ 080-28017000; www.soukya.com; Soukya Rd, Samethanahalli, Whitefield; per day incl treatments, meals & accommodation from US$1400; ⊙ 6am-8.30pm) Very upmarket, internationally renowned retreat on a picture-perfect 12-hectare organic farm running programs in ayurvedic therapy and yoga, as well as medical and therapeutic skin treatments.

Ayurvedagram   AYURVEDA, YOGA
(☑ 080-65651090; www.ayurvedagram.com; Hemmandanhalli, Whitefield; day package from ₹4000) Set over 3 hectares of tranquil gardens with heritage homes transplanted from Kerala, this centre has specifically tailored ayurvedic treatments, yoga and rejuvenation programs. It's in the outer suburb of Whitefield, around 25km from central Bengaluru.

👉 Tours

★ Bangalore Walks   WALKING
(☑ 9845523660; www.bangalorewalks.com; adult/child from ₹500/300; ⊙ 7-10am Sat & Sun) Highly recommended tours including guided walks through Lalbagh Botanical Gardens and Cubbon Park, a medieval Old City history walk or 19th-century Victorian walk. Most walks include a delicious breakfast. Customised tours are also possible.

★ Unhurried Tours   WALKING
(☑ 919880565446; www.unhurried.in; half-day tours ₹2500) Led by Poornima Dasharathi, an author and history enthusiast, these excellent walking tours explore backstreets, temples, streetlife and local cuisine in Bengaluru. Out-of-town trips are also offered.

Bus Tours   TOURS
(www.karnatakaholidays.net; half day ₹255, full day ₹485, without AC ₹230/385) The government tourism department runs city bus tours which are worth considering (though they do cover a lot of places in a short space of time). Basic half-day city tours run twice daily at 7.30am and 2pm, while the full-day tour departs at 7.15am Wednesday to Sunday.

Day trips around Bengaluru are also offered, including a daily departure to Srirangapatna and Mysuru that takes in several temples, palaces and gardens.

🛏 Sleeping

Choosing a place to stay near a metro station is a wise idea for those who want to really explore the city. Decent budget rooms are in short supply but you'll find a stack of dive lodges on Subedar Chatram (SC) Rd, east of the bus stands and around the train station.

🛏 MG Road Area

JüSTa MG Road   BOUTIQUE HOTEL **$$**
(☑ 080-41135555; www.justahotels.com/mg-road-bangalore; 21/14 Craig Park Layout, MG Rd; r/ste incl breakfast ₹3520/4840; ❈ 🛜; Ⓜ Trinity) A stylish alternative to Bengaluru's plethora of generic business hotels, this intimate arty hotel has slick and spacious rooms with Japanese-inspired motifs throughout. It's well located with a metro station and shopping malls close by.

Hotel Ajantha   HOTEL **$$**
(☑ 080-25584321; www.hotelajantha.in; 22A MG Rd; s/d incl breakfast with fan ₹1500/2000, with AC from ₹2300; ❈ 🛜; Ⓜ Trinity) Dependable, affordable budget favourite Ajantha is very close to Trinity metro station and has decent, well-maintained rooms with cable TV. There's a well-regarded restaurant in the compound and the complimentary breakfast is generous.

Tom's Hotel HOTEL $$

(080-25575875; www.hoteltoms.com; 1/5 Hosur Rd; s/d incl breakfast with fan ₹2200/2400, with AC ₹2310/2560; ❄ 🛜 🏊) An excellent place with high cleanliness standards, and bright cheerful rooms, Tom's allows you to stay in a central location (it's a 15-minute walk from MG Rd) and has friendly staff and free wi-fi. There's a restaurant which serves well-priced Indian dishes.

★**Casa Piccola Cottage** HERITAGE HOTEL $$$

(080-22990337; www.casacottage.com; 2 Clapham Rd; r incl breakfast from ₹4400; ❄ 🛜) A tastefully renovated heritage hotel, Casa Piccola's atmospheric rooms offer a tranquil sanctuary. Its personalised brand of hospitality has garnered it a solid reputation and rooms come with tiled floors and traditional bedspreads while the garden boasts papaya and avocado trees.

★**Oberoi** HOTEL $$$

(080-41358222; www.oberoihotels.com; 39 MG Rd; s/d from ₹13,400/14,600; ❄ @ 🛜 🏊 ; M Trinity) Top dog (and top dollar) in Bengaluru, the opulent Oberoi is set in lush gardens around an enchanting 120-year-old tree, yet its central location could not be more convenient. It mixes colonial-era ambience with modern touches like tablet-controlled in-room devices and TVs in the bathrooms. Rooms all have balconies with garden views and the spa and restaurants are superb.

Laika Boutique Stay B&B $$$

(9482806630; www.laikabangalore.in; Rathna Rd; r from ₹4235; ❄ 🛜 ; M Trinity) Hidden down a leafy side street, this welcoming guesthouse is a wonderful choice for those seeking a more local experience combined with style and comfort. Extra touches, including thoughtful service and home-cooked breakfasts, make it a great choice.

St Mark's Inn HOTEL $$$

(080-41122783; www.stmarkshotel.com; St Mark's Rd; s/d incl breakfast ₹4870/5880; ❄ 🛜 ; M MG Rd) Designer hotel with immaculate rooms decked out with modern decor, big comfy beds and sparkling stainless-steel bathroom fittings. The buffet breakfast is quite a spread. Rates vary considerably day to day according to demand.

🛏 Other Areas

★**Electric Cats B&B** HOSTEL $

(9845290679; www.facebook.com/ElectricCats Hostel; 1794 6th Cross Rd; ☉ dm ₹500-600; ❄ 🛜 ;

M Indiranagar) A really well-organised, sociable hostel close to the buzzing Indiranagar area with good dorms (one female-only with a shared bathroom), all beds have good linen, private reading lamps and charging facilities. Drinking water and wi-fi are free, there's no curfew and staff are very switched on to travellers' needs, even organising pub crawls and barbecues.

Cuckoo Hostel HOSTEL $

(9535034683; www.facebook.com/cuckoohostel; 561 17 A Main Rd, Koramangala; dm/s ₹650/850; ❄ @ 🛜) A lot of thought has gone into this new hostel which is run by and attracts a creative crowd, with regular craft, art, music sessions and occasional debates about the environment and global issues. There are cycles for hire, laundry facilities and clean, well-presented dorms. It's about 6km southwest of the centre.

Meditating Monkeys HOSTEL $

(918861459156; http://themeditatingmonkeys. com; 9/24 Lloyd Rd, Cooke Town; dm incl breakfast ₹500; ❄ @ 🛜) Founded by a local musician/traveller this excellent new hostel offers a comfy, social base in a business city. There's a free veg breakfast, wi-fi, tea and coffee, kitchen and washing machine. Dorms are well-presented and communal bathrooms are clean. It's a smoke- and alcohol-free zone. Located 4km north of MG Rd.

Temple Tree Hotel Wilson Garden HOTEL $$

(080-46622000; http://templetreehotel.com; 9th Cross Rd, Mavalli; r ₹3765-4499; ❄ 🛜) Ticking the right contemporary boxes, including hip bathrooms and modish design touches, this sleek hotel won't fail to impress. Garden view rooms have great balconies, and there's a rooftop restaurant and a small gym. It's not far from the Lalbagh Botanical Gardens.

Mass Residency GUESTHOUSE $$

(9945091735; massresidency@yahoo.com; 18, 2nd Main Rd, 11th Cross, JP Nagar; r incl breakfast with fan/AC ₹1600/2000; ❄ 🛜) Welcoming guesthouse,

---

SLEEPING PRICE RANGES

The following price ranges are for a double room with bathroom and are inclusive of tax:

$ less than ₹1500

$$ ₹1500–₹4000

$$$ more than ₹4000

run by two brothers who are world travellers themselves. It has comfortable enough rooms, but wins rave reviews for its warm hospitality and free neighbourhood walking tours. Located 8km south of the centre.

Hotel ABM International HOTEL $$

(☑ 080-41742030; 232 Subedar Chatram Rd, near Anand Rao Circle; r ₹1400-1700, with AC ₹1600-2200; ❋ ☜; Ⓜ Kempegowda) Offering good value for money, this budget hotel has neat, simple, well-presented rooms. There is a popular juice bar and restaurant downstairs and it's walking distance from the Kempegowda Bus Stand and metro.

★ Taj West End HERITAGE HOTEL $$$

(☑ 080-66605660; www.tajhotels.com; Racecourse Rd; s/d incl breakfast from ₹12,600/13,700; ❋ ☜ ☼) Spread over 8 hectares of stunning tropical gardens the West End saga flashbacks to 1887, when it was first established as a base for British officers, and it still oozes colonial class. Some of the city's best dining options include the Blue Ginger for Vietnamese cuisine and the Masala Klub for superb Indian food.

Leela Palace HOTEL $$$

(☑ 080-25211234; www.theleela.com; 23 HAL Airport Rd; s/d from ₹18,800/19,300; ❋ @ ☜ ☼) Modelled on Mysuru Palace, the astonishing Leela isn't actually a palace (it was built in 2003), but it's fit for royalty. Gleaming marble, luxurious carpets, regal balconies and period features are done superbly, as are its beautiful gardens, classy restaurants, bars and boutique galleries. It's within the Leela Galleria complex, 5km east of MG Rd next to a golf course.

Villa Pottipati GUESTHOUSE $$$

(☑ 080-41144725; www.villa-pottipati.neemranaho tels.com; 142 8th Cross, 4th Main, Malleswaram; s/d incl breakfast from ₹4800/7600; ❋ @ ☜ ☼) This heritage building makes an atmospheric base, with antique furniture and kindly staff. Indeed it was once the home of the wealthy expat Andhra family. Its garden is full of ancient trees and has a dunk-sized pool. However, the property is close to a busy intersection and there's some traffic noise.

✘ Eating

Bengaluru's adventurous dining scene keeps pace with the whims and rising standards of its hungry, moneyed locals and IT expats. You'll find high-end dining, gastropubs and cheap local favourites.

✘ MG Road Area

Khan Saheb INDIAN $

(www.khansaheb.co; 9A Block, Brigade Rd; rolls from ₹60; ☺ noon-11.30pm; Ⓜ MG Rd) Famous for its terrific rolls (wholewheat chapatis), filled with anything from charcoal-grilled meats and tandoori prawns to paneer and sweetcorn tikka.

Koshy's Bar & Restaurant INDIAN $$

(39 St Mark's Rd; mains ₹160-350; ☺ 9am-11pm; Ⓜ MG Rd) Serving the city's intelligentsia for decades, this buzzy, decidedly old-school resto-pub is where you can put away tasty North Indian dishes in between fervent discussions and mugs of beer. The decor is all creaky ceiling fans and dusty wooden shuttered windows and lashings of nostalgia. Between lunch and dinner it's 'short eats' only (colonial-era snacks like chicken liver on toast).

Church Street Social GASTROPUB $$

(http://socialoffline.in; 46/1 Church St; mains ₹170-350; ☺ 9am-11pm Mon-Thu, to 1am Fri & Sat; ☜; Ⓜ MG Rd) Bringing hipsterism to Bengaluru, this industrial warehouse-style space serves cocktails in beakers and its napkins are toilet paper–style (on a roll). The menu takes in fine breakfasts, meze platters, southern fried chicken burgers and 'gunpowder' calamari.

Empire NORTH INDIAN $$

(www.facebook.com/hotelempire; 36 Church St; mains ₹120-240; ☺ 11am-11pm; Ⓜ MG Rd) Famous in the city, Empire is all about authentic, inexpensive tandoori and meat dishes in unpretentious surrounds (plastic banquette seating and fake wood); try their butter chicken, kebabs or a mutton biryani. It's busy day and night and its streetside kitchen dishes out tasty shawarma (spit-roasted kebab) to time-pushed peeps on the go. There are numerous other branches around the city.

★ Olive Beach MEDITERRANEAN $$$

(☑ 080-41128400; www.olivebarandkitchen.com; 16 Wood St, Ashoknagar; mains ₹525-795; ☺ noon-3.30pm & 7-11pm; ☜) A whitewashed villa straight from the coast of Santorini, Olive Beach does a menu that evokes wistful memories of sunny Mediterranean getaways. Things change seasonally, but expect Moroccan lamb tagines, prawns *pil pil* (with garlic and hot peppers) and plenty of veg choices. The addition of a new alfresco lounge bar here has only added to Olive Beach's allure.

Karavalli
SEAFOOD $$$

(☑080-66604545; Gateway Hotel, 66 Residency Rd; mains ₹500-1575; ⊙12.30-3pm & 6.30-11.30pm; ⓂMG Rd) For the finest Indian seafood, look no further. The wonderfully atmospheric interior is perfect for a special meal, with subtle lighting, traditional thatched roof, vintage woodwork and beaten brassware – though the garden seating is equally appealing. Choose from fiery Mangalorean fish dishes, spicy Kerala-style prawns, crab Milagu in a pepper masala and superb lobster *balchao* (cooked in a spicy sauce; ₹1495).

Ebony
MULTICUISINE $$$

(☑080-41783333; www.ebonywithaview.com; 13th fl, Barton Centre, 84 MG Rd; mains ₹300-560; ⊙12.30-3pm & 7-11pm; 🖥; ⓂMG Rd) While there's a delectable menu of Indian, Thai and European dishes, here it's all about the romantic views from the 13th-floor rooftop. On weekday lunchtimes two courses are just ₹445. There's a cool lounge zone, too, buzzing with Bengaluru's cocktail-sipping classes on weekends.

Indian Kitchen
MODERN INDIAN $$$

(☑080-25598995; 86 Oak Shot Pl, MG Rd; 250-825; ⊙noon-3pm & 7pm-1am; ⓂMG Rd) Destination restaurant that's a big hit with the city's bright young things. The menu raids the nation for inspiration; standouts include the Chingri Malai (Bengali-style curry with prawns and coconut) and chicken gassi (with spicy tamarind sauce). Doubles as a bar, with a good selection of beers, wines and cocktails.

Fava
MEDITERRANEAN $$$

(www.fava.in; UB City, 24 Vittal Mallya Rd; mains ₹350-850; ⊙11am-11pm; 🖥; ⓂCubbon Park) Dine alfresco on Fava's canopy-covered decking, feasting on large plates of delectable dishes like duck leg confit, fish kebabs or something from the organic menu. The fixed-price Med lunch is great value at ₹475/570 for two/three courses.

Sunny's
ITALIAN $$$

(☑080-41329366; www.sunnysbangalore.in; 50 Lavelle Rd; mains ₹350-730; ⊙12.30-11.30pm; 🖥) A well-established fixture on Bengaluru's restaurant scene, classy Sunny's has a lovely terrace for alfresco dining. On the menu you'll find authentic thin-crust pizzas, homemade pastas, imported cheese and some of the best desserts in the city.

FOOD STREET

For a local eating experience, head to VV Puram, aka **Food Street** (Sajjan Rao Circle, VV Puram; meals from ₹100; ⊙from 5.30pm), with its strip of hole-in-the-wall eateries cooking up classic street-food dishes from across India. It's quite a spectacle, with rotis being handmade and spun in the air and *bhajia* (vegetable fritters) dunked into hot oil before packed crowds.

It's an all-vegetarian affair with a range of dosas, *idli* (fermented rice cake), Punjabi-style snacks and curries.

Other Areas

Mavalli Tiffin Rooms
SOUTH INDIAN $

(MTR; ☑080-22220022; www.mavallitiffinrooms.com; 14 Lalbagh Rd; snacks from ₹50, meals from ₹130; ⊙6.30-11am & 12.30-9.30pm, closed Mon) A legendary name in South Indian comfort food, this super-popular eatery has had Bengaluru eating out of its hands since 1924. Head to the dining room upstairs, queue for a table, and then admire the images of southern beauties etched on smoky glass as waiters bring you delicious *idlis* (fermented rice cakes) and dosas (savoury crêpes), capped by frothing filter coffee served in silverware.

Gramin
INDIAN $

(☑080-41104104; 20, 7th Block, Raheja Arcade, Koramangala; mains ₹136-180; ⊙12.30-11pm) Translating to 'from the village', Gramin offers a wide choice of flavourful rural North Indian fare at this cosy, eclectic all-veg place. Try the excellent range of lentils and curries with oven-fresh rotis, accompanied by sweet rose-flavoured lassi served in a copper vessel. The lunchtime thali (₹136) is always a good bet. Between 3.30pm and 7pm there's a limited snack menu.

Fatty Bao
ASIAN $$$

(☑080-44114499; www.facebook.com/thefatty bao; 610 12th Main Rd, Indiranagar; mains ₹380-650; ⊙noon-3pm & 7-10.30pm; 🖥; ⓂIndiranagar) This hip rooftop restaurant serves up Asian hawker food to a crowd of fashionable, young foodies in a vibrant setting with colourful chairs and wooden bench tables. There's ramen, Thai curries and Malaysian street food, as well as Asian-inspired cocktails such as lemongrass mojitos.

🍷 Drinking & Nightlife

Bengaluru's rock-steady reputation and wide choice of chic watering holes makes it the place to indulge in a spirited session of pub-hopping in what's the original beer town of India. Many microbreweries have sprung up in the past few years, producing quality ales. All serve food too.

The trendiest nightclubs will typically charge a cover of around ₹1000 per couple, but it's often redeemable against drinks or food.

Lassi Shop
CAFE

(41 Church St; drinks ₹30-90; ☺noon-midnight; 🎧) Kitsch-kool cafe on two levels run by a couple of enthusiasts that's perfect for lassis, mocktails and cold-pressed juices: try the ABC (apple, beetroot and carrot). There's ample lounge seating so you can spread out, plus a few streetside tables too.

blueFROG
CLUB, BAR

(www.bluefrog.co.in; 3 Church St; ☺noon-11pm Sun-Thu, to 12.30am Fri & Sat; Ⓜ MG Rd) Upmarket club that draws a hip, lively crowd with

its fine roster of house, techno and trance DJs and live bands. Entrance is free to ₹500 depending on the night.

13th Floor
BAR

(13th fl, Barton Centre, 84 MG Rd; ☺5-11pm Sun-Thu, to 1am Fri & Sat; 🎧) Forget your superstitions and head up to 13th Floor's terrace, with all of Bengaluru glittering at your feet. There's an excellent selection of martini, sangria and mojito combinations. Happy hour is 5pm to 7pm.

Dyu Art Cafe
CAFE

(www.dyuartcafe.yolasite.com; 23 MIG, KHB Colony, Koramangala; ☺10am-10.30pm; 🎧) An atmospheric cafe-gallery in a leafy neighbourhood with a peaceful courtyard reminiscent of a Zen temple. It has coffee beans from Kerala and does good French press, espresso and iced coffee, to go with homemade cakes, sandwiches and mains.

Monkey Bar
PUB

(14/1 Wood St, Ashoknagar; ☺noon-11pm; 🎧) Gastropub that draws a mixed, jovial crowd knocking back drinks around the bar or at wooden booth seating. Otherwise head

BENGALURU'S MICROBREWERIES

Arbor Brewing Company (www.arborbrewing.com/locations/india; 8 Magrath Rd; ☺noon-12.30am Sun-Thu, to 1am Fri & Sat; 🎧) This classic brewpub was one of the first microbreweries to get the craft beer barrel rolling in Bengaluru. Choose from stout, porter, IPA, Belgian beers, spiced, sour and fruit beers.

Toit Brewpub (www.toit.in; 298 100 Feet Rd, Indiranagar; ☺noon-11.30pm Mon-Tue, to 12.30am Wed, Thu & Sun, to 1am Fri & Sat; 🎧) A brick-walled gastropub split over three levels where lively punters sample its quality beers brewed on-site, including two seasonals and a wheat beer on tap. Sample six beers for ₹220.

Vapour (www.vapour.in; 773 100 Feet Rd, Indiranagar; ☺noon-11.30pm; 🎧) Multilevel complex divided into several bars and restaurants, though its highlight is the rooftop with big screen to enjoy its six microbrews, including a rice beer and guest ale.

Prost (www.prost.in; 811 5th Cross Rd, Koramangala; ☺noon-11.30pm Sun-Thu, to 1am Fri & Sat; 🎧) Prost has eclectic industrial decor, a rooftop with several quality craft beers on tap and a tempting food menu. Things kick off on weekend evenings with DJs and dancing.

Brewsky (www.brewsky.in; 4th & 5th Fl Goenka Chambers, 19th Main Rd, JP Nagar; ☺noon-12.30am; 🎧) A very cool spot, with city views from its fine roof terrace, a mezzanine terrace and a funky restaurant with vintage decor. It brews six beers on-site including a golden ale, wheat beer and stout. Tasty 'small bites' and substantial sharing platters are good value.

Biere Club (www.thebiereclub.com; 20/2 Vittal Mallya Rd; ☺11am-11pm Sun-Thu, to midnight Fri & Sat; 🎧) Beer lovers rejoice as South India's first microbrewery serves up handcrafted beers on tap, some of which are brewed on-site. There's plenty on the menu (platters, burgers) to nibble on while you sup.

Barleyz (www.barleyz.com; 100 Feet Rd, Koramangala; ☺11am-11.30pm Sun-Thu, to 1am Fri & Sat; 🎧) A suave rooftop beer garden with potted plants, artificial grass and tables with built-in BBQ grills. Offers free tastings of its six beers, as well as rotating seasonal brews. There's also excellent wood-fired pizza, Indian snacks and Western food.

down to the basement to join the 'party' crew shooting pool, playing foosball and rocking out to bangin' tunes.

Another branch is in **Indiranagar** (925 12th Main Rd; ⏰ noon-11pm, till midnight weekends; 🛜).

Infinitea CAFE
(www.infinitea.in; 2 Shah Sultan Complex, Cunningham Rd; pot of tea from ₹100; ⏰ 11am-11pm; 🛜) This smart yet homely place has an impressive menu including orthodox teas from the best estates, and a few fancy selections. Their food (soups, salads, smoked chicken wings) also scores highly and they sell loose tea by the gram.

Atta Galatta CAFE
(☑ 080-41600677; www.attagalatta.com; 134, KHB Colony, 5th Block, Koramangala; 11am-8.30pm; 🛜) This fine cafe and bakery offers good sandwiches on nutritious bread, cookies and snacks and also doubles as a bookshop and art venue, hosting readings and performances.

Plan B PUB
(20 Castle St, Ashoknagar; ⏰ 11am-11.30pm Sun-Thu, to 1am Fri & Sat; 🛜) This popular student hang-out has 3.5L beer towers, a long cocktail list and is famous for its chicken wings (six for ₹215) which are half-price on Tuesdays.

Also runs industrial-chic gastropub **Plan B Loaded** (https://holycowhospitality.com; 13 Rhenius St, Richmond Town; mains ₹295-475; ⏰ noon-1am; 🛜).

Shiro BAR
(www.shiro.co.in; UB City, 24 Vittal Mallya Rd; ⏰ 12.30-11.30pm Sun-Thu, to 1am Fri & Sat; 🛜) A sophisticated lounge to get sloshed in style, Shiro has elegant interiors complemented by the monumental Buddha busts and *apsara* (celestial nymph) figurines. There's also outdoor deck seating. Has good Japanese food and its 'Special Shiro' cocktails are the bomb.

☆ Entertainment

Humming Tree LIVE MUSIC
(☑ 9945532828; www.facebook.com/thehumming tree; 12th Main Rd, Indiranagar; ⏰ 11am-11.30pm Sun-Thu, to 1am Fri & Sat; Ⓜ Indiranagar) This popular warehouse-style venue has bands (starting around 9pm), DJs and a rooftop terrace. Cover charge is anything from free to ₹300. There's a good finger food menu and happy hour until 7pm.

Ranga Shankara THEATRE
(☑ 080-26592777; www.rangashankara.org; 36/2 8th Cross, JP Nagar) All kinds of interesting theatre (in a variety of languages and spanning various genres) and dance are held at this cultural centre. Hosts an annual minifestival in late October/early November.

M Chinnaswamy Stadium SPECTATOR SPORT
(www.ksca.cricket; MG Rd; Ⓜ Cubbon Park) A mecca for cricket lovers, hosting many matches per year. Check online for upcoming schedule of tests, one-dayers and Twenty20s.

B Flat LIVE MUSIC
(☑ 080-41739250; www.facebook.com/thebflat bar; 776 100 Feet Rd, Indiranagar; cover charge ₹300; ⏰ 11am-3pm & 7pm-1am; Ⓜ Indiranagar) A pub and live music venue that features some of India's best blues and jazz bands.

Indigo Live Music Bar LIVE MUSIC
(☑ 080-25535330; www.facebook.com/IndigoLive MusicBar; 5/6th fl, Elite Bldg, Jyoti Nivas College Rd, Koramangala; 5-11pm Sun-Thu, to 1am Fri & Sat) Hosting bands, DJs, acoustic musicians and even stand-up comedy this popular spot is always lively. On the upper (6th floor) there's a large terrace for dining and lounging.

🛍 Shopping

Bengaluru's shopping options are abundant, ranging from teeming bazaars to glitzy malls. Some good shopping areas include Commercial St, Vittal Mallya Rd and the MG Rd area.

★ Mysore Saree Udyog CLOTHING
(www.mysoresareeudyog.com; 1st fl, 316 Kamaraj Rd; ⏰ 10.30am-8.30pm) A great choice for top-quality silk saris, blouses, fabrics and men's shirts, this fine store has been in business for over 70 years and has something to suit all budgets. Most garments are made with Mysuru silk. Also stocks 100% *pashmina* (wool shawls).

Cauvery Arts & Crafts Emporium GIFTS & SOUVENIRS
(45 MG Rd; ⏰ 10am-8pm; Ⓜ MG Rd) Government-run store famous for its expansive collection of quality sandalwood and rosewood products as well as handmade weavings, silks and bidriware (metallic handicrafts). Fixed prices.

Forest Essentials COSMETICS
(www.forestessentialsindia.com; 4/1 Lavelle Junction Bldg, Vittal Mallya Rd; ⏰ 10am-9pm) High-end natural beauty products including

ⓘ WHAT'S ON, BENGALURU?

The following cover all the latest restaurant openings, cultural events, nightlife and shopping in the city:

➡ Time Out Bengaluru (www.timeout.com/bangalore)

➡ What's Up Bangalore (www.whatsupguides.com)

➡ Explocity (https://bangalore.explocity.com)

potions and lotions for hair, face and body as well as all-organic ayurvedic essential oils.

Fabindia   CLOTHING, HOMEWARES
(Garuda Mall, Magrath Rd; ⊙10am-8pm) Hugely successful chain with a range of stylish traditional clothing, homewares and accessories in traditional cotton prints and silks. Quality skincare products too.

Branches at **Commercial Street** (152 Commercial St; ⊙10am-8.30pm), **MG Road** (www.fabindia.com; 1 MG Rd, Lido Mall, Kensington Rd; ⊙10.30am-9pm; Ⓜ Trinity) and **Koramangala** (www.fabindia.com; 54 17th Main Rd; ⊙10am-8pm).

★ Kynkyny Art Gallery   ART
(www.kynkyny.com; Embassy Sq, 148 Infantry Rd; ⊙10am-7pm Mon-Sat; Ⓜ Cubbon Park) A sophisticated commercial gallery inside a stunning colonial-era building with works by contemporary Indian artists, priced suitably for all budgets. Also sells outstanding designer furniture.

Goobe's Book Republic   BOOKS
(www.goobes.wordpress.com; 11 Church St; ⊙10.30am-9pm Mon-Sat, noon-9pm Sun) Great little bookshop selling new and secondhand, cult and mainstream books and comics. Run by informed, helpful staff.

Garuda Mall   MALL
(www.garudamall.in; McGrath Rd; ⊙10am-10pm, to 10.30pm Fri & Sat) A modern mall in central Bengaluru with a wide selection of clothing chains and a multiplex Inox cinema.

UB City   MALL
(www.ubcitybangalore.in; 24 Vittal Mallya Rd; ⊙10.30am-10pm) Global haute couture (Louis Vuitton, Jimmy Choo, Burberry) and Indian high fashion come to roost at this towering mall in the central district. Also boasts good restaurants and a spa.

Forum   MALL
(www.theforumexperience.com/forumbangalore.htm; Hosur Rd, Koramangala; ⊙10am-11pm) Shiny mall complex in the happening district of Koramangala with lots of fashion stores and a cinema.

Gangarams Book Bureau   BOOKS
(www.facebook.com/Gangaramsbookbureau; 3rd fl, 48 Church St; ⊙10am-8pm Mon-Sat) Excellent selection of Indian titles, guidebooks and Penguin classics. Has knowledgeable staff and author-signing sessions.

Indiana Crockery   HOMEWARES
(97/1 MG Rd; ⊙10.30am-9pm) Good spot to buy thali trays, brass utensils and chai cups for that dinner party back home.

Blossom Book House   BOOKS
(www.blossombookhouse.com; 84/6 Church St; ⊙10.30am-9.30pm; Ⓜ MG Rd) Great deals on new and secondhand books.

ⓘ Orientation

Finding your way around Bengaluru can be difficult at times. In certain areas, roads are named after their widths (eg 80 Feet Rd). The city also follows a system of mains and crosses: 3rd Cross, 5th Main, Residency Rd, for example, refers to the third lane on the fifth street branching off Residency Rd. New affluent pockets are springing up across the city, including the ritzy suburbs of Indirangar, JP Nagar, Koramangala and Whitefield – all with Western-style malls, nightlife and restaurants.

ⓘ Information

LEFT LUGGAGE

The City train station and Kempegowda bus stand have 24-hour cloakrooms (per day ₹15). You need a valid journey ticket and proof of ID. Your bag must be locked.

MEDICAL SERVICES

Hosmat (☑080-25593796; www.hosmatnet.com; 45 Magrath Rd) Hospital for critical injuries and general illnesses.

Mallya Hospital (☑080-22277979; www.mallyahospital.net; 2 Vittal Mallya Rd) Emergency services and 24-hour pharmacy.

MONEY

ATMs are everywhere, as are moneychangers around MG Rd.

TT Forex (☑080-22254337; 33/1 Cunningham Rd; ⊙9.30am-6.30pm Mon-Fri, 9.30am-1.30pm Sat) Changes travellers cheques and foreign currency.

TOURIST INFORMATION

Government of India Tourist Office (GITO; ☑ 080-25585417; indtourblr@dataone.in; 2nd level, 48 Church St; ⊙9.30am-6pm Mon-Fri, 9.30am-1pm Sat; M MG Rd) Very helpful for Bengaluru and beyond.

Karnataka State Tourism Development Corporation (KSTDC; ☑ 080-41329211; www. kstdc.co; Karnataka Tourism House, 8 Papanna Lane, St Mark's Rd; ⊙10am-7pm Mon-Sat; M MG Rd) Bookings can be made for KSTDC city and state tours.

Karnataka State Tourism Development Corporation (KSTDC; ☑ 080-43344334; www.kstdc.co; Badami House, Kasturba Rd; ⊙10am-7pm Mon-Sat) Useful office just south of Cubbon Park.

TRAVEL AGENCIES

Skyway (☑ 080-22111401; www.skywaytour. com; 8 Papanna Lane, St Mark's Rd; ⊙9am-6pm Mon-Sat) Thoroughly professional and reliable outfit for booking long-distance taxis and air tickets.

ⓘ Getting There & Away

AIR

International and domestic flights arrive at Bengaluru's **Kempegowda International Airport** (☑ 1800 4254425; www.bengaluruairport.com), about 40km north from the MG Rd area. Domestic flights also leave here with daily connections to major cities including Chennai (Madras), Mumbai (Bombay), Hyderabad, Delhi and Goa. Carriers include:

Air India (☑ 080-22978427; www.airindia.com; Unity Bldg, JC Rd; ⊙10am-5pm Mon-Sat)

GoAir (☑ 080-47406091; www.goair.in; Bengaluru Airport)

IndiGo (☑ 9910383838; www.goindigo.in)

Jet Airways (☑ 080-39893333; www.jetairways.com; Unity Bldg, JC Rd; ⊙9.30am-6pm Mon-Sat)

BUS

Bengaluru's huge, well-organised **Kempegowda bus stand** (Majestic; Gubbi Thotadappa Rd), also commonly known as both the Majestic and Central, is directly in front of the City train station. Karnataka State Road Transport Corporation (KSRTC; www.ksrtc.in) buses run to destinations in Karnataka and neighbouring states.

Mysuru Road Satellite Bus Stand (Mysuru Rd) 8km southwest of the centre is another important terminal: most KSRTC buses to Mysuru, Mangaluru (Mangalore) and other destinations southwest of Bengaluru leave from here as does the Flybus to Bengaluru airport.

The KSRTC website lists current schedules and fares. Booking online isn't always possible using international credit cards, but travel agents can. Book long-distance journeys in advance.

Private bus operators line the street facing Kempegowda bus stand.

TRAIN

Bengaluru's **City train station** (www.bangalorecityrailwaystation.in; Gubbi Thotadappa Rd) is the main train hub. There's also **Cantonment train station** (Station Rd), a sensible spot to disembark if you're arriving and headed for the MG Rd area, while **Yeshvantpur train station** (Rahman Khan Rd), 8km northwest of downtown, is the starting point for trains to Goa.

The computerised **reservation office** (☑ 139; ⊙8am-8pm Mon-Sat, to 2pm Sun) has separate counters for credit card purchase, women and foreigners. Head to the **Divisional Railway Office** (Gubbi Thotadappa Rd) for last-minute reservations. Luggage can be left at the 24-hour cloakroom on Platform 1 at the City train station.

MAJOR BUSES FROM BENGALURU (BANGALORE)

DESTINATION	FARE (₹)	DURATION (HR)	DEPARTURES
Chennai	398 (R)/491 (V)/693 (S)	6-7	25 daily, 5.35am-11.30pm
Ernakulam	619 (R)/1139 (V)	10-12	7 daily, 4pm-9.45pm
Hampi	629 (R)	7½	1 daily, 11pm
Hosapete	334 (R)/599 (V)/696 (S)	8	17 daily, 4.30pm-11.30pm
Hyderabad	713 (R)/989 (V)/1190 (S)	9-11	27 daily, 7.30am-11.30pm
Mumbai	1383 (V)	18	3 daily, 3pm-8pm
Mysuru*	123 (R)/299 (V)	2-3	51 daily, 24hr
Ooty*	639-839 (V)	7-9½	9 daily, 6.15am-11.15pm
Panaji	919 (V)1800 (S)	11-13	5 daily, 6.30pm-8.30pm
Gokana	549 (R) 789 (V) 882 (S)	9-11½	4 daily, from 8.30pm-10.15pm

Fares: (R) Rajahamsa Semideluxe, (V) Airavath AC Volvo, (S) AC Sleeper
*leave from Mysuru Rd Satellite Bus Stand.

ℹ Getting Around

TO/FROM THE AIRPORT

Metered AC taxis from the airport to the centre cost between ₹750 and ₹1000, while Uber/Ola cab rates are around ₹500 to ₹600; these rates include the ₹120 airport toll charge.

Flybus (www.ksrtc.in) KSRTC runs the Flybus to/from Mysuru (₹739, four hours) departing the airport 10 times daily, it travels via the Mysuru Rd Satellite Bus Stand.

Vayu Vajra (☑ 1800 4251663; www.mybmtc.com) Vayu Vajra's airport shuttle service has regular AC buses to destinations including Kempegowda (Majestic) bus stand, MG Rd and Indiranagar departing 24 hours.

AUTORICKSHAW

Very few autorickshaw drivers use meters but if yours does 50% is added to the metered rate after 10pm.

BUS

Bengaluru has a comprehensive local bus network, operated by the Bangalore Metropolitan Transport Corporation (BMTC; www.mybmtc.com), with a useful website for timetables and fares. Red AC Vajra buses criss-cross the city, while green Big10 deluxe buses connect the suburbs. Ordinary buses run from the **City bus stand** (Sayyali Rao Rd), next to Kempegowda bus stand; a few operate from the City Market bus stand further south.

To get from the City train station to the MG Rd area, catch any bus from Platform 17 or 18 at the City bus stand. For the City Market, take bus 31, 31E, 35 or 49 from Platform 8.

METRO

Bengaluru's shiny new AC metro service, known as Namma Metro, is still a work in progress, but it does have two lines up and running. There was *no* interchange between the two, despite what the official maps indicate, at the time of research. The most relevant route to tourists is the Purple Line, which runs east–west: useful stops include Kempegowda (for the bus terminal), MG Rd (for shopping and bars) and Indiranagar (for restaurants and nightlife). Trains run about every 15 minutes, 6am to 10pm, and tickets are priced at ₹10 to ₹22 for most journeys. For the latest updates on the service, log on to www.bmrc.co.in.

TAXI

There are thousands of Uber and Ola drivers in Bengaluru. To hire a conventional cab for a day allow around ₹2000 for eight hours.

Meru Cabs (☑ 080-44224422; www.merucabs.com) Available at the airport.

Olacabs (☑ 080-33553355; www.olacabs.com) Professional, efficient company with modern air-con cars. Online and phone bookings.

Around Bengaluru

Hesaraghatta

☑ 080 / POP 9200

Located 30km northwest of Bengaluru, the small town of Hesaraghatta is home to Nrityagram, a leading dance academy.

◉ Sights

Nrityagram   ARTS CENTRE
(☑ 080-28466313; www.nrityagram.org; self-guided tour ₹50, children under 12 free; ⊙ 10am-2pm Tue-Sun) This leading dance academy was established in 1990 to revive and popularise Indian classical dance. The brainchild and living legacy of celebrated dancer Protima Gauri Bedi (1948–98), the complex was designed like a village by Goa-based architect Gerard da

MAJOR TRAINS FROM BENGALURU (BANGALORE)

DESTINATION	TRAIN NO & NAME	FARE (₹)	DURATION (HR)	DEPARTURES
Chennai	12658 Chennai Mail	255/910	6	10.40pm
Chennai	12028 Shatabdi	785/1060	5	6am & 4.25pm Wed-Mon
Hosapete	16592 Hampi Exp	255/970	9½	10pm
Hubballi	16589 Rani Chennamma Exp	270/1045	8½	9.15pm
Madgaon, Goa	17311 Mas Vasco Exp	360/1405	15	8.10pm Fri
Mysuru	12007 Shatabdi	300/835	2	11am Thu-Tue
Mysuru	12614 Tippu Exp	90/310	2½	3pm
Trivandrum	16526 Kanyakumari Exp	410/1605	16½	8pm

Fares: Shatabdi fares are AC chair/AC executive; Express (Exp/Mail) fares are 2nd-class/AC chair for day trains and sleeper/2AC for night trains.

WHISKY & WINE

In a country not known for being a big exponent of fine wines and liquors (anyone who has stepped foot into one of India's ubiquitous 'wine shops' can attest to this), Bengaluru is very much an exception to the rule. It's a city that's not only gained a thirst for craft beer, but has on its doorstep one of India's premier wine-growing regions in **Nandi Hills** (per person ₹10, car ₹150; ⊙6am-6pm). While an emerging industry, it's fast gaining a reputation internationally with some 18 wineries in the area. Also a few clicks out of town is India's first single-malt whisky distillery, which allows tastings.

Grover Wineries (✆080-27622826; www.groverzampa.in; 1½hr tour Mon-Fri ₹850, Sat & Sun ₹1000) At an altitude of at 920m this winery produces quality white and red varietals. Tours include tastings of five wines in the cellar rooms accompanied by cheese and crackers, followed by lunch. From February to May you'll also see grape crushing and can visit its vineyards. It's located on the approach to Nandi Hills, around 40km north of Bengaluru.

Amrut (✆080-23100402; www.amrutdistilleries.com; Mysuru Rd) **FREE** Established in 1948, Amrut, India's first producer of single malt whisky, offers free distillery tours run by knowledgeable guides. You get taken through the entire process before tasting its world-class single malts and blends. It's 20km outside Bengaluru on the road to Mysuru; prebookings essential.

Cunha. Long-term courses in classical dance are offered here to deserving students, while local children are taught for free on Sundays. Check their website for upcoming performances (₹1000 per person).

You can also book a tour package that includes a guided tour, lecture, dance demonstration and vegetarian meal (per person ₹1500 to ₹2000, minimum 10 people, advance booking required).

🛌 Sleeping

Taj Kuteeram HOTEL $$$
(✆080-28466326; www.tajhotels.com; d from ₹4660; ❈@⚛) Opposite Nrityagram dance village, Kuteeram isn't as luxurious as other Taj Group hotel offerings, but it's still atmospheric with a balance of comfort and rustic charm, and designs by Gerard da Cunha. It also offers ayurveda and yoga sessions.

ℹ Getting There & Away

From Bengaluru's City Market, buses 266, 253 and 253E run to Hesaraghatta (₹26, one hour), with bus 266 continuing on to Nrityagram. From Hesaraghatta an autorickshaw will cost ₹75 to Nrityagram.

Janapada Loka Folk Arts Museum

Janapada Loka Folk Arts Museum MUSEUM
(www.jaanapadaloka.org; Bengaluru-Mysuru Rd; Indian/foreigner ₹20/100; ⊙9am-5.30pm Wed-Mon)

A worthwhile stopover between Bengaluru and Mysuru, this museum is dedicated to the preservation of rural local culture. It has a wonderful collection of folk-art objects, including 500-year-old shadow puppets, festival costumes, musical instruments, a superb temple chariot and a replica of a traditional village. There's also a children's playground. It's situated 53km south of Bengaluru, 3km from Ramnagar; any Mysuru–Bengaluru bus can drop you here.

Mysuru (Mysore)

✆0821 / POP 912,000 / ELEV 707M
The historic settlement of Mysuru (which changed its name from Mysore in 2014) is one of South India's most enchanting cities, famed for its glittering royal heritage and magnificent monuments and buildings. Its World Heritage–listed palace brings most travellers here, but Mysuru is also rich in tradition with a deeply atmospheric bazaar district littered with spice stores and incense stalls. Ashtanga yoga (p190) is another drawcard and there are several acclaimed schools which attract visitors from across the globe.

History

Mysuru owes its name to the mythical Mahisuru, a place where the demon Mahisasura was slain by the goddess Chamundi. Its regal history began in 1399, when the Wodeyar dynasty of Mysuru was founded, though they remained in service of the Vijayanagar empire until the mid-16th century. With the fall of Vijayanagar in 1565, the Wodeyars declared their sovereignty, which – save for a brief period of Hyder Ali and Tipu Sultan's supremacy in the late 18th century – remained unscathed until Independence in 1947.

◉ Sights

Mysuru isn't known as the City of Palaces for nothing, being home to a total of seven and an abundance of majestic heritage architecture dating from the Wodeyar dynasty and British rule. The majority of grand buildings are owned by the state, and used as anything from hospitals, colleges and government buildings to heritage hotels. Visit www.karnatakatourism.org/Mysore/en for a list of notable buildings.

★ Mysuru Palace   PALACE
(Maharaja's Palace; www.mysorepalace.gov.in; Purandara Dasa Rd; Indian/foreigner/child under 10 incl audio guide ₹40/200/free; ⊘10am-5.30pm) Among the grandest of India's royal buildings, this was the seat of the Wodeyar maharajas. The original palace was gutted by fire in 1897; the one you see today was completed in 1912 by English architect Henry Irwin for ₹4.5 million. The lavish Indo-Saracenic interior – a kaleidoscope of stained glass, mirrors and gaudy colours – is undoubtedly over the top. It's further embellished by carved wooden doors, mosaic floors and a series of paintings depicting life here during the Edwardian Raj era.

The way into the palace takes you past a fine collection of sculptures and artefacts. Don't forget to check out the armoury, with an intriguing collection of 700-plus weapons.

Every Sunday and national holiday, from 7pm to 7.30pm, the palace is illuminated by nearly 100,000 light bulbs that accent its majestic profile against the night.

Entrance to the palace grounds is at the South Gate (Purandara Dasa Rd). While you are allowed to snap the palace's exterior, photography within is strictly prohibited.

Devaraja Market   MARKET
(Sayyaji Rao Rd; ⊘6am-8.30pm) Dating from Tipu Sultan's reign, this lively bazaar has local traders selling traditional items such as flower garlands, spices and conical piles of *kumkum* (coloured powder used for bindi dots), all of which makes for some great photo ops. Refresh your bargaining skills before shopping.

Jaganmohan Palace   PALACE
(Jaganmohan Palace Rd; adult/child ₹120/30; ⊘8.30am-5pm) Built in 1861 as the royal auditorium, this stunning palace just west of the Mysuru Palace now houses the Jayachamarajendra Art Gallery. Set over three floors it has a huge collection of Indian paintings, including works by noted artist Raja Ravi Varma, traditional Japanese art and some rare musical instruments. However, presentation is poor and the building is sadly neglected.

Rail Museum   MUSEUM
(KRS Rd; adult/child ₹15/10, camera/video ₹20/30; ⊘9.30am-6pm) This open-air museum's main exhibit is the Mysuru maharani's saloon, a wood-panelled beauty dating from 1899 that provides an insight into the stylish way in which the royals once rode the railways. There are also steam engines, locomotives and carriages to investigate. A toy train (₹10) rides the track around the museum.

Jayalakshmi Vilas
Mansion Museum Complex   MUSEUM
(Mysore University Campus; ⊘10am-1pm & 3-5pm Tue-Sun) FREE On the university campus west

---

MYSURU (MYSORE) COLONIAL-ERA ARCHITECTURE

Mysuru's colonial heritage is considerable, with numerous grand edifices and quirky reminders to investigate. Dating from 1805, Government House (Irwin Rd), formerly the British Residency, is a Tuscan Doric building set in 20 hectares of gardens. Facing the north gate of Mysuru Palace is the 1927 Silver Jubilee Clock Tower (Dodda Gadiara; Ashoka Rd). The beauty of towering St Philomena's Cathedral (St Philomena St; ⊘8am-5pm), built between 1933 and 1941 in neo-Gothic style, is emphasised by wonderful stained-glass windows. Wellington Lodge is an unassuming early colonial landmark which today houses a museum: Indira Gandhi Rashtriya Manav Sangrahalaya (National Museum of Mankind; www.igrms.com; Wellington Lodge, Irwin Rd; ⊘10am-5.30pm Tue-Sun) FREE.

DUSSEHRA

Mysuru is at its carnivalesque best during the 10-day Dussehra (Dasara; ⊙ Sep/Oct) festival held in September or October. During this time the Mysuru Palace is dramatically lit up every evening, while the town is transformed into a gigantic fairground, with concerts, dance performances, sporting demonstrations and cultural events running to packed houses.

On the last day the celebrations are capped off in grand style. A dazzling procession of richly costumed elephants, garlanded idols, liveried retainers and cavalry march through the streets to the rhythms of clanging brass bands.

Mysuru is chock-a-block with tourists during the festival, especially on the final day. To bypass suffocating crowds, consider buying a Dasara VIP Gold Card (₹7500 for two adults). Only 1000 are available, and though expensive, it assures you good seats at the final day gala and helps you beat the entry queues at other events, while providing discounts on accommodation, dining and shopping. It's also possible to buy tickets (₹250 to ₹1000) just for entering the palace and Bannimantap for the final day's parades.

---

of town, this museum specialises in folklore, with artefacts, stone tablets and sculptures, including rural costumes and a wooden puppet of the 10-headed demon king Ravana. The building itself (restored in 2006) was originally built as a mansion for Princess Jayalakshmi Ammani, the eldest daughter of the Maharaja Chamaraja Wodeyar.

Chamundi Hill VIEWPOINT
This 1062m hill is crowned with the Sri Chamundeswari Temple (http://chamundeswaritemple.kar.nic.in; ⊙ 7am-2pm, 3.30-6pm & 7.30-9pm). It's a fine half-day excursion, offering spectacular views of the city below. Queues are long at weekends, so visit during the week. From Central bus stand take bus 201 (₹28; AC); a return autorickshaw/Uber trip is around ₹450/700.

Alternatively, you can take the foot trail comprising 1000-plus steps that Hindu pilgrims use to visit the temple. One-third of the way down is a 5m-high statue of Nandi (Shiva's bull) that was carved out of solid rock in 1659.

Mysuru Zoo ZOO
(http://mysorezoo.info; Indiranagar; adult/child Mon-Fri ₹50/20, Sat & Sun ₹60/30, camera ₹20; ⊙ 8.30am-5.30pm Wed-Mon) A well-managed zoo set in pretty gardens. Highlights include white tigers, lowland gorillas, giraffes and rhinos. It's situated around 2km southeast of Mysuru Palace.

🏃 Activities

Emerge Spa AYURVEDA, MASSAGE
(☑ 0821-2522500; www.thewindflower.com; Windflower Spa & Resort, Maharanapratap Rd, Nazarbad;

massages from ₹2275; ⊙ 7am-9pm) Wonderful resort spa offering over 30 ayurvedic treatments including hot-stone massages and pampering rituals. Day packages include access to the hotel pool. It's located 3km southeast of Mysuru Palace; rates include pick-up and drop-off.

Indus Valley Ayurvedic Centre AYURVEDA
(☑ 0821-2473263; www.ayurindus.com; Lalithadripura) Set on 10 hectares of gardens, this classy centre derives its therapies from ancient scriptures and prescriptions. The overnight package (single/double including full board from US$180/310) includes one session each of ayurveda, yoga and beauty therapy.

🎵 Courses

Shruthi Musical Works MUSIC
(☑ 9845249518; 1189 3rd Cross, Irwin Rd; per hr ₹400; ⊙ 10.30am-9pm Mon-Sat, to 2pm Sun) Music teacher Jayashankar gets good reviews for his tabla (drum) instruction.

☞ Tours

★ Royal Mysore Walks WALKING, TOURS
(☑ 9632044188; www.royalmysorewalks.com; from ₹500) An excellent way to familiarise yourself with Mysuru's epic history and heritage. Offers a range of weekend walks (themes include royal history and food) as well as cycle and jeep tours.

KSTDC Transport Office BUS
(☑ 080-43344334; www.kstdc.co; city tour ₹210) KSTDC runs a daily Mysuru city tour, taking in city sights (excluding the palace), Chamundi Hill, Srirangapatna and Brindavan

Mysuru Palace

A HALF-DAY TOUR

The interior of Mysuru Palace houses opulent halls, royal paintings, intricate decorative details, as well as sculptures and ceremonial objects. There is a lot of hidden detail and much to take in, so be sure to allow yourself at least a few hours for the experience. A guide can also be invaluable.

After entering the palace the first exhibit is the ❶ **Doll's Pavilion**, which showcases the maharaja's fine collection of traditional dolls and sculptures acquired from around the world. Opposite the ❷ **Elephant Gate** you'll see the seven cannons that were used for special occasions, such as the birthdays of the maharajas. Today the cannons are still fired as part of Dasara festivities.

At the end of the Doll's Pavilion you'll find the ❸ **Golden Howdah**. Note the fly whisks on either side; the bristles are made from fine ivory.

Make sure you check out the paintings depicting the Dasara procession in the halls on your way to the ❹ **Marriage Pavilion** and look into the courtyard to see what was once the wrestling arena. It's now used during Dasara only. In the Marriage Pavilion, take a few minutes to scan the entire space. You can see the influence of three religions in the design of the hall: the glass ceiling represents Christianity, stone carvings along the hallway ceilings are Hindu design and the top-floor balcony roof (the traditional ladies' gallery) has Islamic-style arches.

When you move through to the ❺ **Private Durbar Hall**, take note of the intricate ivory inlay motifs depicting Krishna in the rosewood doors. The ❻ **Public Durbar Hall** is usually the last stop where you can admire the panoramic views of the gardens through the Islamic arches.

Private Durbar Hall
Rosewood doors lead into this hall, which is richly decorated with stained-glass ceilings, steel grill work and chandeliers. It houses the Golden Throne, only on display to the public during Dasara.

Entry to the Palace

Doll's Pavilion
The first exhibit, the Doll's Pavilion, displays the gift collection of 19th- and early-20th-century dolls, statues and Hindu idols that were given to the maharaja by dignitaries from around the world.

Public Durbar Hall

The open-air hall contains a priceless collection of paintings by Raja Ravi Varma and opens into an expansive balcony supported by massive pillars with an ornate painted ceiling of 10 incarnations of Vishnu.

Marriage Pavilion

This lavish hall used for royal weddings features themes of Christianity, Hindu and Islam in its design. The highlight is the octagonal painted glass ceiling featuring peacock motifs, the bronze chandelier and the colonnaded turquoise pillars.

Elephant Gate

Next to the Doll's Pavilion, this brass gate has four bronze elephants inlaid at the bottom, an intricate double-headed eagle up the top and a hybrid lion-elephant creature (the state emblem of Karnataka) in the centre.

Golden Howdah

At the far end of the Doll's Pavilion, a wooden elephant howdah decorated with 80kg of gold was used to carry the maharaja in the Dasara festival. It now carries the idol of goddess Chamundeswari.

Mysuru (Mysore)

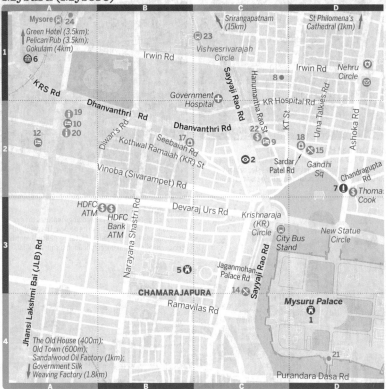

Mysuru (Mysore)

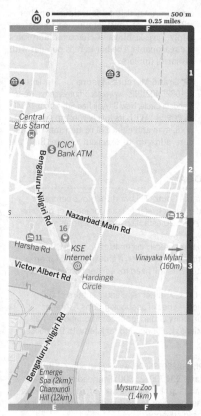

Central
Bus Stand

ICICI
Bank ATM

Bengaluru-Nilgiri Rd

Nazarbad Main Rd

Harsha Rd

KSE
Internet
@

Victor Albert Rd

Hardinge
Circle

Vinayaka Mylari
(160m)

Bengaluru-Nilgiri Rd

Emerge
Spa (2km);
Chamundi
Hill (12km)

Mysuru Zoo
(1.4km)

Gardens. It starts daily at 8.30am, ends at 8.30pm and is likely to leave you breathless! Other tours go to Belur, Halebid and Sravanabelagola (₹550) on Tuesday and Thursday from 7.30am to 9pm.

All tours leave from the KSTDC transport office (p192) next to Hotel Mayura Hoysala, from where bookings are made, or at travel agencies around town.

🛏 Sleeping

Mysuru attracts tourists throughout the year and can fill up very quickly during Dussehra (p185). Booking early is recommended.

⭐ Mansion 1907 HOSTEL $
(☎ 9886523472; www.facebook.com/themansion 1907; 36 Shalivahana Rd; dm with fan/AC ₹500/600, r from ₹1400; ❄ 🛜) Deservedly popular hostel in a historic house that shows Indian and British architectural influences. It's very well set up, with spacious dorms and private rooms, cool communal areas, good bathrooms, a kitchen and speedy wi-fi. And it's a great place to meet other travellers and plan your next journey.

Sonder HOSTEL $
(www.sonderhostel.com; 66, 3rd Block, Jayalaxmipuram; dm incl breakfast ₹500; ❄ 🛜) Backpackers hostel located about 3km from the centre in a tranquil, leafy suburb not far from many yoga schools. It's a well-designed space with comfy dorms, lockers, board games and books, a kitchen and a friendly vibe. There are regular events like movie nights and cooking classes.

Hotel Maurya HOTEL $
(☎ 0821-2426677; 9/5 Hanumantha Rao St; s/d from ₹195/350; ❄ 🛜) Very centrally located, the Maurya is a good budget choice with a wide range of large, unremarkable but very cheap rooms. It offers more upmarket choices with TV and AC too. The manager and his staff are extremely helpful and welcoming.

Anokhi Garden Guest House GUESTHOUSE $$
(☎ 0821-4288923; www.anokhigarden.com; 408 Contour Rd, 3rd Stage, Gokulam; s/d from ₹2200/3200; 🛜) Very popular with yoga students and young travellers, this homely French-run guesthouse offers neat, tidy rooms in a property which also boasts a lovely garden cafe.

Parklane Hotel HOTEL $$
(☎ 0821-4003500; www.parklanemysore.com; 2720 Harsha Rd; r ₹1755-3267; ❄ @ 🛜 ♨) The Parklane is very well located for the palace and city and represents fine value. Decor is over-the-top kitsch but it's hard to dislike with its massive and immaculate rooms, ultracomfortable and thoughtfully outfitted with mobile-chargers and considerate toiletry kits. Its lively open-air restaurant is always buzzing, and there's a small rooftop pool too.

Mystic School Studios HOTEL $$
(☎ 0821-4288490; www.mysoreyoga.in; 100 3rd Main Rd, Gokulam; r with/without kitchen per month ₹25,000/15,000; ❄ 🛜 ♨) This yoga school offers squeaky-clean rooms with private bathrooms and studios with kitchenettes and balconies. There's a great cafe, Finnish sauna, plunge pool and rooftop chill-out zone.

Urban Oasis HOTEL $$
(☎ 0821-4006332; www.urbanoasis.co.in; 7 Contour Rd, 3rd Stage, Gokulam; r ₹1200-2000, monthly from ₹30,000; ❄ 🛜) More of a business

hotel, but popular with yoga students for its clean, functional and modern rooms with cable TV. There are four price categories from compact single to spacious rooms with balconies and AC.

Hotel Mayura Hoysala HOTEL **$$**
(☎ 0821-2426160; www.karnatakaholidays.net; 2 Jhansi Lakshmi Bai Rd; r incl breakfast with fan/AC from ₹1550/2900; ❊ ☎) Near the train station, the potential of this beautiful historic building remains unrealised. Yes, this gov-

ernment-owned hotel is a timewarp, but is still worthy of consideration as rooms certainly have lashings of character, and rates are reasonable. The bar here is popular with Mysuru's tipplers.

★ **Grand Mercure Mysore** HOTEL **$$$**
(☎ 0821-4021212; www.accorhotels.com; Nelson Mandela Circle, New Sayyaji Rao Rd; r from ₹4940; ❊ @ ☎ ❊) With its lovely rooftop swimming pool, gym and choice of restaurants the Mercure adds up to excellent choice. Staff are

MYSURU (MYSORE) ASHTANGA YOGA

What Rishikesh is to North India, Mysuru is to the South. This world-famous centre for yoga attracts thousands of international students each year to learn, practise or become certified in teaching Ashtanga. There are now over 20 established yoga schools in the city.

For the most part students are required to be austerely committed to the art, and will need at least a month. While in more recent times there's been a growing trend for drop-in classes or week-long courses, long-term students will need to register far in advance, as courses are often booked out.

Most foreign yoga students congregate in the upmarket residential suburb of Gokulam. Several schools now offer accommodation – check Facebook groups Ashtanga Community in Mysore and Mysore Yoga Community Group for accommodation rentals.

Yogis in India no longer need a special student visa or need to register with the police.

Yoga Centres

Ashtanga Yoga Research Institute (AYRI; ☎ 9880185500; www.kpjayi.org; 235 8th Cross, 3rd Stage, Gokulam; 1st/2nd month plus taxes ₹34,700/23,300) Founded by the renowned ashtanga teacher K Pattabhi Jois, who taught Madonna her yoga moves. He has since passed away and the reins have been handed over to his grandson, who is proving very popular. You need to register two months in advance.

IndeaYoga (Ānanda Yoga India; ☎ 0821-2416779; www.indeayoga.com; 144E 7th Main Rd, Gokulam; incl food and lodging US$1999) Offering hatha and ashtanga yoga with guru Bharath Shetty (who practised under the late BKS Iyengar) and his wife Archana. Courses include anatomy and yoga philosophy. Drop-in classes and student accommodation are also offered.

Mystic School (☎ 0821-4288490; www.mysoreyoga.in; 100 3rd A Main Rd, Gokulam; drop-in/1-month yoga classes ₹500/17,000) Well-established school with a diverse program covering hatha and ashtanga, meditation and lectures. Suitable for short- and long-term students at all levels, and has drop-in classes. Reiki and massage courses are also offered. There's accommodation (studios with kitchenettes), sauna, plunge pool and cafe.

Atmavikasa Centre (☎ 0821-2341978; www.atmavikasayoga.com; 18 Rd, 6th Cross, Ramakrishnanagar) Classical hatha yoga school set up by Acharya Venkatesh and Acharye Hema offering training, therapy and workshops. Enjoys a garden setting in a peaceful suburb 5km southwest of the palace.

Yogadarshanam (☎ 0821-2412143; http://yogadarshanam.org; 77/A, 4th Main Rd, 3rd Stage; courses ₹6000-29,600) Classical Indian yoga centre offering classes, teacher training, workshops and retreats. Their one-month foundation course covers the yoga fundamentals and is perfect for beginners.

Yoga Bharata (☎ 0821-4242342; www.yogabharata.com; 1st fl, 810 Contour Rd; 20-class pass ₹4500) Professional centre offering ashtanga, vinyasa, hatha and yoga therapy with experienced teachers. Linked to IndeaYoga. Drop-in classes (₹300) are available.

super attentive and rooms are sleek, well-equipped and have a wide selection of international TV channels. Located 4km north of the city centre.

Royal Orchid Metropole   HERITAGE HOTEL **$$$**
(☑ 0821-4255566; www.royalorchidhotels.com; 5 Jhansi Lakshmi Bai Rd; s/d incl breakfast from ₹6880/7250; ❖ 🐾 ☲) Originally built by the Wodeyars to serve as the residence of the maharaja's British guests, this is undoubtedly one of Mysuru's leading heritage hotels. The charming colonial-era structure has 30 rooms oozing historical character, just with all mod cons. There's a fitness centre and lovely outdoor pool area.

Green Hotel   GUESTHOUSE **$$$**
(☑ 0821-4255000; www.greenhotelindia.com; 2270 Vinoba Rd, Jayalakshmipuram; s/d incl breakfast from ₹3880/4480; 🐾) 🍴 The historic Green Hotel was originally built as a palace in the 1920s by the maharajah for his daughters. Today it's a heritage hotel set among charming gardens. Commendably, all 31 rooms run on solar power and have plenty of character, though maintenance could be a little better and some fixtures are looking a tad tired. There's a good cafe (cakes from ₹40, snacks from ₹70; ⊙ 10am-7pm; 🐾) 🍴, restaurant and travel agent here.

Profits are distributed to charity and environmental projects across India.

🍴 Eating

★**Vinayaka Mylari**   SOUTH INDIAN **$**
(769 Nazarbad Main Rd; dosas ₹30-50; ⊙ 6.30-1.30pm & 3-8.30pm) This no-nonsense place is one of the best eateries in town to try South Indian classics of *masala dosa* (large South Indian savoury crêpe stuffed with spiced potatoes), which are beautifully light and fluffy and *idlis*. Locals eat them with coconut chutney and a coffee.

Depth 'n' Green   VEGETARIAN **$**
(www.facebook.com/depthngreen; 228/3, 1st Main Rd, Gokulam; dishes ₹80-170; ⊙ 10.30am-10.30pm; 🐾) Wildly popular with local yogis, this buzzing healthy cafe offers a menu of satisfying Indian and Western dishes, including great salads, served up on tree trunk tables. Their green smoothies and lassis and other drink concoctions (beet and ginger lemonade) are also superb.

Hotel RRR   SOUTH INDIAN **$**
(Gandhi Sq; mains ₹90-135; ⊙ noon-4pm & 6-11pm) Classic Andhra-style food is ladled out at

this ever-busy eatery, and you may have to queue for a table during lunch. Try their famous chicken or mutton biryanis (served on a banana leaf).

Cafe Aramane   SOUTH INDIAN **$**
(Sayyaji Rao Rd; mains ₹90-110; ⊙ 8am-10pm) 🍴 In a character-filled heritage building, this typically busy South Indian eatery rolls out steaming breakfast platters for Mysuru's office-goers, thalis for lunch (from ₹80) and welcomes them back in the evenings with aromatic filter coffee and a convoy of delicious snacks. There are speciality dosas each day of the week.

Parklane Hotel   MULTICUISINE **$$**
(Parklane Hotel, 2720 Harsha Rd; mains ₹100-160; 🐾) Mysuru's most social restaurant with outdoor tables, lit up moodily by countless lanterns, and there's often live traditional music. The menu does delicious regional dishes from across India as well as Chinese and continental options and cold beers.

Anu's Bamboo Hut   HEALTH FOOD **$$**
(☑ 9900909428; www.facebook.com/CafeinGokulam; 367, 2nd Main, 3rd Stage, Gokulam; lunch buffet ₹250; ⊙ 1-3pm & 5-7pm Mon-Sat; 🐾) Rooftop shack cafe catering mainly to yoga students with healthy vegetarian lunch buffets (from 1pm) and evening smoothies. Chef-owner Anu is a great source of info and offers cooking classes (₹700, lunch included).

Tiger Trail   INDIAN **$$$**
(☑ 0821-4255566; Royal Orchid Metropole, 5 Jhansi Lakshmi Bai Rd; mains ₹200-650; ⊙ 7.30-10am, 12.30-3.30pm & 7.30-11pm; 🐾) This sophisticated hotel restaurant works up delectable Indian cuisine in a courtyard that twinkles with fairy lights at night. The North Indian dishes are particularly good; try a Lucknow chicken korma (₹300). Also has a fine lunch buffet.

Old House   ITALIAN **$$$**
(☑ 0821-2333255; 451 Jhansi Rani Lakshmi Bai Rd; mains ₹175-399; ⊙ 7.30am-9.45pm; 🐾) Classy Italian with delightful terrace for tasty salads, pasta and risotto and pizzas (baked in a wood-fired oven). They serve a full range of mocktails and coffees but no alcohol.

🍸 Drinking & Nightlife

Pelican Pub   PUB
(Hunsur Rd; mains ₹100-190; ⊙ 11am-11pm) A venerable, still-popular watering hole located on the fringes of upmarket Gokulam.

Serves draught beer and food (try the chilli pork) at bargain basement rates in the indoor classic pub or alfresco-style garden setting out back. There's live music some nights.

Infinit Doora BAR
(Hotel Roopa, 2724/C, Bangalore Nilgiris Rd; ⊙ noon-11pm; 🛜) The nearest thing to a lounge in Mysuru, this rooftop bar has a classy ambience and comprehensive drinks selection, smoking and nonsmoking zones and fine city views.

🛍 Shopping

Mysuru is a great place to shop for sandalwood products, silk saris and wooden toys. It is also one of India's major incense-manufacturing centres. Look for the butterfly-esque 'Silk Mark' on your purchase; it's an endorsement for quality silk.

The bazaar area around the Devaraja Market is a real highlight for those in search of spices (and photographs).

Government Silk Weaving Factory CLOTHING
(📞 8025586550; www.ksicsilk.com; Mananthody Rd, Ashokapuram; ⊙ 8.30am-4pm Mon-Sat, outlet 10.30am-7pm daily) Given that Mysuru's prized silk is made under its very sheds, this government-run outlet, set up in 1912, is the best and cheapest place to shop for the exclusive textile. Behind the showroom is the factory, where you can drop by to see how the fabric is made. It's around 2km south of town.

Sumangali Silks CLOTHING
(off Gandhi Sq; ⊙ 10.30am-8.30pm) Exceptionally popular with Indian ladies, this multilevel store is another option to pick up a silk sari, with quality of varying degrees depending on how much you want to spend.

Sandalwood Oil Factory GIFTS & SOUVENIRS
(Mananthody Rd, Ashokapuram; ⊙ outlet 9.30am-6.30pm, factory closed Sun) A quality-assured place for sandalwood products including incense, soap, cosmetics and the prohibitively expensive pure sandalwood oil (if in stock). Guided tours are available to show you around the factory.

Sri Sharada Grand Musical Works MUSIC
(2006 Seebaiah Rd) Sells a variety of traditional musical instruments including tabla (drum) sets and assorted percussion instruments.

ℹ Information

MEDICAL SERVICES

Government Hospital (📞 0821-4269806; Dhanvanthri Rd) Centrally located and has a 24-hour pharmacy.

Left Luggage

The city bus stand's left-luggage cloakroom is open from 6am to 11pm and costs ₹15 per bag for 12 hours.

TOURIST INFORMATION

Karnataka Tourism (📞 0821-2422096; www.karnatakatourism.org; 1st fl, Hotel Mayura Hoysala, 2 Jhansi Lakshmi Bai Rd; ⊙ 10am-5pm Mon-Sat) Helpful and has plenty of brochures.

KSTDC Transport Office (📞 0821-2423652; www.karnatakaholidays.net; Yatri Nivas Bldg, 2 Jhansi Lakshmi Bai Rd; ⊙ 8.30am-8.30pm) Main office which offers general tourist information and provides a useful map.

BUSES FROM MYSURU (MYSORE)

DESTINATION	FARE (₹)	DURATION (HR)	DEPARTURES
Bandipur	77 (O)	2	11 daily via Ooty
Bengaluru	123 (O)/209 (R)/299 (V)	2-3	every 30min
Bengaluru Airport	739 (V)	3½-4	12 daily
Channarayapatna	83 (O)/160 (V)	2	hourly
Chennai	632 (R)/1026 (V)	9-11	6 daily from 4.30pm
Ernakulam	739 (V)	8-9	3 daily from 6pm
Gokarna	478 (O)	12	1 daily
Hassan	112 (O)	3	hourly
Hosapete (Hospet)	381 (O)/608 (R)	9-12	7 daily
Mangaluru	245 (O)/390 (R)/502 (V)	6-7	hourly
Ooty	131 (O)/193 (R)/529 (V)	4-5	12 daily

Fares: (O) Ordinary, (R) Rajahamsa Semideluxe, (V) Airavath AC Volvo

TRAINS FROM MYSURU (MYSORE)

DESTINATION	TRAIN NO & NAME	FARE (₹)	DURATION (HR)	DEPARTURES
Bengaluru	16518 Bengaluru Exp	2AC/3AC 695/490	3	5.30am
Bengaluru	12613 Tippu Exp	2nd class/AC chair 90/305	2½	11.15am
Bengaluru	12008 Shatabdi Exp	AC chair/AC executive chair 305/770	2	2.15pm daily except Wed
Chennai	12008 Shatabdi Exp	AC chair/AC executive chair 1280/1845	7	2.15pm daily Thu-Tue
Hosapete (for Hampi)	16592 Hampi Exp	3AC/2AC sleeper 840/1205	12	7pm
Hubballi	17301 Mysore Dharwad Exp	sleeper/2AC 275/1065	9½	10.30pm

❶ Getting There & Away

AIR

Mysuru's airport was not operating at research time, but flights may resume.

BUS

The **central bus stand** (Bengaluru-Nilgiri Rd) handles all KSRTC long-distance buses.

The **city bus stand** (Sayyaji Rao Rd) is for city, Srirangapatna and Chamundi Hill buses.

The **private bus stand** (Sayyaji Rao Rd) serves Hubballi (Hubli), Vijapura (Bijapur), Mangaluru, Ooty (Udhagamandalam) and Ernakulam. You'll find several ticketing agents around the stand.

TRAIN

Train tickets can be bought from Mysuru's **railway reservation office** (☏131; ⊙8am-8pm Mon-Sat, to 2pm Sun).

❶ Getting Around

Uber and Ola cabs are everywhere in Mysuru. Agencies at hotels can organise drivers for around ₹1800 per day in town, or from ₹2500 per day for out of town trips.

Count on around ₹1000 for a day's sightseeing in an autorickshaw.

Around Mysuru

Consider one of KSTDC's (p185) tours for visiting sights around Mysuru.

Srirangapatna (Srirangapatnam)

☏08236 / POP 26,300

Steeped in bloody history, the fort town of Srirangapatna, 16km from Mysuru, is built on an island straddling the Cauvery River. The seat of Hyder Ali and Tipu Sultan's power, this town was the de facto capital of

much of southern India during the 18th century. The ramparts, battlements and some of the gates of the fort still stand, as do a clutch of monuments.

⊙ Sights

Daria Daulat Bagh

PALACE

(Summer Palace; Indian/foreigner ₹20/100; ⊙9am-5pm) Set within lovely manicured grounds, Srirangapatna's star attraction is Tipu's summer palace, 1km east of the fort. Built from teak and rosewood, the lavish decoration that covers every inch of its interiors is impressive. The ceilings are embellished with floral designs, while the walls bear murals depicting courtly life and Tipu's campaigns against the British. There's a small museum within displaying artefacts and interesting paintings.

Gumbaz

MAUSOLEUM

(⊙8am-6.30pm) FREE In a serene garden, the historically significant Persian-style Gumbaz is the resting place of the legendary Tipu Sultan, his equally famed father, Hyder Ali, and his wife. Most inscriptions are in Farsi. The interior of the onion-dome mausoleum is impressive and painted in a tiger-like motif as a tribute to the sultan.

Sri Ranganathaswamy Temple

HINDU TEMPLE

(⊙7.30am-1pm & 4-8pm) Constructed in AD 894, this attractive Vaishnavite temple has a mix of Hoysala and Vijayanagar design. Within are cavernous walkways, pillars and the centrepiece 4.5m-long reclining statue of Ranganatha, a manifestation of Vishnu.

Jamia Masjid

MOSQUE

This cream-coloured mosque with two minarets was built by the sultan in 1787 and features an interesting blend of Islamic and Hindu architecture. Climb the stairs at the back for panoramic views of the site.

Colonel Bailey's Dungeon
HISTORIC SITE

FREE North of the island, on the banks of the Cauvery, is this well-preserved 18th-century white-walled dungeon used to hold British prisoners of war, including Colonel Bailey who died here in 1780. Jutting out from the walls are stone fixtures used to chain the naked prisoners, who were immersed in water up to their necks.

Ranganathittu
Bird Sanctuary
NATURE RESERVE

(Indian/foreigner incl 15min boat ride ₹60/120, long lens camera/video ₹500; ⊙ 8.30am-5.45pm) The Ranganathittu Bird Sanctuary includes six islets and the banks of the Cauvery River. Storks, ibises, egrets, spoonbills and cormorants are best seen in the early morning or late afternoon on an extended boat ride (₹1000 per hour). There are also plenty of crocodiles around, which are quite easy to spot. You'll find a restaurant on-site.

🛏 Sleeping & Eating

Mayura River View
HOTEL $$

(☑ 0823-6252114; www.kstdc.co/hotels; d with fan/AC from ₹2300/3300; ❄) These government rooms and cottages are in pretty decent shape and have a fine location on a quiet patch of riverbank. Day trippers can pop in for lunch (mains ₹150 to ₹180) to gaze at the river while guzzling beer.

ⓘ Getting There & Away

Hourly buses (₹22 to ₹30, 45 minutes) depart from Mysuru's City bus stand. Passenger trains travelling from Mysuru to Bengaluru also stop here. Bus 307 (₹18, 30 minutes) heading to Brindavan Gardens is just across from Srirangapatna's main bus stand. A return autorickshaw from Mysuru is about ₹600, and a taxi around ₹1000.

ⓘ Getting Around

The sights are spread out, so hiring an autorickshaw (around ₹300 for three hours) is the best option for getting around.

Melukote (Melkote)

Life in the devout Hindu town of Melukote (also called Melkote), about 50km north of Mysuru, revolves around the atmospheric 12th-century Cheluvanarayana Temple (Raja St; ⊙ 8am-1pm & 5-8pm), with its rose-coloured *gopuram* (gateway tower) and ornately carved pillars. Get a workout on the hike up to the hilltop Yoganarasimha Temple, which offers fine views of the surrounding hills.

Three KSRTC buses shuttle daily between Mysuru and Melukote (₹100, 1½ hours).

Somnathpur

The astonishingly beautiful Keshava Temple (Indian/foreigner ₹5/100; ⊙ 8.30am-5.30pm) is one of the finest examples of Hoysala architecture, on par with the masterpieces of Belur and Halebid. Built in 1268 AD, this star-shaped temple, 33km from Mysuru, is adorned with superb stone sculptures depicting various scenes from the Ramayana, Mahabharata and Bhagavad Gita, and the life and times of the Hoysala kings.

Somnathpur is 12km south of Bannur and 10km north of Tirumakudal Narsipur. Take one of the half-hourly buses from Mysuru to either village (₹35, 30 minutes) and change there.

Bandipur National Park
☑ 08229

Part of the Nilgiri Biosphere Reserve, Bandipur National Park (http://bandipurtigerreserve.in; Indian/foreigner ₹75/1000, video ₹1000; ⊙ 6am-9.30am & 4-6pm) is one of South India's most famous wilderness areas. Covering 880 sq km, it was once the Mysuru maharajas' private wildlife reserve, and is now a protected zone for over 100 species of mammals, including tiger, elephant, leopard, gaur (Indian bison), chital (spotted deer), sambar, sloth bear, dhole (wild dog), mongoose and langur. It's also home to an impressive 350 species of bird. It's only 80km south of Mysuru on the Ooty road.

🏃 Activities

Only government-approved vehicles are permitted to run safaris within the park.

Bandipur Safari Lodge
JEEP SAFARI

(☑ 08229-233001; www.junglelodges.com; 2hr safari per person ₹2700; ⊙ 8am & 4pm) Bandipur Safari Lodge has open-air 4WDs and minibuses, accompanied by knowledgeable guides.

Forest Department Safari
SAFARI

(☑ 08229-236043; directorbandipur@gmail.com; 1hr safari per person incl permit in bus/jeep/Gypsy

BILIGIRI RANGANNA TEMPLE WILDLIFE SANCTUARY

Much less known than Bandipur or Nagarhole, the **Biligiri Ranganna Temple Wildlife Sanctuary** in the BR Hills makes a great alternative to live out your *Jungle Book* fantasies. Set over 570 sq km, it was declared a tiger reserve in 2011 – but as with most parks, you'd be extremely lucky to spot one. Elephants, leopards, sloth bears and dholes (wild dogs) also roam the hills here.

The **Kyathdevaraya Gudi Wilderness Camp** (☑080-40554055; www.junglelodges.com/kyathadevara-gudi-wilderness-camp; Yelandur; per person incl full board Indian/foreigner from ₹8036/9804) has a fantastic site among the peaceful forest, with grazing warthog and spotted deer. Accommodation (in tented cottages or delightful stilted log cabins) is pricey, but rates include all meals, a safari, guided walk and all taxes.

The wildlife sanctuary is a 4½-hour drive from Bengaluru. It's best to hire a vehicle, although it is theoretically possible to get there by public transport. You can catch a direct 7.45am bus from Mysuru to K Gudi, or a bus to Chamarajanagar and connect to a 1.30pm bus to K Gudi. From Chamarajanagar you can arrange a jeep for ₹700.

₹1200/2000/3000; ⊘departures 6.30-8.30am & 3.30-5.30pm) The forest department has rushed drives on buses (capacity 20) arranged at the park headquarters. It's worth paying extra for a jeep or 4WD. Avoid weekends when it gets very crowded.

🛏 Sleeping & Eating

Hotel Bandipur Plaza　　　　HOTEL $
(☑08229-233200; Ooty-Mysuru Hwy; r ₹1500; ☞) Its highway location is a drawback, but this basic hotel's rooms are affordable and adequate in an otherwise pricey destination. It's nearby to Bandipur Safari Lodge, so convenient for safaris into the park, and has a decent restaurant.

Forest Department Bungalows　　GUESTHOUSE $
(☑08229-236051; www.bandipurtigerreserve.in; 9-/20-bed dm ₹720/1000, bungalow foreigner from ₹3000; ☞) Basic lodging at the park HQ is convenient for location and atmosphere, but the downside is foreigners have to pay an additional ₹1000 per night for park entry fees. Dorms are rented out in the entirety, so you won't need to share with strangers. You can book online.

Tiger Ranch　　　　LODGE $$
(☑8095408505; www.tigerranch.net; Mangala Village; per person incl full board ₹1510) Offering a genuine wilderness experience, the very rustic Tiger Ranch has basic but attractive cottages, an atmospheric thatched-roof dining hall and fine home-cooked food. There's good walking in the surrounding forest, and a you're sure to encounter wildlife. Evenings can be enjoyed around a bonfire. It's located

10km from the park; call ahead to arrange a pick-up (₹300).

⭐**Dhole's Den**　　　　LODGE $$$
(☑9444468376; www.dholesden.com; Kaniyanapura Village; camping/s/d incl full board from ₹3000/11,000/12,000; ☞) 🌿 Flawlessly presented, Dhole's Den offers contemporary design in lovely pastoral surrounds. Stylish, modernist rooms and bungalows are decked out with art and colourful fabrics, plus couches and deckchairs. It's environmentally conscious with solar power, tank water and organic vegies. Camping is available for those on a budget. It's a 20-minute drive from the park headquarters; rates include a guided nature walk.

Serai　　　　RESORT, LODGE $$$
(☑08229-236075; www.theserai.in; Kaniyanapura Village; r incl full board from ₹21,000; ✳☞▣) Set in a coffee plantation that backs onto the national park, this luxurious resort has gorgeous Mediterranean-inspired villas (some with private pool) that are in harmony with the natural surrounds. Thatched-roof rooms feature elegant touches such as copper bathroom fixtures, stone-wall showers and wildlife photography on the walls. Its glassed-in restaurant and infinity pool both maximise outlooks to Nilgiri Hills.

MC Resort　　　　HOTEL $$$
(☑9019954162; www.mcresort.in; Bengaluru-Ooty Rd, Melukamanahally; s/d incl full board from ₹4000/5000; ☞▣) Decent resort-style place with spacious, well-equipped rooms, a large swimming pool, kids' pool, a multicuisine restaurant and a convenient location near the park. Rates are inclusive of meals.

ℹ Getting There & Away

Buses between Mysuru and Ooty can drop you at Bandipur (₹78, 2½ hours), an 88km journey. Taxis from Mysuru are about ₹2000.

Nagarhole National Park

Rich in wildlife, jungle and boasting a scenic lake, the 643-sq-km **Nagarhole National Park** (Rajiv Gandhi National Park; Indian/foreigner ₹200/1000, video ₹1000; ⏰ 6am-6pm) (pronounced *nag*-ar-hole-eh) is one of Karnataka's best wildlife getaways, containing good numbers of animals including tigers and elephants. Flanking the **Kabini River**, it forms an important protected region that includes neighbouring Bandipur National Park (p194) and several other reserves. The lush forests here are home to tigers, leopards, elephants, gaurs, muntjacs (barking deer), wild dogs, bonnet macaques and common langurs, and 270 species of birds. The park can remain closed for long stretches between July and October, when the rains transform the forests into a giant slush-pit.

The Kabini River empties into the Kabini Reservoir, creating a vast watering hole for Nagarhole's wildlife. Herds of wild elephants and other animals gather on the banks, and the high concentration of wildlife has made this one of Karnataka's top wildlife-spotting locations.

The traditional inhabitants of the land, the hunter-gatherer Jenu Kuruba people, still live in the park, despite government efforts to relocate them.

🏃 Activities

Government-Run Safaris   SAFARI
(Kabini River Lodge; 2½hr 4WD safari ₹3000) Leave at 6am and 3pm when conditions permit in the dry season.

20-Seater Motorboat Rides   BOATING, WILDLIFE
(Kabini River Lodge; per person ₹2000) Organised by the Kabini River Lodge for relaxed wildlife viewing, and excellent for birders.

🛏 Sleeping & Eating

Kabini Lake (home to most lodges) makes a wonderful base, but has no real budget hotels. For inexpensive places head to the park HQ.

Karapur Hotel   GUESTHOUSE $$
(☑ 9945904840; Karapura roundabout; r ₹1200) The only budget option close to Kabini is this simple lodge with a few rooms above a shop in the township of Karapura, 3km from the park.

★ **Waterwoods Lodge**   GUESTHOUSE $$$
(☑ 082-28264421; www.waterwoods.in; d incl full board from ₹13,200; ❄ 🛜 🏊) On a grassy embankment overlooking scenic Kabini Lake, Waterwoods is a stunning lodge. Most rooms have balconies with wonderful lake views, swing chairs, hardwood floors and designer flair. It's kid-friendly with trampoline, infinity pool, free canoe hire and wood-fired pizzas. Pamper yourself in the spa which has massage rooms, Jacuzzi and a steam bath.

Serai Kabini   LODGE $$$
(☑ 080-40012200; http://theserai.in/kabini; r incl full board from ₹16,450; ❄ 🛜 🏊) Perfectly set up for wildlife spotting, this luxury lodge has wonderful lake-facing bungalows, and organises tip-top jungle safaris, boat trips and nature walks. The restaurant is beautifully designed and the cuisine excellent. There's a beautiful spa too. Located on the north shore of Kabini Reservoir.

Bison Resort   LODGE $$$
(☑ 080-41278708; www.thebisonresort.com; Gundathur Village; camping per person from ₹2500, s/d incl full board from US$320/370; 🛜 🏊) Inspired by luxury safari lodges in Africa, Bison succeeds in replicating the classic wilderness experience with a stunning waterfront location and choice between canvas-walled cottages, stilted bungalows or bush camping. They offer a wide selection of activities including treks to local tribal villages and sunset boat rides. Service standards are top-notch and there are expert naturalists at hand.

KAAV Safari Lodge   LODGE $$$
(☑ 08228-264492; www.kaav.com; Mallali Cross, Kabini; incl full board s/d from ₹10,400/13,200, tent from ₹12,000; ❄ 🛜 🏊) A kind of designer safari lodge, KAAV has open-plan rooms with polished concrete floors, hip bathrooms and spacious balconies that open directly to the national park. Yes, the attention to detail is superb. Head up to the viewing tower to lounge on plush day beds, or take a dip in the infinity pool. No children under 10.

ℹ Getting There & Away

The park's main entrance is 93km southwest of Mysuru. Two buses depart daily from Mysuru to Karapuram (₹68, 2½ hours), around 3km from Kabini Lake. A taxi from Mysuru is around ₹2000.

Kodagu (Coorg) Region

Nestled amid evergreen hills that line the southernmost edge of Karnataka is the luscious Kodagu (Coorg) region, gifted with emerald landscapes and hectares of plantations. A major centre for coffee and spice production, this rural expanse is also home to the Kodava people, who are divided into 1000 clans. The uneven terrain and cool climate make it a fantastic area for trekking, birdwatching or lazily ambling down little-trodden paths winding around carpeted hills. All in all, Kodagu is rejuvenation guaranteed.

Kodagu was a state in its own right until 1956, when it merged with Karnataka. The region's chief town and transport hub is Madikeri, but for an authentic Kodagu experience, you have to venture into the countryside. Avoid weekends if you can, when places can quickly get filled up by weekenders from Bengaluru.

🏃 Activities

Exploring the region by foot is a highlight for many visitors. Treks are part cultural experience, part nature encounter, involving hill climbs, plantation visits, forest walks and homestays.

The best season for trekking is October to March; there are no treks during monsoon. The most popular peaks are the seven-day trek to Tadiyendamol (1745m), and to Pushpagiri (1712m) and Kotebetta (1620m). Plenty of day hikes are possible too; Rainforest Retreat (p198) organises several. A trekking guide is essential for navigating the labyrinth of forest tracks.

Madikeri (Mercara)

📞 08272 / POP 34,200 / ELEV 1525M

Madikeri (also known as Mercara) is a congested market town spread out along a series of ridges. The only reason for coming here is to organise treks or sort out the practicalities of travel.

👁 Sights

Madikeri Fort   HISTORIC SITE

There are good views from this hilltop fort, built by Tipu Sultan in the 16th century, though today it's the less glamorous site of the municipal headquarters. You can walk a short section of ramparts and within the fort's walls are the hexagonal palace (now the dusty district commissioner's office) and

colonial-era church, which houses a quirky museum (⊙ 10am-5.30pm Sun-Fri) FREE.

Raja's Seat   VIEWPOINT

(MG Rd; ₹5; ⊙ 5.30am-7pm) A very popular spot to enjoy sunset, as the raja himself did, with fantastic outlooks to rolling hills and endless valleys.

Raja's Tombs   HISTORIC BUILDING

(Gaddige) FREE These domed tombs are built in Indo-Sarcenic style and serve as the resting place for Kodava royalty and dignitaries. Located 7km from Madikeri, so take an autorickshaw (₹200).

Abbi Falls   WATERFALL

A spectacular sight after the rainy season, these 21.3m-high falls can pack a punch.

🏃 Activities

Coorg Sky Adventures   SCENIC FLIGHTS

(📞 9448954384; www.coorgskyadventures.com; short/long flight ₹2500/8000) Soar over plantation and paddy valleys on a microlight flight for tremendous views of Coorg's lush scenery. An experienced, professional operator.

Ayurjeevan   AYURVEDA

(📞 944974779; www.ayurjeevancoorg.com; Kohinoor Rd; 1hr from ₹1400; ⊙ 7am-7pm) An ayurvedic 'hospital' that offers a whole range of intriguing and rejuvenating techniques including rice ball massages and oil baths. It's a short walk from the State Bank India.

🛏 Sleeping

With fantastic guesthouses in the surrounding plantations, there's no real reason to stay in Madikeri, unless you arrive very late.

Hotel Chitra   HOTEL $

(📞 08272-225372; www.hotelchitra.co.in; School Rd; dm ₹270, d from ₹780, with AC ₹1760; ❄️) Concrete hotel close to Madikeri's main intersection, so expect some background traffic noise. Provides low-cost, no-frills rooms and friendly service.

Hotel Mayura Valley View   HOTEL $$

(📞 08272-228387; www.kstdc.co/hotels/hotel-mayura-valley-view-madikeri; Stuart Hill; d/ste incl breakfast from ₹3250/4950; ❄️🛜) On the hilltop past Raja's Seat, this government hotel is one of Madikeri's best, with large bright rooms, a peaceful ambience and fantastic valley views. Its restaurant-bar with terrace overlooking the valley is a great spot for a beer.

🍴 Eating

Coorg Cuisine   INDIAN $
(Main Rd; mains ₹100-130; ⊙ noon-4pm & 7-10pm)
Championing unique Kodava specialities
such as *pandhi barthadh* (pork dry fry)
and *kadambuttu* (rice dumplings), this restaurant is well worth trying. It's not exactly
atmospheric, located above a shop on the
main road, but there are a few portraits on
the walls and the seating is comfy.

⭐ **Raintree**   MULTICUISINE $$
(www.raintree.in; 13-14 Pension Lane; meals ₹170-
260; ⊙ 11.30am-10pm) A welcome surprise
in a humdrum town, this cute converted
bungalow makes a homely place for a deli-
cious meal, with solid wooden furniture and
some tribal art. The food does not disap-
point either, with local specialities and dish-
es from the coast. They also sell wine and
great Kodagu coffee. Located just behind
Madikeri Town Hall.

ℹ️ Information

Travel Coorg (☏ 08272-223333; www.travel-
coorg.in; outside KSRTC bus stand; ⊙ 24hr)
Provides a good overview of things to do, as
well as arranging homestays, trekking guides
and other activities. Also offers transport.

ℹ️ Getting There & Away

Very regular buses depart from the KSRTC bus
stand for Bengaluru (fan/AC ₹350/539, 5½ to
seven hours), stopping in Mysuru (₹162/250,
2½ to four hours) en route. Buses go roughly
every two hours in the daytime to Mangaluru
(₹135/283, three to four hours), while infrequent
ordinary buses head to Hassan (₹117, four hours).

Around Madikeri

The beguiling highlands around Madikeri
offer some of the Kodagu's most enchanting
countryside. Dotted around its lush hills are
numerous spice and coffee plantations, and
some tea is grown too.

🏃 Activities

⭐ **Jiva Spa**   AYURVEDA, MASSAGE
(☏ 08272-2665800; www.tajhotels.com/jivaspas/
index.html; Vivanta, Galibeedu; treatments from
₹2700; ⊙ 9am-9pm) Surrounded by rainfor-
est, Jiva Spa at the stunning Vivanta hotel
(p198) is *the* place to treat yourself with a
range of rejuvenating treatments. With soak
tubs, a relaxation lounge, beauty salon and

a yoga and meditation zone, it's one of the
best in South India. Appointments essential.

**Swaasthya Ayurveda
Retreat Village**   AYURVEDA
(www.swaasthya.com; Bekkesodlur Village; per
person per day incl full board & yoga class ₹7000)
For an exceptionally peaceful and refreshing
ayurvedic vacation, head to south Coorg to
soothe your soul among the lush greenery on
1.6 hectares of coffee and spice plantations.
Prices include up to six treatments a day.

🛏️ Sleeping & Eating

Rainforest Retreat   GUESTHOUSE $$
(☏ 08272-265638, 08272-265639; www.rainfores
tours.com; Galibeedu; s/d tent ₹1500/2000, cottage from ₹2500/3000; 📶) 🌿 A great place
to socialise with eco-minded Indians, this
nature-soaked refuge is immersed within forest and plantations and an organic,
sustainable set-up. Accommodation is lazy
camping (prepitched tents with beds) or cottages with solar power. Rates include plantation tours and treks. Check the website
for volunteering opportunities. An autorickshaw from Madikeri is ₹240.

Victorian Verandaz   B&B $$
(☏ 08272-200234; http://victorianverandaz.com;
Modur Estate, Kadagadal Village; d self-catering
₹2000-5500, B&B ₹2950; 📶) Fine family-owned
lodgings on a huge estate that grows coffee,
pepper, cardamom and rice. There's a choice
of accommodation, with two rental cottages
that have kitchens which are available on a
self-catering basis and two rooms in a cottage
which operate on a B&B basis. There's good
birding and trail walking on the estate.

Golden Mist   HOMESTAY $$
(☏ 9448903670, 08272-265629; www.golden-mist.
net; Galibeedu; s/d incl full board ₹2500/4000)
An incredibly peaceful, very rustic Indian-
German-managed tea, coffee and rice-
growing farm. The cottages have character
though they are basic and best suited for
outdoor types rather than those who prize
their creature comforts. Meals are tasty local
dishes made from the farm's organic produce and staff are very hospitable. It's tricky
to find and not signposted, an autorickshaw
costs ₹250 from Madikeri.

⭐ **Vivanta**   HOTEL $$$
(☏ 08272-665800; www.vivantabytaj.com; Gali-
beedu; r from ₹15,800; @ 📶 🏊) Built across 72
hectares of misty rainforest this effortlessly
stylish hotel incorporates principles of space

BYLAKUPPE

The small, beautifully kept village of Bylakuppe, just south of the Mysuru–Mangaluru highway, forms South India's largest Tibetan community. Established in 1961, it was among the first refugee camps set up in South India to house thousands of Tibetans who fled from Tibet following the 1959 Chinese invasion. Over 10,000 Tibetans live here (including 3300 monks).

Foreigners are not allowed to stay overnight without a Protected Area Permit (PAP) from the Ministry of Home Affairs in Delhi, which can take months to process. Contact the **Tibet Bureau Office** (⊙11–26479737; www.tibetbureau.in; New Delhi) for details. Day trippers are welcome to visit, however.

The area's highlight is the atmospheric **Namdroling Monastery** (www.namdroling.org; ⊙7am-6pm), home to the spectacular **Golden Temple** (Padmasambhava Buddhist Vihara; ⊙7am-6pm), presided over by three 18m-high gold-plated Buddha statues. The temple is at its dramatic best when prayers are in session and it rings out with gongs, drums and the drone of hundreds of young monks chanting. You're welcome to meditate. The **Zangdogpalri Temple** (⊙7am-6pm), a similarly ornate affair, is next door.

If you have a permit, the simple **Paljor Dhargey Ling Guest House** (☑08223-258686; pdguesthouse@yahoo.com; r ₹275-375) is opposite the Golden Temple. For delicious *momos* (Tibetan dumplings) or *thukpa* (noodle soup), pop into the Tibetan-run **Malaya Restaurant** (momos ₹60-90; ⊙7am-9pm). **Thirsty Crow** (south of Namdroling Monastery) offers fine fresh juices, milkshakes, lime sodas, teas and coffees. Otherwise there are many hotels in nearby Kushalnagar – including modern, well-presented **Hotel White Wings** (☑9741155900; http://whitewingscoorg.com; 1-86, BM Rd, Kushalnagar; r with AC ₹2100; ❋ 🛜) – and the surrounding countryside.

Autorickshaws (shared/solo ₹15/30) run to Bylakuppe from Kushalnagar, 5km away. Buses frequently do the 34km run to Kushalnagar from Madikeri (₹45, 45 minutes) and Hassan (₹80, 2½ hours). Most buses on the Mysuru–Madikeri route stop at Kushalnagar.

KARNATAKA & BENGALURU KODAGU (COORG) REGION

and minimalism, and effectively blends into its environment. Old cattle tracks lead to rooms, with pricier ones featuring private indoor pools, fireplaces and butlers. There are astonishing highland views from the lobby and infinity pool, and a top-class ayurvedic spa (p198).

Kakkabe

☑ 08272 / POP 580

Surrounded by forested hills, this tranquil village and hiking hot spot is an ideal base to plan an assault on Kodagu's highest peak, Tadiyendamol, or just enjoy a wander along scenic highland trails.

🛏 Sleeping & Eating

★ **Honey Valley Estate** GUESTHOUSE $
(☑08272-238339; www.honeyvalleyindia.in; r from ₹800, without bathroom from ₹550; 🛜) A homestay on a hilltop, this wonderful trekking guesthouse, at 1250m above sea level, transports you into a lovely cool, fresh, natural environment. The owners' friendliness, eco-mindedness and local knowledge of wildlife is excellent. There are 18 local

trekking routes and six different accommodation options. It's accessible by 4WD only (₹200, book via hotel) from Kakkabe.

Chingaara GUESTHOUSE $$
(☑08272-238633; www.chingaara.com; Kabbinakad; r incl half board ₹2300-3200; 🛜) This delightful farmhouse is surrounded by verdant coffee plantations, with good birding in the vicinity. Rooms are spacious, and most have good views – especially room 9. Good home-style cooking is served and staff will light a bonfire at night. It's 2.5km up a rocky steep hill (4WD only); call ahead and Chingaara's jeep will pick you up from Kabbinakad junction.

Tamara Resort RESORT $$$
(☑080-71077700; www.thetamara.com; Yavakapadi Village; r incl meals & activities from ₹23,800; ❋ 🛜 ⛱) Set in a coffee estate, this romantic nature resort has stilted cottages that soar above the lush green surrounds. Luxurious rooms all have teak floorboards, balconies and king-sized beds. Its memorable restaurant is raised above the plantations with a glass-bottom floor to look down upon. There are three good local treks, yoga classes and a spa. No children under 12.

Hassan

📞 08172 / POP 138,000

This sprawling, congested transport hub (with decent accommodation) has minimal appeal other than as a base to visit nearby Belur, Halebid or Sravanabelagola. The helpful **tourist office** (📞08172-268862; AVK College Rd; ⊙10am-5.30pm, Mon-Fri) advises on transport options.

🛏 Sleeping

SS Residency   HOTEL **$$**
(📞08172-233466; www.ssresidency.co.in; BM Rd; r from ₹1960; ❈🛜) Modern, centrally located hotel with a wide choice of rooms, all attractively styled with cream furnishings, cable TV and minibars. There's no restaurant, however.

ℹ Getting There & Away

From the **New Bus Stand** (Hwy 71), 500m south of the town centre, buses depart to Mysuru (₹112, three hours), Bengaluru (₹192 to ₹469, 3½ to 4½ hours) and Mangaluru (₹163 to ₹355, 3½ to 4½ hours). A day tour of Belur and Halebid or Sravanabelagola will cost you about ₹1400.

From Hassan's well-organised train station, three to four trains head to Mysuru daily (sleeper/2AC ₹140/695, two to three hours), all in the dead of night. For Bengaluru, there's the red-eye 3am 16518 Bangalore Express (sleeper/2AC ₹180/695, 5½ hours).

Belur (Beluru)

📞 08177 / POP 9320 / ELEV 968M

The Hoysala temples at Belur (also Beluru) and nearby Halebid are the apex of one of the most artistically exuberant periods of ancient Hindu cultural development. Architecturally, they are South India's answer to Khajuraho in Madhya Pradesh and Konark near Puri in Odisha (Orissa).

⊙ Sights

Channakeshava Temple   HINDU TEMPLE
(Temple Rd; guide ₹250; ⊙7.30am-7.30pm) Commissioned in AD 1116 to commemorate the Hoysalas' victory over the neighbouring Cholas, this temple took more than a century to build, and is currently the only one among the three major Hoysala sites still in daily use – try to be there for the *puja* (offerings or prayer) ceremonies at 9am, 3pm and 7.30pm.

Some parts of the temple, such as the exterior lower friezes, were not sculpted

to completion and are thus less elaborate. However, the work higher up is unsurpassed in detail and artistry, and is a glowing tribute to human skill.

Particularly intriguing are the angled bracket figures depicting women in ritual dancing poses. While the front of the temple is reserved for images depicting erotic sections from the Kama Sutra, the back is strictly for gods. The roof of the inner sanctum is held up by rows of exquisitely sculpted pillars, no two of which are identical in design.

🛏 Sleeping & Eating

Hotel Mayura Velapuri   HOTEL **$$**
(📞0817-7222209; www.kstdc.co/hotels; Kempegowda Rd; d with fan/AC from ₹1200/1550; ❈) A renovated state-run hotel located on the way to Channakeshava Temple with pretty comfortable, spacious rooms. Its restaurant-bar serves a variety of Indian dishes (from ₹80) to go with beer.

ℹ Getting There & Away

There are frequent buses to/from Hassan (₹44 to ₹96, 45 minutes), 38km away, and Halebid (₹25, 30 minutes). It's also possible to visit on day-trip KSTDC tour from Bengaluru or Mysuru.

Halebid

📞 08177 / POP 9348

Halebid (also called Halibidu, or Halebeedu) is a small town that's home to a stunning Hoysala temple and some other minor Jain sites. Most travellers visit on a day trip from Belur, 15km west.

⊙ Sights

Hoysaleswara Temple   HINDU TEMPLE
(⊙dawn-dusk) Construction of the Hoysaleswara Temple, Halebid's claim to fame, began around AD 1121 and went on for more than 80 years. It was never completed, but nonetheless stands today as a masterpiece of Hoysala architecture. The interior of its inner sanctum, chiselled out of black stone, is marvellous. On the outside, the temple's richly sculpted walls are covered with a flurry of Hindu deities, sages, stylised animals and friezes depicting the life of the Hoysala rulers.

Museum   MUSEUM
(₹5; ⊙9am-5pm Sat-Thu) Adjacent to Hoysaleswara Temple is this small museum with a collection of beautiful sculptures from around Halebid.

🛏 Sleeping

Hotel Mayura Shanthala   HOTEL **$$**
(☎ 08177-273224; www.kstdc.co/hotels/; d incl
breakfast from ₹1600; ❄ 🛜) Set in a leafy gar-
den right opposite the temple complex, Hotel
Mayura Shanthala is the best sleeping option.

ℹ️ Getting There & Away

Regular buses depart for Hassan (₹35, one hour),
33km away; buses to Belur are ₹25. KSTDC tours
from Bengaluru and Mysuru also visit Halebid.

Sravanabelagola

📞 08176 / POP 5660

Atop the bare rocky summit of Vindhyagiri
Hill, the 17.5m-high statue of the Jain deity
Gomateshvara (Bahubali) is visible long be-
fore you reach the pilgrimage town of Sra-
vanabelagola (also spelt Shravanabelagola).
Viewing the statue close up is the main rea-
son for heading to this sedate town, whose
name means 'Monk of the White Pond'.

⊙ Sights

Gomateshvara Statue   JAIN SITE
(Bahubali; ⊙ 6.30am-6.30pm) A steep climb up
614 steps takes you to the top of Vindhyagiri
Hill, the summit of which is lorded over by
the towering naked statue of the Jain deity
Gomateshvara (Bahubali). Commissioned
by a military commander in the service of
the Ganga king Rachamalla and carved out
of a single piece of granite by the sculptor
Aristenemi in AD 98, it is said to be the
world's tallest monolithic statue. Leave your
shoes at the foot of the hill.

Bahubali was the son of emperor Vrish-
abhadeva, who later became the first Jain
tirthankar (revered teacher), Adinath.
Embroiled in fierce competition with his
brother Bharatha to succeed his father, Ba-
hubali realised the futility of material gains
and renounced his kingdom. As a recluse, he
meditated in complete stillness in the forest
until he attained enlightenment. His lengthy
meditative spell is denoted by vines curling
around his legs and an ant hill at his feet.

Every 12 years, millions flock here to at-
tend the **Mastakabhisheka** (⊙ Feb) ceremo-
ny, when the statue is dowsed in holy waters,
pastes, powders, precious metals and stones.
The next ceremony is slated for 2018.

🛏 Sleeping & Eating

The local Jain organisation **SDJMI** (☎ 08176-
257258) handles bookings for its 15 guest-

SRAVANABELAGOLA (SHRAVANABELAGOLA) JAIN TEMPLES

Apart from the Gomateshvara statue,
there are several interesting Jain temples
in town. The **Chandragupta Basti**
(Chandragupta Community; ⊙ 6am-6pm),
on Chandragiri Hill opposite Vindhyagiri,
is believed to have been built by Emperor
Ashoka. The **Bhandari Basti** (Bhandari
Community; ⊙ 6am-6pm), in the southeast
corner of town, is Sravanabelagola's
largest temple. Nearby, **Chandranatha
Basti** (Chandranatha Community; ⊙ 6am-
6pm) has well-preserved paintings de-
picting Jain tales.

---

houses (double/triple ₹250/310). The office
is behind the Vidyananda Nilaya Dharamsa-
la, past the post office.

Hotel Raghu   HOTEL **$**
(☎ 08176-257238; s/d from ₹400/500, d with AC
₹900; ❄) Very basic rooms that are some-
thing of a last resort should you be stranded
in town. However, the vegetarian restaurant
downstairs works up an awesome veg thali
(₹90).

ℹ️ Getting There & Away

There are no direct buses from Sravanabelagola
to Hassan or Belur – you must go to Chan-
narayapatna (₹40, 20 minutes) and catch an
onward connection there. One daily bus runs
direct to Mysuru (₹149, 1½ hours).

KARNATAKA COAST

Mangaluru (Mangalore)

📞 0824 / POP 492,500

Alternating between relaxed coastal town
and hectic nightmare, Mangaluru (more
commonly known as Mangalore) has a Jekyll
and Hyde thing going, but it's a useful gate-
way for the Konkan coast and inland Kodagu
region. While there's not a lot to do here, it
has an appealing off-the-beaten-path feel,
and the spicy seafood dishes are sensational.

Mangaluru sits at the estuaries of the pic-
turesque Netravathi and Gurupur Rivers on
the Arabian Sea and has been a major port
on international trade routes since the 6th
century.

Mangaluru (Mangalore)

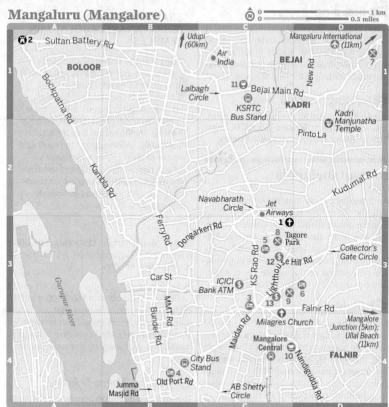

Mangaluru (Mangalore)

⊙ Sights

St Aloysius College Chapel   CHURCH
(Lighthouse Hill; ⊘9am-6pm) Catholicism's
roots in Mangaluru date back to the arrival
of the Portuguese in the early 1500s. One impressive legacy is the 1880 Sistine Chapel–
like St Aloysius chapel, with its walls and

ceilings painted with brilliant frescoes. No
photography is permitted.

Sultan's Battery   FORT
(Sultan Battery Rd; ⊘6am-6pm) The only rem-
nant of Tipu Sultan's fort is this small lookout with views over scenic backwaters. It's
4km from the city centre on the headland
of the old port.

Ullal Beach
BEACH

This stretch of golden sand is a good destination to escape the city heat. It's 12km south of Mangaluru, across the Netravathi estuary. An Uber/autorickshaw is ₹200 one way, or take bus 44A or 44C (₹10) from the City bus stand.

🛏 Sleeping

Hotel Roopa
HOTEL $

(📞0824-2421272; www.roopahotel.com; Balmatta Rd; r with fan/AC from ₹450/1300; 🌫🛜) One of the city's best-value hotels, close to the KSRTC bus stand, and combines good prices with professional management and decent, very affordable rooms. It has an excellent basement restaurant and bar.

Hotel Manorama
HOTEL $

(📞0824-2440306; KS Rao Rd; s/d from ₹620/640, with AC from ₹1120; 🌫) Offering fine value with clean, good-value rooms and a lobby that provides a memorable first impression with its display of Hindu statues and artefacts. It's close to the City Center mall for shopping and a food court.

Adarsh Hotel
HOTEL $

(📞0824-2440878; Market Rd; s/d ₹340/500) Enjoying a good location in the thick of things, this old-school cheapie has very low rates and fairly well-maintained rooms.

Gateway Hotel
HOTEL $$$

(📞0824-6660420; www.tajhotels.com; Old Port Rd; s/d incl breakfast from ₹5840/6260; 🌫@🛜🏊) Owned by the Taj group, this is a well-run hotel where the spacious rooms have plasma TVs and large beds laden with pillows, though bathrooms are somewhat dated. The lovely 20m swimming pool is surrounded by lawn and loungers, and there's a small spa and a fine restaurant.

🍴 Eating

Lalith Bar & Restaurant
SEAFOOD $$

(Balmatta Rd; mains ₹150-400; ⊘11.30am-3.30pm & 6.30-11.30pm; 🌫) Specialising in authentic Mangalorean seafood delights such as spicy masala fish fry smothered in saucy red coconut curry, or scrumptious deep-fried prawn rava fry, this scruffy restaurant is always popular. It all goes beautifully with a cold beer from its fully stocked bar.

Kadal
SOUTH INDIAN $$

(www.kadalrestaurant.in; Nalapad Residency, Lighthouse Hill Rd; mains ₹150-230; ⊘11am-3.30pm & 6.30-11pm; 🛜) This high-rise restaurant affords wonderful city views and elegant and warmly lit interiors. Try the spicy chicken *uruval* (a coconut coastal curry) or the yummy prawn ghee roast. Prices are moderate for the quality and experience.

Gajalee
SEAFOOD $$$

(📞0824-2221900; www.gajalee.com; Circuit House, Kadri Hills; mains ₹160-1280; ⊘10am-11pm) In a town famous for seafood, locals often cite this as the best. Their fish curries are superb, prepared in a spicy coconut sauce, while the clam *koshimbir* is cooked in a rich green masala.

KARNATAKA & BENGALURU MANGALURU (MANGALORE)

WORTH A TRIP

SURFING SWAMIS

While there has always been a spiritual bond between surfer and Mother ocean, the **Surfing Ashram** (Mantra Surf Club; 📞9663141146; www.surfingindia.net; 6-64 Kolachikambla, Mulki; board hire/lessons per day ₹700/2200) at Mulki, 30km north of Mangaluru, takes things to a whole new plane. At this Hare Krishna ashram, which was established by its American guru who's been surfing since 1963, devotees follow a daily ritual of *puja* (prayers), chanting, meditation and vegetarian diet in between catching barrels.

There's surf year-round, but the best waves are May to June and September to October. The swamis can also assist with information on surfing across India. Board hire is ₹700 per day and lessons are ₹2200 per day.

If there are no waves they have SUP boards for the river or ocean, sea kayaks and a jet ski for wakeboarding. Snorkelling trips to offshore islands are also possible.

The centre has a homely beachhouse feel, and rates (per person/couple including full board ₹2800/3900).

All are welcome to visit, but it's important to be aware that it's strictly a place of worship and there are guidelines to abide by, including abstinence from meat, alcohol, tobacco and sex during your stay.

🍷 Drinking & Nightlife

★ Spindrift
MICROBREWERY

(www.facebook.com/SpindriftMangalore; 5th Fl, Bharath Mall, Lalbagh; ⊙11am-11pm; 🛜) The first microbrewery in town is a big space with indoor and outdoor seating and the acoustic artists, indie bands and DJs create quite a vibe on weekend nights. Beers on tap (from ₹230) include a wheat beer, pilsner and IPA and there's good finger food too.

#45
CAFE

(Trinity Commercial Complex, Attavara Rd; ⊙10.30am-10.30pm; 🛜) Very popular with students, this hip little cafe does a wide range of huge milkshakes (including Ferrero Rocher and Nutella flavours), fresh juices, good coffees, wraps, burgers and breakfasts.

❶ Getting There & Away

AIR

Mangaluru International Airport (☑0824-2254252; www.mangaloreairport.com) is about 15km northeast of town. There are daily flights to Mumbai, Delhi, Bengaluru, Hyderabad and Chennai and international connections to Abu Dhabi, Doha and Dubai.

Airlines include:

Air India (☑0824-2451046; Hathill Rd; ⊙9am-5.30pm Mon-Sat)

Jet Airways (☑0824-2441181; Ram Bhavan Complex, KS Rao Rd; ⊙9am-5.30pm Mon-Sat)

BUS

The **KSRTC bus stand** (☑0824-2211243; Bejai Main Rd) is 3km from the city centre. Deluxe buses depart half-hourly to Bengaluru (₹406 to ₹815, seven to nine hours) via Mysuru (₹245 to ₹505, five to six hours).

Dharmasthala ₹49-82, one to two hours, 8.05am and 2.20pm daily

Ernakulam ₹845, nine hours, 9pm

Gokarna ₹234, 5½ hours, 12.45pm daily

Hassan ₹163 to ₹355, three to five hours, 12 daily

Madikeri ₹135 to ₹305, 3½ to four hours, 11 daily

Panaji ₹359 to ₹698, 8-9½ hours, one to three daily

For Udupi (₹58, 1½ hours) head to the **City bus stand** (State Bank stand).

TRAIN

The main train station, Mangaluru Central, is south of the city centre.

❶ Getting Around

To get to the airport, take buses 47B or 47C from the City bus stand. An Uber is around ₹350.

Dharmasthala

📞 08256 / POP 10,340

Inland from Mangaluru are a string of Jain temple towns, such as Venur, Mudabidri and Karkal. The most interesting among them is Dharmasthala village, 75km east of Mangaluru by the Netravathi River. Tens of thousands of pilgrims pass through this tiny settlement every day. During holidays and major festivals, such as the five-day pilgrim festival of **Lakshadeepotsava** (⊙Nov), the footfall can go up tenfold.

⊙ Sights

Manjunatha Temple
HINDU TEMPLE

(⊙6.30am-2.30pm & 5-8.45pm) This striking Kerala-style temple has a pyramidal roof of gold plated copper plates and its wood carvings have recently been meticulously renovated. Three elephants trunk out blessings to pilgrims outside the Manjunatha Temple; men have to enter bare-chested, with legs covered. You can fast-track the queue if you pay ₹200.

Car Museum
MUSEUM

(₹5; ⊙8.30am-1pm & 2-7pm) Don't forget to visit the fantastic Car Museum, home to 48 vintage autos, including a 1903 Renault and 1920s Studebaker President used by Mahatma Gandhi, plus classic Mercedes Benz, Chevrolet and Rolls-Royce models. No photos are allowed.

TRAINS FROM MANGALURU (MANGALORE)

DESTINATION	TRAIN NO & NAME	FARE (₹)	DURATION (HR)	DEPARTURES
Bengaluru	16524 Bangalore Exp	sleeper/2AC 280/1080	11½	8.55pm
Chennai	12686 Chennai Exp	sleeper/2AC 460/1725	15½	4.20pm
Gokarna	16523 Karwar Exp	sleeper/2AC 190/6900	5½	7.55am
Gokarna	12620 Matsyaganda Exp	sleeper/2AC 235/825	4	2.35pm
Thiruvananthapuram	16630 Malabar Exp	sleeper/2AC 340/1320	15	6.15pm

RANI ABBAKKA: THE WARRIOR QUEEN

The legendary exploits of Rani Abbakka, one of India's first freedom fighters – who happened to be a female – is one that gets surprisingly little attention outside the Mangaluru region. An Indian Joan of Arc, her inspiring story is just waiting to be picked up by a Bollywood/Hollywood screenwriter.

As the Portuguese consolidated power along India's western coastline in the 16th century, seizing towns across Goa and down to Mangalore, their attempts to take Ullal proved more of a challenge. This was thanks to its 'fearless queen', who proved to be a major thorn in their grand plans to control the lucrative spice trade. Her efforts to continually repel their advances is the stuff of local legend.

Well trained in the art of war, both in strategy and combat, Rani Abbakka knew how to brandish a sword. And while she was eventually defeated, this wasn't from a loss on the battlefield, but by her treacherous ex-husband, who conspired against her in leaking intelligence to the enemy.

Her efforts to rally her people to defeat the powerful Portuguese is not forgotten by locals: Rani Abbakka is immortalised in a bronze statue on horseback at the roundabout on the road to Ullal beach, and has an annual festival dedicated to her.

The shore temple that looks over the beautiful Someshwara beach a few kilometres south from Ullal was the former site of her fort, but only sections of its wall remains intact.

🛏 Sleeping

There are only very simple sleeping options. Contact the **temple office** (☑ 08256-277121; www.shridharmasthala.org) for help with lodging.

Rajathadri Guest House   LODGE **$**
(www.shridharmasthala.org/online-accommodation; r with fan/AC ₹500/1000) About 700m north of the main temple, this clean guesthouse is used by pilgrims and can be booked online. Rooms sleep up to three.

🍴 Eating

Manjunatha Temple Kitchen   INDIAN
(⊙ 11.30am-2.15pm & 7.30-10pm) FREE Offers simple free meals, attached to a hall that can seat up to 3000. Very efficiently managed.

ℹ Getting There & Away

There are frequent buses to Dharmasthala from Mangaluru (₹75, 2½ hours).

Udupi

☑ 0820 / POP 177,800
Just inland from the coast, Udupi is a holy town home to an ancient Hindu temple and several monasteries.

◎ Sights

Krishna Temple   HINDU TEMPLE
(www.udupisrikrishnamatha.org; Car St; ⊙ 3.30am-10pm) Udupi is home to the atmospheric, 13th-century Krishna Temple, which draws thousands of Hindu pilgrims through the year. Surrounded by eight *maths* (monasteries), it's a hive of activity, with musicians playing at the entrance, elephants on hand for *puja* (prayer rituals) and pilgrims constantly coming and going. Non-Hindus are welcome inside the temple; men must enter bare-chested. Elaborate rituals are also performed in the temple during the Udupi Paryaya festival.

🛏 Sleeping

Shri Vidyasamuda Choultry   HOTEL **$**
(☑ 0820-2520820; Car St; r ₹150-350) There are several pilgrim hotels near the temple, but this simple offering is the best with views looking over the ghat.

Hotel Sriram Residency   HOTEL **$$**
(☑ 0820-2530761; www.hotelsriramresidency.in; Head Post Office Rd; r with fan/AC from ₹1035/1868; ❋ 🛜) A well-run place with good choice of rooms, some on the upper floors overlooking the Krishna temple. There are two bars and a good seafood restaurant here.

🍴 Eating

Udupi is famed for its vegetarian food, and recognised across India for its sumptuous thali and as the birthplace of the humble dosa.

Woodlands   INDIAN **$**
(Dr UR Rao Complex; dosas from ₹60, meals from ₹100; ⊙ 8am-3.15pm & 5.30-10.30pm)

Woodlands is regarded as the best vegetarian place in town and has an AC dining room where you can escape the heat. It's a short walk south of Krishna Temple.

Mitra Samaja INDIAN $
(Car St; meals from ₹80; ⊙8am-9pm) A famous old establishment that serves delicious snacks, dosas and coffee. Can get crowded. It's just south of the Krishna Temple.

❶ Getting There & Away

Udupi is 58km north of Mangaluru along the coast; very regular buses ply the route (₹40 to ₹62, 1½ hours). There's a daily bus to Gokarna (₹180, four hours) at 2pm and many services (mostly at night) to Bengaluru (₹434 to ₹880, eight to 10 hours). Regular buses head to Malpe (₹9, 30 minutes).

Malpe

☑ 0820 / POP 1980
A laid-back fishing harbour on the west coast 4km from Udupi, Malpe has nice beaches ideal for flopping about in the surf (though on weekends and holidays jet skis, banana boats and quad bikes taint the scene).

◉ Sights & Activities

St Mary's Island ISLAND
This tiny island off Malpe is where Portuguese explorer Vasco da Gama supposedly landed in 1498, and has curious hexagonal basalt formations that jut out of the sand. No boats run here between June and mid-October. From Malpe pier you can take a ferry (₹100 return, 45 minutes, departing at 11am or when demand is sufficient) or charter a private boat from Malpe Beach here.

⊨ Sleeping & Eating

Paradise Isle Beach Resort HOTEL $$
(☑ 0820-2538777; www.theparadiseisle.com; r ₹3000-5500; ❈@శ☲) This large concrete

hotel is right on the sands and has comfortable rooms, many with sea views. They offer a lot of ayurvedic packages, which include massages and specialised diet programs, water sports such as banana boat rides and jet skiing, and can organise **boats** (per couple ₹4000; ⊙Oct-Mar) in the backwaters of Hoode nearby.

❶ Getting There & Away

Buses to Udupi are ₹9, and an autorickshaw ₹60.

Jog Falls

☑ 08186
The second-highest waterfalls in India, **Jog Falls** (₹5) only come to life during the monsoon. The tallest of the four falls is the Raja, which drops 293m. For a good view of the falls, bypass the area close to the bus stand and hike to the foot of the falls down a 1200-plus step path. Watch out for leeches during the wet season.

⊨ Sleeping

Hotel Mayura Gerusoppa Jogfalls HOTEL $$
(☑ 08186-244732; www.kstdc.co/hotels/hotel-mayura-gerusoppa-jogfalls; dm ₹300, d with fan/AC incl breakfast from ₹1950/2400; ❈శ) Located near Jog Falls' car park, this government-run hotel has enormous rooms that are in decent shape, all with spectacular views, though they can be a tad musty off-season. The dorm has 10 beds and is more geared to local school groups. Note prices rise weekends and wi-fi is confined to the lobby area only.

❶ Getting There & Away

Most people hire a taxi; a return trip from Gokarna costs ₹2200. Otherwise, you can get a string of buses which head via Kumta and turn off at Honavar (₹68), or Shivamogga (Shimoga) if coming via Bengaluru (₹470, nine hours).

FORMULA BUFFALO
....

Call it an indigenous take on the Grand Prix, Kambla, or traditional buffalo racing, is a hugely popular pastime among villagers along the southern Karnataka coast. Popularised in the early 20th century and born out of local farmers habitually racing their buffaloes home after a day in the fields, the races have now hit the big time. Thousands of spectators attend each edition, and racing buffaloes are pampered and prepared like thoroughbreds.

Kambla events are held between November and March, usually on weekends. Parallel tracks are laid out in a paddy field, along which buffaloes hurtle towards the finish line. In most cases the man rides on a board fixed to a ploughshare, literally surfing his way down the track behind the beasts. The faster creatures can cover the 120m-odd distance through water and mud in around 14 seconds!

Gokarna

📞 08386 / POP 28,880

A regular nominee among travellers' favourite beaches in India, Gokarna attracts a crowd for a low-key, chilled-out beach holiday and not for full-scale parties. Most accommodation is in thatched bamboo huts along its several stretches of blissful coast.

In fact there are two Gokarnas; adjacent to the beaches is the sacred Hindu pilgrim town of Gokarna, full of ancient temples that come to life during important festivals such as Shivaratri and Ganesh Chaturthi (p169). While its lively bazaar is an interesting place to visit, most foreign tourists don't hang around overnight, instead making a beeline straight to the adjoining beaches.

◉ Sights

The best beaches are south of Gokarna town: first Kudle Beach (5km by road from Gokarna), then Om Beach (6.5km by road). Well hidden south of Om Beach lie the small sandy coves of Half Moon Bay and Paradise Beach, without road access. A lovely coastal trail links all the beaches, but, as there have been (very occasional) reports of muggings, it's best not to walk it alone.

★ Om Beach
BEACH

One of Karnataka's best beaches, Gokarna's most famous stretch of sand twists and turns over several kilometres in a form that resembles the outline of an Om symbol. It comprises several gorgeous coves, with wide stretches interspersed with smaller patches of sand, perfect for sunbathing and swimming. There's fine swimming most of the season when the sea is not choppy, though signs officially ban swimming (local tourists have drowned here in rough seas).

Kudle Beach
BEACH

This lovely wide cove, backed by wooded headlands, offers plenty of room to stretch out on along its attractive sands. Restaurants, guesthouses and yoga camps are dotted around the rear of the beach, but they're well spaced and development remains peaceful and attractive.

Half Moon Bay
BEACH

Small, attractive cove with a lovely sweep of powdery sand and basic hut accommodation. There's no road, only a path to this beach. It's about a 30-minute hike from Om Beach (itself 5km from Gokarna town), or boats run here on demand from Gokarna town.

ℹ️ GOKARNA'S TEMPLES

This is a deeply holy town and foreigners should be respectful in and around its many temples: do not try to enter their inner sanctums, which are reserved for Hindus only. It's customary for pilgrims to bathe in the sea and fast, and many shave their heads, before entering Gokarna's holy places.

Paradise Beach
BEACH

Paradise Beach is a mix of sand and rocks, and a haven for the long-term 'turn-on-tune-in-drop-out' crowd. Unfortunately, the government routinely destroys all the huts out this way, leaving it in a ramshackle state – hence it's BYO everything here. If you've a hammock or tent it's a great choice for total isolation.

★ Mahaganapati Temple
HINDU TEMPLE

(Car St; ⊙6am-8.30pm) **FREE** Deeply atmospheric temple complex, encircled by lanes, but peaceful inside. Here there's a (rare) stone statue of an upright, standing Ganesh, said to be over 1500 years old, who is depicted with a flat head – said to mark the spot where the demon Ravana struck him. This is the second-most holy site in Gokarna and it's customary for pilgrims to visit here first before heading to the neighbouring Mahabaleshwara Temple. Foreigners are not allowed inside the inner sanctum.

★ Mahabaleshwara Temple
HINDU TEMPLE

(Car St; ⊙6am-8.30pm) **FREE** Dedicated to Lord Shiva, this is a profoundly spiritual temple, built of granite by Mayurasharma of the Kadamba dynasty and said to date back to the 4th century. Hindus believe it brings blessings to pilgrims who even glimpse it, and rituals are performed for the deceased. A *gopura* (gateway tower) dominates the complex, while inside a stone nandi faces the inner chamber, home to Shiva's lingam. Foreigners may enter the complex but not the inner sanctum.

Koorti Teertha
HINDU SITE

A large temple tank where locals, pilgrims and immaculately dressed Brahmins perform their ablutions.

Gokarna Beach
BEACH

Gokarna's main town beach isn't clean and is not good for casual bathing. The main section is popular with domestic tourists but if you walk away from here to the north you'll

MURUDESHWAR

A worthwhile stopover for those taking the coastal route from Gokarna to Mangaluru, Murudeshwar is a beachside pilgrimage town. It's most notable for its colossal seashore **statue of Lord Shiva**, which sits directly on the shore overlooking the Arabian Sea. For the best views, take the lift 18 storeys to the top of the skyscraper-like **Shri Murudeshwar Temple** (lift ₹10; ⊘ lift 7.45am-12.30pm & 3.15-6.45pm).

Murudeshwar is 3km off the main highway, accessed by train or bus passing up and down the coast. If you'd like to stay overnight, beachfront homestay **Mavalli Beach Heritage Home** (☑ 9901767993; http://mavallibeachheritage.com; r ₹4200; ✳ ✆) has four stylish rooms, a warm ambience and great home-cooked food, though the approach road is in poor shape.

find a long stretch of sand that seems to go forever. There's some surf here in season.

🏃 Activities

Cocopelli Surf School SURFING
(☑ 8105764969; www.cocopelli.org; Gokarna Beach; lesson per person ₹2000, board rental per 2hr ₹750; ⊘ Oct-May) Offers lessons by internationally certified instructors and rents boards.

🎊 Festivals & Events

★**Shivaratri** RELIGIOUS
(⊘ Feb/Mar) A chariot bearing a statue of Lord Shiva and his lingam is pulled through the streets by hundreds of pilgrims to conclude this nine-day festival.

🛏 Sleeping & Eating

For most foreigners Gokarna means sleeping right on the beach in a simple shack. However, there are a growing number of more upmarket lodges and hotels, so if you don't want to rough it you don't have to. Note that most places close from November to March.

🛏 Om Beach

★**Nirvana Café** GUESTHOUSE $
(☑ 9742466481; cottage ₹700-900; ✆) These attractive cottages, towards the eastern

end of the beach, are some of Om's best, all with front porches that face a slim central garden. On the premises you'll find a good beachfront restaurant, laundry and travel agency.

Namaste Café GUESTHOUSE $
(☑ 08386-257141; www.namastegokarna.com; r with fan/AC from ₹1080/1720; ✳ ✆) At the beginning of Om, this long-standing guesthouse is the most upmarket place on the beach, with well-constructed accommodation in leafy gardens and the comforts of AC and wi-fi and hot water.

Dolphin Shanti GUESTHOUSE $
(☑ 9740930133; r from ₹300) Rooms are basic yet appealing at this simple guesthouse at the far eastern end of Om Beach. It's perched upon the rocks with fantastic ocean views, and lives up to its name with dolphins often spotted.

Sangham BUNGALOW $
(☑ 9448101099; Om Beach; r ₹650, without bathroom ₹400) The no-frills concrete bungalows at the back of this beachfront resort are set in a garden area. Rooms are basic and a bit soulless, with OK mattresses and mossie nets.

★**SwaSwara** HOTEL $$$
(☑ 08386-257132; www.swaswara.com; s/d 5 nights from €1820/2450; ✳ @ ✆ ☀) 'Journeying into the self' is the mantra at SwaSwara and you certainly have the infrastructure in place to achieve that here, as this is one of South India's finest retreats. Yoga, ayurveda, treatments, a meditation dome and elegant private villas with open-air showers and lovely sitting areas await. No short stays are possible.

Sunset Point INDIAN $
(mains ₹120-200; ⊘ 7.30am-10pm) Family-run place at the eastern end of Om Beach with a great perch overlooking the waves. There's a long menu that takes in breakfasts, sandwiches, Indian and Chinese dishes; grilled kingfish is around ₹180.

Om Shree Ganesh MULTICUISINE, INDIAN $
(meals ₹80-170; ⊘ 8am-3pm & 6-10.30pm) Across a stream on Om Beach, this atmospheric double-storey restaurant does tasty dishes such as tandoori prawns, mushroom tikka and *momos* (Tibetan dumplings).

Namaste Cafe MULTICUISINE $$
(mains ₹120-230; ⊘ 8.30am-4pm & 6-11pm) The only 'proper' restaurant on Om Beach, this

attractive double-deck affair has dreamy, romantic sea views, cold beer and good seafood, pasta and Indian dishes.

Kudle Beach

Strawberry Farmhouse   GUESTHOUSE $
(📞7829367584; r ₹700-1000; 🌢) A good guesthouse at the northern section of Kudle with spacious cottages (some with AC), all with verandahs and a prime position looking out to the water.

Uma Garden   GUESTHOUSE $
(📞9916720728; www.facebook.com/uma.garden kudlebeach; r without bathroom ₹350) Tucked around the corner at the beginning of Kudle, this bucolic guesthouse has a laid-back owner and sea-facing vegetarian restaurant.

Ganga Cafe   GUESTHOUSE $
(📞8095766058; r from ₹350; 📶) At the north end of Kudle, these concrete rooms are above a popular restaurant and have partial sea views from a shared balcony. Bathrooms are shared.

★Arya Ayurvedic
Panchakarma Centre   SPA HOTEL $$
(📞9611062468; www.ayurvedainindien.com; r from ₹1800; 🌢📶) Some of the best rooms in Gokarna, the simple yet elegant, accommodation on Kudle Beach has been carefully planned and designed using quality furnishings. Priority is given to those booking ayurvedic packages and there's a fine in-house cafe (mains ₹130-200; ☉8am-10pm; 📶).

Namaste Yoga Farm   BUNGALOW $$$
(📞08386-257454; www.spiritualland.com; incl breakfast & yoga r €50-94, cottage €80-104; 📶) On the hillside above the northern end of Kudle this popular place is owned by an excellent, patient German yoga instructor. The accommodation, in a patch of jungle, is pretty functional and does not have a 'wow' factor but the yoga (two daily classes are included) and breakfast (cooked to order) are exceptional and there's a very welcoming vibe.

Half Moon Beach

Half Moon Garden Cafe   BUNGALOW $
(📞9743615820; hut from ₹300) 🍃 A throwback to the hippie days, this hideaway has a blissful beach and pretty decent huts in a coconut grove. It runs on solar power.

Gokarna Town

Shree Shakti Hotel   HOTEL $
(📞9036043088; chidushakti@gmail.com; Gokarna Beach Rd; s/d ₹400/600) On Gokarna's main strip, this friendly hotel is excellent value with immaculate lime-green rooms. There's a popular restaurant downstairs.

Greenland Guesthouse   GUESTHOUSE $
(📞9019651420; r from ₹300; 📶) Hidden down a jungle path on the edge of town, this mellow family-run guesthouse has clean rooms in vibrant colours and a lovely verdant garden to enjoy. There's a daily charge (₹200) for wi-fi.

★Prema   INDIAN, MULTICUISINE $
(Gokarna Beach Rd; meals ₹80-150; ☉8am-10pm) Always packed, this humble-looking place has a prime location just before the beach. Offers Western food but it's best to stick to the South Indian classics. They accept cards for payments.

Shree Shakti   ICE CREAM, INDIAN $
(Gokarna Beach Rd; meals from ₹110; ☉8am-10pm; 📶) Attractive, casual cafe-restaurant in Gokarna town that's rightly renowned for its ice cream, juices and flavoursome local food.

🛍 Shopping

Shree Radhakrishna Bookstore   BOOKS
(Car St, Gokarna Town; ☉10am-6pm) Second-hand novels, postcards and maps.

❶ Information

Post Office (Main St; ☉10am-4.30pm Mon-Sat)
SBI ATM (Main St)

❶ Getting There & Away

Trains from Mumbai or Goa and private buses from Hampi/Hospet may get you into Gokarna at ungodly hours: it's worth notifying your guesthouse.

BUS

Local and private buses depart daily to Bengaluru (₹505 to ₹714, 12 hours) and Mysuru (from ₹570, 12 hours), as well as Mangaluru (from ₹255, 6½ hours) and Hubballi (₹195, four hours).

For Hampi, **Paulo Travels** (📞08394-225867; www.paulobus.com) is a popular choice which heads via Hosapete (Hospet; fan/AC ₹1500/1550, seven hours). Note if you're coming from Hampi, you'll be dropped at Ankola from where there's a free transfer for the 26km journey to Gokarna.

There's also regular buses to Panaji (₹120, three hours) and Mumbai (₹754 to ₹980, 12 hours).

TRAIN

Many express trains stop at Gokarna Rd station, 9km from town. There are other options from Ankola, 26km away. Hotels and travel agencies in Gokarna can book tickets.

The 3am 12619 Matsyagandha Express goes to Mangaluru (sleeper/2AC ₹220/740, 4½ hours); the return train leaves Gokarna Rd at 6.40pm for Madgaon in Goa (sleeper/2AC ₹170/740, two hours) and Mumbai (sleeper/2AC, ₹455/1700, 12 hours).

Autorickshaws charge ₹220 to go to Gokarna Rd station (or ₹450 to Ankola); a bus from Gokarna town charges ₹30 and leaves every 30 minutes.

CENTRAL KARNATAKA

KARNATAKA & BENGALURU HAMPI

Hampi

📞 08394 / POP 3500

The magnificent ruins of Hampi dot an unearthly landscape that has captivated travellers for centuries. Heaps of giant boulders perch precariously over kilometres of undulating terrain, their rusty hues offset by jade-green palm groves, banana plantations and paddy fields. While it's possible to see this World Heritage Site in a day or two, plan on lingering for a while.

The main travellers' ghetto has traditionally been Hampi Bazaar, a village crammed with budget lodges, shops and restaurants, and towered over by the majestic Virupaksha Temple. Tranquil Virupapur Gaddi across the river has become a new popular hang-out. However, recent demolitions (p215) in both areas have seen businesses closed, with the future of Hampi bitterly contested between locals and authorities.

History

Hampi and its neighbouring areas find mention in the Hindu epic Ramayana as Kishkinda, the realm of the monkey gods. In 1336 Telugu prince Harihararaya chose Hampi as the site for his new capital Vijayanagar, which – over the next couple of centuries – grew into one of the largest Hindu empires in Indian history. By the 16th century it was a thriving metropolis of about 500,000 people, its busy bazaars dab-

bling in international commerce, brimming with precious stones and merchants from faraway lands. All this, however, ended in a stroke in 1565, when a confederacy of Deccan sultanates razed Vijayanagar to the ground, striking it a death blow from which it never recovered.

◉ Sights

Set over 36 sq km, there are some 3700 monuments to explore in Hampi, and it would take months if you were to do it justice. The ruins are divided into two main areas: the Sacred Centre, around Hampi Bazaar with its temples, and the Royal Centre, towards Kamalapuram, where the Vijayanagara royalty lived and governed.

◎ Sacred Centre

★ **Virupaksha Temple** HINDU TEMPLE
(Map p214; ₹2, camera/video ₹50/500; ⊙ dawn-dusk) The focal point of Hampi Bazaar is the Virupaksha Temple, one of the city's oldest structures, and Hampi's only remaining working temple. The main *gopuram*, almost 50m high, was built in 1442, with a smaller one added in 1510. The main shrine is dedicated to Virupaksha, an incarnation of Shiva.

An elephant called Lakshmi blesses devotees as they enter in exchange for donations; it doesn't seem hugely rewarding for the pachyderm, but she gets time off for a morning bath down by the river ghats

Hemakuta Hill HISTORIC SITE
(Map p212) To the south, overlooking Virupaksha Temple, Hemakuta Hill has a scattering of early ruins, including monolithic sculptures of Narasimha (Vishnu in his man-lion incarnation) and Ganesh. It's worth the short walk up for the view.

Nandi Statue STATUE
(Map p212) At the east end of Hampi Bazaar is a Nandi statue, around which stand some of the colonnaded blocks of the ancient marketplace. This is the main location for Vijaya Utsav (Hampi Festival; ⊙ Jan), the Hampi arts festival.

★ **Vittala Temple** HINDU TEMPLE
(Map p212; Indian/foreigner/child under 15 ₹30/500/free; ⊙ 8.30am-5.30pm) The undisputed highlight of the Hampi ruins, the 16th-century Vittala Temple stands amid the boulders 2km from Hampi Bazaar. Work

possibly started on the temple during the reign of Krishnadevaraya (r 1509–29). It was never finished or consecrated, yet the temple's incredible sculptural work remains the pinnacle of Vijayanagar art.

The ornate **stone chariot** that stands in the courtyard is the temple's showpiece and represents Vishnu's vehicle with an image of Garuda within. Its wheels were once capable of turning.

The outer 'musical' pillars reverberate when tapped. They were supposedly designed to replicate 81 different Indian instruments, but authorities have placed them out of tourists' bounds for fear of further damage, so no more do-re-mi.

As well as the main temple, whose sanctum was illuminated using a design of reflective waters, you'll find the marriage hall and prayer hall, the structures to the left and right upon entry, respectively.

Lakshimi Narasmiha HINDU TEMPLE
(Map p212) An interesting stop-off along the road to the Virupaksha Temple is the 6.7m monolithic statue of the bulging-eyed Lakshimi Narasmiha in a cross-legged lotus position and topped by a hood of seven snakes.

Krishna Temple HINDU TEMPLE
(Map p212) Built in 1513, the Krishna Temple is fronted by an *apsara* and 10 incarnations of Vishnu. It's on the road to the Virupaksha Temple near Lakshimi Narasmiha.

Sule Bazaar HISTORIC SITE
(Map p212) Halfway along the path from Hampi Bazaar to Vittala Temple, a track to the right leads over the rocks to deserted Sule Bazaar, one of ancient Hampi's principal centres of commerce and reputedly its red-light district. At the southern end of this area is the beautiful 16th-century **Achyutaraya Temple** (Map p212).

◉ Royal Centre & Around

While it can be accessed by a 2km foot trail from the Achyutaraya Temple, the Royal Centre is best reached via the Hampi–Kamalapuram road. A number of Hampi's major sites stand here.

Mahanavami-diiba RUINS
(Map p212) The Mahanavami-diiba is a 12m-high three-tiered platform with intricate carvings and panoramic vistas of the walled complex of ruined temples, stepped tanks and the King's audience hall. The platform was used as a royal viewing area for the Dasara festivities, religious ceremonies and processions.

Zenana Enclosure RUINS
(Map p212; Indian/foreigner ₹30/500; ◉8.30am-5.30pm) Northeast of the Royal Centre within the walled ladies' quarters is the Zenana Enclosure. Its peaceful grounds and manicured lawns feel like an oasis amid the arid surrounds. Here are the **Lotus Mahal** (Map p212) and **Elephant Stables** (Map p212; ◉8.30am-5.30pm).

Hazarama Temple HINDU TEMPLE
(Map p212) Features exquisite carvings that depict scenes from the Ramayana, and polished black granite pillars.

Queen's Bath RUINS
(Map p212; ◉8.30am-5.30pm) South of the Royal Centre you'll find various temples and elaborate waterworks, including the Queen's Bath, deceptively plain on the outside but amazing within, with its Indo-Islamic architecture.

Archaeological Museum MUSEUM
(Map p212; Kamalapuram; ◉10am-5pm Sat-Thu) Boasts a fine collection of sculptures from local ruins, plus neolithic tools, 16th-century weaponry and a large floor model of the Vijayanagar ruins. There's a fine photographic record of the site dating back to 1856.

🏃 Activities

Hampi Waterfalls WATERFALL
About a 2km walk west of Hampi Bazaar, past shady banana plantations, you can scramble over the boulders to reach the attractive Hampi 'waterfalls', a series of small whirlpools among the rocks amid superb scenery.

Bouldering
Hampi is the undisputed bouldering capital of India. The entire landscape is a climber's adventure playground made of granite crags and boulders, some bearing the marks

> **ℹ HAMPI RUINS TICKET**
>
> The ₹500 ticket for Vittala Temple entitles you to same-day admission into most of the paid sites across the ruins (including around the Royal Centre and the Archaeological Museum), so don't lose your ticket.

Hampi & Anegundi

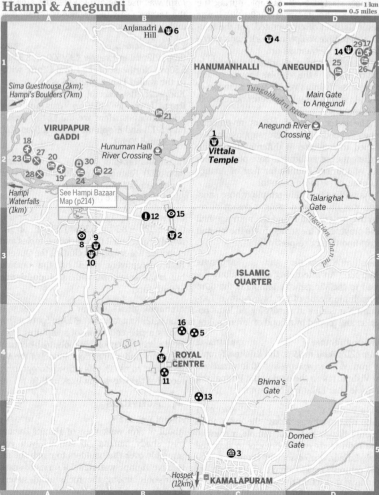

of ancient stonemasons. *Golden Boulders* (2013) by Gerald Krug and Christiane Hupe has a tonne of info on bouldering in Hampi.

Tom & Jerry CLIMBING
(Map p212; ☑9482746697, 8277792588; www.facebook.com/TomJerry-Climbing-Shop; Virupapur Gaddi; 2½hr class ₹500) Two local lads who are doing great work in catering to climbers' needs, providing quality mats, shoes and local knowledge and running climbing classes.

Thimmaclimb CLIMBING
(Map p212; ☑8762776498; www.thimmaclimb.wix.com/hampi-bouldering; Shiva Guesthouse, Virupap-

ur Gaddi; class from ₹400) A small professional operation run by local pro Thimma, who guides, runs lessons and stocks professional equipment for hire and sale. He also runs three-day trips (₹5000) to Badami for sandstone climbing.

Birdwatching

Get in touch with Kishkinda Trust (TKT; ☑08533-267777; http://tktkishkinda.org) in Anegundi for info on birdwatching in the area, which has over 230 species, including the greater flamingo. *The Birds of Hampi* (2014) by Samad Kottur is the definitive guide.

Hampi & Anegundi

☆☆ Festivals & Events

Virupaksha Car Festival RELIGIOUS
(⊙Mar/Apr) The Virupaksha Car Festival is a big event, with a colourful procession characterised by a giant wooden chariot (the temple car from Virupaksha Temple) being pulled along the main strip of Hampi Bazaar.

⌂ Sleeping

Most guesthouses are cosy family-run digs, perfect for the budget traveller. More upmarket places are located further from the centre.

⌂ Hampi Bazaar

This little enclave is a classic travellers' ghetto. However, its existence is under threat as there are plans to demolish it.

★ Manash Guesthouse GUESTHOUSE $
(Map p214; ☎9448877420; manashhampi@gmail.com; r with fan/AC ₹1200/1500; ❋🗐) Owned by the legendary Mango Tree people, this place has only two rooms set off a little yard, but they are the best in Hampi Bazaar, each with quality mattresses, attractive decorative touches and free fast wi-fi.

Thilak Homestay GUESTHOUSE $
(Map p214; ☎9449900964; www.facebook.com/thilak.homestay; r with fan/AC ₹1000/1500; ❋🗐) A commendably clean, orderly place with

eight well-presented rooms (and more in another block) that have spring mattresses and hot water. The owner is helpful and can arrange transport from Hosapete or around Hampi.

Pushpa Guest House GUESTHOUSE $
(Map p214; ☎9448795120; pushpaguesthouse99@yahoo.in; d from ₹900, with AC from ₹1300; ❋🗐) Pushpa is a good all-rounder with comfortable, attractive and spotless rooms that have mossie nets. It has a lovely sit-out on the 1st floor, and reliable travel agency.

Ganesh Guesthouse GUESTHOUSE $
(Map p214; vishnuhampi@gmail.com; r ₹500-800, with AC from ₹1500; ❋🗐) A welcoming place, the small family-run Ganesh has been around for over 20 years, and has four tidy, neat rooms. Also has a nice rooftop restaurant.

Archana Guest House GUESTHOUSE $
(Map p214; ☎08394-241547; addihampi@yahoo.com; d from ₹800; 🗐) On the riverfront, quiet and cheerful Archana has two plain rooms with river views above a restaurant. The others are in a separate block over the street.

Vicky's GUESTHOUSE $
(Map p214; ☎9480561010; vikkyhampi@yahoo.co.in; r from ₹350; 🗐) Dependable cheapie with decent, basic rooms with mossie nets done up in pop purple and green and a friendly owner. There's a good travel agent here too.

Hampi Bazaar

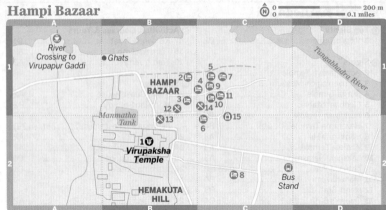

Hampi Bazaar

◎ Top Sights
1 Virupaksha Temple B2

🛏 Sleeping
2 Archana Guest House B1
3 Ganesh Guesthouse B1
4 Gopi Guest House..................................C1
5 Kiran Guest House C1
6 Manash Guesthouse C2
7 Netra Guesthouse C1
8 Padma Guest House C2
9 Pushpa Guest House.............................C1
10 Thilak Homestay....................................C1

11 Vicky's C1

🍴 Eating
12 Mango Tree..B1
13 Moonlight B2
14 Ravi's Rose C1

🛍 Shopping
15 Akash Art Gallery &
   Bookstore C2

ℹ Information
   Tourist Office..................................(see 1)

Padma Guest House GUESTHOUSE $
(Map p214; ☑08394-241331; padmaguesthouse
@gmail.com; d ₹900-1600; ❄🌐) Away from
the main bazaar area, this guesthouse has
a choice of basic, decent rooms, many with
views of Virupaksha Temple, though bathrooms could do with an upgrade. The owners can arrange bus and train tickets.

Kiran Guest House GUESTHOUSE $
(Map p214; ☑9448143906; kiranhampi2012@
gmail.com; r ₹600-800; 🌐) No-frills guesthouse
close to the riverfront and banana groves.
Rooms are basic but clean, the showers are
warmish and the family owners are helpful.

Netra Guesthouse GUESTHOUSE $
(Map p214; ☑9480569326; r from ₹500, without
bathroom from ₹300) Basic, clean rooms for
shoestringers, with an ambient open-air
restaurant.

Gopi Guest House GUESTHOUSE $$
(Map p214; ☑08394-241695; www.gopi-guest
house.com; r with fan/AC ₹2000/2500; ❄@🌐)

Split over two properties on the same street,
long-standing Gopi offers friendly service
and has good-quality rooms that are almost
upscale for Hampi's standards. There are
temple views from its rooftop cafe. Walk-in
rates are usually lower than online bookings.

🛏 Virupapur Gaddi & Around

The rural tranquillity of Virupapur Gaddi,
across the river from Hampi Bazaar, has real
appeal, particularly with Israelis – locals
nickname the place 'Little Jerusalem'. How-
ever, authorities demolished buildings here
in 2016, and its long-term status is unclear.

Sunny Guesthouse GUESTHOUSE $
(Map p212; ☑9448566368; www.sunnyguest
house.com; r ₹450-1200; @🌐) Sunny both in
name and disposition, this popular guest-
house is a hit among backpackers for its
characterful huts, very well-maintained
tropical garden, hammocks and chilled-out
restaurant.

Shanthi
GUESTHOUSE $

(Map p212; ☑ 8533287038; http://shanthihampi. com/; cottages ₹1000-1800; @) Enjoys a stunning, peaceful setting next to rice fields and primed for sunset. Shanthi's attractive earth-themed, thatched cottages have couch swings dangling in their front porches and the restaurant serves good grub.

Hema Guest House
GUESTHOUSE $

(Map p212; ☑ 8762395470; rockyhampi@gmail. com; Virupapur Gaddi; d from ₹600; ☎) Worth considering, with rows of cute and comfy colourful cottages in a shady grove, all with a table or chair for company and a hammock; though mattresses could be better. Its restaurant is perpetually full with lazing tourists.

Manju's Place
GUESTHOUSE $

(Map p212; ☑ 9449247712; r ₹500, without bathroom from ₹250) The place for those who like things quiet, with attractive mud-brick huts in a bucolic setting among rice fields.

★ Hampi's Boulders
LODGE $$$

(☑ 9448034202; www.hampisboulders.com; Narayanpet; r incl full board from ₹5600; ❄ ☎ ✉) Beautifully designed, Hampi Boulders is the only luxury option in these parts, an 'eco-wilderness' resort in leafy gardens 7km west of Virupapur Gaddi. There's a choice of themed rooms and chic cottages with elegant furnishings, river views and outdoor showers. There's a stunning natural pool for chlorine-free swims. Rates include guided walks, and the restaurant's food is from their organic farm.

✖ Eating

Due to Hampi's religious significance, meat is strictly off the menu in all restaurants, and alcohol is banned (though some restaurants can order it for you).

Laughing Buddha
MULTICUISINE $

(Map p212; mains from ₹80; ⊙ 8am-10pm; ☎) Laughing Buddha is perhaps Hampi's most atmospheric place to eat, with serene river views that span beyond the temples and ruins and a loyal crowd of diners. Its menu includes curries, burgers and pizzas but service can be slow.

Gouthami
MULTICUISINE $

(Map p212; mains ₹90-180; ⊙ 8am-11pm) A well-run place with the usual cushioned seating (or dining tables) and an excess of psyche-

HAMPI BAZAAR DEMOLITION

While in 1865 it was the Deccan sultanates who levelled Vijayanagar, today a different battle rages in Hampi, between conservationists bent on protecting Hampi's architectural heritage and the locals who have settled there.

In 1999, Unesco placed Hampi on its list of World Heritage Sites in danger because of 'haphazard informal urbanisation' around the temples, particularly the ancient bazaar area near Virupaksha Temple.

The government consequently produced a masterplan which aimed to classify all of Hampi's ruins as protected monuments. After years of inaction this plan was dramatically and forcefully put into action in July 2011. Shops, hotels and homes in Hampi Bazaar were bulldozed overnight, reducing the atmospheric main strip to rubble in hours, as 1500 villagers who'd made the site a living monument were evicted.

Villagers were compensated with a small plot of land in the village of Kaddirampur, 18km from the bazaar. There's talk of new guesthouses eventually opening up here but such is its distance from Hampi few villagers are keen to start building guesthouses. Meanwhile the displaced await their payout.

Then in May 2016 history repeated itself as homes, guesthouses and shops in the old village of Virupapur Gaddi were demolished. Larger establishments avoided the clearance by contesting eviction orders in court. Angry locals blame HWHAMA (Hampi World Heritage Area Management Authority) and the ASI (Archaeological Survey of India) for the demolitions and argue that the masterplan is causing a lifeless 'museumification' of what was a vibrant cultural monument.

The main temple road today is devoid of buildings and bustle, and legendary hangouts like the (original) Mango Tree have been knocked down. By early 2017 Hampi Bazaar consisted of an enclave of guesthouses and restaurants north of Virupaksha Temple, but its future is in doubt as there are more clearance plans in place.

delic wall hangings. Serves tasty Indian, Israeli and Western food; they've an espresso machine and the bakery at the front has good cakes.

Moonlight   MULTICUISINE $
(Map p214; mains ₹80-150; ⊙7.30am-10pm) Simple, family-owned place that has a good set breakfast, espresso coffee and tasty pancakes and egg dishes and, of course, curries.

Ravi's Rose   MULTICUISINE $
(Map p214; mains from ₹100; ⊙8am-10.30pm; 🛜) This is the bazaar's most social hang-out, with a good selection of dosas and thalis, but most are here for the, erm, special lassis (cough, cough, nudge, nudge).

★ Mango Tree   MULTICUISINE $$
(Map p214; mains ₹140-310; ⊙7.30am-9.30pm) Hampi's most famous restaurant has relocated to the bazaar inside an ambient tented restaurant but is still run by three generations of the same local family. It's an efficiently run place with good service and delicious Indian cuisines including thalis and spinach paneer with chapati (₹160).

🛍 Shopping

Akash Art Gallery & Bookstore   BOOKS
(Map p214; Hampi Bazaar; ⊙6am-9pm) Excellent selection of books on Hampi and India, plus secondhand fiction. It has a free Hampi map.

Gali Djembe Music Shop   MUSIC
(Map p212; ☎9449982586; www.facebook.com/pg/Galidurugappa; Virupapur Gaddi; ⊙10am-7pm) Run by an amiable musician who teaches djembe (drums) and didgeridoo this store sells Indian and Western musical instruments at fair prices.

DAROJI SLOTH BEAR SANCTUARY

About 30km south of Hampi, amid scrubby undulated terrain, lies the **Daroji Sloth Bear Sanctuary** (₹25, vechicle ₹500; ⊙2-6pm), which nurses a large population of free-ranging sloth bears in an area of 83 sq km. You have a good chance of spotting them (but only from afar at the viewing platform), as honey is slathered on the rocks to coincide with the arrival of visitors. Bring binoculars, or there's no point showing up. Late afternoon is the best time to visit.

ℹ Information

DANGERS & ANNOYANCES
Hampi is generally a safe, peaceful place. However, exercise normal precautions and don't wander around the ruins after dark; female travellers should avoid being alone in the site's more remote parts. Alcohol and narcotics are illegal in Hampi.

MONEY
There's no ATM in Hampi; the closest is 3km away in Kamalapuram – an autorickshaw costs ₹80 for a return trip.

TOURIST INFORMATION
Tourist Office (Map p214; ☎08394-241339; ⊙10am-5.30pm Sat-Thu) Has brochures but is more useful for arranging cycling tours (per person ₹400 including bike and guide), walking guides (from ₹600) and bus tours (₹350, seven hours), all of which head to the ruins.

ℹ Getting There & Away

Hosapete (Hospet) is the gateway to Hampi. There's only one daily direct (very slow) bus from Hampi Bazaar to Goa (₹663, 11 hours, 7pm). Travel agents in Hampi Bazaar can book bus tickets to Bengaluru, Hyderabad, Goa and other destinations; many of these include a minibus transfer from Hampi to Hosapete.

Local buses connect Hampi with Hosapete (₹22, 30 minutes, half-hourly) between 5.45am and 7.30pm. An autorickshaw costs around ₹180.

Hosapete is Hampi's nearest train station.

ℹ Getting Around

Bicycles cost ₹30 to ₹50 per day in Hampi Bazaar, while mopeds can be hired for ₹150 to ₹400. Traffic is very light around Hampi, except on the road to Hosapete.

A small boat shuttles frequently across the **river crossing** (Map p214; person/bicycle/motorbike ₹10/10/20; ⊙6am-6pm) to Virupapur Gaddi. After dark it costs ₹50 to ₹100 per person depending on how late you cross. There are also boats to **Anegundi** (Map p212; person/bicycle/motorbike ₹10/10/20; ⊙6am-5.45pm) and **Hunuman Halli** (Map p212; person/bicycle ₹10/10; ⊙6am-5.45pm).

Walking the ruins is possible, but expect to cover at least 7km just to see the major sites. The beautiful river section between Hampi Bazaar and Vittala Temple is a delight to stroll. Autorickshaws and taxis are available for sightseeing, and an autorickshaw for the day costs around ₹750.

Organised tours depart from Hosapete and Hampi.

Around Hampi

Anegundi

⚑ 08394 / POP 5600

Anegundi is an ancient fortified village that's part of the Hampi World Heritage Site, but predates Hampi by way of human habitation. The settlement has been spared the blight of commercialisation, and retains a delightfully rustic feel where the seasons dictate the cycle of change and craft traditions endure.

It's accessed by a river crossing or via a long loop from Virupapur Gaddi.

◉ Sights & Activities

Mythically referred to as Kishkinda, the kingdom of the monkey gods, Anegundi retains many of its historic monuments, such as sections of its defensive wall and gates, and the **Ranganatha Temple** (Map p212; ⊘dawn-dusk) devoted to Rama. Also worth visiting is the **Durga Temple** (Map p212; ⊘dawn-dusk), an ancient shrine closer to the village and the hilltop Hanuman Temple. A new museum is scheduled to open here in 2017 in a meticulously restored old structure and other royal residences are also being renovated.

Hanuman Temple   HINDU TEMPLE
(Map p212; ⊘dawn-dusk) The whitewashed Hanuman Temple, accessible by a 570-step climb up the Anjanadri Hill, has fine views of the rugged terrain around. Many believe this is the birthplace of Hanuman, the Hindu monkey god who was Rama's devotee and helped him in his mission against Ravana. The hike up is pleasant, though you'll be courted by impish monkeys. At the temple you may encounter chillum-puffing sadhus. It's a very popular sunset spot, with panoramic views over the Hampi region.

**Kishkinda
Trust**   CULTURAL PROGRAMS, OUTDOOR ADVENTURE
(TKT; Map p212; ⚑08533-267777; www.tktkishkinda.org; Main Rd) ⚐ For cultural events, activities and volunteering opportunities, get in touch with Kishkinda Trust, an NGO based in Anegundi that works with local people.

🛌 Sleeping & Eating

Anegundi has fantastic homestays in restored heritage buildings. It's ideal for experiencing Indian village life.

Peshegaar Guest House   GUESTHOUSE $
(Map p212; ⚑9449972230; www.urammaheritagehomes.com; Hanumanahalli; s/d ₹500/1000) In the middle of the village this homely, heritage place has five simple yet stylish rooms decorated with tribal textiles around a pleasant common area with courtyard garden. Bathrooms are shared, but there are four.

Uramma House   GUESTHOUSE $$
(Map p212; ⚑9449972230; www.urammaheritagehomes.com; s/d per r ₹2100/4200; ☎) This 4th-century heritage house is a gem, with traditional-style rooms with exposed beams featuring boutique touches. It has two bedrooms and is ideal for a family or small group, with a dining room.

★Uramma Cottage   COTTAGE $$$
(Map p212; ⚑08533-267792; www.urammaheritagehomes.com; s/d incl breakfast from ₹2100/4200; ❄ 🐾 ☎) Close to the river crossing, this wonderfully atmospheric village lodge has thatched-roof cottages with farmhouse charm scattered around a large grassy plot. The attention to detail is all-evident with rustic chic furniture, lovely bed linen and handmade textiles adding a splash of colour. Staff could not be more helpful and the restaurant serves very fine food (and beer).

Machaan Studio   APARTMENT $$$
(Map p212; ⚑9448248658; www.urammaheritagehomes.com; ⊘apt incl breakfast ₹5000; ☎) A gorgeous fully equipped loft-style place with a huge living space, sunken bathtub and terrace. It's been imaginatively designed with a mix of rustic and contemporary touches and has views of the Vittala Temple and river. It's in the neighbouring village of Hunuman Halli.

🛍 Shopping

Banana Fibre Craft Workshop   ARTS & CRAFTS
(Map p212; ⊘10am-1pm & 2-5pm Mon-Sat) Watch on at this small workshop as workers ply their trade making a range of handicrafts and accessories using the bark of a banana tree, and recycled materials. Of course they sell it all too.

ⓘ Getting There & Away

Anegundi is 7km from Hampi, and reached by crossing the river on a boat (₹10) from the pier east of the Vittala Temple. From Hampi get here by moped or bicycle (if you're feeling energetic). An autorickshaw to the Anegundi crossing costs ₹120 from Hampi.

DANDELI

Located in the jungles of the Western Ghats about 100km from Goa, emerging **Dandeli** is a wildlife getaway that promises close encounters with wildlife such as elephants, leopards, sloth bears, gaur, wild dogs and flying squirrels. It's a chosen birding destination too, with resident hornbills, golden-backed woodpeckers, serpent eagles and white-breasted kingfishers. Also on offer are a slew of adventure activities, from kayaking to bowel-churning white-water rafting on the swirling waters of the Kali River.

Kali Adventure Camp (☑ 08284-230266; www.junglelodges.com/kali-adventure-camp; Dandeli; ☺ incl full board Indian/foreigner tent from ₹4168/5052, r from ₹4948/5832; ☎) is a well-managed government lodge adhering to ecofriendly principles, with rooms, tented cottages and accommodating staff. It organises white-water rafting on the Kali (possible most of the year), guided canoe adventures, canyoning and mountain-biking trips.

Frequent buses connect Dandeli to both Hubballi (₹58, two hours) and Dharwad (₹46, 1½ hours), with onward connections to Goa, Gokarna, Hosapete and Bengaluru.

Hosapete (Hospet)

☑ 08394 / POP 168,600

A hectic, dusty regional city, Hosapete (still called Hospet by many) is notable only as a transport hub for Hampi.

🛏 Sleeping & Eating

Hotel Malligi   HOTEL **$$**
(☑ 08394-228101; www.malligihotels.com; Jabunatha Rd; r ₹2200-4000, ste from ₹5000; ❇ @ ☎ ☒) Boasts a choice of modern, well-serviced rooms, an aquamarine swimming pool, spa, a good multicuisine restaurant and lounge bar for TV sports events.

Udupi Sri Krishna Bhavan   SOUTH INDIAN **$**
(Bus Stand; thali ₹45, mains ₹70-90; ☺ 6am-11pm) This bustling place dishes out Indian vegie fare, including thalis and dosas, plus some North Indian dishes. It's opposite the bus stand.

ⓘ Getting There & Away

BUS

Hosapete's bus stand has services to Hampi every half-hour (₹22, 30 minutes). Overnight private sleeper buses ply to/from Goa (₹1200 to 1600, seven to 10 hours), Gokarna (₹700, 6½ hours), Bengaluru (₹510 to ₹660, seven hours), Mysuru (₹380 to ₹605, 8½ hours) and Hyderabad (₹890 to ₹1120, seven to eight hours). **Paulo Travels** (p209) runs overnight buses to Gokarna and Goa.

TRAIN

Hosapete's train station is a ₹20 autorickshaw ride from the town centre. The 18047 Amaravathi Express heads to Magdaon, Goa (sleeper/2AC ₹225/860, 7½ hours) daily at 6.20am. The 16591 Hampi Express departs nightly at 9pm for Bengaluru (3AC/2AC/1AC ₹625/895/1505, nine hours) and Mysuru (₹840/1205/2015, 12 hours). For Hyderabad there's a daily train at 7pm (sleeper/2AC ₹305/1175, 12 hours).

Hubballi (Hubli)

☑ 0836 / POP 958,600

Industrial Hubballi (still called by its old name Hubli by many) is a hub for rail routes for Mumbai, Bengaluru, Goa and northern Karnataka. There's no other reason to visit.

🛏 Sleeping & Eating

Hotel Ajanta   HOTEL **$**
(☑ 0836-2362216; Koppikar Rd; s/d from ₹455/565) A simple crash pad near the train station with a popular ground-floor restaurant that serves delicious regional-style thalis.

Hotel Metropolis   HOTEL **$$**
(☑ 0836-4266666; www.hotelmetropolishubli. com; Koppikar Rd; ☺ s/d with fan ₹1134/1242, with AC ₹1755/1989; ❇ ☎) In the city centre and convenient for the train station, with a choice of clean, attractive, spacious and good-value rooms. Staff are eager to help travellers and there are two restaurants, including a multicuisine rooftop option.

ⓘ Getting There & Away

The train station is 1.5km from the centrally located KSRTC Old Bus Stand, ₹50 in an autorickshaw. There's also a KSRTC New Bus Stand 4km west of the centre where many services originate, but nearly all also stop at the Old Bus Stand too.

AIR

The airport is 6km west of the centre. Currently only Air India Regional operates a daily flight to Bengaluru. Buses (₹6, 20 minutes) run between Gokul Rd, 400m south of the terminal, and the centre; taxis cost ₹180.

BUS

There are very regular services to Bengaluru, most being overnight (₹420 to ₹650, seven to 8½ hours), and plenty daily to Vijapura (₹197 to ₹241, five to six hours) and mainly night-time buses to Hosapete (₹144 to ₹189, four hours). There's an 8am bus to Gokarna (₹158, four hours) and regular connections to Mumbai (₹715 to ₹1300, 11 to 14 hours), Mysuru (₹452 to ₹808, nine hours) and Panaji (₹171 to ₹347, five to six hours).

TRAIN

From the train station, plenty of expresses head to Hosapete (sleeper/2AC ₹140/695, 2½ hours, six daily), Bengaluru (sleeper/2AC ₹270/1045, eight hours, three daily), Mumbai (sleeper/2AC ₹380/1435, 15½ hours) and Goa (sleeper/3AC ₹190/540, 6½ hours, two daily).

NORTHERN KARNATAKA

Badami

📞 08357 / POP 26,600

Once the capital of the mighty Chalukya empire, today Badami is famous for its magnificent rock-cut cave temples, and red sandstone cliffs that resemble the Wild West. While the dusty main road is an eyesore that will have you wanting to get the hell out of there, its backstreets are a lovely area to explore with old houses, carved wooden doorways and the occasional Chalukyan ruin.

History

From about AD 540 to 757, Badami was the capital of an enormous kingdom stretching from Kanchipuram in Tamil Nadu to the Narmada River in Gujarat. It eventually fell to the Rashtrakutas, and changed hands several times thereafter, with each dynasty sculpturally embellishing Badami in their own way.

The sculptural legacy left by the Chalukyan artisans in Badami includes some of the earliest and finest examples of Dravidian temples and rock-cut caves.

⊙ Sights & Activities

The bluffs and horseshoe-shaped red sandstone cliff of Badami offer some great low-altitude climbing. For more information, visit www.indiaclimb.com.

Badami's caves overlook the 5th-century Agastyatirtha Tank and the waterside Bhutanatha temples. The stairway behind the Archaeological Museum climbs to the North Fort.

Cave Temples   CAVE

(Indian/foreigner ₹15/200, children under 15 free, tour guide ₹300; ⊙9am-5.30pm) Badami's highlights are its beautiful cave temples, three Hindu and one Jain, which display exquisite sculptures and intricate carvings. They're a magnificent example of Chalukya architecture and date back to the 6th century. All have a columned verandah, interior hall and a shrine at their rear.

Cave One, just above the entrance to the complex, is dedicated to Shiva. It's the oldest of the four caves, probably carved in the latter half of the 6th century. On the wall to the right of the porch is a captivating image of Nataraja striking 81 dance moves in the one pose. On the right of the porch area is a huge figure of Ardhanarishvara. On the opposite wall is a large image of Harihara, half Shiva and half Vishnu.

Dedicated to Vishnu, Cave Two is simpler in design. As with caves one and three, the front edge of the platform is decorated with images of pot-bellied dwarfs in various poses. Four pillars support the verandah, their tops carved with a bracket in the shape of a *yali* (mythical lion creature). On the left wall of the porch is the bull-headed figure of Varaha, the emblem of the Chalukya empire. To his left is Naga, a snake with a human face. On the right wall is a large sculpture of Trivikrama, another incarnation of Vishnu.

Between the second and third caves are two sets of steps to the right. The first leads to a natural cave with a small image of Padmapani (an incarnation of the Buddha). The second set of steps – sadly, barred by a gate – leads to the hilltop South Fort.

Cave Three, carved in AD 578, is the largest and most impressive. On the left wall is a carving of Vishnu, to whom the cave is dedicated, sitting on a snake. Nearby is an image of Varaha with four hands. The pillars have carved brackets in the shape of *yalis*. The ceiling panels contain images, including Indra riding an elephant, Shiva on a bull and Brahma on a swan. Keep an eye out for the image of drunken revellers, in particular one lady being propped up by her husband. There's also original colour on the ceiling;

the divots on the floor at the cave's entrance were used as paint palettes.

Dedicated to Jainism, **Cave Four** is the smallest of the set and dates to between the 7th and 8th centuries. The right wall has an image of Suparshvanatha (the seventh Jain *tirthankar*) surrounded by 24 Jain *tirthankars*. The inner sanctum contains an image of Adinath, the first Jain *tirthankar*.

Archaeological Museum MUSEUM
(₹5; ⊙9am-5pm Sat-Thu) The archaeological museum houses superb examples of local sculpture, including a remarkably explicit Lajja-Gauri image of a fertility cult that once flourished in the area. There are many sculptures of Shiva in different forms and there's a diorama of the Shidlaphadi cave.

🛏 Sleeping & Eating

Mookambika Deluxe HOTEL $
(☏08357-220067; hotelmookambika@yahoo.com; Station Rd; d with fan/AC from ₹1200/1800; ❄🛜) For 'deluxe' read 'decent' – this hotel offers fair value with rooms done up in matt orange and green. Staff are a good source of travel info. It's opposite the bus stand.

Hotel Mayura Chalukya HOTEL $
(☏08357-220046; www.kstdc.co/hotels; Ramdurg Rd; d with fan/AC from ₹962/1282; ❄🛜) Away from the bustle, this government hotel has large, clean rooms with an OK restaurant serving Indian staples.

Krishna Heritage HOTEL $$$
(☏08357-221300; www.krishnaheritagebadami. com; Ramdurg Rd; s/d incl breakfast ₹4000/6000; ❄🛜) Located 2km west of the centre this attractive hotel is set in landscaped grounds. Rooms are massive with open-air showers and balconies and the large restaurant has delightful views over gardens and fields.

Bridge Restaurant MULTICUISINE $$
(Clarks Hotel, Veerpulakeshi Circle; mains ₹130-320; ⊙7am-10.30pm; 🛜) Just the place when you need some AC relief, this business hotel's restaurant makes a good stab at Western dishes like pasta and pizza as well as Chinese and North Indian fare.

ℹ Getting There & Away

Badami is not served by many direct services. From Badami's bus stand on Station Rd there's one direct bus to both Vijapura (₹157, four hours, 5pm) and Hubballi (₹100, five hours, 3.15pm) but otherwise head on one of the regu-

lar buses to Kerur (₹26, 45 minutes), which has many more connections.

ℹ Getting Around

Theoretically, you can visit Aihole and Pattadakal in a day from Badami by bus if you get moving early. Start with Aihole (₹38, one hour), then move to Pattadakal (₹22, 30 minutes), and finally return to Badami (₹40, one hour). The last bus from Pattadakal to Badami is at 4pm.

However, it's much easier and less stressful to arrange an autorickshaw (₹1000) or taxi (₹2000) for a day trip to Pattadakal, Aihole and nearby Mahakuta.

Around Badami

Pattadakal
☑08357 / POP 1630
A secondary capital of the Badami Chalukyas, Pattadakal is known for its finely carved Hindu and Jain temples, which are collectively a World Heritage Site. The surrounding village of Pattadakal is tiny; most travellers visit the site from nearby Badami.

⊙ Sights

Barring a few that date back to the 3rd century AD, most of Pattadakal's World Heritage Site–listed temples were built during the 7th and 8th centuries AD. The main **Virupaksha Temple** (⊙6am-6pm) is a massive structure, its columns covered with intricate carvings depicting episodes from the Ramayana and Mahabharata. A giant stone sculpture of Nandi sits to the temple's east. The **Mallikarjuna Temple**, next to the Virupaksha Temple, is almost identical in design.

About 500m south of the main enclosure is the Jain **Papanatha Temple**, its entrance flanked by elephant sculptures.

ℹ Getting There & Away

Pattadakal is 20km from Badami, with buses (₹28) departing every 30 minutes until about 5pm. There's a morning and afternoon bus to Aihole (₹20), 13km away.

Aihole
☑08351 / POP 3200
Some 100 temples, built between the 4th and 6th centuries AD, speck the ancient Chalukyan regional capital of Aihole (*ay*-holeh). Most, however, are either in ruins or engulfed by the modern village. Aihole doc-

uments the embryonic stage of South Indian Hindu architecture, from the earliest simple shrines, such as the most ancient Ladkhan Temple, to the later and more complex buildings, such as the Meguti Temple.

Aihole is about 40km from Badami and 13km from Pattadakal.

◉ Sights

The most impressive of all the temples in Aihole is the 7th-century **Durga Temple** (Indian/foreigner ₹5/200, camera ₹25; ⊙ 6am-6pm), notable for its semicircular apse (inspired by Buddhist architecture) and the remains of the curvilinear *sikhara* (temple spire). The interiors house intricate stone carvings. The small **museum** (₹5; ⊙ 9am-5pm Sat-Thu) behind the temple contains further examples of Chalukyan sculpture.

To the south of the Durga Temple are several other temple clusters, including early examples. About 600m to the southeast, on a low hillock, is the Jain **Meguti Temple**. Watch out for snakes if you're venturing up.

ℹ Getting There & Away

Regular buses run from Badami to Aihole (₹38, one hour).

Vijapura (Bijapur)

✆ 08352 / POP 337,200

A historic city epitomising the Deccan's Islamic era, dusty Vijapura (renamed in 2014 but still widely called Bijapur) tells a glorious tale dating back some 600 years. Blessed with a heap of mosques, mausoleums, palaces and fortifications, it was the capital of the Adil Shahi kings from 1489 to 1686, and one of the five splinter states formed after the Islamic Bahmani kingdom broke up in 1482. Despite its strong Islamic character, Vijapura is also a centre for the Lingayat brand of Shaivism, which emphasises a single personalised god. The **Lingayat Siddeshwara Festival** (Jan or Feb) runs for eight days.

◉ Sights

★ **Golgumbaz**   MONUMENT
(Indian/foreigner ₹15/200; ⊙ 10am-5pm) Set in tranquil gardens, the magnificent Golgumbaz mausoleum houses the tombs of emperor Mohammed Adil Shah (r 1627–56), his two wives, his mistress (Rambha), one of his daughters and a grandson. Octagonal seven-storey towers stand at each corner of the monument, which is capped by an enormous dome. Climb the steep, narrow stairs up one of the towers to reach the 'whispering gallery' within the dome, which has terrific acoustics (which excitable schoolchildren love to prove to loud effect).

Archaeological Museum   MUSEUM
(₹5; ⊙ 10am-5pm Sat-Thu) A well-presented archaeological museum set in the Golgumbaz lawns. Skip the ground floor and head upstairs; there you'll find an excellent collection of artefacts, such as oriental carpets, china crockery, weapons, armoury and scrolls.

Jama Masjid   MOSQUE
(Jama Masjid Rd; ⊙ 9am-5.30pm) Constructed by Ali Adil Shah I (r 1557–80), the finely proportioned Jama Masjid has graceful arches, a fine dome and a vast inner courtyard with room for more than 2200 worshippers. Women should make sure to cover their heads and not wear revealing clothing.

Asar Mahal   HISTORIC BUILDING
(⊙ 6am–8.30pm) **FREE** Built by Mohammed Adil Shah in about 1646 to serve as a Hall of Justice, the graceful Asar Mahal once housed two hairs from Prophet Mohammed's beard. The rooms on the upper storey are decorated with frescoes and a square tank graces the front. It's out of bounds for women.

Citadel   FORT
FREE Surrounded by fortified walls and a wide moat, the citadel once contained the palaces, pleasure gardens and durbar (royal court) of the Adil Shahi kings. Now mainly in ruins, the most impressive of the remaining fragments are the colossal arches of the **Gagan Mahal FREE**, built by Ali Adil Shah I around 1561. The gates here are locked, but someone will be on hand to let you in.

The ruins of Mohammed Adil Shah's seven-storey palace, the **Sat Manzil FREE**, are nearby. Across the road stands the delicate **Jala Manzil**, once a water pavilion surrounded by secluded courts and gardens. On the other side of Station Rd (MG Rd) are the graceful arches of **Bara Kaman FREE**, the ruined mausoleum of Ali Roza.

Central Market   MARKET
(Station Rd; ⊙ 9am-9pm) This lively market is an explosion of colour and scents with flowers, spices and fresh produce on sale.

KARNATAKA & BENGALURU VIJAPURA (BIJAPUR)

Vijapura (Bijapur)

Upli Buruj   HISTORIC SITE
FREE Upli Buruj is a 16th-century, 24m-high watchtower near the western walls of the city. An external flight of stairs leads to the top, where you'll find two hefty cannons and good views of other monuments around town.

Malik-e-Maidan   HISTORIC SITE
(Monarch of the Plains) Perched upon a platform is this beast of a cannon – over 4m long, almost 1.5m in diameter and estimated to weigh 55 tonnes. Cast in 1549, it was supposedly brought to Vijapura as a war trophy thanks to the efforts of 10 elephants, 400 oxen and hundreds of men!

★**Ibrahim Rouza**   MONUMENT
(Indian/foreigner ₹15/200; ⊙6am-6pm) The beautiful Ibrahim Rouza is among the most elegant and finely proportioned Islamic monuments in India. Its 24m-high minarets are said to have inspired those of the Taj Mahal, and its tale is similarly poignant: built by emperor Ibrahim Adil Shah II (r 1580–1627) as a future mausoleum for his queen,

Taj Sultana. Ironically, he died before her, and was thus the first person to be rested there. Also interred here with Ibrahim Adil Shah are his queen, children and mother.

For a tip (₹150 is fine), caretakers can show you around the monument, including the dark labyrinth around the catacomb where the actual graves are located.

🛏 Sleeping & Eating

Hotel Tourist   HOTEL $
(☎08352-250655; Station Rd; s/d from ₹220/360) A dive bang in the middle of the bazaar, with no-frills rooms; their 'deluxe' options cost slightly more but are worth it.

★**Sabala Heritage Home**   HERITAGE HOTEL $$
(☎9448118204; www.sabalaheritagehome.org; Bijapur Bypass, NH-13, near Ganesh Nagar; r incl breakfast & dinner ₹3000; 🖥) 🍴 On the edge of the city this heritage hotel has attractive, artistically decorated rooms overlooking farmland. Food is home-cooked, flavoursome and inventive. The hotel is linked to an NGO that empowers women and trades

fine handicrafts (there's a store here too). It's 4km south of the centre.

Hotel Pearl HOTEL $$
(☑08352-256002; www.hotelpearlbijapur.com; 633 Station Rd; d with fan/AC from ₹1600/2200; ❄🛜) Offering good value, this midrange hotel has clean motel-style rooms around a central atrium, and is conveniently located to Golgumbaz. Wi-fi is a bit spotty but its in-house **Qaswa Hills restaurant** (Pearl Hotel, Station Rd; meals ₹120-280; ⊙7am-4pm & 7-10pm) is very popular.

Hotel Madhuvan International HOTEL $$
(☑08352-255571; Station Rd; d with fan/AC ₹1600/2100; ❄🛜) An ongoing renovation program means most rooms are in good shape at this pleasant hotel which has a courtyard garden. It's hidden down a lane off Station Rd and has a great in-house **restaurant** (mains ₹60-100; ⊙9-11am, noon-4pm & 7-11pm). There's no lift, however.

🛍 Shopping

Sabala Handicrafts ARTS & CRAFTS
(http://sabalahandicrafts.com; NH13, Bijapur Bypass; from ₹800; ⊙8am-5.30pm) Beautiful handmade textiles, bags, saris, kurtas and accessories. Profits benefit an NGO that empowers village women. It's 4km south of the centre.

ℹ Information

Tourist Office (☑08352-250359; Hotel Mayura Adil Shahi Annexe, Station Rd; ⊙10am-5.30pm Mon-Sat) Has good Vijapura brochures with map.

ℹ Getting There & Away

BUS
The following services leave from the **bus stand** (☑08352-0251344; Meenakshi Chowk Rd; ⊙24hr):
Bengaluru ordinary/sleeper ₹576/757, 12 hours, four daily
Bidar ₹265, 6½ hours, four evening buses
Kalaburgi (Gubarga) ₹164, four hours, three day buses
Hosapete ₹241, five hours, five daily
Hubballi ₹193 to ₹241, five hours, two daily
Hyderabad ₹373 to ₹729, eight to 10 hours, six daily
Mumbai ₹660, 12 hours, four daily, via Pune (₹428, eight hours)
Panaji (Goa) ₹335 to ₹415, 10 hours, two daily

TRAIN
Trains from Vijapura station go to:
Badami 17320 Hubli-Secunderabad Express, sleeper/2AC ₹140/695, 2½ hours, 1am and two other daily trains
Bengaluru 16536 Golgumbaz Express, sleeper/2AC ₹355/1395, 15½ hours, 5pm
Hyderabad 17319 Secunderabad Express, sleeper/2AC ₹250/960, 11 hours, 1am

ℹ Getting Around

Given the amount to see and distance to cover, ₹700 is a fair price to hire an autorickshaw for a day of sightseeing. Short hops around town cost ₹50.

Bidar
☑08482 / POP 218,500
Despite being home to amazing ruins and monuments, Bidar, hidden away in Karnataka's far northeastern corner, gets very little tourist traffic – which of course makes it all the more appealing. It's a city drenched in Islamic Indian history, with this old-walled town being first the capital of the Bahmani kingdom (1428–87) and later the capital of the Barid Shahi dynasty. This is one of the least Westernised parts of Karnataka, with many niqab-wearing women and turbaned Sikh pilgrims, and though locals are welcoming to visitors, conservative values predominate.

◉ Sights

⭐**Bidar Fort** FORT
(⊙6am-6pm) **FREE** Keep aside a few hours for peacefully wandering around the remnants of this magnificent 15th-century fort, the largest in South India – and once the administrative capital of much of the region. Surrounded by a triple moat hewn out of solid red rock and many kilometres of defensive walls, the fort has a fairy-tale entrance that twists in an elaborate chicane through three gateways.

Information at the site is minimal so consider hiring a guide from the archaeological office (who can unlock the most interesting ruins within the fort). These include the **Rangin Mahal** (Painted Palace), with elaborate tilework, teak pillars and panels with mother-of-pearl inlay, **Solah Khamba Mosque** (Sixteen-Pillared Mosque), and **Tarkash Mahal** with exquisite Islamic inscriptions and wonderful rooftop views.

There's a small **museum** in the former royal bath with local artefacts.

Khwaja Mahmud Gawan Madrasa
RUIN, HISTORIC SITE

(⊙dawn-dusk) **FREE** Dominating the heart of the old town are the ruins of Khwaja Mahmud Gawan Madrasa, a college for advanced learning built in 1472. To get an idea of its former grandeur, check out the remnants of coloured tiles on the front gate and one of the minarets which still stands intact.

Guru Nanak Jhira Sahib
SIKH TEMPLE

(Shiva Nagar; ⊙24hr) **FREE** This large Sikh temple on the northwestern side of town is dedicated to the guru Guru Nanak and was built in 1948. It's centred around the Amrit Kund (a water tank) where pilgrims cleanse their souls.

Bahmani Tombs
HISTORIC SITE

(⊙dawn-dusk) **FREE** The huge domed tombs of the Bahmani kings in Ashtur, 3km east of Bidar, were built to house the remains of the sultans, of which the painted interior of Ahmad Shah Bahman's tomb is the most impressive.

🛏 Sleeping & Eating

Hotel Mayura
HOTEL $

(☑08482-228142; Udgir Rd; d with fan/AC from ₹1100/2200; ❋🛜) Its concrete exterior is unappealing but rooms are cheerful and well-appointed. There's a bar and restaurant and it's opposite the central bus stand. Look out for its NBC-peacock symbol.

Hotel Mayura Barid Shahi
HOTEL $

(☑08482-221740; Udgir Rd; s/d ₹500/600, r with AC ₹900; ❋🛜) Maintenance could be better at this old-timer which has simple, institutional rooms, a central location and a popular garden bar-restaurant.

Jyothi Fort
INDIAN $

(Bidar Fort; mains ₹70-120; ⊙9am-5pm) A peaceful setting at the fort's entry with tables set up on the grass under sprawling tamarind trees has delicious vegetarian meals.

Kamat Hotel
SOUTH INDIAN $

(Udgir Rd; meals ₹80-150; ⊙7.30am-10pm) Scores highly for South Indian classics at very affordable rates. It's busy through the day and there's an AC room.

❶ Getting There & Away

From the bus stand, frequent buses run to Kalaburagi (₹124, three hours) and there are two evening buses to Vijapura (₹280, seven hours). There are also buses to Hyderabad (₹142, four hours, 6.30pm) and Bengaluru (semideluxe/AC ₹750/900, 13 hours, five daily).

Trains head to Hyderabad (sleeper ₹100, five hours, 2am) and Bengaluru (sleeper/2AC ₹370/1435, 13 hours, 6.05pm).

❶ Getting Around

You can arrange a day tour in an autorickshaw for around ₹600.

Telangana & Andhra Pradesh

Best Places to Eat

➡ Sea Inn (p250)

➡ Shah Ghouse Cafe (p237)

➡ SO – The Sky Kitchen (p238)

➡ Hotel Mayura (p253)

➡ Dhaba By Claridges (p239)

➡ TFL (p247)

Best Off the Beaten Track

➡ Ramappa Temple (p244)

➡ Sankaram (p251)

➡ Moula Ali Dargah (p233)

➡ Guntupalli (p247)

Why Go?

Hyderabad, one of Islamic India's greatest cities, is reason enough on its own to visit this region. Its skyline is a sight to behold, defined by the great domes and minarets of ancient mosques, mausoleums and palaces of once-mighty dynasties. Delve inside the city's fabled old quarter for fascinating street markets, teahouses and biryani restaurants, then journey to the city's fringes to the majestic Golconda fort. Meanwhile, Hyderabad's newer districts are awash with the classy restaurants and boutiques of IT-fuelled economic advancement.

The other attractions of these two states (which were one state until they split in 2014) are less brazen, but dig around and you will unearth gems – like the wonderful medieval temple sculptures of Ramappa, the beauty of ancient Buddhist sites such as Sankaram and Guntupalli hidden in deep countryside, the cheery coastal holiday vibe of Visakhapatnam, and the positive vibrations emanating from the vast pilgrim crowds at Tirumala's temple.

When to Go
Hyderabad

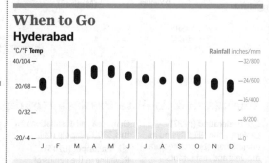

May–Jun Join locals digging into *haleem*, a Ramadan (Ramzan) favourite.

Nov–Feb Explore Hyderabad's sights in balmy 22–28°C weather.

Dec–Apr The best time to enjoy Vizag's coastal attractions – there's little rain and it's not *too* hot.

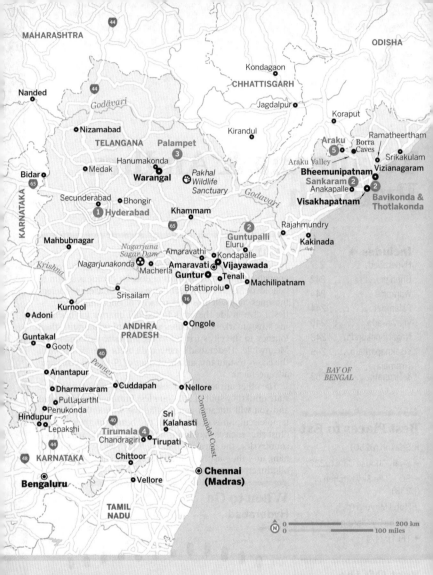

Telangana & Andhra Pradesh Highlights

1 **Hyderabad** (p227)
Exploring the Old City and its
unique markets, architectural
marvels and restaurants.

2 **Monastic trail** (p251)
Absorbing the meditative
ambience at beautiful
Sankaram, as well as
Bavikonda, Thotlakonda and

Guntupalli, all destinations on
this 2300-year-old trail.

3 **Palampet** (p244)
Revelling in the genius of
Kakatiya sculptors at the
temple near this village.

4 **Tirumala** (p252) Going
with the crowd and finding a
spiritual calling with Hindu
pilgrims.

5 **Araku** (p252) Enjoying
the delightful train ride here
through the lush forests and
wide green valleys of the
Eastern Ghats.

History

From the 3rd century BC to 3rd century AD the Satavahana empire, also known as the Andhras, ruled over much of the Deccan plateau from a base in this region. The Satavahanas helped Buddhism to flourish after it arrived with emperor Ashoka's missionary monks, and today Andhra Pradesh has more ancient Buddhist sites than almost any other Indian state.

The Hindu Kakatiyas, based at Warangal, ruled most of Telangana and Andhra Pradesh from the 12th to 14th centuries, a period that saw the rise of Telugu culture and language. Warangal eventually fell to the Muslim Delhi Sultanate and then passed to the Deccan-based Bahmani Sultanate. Then, in 1518, the Bahmanis' governor at Golconda, Sultan Quli Qutb Shah, claimed independence. His Qutb Shahi dynasty developed Golconda into the massive fortress we see today. But a water shortage there caused Sultan Mohammed Quli Qutb Shah to relocate a few kilometres east to the south bank of the Musi River, where he founded the new city of Hyderabad in 1591.

The Qutb Shahis were ousted by the Mughal emperor Aurangzeb in 1687. When the Mughal empire in turn started fraying at the edges, its local viceroy Nizam ul-Mulk Asaf Jah took control of much of the Deccan, launching Hyderabad's second great Muslim dynasty, the Asaf Jahis – the famously fabulously wealthy nizams of Hyderabad – in 1724. His capital was Aurangabad, but his son Asaf Jah II moved to Hyderabad in 1763. Hyderabad rose to become the centre of Islamic India and a focus for the arts, culture and learning. Its abundance of rare gems and minerals – the world-famous Kohinoor diamond is from here – furnished the nizams with enormous wealth.

The whole region was effectively under British control from around 1800, but while Andhra Pradesh was governed from Madras (now Chennai), the princely state of Hyderabad – which included large territories outside the city populated by Telugu-speaking Hindus – remained nominally independent. Come Indian Independence in 1947, nizam Osman Ali Khan wanted to retain sovereignty, but Indian military intervention saw Hyderabad state join the Indian union in 1948.

When Indian states were reorganised along linguistic lines in 1956, Hyderabad was split three ways. What's now Telangana joined other Telugu-speaking areas to form Andhra Pradesh state; other districts became parts of Karnataka and Maharashtra. Telangana was never completely happy with this arrangement, and after prolonged campaigning, it was split off from Andhra Pradesh as a separate state in 2014. Hyderabad remains capital of both states until Andhra Pradesh gets its new capital at Amaravati (next to Vijayawada) up and running. Amaravati, designed by Singapore city planners, should be smart, green and ultramodern – though completion will doubtless take many decades.

HYDERABAD

📞 040 / POP 7.68 MILLION / ELEV 600M

Steeped in history, thronged with people and buzzing with commerce, the Old City of Hyderabad is one of India's most evocative ancient quarters. Exploring the lanes of this district, with its chai shops and spice merchants, you'll encounter a teeming urban masala of colour and commerce. Looming over the Old City is some of Islamic India's most impressive architecture, in varying states of repair. Most visitors concentrate their time in this area, though the magnificent Golconda Fort should not be missed either.

Hyderabad's other pole is far younger and west of the centre – its Hi-Tech City, or 'Cyberabad', and other districts like Banjara Hills and Jubilee Hills are replete with glittery malls, multiplexes, clubs, pubs and sleek restaurants.

TOP STATE FESTIVALS

Sankranti (☉ Jan) This important regionwide Telugu festival marks the end of harvest season. Kite-flying abounds, doorsteps are decorated with colourful *kolams* (rice-flour designs) and men adorn cattle with bells and fresh horn paint.

Brahmotsavam (☉ Sep/Oct) This nine-day festival sees the Venkateshwara temple at Tirumala awash in vast crowds of worshippers. Special *pujas* (offerings) and chariot processions are held, and it's an auspicious time for *darshan* (deity-viewing).

Muharram (☉ Sep/Oct) Commemorates the martyrdom of Mohammed's grandson Hussain. A huge procession throngs the Old City in Hyderabad.

One thing you have to accept wherever you are in Hyderabad: the traffic is appalling. A (long-delayed) Metro Rail rapid-transit system should ease things somewhat in the coming years.

⊙ Sights

⊙ Old City

★**Charminar** MONUMENT
(Map p230; Indian/foreigner ₹5/100; ⊙9am-5.30pm) Hyderabad's principal landmark and city symbol was built by Mohammed Quli Qutb Shah in 1591 to commemorate the founding of Hyderabad and the end of epidemics caused by Golconda's water shortage. The gargantuan four-column, 56m-high structure has four arches facing the cardinal points, with minarets atop each column (hence the name Charminar, 'four minarets'). It's certainly an impressive sight, though the relentless traffic that swirls around the structure, crowds and queues make it somewhat less rewarding to visit.

The Charminar stands at the heart of Hyderabad's main bazaar area (also known as Charminar), a labyrinth of lanes crowded with shops, stalls, markets and shoppers. You can climb to the 1st floor for a view of the district. The 2nd floor, home to Hyderabad's oldest mosque, and the upper columns, are not open to the public. The structure is illuminated from 7pm to 9pm.

★**Chowmahalla Palace** PALACE
(Map p230; http://chowmahalla.co.in; Indian/foreigner ₹50/200, camera ₹50; ⊙10am-5pm Sat-Thu) This opulent 18th- and 19th-century palace compound, the main residence of several nizams, comprises several grandiose buildings and four garden courtyards. Most dazzling is the Khilwat Mubarak, a magnificent durbar hall where nizams held ceremonies under 19 enormous chandeliers of Belgian crystal. Its side rooms today house historical exhibits, arts and crafts and exhibits of nizams' personal possessions. In the southernmost courtyard is a priceless collection of carriages and vintage cars including a 1911 yellow Rolls-Royce and 1937 Buick convertible.

Salar Jung Museum MUSEUM
(Map p230; www.salarjungmuseum.in; Salar Jung Rd; Indian/foreigner ₹20/500, camera ₹50; ⊙10am-5pm Sat-Thu) This vast collection was amassed by Mir Yousuf Ali Khan (Salar Jung III), who was briefly grand vizier to the sev-

enth nizam. The 39 galleries include early South Indian bronzes and wood and stone sculptures, Indian miniature paintings, European fine art, historic manuscripts, a room of jade and the remarkable *Veiled Rebecca* by 19th-century Italian sculptor Benzoni. Note the entrance ticket for foreigners is very steep and the museum is very popular (near bedlam on Sundays).

HEH The Nizam's Museum MUSEUM
(Purani Haveli; Map p230; www.hehnmh.com; off Dur-e-Sharwah Hospital Rd; adult/child ₹80/15, camera ₹150; ⊙10am-5pm Sat-Thu) The Purani Haveli was a home of the sixth nizam, Mahbub Ali Khan (r 1869–1911). He was rumoured to have never worn the same thing twice: hence the 54m-long, two-storey Burmese teak wardrobe. Much of the museum is devoted to personal effects of the seventh nizam, Osman Ali Khan, including his silver cradle, gold-burnished throne and lavish Silver Jubilee gifts. The displays, lighting and information could be improved, but it's still a worthwhile visit.

Mecca Masjid MOSQUE
(Map p230; Shah Ali Banda Rd; ⊙4.30am-9pm) This mosque is one of the world's largest, with 10,000 men praying here at major Muslim festivals, and also one of Hyderabad's oldest buildings, begun in 1617 by the city's founder Mohammed Quli Qutb Shah. Women are not allowed inside the main prayer hall, and male tourists are unlikely to be let in either (they can look through the railings). Female tourists, even with headscarves, may not even be allowed into the vast courtyard if their clothing is judged too skimpy or tight.

Several bricks embedded above the prayer hall's central arch are made with soil from Mecca, hence the mosque's name. An enclosure alongside the courtyard contains the tombs of several Hyderabad nizams.

Badshahi Ashurkhana ISLAMIC SITE
(Map p230; High Court Rd) The 1594 Badshahi Ashurkhana (literally 'royal house of mourning') was one of the first structures built by the Qutb Shahs in their new city of Hyderabad. In a courtyard set back from the road, its walls are practically glowing with intricate, brightly coloured tile mosaics. The Ashurkhana is packed during Muharram, as well as on Thursdays, when local Shiites gather to commemorate the martyrdom of Hussain Ibn Ali. Visitors should remove shoes and dress modestly (including a headscarf for women).

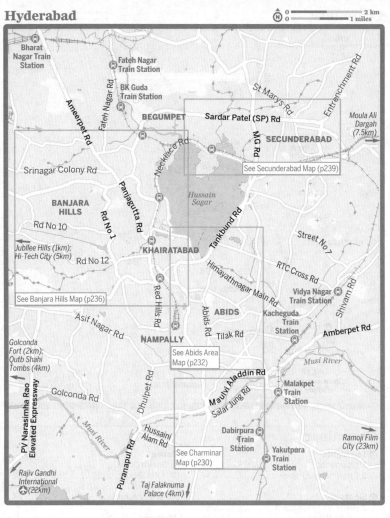

N 0 ——————— 2 km
0 ——————— 1 miles

Bharat Nagar Train Station

Fateh Nagar Train Station

Ameerpet Rd

Fateh Nagar Rd

BK Guda Train Station

BEGUMPET

St Marys Rd

Sardar Patel (SP) Rd

Entrenchment Rd

Moula Ali Dargah (7.5km)

MG Rd

SECUNDERABAD

Srinagar Colony Rd

Necklace Rd

See Secunderabad Map (p239)

Hussain Sagar

BANJARA HILLS

Panjagutta Rd

Rd No 10

Rd No 1

Tankbund Rd

Street No 7

KHAIRATABAD

Jubilee Hills (1km); Hi-Tech City (5km)

Rd No 12

Himayathnagar Main Rd

RTC Cross Rd

Shivam Rd

Red Hills Rd

Vidya Nagar Train Station

See Banjara Hills Map (p236)

Asif Nagar Rd

ABIDS

Abids Rd

Tilak Rd

Kacheguda Train Station

Amberpet Rd

Golconda Fort (2km); Qutb Shahi Tombs (4km)

NAMPALLY

Dhulpet Rd

See Abids Area Map (p232)

Musi River

PV Narasimha Rao Elevated Expressway

Golconda Rd

Maulvi Aladdin Rd

Malakpet Train Station

Hussaini Alam Rd

Salar Jung Rd

Dabirpura Train Station

Ramoji Film City (23km)

Puranapul Rd

Musi River

See Charminar Map (p230)

Yakutpura Train Station

Rajiv Gandhi International

Taj Falaknuma Palace (4km)

TELANGANA & ANDHRA PRADESH HYDERABAD

🔵 Abids Area

State Museum   MUSEUM
(Map p232; Public Gardens Rd, Nampally; ₹10, camera/video ₹100/500; ⏰10.30am-4.30pm Sat-Thu, closed 2nd Sat of month) This sprawling museum is in a fanciful Indo-Saracenic building constructed by the seventh nizam as a playhouse for one of his daughters. It hosts a collection of important archaeological finds as well as an exhibit on the region's Buddhist history. There's an interesting decorative-arts gallery, where you can learn about Bidriware inlaid metalwork and *kalamkari* textile painting, plus a bronze-sculpture gallery and a 4500-year-old Egyptian mummy.

British Residency   HISTORIC BUILDING
(Koti Women's College; Map p232; Koti Main Rd) This palatial Palladian residence, built in 1803–06 by James Achilles Kirkpatrick, the British Resident (official East India Company representative) in Hyderabad, features in William Dalrymple's brilliant historical love story *White Mughals*. Work is ongoing to restore the building to its former glory, a project which will take many years to accomplish. There's no official access but Detours

Charminar

N 0 _____ 500 m
   0 _____ 0.25 miles

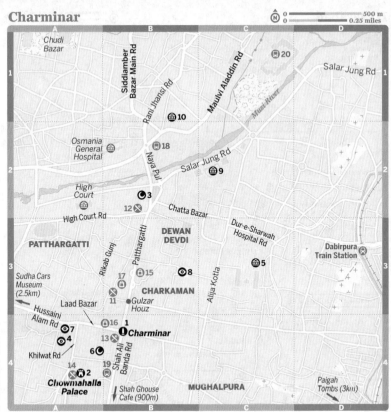

Charminar

◎ Top Sights
| 1 Charminar | B4 |
| 2 Chowmahalla Palace | A4 |

◎ Sights
3 Badshahi Ashurkhana	B2
4 Chiddi Bazar	A4
5 HEH The Nizam's Museum	C3
6 Mecca Masjid	A4
7 Mehboob Chowk	A4
8 Mir Alam Mandi	B3
9 Salar Jung Museum	C2
10 State Library	B1

◎ Activities, Courses & Tours
| Heritage Walks | (see 1) |

◎ Eating
11 Govind Dosa	B3
12 Hotel Shadab	B2
13 Nimrah	B4
14 Taj Restaurant	A4

◎ Shopping
15 Hyderabad Perfumers	B3
16 Laad Bazar	B4
17 Patel Market	B3

◎ Transport
18 Afzalgunj Bus Stop	B2
19 Charminar Bus Stop	B4
20 Mahatma Gandhi Bus Station	C1

(p234) can usually gain entry for those booking one of its fascinating White Mughal tours.

Kirkpatrick became enchanted by Hyderabad courtly culture, converted to Islam and married Khair-un-Nissa, a teenage relative of the Hyderabad prime minister. The Residency and its extensive gardens became the Osmania University College for Women, known as Koti Women's College, in 1949. Beyond the grand classical portico is the (newly renovated) Durbar Hall, with Islamic geometric designs on its high ceiling above the chandeliers and classical columns and an elaborate curving staircase behind. In the overgrown gardens to the southwest you'll find a British cemetery, the surviving entrance to the Residency's zenana (women's quarters) and a model of the Residency building made by Kirkpatrick for Khair-un-Nissa.

Birla Mandir
HINDU TEMPLE

(Map p236; ⊙7am-noon & 3-9pm) The ethereal Birla Mandir, constructed of white Rajasthani marble in 1976, graces Kalapahad (Black Mountain), one of two rocky hills overlooking the lake of Hussain Sagar. Dedicated to Venkateshwara, it's a popular Hindu worship centre, with a relaxed atmosphere, and affords magnificent views over the city, especially at sunset. There are several imposing statues including a huge granite image of Venkateshwara. Disabled access is good: there's a lift in the curious clock tower.

Birla Modern Art Gallery
MUSEUM

(Map p232; www.birlasciencecentre.org; Naubat Pahad Lane, Adarsh Nagar; ₹50; ⊙10.30am-8pm) This skilfully curated collection of modern and contemporary art includes paintings by superstars Jogen Chowdhury, Tyeb Mehta and Arpita Singh.

◉ Banjara Hills

★Lamakaan
CULTURAL CENTRE

(Map p236; ☑9642731329; www.lamakaan.com; next to JVR Park, Banjara Hills; ⊙10am-10.30pm Tue-Sun) This noncommercial 'inclusive cultural space' is an open centre that hosts plays, films, musical events, exhibitions, organic markets and lectures. It also has a great Irani cafe, with cheap tea and snacks and free wi-fi. On a lane off Rd No 1.

Kalakriti Art Gallery
GALLERY

(Map p236; www.kalakritiartgallery.com; Rd No 10, Banjara Hills; ⊙11am-7pm) FREE One of the city's best contemporary galleries, Kalakriti hosts excellent exhibitions by some of India's leading artists, and collaborative programs with the Alliance Française and Goethe Zentrum.

◉ Other Areas

★Golconda Fort
FORT

(Indian/foreigner ₹20/200, 1hr sound-and-light show ₹140; ⊙9am-5.30pm, English-language sound-and-light show 6.30pm Nov-Feb, 7pm Mar-Oct) Hyderabad's most impressive sight, this monumental fort lies on the western edge of town. In the 16th century the Qutb Shahs made Golconda a fortified citadel, built atop a 120m-high granite hill surrounded by mighty ramparts, all ringed by further necklaces of crenellated fortifications, 11km in perimeter. From the summit there are stunning vistas across dusty Deccan foothills and the crumbling outer ramparts, over the domed tombs of Qutb Shahs, past distant shanty towns to the horizon haze of the inner city.

By the time of the Qutb Shahs, Golconda Fort had already existed for at least three centuries under the Kakatiyas and Bahmani sultanate, and was already famed for its diamonds, which were mostly mined in the Krishna River valley, but cut and traded here. The Qutb Shahs moved to their new city of Hyderabad in 1591, but maintained Golconda as a citadel until the Mughal emperor Aurangzeb took it in 1687 after a year-long siege, ending Qutb Shahi rule.

KITSCHABAD

Mixed in with Hyderabad's world-class sights are some attractions that err on the quirkier side.

Ramoji Film City (www.ramojifilmcity.com; adult/child from ₹1000/900; ⊙9am-8pm) The Telangana/Andhra Pradesh film industry, 'Tollywood', is massive, and so is the 6.7-sq-km Film City, where films and TV shows in Telugu, Tamil and Hindi, among others, are made. The day-visit ticket includes a bus tour, funfair rides and shows. **Telangana Tourism** (p234) runs tours here.

Sudha Cars Museum (www.sudhacars.com; 19-5-15/1/D, Bahadurpura; Indian/foreigner ₹50/200, camera ₹50; ⊙9.30am-6.30pm) The eccentric creations of auto-enthusiast K Sudhakar include cars and bikes in the shape of a cricket bat, computer and lipstick, among other wacky designs. And they all work. The museum is 3km west of Charminar.

Abids Area

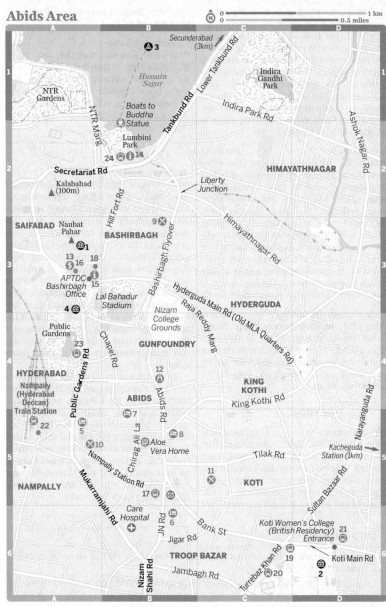

N

0   1 km

0   0.5 miles

Secunderabad (3km)

Lower Tankbund Rd

Indira Gandhi Park

NTR Gardens

Hussain Sagar

Tankbund Rd

Indira Park Rd

Ashok Nagar Rd

Boats to Buddha Statue

NTR Marg

Lumbini Park

24   14

Secretariat Rd

HIMAYATHNAGAR

Liberty Junction

Kalabahad (100m)

Hill Fort Rd

SAIFABAD

Naubat Pahar

BASHIRBAGH

9

Himayathnagar Rd

13   16   18

1

APTDC Bashirbagh Office

15

Bashirbagh Flyover

Hyderguda Main Rd (Old MLA Quarters Rd)

HYDERGUDA

4

Lal Bahadur Stadium

Raja Reddy Marg

Public Gardens

Nizam College Grounds

GUNFOUNDRY

23

Chapel Rd

KING KOTHI

HYDERABAD

Public Gardens Rd

12

King Kothi Rd

Narayanguda Rd

Nampally (Hyderabad Deccan) Train Station

ABIDS

Abids Rd

22

5

7

Chirag Ali La

Aloe Vera Home

8

Tilak Rd

Kacheguda Station (1km)

10

11

KOTI

NAMPALLY

Nampally Station Rd

17

Sultan Bazaar Rd

Mukarramjahi Rd

6

JN Rd

Bank St

Koti Women's College (British Residency) Entrance

21

Care Hospital

Jigar Rd

19

Koti Main Rd

Nizam Shahi Rd

TROOP BAZAR

Jambagh Rd

2

Turrebaz Khan Rd

20

Golconda's massive gates were studded with iron spikes to obstruct war elephants. Within the fort, a series of concealed glazed earthenware pipes ensured a reliable water supply, while the ingenious acoustics guaranteed that even the smallest sound from the entrance would echo across the fort complex.

Allow at least a couple of hours to explore the site. Guides charge at least ₹600 per 90-minute tour. Small ₹20 guide booklets are also available. Inside the citadel gate, an

Abids Area

anticlockwise circuit leads through gardens and up past mostly minor buildings to the top of the hill, where you'll find the functioning Hindu Jagadamba Mahakali Temple and the three-storey durbar hall, with fine panoramas. You then descend to the old palace buildings in the southeastern part of the fort and return to the entrance passing the elegant three-arched Taramati Mosque.

Golconda is about 10km west from Abids or Charminar: an Uber cab or auto is around ₹250 one way. Buses 65G and 66G run from Charminar to Golconda via GPO Abids hourly; the journey takes about an hour.

★ Qutb Shahi Tombs   HISTORIC SITE

(Tolichowki; Indian/foreigner ₹15/100, camera/video ₹50/100; ⊙9.30am-5.30pm Sat-Thu) These 21 magnificent domed granite tombs, with almost as many mosques, sit serenely in landscaped gardens about 2km northwest of Golconda Fort, where many of their occupants spent large parts of their lives. Seven of the eight Qutb Shahi rulers were buried here, as well as family members and a few physicians, courtesans and other favourites. An exhibition near the entrance provides helpful explanatory information (including the ambitious plans to renovate the structures and create a Heritage Park).

The tombs' great domes are mounted on cubical bases, many of which have beautiful colonnades and delicate lime stucco ornamentation. Among the finest is that of Mohammed Quli, the founder of Hyderabad, standing 42m tall on a platform near the edge of the complex, with views back towards Golconda.

The tombs are about 2km from Golconda Fort, ₹30 by autorickshaw or Uber cab.

Paigah Tombs   HISTORIC SITE

(Santoshnagar; ⊙9.30am-5pm) FREE The aristocratic Paigah family, purportedly descendants of the second Caliph of Islam, were fierce loyalists of the nizams, serving as statespeople, philanthropists and generals. The Paigahs' necropolis, in a quiet neighbourhood 4km southeast of Charminar, is a small compound of exquisite mausoleums made of marble and lime stucco. It's signposted down a small lane opposite Owaisi Hospital on the Inner Ring Rd.

The complex contains 27 carved-marble tombs in enclosures with delicately carved walls and pillars, stunning geometrically patterned filigree screens and, overhead, tall, graceful turrets. At the western end a handsome mosque is reflected in its large ablutions pool.

Moula Ali Dargah   ISLAMIC SITE

Out on the city's northeastern fringes, the dramatic rock mound of Moula Ali hill has long-distance views, cool breezes and at the top, up 500 steps, a dargah (shrine to a Sufi saint) containing what's believed to be a handprint of Ali, the son-in-law of the Prophet Mohammed. The dargah's reputed healing properties make it a pilgrimage site for the sick.

Visitors are normally allowed inside the dargah, which is covered in thousands of tiny mirrors, only during the three-day Moula Ali *urs* festival during Muharram, but you can admire them outside at other times.

TELANGANA & ANDHRA PRADESH HYDERABAD

Moula Ali hill is 9km northeast of Secunderabad – around ₹250 in an Uber cab, or take bus 16A or 16C from Rathifile bus stand to ECIL bus stand, and an autorickshaw 2km from there.

Buddha Statue
& Hussain Sagar
BUDDHIST MONUMENT

(Map p232; boats adult/child ₹55/35) Set magnificently on a plinth in the Hussain Sagar, a lake created by the Qutb Shahs, is a colossal stone statue of the Buddha (18m tall). The Dalai Lama consecrated the monument in 2006, which is evocatively illuminated at night.

Frequent boats make the 30-minute return trip to the statue from both Eat Street (⊙launches 3-8pm) and popular Lumbini Park (admission ₹10; ⊙9am-9pm). The Tankbund Rd promenade, on the eastern shore of Hussain Sagar, has great views of the statue.

🏃 Activities

Blue Cross of Hyderabad
VOLUNTEERING

(📞9642229858; www.bluecrosshyd.in; Rd No 35, Jubilee Hills; ⊙9am-5pm) This large shelter rescues animals, and vaccinates and sterilises stray dogs. Volunteers can help in the shelter (grooming and feeding animals), in the adoption centre (walking and socialising dogs) or in the office. A minimum 20 hours is requested.

🧭 Tours

★ Detours
TOURS

(📞9000850505; www.detoursindia.com; per person 3hr walk ₹2500) Outstanding cultural tours led by the enthusiastic, knowledgable Jonty Rajagopalan and her small team. Options cover off-the-beaten-track corners of Hyderabad, Warangal, plus markets, food (including cooking lessons and eating), religion and crafts.

★ Heritage Walks
WALKING

(Map p230; 📞9849728841; www.telanganatourism. gov.in/heritagewalks; per person ₹50; ⊙7.30-9am Sun & every 2nd Sat) Starting at Charminar and ending at the Chowmahalla Palace, these highly informative (and incredibly inexpensive) walks were designed and are sometimes led by architect and historian Madhu Vottery. The price includes breakfast.

SIA Photo Walks
WALKING

(📞8008633354; http://siaphotography.in/tours; group walks from ₹300) Excellent street-photography tours of the city curated by Saurabh Chatterjee, who is a knowledgable guide and experienced photographer. Smartphone users will also benefit from his expertise.

Telangana Tourism
TOURS

(📞1800 42546464; www.telanganatourism.gov.in) Offers fine weekend tours, such as a 'Nizam Palace' trip that includes the Chowmahalla Palace, Falaknuma Palace and the Golconda Fort (for the sound-and-light show) for ₹3100/2000 with/without high tea at Falaknuma. Also has daily bus tours of city sights (from ₹350 plus admission tickets) and evening Golconda sound-and-light trips. Book at any Telangana Tourism office (p241).

📖 Courses

Vipassana International
Meditation Centre
HEALTH & WELLBEING

(Dhamma Khetta; 📞040-24240290; www.khetta. dhamma.org; Nagarjuna Sagar Rd, Km12.6) Intensive 10-day silent meditation courses (10 hours a day) in peaceful grounds 20km outside the city. Apply online. There's no official charge; you donate according to your means.

🎉 Festivals & Events

Pandit Motiram–Maniram
Sangeet Samaroh
MUSIC

(⊙Nov) This four-day music festival, named for two renowned classical musicians, celebrates Hindustani music. It's held in the Chowmahalla Palace.

🛏 Sleeping

The inner-city Abids area is convenient for Nampally station and the Old City. For more space and greenery head to middle-class Banjara Hills, about 4km northwest of Abids.

In addition to the uberluxurious Taj Falaknuma Palace (p235), the swish Taj Group also runs three of Hyderabad's top high-end hotels, in Banjara Hills: the opulent **Taj Krishna** (Map p236; 📞040-66662323; www.tajhotels.com; Rd No 1; s/d from ₹8700/9300; ✴@🛜🏊), stylish **Taj Deccan** (Map p236; 📞040-66669999; www.tajhotels.com; Rd No 1; s/d from ₹7540/7980; ✴@🛜🏊) and lakeside **Taj Banjara** (Map p236; 📞040-66669999; www. tajhotels.com; Rd No 1; s/d from ₹8970/10,280; ✴@🛜🏊).

Golden Glory Guesthouse
GUESTHOUSE $

(Map p236; 📞040-23554765; www.goldenglory guesthouse.com; off Rd No 3, Banjara Hills; s/d incl breakfast ₹1100/1300, with AC ₹1300/1700; ✴🛜) Boasting an enviable location in upmarket Banjara Hills, with ample cafes and eateries close by, this modestly priced place has clean simple rooms, some with balconies. There's free wi-fi throughout and staff are eager to please.

Hotel Rajmata HOTEL $
(Map p232; ☑040-66665555; www.hotelrajma ta.chobs.in; Public Gardens Rd; s/d ₹850/1200, with AC ₹2250/2400; ❊🏵🗺) This popular long-running hotel is only 250m from Nampally station, but set back from the busy main road, which keeps things relatively quiet. Standard quarters are aged but roomy; AC rooms are overpriced but fresh. There's 24-hour room service.

Hotel Suhail HOTEL $
(Map p232; ☑040-24610299; www.hotelsuhail.in; Troop Bazar; s/d/tr from ₹700/850/1200, with AC ₹1200/1400/1700; ❊🏵🗺) Reasonable value if you want to be in the thick of things, though standards of cleanliness could be better. Has friendly staff and large, quiet rooms with balconies and hot water. It's tucked away on a lane off Bank St.

Fresh Living APARTMENT $$
(Map p236; ☑9849563056; www.freshlivingrooms. in; 61 Banjara Green Colony, Rd No 12; ⊙d ₹2166, apt from ₹5130; ❊@🏵) This modern place enjoys a good location off Rd No 12 and has well-presented, comfortable rooms and also spacious apartments (sleeping up to nine) that are ideal for families. Breakfast is included.

Raj Classic Inn HOTEL $$
(Map p239; ☑040-27815291; rajclassicinn@gmail. com; 50 MG Rd, Secunderabad; s/d incl breakfast from ₹1630/2050; ❊🏵) A very good-value hotel, with clean, well-maintained and spacious rooms and friendly, courteous staff. Expect some traffic noise due to its busy location (a short rickshaw ride from Secunderabad station). In-house Chilly's restaurant is recommended for veg food.

Treebo GN International HOTEL $$
(Map p239; ☑9322800100; www.treebo.com; Padmarao Nagar; r ₹2660; ❊🏵) Rooms here give more than a nod to contemporary style, and reliable wi-fi. There's no in-house restaurant facility but lots close by as the location is near Secunderabad station. The Treebo budget chain operates around a dozen other places around town.

Taj Mahal Hotel HOTEL $$
(Map p232; ☑040-24758250; www.hoteltajmahal india.com; Abids Rd; incl breakfast s ₹1840-3010, d ₹2620-3250; ❊🏵) The original 1924 building oozes class and houses the reception and a

few bedrooms ('heritage' rooms have some character, the others are plain); the majority of rooms are in a functional modern block to the side. Staff are ever-helpful but facilities like (spotty) wi-fi are poor and the decor needs an upgrade. Still, it's very convenient for sightseeing.

★Taj Falaknuma Palace HERITAGE HOTEL $$$
(☑040-66298585; www.tajhotels.com; Engine Bowli, Falaknuma; s/d from ₹37,800/40,780; ❊@🏵) One of the nation's most impressive hotels, the former residence of the sixth nizam, this 1884 neoclassical palace now run by the Taj group has nizam-esque embossed-leather wallpaper and 24-karat-gold ceiling trim. The rooms are stunning, and the whole place is astoundingly opulent.

Nonguests can come for lunch/dinner or 'high tea' (₹2340) on the Jade Room terrace. Guests (including those just there to eat) get a free palace tour. Book meals two days ahead, or you won't get past the outer gate of the 1.2km driveway.

Marigold HOTEL $$$
(Map p236; ☑040-67363636; www.marigoldho tels.com; Ameerpet Rd, Greenlands; s/d incl breakfast from ₹6920/7970; ❊@🏵🗺) The Marigold is as practical as it is stylish. Rooms are smart but not try-hard, with golds, neutrals and fresh flowers, while the in-house Mekong restaurant offers good Thai food. The rooftop pool is also a great feature.

Fortune Park Vallabha HOTEL $$$
(Map p236; ☑040-39884444; www.fortunehotels. in; Rd No 12, Banjara Hills; s/d incl breakfast from ₹5180/6300; ❊@🏵🗺) Enjoys a good location and has large contemporary rooms with stained-glass panels, many with balconies. Room service is available at reasonable prices and the South Indian food and breakfast buffet are excellent.

Royalton Hotel HOTEL $$$
(Map p232; ☑040-67122000; www.royaltonhotel. in; Fateh Sultan Lane, Abids; s/d incl breakfast from ₹4460/4750; ❊🏵) In a relatively quiet part

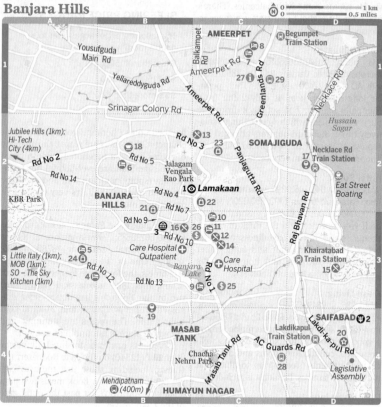

Banjara Hills

of Abids, Royalton's gargantuan black lobby chandelier and mirrored lifts give off a slight Manhattan vibe. Rooms have tasteful textiles, glass showers and tea/coffee makers. The hotel is vegetarian, and alcohol-free.

GreenPark
HOTEL $$$

(Map p236; ☎040-66515151; www.hotelgreenpark. com; Ameerpet Rd, Greenlands; s/d incl breakfast from ₹5320/6550; ❋@☎) The GreenPark has decent standard rooms that have sleek desks, wood flooring and a dash of art; the posher options aren't quite as good value. Staff are attentive and you'll dine well in the in-house Once Upon a Time restaurant.

✕ Eating

In the early evenings, look out for *mirchi bhajji* (chilli fritters), served at street stalls with tea. The Hyderabadi style is famous: chillis are stripped of their seeds, stuffed with tamarind, sesame and spices, dipped in chickpea batter and fried.

Local usage refers to 'thalis' as 'meals'.

✕ Old City & Abids Area

Govind Dosa
STREET FOOD $

(Map p230; Charkaman; snacks ₹40-100; ⊙6am-noon) A famous breakfast spot, cheery Govind's street-corner stand is permanently surrounded by happy Hyderabadis savouring his delicious dosas (try the butter cheese) and *idlis* (spongy, round, fermented rice cake; the *tawa idlis* topped with chilli powder and spices is a great way to kickstart the day). Always very busy, so be prepared to wait.

Nimrah
CAFE $

(Map p230; Charminar; baked goods ₹3-12; ⊙5.30am-11pm) This classic Irani cafe, always packed to the rafters, is located almost underneath the Charminar's arches. It offers a particularly tasty range of Irani baked goods to accompany your chai pick-me-up. The classic dunk is Osmania biscuits (melt-in-

Banjara Hills

the-mouth shortbreads) but there are many other options including sponge breads and plum slices.

Santosh Dhaba
NORTH INDIAN $

(Map p232; Hanuman Tekdi Rd, off Bank St, Abids Circle; mains ₹140-170; ⊙11am-1am) A pure-veg place that serves up tasty North Indian classics (try the paneer butter masala), great roti and naan, plus some Chinese dishes. Prices are easy on the pocket, service is prompt and there's an air-con section upstairs.

Kamat Hotel
SOUTH INDIAN $

(Map p232; Nampally Station Rd; mains ₹110-185; ⊙7am-10pm) Cheap and reliably good for tasty South Indian fare. It's a good option for breakfast or a speedy lunch – try their *idli* or *masala vada* (spicy, deep-fried lentil savoury). There's also a larger AC branch in Saifabad, and two in Secunderabad.

★ Shah Ghouse Cafe
HYDERABADI $$

(Shah Ali Banda Rd; mains ₹120-240; ⊙5am-1am) During Ramadan, Hyderabadis line up for Shah Ghouse's famous *haleem* (a thick soup of pounded spiced wheat, with goat, chicken or beef, and lentils) and at any time of year the biryani is near-perfect. Don't expect ambience: just good, hard-working, traditional food, in a no-frills upstairs dining hall. Wash it down with a delicious lassi (₹60).

Hotel Shadab
HYDERABADI $$

(Map p230; High Court Rd, Charminar; mains ₹170-350; ⊙noon-11.30pm) The timewarp decor looks like it's been based on a 1970s disco but the cuisine is great at this hopping Hyderabadi restaurant. Great for biryani, kebabs and mutton in all configurations and, during Ramadan, *haleem*. Downstairs it's very solo-male; head upstairs to the AC room for more of a family vibe.

Dakshina Mandapa
SOUTH INDIAN $$

(Map p232; Taj Mahal Hotel, Abids Rd; mains & meals ₹170-240; ⊙7am-10.30pm) Highly regarded spot for South Indian vegetarian food. You may have to wait for a lunch table, but order the South Indian thali and you'll be brought heap after heap of rice and refills of authentic dishes. The AC room upstairs does a superb ₹320 lunch buffet (noon to 3.30pm).

Taj Restaurant
HYDERABADI $$

(Map p230; Khilwat Rd; mains ₹100-200; ⊙10am-9pm) Specialising in biryani and delicious chicken and mutton curries, this bustling place is just around the corner from the Chowmahalla Palace. There's an AC room on the upper floor.

Gufaa
NORTH INDIAN $$$

(Map p232; Ohri's Cuisine Court, Bashirbagh Rd; mains ₹210-660; ⊙noon-3.30pm & 7-11pm) For

TELANGANA & ANDHRA PRADESH HYDERABAD

an authentic taste of the north, the great veg and nonveg kebabs and curries at Gufaa will satisfy all. Try a Lahori *mahi* (fish curry) or *dal bukhara* (dhal prepared with cream and tomatoes). The premises are gloriously kitsch, with fake cave walls, goblets and lots of zebra and leopard prints in evidence.

Banjara Hills & Jubilee Hills

Gallery Cafe
CAFE $$

(Map p236; http://gallerycafe.in; Rd No 10, Banjara Hills; meals ₹160-210; ◷ 11.30am-10.30pm; 🛜) A tranquil cafe, well set off busy Rd No 10, with a tempting array of coffees, sandwiches and pasta dishes at moderate prices. It hosts art, musical and stand-up comedy events most Wednesdays and adjoins the excellent Kalakriti Art Gallery.

Chutneys
SOUTH INDIAN $$

(Map p236; Shilpa Arcade, Rd No 3; mains & meals ₹178-272; ◷ 7am-11pm; 🛜) Chutneys is famous for its South Indian meals and all-day dosas, *idlis* and *uttapams* (thick, savoury rice pancake with finely chopped onions, green chillies, coriander and coconut). Its dishes are low on chilli, so you can get the full 'Andhra meals' experience without the pain. It's a bustling place with teams of neatly purple-shirted waiters.

Deli 9
CAFE $$

(Map p236; www.deli9.in; 1st Ave, Rd No 1, Banjara Hills; snacks ₹140-275; ◷ 9am-10pm; 🛜) Renowned for its desserts and cakes, this cafe also offers good breakfasts, wraps, soups, pies, sandwiches and crêpes in a tranquil ambience.

Utupura
KERALAN $$

(Map p236; Rd No 10, Banjara Hills; mains ₹110-200; ◷ 11.30am-4pm & 6-10pm Mon-Fri, noon-10pm Sat

& Sun) Hidden down a lane west of the GVK One mall, this low-key, unpretentious place serves tasty South Indian classics, a mean lunchtime thali (from ₹180), fish curries and *appam* (rice pancake).

★ SO – The Sky Kitchen
ASIAN, MEDITERRANEAN $$$

(☑ 040-23558004; www.notjustso.com; Rd No 92, near Apollo Hospital, Jubilee Hills; mains ₹375-520; ◷ noon-midnight; 🛜) On a quiet Jubilee Hills rooftop, with candles and loungy playlists, this is one of the most atmospheric eating spots in town. The superb menu has been crafted carefully, mixing pan-Asian and Mediterranean dishes and with a nod to healthy eating: most dishes are grilled, baked or stir-fried. It's 4km west of Banjara Hills' Rd No 1.

Fusion 9
MULTICUISINE $$$

(Map p236; ☑ 040-65577722; www.fusion9.in; Rd No 1; mains ₹425-975; ◷ 12.30-3.30pm & 7-11.30pm; 🛜) With a warm ambience and cosy decor, Fusion 9 offers one of the best international menus in town. Food is creatively presented; try a shot of gazpacho blanco and then perhaps the Moroccan veg tagine with lemon couscous. Very popular for Sunday brunch (₹1188).

Southern Spice
SOUTH INDIAN $$$

(Rd No 10, Jubilee Hills; mains ₹215-485; ◷ noon-3.30pm & 7-11pm) Now in new (less intimate) premises in the wealthy western district of Jubilee Hills, Southern Spice offers specialities from across the south. Try *natu kodi iguru* ('country chicken') or a special veg thali (₹325).

Firdaus
INDIAN $$$

(Map p236; ☑ 040-66662323; Taj Krishna hotel, Rd No 1; mains ₹520-1180; ◷ 12.30-3pm & 7.30-

---

HYDERABAD CUISINE

Hyderabad has a food culture all its own and Hyderabadis take great pride and pleasure in it. It was the Mughals who brought the tasty biryanis, skewer kebabs and *haleem* (a thick Ramadan soup of pounded, spiced wheat with goat, chicken or beef, and lentils). Mutton (goat or lamb) is the classic biryani base, though chicken, egg and vegetable biryanis are plentiful too. Biryanis come in vast quantities and one serve may satisfy two people.

If you're in Hyderabad during Ramadan (known locally as Ramzan), look out for the clay ovens called *bhattis*. You'll probably hear them before you see them. Men gather around, taking turns to vigorously pound *haleem* inside purpose-built structures. Come nightfall, the serious business of eating begins. The taste is worth the wait.

Andhra cuisine, found in Telangana and Andhra Pradesh, is more curry- and pilau-based, often with coconut and/or cashew flavours, and famous across India for its delicious spicy hotness. Vegetarians are well catered for, but you'll find plenty of fish, seafood and meat dishes too.

Secunderabad

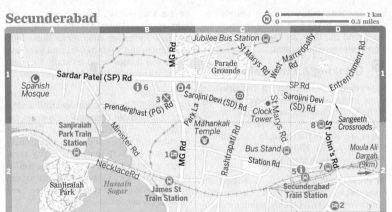

Secunderabad

⊕ Activities, Courses & Tours
APTDC Secunderabad
Office .... (see 6)

⊜ Sleeping
1 Raj Classic Inn.. B2
2 Treebo GN International D2

⊗ Eating
3 Paradise B1

⊜ Shopping
4 Malkha B1

ℹ Information
5 Telangana Tourism D2
6 Telangana Tourism B1

ℹ Transport
7 Rathifile Bus Stand D2
8 Secunderabad Bus Stop
(Pushpak) D2
Secunderabad Junction
Bus Stop ....(see 5)
Secunderabad Reservation
Complex.......................................(see 7)

11.30pm; 🖋) A classy hotel restaurant, Firdaus offers great Hyderabadi (and other) dishes to the strains of live *ghazals* (classical Urdu love songs, accompanied by harmonium and tabla). They even serve *haleem* outside Ramadan and have good vegetarian choices too.

Barbeque Nation INDIAN $$$
(Map p236; 📞 040-64566692; www.barbeque-nation.com; ANR Centre, Rd No 1; veg/nonveg lunch ₹627/752, dinner ₹946/1071; ⏱noon-3.30pm & 6.30-10.30pm; 🖋) All-you-can-eat kebabs, curries, salads and desserts, with many veg and nonveg options. A great-value place to come when you're hungry! Prices fluctuate a little depending on the day and time. Slurp on one of their excellent Indian wines while you dine.

✗ Secunderabad

Paradise HYDERABADI $$
(Persis; Map p239; www.paradisefoodcourt.com; cnr SD & MG Rds; biryani ₹200-254; ⏱11.30am-

11pm) Paradise is synonymous with biryani in these parts. The main Secunderabad location has five different dining areas: head to the attractive 'roof garden', complete with whirring fans, or pay an AC surcharge to eat inside. Also serves lots of (less pleasing) Chinese dishes.

There's a large, modern **branch** (Map p236; 📞 040-67408400; NTR Gardens; mains ₹200-378; ⏱11am-11pm) closer to Abids and Banjara Hills, though we found the biryani there a bit less flavoursome.

✗ Other Areas

★ Dhaba By Claridges MODERN INDIAN $$$
(📞 040-29706704; www.dhababyclaridges.com; Western Pearl Bldg, Survey 13, Kondapur; mains ₹265-445; ⏱noon-11.30pm; 🖋) A good reason to head out west to Hi-Tech City, this hip hang-out offers a contemporary take on North Indian street food (minus the fumes and traffic of course). Dhaba's decor

is kooky, with Bollywood-style murals and bold colours to the fore. House cocktails are wonderful and the ₹599 'Da Lunch Bomb' is a great all-you-can-eat deal.

🍷 Drinking & Entertainment

Hyderabad does not have a big drinking scene, and due to local licensing laws many of the liveliest lounges serve nothing stronger than mocktails. Some of the hottest new places are west of the centre in leafy Banjara Hills and Jubilee Hills, where you'll find a slew of good rooftop venues.

★ Prost Brewpub   MICROBREWERY
(www.prost.in; 882/A Rd No 45, Jubilee Hills; ⊙noon-midnight; 🛜) A highly popular, cavernous brewhouse with five tap beers, including an English ale and a stout, plus cider. There are several zones, all stylishly lit, including ample outdoor space and an extensive East-meets-West pub-grub menu. Rammed on weekend nights. Also hosts comedy and DJs.

★ MOB   BAR
(www.facebook.com/itismob; Aryan's, Rd No 92, near Apollo Hospital, Jubilee Hills; ⊙noon-11.30pm; 🛜) A stylish, sociable Belgium beer house that draws a refreshingly mixed-gender, mixed-age crowd. Order a 'beer platter' for a sample of four choice brews or try the set lunch (₹799), which includes a draught beer. There's live music on Saturday nights. It's on a side road off the south side of KBR National-al Park, 4km west of Banjara Hills' Rd No 1.

Vertigo   BAR
(Map p236; www.vertigothehighlife.in; 5th fl, Shiv Shakti Tower, Rd No 12; ⊙11am-midnight) A roof-top bar that boasts a great terrace, with elegant seating and interior rooms for live music and DJs. The eating 'zone' serves North Indian, Chinese and Western food, and they have an alcohol licence (good cocktails for about ₹400). It's opposite Ratnadeep supermarket.

Coffee Cup   CAFE
(📞040-40037571; www.facebook.com/thecoffee cupp; E 89, off 5th Crescent Rd, Sainikpuri, Secunderabad; ⊙9am-11.30pm; 🛜) Excellent neighbourhood cafe and creative hub that's a magnet for East Hyderabad's arty crew. Offers a fine selection of interesting coffees (try an Ethiopian Khawa), teas, snacks and meals. There's stand-up comedy here most Fridays. It's above Canara Bank.

OCD   CAFE
(Map p236; Rd No 5, Banjara Hills; ⊙10am-10pm) Located on a quiet leafy street in Banjara Hills, OCD (Obsessive Coffee Disorder) attracts a fashionable crowd with its zany decor, pool table and terrace for hookah puffing. There's decent grub (Chinese and Western snacks), great mocktails and, of course, superb coffee.

Kismet   CLUB
(Map p236; 📞040-23456789; www.theparkhotels. com; The Park, Raj Bhavan Rd, Somajiguda; admission per couple ₹700-2000; ⊙9pm-midnight or later Wed-Sun) A sleek, upmarket nightclub, with loungy booth seating, a big dance floor and a pumping bass-driven sound system. Men won't get past the ranks of bouncers without female companions. Drinks are pricey (cocktails around ₹600), not that the wealthy crowd are too bothered. Musically things range from EDM to Bollywood.

CHARMINAR MARKETS

Hyderabadis and visitors of every stripe flock to the Charminar area's labyrinthine lanes to browse, buy and wander. Patthargatti, the broad avenue leading in from the Musi River, is lined with shops selling clothes (especially wedding outfits), perfumes and Hyderabad's famous pearls. **Laad Bazar** (Map p230; ⊙10am-8.30pm), running west from the Charminar, is famed for its sparkling bangle shops: lac bangles, made from a resinous insect secretion and encrusted with colourful beads or stones, are a Hyderabad speciality. In Laad Bazar you'll also find perfumers, wedding goods and fabrics.

Laad Bazar opens into **Mehboob Chowk** (Map p230), a square with shops selling antiquarian books and antiques, a livestock market on its south side, and a market in exotic birds, **Chiddi Bazar** (Map p230; ⊙7am-7pm), just southwest.

A short distance north, the **Patel Market** (Map p230; ⊙approximately 11am-8pm) sells cloth fabrics and cranks into action from around 11am in the back lanes between Patthargatti and Rikab Gunj. Further north again and on the other side of Patthargatti, the wholesale vegetable market **Mir Alam Mandi** (Map p230; Patthargatti Rd; ⊙6.30am-6.30pm) trades in all kinds of fresh stuff from 6.30am to 6.30pm daily.

Ravindra Bharathi Theatre THEATRE
(Map p236; 040-23233672; www.ravindrabhar athi.org; Ladki-ka-pul Rd, Saifabad) Well-curated music, dance and drama performances, and cinema.

Shopping

Charminar is the most exciting place to shop: you'll find exquisite pearls, slippers, gold and fabrics alongside billions of bangles. Upmarket boutiques and malls are scattered around Banjara Hills and the western suburbs.

Bidri Crafts ARTS & CRAFTS
(Map p232; http://bidrihandicraft.com; Gunfoundry, Basheer Bagh; 11am-9pm) *Bidri* is a metal craft (originating in Iran) that involves intricate inlay work. The famous family-run business sells top-quality plates, vases, bowls, jewellery (earrings from ₹180) and accessories at moderate prices.

Malkha CLOTHING
(Map p239; www.malkha.in; 229, 2nd fl, B Wing, Chandralok Complex; 10am-9pm Mon-Sat) Malkha cloth is made near the cotton fields, by hand and with natural dyes, reducing strain on the environment and putting primary producers in control. The result is gorgeous; here you can pick up fabric (from ₹320 per yard), shawls and saris (from ₹2200) at reasonable prices. It's opposite Paradise Hotel.

Fabindia CLOTHING
(Map p236; www.fabindia.com; Rd No 9, Banjara Hills; 11am-9.30pm) Lovely women's (and some men's) clothes in artisanal fabrics with contemporary prints and colours. They also sell homeware including bed linen, cushions and *dhurries* (rugs). Prices are fair.

There's another branch (Fateh Maidan; 10.30am-8.30pm) in Bashirbagh.

Suvasa CLOTHING
(Map p236; www.suvasa.in; Rd No 12, Banjara Hills; 11am-7.30pm) Suvasa's block-printed kurtas (long shirts with a short or no collar), baggy *salwar* pants and dupattas (scarves) are all high quality. They also sell homeware including gorgeous bed and table linen.

Hyderabad Perfumers PERFUME
(Map p230; Patthargatti; 10am-8.30pm Mon-Sat) This fourth-generation family business can conjure something aromatic up for you on the spot. They specialise in *ittar*, natural perfume oils from flowers and herbs; prices

start as low as ₹200 and rise to over ₹7000 per bottle.

GVK One MALL
(Map p236; www.gvkone.com; Rd No 1, Banjara Hills; 11am-11pm) An upmarket mall with a good selection of clothes shops, ATMs, a small food court, cafes and a cinema.

Himalaya Book World BOOKS
(Map p236; Panjagutta Circle, Banjara Hills; 10.30am-10.30pm) A fine selection of English-language fiction and nonfiction by Indian and international authors. They have several other branches in town.

Information

MEDICAL SERVICES
Reputable Care Hospitals are on **Mukarramjahi Road** (Map p232; 040-30417777; www.carehospitals.com) and **Road No 1** (Map p236; 040-30418888; www.carehospitals.com). There's also an outpatient hospital on **Road No 10** (Map p236; 040-39310444; 4th Lane).

POST
General Post Office (Map p232; Abids Circle; 8am-7pm Mon-Sat, 10am-1pm Sun)

TOURIST INFORMATION
Indiatourism (Map p236; 040-23409199; www.incredibleindia.org; Tourism Plaza, Greenlands Rd; 9.30am-6pm Mon-Fri, 9.30am-1pm Sat) A useful office, with good information on Hyderabad, Telangana and beyond.
Telangana Tourism (1800 42546464; www.telanganatourism.gov.in; 7am-8.30pm) Tourist information and bookings for state-government-run tours, heritage walks and hotels in Telangana. Branches at **Bashirbagh** (Map p232; 040-66745986; Shakar Bhavan; 6.30am-8pm), **Tankbund Road** (Map p232; 040-65581555; 6.30am-8pm), **Greenlands Road** (Map p236; 040-23414334; Tourism Plaza; 7am-8pm), **Hyderabad airport** (040-24253215), **Secunderabad** (Map p239; 040-27893100; Yatri Nivas Hotel, SP Rd; 6.30am-8.30pm) and **Secunderabad train station** (Map p239; 040-27801614; 10am-8pm).

Getting There & Away

AIR
Hyderabad's massive, modern, efficient **Rajiv Gandhi International Airport** (040-66546370; http://hyderabad.aero; Shamshabad) is 25km southwest of the city centre. It has direct daily flights, including with **Air India** (Map p232; 040-23389711; www.airindia.com; HACA Bhavan, Saifabad; 9.30am-6pm

BUSES FROM HYDERABAD

DESTINATION	FARE (₹)	DURATION (HR)	FREQUENCY
Bengaluru	687-1040	8-11	22 buses 9am-10.30pm
Chennai	694-1191	11-14	18 buses 6-10.30pm
Hospet	522-850	8-11	3 buses daily
Mumbai	1070-2550	12-14	27 buses 2-11.55pm
Mysore	1050-1733	11-13	9 buses 6.30-9.30pm
Tirupati	652-1485	16	half-hourly 1.30-10pm
Vijayawada	340-480	4-5	half-hourly 5am-11.55pm
Visakhapatnam	660-1650	11-13	hourly 4-11pm
Warangal	180-240	4	half-hourly

Mon-Sat) and **Jet Airways** (Map p232; ☑ 020-39893333; www.jetairways.com; Summit Apartments, Hill Fort Rd; ⊙10am-6pm Mon-Sat), to over 20 Indian cities plus international destinations including Chicago, London and several Southeast Asian and Gulf destinations.

BUS

The main terminal is the vast **Mahatma Gandhi bus station** (MGBS; Imlibun Bus Station; Map p230; ☑ 040-24614406; ⊙ advance booking offices 8am-10.30pm) near Abids. Air-con services by the **TSRTC** (Telangana State Road Transport Corporation; ☑1800 2004599; http://tsrtcbus.in) are quite good; for Karnataka, go with KSRTC near platform 30. Nearly all long-distance services depart in the evening. When booking ahead, women should request seats up front as these are reserved for female passengers.

Secunderabad's **Jubilee bus station** (Map p239; ☑040-27802203; Gandhi Nagar, Secunderabad) is smaller; frequent city buses run here from St Mary's Rd near Secunderabad station. From Jubilee there are buses to cities including Chennai (Madras), Mumbai and these routes:

Bengaluru (Bangalore) ordinary/Volvo AC/sleeper ₹687/from 827/1370, eight to 11 hours, 19 daily

Vijayawada non-AC/AC ₹317/437, four to six hours, 17 daily

Other useful bus stops include the **bus stand** (Map p239) on St Mary's Rd, the **Charminar bus stop** (Map p230; Shah Ali Banda Rd) for the Old City, **Koti bus stand** (Map p232; Turrebaz Khan Rd), **Koti Women's College bus stand** (Map p232) and **Rathifile bus stand** (Map p239; Station Rd) for Secunderabad.

TRAIN

Secunderabad, Nampally (officially called Hyderabad Deccan) and Kacheguda are Hyderabad's three major train stations. Most through trains stop at Kacheguda.

The reservation complexes at **Nampally** (Map p232; ☑040-27829999; Public Gardens Rd;

⊙8am-8pm Mon-Sat, 8am-2pm Sun) and **Secunderabad** (Rathifile; Map p239; St John's Rd; ⊙8am-8pm Mon-Sat, 8am-2pm Sun), both in separate buildings away from the stations, have foreign-tourist-quota counters (bring your passport and visa photocopies, along with originals). For enquiries and PNR status, phone ☑139.

There are 12 daily trains to both Warangal (sleeper/3AC/2AC ₹170/540/735, 2½ hours) and Vijayawada (₹220/650/910, six hours), mostly from Secunderabad.

ⓘ Getting Around

TO/FROM THE AIRPORT
Bus

The TSRTC's Pushpak air-conditioned bus service runs between about 4am or 5am and 11pm to/from various stops in the city including:

AC Guards (Map p236; AC Guards Rd) (₹212, two or three buses hourly) About 1.5km from Abids.

Paryatak Bhavan (Map p236) (₹265, about hourly) On Greenlands Rd.

Secretariat (Map p232; NTR Marg) (₹265, about hourly) About 1.5km from Abids.

Secunderabad (Map p239; Rail Nilayam Rd) (₹265, twice hourly)

The trip takes around one hour. Contact TSRTC or check http://hyderabad.aero for exact timings.

Taxi

The prepaid taxi booth is on the lowest level of the terminal. Fares to Abids or Banjara Hills are ₹600 to ₹750. **Meru Cabs** (☑ 040-44224422) and **Sky Cabs** (☑ 040-49494949) charge similar rates. Uber is cheaper: around ₹350 to ₹500.

AUTORICKSHAW

Expect to pay ₹30 to ₹50 for a short ride, and around ₹120 for 4km. Few drivers use meters.

BUS

Few travellers bother with local buses (₹6 to ₹12 for most rides) but there are some useful routes. Try www.hyderabadbusroutes.com (although it can be inaccurate).

City stops include **Afzalgunj** (Map p230), **GPO Abids** (Map p232; JN Rd), **Koti** (Map p232), **Mehdipatnam**, **Public Gardens** (Map p232) and **Secunderabad Junction** (Map p239).

Hyderabad City Bus Routes

BUS NO	ROUTE
65G, 66G	Charminar–Golconda Fort, via Afzalgunj, GPO Abids; both about hourly
49M	Secunderabad Junction–Mehdipatnam via Rd No 1 (Banjara Hills); frequent
8A	Charminar–Secunderabad Junction via Afzalgunj, GPO Abids; frequent
40, 86	Secunderabad Junction–Koti Bus Stop; both frequent
127K	Koti Bus Stop–Jubilee Hills via GPO Abids, Public Gardens, Rd Nos 1 & 12 (Banjara Hills); frequent

CAR

Arrange car hire through your hotel. The going rate for a small AC car with a driver is ₹1200 to ₹1500 per day for city sightseeing (eight hours/80km maximum), and ₹2800 to ₹3500 per day for out-of-town trips (up to 300km).

METRO RAIL

Hyderabad Metro Rail, a (long-delayed) 72km rapid-transit network is scheduled to start (perhaps) in late 2017 or 2018. Trains will run on elevated tracks above Hyderabad's streets, with 66 stations on three lines.

TAXI

There are thousands of Uber and Ola drivers in Hyderabad and fares are very fair indeed (often cheaper than those quoted by autorickshaw drivers). A 3km ride will be around ₹80 to ₹100.

TRAIN

The suburban **MMTS trains** (www.mmtstrain timings.in; fares ₹5-10) are not very useful for travellers, but infrequent trains (every 30 to 45 minutes) run between Hyderabad (Nampally) and Lingampalli via Necklace Rd, Begumpet and Hi-Tech City. There's also a route between Falaknuma (south of Old City) and Lingampalli via Kacheguda and Secunderabad stations.

TELANGANA

Bhongir

Most Hyderabad–Warangal buses and trains stop at the town of Bhongir, 60km from Hyderabad. It's worth stopping to climb the fantastic-looking 12th-century Chalukyan **hill fort** (off DVK Rd; ₹5, camera ₹10; ⊙10am-5pm), sitting on what resembles a gargantuan

TELANGANA & ANDHRA PRADESH BHONGIR

MAJOR TRAINS FROM HYDERABAD & SECUNDERABAD

DESTINATION	TRAIN NO & NAME	FARE (₹)	DURATION (HR)	DEPARTURE TIME & STATION
Bengaluru	22692 or 22694 Rajdhani	1690/2460 (B)	12	6.50pm Secunderabad
	12785 Bangalore Exp	360/945/1335 (A)	11½	7.05pm Kacheguda
Chennai	12604 Hyderabad-Chennai Exp	400/1055/1495 (A)	13	4.50pm Nampally
	12760 Charminar Exp	425/1115/1590 (A)	14	6.30pm Nampally
Delhi	12723 Telangana Exp	665/1745/2450 (A)	27	6.25am Nampally
	22691 or 22693 Rajdhani	3145/4675 (B)	18	7.50am Secunderabad
Hosapete (Hospet; for Hampi)	17603 Exp	275/740/1065 (A)	11½	9pm Kacheguda
Kolkata	18646 East Coast Exp	615/1645/2415 (A)	31	9.50am Nampally
Mumbai (Bombay)	12702 Hussainsagar Exp	410/1085/1540 (A)	14½	2.45pm Nampally
Tirupati	12734 Narayanadri Exp	385/1005/1425 (A)	12	6.05pm Secunderabad
Visakhapatnam	12728 Godavari Exp	395/1035/1465 (A)	12½	5.15pm Nampally

Fares: (A) – sleeper/3AC/2AC; (B) – 3AC/2AC

stone egg on the eastern side of town. You can leave backpacks at the ticket office.

Warangal

📞 0870 / POP 633,000

Warangal was the capital of the Kakatiya kingdom, which ruled most of present-day Telangana and Andhra Pradesh from the 12th to early 14th centuries. The city merges with the town of Hanumakonda.

⊙ Sights

Ancient temples in Hanumakonda include the lakeside **Bhadrakali Temple** (Bhadrakali Temple Rd), 2km southeast of the 1000-Pillared Temple, whose idol of the mother goddess Kali sits with a weapon in each of her eight hands, and the small **Siddeshwara Temple** on the south side of Hanumakonda Hill.

Fort FORT

(Fort Rd) Warangal's fort, on the southern edge of town, was a massive construction with three circles of walls (the outermost 7km in circumference). Most of it is now either fields or buildings, but at the centre is a huge, partly reassembled Shaivite **Svayambhu Temple** (Indian/foreigner ₹15/100, camera ₹25; ⊙9am-6pm), with handsome, large *torana* (architrave) gateways at its cardinal points. An autorickshaw from Warangal station costs around ₹300 return.

The Svayambhu Temple ticket also covers the Kush Mahal (Shitab Khan Mahal), a 16th-century royal hall 400m west. Almost opposite the Svayambhu entrance is a **park** (₹10; ⊙7am-7pm) containing the high rock Ekashila Gutta, which is topped by another Kakatiya temple overlooking a small lake.

1000-Pillared Temple HINDU TEMPLE

(south of NH163, Hanumakonda; ⊙6am-6pm) FREE The 1000-Pillared Temple, constructed in the 12th century, is in a leafy setting and is a fine example of Kakatiya architecture and sculpture. Unusually, the cross-shaped building has shrines to the sun god Surya (to the right as you enter), Vishnu (centre) and Shiva (left). Despite the name, it certainly does not have 1000 pillars. Behind rises Hanumakonda Hill, site of the original Kakatiya capital.

🛏 Sleeping & Eating

Vijaya Lodge HOTEL $

(📞 0870-2501222; Station Rd; s ₹290, d ₹550-800) Conveniently close (around 350m) to Warangal's bus and train stations, the Vijaya is

certainly basic but has helpful enough staff. Rooms are borderline dreary, with showers by bucket. The upper floors are best.

Hotel Ashoka HOTEL $$

(📞 0870-2578491; www.hotelashoka.in; Main Rd, Hanumakonda; r ₹1760-2650; ❉@) This large hotel, dating from the 1980s, has a selection of AC rooms in several price categories. It's near the Hanumakonda bus stand and 1000-Pillared Temple. Also here is the good veg restaurant **Kanishka** (mains ₹140-260; ⊙6.30am-10.30pm), plus a nonveg restaurant and a bar.

Hotel Landmark HOTEL $$

(📞 0870-2546333, 0870-2546111; landmarkhotel3@yahoo.co.in; Nakkalagutta; r ₹1920; ❉🛜) Behind the mirrored facade you'll find clean if smallish rooms that have a dash of contemporary style. The in-house restaurant serves a wide variety of South Indian dishes.

Sri Geetha Bhavan ANDHRA $

(Market Rd, Hanumakonda; mains ₹90-130; ⊙6am-11pm) Good South Indian meals in pleasant AC surroundings. Follow the Supreme Hotels sign.

Seasons MULTICUISINE $$

(www.facebook.com/seasonsrestauranthnk; NH 163, Hanumakonda, near National Institute of Technology; mains ₹160-240; ⊙1-10.30pm) With subtle lighting, attractive seating and a varied menu that includes popular Chinese, Middle Eastern and Indian dishes, Seasons is a good choice for an atmospheric meal.

❶ Getting There & Around

Buses to Hyderabad (₹135 to ₹215, four hours) leave about three times hourly from **Hanumakonda bus stand** (New Bus Stand Rd), and seven times daily (express/deluxe ₹115/150, seven hours) from **Warangal bus stand** (📞 0870-2565595; Station Rd) opposite the train station.

From Warangal several trains daily run to Hyderabad (sleeper/3AC/2AC ₹170/540/740, three hours), Vijayawada (₹190/535/740, three hours) and Chennai (₹375/985/1395, 10½ to 12 hours).

Shared autorickshaws (₹15) ply fixed routes around Warangal and Hanumakonda.

Palampet

About 70km northeast of Warangal, the stunning **Ramappa Temple** (camera ₹25; ⊙6am-6pm) is near the village of Palampet. Built in the early 13th century, it's the outstanding gem of Kakatiya architecture, covered in wonderfully detailed carvings of animals, lovers, wrestlers, musicians, dancers, deities and Hindu legends. Brackets on its external pillars support superb black-basalt carvings of mythical creatures and sinuous women twined with snakes. The large temple tank, **Ramappa Cheruvu**, 1km south, is popular with migrating birds.

❶ Getting There & Away

The easiest way to get here is by chartered taxi (around ₹2000 return from Warangal), but buses also run half-hourly from Hanumakonda to Mulugu (₹58, one hour), then a further 13km to Palampet (₹20).

ANDHRA PRADESH

The state of Andhra Pradesh stretches 972km along the Bay of Bengal between Tamil Nadu and Odisha, and inland up into the picturesque Eastern Ghats. Its the epicentre of Telugu language and culture, and one of the nation's wealthiest states. Explorers will discover one of India's most visited temples (at Tirumala), some fascinating and remote ancient sites from the earliest days of Buddhism and one of the nicest stretches of India's east coast, north of Visakhapatnam – plus you'll be able to enjoy the spicily delicious Andhra cuisine everywhere.

Andhra's tourism websites are www. aptourism.gov.in and www.aptdc.gov.in.

Vijayawada

📞 0866 / POP 1.12 MILLION

The commercial and industrial city of Vijayawada, on the north bank of the Krishna River, will become Andhra's new state capital. Construction has started on a showpiece capital complex called Amaravati (named after a nearby Buddhist site), encompassing 30 existing villages on the southwest side of the river. It's projected Vijayawada-Amaravati will have 2.5 million inhabitants by 2025.

Right now there's not much of interest for travellers in the city itself, but Vijayawada is a good base for visiting some fascinating old Buddhist sites in the lush and green surrounding area.

❂ Sights

★ **Undavalli Cave Temples**　　HINDU TEMPLE
(Indian/foreigner ₹5/100; ⊙ 9am-5.30pm) This stunning four-storey cave temple was probably originally carved out of the hillside for Buddhist monks in the 2nd century AD, then converted to Hindu use in the 7th century. The shrines are now empty except those on the third level, one of which houses a huge reclining Vishnu. Three gnome-like stone Vaishnavaite gurus/preachers gaze out over the rice paddies from the terrace. It's 6km southwest of downtown Vijayawada: autorickshaws or Ola/Uber cabs here cost ₹125 one way.

Kanaka Durga Temple　　HINDU TEMPLE
(www.kanakadurgatemple.org; Durga Temple Ghat Rd, Indrakeeladri Hill; ⊙ 4am-9pm) Dating back to the 12th century, this important temple is located on Indrakeeladri Hill, close to the Krishna River, and draws many pilgrims.

🛏 Sleeping & Eating

Hotel Sripada　　HOTEL $
(📞 0866-2579641;　hotelsripada@rediffmail.com; Gandhi Nagar; s ₹900-1460, d ₹1010-1690; ❋ 🛜) A short walk from the train station, this is

---

AMARAVATI

On 21 October 2015, the Chief Minister of Andhra Pradesh chartered a helicopter bearing soil and holy water from Mecca, Jerusalem and Hindu holy sites and sprinkled a holy blessing over nondescript flatlands west of the city of Vijayawada. Three days later President Modi laid a founding stone during a grandiose event said to have been witnessed by 500,000 people.

These ceremonies were to mark the founding of Andhra Pradesh's new capital city, Amaravati (named after an important Buddhist site close by). City planners from Singapore and experts from Japan will help in its construction. The main capital area will cover 16.7 sq km and include a vast civic centre, a new business hub dotted with skyscrapers, canals, an island park and a waterfront promenade along the Krishna River. A rapid transit bus system is proposed, plus expressways linking the town to its sister city of Vijayawada.

All this is going to take some time – decades – to achieve. For now Hyderabad remains the joint capital of both Telangana and Andhra Pradesh, but the transfer of power has to occur before 2024.

one of the few budget hotels in Vijayawada authorised to accept foreign guests. Offers small but decent AC rooms in reasonable condition, and helpful staff. However, there's no in-house restaurant.

Hotel Southern Grand
HOTEL $$

(☑ 0866-6677777; www.hotelsoutherngrand.com; Papaiah St, Gandhi Nagar; incl breakfast s ₹2400-2800, d ₹2800-3200; ※ 🕾) A good deal for the tariffs charged, with inviting, spotless and contemporary rooms. Just 600m from the train station, the hotel also has an excellent veg restaurant, **Arya Bhavan** (Hotel Southern Grand, Papaiah St, Gandhi Nagar; mains ₹130-165, thalis ₹110-170; ⊘ 7am-11pm), a useful travel desk, **Southern Travels** (☑ 0866-6677777; Hotel Southern Grand, Papaiah St, Gandhi Nagar), and offers free airport and station transfers.

★ Minerva Hotel
HOTEL $$$

(☑ 0866-6678888; www.minervahotels.in; MG Rd; ⊘ s/d ₹3500/4000; ※ 🕾) Offering excellent value, this renovated hotel has rooms with a pleasing contemporary touch, large flat-screen TVs, wooden floors, safe and minibar. The Blue Fox restaurant here is good, there's a coffee shop and you'll find a cinema and good shopping close by.

Gateway Hotel
HOTEL $$$

(☑ 0866-6644444; www.thegatewayhotels.com; MG Rd; s/d from ₹5220/6160; ※ 🕾 ☎) Part of the Taj Group, this classy hotel has six floors of well-equipped, contemporary rooms around its high atrium lobby, plus two stylish restaurants, a bar, gym and a lovely rooftop pool. Staff are very welcoming and management is helpful. It's 3km southeast of the train station near two malls.

★ Minerva Coffee Shop
INDIAN $$

(Museum Rd; mains ₹170-270; ⊘ 7am-11pm) This outpost of the excellent Minerva chain does great North and South Indian veg cuisine in bright, spotless AC premises. Meals (thalis) are only available from 11.30am to 3.30pm but top-notch dosas, *idlis* and *uttapams* (₹35 to ₹75) are served all day and the biryanis are also good. There's another **branch** (Minerva Hotel, MG Rd; mains ₹180-270; ⊘ 7am-11pm) in airy, sophisticated surrounds on MG Rd.

STATE OF GOOD KARMA

Lying at a nexus of major Indian land routes and sea routes across the Bay of Bengal, Andhra Pradesh played an important role in the early history of Buddhism. Andhra and Telangana have about 150 known Buddhist stupas, monasteries, caves and other sites. They speak of a time when Andhra Pradesh, or 'Andhradesa', was a hotbed of Buddhist activity, when Indian monks set off for Sri Lanka and Southeast Asia to spread the Buddha's teachings, and monks came from far and wide to learn from renowned Buddhist teachers.

Andhradesa's Buddhist culture lasted around 1500 years from the Buddha's own lifetime in the 6th century BC. The dharma really took off in the 3rd century BC under the Mauryan emperor Ashoka, who dispatched monks across his empire to teach and construct stupas enshrining relics of the Buddha. (Being near these was thought to help progress on the path to enlightenment.)

After Ashoka's death in 232 BC, succeeding rulers of central Andhra Pradesh, the Satavahanas and then the Ikshvakus, continued to support Buddhism. At their capital Amaravathi, the Satavahanas adorned Ashoka's stupa with elegant decoration. They built monasteries across the Krishna Valley and exported the dharma through their sophisticated maritime network. It was under Satavahana rule that Nagarjuna, considered the progenitor of Mahayana Buddhism, is believed to have lived, in the 2nd or 3rd centuries AD. The monk, equal parts logician, philosopher and meditator, wrote several ground-breaking works that shaped Buddhist thought.

Today, even in ruins, you can get a sense of how large some of the stupas were, how expansive the monastic complexes, and of how the monks lived, sleeping in caves and fetching rainwater from stone-cut cisterns. Many of the sites have stunning views across seascapes or countryside. The complexes at **Nagarjunakonda** (p248) and **Amaravathi** (p247) have good infrastructure and helpful museums on-site. For a bit more adventure, head out from Vijayawada to **Guntupalli** (p247) or Bhattiprolu, or from Visakhapatnam to **Thotlakonda** (p251), **Bavikonda** (p251) and **Sankaram** (p251).

GUNTUPALLI

Well off the beaten path, the Buddhist site of Guntupalli (Indian/foreigner ₹5/100; ⊙10am-5pm) makes a very scenic adventure. This former monastic compound, high on a hilltop overlooking a vast expanse of forest and paddy fields, is specially noteworthy for its circular rock-cut *chaitya-griha* shrine. The cave's domed ceiling is carved with 'wooden beams' designed to look like those in a hut. The *chaitya-griha* has a well-preserved stupa and, like the monks' dwellings lining the same cliff, a gorgeous arched facade also designed to look like wood. Check out the stone 'beds' in the monks' cells, and the compound's 60-plus votive stupas. The monastery was active from the 2nd century BC to the 3rd century AD.

From Eluru, on the Vijayawada–Visakhapatnam road and railway, take a bus 35km north to Kamavarapukota (₹42, 1½ hours, half-hourly), then an autorickshaw 10km west to Guntupalli. A taxi from Eluru costs around ₹1800 return.

★ **TFL**   MULTICUISINE, ITALIAN $$$
(http://thefoodlounge.in; Santhi Nagar First Lane; mains ₹175-345; ⊙10am-11.30pm; 🛜) This new place is in a stylishly converted suburban bungalow with a great (covered) terrace. Offers great Italian, Mexican, American, European (and East Asian) dishes including risotto, good pizza and excellent Western breakfasts (from ₹110). Don't skip on their desserts.

❶ Information

Department of Tourism (🛜 0866-2578880; Train Station; ⊙10am-5pm) Has helpful staff and can assist with travel planning.

❶ Getting There & Around

The train and bus stations have prepaid autorickshaw stands.

BUS

Services from the large **Pandit Nehru bus station** (Arjuna St; ⊙24hr) include:

Chennai non-AC/AC/semi-sleeper ₹450/760/1050, seven to nine hours, 14 daily

Eluru non-AC/AC ₹70/90, 1½ hours, half-hourly

Hyderabad non-AC/AC ₹335/574, four to six hours, half-hourly

Tirupati non-AC/AC ₹474/698, nine hours, half-hourly

Visakhapatnam non-AC/AC ₹430/674, eight hours, half-hourly

Many private bus companies depart from stops around Benz Circle, 4km east of the centre.

CAR

Southern Travels (p246) Good rates for car-and-driver hire.

TRAIN

Vijayawada Junction station is on the main Chennai–Kolkata (Calcutta) and Chennai–Delhi railway lines. The 12841/12842 Coromandel Express between Chennai and Kolkata is quick for journeys up and down the coast. Typical journey times and frequencies, for sleeper/3AC/2AC fares:

Chennai ₹290/735/1045, seven hours, 12 daily

Hyderabad ₹240/605/880, six hours, 12 daily

Kolkata ₹555/1465/2115, 18 hours, five daily

Tirupati ₹235/670/890, nine hours, seven daily

Warangal ₹190/535/740, three hours, 14 daily

Visit the **Advance-Booking Office** (🛜 enquiries 0866-139; ⊙8am-8pm Mon-Sat, 8am-2pm Sun) at the train station for reservations.

Around Vijayawada

Amaravathi

The historic Buddhist site of Amaravathi (not to be confused with the new state capital, Amaravati) is 43km west of Vijayawada. This was the earliest centre of Buddhism in the southern half of India, with the nation's biggest stupa (Indian/foreigner ₹5/100; ⊙7am-7pm), 27m high and 49m across, constructed here in the 3rd century BC. Amaravathi flourished as a capital of the Satavahana kingdom, which ruled from Andhra across the Deccan for four or five centuries, becoming a fountainhead of Buddhist art. All that remains of the stupa now are its circular base and a few parts of the surrounding stone railing. The great hemispherical dome is gone – but the neighbouring museum (Amaravathi village; ₹5; ⊙9am-5pm Sat-Thu) has a model of the stupa and some of the intricate marble carvings, depicting the Buddha's life, with which the Satavahanas covered and surrounded it. The giant modern **Dhyana Buddha statue** (Amaravathi) of a seated Buddha overlooks the Krishna River nearby.

ℹ Getting There & Away

Bus 301 from Vijayawada bus station runs to Amaravathi (₹64, two hours) every 20 minutes, via Unduvalli. Drivers charge around ₹1800 for a half-day excursion from Vijayawada.

Eluru

📞 08812 / POP 201,050

The city of Eluru, 60km east of Vijayawada on the road and railway to Visakhapatnam, is the jumping-off point for the remote old Buddhist site of Guntupalli (p247) and the Dhamma Vijaya meditation centre at Vijayarai.

🐾 Courses

Dhamma Vijaya   HEALTH & WELLBEING
(📞 9441449044, 08812-225522; www.vijaya.dhamma.org; Eluru-Chintalapudi Rd, Vijayarai) Monthly intensive 10-day *vipassana* silent meditation courses are offered in lush palm- and cocoa-forested grounds; apply in advance. Payment is by donation.

ℹ Getting There & Away

Buses depart Eluru for Vijayarai every 30 minutes (₹16, 20 minutes).

Nagarjunakonda

📞 08680

The unique island of Nagarjunakonda is peppered with ancient Buddhist structures. The Ikshvaku dynasty had its capital here in the 3rd and 4th centuries AD, when the area was probably the most important Buddhist centre in South India.

⊙ Sights

Nagarjunakonda Museum   MUSEUM
(incl monuments Indian/foreigner ₹20/120; ⊙9am-4pm Sat-Thu) The thoughtfully laid-out Nagarjunakonda Museum has Buddha statues and some superbly detailed carvings depicting local contemporary life and the Buddha's lives. The reassembled remains of several buildings, including stupa bases, walls of monastery complexes and pits for horse sacrifice, are arranged on a 1km path running along the island. The largest stupa, in the Chamtasri Chaitya Griha group, con-

tained a bone fragment thought to be from the Buddha himself.

Sri Parvata Arama   BUDDHIST SITE
(Buddhavanam; ⊙9.30am-6pm) FREE This Buddhism Heritage park, featuring a recreation of the huge Amaravathi stupa, is 8km north of the dam. It's been under construction by the state tourism authorities for several years. The 9m replica of the Avukana Buddha statue was donated by Sri Lanka. There's also an attractive meditation area, Dhyanavanam, with fine lake views. Alight at Buddha Park when coming by bus from Hyderabad.

🐾 Courses

Dhamma Nagajjuna   HEALTH & WELLBEING
(📞 9440139329, 9348456780; www.nagajjuna.dhamma.org; Hill Colony) Keeping the Buddha's teachings alive in the region, this centre offers 10-day silent meditation courses in charming flower-filled grounds overlooking Nagarjuna Sagar. Apply in advance; payment is by donation. Alight at Buddha Park when coming by bus from Hyderabad.

🛏 Sleeping & Eating

Nagarjuna Resort   HOTEL $
(📞 08642-242471; Vijayapuri South; r without/with AC ₹800/1500; ▣) Nagarjuna Resort has spacious, though drab, rooms, while the balconies enjoy good views. It's conveniently located just across the road from the boat launch.

Haritha Vijaya Vihar   HOTEL $$
(📞 08680-277362; r with AC incl breakfast Mon-Thu ₹1400-1700, Fri-Sun ₹2400-2700; ▣ 🛜 ▣) Telangana Tourism's Haritha Vijaya Vihar is 6km north of the dam, with decent rooms, nice gardens, a good pool (guest admission ₹50) and lovely lake views. It's a little overpriced, but the location is exceptional, the restaurant is quite decent and there's a bar.

Hotel Siddhartha   INDIAN $$
(Buddhavanam, Hill Colony; mains ₹130-240; ⊙6am-11pm) Beside Sri Parvata Arama, with tasty curries, biryanis, fish dishes and lots of snacks served in a pleasant, airy pavilion.

ℹ Getting There & Away

The easiest way to visit Nagarjunakonda, other than with a private vehicle, is on a bus tour (₹550) from Hyderabad with **Telangana Tourism** (p234), running on weekends only. It's a very long (15 hours!) day trip, however.

Public buses from Hyderabad's Mahatma Gandhi Bus Station run hourly to Hill Colony/

Nagarjuna Sagar (₹220, four hours): alight at Pylon and catch an autorickshaw (shared/private ₹20/120) 8km to Vijayapuri South.

Boats (₹120 return) depart for the island from Vijayapuri South, 7km south of the dam, theoretically at 9.30am, 11.30am and 1.30pm (but they invariably leave late), and stay for one to two hours. The first two boats may not go if not enough people turn up, but the 1.30pm boat goes every day (barring high winds) and starts back from the island around 4.30pm.

Visakhapatnam

📞 0891 / POP 1.76 MILLION

Visakhapatnam – also called Vizag (*vie*-zag) – is Andhra Pradesh's largest city, famous for steel and its big port but also doubling as a beach resort for sea-breeze-seeking domestic tourists. During the main December–February holiday season there's a distinctly kitschy vibe, with camel rides and thousands of bathers (though no swimmers).

The pedestrian promenade along Ramakrishna Beach is pleasant for a stroll, and nearby Rushikonda Beach is Andhra's best. The surrounding area contains one of Andhra's most important Hindu temples, several ancient Buddhist sites and the rural Araku Valley.

Every mid-January the city hosts **Visakha Utsav** (☉ mid-Jan), a festival with food stalls on Ramakrishna Beach, exhibitions and cultural events.

◉ Sights & Activities

Ramakrishna Beach   BEACH
(Beach Rd) Ramakrishna (RK) Beach stretches 4km up the coast from the large port area in the south of town, overlooking the Bay of Bengal with its mammoth ships and brightly painted fishing boats. Its pedestrian promenade is great for strolling. Swimming is officially prohibited (and the sea polluted). On Sunday mornings the adjacent Beach Rd is closed to traffic (from 6am to 9am) in an initiative called 'Happy Streets', as cricket, football and basketball games replace the cars and buses.

★ Submarine Museum   MUSEUM
(Beach Rd; adult/child ₹40/20, camera ₹50; ☉ 2-8.30pm Tue-Sat, 10am-12.30pm & 2-8.30pm Sun) A fantastic attraction located towards the north end of Ramakrishna Beach, the 91m-long, Soviet-built, Indian navy submarine *Kursura* is now a fascinating museum. You're given about 15 minutes to explore the

incredibly confined quarters and check out the torpedoes, kitchens and sleeping areas. Some staff speak a little English.

Rushikonda   BEACH
Rushikonda, 10km north of town, has a wild beauty and is one of the nicest beaches on India's east coast. Swimming is officially prohibited (there have been drownings), but it's the best beach for a knee-high dip. Women should opt for modest beachwear. Weekends are busy and festive. Surfers and kayakers can rent decent boards and kayaks from local surf pioneer **Melville Smythe** (📞 9848561052; per hr surfboard ₹400-600, 2-person kayak ₹300, surf tuition ₹250), by the jet-ski hut.

You can reach Rushikonda by bus 900K from the train station or RTC Complex, or shared autorickshaws from Beach Rd.

Simhachalam Temple   HINDU TEMPLE
(☉ 7-11.30am, 12.30-2.30pm & 3.30-7pm) Andhra's second-most visited temple (after Tirumala) is a 16km drive northwest of town. It's dedicated to Varahalakshmi Narasimha, a combination of Vishnu's boar and lion-man avatars, and can get crowded. A ₹100 ticket will get you to the deity (and a sip of holy water) much quicker than a ₹20 one. Buses 6A and 28 go here from the RTC Complex and train station.

The temple's architecture bears much Odishan influence, including the 13th-century main shrine with its carved stone panels (the lion-man can be seen disembowelling a demon on the rear wall).

🛏 Sleeping

Beach Rd is the best place to stay, but it's low on inexpensive hotels.

SKML Beach Guest House   GUESTHOUSE $
(📞 9848355131; ramkisg.1074@gmail.com; Beach Rd, Varun Beach; r ₹1100-1250, with AC ₹1700-2200; ❋ 🛜) SKML is towards the less select southern end of Ramakrishna Beach but its 12 rooms are clean and decent. Best are the two top-floor 'suites' with sea views, a terrace and a bit of art.

Hotel Morya   HOTEL $
(📞 0891-2731112; www.hotelmorya.com; Bowdara Rd; s/d from ₹490/690, r with AC ₹1390; ❋ 🛜) A good choice, and just 600m south of the train station. Standard rooms here are small and lack ventilation, but their better AC options are quite spacious, bright and relatively smart. There's a lift, but no restaurant.

Dolphin Hotel HOTEL $$
(☑ 0891-2567000; http://dolphinhotelsvizag. com; Dabagardens; r incl breakfast ₹2700-4800; ✷ ☎ ☲) A dependable hotel with quite spacious, well-equipped rooms and an attractive restaurant. Its trump card is the 20m pool and excellent gym, one of the best in the city.

★ **Novotel Visakhapatnam Varun Beach** HOTEL $$$
(☑ 0891-2822222; www.accorhotels.com; Beach Rd; r/ste incl breakfast ₹8230/15,076; ✷ @ ☎ ☲) Novotel Visakhapatnam Varun Beach boasts a commanding position on Beach Rd and its rooms are very well-appointed and immaculately presented, all with direct sea views. Dining options are first class, the bar is great for a tipple, the spa is excellent and the pool area and gym overlook the Bay of Bengal. Both the Indian and English cricket teams stayed here in 2016.

Park HOTEL $$$
(☑ 0891-3045678; www.theparkhotels.com; Beach Rd; s/d incl breakfast from ₹8450/10,880; ✷ @ ☎ ☲) Tasteful seafront property, with lovely beachfront gardens that contain a fine pool and three of the hotel's four restaurants. Guests also have access to a private beach. Rooms are cosy and generally well-maintained, though some furnishings are looking a tad dated.

✗ Eating & Drinking

★ **Sea Inn** ANDHRA $$
(Raju Ka Dhaba; ☑ 9989012102; http://seainn.info; Beach Rd, Rushikonda; meals ₹220-300; ☉ noon-4pm Tue-Sun) This delightful place is owned by chef Devi, who cooks Andhra-style curries the way her mum did. Fish, seafood, chicken and veg are served up in a simple, semi-open-air dining room with bench seating, about 300m north of the Haritha Beach Resort turn-off. Cash only.

★ **Dharani** INDIAN $$
(Daspalla Hotel, off Town Main Rd, Suryabagh; thalis & mains ₹175-240; ☉ noon-3.30pm & 7-10.30pm) Bustling family veg place that's one of the town's best-regarded restaurants, with simply superb South Indian thalis. The hotel has several other restaurants too, including Andhra nonveg and North Indian veg options. Be sure to round off your meal with a Daspalla special filter coffee.

Little Italy ITALIAN $$
(http://littleitaly.in; 1st fl, South Wing, ATR Towers, Vutagedda Rd, Paandurangapuram; mains ₹240-

440; ☉ 11.30am-11pm; ☎) Behind Ramakrishna Beach, this renowned restaurant does fine thin-crust pizza, pasta and reasonable salads in stylish surrounds. No alcohol, but good fruit mocktails.

Vista MULTICUISINE $$$
(The Park, Beach Rd; mains ₹360-960; ☉ dinner 7.30-11pm; ☎) A wonderful setting for a meal, the Vista overlooks the stunning pool in the grand Park hotel. It's a fine choice for its long, truly global menu and excellent all-you-can-eat dinner buffet.

Moksha Restocafé CAFE
(www.facebook.com/moksha.restocafe; Ootagadda Rd, Daspalla Hills; ☉ noon-11pm; ☎) A great independent cafe popular with a hip young Vizag crowd, it has distant sea views. There's fine coffee, including espresso options, and good juices (try the minty lemon). On the menu you'll find Western, Thai, Tibetan and Indian dishes.

ℹ Information

APTDC (☑ 0891-2788820; www.aptdc.gov. in; RTC Complex; ☉ 7am-9pm Mon-Sat) Useful office for tours, hotel bookings and tourist information.

ℹ Getting There & Away

AIR
Vizag airport has direct daily flights to cities including Bengaluru, Bhubaneswar, Chennai, Delhi, Hyderabad, Kolkata, Mumbai and Vijayawada. There are also international connections to Dubai, Kuala Lumpur and Singapore.

BOAT
Boats depart roughly once a month for Port Blair in the Andaman Islands. Call or email for schedules or check www.andamanbeacon.com. Book for the 56-hour journey (bunk ₹2410, cabin berth from ₹4640) at **AV Bhanojirow, Garuda Pattabhiramayya & Co** (☑ 0891-2565597; ops@avbgpr.com; Harbour Approach Rd, next to NMDC, port area; ☉ 9am-5pm). Tickets go on sale two or three days before departure. Bring your passport, two photocopies of its data page, and two passport photos.

BUS
Services from Vizag's well-organised **RTC Complex** (☑ 0891-2746400; RTC Complex Inner Rd) include the following:

Hyderabad non-AC/AC ₹745/1290, 13 hours, almost hourly 2.30pm to 10pm

Jagdalpur non-AC ₹236, eight hours, two daily

Vijayawada general/superluxury/AC ₹375/448/640, eight hours, hourly 5am to midnight

CAR

English-speaking **Srinivasa 'Srinu' Rao** (☑ 7382468137) is a reliable, friendly driver for out-of-town trips. He charges around ₹3000 for an Araku Valley day trip and ₹1600 to Sankaram and back.

Reliable **Guide Tours & Travels** (☑ 9848265559, 0891-2754477; Shop 15, Sudarshan Plaza; ⊙7am-10pm) charges around ₹3200 plus tolls for a day trip up to 300km.

TRAIN

Visakhapatnam station (Station Rd), on the western edge of town, is on the main Kolkata–Chennai line. Typical journey times, frequencies and sleeper/3AC/2AC fares:

Bhubaneswar ₹260/705/1055, six hours, 10 daily

Chennai ₹425/1125/1605, 13 hours, two to three daily

Hyderabad ₹370/1025/1450, 11 hours, five to six daily

Kolkata ₹460/1210/1725, 14 hours, five to six daily

Tirupati ₹410/1070/1520, 10 hours, three to four daily

Vijayawada ₹255/650/910, six hours, 16 to 19 daily

The **railway reservation centre** (Station Approach Rd; ⊙8am-10pm Mon-Sat, 8am-2pm Sun) is 300m south of the main station building.

❶ Getting Around

There are over 2000 Uber (and a similar number of Ola) drivers in Visakhapatnam, so you won't have to wait long for a ride.

For the airport, 12km west of downtown, appcabs or autorickshaws charge about ₹240. Or take bus 38 from the RTC Complex (₹18, 30 minutes). The airport's arrivals hall has a prepaid taxi booth.

The train station has a prepaid autorickshaw booth. Shared autorickshaws run along Beach Rd from the port at the south end of town to Rushikonda, 10km north of Vizag, and Bheemunipatnam, 25km north, charging between ₹5 (for a 1km hop) and ₹40 (Vizag to Bheemunipatnam).

Around Visakhapatnam

Sankaram

Located 40km southwest of Vizag, the stunning Buddhist complex of Sankaram (near Anakapalle; ⊙8am-5pm) 𝗙𝗥𝗘𝗘, also known by the names of its two parts, Bojjannakonda

and Lingalakonda, occupies a rocky outcrop about 300m long. Used by monks from the 2nd to 9th centuries AD, the outcrop is covered with rock-cut caves, stupas, ruins of monastery structures and reliefs of the Buddha. Bojjannakonda, the eastern part, has a pair of rock-cut shrines with several gorgeous carvings of the Buddha inside and outside. Above sit the ruins of a huge stupa and a monastery. Lingalakonda, at the western end, is piled with tiers of rock-cut stupas, some of them enormous. Both parts afford fabulous views over the surrounding rice paddies.

❶ Getting There & Away

A private car from Vizag costs around ₹1600. Or take a frequent train (₹38, one hour), or bus (₹48, 1½ hours) from Vizag's **RTC Complex** (p250), to Anakapalle, 3km away, and then an autorickshaw (₹120 return including waiting).

Bavikonda & Thotlakonda

Bavikonda (⊙9am-5pm) 𝗙𝗥𝗘𝗘 and Thotlakonda (pedestrian/car ₹5/30; ⊙8am-5.30pm) were Buddhist monasteries on scenic hilltop sites north of Vizag that each hosted up to 150 monks, with the help of massive rainwater tanks. Their remains were unearthed in the 1980s and 1990s.

The monasteries flourished from around the 3rd century BC to the 3rd century AD, and had votive stupas, congregation halls, *chaitya-grihas, viharas* and refectories. Thotlakonda has sea views, and Bavikonda has special importance because a relic vessel found in its Mahachaitya stupa contained a piece of bone believed to be from the Buddha himself.

❶ Getting There & Away

Bavikonda and Thotlakonda are reached from turn-offs 14km and 15km, respectively, from Vizag on the Bheemunipatnam road: Bavikonda is 3km off the main road and Thotlakonda 1.25km. Vizag autorickshaw or Uber drivers charge around ₹650 return to see both.

Bheemunipatnam

This former Dutch settlement, 25km north of Vizag, is the oldest municipality in mainland India, with bizarre sculptures on the beach, an 1861 lighthouse, an interesting Dutch cemetery, and Bheemli Beach, where local grommets surf not-very-clean waters on crude homemade boards.

Araku Valley

📞 08936 / ELEV 975M

Andhra's best train ride is through the beautiful, lushly forested Eastern Ghats to the Araku Valley, centred on Araku town, 115km north of Visakhapatnam. The area is home to isolated tribal communities and known for its tasty organic coffee and lovely green countryside. En route you can visit the impressive Borra Caves.

⊙ Sights

Borra Caves CAVE
(adult/child ₹60/45, camera/mobile camera ₹100/25; ⊙10am-1pm & 2-5pm) Illuminated with fancy lighting, the huge million-year-old limestone Borra Caves are 38km before Araku town and can be combined with a visit to the Araku Valley. Watch out for monkeys. There are snack stands close to the entrance.

Museum of Habitat MUSEUM
(₹40; ⊙8am-1.30pm & 2.30-8pm) This museum has extensive exhibits on the tribal peoples of eastern Andhra Pradesh, including full-scale mock-ups of hunting, ceremonial and other scenes, and a few craft stalls. Worthwhile, but displays and information could be better. Located next to the bus station and 2km east of the train station.

🛏 Sleeping & Eating

Hotel Rajadhani HOTEL $
(📞08936-249580; www.hotelrajadhani.com; r without/with AC ₹880/1350; ❄🛜) Budget hotel with over 30 rooms, seven of which have AC, and all have attached bathrooms with hot water. They could all be better presented, but those on the upper floor enjoy valley views from their balconies. There's an **in-house restaurant** (meals ₹130-220; ⊙7am-10pm).

Haritha Valley Resort HOTEL $$
(📞08936-249202; incl breakfast r ₹1200-2150, with AC ₹2350; ❄🛜🏊) The best place to stay in Araku, with a pool and landscaped grounds. It's a government-run hotel and rooms are maintained quite well, though service is very leisurely. Favoured by Tollywood film crews.

Haritha Hill Resort HOTEL $$
(Mayuri; 📞08936-249204; incl breakfast cottage ₹945, r ₹1468-2522; ❄🛜) Not bad for a government hotel, this decent APTDC place is just behind the Museum of Habitat and its cottages offer adequate comfort for the reasonable prices asked.

Star Annapurna INDIAN $
(meals ₹125-240; ⊙7.30am-10pm) Perhaps the best restaurant in the Araka area, offering a wide choice of flavoursome dishes including a good chicken biryani, fish dishes and lots of well-spiced vegetable curries.

Araku Valley Coffee House CAFE $
(coffee ₹25-100; ⊙8.30am-9pm) You can sample and buy local coffee and all kinds of chocolatey goods (brownies, chocolate-covered coffee beans) at Araku Valley Coffee House, which also has a tiny **coffee museum** (₹25; ⊙8.30am-9pm).

🛍 Shopping

Araku Aadiwasi Arts & Crafts ARTS & CRAFTS
(⊙8am-8pm) Located between the Coffee House and bus station, it has a good selection of tribal jewellery, jute bags and ornaments.

ℹ Getting There & Away

From Visakhapatnam a train (₹100, four hours) leaves daily at 7.05am, returning from Araku at 4.10pm. Get to Visakhapatnam early to secure a seat and be aware that the return train often leaves late. Buses (roughly hourly) from Visakhapatnam (from ₹128) take 4½ hours. A taxi day trip costs ₹3000 to ₹4000. The APTDC runs tours that all include the Borra Caves, 38km before Araku; however, its day trips are very rushed.

Tirumala & Tirupati

📞 0877 / POP 292,000 (TIRUPATI) / 7900 (TIRUMALA)

One of the globe's largest pilgrimage destinations, the holy hill of Tirumala is, on any given day, thronged with thousands of devotees who've journeyed to see Lord Venkateshwara here, at his home. Around 60,000 pilgrims come each day, and *darshan* runs 24/7. The **Tirumala Tirupathi Devasthanams** (TTD; 📞0877-2233333, 0877-2277777; www.tirumala.org; KT Rd; ⊙9am-5.30pm Mon-Fri, 9am-1pm Sat) efficiently administers the multitudes, employing 20,000 people to do so. Despite the crowds, a sense of order, serenity and ease mostly prevails, and a trip to the Holy Hill can be fulfilling even if you're not a pilgrim. Queues during the annual nine-day **Brahmotsavam festival** (⊙Sep/Oct) can stretch for kilometres.

Tirupati, the humdrum town at the bottom of the hill, is the gateway to Tirumala.

⊙ Sights

Venkateshwara Temple HINDU TEMPLE
(www.tirumala.org) Devotees flock to Tirumala to see Venkateshwara, an avatar of Vish-

nu. Among the many powers attributed to Venkateshwara is the granting of any wish made at this holy site. 'Ordinary *darshan*' requires a wait of anywhere from two to eight hours in claustrophobic metal cages ringing the temple. Special-entry *darshan* (deity-viewing) tickets (₹300, bookable online) will get you through the queue faster though you'll still have to brave the cages, which is part of the fun, kind of...

There are different hours for special-entry *darshan* each day: check the website. Upon entry, you'll have to sign a form declaring your faith in Lord Venkateshwara.

Legends about the hill itself and the surrounding area appear in the Puranas, and the temple's history may date back 2000 years. The main temple is an atmospheric place, though you'll be pressed between hundreds of devotees when you see it. Venkateshwara inspires bliss and love among his visitors from the back of the dark and magical inner sanctum; it smells of incense and resonates with chanting. You'll have a moment to say a prayer and then you'll be shoved out again. Don't forget to collect your delicious *ladoo* from the counter: Tirumala *ladoos* (sweet balls made with chickpea flour, cardamom and dried fruits) are famous across India.

Many pilgrims donate their hair to the deity – in gratitude for a wish fulfilled, or to renounce ego – so hundreds of barbers attend to devotees. Tirumala and Tirupati are filled with tonsured men, women and children.

Sleeping

Avoid weekends, when Tirupati is uberrammed. The Tirumala Tirupathi Devasthanams (TTD) runs vast **dormitories** (beds free) and **guesthouses** (r ₹50-3000; ❋) near the temple in Tirumala, intended for pilgrims. To stay here, check in at the Central Reception Office.

★ Athidhi Residency · HOTEL $
(☑ 0877-2281222; www.facebook.com/Athidhi-Residency; Peddakapu Layout; r ₹900-1400; ❋🕐) Keenly priced, this is a deservedly popular place with well-presented rooms that have flat-screen TVs, ceiling fans and attractive en suites. It's a short drive from the train station or walkable from the bus stand.

Hotel Annapurna · HOTEL $
(☑ 0877-2250666; www.hotelannapurna.in; 349 G Car St, Tirupati; r without/with AC ₹1180/1980; ❋🕐) Rooms at this long-running place are simply furnished and painted pink. Front

rooms can be noisy. Its **veg restaurant** (mains ₹125-220; 🕐 5.30am-11pm; 🕐) has fresh juices and tasty food. There's a lift.

Minerva Grand · HOTEL $$
(☑ 0877-6688888; http://minervahotels.in; Renigunta Rd, Tirupati; s/d with AC from ₹2300/2700; ❋🕐) A well-run establishment with some of the best rooms in town – comfy business-style abodes with desks, plump pillows and good mattresses. Its two restaurants, both with icy AC, are great too and there's a small gym.

Hotel Regalia · HOTEL $$
(☑ 0877-2238699; www.regaliahotels.com; Ramanuja Circle, Tirupati; r/ste incl breakfast ₹2999/4999; ❋🕐) On the east side of town, 1.5km from the train station, the Regalia provides attractive, inviting, contemporary rooms with sleek en suites. The inclusive breakfast is a generous buffet. Excellent value.

✗ Eating & Drinking

Tirupati is well-endowed with restaurants. Huge **dining halls** (meals free; 🕐 hours vary) on the hill feed thousands of pilgrims daily; veg restaurants also serve meals for ₹25.

★ Hotel Mayura · INDIAN $$
(209 TP Area; meals ₹150-280; 🕐 7am-10pm) Opposite the bus station, this comfortable hotel restaurant is one of the best places in town for South Indian thalis (₹220), with delicious dishes and lots of chutneys neatly arranged on a banana leaf. North Indian dishes are also offered.

★ Minerva Coffee Shop · INDIAN $$
(Minerva Grand, Renigunta Rd; thalis ₹190-230; 🕐 7am-11.30pm; 🕐) The veg-only Minerva Coffee Shop does superb Andhra thalis (with free refills) and dynamite filter coffee. Staff are efficient and the ambience is family orientated. It's a good choice for a local breakfast.

Blue Fox · INDIAN, CHINESE $$
(Minerva Grand, Renigunta Rd; mains ₹220-380; 🕐 7am-11.30pm; 🕐) The Blue Fox 'fine dining bar', with besuited waiters, serves Indian and Chinese veg and nonveg dishes, as well as alcoholic drinks.

Aroma Coffee House · CAFE
(Tirumala Bypass; 🕐 9am–11pm) Hits the spot when you need that espresso or latte. In modern, AC surrounds; they also sell sandwiches and snacks.

❶ Getting There & Away

It's possible to visit Tirumala on a long day trip from Chennai. The Andhra Pradesh State Road Transport Corporation (APSRTC) runs half-hourly buses direct to Tirumala (₹112 to ₹303, three to four hours) from **Chennai's CMBT bus station** (p343).

AIR

Tirupati Airport (www.tirupatiairport.com; Renigunta Airport Rd) is at Renigunta, 14km east of town. There are daily flights to Delhi, Hyderabad and other cities with **Air India** (☐0877-2283981, airport 0877-2283992; www.airindia.in; Srinivasam Pilgrim Amenities Complex,Tirumala Bypass Rd; ⊘9.30am-5.30pm Mon-Sat), SpiceJet, Air Costa and TruJet.

BUS

Tirupati's **bus station** (☐0877-2289900; Tirupati Rd; ⊘24hr) has services, all once or twice hourly, including the following:

Chennai express/Volvo ₹112/293, three to four hours

Bengaluru express/Volvo/semi-sleeper ₹229/323/377, four to six hours

Hyderabad superluxury/Volvo ₹652/1023, nine to 13 hours

Vijayawada express/semi-sleeper ₹474/698, seven to nine hours

TRAIN

There are numerous daily departures; the **reservation office** (Netaji Rd; ⊘8am-8pm Mon-Sat, 8am-2pm Sun) is opposite Tirupati station's east end. Typical journey times and fares for sleeper/3AC/2AC:

Bengaluru ₹210/615/860, seven hours

Chennai ₹140/490/695, three to four hours

Hyderabad ₹380/1035/1495, 12 hours

Vijayawada ₹235/625/935, seven hours

Visakhapatnam ₹380/1035/1490, 15 hours

❶ Getting Around

BUS

There's a stand for buses to Tirumala opposite the train station, with departures every few minutes. The scenic one-hour trip costs ₹48/85 one-way/return; going up, sit on the left side for views.

TAXI

There's a prepaid taxi booth outside the east end of the train station. Ola and Uber cabs are in Tirupati.

WALKING

The Tirumala Tirupathi Devasthanams has constructed probably the best footpath in India, for pilgrims to walk up to Tirumala. It's about 12km from the start of the path at Alipiri on the

north side of Tirupati (₹50 by autorickshaw), and takes three to six hours. You can leave your luggage at Alipiri and it will be transported free to the reception centre. There are shady rest points along the way, and a few canteens.

Around Tirumala & Tirupati

Chandragiri Fort

This fort complex, 15km west of Tirupati, dates back 1000 years but its heyday came in the late 16th century when the rulers of the declining Vijayanagar empire, having fled from Hampi, made it their capital. At the heart of a 1.5km-long stout-walled enclosure beneath a rocky hill, the **palace area** (Indian/foreigner ₹10/100; ⊘9am-5pm Sat-Thu) contains nice gardens and the Raja Mahal, a heavily restored Vijayanagar palace reminiscent of Hampi buildings, with a reasonably interesting **museum** (⊘9am-5pm Sat-Thu) of bronze and stone sculptures. The upper fort on the hillside is (frustratingly) out of bounds.

❶ Getting There & Away

Buses for Chandragiri (₹10) leave Tirupati hourly. Cabs charge around ₹600 return.

Sri Kalahasti

☐08578 / POP 82,521

The holy town of Sri Kalahasti, 37km east of Tirupati, is known for its important **Sri Kalahasteeswara Temple** (www.srikalahasthitemple.com; ⊘6am-9.30pm) and for being, along with Machilipatnam near Vijayawada, a centre for the ancient textile-painting art of *kalamkari*. Cotton cloth is primed with *myrabalam* (resin) and cow's milk; figures are drawn with a pointed bamboo stick dipped in fermented jaggery and water; and the dyes are made from cow dung, ground seeds, plants and flowers. You can see artists at work, and buy some of their products, in the Agraharam neighbourhood, 2.5km from the bus stand. **Sri Vijayalakshmi Fine Kalamkari Arts** (☐9441138380; Door No 15-890; ⊘by appointment) is a 40-year-old family business employing over 60 artists. Dupatta scarves start at around ₹1500.

❶ Getting There & Away

Buses leave Tirupati for Sri Kalahasti every 15 minutes (₹32, one hour). Taxis charge around ₹1400 return including waiting time.

Kerala

Best Places to Eat

➜ Villa Maya (p261)

➜ Dal Roti (p307)

➜ Bait (p274)

➜ Malabar Junction (p307)

➜ Paragon Restaurant (p315)

Best Places to Sleep

➜ Green Woods Bethlehem (p303)

➜ Varnam Homestay (p319)

➜ Kaiya House (p277)

➜ Ashtamudi Villas (p281)

➜ Reds Residency (p303)

Why Go?

For many travellers, Kerala is South India's most serene-ly beautiful state. A slender coastal strip is shaped by its layered landscape: almost 600km of glorious Arabian Sea coast and beaches; a languid network of glistening back-waters; and the spice- and tea-covered hills of the Western Ghats. Just setting foot on this swath of soul-quenching, palm-shaded green will slow your subcontinental stride to a blissed-out amble. Kerala is a world away from the frenzy of elsewhere, as if India had passed through the Looking Glass and become an altogether more laid-back place.

Besides its famous backwaters, elegant houseboats, ayurvedic treatments and delicately spiced, taste-bud-tingling cuisine, Kerala is home to wild elephants, exotic birds and the odd tiger, while vibrant traditions such as Kathakali plays, temple festivals and snake-boat races fre-quently bring even the smallest villages to life. It's hard to deny Kerala's liberal use of the slogan 'God's Own Country'.

When to Go
Thiruvananthapuram

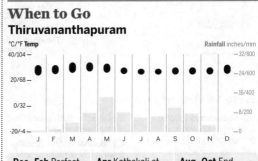

Dec–Feb Perfect beach and back-water weather. Festival season throughout the state.

Apr Kathakali at Kottayam and Kollam festivals, and the elephant procession in Thrissur.

Aug–Oct End of the monsoon period: Onam festival, snake-boat races.

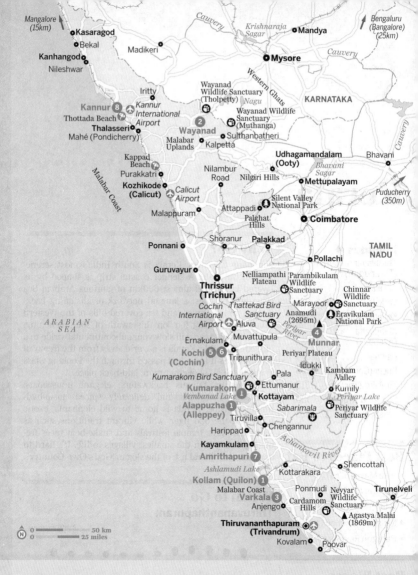

Mangalore
(15km)

Kasaragod
Bekal
Kanhangod
Nileshwar
Madikeri

Cauvery

Krishnaraja
Sagar

Mandya

Bengaluru
(Bangalore)
(25km)

Mysore

Cauvery

Western Ghats

Iritty

Kannur 8
Kannur
International
Airport
Thottada Beach
Thalasseri
Mahé (Pondicherry)

Wayanad
Wildlife Sanctuary
(Tholpetty)

Nagu

Wayanad Wildlife
Sanctuary
(Muthanga)

KARNATAKA

2
Wayanad
Malabar
Uplands
Kalpetta

Sulthanbatheri

Udhagamandalam
(Ooty)

Bhavani
Sagar

Bhavani

Kappad
Beach
Purakkatri
Kozhikode
(Calicut)
Calicut
Airport

Nilambur
Road

Nilgiri Hills

Mettupalayam

Puducherry
(350m)

Malabar Coast

Malappuram

Attappadi

Silent Valley
National Park

Palghat
Hills

Coimbatore

Ponnani

Shoranur

Palakkad

TAMIL
NADU

Guruvayur

Pollachi

ARABIAN
SEA

Thrissur
(Trichur)

Cochin
International
Airport

Nelliampathi
Plateau

Thattekad Bird
Sanctuary

Aluva

Ernakulam
Muvattupula

Kochi 5 6
(Cochin)
Tripunithura

Parambikulam
Wildlife
Sanctuary

Marayoor

Chinnar
Wildlife
Sanctuary

Anamudi
(2695m)

Eravikulam
National Park

Periyar
River

Munnar 4

Kumarakom Bird Sanctuary

Kumarakom
Vembanad Lake
Alappuzha 1
(Alleppey)
Tiruvilla

Harippad

Pala

Ettumanur
Kottayam

Periyar Plateau

Idukki

Kambam
Valley

Kumily

Periyar Lake

Sabarimala

Periyar Wildlife
Sanctuary

Chengannur

Achankovil River

Kayamkulam

Amrithapuri 7

Ashlamudi Lake

Kollam (Quilon) 1

Varkala 3

Kottarakara

Ponmudi

Shencottah

Neyyar
Wildlife
Sanctuary

Tirunelveli

Malabar Coast

Anjengo

Thiruvananthapuram
(Trivandrum)

Cardamom
Hills

Agastya Malai
(1869m)

Kovalam

Poovar

0   50 km
0   25 miles

Kerala Highlights

1 Backwaters (p286)
Cruising in a houseboat or
punted canoe from Alappuzha,
Kollam or Kumarakom.

2 Wayanad (p317) Spotting
wild elephants, trekking and
relaxing in remote forest
accommodation.

3 Varkala (p275) Watching

the days slip-slide away at this
clifftop beach resort.

4 Munnar (p294) Bedding
down in a beautifully remote
resort and trekking through
emerald tea plantations.

5 Fort Cochin (p299)
Feeling the history and
dining with a local family in a
homestay.

6 Kathakali (p312)
Experiencing a performance
in Kochi.

**7 Matha Amrithanandam-
ayi Mission** (p282) Calling in
for a cuddle at the ashram of
Amma, in Amrithapuri.

8 Kannur (p320) Exploring
unspoilt beaches and *theyyam*
rituals in the north.

History

Traders have been drawn to the scent of Kerala's spices for more than 3000 years. The coast was known to the Phoenicians, the Romans, the Arabs and the Chinese, and was a transit point for spices from the Moluccas (eastern Indonesia).

The kingdom of Cheras ruled much of Kerala until the early Middle Ages, competing with kingdoms and small fiefdoms for territory and trade. Vasco da Gama's arrival in 1498 opened the floodgates to European colonialism as Portuguese, Dutch and English interests fought Arab traders, and then each other, for control of the lucrative spice trade.

The present-day state of Kerala was created in 1956 from the former states of Travancore, Kochi and Malabar. A tradition of valuing the arts and education resulted in a post-Independence state that is one of the most progressive in India, with the nation's highest literacy rate.

In 1957 Kerala had the first freely elected communist government in the world, which has gone on to hold power regularly since – though the Congress-led United Democratic Front (UDF) has been in power since 2011. Many Malayalis (speakers of Malayalam, the state's official language) work in the Middle East and their remittances play a significant part in the economy. A big hope for the state's future is the relatively recent boom in tourism, with Kerala emerging in the past decade as one of India's most popular new tourist hot spots. According to Kerala Tourism almost 13.5 million visitors arrived in 2015 – more than double the number of a decade ago – though fewer than a million of these were foreign tourists.

SOUTHERN KERALA

Thiruvananthapuram (Trivandrum)

📞 0471 / POP 958,000

Thiruvananthapuram, Kerala's capital – still usually referred to by its colonial name, Trivandrum – is a relatively compact but energetic city and an easygoing introduction to urban life down south. Most travellers merely springboard from here to the nearby beach resorts of Kovalam and Varkala, but Trivandrum has enough sights – including a zoo and cluster of Victorian museums in glorious neo-Keralan buildings – to justify a stay.

◉ Sights

Zoological Gardens ZOO
(📞0471-2115122; adult/child ₹20/5, camera/video ₹50/75; ⊙9am-5.15pm Tue-Sun) Yann Martel famously based the animals in his novel *Life of Pi* on those he observed here in Trivandrum's zoological gardens. Shaded paths meander through woodland, lakes and native forest, where tigers, macaques and hippos gather in reasonably large open enclosures.

★**Napier Museum** MUSEUM
(adult/child ₹10/5; ⊙10am-5pm Tue & Thu-Sun, 1-5pm Wed) Housed in an 1880 wooden building designed by Robert Chisholm, a British architect whose Fair Isle–style version of the Keralan vernacular shows his enthusiasm for local craft, this museum has an eclectic display of bronzes, Buddhist sculptures, temple carts and ivory carvings. The carnivalesque interior is stunning and worth a look in its own right.

★**Museum of History & Heritage** MUSEUM
(📞9567019037; www.museumkeralam.org; Park View; adult/child Indian ₹20/10, foreigner ₹200/50, camera ₹25; ⊙10am-5.30pm Tue-Sun) In a lovely heritage building within the Kerala Tourism complex, this beautifully presented museum traces Keralan history and culture through superb static displays and interactive

---

TOP STATE FESTIVALS

As well as the major state festivals, Kerala has hundreds of annual temple festivals, *theyyam* rituals, boat-race regattas and street parades. *A Hundred Festivals for You,* a free publication produced by Kochi's Tourist Desk, lists many of them.

Ernakulathappan Utsavam (p303) Eight days of festivities culminating in a parade of elephants, music and fireworks.

Thrissur Pooram (p313) The elephant procession to end all elephant processions.

Nehru Trophy Boat Race (p283) The most popular of Kerala's boat races.

Onam (⊙Aug/Sep) The entire state celebrates the golden age of mythical King Mahabali for 10 days.

Thiruvananthapuram (Trivandrum)

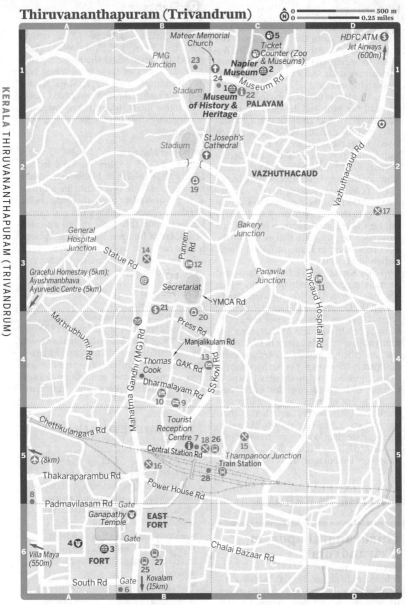

audiovisual presentations. Exhibits range from Iron Age implements to bronze and terracotta sculptures, murals, *dhulichitra* (floor paintings) and recreations of traditional Keralan homes.

Puthe Maliga Palace Museum   MUSEUM
(Fort; Indian/foreigner ₹30/100, camera/video ₹50/250; ⊙ 9.30am-12.30pm & 2-4.45pm Tue-Sun) The 200-year-old palace of the Travancore maharajas has carved wooden ceilings, marble sculptures and imported Belgian

Thiruvananthapuram (Trivandrum)

Top Sights
1 Museum of History & Heritage ... C1
2 Napier Museum ... C1

Sights
3 Puthe Maliga Palace Museum ... A6
4 Shri Padmanabhaswamy Temple ... A6
5 Zoological Gardens ... C1

Activities, Courses & Tours
6 CVN Kalari Sangham ... B6
7 KTDC Tours ... B5
8 Margi Kathakali School ... A5

Sleeping
9 Hotel Regency ... B4
10 Princess Inn ... B4
11 Taj Vivanta ... D3
12 Varikatt Heritage ... B3
13 Vedanta Wake Up Trivandrum ... B4

Eating
14 Ananda Bhavan ... B3
15 Ariya Nivaas ... C5
16 Azad Restaurant ... B5
17 Cherries & Berries ... D2
18 Indian Coffee House ... B5

Shopping
19 Connemara Market ... B2
20 SMSM Institute ... B4

Information
21 State Bank of India ATM ... B3
22 Tourist Facilitation Centre ... C1

Transport
23 Air India ... B1
24 Airtravel Enterprises ... C1
25 East Fort Bus Stand ... B6
26 KSRTC Central Bus Stand ... C5
27 Municipal Bus Stand ... B6
28 Train Station Reservation Office ... B5

glass. Inside you'll find Kathakali images, an armoury, portraits of maharajas, ornate thrones and other artefacts. Admission includes an informative one-hour guided tour, though you can just visit the outside of the palace grounds (free), where you'll also find the **Chitrali Museum** (₹50), containing loads of historical memorabilia, photographs and portraits from the Travancore dynasty.

Shri Padmanabhaswamy Temple HINDU TEMPLE
(Hindu-only inner sanctum 3.30am-7.30pm) Trivandrum's spiritual heart is this 260-year-old temple in the Fort area. The main entrance is the 30m-tall, seven-tier eastern *gopuram* (gateway tower). In the inner sanctum (Hindus only), the deity Padmanabha reclines on the sacred serpent and is made from over 10,000 *salagramam* (sacred stones) that were purportedly transported from Nepal by elephant.

The path around to the right of the gate offers good views of the *gopuram*.

Courses

Ayushmanbhava Ayurvedic Centre AYURVEDA, YOGA
(0471-2556060; www.ayushmanbhava.com; Pothujanam; massage from ₹900; yoga classes 6.30am) This centre, 5km west of MG Rd, offers massage, daily therapeutic-yoga classes, as well as longer ayurvedic treatments and a herbal garden.

Margi Kathakali School CULTURAL PROGRAM
(0471-2478806; www.margitheatre.org; Fort) Conducts courses in Kathakali and Koodiattam (traditional Sanskrit drama) for beginner and advanced students. Fees average ₹300 per two-hour class. Visitors can peek at uncostumed practice sessions held from 10am to noon Monday to Friday. It's in an unmarked building behind the Fort School, 200m west of the fort.

CVN Kalari Sangham MARTIAL ARTS
(0471-2474182; www.cvnkalari.in; South Rd; 15-day/1-month course ₹1000/2000) Offers long-term courses in *kalarippayat* for serious students (aged under 30) with some experience in martial arts. Visitors are welcome to watch training sessions from 7am to 8.30am Monday to Saturday.

Tours

KTDC Tours BUS
(0471-2330031; www.ktdc.com) KTDC runs several tours, all leaving from the Tourist

SLEEPING PRICE RANGES

The following price ranges refer to a double room with bathroom:

$ less than ₹1200

$$ ₹1200–₹5000

$$$ more than ₹5000

Reception Centre at the Hotel Chaithram on Central Station Rd. The City Tour (₹300) includes the zoo, museums and other local sights; the Kanyakumari Day Tour (₹700) visits Padmanabhapuram Palace, Kanyakumari in Tamil Nadu and the nearby Suchindram Temple. Other trips include Neyyar Dam (₹400) and Kovalam (₹200).

🛏 Sleeping

There are several decent budget and midrange hotels along Manjalikulam Rd, north of Central Station Rd.

Vedanta Wake Up Trivandrum HOSTEL $
(☑ 0471-2334351; www.vedantawakeup.com; SS Kovil Rd; dm/d ₹650/1450; ❋ ⊙) A good central bet for backpackers and solo travellers, with spotless air-con dorms and a private double.

Princess Inn HOTEL $
(☑ 0471-2339150; princess_inn@yahoo.com; Manjalikulam Rd; s/d from ₹600/800, with AC from ₹1000/1200; ❋ ⊙) In a glass-fronted building, the Princess Inn promises a relatively quiet budget sleep in a central side street location. It's comfortable, with satellite TV and immaculate bathrooms; it's worth paying a little more for the spacious 'deluxe' rooms.

Hotel Regency HOTEL $
(☑ 0471-2330377; www.hotelregency.com; Manjalikulam Cross Rd; s/d ₹650/800, with AC

THE INDIAN COFFEE HOUSE STORY

The Indian Coffee House is a place stuck in time. Its India-wide branches feature old-India prices and waiters dressed in starched white with peacock-style headdresses. It was started by the Coffee Board in the early 1940s, during British rule. In the 1950s the Board began to close down cafes across India, making employees redundant. At this point, the Keralan-born communist leader Ayillyath Kuttiari Gopalan Nambiar began to support the workers and founded with them the India Coffee Board Workers' Co-operative Society. The Coffee House has remained ever since, always atmospheric, and always offering bargain snacks and drinks such as Indian filter coffee, rose milk and *idlis* (fermented rice cakes). It's still run by its employees, all of whom share ownership.

₹1000/1600; ❋ ⊙) This tidy, welcoming place offers small but spotless rooms with satellite TV; the deluxe rooms are larger and there's wi-fi in the lobby, as well as a rooftop garden.

★ Graceful Homestay HOMESTAY $$
(☑ 9847249556, 0471-2444358; www.graceful homestay.com; Pothujanam Rd, Philip's Hill; incl breakfast downstairs s/d ₹1550/1800, upstairs & ste s/d ₹2450/3000; @ ⊙) In Trivandrum's leafy western suburbs, this lovely, serene family house set in a couple of hectares of garden has four rooms, neatly furnished with individual character and access to kitchen, living areas and balconies. The pick of the rooms has an amazing covered terrace overlooking a sea of palms. Call ahead for directions.

Varikatt Heritage HOMESTAY $$$
(☑ 0471-2336057, 9895239055; www.varikatt heritage.com; Punnen Rd; r/ste incl breakfast ₹5000/6000; ⊙) Trivandrum's most charismatic place to stay is the 250-year-old home of Colonel Roy Kuncheria. It's a wonderful Indo-Saracenic bungalow with four rooms flanked by verandahs facing a pretty garden. Every antique – and the home itself – has a family story attached. Lunch and dinner are available (₹500).

Taj Vivanta HOTEL $$$
(☑ 0471-6612345; vivanta.tajhotels.com; Thycaud Hospital Rd; s/d incl breakfast from ₹8500/11,000; ❋ @ ⊙ ≋) The lobby here is bigger than most hotels in town, so the Taj doesn't disappoint with the wow factor. Rooms are sufficiently plush, the lawn and pool area is well maintained, and there's a spa, 24-hour gym and several good restaurants, including the Smoke on the Water poolside grill.

🍴 Eating

★ Ariya Nivaas SOUTH INDIAN $
(Manorama Rd; mains ₹40-150, thalis ₹100; ⊙ 6.45am-10pm, lunch 11.30am-3pm) Trivandrum's best all-you-can-eat South Indian veg thalis mean Ariya Nivaas is always busy at lunchtime, but service is snappy and the food fresh.

Indian Coffee House INDIAN $
(Maveli Cafe; Central Station Rd; snacks ₹10-60; ⊙ 7am-10.30pm) This branch of Indian Coffee House serves its strong coffee and snacks in a crazy red-brick tower that looks like a cross between a lighthouse and a pigeon coop, and has a spiralling interior lined with

concrete benches and tables. You have to admire the hard-working waiters.

Azad Restaurant INDIAN $
(MG Rd; dishes ₹60-200; ⊙11am-11.30pm) A busy family favourite serving up authentic Keralan seafood dishes such as *molee* (fish pieces in coconut sauce), and excellent biryanis and tandoori. There's a takeaway barbecue on street level and the restaurant is downstairs.

Ananda Bhavan SOUTH INDIAN $
(✆0471-2477646; MG Rd; dishes ₹20-80; ⊙noon-3pm & 6-10pm) Classic cheap veg place specialising in tiffin snacks and dosas.

Cherries & Berries CAFE $$
(✆0471-2735433; www.cherriesandberries.in; Carmel Towers, Cotton Hill; items ₹130-220; ⊙10am-10pm; 🛜) For serious comfort food, icy air-con and free wi-fi that really works, take a trip east of the centre to Cherries & Berries. The menu includes waffles, mini-pizzas, hot dogs, toasties, good coffee and indulgent chocolate-bar milkshakes – try the KitKat shake (₹165).

★**Villa Maya** KERALAN $$$
(✆0471-2578901; www.villamaya.in; 120 Airport Rd, Injakkal; starters ₹200-600, mains ₹400-1500; ⊙11am-11pm) Villa Maya is more an experience than a restaurant. Dining is either in the magnificent 18th-century Dutch mansion or in private curtained niches in the tranquil courtyard garden. The Keralan cuisine is expertly crafted, delicately spiced and beautifully presented. Seafood is a speciality, with dishes like stuffed crab with lobster butter, but there are some tantalising veg dishes too.

Between lunch and dinner (3pm to 7pm) you can order snacks like sandwiches, pizzas and calzones. Ask the friendly staff for a free tour of the historic manor.

🛍 Shopping

Connemara Market MARKET
(MG Rd; ⊙6am-9pm) At the busy Connemara Market vendors sell vegetables, fish, goats, fabric, clothes, spices and more.

SMSM Institute ARTS & CRAFTS
(www.keralahandicrafts.in; YMCA Rd; ⊙9am-8pm Mon-Sat) A Kerala Government–run handicraft emporium with an Aladdin's cave of fix-priced crafts, souvenirs and antiques.

ℹ Information

KIMS (Kerala Institute of Medical Sciences; ✆0471-3041400, emergency 0471-3041144; www.kimskerala.com; Kumarapuram; ⊙24hr) The best choice for treating medical problems; about 7km northwest of Trivandrum railway station.

Tourist Facilitation Centre (✆0471-2321132; Museum Rd; ⊙24hr) Near the zoo; supplies maps and brochures.

Tourist Reception Centre (KTDC Hotel Chaithram; ✆0471-2330031; Central Station Rd; ⊙7am-9pm) Arranges KTDC-run tours.

ℹ Getting There & Away

AIR
Trivandrum International Airport (www.trivandrumairport.com), around 5km west of the city, serves international destinations with direct flights to/from Colombo in Sri Lanka, Malé in the Maldives and major Gulf destinations such as Dubai, Sharjah, Muscat, Bahrain and Kuwait.

BUSES FROM THIRUVANANTHAPURAM (TRIVANDRUM)

DESTINATION	FARE (₹)	DURATION (HRS)	DEPARTURES
Alleppey	132, AC 221	3½	every 15min
Chennai	AC from 850	12	15 daily (overnight)
Ernakulam (Kochi)	177, AC 291	5½	every 15-30min
Kanyakumari	70	2	4 daily
Kollam	63, AC 111	1½	every 15min
Kumily (for Periyar)	226	8	7.30am
Munnar	245	8	3 daily
Neyyar Dam	35	1½	every 40min
Thrissur	224, AC 391	7½	hourly
Varkala	65	1¼	hourly

Within India, **Air India** (☎0471-2317341; www.airindia.com; Mascot Sq; ⏲9am-5pm Mon-Sat), **Jet Airways** (☎0471-2728864; www.jetairways.com; Sasthamangalam Junction; ⏲9am-6pm) and **IndiGo** (☎9212783838; www.indigo.in) fly between Trivandrum and Mumbai (Bombay), Kochi (Cochin), Bengaluru (Bangalore), Chennai (Madras) and Delhi. **SpiceJet** (☎9871803333; www.spicejet.com; Trivandrum Airport) flies to Chennai once a week.

All airline bookings can be made at the efficient travel agency **Airtravel Enterprises** (☎0471-3011300; www.ate.travel; MG Rd, New Corporation Bldg; ⏲9am-7pm).

BUS

State-run and private buses use Trivandrum's giant new concave **KSRTC central bus stand** (☎0471-2462290; www.keralartc.com; Central Station Rd, Thampanoor), opposite the train station.

Buses leave for Kovalam beach (₹17, 30 minutes, every 20 minutes) between 6am and 9pm from the southern end of the **East Fort bus stand** on MG Rd.

TRAIN

Trains are often heavily booked, so it's worth visiting the **reservation office** (☎139; ⏲8am-8pm Mon-Sat, to 2pm Sun) at the main train station or booking online. There's a foreign tourist counter on the 1st floor. While most major trains arrive at Trivandrum Central Station close to the city centre, some express services terminate at Vikram Sarabhai Station (Kochuveli), about 7km north of the city – check in advance.

Within Kerala there are frequent express trains to Varkala (2nd class/sleeper/3AC ₹45/140/490, one hour), Kollam (₹55/140/490, 1¼ hours) and Ernakulam (₹90/165/490, 4½ hours), with trains passing through either Alappuzha (Alleppey; ₹80/140/490, three hours) or Kottayam (₹80/140/490, 3½ hours). There are also numerous daily services to Kanyakumari (2nd class/sleeper/3AC ₹60/140/490, three hours).

Getting Around

For the airport, take local bus 14 from the **East Fort** and **Municipal** bus stands (₹10). Prepaid taxi vouchers from the airport cost ₹350 to the city and ₹500 to Kovalam (13km away).

Autorickshaws are the easiest way to get around, with short hops costing ₹30 to ₹50.

Around Trivandrum

Sights

Neyyar Wildlife Sanctuary NATURE RESERVE
(☎0471-2272182; Indian/foreigner ₹10/100; ⏲9am-4pm Tue-Sun) Surrounding an idyllic lake created by the 1964 Neyyar Dam 35km north of Trivandrum, this sanctuary features a **Lion Safari Park** (☎9744347582, 0471-2272182; Indian/foreigner ₹200/300; ⏲9am-4pm Tue-Sun), deer park and Crocodile Production Centre (named for Australian legend Steve Irwin). The fertile forest lining the shore is home to gaurs, sambar deer, sloth, elephants, lion-tailed macaques and the occasional tiger.

Get here from Trivandrum's KSRTC bus stand by frequent bus (₹35, 1½ hours). A taxi is about ₹1000 return (with two hours' waiting time) from Trivandrum, or ₹1400 from Kovalam. The KTDC office in Trivandrum also runs tours to Neyyar Dam (₹400).

Sivananda Yoga Vedanta Dhanwantari Ashram YOGA
(☎0471-2273093; www.sivananda.org.in/neyyardam; dm/tent ₹800, tw ₹1000-1250, with AC ₹1850) Just before Neyyar Dam, this superbly located ashram established in 1978 is renowned for its hatha yoga courses. Courses start on the 1st and 16th of each month, run for a minimum of two weeks and include various levels of accommodation and vegetarian meals. Low season (May to September) rates are ₹100 less.

MAJOR TRAINS FROM THIRUVANANTHAPURAM (TRIVANDRUM)

DESTINATION	TRAIN NAME & NO	FARE (₹; SLEEPER/3AC/2AC)	DURATION (HRS)	DEPARTURES (DAILY)
Bengaluru	16525 Bangalore Exp	415/1120/1620	18	12.45pm
Chennai	12696 Chennai Exp	470/1240/1775	16½	5.15pm
Coimbatore	17229 Sabari Exp	255/685/980	9¼	7.15am
Mangalura	16604 Maveli Exp	340/915/1320	12½	7.25pm
Mumbai	16346 Netravathi Exp	670/1795/2645	31	9.50am

VLADIMIR ZHOGA / SHUTTERSTOCK ©

Kerala

Serene Kerala is a state shaped by its wonderful natural landscape: a long, luxurious coastline; wandering backwaters; lush palms and spice plantations; and cool mountain escapes. Add the kaleidoscope of culture best experienced in the unique performing arts and you'll understand why Kerala is a destination not to be missed.

Contents

Above Traditional Kathakali dancers (p312), Kerala

Beaches

Goa might pull in the package-holiday crowds, but Kerala's coastline – almost 600km of it – boasts a stunning string of golden-sand beaches, fringed by palms and washed by the Arabian Sea. The southern beaches are the busiest. Less-discovered, wilder choices await in the north.

Southern Beaches

Most established of the resorts along the coast is Kovalam (p271), only a short hop from the capital, Thiruvananthapuram (Trivandrum; p257). Once a quiet fishing village, Kovalam has two sheltered crescents of beach perfect for paddling or novice surfing, overlooked by a solid line of low-rise hotels and restaurants. If you're looking for something less busy, some lovely beaches and resorts cluster south of Kovalam in the area around Pulinkudi and Chowara, where ayurvedic treatments are popular.

North of Trivandrum is Varkala (p275), which straggles along dramatic, russet-and-gold-streaked cliffs. Although a holy town popular with Hindu pilgrims, Varkala has also developed into Kerala's backpacker bolthole and the cliffs are lined with guesthouses, open-front restaurants and bars all moving to a reggae, rock and trance soundtrack. For a quieter scene, travellers are drifting north to Odayam beach.

Even further north, Alappuzha (Alleppey; p282) is best known for its backwaters, but also has a decent coastline up to Marari, while Kochi (Cochin; p298) has Cherai Beach on Vypeen Island, a lovely stretch of white sand, with kilome-

tres of lazy lagoons and backwaters only a few hundred metres from the seafront.

Far North & Islands

Fewer travellers make it to Kerala's far north, which means there are some beautifully deserted pockets of beach, where resorts are replaced by more traditional village life. Among the best are the peaceful white-sand beaches south of Kannur (p320), or further north around the Valiyaparamba backwaters (p322) between Kannur and Bekal.

Even more far flung are the Lakshadweep islands (p323), a palm-fringed archipelago 300km west of Kerala. As well as pristine beaches, the islands boast some of India's best scuba diving and snorkelling.

Best Beach Towns

Varkala (p275) The beautiful cliff-edged coastline of Varkala is a Hindu holy place as well as a lively backpacker-focused resort. Good base for yoga, surfing or just chilling out.

Kovalam (p271) Kerala's most commercial beach resort, but still fun and easily accessible with some good waves and a surf club. Resorts here and further south have a strong focus on ayurvedic treatments.

Kannur (p320) While Kannur itself is not particularly appealing, head 8km south to Thottada for gorgeous beaches and seafront homestays in local villages. Kannur town's 4km-long Payyambalam Beach is popular with locals.

DMITRY RUKHLENKO / SHUTTERSTOCK ©

DANIEL J. RAO / SHUTTERSTOCK ©

1. Papanasham beach, Varkala (p275) **2.** Sunset at a Kannur beach (p320)

Backwaters

Kerala's 900km of waterways spread watery tendrils through a lusciously green landscape. Palm-shaded, winding canals are lined by back-in-time villages, many of which are accessible only by boat. It's an environment unique to Kerala and an unforgettable South India experience.

Houseboats

To glide along the canals in a punted canoe, or sleep under a firmament of stars in a traditional houseboat, is pure enchantment. The distinctive houseboats that cluster around the main hubs of Alleppey (282) and Kollam (Quilon; p279) are designed like traditional rice barges or *kettuvallam* ('boats with knots', so-called because the curvaceous structure is held together by knotted coir).

There are several ways to explore the backwaters. The most popular is to rent a houseboat for a night or two; these sleep anywhere from two to 14 or more people. They vary wildly in luxury and amenities. The hire includes staff (at least a driver and cook, but often additional kitchen staff and crew), so catering is included, and you'll eat traditional Keralan meals of fish and vegetables cooked in coconut milk. The popularity of these tours can mean that the main waterways get very busy – even gridlocked – in peak season.

Ferries, Canoes & Kayaks

The cheapest means of seeing the waterways is to take a public ferry. You can take trips from town to town, though you won't see much of the smaller canals. Two of the most popular trips are the all-day tourist cruise between Kollam and

1. Houseboat, Kerala backwaters
2. Navigating the backwaters
3. Houseboat tour

Alleppey, a scenic but slow trip, and the 2½-hour ferry from Alleppey to Kottayam.

A better way to explore deep into the network and escape the bigger boats is on a canoe tour, which allows you to travel along the narrower canals and see village life in a way that's impossible on a houseboat or ferry. Village tours with a knowledgable guide are another tranquil way to explore the region and understand some of the local culture.

Kayaking the canals is gaining popularity; an operator such as **Kerala Kayaking** (☑9846585674, 8547487701; www.keralakayaking.com; per person 4/7/10hr ₹1500/3000/4500) will take you deep into the backwaters where you can experience a leisurely paddle through villages.

Ecofriendly Cruises

The choice of houseboats can be mind-boggling and your selection can make or break the experience.

➡ Unless it's peak season, avoid booking a houseboat until you arrive at the backwaters; inspect a few boats before committing.

➡ Ask to see the operator's certification: those houseboat owners who have a 'Green Palm' or 'Gold Star' certificate have met requirements such as solar panels, sanitary tanks and low-emission engines.

➡ Visit the houseboat dock in Alleppey, talk to returning travellers or guesthouse owners, and search online to gauge costs and quality.

➡ Avoid peak season (mid-December to mid-January) and domestic holidays when prices peak and the waterways are clogged.

Performing Arts

Kerala has an intensely rich culture of performing arts – living art forms are passed on to new generations in specialised schools and arts centres.

Kathakali

Kathakali – with its elaborate ritualised gestures, heavy make-up, and dramatic stories of love, lust and power based on the Ramayana, the Mahabharata and the Puranas – stems in part from 2nd-century temple rituals, though its current form developed around the 16th century. The actors tell the stories through precise mudras (hand gestures) and facial expressions. Traditionally performances start in temple grounds at around 8pm and go on all night, though versions for those with shorter attention spans are performed in many tourist centres, to give you a taste of the art.

Theyyam

Theyyam is believed to be older than Hinduism, having developed from harvest folk dances. It's performed in *kavus* (sacred groves) in northern Kerala. The word refers to the ritual itself, and to the shape of the deity or hero portrayed, of whom there are around 450. The costumes are magnificent, with face paint, armour, garlands and huge headdresses. The performance consists of frenzied dancing to a wild drumbeat, creating a trancelike atmosphere.

Kalarippayat

Taking its moves from both Kathakali and *theyyam* is the martial art of *kalarippayat*, a ritualistic discipline taught throughout Kerala. It's taught and displayed in

1. Traditional *bharatanatyam* dancer (477) 2. Theyyam performer (p321)

an arena called a *kalari,* which combines gymnasium, school and temple.

Places to See Performing Arts

In the spring there are numerous festivals offering the chance to see Kathakali, with Thirunakkara in Kottayam in March and the Pooram festival in Kollam in April. The easiest places for travellers to see performances are at cultural centres such as Kerala Kathakali Centre (p308) and See India Foundation (p308) in Kochi; Mudra Cultural Centre (p293) and Navarasa Kathakali Centre (p294) in Kumily; and Punarjani Traditional Village (p297) and Thirumeny Cultural Centre (p297) in Munnar. In Kovalam and Varkala there are short versions of the art in season.

If you're interested in learning more about the art of Kathakali, Kerala Kala-

mandalam (p314) near Thrissur and Margi Kathakali School (p259) in Trivandrum offer courses for serious students, or you can attend these schools to see performances and practice sessions.

Both the Kochi and Kumily centres have demonstrations of *kalarippayat,* or you can visit the martial art training centres of CVN Kalari Sangham (p259) in Trivandrum and Ens Kalari (p308) in Nettoor, close to Ernakulam.

The best areas to see *theyyam* performances are around Kannur, Payyanur and Valiyaparamba, in the northern backwater area, where there are more than 500 *kavus.* The season is from October to May. For advice on finding performances, contact the Tourist Desk (p303) in Kochi or homestays at Thottada Beach.

Tea plantation, Munnar (p29...)

Hill Stations & Sanctuaries

Kerala's hill country in the Western Ghats is a sumptuous natural spectacle where narrow roads wind up through jungle-thick vegetation and provide dizzying views over peacock-green tea plantations. A cooling altitude helps to make the towns soothing places to escape from the coast, while the wildlife sanctuaries are largely unspoilt wildernesses offering the chance to spot wild animals and birdlife.

Munnar

Best known of the hill stations is Munnar (p294), with contoured green fields and plantations carpeting the hills as far as the eye can see. This is South India's tea-growing heartland, but also a great place to trek to viewpoints across fine mountain scenery. Some wonderfully remote lodgings are hidden in the hills, tucked deep into spice and flower gardens or cardamom and coffee plantations.

Wayanad & Periyar

The northern area around Wayanad Wildlife Sanctuary (p317) has shimmering green rice paddies and plantations of coffee, cardamom, ginger and pepper. The rolling hills are fragrant with wild herbs and punctuated by mammoth clumps of bamboo. It's one of the best places to spot wild elephants and there are plenty of opportunities for trekking.

At Periyar Wildlife Sanctuary (p290), a tiger reserve since 1978 and Kerala's most visited wildlife sanctuary, you can cruise on Periyar Lake, stay in an island palace, paddle on a bamboo raft or embark on a jungle trek with a trained tribal guide.

Kovalam

📞 0471 / POP 25,700

Once a calm fishing village clustered around its crescent beaches, Kovalam competes with Varkala as Kerala's most developed resort. The touristy main stretch, Lighthouse Beach, has hotels and restaurants built up along the shore, while Hawa Beach to the north is usually crowded with day trippers heading straight from the taxi stand to the sand. Neither beach could be described as pristine, but at less than 15km from the capital it's a convenient place to have some fun by the sea, there are some promising waves (and a surf club), and it makes a good base for ayurvedic treatments and yoga courses.

About 2km further north, Samudra Beach has several upmarket resorts, restaurants and a peaceful but steep beach.

📍 Sights & Activities

Vizhinjam Lighthouse
LIGHTHOUSE

(Indian/foreigner ₹10/25, camera/video ₹20/25; ⊙10am-5pm) Kovalam's most distinguishing feature is the working candy-striped lighthouse at the southern end of Lighthouse Beach. Climb the spiral staircase – or the brand-new elevator – for vertigo-inducing views up and down the coast.

Cool Divers & Bond Safari
DIVING

(📞9946550073; www.bondsafarikovalam.com; introductory dive ₹6000, 3hr ocean safari ₹6000; ⊙9am-7pm) This new dive outfit offers state-of-the-art equipment, PADI courses and guided trips to local dive sites. It also has nifty Bond submarine scooters, where your head is enclosed in a helmet with an airhose to the surface – no diving experience required!

Kovalam Surf Club
SURFING

(📞9847347367; www.kovalamsurfclub.com; 1½hr lesson ₹1000, rental from ₹400) This surf shop and club just back from Lighthouse Beach offers introductory lessons and 'guided surfing' with a community focus.

Ayur Kerala Ayurvedic
Health Care
AYURVEDA

(📞9947027226; www.ayurkerala.org; Lighthouse Beach Rd; massage from ₹1200; ⊙9am-8pm) Recommended massages and ayurvedic treatments.

🛏 Sleeping

Kovalam is tightly packed with hotels and guesthouses, though true budget places are

in the minority in high season. Beachfront properties are the most expensive and sought after, but look out for smaller places in the labyrinth of sandy paths behind Lighthouse Beach among palm groves and rice paddies; they're usually much better value. Samudra Beach has upmarket resorts. All places offer discounts outside the December–January high season; book ahead in peak times.

Vedanta Wake Up Kovalam
HOSTEL $

(📞0471-2484211; www.vedantawakeup.com; behind Lighthouse Beach; dm/d ₹600/1800; ❄🛜) Kovalam's first backpacker hostel is a five-storey joint a short walk back from Lighthouse Beach. The two air-con dorms are very clean, while the private rooms come with TV and bathroom. It has helpful staff, but lacks common areas and personality.

Green Valley Cottages
GUESTHOUSE $

(📞0471-2480636; indira_ravi@hotmail.com; r ₹800-1000) Back among the palm trees and overlooking a lily pond, this serene complex feels a little faded but it's quiet and decent value. The 22 rooms are simple, but the upper rooms have good views from the front terraces.

Hotel Greenland
GUESTHOUSE $

(📞0471-2486442; hotelgreenlandin@yahoo.com; r ₹700-1400) This friendly family-run place has refurbished rooms in a multilevel complex just back from Lighthouse Beach. It's not flash but rooms have lots of natural light and the larger upstairs rooms have balconies.

Paradesh Inn
GUESTHOUSE $$

(📞9995362952; inn.paradesh@yahoo.com; Avaduthura; s/d incl breakfast ₹2300/2700, superior ₹3000/3400; ⊙Oct-Mar; @🛜) Set back from Lighthouse Beach high above the palms, tranquil Italian-run Paradesh Inn resembles a whitewashed Greek island hideaway. Each of the six fan-cooled rooms has a hanging chair outside, there are views from the rooftop, nice breakfasts and *satya* cooking ('yoga food') for guests.

Kovalam

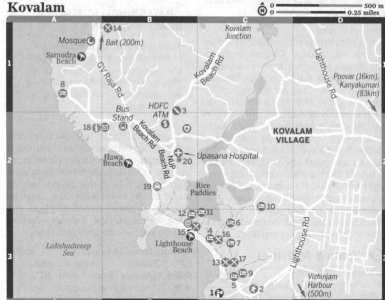

Kovalam

Beach Hotel II   HOTEL $$
(📱9400031243, 0471-2481937; www.thebeach
hotel-kovalam.com; d ₹4400, with AC ₹5500;
❀🛜) Tucked into the southern end of
Lighthouse Beach, this stylish pad has 10
sea-facing rooms all with balcony and large
sliding French windows. Decor is simple
chic. It's also home to the excellent terrace
restaurant Fusion.

Treetops   GUESTHOUSE $$
(📱9847912398; treetopsofkovalam@yahoo.in; d
₹1500; @🛜) Indeed in the treetops high
above Lighthouse Beach, this friendly ex-
pat-owned place is a peaceful retreat from
the action below. The three bright, clean
rooms have hanging chairs on the terraces
and TVs, and there are rooftop views and

a guest kitchen; yoga classes are available. Call ahead to book and get directions.

Beach Hotel
GUESTHOUSE **$$**

(☑ 0471-2481937; www.thebeachhotel-kovalam. com; d ₹3300; ☎) Location alert! Below Waves Restaurant and German Bakery, the eight beach-facing rooms here are designed with minimalist flair, ochre tones and finished with smart, arty touches.

Maharaju Palace
GUESTHOUSE **$$**

(☑ 9946854270; www.maharajupalace.com; s/d incl breakfast from ₹1650/1980, cottage ₹3300/3600, summer house ₹7150; ❄☎) More of a peaceful retreat than a palace, this quirky Dutch-owned place in a lane just back from Lighthouse Beach has more character than most, with timber furnishings, including the odd four-poster bed, and a separate cottage in the garden. The lovely breakfast terrace is hung with chintzy chandeliers.

Wilson Ayurvedic Resort
HOTEL **$$**

(☑ 9847363831; Lighthouse Beach; d ₹1500, with AC ₹2500; ❄☎≋) Wilson has simple but reasonably well-maintained rooms orbiting a shady pool just back from Lighthouse Beach. There's a leafy holiday-resort vibe and it offers ayurvedic treatments.

Leela
HOTEL **$$$**

(☑ 0471-2480101; www.theleela.com; d from ₹18,000, ste from ₹66,000; ❄@☎≋) The sumptuous Leela is set in extensive grounds on the headland north of Hawa Beach. You'll find three swimming pools, an ayurvedic centre, a gym, two 'private beaches', several restaurants and more. Spacious rooms have period touches, colourful textiles and Keralan artwork.

Vivanta By Taj Green Cove
HOTEL **$$$**

(☑ 0471-6613000; vivanta.tajhotels.com; Samudra Beach; d from ₹17,500, ste from ₹28,000; ❄@☎≋) The Kovalam branch of this swanky Indian hotel chain is set among sprawling green grounds and has direct access to a secluded stretch of Samudra Beach. The individual thatched cottages here are simply but tastefully adorned, some with private gardens and others with primo sea views. There are several restaurants and the usual top-end amenities.

🍴 Eating & Drinking

Lighthouse Beach is the main restaurant hub, with lots of seafood places. Samudra Beach, to the north, is quieter but also has some restaurants worth seeking out. For a romantic dining

---

PADMANABHAPURAM PALACE

About 60km southeast of Kovalam, just over the border in Tamil Nadu, **Padmanabhapuram Palace** (p391) is considered the finest surviving example of traditional Keralan architecture. It's accessible by bus or taxi from Kovalam or Kanyakumari, via Thuckalay. A return taxi from Kovalam including waiting time costs ₹2000.

---

splurge, the restaurants at Leela and Vivanta By Taj Green Cove are pricey but top class.

Each evening a dozen or so restaurants lining the Lighthouse Beach promenade display the catch of the day – just pick a fish or lobster, settle on a price and decide how you want it prepared. Market prices vary enormously depending on the day's catch, but at the time of research it was around ₹400 per fish fillet, tiger prawns were ₹900 per half kilo, and lobster was ₹3500 per kilo.

★ Varsha Restaurant
SOUTH INDIAN **$**

(dishes ₹100-200; ⊙8am-10pm; ☎) This little restaurant just back from Lighthouse Beach serves some of Kovalam's best vegetarian food at budget prices. Dishes are fresh and carefully prepared. It's a great spot for breakfast and lunch in particular.

Suprabhatham
KERALAN **$**

(meals ₹90-250; ⊙7am-11pm; ☎) This little veg place hidden back from Lighthouse Beach doesn't look like much, but it dishes up excellent, inexpensive Keralan cooking, vegetarian thalis and fresh fruit juices in a rustic setting.

Waves Restaurant & German Bakery
MULTICUISINE **$$**

(Beach Hotel; mains ₹220-550; ⊙7.30am-11pm; ☎) With its broad, burnt-orange balcony, ambient soundtrack and wide-roaming menu, Waves is usually busy with foreigners. It morphs into the German Bakery, a great spot for breakfast with fresh bread, croissants, pastries and decent coffee, while dinner turns up Thai curries, German sausages, pizza and seafood. There's a small bookshop attached. Wi-fi (unusually) costs ₹30 per half hour.

Fusion
MULTICUISINE **$$**

(mains ₹200-450; ⊙7.30am-10.30pm; ☎) This terrace restaurant at Beach Hotel II is one of the better dining experiences on Lighthouse

Beach, with an inventive East-meets-West menu, a range of Continental dishes, Asian fusion and interesting seafood numbers like lobster steamed in vodka. It also serves French press coffee and herbal teas.

Malabar Cafe
INDIAN $$

(mains ₹110-450; ⊘8am-11pm; 🛜) The busy tables tell a story: with candlelight at night and views through pot plants to the crashing waves, Malabar offers tasty food, including the nightly fresh seafood display, and good service.

Beatles Cafe
MULTICUISINE $$

(Lighthouse Beach; mains ₹100-400; ⊘8am-11pm; 🛜) This sweet little cafe on the promenade has been around for a long time and is a good little spot for breakfast or a burger, but the menu ranges from pizza to *momos* (Tibetan dumplings) and South Indian curries.

Curry Leaf
MULTICUISINE $$

(Samudra Beach; mains ₹100-380; ⊘8am-8.30pm) On a small hilltop overlooking Samudra Beach, this two-storey restaurant boasts enviable ocean and sunset views, eager staff and a menu ranging from fresh seafood and tandoori to Continental dishes. It requires a bit of a walk along paths or uphill from the beach, but the uncrowded location is part of the charm.

★ Bait
SEAFOOD $$$

(Vivanta by Taj Green Cove; mains ₹300-800; ⊘12.30-3pm & 6-10.30pm) The seafood restaurant at the Vivanta (p273) fronts Samudra Beach, a golf-buggy ride from the hotel itself. It's designed as an upmarket alfresco beach shack, where you can watch the waves on one side and the chefs at work in the open kitchen on the other; the seafood and spicy preparations are top-notch.

ℹ Information

About 500m uphill from Lighthouse Beach are HDFC and Axis ATMs, and there are Federal Bank and ICICI ATMs at Kovalam Junction.

Tourist Facilitation Centre (📞0471-2480085; Kovalam Beach Rd; ⊘9.30am-5pm Mon-Sat) This helpful office is in the main entrance to Leela hotel near the bus stand.

Upasana Hospital (📞0471-2480632) Has English-speaking doctors who can take care of minor injuries.

ℹ Getting There & Around

BUS

Buses start and finish at an unofficial bus stand on the main road outside the entrance to Leela hotel, and all buses pass through Kovalam Junction, about 1.5km north of Lighthouse Beach. Buses connect Kovalam and Trivandrum every

AYURVEDIC RESORTS

Between Kovalam and Poovar (16km southeast), amid seemingly endless swaying palms, laid-back village life and empty golden-sand beaches, are a string of upmarket ayurvedic resorts that are worth a look if you're serious about immersing yourself in ayurvedic treatments. They're all between 6km and 10km southeast of Kovalam. A taxi from Kovalam costs between ₹250 and ₹450.

Dr Franklin's Panchakarma Institute (📞0471-2480870; www.dr-franklin.com; Chowara; s/d hut €25/33, r from €30/40, with AC €45/66; @🛜≋) For those serious about ayurvedic treatment, this is a reputable and less expensive alternative to the flashier resorts. Daily treatment with full meal plan costs €75. Accommodation is tidy and comfortable but not resort-style.

Niraamaya Surya Samudra (📞8589982204, 0471-2229400; www.niraamaya.in; Pulinkudi; r incl breakfast ₹16,800-30,000; ❄🛜≋) Surya Samudra offers A-list-style seclusion. The 22 transplanted traditional Keralan homes come with four-poster beds and open-air bathrooms, set in a palm grove above sparkling seas. There's an infinity pool carved out of a single block of granite, renowned Niraamaya Spa, ayurvedic treatments, a gym and spectacular outdoor yoga platforms.

Bethsaida Hermitage (📞0471-2267554; www.bethsaidahermitage.com; Pulinkudi; s/d incl meals ₹1760/5500, with AC ₹4000/6050; ❄🛜≋) This charitable organisation helps support two nearby orphanages and several other worthy causes. As a bonus, it's also a luxurious and remote beachside escape, with sculpted gardens, seductively slung hammocks, putting-green-perfect lawns, palms galore and professional ayurvedic treatments and yoga classes.

POOVAR & KERALA'S DEEP SOUTH BACKWATERS

About 16km southeast of Kovalam, almost at the Tamil Nadu border, Poovar is the gateway to a region of beaches, estuaries, villages and upmarket resorts that comprise the 'mini backwaters' of Kerala's far south.

Numerous 'boat clubs' and operators along the Neyyar River or backwater canals will take you on 1½- to two-hour cruises through the waterways visiting the beach, bird-filled mangrove swamps and forested Poovar Island for ₹1500 to ₹2500 per boat (you can bargain down outside high season). Kovalam travel agents also arrange trips.

Poovar Island Resort (☎0471-2212068, 9895799044; www.poovarislandresorts.com; d cottage from ₹11,400, floating cottage from ₹16,800; ❀❂❄), accessible only by boat, is popular for its romantic 'floating' cottages, though most rooms are on land, in Keralan architectural style.

Local buses head south from Kovalam Junction to Poovar, from where you'll need to take an autorickshaw to the backwaters. A taxi/autorickshaw from Kovalam to Poovar costs ₹1000/800, or hire a scooter.

20 minutes between 7am and 8pm (₹17, 30 minutes).

For northbound onward travel it's easiest to take any bus to Trivandrum and change there, although there is one bus to Varkala at 3.30pm (₹120, 2½ hours).

There are two buses at 9.30am and 5.30pm for Kanyakumari (₹100, 2½ hours).

MOTORCYCLE

K Tours & Travel (☎9847259507; per day scooters/Enfields from ₹400/600; ◷9am-5pm), next door to Devi Garden Restaurant just above Hawa Beach, rents out scooters and Enfields.

TAXI & AUTORICKSHAW

A taxi between Trivandrum and Kovalam Beach is around ₹500; an autorickshaw should cost ₹350. From the bus stand to the north end of Lighthouse Beach costs around ₹50.

The main autorickshaw and taxi stand is at Hawa Beach.

Varkala

☎0470 / POP 42,300

Perched almost perilously along the edge of 15m-high red laterite cliffs, the North Cliff part of Varkala has a naturally beautiful setting that has steadily grown into Kerala's most popular backpacker hang-out. A small strand of beach nuzzles Varkala's cliff edge, where restaurants play innocuous world music and stalls sell T-shirts, baggy trousers and silver jewellery. It's touristy and the sales pitch can be tiring, but Varkala is still a great place to watch the days slowly turn into weeks, and it's not hard to escape the crowds further north or south where the beaches are cleaner and quieter.

Despite its backpacker vibe, Varkala is essentially a temple town, and the main Papanasham Beach is a holy place where Hindus come to make offerings for passed loved ones, assisted by priests who set up shop beneath the Hindustan Hotel. About 2km east of here is busy Varkala town.

◉ Sights

The gently undulating path from the northern clifftop continues for a photogenic 7km to Kappil Beach, passing a subtly changing beach landscape, including Odayam Beach and the fishing village of Edava. The walk is best done early in the morning.

Janardhana Temple   HINDU TEMPLE
Varkala is a temple town and Janardhana Temple is the main event – its technicolour Hindu spectacle hovers above Beach Rd. It's closed to non-Hindus, but you may be invited into the temple grounds where there is a huge banyan tree and shrines to Ayyappan, Hanuman and other Hindu deities.

Sivagiri Mutt   ASHRAM
(☎0470-2602807; www.sivagirimutt.org) Sivagiri Mutt is the headquarters of the Shri Narayana Dharma Sanghom Trust, the ashram devoted to Shri Narayana Guru (1855–1928), Kerala's most prominent guru. This is a popular pilgrimage site and the resident swami is happy to talk to visitors.

Varkala Aquarium   AQUARIUM
(adult/child ₹30/15, camera ₹10; ◷10am-7pm) Varkala's new aquarium, between Black

Varkala

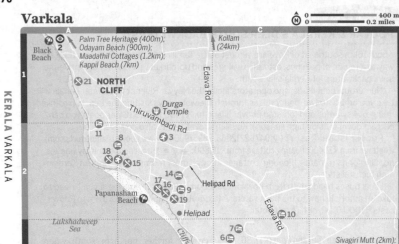

Varkala

Beach and Odayam Beach, has large tanks, viewed from a spiralling walkway, that are full of exotic species including piranha, sea snakes, scorpion fish and the local karimeen. A worthwhile diversion from the beach.

Kappil Beach   BEACH
About 9km north of Varkala by road, Kappil Beach is a pretty and, as yet, undeveloped stretch of sand. It's also the start of a mini network of backwaters.

Ponnumthuruthu (Golden) Island   ISLAND
(boat ride 2/3/4 people ₹500/600/700, island admission per person ₹50) About 10km south of Varkala, this island in the middle of a backwater lake is home to the Shiva-Parvati Hindu temple, also known as the Golden Temple. It's closed to non-Hindus but the main reason to venture down here is the scenic punt-powered boat ride to and around the island. An autorickshaw from Varkala should cost ₹500 with waiting time.

⚡ Activities

Yoga (₹300 to ₹400 per session) is offered at several guesthouses, and boogie boards (₹100) can be hired from places along the beach; be wary of strong currents. Many of the resorts and hotels along the north cliff offer ayurvedic treatments and massage.

Eden Garden MASSAGE
(☑0470-2603910; www.edengarden.in; massages ₹1000-3000) Eden Garden offers an upmarket ayurvedic experience, including single treatments and packages.

Soul & Surf SURFING, YOGA
(☑9895580106; www.soulandsurf.com; South Cliff; surf lessons ₹2300, surf guide ₹1150, board rental half-/full day ₹850/1600; ⊙ Oct-May) This UK outfit organises surfing trips and yoga retreats in season, with accommodation and a garden restaurant at its South Cliff pad. It also offers 1½-hour lessons and board rental. If you already surf and there's space, join one of the regular surf tours (₹1150).

Can Fly PARAGLIDING
(☑9048795781; canflyindia@gmail.com; 20min flight ₹3500) Tandem paragliding from the North Cliff car park, depending on the wind. The French owner also runs stand-up paddleboarding tours and a budget guesthouse, Pooja House.

Haridas Yoga YOGA
(☑9846374231; www.pranayogavidya.com; Hotel Green Palace; classes ₹300; ⊙8am & 4.30pm Aug-May) Recommended drop-in 1½-hour hatha yoga classes with experienced teachers.

🛏 Sleeping

Most places to stay are crammed along and behind the north cliff where backpackers tend to congregate, but there are some nice places down by the southern cliffs. Less-developed Odayam Beach is a tranquil alternative.

Practically all accommodation places can be reached by taxi or autorickshaw via the network of lanes leading to the cliffs, but the commission racket is alive and well – be sure your driver takes you to the place you've asked for.

★ Jicky's GUESTHOUSE $
(☑9846179325, 0470-2606994; www.jickys.com; s ₹600, d ₹800-1500, AC cottage ₹2500-3000; ❄ 🛜) In the palm groves just back from the cliffs and taxi stand, family-run Jicky's is as friendly as they come and has blossomed into several buildings offering plenty of choice for trav-

ellers. The rooms in the main whitewashed building are fresh, and nearby are two charming octagonal double cottages, and some larger air-con rooms. Good off-season discounts.

Wake Up Vedanta Varkala HOSTEL $
(☑0470-2051341; www.vedantawakeup.com; North Cliff; dm/d ₹600/1500, huts ₹1500; ❄ 🛜) This large house on the road to the helipad has spotless six-bed air-con dorms, good-value private rooms and neat bamboo huts. It's a good deal for backpackers.

★ Kaiya House GUESTHOUSE $$
(☑9746126909, 9995187913; www.kaiyahouse.com; d incl breakfast ₹2750, d with AC ₹3300; ❄ 🛜) Not your typical Varkala address, Kaiya House has bags of charm, a warm welcome and sheer relaxation. Each of the five rooms is thoughtfully furnished and themed (African, Indian, Chinese, Japanese and English), with four-poster beds and artworks. There's a lovely rooftop terrace and expat owner Debra welcomes you with tea, advice and free walking tours. The clifftop is a 10-minute walk away.

Eden Garden RESORT $$
(☑0470-2603910; www.edengarden.in; cottages ₹1200-2000, deluxe cottages ₹5500; 🛜) Stylish rooms come with high wooden ceilings and attractive furniture, set around a lush lily pond. There are also bamboo cottages and deluxe cottages organically shaped like white space mushrooms, with intricate paintwork, round beds and mosaic circular baths. All-inclusive ayurvedic packages range from three to 30 days.

InDa Hotel GUESTHOUSE $$
(☑7025029861; North Cliff; s/d incl breakfast ₹1900/2400; 🛜) Tucked away behind the North Cliff restaurants, InDa Hotel is a friendly and highly regarded hotel with ruthlessly clean rooms and individual cottages in a leafy garden. A big plus is the serene cafe serving healthy snacks such as wraps and the Buddha bowl.

Kerala Bamboo House RESORT $$
(☑9895270993; www.keralabamboohouse.com; huts d ₹2000, r with AC ₹3000; ❄ 🛜) For that simple bamboo-hut experience, this popular place squishes together dozens of pretty Balinese-style huts and a neatly maintained garden about halfway along the North Cliff walk. Ayurvedic treatments, yoga and **cooking classes** (☑9895270993; www.keralabamboohouse.com; Kerala Bamboo House; per person ₹1500; ⊙8am-8pm Nov-Mar) are on offer.

Palm Tree Heritage
RESORT **$$**

(📞 9946055036; www.palmtreeheritage.com; Odayam Beach; d from ₹3350, with AC ₹4500-8000, ste from ₹9000; ✳️ 📶) Set in a lovely garden just steps from quiet Odayam Beach, Palm Tree Heritage is an antidote to Varkala's backpacker scene. A wide variety of rooms are neatly furnished and tables and chairs from the restaurant spill out onto the sand.

Omsam Guesthouse
GUESTHOUSE **$$**

(📞 0470-2604455; www.omsamguesthome.com; South Cliff; d ₹2500-2900, d with AC ₹4200; ✳️ 📶) The seven rooms in this beautful Keralan-style guesthouse are a delight, with heavy timber stylings and furniture. Good location south of the main beach.

Maadathil Cottages
GUESTHOUSE **$$**

(📞 9746113495; www.maadathilcottages.com; Odayam Beach; d incl breakfast without/with AC ₹4000/5000; ✳️ 📶) The 10 beachfront cottages here are designed in traditional Keralan style with heritage furniture and big beds. All have sea views from the spacious balconies and some overlook a large lotus pond. Excellent location on quiet Odayam Beach.

Villa Jacaranda
GUESTHOUSE **$$$**

(📞 0470-2610296; www.villa-jacaranda.biz; Temple Rd West; d incl breakfast ₹6850-9600; ✳️ 📶) This understated but romantic retreat back from the southern beach has just four spacious, bright rooms in a large two-storey house, each with a balcony and decorated with a chic blend of minimalist modern and period touches. The divine top-floor room has its own rooftop garden with sea views.

Gateway Hotel Janardhanapuram
HOTEL **$$$**

(📞 0470-6673300; www.thegatewayhotels.com; d incl breakfast from ₹9600; ✳️ @ 📶 ☀️) Varkala's flashiest hotel and part of the Taj group, the Gateway is all gleaming linen and mocha cushions in capacious rooms overlooking the garden, while the more expensive rooms have sea views and private balconies. There's a fantastic pool with bar, a tennis court and the highly regarded GAD restaurant.

🍴 Eating

Most restaurants in Varkala offer a similar traveller menu of Indian, Asian and Western fare but these days some of the cliffside 'shacks' are impressive multilevel hang-outs and most offer free wi-fi and espresso coffee. Join in the nightly Varkala saunter till you find a place that suits.

Coffee Temple
CAFE **$**

(coffee ₹80-110, mains ₹80-350; ⏰ 6am-8pm; 📶) For your early morning coffee fix it's hard to beat this place at the start of the North Cliff trail, where the beans are freshly ground, there's fresh bread and a daily paper. The menu also features crêpes, baguettes and Mexican burritos, fajitas and tacos.

Sreepadman
SOUTH INDIAN **$**

(thalis ₹80; ⏰ 5am-10pm) For cheap and authentic Keralan fare – think dosas and thalis – in a spot where you can rub shoulders with rickshaw drivers and pilgrims rather than tourists, pull up a seat at Sreepadman, opposite the Janardhana Temple and overlooking the large bathing tank.

Juice Shack
MULTICUISINE **$**

(juices from ₹80, mains ₹80-300; ⏰ 7am-11.30pm; 📶) The Juice Shack has moved into less shack-like premises (after the old one burnt down) but still turns out great health juices, smoothies and now has a full menu including good breakfast choices.

Oottupura Vegetarian Restaurant
SOUTH INDIAN **$**

(mains ₹40-180; ⏰ 7am-10pm) Near the taxi stand, this budget eatery has a respectable range of cheap veg dishes, including breakfast *puttu* (flour with milk, bananas and honey) and a good thali (₹100).

God's Own Country Kitchen
MULTICUISINE **$$**

(North Cliff; mains ₹100-500; ⏰ 7am-11pm; 📶) This fun place doesn't really need to play on Kerala Tourism's tagline in its name – the food is good, there's a great little upper-floor deck and there's live music some nights in season.

Trattorias
MULTICUISINE **$$**

(meals ₹100-400; ⏰ 8.30am-11pm) Trattorias sounds Italian and has a decent range of pasta and pizza, but the menu is equally pan-Asian and Indian and the food consistently good. This was one of the original places here with an Italian coffee machine, and the wicker chairs and sea-facing terrace are cosy.

Café del Mar
MULTICUISINE **$$**

(mains ₹100-420; ⏰ 7am-11pm; 📶) It doesn't have the big balcony of some of its neighbours, but Café del Mar is usually busy thanks to efficient service, decent coffee and consistently good food.

Wait n Watch
INDIAN **$$**

(Hindustan Beach Retreat; mains ₹120-280; ⏰ 11am-10.30pm; 📶) The top-floor restaurant

AYURVEDA

With its roots in Sanskrit, the word ayurveda comes from *ayu* (life) and *veda* (knowledge); the knowledge or science of life. Principles of ayurvedic medicine were first documented in the Vedas some 2000 years ago, but may have been practised centuries earlier.

Ayurveda sees the world as having an intrinsic order and balance. It argues that we possess three *doshas* (humours): *vata* (wind or air); *pitta* (fire); and *kapha* (water/earth), known together as the *tridoshas*. Deficiency or excess in any of them can result in disease: an excess of *vata* may result in dizziness and debility; an increase in *pitta* may lead to fever, inflammation and infection. *Kapha* is essential for hydration.

Ayurvedic treatment aims to restore the balance, and hence good health, principally through two methods: panchakarma (internal purification) and herbal massage. Panchakarma is used to treat serious ailments, and is an intense detox regime, a combination of five types of different therapies to rid the body of built-up endotoxins. These include: *vaman* – therapeutic vomiting; *virechan* – purgation; *vasti* – enemas; *nasya* – elimination of toxins through the nose; and *raktamoksha* – detoxification of the blood. Before panchakarma begins, the body is first prepared over several days with a special diet, oil massages *(snehana)* and herbal steam-baths *(swedana)*. Although it may sound pretty grim, panchakarma purification might only use a few of these treatments at a time, with therapies like bloodletting and leeches only used in rare cases. Still, this is no spa holiday. The herbs used in ayurveda grow in abundance in Kerala's humid climate – the monsoon is thought to be the best time of year for treatment, when there is less dust in the air, the pores are open and the body is most receptive to treatment – and every village has its own ayurvedic pharmacy.

and bar at this ugly beachfront hotel block offers tasty-enough Indian fare and seafood, but the main reason to take the elevator is for the view from the balcony (with just a few tables) over the action of the beach. There's another alfresco restaurant by the pool.

ℹ️ Information

An **ATM** (⏰ 24hr) at Temple Junction takes Visa cards; more ATMs and banks in Varkala town.

DANGERS & ANNOYANCES

The beaches at Varkala have strong currents; even experienced swimmers have been swept away. During the monsoon the beach all but disappears, and the cliffs themselves are slowly being eroded. Take care walking on the cliff path, especially at night – some of it is unfenced and it can be slippery in parts.

If women wear bikinis or even swimsuits on the main beach at Varkala, they are likely to feel uncomfortably exposed to stares. Wearing a sarong when out of the water will help avoid offending local sensibilities. Dress conservatively if going into Varkala town.

ℹ️ Getting There & Away

There are frequent local and express trains to Trivandrum (2nd class/sleeper/3AC ₹45/140/490, one hour) and Kollam (₹45/140/490, 40 minutes), as well as seven daily services to Alleppey (₹95/140/490, two hours).

Varkala is off the main highway and the main bus stand is buried in Varkala town; there are frequent buses to Trivandrum and seven daily to Kollam. If you can time it right, three daily buses pass by Temple Junction on their way to Trivandrum (₹65, 1½ to two hours), with one heading to Kollam (₹45, one hour).

If you're opting for a taxi or autorickshaw to Kollam (₹600), Trivandrum or Kovalam (both ₹1300), ask for the scenic coast road rather than the highway.

ℹ️ Getting Around

It's about 3km from the train station to Varkala beach, with autorickshaws going to Temple Junction for ₹80 and North Cliff for ₹100. Taxis and autorickshaws gather at the helipad at the North Cliff and at a stand near the Janardhana Temple. Local buses also travel regularly between the train station and Temple Junction (₹8).

A few places along the cliff hire out scooters/motorbikes for ₹350/450 per day.

Kollam (Quilon)

🔲 0474 / POP 349,000

Kollam (Quilon) is the southern approach to Kerala's backwaters and one end of the popular backwater ferry trip to Alleppey. One of the oldest ports in the Arabian Sea, it was once a major commercial hub that saw Roman, Arab, Chinese and later Portuguese,

Kollam (Quilon)

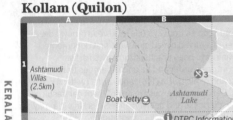

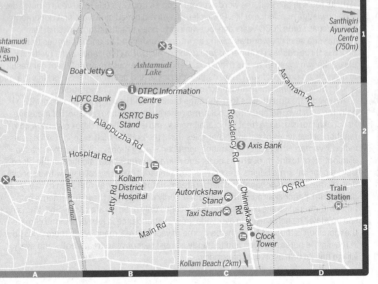

Kollam (Quilon)

Sleeping
- 1 Hotel Sudarsan B2
- 2 Nani Hotel C3

Eating
- 3 8 Point Art Cafe....................................B1
- Prasadam......................................(see 2)
- 4 Wok & Grill A2

Dutch and British traders jostle into port – eager to get their hands on spices and the region's cashew crops. The centre of town is reasonably hectic, but surrounding it are the calm waterways of Ashtamudi Lake, fringed with coconut palms, cashew plantations and traditional villages – a great place to get a feel for the backwaters without the crowds.

Sights

There's a rowdy fish market and harbour north of **Kollam Beach** where customers and fisherfolk alike pontificate on the value of the day's catch. Kollam's beach is 2km south of town but there are better stretches of sand further south at Eravipuram and Mayyanad. The northern end of the harbour is marked by the **Thangassery Lighthouse** (₹10, lift Indian/ foreigner ₹20/50; ⊙10am-1pm & 2-6pm Tue-Sun).

Activities

★ Munroe Island Cruise   BOATING
(www.dtpckollam.com; tours per person ₹500; ⊙9am-1.30pm & 2-6.30pm) Excellent tours through the canals of Munroe Island are organised by the DTPC (p281) and a number of private operators, including Ashtamudi Villas and Munroe Island Backwaters Homestay. The trip begins about 15km north of Kollam, where you take a leisurely three-hour punted canoe ride through a network of canals.

On the canals you can observe daily village life, see *kettuvallam* (rice barge) construction, toddy (palm beer) tapping, coir-making, prawn and fish farming, and do some birdwatching on spice-garden visits.

Houseboat Cruises   BOATING
(www.dtpckollam.com; overnight cruise ₹9200, Kollam-Alleppey cruise ₹20,000-28,000) Kollam has far fewer houseboats than Alleppey, which can mean a less touristy experience. The DTPC organises various houseboat cruise packages, along with two private operators with offices at the jetty who also offers trips from Kollam to Alleppey.

Santhigiri Ayurveda Centre   AYURVEDA
(☏9287242407, 0474-2763014; www.santhigiri ashram.com; Asramam Rd, Kadappakada; massage from ₹1200) An ayurvedic centre with more

of an institutional than a spa vibe, popular for its seven- to 21-day treatment packages.

✲ Festivals & Events

The Kollam region hosts many festivals and boat regattas – from November to March there are temple festivals somewhere in the region virtually every day.

Kottamkulangara
Chamaya Vilakku   RELIGIOUS
(☻Mar/Apr) An unusual festival event in Chavara, 15km north of Kollam, where local men dress as women and carry lamps to the temple.

Kollam Pooram   CULTURAL
(Asraman Shri Krishna Swami Temple, Kollam; ☻Apr) A 10-day festival with full-night Kathakali performances and a procession of 40 ornamented elephants.

President's Trophy Boat Race   SPORTS
(☻1 Nov) Held on Ashtamudi Lake, this is the most prestigious boat regatta in the Kollam region.

🛏 Sleeping

Munroe Island
Backwaters Homestay   HOMESTAY $
(☑9048176186; Chittamula Rd, Munroe Island; d incl breakfast ₹1200; 🛜) The three colourful cottages built in Keralan style and hidden away in the backwaters of Munroe Island north of Kollam are popular with travellers wanting to immerse themselves in the village experience. Vijeesh and his friendly family also run backwater canoe tours (₹450 per person).

Hotel Sudarsan   BUSINESS HOTEL $
(☑0474-2744322; www.hotelsudarsan.com; Hospital Rd; d ₹950, with AC from ₹1900, ste ₹3500; 🌢🛜) Sudarsan is well located near the boat jetty and surprisingly good value. Rooms are arranged around a central courtyard with the Kedar Restaurant and Golden Tavern beer parlour on-site. The suite rooms are particularly spacious.

★ Ashtamudi Villas   GUESTHOUSE $$
(☑9847132449, 0474-2706090; www.ashtamudivillas.com; near Kadavoor Church, Mathilil; d/f ₹1500/2500; 🛜) These charming lakeside cottages are easily the best choice for a relaxing, affordable stay in Kollam. Host Prabhath Joseph offers a warm welcome, with thoughtful architectural design, colourful decor, gleaming bathrooms, hammocks swinging between palm trees by the lake

and a library of books on Kerala. Free kayaks are available, and canoe tours of Munroe Island can be organised from here.

Access is by road or boat – call ahead for directions.

Nani Hotel   HOTEL $$
(☑0474-2751141; www.hotelnani.com; Chinnakkada Rd; d incl breakfast ₹1460, with AC ₹2250-3650, ste ₹7800; 🌢@🛜) This boutique business hotel is a good-value surprise in Kollam's chaotic centre. Built by a cashew magnate, its beautifully designed architecture mixes traditional Keralan elements and modern lines for a sleek look. Even the cheaper rooms have flat-screen TVs, feathery pillows and sumptuous bathrooms.

🍴 Eating

★ 8 Point Art Cafe   CAFE $
(☑0474-2970256; mains ₹70-190; ☻11.30am-9pm) On the fun side of Ashtamudi Lake, this excellent cafe in a restored heritage building is part local art gallery, part trendy hang-out, with changing free exhibitions, good coffee, soups, pasta and a small library.

Wok & Grill   ASIAN $$
(☑0474-2753400; High School Junction Rd; mains ₹185-290; ☻noon-10.30pm) The combination of Indian, Chinese, Thai, Arabic and Chettinad cuisines offers some tasty, meaty dishes at this modern, clean restaurant. Choose from *kung pao* chicken, green curry, ginger garlic prawns and shawarma rolls.

Prasadam   MULTICUISINE $$
(☑0474-2751141; Chinnakkada Rd, Nani Hotel; mains ₹160-280, lunch thali ₹160; ☻noon-2.30pm & 7-10pm) The restaurant at the Nani Hotel has a slightly formal feel with high-backed chairs amid intricate copper-relief artwork depicting Kollam history. Meals, including Keralan dishes, tandoori and Chinese, are well prepared, and the tasty thalis are good value at lunchtime.

ℹ Information

DTPC Information Centre (☑0474-2745625; www.dtpckollam.com; ☻8am-7pm) Helpful and can organise backwater trips and yoga classes; opposite the KSRTC bus stand near the boat jetty.

ℹ Getting There & Away

BOAT
Many travellers take the government canal boat to or from Alleppey (₹400, eight hours,

10.30am); it's not necessary to book, but be at the ferry dock by 9.30am. From the main boat jetty there are frequent public ferry services across Ashtamudi Lake to Guhanandapuram (one hour). Fares are around ₹10 return, or ₹3 for a short hop.

BUS

Kollam is on the Trivandrum–Kollam–Alleppey–Ernakulam bus route, with buses departing every 10 or 20 minutes to Trivandrum (₹84, two hours), Alleppey (₹80, 2½ hours) and Ernakulam (Kochi, standard/AC ₹122/225, 3½ hours). There's a 5am bus to Kumily (₹125, five hours) and a handful of local buses to Varkala (₹40, 30 minutes), though the train is a better option for Varkala.

Buses depart from the **KSRTC bus stand** (☑ 0474-2752008), conveniently near the boat jetty.

TRAIN

There are frequent express trains to Ernakulam (sleeper/3AC ₹140/490, three hours, 20 daily) via Alleppey (₹140/490, 1½ hours) and Trivandrum (₹140/490, 1½ hours, 21 daily) via Varkala (₹140/490, 30 minutes).

Around Kollam

Krishnapuram Palace Museum   MUSEUM
(☑ 0479-2441133;   ₹10,   camera/video ₹25/250;
☺ 9.30am-4.30pm   Tue-Sun)   Two kilometres
south of Kayamkulam (between Kollam and Alleppey), this restored palace is a fine example of grand Keralan architecture. Inside are paintings, antique furniture, sculptures and a renowned 3m-high mural depicting the Gajendra Moksha (the liberation of Gajendra, chief of the elephants) as told in the Mahabharata.

Buses (₹27, one hour) leave Kollam every few minutes for Kayamkulam. Get off at the bus stand near the temple gate, 2km before the palace.

Alappuzha (Alleppey)
☑ 0477 / POP 74,200

Alappuzha – most still call it Alleppey – is the hub of Kerala's backwaters, home to a vast network of waterways and more than a thousand houseboats. Wandering around the small but chaotic city centre and bus-stand area, with its modest grid of canals, you'd be hard-pressed to agree with the 'Venice of the East' tag. But head west to the beach or in practically any other direction towards the backwaters and Alleppey becomes graceful and greenery-fringed, disappearing into a watery world of villages, punted canoes, toddy shops and, of course, houseboats. Float along and gaze over paddy fields of succulent green, curvaceous rice barges and village life along

---

MATHA AMRITHANANDAMAYI MISSION

The incongruously pink Matha Amrithanandamayi Mission (☑ 0476-2897578; www.amritapuri.org; Amrithapuri) is the famous ashram of one of India's few female gurus, Amrithanandamayi, also known as Amma (Mother) or 'The Hugging Mother' because of the *darshan* (audience) she offers, often hugging thousands of people in marathon all-night sessions. The ashram runs official tours at 4pm and 5pm daily – check the website or download the Amma app for details.

It's a huge complex, with about 3500 people living here permanently – monks, nuns, students and families, both Indian and foreign. It offers food, ayurvedic treatments, and a daily schedule of yoga, meditation and *darshan*. Amma travels around for much of the year, so you might be out of luck if in need of a cuddle (check her schedule online). A busy time of year at the ashram is around Amma's birthday on 27 September.

Visitors should dress conservatively and there is a strict code of behaviour. With prior arrangement – register online – you can stay at the ashram in a triple room for ₹250 per person, ₹500 for a single (including simple vegetarian meals).

Since the ashram is on the main canal between Kollam and Alleppey, many travellers break the ferry ride by getting off here, staying a day or two, then picking up another cruise. Alternatively, cross to the other side of the canal and grab a rickshaw 10km south to Karunagappally or 12km north to Kayankulam (around ₹200), from where you can catch onward buses or trains.

If you're not taking the cruise, catch a train to either Karunagappally or Kayankulam and take an autorickshaw (around ₹200) to Vallickavu and cross the pedestrian bridge from there. If you intend to stay a while, you can book online for an ashram taxi – they pick up from as far away as Kochi or Trivandrum.

the banks. This is one of Kerala's most mesmerisingly beautiful and relaxing experiences.

● Sights

Alleppey Beach BEACH
Alleppey's main beach is about 2km west of the city centre; there's no shelter at the beach itself and swimming is fraught due to strong currents, but the sunsets are good and there are a few places to stop for a drink or snack, including a good coffeeshop. The beach stretches up and down the coast.

Alleppey Lighthouse LIGHTHOUSE
(Indian/foreigner ₹10/25, camera/video ₹20/25; ☺ 9-11.45am & 2-5.30pm Tue-Sun) The candy-striped lighthouse is a few blocks back from the beach. There's a small museum containing an original oil lamp and you can climb to the top via the spiralling staircase for 360-degree views of a surprisingly green Alleppey.

RKK Memorial Museum MUSEUM
(☎ 0477-2242923; www.rkkmuseum.com; NH47, near Powerhouse Bridge; Indian/foreigner ₹150/350; ☺ 9am-5pm Tue-Sun) The Revi Karuna Karan (RKK) Memorial Museum, in a grand building fronted by Greco-Roman columns, contains a lavish collection of crystal, porcelain, Keralan antiques, furniture, artworks and (sadly) ivory from the personal collection of wealthy businessman Revi Karuna Karan. The museum was created as a memorial after he passed away in 2003.

🏃 Activities

Kerala Kayaking KAYAKING
(☎ 9846585674, 8547487701; www.keralakayaking.com; per person 4/7/10hr ₹1500/3000/4500) The original and best kayaking outfit in Alleppey. The young crew here offer excellent guided kayaking trips through narrow backwater canals. Paddles in single or double kayaks include a support boat and motorboat transport to your starting point. There are four-hour morning and afternoon trips, seven- or 10-hour day trips, and multiday village tours can also be arranged.

Houseboat Dock BOATING
(dtpcaly@yahoo.com; ☺ prepaid counter 10am-5pm) Where dozens of houseboats gather; this is a good place to wander down and compare a few. There's a government-run prepaid counter where you can see the 'official' posted prices, starting at ₹7000 for two people, up to ₹24,000 for a five-berth boat. Even these prices fluctuate depending on demand.

Shree Krishna Ayurveda Panchkarma Centre AYURVEDA
(☎ 9847119060; www.krishnayurveda.com; 3-/5-/7-day treatments from €275/420/590) For ayurvedic treatments; one-hour rejuvenation massages are ₹1200, but it specialises in three-, five- and seven-night packages with accommodation and yoga classes. Rates are cheaper with two people sharing accommodation. It's near the Nehru boat race finishing point.

☞ Tours
Any guesthouse, hotel, travel agent or the DTPC can and will arrange canoe or houseboat tours of the backwaters.

Kashmiri-style *shikaras* (covered boats) gather along the North Canal on the road to the houseboat dock. They charge ₹300 to ₹400 per hour for motorised canal and backwater trips. Punt-powered dugout canoes are slower but more ecofriendly. They charge from ₹250 per hour and most tours require four to five hours, with village visits, walks and a visit to a toddy bar.

It can be hard to get a good seat for the Nehru Trophy Boat Race, but for the best seat in the house check out Johnson's Houseboat at www.alleppeysnakeboatrace.com.

🎊 Festivals & Events

Nehru Trophy Boat Race SPORTS
(www.nehrutrophy.nic.in; tickets ₹50-2000; ☺ Aug) This is the most renowned and fiercely contested of Kerala's boat-race regattas. Thousands of people, many aboard houseboats, gather around the starting and finishing points on Alleppey's Punnamada Lake to watch snake boats with up to 100 rowers battle it out.

🛏 Sleeping
Even if you're not planning on boarding a houseboat, Alleppey has some of Kerala's most charming and best-value accommodation, from heritage homes and resorts to family-run homestays with backwater views.

The rickshaw-commission racketeers are at work here, particularly at the train and bus stations; ask to be dropped off at a landmark close to your destination, or if you're booked in, call ahead to say you're on the way – some places will pick you up.

Matthews Residency GUESTHOUSE $
(☎ 9447667888, 0477-2235938; www.palmyresidency.com; off Finishing Point Rd; r ₹450-800; @ 🛜) One of the better budget deals in

Alappuzha (Alleppey)

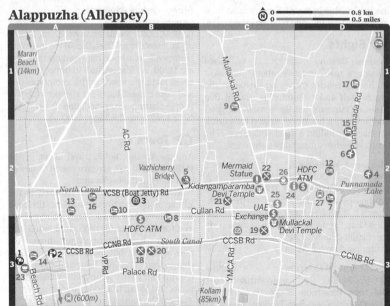

Alappuzha (Alleppey)

Alleppey, this place has six spotless rooms with Italian marble floors, three with garden-facing verandahs. It's north of the canal, five minutes' walk from the bus stand but set well back from the road amid lush greenery.

Johnson's GUESTHOUSE $
(☑ 9846466399, 0477-2245825; www.johnsons-kerala.com; d ₹800-1200, with AC ₹1850; ❄@🤶) This longtime backpacker favourite in a quirky two-storey home is run by the gregarious Johnson Gilbert. It's a rambling res-

idence with themed rooms filled with funky furniture, hanging chairs, outdoor bathtubs and a garden with open-air barbecue and pet horse. Johnson also has an excellent 'eco-houseboat' (www.ecohouseboat.com; ₹8000 to ₹13,000) – book ahead for a spot at the Nehru boat race.

Nanni Backpackers Hostel HOSTEL $
(☑9895039767; www.nannitours.com; Cullan Rd; dm/d ₹250/700) A very good deal, this easy-going backpacker place is a short walk from the beach and 1.5km north of the train station. There are two six-bed dorms and some spacious private rooms upstairs, along with a street cafe and a rooftop lounge. Young owner Shibu is a good source of local information and scooter hire, and works hard at making the place homely.

Vedanta Wake Up! HOSTEL $
(☑0477-2231132; www.vedantawakeup.com; Punnamada Rd; dm ₹400, d with AC from ₹1400; ❀ 🛜) In a quiet location just north of the houseboat dock, this hostel has clean air-con dorms, cosy common areas, a cafe and the usual extras like lockers and wi-fi. It's a good place to meet other travellers, especially if you're looking to get a houseboat group together.

Dream Nest GUESTHOUSE $
(☑9895860716; www.thedreamnest.com; Cullan Rd; d ₹500-900, with AC ₹1200; ❀ 🛜) The colourful rooms set back from the road are a good deal at this budget guesthouse. There's a social communal lounge and a youthful traveller vibe.

Cherukara Nest HOMESTAY $$
(☑0477-2251509, 9947059628; www.cherukara nest.com; d/tr incl breakfast ₹900/1200, with AC ₹1500, AC cottage ₹1500; ❀ @ 🛜) Set in well-tended gardens, this lovely heritage home has the sort of welcoming family atmosphere that makes you want to stay. In the main house there are four large characterful rooms, with high ceilings, lots of polished wood touches and antediluvian doors with ornate locks. Owner Tony also has a good-value houseboat (two/four people ₹6000/8500) and organises village tours (₹900).

Tharavad HOMESTAY $$
(☑0477-242044; www.tharavadheritageresort. com; west of North Police Station; d ₹2500-3500; ❀ 🛜) In a quiet canalside location between the town centre and beach, this charming ancestral home has lots of glossy teak and

antiques, shuttered windows, five characterful rooms and well-maintained gardens.

Malayalam RESORT $$
(☑9496829424, 0477-2234591; malayalamresorts @yahoo.com; Punnamada; r ₹1500-2500; 🛜) This little family-run pad has bamboo cottages and a pair of spacious two-storey four-room houses facing the lake near the Nehru Trophy Boat Race starting point. Views from the upstairs rooms with balcony are sweet. It's a bit hard to find: walk past the Keraleeyam resort reception and along the canal bank.

Canoe Ville COTTAGE $$
(☑9895213162; http://canoeville.com; d cottage incl meals ₹3500) This quirky lakefront place 5km north of Alleppey has created artificial canals and floating mini houseboat cottages for a 'houseboat on land' experience. The comfortable double cottages have attached bath, large verandah and come with meals, free hammocks and activities such as bamboo rafting. There are plans to add budget safari tents (per person ₹500).

Punnamada Homestay HOMESTAY $$
(☑0484-2371761, 9847044688; d incl breakfast & dinner ₹3000; 🛜) This attractive heritage-style family home is north of Alleppey in a peaceful location close to Punnamada Lake. The two rooms are neat, well-furnished, and have private balconies, and the home cooking is first-rate.

Sona Heritage Home GUESTHOUSE $$
(☑0477-2235211; www.sonahome.com; Lakeside, Finishing Point; r ₹900, with AC ₹1400; ❀ 🛜) Run by the affable Joseph, this beautiful old heritage home has high-ceilinged rooms with faded flowered curtains, Christian motifs and four-poster beds overlooking a well-kept garden.

Gowri Residence GUESTHOUSE $$
(☑0477-2236371, 9847055371; www.gowriresidence. com; Mullackall Rd; d ₹600-1200, AC cottages ₹1500-2000; ❀ 🛜) This rambling complex about 800m north of the North Canal has an array of rooms and cottages in a large garden: traditional wood-panelled rooms in the main house, and several types of bungalows made from stone, wood, bamboo or thatch – the best have cathedral ceilings, air-con and flat-screen TVs. Overall the place is looking a little faded.

★Raheem Residency HOTEL $$$
(☑0477-2239767; www.raheemresidency.com; Beach Rd; d ₹9600-12,500; ❀ 🛜 🌊) This thoughtfully renovated beachside 1860s heritage home is a

BOATING KERALA'S BACKWATERS

The undisputed highlight of a trip to Kerala is travelling through the 900km network of waterways that fringe the coast and trickle inland. Long before the advent of roads, these waters were the slippery highways of Kerala, and many villagers still use paddle-power as their main form of transport. Trips through the backwaters traverse palm-fringed lakes studded with cantilevered Chinese fishing nets, and wind their way along narrow, shady canals where coir (coconut fibre), copra (dried coconut kernels) and cashews are loaded onto boats. Along the way are isolated villages where farming life continues as it has for eons.

Tourist Cruises

The popular tourist cruise between Kollam and Alleppey (₹400) departs from either end at 10.30am, arriving at 6.30pm, daily from July to March and every second day at other times, though it may start running later in the season. Generally, there's a 1pm lunch stop and a brief afternoon chai stop. Bring drinks, snacks, sunscreen, a hat and a good book.

It's a scenic and leisurely way – the journey takes eight hours – to get between the two towns, but the boat travels along only the major canals – you won't have many close-up views of the village life that makes the backwaters so magical. Another option is to take the trip halfway (₹200) and get off at the Matha Amrithanandamayi Mission (p282).

Houseboats

If the stars align, renting a houseboat designed like a *kettuvallam* (rice barge) could well be one of the highlights of your trip to India. It can be an expensive experience (depending on your budget) but for a couple on a romantic overnight jaunt or split between a group of travellers, it's usually worth every rupee. Drifting through quiet canals lined with coconut palms, eating delicious Keralan food, meeting local villagers and sleeping on the water – it's a world away from the usual clamour of India.

Houseboats cater for couples (one or two double bedrooms) and groups (up to seven bedrooms!). Food (and an onboard chef to cook it) is generally included in the quoted cost, as is a driver/captain. Houseboats can be chartered through a multitude of private operators in Alleppey, Kollam and Kottayam. This is the biggest business in Kerala and the quality of boats varies widely, from ageing boats to floating palaces – try to inspect the boat before agreeing on a price. Travel-agency reps will be pushing you to book a boat as soon as you set foot in Kerala, but it's better to wait till you reach a backwater hub: choice is greater in Alleppey (an extraordinary 1000-plus boats), and you're much more likely to be able to bargain down a price if you turn up and see what's on offer. Most guesthouses and homestays can also book you on a houseboat.

---

joy. The 10 rooms have been restored to their former glory by owner and Irish personality Bibi Baskin and have bathtubs, antique furniture and period fixtures. The common areas include pretty indoor courtyards, a great pool and an excellent restaurant.

✖ Eating & Drinking

★ **Mushroom**   ARABIAN, INDIAN $
(CCSB Rd; mains ₹70-150; ⊙noon-midnight) A breezy open-air restaurant with wrought-iron chairs, specialising in cheap, tasty and spicy halal meals like chicken *kali mirch*, fish tandoori and chilli mushrooms. Lots of locals and travellers give it a good vibe.

Kream Korner Art Cafe   MULTICUISINE $
(☑0477-2260005; www.kreamkornerartcafe.com; Mullackal Rd; dishes ₹40-160; ⊙9am-10pm) The most colourful dining space in town, this food-meets-art restaurant greets you with brightly painted tables and contemporary local art on the walls. It's a relaxed, airy place popular with Indian and foreign families for its inexpensive and tasty menu of Indian and Chinese dishes.

Thaff   INDIAN $
(VCNB Rd; meals ₹45-120; ⊙9am-9pm Sun-Thu, 9am-10pm Sat & Sun) This popular restaurant serves tasty South Indian bites, with some North Indian and Chinese flavours mixed in. It does succulent roast spit-chicken, biryanis and brain-freezing ice-cream shakes.

Halais   INDIAN, ARABIAN $$
(☑9447053338; www.halaisrestaurant.com; mains ₹70-400, biryani from ₹170; ⊙24hr) Famous for its chicken and mutton biryanis, Halais

In the busy high season or during domestic holidays (such as Pooja, Onam or Diwali) when prices peak, you're likely to get caught in backwater-gridlock – some travellers are disappointed by the number of boats on the water. It's possible to travel by houseboat between Alleppey and Kollam and part way to Kochi – though these trips spend more time on open lakes and large canals than true backwaters and take longer than most travellers expect. Expect a boat for two people for 24 hours to cost about ₹6000 to ₹8000 at the budget level; for four people ₹10,000 to ₹12,000; for larger boats or for air-conditioning expect to pay ₹15,000 to ₹30,000. Shop around to negotiate a bargain – though this will be harder in the peak season. Prices triple from around 20 December to 5 January.

Village Tours & Canoe Boats

Village tours are an excellent way to see the backwaters at a slow pace by day. Village tours usually involve small groups of five to six people, a knowledgable guide and an open canoe or covered *kettuvallam*. The tours (from Kochi, Kollam or Alleppey) last 2½ to six hours and cost around ₹400 to ₹1000 per person. They include visits to villages to watch coir-making, boat building, toddy (palm beer) tapping and fish farming. The Munroe Island trip from Kollam is an excellent tour of this type; the Tourist Desk (p303) in Kochi also organises recommended tours.

Public Ferries

If you want the local backwater transport experience for just a few rupees, there are State Water Transport (www.swtd.gov.in) boats between Alleppey and Kottayam (₹15, 2½ hours) five times daily starting from Alleppey at 7.30am. The trip crosses Vembanad Lake and has a more varied landscape than the Kollam–Alleppey cruise. Other ageing boats operate from the boat jetty at Alleppey, ferrying locals around to backwater villages.

Environmental Issues

Pollution from houseboat motors is becoming a major problem as boat numbers increase. The Keralan authorities have introduced an ecofriendly and safety accreditation system for houseboat operators. Among the criteria an operator must meet before being issued with the Gold Star, Silver Star or Green Palm certificate are the installation of solar panels and sanitary tanks for the disposal of waste – ask operators whether they have the requisite certification. Consider choosing one of the few remaining punting, rather than motorised, boats if possible, though these can only operate in shallow water.

packs them in at this clean restaurant behind the street-front sweet shop. It's also popular for Arabian and Yemeni dishes.

Harbour Restaurant   MULTICUISINE $$
(☑0484-2230767; Beach Rd; meals ₹110-300; ☺10am-10pm) This enjoyable beachside place is run by the nearby Raheem Residency. It's more casual and budget-conscious than the hotel's restaurant, but promises a range of well-prepared Indian, Chinese and Continental dishes, and the coldest beer in town.

Royale Park Hotel   INDIAN $$
(YMCA Rd; meals ₹130-310; ☺7am-10.30pm, bar from 10am; ☎) There's an extensive menu at this air-con hotel restaurant, and the food, including veg and fish thalis, is consistently good. You can order from the same menu

in the surprisingly nice upstairs beer parlour and wash down your meal with a cold Kingfisher.

★Chakara Restaurant   MULTICUISINE $$$
(☑0477-2230767; Beach Rd; mini Kerala meal ₹500, mains from ₹450; ☺12.30-3pm & 7-10pm) The restaurant at Raheem Residency is Alleppey's finest, with seating on a bijou open rooftop, reached via a spiral staircase, with views over to the beach. The menu creatively combines traditional Keralan and European cuisine, specialising in locally caught fish.

Le Coffee Time   CAFE
(Alleppey Beach; coffee & snacks ₹70-150; ☺8am-9pm; ☎) A friendly beachfront place with a genuine Italian espresso machine, some shady tables, good breakfasts and free wi-fi.

GREEN PALM HOMES

Around 12km from Alleppey on a back-water island, **Green Palm Homes** (☑9495557675, 0477-2724497; www.greenpalmhomes.com; Chennamkary; r incl full board ₹3500-5000; ❄) is a series of homestays in a picturesque village, where you sleep in simple rooms in villagers' homes among rice paddies (though 'premium' rooms with attached bathroom and air-con are available). There are no roads but you can take a guided walk, hire bicycles or canoes and take cooking classes.

To get here, call ahead and catch one of the hourly ferries from Alleppey to Chennamkary (₹10, 1¼ hours).

❶ Information

DTPC Tourist Reception Centre (☑0477-2253308; www.dtpcalappuzha.com; Boat Jetty Rd; ⊙9am-5pm) Close to the bus stand and boat jetty. Staff can advise on local tours.
Tourist Police (☑0477-2251161; ⊙24hr) Next door to the DTPC Tourist Reception Centre.

❶ Getting There & Away

BOAT
Ferries run to Kottayam (₹15) and daily at 10am to Kollam (₹400) from the boat jetty on VCSB (Boat Jetty) Rd.

BUS
From the KSRTC bus stand, frequent buses head to Trivandrum (₹132, 3½ hours, every 20 minutes), Kollam (₹73, 2½ hours) and Ernakulam (Kochi; ₹55, 1½ hours). Buses to Kottayam (₹40, 1¼ hours, every 30 minutes) are much faster than the ferry. Three buses leave for Kumily at 6.40am, 1.10pm and 2.50pm (₹126, 5½ hours) and Munnar at 4.30am, 7am and 2pm (₹132, five hours). The Varkala bus (₹90, 3½ hours) leaves daily at 8.15am, 8.45am and 10.40am.

TRAIN
There are numerous daily trains to Ernakulam (2nd class/sleeper/3AC ₹50/140/490, 1½ hours) and Trivandrum (₹80/140/490, three hours) via Kollam (₹60/140/490, 1½ hours). Six trains a day stop at Varkala (2nd class/AC chair ₹65/260, two hours). The train station is 4km southwest of town.

❶ Getting Around

An autorickshaw from the train station to the boat jetty and KSRTC bus stand is around ₹60.

Several guesthouses around town hire out scooters for ₹300 per day, or try the reliable **Nanni Tours & Travel** (☑9895039767; Cullan Rd).

Around Alleppey

Kattoor & Marari Beaches

The beaches at Kattoor and Marari, 10km and 14km north of Alleppey respectively, are popular beachside alternatives to the backwaters.

Marari is the flashier of the two, with some exclusive five-star beachfront accommodation, while Kattoor, sometimes known as 'Secret Beach', is more of a fishing village, where development is at a minimum and sandy back lanes lead down to near-deserted sands.

🛏 Sleeping

⭐ **Secret Beach Yoga Homestay**   HOMESTAY $
(☑9447786931; www.secretbeach.in; Kattoor Beach; d ₹1000-1500; ☎) The location is sublime at this three-room homestay, with a small lagoon separating the property from a near-deserted piece of Kattoor Beach; get here by floating mat or walking through the village. Home-cooked meals are available and the talented and welcoming young owner Vimal is an accredited yoga and *kalari* instructor; yoga lessons and free bikes available.

A Beach Symphony   COTTAGE $$$
(☑9744297123; www.abeachsymphony.com; cottages ₹14,000-17,900; ⊙Sep-May; ❄☎☀) With just four individually designed cottages at the main beach entrance, this is one of Marari's most exclusive beachfront resorts. The Keralan-style cottages are plush and private – Violin Cottage even has its own plunge pool in a private garden.

Kottayam

☑0481 / POP 335,000

Between the backwaters and the Western Ghats, Kottayam is renowned for being the centre of Kerala's spice and rubber trade, rather than for its aesthetic appeal. For most travellers it's a hub town, well connected to both the mountains and the backwaters, with many travellers taking the public canal cruise to or from Alleppey before heading east to Kumily or north to Kochi. The city itself has an unappealing, crazy, traffic-clogged centre.

🛏 Sleeping

There's enough accommodation in Kottayam to justify a stay if you're coming off the Alleppey ferry, but there are better lakeside stays (at a price) at Kumarakom.

Ambassador Hotel   HOTEL $
(✆ 0481-2563293; ambassadorhotelktm@yahoo. in; KK Rd; s/d from ₹550/950, d with AC from ₹1100; ❇) This old-school place is one of the better budget hotels in the town centre. Rooms with TV are spartan but fairly clean, spacious and quiet for this price. It has a bar, an adequate restaurant and a boat-shaped fish tank in the lobby.

Windsor Castle & Lake Village Resort   HOTEL $$
(✆ 0481-2363637; www.thewindsorcastle.net; MC Rd; s/d from ₹3300/3850, Lake Village cottages ₹6600; ❇ 🛜 🏊) This grandiose white box has some of Kottayam's best hotel rooms, but the more impressive accommodation is in the Lake Village behind the hotel. Deluxe cottages, strewn around the private backwaters and manicured gardens, are top-notch. There's a pleasant restaurant overlooking landscaped waterways.

🍴 Eating

Thali   SOUTH INDIAN $
(KK Rd; meals ₹40-175; ⊙ 8am-8pm) A lovely, spotlessly kept 1st-floor dining room with slatted blinds, Thali is a swankier version of the typical Keralan set-meal place. The food here is great, including Malabar fish curry and thalis.

Meenachil   MULTICUISINE $
(KK Rd; dishes ₹60-180; ⊙ noon-3pm & 6-9.30pm) A favourite place in Kottayam to fill up on Indian and Chinese fare. There's a friendly, family atmosphere, the dining room is modern and tidy, and the menu expansive.

★ Nalekattu   SOUTH INDIAN $$$
(MC Rd, Windsor Hotel; dishes ₹200-550; ⊙ noon-3pm & 7-10pm) This traditional Keralan restaurant at the Windsor Castle overlooks some picturesque backwaters and serves tasty Keralan specialities like *chemeen* (prawn curry). Buffet deals are offered on weekends.

ℹ Information

DTPC office (✆ 0481-2560479; www.dtpckot tayam.com; ⊙ 10am-5pm Mon-Sat) At the boat jetty; has local information and can arrange pricey backwater cruises. Private operators

nearby charge around ₹4000 for a full-day cruise to Alleppey.

ℹ Getting There & Away

BOAT
Daily ferries run to Alleppey from the boat jetty (₹15) five times a day.

BUS
The KSRTC bus stand has buses to Trivandrum (₹127, four hours, every 20 minutes), Alleppey (₹37, 1¼ hours, hourly), Ernakulam (Kochi; ₹60, two hours, every 20 minutes), Kumily for Periyar Wildlife Sanctuary (₹97, four hours, every 30 minutes) and Munnar (₹130, five hours, five daily). There are also frequent buses to nearby Kumarakom (₹9, 30 minutes, every 15 minutes) and to Kollam (₹85, three hours, four daily), where you can change for Varkala.

TRAIN
Kottayam is well served by frequent trains running between Trivandrum (2nd class/sleeper/3AC ₹80/140/490, 3½ hours) and Ernakulam (₹50/140/490, 1½ hours).

ℹ Getting Around

The KSRTC bus stand is 1km south of the centre, with the boat jetty a further 2km (at Kodimatha). An autorickshaw from the jetty to the KSRTC bus stand is around ₹50, and from the bus stand to the train station about ₹40.

Around Kottayam

Kumarakom
✆ 0481
Kumarakom, 16km west of Kottayam and on the shore of vast Vembanad Lake – Kerala's largest lake – is an unhurried backwater village with a smattering of dazzling top-end sleeping options and a renowned bird sanctuary. You can arrange houseboats through Kumarakom's less-crowded canals, but expect to pay considerably more than in Alleppey.

Arundhati Roy, author of the 1997 Booker Prize–winning *The God of Small Things*, was raised in the nearby Aymanam village.

◉ Sights

Kumarakom Bird Sanctuary   NATURE RESERVE
(✆ 0481-2525864; Indian/foreigner ₹50/150; ⊙ 6am-5pm) This reserve on the 5-hectare site of a former rubber plantation on Lake Vembanad is the haunt of a variety of domestic and migratory birds. October to February is the time for travelling birds like the garganey

teal, osprey, marsh harrier and steppey eagle; May to July is the breeding season for local species such as the Indian shag, pond herons, egrets and darters. A guide costs ₹300 for a two-hour tour (₹400 from 6am to 8am).

🛏 Sleeping

Cruise 'N Lake　　　　　　　　RESORT $$
(📞9846036375, 0481-2525804; www.homestay kumarakom.com; Puthenpura Tourist Enclave, Cheerpunkal; d ₹1500, with AC ₹2000; ❄ 🛜) Location, location, location. Surrounded by backwaters on one side and a lawn of rice paddies on the other, this is the affordable Kumarakom getaway. The rooms in two separate buildings are plain but all have verandahs facing the water. Go a couple of kilometres past the sanctuary to Cheerpunkal and take a left; it's then 2km down a rugged dirt road.

Tharavadu Heritage Home　　GUESTHOUSE $$
(📞0481-2525230; www.tharavaduheritage.com; d from ₹1200, with AC ₹2000-2200, bamboo cottage ₹1100; ❄ @) Rooms here are either in the superbly restored 1870s teak family mansion or in equally comfortable individual creekside bamboo cottages. All are excellently crafted and come with arty touches. It's 4km before Kumarakom Bird Sanctuary.

ℹ Getting There & Away

Kumarakom is an easy bus ride from Kottayam (₹15, 30 minutes, every 15 minutes).

Sree Vallabha Temple

Devotees make offerings at **Sree Vallabha Temple**, 2km from Tiruvilla, in the form

SABARIMALA

Deep in the Western Ghats, about 20km west of Gavi and some 50km from the town of Erumeli, is a place called Sabarimala, home to the Ayyappan temple. It's said to be one of the world's most visited pilgrimage centres, with anywhere between 40 and 60 million Hindu devotees trekking here each year. Followers believe the god Ayyappan meditated at this spot. Non-Hindus can join the pilgrimage but strict rules apply, and women aged 12 to 50 are only allowed as far as the Pampa checkpoint. For information see www.sabarimala.kerala.gov.in or www.sabarimala.org.

of regular, traditional all-night Kathakali performances that are open to all. Around 10km east of here, the **Aranmula Boat Race** (near Shri Parthasarathy Temple; ⊘ Aug/Sep), one of Kerala's biggest snake-boat races, is held during Onam in August/September.

THE WESTERN GHATS

Periyar Wildlife Sanctuary

📞04869 / POP KUMILY 30,300

South India's most popular wildlife sanctuary, **Periyar** (📞04869-224571; www.periyartiger reserve.org; Indian/foreigner adult ₹33/450, child ₹5/150, camera/video ₹38/300; ⊘6am-6pm, last entry 5pm), also called Thekkady, encompasses 777 sq km and a 26-sq-km artificial lake created by the British in 1895. The vast region is home to bison, sambar, wild boar, langur, 900 to 1000 elephants and 35 to 40 hard-to-spot tigers. It's firmly established on both the Indian and foreigner tourist trails and has a typical boat cruise that doesn't scream 'wildlife experience', but if you dig deeper and do a trek led by a tribal villager, the hills and jungle scenery make for a rewarding visit. Bring warm and waterproof clothing.

Kumily is the closest town and home to a growing strip of hotels, homestays, spice shops, chocolate shops and Kashmiri emporiums. Thekkady, 4km from Kumily, is the sanctuary centre with the KTDC hotels and boat jetty. Confusingly, when people refer to the sanctuary they tend to use Thekkady, Kumily and Periyar interchangeably.

👁 Sights & Activities

Various tours and trips access Periyar Wildlife Sanctuary, all arranged through the Ecotourism Centre. Most hotels and homestays around town can arrange three-hour jeep **jungle safaris** (per jeep ₹1800), which cover around 40km of trails and viewpoints in jungle bordering the park, though many travellers complain that at least 30km of the trip is on sealed roads.

Connemara Tea Factory　　　　FACTORY
(📞04869-252233; Vandiperiyar; tours ₹150; ⊘tours hourly 9am-4pm) About 13km from Kumily, this 77-year-old working tea factory and plantation offers guided tours of the tea-making process and tea garden, and ends with some tea tastings. Regular buses

from Kumily pass by the entrance; ask to be let off at the tea factory or Vandiperiyar.

Ecotourism Centre OUTDOORS

(☑ 8547603066, 04869-224571; www.periyartiger reserve.org; Thekkady Rd; ⊙ 9am-1pm & 2-5pm) The Forest Department's Ecotourism Centre runs all tours within the park. These include border hikes (₹1000 per person), 2½-hour nature walks (from ₹800), bamboo rafting (₹1500) and night 'jungle scouts' (₹750), accompanied by trained tribal guides. Rates are per person and trips usually require a minimum of four.

There are also overnight 'tiger trail' treks (per person ₹4000), covering 20km to 30km, which are run by former poachers retrained as guides.

Periyar Lake Cruise BOATING

(₹225; ⊙ departures 7.30am, 9.30am, 11.15am, 1.45pm & 3.30pm) These 1½-hour boat trips around the lake are the main way to tour the sanctuary without taking a guided walk. You might see deer, boar, otters and birdlife but it's generally more of a cruise than a wildlife-spotting experience. Boats are operated by the KTDC – you need to buy a ticket from the main building above the boat jetty before boarding the boat.

In high season get to the ticket office 1½ hours before each trip to buy tickets. The first and last departures offer the best prospects for wildlife spotting, and October to March is generally the best time to see animals.

Santhigiri Ayurveda AYURVEDA

(☑ 8113018007, 04869-223979; www.santhigiri ashram.org; Munnar Rd, Vandanmedu Junction; ⊙ 9am-8pm) An authentic place for an ayurvedic experience, offering top-notch massage (₹900 to ₹1800) and long-term treatments lasting seven to 14 days.

Cooking Classes

Cooking classes are offered by many local homestays for around ₹400 to ₹600. There are recommended two-hour classes at Bar-B-Que (☑ 9895613036; KK Rd; ₹500; ⊙ 6.30pm), about 1km from the bazaar on the road to Kottayam.

Spice Plantations

Several spice plantations are open to visitors and most hotels can arrange tours (₹450/750 by autorickshaw/taxi for two to three hours).

Abraham's Spice Garden FARM

(☑ 04869-222919; www.abrahamspice.com; Spring Valley; tours ₹100; ⊙ 7.30am-5.30pm) Abraham's

Spice Garden, 3km from Kumily, is a family-run farm that's been operating for more than 50 years. Informative one-hour tours here take you through the spice gardens.

Spice Walk TOURS

(☑ 04869-222449; www.spicewalk.com; Churakulam Coffee Estate; 1hr tour ₹150; ⊙ 9am-5pm) Part of Churakulam Coffee Estate, Spice Walk is a 44-hectare plantation surrounding a small lake. Informative walks take around one hour and include explanations of coffee and cardamom processing, but there's also fishing and boating and a small cafe at the front. It's 2km from Kumily.

🛏 Sleeping

🛏 Inside the Park

The KTDC runs three steeply priced hotels in the park: Periyar House, Aranya Nivas and the grand Lake Palace. Note that there's effectively a curfew at these places – guests are not permitted to roam the sanctuary after 6pm.

The Ecotourism Centre can arrange tented accommodation inside the park at the Jungle Camp (d incl meals ₹6000). Another option is Bamboo Grove (d incl breakfast ₹1500), a group of basic cottages and tree houses not far from Kumily town.

Lake Palace HOTEL $$$

(☑ 04869-223887; www.lakepalacethekkady.com; r incl all meals ₹24,000-30,000) There's a faint whiff of royalty at this restored old summer palace, located on Periyar Lake and accessible only by boat. The six charismatic rooms are decorated with flair and antique furnishings. Staying in the sanctuary gives you a good chance of seeing wildlife from your private terrace, and rates include meals, boat trip and trekking.

🛏 Kumily

Mickey Homestay GUESTHOUSE $

(☑ 9447284160, 04869-223196; www.mickey homestay.com; Bypass Rd; r & cottages ₹750-1000; ☎) Mickey is a genuine homestay with just a handful of intimate rooms in a family house and a rear cottage, all with homely touches that make them some of the cosiest in town. Balconies have rattan furniture and hanging bamboo seats and the whole place is surrounded by greenery.

KERALA PERIYAR WILDLIFE SANCTUARY

Kumily & Periyar Wildlife Sanctuary

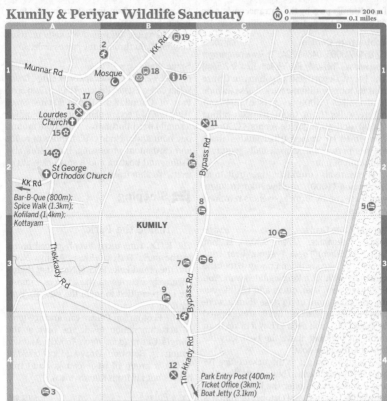

Kumily & Periyar Wildlife Sanctuary

○ Activities, Courses & Tours
1 Ecotourism Centre B4
  Jungle Safaris .... (see 18)
2 Santhigiri Ayurveda B1

⊜ Sleeping
3 Bamboo Grove A4
4 Chrissie's Hotel B2
5 Claus Garden D2
6 El-Paradiso C3
7 Green View Homestay B3
8 Mickey Homestay C2
9 Spice Village B3
10 Tranquilou C3

⊗ Eating
  Chrissie's Cafe .... (see 4)
11 Ebony's Cafe C2

12 French Restaurant & Bakery B4
13 Shri Krishna A1

○ Entertainment
14 Kadathanadan Kalari & Navarasa
    Kathakali Centre A2
15 Mudra Cultural Centre A2

ⓘ Information
16 DTPC Office B1
  Ecotourism Centre .... (see 1)
17 Federal Bank ATM A1

ⓘ Transport
18 Kumily Bus Stand B1
19 Tamil Nadu Bus Stand B1

Tranquilou HOMESTAY **$**
(☏ 04869-223269; off Bypass Rd; r incl breakfast ₹600-1200; ⛱) One of Kumily's friendly, fam-

ily homestays, Tranquilou is in a peaceful location with seven neatly furnished rooms surrounding a pleasant garden; the two douﬁ

bles that adjoin a shared sitting room are a good family option.

★ Green View Homestay   HOMESTAY $$
(☑ 9447432008, 04869-224617; www.sureshgreen view.com; Bypass Rd; r incl breakfast ₹500-1750; ☎) It's grown from its humble homestay origins but Greenview is a lovely place that manages to retain its personal and friendly family welcome from owners Suresh and Sulekha. The two buildings house several classes of well-maintained rooms with private balconies – the best are the upper-floor rooms overlooking a lovely rear spice garden. They also have excellent vegetarian meals and cooking lessons (veg/nonveg ₹450/600).

Claus Garden   HOMESTAY $$
(☑ 04869-222320, 9567862421; www.homestay.in; Thekkumkadu; d/tr/f ₹1600/1800/2000; ☎) Set well away from the hustle and bustle and up a steep hill with good views, this German-run place has gently curving balconies, spotless rooms and a rooftop overlooking a lush green garden. The 'family room' comprises two adjoining rooms sharing a bathroom. Organic breakfast with fresh-baked bread is available for ₹300.

El-Paradiso   HOMESTAY $$
(☑ 04869-222350, 9447431950; www.goelparad iso.com; Bypass Rd; d ₹1500-2500; @☎) This immaculate family homestay has fresh rooms that have balconies and hanging chairs, or open onto a terrace overlooking greenery at the back. Cooking classes (₹500) are a speciality here.

Chrissie's Hotel   GUESTHOUSE $$
(☑ 9447601304, 04869-224155; www.chrissies.in; Bypass Rd; s/d/f from ₹2200/2400/3900; ☎⋇) This four-storey building behind the popular restaurant of the same name somehow manages to blend in with the forest-green surrounds. The chic rooms are spacious and bright, with cheery furnishings, lamps and colourful pillows. Yoga classes are offered and a rooftop pool was being installed when we visited. Wi-fi in the lobby only.

Spice Village   HOTEL $$$
(☑ 0484-3011711; www.cghearth.com; Thekkady Rd; villas ₹18,400-30,900; ☎⋇) ✐ This CGH Earth place takes its green credentials very seriously and has captivating, spacious cottages that are smart yet cosily rustic, in pristinely kept grounds. Its restaurant does lavish lunch and dinner buffets, there's a colonial-style bar and the Wildlife Interpreta-tion Centre has a resident naturalist. Better value out of high season when rates halve.

✗ Eating

There are a few good cheap veg restaurants in Kumily's busy bazaar area, and some decent traveller-oriented restaurants on the road to the wildlife sanctuary. Most homestays offer home-cooked meals on request.

Shri Krishna   INDIAN $
(KK Rd; meals ₹70-140; ⊙ noon-2pm & 6-10pm) A local favourite in the bazaar, serving spicy pure-veg meals including several takes on the lunchtime thali.

Chrissie's Cafe   MULTICUISINE $$
(www.chrissies.in; Bypass Rd; meals ₹120-350; ⊙ 8am-9pm) A perennially popular traveller haunt, this 1st-floor rooftop cafe is clean and airy and satisfies with cakes and snacks, excellent coffee, well-prepared Western faves like pizza and pasta, and even a Middle Eastern meze platter or falafel.

Ebony's Cafe   MULTICUISINE $$
(Bypass Rd; meals ₹120-275; ⊙ 8am-10.30pm) This long-standing breezy rooftop joint has lots of pot plants and traveller-friendly tunes, while the menu serves up a simple assortment of Indian and Western food from mashed potato to basic pasta dishes and cold beer.

French Restaurant & Bakery   CAFE, BAKERY $$
(☑ 9961213107; meals ₹100-300; ⊙ 8am-9pm) This family-run shack set back from the main road is a good spot for breakfast or lunch, mainly for the fluffy tuna or cheese baguettes baked on-site, but also for pasta, pizza and noodle dishes.

Kofiland   MULTICUISINE $$$
(www.kofiland.in; mains ₹210-650; ⊙ 8am-9pm) For a dining splurge, head to the cavernous *palapa*-style restaurant at the new Kofiland Resort on the outskirts of town. Overlooking the pool and lagoon through floor-to-ceiling glass windows, it has a vast menu of North and South Indian dishes with an emphasis on Keralan cuisine.

☆ Entertainment

Mudra Cultural Centre   LIVE PERFORMANCE
(☑ 9061263381; www.mudraculturalcentre.com; Lake Rd; entry ₹200, video ₹200; ⊙ Kathakali 5pm & 7pm, kalarippayat 6pm & 7.15pm) Kathakali shows at this cultural centre are highly entertaining.

PARAMBIKULAM TIGER RESERVE

Possibly the most protected environment in South India – nestled behind three dams in a valley surrounded by Keralan and Tamil Nadu sanctuaries – Parambikulam (☑9442201690; www.parambikulam.org; Indian/foreigner ₹10/150, camera/video ₹25/150; ⊙7am-6pm, last entry 4pm) constitutes 285 sq km of Kipling-storybook scenery and wildlife-spotting goodness. Far less touristed than Periyar, it's home to elephants, bison, gaur, sloths, sambar, crocodiles, tigers, panthers and some of Asia's largest teak trees. The sanctuary is best avoided during monsoon (June to August) and sometimes closes in March and April.

Contact the sanctuary office in Anappady to arrange tours of the park's buffer zones, including treks from ₹500 per person, bamboo rafting (₹8800 for 10 people) and jungle safaris (₹8000 for 10 people). Park accommodation includes treetop huts (₹2750 to ₹3300) or niche tents (from ₹5500), inclusive of some activities. Entry to the reserve is via Pollachi (40km from Coimbatore and 49km from Palakkad) in Tamil Nadu. There are two buses in either direction between Pollachi and Parambikulam via Annamalai daily (₹20, 1½ hours). A taxi costs around ₹2400.

Make-up and costume starts 30 minutes before each show; use of still cameras is free and welcome. Arrive early for a good seat. There also two *kalarippayat* performances nightly.

**Kadathanadan Kalari &
Navarasa Kathakali Centre** LIVE PERFORMANCE
(☑9961740868; www.kalaripayattu.co.in; Thekkady Rd; ₹200; ⊙kalarippayat 6-7pm, Kathakali 7-8pm) Hour-long demonstrations of the exciting Keralan martial art of *kalarippayat*, as well as Kathakali, are staged here every evening. Tickets are available from the box office throughout the day.

⊕ Information

DTPC Office (☑04869-222620; ⊙10am-5pm Mon-Sat) Uphill behind the main bus stand; you can pick up a map and have a chat but that's about it.

Ecotourism Centre (☑8547603066, 04869-224571; www.periyartigerreserve.org; ⊙6.30am-1pm & 2-8.30pm) For park tours, information and guided walks.

⊕ Getting There & Away

Kumily's **bus stand** is at the northeastern edge of town. Eleven buses daily operate between Ernakulam (Kochi) and Kumily (₹150, five hours). Buses leave every 30 minutes for Kottayam (₹87, four hours), with three direct buses to Trivandrum (₹190, eight hours) and two to Alleppey (₹130, 5½ hours). Private buses to Munnar (₹100, four to five hours) also leave from this bus stand.

Tamil Nadu buses leave every 30 minutes to Madurai (₹100, four hours) from the **Tamil Nadu bus stand** just over the border.

⊕ Getting Around

It's only about 1.5km from **Kumily bus stand** (p294) to the main park entrance, but it's another 3km from there to Periyar Lake; an autorickshaw from the entry post is around ₹70, or set off on foot – but bear in mind there's no path so you'll have to walk on the road. Autorickshaws will take you on short hops around town for ₹30.

Kumily town is small enough to explore on foot but some guesthouses rent out bicycles (₹200) and most can arrange scooter hire (₹500) if you want to explore further afield.

Munnar

☑04865 / POP 68,200 / ELEV 1524M

The rolling hills around Munnar, South India's largest tea-growing region, are carpeted in emerald-green tea plantations, contoured, clipped and sculpted like ornamental hedges. The low mountain scenery is magnificent – you're often up above the clouds watching veils of mist clinging to the mountaintops. Munnar town itself is a scruffy, traffic-clogged administration centre, not unlike a North Indian hill station, but wander just a few kilometres out of town and you'll be engulfed in a sea of a thousand shades of green.

Once known as the High Range of Travancore, today Munnar is the commercial centre of some of the world's highest tea-growing estates. The majority of the plantations are operated by corporate giant Tata, with some in the hands of local cooperative Kannan Devan Hills Plantation Company (KDHP).

⊙ Sights & Activities

The main reason most travellers visit Munnar is to explore the lush, tea-filled hillocks that surround it. Hotels, homestays, travel agencies, autorickshaw drivers and practically every passerby will want to organise a day of sightseeing for you: shop around, though rates are fairly standard.

Tea Museum MUSEUM
(☑04865-230561; adult/child ₹125/40, camera ₹20; ⊙9am-7pm Tue-Sun) About 1.5km northwest of town, this museum is a demo model of a working tea factory, but it still shows the basic process. A collection of old bits and pieces from the colonial era, including photographs and a 1905 tea-roller, are also kept here. The walk to or from town follows the busy road with views of tea plantations; an autorickshaw charges ₹25 from the bazaar.

★Nimi's Lip Smacking Classes COOKING
(☑9745513373, 9447330773; www.nimisrecipes.com; ₹2000; ⊙3pm Mon-Fri, 2pm Sat & Sun) Nimi Sunilkumar has earned a solid reputation for Keralan cooking, publishing her own cookbooks, website and blog, and offers popular daily hands-on cooking classes in her home (next to Munnar's DTPC). You'll learn traditional Keralan recipes and the class includes a copy of her book *Lip Smacking Dishes of Kerala*.

Trekking

The best way to experience the hills is on a guided trek, which can range from a half-day 'soft trekking' around tea plantations (from ₹600 per person) to more arduous full-day mountain treks (from ₹800), which open up some stupendous views when the mist clears. Trekking guides can easily be organised through your accommodation, or ask at the DTPC Tourist Information Office (p298).

Bear in mind that the tea plantations are private property and trekking around without a licensed guide is trespassing.

⌖ Tours

The DTPC (p298) runs three fairly rushed but inexpensive full-day tours to points around Munnar. The **Sandal Valley Tour** (per person ₹400; ⊙tour 9am-6pm) visits Chinnar Wildlife Sanctuary, several viewpoints, waterfalls, plantations, a sandalwood forest and villages. The **Tea Valley tour** (per person ₹400; ⊙tour 10am-6pm) visits Echo Point, Top Station and Rajamalai (for Eravikulam National Park), among other places. The

Village Sightseeing Tour (₹400; ⊙9.30am-6pm) covers Devikulam, Anayirankal Dam, Ponmudy and a farm tour, among others. You can hire a taxi to visit the main local sights for around ₹1100 to ₹1500.

🛏 Sleeping

Munnar has plenty of accommodation but it seems a shame to stay in Munnar town when the views and peace are out in the hills and valleys. There are some good budget options just south of the town centre; if you really want to feel the serenity and are willing to pay a bit more, head for the hills.

🛏 Around Town

JJ Cottage HOMESTAY $
(☑9447228599, 04865-230104; jjcottagemnr@gmail.com; d ₹350-800; @ 🛜) The sweet family at this little purple place 2km south of town

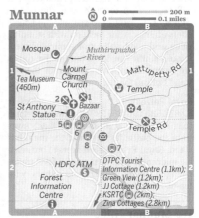

Munnar

⊗ Eating
1 Rapsy Restaurant A1
2 Saravana Bhavan A1
3 Sree Mahaveer Bhojanalaya B2

⊛ Entertainment
4 Thirumeny Cultural Centre B1

ⓘ Transport
Autorickshaw Stand .... (see 8)
5 Buses to Coimbatore A2
6 Buses to Ernakulam &
  Trivandrum A2
7 Buses to Kumily & Madurai B2
8 Buses to Top Station A2

(easy walking distance from the main bus stand) offers a varied and uncomplicated set of clean, bright, great-value rooms with TV and hot water. The one deluxe room on the top floor has a separate sitting room and sweeping views.

Green View
GUESTHOUSE $

(☑ 9447825447, 04865-230940; www.greenview munnar.com; d ₹600-850; @ 🛜) This tidy guesthouse has 10 fresh budget rooms, a friendly welcome and reliable tours and treks. The best rooms are on the upper floor and there's a super rooftop garden where you can sample 15 kinds of tea. Young owner Deepak organises trekking trips (www. munnartrekking.com) and also runs **Green Woods Anachal** (☑ 04865-230189; Anachal; d incl breakfast ₹900; 🛜).

Zina Cottages
GUESTHOUSE $

(☑ 04865-230349; r ₹900-1200; 🛜) If you want to be immersed in lush tea plantations but still be close to town, Zina is the budget choice. This fading 50-year-old bungalow offers an interesting location with stunning views and good walks from your doorstep; it looks a little run down but the five rooms are clean. It's an easy walk from the bus stand but call for directions.

Royal Retreat
HOTEL $$

(☑ 8281611100, 04865-230240; www.royalretreat. co.in; d ₹3030-4230, ste ₹4830; ✲ @ 🛜) Away from the bustle just south of the main bus stand, Royal Retreat is an average but reliable midranger with neat ground-level rooms facing a pretty garden and others with tea-plantation views.

🛏 Munnar Hills

★ Green Valley Vista
GUESTHOUSE $$

(☑ 9447432008, 04865-263261; www.greenvalley vista.com; Chithirapuram; d incl breakfast ₹2200-3850; 🛜) The valley views are superb, accommodation top-notch and the welcome warm. Rooms on three levels all face the valley and have private balconies with dreamy greenery views, as well as flat-screen TVs and modern bathrooms. Staff can organise trekking, jeep safaris and tours to the wild elephant village. It's 11km south of Munnar on the back road to Kochi.

★ Rose Gardens
HOMESTAY $$

(☑ 9447378524, 04864-278243; www.munnar homestays.com; NH49 Rd, Karadipara; r incl breakfast ₹5000; @🛜) This is a true family homestay in a peaceful spot overlooking owner Tomy's idyllic plant nursery and organic mini spice and fruit plantation. The five rooms are large and immaculate with balconies overlooking the valley, and the family is charming. Cooking lessons are free, and include fresh coconut pancakes for breakfast and delicately spiced Keralan dishes for dinner.

Its handy location is on the main road to Kochi, around 10km south of Munnar and with good bus connections.

Aranyaka
RESORT $$

(☑ 9443133722, 04865-230023; www.aranyaka resorts.com; Pallivasal Tea Estate; cottages ₹4800-6000; 🛜) These neat modern cottages set in a landscaped garden have fine views over the Pallivasal Tea Estate, one of Tata's largest tea holdings. The valley setting, with views of waterfalls and the Muthirappuzhayar River, feels remote but is only 8km from Munnar town.

Anna Homestay
HOMESTAY $$

(☑ 8156980088; www.annahomestay.com; d incl breakfast ₹2800, with AC ₹5000; ✲ 🛜) Near Anachal village, Anna Homestay is a welcoming family home with nine very tidy rooms and spacious rooftop common areas. The best are the corner rooms with balconies and there are a couple of large air-con rooms.

British County
GUESTHOUSE $$

(☑ 0484-2371761; http://touristdesk.in/british county.htm; d incl meals ₹3500) Around 11km southeast of Munnar, this appealing little guesthouse has four fresh rooms with balconies facing a stunning valley panorama. Steps lead down to the valley for treks. Rates include meals and the owners offer packages from Kochi.

Windermere Estate
RESORT $$$

(☑ 04865-230512; www.windermeremunnar.com; Pothamedu; d incl breakfast ₹10,100-12,200; ✲ @ 🛜) Windermere is a charming boutique-meets-country-retreat and cardamom plantation 4km southeast of Munnar. There are supremely spacious garden- and valley-view rooms, but the best are the suite-like 'Plantation Villas', surrounded by 26 hectares of cardamom and coffee plantations, with spectacular views. There's a cosy library above the country-style restaurant.

Bracknell Forest
GUESTHOUSE $$$

(☑ 9446951963; www.bracknell.in; Bison Valley Rd, Ottamaram; r incl breakfast ₹5000-6000; @ 🛜)

WORTH A TRIP

THATTEKKAD BIRD SANCTUARY

Thattekkad Bird Sanctuary (☏9048355288; Indian/foreigner ₹35/175, camera/video ₹38/225; ⊙6.30am-5.30pm) is a serene 25-sq-km park in the foothills of the Western Ghats and home to over 320 fluttering species, which are unusually mostly forest, rather than water birds, and include Malabar grey hornbills, Ripley owls, jungle nightjars, grey drongos, darters and rarer species like the Sri Lankan frogmouth. Also here are kingfishers, flycatchers, warblers, sunbirds and tiny 4g flowerpeckers. Boating on the river (₹250 per person) can be organised at the park office; accommodation places offer guided birdwatching trips.

Park accommodation includes the **Frogmouth Watchtower** (Thattekkad Bird Sanctuary; d ₹2500) and **Hornbill View Tower** (Thattekkad Bird Sanctuary; per person ₹1000). Better budget options are **Jungle Bird Homestay** (☏0485-2588143, 9947506188; www.junglebirdhomestay.blogspot.com.au; per person incl meals ₹1300; ❀ 🛈) or **Bird Song Homestay** (d incl meals ₹2500, with AC ₹3250; ❀ 🛈), both inside the main park boundary.

For more luxury, visit the lovely **Soma Birds Lagoon** (☏0471-2268101, 8113876665; www.somabirdslagoon.com; Palamatton; s/d incl breakfast €60/70, with AC from €75/90; ❀ 🛈 ❀). Set deep in the villages near Thattekkad, this low-key ecoresort lies on a seasonal lake among spacious and manicured grounds. The basic rooms here are roomy and the whole place feels refreshingly remote although it's just 16km from Kothamangalam.

The tented **Hornbill Camp** (☏0484-2092280; www.thehornbillcamp.com; d incl full board US$100) has accommodation in large permanent tents and a sublimely peaceful location facing the Periyar River. Kayaking, cycling, a spice-garden tour and all meals are included. It's about 8km from Thattekkad by road.

Thattekkad is on the Ernakulam–Munnar road. Take a bus from Ernakulam (₹35, two hours) or Munnar (₹60, three hours) to Kothamangalam, from where a Thattekkad bus travels the final 12km (₹12, 25 minutes), or catch an autorickshaw (₹300).

The 11 neat rooms here have balconies and views of a lush valley and cardamom plantation. It's surrounded by deep forest on all sides. The small restaurant has wraparound views. A transfer from Munnar costs around ₹400 but call ahead for directions. It's 9.5km southeast of Munnar.

🍴 Eating

Early morning food stalls in the bazaar serve breakfast snacks and cheap meals, but some of the best food is served up at the homestays and resorts.

⭐ **Rapsy Restaurant** INDIAN $
(Bazaar; dishes ₹50-150; ⊙7am-10pm) This spotless glass-fronted sanctuary from the bazaar is packed at lunchtime, with locals lining up for Rapsy's famous *paratha* (Indian-style flaky bread) or biryani. It also makes a decent stab at fancy international dishes like Spanish omelette and Israeli *shakshuka* (eggs with tomatoes and spices).

Saravana Bhavan SOUTH INDIAN $
(mains ₹25-110; ⊙7am-9.30pm) Branch of the popular South Indian pure-veg chain serving all the *idlis* and dosas you could want.

Taste the Brews CAFE $
(drinks ₹30-50; ⊙8am-noon & 3-8pm) A cool cafe near the bus stand for Continental-style breakfasts and tastings of local tea and coffee.

Sree Mahaveer Bhojanalaya NORTH INDIAN $$
(Mattupetty Rd; thalis ₹130-220; ⊙7.30am-9.30pm) This pure-veg restaurant in SN Annex Hotel is madly popular with families for its great range of thalis: take your pick from Rajasthani, Gujarati, Punjabi and more, plus a dazzling array of veg dishes.

☆ Entertainment

Punarjani Traditional Village LIVE PERFORMANCE
(☏04865-216161; www.punarjanimunnar.org; 2nd Mile, Pallivasal; ₹200-300; ⊙shows 5pm & 6pm) Touristy but entertaining daily performances of Kathakali (5pm) and *kalarippayat* (6pm). Arrive at 4pm if you want to see the ritual Kathakali make-up session. Tickets are available on the day but for the best seats consider bookings a day in advance. It's about 8km south of Munnar town.

Thirumeny Cultural Centre LIVE PERFORMANCE
(☏9447827696; Temple Rd; shows ₹300; ⊙Kathakali shows 5-6pm & 7-8pm, kalarippayat 6-7pm &

WORTH A TRIP

CHINNAR WILDLIFE SANCTUARY

About 60km northeast of Munnar, **Chinnar Wildlife Sanctuary** (www.chinnar.org; entry with 3hr trek Indian/foreigner ₹230/600; ⊙8am-5pm) protects deer, leopards, elephants and the endangered grizzled giant squirrel. Trekking and **tree house** (d ₹2600) or **hut** (d ₹2600-3100) accommodation within the sanctuary are available, as well as ecotour programs like river-trekking, cultural visits (two tribal groups inhabit the sanctuary) and waterfall treks (around ₹600 per person). For details contact the Forest Information Centre (p298) in Munnar. Buses from Munnar can drop you off at Chinnar (₹40, 1½ hours), or a taxi costs around ₹1500.

8-9pm) On the road behind the Eastend hotel, this small theatre stages one-hour Kathakali shows and *kalarippayat* martial arts demonstrations twice nightly.

ℹ Information

DTPC Tourist Information Office (☑ 04865-231516; www.dtpcidukki.com; Munnar Rd; ⊙8.30am-7pm) Marginally helpful; operates a number of tours and can arrange trekking guides.

Forest Information Centre (☑ 8301024187; ⊙9am-3pm) Advance bookings for Chinnar Wildlife Sanctuary and information on Chinnar and Eravikulam National Park.

ℹ Getting There & Away

Roads around Munnar are winding and often in poor condition following monsoon rains, so bus times may vary. The main **KSRTC bus station** (AM Rd) is south of town, but it's easier to catch buses from stands in Munnar town (where more frequent private buses also depart). The main stand is in the bazaar.

There are around 18 daily **buses** to Ernakulam (Kochi; ₹124, 5½ hours), six buses to Trivandrum (ordinary/deluxe ₹251/371, nine hours) and two to Alleppey (₹168/226, five hours). **Private buses** go to Kumily (₹80, four hours) at 11.25am, 12.20pm and 2.25pm. There are separate stands for buses to **Top Station** and **Coimbatore**.

A taxi to Ernakulam costs around ₹2800; to Alleppey is ₹3800 and to Kumily ₹2400.

ℹ Getting Around

Gokulam Bike Hire (☑ 9447237165; per day ₹400-500; ⊙9am-6pm), in the former bus stand south of town, has motorbikes and scooters for hire. Call ahead.

Autorickshaws ply the hills around Munnar with bone-shuddering efficiency; they charge up to ₹850 for a day's sightseeing.

Around Munnar

Top Station

High above Kerala's border with Tamil Nadu, Top Station (elevation 1880m) is popular for its spectacular views over the Western Ghats. From Munnar, four daily buses (₹40, 1½ hours, from 7.30am) make the steep 32km climb in around an hour, or you could book a return taxi (₹1200). You may see wild elephants on the way up.

Eravikulam National Park

Eravikulam National Park   NATIONAL PARK
(☑ 04865-208255; www.eravikulam.org; Indian/foreigner ₹95/360, camera/video ₹38/300; ⊙7.30am-4pm Apr-Jan) This park, 13km from Munnar, is home to the endangered, but almost tame, Nilgiri tahr (a type of mountain goat). A safari bus will take you into the Rajamala tourist zone where the likelihood of a sighting is high. Guided treks cost ₹300. The park is also home to Anamudi, Kerala's highest peak (2695m), though it was closed to climbers at the time of research.

From Munnar, an autorickshaw/taxi costs around ₹300/400 return; a government bus will take you the final 4km from the checkpoint (₹40).

CENTRAL KERALA

Kochi (Cochin)

☑ 0484 / POP 601,600

Serene Kochi has been drawing traders, explorers and travellers to its shores for over 600 years. Nowhere else in India could you find such an intriguing mix: giant fishing nets from China, a 400-year-old synagogue, ancient mosques, Portuguese houses and the crumbling remains of the British Raj. The result is an unlikely blend of medieval Portugal, Holland and an English village grafted onto the tropical Malabar Coast. It's a delightful place to spend some time and nap in some of India's finest homestays and heritage accommodation. Kochi is also a

Kochi (Cochin)

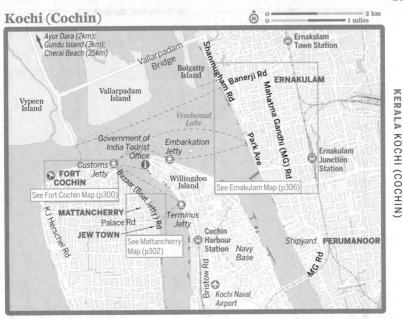

centre for Keralan arts and one of the best places to see Kathakali and *kalarippayat*.

Mainland Ernakulam is the hectic transport and cosmopolitan hub of Kochi, while the historical towns of Fort Cochin and Mattancherry, though well-touristed, remain wonderfully atmospheric – thick with the smell of the past. Other islands, including Willingdon and Vypeen, are linked by a network of ferries and bridges.

◉ Sights

◉ Fort Cochin

Fort Cochin has a couple of small, sandy beaches, which are only really good for people-watching in the evening and gazing out at the incoming tankers. A popular promenade winds around from Mahatma Gandhi Beach to the Chinese fishing nets and fish market.

Look out along the shore for the scant remains of Fort Immanuel, the 16th-century Portuguese fort from which the area takes its name.

Chinese Fishing Nets   LANDMARK
(Map p300) The unofficial emblems of Kerala's backwaters, and perhaps the most photographed, are the half dozen or so giant cantilevered Chinese fishing nets on

Fort Cochin's northeastern shore. A legacy of traders from the AD 1400 court of Kublai Khan, these enormous, spider-like contraptions require at least four people to operate their counterweights at high tide.

Modern fishing techniques are making these labour-intensive methods less and less profitable, but they supply much of the fresh lake fish you'll see on display for sale. Smaller fishing nets are dotted around the shores of Lake Vembanad – some of the best are north of Cherai Beach on Vypeen Island.

Indo-Portuguese Museum   MUSEUM
(Map p300; ☏0484-2215400; Indian/foreigner ₹10/25; ⊗9am-1pm & 2-6pm Tue-Sun) This museum in the garden of the Bishop's House preserves the heritage of one of India's earliest Catholic communities, including vestments, silver processional crosses and altarpieces from the Cochin diocese. The basement contains remnants of Fort Immanuel.

Maritime Museum   MUSEUM
(Beach Rd; adult/child ₹40/20, camera/video ₹100/150; ⊗10am-3.30pm & 4.30-5.30pm Tue-Sun) In a pair of former bomb shelters, this museum traces the history of the Indian navy, as well as maritime trade dating back to the Portuguese and Dutch, through

Fort Cochin

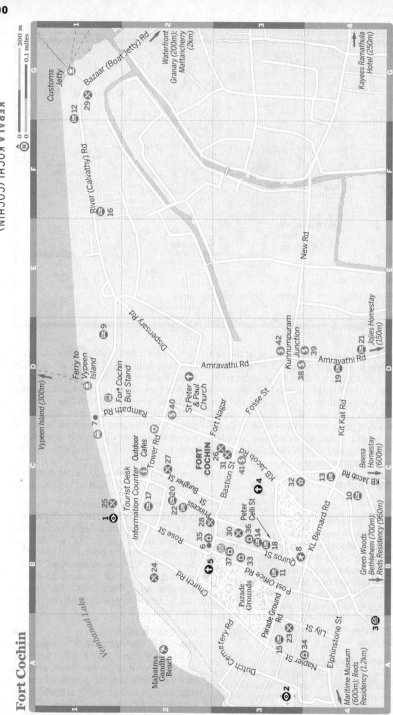

Fort Cochin

⊙ Sights
1	Chinese Fishing Nets	B1
2	Dutch Cemetery	A3
3	Indo-Portuguese Museum	A4
4	Santa Cruz Basilica	C3
5	St Francis Church	B2

⊙ Activities, Courses & Tours
6	Art of Bicycle Trips	B2
	Cook & Eat	(see 14)
7	KTDC	C1
8	SVM Ayurveda Centre	B3

🛏 Sleeping
9	Brunton Boatyard	D1
10	Daffodil	C4
11	Delight Home Stay	B3
12	Fort House Hotel	G1
13	Happy Camper	C4
14	Leelu Homestay	B3
15	Malabar House	A3
16	Maritime	F1
17	Old Harbour Hotel	C2
18	Raintree Lodge	B3
19	Saj Homestay	D4
20	Spice Fort	C2
21	Tea Bungalow	D4
22	Walton's Homestay	C2

⊗ Eating
23	Dal Roti	A3
24	Drawing Room	B2
25	Fishmongers	C1
26	Fusion Bay	C3
27	Kashi Art Cafe	C2
28	Loafers Corner	B2
	Malabar Junction	(see 15)
29	Solar Cafe	G1
30	Teapot	B3
31	Upstairs Italian	C3

✪ Entertainment
32	Kerala Kathakali Centre	C3

🛍 Shopping
33	Cinnamon	B3
34	Fabindia	A4
35	Idiom Bookshop	B2
36	Niraamaya	B3
37	Tribes India	B3

ℹ Information
38	Federal Bank ATM	D3
39	ICICI ATM	D4
40	SBI ATM	D2
41	South India Bank ATM	C3
42	UAE Exchange	D3

a series of rather dry relief murals and information panels. There's plenty of naval memorabilia, including a couple of model battleships outside in the garden.

St Francis Church CHURCH
(Map p300; Church Rd; ⊙8.30am-5pm) Constructed in 1503 by Portuguese Franciscan friars, this is believed to be India's oldest European-built church. The edifice that stands here today was built in the mid-16th century to replace the original wooden structure. Explorer Vasco da Gama, who died in Cochin in 1524, was buried in this spot for 14 years before his remains were taken to Lisbon – you can still visit his tombstone in the church.

Santa Cruz Basilica CHURCH
(Map p300; cnr Bastion St & KB Jacob Rd; ⊙9am-1pm & 2.30-5.30pm Mon-Sat, 10.30am-1pm Sun) The imposing Catholic basilica was originally built on this site in 1506, though the current building dates to 1902. Inside you'll find artefacts from the different eras in Kochi and a striking pastel-coloured interior.

Dutch Cemetery CEMETERY
(Map p300; Beach Rd) Consecrated in 1724, this cemetery near Kochi beach contains the worn and dilapidated graves of Dutch traders and soldiers. Its gates are normally locked but a caretaker might let you in, or ask at St Francis Church.

⊙ Mattancherry & Jew Town

About 3km southeast of Fort Cochin, Mattancherry is the old bazaar district and centre of the spice trade. These days it's packed with spice shops and pricey Kashmiri-run emporiums that autorickshaw drivers will fall over backwards to take you to for a healthy commission – any offer of a cheap tour of the district will inevitably lead to a few shops. In the midst of this, Jew Town is a bustling port area with a fine synagogue. Scores of small firms huddle together in dilapidated old buildings and the air is filled with the biting aromas of ginger, cardamom, cumin, turmeric and cloves, though the lanes around the Dutch Palace and synagogue are packed with antique and tourist-curio shops rather than spices.

★ Mattancherry Palace MUSEUM
(Dutch Palace; Map p302; ☑0484-2226085; Palace Rd; adult/child ₹5/free; ⊙9am-5pm Sat-Thu) Mattancherry Palace was a generous gift presented to the Raja of Kochi, Veera Kerala

Mattancherry

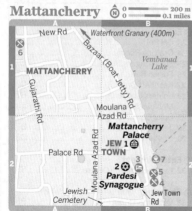

Mattancherry

Varma (1537–61), as a gesture of goodwill by the Portuguese in 1555. The Dutch renovated the palace in 1663, hence its alternative name, the Dutch Palace. The star attractions here are the astonishingly preserved Hindu murals, depicting scenes from the Ramayana, Mahabharata and Puranic legends in intricate detail.

★ **Pardesi Synagogue**   SYNAGOGUE
(Map p302; ₹5; ⊙10am-1pm & 3-5pm Sun-Thu, closed Jewish holidays) Originally built in 1568, this synagogue was partially destroyed by the Portuguese in 1662, and rebuilt two years later when the Dutch took Kochi. It features an ornate gold pulpit and elaborate hand-painted, willow-pattern floor tiles from Canton, China, which were added in 1762. It's magnificently illuminated by Belgian chandeliers and coloured-glass lamps. The graceful clock tower was built in 1760. There's an upstairs balcony for women, who worshipped separately according to Orthodox rites.

Note that shorts, sleeveless tops, bags and cameras are not allowed inside.

⊙ Ernakulam

Kerala Folklore Museum   MUSEUM
(✆0484-2665452; www.keralafolkloremuseum.org; Folklore Junction, Thevara; Indian/foreigner ₹100/200, camera ₹100; ⊙9am-6pm) Created in Keralan style from ancient temples and beautiful old houses collected by its owner, an antique dealer, this museum includes over 4000 artefacts and covers three architectural styles: Malabar on the ground floor, Kochi on the 1st and Travancore on the 2nd. There's a beautiful wood-lined theatre, with a 17th-century wooden ceiling. It's about 6km south of Ernakulam Junction train station.

A rickshaw from Ernakulam should cost ₹90, or you can take any bus to Thevara from where it's a ₹25 rickshaw ride. An autorickshaw from Fort Cochin should cost ₹200.

🏃 Activities

Ayur Dara   AYURVEDA
(✆0484-2502362, 9447721041; www.ayurdara.com; Murikkumpadam, Vypeen Island; ⊙9am-5.30pm) Run by third-generation ayurvedic practitioner Dr Subhash, this delightful waterside treatment centre specialises in treatments of one to three weeks (₹1650 per day). By appointment only. It's 3km from the Vypeen Island ferry.

SVM Ayurveda Centre   AYURVEDA
(Kerala Ayurveda Pharmacy Ltd; Map p300; ✆9847371667; www.svmayurveda.com; Quiros St; massage from ₹900, rejuvenation from ₹1200; ⊙9.30am-7pm) This small Fort Cochin centre offers daily therapeutic massages and Hatha yoga classes (₹500). Longer rejuvenation packages are also available.

🎓 Courses

The Kerala Kathakali Centre (p308) has lessons in classical Kathakali dance, music and make-up (short and long-term courses from ₹350 per hour).

For a crash course in the martial art of *kalarippayat,* head out to Ens Kalari (p308), a famed training centre, which offers short intensive courses from one week to one month.

Cook & Eat   COOKING
(Map p300; ✆0484-2215377; www.leeluhomestay.com; Quiros St; classes veg/nonveg ₹700/750; ⊙4-6pm) Mrs Leelu Roy runs popular two-hour cooking classes in her big family kitch-

en at Leelu Homestay (p304), teaching five dishes and her homemade garam masala to classes of five to 10 people.

Tours

Tourist Desk
TOURS

(Map p306; ☑ 0484-2371761, 9847044688; www.touristdesk.in; Ernakulam Boat Jetty; ◉ 8am-6pm) This high-profile private tour agency runs the popular full-day Water Valley Tour (₹1250, departs 8am) by houseboat through local backwater canals and lagoons. A canoe trip through smaller canals and villages is included. It also offers a sunset dinner cruise (₹850 per person) by canoe from Narakkal Village on Vypeen Island, with the option of an overnight stay at a beach bungalow.

Art of Bicycle Trips
CYCLING

(Map p300; ☑ 08129945707; www.artofbicycletrips.com; Bastion St; 3hr/half-day tours ₹1450/2500; ◉ 9am-6pm) Guided bicycle tours on quality mountain bikes include a morning tour of the historic Fort area and a half-day ride around the backwaters. A great way to see the area at a slow pace.

Kerala Bike Tours
MOTORCYCLING

(☑ 0484-2356652, 9388476817; www.keralabiketours.com; Kirushupaly Rd, Ravipuram) Organises motorcycle tours around Kerala and the Western Ghats, and hires out touring-quality Enfield Bullets (from US$155 per week) for serious riders with unlimited mileage, full insurance and free recovery/maintenance options.

KTDC
BOATING

(Map p300; ☑ 0484-2353234; Marine Dr, Kochi; backwater tours half-/full day ₹750/1250; ◉ 10am-5pm Mon-Sat) The KTDC has half-day backwater tours at 8.30am and 2pm, and full-day trips visiting village weaving factories, spice gardens and toddy tappers, as well as local cruises and city tours.

Festivals & Events

Ernakulathappan Utsavam
RELIGIOUS

(◉ Jan/Feb) At the Shiva Temple, Ernakulam; eight days of festivities culminating in a parade of 15 splendidly decorated elephants, plus music and fireworks.

Cochin Carnival
CARNIVAL

(www.cochincarnival.org; ◉ 21 Dec) The Cochin Carnival is Fort Cochin's biggest bash, a 10-day festival culminating on New Year's Eve. Street parades, colourful costumes, embellished elephants (which won't appeal to all), music, folk dancing and lots of fun.

Sleeping

Fort Cochin is the homestay capital of India with some 200 to choose from, but it also has some of Kerala's best heritage accommodation. It can feel a bit touristy and crowded in season, but it's a great place to escape the noise and chaos of the mainland. Ernakulam is cheaper and more convenient for onward travel, but the ambience and accommodation choices are less inspiring.

Book ahead during December and January. At other times you may snag a discount.

Fort Cochin

Happy Camper
HOSTEL $

(Map p300; ☑ 9742725668; KB Jacob Rd; dm incl breakfast ₹550; ❄ 🛜) Billing itself as a boutique hostel, Happy Camper is a relaxed place with just three air-con dorms (one female-only), a small kitchen, an excellent little cafe and rooftop area and friendly staff. Good location just south of the main tourist hub.

Maritime
HOSTEL $

(Map p300; ☑ 0484-6567875; www.thehostelcrowd.com; 2/227 Calvathy Rd; dm ₹500, d ₹1200-1600; ❄ 🛜) This Goan hostel chain has now opened in Kochi with a great location not far from Customs jetty. The nautical theme is a nice touch, the air-con dorms and double rooms are clean and well-kept, and there's a small kitchen, laundry and library.

Jojies Homestay
HOMESTAY $

(☑ 9995396543; 1/1276 Chirattapallam Rd, off KB Jacob Rd; d/tr ₹800/1200; 🛜) Clean, friendly and welcoming homestay popular with travellers thanks to helpful owners and big breakfasts served on the rooftop garden.

★ Reds Residency
HOMESTAY $$

(☑ 0484-3204060, 9388643747; www.redsresidency.in; 11/372 A KJ Herschel Rd; d incl breakfast ₹900-1200, with AC from ₹1200, AC rooftop cottage ₹1500; ❄ 🛜) Reds is a lovely homestay with hotel-quality rooms but a true family welcome from knowledgable hosts Philip and Maryann. The five rooms – including a triple and four-bed family room – are modern and immaculate, and there's a brilliant self-contained 'penthouse' cottage with kitchen on the rooftop. It's in a peaceful location south of the centre.

★ Green Woods Bethlehem
HOMESTAY $$

(☑ 9846014924, 0484-3247791; greenwoodsbethlehem1@vsnl.net; opposite ESI Hospital; d incl breakfast ₹1200-1400, with AC ₹1500-1800; ❄ 🛜)

With a smile that brightens weary travellers, welcoming owner Sheeba looks ready to sign your adoption papers the minute you walk through her front door. Down a quiet laneway and with a walled garden thick with plants and palms, this is one of Kochi's most serene homestays. The rooms are humble but cosy; breakfast is served in the fantastic, leafy rooftop cafe.

Raintree Lodge BOUTIQUE HOTEL $$

(Map p300; 9847029000, 0484-3251489; http://raintree-lodge.viewhotel.co; 1/618 Peter Celli St; r ₹3100; ❋ 🛜) The intimate and elegant rooms at this historic place flirt with boutique-hotel status. Each of the five rooms has a great blend of contemporary style and heritage carved-wood furniture, and the front upstairs rooms have gorgeous vine-covered Romeo-and-Juliet balconies. Good value.

Delight Home Stay GUESTHOUSE $$

(Map p300; 98461121421, 0484-2217658; www.delightfulhomestay.com; Post Office Rd; r incl breakfast ₹2500-4500; ❋ 🛜) One of Fort Cochin's original homestays, this grand house's exterior is adorned with frilly white woodwork, and the six rooms are spacious and polished. There's a charming little garden, elegant breakfast room and an imposing sitting room covered in wall-to-wall teak. Good food is served and cooking classes are offered in the open kitchen.

Beena Homestay HOMESTAY $$

(homestaykochi.com; XI/359B KB Jacob Rd; d incl breakfast & dinner ₹3000; ❋ 🛜) Beena has been feeding and sheltering travellers in the family homestay for quite a few years and maintains a high standard with six spotless air-con rooms and home-cooked meals taken in the dining room.

Walton's Homestay GUESTHOUSE $$

(Map p300; 9249721935, 0484-2215309; www.waltonshomestay.com; Princess St; r incl breakfast ₹1600-3500; ❋ 🛜) The fastidious Mr Walton offers big wood-furnished rooms in his lovely old house that's painted a nautical white with blue trim and buried behind a bookstore. Downstairs rooms open onto a lush garden while upstairs rooms have a balcony, and there's a nice communal breakfast room.

Saj Homestay HOMESTAY $$

(Map p300; 8086565811, 9847002182; www.sajhome.com; Amravathi Rd, near Kunnumpuram Junction; d incl breakfast from ₹2500; ❋ 🛜) There are six upstairs rooms at this welcoming and spotless homestay run by helpful Saj. It can be a bit street-noisy at the front but the air-con rooms are well soundproofed and travellers rave about the balcony breakfasts.

Leelu Homestay HOMESTAY $$

(Map p300; 0484-2215377; www.leeluhomestay.com; 1/629 Quiros St; s/d incl breakfast ₹1500/2500; ❋ 🛜) Central and very homely, Leelu has four air-con rooms upstairs, a rooftop terrace (yoga can be arranged) and sociable lounge areas with nanna furniture. The kitchen is a popular venue for Leelu's Cook & Eat cooking classes (p302).

Daffodil GUESTHOUSE $$

(Map p300; 9895262296, 0484-2218686; www.daffodilhomestay.com; Njaliparambu Junction; d incl breakfast without/with AC ₹1800/2500; ❋ @ 🛜) Run by a welcoming local couple, Daffodil has eight big and brightly painted modern rooms with a sense of privacy, but the best feature is the carved-wood Keralan balcony upstairs.

★ Malabar House HOTEL $$$

(Map p300; 0484-2216666; www.malabarhouse.com; Parade Ground Rd; r €275, ste incl breakfast €300-400; ❋ @ ≋) What may just be one of the fanciest boutique hotels in Kerala, Malabar flaunts its uberhip blend of modern colours and period fittings like it's not even trying. While the suites are huge and lavishly appointed, the standard rooms are more snug. The award-winning restaurant and wine bar are top-notch.

★ Brunton Boatyard HOTEL $$$

(Map p300; 0484-2215461; www.cghearth.com/brunton-boatyard; River Rd; d from ₹22,000; ❋ @ 🛜 ≋) This imposing hotel faithfully reproduces grand 16th- and 17th-century Dutch and Portuguese architecture. All of the rooms look out over the harbour, and have bathtubs and balconies with a refreshing sea breeze that beats air-con. The hotel is also home to the excellent History Restaurant and Armoury Bar, along with a couple of open-air cafes.

Spice Fort BOUTIQUE HOTEL $$$

(Map p300; 9364455440; www.duneecogroup.com; Princess St; r ₹10,500-12,600; ❋ 🛜 ≋) The chic red-and-white spice-themed rooms here have TVs built into the bed heads, cool tones and immaculate bathrooms. They all orbit an inviting pool in a heritage courtyard shielded from busy Princess St. Great location, excellent restaurant, friendly staff.

Tea Bungalow HOTEL $$$
(Map p300; ☑0484-2216337; www.teabunga
low.in; 1/1901 Kunumpuram; r incl breakfast from
₹10,500; ❀@🏊💺) This mustard-coloured
colonial building was built in 1912 as head-
quarters of a UK spice trading company be-
fore being taken over by Brooke Bond tea.
The 10 graceful boutique rooms – all named
after sea ports – are decorated with flashes
of strong colour and carved colonial wood-
en furniture, and have Bassetta-tiled bath-
rooms. Off-season rates drop by 60%.

Old Harbour Hotel HOTEL $$$
(Map p300; ☑0484-2218006; www.oldharbour
hotel.com; 1/328 Tower Rd; r ₹12,700-15,700, ste
₹16,500; ❀@💺) Set around an idyllic garden
with lily ponds and a small pool, the digni-
fied Old Harbour is housed in a 300-year-old
Dutch/Portuguese heritage building. The
elegant mix of period and modern styles
lends it a more intimate feel than some of
the more grandiose competition. There are
13 rooms and suites, some facing directly
onto the garden, and some with plant-filled,
open-air bathrooms.

Fort House Hotel HOTEL $$$
(Map p300; ☑0484-2217103; www.hotelfort
house.com; 2/6A Calvathy Rd; r incl breakfast
₹6500; ❀@) Close to the ferry point, this is
one of Fort Cochin's few truly waterfront ho-
tels, though the 16 smart air-con rooms are
set back in a lush garden, with the restau-
rant taking prime waterside position.

🏠 Mattancherry & Jew Town

Caza Maria HERITAGE HOTEL $$
(Map p302; ☑9846050901; cazamaria@rediff
mail.com; Jew Town Rd, Mattancherry; r incl breakfast ₹5000; ❀🏠) Right in the heart of Jew
Town, this unique unsigned place has just
two large heritage rooms above shops overlooking the bazaar. Fit for a maharaja, the
rooms feature an idiosyncratic style, with
each high-ceilinged room painted in bright
colours, filled to the brim with antiques.

Waterfront Granary BOUTIQUE HOTEL $$$
(☑98952847000, 0484-2211177; www.thewater
frontgranary.com; 6/641 Bazaar Rd, Mattancher-
ry; d ₹10,200-14,400, ste ₹21,600; ❀🏠🏊) The
first thing you'll notice when entering the
Waterfront Granary is the 1928 Ford vintage
car in the lounge. This is a museum hotel,
where many relics from the owner's person-
al collection are on show. The main building
itself, a former granary, dates to 1877, while

the 16 spacious room have a heritage feel
with modern touches.

The location on the lakefront is superb,
with a large terrace and small pool looking
out to Willingdon Island.

🏠 Ernakulam

John's Residency HOTEL $
(Map p306; ☑8281321395, 0484-2355395; TG
Rd; s/d from ₹550/750, with AC ₹1550; ❀) John's
is a genuine backpacker place and the best
budget bet in Ernakulam, especially if John
is in residence. Quiet location but a short
walk from the boat jetty. Rooms are small
(deluxe rooms are bigger) but decorated
with flashes of colour that give them a wel-
coming funky feel in this price bracket.

Boat Jetty Bungalow HOTEL $$
(Map p306; ☑0484-2373211; www.boatjetty
bungalow.com; Cannon Shed Rd, Ernakulam;
s/d ₹650/950, with AC ₹1400/1900; ❀) This
140-year-old former jetty manager's house
has been refurbished with 22 compact and
very clean rooms with TV. It's a short walk
from here to the boat jetty for Fort Cochin.

Grand Hotel HOTEL $$
(Map p306; ☑9895721014, 0484-2382061; www.
grandhotelkerala.com; MG Rd; s/d incl breakfast from
₹3500/4300, ste ₹6500; ❀@🏠) This 1960s ho-
tel, with its polished original art deco fittings,
exudes the sort of retro cool that modern
hotels would love to recreate. The spacious
rooms have gleaming parquet floors and large
modern bathrooms, and there's a good restau-
rant and Ernakulam's most sophisticated bar.

🏠 Around Kochi

Kallanchery Retreat HOMESTAY $$
(☑9847446683, 0484-2240564; www.kallanchery
retreat.com; Kumbalanghi Village; r & cottage with-
out/with AC ₹2000/2500; ❀🏠) Escape the
Kochi tourist crowds at this serene budget
waterfront homestay and expansive garden
in the village of Kumbalanghi about 15km
south of Fort Cochin. Rooms are either in
the family home or in a sublime lakefront
cottage. Chinese fishing nets are on your
doorstep, and boat trips, village tours and
home-cooked meals are available.

The Bungalow HOMESTAY $$
(☑9846302347; www.thebungalow.in; Vypeen Is-
land; d incl breakfast ₹4500-5500; ❀🏠) A short
walk from the ferry dock on Vypeen Island,
this beautiful old Keralan heritage home

Ernakulam

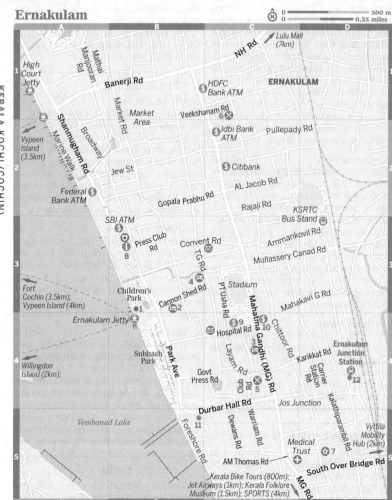

Ernakulam

⊕ Activities, Courses & Tours
1 Tourist Desk...B3

🛏 Sleeping
2 Boat Jetty Bungalow.............................B3
3 Grand Hotel..C4
4 John's Residency B3

🍴 Eating
5 Chillies C4
6 Frys Village Restaurant C1
Grand Pavilion ....(see 3)

🎭 Entertainment
7 See India Foundation D5

ℹ Information
8 KTDC Tourist Reception Centre...........B3
Tourist Desk Information
Counter ....(see 1)
9 UAE Exchange...C4
10 UAE Exchange...C4

ℹ Transport
11 Air India B5
12 Reservations Office D4

has just two large connecting rooms with four-poster beds and quaint furnishings. Owner Neema is a great cook and offers cooking lessons (₹500).

Olavipe HOMESTAY $$$
(☑ 0478-2522255; www.olavipe.com; Olavipe; s/d incl meals ₹6000/10,000; 🕲) This gorgeous 1890s traditional Syrian-Christian home is on a 16-hectare farm surrounded by backwaters, 28km south of Kochi. A restored mansion of rosewood and glistening teak, it has several large and breezy rooms beautifully decorated in original period decor.

🍴 Eating & Drinking

Some of Fort Cochin's best cooking can be found in the homestays, but there are lots of good restaurants and cafes.

🍽 Fort Cochin

Behind the Chinese fishing nets are **fishmongers** (Map p300; Fort Cochin; seafood ₹400-1000; ⊘ restaurants 8am-9pm), from whom you can buy the day's catch – fresh fish, prawns, crab and lobster – then take your selection to one of the simple but popular restaurants on nearby Tower Rd where they will cook it and serve it to you for an additional charge. Market prices vary but you'll easily get a feel for prices if you wander along and bargain.

Loafers Corner CAFE $
(Map p300; ☑ 0484-2215351; Princess St; snacks from ₹60; ⊘ 9am-9pm) If you get a window seat there are few better people-watching spots on Princess St than this. It's a good spot for a coffee, lassi, breakfast or light snack.

Solar Cafe CAFE $
(Map p300; Calvathy Rd; meals ₹60-240; ⊘ 8am-6pm) This arty upstairs cafe serves organic breakfasts and lunches, cinnamon coffee and fresh juice in a lime-bright, book-lined setting opposite the Customs Jetty.

★ **Dal Roti** INDIAN $$
(Map p300; ☑ 9746459244; 1/293 Lily St; meals ₹150-250; ⊘ noon-3pm & 6.30-10pm Wed-Mon) There's a lot to like about busy Dal Roti. Friendly and knowledgable owner Ramesh will hold your hand through his expansive North Indian menu, which even sports its own glossary, and help you dive into his delicious range of vegetarian, eggetarian and non-vegetarian options. From *kati* rolls (kebabs wrapped in a hot *paratha*) to seven types of thali, you won't go hungry. No alcohol.

★ **Kashi Art Cafe** CAFE $$
(Map p300; Burgher St; breakfast & snacks ₹160-280; ⊘ 8.30am-10pm) An institution in Fort Cochin, this natural-light-filled place has a Zen, casual vibe and solid wood tables that spread out into a semi-courtyard space. The coffee is strong and the daily Western breakfast and lunch specials are excellent. A small gallery shows off local artists.

Teapot CAFE $$
(Map p300; Peter Celli St; tea ₹50-120, mains ₹200-300; ⊘ 8.30am-8.30pm) This atmospheric cafe is the perfect venue for 'high tea', with 16 types of tea, sandwiches, cakes and a few meals served in chic, airy rooms. Witty tea-themed accents include loads of antique teapots, tea chests for tables and a gnarled, tea-tree-based glass table.

Drawing Room CAFE $$
(Map p300; Church Rd; mains ₹150-450; ⊘ noon-10.30pm) In the Grand Cochin Club, this slick new restaurant enjoys a wonderful location with large windows facing out to the water. The light menu features platters, salads and pasta dishes. Occasional live music in the evenings.

Fusion Bay SEAFOOD $$
(Map p300; ☑ 9995105110; KB Jacob Rd; mains ₹250-400; ⊘ noon-10.30pm) This unassuming little family restaurant in central Fort Cochin is renowned locally for its Kerala Syrian fish delicacies cooked in the *pollichathu* style (masala spiced and grilled in a banana leaf), and assorted seafood dishes such as spicy fish pappas and fish in mango curry.

★ **Malabar Junction** INTERNATIONAL $$$
(Map p300; ☑ 0484-2216666; Parade Ground Rd; mains ₹420-750, 5-course degustation ₹2000; ⊘ 12.30-3pm & 7-11pm) Set in an open-sided pavilion, the restaurant at Malabar House (p304) is movie-star cool, with white-tableclothed tables in a courtyard close to the small pool. There's a seafood-based, European-style menu – the signature dish is the impressive seafood platter with grilled vegetables. Upstairs, the wine bar serves upmarket tapas-style snacks and fine wine by the glass.

Upstairs Italian ITALIAN $$$
(Map p300; ☑ 9745682608; Bastion St; mains ₹250-600; ⊘ 10am-11pm) For authentic Italian – imported gorgonzola, prosciutto, olive oil, parmesan – head upstairs to this cosy little place serving Kochi's best pizza, pasta and antipasto. Pricey but worth the effort.

✗ Mattancherry & Jew Town

Kayees Ramathula Hotel   INDIAN $
(Map p302; Kayees Junction, Mattancherry; biryani ₹60-145; ☉noon-2.30pm) This place is legendary among locals for its lunchtime chicken and mutton biryanis – get here early or miss out. Don't be confused by the lime-green biryani place on the corner – Kayees is next door.

Cafe Crafters   CAFE $$
(Map p302; ☑ 0484-2223345; www.crafters. in; Jew Town Rd, Mattancherry; mains ₹100-350; ☉9.30am-6.30pm) In the heart of Mattancherry's Jewish Quarter and above a large antique store, this charming little 1st-floor restaurant cooks up Keralan seafood and Western efforts like sandwiches and burgers. Prime position is the small balcony overlooking the street.

★ Ginger House   INDIAN $$$
(Map p302; ☑ 8943493648; www.gingerhouse cochin.com; Jew Town Rd, Jew Town; mains ₹200-720; ☉9am-6.30pm, to 10pm Dec-May) Hidden behind a massive antique-filled godown (warehouse) is this weird and wonderful waterfront restaurant, where you can feast on Indian dishes and snacks – ginger prawns, ginger ice cream, ginger lassi...you get the picture. To get to the restaurant, walk through the astonishing Heritage Arts showroom with amazing sculptures and antiques – check out the giant snake-boat canoe.

Caza Maria   MULTICUISINE $$$
(Map p302; Bazaar Rd; mains ₹200-700; ☉9am-8pm) This enchanting 1st-floor place is a bright-blue, antique-filled heritage space with soft music and a changing daily menu of North Indian, South Indian and French dishes.

✗ Ernakulam

Ernakulam's mega shopping malls provide food-court dining. Another interesting development is the leafy Panampilly Ave, in a residential area south of the main train station, which is lined with modern fine-dining and fast-food restaurants.

Frys Village Restaurant   KERALAN $
(Map p306; Chittoor Rd; mains ₹90-180; ☉noon-3.30pm & 7-10.30pm) This brightly decorated and breezy place with an arched ceiling is a great family restaurant with authentic Keralan food, especially seafood like pol-

lichathu or crab roast. Fish/veg thalis are available for lunch.

Chillies   INDIAN $$
(Map p306; Layam Rd; meals ₹140-280, thali ₹150; ☉11.30am-3.30pm & 7.30-11pm) A dark, buzzing 1st-floor place, serving Kochi's best spicy Andhra cuisine on banana leaves. Try a thali, for all-you-can-eat joy.

Grand Pavilion   INDIAN $$$
(Map p306; MG Rd; meals ₹260-390; ☉noon-3pm & 6-9pm) The restaurant at the Grand Hotel (p305) is as elegant and retro-stylish as the hotel itself, with cream-coloured furniture and stiff tablecloths. It serves a tome of a menu that covers dishes from the West, North India, South India and most of the rest of the Asian continent.

☆ Entertainment

There are several places where you can view Kathakali. Performances are designed for tourists, but they're a good introduction. Standard programs start with the intricate make-up application and costume-fitting, followed by a demonstration and commentary on the dance and then the performance – usually two hours in all. The fast-paced traditional martial art of *kalarippayat* can also be easily seen, often at the same theatres.

Kerala Kathakali Centre   LIVE PERFORMANCE
(Map p300; ☑ 0484-2217552; www.kathakali centre.com; KB Jacob Rd, Fort Cochin; shows ₹250-300; ☉make-up from 5pm, show 6-7.30pm) In an intimate, wood-lined theatre, this recommended place provides a useful introduction to Kathakali, complete with handy translations of the night's story. The centre also hosts performances of classical music from 8pm to 9pm Sunday to Friday and traditional dance on Saturday.

See India Foundation   LIVE PERFORMANCE
(Map p306; ☑ 0484-2376471; devankathakali@ yahoo.com; Kalathiparambil Lane, Ernakulam; entry ₹300; ☉make-up 6pm, show 7-8pm) One of the oldest Kathakali theatres in Kerala, this intimate venue has small-scale shows with an emphasis on the religious and philosophical roots of Kathakali.

Ens Kalari   LIVE PERFORMANCE
(☑0484-2700810; www.enskalari.org.in; Nettoor; entry by donation; ☉demonstrations 7.15-8.15pm, training from 5.30pm) If you want to see real professionals practising *kalarippayat,* travel

out to this renowned *kalarippayat* training centre, 8km southeast of Ernakulam. There are daily one-hour demonstrations (one day's notice required) or you can watch training sessions from 5.30pm daily except Sunday.

Shopping

Broadway in Ernakulam is good for local shopping, spice shops and clothing. On Jew Town Rd in Mattancherry you'll find Gujarati-run shops selling genuine antiques mingled with knock-offs. Most shops in Fort Cochin are identikit Kashmiri-run stores selling North Indian crafts. Many shops around Fort Cochin and Mattancherry operate lucrative commission rackets, with autorickshaw drivers getting kickbacks (added to your price) for dropping tourists at their door.

Lulu Mall MALL
(📞0484-2727777; www.lulumall.in; NH47, Edapally; ⏰9am-11pm; 🛜) India's largest shopping mall, Lulu is an attraction in its own right with people coming from all over to shop here, hang out in the food courts or cinema, go ice-skating or tenpin bowling. Sprawling over 7 hectares, this state-of-the-art air-con, wi-fi-connected mall has more than 215 brand outlets from Calvin Klein to KFC. It's in Edapally, about 9km from the Ernakulam boat jetty.

Niraamaya CLOTHING
(Map p300; 📞0484-3263465; www.ayurvastraonline.com; Quiros St, Fort Cochin; ⏰10am-5.30pm Mon-Sat) Popular throughout Kerala, Niraamaya sells 'ayurvedic' clothing and fabrics – all made of organic cotton, coloured with natural herb dyes, or infused with ayurvedic oils. There's another branch in Mattancherry.

Idiom Bookshop BOOKS
(Map p300; Bastion St; ⏰9am-8pm) Huge range of quality new and used books in Fort Cochin.

Cinnamon CLOTHING
(Map p300; 📞0484-2217124; www.cinnamonthestore.com; 1/658 Ridsdale Rd, Parade Grounds; ⏰10am-7pm Mon-Sat) Cinnamon sells gorgeous Indian-designed clothing, jewellery and homewares in an ultrachic white retail space.

Fabindia CLOTHING, HOMEWARES
(Map p300; 📞0484-2217077; www.fabindia.com; Napier St, Fort Cochin; ⏰9.30am-9pm) This renowned brand has fine Indian textiles, fabrics, clothes and household linen.

Tribes India ARTS & CRAFTS
(Map p300; 📞0484-2215077; Ridsdale Rd; ⏰10am-6.30pm Mon-Sat) Tucked behind the post office, this Trifed (Tribal Cooperative Marketing Development Federation of India) enterprise sells tribal artefacts, paintings, shawls, figurines and more at reasonable fixed prices, with the profits going towards supporting the artisans.

Information

DANGERS & ANNOYANCES

Tourist police are at **Ernakulam** (Map p306; 📞0484-2353234; Shanmugham Rd, Ernakulam; ⏰8am-6pm) and **Fort Cochin** (Map p300; 📞0484-2215055; Tower Rd, Fort Cochin; ⏰24hr).

MEDICAL SERVICES

Lakeshore Hospital (📞0484-2701032; www.lakeshorehospital.com; NH Bypass, Marudu) Modern hospital 8km southeast of central Ernakulam.

Medical Trust (Map p306; 📞0484-2358001; www.medicaltrusthospital.com; MG Rd) Central hospital in Ernakulam.

MONEY

UAE Exchange Foreign exchange and travellers cheques. Has branches on **MG Road** (Map p306; 📞0484-2383317; MG Rd, Perumpillil Bldg, Ernakulam; ⏰9.30am-6pm Mon-Fri, to 2pm Sat) and **PT Usha Road** (Map p306; 📞0484-3067008; Chettupuzha Towers, PT Usha Rd Junction, Ernakulam; ⏰9.30am-6pm Mon-Fri, to 2pm Sat) in Ernakulam and in **Fort Cochin** (Map p300; 📞0484-2216231; Amravathi Rd, Fort Cochin; ⏰9.30am-6pm Mon-Fri, to 2pm Sat).

TOURIST INFORMATION

There's a tourist information counter at the airport. Many places distribute a free brochure that includes a map and walking tour entitled *Historical Places in Fort Cochin*.

Government of India Tourist Office (📞0484-2669125; indtourismkochi@sify.com; Willingdon Island; ⏰9am-5.30pm Mon-Fri, to 1pm Sat) On Willingdon Island.

KTDC Tourist Reception Centre (Map p306; 📞0484-2353234; Shanmugham Rd, Ernakulam; ⏰8am-7pm) Near Ernakulam's main jetty.

Tourist Desk Information Counter At this private tour agency, with offices at **Ernakulam's ferry terminal** (Map p306; 📞0484-2371761, 9847044688; www.touristdesk.in; Boat Jetty, Ernakulam; ⏰8am-6pm) and in **Fort Cochin** (Map p300; 📞0484-2216129; Fort Cochin; ⏰8am-7pm), the staff are extremely knowledgable and helpful about Kochi and beyond. They run several popular and recommended tours, including a festival tour, and publish information on festivals and cultural events.

ⓘ Getting There & Away

AIR

Cochin International Airport (☏ 0484-2610115; http://cial.aero) is at Nedumbassery, 30km northeast of Ernakulam. It's a popular hub, with international flights to/from the Gulf states, Sri Lanka, the Maldives, Malaysia, Bangkok and Singapore.

On domestic routes, **Jet Airways** (☏ 0484-2359633; www.jetairways.com; MG Rd; ☺ 9am-6pm Mon-Sat), **Air India** (Map p306; ☏ 0484-2371141; www.airindia.com; Durbar Hall Rd; ☺ 9am-5pm Mon-Sat), Indigo, SpiceJet and GoAir fly direct daily to Chennai (Madras), Mumbai (Bombay), Bengaluru (Bangalore), Hyderabad, Delhi and Trivandrum (but not Goa). Air India flies to Delhi daily and to Agatti in the Lakshadweep islands six times a week.

BUS

All long-distance services operate from Ernakulam. The **KSRTC bus stand** (Map p306; ☏ 0484-2372033; ☺ reservations 6am-10pm) still has a few services but most state-run and private buses pull into the massive **Vyttila Mobility Hub** (☏ 0484-2306611; www.vyttila mobilityhub.com; ☺ 24hr), a state-of-the-art transport terminal about 2km east of Ernakulam Junction train station. Numerous private bus companies have super-deluxe, air-con, video and Volvo buses to long-distance destinations such as Bengaluru, Chennai, Mangaluru (Mangalore), Trivandrum and Coimbatore; prices vary depending on the standard. Agents in Ernakulam

and Fort Cochin sell tickets. Private buses also use the Kaloor bus stand, 1km north of the city.

A prepaid autorickshaw from Vyttila costs ₹86 to the boat jetty, ₹215 to Fort Cochin and ₹400 to the airport.

TRAIN

Ernakulam has two train stations, Ernakulam Town and Ernakulam Junction. Reservations for both are made at the **reservations office** (Map p306; ☏ 132; ☺ 8am-8pm Mon-Sat, 8am-2pm Sun) at Ernakulam Junction.

There are local and express trains to Trivandrum (2nd class/sleeper/3AC ₹95/165/490, 4½ hours), via either Alleppey (₹50/140/490, 1½ hours) or Kottayam (₹50/140/490, 1½ hours). Trains also run to Thrissur (2nd class/AC chair ₹60/260, 1½ hours), Kozhikode (sleeper/3AC/2AC ₹170/540/740, 4½ hours) and Kannur (₹220/490/695, 6½ hours).

ⓘ Getting Around

TO/FROM THE AIRPORT

AC Volvo buses run between the airport and Fort Cochin (₹80, one hour, eight daily) via Ernakulam. Taxis to/from Ernakulam cost around ₹850, and to/from Fort Cochin around ₹1200, depending on the time of night.

BOAT

Ferries are the fastest and most enjoyable form of transport between Fort Cochin and the mainland. The main stop at Fort Cochin is called **Customs** (Map p300), with another stop at the **Mattancherry Jetty** near the synagogue. **Ferries** (Map p302)

MAJOR BUSES FROM ERNAKULAM (KOCHI)

The following bus services operate from the KSRTC bus stand and Vyttila Mobility Hub. In addition, private buses operate on long-haul routes.

DESTINATION	FARE (₹)	DURATION (HR)	DEPARTURES
Alleppey	55	1½	every 10min
Bengaluru	530-890	14	8 daily
Calicut	170	5	hourly
Chennai	600	16	1 daily, 2pm
Coimbatore	162	4½	10 daily
Kannur	260	8	5 daily
Kanyakumari	237	8	1 daily, 7pm
Kollam	124	3½	every 30min
Kottayam	60	2	every 30min
Kumily (for Periyar)	135	5	8 daily
Mangaluru	400	12	3 daily
Munnar	124	4½	every 30min
Thrissur	68	2	every 15min
Trivandrum	177-290	5	every 30min

MAJOR TRAINS FROM ERNAKULAM (KOCHI)

DESTINATION	TRAIN NO & NAME	FARES (₹)	DURATION (HR)	DEPARTURES (DAILY)
Bengaluru	16525 Bangalore Exp (A)	345/940/1345	13	6pm
Chennai	12624 Chennai Mail (A)	395/1045/1480	12	7.25pm
Delhi	12625 Kerala Exp (B)	885/2290/3400	46	3.45pm
Goa (Madgaon)	16346 Netravathi Exp (B)	445/1175/1630	15	2.10pm
Mumbai	16346 Netravathi Exp (B)	615/1645/2465	27	2.10pm

Trains: (A) departs from Ernakulam Junction; (B) departs from Ernakulam Town
Fares: Sleeper/3AC/2AC

also run from Mattancherry to Willingdon Island. The jetty on the eastern side of Willingdon Island is called Embarkation; the west one, opposite Mattancherry, is Terminus. One-way fares are ₹4 (₹6 between **Ernakulam** (Map p306) and Mattancherry). Ferries run to Vypeen Island from **Ernakulam** (Map p306) and **Fort Cochin** (Map p300). Ferries to Bolgatty Island depart from **High Court Jetty** (Map p306).

Ernakulam

There are services to both Fort Cochin jetties (Customs and Mattancherry) every 25 to 50 minutes from Ernakulam's main jetty between 4.40am and 9.10pm. Ferries run every 20 minutes or so to Willingdon and Vypeen Islands.

Fort Cochin

Ferries run from Customs Jetty to Ernakulam regularly between 5am and 9.50pm. Ferries also hop between Customs Jetty and Willingdon Island 18 times a day. Car and passenger ferries cross to Vypeen Island from Fort Cochin virtually nonstop.

LOCAL TRANSPORT

There are no regular bus services between Fort Cochin and Mattancherry Palace, but it's an enjoyable 30-minute walk through the busy warehouse area along Bazaar Rd. Autorickshaws should cost around ₹80, much less if you promise to look in a shop. Most short autorickshaw trips around Ernakulam shouldn't cost more than ₹50.

To get to Fort Cochin after ferries (and buses) stop running you'll need to catch a taxi or autorickshaw – Ernakulam Town train station to Fort Cochin should cost around ₹400; prepaid autorickshaws during the day cost ₹250.

Local buses from Ernakulam and airport buses use the **Fort Cochin bus stand** (Map p300).

Uber drivers are becoming a popular alternative to **taxis** (Map p300) for trips around Kochi.

Scooters (₹300 per day) or Enfields (₹400 to ₹600 per day) can be hired from a number of agents in Fort Cochin.

METRO

An elevated metro (www.kochimetro.org) is under construction in Ernakulam, with the first phase expected to be completed mid-2017. It will connect bus and train stations and suburbs including Edappally, and will eventually connect the airport with the city.

Around Kochi

Cherai Beach

On Vypeen Island and 25km from Fort Cochin, Cherai Beach makes a fun day trip or getaway from Kochi, especially if you hire a scooter or motorbike in Fort Cochin. The main beach entrance can get busy at times but with kilometres of lazy backwaters just a few hundred metres from the seafront, it's a pleasant place to explore.

🛏 Sleeping & Eating

Brighton Beach House   GUESTHOUSE **$$**
(☑ 9946565555; www.brightonbeachhouse.org; d ₹2400-3300; ❄☎) Brighton Beach House has a handful of basic rooms in a small building right near the shore. The beach is rocky here, but the garden is filled with hammocks to loll in, and has a neat, elevated stilt-restaurant that serves perfect sunset views with dinner.

★ Les 3 Elephants   RESORT **$$$**
(☑ 9349174341, 0484-2480005; www.3elephants.in; Convent St; cottages incl breakfast ₹6000-10,000, with AC ₹12,500; ❄☎) Hidden back from the beach but with the backwaters on your doorstep, Les 3 Elephants is a superb French-run ecoresort. The 11 beautifully designed boutique cottages are all different but have private sit-outs, thoughtful personal touches and lovely backwater views out to Chinese fishing nets. The restaurant serves home-cooked French-Indian fare. Worth the trip.

Chilliout Cafe   CAFE **$$**
(mains ₹180-450; ⊙9.30am-11pm Thu-Tue Oct-May) For European-style comfort food by

TRADITIONAL KERALAN ARTS

Kathakali

The art form of Kathakali crystallised at around the same time as Shakespeare was scribbling his plays. The Kathakali performance is the dramatised presentation of a play, usually based on the Hindu epics the Ramayana, the Mahabharata and the Puranas. All the great themes are covered – righteousness and evil, frailty and courage, poverty and prosperity, war and peace.

Drummers and singers accompany the actors, who tell the story through their precise movements, particularly *mudras* (hand gestures) and facial expressions.

Preparation for the performance is lengthy and disciplined. Paint, fantastic costumes, ornamental headpieces and meditation transform the actors both physically and mentally into the gods, heroes and demons they are about to play. Dancers even stain their eyes red with seeds from the *chundanga* plant to maximise the drama.

Traditional performances can last for many hours, but you can see cut-down performances in tourist destinations such as Kochi, Munnar and Kumily, and there are Kathakali schools in Thiruvananthapuram (Trivandrum; p259) and near Thrissur (p312) that encourage visitors.

Kalarippayat

Kalarippayat (or *kalari*) is an ancient tradition of martial arts training and discipline, still taught throughout Kerala. Some believe it is the forerunner of all martial arts, with roots tracing back to the 12th-century skirmishes among Kerala's feudal principalities.

Masters of *kalarippayat,* called Gurukkal, teach their craft inside a special arena called a *kalari.* You often can see *kalarippayat* performances at the same venues as Kathakali.

The three main schools of *kalarippayat* can be divided into northern and central, both practised in northern Kerala and the Malabar region, and southern *kalarippayat.* As well as open hand combat and grappling, demonstrations of the martial art are often associated with the use of weapons, including sword and shield *(valum parichayum),* short stick *(kurunthadi)* and long stick *(neduvadi).*

the beach – think burgers, pizzas, crêpes and barbecue – Chilliout Cafe is a breezy open-sided hang-out with sea views and a relaxed vibe. No alcohol.

ⓘ Getting There & Away

From Fort Cochin, catch the vehicle-ferry to Vypeen Island (per person ₹3, two-wheeler ₹9) and hire an autorickshaw from the jetty (around ₹400) or catch one of the frequent buses (₹15, one hour) and get off at Cherai village, 1km from the beach. Buses also go here direct from Ernakulam via the Vallarpadam bridge.

North Paravur & Chennamangalam

Nowhere is the tightly woven religious cloth that is India more apparent than in North Paravur, 35km north of Kochi. Here, one of the oldest synagogues (₹5; ⊙9am-5pm Tue-Sun) in Kerala, at Chennamangalam, 8km from Paravur, has been fastidiously renovated. Inside you can see door and ceiling wood-reliefs in dazzling colours, while just outside lies one

of the oldest tombstones in India – inscribed with the Hebrew date corresponding to 1269. The Jesuits first arrived in Chennamangalam in 1577 and there's a Jesuit church and the ruins of a Jesuit college nearby. Nearby are a Hindu temple on a hill overlooking the Periyar River, a 16th-century mosque, and Muslim and Jewish burial grounds.

In Paravur town, you'll find the *agraharam* (place of Brahmins) – a small street of closely packed and brightly coloured houses originally settled by Tamil Brahmins.

Travel agencies in Fort Cochin can organise tours to both places.

Thrissur (Trichur)

☑ 0487 / POP 315,600

While the rest of Kerala has its fair share of celebrations, untouristy, slightly chaotic Thrissur is the cultural cherry on the festival cake with a list of energetic festivals as long as a temple-elephant's trunk. Centred around a large park (known as the 'Round') and Hindu temple complex, Thrissur is also home to a Nestorian Christian community whose denomination dates to the 3rd century AD.

◎ Sights

Thrissur is renowned for its central temple, as well as for its numerous impressive churches, including the massive **Our Lady of Lourdes Cathedral**, towering, white-washed **Puttanpalli (New) Church** and the **Chaldean (Nestorian) Church**.

Vadakkunathan
Kshetram Temple HINDU TEMPLE

Finished in classic Keralan architecture and one of the oldest Hindu temples in the state, Vadakkunathan Kshetram Temple crowns the hill at Thrissur. Only Hindus are allowed inside, though the mound surrounding the temple has sweeping views and the surrounding park is a popular spot to linger.

Archaeology Museum MUSEUM
(adult/child ₹20/5, camera/video ₹50/250; ⊙9.30am-1pm & 2-4.30pm Tue-Sun) The refurbished Archaeology Museum is housed in the wonderful 200-year-old Sakthan Thampuran Palace. Its mix of artefacts includes 12th-century Keralan bronze sculptures and giant earthenware pots, weaponry, coins and a lovely carved chessboard. To the side is a shady heritage garden.

✪ Festivals & Events

Thypooya Maholsavam RELIGIOUS
(⊙Jan/Feb) This festival stars a procession of *kavadiyattam* (a form of ritualistic dance), in which dancers carry tall, ornate structures called *kavadis*.

Uthralikavu Pooram RELIGIOUS
(⊙Mar/Apr) The climactic day of this event sees 20 elephants circling the Uthralikavu Temple shrine.

Thrissur Pooram RELIGIOUS
(⊙Apr/May) The most colourful and largest of Kerala's temple festivals, with huge processions of caparisoned elephants. Held at the Vadakkunathan Kshetram Temple.

🛏 Sleeping

Gurukripa Heritage HERITAGE HOTEL $
(☑0487-2421895; http://gurukripaheritage.in; Chembottil Lane; d without/with AC ₹930/1470, AC cottage ₹2800; ❄🖥) Almost a century old but recently refurbished, Gurukripa is a fine budget heritage hotel in an excellent location just off the Round. Simple rooms and family cottages are unpretentious but clean.

Thrissur (Trichur)

KERALA THRISSUR (TRICHUR)

Thrissur (Trichur)

Pathans Hotel HOTEL $
(☑0487-2425620; www.pathansresidentialhotel.in; Round South; s/d from ₹600/800, with AC ₹1100/1500; ❄) No-frills rooms at no-frills

prices and the location is handy, though chaotic, across from the central park. The basic, cleanish and secure rooms are on the 5th and 6th floors (served by a painfully slow lift) and have TVs and occasional hot water.

★**Hotel Luciya Palace** HOTEL **$$**
(📞0487-2424731; www.hotelluciyapalace.com; Marar Rd; s/d with AC ₹3000/4000, ste ₹7200; ❊ 🛜) In a cream, colonial-themed building, this is one of the few midrange places in town that has some character, and the spacious, modern air-con rooms are great value. It's in a quiet cul-de-sac but close to Vadakkunathan Kshetram Temple and town-centre action, and has a decent restaurant and busy bar.

🍴 Eating

★**Hotel Bharath** SOUTH INDIAN **$**
(📞0487-2421720; Chembotil Lane; mains ₹85-110, thalis ₹90; ⊘6.30am-10.30pm) The air-conditioned and spotless Bharath is regarded by most locals as the best veg restaurant in town and the place for a lunchtime thali meal, Keralan breakfast or spicy curry.

India Gate INDIAN **$**
(Palace Rd; dishes ₹60-170; ⊘8am-10pm) In the Kalliath Royal Square building, this pure-veg place has a vintage feel and an extraordinary range of dosas, including jam, cheese and cashew versions. In the same complex is a Chinese restaurant (China Gate) and a fast-food joint (Celebrations).

Navaratna Restaurant MULTICUISINE **$$**
(Round West; dishes ₹100-200; ⊘noon-9.30pm) Cool, dark and intimate, this is one of the classier dining experiences in the town centre, with seating on raised platforms. Downstairs is veg and upstairs is nonveg, with lots of North Indian specialities, Chinese and a few Keralan dishes.

ℹ️ Information

DTPC Office (📞0487-2320800; Palace Rd; ⊘10am-5pm Mon-Sat) You might be able to pick up some local brochures from this tourist office.

ℹ️ Getting There & Away

BUS
State buses leave around every 30 minutes from the **KSRTC bus stand** bound for Trivandrum (₹235, 7½ hours), Ernakulam (Kochi; ₹68, two hours), Calicut (₹112, 3½ hours), Palakkad (₹60, 1½ hours) and Kottayam (₹115, four hours). Hourly buses go to Coimbatore (₹98, three hours).

Local services also chug along to Guruvayur (₹27, one hour), Irinjalakuda (₹27, one hour) and Cheruthuruthy (₹30, 1½ hours). Two private bus stands – **Sakthan Thampuran** and **Priyadarshini (North)** – have more frequent buses to these destinations, though the chaos involved in navigating each station hardly makes using them worthwhile.

TRAIN
Services run regularly to Ernakulam (2nd class/AC chair ₹60/260, 1½ hours), Calicut (₹70/260, three hours) and Coimbatore (₹90/305, three hours).

ℹ️ Getting Around
Hundreds of autorickshaws gather at the Round and are usually happy to use the meter. Short trips are ₹20.

Around Thrissur
The Thrissur region supports several institutions that are nursing the dying classical Keralan performing arts back to health.

📖 Courses

Kerala Kalamandalam CULTURAL PROGRAMS
(📞0488-4262418; www.kalamandalam.org; courses per month ₹600; ⊘Jun-Mar) Using an ancient Gurukula system of learning, students undergo intensive study in Kathakali, *mohiniyattam* (dance of the enchantress), Kootiattam, percussion, voice and violin. A Day with the Masters (₹1400, including lunch) is a morning program allowing visitors to tour the theatre and classes and see various art and cultural presentations. Email to book in advance. It's 26km north of Thrissur.

Natana Kairali Research & Performing Centre for Traditional Arts CULTURAL PROGRAMS
(📞0480-2825559; www.natanakairali.org) This school, 20km south of Thrissur near Irinjalakuda, offers training in traditional arts, including rare forms of dance and puppetry. Short appreciation courses lasting up to a month are sometimes available to interested foreigners.

🛏️ Sleeping

River Retreat GUESTHOUSE **$$**
(📞0488-4262244; www.riverretreat.in; Palace Rd, Cheruthuruthy; s/d from ₹3600/4900, ste ₹7200-9200; ❊🛜🏊) River Retreat is an excellent heritage hotel and ayurvedic resort in the

former summer palace of the Maharajas of Cochin. Along with ayurvedic treatments, it includes a pool, gym and business centre. It's about 30km north of Thrissur.

NORTHERN KERALA

Kozhikode (Calicut)

☑ 0495 / POP 432,100

Northern Kerala's largest city, Kozhikode (still widely known as Calicut), was always a prosperous trading town and was once the capital of the formidable Zamorin dynasty. Vasco da Gama first landed near here in 1498, on his way to snatch a share of the subcontinent for king and country (Portugal that is). These days, trade depends mostly on exporting Indian labour to the Middle East, while agriculture and the timber industry are economic mainstays. For travellers it's mainly a jumping-off point for Wayanad or for the long trip over the ghats to Mysuru (Mysore) or Bengaluru.

◎ Sights

Mananchira Square, a large central park, was the former courtyard of the Zamorins and preserves the original spring-fed tank. South of the centre, the 650-year-old Kuttichira Mosque is in an attractive wooden four-storey building that is supported by impressive wooden pillars and painted brilliant aquamarine, blue and white. The central **Church of South India** was established in 1842 by Swiss missionaries and has unique Euro-Keralan architecture.

About 1km west of Mananchira Sq, Kozhikode Beach is good enough for a sunset promenade.

⌂ Sleeping

Beach Hotel   HOTEL $$
(☑ 0495-2762055, 9745062055; www.beachheritage.com; Beach Rd; r incl breakfast ₹3550-3850; ❄ @ 🛜) Built in 1890 to house the Malabar British Club, this is a slightly worn but charming 10-room hotel. Some rooms have bathtubs and secluded sea-facing verandahs; others have original polished wooden floors and private balconies. Restaurant and bar on-site.

Hyson Heritage   HOTEL $$
(☑ 0495-4081000; www.hysonheritage.com; Bank Rd; s/d incl breakfast from ₹3600/4200; ❄ 🛜) You get a bit of swank for your rupee at this central business hotel. Rooms are spick

and span and shielded from the main road. There's a good restaurant and a gym.

Alakapuri   HOTEL $$
(☑ 0495-2723451; www.hotelalakapuri.com; MM Ali Rd; s/d from ₹750/1800, with AC from ₹1350/1900; ❄ 🛜) Built motel-style around a green lawn (complete with fountain!), this place is set back from a busy market area. Various rooms are a little scuffed, but reasonable value, and there's a restaurant and modern bar.

★Harivihar   HOMESTAY $$$
(☑ 9388676054, 0495-2765865; www.harivihar.com; Bilathikulam; s/d incl meals & yoga €150/230; 🛜) In northern Calicut, the ancestral home of the Kadathanadu royal family is as serene as it gets – a traditional Keralan family compound with pristine lawns. The seven rooms are large and beautifully furnished with dark-wood antiques, but this is primarily an ayurvedic and yoga centre, with packages available.

✗ Eating

Famous for its Malabar cuisine, Calicut is regarded as the foodie capital of northern Kerala.

Zains   SOUTH INDIAN $
(☑ 0495-2366311; dishes ₹40-180; ⊙ 6am-10pm) A local favourite for its Malabar dishes, biryanis and snacks, Zains is usually busy in the afternoons and evenings.

★Paragon Restaurant   INDIAN $$
(Kannur Rd; dishes ₹120-350; ⊙ 8am-midnight, lunch from noon) You might struggle to find a seat at this always-packed restaurant, founded in 1939. The overwhelming menu is famous for fish dishes such as fish in tamarind sauce, and its legendary chicken biryani.

Salkaram & Hut   INDIAN $$
(Beach Rd; mains ₹110-300; ⊙ 7am-10.30pm) At the back of the Beach Hotel are two restaurants with the same menu: the air-con Salkaram, and the cool open-sided bamboo 'hut' restaurant-bar serving a big range of fish and chicken dishes, and Malabari cuisine. It's a breezy place for an informal lunch or cold beer. Snacks are also served out on the front lawn.

ⓘ Getting There & Away

AIR

Kozhikode Airport (www.kozhikodeairport.com) is about 25km southeast of the city in Karipur. It serves major domestic routes as well as international flights to the Gulf.

Kozhikode (Calicut)

Kozhikode (Calicut)

Sights

1 Church of South India C1
2 Mananchira Square C1

Sleeping

3 Alakapuri C2
4 Beach Hotel B2
5 Hyson Heritage C1

Eating

6 Paragon Restaurant B1
Salkaram & Hut .... (see 4)
7 Zains B1

Information

8 State Bank of India C1

Transport

9 Air India C1
10 KSRTC Bus Stand C1

SpiceJet (www.spicejet.com; Kozhikode Airport) has the best domestic connections, with direct flights to Mumbai, Bengaluru and Chennai. **Air India** (☎0495-2771974; 5/2521 Bank Rd, Eroth Centre; ⏰9am-5pm) flies to Kochi and Coimbatore. **Jet Airways** (☎0495-2712375; Kozhikode Airport) has one daily flight to Mumbai. Flights to Goa go via Bengaluru or Mumbai.

BUS

The new **KSRTC bus stand** (Mavoor Rd) has government buses to Bengaluru (₹326 to ₹700, eight hours, 14 daily) via Mysuru (₹195 to ₹400, five hours), Mangaluru (₹240 to ₹340, seven hours, three daily) and to Ooty (Udhagamandalam; ₹130, 5½ hours, 5am and 6.45am). There are frequent buses to Thrissur (₹112, 3½ hours) and Kochi (₹170 to ₹280, four hours, 14 daily). For Wayanad district, buses leave every 15 minutes heading to Sultanbatheri (₹80, three hours) via Kalpetta (₹55, two hours). Private buses for various long-distance locations also use this bus stand.

TRAIN

The train station is 1km south of Mananchira Sq. There are frequent trains to Kannur (2nd class/sleeper/3AC ₹75/140/490, two hours), Mangaluru (sleeper/3AC/2AC ₹165/490/695, five hours), Ernakulam (₹170/490/695, 4½ hours), and all the way to Trivandrum (₹240/650/930, 11 hours).

Heading southeast, trains go to Coimbatore (sleeper/3AC/2AC ₹140/490/695, 4½ hours), via Palakkad.

Getting Around

Calicut has a glut of autorickshaws and most are happy to use the meter. It costs about ₹40 from the station to the KSRTC bus stand or most hotels. An autorickshaw/taxi to the airport costs around ₹450/650.

Wayanad Region

☎04935 & 04936 / POP 816,600

Many Keralans rate the elevated Wayanad region as the most beautiful part of their state. Encompassing part of a remote forest reserve that spills into Tamil Nadu and Karnataka, Wayanad's landscape combines mountain scenery, rice paddies of ludicrous green, skinny betel nut trees, bamboo, red earth, spiky ginger fields, and rubber, cardamom and coffee plantations. Foreign travellers stop here on the bus route between Mysuru, Bengaluru or Ooty and Kerala, but

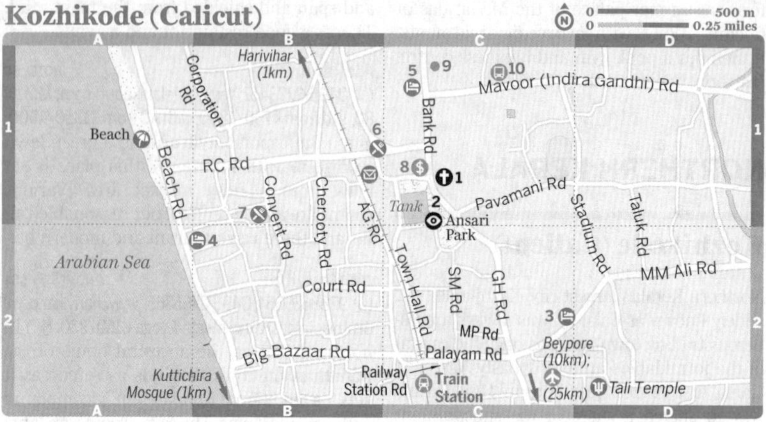

it's still fantastically unspoilt and satisfyingly remote. It's also an excellent place to spot wild elephants.

The 345-sq-km sanctuary has two separate pockets – **Muthanga** in the east bordering Tamil Nadu, and **Tholpetty** in the north bordering Karnataka. Three main towns in Wayanad district make good bases and transport hubs for exploring the sanctuary – **Kalpetta** in the south, **Sultanbatheri** (Sultan Battery) in the east and **Mananthavadi** in the northwest – though the best of the accommodation is scattered throughout the region.

◉ Sights & Activities

★ Wayanad
Wildlife Sanctuary   NATURE RESERVE
(www.wayanadsanctuary.org; entry to each part Indian/foreigner ₹115/300, camera/video ₹40/225; ⊙7-10am & 3-5pm) Entry to both parts of the sanctuary is only permitted as part of a two-hour jeep safari (₹650), which can be arranged at the sanctuary entrances. At the time of research the government was planning to introduce minibuses to supplement the jeeps. Trekking is no longer permitted in the sanctuary. Both Tholpetty and Muthanga close during April, but remain open during the monsoon.

Whether you go to Tholpetty or Muthanga essentially depends on whether you're staying in the north or south of Wayanad, as there's no difference in the chances of spotting wildlife. At both locations arrive at least an hour before the morning or afternoon openings to register and secure a vehicle, as there are a limited number of guides and jeeps permitted in the park at one time.

Thirunelly Temple   HINDU TEMPLE
(⊙dawn-dusk) Thought to be one of the oldest temples on the subcontinent, Thirunelly Temple is 10km from Tholpetty. Non-Hindus cannot enter, but it's worth visiting for the otherworldly cocktail of ancient and intricate pillars. Follow the path behind the temple to the stream known as Papanasini, where Hindus believe you can wash away all your sins.

Edakkal Caves   CAVE
(adult/child ₹20/10, camera ₹30; ⊙9am-4pm Tue-Sun) The highlight of these remote hilltop 'caves' – more accurately a small series of caverns – is the ancient collection of petroglyphs in the top cave, thought to date back over 3000 years. From the car park near Ambalavayal it's a steep 20-minute walk up

a winding road to the ticket window, then another steep climb up to the light-filled top chamber. On a clear day there are exceptional views out over the Wayanad district. The caves get crowded on weekends.

Wayanad Heritage Museum   MUSEUM
(Ambalavayal; adult/child ₹20/10, camera/video ₹20/150; ⊙9am-5.30pm) In the small village of Ambalavayal, about 5km from Edakkal Caves, this museum exhibits tools, weapons, pottery, carved stone and other artefacts dating back to the 14th century, shedding light on Wayanad's significant Adivasi population.

Uravu   HANDICRAFTS WORKSHOP
(☑04936-231400; www.uravu.net; Thrikkaippetta; ⊙8.30am-5pm Mon-Sat) ✦ Around 6km from Kalpetta a collective of workers creates all sorts of artefacts from bamboo. You can visit the artists' workshops, where they work on looms, painting and carving, and support their work by buying vases, lampshades, bangles and baskets.

Kannur Ayurvedic Centre   AYURVEDA
(☑9497872562, 9495260535; www.ayurvedawayanad.com; Kalpetta; massage from ₹1200, yoga & meditation ₹1200) For rejuvenation and curative ayurvedic treatments, visit this excellent small, government-certified and family-run clinic in the leafy backstreets of Kalpetta. Accommodation and yoga classes are available.

Trekking
There are some good opportunities for trekking around the district (though not in

KERALA WAYANAD REGION

MAHÉ
Mahé is an anomaly in Kerala. On the Malabar Coast about 10km south of Thalassery, Mahé is surrounded by, but not actually part of, Kerala – it's part of the Union Territory of Puducherry (Pondicherry), formerly under French India. Apart from the riverfront promenade with its Parisian-style street lamps, the province is similar to other towns along the Keralan coast, and Malayalam and English are the main languages. The other obvious difference is that there is no restriction on the sale of alcohol here (unlike in Kerala) and sales tax is low. Unsurprisingly, every third shop is an open-fronted liquor store with giant brandname signs!

the wildlife sanctuary itself), but it's tightly controlled by the Forest Department and various trekking areas open and close depending on current environmental concerns. At the time of research three treks were open: Chembra Peak (but only to the midway point) and Banasura Hills in the south, and Brahmagiri Hills in the north. Permits and guides are mandatory and can be arranged at forest offices in south or north Wayanad or through your accommodation. The standard cost for a permit and guide is ₹2500 for up to five people – try to arrange a group in advance.

🛌 Sleeping & Eating

There's plenty of accommodation in Wayanad's three main towns of Kalpetta, Sultanbatheri and Mananthavadi, but the isolated homestays and resort accommodation scattered throughout the region are much better choices.

🛏 Kalpetta

PPS Residency   HOTEL $
(☑ 04936-203431; www.ppsresidency.com; Kalpetta; s/d ₹400/500, with AC ₹1320/1540; ❄) This friendly budget place in the middle of Kalpetta has a variety of reasonably clean rooms in a motel-like compound, which in-

cludes the reasonably popular multicuisine Pankaj restaurant and a beer parlour. Helpful management can arrange trips around Wayanad.

Haritagiri   HOTEL $$
(☑ 04936-203145; www.hotelharitagiri.com; Kalpetta; s/d incl breakfast from ₹1650/2100, with AC from ₹2100/2750; ❄ 🛜 🏊) Set back from Kalpetta's busy main streets, this is a comfortable midrange option, with balconied rooms and more private garden cottages. There are two good restaurants, a pool, gym and an ayurvedic 'village' on-site.

🛏 Sultanbatheri

Mint Flower Residency   HOTEL $$
(☑ 04936-222206, 9745222206; www.mintflower residency.com; Sultanbatheri; s/d ₹830/1375, with AC ₹1075/1670) The budget annexe of Mint Flower Hotel is in great condition. It's no frills but rooms are spotless and come with hot water and TV.

Issac's Hotel Regency   HOTEL $$
(☑ 04936-220512; www.issacsregency.com; Sultanbatheri; dm ₹250, s/d/tr from ₹1150/1600/1800, with AC from ₹1550/2000/2250; ❄ @ 🛜 🏊) This remarkably well-equipped complex near the private bus stand in the town centre has everything from a cinema to a swim

Wayanad District

0 ———— 10 km
0 ———— 5 miles

Pakshipathalam
KANNUR
Thirunelly Temple
Jungle Retreat Wayanad
Sanctuary Entrance
Pachydrama Palace
Mysore (107km)
Wayanad Wildlife Sanctuary (Tholpetty)
KARNATAKA
Katikulam
Periya
Kannur (64km)
Varnam Homestay
Kuruva Island
Pulpally
Mananthavadi
Wayanad Wildlife Sanctuary (Muthanga)
WAYANAD
Mysore (86km)
Koroth
Ente Veedu
Panamaram
Kaniyambetta
Sanctuary Entrance
Tariyod
Minangadi
Sultanbatheri
Kalpetta
Wayanad Heritage Museum
Tranquil
Greenex Farms
Chundale
Uravu
Edakkal Caves
Pookot Lake
Vythiri
Chembra Peak (2100m)
Kozhikode (45km)
KOZHIKODE
Vellarimala Peak
Ooty (40km)

ming pool at a reasonable price. The air-con 'dorm' has only mattresses on the floor.

Wilton Restaurant
MULTICUISINE $$

(☑ 04936-226444; Kalpetta Rd; mains ₹120-440; ⊙ 7am-10pm) Wilton's is a stand-out restaurant in Sultanbatheri with an eclectic menu of Indian, Arabian, Asian and burgers served in the air-con upstairs dining room. Downstairs is a snack and sweet shop with pastries, dried fruits and coffee. Snappy service.

Around Wayanad

★ Varnam Homestay
HOMESTAY $$

(☑ 9745745860, 04935-215666; www.varnamhome stay.com; Kurukanmoola, Kadungamalayil House; s/d r incl meals ₹1500/2600, villa ₹1800/3000; ✳ 🛜) This oasis of peace and calm is a lovely place to stay a few kilometres from Katikulam in northern Wayanad. Varghese and Beena will look after you with Wayanad stories, local information and delicious home cooking with organic farm-fresh ingredients. Rooms are in a traditional family home or a newer elevated 'tree-house' villa, and the property is surrounded by jungle and spice plantations.

Ente Veedu
HOMESTAY $$

(☑ 9446834834, 04935-5220008; www.enteveedu. co.in; Panamaram; r incl breakfast ₹2500-5500, with AC ₹3500-4000; ✳ @ 🛜) Secluded and set in a lovely location overlooking sprawling banana plantations and rice paddies, this homestay halfway between Kalpetta and Mananthavadi is definitely worth seeking out. There are several large rooms, two bamboo-lined ones with private balconies, hammocks and wicker lounges to enjoy the sensational views. Lunch and dinner are available. Call to arrange a pick-up.

Greenex Farms
RESORT $$

(☑ 9645091512; www.greenexfarms.com; Chundale Estate Rd, Moovatty; r ₹2250-7800; 🛜 🏊) Greenex Farms is a wonderfully remote-feeling place surrounded by spice, coffee and tea plantations about 8km southwest of Kalpetta. Each of the private cottages is individually designed with separate lounge, bathroom, balcony and superb views. Restaurants, campfire, walks and activities.

Jungle Retreat Wayanad
GUESTHOUSE $$

(☑ 9742565333; www.jungleretreatwayanad.com; d incl breakfast ₹2500; 🛜) The location on the boundary of Tholpetty Wildlife Sanctuary is exceptional and the rooms and cottages

comfortable at this jungle guesthouse. The best rooms are the rustic cottages with terraces facing the reserve. Meals are ₹500 extra and a host of activities can be arranged.

★ Tranquil
HOMESTAY $$$

(☑ 04936-220244; www.tranquilresort.com; Kuppamudi Estate, Kolagapara; d incl breakfast ₹11,900-16,500, tree house ₹18,800, tree villa ₹19,350; 🛜 🏊) This wonderfully serene and exclusive homestay is in the middle of an incredibly lush 160 hectares of pepper, coffee, vanilla and cardamom plantations. The elegant house has sweeping verandahs filled with plants and handsome furniture, and there are two tree houses that may be the finest in the state. A network of marked walking trails meanders around the plantation.

❶ Information

International ATMs can be found in each of Wayanad's three main towns.

DTPC Office (☑ 9446072134; www.wayanad tourism.org; Kalpetta; ⊙ 9.30am-5.30pm Mon-Sat) The DTPC has two useful offices in Kalpetta: one in town and the other upstairs at the new bus stand. They have a map and can advise on trekking.

❶ Getting There & Away

Although remote, Wayanad is easily accessible by bus from Calicut and Kannur in Kerala, and from Mysuru (Karnataka) and Ooty (Tamil Nadu). Buses brave the winding roads – including a series of nine spectacular hairpin bends – between Calicut and Kalpetta (₹65 to ₹95, two hours) every 15 minutes, with some continuing on to Sultanbatheri (₹80 to ₹150, three hours) and others to Mananthavadi (₹87, three hours). Hourly buses run between Kannur and Mananthavadi (₹55, 2½ hours).

From Sultanbatheri, an 8am bus heads out for Ooty (₹100, four hours), with a second one passing through town at around 12.45pm. The Ooty bus leaves Mananthavadi at 11.15am. Buses run from Kalpetta to Mysuru (₹143, four hours, hourly) via Sultanbatheri, but note that the border gate is closed between 7pm and 6am. There are six daily buses to Mysuru (₹167, three hours) on the alternative northern route from Mananthavadi, where the border is open 24 hours.

❶ Getting Around

The Wayanad district is quite spread out but plenty of private buses connect the main towns of Mananthavadi, Kalpetta and Sultanbatheri every 10 to 20 minutes during daylight hours (₹15 to ₹25, 45 minutes to one hour). From Mananthavadi, regular buses also head to

Tholpetty (₹15, one hour). You can hire jeeps or taxis to get between towns for ₹600 to ₹800 each way, or hire a vehicle to tour the region for around ₹2000 per day.

There are plenty of autorickshaws and taxis for short hops within the towns.

Kannur & Around

📞 0497 / POP 1.2 MILLION

Kerala's northern coast is far less touristed than the south, which for many is an attraction in its own right. The main draws in this part of coastal Kerala are the beautiful, undeveloped beaches and the enthralling theyyam possession rituals (p321).

Under the Kolathiri rajas, Kannur (formerly Cannanore) was a major port bristling with international trade – explorer Marco Polo christened it a 'great emporium of spice trade'. Since then, the usual colonial suspects, including the Portuguese, Dutch and British, have had a go at exerting their influence on the region, leaving behind the odd fort. Today it is an unexciting, though agreeable, town known mostly for its weaving industry and cashew trade.

This is a predominantly Muslim area, so local sensibilities should be kept in mind: wear a sarong over your bikini on the beach.

◉ Sights

Kannur's main town beach is the 4km-long **Payyambalam Beach** (beach park ₹10, camera/video ₹25/150; ⏰ 8am-8pm), which starts about 1.5km east of the train station, just past the military cantonment. The beach park gets busy in the evening when families and couples come down to watch the sunset and picnic.

Arakkal Museum   MUSEUM
(Indian/foreigner ₹20/100, camera ₹25; ⏰ 9.30am-5.15pm Mon-Sat) Housed in part of the royal palace of the Arakkal family, a 16th-century Kannur dynasty, this harbourfront museum features antiques, furniture, weapons, silver and portraits. It's a fascinating look into the life of Kerala's only Muslim royal family.

Kerala Dinesh Beedi
Co-Operative   WORKSHOP
(📞 0497-2701699; www.keraladinesh.com; ⏰ 8am-6pm Mon-Sat) FREE The Kannur region is known for the manufacture of *beedis*, those tiny Indian cigarettes deftly rolled inside green leaves. This is one of the largest and purportedly best manufacturers, with a fac-

tory at Thottada, 7km south of Kannur and about 4km from Thottada beach. A skilled individual can roll up to 1000 a day! Visitors are welcome to look around; an autorickshaw should cost around ₹120 return from Kannur town.

🛏 Sleeping & Eating

Although there are plenty of hotels in Kannur town, the best places to stay are homestays near the beach at Thottada (8km south) and towards Thalassery.

🛏 Kannur Town

Hotel Meridian Palace   HOTEL $
(📞 9995999547, 0497-2701676; www.hotelmeridianpalace.com; Bellard Rd; s/d from ₹550/700, deluxe ₹935/1100, with AC ₹1425-1650; ❄) In the market area opposite the main train station, this place is hardly palatial but it's friendly enough and offers a cornucopia of clean budget rooms and a Punjabi restaurant.

Hotel Odhen's   INDIAN $
(Onden Rd; mains ₹30-100; ⏰ 8.30am-5pm) This popular local restaurant in Kannur's market area is usually packed at lunchtime. The speciality is Malabar cuisine, including tasty seafood curries and banana-leaf thalis.

🛏 Thottada Beach & Around

Blue Mermaid Homestay   HOMESTAY $$
(📞 9497300234; www.bluemermaid.in; Thottada Beach; s/d incl breakfast & dinner ₹2500/3500, cottage ₹4000; ❄ 🖥) With a prime location among the palms facing Thottada Beach, Blue Mermaid is a charming and immaculate guesthouse with rooms in a traditional home, bright air-con rooms in a newer building and a whimsical stilted 'honeymoon cottage'. Friendly young owners cook up fine Keralan meals.

Waves Beach Resort   HOMESTAY $$
(📞 9495050850, 9447173889; www.wavesbeachresort.co.in; Adikadalayi, Thottada Beach; s/d incl meals ₹2000/3500; 🖥) Crashing waves will lull you to sleep at these very cute hexagonal laterite huts overlooking a semi-private little crescent beach. The welcoming owners, Seema and Arun, also have rooms in two other nearby properties, including cheaper rooms in an old Keralan house.

Costa Malabari   GUESTHOUSE $$
(📞 0944-7775691, reservations 0484-2371761; www.touristdesk.in; Thottada Beach; d incl meals

THEYYAM

Kerala's most popular ritualistic art form, *theyyam* is believed to predate Hinduism, originating from folk dances performed during harvest celebrations. An intensely local ritual, it's often performed in *kavus* (sacred groves) throughout northern Kerala.

Theyyam refers both to the shape of the deity/hero portrayed, and to the actual ritual. There are around 450 different *theyyams*, each with a distinct costume, made up of face paint, bracelets, breastplates, skirts, garlands and exuberant, intricately crafted headdresses that can be up to 6m or 7m tall. During performances, each protagonist loses his physical identity and speaks, moves and blesses the devotees as if he were that deity. Frenzied dancing and wild drumming create an atmosphere in which a deity indeed might, if it so desired, manifest itself in human form.

From November to April there are annual rituals at each of the hundreds of *kavus*. *Theyyams* are often held to bring good fortune to important events such as marriages and housewarmings.The best place for visitors to see *theyyam* is in village temples in the Kannur region of northern Kerala. In peak times (December to February) there should be a *theyyam* ritual happening somewhere almost every night.

Although tourists are welcome to attend, this is not a dance performance but a religious ritual, and the usual rules of temple behaviour apply: dress appropriately, avoid disturbing participants and villagers; refrain from displays of public affection. Photography is permitted, but avoid using a flash. For details on where and when, ask at your guesthouse or contact Kurien at Costa Malabari.

₹3000-4000; ❄ 🛜) Costa Malabari pioneered tourism in this area and there are three lovely homestay properties just back from Thottada Beach. Costa Malabari 1 has spacious rooms in an old hand-loom factory, while rooms are offered in two other nearby bungalows. The home-cooked Keralan food is included. Manager Kurien is an expert on the *theyyam* ritual and can help arrange a visit.

Kannur Beach House HOMESTAY $$
(📞 0497-2708360, 9847184535; www.kannurbeach house.com; Thottada Beach; s/d ₹2600/3600) This original beachfront homestay is a traditional Keralan building with handsome wooden shutters. Rooms are looking a little worn but you can enjoy sensational ocean sunset views from your porch or balcony. A small lagoon separates the house from the beach. Breakfast and dinner included.

Ezhara Beach House HOMESTAY $$
(📞 0497-2835022; www.ezharabeachhouse.com; 7/347 Ezhara Kadappuram; s/d incl meals from ₹1500/3000; 🛜) Fronting the unspoilt Kizhunna Ezhara beach, midway between Kannur and Thalassery railway stations (11km from each), Ezhara Beach House is run by welcoming and no-nonsense Hyacinth. Rooms are simple but the house has character and guests rave about the meals.

🛏 Thalassery

Ayisha Manzil HOMESTAY $$$
(📞 9496189296; www.ayishamanzil.com; Thalassery; d incl meals ₹15,500; ❄🛜▦) The four rooms in this 150-year-old heritage homestay are enormous and filled with antique furniture, but most guests come for the Mappila (Muslim) cuisine and the famous cooking classes (₹2500) overseen by Mrs Faiza Moosa. A visit to the local market is part of the culinary experience. Book well ahead.

ℹ Getting There & Away

AIR
Kannur International Airport, 25km east of Kannur, is due to open in 2017 and will be the largest in Kerala.

BUS
Kannur has several bus stands: the enormous central bus stand – one of the largest in Kerala – is the place to catch private and some government buses, but most long-distance state buses still also use the KSRTC bus stand near the Caltex junction, 1km northeast of the train station.

There are daily buses to Mysuru (₹203 to ₹298, eight hours, five daily), Madikeri (₹85, 2½ hours, 11am) and Ooty (via Wayanad; ₹221, nine hours, 7.30am and 10pm).

For the Wayanad region, buses leave every hour from the central bus stand to Mananthavadi (₹80, 2½ hours).

For Thottada Beach, take bus 22 or 29 (₹9) from Plaza Junction opposite the train station and get off at Adikadalayi village.

TRAIN

There are frequent daily trains to Calicut (2nd class/AC chair ₹60/295, 1½ hours), Ernakulam (sleeper/3AC/2AC ₹220/540/740, 6½ hours) and Alleppey (₹215/580/830). Heading north there are express trains to Mangaluru (sleeper/3AC/2AC ₹170/540/740, three hours) and up to Goa (sleeper/3AC/2AC ₹350/915/1295, eight hours).

Bekal & Around

📞 0467

Bekal and nearby Palakunnu and Udma, in Kerala's far north, have long, white-sand beaches begging for DIY exploration. The area is gradually being colonised by glitzy five-star resorts catering to fresh-from-the-Gulf millionaires, but it's still worth the trip for off-the-beaten-track adventurers.

◉ Sights & Activities

The laterite-brick **Bekal Fort** (Indian/foreigner ₹15/200; ⊙ 8am-5pm), built between 1645 and 1660, sits on Bekal's rocky headland. Next door, **Bekal Beach** (₹5) encompasses a grassy park and a long, beautiful stretch of sand that turns into a circus on weekends and holidays when local families descend for rambunctious leisure time. Isolated **Kappil Beach**, 6km north of Bekal, is a lonely stretch of fine sand and calm water, but beware of shifting sandbars.

🛌 Sleeping & Eating

Apart from the five-star Vivanta Taj and Lalit hotels, there are lots of cheap, average-quality hotels scattered between Kanhangad (12km south) and Kasaragod (10km north), with a few notable exceptions.

Nirvana@Bekal   COTTAGE $$

(📞 0467-2272900, 9446463088; www.nirvana bekal.com; Bekal Fort Rd; d incl breakfast ₹1800-4700; ❄️🛜) Right below the walls of Bekal Fort, these laterite-brick cottages in a beachfront palm-filled garden are the best value in town. Rooms come with air-con and TV, there's a good restaurant, ayurvedic treatments and even a cricket bowling machine!

★**Neeleshwar Hermitage**   RESORT $$$

(📞 0467-2287510; www.neeleshwarhermitage.com; Ozhinhavalappu, Neeleshwar; s/d cottages from ₹13,900/16,600; ❄️🛜🏊) This spectacular beachfront ecoresort consists of 18 beautifully designed thatch-roof cottages modelled on Keralan fisherman's huts but with modern touches like iPod docks and a five-star price tag. Built according to the principles of Kerala Vastu, the resort has an infinity pool, nearly 5 hectares of lush gardens fragrant with frangipani, superb organic food and ayurvedic massage, meditation and yoga programs.

ℹ️ Getting There & Away

A couple of local trains stop at Fort Bekal station, right on Bekal beach. Kanhangad, 12km south, and Kasaragod, 10km to the north, are major train stops. Frequent buses run from

---

OFF THE BEATEN TRACK

VALIYAPARAMBA BACKWATERS

Kerala's 'northern backwaters' offer an intriguing alternative to better-known waterways down south. This large body of water is fed by five rivers and fringed by ludicrously green groves of nodding palms. One of the nearest towns is **Payyanur**, 50km north of Kannur. It's possible to catch the ferry from Kotti, from where KSWTD operates local ferries to the surrounding islands. It's five minutes' walk from Payyanur railway station. The 2½-hour trip (₹10) from Kotti takes you to the Ayitti Jetty, 8km from Payyanur, from where you can also catch the return ferry.

You can stay at the peaceful **Valiyaparamba Retreat** (📞 0484-2371761; www.tourist desk.in/valiyaparambaretreat.htm; d incl meals ₹4000), a secluded homestay with simple rooms and stilted bungalows 15km north of Payyanur and 3km from Ayitti Jetty. Kochi's Tourist Desk (p303) also runs day trips on a traditional houseboat around the Valiyaparamba Backwaters.

Bekal Boat Stay (📞 0467-2282633, 9447469747; www.bekalboatstay.com; Kottappuram, Nileshwar; 24hr cruise ₹6000-8000) is one of the few operators around here to offer overnight houseboat trips in the Valiyaparamba Backwaters. Day cruises (₹4000 for up to six people) are also available. It's around 22km south of Bekal and about 2km from Nileshwar – get off any bus between Kannur and Bekal and take an autorickshaw from there (₹30).

Bekal to both Kanhangad and Kasaragod (around ₹15, 20 minutes), from where you can pick up major trains to Mangaluru, Goa or south to Kochi. An autorickshaw from Bekal Junction to Kappil beach is around ₹80.

LAKSHADWEEP

POP 64,500

Comprising a string of 36 palm-covered, white-sand-skirted coral islands 300km off the coast of Kerala, Lakshadweep is as stunning as it is isolated. Only 10 of these islands are inhabited, mostly by Sunni Muslim fishermen, and foreigners are only allowed to stay on a few of these. With fishing and coir production the main sources of income, local life on the islands remains highly traditional, and a caste system divides the islanders between Koya (land owners), Malmi (sailors) and Melachery (farmers). Electricity is supplied by generator.

The real attraction of the islands lies under the water: the 4200 sq km of pristine archipelago lagoons, unspoilt coral reefs and warm waters are a magnet for scuba divers and snorkellers.

Lakshadweep can only be visited on a prearranged package trip. At the time of research, resorts on Kadmat, Minicoy, Kavaratti and Bangaram Islands were open to tourists – though most visits to the islands are boat-based packages that include a cruise from Kochi, island visits, water sports, diving and nights spent on board the boat. At the time of research foreigners were not permitted to stay on Agatti Island but can fly there and take a boat transfer to other islands. Packages include permits and meals, and can be arranged through SPORTS.

Sleeping & Eating

You can stay on the remote island of Minicoy, the second-largest island and the closest to the Maldives, in modern cottages or a 20-room guesthouse at Minicoy Island Resort (0484-2668387; www.lakshadweeptourism.com; s/d with AC from ₹5000/7000;); book via SPORTS (p323).

Kadmat Beach Resort (0484-4011134; www.kadmat.com; 2 night s/d incl meals from ₹11,450/16,050;) on Kadmat Island has 28 modern, beach-facing cottages, reachable by overnight boat from Kochi or boat transfer from Agatti airport.

There are basic cottages (www.lakshadweeptourism.com; s/d ₹10,000/15,000) and Lakshadweep's most upmarket, newly reo-

DIVING LAKSHADWEEP

Lakshadweep is a scuba diver's dream, with excellent visibility and an embarrassment of marine life living on undisturbed coral reefs. The best time to dive is between November and mid-May when the seas are calm and visibility is 20m to 40m. There are dive centres on Bangaram, Kadmat, Kavaratti, Minicoy and Agatti islands (though the last was closed to foreigners at the time of research). SPORTS in Kochi can organise dive packages or courses.

pened Bangaram Island Resort (0484-2397550; www.bangaram.org; s/d incl meals ₹11,150/16,900) on otherwise uninhabited Bangaram Island, reached by boat from Agatti.

Information

PERMITS

All visits require a special permit (one month's notice), which can be organised by tour operators or SPORTS in Kochi. At the time of research foreigners were allowed to stay at the government resorts on Kadmat, Minicoy, Kavaratti and Bangaram; enquire at SPORTS.

TOURIST INFORMATION

Mint Valley Travel (0484-2397550; www.mintvalley.com; Kochi) Reliable private tour operator.

SPORTS (Society for the Promotion of Recreational Tourism & Sports; 9495984001, 0484-2668387; www.lakshadweeptourism.com; PS Parameswaran Rd, Willingdon Island; 10am-5pm Mon-Sat) In Kochi; the main organisation for tourist information and booking package tours.

Getting There & Away

Air India flies between Kochi and Agatti Island (from ₹9700 return) daily except Sunday. Boat transport between Agatti and Kadmat, Kavaratti and Bangaram is included in the package tours available.

Six passenger ships – MV Kavaratti, MV Arabian Sea, MV Lakshadweep Sea, MV Bharat Seema, MV Amindivi and MV Minicoy – operate between Kochi and Lakshadweep, taking 14 to 20 hours.

Cruise packages start from a weekend package (adult/child ₹7216/6185) to a five-day, three-island cruise from ₹25,000/18,000.

See the package tour section of www.lakshadweeptourism.com for more details.

Tamil Nadu & Chennai

Best Places to Sleep

➡ Saratha Vilas (p380)

➡ Les Hibiscus (p363)

➡ Bungalow on the Beach (p369)

➡ Visalam (p380)

➡ 180° McIver (p399)

Best Temples

➡ Meenakshi Amman Temple (p381)

➡ Brihadishwara Temple (p372)

➡ Arunachaleshwar Temple (p356)

➡ Nataraja Temple (p368)

➡ Sri Ranganathaswamy Temple (p375)

Why Go?

Tamil Nadu is the homeland of one of humanity's living classical civilisations, stretching back uninterrupted for two millennia and very much alive today in the Tamils' language, dance, poetry and Hindu religion.

But this deep-South state, with its age-old trading vocation, is as dynamic as it is immersed in tradition. Fire-worshipping devotees who smear tikka on their brows in Tamil Nadu's famously spectacular temples might rush off to IT offices – and then unwind at a glitzy night-time haunt in rapidly modernising Chennai (Madras) or with sun salutations in bohemian Puducherry (Pondicherry).

When the hot chaos of Tamil temple towns overwhelms, escape to the southernmost tip of India where three seas mingle; to the splendid mansions sprinkled across arid Chettinadu; or up to the cool, forest-clad, wildlife-prowled Western Ghats. It's all packed into a state that remains proudly distinct from the rest of India, while also being among the most welcoming.

When to Go
Chennai

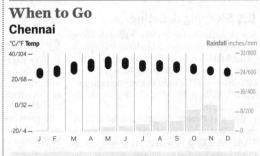

Jan–Mar The weather is at its (relative) coolest and the monsoon is over.

Jul–Sep Hit the hill stations after the crowded 'season' but while the weather is still good.

Nov–Dec The full-moon festival of lights.

Tamil Nadu & Chennai Highlights

1 Puducherry (p359)
Soaking up the unique Franco-Indian flair, boho boutiques and lively yoga scene.

2 Hill Stations (p390)
Escaping to the cool, mist-cloaked mountains and heritage hotels at Kodaikanal or Ooty.

3 Thanjavur (p372)
Admiring the Chola temple architecture of Brihadishwara Temple.

4 Chettinadu (p379)
Spending the night in an opulent mansion and feasting on fiery cuisine.

5 Madurai (p381) Getting lost in the colourful chaos of Tamil temple life at Madurai's Meenakshi Amman Temple.

6 Tranquebar (p369)
Losing track of time at a quirky old Danish seaside colony.

7 Mudumalai Tiger Reserve (p406) Tracking down rare exotic wildlife between mountain panoramas.

8 Chennai (p327) Exploring the countless faces of Tamil Nadu's capital.

History

The Tamils consider themselves the standard bearers of Dravidian – pre-Aryan Indian – civilisation. Dravidians are defined as speakers of languages of the Dravidian family, the four most important of which are all rooted in South India – Tamil, Malayalam (Kerala), Telugu (Telangana and Andhra Pradesh) and Kannada (Karnataka). South Indian cultures and history are distinct from Aryan North India, and Tamils' ability to trace their identity back in an unbroken line to classical antiquity is a source of considerable pride.

Despite the Dravidians' long-standing southern location, elements of Dravidian culture – including a meditating god seated in the lotus position, possibly the world's first depiction of the yogi archetype – existed in the early Indus civilisations of northwest India some 4000 years ago. Whether Dravidian culture was widespread around India before Aryan cultures appeared in the north in the 2nd millennium BC, or whether the Dravidians only reached the south because the Aryans drove them from the north, is a matter of debate. But the cushion of distance has undoubtedly allowed South Indian cultures to develop with little interruption from northern influences or invasions for more than 2000 years.

The Tamil language was well established in Tamil Nadu by the 3rd century BC, the approximate start of the Sangam Age, when Tamil poets produced the body of classical literature known as Sangam literature. The Sangam period lasted until about AD 300, with three main Tamil dynasties arising in different parts of Tamil Nadu ('Tamil Country'): the early Cholas in the centre, the Cheras in the west and the Pandyas in the south.

By the 7th century the Pallavas, also Tamil, established an empire based at Kanchipuram extending from Tamil Nadu north into Andhra Pradesh. They take credit for the great stone carvings of Mamallapuram (Mahabalipuram) and constructed the region's first free-standing temples.

Next in power were the medieval Cholas (whose connection with the early Cholas is hazy). Based in the Cauvery valley of central Tamil Nadu, at their peak the Cholas ruled Sri Lanka and the Maldives plus much of South India, and extended their influence to Southeast Asia, spreading Tamil ideas of reincarnation, karma and yogic practice.

The Cholas raised Dravidian architecture to new heights with the magnificent towered temples at Thanjavur and Gangaikondacholapuram, and carried the art of bronze image casting to its peak, especially in their images of Shiva as Nataraja, the cosmic dancer. *Gopurams,* the tall temple gate towers characteristic of Tamil Nadu, made their appearance in late Chola times.

By the late 14th century much of Tamil Nadu was under the sway of the Vijayanagar empire based at Hampi (Karnataka). As the Vijayanagar state weakened in the 16th cen-

TOP STATE FESTIVALS

International Yoga Festival (p363; 4–7 Jan, Puducherry) Shows, workshops and competitions.

Pongal (statewide; mid-Jan) Marks the end of the harvest season and is one of Tamil Nadu's most important festivals, named after a rice-and-lentil dish cooked in new clay pots. Animals, especially cows, are honoured for their contributions.

Thyagaraja Aradhana (p374; Jan, Thiruvaiyaru) Carnatic music.

Teppam (Float) Festival (p384; Jan/Feb, Madurai) Meenakshi temple deities are paraded around town.

Natyanjali Dance Festival (p368; Feb/Mar, Chidambaram) Five days of professional classical dance.

Chithirai Festival (p384; Apr/May, Madurai) Two-week event celebrating the marriage of Meenakshi to Sundareswarar (Shiva).

Karthikai Deepam Festival (p357; Nov/Dec, statewide) Festival of lights.

Chennai Festival of Music & Dance (p333; mid-Dec–mid-Jan, Chennai) A huge celebration of South Indian music and dance.

Mamallapuram Dance Festival (p350; Dec–Jan, Mamallapuram) Four weeks of classical and folk dance from across India on open-air stages.

tury, some of their local governors, the Nayaks, set up strong independent kingdoms, notably at Madurai and Thanjavur. Vijayanagar and Nayak sculptors carved wonderfully detailed temple statues and reliefs.

Europeans first landed on Tamil shores in the 16th century, when the Portuguese settled at San Thome. The Dutch, British, French and Danes followed in the 17th century, striking deals with local rulers to set up coastal trading colonies. Eventually it came down to the British, based at Chennai (then Madras), against the French, based at Puducherry (then Pondicherry). The British won out in the three Carnatic Wars, fought between 1744 and 1763. By the end of the 18th century British dominance over most Tamil lands was assured.

The area governed by the British from Madras, the Madras Presidency, included parts of Andhra Pradesh, Kerala and Karnataka, an arrangement that continued (as Madras State) after Indian independence in 1947, until Kerala, Karnataka, Andhra Pradesh and present-day Tamil Nadu (130,058 sq km) were created on linguistic lines in the 1950s. It wasn't until 1968 that the current state (population 72.1 million) was officially named Tamil Nadu.

Tamil Nadu's political parties are often headed up by former film stars, most prominent among them controversial former Chief Minister and AIADMK (All India Anna Dravida Munnetra Kazhagam) leader Jayalalithaa Jayaram. Known as 'Amma' (mother), Jayalalithaa was worshipped with almost deity-like status across the state until her death on 5 December 2016.

CHENNAI (MADRAS)

🎵 044 / POP 8.7 MILLION

If you have time to explore Chennai (formerly Madras), this 400-sq-km conglomerate of urban villages and diverse neighbourhoods making up Tamil Nadu's capital will pleasantly surprise you. Its role is as keeper of South Indian artistic, religious and culinary traditions.

Among Chennai's greatest assets are its people, infectiously enthusiastic about their hometown; they won't hit you with a lot of hustle and hassle. Recent years have thrown in a new layer of cosmopolitan glamour: luxe hotels, sparkling boutiques, quirky cafes, smart contemporary restaurants and a sprinkling of swanky bars and clubs.

With its sweltering southern heat, roaring traffic and lack of outstanding sights, Chennai has often been seen as the dowdier sibling among India's four biggest cities. But even if you're just caught here between connections, it's well worth poking around the museums, exploring the temples, savouring deliciously authentic South Indian delicacies or taking a sunset saunter along Marina Beach.

History

The southern neighbourhood of Mylapore existed long before the rest of Chennai; there is evidence that it traded with Roman and even Chinese and Greek merchants. In 1523, the Portuguese established their nearby coastal settlement San Thome. Another century passed before Francis Day and the British East India Company rocked up in 1639, searching for a good southeast-Indian trading base, and struck a deal with the local Vijayanagar ruler to set up a fort-cum-trading-post at Madraspatnam fishing village. This was Fort St George, built from 1640 to 1653.

The three Carnatic Wars between 1744 and 1763 saw Britain and its colonialist rival France allying with competing South Indian princes in their efforts to get the upper hand over local rulers – and each other. The French occupied Fort St George from 1746 to 1749 but the British eventually triumphed, and the French withdrew to Pondicherry.

As capital of the Madras Presidency, one of the four major divisions of British-era India, Madras grew into an important naval and commercial centre. After Independence, it became capital of Madras State and its successor Tamil Nadu. The city was renamed Chennai in 1996. Today, it's a major IT hub, and is often called 'the Detroit of India' for its booming motor-vehicle industry.

💿 Sights

◉ Central Chennai

⭐ **Government Museum**   MUSEUM
(Map p334; www.chennaimuseum.org; Pantheon Rd, Egmore; Indian/foreigner ₹15/250, camera/video ₹200/500; ⊙9.30am-5pm Sat-Thu) Housed across the striking British-built Pantheon Complex, this excellent museum is Chennai's best. The big highlight is building 3, the **Bronze Gallery**, with a superb collection of South Indian bronzes from the 7th-century Pallava era through to modern times (and English-language explanatory material).

It was from the 9th to 11th centuries, in the Chola period, that bronze sculpture

Chennai (Madras)

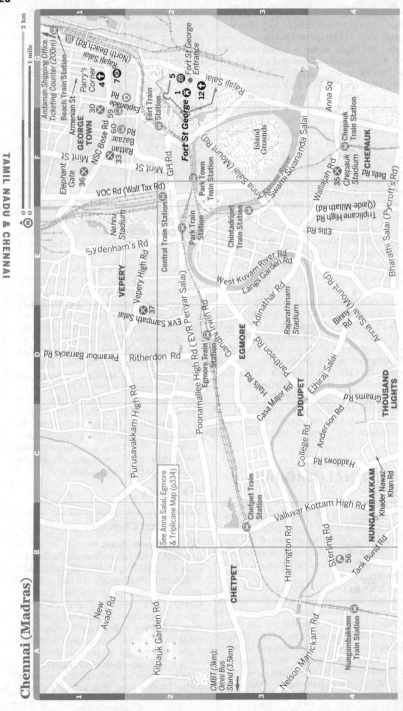

Andaman Shipping Office
Ticketing Counter (200m)

Rajaji Salai (North Beach Rd)

Parry's Corner

Beach Train Station

Esplanade Rd

Armenian St

GEORGE TOWN

NSC Bose Rd

Rattan Bazaar Rd

Mint St

Elephant Gate

Fort Train Station

Fort St George Entrance

Fort St George

Rajaji Salai

Anna Sq

Chepauk Train Station

CHEPAUK

Chepauk Stadium

Wallajah Rd

Bells Rd

GH Rd

VOC Rd (Wall Tax Rd)

Park Town Train Station

Island Grounds

Anna Salai (Mount Rd)

Swami Sivananda Salai

Triplicane High Rd (Qaide-Millath Rd)

Ellis Rd

Bharathi Salai (Pycroft's Rd)

Nehru Stadium

Sydenham's Rd

Central Train Station

Park Train Station

Chintadripet Train Station

West Kuvam River Rd

Langs Garden Rd

VEPERY

Vepery High Rd

EVK Sampath Salai

Perambur Barracks Rd

Ritherdon Rd

Gandhi Irwin Rd

Egmore Train Station

Poonamallee High Rd (EVR Periyar Salai)

EGMORE

Adinathar Rd

Rajarathinam Stadium

Halls Rd

Pantheon Rd

PUDUPET

Casa Major Rd

Ethiraj Salai

Anna Salai (Mount Rd)

Binny Rd

THOUSAND LIGHTS

Greams Rd

Anderson Rd

Purusavakkam High Rd

See Anna Salai, Egmore & Triplicane Map (p334)

College Rd

Haddows Rd

NUNGAMBAKKAM

Khader Nawaz Khan Rd

Chetpet Train Station

Valluvar Kottam High Rd

CHETPET

Harrington Rd

Sterling Rd

Tank Bund Rd

New Avadi Rd

Kilpauk Garden Rd

CMBT (3km); Omni Bus Stand (3.5km)

Nelson Manickam Rd

Nungambakkam Train Station

2 km
1 mile

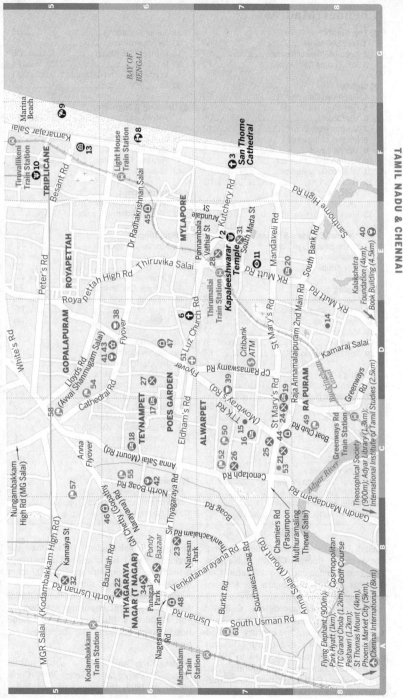

BAY OF BENGAL

Marina Beach

Kamarajar Salai

9

Tiruvallikeni Train Station

TRIPLICANE

10

13

Besant Rd

Light House Train Station

8

Dr Radhakrishnan Salai

San Thome Cathedral

3

MYLAPORE

Kutchery Rd

45

Santhome High Rd

Pennambala Vathiar St

Arundale St

2

31

South Mada St

28

Kapaleeshwarar Temple

11

Mandaveli Rd

RK Mutt Rd

20

South Bank Rd

Thiruvika Salai

ROYAPETTAH

Peter's Rd

Royapettah High Rd

Roya

Thirumailai Train Station

6

Citibank ATM

RK Mutt Rd

GOPALAPURAM

Lloyds Rd (Avvai Shanmugam Salai)

38

Flyover

41 43

Luz Church Rd

51

47

CP Ramaswamy Rd

St Mary's Rd

14

Kamaraj Salai

RA PURAM

Raja Annamalaipuram 2nd Main Rd

Kalakshetra Foundation (4km); Book Building (4.5km)

40

White's Rd

Cathedral Rd

54

Flyover

27

17

POES GARDEN

Eldham's Rd

TTK Rd (Mowbray's Rd)

39

52 50

15

16

St Mary's Rd

24

19

25

44

21

53

Boat Club Rd

49

Greenways Rd Train Station

Buckingham Canal

Greenways Rd

Adyar River

Theosophical Society (900m); Adyar Library (1.3km); International Institute of Tamil Studies (2.5km)

Nungambakkam High Rd (MG Salai)

Anna Flyover

57

TEYNAMPET

18

Anna Salai (Mount Rd)

ALWARPET

Cenotaph Rd

26

52

Gandhi Mandapam Rd

MGR Salai (Kodambakkam High Rd)

North Usman Rd

32

Bazullah Rd

22

GN Chetty (Rd)

46

North Boag Rd

55

42

Sir Thyagaraya Rd

Boag Rd

Chamiers Rd (Pasumpon Muthuramaling Thewar Salai)

Anna Salai (Mount Rd)

Southwest Boag Rd

Kodambakkam Train Station

THYAGARAYA NAGAR (T NAGAR)

34

Panagal Park

29

23

Thanikachalam Rd

Natesan Park

Venkatanarayana Rd

Burkit Rd

Flying Elephant (900m); Park Hyatt (1km); ITC Grand Chola (1.2km); Golf Course

Nageswaran Rd

48

Usman Rd

South Usman Rd

61

Mambalam Train Station

St Thomas Mount (4km); Phoenix Market City (5km); Peshawri (1.2km); Chennai International (8km)

Cosmopolitan

Chennai (Madras)

peaked. Among the Bronze Gallery's impressive pieces are many of Shiva as Nataraja, the cosmic dancer, and an outstanding Chola bronze of Ardhanarishvara, the androgynous incarnation of Shiva and Parvati.

The main **Archaeological Galleries** (building 1) represent all the major South Indian periods from 2nd-century BC Buddhist sculptures to 16th-century Vijayanagar work, with rooms devoted to Hindu, Buddhist and Jain sculpture. Building 2, the **Anthropology Galleries**, traces South Indian human history back to prehistoric times,

displaying tribal artefacts from across the region; outside it is a tiger-head cannon captured from Tipu Sultan's army in 1799 upon his defeat at Srirangapatnam.

The museum also includes the **National Art Gallery**, **Contemporary Art Gallery** and **Children's Museum**, on the same ticket. Some sections may be closed for renovation.

Madras High Court   NOTABLE BUILDING
(Map p328; Parry's Corner, George Town) Completed in 1892, this imposing red Indo-

Saracenic structure is said to be the world's largest judicial building after the Courts of London. The central tower was added in 1912. At research time, visitors were not permitted to wander the grounds, but if you fancy trying, take your passport.

★ **Fort St George**   FORT
(Map p328; Rajaji Salai; ⊙10am-5pm) FREE Finished in 1653 by the British East India Company, the fort has undergone many facelifts. Inside the vast perimeter walls (the ramparts are 18th-century replacements) is now a precinct housing Tamil Nadu's Legislative Assembly & Secretariat, and a smattering of older buildings. The **Fort Museum** (Map p328; Indian/foreigner ₹15/200; ⊙9am-5pm Sat-Thu) has displays on Chennai's origins and the fort, and interesting military memorabilia and artwork from colonial times. The 1st-floor portrait gallery of colonial-era VIPs includes a very assured-looking Robert Clive (Clive of India).

Also within the fort is **St Mary's Church** (Map p328; ⊙10am-5pm Mon-Sat), completed in 1680, and India's oldest surviving British church, surrounded by even earlier gravestones; Clive was married here. To its right (west) is the neoclassical former **Admiralty House** (Clive's House).

Marina Beach   BEACH
(Map p328) Take an early morning or evening stroll (you don't want to roast here at any other time) along the 3km-long main stretch of Marina Beach and you'll pass cricket matches, flying kites, fortune-tellers, fish markets, corn-roasters and families enjoy-ing the sea breeze. But don't swim: strong rips make it dangerous. At the southern end, the ridiculously popular **Madras Lighthouse** (Map p328; adult/child ₹20/10, camera ₹25; ⊙10am-1pm & 3-5pm Tue-Sun) is India's only lighthouse with a lift; the panoramic city and beach views are fabulous.

Parthasarathy Temple   HINDU TEMPLE
(Map p328; Singarachari St, Triplicane; ⊙5.30am-noon & 4-9.30pm) Built under the 8th-century Pallavas and unusually dedicated to Krishna (a form of Vishnu) as the charioteer Parthasarathy, this is one of Chennai's oldest temples. Most of its elaborate carvings, however, date from its 16th-century Vijayanagar expansion, including the fine stone-carved colonnade fronting the entrance. It's special for its shrines dedicated to five of the incarnations of Vishnu.

Vivekananda House   MUSEUM
(Vivekanandar Illam, Ice House; Map p328; www.vivekanandahouse.org; Kamarajar Salai; adult/child ₹20/10; ⊙10am-12.15pm & 3-7.15pm Tue-Sat) The marshmallow-pink Vivekananda House is interesting not only for its displays on the famous 'wandering monk', Swami Vivekananda, but also for its semicircular form, built in 1842 to store ice imported from the USA. Vivekananda stayed here briefly in 1897, preaching his ascetic Hindu philosophy to adoring crowds. Displays include a photo exhibition on the swami's life, a 3D reproduction of Vivekananda's celebrated 1893 Chicago World's Parliament of Religions speech, and the room where he stayed, now used for meditation.

DRAVIDIAN PRIDE

Since before Indian independence in 1947, Tamil politicians have railed against caste (considered to favour light-skinned Brahmins) and the Hindi language (seen as North Indian cultural imperialism). The pre-Independence 'Self Respect' movement and Justice Party, influenced by Marxism, mixed South Indian communal values with class-war rhetoric, and spawned Tamil political parties that remain the major powers in Tamil Nadu today. In the early post-Independence decades there was even a movement for an independent Dravida Nadu nation comprising the four main South Indian peoples, but there was little solidarity between different groups. Today Dravidian politics is largely restricted to Tamil Nadu, where parties are often led by former film stars (who often have immense, passionate followings).

During the conflict in nearby Sri Lanka, many Indian Tamil politicians loudly defended the Tamil Tigers, the organisation that assassinated Rajiv Gandhi in Sriperumbudur near Chennai in 1991. There is still considerable prejudice among the generally tolerant Tamils towards anything Sinhalese. The most obvious sign of Tamil pride you'll see today is the white shirt and white *mundu* (sarong), worn by most Tamil public figures.

TAMIL NADU & CHENNAI (MADRAS)

⊙ Southern Chennai

★**Kapaleeshwarar Temple**   HINDU TEMPLE
(Map p328; Ponnambala Vathiar St, Mylapore; ⊙6am-noon & 4-9.30pm) Mylapore is one of Chennai's most characterful and traditional neighbourhoods; it predated colonial Madras by several centuries. Its Kapaleeshwarar Temple is Chennai's most active and impressive, believed to have been built after the Portuguese destroyed the seaside original in 1566. It displays the main architectural elements of many a Tamil Nadu temple – a rainbow-coloured *gopuram*, pillared *mandapas* (pavilions), and a huge tank – and is dedicated to the state's most popular deity, Shiva.

Legend tells that in an angry fit Shiva turned his consort Parvati into a peacock, and commanded her to worship him here to regain her normal form. Parvati supposedly did so at a spot just outside the northeast corner of the temple's central block, where a shrine commemorates the event. Hence the name Mylapore, 'town of peacocks'. The story is depicted at the west end of the inner courtyard, on the exterior of the main sanctum.

The temple's colourful **Brahmotsavam festival** (March/April) sees the deities paraded around Mylapore's streets.

Sri Ramakrishna Math   RELIGIOUS SITE
(Map p328; www.chennaimath.org; 31 RK Mutt Rd, Mylapore; ⊙Universal Temple 4.30-11.45am & 3-9pm, evening prayers 6.30-7.30pm) The tranquil, flowery grounds of the Ramakrishna Math are a world away from Mylapore's chaos. Orange-robed monks glide around and there's a reverential feel. The Math is a monastic order following the teachings of the 19th-century sage Sri Ramakrishna, who preached the essential unity of all religions. Its Universal Temple is a handsome, modern, salmon-pink building incorporating architectural elements from different religions, and is open to all, to worship, pray or meditate.

★**San Thome Cathedral**   CATHEDRAL
(Map p328; Santhome High Rd, Mylapore; ⊙5.30am-8.30pm) This soaring Roman Catholic cathedral, a stone's throw from the beach, was founded by the Portuguese in 1523, then rebuilt by the British in neo-Gothic style in 1896, and is said to mark the final resting place of St Thomas the Apostle. It's believed 'Doubting Thomas' brought Christianity to the subcontinent in AD 52 and was killed at St Thomas Mount (p333), Chennai, in AD 72. Behind the cathedral is the **tomb of St Thomas** (Map p328; ⊙5.30am-8.30pm) FREE.

Although most of St Thomas' mortal remains now apparently lie in Italy, a cross on the tomb wall contains a tiny bone fragment marked 'Relic of St Thomas'. The museum above displays Thomas-related artefacts including the lancehead believed to have killed him.

St Thomas' Pole, at the beach end of the street on the cathedral's south side, is said to have miraculously saved the cathedral from the 2004 tsunami.

Theosophical Society   GARDENS
(www.ts-adyar.org; south end of Thiru Vi Ka Bridge, Adyar; ⊙grounds 8.30-10am & 2-4pm Mon-Sat) FREE Between the Adyar River and the coast, the 100-hectare grounds of the Theosophical Society provide a peaceful, green, vehicle-free retreat from the city. Despite restricted opening hours, it's a lovely spot to wander, containing a church, mosque, Buddhist shrine, Zoroastrian temple and Hindu temple as well as a huge variety of native and introduced flora, including the offshoots of a 450-year-old banyan tree severely damaged by a storm in the 1980s.

The **Adyar Library** (www.ts-adyar.org; Theosophical Society, off Besant Ave Rd, Adyar; 1yr reader's card ₹50, deposit ₹250; ⊙9am-5pm Tue-Sun) here has an impressive collection of religion and philosophy books (some on display), from 1000-year-old Buddhist scrolls to handmade 19th-century Bibles.

Kalakshetra Foundation   ARTS CENTRE
(☑044-24521169; www.kalakshetra.in; Muthulakshmi St, Thiruvanmiyur; Indian/foreigner incl craft centre ₹100/500; ⊙campus 8.30-11.30am Mon-Fri Jul-Feb, craft centre 9am-1pm & 2-5pm Mon-Sat, all closed 2nd & 4th Sat of month) Founded in 1936, Kalakshetra is a leading serious school of Tamil classical dance and music (sponsoring many students from disadvantaged backgrounds), set in beautiful, shady grounds in south Chennai. During morning class times visitors can (quietly) wander the complex and its **Rukmini Devi Museum**. Across the road is the **Kalakshetra Craft Centre**, where you can see Kanchipuram-style hand-loom weaving, textile block-printing and the fascinating, rare art of *kalamkari* (hand-painting on textiles with vegetable dyes). For upcoming performances, check the website.

The Thiruvanmiyur bus stand, terminus of many city bus routes, is 500m southwest of the Kalakshetra entrance.

CHENNAI'S OTHER CHURCHES

Armenian Church (Map p328; Armenian St, George Town; ◷9.30am-2.30pm, hours vary) A frangipani-scented haven in the midst of George Town, this 18th-century church is testament to the city's once-flourishing Armenian merchant community. Its courtyard displays ancient gravestones covered in Armenian script.

St Andrew's Church (St Andrew's Kirk; Map p334; www.thekirk.in; 37 Poonamallee High Rd, Egmore; ◷9.30am-5pm) This 1821 neoclassical Scottish Presbyterian church stands in leafy Egmore grounds. Inspired by London's St Martin-in-the-Fields, it has an exquisite columned portico, an unusual oval colonnade under a domed ceiling supported by Corinthian columns, and a slim multilevel spire.

Luz Church (Shrine of our Lady of Light; Map p328; www.luzchurch.org; off Luz Church Rd, Mylapore; ◷dawn-dusk) Styled with blue-and-white baroque elegance, palm-fringed 1516 Luz Church is Chennai's oldest European building.

Book Building GALLERY
(🖉044-24426696; www.tarabooks.com; Plot 9, CGE Colony, Kuppam Beach Rd, Thiruvanmiyur; ◷10am-7.30pm Mon-Sat) FREE Within this mural-covered space, Tara Books stages free exhibitions, author talks and workshops with visiting artists, and displays its own highly original handmade books. With prior notice, you can visit the workshop where the books are created (20 minutes' drive away).

St Thomas Mount RELIGIOUS SITE
(Parangi Malai; off Lawrence Rd, Guindy; ◷6am-8pm) FREE The reputed site of St Thomas' martyrdom in AD 72 rises in the southwest of Chennai, 2.5km north of St Thomas Mount train station and metro station. The **Church of Our Lady of Expectation**, built atop the 'mount' by the Portuguese in 1523, contains what are supposedly a fragment of Thomas' finger bone and the 'Bleeding Cross' he carved. The city and airport views are wonderful.

🏃 Activities

Krishnamacharya Yoga Mandiram YOGA, MEDITATION
(KYM; Map p328; 🖉044-24937998; www.kym.org; 31 4th Cross St, RK Nagar; class US$30; ◷8am-7pm) Highly regarded, serious two-week and month-long yoga courses, yoga therapy, and intensive teacher training.

🐚 Courses

Run by Storytrails, the four-hour Spice Trail (per person ₹2500) is a fascinating introduction to South Indian cooking, with hands-on, small-group cookathons.

Kalakshetra Foundation ART
(🖉044-24525423; www.kalakshetra.in; Muthulakshmi St, Thiruvanmiyur; per day ₹500) Kalakshetra's crafts centre offers one-month to two-month courses in the intricate old art of *kalamkari*, which survives in only a handful of places. Courses run 10am to 1pm Monday to Friday.

International Institute of Tamil Studies LANGUAGE
(🖉044-22542992, 9952448862; www.ulakaththamizh.org; CIT Campus, 2nd Main Rd, Tharamani; 3-/6-month course ₹5000/10,000) Intensive three-month and six-month Tamil-language courses.

☞ Tours

Storytrails WALKING
(Map p328; 🖉044-45010202, 9940040215; www.storytrails.in; 21/2 1st Cross St, TTK Rd, Alwarpet; 3hr tour for up to 4 people from ₹4400) Entertaining neighbourhood walking tours on themes like dance, temples, jewellery and bazaars. Also runs popular food-tasting tours through George Town and in-house cooking classes.

🎊 Festivals & Events

Madras Week CULTURAL
(www.themadrasday.in; ◷Aug) An inspired series of heritage walks, talks and exhibitions held across town to honour the 1639 founding of then-Madras.

Chennai Festival of Music & Dance MUSIC, DANCE
(Madras Music & Dance Season; ◷mid-Dec–mid-Jan) One of the largest of its type in the world, this festival celebrates South Indian music and dance.

🛏 Sleeping

Hotels in Chennai are pricier than elsewhere in Tamil Nadu and don't offer particularly good value. The Triplicane High Rd area is

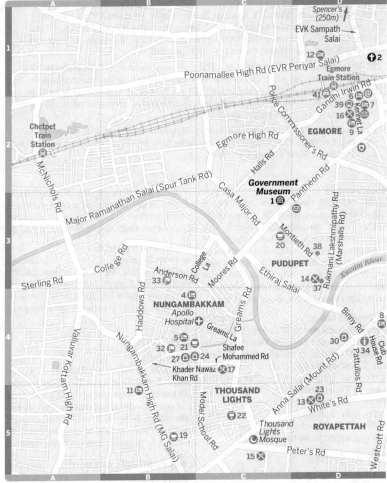

TAMIL NADU & CHENNAI CHENNAI (MADRAS)

best for budget accommodation. There are some cheapies in Egmore, plus a few mid-range options. You'll find upper-midrange B&Bs in Nungambakkam, Poes Garden and Alwarpet. Top-end hotels have become plentiful, especially in southern areas.

Many hotels have 24-hour checkout and fill up by noon; call ahead.

☞ Egmore

New Lakshmi Lodge HOTEL **$**
(Map p334; ☎ 044-28194576, 9840900343; 16 Kennet Lane; s/d ₹500/900, r with AC ₹1460-1580; ▣) With small and bare but spotless, pas-

tel-walled rooms spread over four floors around a parking courtyard, this huge block is not a bad budget choice. Book ahead, as it's often full. Upper floors offer more privacy.

YWCA International
Guest House GUESTHOUSE **$$**
(Map p334; ☎ 044-25324234; http://ywcamadras.org/international-guest-house; 1086 Poonamallee High Rd; incl breakfast s ₹1760-2380, d ₹2170-2850, s/d without AC ₹1020/1560; ▣@⊜) Chennai's YWCA guesthouse, set in shady grounds just north of Egmore station, offers excellent value combined with a calm atmosphere. Effi-

lite service, 24-hour checkout and free wi-fi, and this is good value by Egmore standards.

Hotel Victoria
HOTEL **$$**

(Map p334; ☑ 044-28193638; www.empeehotels. com; 3 Kennet Lane; incl breakfast s ₹2500-4300, d ₹2800-4700; ※ ☜) Easily your smartest choice on hectic Kennet Lane. Rooms are clean and decent (with kettles, wi-fi and TVs), though not as exciting as the shiny lobby and cordial service suggest.

Nungambakkam & Around

Frangi House
B&B **$$**

(Map p334; ☑ 044-43084694; www.frangihouse. com; 6B Nawab Habibullah Ave, 1st St, off Anderson Rd; r incl breakfast ₹3940-4280; ※ ☜) This elegant, immaculate retreat is tucked into a tranquil street in upmarket Nungambakkam, offering grassy gardens, comfy lounges and eight airy, all-different rooms. 'Boutique' rooms mix vintage four-poster beds with modern bathrooms sporting stylish square sinks. 'Old world' pads are styled in florals and pastels; the pick is blue-hued 'Dew', with its four-poster and shared balcony.

Hanu Reddy Residences
B&B **$$**

(Map p334; ☑ 9176869926, 044-43084563; www. hanureddyresidences.com; 6A/24 3rd St, Wallace Garden; incl breakfast s ₹3600-4200, d ₹4200-4800; ※ ☜) Spread across two residential buildings engulfed by greenery in upscale Wallace Garden, this is exactly the kind of homey hideaway that central Chennai needs. The 13 unpretentious rooms come with air-con, free wi-fi, tea/coffee sets, splashes of colourful artwork – and anti-mosquito racquets! Terraces have bamboo lounging chairs. Service hits that ideal personal-yet-professional balance. There's another **branch** (Map p328; ☑ 044-24661021; 41/19 Poes Garden; incl breakfast s ₹4200-5400, d ₹4800-7800; ※ ☜) in exclusive Poes Garden.

Taj Coromandel
HOTEL **$$$**

(Map p334; ☑ 044-66002827; www.tajhotels. com; 37 Nungambakkam High Rd; r from ₹12,000; ※ ☜ ☒) Luxurious without going overly ostentatious, the glittering Coromandel offers a sensibly central top-end retreat from the city. Rooms flaunt a smart stripped-back style and there's a lovely palm-shaded pool. The marble-effect lobby hosts fine-dining South Indian restaurant **Southern Spice** (Map p334; mains ₹550-900, thalis ₹1500-2200; ⊙12.30-2.45pm & 7-11pm), along with a busy cocktail bar.

ciently run by helpful staff, it has good-sized, brilliantly clean rooms, spacious common areas and solid-value meals (veg/nonveg ₹225/330). Lobby-only wi-fi costs ₹150 per day.

Hotel Chandra Park
HOTEL **$$**

(Map p334; ☑ 044-40506060; www.hotelchandra park.com; 9 Gandhi Irwin Rd; incl breakfast s ₹1580-2560, d ₹1820-3020; ※ ☜) Chandra Park's prices remain mysteriously lower than most similar establishments. 'Standard' rooms are small and a bit dated but have air-con, clean towels and tight, white sheets. Throw in po-

TAMIL NADU & CHENNAI CHENNAI (MADRAS)

Anna Salai, Egmore & Triplicane

🛏 Triplicane & Around

Paradise Guest House   GUESTHOUSE $
(Map p334; ☑044-28594252; www.paradise
guesthouse.co.in; 17/1 Vallabha Agraharam St; s/d
₹600/700, with AC ₹1000/1100; 🅿🛜) Paradise
offers some of Triplicane's best-value digs:
simple rooms with clean tiles, a breezy
rooftop, friendly staff and hot water by the
steaming bucket.

Broad Lands Lodge   GUESTHOUSE $
(Map p334; ☑044-28545573; broadlandshotel@
yahoo.com; 18 Vallabha Agraharam St; s ₹400-750,
d ₹450-800; 🛜) In business since 1951, Broad
Lands was a hippie-era stalwart. This laid-
back colonial-era mansion, with leafy courtyards and rooms up rambling staircases, still
has its devotees, who don't seem to mind the
44 bare-bones, idiosyncratic rooms, dank
bathrooms, or high-volume muezzins of
Wallajah Big Mosque. The cheapest rooms
share bathrooms; wi-fi costs ₹50. The red-
banistered back block has breezier rooms.

La Woods   HOTEL $$
(Map p334; ☑044-28608040; www.lawoodshotel.
com; 1 Woods Rd; r incl breakfast ₹3600; 🅿🛜)
Wonderfully erratic colour schemes throw
fresh whites against lime greens and bright
turquoises at this friendly, well-managed
modern hotel. The shiny, spotless, contemporary rooms are perfectly comfy, with
mountains of pillows, kettles, hairdryers and
'global' plug sockets.

🛏 Southern Chennai

Red Lollipop Hostel   HOSTEL $
(Map p328; ☑044-24629822; www.redlollipop.in;
129/68 RK Mutt Rd, Mandavelli; dm ₹650; 🅿🛜)
Saving the day for Chennai's budget travellers, Red Lollipop is a genuine, sociable
hostel, 700m south of Mylapore's temple.
Boldly colourful walls are scrawled with inspirational messages. Each of the spotless,
locker-equipped six- to 10-bed dorms (one
women-only) has its own bathroom. There's

a rooftop terrace, plus a shared kitchen, a lounge, towel rental (₹30) and Chennai tips.

★Footprint B&B
B&B $$

(Map p328; ☑9840037483; www.chennaibed andbreakfast.com; Gayatri Apartments, 16 South St, Alwarpet, behind Crowne Plaza Hotel; r incl break-fast ₹3900; ❄☎) A beautifully comfortable, relaxed base occupying three apartments on a quiet street in a leafy south-Chennai neighbourhood. Bowls of wild roses, organic Auroville soaps and old-Madras photos set the scene for nine cosy, pristine rooms with king-size or wide twin beds. Home-cooked breakfasts are generous, service is excellent, and the welcoming owners are full of Tamil Nadu tips. Book ahead.

Madras B&B
B&B $$

(Map p328; ☑9840037483; www.madrasbed andbreakfast.com; Flat 1/3, Nandini Apartments, 72/45 1st Main Rd, RA Puram; r incl breakfast ₹3040; ❄☎) Popular with yoga students, this multilocation operation offers good-sized, straightforward but comfy, stylish rooms in peaceful private apartments that feel like cosy self-service lodges, dotted around RA Puram and Alwarpet. Help yourself to fully equipped kitchens, washing machines, small libraries and relaxed communal lounges full of flower bowls. No walk-ins: book ahead.

★Raintree
HOTEL $$$

(Map p328; ☑044-42252525; www.raintree hotels.com; 120 St Mary's Rd, Alwarpet; s/d ₹9590/10,790; ❄@☎) At this 'eco-sensitive' business-style hotel, floors are bamboo or rubber, water and electricity conservation hold pride of place, and AC-generated heat warms the bathroom water. Sleek, fresh, minimalist rooms are bright, comfy and stylish, with wonderful city vistas. A sea-view infinity pool (doubling as insulation) and an open-air bar-restaurant grace the rooftop. Downstairs is excellent pan-Asian restaurant **Chap Chay** (Map p328; mains ₹500-900, set menu ₹1900; ☺noon-3pm & 7-11pm).

Hyatt Regency
HOTEL $$$

(Map p328; ☑044-61001234; http://chennai. regency.hyatt.com; 365 Anna Salai, Teynampet; r ₹9720-15,800; ❄@☎) Smart, swish and bang up to date, this towering, triangular hotel is the most central of Chennai's newer top-end offerings. Contemporary art surrounds the sun-flooded atrium, local chefs head up three good restaurants and an insanely popular bar (p340), and glossy rooms have walk-through bathrooms and fabulous sea/city panoramas through massive picture windows. Flowers fringe the pool, and there's a luxury spa.

ITC Grand Chola
HOTEL $$$

(☑044-22200000; www.itchotels.in; 63 Mount Rd, Guindy; r incl breakfast from ₹13,970; ❄☎) Chennai's most talked-about hotel is this ultraluxurious, 600-room, temple-inspired beauty in the city's southwest. A maze of sumptuous iPad-operated rooms, complete with soaking tubs and French press coffee kits, unfolds beyond the sweeping lantern-lit marble lobby. One corridor caters exclusively to women travellers. Also here are seven swish restaurants, two glitzy bars, three gyms, a spa and five pools.

Park Hyatt
HOTEL $$$

(☑044-71771234; http://chennai.park.hyatt.com; 39 Velachery Rd, Guindy; s/d incl breakfast from ₹9720/10,940; ❄☎) The gleaming, ultra-modern Park Hyatt has swanky, straight-lined rooms kitted out with Nespresso machines, iPod docks and king-size beds; a divine spa; and a rooftop infinity pool overlooking Guindy National Park. The multi-floor **Flying Elephant** (☑044-71771234; per couple ₹3300 incl ₹2000 drink credit, women free; ☺7pm-late Mon-Sat, noon-3pm & 7pm-late Sun) restaurant doubles as a popular party pad. It's a hike from central Chennai, but perfect if you're after a plush stay near the airport.

✕ Eating

Chennai is packed with inexpensive 'meals' joints ('messes'), serving lunch and dinner thalis (all you can eat meals), and tiffin (snacks) like *idlis* (spongy, round fermented rice cakes), *vadas* (doughnut-shaped deep-fried lentil savoury) and dosas (savoury crêpe). Hotel Saravana Bhavan (p338) is always a quality veg choice. In the Muslim Triplicane High Rd area, you'll find great biryanis (fragrant, spiced steamed rice with meat and vegetables).

There's plenty of upmarket dining: classier Indian restaurants are on the rise, and international cuisines are soaring in popularity.

Useful, well-stocked supermarkets include **Spencer's** (Map p328; 15 EVK Sampath Salai, Vepery; ☺7.30am-10pm), near Egmore and Central stations, Big Bazaar at **T Nagar** (Map p328; 34 Sir Thyagaraya Rd, Pondy Bazaar, T Nagar; ☺10.30am-10pm) and **Express Avenue mall** (Map p334; Express Avenue, White's Rd; ☺10am-9.30pm Mon-Fri, to 10pm Sat & Sun),

Nilgiri's (Map p334; 25 Shafee Mohammed Rd, Nungambakkam; ⊙7.30am-10pm) off Nungambakkam's Khader Nawaz Khan Rd and **Amma Naana** (Map p328; www.ammanaana. com; 82/100 Chamiers Rd, Alwarpet; ⊙10am-9pm Mon-Sat) in Alwarpet.

✕ Egmore

★Hotel Saravana Bhavan
INDIAN $
(Map p334; ☑044-28192055; www.saravanabha van.com; 21 Kennet Lane; mains ₹70-140; ⊙6am-10.30pm) Dependably delish, Chennai's famous vegetarian chain doles out epically good South Indian thalis and breakfasts (*idlis* and *vadas* ₹15 to ₹35, dosas ₹20 to ₹40), filter coffee and other Indian vegetarian fare. This branch is handy for Egmore station. Others include **George Town** (Map p328; ☑044-25387766; 209 NSC Bose Rd; mains ₹60-100, thalis ₹60-145; ⊙7am-10pm), **Mylapore** (Map p328; ☑044-24611177; 70 North Mada St; mains ₹60-100, thalis ₹60-145; ⊙6am-10.30pm), **Pondy Bazaar** (Map p328; ☑044-281576677; 102 Sir Thyagaraya Rd; mains ₹60-100, thalis ₹170-210; ⊙6am-11pm) and, more upscale with a ₹320 buffet, **Thousand Lights** (Map p334; ☑044-28353377; 293 Peter's Rd; mains ₹100-180, thalis ₹60-150; ⊙8am-10.30pm), plus London, Paris and New York!

Annalakshmi
INDIAN $$
(Map p334; ☑044-28525100; www.annalaksh michennai.co.in; 1st fl, Sigapi Achi Bldg, 18/3 Rukmani Lakshmipathy Rd, Egmore; mains ₹180-280, set menus ₹700-1200, buffet weekday/weekend ₹420/470; ⊙noon-2.30pm & 7-9pm Tue-Sun) Very fine South and North Indian vegetarian fare, plus glorious fresh juices, in a beautiful dining room decorated with carvings and paintings, inside a high-rise behind the Air India building. Buffet lunches and dinners are served in another part of the same block. Annalakshmi is run by devotees of Swami Shanthanand Saraswathi; proceeds support medical programs for the poor.

✕ Nungambakkam & Around

★Amethyst
MULTICUISINE, CAFE $$$
(Map p334; ☑044-45991633; www.amethystchen nai.com; White's Rd, Royapettah; mains ₹250-470; ⊙10am-11.30pm; 🖘) Set in an exquisitely converted warehouse with a wraparound verandah from which tables spill out into lush gardens, Amethyst is a nostalgically posh haven that's outrageously popular with expats and well-off Chennaiites. Well-executed European-flavoured dishes range over

quiches, pastas, sandwiches, crepes, creative salads, all-day breakfasts and afternoon teas. Fight for your table, then check out the stunning Indian couture **boutique** (Map p334; ⊙11am-7.30pm).

✕ Triplicane & Around

Ratna Café
SOUTH INDIAN $
(Map p334; 255 Triplicane High Rd, Triplicane; dishes ₹70-110; ⊙6am-11pm) Often crowded and cramped, Ratna is famous for its scrumptious *idlis* accompanied by hearty doses of its signature *sambar* (soupy lentil dish with cubed vegetables). People have been sitting down to this ₹45 dish at all hours since 1948. There are also North Indian mains, and an air-con room out the back.

Nair Mess
SOUTH INDIAN $
(Map p328; 22 Mohammed Abdullah Sahib, 2nd St, Chepauk; meals ₹60-75; ⊙11.30am-3pm & 7-10pm) Big flavours are rustled up in a starkly simple setting at this no-nonsense, forever-busy meals spot, pocketed away in a lane opposite the Chepauk cricket stadium since 1961. Loaded banana-leaf thalis complemented by fish-fry dishes are the speciality.

✕ Southern Chennai

Murugan Idli Shop
SOUTH INDIAN $
(Map p328; http://muruganidlishop.com; 77 GN Chetty Rd, T Nagar; dishes ₹50-85; ⊙7am-11.30pm) Those in the know generally agree that this particular branch of the small Madurai-born Murugan chain serves some of the best *idlis*, dosas, *uttapams* and South Indian meals in town.

Double Roti
BURGERS $$
(Map p328; ☑044-30853732; http://doubleroti. in; 4/27 1st St, Cenotaph Rd, Teynampet; mains ₹245-395; ⊙11am-11pm; 🖘) 'Double roti' refers to burger buns – the semi-open kitchen at this always-packed industrial-chic cafe plates them up with fun, flair and buckets of flavour. Lemonades and milkshakes are served in jars; burgers arrive in mini-frying pans; buckets come filled with masala fries; and witty slogans are chalked up on boards. There's plenty for vegetarians too, including fantastic spicy-falafel burgers.

Junior Kuppanna
SOUTH INDIAN $$
(Map p328; ☑044-28340071; 4 Kannaiya St, North Usman Rd, T Nagar; mains ₹130-220, thalis ₹200; ⊙noon-4pm & 6.30-11.30pm) From an impeccably clean kitchen (which you're welcome

CHENNAI STREET FOOD

Chennai may not have the same killer street-food reputation as Mumbai, but there are some sensational South Indian street-side delicacies around, especially in Mylapore, George Town, Egmore and T Nagar, and along Marina Beach. **Storytrails** (p333) runs George Town **food-tasting tours** (for one or two people ₹4000).

Mehta Brothers (Map p328; 310 Mint St, George Town; dishes ₹15-25; ⏱7.30am-9.30pm Mon-Sat, to 2pm Sun) This tiny spot pulls in the crowds with the deep-fried delights of its signature Maharashtrian *vada pavs* – spiced potato fritters in buns, doused in garlicky chutney.

Seena Bhai Tiffin Centre (Map p328; 111/1 NSC Bose Rd, George Town; idlis & uttapams ₹40; ⏱6pm-midnight) It's all about deliciously griddled, ghee-coated *idlis* and *uttapams* at this 37-year-old eatery in the thick of George Town.

Jannal Kadai (Map p328; Ponnambala Vathiar St, Mylapore; items ₹20-30; ⏱8.30-10am & 5.30-8.30pm Mon-Sat) You take what you're given from the chap in the 'window shop', a fast-and-furious hole-in-the-wall famous for its hot crispy *bajjis* (vegetable fritters), *bondas* (battered potato balls) and *vadas*. Look for the blue windows opposite Pixel Service, just south of the Mylapore temple.

to tour), come limitless, flavour-packed lunchtime thalis, dished up traditional-style on banana leaves. This typical, frenzied Chennai 'mess' also has a full menu. Carnivores tiring of the pure-veg lifestyle can seek solace in specialities like mutton brains and pan-fried seer fish. Arrive early: it's incredibly popular. Branches across Chennai.

Enté Keralam
KERALAN $$
(Map p328; ✆07604915091; http://entekeralam.in; 1 Kasturi Estate, 1st St, Poes Garden; mains ₹200-565; ⏱noon-3pm & 7-11pm) A calm ambience seeps through the four orange-toned, three-to four-table rooms of this elegant Keralan restaurant. Lightly spiced *pachakkari* vegetable stew is served with light, fluffy *appam* (rice pancake), the Alleppey curry is rich with mango, and there are plenty of fish dishes. Wind up with tender coconut ice cream. Set meals (veg/nonveg ₹795/1195) give a multidish miniformat taster.

Barbeque Nation
INDIAN, BARBECUE $$
(Map p328; ✆044-60600000; www.barbeque-nation.com; Shri Devi Park Hotel, 1 Hanumantha Rd, off North Usman Rd, T Nagar; veg/nonveg lunch ₹705/780, dinner ₹900/1050; ⏱12.30-4.30pm & 6.30-11.30pm) For an incredible-value red-hot BBQ blow-out, hunt down this busy-busy all-you-can-eat spot. The highlights are the spicy meat, seafood and veg (paneer, pineapple) skewers that you sizzle to personal taste on live-grills set into the middle of your table. And *then* there's a full-fledged pan-Indian buffet.

★Peshawri
NORTH INDIAN $$$
(✆044-22200000; www.itchotels.in; ITC Grand Chola, 63 Mount Rd, Guindy; mains & set meals ₹3240-4140; ⏱noon-3pm & 7-11.30pm) Perfect for a five-star splash-out, the ITC's signature Northwest Frontier restaurant serves inventive, flavour-popping creations at intimate booths alongside a glassed-in kitchen that gets you right in on the culinary action. Try huge hunks of pillowy chilli-grilled paneer, expertly spiced kebabs, or the deliciously rich house-special *dhal bukhara*, simmered overnight. There's an astounding international wine/cocktail list.

★Copper Chimney
NORTH INDIAN $$$
(Map p328; ✆044-28115770; 74 Cathedral Rd, Gopalapuram; mains ₹300-700; ⏱noon-3pm & 7-11.30pm) Meat-eaters will drool over the yummy North Indian tandoori dishes served in stylishly minimalist surroundings, but the veg food here is fantastic too. Jain specialities mingle with biryanis, chicken kebabs, chargrilled prawns and fluffy-fresh naan. The *machchi* tikka – skewers of tandoori-baked fish – is superb, as is the spiced paneer kebab.

Chamiers
MULTICUISINE, CAFE $$$
(Map p328; ✆044-42030734; www.chamiershop.com; 106 Chamiers Rd, RA Puram; mains ₹300-500; ⏱8.30am-11pm; 📶) This bubbly 1st-floor cafe feels a continent away from Chennai, except that Chennaiites love it too. Flowery wallpaper, printed cushions, wicker chairs, wi-fi (per hour ₹100), wonderful carrot cake, croissants and cappuccino, English

breakfasts, American pancakes, pastas, quiches, quesadillas, salads...

Dakshin
SOUTH INDIAN $$$

(Map p328; ☑ 044-24994101; www.ihg.com; Crowne Plaza, 132 TTK Rd, Alwarpet; mains ₹690-1500, thalis ₹1800-2300; ⊘12.30-2.45pm & 7-11.15pm) Dakshin specialises in the cuisines of Kerala, Tamil Nadu, Andhra Pradesh, Telangana and Karnataka. Traditional sculptures, mirrored pillars and flute and tabla musicians set the temple-inspired scene. Food suggestion: the Andhra Pradesh fish curry – and perhaps a little something from the impressive whisky and wine list. Lunch revolves around fancy thalis.

🍷 Drinking & Nightlife

Chennai nightlife is on the up, with a smattering of lively new openings, but you'll need a full wallet for a night out here. Continental-style cafes are growing in number, and, yes, Starbucks has arrived.

Bars and clubs in five-star hotels serve alcohol 24 hours a day, seven days a week, so that's where most of the after-dark fun happens. Solo guys ('stags') can be turned away, and there's usually a hefty admission charge for couples and men. Dress codes are strict: no shorts or sandals.

Other hotel bars, mostly male-dominated, generally close by midnight. If you're buying your own alcohol, look for 'premium' or 'elite' government-run TASMAC liquor stores inside malls.

365 AS
LOUNGE, CLUB

(Map p328; ☑ 044-61001234; https://chennai.regency.hyatt.com; Hyatt Regency, 365 Anna Salai, Teynampet; drinks ₹400-700; ⊘3pm-2am) In the glamorous Hyatt Regency, Chennai's hottest party spot bursts into life on Friday and Saturday nights, when wild DJ sets kick off on the terrace. Otherwise, it's a swish, sultry lounge serving carefully crafted cocktails alongside Indian and international wines, beers and spirits. Dress code is smart casual (for guys, trousers and closed shoes).

Sera the Tapas Bar
BAR

(Map p328; ☑ 044-28111462; www.facebook.com/zaratapasbar; 71 Cathedral Rd, Gopalapuram; cocktails ₹400-500, tapas ₹220-330; ⊘12.30-11.30pm) Where else in the world can you find DJs playing club music beneath bullfight posters next to TVs showing cricket? Sera is packed most nights with a young, fashionable crowd sipping *sangría* and cocktails.

It's a good idea to book. Tapas include garlic prawns, fried calamari and aubergine dips; the *tortilla española* (potato omelette) is authentically good.

Radio Room
BAR

(Map p328; ☑ 8500005672; www.facebook.com/radioroomchennai; Somerset Greenways, 94 Sathyadev Ave, MRC Nagar, RA Puram; cocktails ₹450-600, dishes ₹200-300; ⊘6-11.30pm Mon-Fri, 4-11.30pm Sat & Sun) From a keen young team comes this incredibly popular radio-themed bar in southeast Chennai. It's all about mismatched furniture, a bar made of speakers and carefully mixed, inspired cocktails and pitchers – some full of local flavour, like chai punch. Creative twists on Chennai's culinary favourites include mozzarella-stuffed *bajjis* (vegetable fritters) delivered in bicycle-shaped baskets.

Sudaka
COCKTAIL BAR

(Map p328; ☑ 044-42004355; www.facebook.com/besudaka; 37 North Boag Rd, T Nagar; cocktails ₹400-500, dishes ₹200-500; ⊘noon-3pm & 6pm-midnight Mon-Fri, noon-midnight Sat) A genuine, sassy cocktail bar where expertly concocted, wittily named liquid mixes are served in a moodily lit lounge alongside artful Latin American and international cooking. Just name your spirit and they'll whip up something special.

Plan B
BAR

(Map p334; https://holycowhospitality.com; 65/5 Murugesan Naicker Complex, Greams Rd; cocktails ₹320-400, dishes ₹230-350; ⊘noon-11pm) Like its studenty same-name Bengaluru (Bangalore) sibling, this easygoing, industrial-feel bar is a hit with young crowds for its reasonably priced cocktails, wines and beers (mugs, pints or 'towers'), pub-style food (burgers, nachos, chilli-cheese chips) and belting chart-toppers.

Brew Room
CAFE

(Map p328; www.saverahotel.com; Savera Hotel, Dr Radhakrishnan Salai; coffees ₹120-180, dishes ₹250-350; ⊘8am-10.30pm; 🛜) Decked out in neo-rustic style, Brew Room does coffee like you've never had in Chennai, from double espresso and Italian cappuccino to Americano, French press and 'iceberg' coffee with ice cream. The contemporary Continental menu includes all-day breakfasts and brilliant vegetarian and vegan choices – even tofu!

Café Coffee Day
CAFE

(Map p334; www.cafecoffeeday.com; Ispahani Centre, 123 Nungambakkam High Rd, Nungambakkam; drinks

₹60-120; ⊙10am-10pm Mon-Fri, to 11pm Sat & Sun) Reliably good hot and cold coffees and teas. Also at **Egmore** (Map p334; Alsa Mall, Montieth Rd; drinks ₹60-120; ⊙11am-9pm), **Nungambakkam** (Map p334; KNK Sq, Khader Nawaz Khan Rd; drinks ₹60-120; ⊙9am-11pm; 🛜), **Express Avenue Mall** (Map p334; 1st fl & 3rd fl, White's Rd; drinks ₹60-120; ⊙10am-9pm Mon-Fri, to 10pm Sat & Sun), **Alwarpet** (Map p328; Ramakrishnan Towers, TTK Rd; drinks ₹60-120; ⊙10am-10pm) and **Phoenix Market City** (Basement, Phoenix Market City, Velachery; drinks ₹60-120; ⊙10am-11pm).

☆ Entertainment

There's *bharatanatyam* (Tamil classical dance) and/or a Carnatic music concert going on in Chennai almost every evening. Check listings in the *Hindu* or *Times of India,* or on www.timescity.com/chennai.

The **Music Academy** (Map p328; 📞044-28112231; www.musicacademymadras.in; 168/306 TTK Rd, Royapettah) is the most popular venue. The Kalakshetra Foundation (p332) and **Bharatiya Vidya Bhavan** (Map p328; 📞044-24643420; www.bhavanchennai.org; East Mada St, Mylapore) also stage many events, often free.

🔒 Shopping

T Nagar has great shopping, especially at Pondy Bazaar and in the Panagal Park area. Many of Kanchipuram's finest silks turn up in Chennai, and the streets around Panagal Park are filled with silk shops; *this* is where you buy your sari.

Nungambakkam's shady Khader Nawaz Khan Rd is a lovely lane of increasingly upmarket designer boutiques, cafes and galleries.

Chennai's shopping malls are full of major international and Indian fashion chains. The best include **Express Avenue** (Map p334; www.expressavenue.in; White's Rd, Royapettah; ⊙10am-10pm), **Chennai Citi Centre** (Map p328; http://chennaiciticenter.com; 10 Dr Radhakrishnan Salai, Mylapore; ⊙10am-10pm), **Spencer Plaza** (Map p334; 769 Anna Salai; ⊙10am-10pm) and the newer, glitzier **Phoenix Market City** (www.phoenixmarketcity.com; 142 Velachery Main Rd, Velachery; ⊙11am-10pm) in the city's south. Spencer Plaza is a bit downmarket, good for smaller craft and souvenir shops.

🔒 Central Chennai

★**Higginbothams** BOOKS
(Map p334; higginbothams@vsnl.com; 116 Anna Salai; ⊙9am-8pm Mon-Sat, 10.30am-7.30pm Sun)

Open since 1844, this grand white building is reckoned to be India's oldest bookshop. It has a brilliant English-language selection, including travel and fiction books, and a good range of maps.

Naturally Auroville ARTS & CRAFTS
(Map p334; http://naturallyaurovillechennai.com; 8 Khader Nawaz Khan Rd, Nungambakkam; ⊙10.15am-9pm) Colourful handicrafts and home-decor trinkets, including bedspreads, cushions, incense, scented candles and handmade-paper notebooks, all from Auroville, near Puducherry.

Poompuhar ARTS & CRAFTS
(Map p334; http://tnpoompuhar.org; 108 Anna Salai; ⊙10am-8pm Mon-Sat, 11am-7pm Sun) This large branch of the fixed-price state-government handicrafts chain is good for everything from cheap technicolour plaster deities to a ₹700,000 bronze Nataraja.

Evoluzione CLOTHING
(Map p334; www.evoluzionestyle.com; 3 Khader Nawaz Khan Rd, Nungambakkam; ⊙10.30am-7.30pm Mon-Sat, 11am-6pm Sun) This sparkly high-end boutique showcases neotraditional creations by cutting-edge Indian designers. Great for browsing, even if your budget doesn't allow the fabulously glittery wedding gowns!

🔒 Southern Chennai

★**Nalli Silks** TEXTILES
(Map p328; www.nallisilks.com; 9 Nageswaran Rd, T Nagar; ⊙9.30am-9.30pm) Set up in 1928, the enormous, supercolourful granddaddy of Chennai silk shops sparkles with wedding saris and rainbows of Kanchipuram silks, as well as silk dhotis (long loincloths) for men.

TRADITIONAL TRADERS

Even as Chennai expands relentlessly to the south, west and north, George Town, the local settlement that grew up near British Fort St George, remains the city's wholesale centre. Many of its narrow streets are entirely devoted to selling one particular product, as they have for hundreds of years – jewellery on NSC Bose Rd, paper goods in Anderson St. Even if you aren't buying, wander the maze-like streets to see Indian life flowing seamlessly from the past into the present.

TAMIL NADU & CHENNAI CHENNAI (MADRAS)

Fabindia CLOTHING, HANDICRAFTS

(Map p328; www.fabindia.com; 2nd fl, 35 TTK Rd, Alwarpet; ⊙10.30am-8.30pm) 🌿 This fair-trade, nationwide chain sells stylishly contemporary village-made clothes and crafts. Perfect for picking up a kurta (long shirt with short/no collar) to throw over trousers. This branch has incense, ceramics, table and bed linen, and natural beauty products too. Also at **Woods Road** (Map p334; 3 Woods Rd; ⊙10.30am-8.30pm), **Express Avenue** (Map p334; 1st fl, White's Rd, Royapettah; ⊙11.30am-9pm), **Nungambakkam** (Map p334; 2nd fl, 9/15 Khader Nawaz Khan Rd; ⊙10.30am-8.30pm), **T Nagar** (Map p328; 44 GN Chetty Rd; ⊙10.30am-8.30pm) and **Besant Nagar** (T-25, 7th Ave, Besant Nagar; ⊙10.30am-8.30pm).

Chamiers CLOTHING, HANDICRAFTS

(Map p328; http://chamiershop.com; 106 Chamiers Rd, RA Puram; ⊙10.30am-7.30pm) On the ground floor of this popular cafe-and-boutique-complex, **Anokhi** (Map p328; www.anokhi.com; ⊙10.30am-7.30pm) has wonderful, East-meets-West hand-block-printed clothes, bedding, bags and accessories in floaty fabrics, at good prices. Elegant **Amethyst Room** (Map p328; www.amethystchennai.com; ⊙10.30am-7pm) next door takes things upmarket with beautiful Indian-design couture. Upstairs is **Chamiers for Men** (Map p328; ⊙10.30am-7.30pm).

Starmark BOOKS

(Map p334; www.starmark.in; 2nd fl, Express Avenue, White's Rd, Royapettah; ⊙10.30am-9.30pm Mon-Fri, 10am-10pm Sat & Sun) Smart bookshop with an excellent collection of English, Indian and Tamil fiction and nonfiction, India travel books and Lonely Planet guides. Also at Phoenix Market City (p341).

❶ Orientation

The old British Fort St George and George Town's jumble of narrow streets and bazaars constitute Chennai's historic hub. The two main train stations, Egmore and Central, sit inland (west) from the fort. Much of the best eating, drinking, shopping and accommodation lies in the city's leafier southern and southwestern suburbs such as Nungambakkam, T Nagar (Thyagaraya Nagar), Alwarpet, Guindy and Velachery. The hectic major thoroughfare linking northern with southern Chennai is Anna Salai (Mount Rd).

❶ Information

INTERNET ACCESS

Many cafes and hotels have wi-fi. 'Browsing centres' (per hour ₹25 to ₹30) are everywhere; take your passport.

LEFT LUGGAGE

Egmore and Central train stations have left-luggage offices ('Cloakroom') for people with journey tickets. The airport also has left-luggage facilities.

MEDICAL SERVICES

Apollo Hospital (Map p334; ☑044-28290200, emergency 044-28293333; www.apollohospitals.com; 21 Greams Lane, Nungambakkam; ⊙24hr) State-of-the-art, expensive hospital, popular with 'medical tourists'.

Kauvery Hospital (Map p328; ☑044-40006000; www.kauveryhospital.com; 199 Luz Church Rd, Mylapore; ⊙24hr) Good, private, general hospital.

MONEY

Citibank ATMS are best for withdrawing large amounts of cash with foreign cards in Tamil Nadu. Axis Bank, Canara Bank, HDFC Bank, ICICI Bank and State Bank of India ATMs are other options.

NONSTOP DOMESTIC FLIGHTS FROM CHENNAI

DESTINATION	AIRLINES	TIME (HR)	DEPARTURES (DAILY)
Bengaluru	AI, SG, 6E, 9W	1	19
Delhi	AI, SG, 6E, 9W	2¾-3	23
Goa	AI, SG	1¼-2	2
Hyderabad	AI, G8, SG, 6E, 9W	1-1½	23
Kochi	AI, SG, 6E	1-1½	7
Kolkata	AI, SG, 6E	2-2¾	10
Mumbai	AI, G8, SG, 6E, 9W	2	22
Port Blair	AI, G8, SG, 6E, 9W	2-2¼	6
Trivandrum	AI, 6E	1-1½	3

Airline codes: AI – Air India, G8 – Go Air, SG – SpiceJet, 6E – IndiGo, 9W – Jet Airways

GOVERNMENT BUSES FROM CHENNAI'S CMBT

DESTINATION	FARE (₹)	TIME (HR)	DEPARTURES
Bengaluru	360-580	7-8	at least 40 daily
Coimbatore	40	11	11 daily
Ernakulam (Kochi)	590	12-16	3pm
Hyderabad	825-1500	14	5.30pm, 6.30pm, 7pm
Kodaikanal	380	10-13	5pm
Madurai	325	9-10	42 daily
Mamallapuram	40	2-2½	every 10min
Mysuru	550-900	10	7pm, 7.45pm, 8.40pm, 10.05pm
Ooty	435	12	4.30pm, 5.45pm, 7.15pm
Puducherry	125	4	36 daily
Thanjavur	250	8½	12 daily
Tirupati	150-320	4	every 30min
Trichy	235	6½-7	45 daily
Trivandrum	570	14	9 daily

POST

DHL (Map p334; ☑ 044-42148886; www.
dhl.com; 85 VVV Sq, Pantheon Rd, Egmore;
⊙ 9am-9pm) Secure international parcel delivery; branches around town.

Main Post Office (Map p328; Rajaji Salai,
George Town; ⊙ 8am-9pm Mon-Sat, 10am-4pm
Sun)

TOURIST INFORMATION

Indiatourism (Map p334; ☑ 044-28460285,
044-28461459; http://incredibleindia.org; 154
Anna Salai; ⊙ 9.15am-5.45pm Mon-Fri) Helpful
on all of India, as well as Chennai.

**Tamil Nadu Tourism Development Corpo-
ration** (TTDC; Map p334; ☑ 044-25333333;
www.tamilnadutourism.org; Tamil Nadu
Tourism Complex, 2 Wallajah Rd, Triplicane;
⊙ 24hr) The state tourism body's main office
takes bookings for its own bus tours, answers
questions and hands out leaflets. In the same
building are state tourist offices from all over
India, mostly open 10am to 6pm. The TTDC has
a counter at Egmore station.

TRAVEL AGENCIES

Milesworth Travel (Map p328; ☑ 044-
24338664; http://milesworth.com; RM Towers,
108 Chamiers Rd, Alwarpet; ⊙ 9.30am-6pm
Mon-Fri, to 4pm Sat) Very professional, welcoming agency that will help with all your travel
needs.

🛈 Getting There & Away

AIR

Chennai International Airport (☑ 044-
22560551; Tirusulam) is in the far southwest

of the city. The international terminal is 500m
west of the domestic terminal; walkways link
the two terminals.

There are direct flights to cities all over India,
including Trichy (Tiruchirappalli), Madurai,
Coimbatore and Thoothikudi (Tuticorin) within
Tamil Nadu. Internationally, Chennai has many
direct flights to/from Colombo, Singapore,
Kuala Lumpur and the Gulf states. The best
fares from Europe are often on Jet Airways (via
Mumbai or Delhi), Qatar Airways (via Doha),
Emirates (via Dubai) or Oman Air (via Muscat).
Cathay Pacific flies to Hong Kong, and Maldivian
to Male.

BOAT

Passenger ships sail from George Town harbour
direct to Port Blair in the Andaman Islands once
weekly. The **Andaman Shipping Office Ticketing Counter** (☑ 044-25226873; 2nd fl, Shipping
Corporation of India, Jawahar Bldg, 17 Rajaji
Salai, George Town; ⊙ 10am-4pm Mon-Fri, to
noon Sat) sells tickets (₹2500 to ₹6420) for the
60-hour trip. Book several days ahead, and take
three copies each of your passport data page
and Indian visa along with the original. It can be
a long process.

BUS

Most government buses operate from the
large but surprisingly orderly **CMBT** (Chennai
Mofussil Bus Terminus; Jawaharlal Nehru Rd,
Koyambedu), 6km west of the centre. The most
comfortable and expensive are the air-con buses
(best of these are Volvo AC services), followed
by the UD ('Ultra Deluxe'); these can generally
be reserved in advance. You can book up to 60
days ahead at the computerised reservation

MAJOR TRAINS FROM CHENNAI

DESTINATION	TRAIN NO & NAME	FARE (₹)	TIME (HR)	DEPARTURE
Agra	12615 Grand Trunk Exp	745/1960/2865 (C)	31½	7.15pm CC
Bengaluru	12007 Shatabdi Exp*	710/1435 (A)	5	6am CC
	12609 Bangalore Exp	150/540 (B)	6½	1.35pm CC
Coimbatore	12675 Kovai Express	180/660 (B)	7½	6.15am CC
	12671 Nilgiri Exp	315/810/1140 (C)	7¾	9.15pm CC
Delhi	12621 Tamil Nadu Exp	780/2040/2990 (C)	33	10pm CC
Goa	17311 Vasco Exp (Friday only)	475/1285/1865 (C)	21	3pm CC
Hyderabad	12759 Charminar Exp	425/1125/1605 (C)	13¾	6.10pm CC
Kochi	22639 Alleppey Exp	395/1045/1480 (C)	11½	8.45pm CC
Kolkata	12842 Coromandel Exp	665/1745/2540 (C)	27	8.45am CC
Madurai	12635 Vaigai Exp	180/660 (B)	7¾	1.30pm CE
	12637 Pandian Exp	315/810/1140 (C)	8¾	9.20pm CE
Mumbai	11042 Mumbai Exp	540/1450/2115 (C)	25¾	11.55am CC
Mysuru	12007 Shatabdi Exp*	930/1825 (A)	7	6am CC
	16021 Kaveri Exp	315/810/1140 (C)	9¾	9pm CC
Tirupati	16053 Tirupathi Exp	80/285 (B)	3½	2.15pm CC
Trichy	12635 Vaigai Exp	145/515 (B)	5	1.30pm CE
Trivandrum	12695 Trivandrum Exp	470/1240/1775 (C)	16	3.25pm CC

Departure Codes: CC – Chennai Central, CE – Chennai Egmore
*Daily except Wednesday
Fares: (A) chair/executive; (B) 2nd class/chair; (C) sleeper/3AC/2AC

centre at the left end of the main hall, or online (www.tnstc.in).

The **T Nagar Bus Terminus** (Map p328; South Usman Rd, T Nagar) is handy for bus 599 to Mamallapuram (₹40, 1½ hours, hourly 5am to 7.30pm).

Private buses generally offer greater comfort than non-AC government buses, at up to double the price. Their main terminal is the **Omni Bus Stand** (off Kaliamman Koil St, Koyambedu), 500m west of the CMBT, but some companies also pick up and drop off elsewhere in the city. Service information is at www.redbus.in; tickets can be booked through travel agencies. **Parveen Travels** (Map p334; ☑ 044-28192577; www.parveentravels.com; 11/5 Kennet Lane, Egmore) Services to Bengaluru, Ernakulam (Kochi; Cochin), Kodaikanal, Madurai, Ooty (Udhagamandalam), Puducherry, Trichy and Thiruvananthapuram (Trivandrum) depart from its Egmore office.

CAR

Renting a car with a driver is the easiest form of transport and easily arranged through most travel agents, midrange or top-end hotels, or the airport's prepaid taxi desks. Sample rates for non-AC/AC cars are ₹700/900 for up to five

hours and 50km, and ₹1400/1800 for up to 10 hours and 100km.

TRAIN

Interstate trains and those heading west generally depart from Central station, while trains heading south mostly leave from Egmore. The **Advanced Reservation Office** (Map p334; 1st fl, Chennai Central suburban station; ☑ 8am-2pm & 2.15-8pm Mon-Sat, 8am-2pm Sun), with its incredibly helpful Foreign Tourist Cell, is on the 1st floor in a separate 11-storey building just west of the main Central station building. Bring photocopies of your passport visa and photo pages. Egmore station has its own **Passenger Reservation Office** (Map p334; 1st fl, Egmore station, Egmore; ☑ 8am-2pm & 2.15-8pm Mon-Sat, 8am-2pm Sun).

① Getting Around

TO/FROM THE AIRPORT

The cheapest airport transport are suburban trains to/from Tirusulam station opposite the domestic terminal parking areas, accessed via a signposted pedestrian subway under the highway. Trains run roughly every 15 minutes from 4.53am to 11.43pm to/from Chennai Beach station (₹10, 40 minutes); stops include Nungambakkam, Egmore, Chennai Park and Chennai Fort.

Prepaid taxi kiosks outside the airport's international terminal charge ₹550/600 for a non-AC/AC cab to Egmore, and ₹450/500 to T Nagar. Rates are slightly lower at prepaid taxi kiosks outside the domestic terminal. Both terminals have **Fast Track** (☑ 60006000) taxi booking counters.

The Chennai Metro Rail system provides cheap, easy transport between the airport and, at the time of writing, the CMBT only (₹50; possibly changing at Alandur). The metro station is between the two airport terminals. A metro branch connecting the airport with central Chennai isn't due until 2018.

From the CMBT, city buses 70 and 170 to Tambaram stop on the highway across from the airport (₹12 to ₹15, 30 to 40 minutes).

AUTORICKSHAW

Most autorickshaw drivers refuse to use their meters and quote astronomical fares. Avoid paying upfront, and always establish the price before getting into a rickshaw. Rates rise by up to 50% from 11pm to 5am.

There are prepaid autorickshaw booths outside the CMBT (₹125 to Egmore), and 24-hour prepaid stands on the south side of Central station and outside the north and south exits of Egmore station.

Tempting offers of ₹50 autorickshaw 'city tours' sound too good to be true. They are. You'll spend the day being dragged from one shop to another.

BUS

Chennai's city bus system is worth getting to know, although buses get packed to overflowing at busy times. Fares are between ₹3 and ₹14 (up to double for express and deluxe services, and multiplied by five for Volvo AC services). Route information is on www.mtcbus.org.

METRO RAIL

Chennai Metro Rail, a much-awaited, part-underground rapid transit system, partly opened in late 2016. At the time of writing, the only operational section was a part of Line 2 (Green) that runs from the CMBT south to St Thomas Mount and the airport. When completed, Line 2 will continue east from the CMBT to Egmore and Central train stations. Line 1 (Blue) goes from the airport to Teynampet, Thousand Lights, Central train station, the High Court and Washermanpet in northern Chennai, running beneath Anna Salai for several kilometres, but isn't due to be completed until 2018. Trains run from 5am to 10pm; tickets cost ₹10 to ₹50.

TAXI

Both airport terminals have prepaid taxi kiosks. There are prepaid taxi stands outside the south side of **Egmore** (Map p334; Egmore station, Egmore; ☺24hr) and **Central** (Map p334; Central station; ☺24hr) stations; a ride of 8km or 9km, such as to the CMBT, costs around ₹450.

CHENNAI BUS ROUTES

BUS NO	ROUTE
A1	Central–Anna Salai–RK Mutt Rd (Mylapore)–Theosophical Society–Thiruvanmiyur
1B	Parry's–Central–Anna Salai–Airport
10A	Parry's–Central–Egmore (S)–Pantheon Rd–T Nagar
11	Rattan–Central–Anna Salai–T Nagar
12	T Nagar–Pondy Bazaar–Eldham's Rd–Dr Radhakrishnan Salai–Vivekananda House
13	T Nagar–Royapettah–Triplicane
15B & 15F	Broadway–Central–CMBT
M27	CMBT–T Nagar
27B	CMBT–Egmore (S)–Bharathi Salai (Triplicane)
27D	Egmore (S)–Anna Salai–Cathedral Rd–Dr Radhakrishnan Salai–San Thome Cathedral
32A	Central–Vivekananda House
102	Broadway–Fort St George–Kamarajar Salai–San Thome Cathedral–Theosophical Society

Routes operate in both directions.
Broadway – Broadway Bus Terminus, George Town
Central – Central Station
Egmore (S) – Egmore station (south side)
Parry's – Parry's Corner
Rattan – Rattan Bazaar Rd Bus Stop
T Nagar – T Nagar Bus Terminus

TAMIL NADU & CHENNAI CHENNAI (MADRAS)

ℹ️ HOLIDAY TRANSPORT

All kinds of transport in, to and from Tamil Nadu get booked up weeks in advance for periods around major celebrations, including Pongal, Karthikai Deepam, Gandhi Jayanti and Diwali. Plan ahead.

Relatively reliable **Fast Track** (p345) taxis charge ₹100 for up to 4km, then ₹18 per kilometre (with a 25% hike in rates between 11pm and 5am); bookings by phone.

The Uber taxi app offers reliable, sensibly priced transport around town, as does the near-identical Ola Cabs app (for which you need an Indian mobile number).

TRAIN

Efficient, cheap suburban trains run from Beach station to Fort, Park (near Central station), Egmore, Chetpet, Nungambakkam, Kodambakkam, Mambalam, Saidapet, Guindy, St Thomas Mount, Tirusulam (for the airport), and on south to Tambaram. At Egmore station, the suburban platforms (10 and 11) and ticket offfice are on the station's north side. A second line branches south after Fort to Park Town, Chepauk, Tiruvallikeni (for Marina Beach), Light House and Thirumailai (near the Kapaleeshwarar Temple). Trains run several times hourly from 4am to midnight, costing ₹5 to ₹10.

NORTHERN TAMIL NADU

South of Chennai

Chennai's sprawl peters out after an hour or so heading south on the East Coast Rd (ECR), at which point Tamil Nadu becomes red dirt, blue skies, palm trees and green fields, sprinkled with towns and villages (or, if you take the 'IT Expressway' inland, enormous new buildings).

There are several worthwhile ECR stops if you're travelling between Chennai and Mamallapuram, 50km south. Among these is the low-key fishing-turned-surfing village of Kovalam (Covelong). Swimming along the coast is dangerous due to strong currents.

👁 Sights

Cholamandal Artists' Village　　　ARTIST COLONY, MUSEUM
(☑044-24490092; www.cholamandalartistvillage.com; Injambakkam; museum adult/child ₹20/5; ☺museum 9.30am-6.30pm) There's a tropical bohemian groove floating around Injambakkam village, site of the Cholamandal Artists' Village, 10km south of Chennai's Adyar River. This 4-hectare artists' cooperative – founded in 1966 by artists of the Madras Movement, pioneers of modern art in South India – is a serene muse away from the world. The art in its museum is very much worth lingering over; look especially for work by KCS Paniker, SG Vasudev, M Senathipathi and S Nandagopal.

DakshinaChitra　　　ARTS/CRAFTS CENTRE
(☑044-27472603; www.dakshinachitra.net; East Coast Rd, Muttukadu; adult/student Indian ₹100/50, foreign ₹250/70; ☺10am-6pm Wed-Mon) DakshinaChitra, 22km south of Chennai's Adyar River, offers a fantastic insight into South India's traditional arts and crafts. Like a treasure chest of local art and architecture, this jumble of open-air museum, preserved village, artisan workshops (pottery, silk-weaving, basket-making) and galleries is strewn among an exquisite collection of real-deal traditional South Indian homes. You can see silk-weavers in action, have *mehndi* (ornate henna designs) applied and enjoy an array of shows.

Madras Crocodile Bank　　　ZOO
(☑044-27472447; www.madrascrocodilebank.org; Vadanemmeli; adult/child ₹40/20; ☺8.30am-5.30pm Tue-Sun) 🌿 Just 6km south of Kovalam, this incredible conservation and research trust is a fascinating peek into the reptile world. Founded by croc/snake-expert Romulus Whitaker, the bank has thousands of reptiles, including 17 of the world's 23 species of crocodilian (crocodiles and similar creatures), and does crucial work in maintaining genetic reserves of these animals, several of which are endangered. There are openings for volunteers (minimum two weeks).

Tiger Cave　　　HINDU SITE
(Saluvankuppam; ☺6am-6pm) `FREE` The Tiger Cave, 5km north of Mamallapuram, is an unfinished but impressive rock-cut shrine, dedicated to Durga (a form of Devi, Shiva's wife) and probably dating from the 7th century. What's special is the 'necklace' of 11 monstrous tiger-like heads framing its central shrine-cavity, next to two elephant-carved heads. At the north end of the park-like complex is a same-era rock-cut **Shiva shrine**. Beyond the fence lies the **Subrahmanya Temple**: an 8th-century granite shrine built over a brick, Sangam-era Murugan temple.

ⓘ Getting There & Away

To reach the ECR sights, take any Chennai–Mamallapuram bus, and hop off at the appropriate point(s). The **TTDC** (p343) Chennai–Mamallapuram round-trip bus tour (₹625, 10 hours) visits several of these sights and Mamallapuram. A full-day taxi tour from Chennai costs ₹2500 to ₹3000.

Mamallapuram (Mahabalipuram)

📞 044 / POP 15,170

Mamallapuram, 50km south of Chennai, was the major seaport of the ancient Pallava kingdom based at Kanchipuram. A wander round the town's magnificent, World Heritage–listed temples and carvings inflames the imagination, especially at sunset.

In addition to ancient archaeological wonders, salty air and coastal beauty, there's also the traveller hub of Othavadai and Othavadai Cross Sts, where restaurants serve pasta, pizza and pancakes, and shops sell Tibetan trinkets. The town's buzzing, growing surf scene is another attraction.

'Mahabs', as most call it, is less than two hours by bus from Chennai, and many travellers make a beeline straight here. It's small and laid-back, and sights can be explored on foot or by bicycle.

◉ Sights

You can easily spend a full day exploring Mamallapuram's marvellous temples, caves and rock carvings. Most were carved from the rock during the 7th-century reign of Pallava king Narasimhavarman I, whose nickname Mamalla (Great Wrestler) gave the town its name. Official Archaeological Survey of India guides can be hired at sites.

★ **Shore Temple**   HINDU TEMPLE
(Beach Rd; combined 1-day ticket with Five Rathas Indian/foreigner ₹30/500, video ₹25; ⊙ 6am-6pm) Standing like a magnificent fist of rock-cut elegance overlooking the sea, surrounded by gardens and ruined courts, the two-towered Shore Temple symbolises the heights of Pallava architecture and the maritime ambitions of the Pallava kings. Its small size belies its excellent proportion and the supreme quality of the carvings, many now eroded into vaguely Impressionist embellishments. Built under Narasimhavarman II in the 8th century, it's the earliest significant free-standing stone temple in Tamil Nadu.

The two towers rise above shrines to Shiva and their original linga captured the sunrise and sunset. Between the Shiva shrines is one to Vishnu, shown sleeping. Rows of Nandi (Shiva's vehicle) statues frame the temple courtyard. A boulder-carved Durga sits on her lion-vehicle's knee on the temple's south side.

★ **Five Rathas**   HINDU TEMPLE
(Pancha Ratha; Five Rathas Rd; combined 1-day ticket with Shore Temple Indian/foreigner ₹30/500, video ₹25; ⊙ 6am-6pm) Huddled together at the southern end of Mamallapuram, the Five Rathas were, astonishingly, all carved from single large rocks. Each of these fine 7th-century temples was dedicated to a

DON'T MISS

SURF & SEA: KOVALAM (COVELONG)

Low-key fishing village **Kovalam** (Covelong), 30km south of Chennai, has sprung into the spotlight for having the best surfing waves in Tamil Nadu. It's now an increasingly popular travellers' hang-out, hosting the high-profile **Covelong Point Surf & Music Festival** (www.covelongpoint.com; ⊙ Aug-Sep) and offering all kinds of water sports plus beachfront yoga.

For classes, head to 'social surfing school' **Covelong Point** (📞 9840975916; www.covelongpoint.com; 10 Pearl Beach, Ansari Nagar; per hour board rental/surf class ₹300/500; ⊙ hours vary), under the watch of Kovalam's original local surf pioneer Murthy. It also provides kayaking, diving, windsurfing and stand-up paddleboarding.

The same team runs stylish, surf-mad B&B **Surf Turf** (📞 9884272572; www.surfturf.in; 10 Pearl Beach, Ansari Nagar; r incl breakfast ₹2810-4950; 2-person 'surf & stay' package from ₹9500; ❄ 🛜) and its breezy beach-facing cafe. The five tastefully unfussy rooms here have stripped-back contemporary decor, aqua-toned bedding and delicious sand-and-sea views from private balconies; 'standards' share a bathroom. Kovalam's luxury choice is beachside **Vivanta by Taj – Fisherman's Cove** (📞 044-67413333; www.vivanta.tajhotels.com; Kovalam Beach; r incl breakfast ₹12,090-21,760; ❄ 🛜 🏊).

Mamallapuram (Mahabalipuram)

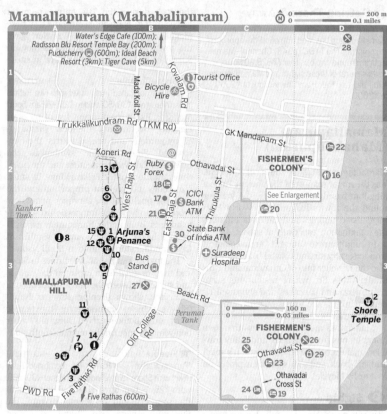

Hindu god and is now named after one or more of the Pandavas, the five hero-brothers of the epic Mahabharata, or their common wife, Draupadi. The *rathas* were hidden in the sand until excavated by the British 200 years ago.

Ratha is Sanskrit for 'chariot', and may refer to the temples' form or to their function as vehicles for the gods. It's thought they didn't originally serve as places of worship, but as architectural models.

The first *ratha* on the left after you enter is the Draupadi Ratha, in the form of a stylised South Indian hut. It's dedicated to the demon-fighting goddess Durga, who looks out from inside, standing on a lotus, and is depicted on the outside walls. Female guardians flank the entrance; a huge sculpted lion, Durga's mount, stands outside.

Next, on the same plinth, is the 'chariot' of the most important Pandava, the Arjuna Ratha, dedicated to Shiva. Its pilasters, minia-

ture roof shrines, and small octagonal dome make it a precursor of many later South Indian temples. A huge Nandi stands behind. Shiva (leaning on Nandi, south side) and other gods are depicted on the temple's outer walls.

The barrel-roofed Bhima Ratha was never completed, as evidenced by the missing north-side colonnade; inside is a shrine to Vishnu. The Dharmaraja Ratha, tallest of the temples, is similar to the Arjuna Ratha but one storey higher, with lion pillars. The carvings on its outer walls mostly represent gods, including the androgynous Ardhanarishvara (half Shiva, half Parvati) on the east side. King Narasimhavarman I appears at the west end of the south side.

The Nakula-Sahadeva Ratha (named after two twin Pandavas) stands aside from the other four and is dedicated to Indra. The life-size stone elephant beside it is one of India's most perfectly sculpted elephants. Approaching from the gate to the north you

Mamallapuram (Mahabalipuram)

see its back end first, hence its nickname Gajaprishthakara (elephant's backside).

★ **Arjuna's Penance**   HINDU MONUMENT
(West Raja St; ⊙ 24hr) **FREE** The crowning masterpiece of Mamallapuram's stonework, this giant relief carving is one of India's greatest ancient artworks. Inscribed on two huge, adjacent boulders, the Penance bursts with scenes of Hindu myth and everyday South Indian life. In the centre, *nagas* (snake-beings) descend a once water-filled cleft, representing the Ganges. To the left Arjuna (hero of the Mahabharata) performs self-mortification (fasting on one leg), so that the four-armed Shiva will grant him his most powerful weapon, the god-slaying Pasupata.

Some scholars believe the carving actually shows the sage Bagiratha, who did severe penance to obtain Shiva's help in bringing the Ganges to earth. Shiva is attended by dwarves, and celestial beings fly across the carving's upper sections. Below Arjuna/Bagiratha is a temple to Vishnu (mythical ancestor of the Pallava kings), with sages, deer and a lion. The many wonderfully carved animals include a herd of elephants and – humour amid the holy – a cat mimicking Arjuna's penance to a crowd of mice.

South along the road from Arjuna's Penance are the unfinished **Panch Pandava Mandapa** (West Raja St; ⊙ 6am-6pm) **FREE** cave

temple; the **Krishna Mandapa** (West Raja St; ⊙ 6am-6pm) **FREE**, which famously depicts Krishna lifting Govardhana Hill to protect cows and villagers from a storm sent by Indra; an **unfinished relief carving** (West Raja St; ⊙ 24hr) **FREE** of similar size to Arjuna's Penance; and the empty **Dharmaraja Cave Temple** (Five Rathas Rd; ⊙ 6am-6pm) **FREE**.

🏃 Activities

Beaches
The beach fronting the village isn't exactly pristine, but south of the Shore Temple it clears into finer sand. You'll also be further away from the leers of men who spend their days gawking at tourists. Like most of Tamil Nadu's coast, these beaches aren't great for swimming, due to dangerous rips.

Surfing
Mumu Surf School   SURFING
(☑ 9789844191; http://mumusurfer.wixsite.com/indiasurfing; Othavadai St; 90min group/private class ₹750/1300; ⊙ 7.30am-6pm) Popular, well-organised school for all levels and board rental (per hour ₹250 to ₹300); also runs beach clean-ups and the relaxed Sandy Bottom cafe.

Yoga, Ayurveda & Massage
Numerous places offer massage (₹750 to ₹1500), yoga (₹300) and ayurvedic treatments, at similar rates.

🧭 Tours

Travel XS CYCLING, BIRDWATCHING
(☑044-27443260; www.travel-xs.com; 123 East Raja St; bicycle tour per person ₹500; ⊙9.30am-6pm Mon-Fri, to 2pm Sat) Runs half-day bicycle tours (minimum two people) to nearby villages, visiting local potters and observing *kolam* drawing (elaborate chalk, rice-paste or coloured powder designs, also called *rangoli*), and organises day trips, including to Kanchipuram and (seasonally) Vedanthangal Bird Sanctuary.

✨ Festivals & Events

Mamallapuram Dance Festival DANCE
(⊙Jan-Feb) A four-week dance festival showcasing classical and folk dances from all over India, with many performances on an open-air stage. Dances include *bharatanatyam* (Tamil Nadu), Kuchipudi dance-drama (Andhra Pradesh) and Kathakali (Kerala drama).

🛏 Sleeping

Sri Harul Guest House GUESTHOUSE $
(☑9941070343; www.facebook.com/sriharul-guesthouse; 181 Bajanai Koil St, Fishermen's Colony; r ₹800-1200) The beach sits right below your balcony if you land one of the half-dozen seaview rooms at Sri Harul, one of Mamallapuram's better seafront budget deals. Rooms are basic, medium-sized and quite clean.

Vinodhara Guesthouse GUESTHOUSE $
(☑9444135118, 044-27442694; www.vinodhara.com; 9/4 Othavadai Cross St; s/d ₹600/700, r with AC ₹1200-1800; ❀🐾) An ever-growing collection of varied, clean-enough, no-frills rooms, from boxy fan-cooled singles to spacious, modernish air-con doubles, all under helpful management. Check out a few rooms first.

Greenwoods Beach Resort GUESTHOUSE $
(☑044-27442212, 9791145729; greenwoods_resort@yahoo.com; 7 Othavadai Cross St; r ₹700-900, with AC ₹1300-1700; ❀🐾) Perhaps the most char-

MAMALLAPURAM HILL

Many interesting monuments, mostly dating from the late 7th and early 8th centuries, are scattered across the rock-strewn hill on the west side of town. It takes about an hour to walk round the main ones. The hill is open from 6am to 6pm and has entrances on West Raja St and just off Five Rathas Rd.

Straight ahead inside the northernmost West Raja St entrance stands a huge, impossible-to-miss boulder with the inspired name of **Krishna's Butterball** (Mamallapuram Hill; ⊙6am-6pm) FREE, immovable but apparently balancing precariously. Beyond the rocks north of here is the **Trimurti Cave Temple** (Mamallapuram Hill; ⊙6am-6pm) FREE, honouring the Hindu 'trinity': Brahma (left), Shiva (centre) and Vishnu (right), flanked by guardians. On the back of this rock is a beautiful group of carved elephants.

South of Krishna's Butterball you reach the **Ganesh Ratha** (Mamallapuram Hill; ⊙6am-6pm) FREE, carved from a single rock, with lion-shaped pillar bases. Once a Shiva temple, it became a shrine to Ganesh (Shiva's elephant-headed son) after the original lingam was removed. Southwest of here, the **Varaha Mandapa** (Mamallapuram Hill; ⊙6am-6pm) FREE houses some of Mamallapuram's finest carvings, including columns with sitting lions. The left panel shows Vishnu's boar avatar, Varaha, lifting the earth out of the oceans. The outward-facing panels show Vishnu's consort Lakshmi (washed by elephants) and Durga, while the right-hand panel has Vishnu in his eight-armed giant form, Trivikrama, overcoming the demon king Bali.

A little further south, then east (up to the left), is the 16th-century **Raya Gopura** (Olakkanatha Temple; Mamallapuram Hill; ⊙6am-6pm) FREE, probably an unfinished *gopuram* (gateway tower). West just up the hill is the finely carved **Lion Throne** (Mamallapuram Hill; ⊙6am-6pm) FREE (depicted roaring). The main path continues south to the **Ramanuja Mandapa** (Mamallapuram Hill; ⊙6am-6pm) FREE and up to Mamallapuram's **lighthouse** (Mamallapuram Hill; Indian/foreigner ₹10/25, camera/video ₹20/25; ⊙10am-1pm & 2-5.30pm). Southwest of the lighthouse is the rock-carved **Mahishamardini Mandapa** (Mamallapuram Hill; ⊙6am-6pm) FREE, with excellent scenes from the Puranas (Sanskrit stories from the 5th century AD). The left-side panel shows Vishnu sleeping on the coils of a snake; on the right, Durga bestrides her lion vehicle while killing the demon-buffalo Mahisha. Inside the central shrine, Murugan sits between his parents Shiva and Parvati.

acterful of the Othavadai Cross St cheapies and definitely not on the beach, Greenwoods is run by an enthusiastic family who put up backpackers in plain, cleanish rooms (some with balconies and/or outdoor showers) up staircases around a leafy courtyard.

Tina Blue View
Lodge & Restaurant
GUESTHOUSE $

(📞 044-27442319; 48 Othavadai St; r ₹600-700, with AC ₹1200) Frayed and faded Tina is one of Mamallapuram's originals and looks it, but still remains deservedly popular for its whitewashed walls, blue flourishes, little porches and shady tropical garden, as well as tireless original owner Xavier.

Butterball Bed 'n Breakfast
B&B $$

(📞 9094792525; http://butterball-bnb.in; 9/26 East Raja St; s/d incl breakfast ₹1700/2000; 🟦🛜🛏) Smallish but pleasant, white-walled, spotlessly maintained rooms have old English prints, writing desks, big mirrors and blue-tiled bathrooms. There's a great view of the eponymous giant rock from the roof terrace, plus a lovely lawn, a massage centre, a little pool and daily yoga (₹300). Breakfast is in the attached **Burger Shack** (📞 9094792525; http://butterball-bnb.in; 9/26 East Raja St; mains ₹120-300; ⏱10am-10pm).

Hotel Daphne
HOTEL $$

(📞 9894282876; www.moonrakersrestaurants.com; 24 Othavadai Cross St; r without/with AC ₹900/1700; 🟦🛜) Non-AC rooms are perfectly acceptable and clean if nothing fancy, but the Daphne's seven air-con rooms are great value (especially top-floor rooms 13 and 14), most with four-poster beds, balconies and cane swing chairs. The shaded fairy-lit courtyard, cordial staff and free wi-fi are other drawcards.

Hotel Mamalla Heritage
HOTEL $$

(📞 044-27442060; www.hotelmamallaheritage.com; 104 East Raja St; incl breakfast s ₹2920-3160, d ₹3160-3400; 🟦🛜🛏) King of tour-group packages, the Mamalla has 43 big, comfortable, forgettable rooms rising around a cool-blue pool, and a quality rooftop veg restaurant. 'Deluxe' rooms are more up-to-date than 'standards'.

Radisson Blu Resort Temple Bay
RESORT $$$

(📞 044-27443636; http://radissonblu.com/hotel mamallapuram; 57 Kovalam Rd; r incl breakfast from ₹11,100; 🟦@🛜🛏) The Radisson's luxurious chalets, villas and bungalows are strewn across manicured gardens stretching 500m to the beach. Somewhere in the middle is In-

dia's longest swimming pool (220m). Rooms range from large to enormous; the most expensive have private pools. The Radisson also offers Mamallapuram's finest (priciest) dining and a top-notch ayurvedic spa (massage ₹2500). It's ridiculously popular. Best rates online.

Ideal Beach Resort
RESORT $$$

(📞 044-27442240; www.idealresort.com; East Coast Rd; incl breakfast s ₹6600-13,200, d ₹7200-14,400; 🟦@🛜🛏) With flowery landscaped gardens and its own stretch of beach, this laid-back resort, 3km north of town, is popular with weekending families and couples. Though dated in parts, it's quiet and secluded, there's a lovely poolside restaurant, and comfy rooms come with tea/coffee sets, hairdryers and, for some, open-air showers. Nonguest pool/beach day passes cost ₹500.

🍴 Eating

Restaurants on Othavadai and Othavadai Cross Sts provide semi-open-air settings, decent Continental mains and bland Indian curries. For real Indian food, try the cheap veg places near the bus stand.

Mamalla Bhavan
SOUTH INDIAN $

(South Mada St; mains ₹65-80, meals ₹70-125; ⏱6am-9.15pm) For an authentically good, wallet-friendly South Indian fill-up, swing by this simple, packed-out veg restaurant pumping out morning *idlis, vadas* and dosas, ₹18 filter coffee and banana-leaf lunchtime thalis. It's right beside the bus stand.

Le Yogi
MULTICUISINE $$

(📞 9840706340; 19 Othavadai St; mains ₹190-300; ⏱7.30am-11pm; 🛜) Some of Mamallapuram's best Continental food. The pasta, pizza, sizzlers, crepes and *momos* (Tibetan dumplings) are genuine and tasty (if small), service is good, and the chilled-out setting, with bamboo posts, floor cushions and lamps dangling from a thatched roof, has a touch of the romantic.

Gecko Restaurant
MULTICUISINE $$

(www.gecko-web.com; 37 Othavadai St; mains ₹180-320; ⏱9am-9.30pm; 🛜) Two friendly brothers run this cute blue-and-yellow-walled spot sprinkled with colourful artwork and wood carvings, and with daily seafood specials chalked up on boards. The offerings and prices aren't that different from other tourist-oriented restaurants, but there's a little more love put into the cooking here and it's tastier.

Water's Edge Cafe
MULTICUISINE $$$

(📞044-27443636; www.radissonblu.com/hotel-mamallapuram; Radisson Blu Resort Temple Bay, 57 Kovalam Rd; mains ₹545-800; ⏰24hr) The Radisson's pool-side 'cafe' offers everything from American pancakes to grilled tofu, Indian veg dishes, pan-Asian cuisine and a fantastic breakfast buffet (₹1190). It's expensive, but smart and popular.

Wharf
MULTICUISINE $$$

(📞044-27443636; www.radissonblu.com/hotel-mamallapuram; Radisson Blu Resort Temple Bay, 57 Kovalam Rd; mains ₹695-2575; ⏰noon-3pm & 7-11pm) Though it looks like a beach shack, the Wharf is actually the Radisson's gourmet multicuisine seaside restaurant, with a strong emphasis on fresh seafood.

🛍 Shopping

The roar of electric stone-grinders has just about replaced the tink-tink of chisels in Mamallapuram's stone-carving workshops, enabling sculptors to turn out ever more granite sculptures (of varying quality), from ₹100 pendants to ₹400,000 Ganesh. There are also some decent art galleries, tailors and antique shops.

Apollo Books
BOOKS

(150 Fishermen's Colony; ⏰9am-9.30pm) Good collection of books in several languages, to sell and swap.

ℹ Information

Suradeep Hospital (📞044-27442448; 15 Thirukula St; ⏰24hr) Recommended by travellers.
Tourist Office (📞044-27442232; Kovalam Rd; ⏰10am-5.45pm Mon-Fri)

ℹ Getting There & Away

From the **bus stand** (East Raja St), bus 599 heads to Chennai's T Nagar Bus Terminus (₹40,1½ hours) every 30 minutes from 6.50am to 8.30pm; bus 118 runs to Chennai's CMBT (₹40, two hours) hourly, 4am to 8pm. For Chennai Airport take bus 515 to Tambaram (₹27, 1½ hours, every 30 minutes), then a taxi, autorickshaw or suburban train. There are also seven daily buses to Kanchipuram (₹42 to ₹45, two hours). Buses to Puducherry (₹90 to ₹150, two hours) stop roughly every 15 minutes at the junction of Kovalam Rd and the Mamallapuram bypass, 1km north of Mamallapuram centre.

You can make train reservations at the **Southern Railway Computerised Passenger Reservation Centre** (32 East Raja St, 1st fl; ⏰8am-2pm).

Taxis are available from the bus stand, travel agents and hotels. It's ₹1500 to Chennai or the airport, or ₹2500 to Puducherry.

ℹ Getting Around

The easiest way to get around is by walking.
Bicycle hire (per day ₹100; ⏰8am-8pm) is available on Kovalam Rd.

Kanchipuram
📞044 / POP 164,384

Kanchipuram, 80km southwest of Chennai, was capital of the Pallava dynasty during the 6th to 8th centuries, when the Pallavas created the great stone monuments of Mamallapuram. Today a typically hectic modern Indian town, it's famous for its numerous important and vibrant temples (and their colourful festivals), some dating from Pallava, Chola or Vijayanagar times. It's also known for its high-quality silk saris, woven on hand looms by thousands of families in the town and nearby villages. Silk and sari shops are strung along Gandhi Rd, southeast of the centre, though their wares are generally no cheaper than at Chennai silk shops.

Kanchipuram is easily visited in a day trip from Mamallapuram or Chennai.

🔘 Sights

All temples have free admission, though you may have to pay small amounts for shoe-keeping and/or cameras. Ignore claims that there's an entrance fee for non-Hindus.

Kailasanatha Temple
HINDU TEMPLE

(SVN Pillai St; ⏰6am-6.30pm, inner sanctum 6am-noon & 4-6.30pm) Kanchipuram's oldest temple is its most impressive, not for its size but for its weight of historical presence and the intricacy of its stonework. As much monument as living temple, Kailasanatha is quieter than other temples in town, and has been heavily restored. Dedicated to Shiva, it was built in the 8th century by Pallava king Narasimhavarman II (Rajasimha), who also created Mamallapuram's Shore Temple.

The low-slung sandstone compound, in oleander-dotted grounds, has fascinating carvings, including many of the half-animal deities in vogue in early Dravidian architecture. It's framed by walls of subshrines topped by domed roofs and carved elephants and Nandis. Note the rearing lions on the outer walls and the large Nandi facing the compound from outside. The inner sanctum is centred on a large 16-sided lingam, which non-Hindus can view from about 8m away. The tower rising above is a precursor of the great *vimanas* of later Chola temples.

An autorickshaw from central Kanchipuram costs ₹50, but walking is nice.

Ekambareshwara Temple HINDU TEMPLE
(Ekambaranathar Temple; Ekambaranathar Sannidhi St; phone-camera/camera/video ₹10/20/100; ☉6am-12.30pm & 4-8.30pm) Of South India's five Shiva temples associated with the five elements, this 12-hectare precinct is the shrine of earth. You enter beneath the 59m-high, unpainted south *gopuram,* whose lively carvings were chiselled in 1509 under Vijayanagar rule. Inside, a columned hall leads left into the central compound, which Nandi faces from the right. The inner sanctum (Hindus only) contains a lingam made of earth and a mirror chamber whose central Shiva image is reflected in endless repetition.

According to legend, the goddess Kamakshi (She Whose Eyes Awaken Desire; a form of Parvati, Shiva's consort) worshipped Shiva under a mango tree here, before the two were married on the same spot. In a courtyard behind the inner sanctum stands a mango tree said to be 2500 years old, with four branches representing the four Vedas (sacred Hindu texts). Also of note, in the temple's northwest corner, is the Sahasra Lingam, made of minilinga.

Kamakshi Amman Temple HINDU TEMPLE
(Kamakshi Amman Sannidhi St; ☉5.30am-noon & 4-8pm) This imposing temple, dedicated to Kamakshi/Parvati, is one of India's most important places of *shakti* (female energy/deities) worship, said to mark the spot where Parvati's midriff fell to earth. It's thought to have been founded by the Pallavas. The entire main building, with its gold-topped sanctuary, is off imits to non-Hindus, but the small, square, 16th-century marriage hall, to the right inside the temple's southeast entrance, has wonderfully ornate pillars. No cameras allowed.

Vaikunta Perumal Temple HINDU TEMPLE
(Vaikundaperumal Koil St; ☉6am-noon & 4-8pm) This 1200-year-old Vishnu temple is a Pallava creation. The passage around the central shrine has lion pillars and a wealth of weathered wall panels, some depicting historical events. The main shrine, uniquely spread over three levels and with jumping *yalis* (mythical lion creatures) on the exterior, contains images of Vishnu standing,

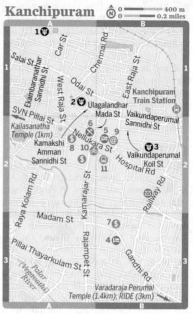

TAMIL NADU & CHENNAI KANCHIPURAM

Kanchipuram

◎ Sights
1 Ekambareshwara Temple A1
2 Kamakshi Amman Temple A1
3 Vaikunta Perumal Temple B2

🛏 Sleeping
4 GRT Regency B3
5 Sree Sakthi Residency B2

🍴 Eating
Dakshin .... (see 4)
Hotel Saravana Bhavan .... (see 4)
6 Hotel Saravana Bhavan A2
Upashana Veg Restaurant .... (see 5)

ℹ Information
7 Axis Bank ATM B3
8 State Bank of India ATM A2
9 State Bank of India ATM A2

ℹ Transport
10 Bicycle Hire A2
11 Bus Stand B2

sitting, reclining and riding his preferred mount, Garuda (half-eagle, half-man).

Varadaraja Perumal Temple HINDU TEMPLE
(Devarajaswami Temple; off Kanchipuram-Chengalpattu Rd, Little Kanchipuram; 100-pillared hall ₹1, camera/video ₹5/100; ☉7.30am-12.30pm & 3.30-

8pm) This enormous 11th-century Chola-built temple in southeast Kanchipuram is dedicated to Vishnu. Non-Hindus cannot enter the central compound, but the artistic highlight is the 16th-century '100-pillared' marriage hall, just inside the (main) western entrance. Its pillars (actually 96) are superbly carved with animals, monsters, warriors and several erotic sculptures. *Yalis* frame its inner southern steps and at its corners hang four stone chains, each carved from a single rock.

Tours

RIDE CULTURAL
(Rural Institute for Development Education; ☑ 044-27268223; www.rideindia.org; 48 Periyar Nagar, Little Kanchipuram) Kanchipuram's famous silk-weaving industry has traditionally depended heavily on child labour. This long-standing NGO helps reduce the industry's child-labour numbers, from over 40,000 in 1997 to under 4000 by 2007 (its own estimates), and empower the rural poor, especially women. It also runs some interesting tours that provide insights into the lives of people working in the industry.

Sleeping & Eating

RIDE GUESTHOUSE $
(Rural Institute for Development Education; ☑ 044-27268223; www.rideindia.org; 48 Periyar Nagar, Little Kanchipuram; per person ₹750-1000; ❄) This NGO offers simple, clean rooms at its base in a residential area, 5km southeast of central Kanchipuram. If things are quiet, the friendly owners put you up in their own colourful home next door. Home-cooked breakfast (₹150), lunch (₹250) and dinner (₹250) available. Book a day ahead. It's signposted 1km east of the Varadaraja Perumal Temple.

GRT Regency HOTEL $$
(☑ 044-27225250; www.grthotels.com; 487 Gandhi Rd; incl breakfast s ₹2470-4010, d ₹4940; ❄ 🕸) The cleanest, comfiest and most stylish rooms in Kanchi, boasting marble floors, tea/coffee makers and glass-partitioned

showers. The GRT's smart-ish **Dakshin** (mains ₹300-550; ⊙7am-11pm; 🕸) restaurant is overpriced, but offers a lengthy multicuisine menu of breakfast omelettes, South Indian favourites and tasty tandoori.

Sree Sakthi Residency HOTEL $$
(☑ 044-27233799; www.sreesakthiresidency.com; 71 Nellukara St; s ₹1820-2065, d ₹2190-2675; 🕸 🕸) Simple blonde-wood furniture and in-room kettles make the clean 'standard' rooms perfectly comfy, while newer 'premiums' have hairdryers, glassed-in showers and more modern decor. The popular ground-floor **Upashana Veg Restaurant** (dishes ₹50-110; ⊙7am-10pm) does good vegetarian food, including thalis (₹90 to ₹175).

Hotel Saravana Bhavan SOUTH INDIAN $$
(☑ 044-27226877; www.saravanabhavan.com; 66 Nellukara St; mains ₹60-130, meals ₹95-125; ⊙6am-10.30pm) A reliably good pure-veg restaurant with delicious dosas, a few North Indian surprises, a welcome air-con hall, and thalis on the 1st floor. There's another (scruffier) **branch** (☑ 044-27222505; www.saravanabhavan.com; 504 Gandhi Rd; mains ₹60-130, meals ₹95-125; ⊙6am-10.30pm) just west off Gandhi Rd.

❶ Getting There & Away

Suburban trains to Kanchipuram (₹25, 2½ hours) leave Chennai's Egmore station (platform 10 or 11) roughly hourly from 4.30am to 8.30pm. A full-day return taxi from Mamallapuram costs ₹2700. The busy **bus stand** (Kamarajar St) is in the town centre.

❶ Getting Around

An autorickshaw for a half-day tour of the five main temples (around ₹500) will inevitably involve stopping at a silk shop.

Vellore

☑ 0416 / POP 185,800

For a dusty bazaar town, Vellore feels pretty cosmopolitan, thanks to a couple of ter-

BUSES FROM KANCHIPURAM

DESTINATION	FARE (₹)	TIME (HR)	DEPARTURES
Chennai	47	2	every 10min 3.30am-10.30pm
Mamallapuram	42	2	every 2hr 5.30am-8.30pm
Puducherry	68	3	every 30min 5.45am-9.20pm
Tiruvannamalai	63-72	3	every 30min 5.10am-9.30pm
Vellore	41	2	every 10min 3.30am-11pm

tiary institutions and the American-founded Christian Medical College (CMC), one of India's finest hospitals, which attracts both medical students and patients from across the country. On the main Chennai–Bengaluru road, Vellore is worth a visit mainly for its massive Vijayanagar fort and temple. Many Indians come to visit the golden Sripuram Temple, 10km southwest of town.

Central Vellore is bounded on the north by Arcot Rd (Ida Scudder Rd), home to the hospital and cheap hotels and restaurants; and on the west by Anna Salai (Officer's Line), with Vellore Fort on its west side.

◉ Sights

Vellore Fort   FORT
(off Anna Salai; ⊘ 24hr) Vellore's splendid fort, with nearly 2km of moat-surrounded ramparts, was built in the 16th century and passed through Maratha and Mughal hands before the British occupied it in 1760. These days it houses, among other things, the magnificent Jalakantesvara Temple, two **museums** (⊘ 9am-5pm Sat-Thu) `FREE`, two parade grounds, a **church** (⊘ 7.30am-6pm Sun), government offices and a police recruiting school. A stroll around it is the most peaceful experience in town.

Jalakantesvara Temple   HINDU TEMPLE
(Vellore Fort; ⊘ 6.30am-1pm & 3-8.30pm) The Jalakantesvara Temple, a gem of late Vijayanagar architecture, dates from around 1566, and was once occupied as a garrison. Check out the small, beautifully detailed sculptures – especially the leaping *yali* – on the walls and columns of the **marriage hall** in the southwest corner.

🛏 Sleeping & Eating

Vellore's cheap hotels cluster along Ida Scudder Rd and in the busy, narrow streets just south. Many won't take foreigners; the better options fill up fast.

Vimal Lodge   HOTEL $
(☑ 9500531686; 6/83 Babu Rao St; r ₹715, with AC ₹1090-1200; ✱) Plain, clean budget rooms, neat sheets and a *relatively* helpful reception desk, in the busy bazaar area just south of Ida Scudder Rd.

Darling Residency   HOTEL $$
(☑ 0416-2213001; www.darlingresidency.com; 11/8 Anna Salai; incl breakfast s ₹2670-2920, d ₹3040-3280; ✱ @ �) It's no five-star property but the Darling has clean, comfortable, forgettable rooms (those at the back are quieter), as

well as friendly reception and four in-house restaurants, including the breezy, multicuisine **Aaranya Roof Garden Restaurant** (mains ₹160-400; ⊘ 11.30am-10.30pm). It's 1.5km south of Vellore Fort entrance.

GRT Regency Sameera   HOTEL $$$
(☑ 0416-2206466; www.grthotels.com; 145 Green Circle, New Bypass Rd; incl breakfast s ₹4320-6790, d ₹5560-6790; ✱ �) Mirrored cupboards, in-room tea/coffee sets and splashes of colour make the GRT's smart modern rooms pretty characterful for Vellore. The free wi-fi, upscale multicuisine **Gingee Restaurant** (mains ₹260-400; ⊘ 7-10am, 12.30-3pm & 7-10.30pm) and 24-hour cafe are extra bonuses. It's 1.5km north of central Vellore, just off the Chennai–Bengaluru road (and surprisingly not too noisy).

Hotel Saravana Bhavan   SOUTH INDIAN $
(☑ 0416-2217755; www.saravanabhavan.com; Sri Siva AVM Grande Hotel, 58/2 Katpadi Rd; dishes ₹60-125, meals ₹110-150; ⊘ 6am-11pm) Tamil Nadu's favourite veg chain is a welcome addition, turning out delectably simple *idlis*, dosas, thalis and other South Indian staples. The air-con hall does North Indian fare, too. It's opposite the New Bus Stand. There's another **branch** (☑ 0416-2217433; www.saravanabhavan.com; 25B/25C Jeevarathnam Maaligai, Arcot Rd; dishes ₹60-140, meals ₹110-150; ⊘ 10am-6pm) in town.

ⓘ Information

Canara Bank ATM (Anna Salai) Opposite Vellore Fort entrance.

ⓘ Getting There & Away

BUS
Buses use the **New Bus Stand** (Katpadi Rd), 1.5km north of central Vellore.
Bengaluru ₹156, five hours, every 30 minutes
Chennai AC Volvo buses ₹160, 2½ hours, noon & 2pm; other buses ₹81 to ₹105, three hours, every five minutes
Kanchipuram ₹40, two hours, every 10 minutes
Tiruvannamalai ₹37 to ₹40, three hours, every 10 minutes

TRAIN
Vellore's train station is 5km north at Katpadi. There are at least 22 daily superfast or express trains to/from Chennai Central (sleeper/3AC ₹170/540, two to three hours) and 10 to/from Bengaluru's Bangalore City station (₹170/490, three to five hours).

Buses 1 and 2 (₹4) shuttle between the train station and the **Town Bus Stand** (Anna Salai).

TAMIL NADU & CHENNAI VELLORE

TAMIL NADU TEMPLES

Tamil Nadu is a gold mine for anyone wanting to explore Indian temple culture. It's home to some of the country's most spectacular temple architecture and sculpture, and few parts of India are as fervent in their worship of the Hindu gods as Tamil Nadu. Its 5000-odd temples are constantly abuzz with worshippers flocking in for *puja* (offering or prayer), and colourful temple festivals abound. Among the plethora of Hindu deities, Shiva has the most Tamil temples dedicated to him, in a multitude of forms including Nataraja, the cosmic dancer, who dances in a ring of fire with two of his four hands holding the flame of destruction and the drum of creation. Tamils also have a soft spot for Shiva's peacock-riding son Murugan (also Kartikeya or Skanda), who is intricately associated with their cultural identity.

The special significance of many Tamil temples makes them goals of countless Hindu pilgrims from all over India. The Pancha Sabhai Sthalangal are the five temples where Shiva is believed to have performed his cosmic dance (chief among them Chidambaram). Then there's the Pancha Bootha Sthalangal, the five temples where Shiva is worshipped as one of the five elements: Tiruvannamalai's Arunachaleshwar Temple (fire; p356), Kanchipuram's Ekambareshwara Temple (earth; p353), Chidambaram's Nataraja Temple (space; p368), Trichy's Sri Jambukeshwara Temple (water; p376) and, in Andhra Pradesh, Sri Kalahasteeswara Temple (air). Each of Kumbakonam's nine Navagraha temples is the abode of one of the nine celestial bodies of Hindu astronomy – key sites given the importance of astrology in Hindu faith.

Typical Tamil temple design features tall layered entrance towers (*gopurams*), encrusted with often colourfully painted sculptures of gods and demons; halls of richly carved columns (*mandapas*); a sacred water tank; and a series of compounds (*prakarams*), one within the next, with the innermost containing the central sanctum where the temple's main deity resides. The earliest Tamil temples were small rock-cut shrines; the first free-standing temples were built in the 8th century AD; *gopurams* first appeared around the 12th century.

Admission to most temples is free, but non-Hindus are often not allowed inside inner sanctums. At other temples priests may invite you in and in no time you are doing *puja*, having an auspicious *tilak* mark daubed on your forehead and being hassled for a donation.

Temple touts can be a nuisance, but there are also many excellent guides; use your judgement and be on the lookout for badge-wearing official guides.

A South Indian Journey by Michael Wood and *Southern India: A Guide to Monuments, Sites & Museums* by George Michell are great reads if you're interested in Tamil temple culture. TempleNet (www.templenet.com) is one of the best online resources.

Tiruvannamalai

📞 04175 / POP 145,280

There are temple towns, there are mountain towns, and then there are temple-mountain towns where God appears as a phallus of fire. Welcome to Tiruvannamalai, one of Tamil Nadu's holiest destinations.

Set below boulder-strewn Mt Arunachala, this is one of South India's five 'elemental' cities of Shiva; here the god is worshipped in his fire incarnation as Arunachaleshwar. At every full moon, 'Tiru' swells with thousands of pilgrims who circumnavigate Arunachala's base in a purifying ritual known as Girivalam; at any time you'll see Shaivite priests, sadhus (spiritual men) and devotees gathered around the Arunachaleshwar Temple.

Tiru's reputation for strong spiritual energies has produced numerous ashrams, and the town now attracts ever-growing numbers of spiritual-minded travellers.

⊙ Sights & Activities

Yoga, meditation and ayurveda sessions are advertised everywhere in the main ashram area.

★ **Arunachaleshwar Temple**   HINDU TEMPLE
(Annamalaiyar Temple; www.arunachaleswarartemple.tnhrce.in; ⊙ 5.30am-12.30pm & 3.30-9.30pm) This 10-hectare temple is one of India's largest. Its oldest parts date to the 9th century, but the site was a place of worship long before that. Four huge, unpainted white *gopurams* mark the entrances; the main,

17th-century eastern one rises 13 storeys (an astonishing 66m), its sculpted passageway depicting dancers, dwarves and elephants. During festivals the Arunachaleshwar is awash with golden flames and the scent of burning ghee, as befits the fire incarnation of Shiva, Destroyer of the Universe.

Inside the complex are five more *gopurams*, a 17th-century 1000-pillared hall with impressive carvings, two tanks and a profusion of sub-temples and shrines. There's a helpful temple model inside the second *gopuram* from the east, where the temple elephant gives blessings. To reach the innermost sanctum, with its huge lingam, worshippers must pass through five surrounding *prakarams* (compounds).

Mt Arunachala   MOUNTAIN

This 800m-high extinct volcano dominates Tiruvannamalai – and local conceptions of the element of fire, which supposedly finds its sacred abode in Arunachala's heart. Devout barefoot pilgrims, especially on full-moon and festival days, make the 14km (four-hour) circumambulation of the mountain, stopping at eight famous linga. The inner path was closed at research time, but it's possible to circle around on the main road, or climb the hill past two caves where Sri Ramana Maharshi lived and meditated (1899–1922).

The hot ascent to the top opens up superb views of Tiruvannamalai, and takes five or six hours round-trip: start early and take water. An unsigned path across the road from the northwest corner of the Arunachaleshwar Temple leads the way up past homes and the two caves, **Virupaksha** (about 20 minutes up) and **Skandasramam** (30 minutes). Women are advised not to hike alone.

If you aren't that devoted, buy a Giripradakshina map (₹15) from the bookshop at Sri Ramana Ashram (p357), hire a bicycle on the roadside opposite (per hour/day ₹10/40) and ride around. Or make an autorickshaw circuit for about ₹300 (up to double at busy times).

Sri Ramana Ashram   MEDITATION

(Sri Ramanasramam; ☑ 04175-237200; www.sriramanamaharshi.org; Chengam Rd; ⊙ office 7.30am-12.30pm & 2-6.30pm) This tranquil ashram, 2km southwest of Tiruvannamalai centre amid green, peacock-filled grounds, draws devotees of Sri Ramana Maharshi, one of the first Hindu gurus to gain an international following; he died here in 1950 after half a century in contemplation. Visitors can meditate and attend daily *pujas* (prayers) and chantings, mostly in the **samadhi hall** where the guru's body is enshrined.

A limited amount of free accommodation (donations accepted) is available for *devotees only:* email a month ahead or write six weeks in advance.

Sri Seshadri Swamigal Ashram   MEDITATION

(☑ 04175-236999; www.tiruvarunaimahan.org; Chengam Rd; ⊙ 6am-9.30pm) Dedicated to a contemporary and helper of Sri Ramana, with meditation platforms and some accommodation (by donation; book at least two weeks ahead). It's in the southwest of town next to Sri Ramana Ashram.

Sri Anantha Niketan   MEDITATION

(☑ 9003480013; www.sriananthaniketan.com; Periya Paliyapattu village; by donation) A place for organised retreats rather than a permanent community, Sri Anantha Niketan has tree-shaded grounds, wonderful Arunachala views and homey rooms, and guests are welcome to join daily chanting in an attractive meditation hall. It's just off the Krishnagiri road, 7km west of Tiruvannamalai. Book at least three months ahead for December to February.

THE LINGAM OF FIRE

According to legend, Shiva appeared as the original lingam (phallic image of Shiva) of fire on Mt Arunachala to restore light to the world after his consort Parvati playfully plunged everything into darkness by closing his eyes. The **Karthikai Deepam Festival** (statewide; ⊙ Nov/Dec) celebrates this legend throughout India but is particularly significant at Tiruvannamalai. The lighting of a huge fire atop Mt Arunachala on the full-moon night, from a 30m wick immersed in 3 tonnes of ghee, culminates a 10-day festival for which hundreds of thousands of people converge on Tiruvannamalai. Huge crowds scale the mountain or circumnavigate its base, chanting Shiva's name. The sun is relentless, the rocks are jagged and the journey is barefoot – none of which deters the thousands of pilgrims who joyfully make their way to the top.

🏃 Activities

Arunachala Animal Sanctuary VOLUNTEERING
(☑ 9442246108; www.arunachalasanctuary.com;
Chengam Rd; ⊙ 9am-5pm) 🍴 Aimed at steri-
lisation, castration, rabies control, rehoming
and affordable treatments, this nonprofit
sanctuary, at the western end of Tiruvannamalai's ashram area, provides shelter to
over 200 homeless and/or injured dogs, plus
a few cats. Travellers can help with bathing,
feeding, applying creams or simply playing
with the animals – just show up. Possible
openings for longer-term volunteers.

🛏 Sleeping & Eating

Rainbow Guest House GUESTHOUSE $
(☑ 9443886408, 04175-236408; rainbowguest
housetiru@gmail.com; 27/28 Lakshmanan Nagar, Perumbakkam Rd; s ₹450, d ₹900-1000; 🛜)
A great-value, spick-and-span spot 800m
southwest off Chengam Rd. Beyond the psychedelic exterior, wood-carved doors reveal
simple, immaculate, fan-cooled rooms with
hot water and tiled floors. Staff are gracious,
cane chairs dangle along corridors and there
are fantastic Mt Arunachala views from the
spartan rooftop terrace.

Arunachala Ramana Home HOTEL $
(☑ 9626044492, 04175-236120; www.arunachala
ramanahome.com; 70 Ramana Nagar; s/d ₹500/
800, with AC r ₹1300; ❄🛜) Basic, clean and
friendly, this popular place is down a lane
south off Chengam Rd.

Sunshine Guest House GUESTHOUSE $$
(☑ 04175-235335; www.sunshineguesthouseindia.
com; 5 Annamalai Nagar, Perumbakkam Rd; s/d
₹600/800, with AC ₹1400/1970; ❄🛜) In a bliss-
fully quiet spot 1km southwest of the main
ashram area, this colourful new building
fronted by gardens offers excellent value.
Tasteful, spotless rooms, each styled after a
Hindu god, give the feel of an Indian trin-
kets shop: print-design sheets, sequined fab-
rics, cane swing-chairs and in-room water

filters. The upstairs hall is perfect for yoga.
Fresh breakfasts cost ₹150.

Hotel Arunachala HOTEL $$
(Arunachala Inn; ☑ 04175-228300; www.hotel
arunachala.com; 5 Vada Sannathi St; r ₹990, with
AC s/d ₹1125/1690, deluxe d ₹2250; ❄) Right
next to the Arunachaleshwar Temple's east
entrance, Hotel Arunachala is clean and
decent with pretensions to luxury in the
marblesque floors, ugly furniture, keen
management and lobby fish pond. The revamped 'deluxe' rooms are the best. Downstairs, pure-veg **Hotel Sri Arul Jothi** (dishes
₹40-80; ⊙ 6am-10.30pm) provides good South
Indian dishes (thalis ₹80 to ₹100).

⭐ **Dreaming Tree** CAFE $$
(☑ 8870057753; www.dreamingtree.in; Ramana
Nagar; mains ₹150-250; ⊙ 8.30am-10pm) 🍴 Su-
per-chilled Dreaming Tree dishes out huge
portions of exquisite, health-focused veg
fare, prepped with mostly organic ingredi-
ents, on a breezy thatched rooftop loaded
with low-slung purple-cushioned booths.
Expect fabulous 'hippie salads' and tofu stir-
fries, luscious breakfasts, and all kinds of
cakes, juices, lassis, lemonades and organic
coffees. Signs lead the way (500m) across the
road from Sri Ramana Ashram.

Shanti Café CAFE $$
(www.facebook.com/shanticafetiru; 115A Chengam
Rd; dishes ₹60-200, drinks ₹30-80; ⊙ 8.30am-
8.30pm; 🛜) This popular and relaxed cafe
with floor-cushion seating, up a lane off
Chengam Rd, serves wonderful croissants,
cakes, baguettes, pancakes, juices, coffees,
teas, breakfasts and Indian meals with an
extra-healthy twist. It's run by a delightful
team and there's an **internet cafe** (www.shan-
tionline.com; per hour ₹25; ⊙ 8.30am-1.30pm &
3-7pm Mon-Sat, 8.30am-1.30pm Sun) downstairs.

Tasty Café CAFE $$
(Lakshmanan Nagar, Perumbakkam Rd; mains
₹100-210; ⊙ 7am-10pm) In a peaceful, shady
courtyard of plastic chairs and wooden ta-

BUSES FROM TIRUVANNAMALAI

DESTINATION	FARE (₹)	TIME (HR)	DEPARTURES
Chennai	120-140	5	every 10min
Kanchipuram	63	3	hourly
Puducherry	63	3	hourly
Trichy	123	5	every 45min
Vellore	37-50	2½	every 10min

bles, friendly Tasty Café does well-prepared Indian and Continental food, including pizza, pasta, pancakes and salads. It's 700m southwest off Chengam Rd.

🛍 Shopping

Shantimalai Handicrafts Development Society ARTS & CRAFTS
(www.smhds.org; 83/1 Chengam Rd; ⊙9am-7pm) Beautiful bedspreads, bags, incense, candles, oils, bangles, scarves and cards, all made by local village women.

ℹ Getting There & Away

The **bus stand** (Polur Rd) is 800m north of the Arunachaleshwar Temple, and a ₹50 to ₹60 autorickshaw ride from the main ashram area. For Chennai, the best options are the hourly Ultra Deluxe services.

Gingee (Senji)

☑ 04145 / POP 27,000

Straddling the main Tiruvannamalai–Puducherry road, Gingee is mainly worth a visit for the fantastical ruins of 16th-century Gingee Fort, on the western edge of town.

⊙ Sights

Gingee Fort FORT
(☑04145-222072; Gingee; Indian/foreigner ₹15/200; ⊙8am-5pm) With three separate hilltop citadels and a 6km perimeter of cliffs and thick walls, the ruins of enormous Gingee Fort rise out of the Tamil plain, 37km east of Tiruvannamalai, like castles misplaced by the Lord of the Rings. It was constructed mainly in the 16th century by the Vijayanagars and was later occupied by the Marathas, Mughals, French and British, then abandoned in the 19th century. The fort's sheer scale, dramatic beauty and peaceful setting make it a very worthwhile stop.

Today, few foreigners make it here, but Gingee is popular with domestic tourists for its starring role in various films. The main road between Tiruvannamalai and Puducherry slices through the fort, just west of Gingee town. Of the three citadels, the easiest to reach, **Krishnagiri**, rises north of the road. To the south are the highest of the three, **Rajagiri**, and the most distant and least interesting, **Chakklidurg** (which you can't climb). Ticket offices (with maps) are at the foot of Krishnagiri and Rajagiri.

Remains of numerous buildings stand in the site's lower parts, especially at the bottom

of Rajagiri in the old palace area, where the main landmark is the white, restored, seven-storey **Kalyana Mahal** (Marriage Hall). Just east (outside) of the palace area is the 18th-century **Sadat Ullah Khan Mosque**; southeast of this lies the abandoned 16th-century **Venkatarama Temple**.

It's a one-hour round-trip hike up Krishnagiri and a two-hour round-trip hike for Rajagiri (more than 150m above the plain); allow at least half a day to cover both hills. Most visitors climb Rajagiri, which makes Krishnagiri quieter. Start early and bring water. Hill-climbing entry ends at 3pm.

ℹ Getting There & Away

A taxi between Tiruvannamalai and Puducherry with a two- to three-hour stop at Gingee costs around ₹3000.

Gingee is on the Tiruvannamalai–Puducherry bus route, with buses from Tiruvannamalai (₹25 to ₹35, one hour) every 10 minutes. Hop off at the fort to save a trip back out from Gingee town.

Puducherry (Pondicherry)

☑ 0413 / POP 244,380

The union territory of Puducherry (formerly Pondicherry; generally known as 'Pondy') was under French rule until 1954. Some people here still speak French (and English with French accents). Hotels, restaurants and 'lifestyle' shops sell a seductive vision of the French-subcontinental aesthetic, enhanced by Gallic creative types and Indian artists and designers. The internationally famous Sri Aurobindo Ashram and its offshoot just north of town, Auroville, draw large numbers of spiritually minded visitors. Thus Pondy's vibe: less faded colonial-era *ville,* more bohemian-chic, New Age-meets–Old World hang-out on the international travel trail.

The older 'French' part of town (where you'll probably spend most of your time) is full of quiet, clean streets, lined with bougainvillea-draped colonial-style townhouses numbered in an almost logical manner. Newer Pondy is typically, hectically South Indian.

Enjoy fabulous shopping, French food (hello steak!), beer (*au revoir* Tamil Nadu alcohol taxes), and plenty of yoga and meditation.

Puducherry is split from north to south by a partially covered canal. The 'French' part of town is on the east side (towards the sea). Nehru (JN) St and Rue Bussy (Lal Bahadur Shastri St) are the main east-west streets;

Puducherry (Pondicherry)

Mahatma Gandhi (MG) Rd and Mission St (Cathedral St) are the chief north–south thoroughfares. Many streets change names as they go along and often have English, French and Tamil names simultaneously.

☉ Sights

Seafront WATERFRONT
(Goubert Ave) Pondy is a seaside town, but that doesn't make it a beach destination; the city's sand is a thin strip of dirty brown that slurps into a seawall of jagged rocks. But Goubert Ave (Beach Rd) is a killer stroll, especially at dawn and dusk when half the town takes a romantic wander. In a stroke of genius, authorities have banned traffic here from 6pm to 7.30am.

Sri Aurobindo Ashram ASHRAM
(☎ 0413-2233649; www.sriaurobindoashram.org; Marine St; ⊗ 8am-noon & 2-6pm) FREE Founded in 1926 by Sri Aurobindo and a French-born woman, 'the Mother', this famous spiritual community has about 2000 members in its many departments. Aurobindo's teachings focus on 'integral yoga' that sees devotees work in the world, rather than retreat from it. Visits to the main, grey-walled ashram

Puducherry (Pondicherry)

building are cursory: you see the flower-festooned samadhi of Aurobindo and the Mother, then the bookshop. Ashram-accommodation guests can access other areas and activities. Evening meditation around the samadhi is for everyone.

There are daily weekday ashram tours (per person ₹50); enquire online (www.sriaurobindoautocare.com) or at the ashram's **Bureau Central** (☑ 0413-2233604; bureaucentral@sriaurobindoashram.org; Ambour Salai; ☺ 6am-noon & 4-6pm).

Sri Manakula
Vinayagar Temple   HINDU TEMPLE
(www.manakulavinayagartemple.com; Manakula Vinayagar Koil St; ☺ 5.45am-12.30pm & 4-9pm) Pondy may have more churches than most Indian towns, but the Hindu faith still reigns supreme. Pilgrims, tourists and the curious get a head pat from the temple elephant at this centuries-old temple dedicated to Ganesh, which contains around 40 skilfully painted friezes.

Puducherry Museum   MUSEUM
(http://art.puducherry.gov.in/museum.html; St Louis St; Indian/foreigner ₹10/50; ☺ 9am-6.30pm Tue-Sun) God knows how this converted late-18th-century villa keeps its artefacts from disintegrating, considering there's a whole floor of French-era furniture sitting in the South Indian humidity. On the ground floor look especially for Chola, Vijayanagar and Nayak bronzes, and pieces of ancient Greek and Spanish pottery and amphorae (storage vessels) excavated from Arikamedu, a once-major trading port just south of Puducherry. Upstairs is Governor Dupleix' bed.

Institut Français de Pondichéry   LIBRARY
(☑ 0413-2231616; www.ifpindia.org; 11 St Louis St; ☺ 9am-1pm & 2-5.30pm Mon-Fri) [FREE] This grand 19th-century neoclassical building is also a flourishing research institution devoted to Indian culture, history and ecology. Visitors can browse books in the beach-facing library.

⊙ French Quarter

Pocketed away just behind the seafront is a series of cobbled bougainvillea-wrapped streets and white-and-mustard buildings in various states of romantic *déshabillé*, otherwise known as Puducherry's French Quarter. A do-it-yourself heritage walk could start at the French consulate (p1185) near the north end of Goubert Ave, the seafront promenade (p360). Head south, passing the 1836 **lighthouse** (Goubert Ave), then turn inland to shady, landscaped **Bharathi Park** (Compagnie St; ⊙ 6am-7pm) FREE. The neoclassical governor's residence, **Raj Nivas** (Rangapillai St), faces the park's north side. Return to the seafront at the **Gandhi Memorial** (Goubert Ave), wander south past Notre Dame des Anges (p362) church, and then potter south through the 'white town' – Dumas, Romain Rolland, Suffren and Labourdonnais Sts. Towards the southern end of Dumas St, pop into the beautiful **École Française d'Extrême-Orient** (www.efeo.fr; 16-19 Dumas St; ⊙ 8.30am-12.30pm & 2.30-5.30pm Mon-Fri) FREE.

A lot of restoration has been happening in this area: if you're interested in Pondy's architectural heritage, check out INTACH Pondicherry (www.intachpondicherry.org). The tourist office (p366) website details heritage walks.

PUDUCHERRY'S CATHEDRALS

Pondy hosts one of India's best collections of over-the-top cathedrals. *Merci*, French missionaries. **Our Lady of Immaculate Conception Cathedral** (Mission St; ⊙ 7am-noon & 3-8.30pm), completed in 1791, is a sky-blue, hot-yellow and cloud-white typically Jesuit edifice in a Goa-like Portuguese style. The brown-and-white grandiosity of the **Sacred Heart Basilica** (Subbaiah Salai; ⊙ 5.30am-1pm & 6-8pm) is set off by beautifully restored stained glass and a Gothic sense of proportion. The twin towers and dome of the mellow-pink-and-yellow **Notre Dame des Anges** (Dumas St; ⊙ 6-10am & 4-7pm), built in the 1850s, look sublime in the late-afternoon light. Its smooth limestone interior was made using eggshell plaster; in the square opposite, there's a Joan of Arc statue.

🏃 Activities

Sita   CULTURAL PROGRAMS
(🗹 0413-4200718; www.pondicherry-arts.com; 22 Candappa Moudaliar St; class ₹300-1200; ⊙ 9am-1pm & 3-7.30pm) This energetic Franco-Indian cultural centre runs a host of activities, open to visitors (even for a single session): Indian cooking, *bharatanatyam* or Bollywood dance, *kolam* making, *mehndi* (henna 'tattoos'), yoga, pilates, ayurveda and sari 'workshops', plus brilliant cycling and photography tours.

Kallialay Surf School   SURFING
(🗹 9442992874; www.surfschoolindia.com; Serenity Beach, Tandriankuppam; 1hr private class ₹1500, board rental per 90min ₹400-600; ⊙ hours vary) Surfing continues to soar in popularity along Tamil Nadu's coast, and this long-standing, well-equipped, Spanish-run school, 5km north of Puducherry, offers everything from beginner sessions to intensive two-week courses.

Pondy Nautic   BOATING
(🗹 8220125027; www.pondynautic.com; Thengaithittu; per person from ₹900; ⊙ 9am-1pm & 3-7.30pm) One-hour speedboat jaunts whizz you across the Bay of Bengal, offering the unique chance of a 30-minute out-in-the-open swim; sailing tours head into the backwaters. Book tickets ahead through Sita.

Yoga & Ayurveda

You can practise and study yoga at Sri Aurobindo Ashram (p360) and Auroville. Sita offers yoga, ayurvedic massages, and courses in practising ayurveda.

International Centre for Yoga Education & Research   YOGA
(Ananda Ashram; 🗹 0413-2622902; www.icyer.com; 16A Mettu St, Chinnamudaliarchavady, Kottukuppam; ⊙ 10am-2pm) Rigorous six-month yoga-teacher-training, and 10-lesson, one-to-one introductory courses (₹8000), these last at the **city-centre branch** (🗹 0413-2241561; 25 II Cross, Iyyanar Nagar; ⊙ 9am-6pm).

👉 Tours

A wonderful way to explore Pondy is on the Sita (p362) popular early morning guided Wake Up Pondy bicycle tours (per person ₹1200), which include breakfast.

Shanti Travel (p366) offers recommended two-hour walking tours (per person ₹500) of Puducherry with English- or French-speaking guides.

✦ Festivals & Events

International Yoga Festival   YOGA
(◉4-7 Jan) Puducherry's ashrams and yoga culture are put on show with workshops, demonstrations and competitions, attracting experts from across India and beyond.

Bastille Day   PARADE
(◉14 Jul) Street parades, fireworks and French pomp and ceremony are part of the fun at this celebration.

🛏 Sleeping

If you've been saving for a splurge, this is the place: Puducherry's lodgings are as good as South India gets. Local heritage houses combine colonial-era romanticism with modern comfort and chic French-inspired styling, and there are some beautifully updated properties. Most of these rooms would cost five times as much in Europe. Book ahead for weekends.

Sri Aurobindo Ashram (p360) runs several simple but clean guesthouses. They're primarily for ashram guests, but many accept other travellers who'll follow their rules: 10.30pm curfew and no smoking, alcohol or drugs. The ashram's Bureau Central (p361) has a list.

Park Guest House   ASHRAM GUESTHOUSE $
(✆0413-2233644; parkgh@sriaurobindoashram.org; 1 Goubert Ave; r without/with AC ₹900/1400; ❄) Pondy's most sought-after ashram guesthouse thanks to its wonderful seafront position, with the best-value air-con rooms around, but no advance bookings. All front rooms face the sea and have a porch or balcony. There's a garden for yoga or meditation, plus vegetarian buffet lunches (₹125) and bicycle hire (per day ₹50).

International Guest House   ASHRAM GUESTHOUSE $
(INGH; ✆0413-2336699; ingh@aurosociety.org; 47 NSC Bose St; s ₹450, d ₹550-700, with AC s ₹750, d ₹1300-1630; ❄) The sparse, spotless rooms here, adorned with a single photo of the Mother, make for good-value ashram lodgings. It's very popular: book three weeks ahead.

Kailash Guest House   GUESTHOUSE $
(✆0413-2224485; http://kailashguesthouse.in; 43 Vysial St; s/d ₹1000/1200, with AC ₹1500; ❄) Good-value Kailash has simple, superclean rooms with well-mosquito-proofed windows, friendly management, and superb city views from top floors. It's geared to traveller needs, with loungey communal areas, clothes-drying facilities and a cafe-bar.

★Les Hibiscus   GUESTHOUSE $$
(✆9442066763, 0413-2227480; www.leshibiscus.in; 49 Suffren St; s/d incl breakfast ₹2725/2940; ❄@🛈) A strong contender for our favourite Tamil Nadu hotel, mango-yellow Les Hibiscus has just a handful of fabulous high-ceilinged rooms with antique beds, coffee-makers and a mix of quaint Indian art and old-Pondy photos, at astoundingly reasonable prices. The whole place is immaculately styled, fresh breakfasts are fantastic and management is genuinely friendly and helpful. Book well ahead.

Gratitude   GUESTHOUSE $$
(✆0413-2225029; www.gratitudeheritage.in; 52 Romain Rolland St; incl breakfast s ₹4200-6500, d ₹5000-7800; ❄🛈) A wonderfully tranquil 19th-century house (no shoes, no TVs, no children), sun-yellow Gratitude has been painstakingly restored to a state probably even more delightful than the original. Nine individually styled rooms sprawl across two floors around a tropically shaded courtyard, beside which delicious breakfasts are served. There's a roof terrace for yoga and massages.

Hotel de Pondichéry   HERITAGE HOTEL $$
(✆0413-2227409; www.hoteldepondichery.com; 38 Dumas St; incl breakfast s ₹2500, d ₹3000-5000; ❄🛈) A colourful heritage spot with 14 comfy, quiet, airy colonial-style rooms (some sporting semi-open bathrooms) and splashes of original modern art. The excellent restaurant, Le Club (p365), takes up the charming front courtyard and staff are lovely.

Nila Home Stay   GUESTHOUSE $$
(✆9994653006; www.nilahomestay.com; 18 Labourdonnais St; r ₹1300-1800, with AC ₹2000-3000; ❄🛈) A simple but brilliantly characterful and well-kept French Quarter guesthouse run by welcoming hosts, with a range of fresh, colourful, heritage-style rooms (some with kitchens and/or terraces), handy communal kitchens and a low-key lounge area.

Coloniale Heritage Guest House   GUESTHOUSE $$
(✆0413-2224720; http://colonialeheritage.com; 54 Romain Rolland St; r incl breakfast ₹2900-3500; ❄🛈) This leafy colonial-era haven with six comfy rooms (some up steep stairs) is crammed with character thanks to the owner's impressive collection of gem-studded Tanjore paintings, Ravi Varma lithographs

and other 19th- and 20th-century South Indian art. One room has a swing, another its own balcony. Breakfast is laid out in the sunken garden-side patio.

★ Villa Shanti
HERITAGE HOTEL $$$

(☑ 0413-4200028; www.lavillashanti.com; 14 Suffren St; r incl breakfast ₹7960-12,500; ❋ 🛜) Occupying a 100-year-old building revamped by two French architects, Villa Shanti puts an exquisitely contemporary twist on the French Quarter heritage hotel. Beautiful modern rooms combine superchic design with typically Tamil materials and colonial-style elegance: four-poster beds, Chettinadu tiles, walk-through bathrooms, Tamil-language murals. The sunken courtyard houses a hugely popular restaurant (p365) and bar.

The owners are also behind uberchic top-end La Villa (☑ 0413-2338555; www.lavilla pondicherry.com; 11 Surcouf St; r incl breakfast ₹15,960-19,380; ❋ 🛜 🏊).

Villa Helena
HERITAGE HOTEL $$$

(☑ 0413-2226789; www.villa-helena-pondicherry. com; 13 Rue Bussy; incl breakfast s ₹4000, d ₹5500-7000; ❋ 🛜) A smart revamp has infused this gorgeous 19th-century French-run mansion with contemporary character. Spread along plant-dotted galleries, freshly updated, soft-toned rooms are done up in tasteful minimalist style, with stripy bedding, printed cushions, vintage furniture and stylish modern bathrooms. There's wonderful Continental cooking in the romantic courtyard restaurant (☑ 0413-4210806; mains ₹350-520; ⊙ noon-3pm & 7-10.30pm).

Dune Mansion Calvé
HERITAGE HOTEL $$$

(☑ 0413-2656351; http://dunewellnessgroup.com; 44 Vysial St; r incl breakfast ₹6870-8180; ❋ 🛜) 🍃 The old Tamil Quarter has almost as many mansions as the French Quarter but is off most tourists' radars. Reincarnated under environmentally friendly management, this 150-year-old heritage choice, on a quiet, tree-shaded street, mixes a soaring sense of space with a teak-columned atrium, Chettinadu-tiled floors, and 10 elegantly styled rooms featuring free-standing bathtubs and solar-powered hot-water systems.

Palais de Mahé
HERITAGE HOTEL $$$

(☑ 0413-2345611; www.cghearth.com; 4 Rue Bussy; r incl breakfast ₹14,500-18,100; ❋ 🛜 🏊) Three colonnaded floors of swish soaring-ceilinged rooms with colonial-style wood furnishings and varnished-concrete floors rise around a seductive turquoise pool at this imposing heritage hotel. The first-rate rooftop restaurant (☑ 0413-2345611; www.cghearth.com; 4 Rue Bussy; mains ₹300-600; ⊙ 7.30-10.30am, 12.30-3pm & 7-11pm) serves impressive, creative fusion cuisine, including cooked-to-order breakfasts. Good value May to September, when rates drop by 30%.

Maison Perumal
HERITAGE HOTEL $$$

(☑ 0413-2227519; www.cghearth.com; 44 Perumal Koil St; r incl breakfast ₹8360-10,450; ❋ 🛜) Secluded rooms with colourful flourishes, antique beds and photos of original owners surround two pillared patios at this renovated 130-year-old home, pocketed away in Pondy's less touristic Tamil Quarter. The excellent Tamil/French restaurant (dinner ₹1200, lunch mains ₹350-550; ⊙ 12.30-3pm & 7.30-9.30pm) cooks everything to order from market-fresh ingredients. From May to September rates drop by 50%. Guests can use the pool at sister property Palais de Mahé.

🍴 Eating

Puducherry is a culinary highlight of Tamil Nadu. You can get great South Indian cooking, well-prepped French and Italian cuisine, and delicious fusion food. If you've been missing cheese or have a craving for croissants, you're in luck, and *everyone* in the French Quarter does good brewed coffee and crepes. There are some fabulous artsy cafes too.

Surguru
SOUTH INDIAN $

(☑ 0413-4308083; www.hotelsurguru.com; 235 Mission St; mains ₹65-140; ⊙ 7am-10.40pm) Simple South Indian in a relatively posh setting. Surguru is the fix for thali (lunchtime only) and dosa addicts who like their veg with good strong AC. The *slightly* more refined Surguru Spot branch (☑ 0413-4308084; 12 Nehru St; mains ₹60-140; ⊙ 6.30am-11pm) is near the ashram.

Baker Street
CAFE $

(123 Rue Bussy; dishes ₹40-200; ⊙ 7am-9pm; 🛜) A popular upmarket French-style bakery that does delectable cakes, croissants and biscuits. The baguettes, brownies and quiches aren't bad either. Eat in or takeaway.

Indian Coffee House
SOUTH INDIAN $

(125 Nehru St; dishes ₹30-55; ⊙ 6.30am-9.30pm) Snack to your heart's content on cheap, South Indian favourites – dosas, *vadas, uttapams* and ₹20 filter coffee – at this Pondy institution. It's also, incidentally, where Yann Martel's novel *Life of Pi* begins.

Nilgiri's SUPERMARKET **$**
(23 Rangapillai St; ⊙ 9.30am-9pm) Well-stocked, central air-con shop for groceries and toiletries.

★**Domus** CAFE, CONTINENTAL **$$**
(📞 0413-4210807; www.facebook.com/domus-pondicherry-708267965970400; 59 Suffren St; dishes ₹210-350; ⊙ 10am-7pm; 🛜) A laid-back, health-focused, all-veg hideaway cafe in the hushed garden of a zany design shop, where faded turquoise pillars clash beautifully against red walls. Dig into wholesome muesli breakfasts, build your own sandwich from a choice of breads, fillings and seasonings, or try the creative European-salad 'thalis', served traditional-style on stainless-steel dishes. Delicious espresso, smoothies and juices.

★**La Pasta World** ITALIAN **$$**
(📞 9994670282; www.facebook.com/lapastaworld; 55 Vysial St; mains ₹295-355; ⊙ 10am-2pm & 5-10pm Thu-Sat, 5-10pm Sun-Wed) Pasta lovers should make a pilgrimage to this little Tamil Quarter spot with just a few check-cloth tables, where a real Italian concocts her own authentically yummy sauces and bubbles up her own perfect pasta in an open-plan kitchen as big as the dining area. No alcohol: it's all about the food.

Café des Arts CAFE **$$**
(www.facebook.com/café-des-arts-155637583166; 10 Suffren St; dishes ₹150-260; ⊙ 8.30am-7pm Wed-Mon; 🛜) This bohemian cafe would look perfectly at home in Europe, but this is Pondy, so there's a cycle rickshaw in the garden. Refreshingly light dishes range from crisp salads to crepes, baguettes, omelettes and toasties. Coffees and fresh juices are great. The old-townhouse setting is lovely, with low tables and lounge chairs spilling out in front of a vintage boutique.

Kasha Ki Aasha CAFE **$$**
(www.kkapondy.com; 23 Surcouf St; mains ₹150-250; ⊙ 10am-8pm Thu-Tue; 🛜) A friendly all-female team whips up great pancake breakfasts, lunches and cakes on the thatched rooftop of this colonial-era-house-turned-craft-shop-and-cafe, where fusion food includes 'European thalis' and 'Indian enchiladas'. The floaty fabrics and leather sandals downstairs come direct from their makers. Live music Saturday night.

Le Café CAFE **$$**
(📞 0413-2334949; Goubert Ave; dishes ₹80-240; ⊙ 24hr) Pondy's only seafront cafe is good for croissants, cakes, salads, baguettes, breakfasts and organic South Indian coffee (hot or iced), plus welcome fresh breezes from the Bay of Bengal. It's popular, so you often have to wait for, or share, a table. But hey, it's all about the location.

★**Villa Shanti** CONTINENTAL, INDIAN **$$$**
(📞 0413-4200028; www.lavillashanti.com; 14 Suffren St; mains ₹225-495; ⊙ 12.30-2.30pm & 7-10.30pm) Smart candlelit tables in a palm-dotted pillared courtyard attached to a colourful cocktail bar create a casually fancy vibe at this packed-out hotel restaurant, one of Pondy's hottest dining spots. The building's contemporary Franco-Indian flair runs right through the North Indian/European menu. While portions are small, flavours are exquisite, and there are some deliciously creative veg dishes. No bookings beyond 7.30pm.

Le Club CONTINENTAL, INDIAN **$$$**
(📞 0413-2227409; www.leclubraj.com; 38 Dumas St; mains ₹200-530; ⊙ 11.45am-3pm & 6-10pm) The steaks (with sauces like blue cheese or Béarnaise), pizzas, pastas and crepes are all top-class at this romantically lit garden restaurant. Tempting local-themed options include creole prawn curry, veg-paneer kebabs and Malabar-style fish. There are plenty of wines, mojitos and margaritas to wash it all down.

🍷 Drinking & Nightlife

Although Pondy is one of the better places in Tamil Nadu to knock back beers, closing time is a strictly enforced 11pm. Despite low alcohol taxes, you'll only really find cheap beer in 'liquor shops' and their darkened bars. Hotel restaurants and bars make good drinking spots.

L'e-Space BAR
(2 Labourdonnais St; cocktails ₹200, dishes ₹150-300; ⊙ 5-11.30pm) A quirky little semi-open-air rooftop bar/cafe lounge that's friendly, laid-back and sociable, and does good cocktails (assuming the barman hasn't disappeared).

🛍 Shopping

With all the yogis congregating here, Pondy specialises in boutique-chic-meets-Indian-bazaar fashion and souvenirs. There's some beautiful and original stuff, a lot of it produced by Sri Aurobindo Ashram or Auroville. Nehru St and MG Rd are the shopping hot spots; boutiques line the French Quarter.

TAMIL NADU & CHENNAI PUDUCHERRY (PONDICHERRY)

★ Kalki
FASHION & ACCESSORIES

(www.maroma.com; 134 Mission St; ⊙10am-8.30pm) Dazzling, jewel-coloured silk and cotton fashion, as well as accessories, incense, oils, scented candles, handmade-paper trinkets and more, mostly made at Auroville, where there's another **branch** (visitors centre; ⊙9.30am-6pm).

Anokhi
FASHION & ACCESSORIES

(www.anokhi.com; 1 Caserne St; ⊙10am-7.30pm) A sophisticated Jaipur-born boutique popular for its beautiful, bold block-printed garments with a traditional-turns-modern twist, and gorgeous colourful bedspreads, tablecloths, scarves, bags, homewares and accessories.

Auroshikha
INCENSE

(www.auroshikha.com; 28 Marine St; ⊙9am-1pm & 3-7pm Tue-Sun) An endless array of incense, perfumed candles, essential oils and other scented trinkets, made by Sri Aurobindo Ashram.

Fabindia
CLOTHING, TEXTILES

(www.fabindia.com; 223 Mission St; ⊙10.30am-8.30pm) 🖉 Going strong since 1960, the Fabindia chain stocks stunning handmade, fair-trade products made by villagers using traditional craft techniques, and promotes rural employment. This branch has wonderful cotton and silk contemporary-Indian clothing, along with high-quality fabrics, tablecloths, beauty products and furniture.

La Boutique d'Auroville
ARTS & CRAFTS

(www.auroville.com; 38 Nehru St; ⊙9.30am-8pm) Perfect for browsing through Auroville-made crafts: jewellery, pottery, clothing, shawls, handmade cards and herbal toiletries.

LivingArt Lifestyles
FASHION & ACCESSORIES

(www.facebook.com/livingartlifestyles; 14 Rue Bazar St Laurent; ⊙10am-2pm & 3-8pm Tue-Sat) Breezy, boho-chic block-printed dresses, skirts, trousers and crop-tops in fun-but-fashionable geometric patterns (all handmade at Auroville) sit side-by-side with beautifully crafted saris from across India.

Focus
BOOKS

(204 Mission St; ⊙9.30am-1.30pm & 3.30-9pm Mon-Sat) Good collection of India-related and other English-language books (including Lonely Planet guides).

❶ Information

Rue Bussy between Bharathi St and MG Rd is packed with clinics and pharmacies.

New Medical Centre (🖉0413-2225287; www.nmcpondy.com; 470 MG Rd; ⊙24hr) Recommended private clinic and hospital.

Shanti Travel (🖉0413-4210401; www.shanti-travel.com; 44 Vysial St; ⊙10am-6pm) Professional agency offering walking tours, day trips and Chennai airport pick-ups.

Tourist Office (🖉0413-2339497; www.pondy-tourism.in; 40 Goubert Ave; ⊙10am-5pm)

❶ Getting There & Away

AIR

Puducherry's airport is 6km northwest of the centre, but has been in and out of action for several years. At the time of writing, it was scheduled to reopen in early 2017 with flights to Bengaluru via Trichy, plus, possibly, to other domestic destinations.

BUS

The **bus stand** (Maraimalai Adigal Salai) is 2km west of the French Quarter. Further services run from Villupuram (₹20, one hour, every 15 minutes), 38km west of Puducherry. Private bus companies, operating mostly overnight to various destinations, have offices along Maraimalai Adigal Salai west of the bus stand. **Parveen Travels** (🖉0413-2201919; www.parveentravels.com; 288 Maraimalai Adigal Salai; ⊙24hr) runs an 11pm semi-sleeper service to Kodaikanal (₹650, eight hours).

TAXI

Air-conditioned taxis to/from Chennai airport cost ₹4000.

TRAIN

Puducherry train station has just a few services. Two daily trains go to Chennai Egmore, unreserved seating only (₹45 to ₹90, four to five hours). Connect at Villupuram for many more services. The station has a computerised booking office for trains throughout India.

❶ Getting Around

Pondy's flat streets are great for getting around on foot. Autorickshaws are plentiful, but drivers usually refuse to use meters. A trip from the bus stand to the French Quarter costs ₹60.

A good way to explore Pondy and Auroville is by rented bicycle or motorbike from **outlets** (Mission St; per day bicycle ₹75, scooter or motorbike ₹250-400) on northern Mission St, between Nehru and Chetty Sts.

Auroville

🖉 0413 / POP 2570

Auroville, 'the City of Dawn', is a place that anyone with idealistic leanings will love:

an international community dedicated to peace, sustainability and 'divine consciousness', where people from across the globe, ignoring creed, colour and nationality, work together to build a universal, cash-free, non-religious township.

Outside opinions of Auroville's inhabitants range from admiration to accusations of self-indulgent escapism. Imagine over 100 small scattered countryside settlements, with 2500-odd residents of 52 nationalities. Nearly 60% of Aurovillians are foreign; most new members require more funds than most Indians may ever have. But the energy driving the place is palpable and, on a visit, you'll receive a positive vibe.

Some 12km northwest of Puducherry, Auroville was founded in 1968 by 'the Mother', cofounder of Puducherry's Sri Aurobindo Ashram. Aurovillians run a wide variety of projects, from schools and IT to organic farming, renewable energy and handicrafts production, employing 4000 to 5000 local villagers.

The Auroville website (www.auroville. org) is an encyclopedic resource.

◎ Sights & Activities

Auroville isn't directly geared for tourism – most inhabitants are just busy getting on with their lives – but it does have a good **visitors centre** (☏ 0413-2622239; www.facebook. com/aurovillevisitorscentre; ⊙ 9.30am-1pm & 1.30-5pm) with information desks, exhibitions and Auroville products. You can buy a handbook and map (₹20), and watch a 10-minute video. Free passes for external viewing of the Matrimandir, Auroville's 'soul', a 1km woodland walk away, are handed out here.

Visitors are free to wander Auroville's 10-sq-km network of roads and tracks. With two million trees planted since Auroville's foundation, it's a lovely shaded space.

If you're interested in getting to know Auroville, authorities recommend you stay at least 10 days and join an introduction and orientation program. To get properly involved, you'll need to come as a volunteer for six to 12 months. Contact the **Auroville Guest Service** (☏ 0413-2622675; guestservice@ auroville.org.in; Solar Kitchen Bldg, 2km east of visitors centre; ⊙ 9.30am-12.30pm & 1-4pm Mon-Fri, 9.30am-12.30pm Sat) for advice on active participation.

Matrimandir　　　　　NOTABLE BUILDING
(1km east of visitors centre; ⊙ passes issued 9.45am-1pm & 1.30-4.30pm Mon-Sat, 9.45am-12.30pm Sun) FREE The large, golden, almost spherical Matrimandir (Auroville's focal

point) is often likened to a golf ball, on a bed of lotus petals. You might equally feel that its grand simplicity of form, surrounded by pristine green parkland, does indeed evoke the divine consciousness it's intended to represent. The main inner chamber, lined with white marble, houses a large glass crystal orb that suffuses a beam of sunlight around the space. It's conceived as a place for individual silent concentration.

If, after viewing the Matrimandir from the gardens, you want to meditate inside, you must reserve one to four days ahead at Auroville's **Matrimandir Access Office** (☏ 0413-2622239, 0413-2622204; mmconcentration@auroville.org.in; visitors centre; ⊙ 10-11am & 2-3pm Wed-Mon).

🛏 Sleeping

Auroville has over 80 guesthouses and homestays of hugely varied comfort levels and budgets, from ₹200 dorm beds to ₹5400 two-person cottages with pools. The **Guest Accommodation Service** (☏ 0413-2622704; www.aurovilleguesthouses.org; visitors centre; ⊙ 9.30am-12.30pm & 2-5pm) offers advice, but bookings are direct with individual guesthouses. For peak seasons (August, September and December to March) book three or four months ahead.

❶ Getting There & Away

The main turning to Auroville from the East Coast Rd is at Periyar Mudaliarchavadi village, 6km north of Puducherry. From there it's 6km west to the visitors centre.

A one-way autorickshaw from Puducherry costs ₹270. Or you can take a Kottukuppam bus northbound from Puducherry's Ambour Salai to the Auroville turn-off (₹10 to ₹20, every 10 minutes), then an autorickshaw for ₹150. There are direct buses (₹10) from Puducherry bus station to Auroville visitors centre at 7.30am, 1.45pm and 4.30pm, returning at 8.15am, 2.20pm and 5.15pm.

Otherwise, rent a bicycle or motorcycle from **outlets** on northern Mission St in Puducherry.

CENTRAL TAMIL NADU

Chidambaram

☏ 04144 / POP 62,150

There's one reason to visit Chidambaram: the great temple complex of Nataraja, Shiva as the Dancer of the Universe. One of the holiest of all Shiva sites, this also happens to be a Dravidian architectural highlight. It's easily visited on a day trip from Puducherry, or en route between Puducherry and Tranquebar or Kumbakonam.

Most accommodation is near the temple or the bus stand (500m southeast of the temple). The train station is 1km further southeast.

⊙ Sights

★ Nataraja Temple   HINDU TEMPLE
(East Car St; ⊙ inner compound 6am–noon & 4.30–10pm) According to legend, Shiva and Kali got into a dance-off judged by Vishnu. Shiva dropped an earring and picked it up with his foot, a move that Kali could not duplicate, so Shiva won the title Nataraja (Lord of the Dance). It's in this form that endless streams of people come to worship him at this great temple. It was built during Chola times (Chidambaram was a Chola capital), but the main shrines date to at least the 6th century.

The high-walled 22-hectare complex has four towering 12th-century *gopurams* decked out in schizophrenic Dravidian stone and stucco work. The main entrance is through the east (oldest) *gopuram*. The 108 sacred positions of classical Tamil dance are carved in its passageway. To your right through the *gopuram* are the 1000-pillared 12th-century Raja Sabha (King's Hall; open only festival days), with carved elephants, and the large Sivaganga tank.

You enter the central compound (no cameras) from the east. In its southern part (left from the entrance) is the 13th-century Nritta Sabha (Dance Hall), shaped like a chariot with 56 finely carved pillars. Some say this is the spot where Shiva out-danced Kali.

North of the Nritta Sabha, through a door, you enter the inner courtyard, where most temple rituals are performed. Right in front are the attached hut-like, golden-roofed Kanaka Sabha and Chit Sabha (Wisdom Hall). The Chit Sabha, the innermost sanc-

tum, holds the temple's central bronze image of Nataraja – Shiva the cosmic dancer, ending one cycle of creation, beginning another and uniting all opposites. Shiva's invisible 'space' form is also worshipped here.

At *puja* times devotees crowd into the encircling pavilion to witness rites performed by the temple's hereditary Brahmin priests, the Dikshithars, who shave off some of their hair but grow the rest of it long (thus representing both Shiva and Parvati) and tie it into topknots.

On the south side of the two inner shrines is the Govindaraja Shrine with a reclining Vishnu. Overlooking the tank from the west, the Shivakamasundari Shrine displays fine ochre-and-white 17th-century Nayak ceiling murals.

Priests may offer to guide you around the temple for ₹200 to ₹300. Unusually for Tamil Nadu, this magnificent temple is privately funded and managed, so you may wish to support it by hiring one, but there are no official guides.

★☆ Festivals & Events

Chariot Festivals   RELIGIOUS
(⊙ Jun-Jul & Dec-Jan) Of Chidambaram's many festivals, the two largest are the 10-day chariot festivals.

Natyanjali Dance Festival   DANCE
(http://natyanjalichidambaram.com; ⊙ Feb-Mar) Chidambaram's five-day dance festival attracts 300 to 400 classical dancers from all over India to the Nataraja Temple.

🛏 Sleeping & Eating

Many cheap pilgrims' lodges are clustered around the temple (some pretty grim). There are a couple of decent-ish lower-midrange hotels (with restaurants) nearby.

Hotel Saradharam   HOTEL $$
(📞04144-221336; www.hotelsaradharam.co.in; 19 VGP St; r incl breakfast ₹1100, with AC ₹2200; ❋@🛜) Opposite the bus stand, the busy,

BUSES FROM CHIDAMBARAM

DESTINATION	FARE (₹)	TIME (HR)	DEPARTURES
Chennai	140	6	every 10min
Kumbakonam	42	3	every 30min
Puducherry	75	2	every 10min
Thanjavur	60	3-4	every 30min
Tranquebar	75	2-3	every 30min

TRANQUIL TRANQUEBAR (THARANGAMBADI)

South of Chidambaram, the Cauvery River's many-armed delta stretches 180km along the coast and into the hinterland. The Cauvery is the beating heart of Tamil agriculture and its valley was the heartland of the Chola empire. Today the delta is one of Tamil Nadu's prettiest, poorest and most traditional areas.

The tiny seaside town of **Tharangambadi**, still known as Tranquebar, is easily the most appealing base. A great place to recharge from the crowded towns inland, this quiet former Danish colony is set right on a long sandy beach with fishing boats and delicious sea breezes. Denmark sold it to the British East India Company in 1845.

The old town inside the 1792 **Landporten Gate**, with its colonial-era buildings, has been significantly restored since the 2004 tsunami, which killed about 800 people here. INTACH Pondicherry (www.intachpondicherry.org) has a good downloadable map. The peach-hued, seafront Danish fort, **Dansborg** (Parade Ground, King's St; Indian/foreigner ₹5/50, camera/video ₹30/100; ☺10am-5.45pm Sat-Thu), dates from 1624 and was occupied by the British in 1801; it now houses a small but fascinating museum. Among other notable buildings is the 1718 **New Jerusalem Church** (Tamil Evangelical Lutheran Church; King's St; ☺dawn-dusk), in mixed Indian and European styles; it contains the tomb of German-born Bartholomäus Ziegenbalg, the first Lutheran missionary to arrive in South India and first ever translator of the New Testament into Tamil. Tranquebar's **post office** (Post Office St; ☺8.30am-6pm Mon-Sat) has occupied the same dishevelled little building since 1884, while the 14th-century seafront **Masilamani Nathar Temple** (☺6am-noon & 4-8pm, hours vary) is now painted in kaleidoscopic colours.

Most Tranquebar accommodation is run by the sea-fronting **Bungalow on the Beach** (☎04364-289036; http://neemranahotels.com; 24 King's St; r incl breakfast ₹6080-10,320; ✵☎✦) , in the exquisitely restored 17th-century former residence of the British administrator. There are 17 beautiful old-world rooms in the main building and two other heritage locations in town; book ahead. The main block has a good **restaurant** (☎04364-289036; http://neemranahotels.com; 24 King's St; mains ₹150-300; ☺7.30-9.30am, 12.30-2.30pm, 7-9.30pm), a dreamy swimming pool and a fantastic wraparound terrace.

Tranquebar has regular (crowded) buses to/from Chidambaram (₹75, two hours, hourly) and Karaikal (₹12, 30 minutes, half-hourly). From Karaikal buses go to Kumbakonam (₹26 to ₹34, two hours, every two hours 4am to 10.15pm), Thanjavur (₹62, three hours, every two hours 4am to 10.15pm) and Puducherry (₹85, four hours, half-hourly 4.15am to midnight).

friendly Saradharam is as good as it gets. It's a bit worn and stuffy but comfortable enough, and a welcome respite from the town-centre frenzy. There's free wi-fi in the lobby, plus three restaurants – two vegetarian, and the good multicuisine, air-con **Anupallavi** (mains ₹150-225; ☺7-10am, noon-3pm & 7-10pm).

ⓘ Getting There & Away

BUS

Government buses depart from the **bus stand** (VGP St). **Universal Travels** (☎044-9842440926; VGP St; ☺9am-10pm), opposite the bus stand, runs Volvo AC buses to Chennai (₹500, five hours) at 8am and 4.30pm.

TRAIN

Three or more daily trains head to Trichy (2nd class/3AC/2AC ₹80/490/695, 3½ hours) via Kumbakonam (₹55/490/695, 1½ hours) and

Thanjavur (₹65/490/695, two hours), and seven to Chennai Egmore (₹105/490/695, 5½ hours).

Kumbakonam

☎0435 / POP 140,160

At first glance Kumbakonam is just another chaotic Indian junction town, but then you notice the dozens of colourful *gopurams* pointing skyward from its 18 temples – a reminder that this was once a seat of medieval South Indian power. With another two magnificent World Heritage–listed Chola temples (p371) nearby, it's worth staying the night.

◉ Sights

Nageshwara Temple　　HINDU TEMPLE
(Nageswaran Koil St;　☺6.30am-12.30pm & 4-8.30pm) Founded by the Cholas in 886, this is Kumbakonam's oldest temple, dedicated

Kumbakonam

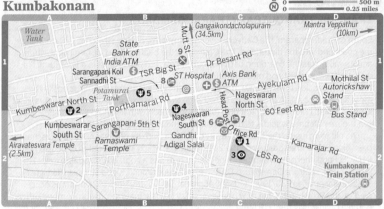

to Shiva as Nagaraja, the serpent king. On three days of the year (April or May) the sun's rays fall on the lingam. The elevated Nataraja shrine on the right in front of the inner sanctum is fashioned, in typical Chola style, like a horse-drawn chariot; colourful modern elephants stand beside it.

Sarangapani Temple   HINDU TEMPLE

(Sarangapani Koil Sannadhi St; ⊘ 6.30am-12.30pm & 4-8.30pm) Sarangapani is Kumbakonam's largest Vishnu temple, with a 45m-high eastern *gopuram* embellished with low-level dancing panels as its main entrance. Past the temple cowshed (Krishna the cowherd is one of Vishnu's forms), another *gopuram* and a pillared hall, you reach the inner sanctuary, a 12th-century Chola creation styled like a chariot with big carved elephants, horses and wheels. Photography is not permitted inside.

Kumbeshwara Temple   HINDU TEMPLE

(off Kumbeswarar East St; ⊘ 6.30am-12.30pm & 4-8.30pm) Kumbeshwara Temple, entered via a nine-storey *gopuram,* a small bazaar and a long porticoed *mandapa,* is Kumbakonam's biggest Shiva temple. It dates from the 17th and 18th centuries and contains a lingam said to have been made by Shiva himself when he mixed the nectar of immortality with sand.

Mahamaham Tank   RELIGIOUS SITE

(LBS Rd) Surrounded by 16 pavilions, the huge Mahamaham Tank is one of Kumbakonam's most sacred sites. It's believed that every 12 years the waters of India's holiest rivers, including the Ganges, flow into it, and at this time a festival is held (next due: 2028). On the tank's north side, the **Kashivishvanatha Temple** (LBS Rd; ⊘ 6.30am-12.30pm & 4-8.30pm) contains an intriguing trio of river goddesses, the central of which embodies the Cauvery River.

🛏 Sleeping & Eating

Pandian Hotel   HOTEL $

(☑ 0435-2430397; 52 Sarangapani Koil Sannadhi St; s/d ₹350/660, d with AC ₹990; ❄) It feels institutional, but you're generally getting fair value at this clean-enough budget standby.

Hotel Raya's   HOTEL $$

(☑ 0435-2423170; www.hotelrayas.com; 18 Head Post Office Rd; r ₹1200, with AC ₹1560; ❄) Friendly service and spacious, spotless rooms make Raya's your top lodging option in town. Its newer **Hotel Raya's Annexe** (☑ 0435-2423270; 19 Head Post Office Rd; r ₹2000; ❄ 🛜) has the best, brightest rooms, and a mural-lined lobby. The hotel runs a convenient car service for out-of-town trips. **Sathars Restaurant** (☎0435-2423170; mains ₹120-240; ⊙11.30am-11.30pm) here does good veg and nonveg fare in clean surroundings.

Mantra Veppathur   RESORT $$$
(☎0435-2462261;   www.mantraveppathur.com; 536/537 A, 1 Bagavathapuram Main Rd Extension, Srisailapathipuram Village; incl breakfast s ₹8500-9720, d ₹9720-10,940; ❇🛏❄) 🅿 Lost in the riverside jungle, 10km northeast of Kumbakonam, this is a wonderful retreat from temple-town chaos. Comfy modern-rustic rooms fronted by porches with rocking chairs have open-air showers and carved-teak doors; ayurveda is offered; there's rain-water

harvesting; and the organic farm fuels the Indian-focused restaurant, where you can eat out on a turquoise-tiled verandah.

Hotel Sri Venkkatramana   SOUTH INDIAN $
(TSR Big St; thalis ₹70-110; ⊙6am-10pm Mon-Sat) Good fresh veg food and an air-con hall; very popular with locals.

ℹ️ Getting There & Away

Government buses depart from the **bus stand** (60 Feet Rd).

Thirteen daily trains head to Thanjavur (2nd class/3AC/2AC ₹45/490/695, 30 minutes to one hour) and nine to Trichy (₹60/490/695, 1½ to 2½ hours). Five daily trains to/from Chennai

---

DON'T MISS

CHOLA TEMPLES NEAR KUMBAKONAM

Two of the three great monuments of Chola civilisation stand in villages just outside Kumbakonam: Darasuram's Airavatesvara Temple and the Gangaikondacholapuram temple. Unlike the also World Heritage–listed Brihadishwara Temple at Thanjavur, today these two temples receive relatively few worshippers (and visitors). They are wonderful both for their overall form (with pyramidal towers rising at the heart of rectangular walled compounds) and for the exquisite detail of their carved, unpainted stone.

From Kumbakonam bus stand (p371), frequent buses to nearby villages will drop you at Darasuram; buses to Gangaikondacholapuram (₹20, 1½ hours) run every 15 minutes. A return autorickshaw to Darasuram costs about ₹150. A half-day car trip to both temples, through Kumbakonam's reliable Hotel Raya's (p370), costs ₹1100 (₹1250 with AC).

Airavatesvara Temple (Darasuram; ⊙6am-8pm, inner shrine 6am-1pm & 4-8pm) Only 3km west of Kumbakonam, this late-Chola Shiva temple was constructed by Raja Raja II (1146–73). The steps of the **Rajagambhira Hall** are carved with vivid elephants and horses pulling chariots. This pavilion's 108 all-different pillars have detailed carvings including dancers, acrobats and the five-in-one beast *yali* (elephant's head, lion's body, goat's horns, pig's ears and a cow's backside). Inside the **main shrine** (flanked by guardians), you can honour the central lingam and get a *tilak* (auspicious forehead mark) for ₹10.

Gangaikondacholapuram Temple (Brihadishwara Temple; Gangaikondacholapuram; ⊙6am-noon & 4-8pm) The temple at Gangaikondacholapuram ('City of the Chola who Conquered the Ganges'), 35km north of Kumbakonam, is dedicated to Shiva. It was built by Rajendra I in the 11th century when he moved the Chola capital here from Thanjavur, and has many similarities to Thanjavur's earlier Brihadishwara Temple. Its beautiful 49m-tall tower, however, has a slightly concave curve, making it the 'feminine' counterpart to the mildly convex Thanjavur one. The artistic highlights are the wonderfully graceful sculptures around the tower's exterior.

A massive Nandi (Shiva's vehicle) faces the temple from the tranquil surrounding gardens; a lion stands guard nearby. The main shrine, beneath the tower, contains a huge lingam and is approached through a long 17th-century hall. The fine carvings on the tower's exterior include Shiva as the beggar Bhikshatana, immediately left of the southern steps; Ardhanarishvara (Shiva as half-man, half-woman), and Shiva as Nataraja, on the south side; Shiva with Ganga, Shiva emerging from the lingam, and Vishnu with Lakshmi and Bhudevi (southernmost three images on the west side); and Shiva with Parvati (northernmost image on the west side). Most famous is the masterful panel of Shiva garlanding the head of his follower, Chandesvara, beside the northern steps.

BUSES FROM KUMBAKONAM

DESTINATION	FARE (₹)	TIME (HR)	DEPARTURES
Chennai (AC)	300	8	1.50pm
Chidambaram	50	2½-3	every 30min
Karaikal	40	2¼	every 15min
Thanjavur	30	2	every 5min
Trichy	60	4	every 5min

Egmore include the overnight Mannai Express (sleeper/3AC/2AC/1AC ₹210/555/795/1325, 6½ hours) and the daytime Chennai Express/Trichy Express (₹210/555/795/1325, six to seven hours).

Thanjavur (Tanjore)

📞 04362 / POP 222,940

Here are the ochre foundation blocks of perhaps the most remarkable civilisation of Dravidian history, one of the few kingdoms to expand Hinduism beyond India, a bedrock for aesthetic styles that spread from Madurai to the Mekong. A dizzying historical legacy was forged from Thanjavur, capital of the great Chola empire during its heyday. Today Thanjavur is a crowded, hectic, modern Indian town – but the past is still very much present. Every day thousands of people worship at the Cholas' grand Brihadishwara Temple, and the city's labyrinthine royal palace preserves memories of other, later powerful dynasties.

🅞 Sights

⭐ **Brihadishwara Temple**   HINDU TEMPLE
(Big Temple St; ⊙6am-8.30pm, central shrine 8.30am-12.30pm & 4-8.30pm) Come here twice: in the morning, when the honey-hued granite begins to assert its dominance over the white dawn sunshine, and in the evening, when the rocks capture a hot palette of reds, oranges, yellows and pinks on the crowning glory of Chola temple architecture. The World Heritage–listed Brihadishwara Temple was built between 1003 and 1010 by Raja Raja I ('king of kings'). The outer fortifications were put up by Thanjavur's later Nayak and British regimes.

You enter through a Nayak gate, followed by two original *gopurams* with elaborate stucco sculptures. You might find the temple elephant under one of the *gopurams*. Several shrines are dotted around the extensive grassy areas of the walled temple compound, including one of India's largest statues of Nandi (Shiva's sacred bull), facing the main temple building. Cut from a single rock and framed by slim pillars, this 16th-century Nayak creation is 6m long.

A long, columned assembly hall leads to the **central shrine** with its 4m-high Shiva lingam, beneath the superb 61m-high *vimana* (tower). The assembly hall's southern steps are flanked by two huge *dvarapalas* (temple guardians). Many graceful deity images stand in niches around the *vimana's* lower outer levels, including Shiva emerging from the lingam (beside the southern steps); Shiva as the beggar Bhikshatana (first image, south side); Shiva as Nataraja, the cosmic dancer (west end of south wall); Harihara (half Shiva, half Vishnu) on the west wall; and Ardhanarishvara (Shiva as half-man, half-woman), leaning on Nandi, on the north side. Between the deity images are panels showing classical dance poses. On the *vimana's* upper east side is a later Maratha-period Shiva within three arches.

The compound also contains an interpretation centre along the south wall and, in the colonnade along the west and north walls, hundreds more linga. Both west and north walls are lined with exquisite lime-plaster Chola frescoes, for years buried under later Nayak-era murals. North of the temple compound, but still within the outer fortifications, are 18th-century neoclassical **Schwartz's Church** (⊙dawn-dusk) and a park containing the **Sivaganga tank** (₹5, camera/video ₹10/25; ⊙dawn-dusk).

⭐ **Royal Palace**   PALACE
(East Main St; Indian/foreigner ₹50/200, camera ₹30/100; ⊙9am-1pm & 1.30-5.30pm, Art Gallery 9am-1pm & 3-6pm, Sarawasti Mahal Library Museum closed Wed) Thanjavur's royal palace is a mixed bag of ruin and renovation, superb art and random royal paraphernalia. The maze-like complex was constructed partly by the Nayaks who took over Thanjavur in 1535, and partly by a local Maratha dynasty that ruled from 1676 to 1855. The two don't-

Thanjavur (Tanjore)

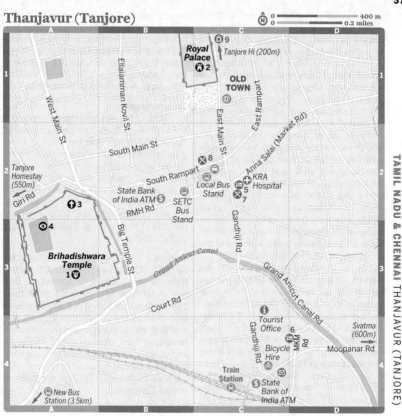

miss sections are the Saraswati Mahal Library Museum and the Art Gallery.

Seven different sections of the palace can be visited. 'Full' tickets include the Art Gallery and Saraswati Mahal Library Museum, along with the Mahratta Dharbar Hall, bell tower and Saarjah Madi; other sections require extra tickets. The main entrance is from the north, off East Main St. On the way in you'll come to the main ticket office, followed by the Maratha Palace complex.

Past the ticket office, a passage to the left leads to, first, the **Royal Palace Museum** (₹2), a small miscellany of sculptures, weaponry, elephant bells and rajas' headgears; second, the **Maharaja Serfoji Memorial Hall** (₹4), commemorating the enlightened Maratha scholar-king Serfoji II (1798–1832), with a better collection overlooking a once-splendid, now crumbling courtyard; and third, the **Mahratta Dharbar Hall**, where Maratha rulers gave audience in a

Thanjavur (Tanjore)

◎ Top Sights
1	Brihadishwara Temple	A3
2	Royal Palace	C1

◎ Sights
3	Schwartz's Church	A2
4	Sivaganga Tank	A3

🛏 Sleeping
5	Hotel Gnanam	C2
6	Hotel Valli	D4

⊗ Eating
	Diana	(see 5)
	Sahana	(see 5)
7	Sri Venkata Lodge	C2
8	Vasanta Bhavan	C2

🛍 Shopping
9	Kandiya Heritage	C1

grand but faded pavilion adorned with colourful murals (including their own portraits behind the dais) and sturdy pillars topped by arches filled with gods.

Exiting the passage, the fabulous **Sarawasti Mahal Library Museum** is on your left, through a vibrant entranceway. Perhaps Serfoji II's greatest contribution to posterity, this is testimony both to the 19th-century obsession with knowledge accumulation and to an eclectic mind that collected prints of Chinese torture methods, Audubon-style paintings of Indian flora and fauna, world atlases, dictionaries and rare medieval books. Serfoji amassed more than 65,000 books and 50,000 palm-leaf paper manuscripts in Indian and European languages, though most aren't displayed. Hourly **audiovisual displays** (10.30am to 4.30pm) highlight Thanjavur's sights, history and traditions in the attached cinema room.

Leaving the library, turn left for the **Art Gallery**, set around the Nayak Palace courtyard behind the **bell tower**. It contains a collection of superb, mainly Chola, bronzes and stone carvings; its main room, the 1600 Nayak Durbar Hall, has a statue of Serfoji II. From the courtyard, steps lead part of the way up a large *gopuram*-like tower to a whale skeleton that washed up in Tranquebar.

The renovated **Saarjah Madi** is best admired from East Main Rd for its ornate balconies.

✹ Festivals & Events

Thyagaraja Aradhana   MUSIC
(☉Jan) At Thiruvaiyaru, 13km north of Thanjavur, this important five-day Carnatic music festival honours the saint and composer Thyagaraja.

🛏 Sleeping & Eating

Thanjavur has nondescript, cheap lodges opposite the SETC and local bus stands.

Hotel Valli   HOTEL $
(☏04362-231584; www.hotelvalli.in; 2948 MKM Rd; s/d ₹610/770, r with AC ₹1090; ✱) Near the train station, green-painted Valli offers good-value, spick-and-span rooms, friendly staff and a basic restaurant. It's in a reasonably peaceful leafy spot beyond a bunch of greasy backstreet workshops and a booze shop.

Hotel Gnanam   HOTEL $$
(☏04362-278501; www.hotelgnanam.com; Anna Salai; s/d incl breakfast ₹2920/3280; ✱🛜) Easily the best value in town, the Gnanam has

comfy, stylish rooms (some with balconies) and ultra-efficient receptionists, and is perfect for anyone needing modern amenities in Thanjavur's geographic centre. Its **Diana** (mains ₹160-350; ☉11am-3pm & 6.30-10.30pm) and **Sahana** (mains ₹120-185; ☉7am-11pm) restaurants are both good. Book ahead.

Tanjore Homestay   HOMESTAY $$
(☏9443157667; www.tanjorehomestay.blogspot. in; 64A Giri Rd, Srinivasa Puram; s/d incl breakfast ₹1800/2300; @🛜) Under the watch of a welcoming Indian couple who serve tasty home-cooked meals, this low-key homestay offers four simple, modern rooms with splashes of art. Breakfast is served in the pretty back garden and there's a rooftop terrace, plus hot water, air-con and wi-fi. It's in a residential area, 1.5km west of Thanjavur's main temple; no sign.

Svatma   HERITAGE HOTEL $$$
(☏04362-273222; www.svatma.in; 4/1116 Blake Higher Secondary School Rd, Maharnonbu Chavadi; r incl breakfast ₹12,150-21,870; ✱🛜✱) This fresh luxury arrival is a gorgeous boutique-heritage blend with an elegant, uncluttered look inspired by and incorporating traditional local arts and crafts. Of the 38 rooms, those in the revamped heritage wing have most character. Enjoy the dance shows, spa and divine pool. It's 1.5km southeast of central Thanjavur.

Vasanta Bhavan   INDIAN $
(1338 South Rampart; mains ₹70-110; ☉6am-10.45pm) The busiest of several veg places facing the local bus stand, Vasanta Bhavan doles out biryanis and North Indian curries as well as smoothies, juices and your usual southern favourites.

Sri Venkata Lodge   SOUTH INDIAN $
(Gandhiji Rd; thalis ₹60; ☉6.30am-9pm) A friendly, popular, veg-only place near the centre of everything, that does afternoon dosas and a nice thali.

Tanjore Hi   MULTICUISINE $$
(☏04362-252111; www.duneecogroup.com; 464 East Main St; mains ₹230-360; ☉7.30-10am, 12.30-2.30pm & 7.30-10.30pm) 🌱 On a boutique-hotel rooftop, this industrial-chic restaurant is a welcome surprise in traditional Thanjavur. The world-wandering menu is fuelled by fresh, organic ingredients grown at the hotel's sister property in Kodaikanal. Dine at terrace tables outside or in the glassed-in air-con room.

🛍 Shopping

Kandiya Heritage ANTIQUES, HANDICRAFTS
(634 East Main St; ⊙9.30am-8pm) Opposite the palace, Kandiya Heritage sells antiques, re-production bronzes, brightly painted wooden horses and dolls, old European pottery and jewellery.

ⓘ Information

Tourist Office (📞04362-230984; Hotel Tamil Nadu, Gandhiji Rd; ⊙10am-5.45pm Mon-Fri) One of Tamil Nadu's more helpful offices.

ⓘ Getting There & Away

BUS

The downtown **SETC Bus Stand** (RMH Rd) has hourly express buses to Chennai (₹265, 8¼ hours) from 7.30am to 12.30pm and 8pm to 11pm. Buses for most other cities leave from the **New Bus Station** (Trichy Main Rd), 5km southwest of the centre. Many arriving buses will drop you off in the city centre on the way out there. Services from the New Bus Station:

Chidambaram ₹72, four hours, hourly

Kumbakonam ₹29, 1½ hours, every five minutes

Madurai ₹90, four hours, every 15 minutes

Trichy ₹31, 1½ hours, every five minutes

TRAIN

The train station is at the southern end of Gandhiji Rd. Five daily trains head to Chennai Egmore (seven hours) including the 10.45pm Mannai Express (sleeper/3AC/2AC/1AC ₹225/605/860/1445). Eighteen daily trains go to Trichy (2nd class/3AC/2AC ₹45/490/695, 1½ hours) and 12 to Kumbakonam (₹45/490/695, 30 minutes to 1¼ hours). Two go to Madurai (sleeper/3AC/2AC ₹160/490/695, four to five hours).

ⓘ Getting Around

Bus 74 (₹6) shuttles between the New Bus Station and the central **local bus stand** (South Rampart); autorickshaws cost ₹120.

Trichy (Tiruchirappalli)

📞0431 / POP 847,390

Welcome to (more or less) the geographic centre of Tamil Nadu. Tiruchirappalli, universally called Trichy or Tiruchi, isn't just a travel junction: it also mixes up a heaving bazaar with some major temples. It's a huge, crowded, busy city, and the fact that most hotels are clumped together around the big bus station isn't exactly a plus point. But Trichy has a strong character and long history, and a way of overturning first impressions.

Trichy may have been a capital of the early Cholas in the 3rd century BC. It passed through the hands of the Pallavas, medieval Cholas, Pandyas, Delhi Sultanate and Vijayanagars before the Madurai Nayaks brought it to prominence, making it a capital in the 17th century and building its famous Rock Fort Temple. Under British control, it became an important railway hub known as Trichinopoly.

Trichy stretches a long way from north to south. Most of what's interesting to travellers is split into three distinct areas. The Trichy Junction, or Cantonment, area in the south has most of the hotels and restaurants and the main bus and train stations. The Rock Fort Temple and main bazaar are 4km north of here; the other important temples are on Srirangam island, a further 4km north, across the Cauvery River. Luckily, it's all connected by a good bus service.

◉ Sights

★**Sri Ranganathaswamy Temple** HINDU TEMPLE
(Map p376; Srirangam; camera/video ₹50/100; ⊙6am-9.30pm) So large it feels like a self-enclosed city, Sri Ranganathaswamy is quite possibly India's biggest temple. It has 49 separate Vishnu shrines, and reaching the inner sanctum from the south, as most worshippers do, requires passing through seven *gopurams*. The first (southernmost), the **Rajagopuram** (Map p376), was added in 1987, and is one of Asia's tallest temple towers at 73m high. Non-Hindus cannot pass the sixth *gopuram* so won't see the innermost sanctum, where Vishnu as Ranganatha reclines on a five-headed snake.

You pass through streets with shops, restaurants, motorbikes and cars until you reach the temple proper at the fourth *gopuram*. Inside on the left is an information counter selling tickets for the **roof viewpoint** (₹20), which affords semi-panoramic views. Take no notice of would-be guides who spin stories to get hired. Also here, in the southwest corner, is the beautiful 16th-century **Venugopal Shrine**, adorned with superbly detailed Nayak-era carvings of preening *gopis* (milkmaids) and the flute-playing Krishna (Vishnu's eighth incarnation).

Turn right just before the fifth *gopuram* to the small **Art Museum** (Map p376; ₹5; ⊙9am-1pm & 2-6pm), displaying fine bronzes,

TAMIL NADU & CHENNAI TRICHY (TIRUCHIRAPPALLI)

Trichy (Tiruchirappalli)

to Vishnu's man-eagle vehicle and four remarkable sculptures of Nayak donors (with daggers on the hip).

Bus 1 to/from the Central Bus Station or the Rock Fort stops just south of the Rajagopuram.

Sri Jambukeshwara Temple HINDU TEMPLE
(Tiruvanakoil, Srirangam; ⊙ 5am-8pm) Of Tamil Nadu's five Shiva elemental temples, Sri Jambukeshwara is dedicated to Shiva, Parvati and the medium of water. The liquid theme is realised in the central shrine (closed to non-Hindus), whose Shiva lingam reputedly issues a nonstop trickle of water. In the north part of the complex is a shrine dedicated to Akilandeswari, Jambukeshwara's consort.

If you're taking bus 1, ask for 'Tiruvanakoil'; the temple is 350m east of the main road.

★ Rock Fort Temple HINDU TEMPLE
(Map p376; NSB Rd; ₹5, camera/video ₹20; ⊙ 6am-8pm) The Rock Fort Temple, perched 83m high on a massive outcrop, lords over Trichy with stony arrogance. The ancient rock was first hewn by the Pallavas and Pandyas, who cut small cave temples on its south side, but it was the war-savvy Nayaks who later made strategic use of the naturally fortified position. Reaching the top requires climbing over 400 stone-cut steps.

From NSB Rd on the south side, you pass between small shops and cross a street before entering the temple precinct itself, where there's a shoe stand. You might meet the **temple elephant** here. Then it's 180

tusks of bygone temple elephants, and a collection of exquisite 17th-century Nayak ivory figurines depicting gods, demons, and kings and queens (some in erotic poses). Continue left past the museum to the **Sesha Mandapa**, a 16th-century pillared hall with magnificently detailed monolithic Vijayanagar carvings of rearing battle horses and Vishnu's 10 incarnations sculpted on pillars. Immediately north is the **1000-pillared hall**, whose recently unearthed lower base is carved into dance positions.

Inside the fifth *gopuram* is the **Garuda Mandapa**, containing an enormous shrine

steps up to the **Thayumanaswamy Temple**, the rock's biggest temple, on the left (closed to non-Hindus); a gold-topped tower rises over its sanctum. Further up, you pass the 6th-century Pallava **upper cave temple** on the left (usually railed off); on the left inside is a famous Gangadhara panel showing Shiva restraining the Ganges with a single strand of his hair. From here it's another 183 steps to the summit's small **Uchipillaiyar Temple**, dedicated to Ganesh. The views are wonderful, with eagles wheeling beneath and Trichy sprawling all around.

Back at the bottom, check out the 8th-century Pandya **lower rock-cut cave temple**, with particularly fine pillars (turn right as you exit the temple precinct, past five or six houses, then right again down a small lane).

The stone steps get scorching-hot in the midday sun and it's a barefoot climb, so time your visit carefully.

Railway Museum   MUSEUM

(Bharatiyar Salai; adult/child ₹10/5, camera/video ₹20/40; ⊙ 9.30am-5.30pm Tue-Sun) Trichy's Railway Museum is a fascinating jumble of disused train-related equipment (phones, clocks, control boards), British-era railway construction photos, old train-line maps (including a 1935 pre-Independence Indian Railway map) – and even modern-day London Underground tickets. It's 500m east of Trichy Junction.

🛏 Sleeping & Eating

Most hotels are near the Central Bus Station (p379), a short walk north from Trichy Junction train station. There are also a few options in the Rock Fort area.

Hotel Abbirami   HOTEL $

(Map p378; ☑ 0431-2415001; 10 McDonald's Rd; r ₹770-990, with AC ₹1460-2430; ✳) Most appealing are the 1st- and 4th-floor renovated rooms, with light wood and colourful glass panels. Older rooms are a bit worn, but still well kept. It's a busy, fair-value place with friendly staff.

Ashby Hotel   HOTEL $

(Map p378; ☑ 0431-2460652; 17A Rockins Rd; s ₹630-890, d ₹760-950, with AC s ₹1100-1380, d ₹1700-1930; ✳) Wedged between the train station and the Central Bus Station, this long-running budget spot has a seedy location, but you could do worse at these prices. Behind a fiery-orange facade are plain, clean rooms around a patio.

Tranquility   GUESTHOUSE $$

(☑ 9443157667; www.tranquilitytrichy.com; Anakkarai, Melur, Srirangam; s/d incl breakfast ₹3200/4000; ✳ 🛜) This charming rustic-chic guesthouse sits in a gloriously rural setting 6km west of Sri Ranganathaswamy Temple. Elegant, unfussy rooms are sprinkled with terracotta-horse statuettes, sparkly cushions, recycled wood-carved doors and custom-made furniture. Terrace swing-chairs overlook a sea of palms. Rates include bicycles and transfers. The knowledgeable owners also offer a thatched-roof homestay **room** (Map p376; 43C Raghavendra Puram, Srirangam; r incl breakfast ₹2000; 🛜) just southwest of the temple's outermost wall.

Ramyas Hotel   HOTEL $$

(Map p378; ☑ 0431-2414646; www.ramyas.com; 13D/2 Williams Rd; incl breakfast s ₹2240-3020, d ₹2670-3630; ✳ @ 🛜) Comfortable rooms and good service and facilities make this business-oriented hotel excellent value, though 'business-class' rooms are ironically small. Turquoise-clad **Meridian** (Map p378; mains ₹130-250; ⊙ noon-3.30pm & 7-11.30pm) does tasty multicuisine fare, breakfast is a nice buffet and the breezy **Thendral** (Map p378; mains ₹130-245; ⊙ 7-10.30pm) roof-garden restaurant is brilliant.

Grand Gardenia   HOTEL $$

(☑ 0431-4045000; www.grandgardenia.com; 22-25 Mannarpuram Junction; incl breakfast s ₹3020, d ₹3630-4840; ✳ 🛜) Elegant, modern rooms provide comfy beds and glassed-in showers at this corporate-style hotel, one of Trichy's smartest options. Nonveg **Kannappa** (mains ₹100-200; ⊙ 11.30am-11.30pm) serves up excellent Chettinadu food; the rooftop terrace hosts a multicuisine **restaurant** (mains ₹120-240; ⊙ 7-10.30am, 11.30am-3pm & 7-10.30pm). Comfort and amenities outweigh the uninspiring highway-side location, 1km south of Trichy Junction.

Femina Hotel   HOTEL $$

(Map p378; ☑ 0431-2414501; www.feminahotel. net; 109 Williams Rd; incl breakfast s ₹1690-4230, d ₹2240-4840; ✳ 🛜 ⛱) From outside the enormous Femina looks 1950s, but renovations have turned parts of the interior quite contemporary. Facilities are good and staff helpful. Renovated deluxe rooms are cosy and modern; standard rooms are worn but spacious. There's an outdoor pool, plus a food court and supermarket.

Trichy Junction Area

Sangam Hotel (450m); Rock Fort Area (3km); Srirangam (7km)

KMC Speciality Hospital

Canara Bank ATM

Guard's Park

Central Bus Station

CANTONMENT

McDonald's Rd

Williams Rd

Royal Rd

VOC Rd

Rockins Rd

State Bank Rd

Bharativar Salai (Madurai Rd)

Flyover (under construction)

St John's Church

Railway Museum (350m)

Grand Gardenia (1.2km); Tiruchirappalli International (5km)

Trichy Junction Train Station

Sangam Hotel   HOTEL $$$
(☎ 0431-2414700; www.sangamhotels.com; Collector's Office Rd; incl breakfast s ₹3950-6990, d ₹4740-7590, ste ₹11,540-18,230; ❄️🛜🏊) With its well-equipped rooms, smartly outfitted staff and guests-only pool, the Sangam offers a good upmarket-angled package. It's faded in parts, but service and facilities are good,

including a 24-hour cafe, on-site bar and multicuisine restaurant. 'Deluxe' rooms are the most spacious and characterful, though they're all perfectly comfy.

Shri Sangeetas   INDIAN $
(Map p378; www.shrisangeetas.com; 2 VOC Rd; mains ₹95-130, thalis ₹85-150; ⊗ 5.30am-12.30am) Don't let the behind-the-bus-station address put you off. Super-popular Sangeetas has tables in a buzzing, fairy-lit courtyard (or inside in air-con comfort) and a tantalising menu of pure-veg North and South Indian favourites – everything from *idlis* and dosas to samosas, thalis and paneer tikka.

Vasanta Bhavan   INDIAN $
(Map p376; 3 NSB Rd; mains ₹40-90, thalis ₹70-150; ⊗ 8am-10pm) A great spot for a meal with views, near the Rock Fort. Tables on the outer gallery overlook the Teppakulam Tank, or there's an air-con hall. It's good for both North Indian veg food (of the paneer and naan genre) and South Indian. People crowd in for lunchtime thalis. There's another **branch** (Map p378; Rockins Rd; mains ₹40-90, thalis ₹70-150; ⊗ 6am-11pm) in the Cantonment.

ℹ Information

Indian Panorama (☎ 0431-4226122; www.indianpanorama.in; 5 Annai Ave, Srirangam; ⊗ 10am-6pm) Trichy-based and covering all of India, this professional, reliable travel agency/tour operator is run by an Indian–New Zealander couple.

KMC Speciality Hospital (Kauvery Hospital; Map p378; ☎ 0431-4077777; www.kauveryhospital.com; 6 Royal Rd; ⊗ 24hr) Large, well-equipped, private hospital.

ℹ Getting There & Away

AIR

Trichy's airport is 6km southeast of Trichy Junction and the Central Bus Station.

AirAsia (www.airasia.com) Flies to Kuala Lumpur three times daily.

Air India Express (☎ 0431-2341744; www.airindiaexpress.in) Chennai, Dubai and Singapore daily.

Jet Airways (www.jetairways.com) Chennai three times daily; Abu Dhabi daily.

SriLankan Airlines (Map p378; ☎ 0431-2460844; www.srilankan.com; 14C Williams Rd; ⊗ 9am-5.30pm Mon-Sat, to 1pm Sun) Colombo daily.

Tiger Air (www.tigerair.com) Singapore twice daily.

BUS

Government buses use the busy but orderly **Central Bus Station** (Map p378; Rockins Rd). The best services for longer trips are the UD ('Ultra Deluxe') buses; there's a booking office for these in the southwest corner of the station. For Kodaikanal, you can also take a bus to Dindigul (₹57, two hours, every 15 minutes) and change there.

Private bus companies have offices near the Central Bus Station.

Parveen Travels (Map p378; ☑ 0431-2419811; www.parveentravels.com; 12B Ashby Complex, Rockins Rd; ⊙ 24hr) AC buses to Chennai (₹815, six hours, five daily) and Trivandrum (₹1300, seven hours, 12.30am and 1.30am), plus non-AC semi-sleeper buses to Puducherry (₹535, four hours, 12.15am) and Kodaikanal (₹510, 4½ hours, 2.15am).

TAXI

Travel agencies and hotels provide cars with drivers. Reasonably priced **Femina Travels** (Map p378; ☑ 0431-2418532; www.feminahotel.net; 109 Williams Rd; ⊙ 6.30am-9.30pm) charges ₹2000 for up to eight hours and 100km (AC car).

TRAIN

Trichy Junction station is on the main Chennai–Madurai line. Of the 17 daily express services to Chennai, the best daytime option is the 9.05am Vaigai Express (2nd/chair class ₹145/515, 5½ hours). The overnight Pandian Express (sleeper/3AC/2AC/1AC ₹245/625/875/1460, 6¼ hours) leaves at 11.10pm.

Thirteen daily trains to Madurai include the 7.15am Tirunelveli Express (2nd class/chair class ₹95/345, 2¼ hours) and the 1.20pm Guruvayur Express (2nd class/sleeper/3AC/2AC ₹80/140/490/695, 2¾ hours).

Eighteen trains head to Thanjavur (2nd class/sleeper/3AC ₹45/140/490, 40 minutes to 1½ hours).

❶ Getting Around

Taxis between the airport and Central Bus Station area cost ₹300 and autorickshaws ₹200. From the Central Bus Station, Pudukkottai-bound buses will drop you at the airport.

Bus 1 from Rockins Rd outside the Central Bus Station goes every few minutes to the Sri Ranganathaswamy Temple (₹6) and back, stopping near the Rock Fort Temple and Sri Jambukeshwara Temple en route.

Autorickshaws from the Central Bus Station cost ₹170 to the Sri Ranganathaswamy Temple and ₹120 to the Rock Fort Temple.

SOUTHERN TAMIL NADU

Chettinadu

The Chettiars, a community of traders based around Karaikkudi (95km south of Trichy), hit the big time in the 19th century as financiers and entrepreneurs in colonial-era Sri Lanka and Southeast Asia. They lavished their fortunes on building 10,000 (maybe even 30,000) ridiculously opulent mansions in the 75 towns and villages of their arid rural homeland, Chettinadu. No expense was spared on finding the finest materials for these palatial homes: Burmese teak, Italian marble, Indian rosewood, English steel, and art and sculpture from everywhere.

After WWII, the Chettiars' businesses crashed. Many families left Chettinadu, and disused mansions decayed and were demolished or sold. Awareness of their value started to revive around the turn of the 21st century, with Chettinadu making it on to Unesco's tentative World Heritage list in

TAMIL NADU & CHENNAI CHETTINADU

GOVERNMENT BUSES FROM TRICHY (TIRUCHIRAPPALLI)

DESTINATION	FARE (₹)	TIME (HR)	DEPARTURES
Bengaluru	380 (A)	8	20 UD daily
Chennai	188/260/325 (B)	6-7	15 UD, 2 AC daily
Coimbatore	116-155 (C)	4½-6	every 10min
Kodaikanal	116 (C)	5½	6.40am, 8.30am, 11am, 12.15pm
Madurai	80 (C)	2½	every 15min
Ooty	260 (A)	8½	UD 10.15pm
Rameswaram	170 (C)	6	hourly
Thanjavur	31 (C)	1½	every 5min
Trivandrum	365 (A)	8	UD 8am, 7.30pm, 9.30pm, 10.30pm

Fares: (A) Ultra Deluxe (UD), (B) regular/UD/AC, (C) regular

2014. Several mansions have now been converted into gorgeous heritage hotels that are some of Tamil Nadu's best.

◉ Sights & Activities

Hotels give cooking demos or classes, and provide bicycles or bullock carts for rural rambles. They also arrange visits to sari-weavers, temples, mansions, Athangudi's tileworkers (producing the colourful handmade tiles you'll see in Chettiar mansions), and shrines of the popular pre-Hindu deity Ayyanar (identifiable by large terracotta horses, Ayyanar's vehicle).

Vijayalaya Cholisvaram   HINDU TEMPLE
(Narthamalai; ⊙ dawn-dusk) This small but stunning temple stands on a dramatically deserted rock slope 1km southwest of Narthamalai village (16km north of Pudukkottai). Reminiscent of the Shore Temple at Mamallapuram, without the crowds, it was probably built in the 8th or 9th century AD. Two (often locked) rock-cut shrines adorn the rock face behind, one with 12 impressively large reliefs of Vishnu. The Narthamalai turn-off is 7km south of Keeranur on the Trichy–Pudukkottai road; it's 2km west to Narthamalai itself.

Ellangudipatti   SHRINE
(Namunasamudram; ⊙ dawn-dusk) Just 8km southwest of Pudukkottai, this is an outstanding village shrine dedicated to the pre-Hindu guardian-god Ayyanar, worshipped only in rural Tamil Nadu and Sri Lanka. Hundreds of majestic terracotta horses and other beasts – offerings from local families, in various states of dishevelment – line a jungle-shrouded path leading to a modest altar.

Pudukkottai Museum   MUSEUM
(Thirukokarnam, Pudukkottai; Indian/foreigner ₹5/100, camera/video ₹20/100; ⊙ 9.30am-5pm Sat-Thu) The relics of Chettinadu's bygone days are on display at this wonderful museum, 4km north of Pudukkottai train station. Its eclectic collection includes musical instruments, stamps, jewellery, megalithic burial artefacts, and some remarkable paintings, sculptures and miniatures.

🛏 Sleeping & Eating

★ Saratha Vilas   BOUTIQUE HOTEL $$$
(☑ 9884203175, 9884936158; www.sarathavilas. com; 832 Main Rd, Kothamangalam; r incl breakfast ₹7460-11,750; ✳@🛜🏊) A different Chettiar charm inhabits this stylishly renovated, French-run mansion from 1910, 6km east of Kanadukathan. Rooms combine traditional and contemporary with distinct French panache; the food is an exquisite mix of Chettiar and French; and there's a chic salt-water pool. Most furnishings were personally designed by the knowledgeable architect owners, hugely active players in the preservation of Chettinadu heritage.

They're also founders of local conservation NGO ArcHeS (www.arche-s.org; 832 Main Rd, Kothamangalam).

★ Visalam   HERITAGE HOTEL $$$
(☑ 04565 273301; www.cghearth.com; Local Fund Rd, Kanadukathan; r incl breakfast ₹13,800-18,500; ✳@🛜🏊) Stunningly restored and professionally run by a Malayali hotel chain, Visalam is a relatively young Chettiar mansion, done in a fashionable 1930s art deco style. It's still decorated with the original owners' photos, furniture and paintings. The garden is exquisite, the 15 large rooms full of character, and the pool setting magical, with

---

CHETTINADU'S MANSIONS

Lakshmi House (Athangudi Periya Veedu; Athangudi Rd, Athangudi; ₹100; ⊙ 9am-5pm) With perhaps the most exquisitely painted wood-carved ceilings in Chettinadu, Lakshmi House is a popular film set. Take in the especially fine materials (Belgian marble, English iron), Chettiar history panels, chequered floors, and curious statues of British colonials and Hindu gods looming above the entrance.

CVRMCT House (CVRMCT St, Kanadukathan; ₹50; ⊙ 9am-5pm) Backed by the typical succession of pillar-lined courtyards, the impressive reception hall of this 'twin house' is shared by two branches of the same family. Don't miss the fabulous views over neighbouring mansions from the rooftop terrace.

VVRM House (CVRMCT St, Kanadukathan; ⊙ 9am-5pm, hours vary) One of Chettinadu's oldest mansions, built in 1870 with distinctive egg-plaster walls, Burmese-teak columns, patterned tiled floors and intricate wood carvings. A ₹50 group 'donation' is expected.

overflowing bougainvillea and a low-key restaurant alongside.

★ Bangala HERITAGE HOTEL $$$

(✆ 04565-220221; www.thebangala.com; Devakottai Rd, Karaikkudi; r incl breakfast ₹7050-8600; ❀ ☎ 🛏) Chettinadu's original heritage hotel, this lovingly revamped, efficiently managed whitewashed 'bungalow' isn't a typical mansion but has all the requisite charm: colour-crammed rooms, antique furniture, old family photos and a beautiful tile-fringed pool. It's famous for its food: banana-leaf 'meals' (veg/nonveg ₹850/1000) are actually Chettiar wedding feasts (12.30pm to 2.30pm and 8pm to 10pm; book two hours ahead).

Chettinadu Mansion HERITAGE HOTEL $$$

(✆ 04565-273080; www.chettinadmansion.com; SARM House, 11 AR St, Kanadukathan; s/d incl breakfast ₹6050/7950; ❀ ☎ 🛏) Slightly shabbier than Chettinadu's other heritage hotels, but friendly, well run and packed with character, this colourful century-old house is still owned (and lived in) by the original family. Of its 126 rooms, 12 are open to guests – all sizeable, with wacky colour schemes and private balconies gazing out over other mansions.

The owners also run nearby **Chettinadu Court** (✆ 04565-273080; www.deshadan.com; Raja's St, Kanadukathan; s/d incl breakfast ₹4250/5500; ❀ ☎ 🛏), which has eight heritage-inspired rooms. The two share an off-site pool.

❶ Getting There & Around

Car is the best way to get to and around Chettinadu. Renting one with a driver from Trichy, Thanjavur or Madurai for two days costs around ₹5000.

From Trichy, buses run every five or 10 minutes to Pudukkottai (₹31, 1½ hours) and Karaikkudi (₹75, two hours); you can hop off and on along the way. From Madurai, buses run to Karaikkudi (₹80, two hours) every 30 minutes. There are also buses from Thanjavur and Rameswaram.

Three daily trains connect Chennai Egmore with Pudukkottai (sleeper/2AC/3AC ₹265/720/1030, six hours) and Karaikkudi (₹285/730/1025, 6¾ hours). One train connects Chennai with Chettinad Station, for Kanadukathan (₹275/740/1065, nine hours).

Madurai

📞 0452 / POP 1.02 MILLION

Chennai may be the capital of Tamil Nadu, but Madurai claims its soul. Madurai is Tamil-born and Tamil-rooted, one of the oldest cities in India, a metropolis that traded with ancient Rome and was a great capital long before Chennai was even dreamed of.

Tourists, Indian and foreign, come here for the celebrated Meenakshi Amman Temple, a dazzling maze-like structure ranking among India's greatest temples. Otherwise, Madurai, perhaps appropriately given its age, captures many of India's glaring dichotomies: a centre dominated by a medieval temple and an economy increasingly driven by IT, all overlaid with the hustle, energy and excitement of a big Indian city and slotted into a much more manageable package than Chennai's sprawl.

History

Legend has it that Shiva showered drops of nectar *(madhuram)* from his locks on to the city, giving rise to the name Madurai – 'the City of Nectar'.

Ancient documents record the existence of Madurai from the 3rd century BC. It was a trading town, especially in spices, and according to legend was home to the third *sangam* (gathering of Tamil scholars and poets). Over the centuries Madurai came under the sway of the Cholas, Pandyas, local Muslim sultans, Hindu Vijayanagar kings and the Nayaks, who ruled until 1736 and set out the old city's lotus shape. Under Tirumalai Nayak (1623–59) the bulk of the Meenakshi Amman Temple was built, and Madurai became the hub of Tamil culture, playing an important role in the development of the Tamil language.

In 1840 the British East India Company razed Madurai's fort and filled in its moat. The four broad Veli streets were constructed on top and to this day define the old city's limits.

❂ Sights

★ Meenakshi Amman Temple HINDU TEMPLE

(East Chitrai St; Indian/foreigner ₹5/50; phone camera ₹50; ☉ 5am-noon & 4-9.30pm) The colourful abode of the triple-breasted warrior goddess Meenakshi ('fish-eyed' – an epithet for perfect eyes in classical Tamil poetry) is generally considered to be the peak of South Indian temple architecture, as vital to this region's aesthetic heritage as the Taj Mahal to North India. It's not so much a 17th-century temple as a 6-hectare complex with 12 tall *gopurams,* encrusted with a staggering array of gods, goddesses, demons and heroes (1511 on the 55m-high south *gopuram* alone).

TAMIL NADU & CHENNAI MADURAI

Madurai

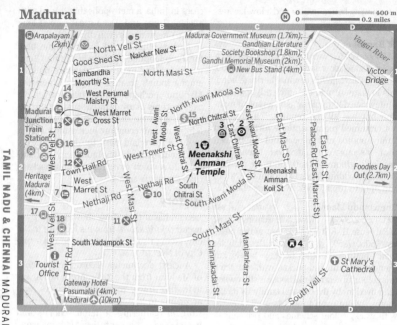

According to legend, the beautiful Meenakshi (a version of Parvati) was born with three breasts and this prophecy: her superfluous breast would melt away when she met her husband. This happened when she met Shiva and took her place as his consort. The existing temple was mostly built during the 17th-century reign of Tirumalai Nayak, but its origins go back 2000 years to when Madurai was a Pandyan capital.

The four streets surrounding the temple are pedestrian-only. Temple dress codes and security are airport-strict: no shoulders or legs (of either gender) may be exposed, and no bags or cameras are allowed inside (but you *can* use phone cameras). Despite this, the temple has a happier atmosphere than some of Tamil Nadu's more solemn shrines, and is adorned with especially vibrant ceiling and wall paintings. Every evening at 9pm, a frenetic, incense-clouded procession carries an icon of Sundareswarar (Shiva) to Meenakshi's shrine to spend the night; visitors can follow along.

Before or after entering the temple, look around the Pudhu Mandapa. The main temple entrance is through the eastern (oldest) *gopuram*. First, on the right, you'll come to the Thousand Pillared Hall, now housing the fascinating Temple Art Museum (p382).

Moving on into the temple, you'll reach a Nandi shrine surrounded by more beautifully carved columns. Ahead is the main Shiva shrine, flanked on each side by massive *dvarapalas*, and further ahead to the left in a separate enclosure is the main Meenakshi shrine, both off limits to non-Hindus. Anyone can however wander round the **Golden Lotus Tank**, where a small pavilion jutting out at the western end has ceiling murals depicting Sundareswarar and Meenakshi's marriage. Leave the temple via a hall of flower sellers and the arch-ceilinged **Ashta Shakti Mandapa** – lined with relief carvings of the goddess' eight attributes and displaying the loveliest of all the temple's elaborately painted ceilings, this is actually the temple entrance for most worshippers.

➡ **Temple Art Museum**

(East Chitrai St; Indian/foreigner ₹5/50, phone camera ₹50; ⊗6am-2pm & 3-9pm) Inside the Meenakshi Amman Temple's eastern *gopuram*, you'll find the Nayak-period Thousand Pillared Hall (with 985 columns) on your right. Now the Art Museum, it contains a Shiva shrine with a large bronze Nataraja at the end of a corridor of superbly carved pillars, plus many other fine bronzes and colourfully painted panels. Some of the best carvings, including Krishna with his flute and Ganesh

Madurai

dancing with a woman on his knee, are immediately inside the museum entrance.

Pudhu Mandapa NOTABLE BUILDING

(East Chitrai St; ☉dawn-dusk) FREE This 16th-century pillared hall stands outside the Meenakshi Amman Temple, opposite the eastern *gopuram*. It's crammed with colourful textile and crafts stalls and tailors at sewing machines, partly hiding some of the fine pillar sculptures, but it's easy to spot the triple-breasted Meenakshi near the southeast corner, facing Sundareswarar (opposite), and their marriage, accompanied by Vishnu, just inside the western entrance. A handsome pale-blue Nandi (Shiva's vehicle) sits outside the *mandapa's* eastern entrance.

Tirumalai Nayak Palace PALACE

(Palace Rd; Indian/foreigner ₹10/50, camera/video ₹30/100; ☉9am-1pm & 1.30-5pm) What Madurai's Meenakshi Amman Temple is to Nayak religious architecture, Tirumalai Nayak's crumbling palace is to the secular. It's said to be only a quarter of its original size, but its

massive scale and hybrid Dravidian-Islamic style still testify to the lofty aspirations of its creator. From the east-side entrance, a large courtyard surrounded by tall, thick columns topped with fancy stucco work leads to the grand throne chamber with its 25m-high dome; two stone-carved horses frame the steps up.

Off the chamber's northwest corner is the Natakasala (Dance Hall), with a small archaeological collection.

Gandhi Memorial Museum MUSEUM

(www.gandhimmm.org; Gandhi Museum Rd; camera ₹50; ☉10am-1pm & 2-5.45pm) FREE Housed in a 17th-century Nayak queen's palace, this impressive museum contains a moving, comprehensive account of Gandhi's life and India's struggle for independence from 1757 to 1947; the English-language displays spare no detail about British rule. They include the blood-stained dhoti that Gandhi was wearing when he was assassinated in Delhi in 1948; it was here in Madurai, in 1921, that he first took up wearing the dhoti as a sign of native pride.

The small **Madurai Government Museum** (Indian/foreigner ₹5/100, camera ₹20; ☉9.30am-5pm Sat-Thu) is next door, and the **Gandhian Literature Society Bookshop** (☉10am-1pm & 2.30-5.45pm Mon-Sat) behind. Buses 3, 66, 75 and 700 from the **Periyar Bus Stand** (West Veli St) go to the Tamukkam bus stop on Alagarkoil Rd, 600m west of the museum.

🏃 Activities

Sivananda Vedanta Yoga Centre YOGA

(☑0452-2521170; http://sivananda.org.in; 444 KK Nagar, East 9th St; class ₹500; ☉6am-8.30pm Mon-Sat, 6.30am-5.30pm Sun) Offers daily drop-in yoga classes (6am, 10am, 4pm, 6pm; book a day ahead) and one-week programs. Also runs rigorous extended courses at its ashram, 22km north of Madurai.

🗣 Tours

Foodies Day Out FOOD & DRINK

(☑9840992340; www.foodiesdayout.com; 2nd fl, 393 Anna Nagar Main Rd; per person from ₹2000) The best way to delve into Madurai's famous foodie culture is on a fantastic evening tour with these local culinary enthusiasts. Vegetarian and vegan options available.

Storytrails WALKING

(☑7373675756; www.storytrails.in; 35 Krishnarayar Tank Rd; up to 4 people tour ₹4000) This Chennai-

TAMIL NADU & CHENNAI MADURAI

born organisation runs highly rated story-based neighbourhood walking tours.

✦ Festivals & Events

Teppam (Float) Festival
RELIGIOUS

(☉ Jan/Feb) A popular 12-day event held on the full moon of the Tamil month of Thai, when Meenakshi Amman Temple deities are paraded around town in elaborate procession and floated in a brightly lit 'minitemple' on the huge **Mariamman Teppakkulam Tank** (Kamarajar Rd), 3km east of the old city.

Chithirai Festival
RELIGIOUS

(☉ Apr/May) The highlight of Madurai's action-packed festival calendar is this two-week celebration of the marriage of Meenakshi to Sundareswarar (Shiva). The deities are wheeled around the Meenakshi Amman Temple in massive chariots forming part of long, colourful processions.

🛏 Sleeping

Budget hotels in central Madurai are mostly dreary and unloved, but there's a big choice of perfectly fine, near-identical midrange hotels along West Perumal Maistry St, near the train station. Higher-end hotels are outside the centre.

YMCA International Guest House
GUESTHOUSE $

(☎ 0452-2346649; www.ymcamadurai.com; Main Guard Sq, Nethaji Rd; incl breakfast s/d ₹850/1110, with AC ₹1300/1450) Madurai's well-managed YMCA guesthouse offers sparse, clean, decent-value rooms. Proceeds help fund the organisation's charitable work.

TM Lodge
HOTEL $

(☎ 0452-2341651; www.tmlodge.in; 50 West Perumal Maistry St; s/d ₹470/720, r with AC ₹1300; ✱) The walls are a bit grubby, but the sheets are clean and TM is efficiently run.

Madurai Residency
HOTEL $$

(☎ 0452-4380000; www.madurairesidency.com; 15 West Marret St; incl breakfast s ₹2640-3120, d ₹3000-3480; ✱ 🖥) The service is stellar and the rooms are comfy and fresh at this winner, which has a handy transport desk and one of the the highest rooftop restaurants in town. It's very popular, particularly with Indian businessmen: book at least a day ahead.

Berrys Boutique
HOTEL $$

(☎ 0452-2340256; www.berrysboutique.in; 25 West Perumal Maistry St; incl breakfast s ₹2130-3220, d ₹2430-3220; ✱ 🖥) Just three months

old at research time, Berrys' 15 smart, contemporary, minimalist fruit-named rooms are the most stylish on this hotel-packed street. There's a soothing atmosphere, plus a friendly welcome and in-house restaurant.

Royal Court
HOTEL $$

(☎ 0452-4356666; www.royalcourtindia.com; 4 West Veli St; incl breakfast s ₹4110-4960, d ₹5080-5690; ✱ 🖥) The Royal Court blends a bit of white-sheeted, hardwood-floored colonial-style elegance with comfort, good eating options and friendly yet professional service. Rooms come with tea/coffee sets. It's an excellent, central choice for someone in need of a bit of a treat.

Gateway Hotel Pasumalai
HERITAGE HOTEL $$$

(☎ 0452-6633000; www.gateway.tajhotels.com; 40 TPK Rd, Pasumalai; s ₹6260-12,710, d ₹7470-13,920; @ 🖥🏊) A stunning escape from the city scramble, the Taj-group Gateway sprawls across hilltop gardens 6km southwest of Madurai centre. The views, outdoor pool and 60 resident peacocks are wonderful, and rooms are luxuriously comfy and well equipped, with glassed-in showers and do-it-yourself yoga kits. The Garden All Day (p385) restaurant is excellent.

Heritage Madurai
HERITAGE HOTEL $$$

(☎ 0452-3244187; www.heritagemadurai.com; 11 Melakkal Main Rd, Kochadai; s ₹4030-8820, d ₹5370-11,600; ✱ 🖥🏊) This leafy haven, 4km northwest of central Madurai, originally housed the old Madurai Club. It's been impeccably tarted up, with intricate Kerala-style woodwork, a sultry sunken pool and airy, terracotta-floored 'deluxe' rooms. Best are the 'villas' featuring private plunge pools. There's a good upscale North and South Indian **restaurant** (mains ₹200-450; ☉ 7am-10.30pm), along with a spa, bar and 24-hour cafe.

🍴 Eating

The hotel-rooftop restaurants along West Perumal Maistry St offer breezy night-time dining and temple views; most hotels also have air-con restaurants for breakfast and lunch. Keep an eye out for Madurai's famous summer drink *jigarthanda* (boiled milk, almond essence, rose syrup and vanilla ice cream).

★ Murugan Idli Shop
SOUTH INDIAN $

(http://muruganidlishop.com; 196 West Masi St; dishes ₹15-75; ☉ 7am-11pm) Though it now has multiple Chennai branches, Murugan is Madurai born and bred. Here you can put the fluffy signature *idlis* and chutneys to the test, and feast on South Indian favourites like dosas, *vadas* and *uttapams*.

Sri Sabareesh   INDIAN $
(49A West Perumal Maistry St; mains ₹65-90; ⊙6am-11pm) Decked with old-Madurai photos, Sri Sabareesh is a popular pure-veg cheapie that rustles up good South Indian thalis (₹80), dosas, *idlis, uttapams* and *vadas*, plus sturdy mains.

Surya   MULTICUISINE $
(www.hotelsupreme.in; Hotel Supreme, 110 West Perumal Maistry St; mains ₹80-160; ⊙4pm-midnight) The Hotel Supreme's rooftop restaurant offers excellent service, good pure-veg food and superb city and temple views. The iced coffee might have been brewed by the gods when you sip it on a hot, dusty day.

Garden All Day   MULTICUISINE $$$
(☑0452-6633000; www.gateway.tajhotels.com; Gateway Hotel Pasumalai, 40 TPK Rd, Pasumalai; mains ₹300-700; ⊙6.30am-11pm) If you're splashing out, the Gateway Hotel's panoramic all-day restaurant (6km southwest of central Madurai) works up an astounding array of delicious global dishes ranging from Chettinadu curries to fancy salads, pastas and burgers.

🛍 Shopping

Madurai teems with cloth stalls and tailors' shops, as you might notice upon being approached by tailor touts. Drivers, guides and touts will also be keen to lead you to the craft shops in North and West Chitrai Sts, offering to show you the rooftop temple view – the views are good, and so is the inevitable sales pitch.

ℹ Information

Tourist Office (☑0452-2334757; 1 West Veli St; ⊙10am-5.30pm Mon-Fri) Also branches at the airport and train station.

ℹ Getting There & Away

AIR
Madurai Airport is 12km south of town. **SpiceJet** (www.spicejet.com) flies once daily to Colombo, Dubai and Hyderabad, and four times daily to Chennai. **Jet Airways** (www.jetairways.com) has one daily flight to Bengaluru and five to Chennai. **Air India** (www.airindia.in) flies daily to Chennai and Mumbai.

BUS
Most government buses arrive and depart from the **New Bus Stand** (Melur Rd), 4km northeast of the centre. Services to Coimbatore, Kodaikanal, Ooty and Munnar go from the **Arapalayam Bus Stand** (Puttuthoppu Main Rd), 2km northwest of the old city. Tickets for more expensive (more comfortable) private buses are sold by agencies on the south side of the **Shopping Complex Bus Stand** (btwn West Veli St & TPK Rd); most travel overnight.

TRAIN
From Madurai Junction station, 12 daily trains head to Trichy and 10 to Chennai; fastest is the 7am Vaigai Express (Trichy 2nd/chair class ₹95/345, two hours; Chennai ₹180/660, 7¾ hours). A good overnight Chennai train is the 8.35pm Pandian Express (sleeper/3AC/2AC/1AC ₹315/810/1140/1930, nine hours). To Kanyakumari the only daily train departs at 1.30am (sleeper/3AC/2AC/1AC ₹210/540/740/1235, five hours); there's a later train some days.

TAMIL NADU & CHENNAI MADURAI

GOVERNMENT BUSES FROM MADURAI

DESTINATION	FARE (₹)	TIME (HR)	DEPARTURES
Bengaluru	420-730	9-10	7am, 6pm, 8.30pm, 9pm, 9.15pm, 9.30pm, 9.35pm, 9.45pm
Chennai	325-420	9-10	every 15min, AC 9am, 8.30pm, 9pm
Kodaikanal	62	4	13 buses 1.30am-2.50pm, 5.50pm, 8.30pm
Coimbatore	125	5	every 10min
Ernakulam (Kochi)	325	9½	9am, 8pm, 9pm
Kanyakumari	200	6	every 30min
Munnar	115	6	5.55am, 8am, 10.40am
Mysuru	300-430	9-12	4.35pm, 6pm, 8pm, 9pm
Ooty	200	8	7.30am, 9.20pm
Puducherry	240-260	7½	9.05pm, 9.30pm
Rameswaram	150	4-5	every 30min
Trichy	90	2¼-3	every 5min

KATHADI WATER SPORTS

Launched by a team of Mumbaikar adventure-activity experts, laid-back water-sports centre **Kathadi North** (☑ 9820367412; www.quest-asia.com; Pirappan Valasai, off Madurai–Rameswaram Hwy; 2-day kitesurfing package incl accommodation ₹9250) 🏄 offers kite-surfing, kayaking, windsurfing, snorkelling, stand-up paddleboarding, sailing, camping, beach clean-ups and after-dark wildlife walks. It's based on the mainland, 18km west of the Pamban Island bridge (which leads to Rameswaram). There's **accommodation** (☑ 9820367412; www.quest-asia.com; Pirappan Valasai, off Madurai–Rameswaram Hwy; s/d incl breakfast ₹3000/3500; 🛜) 🏄 in four fan-cooled, beach-chic concrete huts with thatched roofs and open-air bathrooms, just inland from salt-white sands. Rainwater is harvested, power is solar, doors are recycled, palm fences use on-site materials, and the open kitchen serves communal meals (₹450).

On Pamban Island's southwest coast, budget-oriented branch **Kathadi South** (☑ 9820367412; www.quest-asia.com; off Old Dhanushkodhi Rd, Pamban Island; 2-day kitesurfing package incl accommodation ₹8250) has near-identical activities, plus simple shared -bathroom **huts** (☑ 9820367412; www.quest-asia.com; off Old Dhanushkodhi Rd, Pamban Island; s/d incl breakfast ₹1250/1500) 🏄 and **tents** (single/double ₹650/1000).

Trivandrum (three daily; sleeper/3AC/2AC ₹205/545/775), Coimbatore (three daily; ₹235/590/825), Bengaluru (two daily; ₹1080/750/280) and Mumbai (one daily; ₹2540/1730/645) are other destinations.

ℹ Getting Around

Taxis cost ₹500 between the centre and the airport. Alternatively, bus 10 (₹13) runs to/from the Shopping Complex Bus Stand.

From the **New Bus Stand** (p385), buses 3, 48 and 700 shuttle into the city; autorickshaws cost ₹120.

There's a fixed-rate taxi **stand** (Madurai Junction) outside Madurai Junction train station, with fare boards (one day around Madurai ₹1400 to ₹1800). Fast Track also has a **taxi booking counter** (☑ 0452-2888999; Madurai Junction; ⏱ 24hr) here; rates are ₹90 for the first 3km, then ₹14 to ₹16 per kilometre.

Rameswaram

☑ 04573 / POP 44,860

Rameswaram was once the southernmost point of sacred India; leaving its boundaries meant abandoning caste and falling below the status of the lowliest skinner of sacred cows. Then Rama (incarnation of Vishnu, hero of the Ramayana) led a monkey-and-bear army across a monkey-built bridge to (Sri) Lanka, defeating the demon Ravana and rescuing his wife, Sita. Afterwards, prince and princess offered thanks to Shiva here. Today, millions of Hindus flock to the Ramanathaswamy Temple to worship where a god worshipped a god.

Otherwise, Rameswaram is a small, scruffy fishing town on conch-shaped Pamban Island, connected to the mainland by 2km-long bridges. If you aren't a pilgrim, the temple alone barely merits the journey here. But the island's eastern tip, Dhanushkodi, only 30km from Sri Lanka, has a magical natural beauty that adds to Rameswaram's appeal. And for activity-loving travellers, the island's western edge is buzzing as a low-key water-sports destination.

Most hotels and eateries are clustered around the Ramanathaswamy Temple, which is surrounded by North, East, South and West Car Sts.

⊙ Sights

Ramanathaswamy Temple   HINDU TEMPLE
(East Car St; ⏱ 5am-noon & 3-8.30pm) Housing the world's most sacred sand mound (a lingam said to have been created by Rama's wife Sita, so he could worship Shiva), this temple is one of India's holiest shrines. Dating mainly from the 16th to 18th centuries, it's notable for its lengthy 1000-pillar halls and 22 *theerthams* (temple tanks), in which pilgrims bathe before visiting the deity. Attendants tip pails of water over the (often fully dressed) faithful, who rush from *theertham* to *theertham*.

🛏 Sleeping & Eating

Most Rameswaram hotels are geared towards pilgrims. Some cheapies (mostly pretty grim) won't accept single travellers, but there are tolerable midrange hotels. Budgeteers can try the **rooms booking office** (East Car St; r ₹300-500; ⊙24hr).

Daiwik Hotel HOTEL **$$**
(☑04573-223222; www.daiwikhotels.com; Madurai–Rameswaram Hwy; r ₹4830-6040; ❋ 🛜)
Gleaming, comfy and welcoming, 'India's first four-star pilgrim hotel', 200m west of the bus station, is your classiest choice in Rameswaram. Airy rooms come smartly decked out with huge mirrors and local-life photos, there's a spa, and the pure-veg **Ahaan** (www.daiwikhotels.com; Daiwik Hotel, Madurai–Rameswaram Hwy; mains ₹145-270; ⊙7am-10pm) restaurant is good.

ℹ Getting There & Around

Rameswaram's **bus stand** (Madurai–Rameswaram Hwy) is 2.5km west of town. Buses run to Madurai (₹100, four hours) every five minutes and to Trichy (₹145, seven hours) every 30 minutes. 'Ultra Deluxe' (UD) services are scheduled to Chennai (₹435, 13 hours) at 4pm and 4.30pm, Kanyakumari (₹270, eight hours) at 7.15am and 7.30pm, and Bengaluru (₹580, 12 hours) at 4.30pm, but don't always run. There's also a 5pm AC bus to Chennai (₹565, 13 hours).

The train station is 1.5km southwest of the temple. Three daily trains to/from Madurai (₹35, four hours) have unreserved seating only. The Rameswaram–Chennai Express departs daily at 8.15pm (sleeper/3AC/2AC ₹360/945/1335, 11 hours) via Trichy (₹215/535/740, 4¾ hours). The Rameswaram–Kanyakumari Express leaves at 8.45pm Monday, Thursday and Saturday, reaching Kanyakumari (sleeper/3AC ₹275/710) at 4.05am.

Bus 1 (₹5) shuttles between the bus stand and East Car St. Autorickshaws into town from the bus stand or train station cost ₹50.

Kanyakumari (Cape Comorin)

☑04652 / POP 22,450

This is it, the end of India. There's a sense of accomplishment on making it to the tip of the subcontinent's 'V', past the final dramatic flourish of the Western Ghats and the green fields, glinting rice paddies and slow-looping wind turbines of India's deep south. Kanyakumari can feel surreal; at certain times of year you'll see the sun set and the moon rise over three seas (Bay of Bengal, Arabian Sea, Indian Ocean) simultaneously. The Temple of the Virgin Sea Goddess, Swami Vivekananda's legacy and the 'Land's End' symbolism draw crowds of pilgrims and tourists to Kanyakumari, but it remains a small-scale, refreshing respite from the hectic Indian road.

◉ Sights

Kumari Amman Temple HINDU TEMPLE
(Sannathi St; ⊙4.30am-noon & 4-8.30pm) The legends say the *kanya* (virgin) goddess Kumari, a manifestation of the Great Goddess Devi, single-handedly conquered demons and secured freedom for the world. At this temple

TAMIL NADU & CHENNAI KANYAKUMARI (CAPE COMORIN)

WORTH A TRIP

DHANUSHKODI

Pamban Island's promontory stretches 22km southeast from Rameswaram, narrowing to a thin strip of dunes halfway along. Near the southeasternmost tip stands the ghost town of **Dhanushkodi**. Once a thriving port, Dhanushkodi was washed away by a monster cyclone in 1964. The shells of its train station, church, post office and other ruins stand among fishers' shacks; Adam's Bridge (Rama's Bridge), the chain of reefs, sandbanks and islets that almost connects India with Sri Lanka, stretches away to the east. The atmosphere is at its most magical at sunrise, with pilgrims performing *pujas* (offerings).

Autorickshaws charge ₹500 round-trip (including waiting time) to Moonram Chattram, 14km southeast of Rameswaram. Buses run here from Rameswaram's bus stand every 30 minutes (₹12). From Moonram Chattram to Dhanushkodi it's a 4km walk, or a ₹180 to ₹200 two-hour round trip in a truck or minibus which departs when it fills up with 16 customers (6am to 6pm). You can also hire an entire bus/jeep (₹1500 to ₹2000 return). It's tempting to swim, but beware of strong rips.

At the time of writing, a new tarmac road traversing the once-wild dunes from Moonram Chattram to Dhanushkodi had been completed but not inaugurated. Visiting arrangements may change, and there are concerns that easy road access will ruin the ghost town's spectacularly secluded appeal.

Kanyakumari (Cape Comorin)

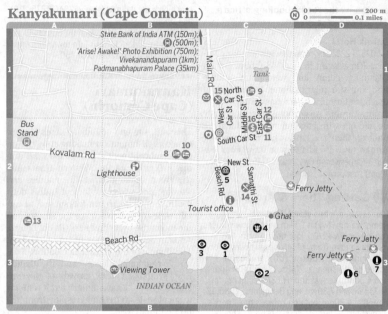

Kanyakumari (Cape Comorin)

on the tip of the subcontinent, pilgrims give her thanks in an intimately spaced, beautifully decorated temple, where the crash of waves from three seas can be heard beyond the twilight glow of oil fires clutched in vulva-shaped votive candles (referencing the sacred femininity of the goddess).

It's said that the temple's east-facing door stays locked to prevent the shimmer of the goddess' diamond nose-stud leading ships astray. From the main north-side gate, you'll be asked for a ₹10 donation to enter the 18th-century inner precinct, where men must remove their shirts, and cameras are forbidden.

The shoreline around the temple has a couple of tiny beaches, and bathing **ghats** where worshippers immerse themselves before visiting the temple. The *mandapa* just south of the temple is popular for sunset-watching and daytime shade.

Vivekananda Memorial   MONUMENT
(₹20; ⊙7.45am-4pm) Four hundred metres offshore is the rock where famous Hindu apostle Swami Vivekananda meditated from 25 to 27 December 1892, and decided to take his moral message beyond India's shores. A two-*mandapa* 1970 memorial to Vivekananda reflects temple architectural styles from

across India. The lower *mandapa* contains what's believed to be goddess Kumari's footprint. With the constant tourist crowds this brings, Vivekananda would no doubt choose somewhere else to meditate today. Ferries shuttle out to the rock (₹34 return).

Thiruvalluvar Statue MONUMENT
(⊙7.45am-4pm) FREE Looking like an Indian Colossus of Rhodes, the towering statue on the smaller island next to the Vivekananda Memorial is of the ancient Tamil poet Thiruvalluvar. The work of more than 5000 sculptors, it was erected in 2000 and honours the poet's 133-chapter work Thirukural – hence its height of exactly 133ft (40.5m). Tides permitting, Vivekananda Memorial ferries (₹34 return) continue to Thiruvalluvar.

Swami Vivekananda
Wandering Monk Exhibition MUSEUM
(Beach Rd; ₹10; ⊙8am-noon & 4-8pm) In lovely leafy grounds, this excellent exhibition details Swami Vivekananda's wisdom, sayings and encounters with the mighty and the lowly during his five years as a wandering monk around India from 1888 to 1893. Tickets also cover the Vivekananda-inspired 'Arise! Awake!' exhibition in Vivekanandapuram, 1km north of town.

Gandhi Memorial MEMORIAL, MONUMENT
(Beach Rd; ⊙7am-7pm) FREE Poignantly placed at the end of the nation that Gandhi fathered, this cream-coloured memorial is designed in the form of an Odishan (Orissan) temple embellished by Hindu, Christian and Muslim architects. The central plinth stored some of the Mahatma's ashes before they were immersed in the sea; each year, on Gandhi's birthday (2 October), the sun's rays fall on the stone. The tower is also a popular sunset-gazing spot.

Kamaraj Memorial MEMORIAL, MONUMENT
(Beach Rd; ⊙7am-7pm) FREE This memorial near the shoreline commemorates K Kamaraj, the 'Gandhi of the South'. One of the most powerful and respected politicians of post-Independence India, Kamaraj held the chief ministership of both Madras State and its successor, Tamil Nadu. The dusty photos inside have English-language captions.

Vivekanandapuram ASHRAM
(☎04652-247012; www.vivekanandakendra.org; Vivekanandapuram; ⊙9am-8pm) Just 1km north of Kanyakumari, this peaceful ashram (offering a variety of yoga retreats) is

the headquarters of spiritual organisation **Vivekananda Kendra**, devoted to carrying out Vivekananda's teachings. Its Vivekananda-focused 'Arise! Awake!' (₹10; ⊙9am-1pm & 4-8pm Wed-Mon, 9am-1pm Tue) exhibition is worth a visit, and you can stroll to the sea past a beautiful lotus-pool-lined **memorial** to the swami.

🛏 Sleeping

Hotel Narmadha HOTEL $
(☎04652-246365; Kovalam Rd; r ₹500-700) This long, colourful concrete block conceals friendly staff, a back-up generator and a range of budget rooms, some of them cleaner and with less grim bathrooms than others. The cheapest are bucket-water only, but the ₹700 sea-view doubles with spearmint-stripe sheets are good value.

Lakshmi Tourist Home HOTEL $
(☎04652-246333; East Car St; r ₹1000, with AC ₹1500) Simple but well-kept, this relatively helpful family hotel is a decent town-centre deal. The better (pricier) rooms come with sea views and hot water, but most are neat and clean.

Hotel Tri Sea HOTEL $$
(☎04652-246586; www.hoteltrisea.in; Kovalam Rd; r ₹1170-2220, with AC ₹2340-2580; ❄🗑🌐) You can't miss the high-rise Tri Sea, whose sea-view rooms are spacious, spotless and airy, with particularly hectic colour schemes. Reception is efficient and the rooftop pool, sunrise/sunset-viewing platforms and free in-room wi-fi are welcome bonuses.

Hotel Sivamurugan HOTEL $$
(☎04652-246862; www.hotelsivamurugan.com; 2/93 North Car St; r ₹1375, with AC ₹2280-2740; ❄🗑) A welcoming, well-appointed hotel, with spacious, spotless, marble-floored rooms and lobby-only wi-fi. 'Super-deluxes' have sea glimpses past a couple of buildings. Rates stay fixed year-round (a novelty for Kanyakumari) and there's 24-hour hot water.

Sparsa Resort RESORT $$$
(☎04652-247041; www.sparsaresorts.com; 6/112B Beach Rd; r incl breakfast ₹4800-7200; ❄🗑🌐) Away from the temple frenzy on the west edge of town, elegant Sparsa is a good few notches above Kanyakumari's other hotels. Fresh, orange-walled rooms with low dark-wood beds, lounge chairs and mood-lighting make for a contemporary-oriental vibe, and there's a lovely pool surrounded by palms,

TAMIL NADU & CHENNAI KANYAKUMARI (CAPE COMORIN)

as well as good Indian cooking at **Auroma** (mains ₹150-400; ⊘ 7-10am, noon-3pm, 7-11pm).

Seashore Hotel
HOTEL $$$

(⌨ 04652-246704; www.theseashorehotel.com; East Car St; r ₹4140-7800; ❀ 🏠) The fanciest town-centre hotel has shiny, roomy chambers with golden curtains and cushions, glassed-in showers and kettles. It's lost its original sparkle, but all rooms except the cheapest offer panoramic sea views, and the 7th-floor restaurant is one of Kanyakumari's best.

✕ Eating

Hotel Anapoorna
INDIAN $

(Sannathi St; mains ₹110-150, thalis ₹120-180; ⊘ 7am-9.30pm) A popular pan-Indian budget spot serving breakfast *idlis,* filter coffee and South Indian thalis alongside curries and biryanis, in a clean, friendly setting.

Seashore Hotel
MULTICUISINE $$

(www.theseashorehotel.com; East Car St; mains ₹210-320; ⊘ 7-10am & 12.30-10pm) Amazingly, this spruced-up 7th-floor hotel restaurant is the only one in Kanyakumari with a proper sea view. There's great grilled fish and plenty of Indian veg and nonveg choices, plus the odd Continental creation. Service is spot-on and it's a good breakfast bet (buffet ₹270).

Sangam Restaurant
INDIAN $$

(Main Rd; mains ₹95-300, thalis ₹100-135; ⊘ 7am-10.30pm) It's as if the Sangam started in Kashmir, trekked south across India, and stopped here to offer tasty veg and nonveg picks from every province along the way. The seats are soft and the food is good.

ⓘ Information

Tourist office (⌨ 04652-246276; Beach Rd; ⊘ 10am-5.30pm Mon-Fri)

ⓘ Getting There & Away

BUS

Kanyakumari's sedate **bus stand** (Kovalam Rd) is a 10-minute walk west of the centre. Most comfortable are the 'Ultra Deluxe' (UD) buses.

TRAIN

The train station is 800m north of Kanyakumari's centre. One daily northbound train, the Kanyakumari Express, departs at 5.20pm for Chennai (sleeper/3AC/2AC/1AC ₹415/1095/1555/2630, 13½ hours) via Madurai (₹210/540/740/1235, 4½ hours) and Trichy (₹275/710/995/1670, seven hours). Two daily express trains depart at 6.40am and 10.30am for Trivandrum (sleeper/3AC/2AC ₹140/490/695, 2¼ hours), continuing to Kollam (Quilon; ₹140/490/695, 3½ hours) and Ernakulam (Kochi; ₹205/545/775, seven hours). More trains go from Nagercoil Junction, 20km northwest of Kanyakumari.

For real train buffs, the Vivek Express runs to Dibrugarh (Assam), 4236km and 80 hours – India's longest single train ride. It departs Kanyakumari at 11pm Thursday (₹1085/2830/4265).

THE WESTERN GHATS

Welcome to the lush Western Ghats, some of the most welcome heat relief in India. Rising like an impassable bulwark of evergreen and deciduous tangle from north of Mumbai to the tip of Tamil Nadu, the World Heritage-listed Ghats (with an average elevation of 915m) contain 27% of India's flowering plants and an incredible array of endemic wildlife. In Tamil Nadu they rise to over 2000m in the Palani Hills around Kodaikanal and the Nilgiris around Ooty. British influence lingers a little stronger up in these hills, where colonists built 'hill stations' to escape the sweltering plains and covered slopes in neatly trimmed tea plantations. It's not just the air and (relative) lack of pollution that's

BUSES FROM KANYAKUMARI

DESTINATION	FARE (₹)	TIME (HR)	DEPARTURES
Bengaluru (UD)	635	12-14	4.45pm, 5.30pm
Chennai (UD)	530	12-14	8 daily
Kodaikanal (UD)	310	10	8.15pm
Kovalam	120	3	6am, 2pm
Madurai	100, UD 210	8	9 daily; UD 2pm, 3pm
Rameswaram	250	8	7.30am, 7pm
Trivandrum	75-80	2½	9 daily

PADMANABHAPURAM PALACE

With a forest's worth of intricately carved rosewood ceilings and polished-teak beams, labyrinthine **Padmanabhapuram Palace** (☑04651-250255; Padmanabhapuram; Indian/foreigner ₹35/300, camera/video ₹50/2000; ⊙9am-1pm & 2-4.30pm Tue-Sun), 35km northwest of Kanyakumari near the Kerala border, is considered the finest example of traditional Keralan architecture today. Asia's largest wooden palace complex, it was once capital of Travancore, an unstable princely state taking in parts of both Tamil Nadu and Kerala. Under successive rulers it expanded into a magnificent conglomeration of corridors, courtyards, gabled roofs and 14 palaces. The oldest sections date to 1550.

Direct buses leave from Kanyakumari's bus stand at 7.30am, 10.45am, 1.30pm and 3.20pm (₹25, two hours); buses also run every 20 minutes from Kanyakumari to Thuckalay (₹25), from where it's an autorickshaw ride or 15-minute walk to the palace. Return taxis from Kanyakumari cost ₹1200.

From Trivandrum (Thiruvananthapuram), take any bus towards Kanyakumari (₹70, three hours, four daily) and get off at Thuckalay. The Kerala Tourist Development Corporation (KTDC; p945) runs full-day Kanyakumari tours from Trivandrum covering Padmanabhapuram (₹700; minimum four people).

refreshing – there's a certain acceptance of quirkiness and eccentricity here. Expect organic farms, handlebar-moustached trekking guides and leopard-print earmuffs.

Kodaikanal (Kodai)

☑04542 / POP 36,500 / ELEV 2100M

There are few more refreshing Tamil Nadu moments than leaving the heat-soaked plains for the sharp pinch of a Kodaikanal night or morning. This misty hill station, 120km northwest of Madurai in the protected Palani Hills, is more relaxed and intimate than its big sister Ooty (Kodai is the 'Princess of Hill Stations', Ooty the Queen). It's not all cold either; days feel more like deep spring than early winter.

Centred on a beautiful star-shaped lake, Kodai rambles up and down hillsides with patches of *shola* (virgin forest), unique to South India's Western Ghats, and evergreen broadleaf trees like magnolia, mahogany, myrtle and rhododendron. Another plant speciality is the *kurinji* shrub, whose lilac-blue blossoms appear every 12 years (next due 2018).

Kodai is popular with honeymooners and groups, who flock to its spectacular viewpoints and waterfalls. The renowned Kodaikanal International School provides some cosmopolitan flair. Visit midweek for peace and quiet.

◉ Sights & Activities

Sacred Heart Natural Science Museum   MUSEUM

(Kodaikanal Museum; Sacred Heart College, Law's Ghat Rd; adult/child ₹20/10, camera ₹20; ⊙9am-

6pm) In the grounds of a former Jesuit seminary 4km downhill east of town, this museum has a ghoulishly intriguing miscellany of flora and fauna put together over more than 100 years by priests and trainees. Displays range over bottled snakes, human embryos (!), giant moths and stuffed animal carcasses. You can also see pressed famous *kurinji* flowers (*Strobilanthes kunthiana*).

Parks & Viewpoints

Several natural beauty spots around Kodai (crowded with souvenir and snack stalls) are very popular with Indian tourists. They're best visited by taxi; drivers offer three-hour 12-stop tours for ₹1500 to ₹1800. On clear days, **Green Valley View** (⊙dawn-dusk) FREE, 6km from the centre), **Pillar Rocks** (₹20; ⊙9am-4pm) FREE, 7km from the centre, and less-visited **Moir's Point** (₹10; ⊙10am-5pm), 13km from the centre, all along the same road west of town, have spectacular views to the plains below.

Bryant Park   PARK

(off Lake Rd; adult/child ₹30/15, camera/video ₹50/100; ⊙9am-6pm) Landscaped and stocked by the British officer after whom it's named, pretty Bryant Park is usually full of tourists and canoodling couples.

Berijam Lake   LAKE

(⊙9am-3pm) FREE Visiting forest-fringed Berijam Lake, 21km southwest of Kodaikanal, requires a Forest Department permit. Taxi drivers will organise this, if asked the day before, and do half-day 'forest tours' to Berijam, via other lookouts, for ₹1800.

Kodaikanal (Kodai)

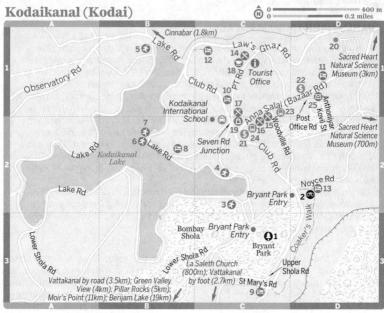

Walking

The 5km **Kodaikanal Lake circuit** is lovely in the early morning before the crowds roll in. A walk along Lower Shola Rd takes you through the **Bombay Shola**, the nearest surviving patch of *shola* to central Kodai.

Officially, you're free to hike anywhere within 19km of Kodai, but not beyond. Forest Department permits for more serious trekking routes in protected areas *may* be obtained with time, patience and luck; if you fancy trying, contact Kodai's **District Forest Office** (☑ 04542-241287; Muthaliarpuram; ☺ 10am-5.45pm Mon-Fri). The tourist office (p395) and guesthouses like Greenlands Youth Hostel (p392) can put you in touch with local guides, who help with permits and offer interesting off-road routes (₹600 to ₹1000 per half-day). The tourist office stocks a leaflet outlining 17 local treks.

A good trek, if you can organise it, is the two-day Kodai–Munnar route into Kerala via Top Station (involving some bus/rickshaw transport). Guides charge ₹5000 per person.

Coaker's Walk
VIEWPOINT

(₹10; ☺ 7am-7pm) Assuming it isn't cloaked in opaque mist, the views from paved Coaker's Walk are beautiful, all the way down to the plains 2000m below. The stroll takes five minutes.

Trails & Tracks
TREKKING

(☑ 9965524279; thenaturetrails@gmail.com; day walk per person per hr ₹200) A reliable, well-established trekking outfit run by very experienced local guide Vijay Kumar, offering day walks, longer hikes and overnight treks.

Boating & Cycling

If you're sappy in love like a bad Bollywood song, the thing to do in Kodai is rent a pedal boat, rowboat or Kashmiri *shikara* ('honeymoon boat') from the **Kodaikanal Boat & Rowing Club** (Lake Rd; per 30min pedal boat/rowboat ₹90/170, shikara incl boatman ₹480; ☺ 9am-6pm) or **TTDC Boat House** (Lake Rd; per hour pedal boat ₹180, rowboat/shikara incl boatman ₹640/970; ☺ 9am-5.30pm).

Bicycle-rental (per hour ₹50) stands are dotted around the lake.

🛏 Sleeping

Some hotels hike prices by up to 100% during the 'season' (April to June). There are some gorgeous heritage places, and good-value midrange options if you can live without colonial-era ambience. Most hotels have a 9am or 10am checkout April to June.

Greenlands Youth Hostel
HOSTEL $

(☑ 04542-240899; www.greenlandskodaikanal. com; St Mary's Rd; dm ₹400, d ₹900-2500; ☎)

Kodaikanal (Kodai)

This long-running, sociable budget favourite has a pretty garden and wonderful views. Accommodation is very bare and basic and hot water runs only from 8am to 10am. Dorms may be available, but are aimed at groups, while newer, comfier 'superdeluxes' and 'suites' have colourful decor and balconies.

Sri Vignesh Guest House GUESTHOUSE $
(☑ 9094972524; umaarkrishnan@gmail.com; Lake Rd; r ₹700-1200) Up a steep driveway, surrounded by neat flowery gardens with a swing, this simple but characterful Raj-era home is run by a friendly local couple, who welcome 'peaceful' guests (no packs of boys!). Rooms are clean and very basic; hot water until noon.

Snooze Inn HOTEL $
(☑ 04542-240837; www.jayarajgroup.com; Anna Salai; dm ₹330, r ₹880-1045; ☎) Rooms don't have quite as much character as the exterior suggests, but this is a decent-value budget choice sporting clean bathrooms and plenty of blankets. There's also a 12-bed dorm with lockers and one shared bathroom.

Cinnabar HOMESTAY $$
(☑ 9842145220; www.cinnabar.in; Chettiar Rd; r incl half-board ₹6000; ☎) 🌱 Cinnabar's two elegant yet homey rooms offer a blissful escape, with 24-hour hot water, tea/coffee kits, glassed-in showers and lovely wooden floors and ceilings. Homemade cheese, bread, granola, jams and 'world' cuisine come courtesy of the clued-up owners, who recommend local hikes and source all ingredients for their organic fruit-and-veg garden out front. It's 2km north of town.

Villa Retreat HOTEL $$
(☑ 04542-240940; www.villaretreat.com; Club Rd; r incl breakfast ₹4740-7900; ☎) Take in the fantastic Coaker's Walk views from your garden breakfast table at this lovely old stone-built hotel, right next to the walk's northern end. It's a friendly place with comfy, good-sized rooms and, when it's cold, a roaring fire in the dining room. Prices are steep, but service is attentive.

Hilltop Towers HOTEL $$
(☑ 04542-240413; www.hilltopgroup.in; Club Rd; r incl breakfast ₹2860-3440; ☎) Although it's bland on the outside, rustic flourishes like polished-teak floors, plus keen staff, in-room tea/coffee sets and a central location make the Hilltop a good-value midranger.

★ Carlton HERITAGE HOTEL $$$
(☑ 04542-240056; www.carlton-kodaikanal. com; Lake Rd; incl half-board s ₹10,350-11,630, d ₹11,820-12,880, cottage ₹17,430; ☎) The cream of Kodai's hotels is a magnificent five-star colonial-era mansion overlooking the lake. Rooms are spacious with extra-comfy beds and, for some, huge private balconies. The grounds and common areas get the old hill-station ambience spot on: open-stone walls, billiards, evening bingo, fireplaces, a hot tub, and a bar that immediately makes you want to demand a Scotch.

WORTH A TRIP

DOLPHIN'S NOSE WALK

This is a lovely walk of 4.5km (each way) from central Kodai, passing through budget-traveller hang-out Vattakanal to reach the Dolphin's Nose, a narrow rock lookout overhanging a precipitous drop. You might spot gaur (bison) or giant squirrels in the forested bits.

From the south end of Coaker's Walk, follow St Mary's Rd west then southwest, passing 19th-century La Saleth Church after 1.2km. At a fork 400m after the church, go left downhill on what quickly becomes an unpaved track passing through the Pambar Shola forest. After 450m you emerge on a bridge above some falls. Across the bridge, stalls sell fruit, tea, coffee, bread omelettes and roasted corn with lime and masala. Follow the road 1km downhill, with panoramas opening up as you go, to Vattakanal village. Take the steep path down past Altaf's Cafe and in 15 minutes you'll reach the Dolphin's Nose.

Vattakanal

Little Vattakanal village ('Vatta'), 4.5km southwest of Kodai, is a wonderful rural retreat for budget travellers. It's very popular, particularly with groups of Indian and Israeli travellers, and there's a mellow party vibe when things gets busy.

Altaf's Cafe GUESTHOUSE $
(☑ 9487120846; www.altafscafe.com; Vattakanal; r ₹1200-2000) Popular little Middle Eastern–Italian Altaf's Cafe runs a few sizeable doubles and three-bed rooms for six people (sometimes more!) with private bathroom, scattered across Vattakanal's hillside.

Kodai Heaven GUESTHOUSE $$
(☑ 9865207207; www.kodaiheaven.com; 6 Dolphin's Nose Rd, Vattakanal; r ₹2000-3200; 🛜) Simple hillside sharing rooms for two to six people, with splashes of colour and fabulous mountain views.

Eating & Drinking

PT Rd is the place for restaurants. Many Kodai eateries have organic and/or international tendencies, and you'll enjoy locally produced cheese, bread, coffee and avocados.

Pastry Corner BAKERY $
(3 Maratta Shopping Complex, Anna Salai; ⊙ 10.30am-2pm & 3-5.30pm) Pick up oven-fresh muffins, croissants, cakes, cinnamon swirls and sandwiches at this popular bakery, or squeeze on to the benches with a cuppa.

Tava INDIAN $
(PT Rd; mains ₹70-140; ⊙ 11.30am-8.45pm Thu-Tue) Cheap, fast and clean, pure-veg Tava has a wide all-Indian menu; try the spicy, cauliflower-stuffed *gobi paratha* or *sev puri* (crisp, puffy fried bread with potato and chutney).

Ten Degrees MULTICUISINE $$
(PT Rd; mains ₹200-360; ⊙ noon-10pm) Honey-coloured wood and monochrome Kodai photos set the tone for tasty, elegantly prepared Indian and Continental food at this lively new PT Rd arrival. It does mouth-meltingly spicy wraps, homemade-bread sandwiches, burgers, salads, sizzlers, egg-based breakfasts and drinks served in jars.

Altaf's Cafe MULTICUISINE $$
(☑ 9487120846; www.altafscafe.com; Vattakanal; dishes ₹70-200; ⊙ 8am-8.30pm) This open-sided cafe whips up soulful Italian, Indian and Middle Eastern dishes including breakfasts and *sabich* (Israeli aubergine-and-egg pita sandwiches), plus teas, coffees, juices and lassis, for hungry travellers at Vattakanal.

Hotel Astoria INDIAN $$
(Anna Salai; mains ₹110-150, thalis ₹115-155; ⊙ 7am-10pm) This pure-veg restaurant is always packed with locals and tourists, especially at lunchtime when it serves fantastic all-you-can-eat thalis.

Cloud Street MULTICUISINE $$$
(www.cloudstreetcafe.com; PT Rd; mains ₹260-550; ⊙ 12.30-9pm Wed-Mon; 🛜) Why yes, that is a real Italian-style wood-fire pizza oven. And yes, that's hummus and falafel on the menu, along with oven-baked pasta and homemade cakes. It's all great food in a simple, relaxed, family-run setting with scattered candles and a crackling fire on cold nights. Live music every other Saturday.

Carlton MULTICUISINE $$$
(Lake Rd; buffet ₹950; ⊙ 7.30-10.30am, 1-3pm & 7.30-10.30pm) Definitely the place to come for a splash-out buffet-dinner fill-up: a huge variety of excellent Indian and Continental dishes in limitless quantity. Lunch is à la carte.

★ Cafe Cariappa   CAFE
(www.facebook.com/cafecariappa; PT Rd; coffees ₹80-100; ⊙10.30am-6.30pm Tue-Sun; 🛜) A caffeine addict's dream, this rustic-chic wood-panelled shoe-box of a cafe crafts fantastic brews from its own locally grown organic coffee. It also does homemade carrot cake, crepes, sandwiches and fresh juices, and sells Kodai-made cheeses.

🛍 Shopping
Shops and stalls all over town sell homemade chocolates, spices, natural oils and handicrafts. Some also reflect a low-key but long-term commitment to social justice.

Re Shop   ARTS & CRAFTS
(www.facebook.com/bluemangotrust; Seven Rd Junction; ⊙10am-7pm Mon-Sat) 🖋 Stylish jewellery, fabrics, cards and more, at reasonable prices, made by and benefiting marginalised village women around Tamil Nadu.

ℹ Information
Tourist Office (☑04542-241675; PT Rd; ⊙10am-5.30pm Mon-Fri) Doesn't look too promising but it's helpful enough.

ℹ Getting There & Away

BUS
For most destinations, it's quickest and easiest to take a bus from Kodai's **bus stand** (Anna Salai).
Raja's Tours & Travels (http://rajastours.com; Anna Salai; ⊙8am-9pm) Runs 20-seat minibuses with push-back seats to Ooty (₹500, eight hours, 7.30pm), plus overnight AC sleeper and semisleeper buses to Chennai (₹650 to ₹950, 12 hours, 6pm and 6.30pm) and Bengaluru (₹650 to ₹850, 12 hours, 6.30pm).

TRAIN
The nearest train station is Kodai Rd, down in the plains 80km east of Kodaikanal. There are four daily trains to/from Chennai Egmore including the overnight Pandian Express (sleeper/3AC/2AC/1AC ₹295/765/1075/1815, 7½ hours), departing Chennai at 9.20pm and de-

parting Kodai Rd northbound at 9.10pm. Kodai's post office has a **train booking office** (Post Office, Post Office Rd; ⊙9am-4pm Mon-Fri, to 2pm Sat).

Direct buses from Kodaikanal to Kodai Rd leave daily at 10.20am and 4.25pm (₹55, three hours); there are also plenty of buses between the train station and Batlagundu, on the Kodai–Madurai bus route. Taxis to/from the station cost ₹1200.

ℹ Getting Around
Central Kodaikanal is compact and easily walkable. There are no autorickshaws (believe it or not), but plenty of taxis. The minimum charge is ₹150 for up to 3km; to/from Vattakanal costs ₹300.

Around Kodaikanal
There are some lovely country retreats in the **Palani Hills** below Kodaikanal.

Elephant Valley   FARMSTAY $$
(☑7867004398; www.duneecogroup.com; Ganesh Puram, Pethupari; r incl breakfast ₹4010-8750; 🛜) 🖋 Deep in the valley 22km northeast of Kodaikanal, off the Kodaikanal–Palani Rd, this ecofriendly French-run retreat sprawls across 48 hectares of mountain jungle and organic farm. Elephants, peacocks and bison wander through, and comfy local-material cottages, including a tree house, sit either side of a river. The French-Indian restaurant does wonderful meals packed with garden-fresh veg, and home-grown coffee.

Coimbatore
☑0422 / POP 1.05 MILLION
This big business and junction city – Tamil Nadu's second largest, often known as the Manchester of India for its textile industry – is friendly enough and increasingly cosmopolitan, but the lack of interesting sights means that for most travellers it's just a stepping stone towards Ooty or Kerala. There

GOVERNMENT BUSES FROM KODAIKANAL (KODAI)

DESTINATION	FARE (₹)	TIME (HR)	DEPARTURES
Bengaluru	560-760	12	5.30pm, 6pm
Chennai	480	12	6.30pm
Coimbatore	130	6	8.30am, 4.30pm
Madurai	65	4	15 daily
Trichy	120	6	1.30pm, 3.30pm, 5.40pm, 6pm

Coimbatore

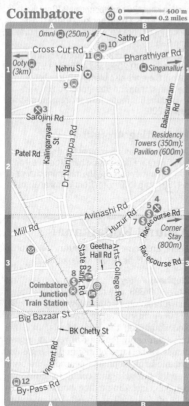

Coimbatore

🛏 Sleeping
1 Legend's Inn..A3
2 Sree Subbu A3

🍴 Eating
3 Junior Kuppanna A1
4 On The Go B2

ℹ Information
5 HSBC ATM B2
6 State Bank of India ATM B2
7 State Bank of India ATM B3
8 State Bank of India ATM A3

🚌 Transport
9 Central Bus Stand A1
10 SETC Bus Stand B1
11 Town Bus Stand A1
12 Ukkadam Bus Stand..........................A4

are plenty of accommodation and eating options if you're staying overnight.

🛏 Sleeping

Sree Subbu
HOTEL $

(☎0422-2300006; Geetha Hall Rd; s/d ₹550/660) If price is the priority, Sree Subbu is a clean-enough, nonair-con budget spot.

Corner Stay
GUESTHOUSE $$

(☎9842220742; www.cornerstay.in; 4/1 Abdul Rahim Rd, off Racecourse Rd; r ₹2000-3000; ❄🛜) On a quiet Racecourse-area lane, this homey guesthouse offers three impeccable, tastefully styled rooms with a communal lounge and balcony. Two share a kitchen, the other has its own, and there are home-cooked meals. It's 2km northeast of the train station.

Legend's Inn
HOTEL $$

(☎0422-4350000; www.legendsinn.com; Geetha Hall Rd; r ₹1460, s/d with AC ₹1820/2070; ❄) One of at least 10 places on this lane opposite the train station, this is a good-value midrange choice, with spacious, clean, comfortable rooms, 24-hour checkout and helpful receptionists. It gets busy: book ahead.

Residency Towers
HOTEL $$$

(☎0422-2241414; www.theresidency.com; 1076 Avinashi Rd; s/d incl breakfast from ₹6800/7600; ❄@🛜🏊) Opening through a soaring lobby, the Residency is a top choice for its professional staff, well-equipped rooms, swimming pool, and excellent eating and drinking options, including great-value buffet meals at the **Pavilion** (www.theresidency.com; Residency Towers, 1076 Avinashi Rd; buffet breakfast/lunch/dinner ₹475/820/930; ⊙7-10am, 12.30-3pm & 7pm-midnight). Check discounts online.

🍴 Eating

Junior Kuppanna
SOUTH INDIAN $$

(☎0422-235773; www.hoteljuniorkuppanna.com; 177 Sarojini Rd, Ram Nagar; mains ₹160-200, thalis ₹170; ⊙noon-4pm & 6.30-11pm) Your favourite South Indian thalis come piled on to banana leaves with traditional flourish, and starving carnivores will love the long menu of famously nonveg southern specialities, all from a perfectly spotless kitchen. Three branches across town.

On The Go
MULTICUISINE $$$

(☎0422-4520116; www.onthegocbe.com; 167 Racecourse Rd; mains ₹275-575; ⊙12.30-2.45pm & 7-10.30pm) Colourful, contemporary, and filled with cartoons and turquoise sofas, this is a great place for tasty (if pricey) global fare from Italian and Middle Eastern to Sri Lankan and North Indian.

ANAMALAI TIGER RESERVE

Anamalai Tiger Reserve (Indira Gandhi Wildlife Sanctuary & National Park; ₹30, camera/video ₹80/200; ⏱6am-noon & 3-5pm) is a 950-sq-km reserve of tropical jungle, *shola* forest and grassland rising to 2400m and spilling over the Western Ghats into Kerala between Kodaikanal and Coimbatore. A tiger reserve since 2007, it's home to all kinds of exotic endemic wildlife, much of it rare and endangered – including leopards and around 30 elusive tigers, plus lion-tailed macaques, peacocks, langurs, crocodiles, spotted deer and elephants.

The reserve's **Reception & Interpretation Centre** (☑04259-238360; Topslip; ⏱7am-6pm) at Topslip (35km southwest of Pollachi) runs official 45-minute **minibus safaris** (Topslip; per person from ₹130; ⏱7-10am & 3-5pm) and **guided treks** (Topslip; 2hr trek per person ₹500; ⏱7am-2pm). Topslip has simple **Forest Department accommodation** (☑bookings 04259-238360; Topslip; r ₹1500-4000); book ahead through Pollachi's **District Forest Office** (☑04259-225356, accommodation bookings 04259-238360; www.forests.tn.nic.in; 365/1 Meenkarai Rd, Pollachi; ⏱10am-5.45pm Mon-Fri).

Tiny tea-plantation town **Valparai**, on the reserve's fringes 65km south from Pollachi, makes a much more comfortable Anamalai base. Wonderful **Sinna Dorai's Bungalow** (☑7094739309; www.sinnadorai.com; Valparai; incl full-board s ₹7650-8650, d ₹9750-11,000; ☎) is exquisitely located on a rambling tea estate here, offering guided walks, after-dark wildlife-spotting drives, homemade meals and six huge rooms bursting with local early-20th-century history.

Buses connect Pollachi with Topslip (₹35, two hours, hourly) and Valparai (₹30, three hours, half-hourly). Buses to Pollachi (₹17 to ₹23, one hour, every five minutes) run from Coimbatore's Ukkadam Bus Stand, which also has one daily service to Valparai (₹65, four hours, 3pm). From Kodaikanal, buses serve Pollachi (₹110, six hours) at 8.30am and 4.30pm.

ⓘ Getting There & Away

AIR

The airport is 10km east of town. Direct daily flights to domestic destinations include Bengaluru, Chennai, Delhi, Hyderabad and Mumbai on **Air India** (www.airindia.in), **IndiGo** (www.goindigo.in), **Jet Airways** (www.jetairways.com) or **SpiceJet** (www.spicejet.com). **SilkAir** (www.silkair.com) flies four times weekly to/from Singapore.

BUS

The **Ooty Bus Stand** (New Bus Stand; Mettupalayam (MTP) Rd), 5km northwest of the train station, has services to Ooty (₹53, four hours) via Mettupalayam (₹14 to ₹18, one hour) and Coonoor (₹40, three hours) every 10 minutes, plus half-hourly buses to Kotagiri (₹30, three hours), 28 buses daily to Mysuru (Mysore; ₹160 to ₹400, six hours) and 11 to Bengaluru (₹400 to ₹650, nine hours).

From **Singanallur Bus Stand** (Kamaraj Rd), 6km east of the centre, buses go to Trichy (₹116, five hours), Thanjavur (₹180, 7¼ hours) and Madurai (₹125, five hours) every 10 minutes. Bus 140 (₹11) shuttles between here and the **Town Bus Stand** (cnr Dr Nanjappa & Bharathiyar Rds), not to be confused with the **Central Bus Stand** (Dr Nanjappa Rd).

Ukkadam Bus Stand (NH Rd), 1.5km southwest of the train station, has buses to southern destinations including Pollachi (₹17 to ₹23, 1¼ hours, every five minutes), Kodaikanal (₹180, six hours, 10am) and Munnar (₹180, 6½ hours, 8.15am).

Express or superfast AC and Volvo government buses go from the **SETC Bus Stand** (Thiruvalluvar Bus Stand; Bharathiyar Rd).
Bengaluru ₹375 to ₹700, nine hours, 12 daily
Chennai ₹400 to ₹460, 11 hours, eight buses 5.30pm to 10.30pm
Ernakulam ₹170, 5½ hours, eight daily
Mysuru ₹160 to ₹400, six hours, 27 daily
Trivandrum ₹322, 10½ hours, seven daily

Private buses to destinations such as Bengaluru, Chennai, Ernakulam, Puducherry, Trichy and Trivandrum start from the **Omni Bus Stand** (Sathy Rd), 500m north of the Town Bus Stand, or from ticket-selling agencies on Sathy Rd.

TAXI

Taxis up to Ooty (three hours) cost ₹2500; Ooty buses often get so crowded that a taxi is worth considering.

TRAIN

Coimbatore Junction is on the main line between Chennai and Ernakulam (Kochi, Kerala), with at least 13 daily trains in each direction. The 5.15am Nilgiri Express to Mettupalayam (sleeper/2AC/3AC ₹170/535/740, one hour) connects with the miniature railway departure from Mettupalayam to Ooty at 7.10am. The whole trip to Ooty takes seven hours.

ℹ Getting Around

Buses 20A, 40, 41D or 44 (₹11) from the **Town Bus Stand** (p397) drop you 1km from the airport. Taxis from the centre charge ₹300 to ₹400.

Many buses run between the train station and the **Town Bus Stand** (p397). Autorickshaws charge ₹60 from the train station to the **Ukkadam Bus Station** (p397), ₹80 to the **SETC** (p397) or **Town Bus Stands** (p397), and ₹150 to the **Ooty Bus Stand** (p397).

Uber and Ola Cabs taxi apps work well here.

Around Coimbatore

The commercial town of **Mettupalayam**, 40km north of Coimbatore, is the starting point for the 7.10am miniature train to Ooty. If you need to stay the night, Mettupalayam has plenty of accommodation.

Coonoor

📞 0423 / POP 45,490 / ELEV 1720M

Coonoor is one of the three Nilgiri hill stations – Ooty, Kotagiri and Coonoor – that sit high above the southern plains. Smaller and quieter than Ooty (20km northwest), it has some fantastic heritage hotels and guesthouses, from which you can do exactly the same things (hike, visit tea plantations, marvel at mountain views) you would do from bigger, busier Ooty. From upper Coonoor, 1km to 3km northeast (uphill) from the town centre, you can look down over a sea of red-tile rooftops to the slopes beyond and soak up the cool climate, quiet environment and beautiful scenery. But you get none of the above in lower (central) Coonoor, which is a bustling, honking mess.

◉ Sights

The best way to see Coonoor's out-of-town sights is by autorickshaw (₹600) or taxi (₹800) tour.

Sim's Park   PARK
(Upper Coonoor; adult/child ₹30/15, camera/video ₹50/100; ⊘ 7am-6.30pm) Upper Coonoor's 12-hectare Sim's Park, established in 1874, is a peaceful oasis of sloping manicured lawns with more than 1000 plant species from several continents, including magnolia, tree ferns, roses and camellia. Kotagiri-bound buses drop you here.

Highfield Tea Estate   PLANTATION
(Walker's Hill Rd; ⊘ 8am-9pm) **FREE** This 50-year-old estate (2km northeast of upper Coonoor) is one of few working Nilgiri tea factories open to visitors. Guides jump in quickly, but you're perfectly welcome to watch the full tea-making process independently. You can also, of course, taste and buy.

Lamb's Rock   VIEWPOINT
(Dolphin's Nose Rd; ₹10, camera/video ₹20/50; ⊘ 8.30am-6.30pm) A favourite picnic spot in a patch of monkey-patrolled forest, Lamb's Rock has incredible views past glimmering tea and coffee plantations to the hazy plains below. It's 5km east of upper Coonoor – walkable, if you like.

Dolphin's Nose   VIEWPOINT
(Dolphin's Nose Rd; ₹10, camera/video ₹20/50; ⊘ 8.30am-6.30pm) About 10km west of town, this popular viewpoint exposes vast panoramas encompassing Catherine Falls (p400) across the valley.

🛏 Sleeping & Eating

You'll need a rickshaw, car or great legs to reach Coonoor's best accommodation. Cheap South Indian restaurants cluster around the bus stand.

MAJOR TRAINS FROM COIMBATORE

DESTINATION	TRAIN NO & NAME	FARE (₹)	DURATION (HR)	DEPARTURE
Bengaluru	16525 Bangalore Exp	260/695/995 (B)	8½	10.55pm
Chennai Central	12676 Kovai Exp	180/660 (A)	7½	2.55pm
	22640 Chennai Exp	315/810/1140 (B)	7½	10.15pm
Ernakulam (Kochi)	12677 Ernakulam Exp	105/390 (A)	3¾	1.10pm
Madurai	16610 Nagercoil Exp	205/545 (C)	5½	8.30pm
Trivandrum	12695 Trivandrum Exp	285/730/1025 (B)	8½	11.10pm

Fares: (A) 2nd class/AC chair; (B) sleeper/3AC/2AC; (C) sleeper/3AC

THE NILGIRIS & THEIR TRIBES

The forest-clothed, waterfall-threaded Nilgiris (Blue Mountains) rise abruptly from the surrounding plains between the lowland towns of Mettupalayam (southeast) and Gudalur (northwest), ascended only by winding ghat roads and the famous Nilgiri Mountain Railway. The upland territory, a jumble of valleys and hills with more than 20 peaks above 2000m, is a botanist's dream, with over 2300 flowering plant species, although much of the native *shola* forest and grasslands have been displaced by tea, coffee, eucalyptus and cattle.

The Unesco-designated Nilgiri Biosphere Reserve is a larger, 5520-sq-km area that also includes parts of Kerala and Karnataka. One of the world's biodiversity hot spots, it contains several important tiger reserves, national parks and wildlife sanctuaries.

The Nilgiris' tribal inhabitants were left pretty much to themselves until the British arrived two centuries ago. Today, colonialism and migration have reduced many tribal cultures to the point of collapse, and some have assimilated to the point of invisibility. Others, however, continue at least a semitraditional lifestyle.

Best known, thanks to their proximity to Ooty, are the Toda (around 1500). Some still inhabit tiny villages (*munds*) of traditional barrel-shaped huts made of bamboo, cane and grass. Toda women style their hair in long, shoulder-length ringlets; both sexes wear distinctive black-and-red-embroidered shawls. Central to Toda life is the water buffalo, which provides milk and ghee. Traditionally, it is only at funerals that the strictly vegetarian Toda kill a buffalo, to accompany the deceased.

The 200,000-strong Badaga are thought to have migrated into the Nilgiris from Karnataka around 1600 AD. Their traditional dress is of white cloth with a border of narrow coloured stripes. They worship the mother goddess Hetti Amman, to whom their December/January Hettai Habba festival is dedicated.

The Kota, traditionally artisans, live in seven settlements in the Kotagiri area. They have adapted relatively well to modernity; a significant number hold government jobs.

The Kurumba, traditionally known for their sorcery, inhabit the thick forests of the south and are food-gatherers (particularly of wild honey), though many now work in agriculture. The Irula specialise in food gathering, too, and are botanical experts.

If you're interested in the Nilgiris' tribes, don't miss the **Tribal Research Centre Museum** (Muthorai Palada; Indian/foreigner ₹5/100; ⏱10am-1pm & 2-5pm Mon-Fri, hours vary), 10km southwest of Ooty. Organisations such as Kotagiri's **Keystone Foundation** (p400) work to promote traditional crafts and activities.

YWCA Wyoming Guesthouse
HERITAGE GUESTHOUSE $
(✆0423-2234426; http://ywcaagooty.com; Bedford; dm ₹220, s ₹600-720, d ₹1300) A ramshackle, 150-year-old gem, the good-value Wyoming is draughty and creaky but oozes colonial character with wooden terraces and serene town views through trees. Rooms are good and clean, with geysers, and simple meals are available on request.

★180° McIver
HERITAGE HOTEL $$
(✆0423-2233323; http://serendipityo.com; Orange Grove Rd, Upper Coonoor; r incl breakfast ₹4560-7300; ☎) A classic 1900s British bungalow at the top of town has been transformed into something special. The six handsome, airy rooms sport antique furniture, working fireplaces and big fresh bathrooms. On-site restaurant **La Belle Vie** (mains ₹260-500; ⏱12.30-3.30pm & 7.30-10.30pm) has guests driving miles for its European-Indian food, and panoramas from the wraparound lawn (where you can dine) are fabulous.

Acres Wild
FARMSTAY $$
(✆9443232621; www.acres-wild.com; 571 Upper Meanjee Estate, Kanni Mariamman Kovil St; r incl breakfast ₹3650-5460; ☎) This beautifully positioned farm on Coonoor's southeast edge is sustainably run with solar heating, rainwater harvesting and cheese like you've never tasted in India from the milk of its own cows. The five large, stylish rooms, in three cottages, include kitchens and fireplaces. Your friendly Mumbaikar hosts are full of ideas for things to do away from the tourist crowds. Book ahead.

Gateway
HERITAGE HOTEL $$$
(✆0423-2225400; https://gateway.tajhotels.com; Church Rd, Upper Coonoor; incl breakfast s ₹7120-14,930, d ₹7800-16,280; ☎) A colonial-era

priory turned gorgeous heritage hotel, the Taj-group Gateway has homey cream-coloured rooms immersed in greenery, most graced by working fireplaces. You get mountain views from those at the back. Evening bonfires are lit on the lawn, the good **Gateway All Day restaurant** (mains ₹400-600; ☉7.30-10.30am, 12.30-3pm & 7.30-10.30pm) overlooks the gardens, and there's free yoga along with Keralan ayurvedic massages.

🛍 Shopping

Green Shop   HANDICRAFTS, FOOD
(www.lastforest.in; Jograj Bldg, Bedford Circle; ☉9.30am-7.30pm Mon-Sat) 🗫 Beautiful fair-trade local tribal crafts, clothes, fabrics and notebooks, plus organic wild honey, nuts, chocolates, soaps and teas.

ℹ Getting There & Away

Coonoor's **bus stand** (Lower Coonoor) has services to/from Ooty (₹10, one hour) every 10 minutes. Buses to Kotagiri (₹12, 50 minutes) and Coimbatore (₹35, three hours) go every 30 minutes.

Coonoor is on the miniature train line between Mettupalayam (1st/2nd class ₹185/25, 2¼ to 3¼ hours) and Ooty (₹150/25, 1¼ hours), with three daily trains just to/from Ooty, as well as the daily Mettupalayam–Ooty–Mettupalayam service.

Taxis to/from Ooty cost ₹900.

Kotagiri

☏ 04266 / POP 28,200 / ELEV 1800M

The oldest and smallest of the three Nilgiri hill stations, Kotagiri lies 30km east of Ooty, beyond one of Tamil Nadu's highest passes. It's a quiet, unassuming place with a forgettable town centre – its appeal is the escape to red dirt tracks in the pines, the blue skies and the high green walls of the Nilgiris.

◉ Sights

A half-day taxi tour encompassing **Catherine Falls** (Kotagiri–Mettupalayam Rd) and **Kodanad Viewpoint** (Kodanad; ☉dawn-dusk) costs around ₹1200.

Sullivan Memorial   MUSEUM
(☏9488771571; Kannerimukku; adult/child ₹20/10; ☉10am-5pm Fri-Wed) Just 2km north of Kotagiri centre, the house built in 1819 by Ooty founder John Sullivan has been refurbished in bright red and filled with fascinating photos, newspaper cuttings and artefacts related to local tribal groups, European settlement

and icons like the miniature train. Also here is the **Nilgiri Documentation Centre** (www.nilgiridocumentation.com), dedicated to preserving the region's beauty and heritage.

Volunteering

Keystone Foundation   VOLUNTEERING
(☏04266-272277; http://keystone-foundation.org; Groves Hill Rd) 🗫 This Kotagiri-based NGO works to improve environmental conditions in the Nilgiris while involving, and improving living standards for, indigenous communities. Occasional openings for volunteers.

🛏 Sleeping & Eating

La Maison   HERITAGE HOTEL $$$
(☏9585857732; www.lamaison.in; Hadatharai; s ₹5630-7430, d ₹6750-8910; 🖥) Flower-draped, French-owned La Maison is a beautifully renovated 1890s Scottish bungalow superbly positioned on a hilltop surrounded by tea plantations, 5km southwest of Kotagiri. The design is all quirky French-chic: antique furniture, tribal handicrafts, old-Ooty paintings. Hike to waterfalls, visit tribal villages, tuck into home-cooked meals (₹800), or laze in the valley-facing hot tub.

🛍 Shopping

Green Shop   FOOD, HANDICRAFTS
(http://lastforest.in; Johnstone Sq; ☉9.30am-7pm) 🗫 The ecofriendly Keystone Foundation's shop has goodies for picnics (local chocolates, wild honey) plus lovely tribal crafts.

ℹ Getting There & Away

Buses run half-hourly to/from Ooty (₹15, 1½ hours) and every 15 minutes to/from Coonoor (₹11, one hour) and Mettupalayam (₹16, 1½ hours). Buses to Coimbatore (₹34, 2½ hours) leave every 45 minutes. Taxis to/from Ooty cost ₹900.

Ooty (Udhagamandalam)

☏ 0423 / POP 88,430 / ELEV 2240M

Ooty may be a bit hectic, especially its messy centre, but it doesn't take long to escape into quieter, greener areas where tall pines rise above what could almost be English country lanes. Ooty, 'Queen of Hill Stations', mixes Indian bustle and Hindu temples with beautiful gardens, an international school and charming Raj-era bungalows (which provide its most atmospheric accommodation).

Memorably nicknamed 'Snooty Ooty', it was established by the British in the early

Nilgiri Hills

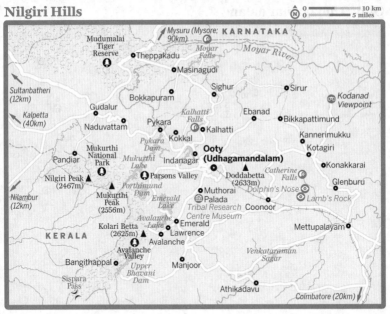

19th century as the summer headquarters of the Madras government. Development ploughed through a few decades ago, but old Ooty survives in patches – you just have to walk further out to find it.

The journey up here on the celebrated miniature train is romantic and the scenery stunning. Even the road up is impressive. During the April-to-June 'season', Ooty is a welcome relief from the steaming plains. Between October and March, overnight temperatures occasionally drop to 0°C.

The train and bus stations are at the west end of Ooty's racecourse, in almost the lowest part of town. To their west is the lake, while the streets of the town twist upwards all around. From the bus station it's a 20-minute walk east to Ooty's commercial centre, Charing Cross.

⊙ Sights

Botanical Gardens GARDENS
(Garden Rd; adult/child ₹30/15, camera/video ₹50/100; ⊙7am-6.30pm) Established in 1848, these pretty 22-hectare gardens are a living gallery of the Nilgiris' natural flora. Keep an eye out for a typical Toda *mund* (village), a fossilised tree trunk believed to be 20 million years old and, on busy days, around 20 million Indian tourists.

St Stephen's Church CHURCH
(Church Hill Rd; ⊙10am-6pm) Perched above Ooty's centre, immaculate pale-yellow St Stephen's, built in 1829, is the Nilgiris' oldest church. It has lovely stained glass, huge wooden beams hauled by elephant from the palace of Tipu Sultan 120km away, and slabs and plaques donated by colonial-era churchgoers. In the overgrown cemetery you'll find headstones commemorating many an Ooty Brit, including Ooty founder John Sullivan's wife and daughter.

Nilgiri Library LIBRARY
(☑0423-2441699; Hospital Rd; ⊙10am-1pm & 2.30-6pm) This quaint little haven in a crumbling, earthy-red 1867 building houses more than 30,000 books, including rare titles on the Nilgiris and hill tribes and 19th-century British journals. Visitors can consult books in the reading room with a temporary one-month membership (₹500). Upstairs is a portrait of Queen Victoria presented to Ooty on her 1887 Golden Jubilee.

In 2016, the library hosted the first-ever Ooty Literary Festival (www.ootylitfest.com).

Doddabetta VIEWPOINT
(Ooty-Kotagiri Rd; ₹6, camera/video ₹10/50; ⊙8am-5pm) About 7km east of Ooty, Doddabetta is the highest point (2633m) in the

Ooty (Udhagamandalam)

Earl's Secret (700m);
King's Cliff (700m)

Nilgiris. On clear days, it's one of the best viewpoints around; go early for better chances of mist-free views. Kotagiri buses will drop you at the Doddabetta junction, then it's a steep 3km walk or a quick jeep ride. Taxis do return trips from Charing Cross (₹700).

🏃 Activities

Hiking & Trekking

The best of Ooty is out in the beautiful **Nilgiri Hills**. Most hotels can put you in touch with local guides who do half-day hikes for around ₹500 per person. You'll normally drive out of town and walk through hills, tribal villages and tea plantations.

More serious treks in the best forest areas with plenty of wildlife – such as beyond Avalanche to the southwest or Parsons Valley to the west, in Mukurthi National Park, or down to Walakkad and Sairandhri in Kerala's Silent Valley National Park – require Tamil Nadu Forest Department permits. At

the time of research, the **Office of the Field Director** (☎ 0423-2444098, Mudumalai accommodation bookings 0423-2445971; fdmtr@tn.nic.in; Mount Stuart Hill; ⊙10am-5.45pm Mon-Fri) was not issuing permits due to rising concerns about human–animal conflict in the region; in recent years there have been several elephant-related foreigner fatalities and multiple tiger attacks on local villagers (several fatal). But if you fancy trying, contact the Office of the Field Director in advance.

The **Nilgiri Wildlife & Environment Association** (☎ 0423-2447167; www.nwea.org.in; Mount Stuart Hill; ⊙10am-1.30pm & 2-5pm Mon-Fri, 10am-1.30pm Sat), the **District Forest Office Nilgiris South Division** (☎ 0423-2444083; www.ootyavalanche.com; Mount Stuart Hill; ⊙10am-5.45pm Mon-Fri) and the **District Forest Office Nilgiris North Division** (☎ 0423-2443968; dfonorth_ooty@yahoo.co.in; Mount Stuart Hill; ⊙10am-5.45pm Mon-Fri) can help with trekking updates and advice.

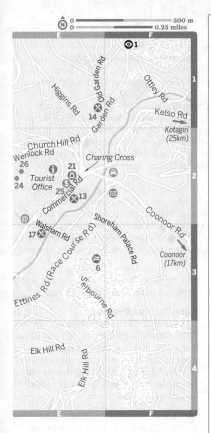

Ooty (Udhagamandalam)

⊙ Sights
1 Botanical Gardens F1
2 Nilgiri Library D2
3 St Stephen's Church..........................D1
4 St Thomas' Church B4

Activities, Courses & Tours
5 Boathouse...A3

Sleeping
6 Fortune Sullivan Court E3
7 Hotel Welbeck Residency C2
8 Lymond House B1
9 Reflections Guest House....................B4
10 Savoy B1
11 Wyoming D1
12 YWCA Anandagiri..............................D4

Eating
13 Adyar Ananda Bhavan.......................E2
14 Modern Stores.................................. E1
15 Place to Bee C2
Savoy ....(see 10)
16 Shinkow's Chinese Restaurant D2
17 Willy's Coffee Pub E3

Drinking & Nightlife
18 Café Coffee Day................................ D2
Café Coffee Day.........................(see 14)

Entertainment
19 Ooty Racecourse...............................D4

Shopping
Green Shop ....(see 15)
20 Higginbothams..................................D2
21 Higginbothams..................................E2
22 K Mahaveer Chand............................C4

Information
23 Canara Bank ATM C4
24 District Forest Office Nilgiris
North Division...................................E2
District Forest Office
Nilgiris South Division............ (see 24)
25 Indian Overseas Bank ATM.................E2
26 Nilgiri Wildlife & Environment
Association E2
Office of the Field Director........ (see 26)
27 State Bank of India ATM D2

TAMIL NADU & CHENNAI OOTY (UDHAGAMANDALAM)

Boating

The **boathouse** (North Lake Rd; ₹12, camera/video ₹25/145; ⊙9am-6pm) by Ooty Lake rents rowboats and pedal boats. Prices start from ₹170 (plus ₹170 deposit) for a two-seater pedal boat (30 minutes).

☞ Tours

Fixed taxi-tour rates are ₹1300 for four hours tootling around Ooty, ₹1400 to Coonoor (four hours) or ₹2500 to Mudumalai Tiger Reserve (full-day).

Sleeping

Ooty has some gorgeous colonial-era homes at the high end and some decent backpacker crashpads, but there isn't much in the lower midrange. During the 'season' (1 April to 15 June) hotels hike rates and checkout time is often 9am. Book well ahead for public holidays.

YWCA Anandagiri GUESTHOUSE $
(☏0423-2444262; www.ywcaagooty.com; Ettines Rd; dm ₹250, s ₹400-2240, d ₹800-2240) This former brewery and sprawling complex of cottages is dotted with flower gardens. With clean, characterful, freshly painted rooms, helpful staff, spacious common areas and a good restaurant (book ahead), you've got some excellent-value budget accommodation.

AVALANCHE VALLEY

The serene, protected **Avalanche Valley** – which extends towards Kerala from around 20km southwest of Ooty – provides the perfect antidote to Ooty's crowds. Rolling farmlands and twinkling tea plantations give way to hushed hills thick with orchids and native *shola* (virgin forest).

Access is restricted, so the only way to explore this blissfully peaceful area is by official two-hour forest department **minibus 'ecotours'** (www.ootyavalanche.com; per person ₹150; ⊙9.30am-3pm) or private-hire jeep trips (₹1200). Sturdy 20-person minibuses trundle up semi-paved tracks southwest into the forest, with the scenery getting wilder and increasingly dramatic as you go. There are stops at a *shola* viewpoint, a waterfall-side Lakshmi temple and, finally, the Lakkidi section of Upper Bhavani Dam, where you get 30 minutes to stroll around.

Minibuses depart from the southern side of Avalanche Lake – officially at 10am, noon and 2pm, but more frequently on demand, and only when numbers reach 20 people (just show up 30 minutes ahead). If there are fewer than 20 people, you might be offered a jeep trip instead. The turn-off to the forest checkpoint, ticket office and minibus departure point is at hairpin bend 6/34, 1km south of Emerald village; then it's 5km west. Ooty taxi drivers charge ₹1600 (return) to the ecotour starting point, including waiting time.

The cheapest rooms have private bathrooms across the corridor. High ceilings can mean cold nights, but you can ask for extra blankets.

Reflections Guest House GUESTHOUSE $
(☑0423-2443834; reflectionsin@yahoo.co.in; 1B North Lake Rd; r ₹800-1200; ☎) A long-standing budget haunt, recently partly revamped, Reflections sits across the road from Ooty Lake. Most of its 12 spotless, good-value rooms have lake views; the best come with freshly updated bathrooms. The attentive owners serve snacks on request and can organise guided treks. Hot water is available once daily.

★**Lymond House** HERITAGE HOTEL $$
(☑9843149490; www.serendipityo.com; Sylks Rd; r incl breakfast ₹4200-5470; ☎) What is it about this 1855 British bungalow that gives it the edge over its peers? The cosy cottage set-up with garden-fresh flowers, four-poster beds, working fireplaces and antique-lined lounges? The contemporary fittings combined with rich, old-world style in the spacious, dramatic rooms? The good multicuisine food and beautiful gardens? All that, no doubt – plus informal yet efficient management.

Wyoming HERITAGE HOTEL $$
(☑0423-2452008; www.wyoming.in; 46 Sheddon Rd; r incl breakfast ₹3150-3680) Six simple, wonderfully spacious colonial-feel rooms open up to classic Nilgiri panoramas at this delightful sun-yellow heritage house high above Ooty. All have kettles, bottled water and pretty wood-panelled floors. It's well

run by friendly hosts and you can enjoy breakfast in the table-dotted garden.

Hotel Welbeck Residency HOTEL $$
(☑0423-2223300; www.welbeck.in; Welbeck Circle, Club Rd; r ₹3650-5040; ☎) An attractive older building that's been thoroughly spruced up with comfortable rooms, a touch of colonial-era class (a 1920 Austin saloon car at the front door!), a decent restaurant and very keen staff.

★**Savoy** HERITAGE HOTEL $$$
(☑0423-2225500; www.gateway.tajhotels.com; 77 Sylks Rd; r incl breakfast from ₹7500; ☎) The Savoy is one of Ooty's oldest hotels, with parts dating back to 1829. Cottages and swing-chairs are set around a charming lawn and garden. Discreetly colonial-style rooms have huge marble-clad bathrooms, log fires, bay windows and hot-water bottles. Welcome touches include a cocktail bar, an ayurveda centre and an excellent multicuisine dining room. Compulsory half-board April to June.

King's Cliff HERITAGE HOTEL $$$
(☑0423-2244000; www.littlearth.in; Havelock Rd; r incl breakfast ₹4200-9410; ☎) Hidden away above Ooty on Strawberry Hill is this classic colonial-era house with wood panelling, antique furnishings, a snug lounge and good Indian/Continental cooking at **Earl's Secret** (☑0423-2452888; mains ₹340-600; ⊙8-10am, noon-3pm & 7-10pm; ☎), partly in a glassed-in conservatory. Cheaper rooms don't have the same old-world charm as the most expensive ones.

Fortune Sullivan Court
HOTEL $$$

(☑0423-2441415; www.fortunehotels.in; 123 Selbourne Rd; incl breakfast s ₹6000-7200, d ₹6600-7800; 🐾) In a quiet spot on the southern fringe of town, the Fortune is no Raj-era mansion, but twirling staircases around a grand lobby lead to comfy, colourful rooms with big beds, light woods and writing desks. Service is perfectly polished, and the hotel has its own bar, spa, small gym and multicuisine restaurant.

🍴 Eating & Drinking

Adyar Ananda Bhavan
INDIAN $

(www.aabsweets.in; 58 Commercial Rd; mains ₹130-200, thalis ₹100-200; ⊘7.30-11.30am, noon-3.30pm & 6-10.30pm) This sparkly new Ooty favourite is constantly crammed with locals and tourists filling up on delicious, swiftly delivered South Indian staples (dosas, *vadas, idlis*), North Indian classics (try the paneer tikka), fresh juices, and thalis heaped onto plastic yellow trays.

Willy's Coffee Pub
CAFE $

(KCR Arcade, Walsham Rd; dishes ₹40-90; ⊘10am-9.30pm; 🐾) Climb the stairs and join Ooty's international students for board games, wi-fi, a lending library and well-priced pizzas, chips, toasties, cakes and cookies.

Modern Stores
SUPERMARKET $

(144 Garden Rd; ⊘9.40am-9pm) Stocks all kinds of international foods, from muesli to marmalade, along with particularly good Western Ghats produce, such as breads, cheeses and chocolates.

Place to Bee
ITALIAN $$

(☑0423-2449464; www.facebook.com/placetObee; 176A Club Rd; mains ₹200-400; ⊘12.30-3pm & 6.30-9.30pm Wed-Mon) 🍴 Brush up on Nilgiri-bee facts over meals at this arty, fairy-lit restaurant tucked inside the Keystone Foundation's (p400) little Bee Museum. It might sound bizarre, but the concept works, ingredients are locally sourced, and the divinely fresh dishes – many involving wild honey – don't disappoint. Choose from expertly executed pastas, Mediterranean-inspired salads and real-deal, build-your-own wood-fired pizzas.

Shinkow's Chinese Restaurant
CHINESE $$

(38/83 Commissioner's Rd; mains ₹100-250; ⊘noon-3.45pm & 6.30-9.45pm) Shinkow's is an Ooty institution. The simple but tasty chicken, pork, beef, seafood, veg, noodle and rice dishes are reliably good and quick to arrive at your chequer-print table.

Savoy
MULTICUISINE $$$

(☑0423-2225500; www.gateway.tajhotels.com; 77 Sylks Rd; mains ₹260-650; ⊘7.30-10am, 12.30-3pm & 7.30-10.30pm) All wood walls, intimate lighting, live piano and plush orange velvets, the Savoy's (p404) candle-lit dining room dishes up fabulous contemporary Continental, Indian and pan-Asian cuisine – including all-day breakfasts, yummy salads, pastas and kebabs, and some unique tribal-inspired dishes.

Café Coffee Day
CAFE

(www.cafecoffeeday.com; Garden Rd; drinks ₹60-120; ⊘9am-10pm) Reliably good coffee, tea and cakes. There's another branch (drinks ₹70-110; ⊘9am-10pm) on Church Hill Rd.

🛍 Shopping

K Mahaveer Chand
JEWELLERY

(291 Main Bazaar Rd; ⊘10am-8pm) K Mahaveer Chand has been selling particularly beautiful Toda tribal and silver jewellery for 45 years.

Green Shop
HANDICRAFTS, FOOD

(www.lastforest.in; Sargan Villa, off Club Rd; ⊘10am-7pm) 🍴 Run by Kotagiri's Keystone Foundation (p400), this fair-trade, organic-oriented shop sells gorgeous tribal crafts and clothes (including Toda embroidery) and wild honey harvested by local indigenous farmers.

Higginbothams
BOOKS

(Commercial Rd; ⊘9am-1pm & 3.30-7.30pm) Well-known outlet with a good stash of English-language books and another branch (Commissioner's Rd; ⊘9am-1pm & 2-6pm Mon-Sat) up the hill.

ℹ Information

Tourist Office (☑0423-2443977; Wenlock Rd; ⊘10am-5pm)

ℹ Getting There & Away

The fun way to arrive in Ooty is on the miniature train from Mettupalayam. Buses also run regularly up and down the mountain from across Tamil Nadu, from Kerala, and from Mysuru and Bengaluru in Karnataka.

BUS

The Tamil Nadu and Karnataka state bus companies have reservation offices at Ooty's busy **bus station**. For Kochi take a bus to Palakkad (₹96, six hours, 7am, 8am, 2pm) and change.

TAXI

Taxis cluster at stands around town. Fixed one-way fares include Coonoor (₹900), Kotagiri (₹900), Coimbatore (₹2000) and Mudumalai Tiger Reserve (₹1300).

TRAIN

The miniature ('toy') train from Mettupalayam to Ooty – one of the Mountain Railways of India given World Heritage status by Unesco – is the best way to get here. The **Nilgiri Mountain Railway** requires special cog wheels on the locomotive, meshing with a third, 'toothed' rail on the ground, to manage the exceptionally steep gradients. There are wonderful forest, waterfall, mountainside and tea-plantation views along the way. The section between Mettupalayam and Coonoor uses steam engines, which push, rather than pull, the train up the hill.

For high season, book several weeks ahead; at other times a few days ahead is advisable (though not always essential). The train departs Mettupalayam for Ooty at 7.10am daily (1st/2nd class ₹205/30, 4¾ hours). From Ooty to Mettupalayam the train leaves at 2pm (3½ hours). There are also three daily trains each way just between Ooty and Coonoor (₹150/25, 1¼ hours). Departures and arrivals at Mettupalayam connect with the Nilgiri Express to/from Chennai Central (sleeper/2AC/3AC ₹340/890/1250, 9¼ hours).

Ooty is often listed as Udhagamandalam in train timetables.

ⓘ Getting Around

Autorickshaws and taxis are everywhere. You'll find taxi fare charts at Charing Cross and outside the bus station. Autorickshaw fare charts are posted outside the bus station and botanical gardens and elsewhere. An autorickshaw from the train or bus station to Charing Cross costs ₹60.

There are jeep taxi stands near the **bus station** (Avalanche Rd) and **municipal market** (Hobert Park Cross Rd); expect to pay about 1½ times the local taxi fares.

Mudumalai Tiger Reserve

📳 0423

In the Nilgiris' foothills, the 321-sq-km **Mudumalai Tiger Reserve** (www.mudumalait igerreserve.com; ⊙ sometimes closed Apr, May or Jun) is like a classical Indian landscape painting given life: thin, spindly trees and light-slotted leaves concealing spotted chital deer and grunting wild boar. Also here are around 50 tigers, giving Mudumalai one of India's highest tiger population densities (though you'd be lucky to see one). Overall the reserve is Tamil Nadu's top wildlife-spotting place. You're most likely to see deer, peacocks, wild boar, langurs, jackals, Malabar giant squirrels, wild elephants (the park has several hundred) and gaur (Indian bison).

Along with Karnataka's Bandipur and Nagarhole, Kerala's Wayanad and Tamil Nadu's Sathyamangalam Tiger Reserve, Mudumalai forms part of an unbroken chain of reserves comprising an important wildlife refuge home to approximately 570 tigers – the world's single largest tiger population.

Mudumalai sometimes closes for fire risk in April, May or June. Rainy July and August are the least favourable months for visiting.

The reserve's **reception centre** (📳 0423-2526235; Theppakadu; ⊙ 6.30am-6pm), and some reserve-run accommodation, is at Theppakadu, on the main road between Ooty and Mysuru. The closest village to Theppakadu is Masinagudi, 7km east.

⊙ Sights & Activities

Hiking in the reserve is banned and private vehicles are only permitted on the main Ooty-Gudalur-Theppakadu–Mysuru road and the Theppakadu–Masinagudi and Masinagudi-Moyar River roads. Official minibus 'safaris' are the only way to get inside the reserve.

Some operators may offer hikes in the buffer zone around the reserve, but reserve authorities advise strongly against them; tourists have died from getting too close to wild elephants on illegal hikes. Expert-led jeep safaris organised through the better resorts are a safer option.

Elephant Camp   LANDMARK
(Theppakadu; ₹15; ⊙ 8.30-9am & 5.30-6pm) In the mornings and evenings, you can see the reserve's working elephants being fed at the

BUSES FROM OOTY (UDHAGAMANDALAM)

DESTINATION	FARE (₹)	TIME (HR)	DEPARTURES
Bengaluru	250-670	8	Volvo 10am, 11.15am, 5.45pm, 10.30pm
Chennai	450	14	4.30pm, 5.45pm, 6.30pm
Coimbatore	53	4	every 20min 5.50am-8.40pm
Coonoor	10	1	every 10min 5.30am-10pm
Kotagiri	15	1½	every 20min 6.30am-7pm, 7.40pm, 8.20pm
Mysuru	136-420	5	Volvo 10am, 11.15am, 5.45pm

elephant camp just east of Theppakadu's reception centre (p406), where you'll need to buy tickets. Most elephants here are rescues or old timber-trade elephants unfit to return to the wild.

Minibus Safaris WILDLIFE-WATCHING
(per person ₹135; ⊘ hourly 6-10am & 2-6pm) The only way to access the reserve is on official one-hour minibus 'safaris', which make a 15km loop in camouflage-striped 20- to 30-person minibuses. There's a good chance you'll spot some wildlife, though it's down to luck. Book at Theppakadu's reception centre (p406) several hours ahead.

Sleeping & Eating

The reserve runs simple lodgings along a track just above the Moyar River at Theppakadu. Better accommodation is provided by numerous lodges and forest resorts outside the park's fringes, many of them welcoming, high-standard family-run businesses. Most of the best cluster at **Bokkapuram** village, 5km south of Masinagudi at the foot of the mountains.

Theppakadu

Reserve-run accommodation must be booked in advance; some may be available for booking online. For the rest, book ahead by phone or in person with Ooty's Office of the Field Director (p402). The reception centre accepts walk-ins if there are vacancies.

Hotel Tamil Nadu LODGE $
(☑ bookings 0423-2445971; www.mudumalaitiger reserve.com; Theppakadu; dm ₹2620) This government-run lodge provides basic, clean, new-build dorms with bathroom, for up to eight people, plus simple meals (₹80).

Theppakadu Log House LODGE $$
(☑ bookings 0423-2445971; Theppakadu; d ₹2510) The best of Theppakadu's reserve-owned accommodation: well-maintained rooms, private bathrooms and ₹70 meals.

Bokkapuram & Around

Wilds at Northernhay LODGE $$
(☑ 9843149490; http://serendipityo.com; Singara; r incl breakfast ₹4800-5400; ▣ 🕸) A wonderful lodge 8km southwest of Masinagudi, in a converted coffee warehouse on a working coffee plantation filled with tall trees that give it a deep-in-the-forest feel. Seven cosy rooms (one up in the trees, another a trib-

al-inspired mud-house) and excellent meals complement jeep safaris, nature walks and birdwatching expeditions, on which you should see a good variety of wildlife.

Bamboo Banks Farm LODGE $$
(☑ 0423-2526211; www.bamboobanks.com; Masinagudi; full board d ₹7870; ▣ 🕸 🕸) This family-run operation has seven simple, comfy cottages tucked into its own patch of unkempt jungle, 2km south of Masinagudi. Geese waddle around; there's a peaceful pool area with hammocks, swing-chairs and a treetop viewing platform; meals are good Indian buffets; and the efficient owners organise biking and horse riding.

★ **Jungle Retreat** RESORT $$$
(☑ 0423-2526469; www.jungleretreat.com; Bokkapuram; dm ₹3800, r ₹5470-12,150; 🕸 🕸) Arguably Mudumalai's most stylish resort, with accommodation in lovingly built stone cottages, two tree houses or a dorm (minimum four people), all spread out for maximum seclusion. The bar, lounge and restaurant (three daily meals ₹2000) are great for meeting travellers, and staff are knowledgeable. The pool has a stunning setting – leopards and elephants often pop in for a drink.

Jungle Hut RESORT $$$
(☑ 0423-2526463; www.junglehut.in; Bokkapuram; full board r ₹7310-9730; ▣ 🕸 🕸) 🖋 Along with ecofriendly touches (solar power, rainwater harvesting) and a sociable lounge, 30-year-old Jungle Hut has probably the best food in Bokkapuram (if you're visiting from another resort after dark, don't walk home alone!). Spacious rooms – the loveliest in semitented safari-style cottages – sprawl across large grounds, where 200-odd chital deer graze. Jeep safaris, treks and birdwatching can be arranged.

Getting There & Around

Taxi day trips to Mudumalai from Ooty cost ₹2000, usually via the alternative Sighur Ghat road with its spectacular 36-hairpin-bend hill. One-way taxis from Ooty to Theppakadu cost ₹1300.

Small buses that can handle the Sighur Ghat road run from Ooty to Masinagudi (₹17, 1½ hours, 12 daily 6.50am to 7.30pm), from where there are a few slow local buses daily to Theppakadu (₹5).

Shared jeeps also run between Masinagudi and Theppakadu for ₹10 per person (or you can have one to yourself for ₹120). Costs are similar for jeeps between Masinagudi and Bokkapuram.

Andaman Islands

Best Beaches

➜ Radhanagar (p417)

➜ Merk Bay (p424)

➜ Ross & Smith Islands (p424)

➜ Butler Bay (p426)

➜ Lalaji Bay (p424)

Best Places to Sleep

➜ Barefoot at Havelock (p419)

➜ Silversand (p420)

➜ Pristine Beach Resort (p425)

➜ Hotel Sinclairs Bayview (p414)

➜ Blue View (p426)

Why Go?

With breathtakingly beautiful coastline, lush forested interior, fantastic diving possibilities and a far-flung location, the Andaman Islands are a perfect place to ramble around or simply chill out on sun-toasted beaches.

Shimmering turquoise waters are surrounded by primeval jungle and mangrove forest, and its sugar-white beaches melt under glorious flame-and-purple sunsets. The population is a friendly mix of South and Southeast Asian settlers, as well as Negrito ethnic groups whose arrival here still has anthropologists somewhat baffled. Adding to the intrigue is its remote location, some 1370km from the Indian mainland, meaning the islands are geographically more Southeast Asia – just 150km from Indonesia and 190km from Myanmar.

Comprising 572 islands, only a dozen or so are open to tourists, Havelock by far being the most popular for its splendid beaches and diving. The Nicobar Islands are strictly off limits to tourists, as are the various patches of tribal areas.

When to Go
Port Blair

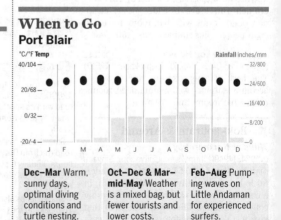

Dec–Mar Warm, sunny days, optimal diving conditions and turtle nesting.

Oct–Dec & Mar–mid-May Weather is a mixed bag, but fewer tourists and lower costs.

Feb–Aug Pumping waves on Little Andaman for experienced surfers.

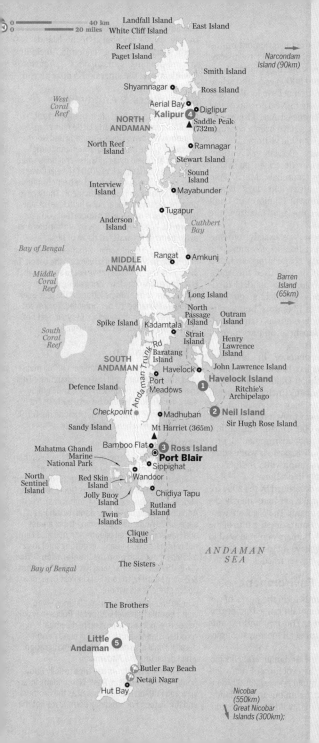

0 — 40 km
0 — 20 miles

Landfall Island
East Island
White Cliff Island
Reef Island
Paget Island
Narcondam Island (90km)
Smith Island
Shyamnagar
Ross Island
West Coral Reef
Aerial Bay
Kalipur ❹ ● Diglipur
NORTH ANDAMAN
Saddle Peak (732m) ▲
North Reef Island
Ramnagar
Stewart Island
Sound Island
Interview Island
Mayabunder
Anderson Island
Tugapur
Cuthbert Bay
Bay of Bengal
Middle Coral Reef
MIDDLE ANDAMAN
Rangat ● Amkunj
Barren Island (65km)
Long Island
North Passage Island
Outram Island
Spike Island
Kadamtala
Strait Island
Henry Lawrence Island
South Coral Reef
Rd
Baratang Island
John Lawrence Island
SOUTH ANDAMAN
● Havelock
Havelock Island
Defence Island
Port Meadows
❶
Ritchie's Archipelago
Checkpoint ●
● Madhuban
❷ **Neil Island**
Sandy Island
Mt Harriet (365m) ▲
Sir Hugh Rose Island
Bamboo Flat
❸ ● **Ross Island**
Mahatma Ghandi Marine National Park
◉ **Port Blair**
● Sippighat
North Sentinel Island
Red Skin Island
● Wandoor
Jolly Buoy Island
● Chidiya Tapu
Twin Islands
Rutland Island
Clique Island
ANDAMAN SEA
Bay of Bengal
The Sisters
The Brothers
Little Andaman ❺
Butler Bay Beach
● Netaji Nagar
Hut Bay
Nicobar (550km)
Great Nicobar Islands (300km);

Andaman Islands Highlights

❶ **Havelock Island** (p417) Snorkelling, diving and socialising on this picturesque island.

❷ **Neil Island** (p421) Easing into a blissfully mellow pace of life.

❸ **Ross Island** (p414) Learning about Port Blair's colonial past.

❹ **Kalipur** (p424) Experiencing the wilds of northern Andaman while island-hopping to pristine beaches and coral reefs.

❺ **Little Andaman** (p425) Finding Butler Bay and a little piece of paradise.

History

The date of initial human settlement on the Andamans and Nicobars is lost to history. Anthropologists say stone-tool crafters have lived here for around 2000 years, and scholars of human migration believe local indigenous tribes have roots in Negrito and Malay ethnic groups in Southeast Asia. Otherwise, these specks in the sea have been a constant source of legend to outside visitors.

The 10th-century Persian adventurer Buzurg Ibn Shahriyar described an island chain inhabited by cannibals, Marco Polo added that the natives had dogs' heads, and tablets in Thanjavur (Tanjore) in Tamil Nadu named the archipelago Timaittivu: the Impure Islands.

None of the above was exactly tourism-brochure stuff, but visitors kept coming: the Marathas in the late 17th century and, 200 years later, the British, who used the Andamans as a penal colony for political dissidents. In WWII some islanders greeted the invading Japanese as liberators, but despite installing Indian politicians as (puppet) administrators, the Japanese military proved to be harsh occupiers.

Following Independence in 1947, the Andaman and Nicobar Islands were incorporated into the Indian Union. With migration from the mainland (including Bengali refugees fleeing the chaos of partition), the population has grown from a few thousand to more than 350,000. During this influx, tribal land rights and environmental protection were often disregarded; while some conditions are now improving, indigenous tribes remain largely in decline.

The islands were devastated by the 2004 Indian Ocean earthquake, offshore aftershocks and the resulting tsunami. The Nicobars were especially hard hit; some estimate a fifth of the population was killed, others were relocated to Port Blair and many have yet to return. But by and large normalcy has returned.

Geography & Environment

Incredibly, the islands form the peaks of the Arakan Yoma, a mountain range that begins in Western Myanmar (Burma) and extends into the ocean, running all the way to Sumatra in Indonesia.

The isolation of the Andaman and Nicobar Islands has led to the evolution of many endemic plant and animal species. Of 62 identified mammals, 32 are unique to the islands, including the Andaman wild pig, crab-eating macaque, masked palm civet, and species of tree shrews and bats. Of the islands' 250 bird species, 18 are endemic, including ground-dwelling megapodes, *hawabills* (swiftlets) and the emerald Nicobar pigeon.

ⓘ Dangers & Annoyances

Crocodiles are a way of life in many parts of the Andamans, particularly Little Andaman, Wandoor, Corbyn's Cove, Baratang and North Andamans. The death of an American tourist who was attacked by a saltwater crocodile while snorkelling in Havelock in 2010 (at Neils Cove near Beach 7) was considered extremely unusual, and remains an isolated incident. There have been no sightings since, but a high level of vigilance remains in place. It's important you keep informed, heed any warnings by authorities and avoid being in the water at dawn or dusk.

Sandflies can be irksome, with these small biting insects sometimes causing havoc on the beach. To avoid infection, it's imperative not to scratch what is an incredibly itchy bite. Bring along hydrocortisone cream and calamine lotion for the bite. Seek medical assistance if it gets infected. To prevent bites, repellent containing DEET is your best bet, and avoid the beach at dawn and dusk.

ⓘ Information

Even though they are 1000km east of the mainland, the Andamans still run on Indian time. This means that it can be dark by 5pm and light by 4am; people here tend to be very early risers.

All telephone numbers must include the 03192 area code, even when dialling locally.

PERMITS

All foreigners need a permit to visit the Andaman Islands; it's issued free on arrival from Port Blair's airport or Haddo Jetty. The 30-day permit allows foreigners to stay in Port Blair, South and Middle Andaman (excluding tribal areas), North Andaman (Diglipur), Long Island, North Passage, Little Andaman (excluding tribal areas), and Havelock and Neil Islands. It's possible (but not routine, so don't bank on getting one) to get a 15-day extension from the **Immigration Office** (⏍ 03192-237793; Kamaraj Rd; ⏍ 8.30am-1pm & 2-5pm Mon-Fri, to 1pm Sat) in Port Blair, or at police stations elsewhere.

Keep your permit on you at all times – you won't be able to travel without it. Police may ask to see it, especially when you're disembarking on other islands, and hotels will need permit details. You'll also need it to pass immigration when departing the Andamans.

The permit also allows day trips to Jolly Buoy, South Cinque, Red Skin, Ross, Narcondam, Interview and Rutland Islands, as well as the Brothers and the Sisters. For most day permits it's not the hassle but the cost. For areas such as Mahatma Gandhi Marine National Park, and Ross and Smith Islands near Diglipur, the permits cost ₹50/500 for Indians/foreigners. Students with valid ID pay minimal entry fees, so bring your card.

The Nicobar Islands are off-limits to all except Indian nationals engaged in approved research, government business or trade.

ⓘ Getting There & Away

AIR

There are daily flights to Port Blair from Delhi, Kolkata, Bengaluru, Mumbai and Chennai. Carriers that service Port Blair include, **Jet Airways** (☑ 03192-230545, 1800225522; www.jetairways.com), **Air India** (☑ 03192-233108; www.airindia.in), **SpiceJet** (☑ 0987-1803333; www.spicejet.com) and **GoAir** (☑ reservations 092-23222111; www.goair.in). Round-trip fares vary in price depending on how early you book. A 15kg check-in luggage limit exists. There are no international flights from Port Blair.

BOAT

Depending on who you ask, the infamous boat to Port Blair is either the only *real* way to get to the Andamans or a hassle and a half. The truth lies somewhere in between. There are usually three to four sailings a month between Port Blair and Chennai (three days) and Kolkata (four to five days), plus a monthly ferry to Visakhapatnam (four days). All arrive at Haddo Jetty.

Take sailing times with a large grain of salt – travellers have reported sitting on the boat at Kolkata harbour for up to 12 hours, or waiting to dock near Port Blair for several hours. With hold-ups and variable weather and sea conditions, the trip can take a day or two extra. **Andaman Shipping Office** (☑ 044-25226873; 2nd fl, Jawahar Bldg, 17 Rajaji Salai George Town, Chennai; ☺10am-4pm Mon-Fri, to noon Sat) has boats from Chennai, **Shipping Corporation of India** (☑ 033-22482354; www.shipindia. com; Strand Rd, Kolkata; ☺10am-1pm & 2-4pm Mon-Fri) departs from Kolkata, and **AV Bhano-jirow, Garuda Pattabhiramayya & Co** (☑ 0891-2565597; ops@avbgpr.com; Harbour Approach Rd, next to NMDC, Port Area, Visakhapatnam; ☺9am-5pm) from Visakhapatnam.

You can organise your return ticket at the **ferry booking office** (p415) at Phoenix Bay. Bring three passport photos and a photocopy of your permit. Updated schedules and fares can be found at www.andamans.gov.in or www.shipindia.com. Otherwise enquire at Phoenix Bay's info office.

Classes vary slightly between boats, but the cheapest is bunk (₹2500), followed by 2nd-class (six beds, ₹6420), 1st class (four beds, ₹8080) and deluxe cabins (two beds, ₹9750). Higher-end tickets cost as much as, if not more than,

a plane ticket. If you go bunk, prepare for little privacy and toilets that tend to get...unpleasant after three days at sea.

Food (tiffin for breakfast, thalis for lunch and dinner) costs around ₹150/200 per day for bunk/cabin class, though bring something (fruit in particular) to supplement your diet. Some bedding is supplied, but if you're travelling bunk class bring a sleeping sheet. Some travellers take a hammock to string up on deck.

There is no ferry between Port Blair and Thailand, but private yachts can usually get clearance. You can't legally get from the Andamans to Myanmar (Burma) by sea. Be aware you risk imprisonment or worse from the Indian and Burmese navies if you give this a go.

ⓘ Getting Around

AIR

At the time of writing, inter-island sea planes were no longer operating and it was uncertain whether they would resume.

While the interisland helicopter service isn't generally for tourists, you can chance your luck by applying one day before at the **Directorate of Civil Aviation office** (☑ 03192-233601; Port Blair Helipad, VIP Rd) at the helipad near the airport. The 5kg baggage limit precludes most tourists from using this service.

BOAT

Most islands can only be reached by water. While this sounds romantic, ferry ticket offices can be utter chaos: expect hot waits, slow service, queue-jumping and a rugby scrum to the ticket window. Have your passport (for photo ID), permit and ticket handy. To hold your spot and advance in line, you need to be a little aggressive (but not a jerk) or be a woman; ladies' queues are a godsend, but they really only apply in Port Blair. You can buy tickets the day you travel by arriving at the appropriate jetty an hour beforehand, but this is risky, and normally one or two days in advance is recommended. You can't pre-book ferry tickets until you've been issued your island permit (p410) upon arrival in the Andamans. Hotels can usually book ferry tickets for you.

Porters can be hired at jetties (expect to pay around ₹50 for an average-size bag), but if your

> **ⓘ FERRY CANCELLATIONS**
>
> Bad weather can play havoc with your itinerary, with ferry services cancelled if the sea is too rough. It's wise to build in a few days' buffer to avoid being marooned and missing your flight.

luggage isn't too heavy it's not a long walk to/from jetties.

There are regular boat services to Havelock and Neil Islands (three to four per day), as well as Rangat, Mayabunder, Diglipur and Little Andaman. A schedule of interisland sailing times can be found at www.andamans.gov.in.

Several private ferry companies also run to Havelock and Neil Islands from Port Blair.

BUS

All roads – and ferries – lead to Port Blair, and you'll inevitably spend a night or two here booking onward travel. The main island group – South, Middle and North Andaman – is connected by road, with ferry crossings and bridges. Buses run south from Port Blair to Wandoor, and north to Baratang, Rangat, Mayabunder and finally to Diglipur.

CAR & MOTORCYCLE

A car with driver costs ₹550 per 35km, or around ₹10,000 for a return trip to Diglipur from Port Blair (including stopovers along the way). Motorbikes are available for hire from Port Blair and all the islands from around ₹300 to ₹400 per day. Due to restrictions in travel within tribal areas, it's not permitted for foreigners to drive their own vehicles to North and Middle Andaman.

Port Blair

POP 108.060

Surrounded by tropical forest and rugged coastline, lively Port Blair serves as the provincial capital of the Andamans. It's a vibrant mix of Indian Ocean inhabitants – Bengalis, Tamils, Telugus, Nicobarese and Burmese. Most travellers don't hang around any longer than necessary (usually one or two days while waiting to book onward travel in the islands, or returning for departure), but PB's fascinating history warrants extended exploration.

◎ Sights

★ **Cellular Jail**
National Memorial   HISTORIC BUILDING
(GB Pant Rd; ₹30, camera/video free/₹200, sound-and-light show adult/child ₹50/25; ⊙8.45am-12.30pm & 1.30-4.15pm) A former British

prison, the Cellular Jail National Memorial now serves as a shrine to the political dissidents it once jailed. Construction began in 1896 and it was completed in 1906 – the original seven wings (several of which were destroyed by the Japanese during WWII) contained 698 cells radiating from a central tower. Like many political prisons, Cellular Jail became something of a university for freedom fighters, who exchanged books, ideas and debates despite walls and wardens.

Anthropological Museum   MUSEUM
(MG Rd; ₹10, camera ₹20; ⊙9am-1pm & 1.30-4.30pm Tue-Sun) This museum provides a thorough and sympathetic portrait of the islands' indigenous tribal communities. The glass display cases may be a tad old school, but they don't feel anywhere near as ancient as the simple geometric patterns etched into a Jarawa chest guard, a skull left in a Sentinelese lean-to, or the totemic spirits represented by Nicobarese shamanic sculptures.

Samudrika Naval Marine Museum   MUSEUM
(Haddo Rd; adult/child ₹50/25, camera/video ₹20/50; ⊙9am-1pm & 2-5pm Tue-Sun) Run by the Indian Navy, this museum has a diverse range of exhibits with informative coverage of the islands' ecosystem, tribal communities, plants, animals and marine life (including a small aquarium). Outside is a skeleton of a young blue whale washed ashore on the Nicobars.

Corbyn's Cove   BEACH
No one comes to Port Blair for the beach, but if you need a break from town, Corbyn's Cove has a small curve of sand backed by palms. The coastal road here is a scenic journey, and passes several **Japanese WWII bunkers** along the way. Located 7km south of town, an autorickshaw costs ₹150, or you can rent a motorcycle. Crocodiles are occasionally spotted in the area.

⚓ Activities

Infinity Scuba   DIVING
(☑03192-281183; www.infinityscubandamans.wordpress.com) Set up by Baath, an ex-Navy commander who has extensively dived in the Andamans, Infinity arranges diving and other day trips including fishing.

🛏 Sleeping

Homestays are an affordable alternative to standard accommodation options; the tourist office provides a list of approved Port Blair homestays (doubles ₹1000 to ₹2000).

Port Blair

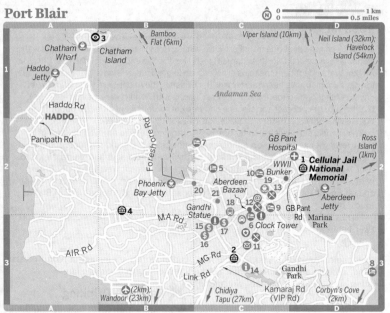

Port Blair

◎ Top Sights
1 Cellular Jail National Memorial............D2

◎ Sights
2 Anthropological Museum....................C3
3 Chatham Saw Mill................................A1
4 Samudrika Naval Marine Museum.......B2

🛏 Sleeping
5 Aashiaanaa Rest Home.......................C2
Amina Lodge.................................(see 6)
6 Azad Lodge...C3
7 Fortune Resort – Bay Island..............C2
8 Hotel Sinclairs Bayview.....................D3
9 J Hotel..C2
10 Lalaji Bay View Hotel.........................C2

🍽 Eating
11 Annapurna...C3
Bayview...(see 8)
Excel Restaurant........................(see 10)
12 Gagan Restaurant..............................C2
13 Lighthouse Residency........................C2

🍷 Drinking & Nightlife
Nico Bar..(see 7)

ℹ Information
14 Andaman & Nicobar Tourism..............C3
Axis Bank ATM.............................(see 9)
15 Axis Bank ATM....................................C3
E-Cafe..(see 12)
16 ICICI ATM..C3
Immigration Office.....................(see 14)
Island Travels..............................(see 13)
17 State Bank of India............................C3

ℹ Transport
18 Bus Stand..C2
19 Coastal Cruise....................................C2
20 Directorate of Shipping
Information Office.............................C2
Ferry Booking Office..................(see 20)
21 Saro Tours & Travels..........................C2

Aashiaanaa Rest Home GUESTHOUSE $
(☏ 09474217008; shads_maria@hotmail.com; Marine Hill; r without bathroom ₹600, r ₹750, with AC from ₹1300; ❄ 🛜) A reliable budget choice, Aashiaanaa has homely rooms and a convenient location uphill from Phoenix Bay jetty. Pricier rooms get you a balcony and air-con. Wi-fi is ₹60 per hour.

Amina Lodge GUESTHOUSE $
(☏ 9933258703; aminalodge@ymail.com; MA Rd, Aberdeen Bazaar; s/d ₹550/700; 🛜) A popular

DON'T MISS

ROSS ISLAND

Just a 20-minute boat ride from Port Blair, visiting Ross Island (not to be confused with its namesake island in North Andaman) feels like discovering a jungle-clad Lost City, à la Angkor Wat, except here the ruins are Victorian English rather than ancient Khmer. The former administrative headquarters for the British in the Andamans, Ross Island in its day was fondly called the 'Paris of the East' (along with Pondicherry, Saigon etc etc...), but the cute title, vibrant social scene and tropical gardens were all wiped out by the double whammy of a 1941 earthquake and invasion by the Japanese.

The island's old English architecture is still standing, despite an invading wave of fast-growing jungle vegetation. Landscaped paths cross the island and most of the buildings are labelled. There's a small **museum** with historical displays and resident spotted deer. A good **sound-and-light show** takes place daily except Wednesday (₹275 per person including ferry return ticket); the boat departs Port Blair's Aberdeen Jetty at 4pm and returns at 7pm at the conclusion of the show; tickets can be bought at Port Blair's tourist office.

Ferries to Ross Island depart hourly from Aberdeen Jetty behind the aquarium in Port Blair, between 8.30am and 2pm every day except Wednesday.

---

budget choice, Amina has good rooms with TV and a handy, although somewhat noisy, location in Aberdeen Bazaar. No meals served. Free wi-fi.

Azad Lodge GUESTHOUSE $
(☏ 03192-242646; MA Rd, Aberdeen Bazaar; s/d without bathroom ₹400/500, d ₹700, with AC ₹900; ❋) Basic but adequately habitable rooms, some sporting colourful paint jobs, in a central location.

Lalaji Bay View Hotel GUESTHOUSE $$
(☏ 9476005820, 03192-233322; www.lalajibay-view.com; RP Rd; d from ₹800, with AC from ₹1200; ❋ 🞔) This popular backpacker hotel has decent rooms, but it's the sociable rooftop restaurant-bar that makes the place tick.

★ **Hotel Sinclairs Bayview** HOTEL $$$
(☏ 03192-227824; www.sinclairshotels.com/portblair; South Point; r incl breakfast from ₹12,000; ❋ 🞔 🞔) Located on the road to Corbyn's Cove, 2km outside town, Sinclairs' large modern rooms open right out to the water. There's a pleasant seaside garden, good multicuisine restaurant and a Japanese WWII bunker on-site.

Fortune Resort – Bay Island HOTEL $$$
(☏ 03192-234101; www.fortunehotels.in; Marine Hill; d incl breakfast from ₹9000; ❋ 🞔 🞔) One of PB's finest hotels, with panoramic bay views, pretty gardens, and modern rooms with polished floors; ask for one that's sea-facing.

J Hotel HOTEL $$$
(☏ 03192-246000; www.jhotel.in; r incl breakfast from ₹5000; ❋ 🞔) A slick designer-esque hotel in the heart of Aberdeen Bazaar, with

contemporary rooms and a rooftop restaurant serving multicuisine fare.

✖ Eating & Drinking

★ **Excel Restaurant** INTERNATIONAL, INDIAN $
(Lalaji Bay View Hotel, RP Rd; mains from ₹100; ⊙ 7am-11pm) This atmospheric bamboo-rooftop restaurant above Lalaji Bay View Hotel brings a 'Havelock' menu to the city, with grilled fish, burgers and more. A cool place to chill out over a beer.

Gagan Restaurant INDIAN $
(Clock Tower, Aberdeen Bazaar; mains from ₹100-200; ⊙ 7am-10pm) Popular with locals, this hole-in-the-wall Bengali restaurant serves great food at good prices, including Nicobari fish, crab curries and coconut chicken.

Annapurna INDIAN $
(MG Rd; mains ₹100-160; ⊙ 6.30am-10.30pm) A good veg option, that looks rather like a high-school cafeteria, serving delicious dosas and rich North Indian-style curries.

Lighthouse Residency SEAFOOD $$
(MA Rd; mains ₹150-800; ⊙ 11am-11pm) Select your meal from the display of red snapper, crab or tiger prawns to barbecue (served with rice and chips), and head to the rooftop for a cold Kingfisher beer.

Bayview MULTICUISINE $$$
(Hotel Sinclairs Bayview, South Point; mains ₹300-550; ⊙ 11am-11pm) Right on the water, with fine sea views, the Bayview is a relaxing place for an unhurried meal. The menu offers a good selection of multicuisine fare.

Nico Bar
BAR

(Marine Hill; ⊙11am-11pm) The closest you'll get to the Nicobars, Fortune Bay Hotel's bar is the spot for sea breezes and scenic views (the picture on the ₹20 note is based on this spot). A pleasant place to while away an afternoon or balmy evening with a frosty cocktail.

ℹ️ Information

Port Blair is the only place in the Andamans where you can reliably change cash or travellers cheques and find enough ATMs. There are several ATMs around town including Axis Bank ones in **Aberdeen Bazaar** (Netaji Rd) and on **MG Rd**; **ICICI** (cnr Foreshore & MA Rds); and at the **State Bank of India** (MA Rd; ⊙9am-noon & 1-3pm Mon-Sat, 10am-noon Sat, closed 2nd & 4th Sat each month), where foreign currency can be changed.

Andaman & Nicobar Tourism (☑03192-232694; www.andamans.gov.in; Kamaraj Rd; ⊙8.30am-1pm & 2-5pm) The main island tourist office has brochures and is the place to book permits for areas around Port Blair.

GB Pant Hospital (☑03192-233473, emergency 03192-232102; GB Pant Rd) The premier public hospital in the Andamans.

Island Travels (☑03192-233358; www.islandtravelsandaman.com; MA Rd, Aberdeen Bazaar; ⊙10am-1pm & 2-6pm Mon-Sat) Come here to book flights, boat charters and guides.

Main Post Office (MG Rd; ⊙9am-5pm Mon-Sat)

ℹ️ Getting There & Away

BOAT

Most interisland ferries depart from Phoenix Bay Jetty. Tickets can be purchased from its **ferry booking office** (⊙9am-1pm & 2-4pm Mon-Fri, to noon Sat). Ferries can be pre-booked one to three days in advance; if they are sold out you can chance your luck with a same-day ticket issued an hour before departure from outside the ticket office. There's a **ferry information office** (☑03192-245555; Phoenix Bay Jetty; ⊙5.30am-6.30pm) outside the ticket office.

Ferries to Havelock (₹195, 2½ hours) depart daily at 6.20am, 11am, 1pm and 2pm, with several heading via Neil Island, all of which book out fast. Otherwise there are some private, pricier ferries. **Makruzz** (☑03192-212355; www.makruzz.com) has daily departures to Havelock (₹900 to ₹1250, two hours) at 6.15am and 2pm, which continue to Neil Island (₹700 to ₹1000, 1½ hours). **Coastal Cruise** (☑03192-230777; 13 RP Rd, Aberdeen Bazaar) heads to Neil Island (₹800 to ₹1100) via Havelock (₹700 to ₹1000) at 7.30am.

There are also daily boats to Little Andaman, which regularly sell out, and several boats a week to Diglipur and Long Island.

New arrivals should make the jetty their first port of call to book tickets. Hotels can usually book tickets, too, if you want to save time.

BUS

Government buses run all day from the **bus stand** (MA Rd) at Aberdeen Bazaar to Wandoor (₹20, one hour) and Chidiya Tapu (₹20, one hour). Buses to Diglipur run at 4am (to Aerial Bay) and 7am (₹270, 12 hours), and 9.30am for Mayabunder (₹200, 10 hours) all via Rangat (₹160, six hours) and Baratang (₹190, three hours). More comfortable, but pricier (around ₹50 to ₹100 extra), private buses have 'offices' (a guy with a ticket book) across from the main bus stand.

ℹ️ Getting Around

TO/FROM THE AIRPORT

A taxi or autorickshaw from Port Blair's airport to Aberdeen Bazaar costs around ₹100 for the 4km trip. There are also hourly buses (₹10) to/from the airport (100m outside the complex) to the main bus stand.

AUTORICKSHAW

An **autorickshaw** from Aberdeen Bazaar to Phoenix Bay Jetty is about ₹30, and to Haddo Jetty it's around ₹50.

MOTORCYCLE

You can hire a motorcycle from various spots in Port Blair for around ₹400 per day. One option is **Saro Tours & Travels** (☑9933291466; www.rentabikeandaman.com; Marine Rd, Aberdeen Bazaar).

Around Port Blair

Wandoor

Wandoor, a tiny speck of a village 29km southwest of Port Blair, is a good spot to see the interior of the island. It's best known as a jumping-off point for snorkelling at Mahatma Gandhi Marine National Park.

SLEEPING PRICE RANGES

The following price ranges refer to a double room with bathroom during high season (December to March).

$ less than ₹800

$$ ₹800 to ₹2500

$$$ more than ₹2500

ANDAMAN ISLANDS AROUND PORT BLAIR

CINQUE ISLAND

The uninhabited islands of North and South Cinque, connected by a sandbar, are part of the wildlife sanctuary south of Wandoor. Surrounded by coral reefs, the islands are among the Andamans' most beautiful. They're two hours by boat from Chidiya Tapu or 3½ hours from Wandoor.

Only day visits are allowed. Unless you're on one of the day trips occasionally organised by travel agencies, you'll need to get permission in advance from the Chief Wildlife Warden by purchasing the Mahatma Gandhi Marine National Park permit (p410).

🏃 Activities

Wandoor has a nice beach, though at the time of research, swimming was prohibited due to crocodiles.

Mahatma Gandhi Marine National Park   SNORKELLING
(permit Indian/foreigner ₹50/500, camera/video ₹25/500; ☉Tue-Sun) The half-day snorkelling trips to Mahatma Gandhi Marine National Park are a fine option for those keen to get underwater while in Port Blair. The park comprises 15 islands of mangrove creeks, tropical rainforest and reefs supporting 50 types of coral and plenty of colourful fish. Boats depart at 9am and 10.30am from Wandoor Jetty, costing ₹750 in addition to the ₹500 permit which you need to pre-arrange from the tourist office in Port Blair.

Depending upon the time of year, the marine park's snorkelling sites alternate between Jolly Buoy and Red Skin, allowing the other to regenerate.

ANET   VOLUNTEERING
(Andaman & Nicobar Environmental Team; ☏03192-280081; www.anetindia.org; North Wandoor) Led by an inspiring team of dynamic Indian ecologists, this is the place to gain a sense of the Andamans' wilderness as you learn about the mangroves, intertidal zones, snakes, crocs and much more. Call ahead for further details.

🛏 Sleeping

Sea Princess Beach Resort   RESORT $$$
(☏03192-280002; www.seaprincessandaman.com; New Wandoor Beach; r incl breakfast ₹7000; ❋ 🛜 🌀) Just a short walk from the beach, Sea Princess'

rooms are decked out in attractive wood tones and come in a range of categories with the beachfront suites being the pick of the bunch.

Anugama Resort   RESORT $$$
(☏03192-280068; www.anugamaresort.com; r incl breakfast from ₹3400; ❋🛜) Anugama has basic but adequately comfortable cottages in a bucolic setting among forest and mud flats.

ℹ Getting There & Away

Catch the bus from Port Blair (₹20, one hour) or hire an autorickshaw for ₹200.

Chidiya Tapu

Chidiya Tapu, 30km south of Port Blair, is a tiny settlement fringed by beaches and mangroves, and famous for celestial sunsets. It also has **Munda Pahar Beach**, popular with day-trippers for its wonderfully natural setting but it's not so crash hot for swimming due to a rocky seabed.

◉ Sights & Activities

Dive companies based in Chidiya Tapu can arrange trips to Cinque and Rutland Islands, known for their abundance of fish, colourful soft corals and excellent visibility.

Chidiya Tapu Biological Park   ZOO
(Indian/foreigner ₹20/50; ☉9am-4pm Tue-Sun) A pleasant place to stroll in a forested setting with natural enclosures for indigenous species such as crab-eating macaques, Andaman wild pig and salt-water crocs.

Lacadives   DIVING
(☏03192-281013; www.lacadives.com; ☉Oct-May) Long-established dive company.

Reef Watch Marine Conservation   VOLUNTEERING
(☏9867437640; www.reefwatchindia.org; Lacadives) NGO with a focus on marine conservation that accepts volunteers to be involved in beach clean ups, fish surveys and more; contact them directly to discuss possibilities that best match your skills with their needs.

🛏 Sleeping & Eating

Wild Grass Resort   RESORT $$$
(☏011-65660202; www.wild-grass-resort-port-blair.hotelsgds.com; r incl breakfast ₹4250; ❋) Unfussy double-storey cottages with an easygoing ambience and verdant jungle backdrop. It also has an atmospheric bamboo restaurant that's good for day-trippers.

ⓘ Getting There & Away

Hourly buses head from Port Blair (₹20, one hour); the last bus back is at 6pm.

Havelock Island

POP 5500

With sublime silken beaches, twinkling teal shallows and some of the best diving in South Asia, Havelock has the well-deserved reputation of being a travellers paradise. Indeed for many, Havelock is *the* Andamans, and it's what lures most tourists across the Bay of Bengal, many of whom are content to stay here for the entirety of their trip.

◉ Sights & Activities

Beaches

Radhanagar BEACH

(Beach 7) One of India's prettiest and most famous stretches of sand is the acclaimed Radhanagar. It's a beautiful curve of sugar fronted by perfectly spiraled waves, all backed by native forest. It's on the northwestern side of the island, about 12km from the jetty.

Late afternoon is the best time to visit to avoid the heat and crowds, as well as for its sunset. The further you walk from the main entry the more privacy you'll get.

Neils Cove BEACH

Northwest of Radhanagar is the gorgeous 'lagoon' at Neils Cove, a gem of sheltered sand and crystalline water. Swimming is prohibited at dusk and dawn; take heed of any warnings regarding crocodiles.

Beach 5 BEACH

On the north-eastern coast of the island, the palm-ringed Beach 5 has your more classic tropical vibe, with the bonus of shady patches and fewer sandflies. However, swimming is very difficult in low tide when the water becomes shallow for miles. Most of the island's accommodation is out this way.

Kalapathar BEACH

Hidden away 5km south of Beach 5, you'll find Kalapathar, a pristine beach. You may have to walk a bit to get away from throngs of package tourists.

Diving & Snorkelling

Havelock is the premier spot for diving in the Andamans. It's famed for its crystal-clear waters, deep-sea corals and kaleidoscope of marine life, including turtles. Diving here is suitable for all levels.

The main dive season is roughly November to April, but trips run year-round.

All companies offer fully equipped boat dives, and prices vary depending on the location, number of participants and duration of the course. Diving starts from around ₹5000 to ₹6000 for a two-tank dive, with options of PADI scuba diver (two dives ₹18,000), open-water (four dives ₹24,000) and advanced (five dives ₹19,500) courses.

While coral bleaching has been a major issue since 2010 (said to be linked to El Niño weather patterns), diving remains world-class. The shallows may not have particularly bright corals, but all the colourful fish are still here, and for depths beyond 16m, corals remain as vivid as ever. The Andamans recovered from a similar bleaching in 1998, and today things are, likewise, slowly repairing themselves.

Popular sites include **Dixon's Pinnacle** and **Pilot Reef** with colourful soft coral, **South Button** for macro dives (to see small critters) and rock formations, **Jackson Bar** or **Johnny's Gorge** for deeper dives with schools of snapper, sharks, rays and turtles, and **Minerva's Delight** for a bit of everything.

ANDAMAN ISLANDS HAVELOCK ISLAND

PROTECTING MARINE LIFE

If you plan on diving or snorkelling in the Andamans, play your part to protect its fragile marine ecosystem. Only snorkel when it's high tide: during low tide it's very easy to step on coral or sea sponges, which can irreparably damage them. In areas of reefs with very shallow water, avoid wearing flippers so as to protect marine life – even the gentle sweep of a flipper kick can result in damage to decades' worth of growth. Divers need to be extra cautious about descents near reefs; colliding with the coral at a strong pace with full gear can be environmentally disastrous. Choose ecologically responsible dive operators.

Avoid touching marine life, including coral, as doing so may not only cause stress and damage (some organisms have a protective coating that is rubbed off if touched, thus making them more vulnerable to parasites and disease), but they could also be toxic.

Finally, clear any rubbish you come across and refrain from taking souvenir shells or coral out of the ocean (it's ecologically detrimental but possibly also illegal).

Havelock Island

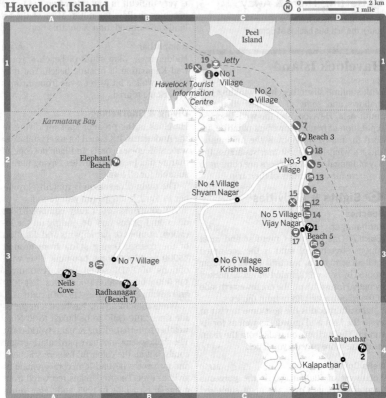

ANDAMAN ISLANDS HAVELOCK ISLAND

There's also a **wreck dive** to SS *Incheket,* a 1950s cargo carrier. Keep an eye out for trips further afield such as **Barren Island**, home to India's only active volcano, whose ash produces an eerie underwater spectacle for divers.

Dive companies arrange **snorkelling** trips, but it can be cheaper to organise a boat through your hotel or guesthouse. Snorkelling gear is widely available on Havelock but is generally mediocre quality, so consider bringing your own if you intend doing a lot of snorkelling.

Most boats head to **Elephant Beach** for snorkelling, which can also be reached by a 40-minute walk through a muddy elephant logging trail; it's well marked (off the cross-island road), but turns to bog if it has been raining. At high tide it's also impossible to reach – ask locally for more information. Lots of snorkelling charters come out this way, so be prepared as it can be a bit of a circus. If you head here around 6am, you'll have a better chance of getting the place to yourself.

Prices are standardised, so it's a matter of finding a dive operator you feel comfortable with.

Ocean Tribe   DIVING
(☎ 03192-282255; www.ocean-tribe.com; No 3 Village) Run by legendary local Karen divers, including Dixon and Jackson, all who have had dive sites named after them.

Dive India   DIVING
(☎ 03192-214247; www.diveindia.com; btwn No 3 & 5 Village; 1/2 dives ₹4500/₹6000) The original PADI company in Havelock, and still one of the best.

Barefoot Scuba   DIVING
(☎ 9566088560; www.diveandamans.com; No 3 Village) Popular, long-established company with dive-and-accommodation packages.

Andaman Bubbles   DIVING
(☎ 03192-282140; www.andamanbubbles.com; No 5 Village; 1hr dive ₹4500, 2-day 4-dive package

Havelock Island

₹10,500) Quality outfit with professional, personable staff.

Other Activities

Some resorts organise guided **jungle treks** for keen walkers or birdwatchers, though the forest floor turns to mush after rain. The inside rainforest is a spectacular, emerald-coloured hinterland cavern, and the **birdwatching** is rewarding (especially on the forest fringes); look out for the blue-black racket-tailed drongo or golden oriole.

High-season yoga lessons (per 1½ hours ₹300 to ₹500) are available at Flying Elephant (p420).

Andaman Kayak Tours KAYAKING
(☑ 9933269653; www.andamanhomestay.com/kayak-and-snorkel; min 2 people 2½hr kayak ₹2500) Weather permitting, Andaman Kayak Tours explore Havelock's mangroves by sea kayak, and run memorable night trips gliding among bio-luminescence.

⊜ Sleeping

Pellicon Beach Resort BUNGALOW $
(☑ 9932081673; www.pelliconbeachresort.com; Beach 5; hut from ₹700; ☎) Attractive beachside bungalows as well as Nicobari huts with private porches on a peaceful plot of land close to the beach.

Coconut Grove Beach Resort GUESTHOUSE $
(☑ 9531835592; www.coconutgrovebeachresort.com; Beach 5; hut ₹600, without bathroom ₹300; ☒) Particularly popular with Israeli travellers, Coconut Grove has an appealingly re-

laxed communal vibe with huts arranged in a circular outlay.

Sunrise Beach Resort BUNGALOW $
(☑ 9474206183; Beach 5; r ₹600-1000, with AC ₹5100) Offers the same thatched goodness as almost every other resort – what sets it apart is its budget A-frame huts with water views.

Emerald Gecko BUNGALOW $$
(☑ 9474286953; www.emerald-gecko.com; Beach 5; hut ₹1500-3000) Double-storey bungalows look to the water, while pricier rooms have ambient lighting and outdoor bathrooms constructed from bamboo rafts that have drifted ashore from Myanmar.

Orient Legend Resort GUESTHOUSE $$
(☑ 9434291008; www.havelockbeachresort.in; Beach 5; hut without bathroom ₹500, r ₹1200, with AC ₹2500) This popular place on Beach 5 covers most budgets, from doghouse A-frame huts and concrete rooms to double-storey cottages that offer a glimpse of the ocean.

Sea View Beach Resort BUNGALOW $$
(☑ 943429877; Beach 3; r ₹800-1000) Chilled-out beach bungalows, backing on to the Ocean Tribe (p418) dive shop, a bit away from the crowds.

⭐ **Barefoot at Havelock** RESORT $$$
(☑ 03192-214534; www.barefootindia.com; Beach 7; tented cottage incl breakfast ₹9500, Nicobari cottage ₹13,500; ❄) ⌀ Thoughtfully designed, eco-conscious resort boasting elegantly comfortable timber and bamboo-thatched cottages just back from the famed Radhanagar Beach.

★ Silversand
RESORT $$$

(☎ 03192-211073; www.silversandhavelock.com; Beach 5; r incl breakfast ₹12,000; ❋ 🛜 ❊) The highlight of this hotel is its location on a lovely stretch of beach, away from the crowds. Rooms are comfortable with the more expensive ones positioned closer to the sea. There's a good bar and restaurant.

Flying Elephant
BUNGALOW $$$

(☎ 9474250821; www.flying-elephant.in; Kalapathar; r ₹4000) Hidden away on Kalapathar beach, in a pastoral setting among rice paddies and betel palms, this serene retreat has simple, earthy bamboo duplexes that feature landscaped outdoor stone-garden bathrooms.

Wild Orchid
RESORT $$$

(☎ 03192-282472; www.wildorchidandaman.com; Beach 5; r incl breakfast from ₹6125; ❋ 🛜) Modern Andamanese-style cottages, all set around a tropical garden a stone's throw from the beach.

✗ Eating & Drinking

Most people eat at, or near, their hotel but there are *dhabas* (snack bars) near the jetty or you can head to the main bazaar (No 3 Village) for local meals.

Alcohol is available from a store (Beach 3; ⊙ 9am-noon & 3-8pm) next to the ATM at No 3 Village.

Fat Martin's
INDIAN $

(Beach 5; mains ₹70-140; ⊙ 7.30am-10pm) Popular open-air cafe with a good selection of Indian dishes and some particularly impressive dosas including paneer tikka and nutella.

Anju-coco Resto
INDIAN, CONTINENTAL $$

(Beach 5; mains ₹200-800; ⊙ 8am-10.30pm) One of Havelock's faves, down-to-earth Anju-coco offers a varied menu with standouts being its hearty breakfasts, yummy barbecue dishes and platters.

★ Red Snapper
SEAFOOD $$$

(Wild Orchid Resort, Beach 5; mains ₹250-850; ⊙ 7.30-10am, noon-2.30pm & 6-9.30pm) This appealing thatched-roof restaurant with polished-bamboo decor exudes a romantic island ambience. Menu items include lavish seafood platters, pepper-crust tuna and handmade pasta. The outdoor deck seating is a good spot for a beer.

Full Moon Cafe
MULTICUISINE $$$

(Dive India, Beach 5; mains ₹200-490; 🖊 Run by an Irish-Indian couple, this cool thatched-roof restaurant shares a site with Dive India on Beach 5. It does fabulous seafood and salads and a refreshing ginger-honey lemonade. Free water refills.

B3 – Barefoot Bayside & Brasserie
MULTICUISINE $$$

(Village No 1; mains ₹350-500; ⊙ noon-9.30pm) Come here for the best pizzas in Havelock or scrumptious handmade pasta. There's good gelato, too! Its breezy outside decking, with sea views, makes this a great place to wait for your ferry. Downstairs is Dakshin (mains ₹80-270; ⊙ 6.30am-10am & noon-3.30pm), specialising in South Indian cuisine.

Cicada
LIVE MUSIC

(Beach 5; ⊙ hours variable) Run by the team from Emerald Gecko, this live-music/hangout venue has a groovy jungle location accessed down a path off the main road across from Beach 5.

❶ Information

Satellite internet is insanely slow and pricey at around ₹300 per hour.

Havelock Tourist Information Centre
(☎ 03192-282117; next to jetty, Village No 1; ⊙ 8am-4.30pm) The official government tourist office provides brochures and information but does not book any tours.

❶ Getting There & Away

Government ferries run from Havelock **jetty** at No 1 Village to Port Blair three times a day (₹420, 2½ hours) at 9am, 2.45pm and 4.30pm. It's best to book tickets from the **ferry ticket office** (⊙ 9.15am-noon & 2-4pm Mon-Fri, to noon Sat) at least two days in advance (most hotels can arrange this for a small fee). One to two ferries a day link Havelock with Neil Island (₹335, 1¼ hours), while four boats a week (9.30am on Monday, Wednesday, Friday, and Saturday) head to Long Island (₹335, two hours) en route to Rangat.

Private (more comfortable) ferries such as **Makruzz** (p415) and **Coastal Cruise** (p415) have daily services to Port Blair via Neil Island.

❶ Getting Around

A local bus (₹10, 40 minutes) connects the jetty, villages and Radhanagar on a roughly hourly circuit from 10am until 5.30pm. Otherwise you can rent a scooter (per 24 hours from around ₹490) or bicycle (per day ₹100) – your guesthouse/hotel should be able to arrange this or point you in the right direction.

An autorickshaw from the jetty to No 3 Village is ₹50, to No 5 ₹90 and to No 7 ₹500.

Neil Island

Although its beaches are not as luxurious as its more famous island neighbour, Havelock, tranquil Neil has its own unique charm. There's a wonderfully unhurried pace of life here; cycling through picturesque little villages is a stellar way to soak up the island's character. The main bazaar has a mellow vibe and is a popular gathering spot in the early evening. On Neil Island you're about 40km from Port Blair, a short ferry ride from Havelock and several universes away from the bustle of life back home.

◉ Sights & Activities

Beaches

Neil Island's five beaches (numbered one to five) all have their own personality, though they aren't necessarily great for swimming due to shallow, rocky sea floors.

Beach 1   BEACH
(Laxmanpur) Beach 1 is a long sweep of sandy coastline and mangrove, a 40-minute walk west of the jetty and village. There's a good sunset viewpoint out this way accessed via Pearl Park Beach Resort (p421). Dugongs are sometime spotted here.

Beach 2   BEACH
On the north side of the island, Beach 2 has the Natural Bridge rock formation, accessible only at low tide by walking around the rocky cove. To get here by bicycle, take the side road that runs through the bazaar, then take a left where the road forks.

Beach 3   BEACH
(Ram Nagar) Beach 3 is a secluded rocky cove with powdery sand. There's also good snorkelling here.

Beach 4   BEACH
(Bharatpur) Beach 4 is Neil Island's best swimming beach, though its proximity to the jetty is a turn-off, as are rowdy day-trippers who descend upon the beach in motorised boats.

Beach 5   BEACH
(Sitapur) The more rugged Beach 5, 5km from the village on the eastern side of Neil, is a nice place to walk along the sand, with small limestone caves accessible at low tide.

Diving & Snorkelling

Neil offers some brilliant dive sites, with colourful fish, large schools of Jack, turtles, rays, and soft and hard corals. There are several dive operators on Neil Island and open-water courses, among others, are also available.

The island's best snorkelling is around the coral reef at the far (western) end of Beach 1 at high tide; if you're extremely lucky you may spot a dugong feeding in the shallows. Beach 3 also has good snorkelling. Gear costs around ₹200 to hire and is available from many guesthouses.

India Scuba Explorers   DIVING
(☑ 9933271450; www.indiascubaexplorers.com; Beach 1; 1 dive ₹4500) Neil's first dive shop, set up by a husband-wife team, is popular for its personalised service.

Dive India   DIVING
(☑ 8001122205; www.diveindia.com; per 1/2 dives ₹4500/6000) Established in Havelock, this professional company also has a branch in Neil. It's based just near the jetty.

🛏 Sleeping

🛏 Beach 1

Sunset Garden Guesthouse   BUNGALOW $
(☑ 9933294573; hut ₹800, without bathroom ₹300) Ideal for those wanting to get away from it all, these basic bamboo huts have a secluded spot accessed via a 15-minute walk through rice fields.

Seashell   RESORT $$$
(☑ 9933239625; www.seashellhotels.net; cottage incl breakfast ₹9000; ❄) Seashell has contemporary, well-appointed cottages that lead down to a mangrove-lined beach. Rooms have TVs and tea-and-coffee-making facilities.

Pearl Park Beach Resort   BUNGALOW $$$
(☑ 9434260132; www.andamanpearlpark.com; r incl breakfast with fan from ₹3500, with AC from ₹5500; ❄ 🛜) Comfortable bamboo huts arranged around a flower-filled garden.

🛏 Beach 3

★**Kalapani**   BUNGALOW $
(☑ 9474274991; hut ₹600, without bathroom ₹300) Run by the lovely Prakash and Bina, laid-back Kalapani has simple bungalows. Motorbikes, bicycles and snorkelling gear are available for hire, and the owners have plenty of suggestions about things to do.

Breakwater Beach Resort   BUNGALOW $
(☑ 9933292654; hut ₹500-1000, without bathroom ₹300) Easygoing ambience, acceptable rooms, attractive garden and delicious food.

Beach 5

Sunrise Beach Resort
BUNGALOW $

(☑ 9933266900; r ₹400, without bathroom ₹300) Sunrise has simple thatched bungalows, a short walk from the beach. There's a sweet little restaurant among flowers serving up tasty dishes such as coconut fish masala (₹150).

Emerald Gecko
BUNGALOW $$

(☑ 9474286953; www.emerald-gecko.com; r ₹2000-4000) Simple, eco-friendly bungalows, with ceiling fans and mosquito nets, set in a coconut plantation.

Neil Kendra

Silversand
RESORT $$$

(☑ 03192-244914; www.silversandneil.com; r incl breakfast from ₹12,000; ❄ ☀) One of Neil's most upmarket places to stay, Silversand has cosy contemporary cottages set among shady palms just a short walk from the water.

✕ Eating

Garden View Restaurant
INDIAN, CONTINENTAL $

(Beach 5; ₹50-130; ⏱ 6am-10pm) Set in a cool garden, this is a relaxing little spot to drink Kingfisher beer (₹170 per bottle) or papaya lassi (₹60) and tuck into fish curry, prawn fried rice and much more.

Blue Sea
SEAFOOD, INDIAN $$

(Beach 3; mains ₹120-300; ⏱ 6am-11pm) Small, quirky beach shack with sandy floor, dangling beach curios and a blue whale skull centrepiece that serves simple, tasty Indian fare as well as some continental dishes. A path leads to, arguably, Neil's best beach. Come here for the unpretentious, chilled-out character and nearby beach.

Moonshine
INTERNATIONAL, INDIAN $$

(Beach 1; mains ₹100-400; ⏱ 8-11am, noon-1pm, 4-9.30pm) On the road to Beach 1, this backpacker favourite cooks up satiating homemade pasta and fish thalis. Cold beer can be arranged.

ℹ Information

There's no ATM or moneychanging facilities on Neil, so bring plenty of cash.

There's wi-fi access at **Pearl Park Beach Resort** (p421) on Beach 1 (₹200 for two hours).

ℹ Getting There & Around

A ferry heads to Port Blair two or three times a day (₹400, two hours). There are also one or two daily ferries to Havelock (₹400, one hour), and three ferries a week to Long Island (₹400, five hours). **Makruzz** (p415) and **Coastal Cruise** (p415) also have ferries to/from Port Blair (from ₹875, one hour) and Havelock (from ₹710).

Hiring a bicycle (per day from ₹100) is the best way to get about; roads are flat and distances short. You'll be able to find one in the bazaar or at a guesthouse. An autorickshaw will take you from the jetty to Beach 1 or 3 for between ₹75 to ₹100.

Middle & North Andaman

The Andamans aren't just sun and sand. They are also jungle that feels as primeval as the Jurassic, a green tangle of ancient forest that could have been birthed in Mother Nature's subconscious. This wild, antediluvian side of the islands can be seen on a long, loping bus ride up the Andaman Trunk Rd (ATR), crossing tannin-red rivers prowled by saltwater crocodiles on roll-on, roll-off ferries.

But there's a negative side to riding the ATR: the road cuts through the homeland of the Jarawa (p423) and has brought the tribe into incessant contact with the outside world. Modern India and tribal life do not seem able to coexist – every time Jarawa and settlers interact, misunderstandings have led to friction, confusion and, at worst, violent attacks and death. Indian anthropologists and indigenous rights groups such as Survival International have called for the ATR to be closed; its status continues to be under review. At present, vehicles are permitted to travel only in convoys at set times from 6am to 3pm. Photography is strictly prohibited, as is stopping or any other interaction with the Jarawa people who are becoming increasingly reliant on handouts from passing traffic.

The first point of interest north of Port Blair are the limestone caves (Baratang; ⏱ Tue-Sun) at Baratang. It's a scenic 45-minute boat trip (₹450) from the jetty, through mangrove forest. A permit is required, and can be organised at the jetty.

Rangat & Around

Travelling north on the Andaman Trunk Rd, Rangat is the first main town in Middle Andaman after Baratang Island. It's primarily a transport hub with not much else going for it on the tourism front. The turtle breeding grounds at Dhaninallah Mangrove is the most popular sight, viewed early evening

ISLAND INDEGENES

The Andaman and Nicobar Islands' indigenous peoples constitute 12% of the population and, in most cases, their numbers are decreasing. The Onge, Sentinelese, Andamanese and Jarawa are all of Negrito ethnicity, and share a strong resemblance to people from Africa. Tragically, numerous groups have become extinct over the past century. In February 2010 the last speaker of the Bo language passed away, bringing an end to a culture and language that originated 65,000 years ago.

It's important to note that these tribal groups live in areas strictly off limits to foreigners – for their protection and dignity – and people have been arrested for trying to visit the regions.

Jarawa

The 300 or so remaining Jarawa occupy the 639-sq-km reserve on South and Middle Andaman Islands (p422). In 1953 the chief commissioner requested that an armed sea plane bomb Jarawa settlements, and their territory has been consistently disrupted by the Andaman Trunk Rd, forest clearance and settler and tourist encroachment. In 2012, a video went viral showing an exchange between Jarawa and tourists, whereby a policeman orders them to dance in exchange for food. This resulted in a government inquest that saw to the end of the so-called 'human safari' tours.

Nicobarese

The 30,000 Nicobarese are the only indigenous people whose numbers are not decreasing. The majority have converted to Christianity and been partly assimilated into contemporary Indian society. Living in village units led by a head man, they farm pigs and cultivate coconuts, yams and bananas. The Nicobarese, who probably descended from people of Malaysia and Myanmar, inhabit a number of islands in the Nicobar group, centred on Car Nicobar, the region worst affected by the 2004 tsunami.

Onge

Two-thirds of Little Andaman's Onge Island was taken over by the Forest Department and 'settled' in 1977. The 100 or so remaining members of the Onge tribe live in a 25-sq-km reserve covering Dugong Creek and South Bay. Anthropologists say the Onge population has declined due to demoralisation through loss of territory.

Sentinelese

The Sentinelese, unlike the other tribes on these islands, have consistently repelled outside contact. For years, contact parties arrived on the beaches of North Sentinel Island, the last redoubt of the Sentinelese, with gifts of coconuts, bananas, pigs and plastic buckets, only to be showered with arrows, though some encounters have been a little less hostile. About 150 Sentinelese remain.

Andamanese

There were around 7000 Andamanese in the mid-19th century, but friendliness to colonisers was their undoing, and by 1971 all but 19 of the population had been wiped away by measles, syphilis and influenza epidemics. Their population now numbers only about 50 and they have been resettled on tiny Strait Island.

Shompen

Only about 250 Shompen remain in the forests on Great Nicobar. Seminomadic hunter-gatherers who live along the riverbanks, they have resisted integration and avoid areas occupied by Indian immigrants.

ANDAMAN ISLANDS MIDDLE & NORTH ANDAMAN

(mid-December to April) from the approximately 1km-long boardwalk, a 45-minute drive from Rangat.

❶ Getting There & Away

Ferries depart for Long Island (₹11) from Yeratta Jetty, 8km from Rangat (accessed by local bus), at 9am and 3pm. Rangat Bay, 5km outside town, has ferries to/from Port Blair (₹378, six hours) and Havelock (₹378, two hours). A daily bus goes to Port Blair (₹145, seven hours) and Digli-pur (₹65, four hours).

Long Island

With its friendly island community and deliciously slow pace of life, Long Island is perfect for those seeking to take the pace down a few more notches. Other than the odd motorcycle, there's no motorised vehicles on the island, and at certain times you may be the only tourist here.

◉ Sights & Activities

Beaches

There's a lovely beach close to Blue Planet (p424), a 15-minute walk from the jetty.

A 1½-hour trek (or cross-trail jog if you're feeling energetic) in the jungle will lead you to the secluded **Lalaji Bay**, a beautiful white-sand beach with good swimming and snorkelling; follow the red arrows from the jetty to get here. Hiring a boat (₹2500 return for two persons) is also an option. Inconveniently, you need a permit (free) from the Forest Office near the jetty to visit.

Diving & Snorkelling

Blue Planet has a dive shop (December to March) and hires snorkelling gear for around ₹100. Trips head to Campbell Shoal for its schools of trevally and barracuda.

You can also get a boat to North Passage Island for snorkelling at the stunning **Merk Bay** (₹3500 for two people) with blinding white sand and translucent waters.

There's terrific offshore **snorkelling** at Lalaji Bay with colourful corals out front from the rest huts. There's also good snorkelling at the beach near Blue Planet guesthouse, di-

DON'T MISS

TURTLE NESTING IN KALIPUR

Reputedly the only beach in the world where leatherback, hawksbill, olive ridley marine and green turtles all nest along the same coastline, Kalipur is a fantastic place to observe this evening show from mid-December to April. Turtles can be witnessed most nights, and you may be able to assist with collecting eggs, or with the release of hatchlings. Contact Pristine Beach Resort for more information.

rectly out from the blue Hindu temple; swim beyond the sea grass to get to the coral.

🛏 Sleeping & Eating

★ **Blue Planet**　　　　　　　GUESTHOUSE $$
(☑ 9474212180; www.blueplanetandamans.com; r from ₹1500, without bathroom from ₹500; @) An old favourite, Blue Planet has thatched-bamboo rooms and hammocks set around a Padauk tree. Food is delicious and there's free filtered water. It's a 15-minute walk from the jetty. They also have bamboo cottages (from ₹3200) at a nearby location.

❶ Getting There & Away

There are four ferries a week to Havelock, Neil and Port Blair (₹195). If you can't get a ferry here from Port Blair, jump on a bus to Rangat to get the ferry from Yeratta, 8km from Rangat, from where two daily boats run to Long Island (₹11, one hour) at 9am and 3.30pm.

Diglipur & Around

Those who make it this far north are rewarded with some impressive attractions in the area. It's a giant outdoor adventure playground designed for nature lovers: home to a world-famous turtle nesting site, the Andamans' highest peak and a network of caves to go with white-sand beaches and some of the best snorkelling in the Andamans.

However, don't expect much of Diglipur (population 70,000), the second largest urban hub in the Andamans, a sprawling, gritty bazaar town. Instead head straight for the tranquil coastal village of **Kalipur**.

🏃 Activities

In season most people come to see the turtles.

★ **Ross & Smith Islands**　BEACH, SNORKELLING
Like lovely tropical counterweights, the twin islands of Smith and Ross are connected by a narrow sandbar of dazzling white sand, and are up there with the best in the Andamans for both swimming and snorkelling.

No permits are required for Smith Island, which is accessed by boat (₹2500 per boat, fits five people) from Aerial Bay. While theoretically you need a permit for Ross Island (₹500), as it's walkable from Smith, permits generally aren't checked. Enquire with Pristine Resort for more information.

Saddle Peak　　　　　　　　TREKKING
(Indian/foreigner ₹25/250) At 732m Saddle Peak is the Andamans' highest point. You

MAYABUNDER & AROUND

In 'upper' Middle Andaman, Mayabunder is best known for its villages inhabited by Karen, members of a Burmese hill tribe who were relocated here during the British colonial period. It's a low-key destination, away from the crowds.

You can go on a range of day tours, with the highlight being jungle trekking at creepy **Interview Island** (boat hire ₹3000, fits six people), inhabited by a population of around 35 wild elephants, released after a logging company closed for business in the 1950s. Armed guards accompany you in case of elephant encounters. A permit (₹500) is required, which is best organised by emailing a copy of your arrival permit to Sea'n'Sand guesthouse. Other trips include **turtle nesting** at Dhaninallah Mangrove (December to March); **Forty One Caves**, where *hawabills* (swiftlets) make their highly prized edible nests; and snorkelling off **Avis Island** (boat hire ₹1500).

Sea'n'Sand (☏03192-273454; titusinseansand@yahoo.com; r from ₹850; ❇) is easily the best place to stay. Hosts Titus and Elizabeth (and their extended Karen family) are an excellent source for everything Mayabunder, and the food here is a treat.

Mayabunder, 71km north of Rangat (₹75, two hours), is linked by daily buses from Port Blair (₹200, 10 hours) and Diglipur (₹60, two hours) and by thrice-weekly ferries.

can trek through subtropical forest to the top and back from Kalipur in about six to seven hours; the views across the archipelago are incredible. It's a demanding trek, so bring plenty of water (around 4L). A permit (₹250) is required from the Forest Office at the trailhead, open 6am to 2pm.

A local guide (300₹) will make sure you don't get lost, but otherwise follow the red arrows marked on the trees.

Craggy Island   SNORKELLING
A small island off Kalipur, Craggy is a good spot for snorkelling. Strong swimmers can make it across (flippers recommended), otherwise a motorised boat is available (₹3000 return).

Excelsior Island   SNORKELLING
Excelsior has beautiful beaches, snorkelling plus resident spotted deer. Permits are required (₹500); boats cost ₹4500 and fit seven people.

🛏 Sleeping & Eating

⭐**Pristine Beach Resort**   GUESTHOUSE $$$
(☏9474286787; www.andamanpristineresorts.com; Kalipur Beach; hut ₹1500, r ₹3500-4500; ❇@) Huddled among the palms between paddy fields and the beach, this relaxing resort has simple bamboo huts as well as more upmarket rooms. Its restaurant-bar serves delicious fish Nicobari.

Sion   INDIAN $
(Kalipur Beach; mains ₹60-150; ⊙10am-10pm) This rooftop restaurant gets the thumbs up for its seafood dishes.

❶ Getting There & Away

Diglipur, located about 80km north of Mayabunder, is served by daily buses to Port Blair (₹265, 12 hours) at 5am and 7am, plus a 10.40pm night bus. There are also buses to Mayabunder (₹55, 2½ hours) and Rangat (₹100, 4½ hours).

Ferries to Port Blair (seat/bunk ₹110/350, nine hours) depart three times a week (Tuesday, Thursday and Saturday).

❶ Getting Around

Ferries and some buses arrive at Aerial Bay, from where it's 11km to Diglipur, and 8km to Kalipur in the other direction.

Buses run the 18km journey from Diglipur to Kalipur (₹15, 30 minutes) every 45 minutes; an autorickshaw costs ₹200.

Little Andaman

As far south as you can go in the islands, Little Andaman has an appealing end-of-the-world feel. It's a gorgeous fist of mangroves, jungle and teal, ringed by beaches as fresh as bread out of the oven. It rates highly as many travellers' favourite spot in the Andamans.

Badly hit by the 2004 tsunami, Little Andaman has slowly rebuilt itself. Located about 120km south of Port Blair, the main settlement here is **Hut Bay**, a pleasant small town.

❂ Sights & Activities

Little Andaman Lighthouse   LIGHTHOUSE
Located 14km east of Hut Bay, Little Andaman lighthouse makes for a worthwhile ex-

cursion. Standing 41m high, 200 steps spiral up to magnificent views over the coastline and forest. The easiest way to get here is by motorcycle. Otherwise take a sweaty bicycle journey or autorickshaw until the road becomes unpassable; from there, walk for an hour along the blissful stretch of deserted beach.

Beaches

Come prepared for sandflies; crocodiles also lurk about (seek local advice as to where crocs may be currently congregating).

Netaji Nagar   BEACH
The sprawling and rugged Netaji Nagar, stretching 8km to 12km north of Hut Bay, is the beach where most accommodation is located.

Butler Bay   BEACH
(₹20) Little Andaman's best beach is Butler Bay, a spectacular curved beach with lifeguards and good surf. It's located at the 14km mark.

Kalapathar   BEACH
Located before Butler Bay is Kalapathar lagoon, a popular enclosed swimming area with shady patches of sand. Look for the cave in the cliff face that you can scramble through for stunning ocean views. It's accessed via a side road that runs past modern housing constructed after the 2004 tsunami.

Surfing

Intrepid surfing travellers have been whispering about Little Andaman since it first opened to foreigners some years back. The reef breaks are legendary, but best suited for more experienced surfers. The most accessible is **Jarawa Point**, a left reef break at the northern point of Butler Bay. Beginners should stick to beach breaks along Km8 to Km11. February to April generally bring the best waves.

Surfing Little Andaman   SURFING
(☑ 9531877287; www.surfinglittleandaman.com; Hut Bay; 2hr lesson ₹1000) Here you can hire boards, arrange lessons and get the lowdown on everything about surfing in Little Andaman.

Waterfalls

Inland, the **White Surf** and **Whisper Wave** waterfalls offer a jungle experience for when

you're done lazing on the beach. The latter involves a 4km forest trek and a guide is highly recommended. They are pleasant falls and you may be tempted to swim in the rock pools, but beware of crocodiles.

🛏 Sleeping & Eating

There are cheap and tasty thali places in Hut Bay.

Blue View   BUNGALOW $
(☑ 9734480840; Km11.5, Netaji Nagar; r without bathroom from ₹300; ☺ Oct-May) With its relaxing atmosphere, Blue View's simple thatched bungalows are popular mainly for the warm hospitality of its hosts. Surfboards, bicycles and motorbikes can be hired.

Aastha Eco Resort   BUNGALOW $
(Km10, Netaji Nagar; r ₹600) Set among betel and coconut palms, Aastha is a calm choice with its atmospheric Nicobari huts and thatched cottages.

Hawva Beach Resort   BUNGALOW $
(☑ 9775181290; Km8, Netaji Nagar; r from ₹400) This laid-back family-run lodging has just a handful of simple cottages. Flavoursome home-cooked food is available.

Palm Groove   INDIAN $
(Hut Bay; mains ₹60-140; ☺ 7am-9pm) Set in a heritage-style bungalow, with an outdoor garden gazebo, Palm Grove dishes up a selection of tasty biriyanis and curries.

ℹ Information

There's an ATM in Hut Bay and village at 16Km.

ℹ Getting There & Away

Ferries land at Hut Bay Jetty. Buses (₹10, depart hourly) to Netaji Nagar usually coincide with ferry arrivals, but often leave before you clear immigration, leaving more pricey jeeps (per person ₹100) as the other option. An autorickshaw from the jetty to Netaji Nagar is around ₹250, or ₹80 to town. Motorbikes and bicycles are popular for getting around, and are available from most lodges; otherwise, shared jeeps (₹25) and buses are very handy.

Boats sail to Port Blair daily, alternating between afternoon and evening departures on vessels ranging from big ferries with four-/two-bed rooms (₹240/330, six to 8½ hours) to faster 5½-hour government boats (₹35); all have air-con. The ferry office is closed Sunday.

Understand South India & Kerala

South India & Kerala Today

While South India is very much part of the Indian nation, subject to Delhi-based decisions, there is a sense that, with its locally focused politics, the south is different – some would say more progressive – with booming IT, tourism, film and automotive industries, and above-average employment, literacy and life expectancy. However, South India also faces major issues. Violence against women frequently hits headlines, alcoholism is an enormous problem, and there is ever-growing concern about climate change, pollution and lack of water resources.

Best on Film

Fire (1996), **Earth** (1998) and **Water** (2005) The Deepa Mehta–directed trilogy on social issues; popular abroad, but controversial in India.
Dhobi Ghat (2011) Understated, absorbing story, directed by Kiran Rao, touching on many levels of life in Mumbai and India.
Gandhi (1982) The classic, directed by Richard Attenborough and starring Ben Kingsley.
Sairat (2016) Realistic, anti-Bolly-wood Marathi-language hit.

Best in Print

Midnight's Children (Salman Rushdie; 1981) Allegory on Independence and Partition.
White Tiger (Aravind Adiga; 2008) Page-turner about class injustice, partly in Bengaluru.
Shantaram (Gregory David Roberts; 2003) Vivid autobiography of Roberts' life in India.
A Fine Balance (Rohinton Mistry; 1995) Tragic, heart-warming tale of Mumbai survival.
The God of Small Things (Arundhati Roy; 1997) Magically written Kerala-based novel of passion and caste.
White Mughals (William Dalrymple; 2002) Historical investigation into 18th- and 19th-century Hyderabad.

The Balance Tilts Southward

In the decades after Independence in 1947, many South Indians headed north for work. Today, the trend is in the opposite direction. Some argue that better, more stable governance in southern states (despite deep-seated corruption) and a less rigid caste system have contributed to the south's upswing. Nearly all South Indian states now have above-average literacy, employment, life expectancy, income per head and female-to-male population ratio. Kerala has India's highest literacy rate.

Mumbai (Bombay) has long been India's financial, commercial and industrial powerhouse, and its film and fashion capital. Chennai (Madras) makes one-third of India's cars. Goa and Kerala are huge tourism success stories. But the biggest story is the technology boom, sparked by India's 1991 economic liberalisation and globalisation. Bengaluru (Bangalore) is India's 'Silicon Valley', and, with Hyderabad and Pune, forms the 'Deccan Triangle' at the heart of India's thriving IT industry, fuelled by well-educated, English-speaking, young professionals. Chennai (Madras), Mumbai (Bombay) and Delhi round off India's IT big six.

Problems intertwined with economic progress include the growth of city slums (60% of Mumbai's population lives in slums) and dreadful traffic and pollution – though new metro systems in Mumbai, Bengaluru, Chennai and Hyderabad are slowly modernising transport. Kerala, despite its education and health successes, has high unemployment and, until recently, India's highest alcohol-consumption rates (now claimed by Andhra Pradesh); in 2014 Kerala removed liquor licences from 700 bars, though full prohibition now looks unlikely. Chennai and Bengaluru unfortunately often top 'suicide capital' lists.

The Political Landscape

Regional parties focused on local issues and personalities dominate South Indian politics; national parties have to strike alliances with them to gain their support in Delhi or a foothold in the regions. Maharashtra shows more support for a national party – the Hindu-nationalist-oriented Bharatiya Janata Party (BJP) – than any state further south, but the BJP has long had to ally with Shiv Sena, a reactionary local party that opposes migration into Maharashtra from other states. Tamil Nadu has had a string of ex–film stars as chief ministers, including Jayalalithaa Jayaram, who received a four-year jail sentence for corruption in 2014, only to be acquitted and return to office (immensely popular) until her death in December 2016.

But the south has certainly sat up and taken notice of national politics since 2014, when Narendra Modi, from the western state of Gujarat, led the BJP to a stunning general election victory – the first time since 1984 that one party won an outright parliament majority. It was a humiliation for the Congress Party (the party of independent India's first prime minister Jawaharlal Nehru, his daughter Indira Gandhi and their descendants) which had then ruled India for 55 of the 67 years since Independence.

Modi's charisma, derived from his economic reputation as former chief minister of Gujarat and his appeal to 'ordinary' Indians due to his working-class origins, has much to do with the BJP's triumph, though accusations linger about Modi's role in religious riots in Gujarat in 2002 in which at least 1000 people, mostly Muslims, were killed. He is a masterful politician, making savvy use of digital technology (he currently has 26.3 million Twitter followers). At the time of writing, Modi remains popular, offering vision, hope and inspiration. His aims to resurrect India's economy but also to address social issues such as sanitation, gender equality, poverty and health are well underway, including the Swachh Bharat Abhiyan (Clean India Mission), which, launched in 2014, has seen politicians, celebrities and the PM himself publicly clearing rubbish.

In 2016 India's economy overtook China's as the world's fastest-growing, partly thanks to renewed investment confidence under the business-friendly Modi. In 2015 India broke a Guinness World Record for the most bank accounts opened in one week (18,096,130) in a scheme aimed at offering scio-economic opportunities to the poor. However, Modi's sudden demonetisation of ₹500 and ₹1000 notes in November 2016 (a crackdown on corruption) received mixed responses.

POPULATION: 366 MILLION

AREA: 956,000 SQ KM

GDP: US$6700 PER CAPITA (PPP)

LITERACY RATE: 78%

GENDER RATIO: FEMALE/ MALE 964/1000

if India were 100 people

55 would speak one of 21 other official languages
41 would speak Hindi
4 would speak one of 400 other official languages

belief systems
(% of population)

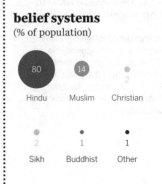

population per sq km

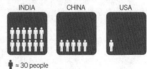

Etiquette

Indian culture is quite conservative by many world standards; tradition and social norms are usually strictly followed.

Greetings Always shake hands and eat with your right hand (the left is reserved for far more unsavoury activities). Saying *namaste* with hands together in a prayer gesture is a traditional, respectful Hindu greeting and is the best greeting for someone of the opposite gender.

Dress Tight or revealing clothing, with few exceptions, is likely to attract unwanted attention. Head cover (for women and sometimes men) is required at some places of worship – especially gurdwaras (Sikh temples) and mosques.

Religion Religious etiquette advises against touching locals on the head, or directing the soles of your feet at a person, religious shrine or image of a deity. Protocol also advises against touching someone with your feet or touching a carving of a deity.

Shoes It's considered bad manners to enter someone's home without removing your shoes, and shoes are also prohibited in many temples and shrines.

Photography Photography inside religious shrines is generally prohibited; photography of funerals or processions of the dead is also likely to cause offence. Ask before photographing people, ceremonies or sacred sites.

Violence Against Women

In December 2012, 23-year-old physiotherapy student Jyoti Singh and her male friend boarded a bus home in Delhi, only to find that it was fake. The six men aboard brutally raped Singh and she died 12 days later, becoming known across India as Nirbhaya ('Fearless One'). The event set off massive protests and soul-searching nationwide.

Within weeks India passed new, but controversial, laws to deter violence against women. Rape now carries a seven-year minimum sentence (20 years for gang rape), or the death penalty if the victim dies; new fast-track courts deal exclusively with rape prosecutions. But violence against women continues to make headlines all too often, while conviction rates remain low (27.1% in 2013). A 22-year-old photojournalist was gang raped in Mumbai in 2013, as was a 51-year-old Danish woman in Delhi in 2014. Most recently, there has been outrage over the 'mass molestation' of women by mobs of men on New Year's Eve 2016 in Bengaluru (usually considered a safe city).

Since being elected, Modi has been actively trying to change the national psyche regarding gender equality. In 2015 Modi launched the Beti Bachao, Beti Padhao (Save the Daughter, Teach the Daughter) campaign, which works towards gender equality by discouraging female infanticide and encouraging education to change male attitudes from a young age. Many Indians are also now reflecting on other abuses of women (a woman is murdered every hour over dowry demands), widespread police and justice-system mishandling of cases, and larger gender-equality problems.

Sadly, reports of sexual assaults against women and girls, including tourists, are on the increase all over India. The saving grace is that, now in the spotlight, India's gender-based violence is finally being discussed.

Climate Change

Despite Modi's pledges to increase India's use of solar power and end water issues (which includes controversial plans for a countrywide river-linking scheme), climate change is a growing South Indian concern. Devastating heatwaves, cyclones and droughts are wreaking havoc across the region with increasing frequency; Lakshadweep's islands are at risk of rising sea levels. In 2015 a deadly heatwave and South India's heaviest floods in 100-plus years killed, officially, around 3000 people (but probably more). Predictably, there is growing conflict over limited water resources. In 2016 Bengaluru experienced much-publicised drinking-water shortages, Maharashtra received emergency water by train, and long-running disputes between drought-hit Karnataka and Tamil Nadu over the Cauvery River erupted into strikes and violent protests in both states.

History

South India has always laid claim to its own unique history, largely resulting from its insulation, by distance, from political developments up north. The cradle of Dravidian culture, it has a long and colourful historical tapestry of wrangling dynasties and empires, interwoven with an influx of traders and conquerors arriving by sea, all of which have richly contributed to a remarkable mix of southern traditions that persists to the present day.

Indus Valley Civilisation

India's first major civilisation flourished between about 3000 and 1700 BC in the Indus Valley, much of which lies within present-day Pakistan. Known as the Harappan culture, it appears to have been the culmination of thousands of years of settlement. Some historians attribute its eventual demise to floods or decreased rainfall, which threatened the Harappans' agricultural base. A more enduring theory, though with little archaeological proof or evidence from ancient Indian texts, is that an invasion from the northwest by Aryans (peoples speaking languages of the Indo-Iranian branch of the Indo-European language family) put paid to the Harappans. Others say that the arrival of the Aryans was more of a gentle migration that gradually subsumed Harappan culture, rather than an invasion. Some nationalist historians argue that the Aryans (the term comes from a Sanskrit word meaning 'noble') were in fact the original inhabitants of India and that the invasion theory was invented by later, self-serving foreign conquerors. Invasion theorists believe that from around 1500 BC Aryan tribes from Afghanistan and Central Asia began to gradually filter into northwest India, eventually controlling northern India as far south as the Vindhya Range (just north of central India's Narmada River), and that, as a consequence, many of the original inhabitants, the Dravidians, were pushed south.

Influences from the North

Aryan culture had a gradual but profound effect on the social order and ethos of South India as well as the north – among other things in

To learn more about the ancient Indus Valley civilisation, ramble around Harappa (www.harappa.com), which presents an illustrated yet scholarly overview.

India: A History, by John Keay, is an astute, readable account of subcontinental history, spanning the Harappan civilisation to post-Independence India.

TIMELINE	2600–1700 BC	1500 BC	1500–1200 BC
	The heyday of the Indus Valley civilisation, spanning parts of Rajasthan, Gujarat and the Sindh province in present-day Pakistan, and including cities such as Harappa and Moenjodaro.	The Indo-Aryan civilisation takes root in the fertile Indo-Gangetic basin. Settlers speak an early form of Sanskrit, from which several Indian vernaculars, including Hindi, later evolve.	The Rig-Veda, the first and longest of Hinduism's canonical texts, the Vedas, is written; three more books follow. Earliest forms of priestly Brahmanic Hinduism emerge.

literature (the four Vedas, a collection of sacred Hindu hymns), religion (gods such as Agni, Varuna, Shiva and Vishnu), language (Sanskrit) and a social structure that organised people into castes, with Brahmins at the top.

George Michell's *Southern India: A Guide to Monuments, Sites & Museums* looks at South India's history from an architectural perspective, providing plenty of regional detail.

Over the centuries other influences flowed from north to south, including Buddhism and Jainism. Sravanabelagola in modern-day Karnataka (an auspicious place of pilgrimage to this day) is where, tradition says, the northern ruler Chandragupta Maurya, who had embraced Jainism and renounced his kingdom, arrived with his guru around 300 BC. Jainism was then adopted by the trading community (its tenet of ahimsa – nonviolence – disqualified occupations tainted by the taking of life), who spread it across South India.

Emperor Ashoka (p434), a successor of Chandragupta who ruled for 40 years from about 272 BC, was a major force behind Buddhism's inroads into the south. Once a campaigning king, his epiphany came in 260 BC when, overcome by the horrific carnage and suffering caused by his campaign against the powerful Kalinga kingdom of Odisha, he renounced violence and embraced Buddhism. He sent Buddhist missionaries far and wide, and his edicts (carved into rock and incised into specially erected pillars) have been found in Andhra Pradesh and Karnataka. Stupas were also built in South India under Ashoka's patronage, mostly in Andhra Pradesh, although at least one was constructed as far south as Kanchipuram in Tamil Nadu.

The appeal of Jainism and Buddhism was that they rejected the Vedas and condemned the caste system. Buddhism, however, gradually lost favour with its devotees, and was replaced with a new brand of Hinduism, which emphasised devotion to a personal god. This bhakti (surrendering to the gods) order developed in South India around AD 500. Bhakti adherents opposed Jainism and Buddhism, and the movement hastened the decline of both in South India.

Mauryan Empire & Southern Kingdoms

The concepts of zero and infinity are widely believed to have been devised by eminent Indian mathematicians during the reign of the North Indian Guptas.

Chandragupta Maurya was the first in a line of Mauryan kings who ruled what was effectively the first Indian empire. The empire's capital was in present-day Patna in Bihar. Chandragupta's son, Bindusara, who came to the throne around 300 BC, extended the empire as far as Karnataka. He seems to have stopped there, possibly because the Mauryan empire was on cordial terms with the southern chieftains of the day.

The identity and customs of these southern chiefdoms have been gleaned from various sources, including archaeological remains and ancient Tamil literature. These literary records describe a land known as the 'abode of the Tamils', within which resided three major ruling families: the Pandyas (centred on Madurai), the Cheras (in what is now Ker-

599–528 BC	563–483 BC	326 BC	321–185 BC
The life of Mahavir, the 24th and last *tirthankar* (enlightened teacher), who established Jainism. Like the Buddha, he preaches compassion and a path to enlightenment for all castes.	The life of Siddhartha Gautama. The prince is born in modern-day Nepal and attains enlightenment beneath the Bodhi Tree in Bodhgaya (Bihar), transforming into the Buddha (Awakened One).	Alexander the Great invades India. He defeats King Porus in Punjab to enter the subcontinent, but a rebellion within his army keeps him from advancing beyond Himachal Pradesh's Beas River.	Rule of the Mauryan kings. Founded by Chandragupta Maurya, this pan-Indian empire is ruled from Pataliputra (present-day Patna), briefly adopting Buddhism during the reign of Emperor Ashoka.

ala and western Tamil Nadu) and the Cholas (Thanjavur and the Cauvery Valley). The region described in classical Sangam literature (written between 300 BC and AD 300) was still relatively insulated from Sanskrit culture, but the literature indicates that Sanskrit traditions were starting to take root in South India around 200 BC.

A degree of rivalry characterised relations between the main chiefdoms and the numerous minor chiefdoms, and there were occasional clashes with Sri Lankan rulers. Ultimately, the southern powers all suffered at the hands of the Kalabhras, about whom little is known except that they appear to have originated from somewhere north of the Tamil region.

By around 180 BC the Mauryan empire, which had started to disintegrate soon after the death of Emperor Ashoka in 232 BC, had been overtaken by a series of rival kingdoms that were subjected to repeated invasions from the northwest by the Bactrian Greeks and others. The post-Ashokan era did, however, produce at least one line of royalty whose patronage of the arts and ability to maintain a relatively high degree of social cohesion have left an enduring legacy. This was the Satavahanas, who eventually controlled all of modern-day Maharashtra, Madhya Pradesh, Chhattisgarh, Karnataka, Telangana and Andhra Pradesh. Under their rule, between about 200 BC and AD 200, the arts blossomed, especially literature, sculpture and philosophy. Buddhism reached a peak in Maharashtra under the Satavahanas, although the greatest of the Buddhist cave temples at Ajanta and Ellora were built later by the Chalukya and Rashtrakuta dynasties. Most of all, the subcontinent enjoyed a period of considerable prosperity. South India may have lacked North India's vast and fertile agricultural plains, but it compensated by building strategic trade links via the Indian Ocean.

The Chalukyas & Pallavas

Following the suppression of the Tamil chiefdoms by the Kalabhras, South India split into numerous warring kingdoms. The Cholas virtually disappeared and the Cheras on the west coast seem to have prospered through trading, although little is known about them. It wasn't until the late 6th century AD, when the Kalabhras were overthrown, that the political uncertainty in the region ceased. For the next 300 years the history of South India was dominated by the fortunes of the Chalukyas of Badami in northern Karnataka, the Pallavas of Kanchi (Kanchipuram) and the Pandyas of Madurai (these last two in modern-day Tamil Nadu).

The Badami Chalukyas controlled most of the Deccan at their peak under King Pulakesi II in the early 7th century. A related clan, known as the eastern Chalukyas, ruled Andhra Pradesh from Vengi near Eluru. It's unclear where the Pallavas originated, but it's thought they may have

Best Buddhist Sites
Ajanta (Maharashtra)
Ellora (Maharashtra)
Amaravathi (Andhra Pradesh)
Nagarjunakonda (Andhra Pradesh)
Guntupalli (Andhra Pradesh)
Karla & Bhaga Caves (Maharashtra)
Aurangabad Caves (Maharashtra)

Chalukya Sites
Ellora Cave Temples (Maharashtra)
Badami Cave Temples (Karnataka)
Pattadakal (Karnataka)
Aihole (Karnataka)
Bhongir Fort (Telangana)

300 BC–AD 300	200 BC–AD 200	AD 52	319–467
Sangam Age, during which Tamil poets produce a body of classical Tamil literature and the Tamil area is dominated by three dynasties, the Pandyas, Cheras and early Cholas.	The Satavahana empire, of Andhra origin, rules over much of the Deccan plateau. Buddhism flourishes and literature, sculpture and philosophy blossom.	Possible arrival of St Thomas the Apostle on the coast of Kerala. Christianity is believed to have been introduced to India with his preaching in Kerala and Tamil Nadu.	The golden era of the North India–based Gupta dynasty, the second of India's great empires after the Mauryas. This era is marked by a creative surge in literature and the arts.

emigrated to Kanchi from Andhra Pradesh. After their successful defeat of the Kalabhras, the Pallavas extended their territory as far south as the Cauvery River, and in the 7th and 8th centuries were at the height of their power, building major monuments such as the Shore Temple (p347) and Arjuna's Penance (p349) at Mamallapuram (Mahabalipuram). They engaged in long-running clashes with the Pandyas, who extended their control into Kerala and, in the 8th century, allied themselves with the Gangas of Mysore. By the 9th century significant Pallava power had been snuffed out by the Pandyas and the Rashtrakutas, a dynasty based in Gulbarga, Karnataka, who replaced the Chalukyas as the dominant force on the Deccan from the 8th to 10th centuries.

The Chola Empire

As the Pallava dynasty came to an end, a new Chola dynasty was laying the foundations for what would be one of the subcontinent's most significant empires. From their Tamil capitals at Thanjavur (Tanjore) and, briefly, Gangaikondacholapuram (p371), the Cholas spread north absorbing what was left of the Pallavas' territory, and made inroads southward. Under Raja Raja Chola I (r 985–1014) the Chola kingdom really started to emerge as a great empire. Raja Raja Chola I successfully waged war against the Pandyas in the south, the Gangas of Mysore and the Eastern

ASHOKA: AN ENLIGHTENED EMPEROR

Apart from the Mughals and the British (many centuries later), no other power controlled more Indian territory than the Mauryan empire. It also provided India with one of its most significant historical figures: Emperor Ashoka, grandson of Chandragupta Maurya.

Emperor Ashoka's rule was characterised by flourishing art and sculpture, while his reputation as a philosopher-king was enhanced by the rock-hewn edicts he used both to instruct his people and to delineate the enormous span of his territory (they are found from Afghanistan to Nepal to Andhra Pradesh).

Ashoka's reign also represented an undoubted historical high point for Buddhism: he embraced the religion in 260 BC, declaring it the state religion and cutting a radical swath through the spiritual and social body of Hinduism. The emperor also built thousands of stupas and monasteries across the region. Ashoka sent missions to Thailand, Greece, the Middle East and North Africa, and is revered in Sri Lanka because his son and daughter carried Buddhism to the island.

The long shadow this emperor of the 3rd century BC still casts over India is evident in the fact that the central motif of the Indian national flag is the Ashoka Chakra, a wheel with 24 spokes. Ashoka's standard (four lions sitting back to back atop an abacus decorated with a frieze and the inscription 'truth alone triumphs'), which topped many pillars, is also the seal of modern-day India and its national emblem.

6th–8th Centuries	10th–12th Centuries	1001–1025	13th Century
The heyday of the Pallava dynasty, which dominates Andhra Pradesh and northern Tamil Nadu from their southern capital, Kanchipuram, and creates marvellous carvings at Mamallapuram.	The Chola empire, based in and around Thanjavur, spreads its influence over much of South India and Southeast Asia, leaving a superb legacy in the arts including sculpture and architecture.	Mahmud of Ghazni (in today's Afghanistan) leads 17 raids into northern India, the very first of several invasions by Muslims over the following years.	The Pandyas, a Tamil dynasty dating back to the 6th century BC, assume control of Chola territory, expanding into Andhra Pradesh, Kalinga (Odisha) and Sri Lanka from their Tamil capital, Madurai.

Chalukyas. He also launched a series of naval campaigns that captured the Maldives, the Malabar Coast (coasts of Kerala and Karnataka) and northern Sri Lanka, which became a province of the Chola empire. These conquests gave the Cholas control over critical ports and trading links between India, Southeast Asia, Arabia and East Africa. They were therefore in a position to grab a share of the huge profits made from selling spices to Europe.

Raja Raja Chola's son, Rajendra Chola I (r 1014–44), continued to expand Chola territory, conquering the remainder of Sri Lanka and campaigning up the east coast as far as Bengal and the Ganges River. Rajendra also launched a campaign in Southeast Asia against the Sumatra-based Srivijaya kingdom, and sent trade missions as far as China. Furthermore, the Chola empire produced a brilliant blossoming of the arts. Its legacy includes three magnificent Shiva temples at Thanjavur and near Kumbakonam. Bronze sculpture reached astonishing heights of aesthetic and technical refinement. Music, dance and literature flourished and developed a distinctly Tamil flavour, enduring in South India long after the Cholas had faded from the picture. The Cholas also took their culture to Southeast Asia, where it lives on in Myanmar (Burma), Thailand, Bali and Cambodia in dance, religion and mythology.

But the Cholas, weakened by constant campaigning, eventually succumbed to expansionist pressure from the Hoysalas of Halebid (Karnataka) and the resurgent Pandyas of Madurai; by the 13th century they were finally supplanted by the Pandyas. The Hoysalas were themselves eclipsed by the Vijayanagar empire, which arose in the 14th century. The Pandyas prospered and were much admired by Marco Polo when he visited in 1288 and 1293. But their glory was short-lived, as they were unable to fend off Muslim invaders from the north. Meanwhile, the Rashtrakutas were replaced by the Yadavas based at Devagiri (Daulatabad) in Maharashtra.

Muslim Expansion & the Vijayanagar Empire

Muslim raiders from the northwest began incursions into northern India in the 11th century and the powerful Delhi sultanate was established in 1206. The sultanate's expansion towards South India began in the 1290s, and by 1323 it was established at Madurai.

In 1328 Sultan Mohammed Tughlaq, in pursuit of his dream of conquering the whole of India, moved his capital 1100km south to Devagiri in Maharashtra, renaming it Daulatabad and forcing the entire Delhi population to move with him, but had to revert to Delhi after two years because of a water shortage. Though Mohammed Tughlaq controlled

---

Chola Bronzes

Government Museum (Chennai)

Royal Palace (Thanjavur)

Puducherry Museum

Architecture of the Deccan Sultanates

Hyderabad (Telangana) Golconda Fort, Qutb Shahi Tombs, Charminar, Mecca Masjid

Vijapura (Bijapur; Karnataka) Citadel, Golgumbaz, Ibrahim Rouza, Jama Masjid

Bidar (Karnataka) Bidar Fort, Bahmani Tomb

1290s	1336	1345	1480s
The Delhi sultanate starts its southward expansion, bringing parts of the Deccan under northern Muslim rule for the first time and reaching Madurai by 1323.	The mighty Vijayanagar empire (Hindu), named after its capital city, is founded. Its ruins can be seen today in the vicinity of Hampi (in modern-day Karnataka).	Bahmani sultanate (Muslim) is established in the Deccan following a revolt against the Tughlaqs of Delhi. The capital is set up at Gulbarga, in today's northern Karnataka, later shifting to Bidar.	Bahmani sultanate begins to break up. By 1528 there are five Deccan sultanates: Berar, Ahmadnagar, Bidar, Bijapur and Golconda.

A History of South India: from Prehistoric Times to the Fall of Vijayanagar, by KA Nilakanta Sastri, is arguably the most thorough history of this region; especially recommended if you're heading for Hampi.

The Career and Legend of Vasco da Gama, by Sanjay Subrahmanyam, is one of the better investigations of the explorer credited with finding the sea route from Europe to India.

a very large part of the subcontinent by 1330, his forces became overstretched and scattered revolts had begun by 1327. From 1335 his empire started shrinking. Not only did local Muslim rulers in places such as Madurai and Daulatabad declare independence, but the foundations of what was to become one of South India's greatest empires, Vijayanagar, were being laid by Hindu chiefs at Hampi.

The Vijayanagar empire is said to have been founded by two brothers who, having been captured and taken to Delhi, converted to Islam and were sent back south to serve as governors for the sultanate. The brothers, however, reconverted to Hinduism and around 1336 established a kingdom that eventually encompassed most of Karnataka and Andhra Pradesh, and all of Tamil Nadu and Kerala. Over seven centuries later, the centre of this kingdom – the ruins and temples of Hampi – is one of South India's biggest tourist drawcards.

The Muslim Bahmani sultanate, initially based at Daulatabad, established its capital at Gulbarga in Karnataka, relocating to Bidar in the 15th century. Its territory eventually included Maharashtra, Telangana and northern Karnataka – and the sultanate took pains to protect it.

Ongoing rivalry characterised the relationship between Vijayanagar and the Bahmani sultanate. Much of the conflict centred on control of trading ports and the fertile agricultural land between the Krishna and Tungabhadra Rivers; at one stage the Bahmanis wrested the important port of Goa from their rivals, but the Vijayanagars seized it back in 1378. The Bahmani empire was eventually torn apart by factional fighting and, between 1490 and 1528, broke into five separate sultanates: Bidar, Bijapur, Berar, Ahmadnagar and Golconda. In 1565 the combined forces of the five sultanates laid waste to Vijayanagar's vibrant capital at Hampi, terminating Vijayanagar power.

The Vijayanagar empire is notable for its prosperity, which was the result of a deliberate policy of giving every encouragement to traders from afar, combined with the development of an efficient administrative system and access to important trading links, including west-coast ports. Hampi became quite cosmopolitan, with people from various parts of India as well as from abroad mingling in the bazaars.

Portuguese chronicler Domingo Paez arrived in Vijayanagar during the reign of one of its greatest kings, Krishnadevaraya (r 1509–29), under whom Vijayanagar enjoyed a period of unparalleled prosperity and power. Paez recorded the achievements of the Vijayanagars and described how they had constructed large water tanks and irrigated their fields. He also described how human and animal sacrifices were carried out to propitiate the gods after one of the water tanks had burst repeatedly. He included detail about the fine houses of wealthy merchants and the

1498	1510	1526	1542–45
Vasco da Gama, a Portuguese voyager, finds the sea route from Europe to India via East Africa. He arrives in present-day Kerala and engages in trade with the local nobility.	Portuguese forces capture Goa under the command of Alfonso de Albuquerque, whose initial attempt was thwarted by then-ruler Sultan Adil Shah of Bijapur. He succeeds following Shah's death.	The central Asian conqueror Babur becomes the first Mughal emperor after conquering Delhi. Within a century the Mughal empire extends from Afghanistan to Bengal and into the northern Deccan.	St Francis Xavier's first mission to India. He preaches Catholicism in Goa, Tamil Nadu and Sri Lanka, returning in 1548–49 and 1552 in between travels in the Far East.

ENTER THE PORTUGUESE

On 20 May 1498 Vasco da Gama dropped anchor off the southwest Indian coast near the town of Calicut (now Kozhikode, in modern-day Kerala). It had taken him 23 days to sail from the east coast of Africa, guided by a pilot named Ibn Majid, sent by the ruler of Malindi in Gujarat – the first time Europeans had made the voyage across the Indian Ocean from Africa to India. The Portuguese sought a sea route between Europe and the east so they could trade directly in spices. They also hoped they might find Christians cut off from Europe by the Muslim dominance of the Middle East, including the legendary kingdom of Prester John, a supposedly powerful Christian ruler with whom they could unite against the Middle East's Muslim rulers. In India they found spices and the Syrian Orthodox community, but no Prester John.

Vasco da Gama was well received by the ruler of Calicut. The Portuguese engaged in a limited amount of trading, but became increasingly suspicious that Muslim traders were turning the Calicut ruler against them. They resolved to leave Calicut, in August 1498. Within a few years other Portuguese expeditions began arriving on India's west coast not just to trade but also to conquer, resulting in an empire of scattered Portuguese possessions around India's coasts which lasted until 1961 when India invaded Goa, Daman and Diu.

bazaars full of precious stones (rubies, diamonds, emeralds, pearls) and textiles (including silk).

Like the Bahmanis, the Vijayanagar kings invested heavily in protecting their territory and trading links. Krishnadevaraya employed Portuguese and Muslim mercenaries to guard the forts and protect his domains. He also fostered good relations with the Portuguese, upon whom he depended for access to trade goods, especially the Arab horses he needed for his cavalry.

As a result of the weakening of Vijayanagar, governors at Gingee, Thanjavur and Madurai in Tamil Nadu – the Nayaks – began to proclaim their independence from the second half of the 16th century. The Nayaks ruled until the early 18th century, with Madurai's Tirumalai Nayak being their most important leader, responsible for such architectural gems as Madurai's Meenakshi Amman Temple (p381).

Arrival of the Europeans & Christianity

Vasco da Gama's arrival in Kerala (p437) in 1498 ushered in a new era of European contact. He was followed by Francisco de Ameida and Alfonso de Albuquerque, who established an eastern Portuguese empire that included Goa (first taken in 1510). Albuquerque waged a constant battle against the local Muslims in Goa, finally defeating them. But perhaps his greatest achievement was in playing off two deadly threats against

Vasco da Gama died in Kochi (Cochin) in 1524. He was originally buried at Kochi's St Francis Church, where you can still visit his tombstone. His remains were transferred to Portugal 14 years later and entombed at Lisbon's Mosteiro dos Jerónimos.

1565	1560–1812	1600	1639
The great Vijayanagar empire collapses and its vibrant capital, Hampi, is destroyed, at the hands of the five combined Deccan sultanates of Berar, Ahmadnagar, Bidar, Bijapur and Golconda.	Portuguese Inquisition in Goa. Trials focus on converted Hindus and Muslims thought to have 'relapsed'. Thousands were tried and several dozen were executed before it was abolished.	Britain's Queen Elizabeth I grants the first trading charter to the East India Company, with the maiden voyage taking place in 1601 under the command of Sir James Lancaster.	Francis Day and the British East India Company strike a deal to set up a fort-cum-trading-post at Madraspatnam fishing village, which goes on to become Madras (now Chennai).

Goan Churches

Basilica of Bom Jesus (Old Goa)

Church of Our Lady of the Immaculate Conception (Panaji; Panjim)

Church & Convent of St Cajetan (Old Goa)

Church of Our Lady of the Rosary (Old Goa)

Church of the Holy Spirit (Margao)

Amar Chitra Katha, a popular publisher of comic books about Indian folklore, mythology and history, has several books about Shivaji, including *Shivaji: The Great Maratha*, *Tales of Shivaji* and *Tanaji, the Maratha Lion*, about Shivaji's close friend and fellow warrior.

each other: the Vijayanagar empire (for whom access to Goa's ports was extremely important) and the Bijapur sultanate (which controlled part of Goa).

The Bijapuris and Vijayanagars were sworn enemies, and Albuquerque skilfully exploited this by supplying both sides with Arab horses for their warring cavalries. The horses died in alarming numbers once on Indian soil, so a constant supply had to be imported, keeping Portugal's Goan ports busy and profitable.

The Portuguese also introduced and forcefully spread Catholicism, and the arrival of the Inquisition in 1560 marked the beginning of 250 years of religious suppression in the Portuguese-controlled areas on the west coast of India.

Today the Portuguese influence is most obvious in Goa, with its chalk-white Catholic churches, Christian festivals and unique cuisine, although the Portuguese also had some influence in Kerala in towns such as Cochin (now Kochi), and landed at what was to become Madras (now Chennai) in the 16th century, before the British. By the mid-16th century Old Goa had grown into a thriving city said to rival Lisbon in magnificence: now only a ruined shadow of that time, its churches and buildings are still a stunning reminder of Portuguese rule.

In 1580 Spain annexed Portugal and, until Portugal regained its independence in 1640, its interests were subservient to Spain's. After the English defeat of the Spanish Armada in 1588, the sea route to the east lay open to the English and the Dutch. The Dutch were more interested in trade than in religion and empire. Indonesia was their main source of spices; trade with South India was primarily for pepper and cardamom. The Dutch East India Company set up a string of trading posts (called factories), which allowed them to maintain a complicated trading structure all the way from the Persian Gulf to Japan. They set up trading posts at Surat (Gujarat) and on southeast India's Coromandel Coast, and entered into a treaty with the ruler of Calicut (now Kozhikode). In 1660 they captured the Portuguese forts at Cochin and Kodungallor.

The English also set up a trading venture, the British East India Company, to which in 1600 Queen Elizabeth I granted a monopoly on trade east of Africa's Cape of Good Hope. Like the Dutch, the English were initially mainly interested in Indonesian spices. But the Dutch proved too strong there and the English turned instead to India, setting up a trading post at Madras in 1639. The Danes traded at Tranquebar (Tharangambadi; on Tamil Nadu's Coromandel Coast) from 1616, and the French acquired Pondicherry (now Puducherry) in 1673.

1661	1673	1674	1707
Britain acquires Bombay (now Mumbai) from Portugal in the marriage settlement between King Charles II and Catherine of Braganza. The East India Company moves its headquarters to Bombay in 1687.	The French East India Company establishes a post at Pondicherry (now Puducherry), which the French, Dutch and British fight over repeatedly in the following century.	Shivaji establishes the Maratha kingdom in modern Maharashtra, assuming the imperial title Chhatrapati. Within half a century the Marathas dominate much of northern and central India.	Death of Aurangzeb, the last of the Mughal greats. His demise triggers the gradual collapse of the Mughal empire, as anarchy and rebellion erupt across its territory.

The Mughals & Their Legacy

During the 17th century the Delhi-based Mughal empire made inroads into South India, especially under Emperor Aurangzeb (r 1658–1707), gaining the sultanates of Ahmadnagar, Bijapur and Golconda (including Hyderabad) before moving into Tamil Nadu. Among the rivals the Mughals came up against were the Marathas – Hindu warriors originating from near Pune in Maharashtra, who controlled much of the Deccan by 1680, the year their first emperor Shivaji (p439) died. Pressing on southward in a series of guerrilla-like raids, the Marathas captured Thanjavur and in the 1690s set up a capital at Gingee near Madras. The Mughal-Maratha wars (1680 to 1707) ended with the Marathas very much on top. By the mid-18th century the Marathas controlled a huge swath of territory extending from the Punjab and Gujarat in the northwest to Odisha in the east and Karnataka in the south; Mughal power barely extended beyond Delhi.

Several dozen people were burned at the stake during the Goa Inquisition, which lasted more than 250 years. The judgement ceremonies took place outside the Sé Cathedral in Old Goa.

MIGHTY SHIVAJI

The name Chhatrapati Shivaji is revered in Maharashtra, with statues of the great warrior astride his horse gracing towns, and many streets and monuments being named – or renamed, as in the case of Mumbai's Victoria Terminus – after him.

Shivaji founded the powerful Hindu Maratha kingdom, which controlled much of the Deccan region and beyond from the late 17th to early 19th centuries, and which played a big part in the decline of the mighty Delhi-based Mughal empire in the early 18th century. A courageous warrior and charismatic leader, Shivaji was born in 1627 to a prominent Maratha family at Shivneri. As a child he was sent to Pune with his mother, where he was given land and forts and groomed as a future leader. With a very small army, Shivaji seized his first fort at the age of 20 and over the next three decades continued to expand Maratha power around his base in Pune, holding out against Muslim rivals from the north (the Mughal empire) and the south (the sultanate of Bijapur), and eventually ruling much of the Deccan. He was shrewd enough to play his enemies (among them Mughal emperor Aurangzeb) off against each other. In a famous 1659 incident, he killed Bijapuri general Afzal Khan in a face-to-face encounter at Pratapgad Fort.

In 1674 Shivaji was crowned Chhatrapati (Emperor or Great Protector) of the Marathas at Raigad Fort. He died six years later. His son and successor, Sambhaji, suffered serious reversals at the hands of the Mughals, but the resilient Marathas bounced back and by the mid-18th century controlled a large proportion of the subcontinent.

Shivaji is an icon to the modern Maharashtrian-nationalist and Hindu-nationalist political party Shiv Sena (Shivaji's Army) which, among other things, opposes immigration into Maharashtra by non-Maharashtrians. For this reason the widespread use of his name is not wholly welcomed by everybody in Maharashtra.

1757	1775–1818	1857	1858
The East India Company registers its first military victory on Indian soil. Siraj-ud-Daulah, Nawab of Bengal, is defeated by Robert Clive in the Battle of Plassey.	The three Anglo-Maratha Wars (1775–82, 1803–05 and 1817–18) between the East India Company and the Marathas. The third war terminates the Maratha empire, leaving most of India under British control.	The First War of Independence (Indian Uprising) against the British. In the absence of a national leader, freedom fighters coerce the Mughal king to proclaim himself emperor of India.	British government assumes control over India, with power officially transferred from the East India Company to the Crown – beginning the period known as the British Raj.

In the Deccan and the south the Marathas had plenty of rivals. One was the Asaf Jahi dynasty (later the nizams of Hyderabad), which broke away from the Mughal empire in 1724 to control much of the Deccan, with its capital initially at Aurangabad (Maharashtra) and then, from 1763, at Hyderabad. Another was Mysore, a landlocked kingdom until a cavalry officer, Hyder Ali, assumed power in 1761 and set about acquiring coastal territory. Hyder Ali and his son Tipu Sultan eventually ruled a kingdom that included southern Karnataka and northern Kerala. Tipu conducted trade directly with the Middle East through the west-coast ports he controlled. The other important players were the British East India Company, based at Madras, and the French, at Pondicherry. The 18th century saw a constantly shifting succession of alliances and conflicts between these five rivals. The British won out over the French in the three Carnatic Wars fought between 1744 and 1763, and their control over the eastern seaboard denied both Hyderabad and Mysore access to trading ports there. Meanwhile, the Portuguese retained control of Goa.

> The princely ruling family of Mysore, the Wodeyars, were so popular with their subjects that the maharaja became the first governor of the post-Independence state of Mysore.

Down in the far south, the kingdom of Travancore (occupying what is now the southern half of Kerala and a bit of Tamil Nadu) was also trying to consolidate its power by gaining control of strategic trade links. Ruler Martanda Varma (r 1729–58) created his own army and tried to keep the local Syrian Orthodox trading community onside by limiting the activities of European traders. Trade in many goods, with the exception of pepper, became a royal monopoly, especially under Martanda's son Rama Varma (r 1758–98).

The British Take Hold

Initially the British East India Company was supposedly interested only in trade, not conquest. But Mysore's rulers proved something of a vexation. In 1780 Hyder Ali formed an alliance with the nizam of Hyderabad and the Marathas to attack all three British bases in India (Bombay, Madras and Bengal). It came to nothing but left the British keen to quash the Mysore menace. This time the Marathas and Hyderabad allied with the British against Mysore, now led by Tipu Sultan, whose river-island citadel, Seringapatam (now Srirangapatnam), fell in 1793 after a year-long siege.

> The British never actually attempted to annex Goa but, in 1839, the British government offered to buy Goa from the Portuguese for half a million pounds.

Within the East India Company there was a growing opinion that only total control of India would satisfy British trading interests. This was reinforced by fears of a renewed French bid for land in India following Napoleon's Egyptian expedition of 1798–99. The company's governor-general, Lord Richard Wellesley, ordered a new strike against Mysore, with an ally in the nizam of Hyderabad (who was required to disband his French-trained troops in return for British protection). Tipu Sultan,

1869	1885	1891	1919
The birth of Mohandas Karamchand Gandhi in Porbandar (Gujarat) – the man who would later become popularly known as Mahatma Gandhi, 'Father of the Nation'.	The Indian National Congress, India's first home-grown political organisation, is set up. It brings educated Indians together and plays a key role in India's enduring freedom struggle.	BR Ambedkar, activist, economist, lawyer and writer, is born to a poor outcast family. He earns several advanced degrees, becomes a Buddhist and advocates forcefully for Dalit rights.	The massacre, on 13 April, of unarmed Indian protesters at Jallianwala Bagh in Amritsar (Punjab). Gandhi responds with his program of civil (non-violent) disobedience against British rule.

who may have counted on support from the French, was killed when the British stormed Seringapatam in 1799.

Wellesley restored the old ruling family, the Wodeyars, to half of Tipu's kingdom; the rest went to Hyderabad and the East India Company. Thanjavur and Karnataka were also absorbed by the British, who, when the rulers of the day died, pensioned off their successors. By 1818 the Marathas, racked by internal strife, had collapsed and most of India was under British influence. In the south, the East India Company had direct control over the Madras Presidency, which stretched from present-day Andhra Pradesh to the southern tip of the subcontinent, and across to northern parts of the Kerala coast. Travancore, Hyderabad and Mysore and other, smaller, chunks of the interior kept their nominal independence as 'princely states', but they were closely watched by their British Residents (de facto governors). Similarly, much of Maharashtra was part of the Bombay Presidency, but there were a dozen or so small princely states scattered around, including Kolhapur, Sawantwadi, Aundh and Janjira.

The First War of Independence (Indian Uprising)

In 1857, half a century after establishing firm control over India, the British suffered a serious setback. To this day, the causes of the Uprising (known at the time as the Indian Mutiny and subsequently labelled by nationalist historians as a War of Independence) are the subject of debate. Key factors included the influx of cheap goods, such as textiles, from Britain that destroyed many livelihoods; the dispossession of territories from many rulers; and taxes imposed on landowners.

The incident that's popularly held to have sparked the Uprising, however, took place at an army barracks in Meerut in Uttar Pradesh on 10 May 1857. A rumour leaked out that a new type of bullet was greased with what Hindus claimed was cow fat, while Muslims maintained that it came from pigs; pigs are considered unclean to Muslims, and cows are sacred to Hindus. Since loading a rifle involved biting the end off the waxed cartridge, these rumours provoked considerable unrest.

The commanding officer in Meerut lined up his soldiers and ordered them to bite off the ends of their issued bullets. Those who refused were marched off to prison. The following morning, the garrison's soldiers rebelled, shot their officers and marched to Delhi. Of the 74 Indian battalions of the Bengal army, seven (one of them Gurkhas) remained loyal, 20 were disarmed and the other 47 mutinied. The soldiers and peasants rallied around the ageing, reluctant Mughal emperor Bahadur Shah Zafar in Delhi. They held Delhi for some months and besieged the British Res-

HISTORY THE FIRST WAR OF INDEPENDENCE (INDIAN UPRISING)

Two fascinating books on princely Hyderabad are John Zubrzycki's *The Last Nizam*, tracing the Asaf Jahi dynasty from its 18th-century beginnings to the present day, and William Dalrymple's *White Mughals*, focusing on the love affair and marriage between British Resident James Achilles Kirkpatrick and local woman Khair-un-Nissa two centuries ago.

The Story of India with Michael Wood is an excellent BBC television series in DVD form with six 50-minute episodes. Also available as a book.

1940	1942	1947	1947–48
The Muslim League adopts its Lahore Resolution, which champions greater Muslim autonomy in India. Campaigns for the creation of a separate Islamic nation follow.	Mahatma Gandhi launches the nonviolent Quit India campaign, demanding that the British leave India without delay and allow the country to get on with self-governance.	India gains independence on 15 August. Pakistan is formed a day earlier. Partition brings a mass cross-border exodus and massacres, as Hindus, Muslims and Sikhs migrate to their respective nations.	First war between India and Pakistan takes place after the (procrastinating) Maharaja of Kashmir signs the Instrument of Accession that cedes his state to India. Pakistan challenges the document's legality.

idency in Lucknow for five months before they were finally suppressed. The incident left festering sores on both sides.

Almost immediately the East India Company was wound up, and direct control of the country was assumed by the British government, which announced its support for the existing rulers of the princely states, claiming they would not interfere in local matters as long as the states remained loyal to the British. Though not felt as strongly in the south as in the north, the First War of Independence kicked off calls for self-rule all over India.

David Davidar's novel The House of Blue Mangoes weaves the story of three generations of a family at the southern tip of India against the backdrop of the decades leading up to Independence.

The Road to Independence & the Partition of India

The desire of many Indians to be free from foreign rule remained. Opposition to the British began to increase at the turn of the 20th century, spearheaded by the Indian National Congress (Congress Party), the nation's oldest political party, formed in 1885. The fight for independence gained momentum when, in April 1919, following riots in Amritsar (Punjab), a British army contingent was sent to quell the unrest. The army ruthlessly fired into a crowd of unarmed protesters attending a meeting, killing an estimated 1500 people. News of the massacre spread rapidly throughout India, turning huge numbers of otherwise apolitical Indians into Congress supporters. The Congress movement found a new leader in Mohandas Gandhi, better known as Mahatma Gandhi.

After three decades of intense nonviolent campaigning for an independent India, Gandhi's dream finally materialised. However, despite his plea for a united India, the Muslim League's leader, Mohammed Ali Jinnah, demanded a separate state for India's sizeable Muslim population, and the decision was made to split the country.

Indian Summer, by Alex von Tunzelmann, is a brilliant, detailed account of the road to Independence, with much focus on the personal lives of the main protagonists including the love affair between Jawaharlal Nehru, independent India's first prime minister, and Edwina Mountbatten, wife of the last British viceroy.

The Partition of India in 1947 contained all the ingredients for an epic disaster, but the resulting bloodshed was far worse than anticipated. Massive population exchanges took place. Train-fulls of Muslims, fleeing westward into Pakistan, were held up and slaughtered by Hindu and Sikh mobs. Hindus and Sikhs fleeing to the east into India suffered the same fate at Muslim hands. By the time the chaos had run its course, more than 10 million people had changed sides and at least 500,000 had been killed.

India and Pakistan became sovereign nations under the British Commonwealth in August 1947, but the violence, migrations and uncertainty over a few states, especially Kashmir, continued. The violence over Kashmir – then a predominantly Muslim-populated state with a Hindu maharaja, which officially became part of India in October 1947 – continues today, and is estimated to have killed around 47,000 people so far.

1948	17 September 1948	November 1949	26 January 1950
Mahatma Gandhi is assassinated in New Delhi by Nathuram Godse on 30 January. Godse and his co-conspirator Narayan Apte are later tried, convicted and executed (by hanging).	Asaf Jah VII, the last nizam of Hyderabad, surrenders to the Indian government. His Muslim dynasty was receiving support from Pakistan but had refused to join either new nation.	The Constitution of India, drafted over two years by a 308-member Constituent Assembly, is adopted. The Assembly included dozens of members from the Scheduled Castes (Dalits).	India becomes a republic. Date commemorates the Purna Swaraj Declaration, or Declaration of Independence, put forth by the Indian National Congress in 1930.

Many of the terrorist attacks that have hit tourist spots in India have a Kashmiri link, including the 2008 Mumbai terror attacks.

The Constitution of India was at last adopted in November 1949 and went into effect on 26 January 1950 when, after untold struggle, independent India officially became a republic.

Mahatma Gandhi

One of the great figures of the 20th century, Mohandas Karamchand Gandhi was born on 2 October 1869 in Porbandar, Gujarat. After studying in London (1888–91), he worked as a barrister in South Africa. Here, the young Gandhi became politicised, railing against the racial discrimination he encountered. He soon became the spokesperson for South Africa's Indian community, championing equality for all.

Gandhi returned to India in 1915 with the doctrine of ahimsa (nonviolence) central to his political plans, and committed to a simple and disciplined lifestyle. He set up the Sabarmati Ashram in Ahmedabad, which was innovative for its admission of Untouchables (now known as Dalits).

Within a year, Gandhi had won his first victory, defending farmers in Bihar from exploitation. It's said that this was when he first received the title 'Mahatma' (Great Soul) from an admirer. The passage of the discriminatory Rowlatt Acts (which allowed certain political cases to be tried without juries) in 1919 spurred him to further action and he organised a national protest. In the days following this hartal (strike), feelings ran high throughout the country. After the massacre of unarmed protesters in Amritsar (Punjab), a deeply shocked Gandhi immediately called off the movement.

By 1920 Gandhi was a key figure in the Indian National Congress, and he coordinated a national campaign of satyagraha (passive resistance) to British rule, with the effect of raising nationalist feeling while earning the lasting enmity of the British. In early 1930 Gandhi captured the imagination of the country, and the world, when he led a march of several thousand followers from Ahmedabad to Dandi on the coast of Gujarat. On arrival, Gandhi ceremoniously made salt by evaporating seawater, thus publicly defying the much-hated British-imposed salt tax; not for the first time, he was imprisoned. Released in 1931 to represent the Indian National Congress at the second Round Table Conference in London, he won the hearts of many British people but failed to gain any real concessions from the government.

Disillusioned with politics, Gandhi resigned from the Congress Party in 1934. He returned spectacularly to the fray in 1942 with the Quit India campaign, in which he urged the British to leave India immediately. His actions were deemed subversive and he and most of the Congress leader-ship were imprisoned.

The Nehrus and the Gandhis is Tariq Ali's astute portrait-history of these families and the India over which they cast their long shadow.

Gandhi in South India

Sevagram (Maharashtra)

Mani Bhavan (Mumbai)

Gandhi National Memorial (Pune)

Gandhi Memorial Museum (Madurai)

Gandhi Memorial (Kanyakumari)

1956–60	1961	1965	1966
Indian states are reorganised on linguistic lines, giving birth to modern Maharashtra, Andhra Pradesh, Kerala, Mysore (Karnataka) and Madras (Tamil Nadu) states.	In a military action code-named 'Operation Vijay' the Indian government sends armed troops into Goa and – with surprisingly little resistance – ends over four centuries of Portuguese colonial rule in the region.	Skirmishes in Kashmir and the disputed Rann of Kutch in Gujarat flare into the Second India-Pakistan War, said to have involved the biggest tank battles since WWII. The war ends with a UN-mandated ceasefire.	Indira Gandhi, daughter of independent India's first prime minister, Jawaharlal Nehru, becomes prime minister of India. She has so far been India's only female prime minister.

In the frantic Independence bargaining that followed the end of WWII, Gandhi was largely excluded and watched helplessly as plans were made to partition the country – a dire tragedy in his eyes. Gandhi stood almost alone in urging tolerance and the preservation of a single India, and his work on behalf of members of all communities drew resentment from some Hindu hardliners. On his way to a prayer meeting in Delhi on 30 January 1948, he was assassinated by a Hindu zealot, Nathuram Godse.

In 21st-century India, including the south, Mahatma Gandhi continues to be an iconic figure, still widely revered as the 'Father of the Nation'.

> A golden oldie, *Gandhi* (1982), directed by Richard Attenborough, is one of few films to engagingly capture the grand canvas that is India in tracing the country's bumpy road to Independence.

Carving up the South

While the chaos of Partition was mostly felt in the north – mainly in Punjab, Kashmir and Bengal – the south faced its own problems. Though most of the princely states acceded to India peacefully, an exception was Hyderabad state, where the Indian army moved in and forcibly took control in 1948. Tens of thousands of Muslims were massacred by Hindus during and after this so-called 'police action' (p445).

In the 1950s the princely states and British-delineated provinces were dismantled and South India was reorganised into states along linguistic lines. Mysore state was extended in 1956 into the Kannada-speaking state of Greater Mysore, which was renamed Karnataka in 1972.

Malayalam-speaking Kerala was created in 1956 from Travancore (except for its Tamil-speaking far south), Cochin (now Kochi) and Malabar (formerly part of the Madras Presidency). The maharajas in both Travancore and Cochin were especially attentive to the provision of basic services and education, and their legacy today is India's most literate state. Kerala also blazed a trail in post-Independence India by becoming the first state in the world to freely elect a communist government in 1957.

> In 1997 KR Narayanan became India's president, the first member of the lowest Hindu caste (the Dalits; formerly known as Untouchables) to hold the position.

Andhra Pradesh was created in 1956 by combining the Telugu-speaking Andhra state (the northern parts of the old Madras Presidency) with Telugu-speaking areas of the old Hyderabad state. In 2014 the latter were separated off as the new state of Telangana, after years of complaints that they were neglected and exploited within Andhra Pradesh; Hyderabad remains capital of both states until Andhra Pradesh's new capital, Amaravati, is eventually completed.

Tamil Nadu was the name given in 1968 to the former Madras state, which since 1956 had comprised the Tamil-speaking areas of the old Madras Presidency plus the southernmost areas of the former Travancore kingdom (also Tamil-speaking).

The creation of Maharashtra was one of the most contested issues of the language-based demarcation of states. After Independence, western Maharashtra and Gujarat were joined to form Bombay state, to which Marathi-speaking parts of Hyderabad and Madhya Pradesh states were added

1971	1984	1991	2004
East Pakistan seeks independence from West Pakistan. India gets involved, sparking the Third India-Pakistan War. West Pakistan surrenders, losing sovereignty of East Pakistan, which becomes Bangladesh.	Prime Minister Indira Gandhi is assassinated by two of her Sikh bodyguards after her highly controversial decision to have Indian troops storm Amritsar's Golden Temple, the Sikhs' holiest shrine.	Former prime minister Rajiv Gandhi, son of Indira Gandhi, is assassinated by a suicide bomber believed to belong to Sri Lanka's Tamil Tigers, at Sriperumbudur near Chennai (formerly Madras).	A tsunami batters coastal parts of eastern and South India as well as the Andaman and Nicobar Islands, killing over 10,000 people and leaving hundreds of thousands homeless.

THE 1948 HYDERABAD STATE MASSACRE

Upon Independence in 1947, the Muslim nizam of Hyderabad refused to join India. Although only he and about 10% of his subjects were Muslims, the nizam was friendlier with Islamic Pakistan than with India, and favoured the idea of Hyderabad remaining an independent state (a concept that independent India's new Nehru-led government opposed). Following a communist-led rebellion and attacks on Hindus by the Muslim Razakar Militia, the Indian Army seized power in Hyderabad state in September 1948 in what was called 'police action'. The nizam quickly surrendered, but, during and after the 'police action', Muslims across Hyderabad state were terrorised, with allegations of looting, arson, abduction, mass rape and mass murder at the hands of some members of the Indian Army and, mostly, local Hindus. However, an investigating team of mixed religion, led by Hindu congressman Pandit Sunderlal, also reported that most Indian Army soldiers had protected Muslims. According to BBC reporting, an estimated 27,000 to 40,000 people are believed to have died, though others claim the figures may have reached 200,000.

It is only in recent years that details about this massacre – a seemingly forgotten, violent chapter of Indian history – have started to trickle out. In its immediate aftermath, Sunderlal's team rushed to Hyderabad to put together a report on the carnage – but it was never published. Some historians argue that Nehru's government covered up what happened, probably because it feared the revelation would lead to retaliatory attacks on Hindus by Muslims and yet more widespread violence across India. There have been some recent calls from the Indian press to make the Sunderlal report more widely available, but, in general, the 1948 Hyderabad events remain surprisingly untalked about in modern-day India.

in 1956. In 1960, after agitation by both Marathis and Gujaratis, Bombay state was divided into the existing states of Maharashtra and Gujarat.

The French relinquished Puducherry (Pondicherry) in 1954 – 140 years after reclaiming it from the British. It's a Union Territory (controlled by the government in Delhi), though largely self-governing. Lakshadweep was granted Union Territory status in 1956, as were the Andaman and Nicobar Islands.

Throughout most of this carve-up, Goa was still under Portuguese rule. Although a rumbling independence movement had existed in Goa since the early 20th century, the Indian government was reluctant to take Goa by force, hoping the Portuguese would leave of their own volition. The Portuguese refused, so in December 1961 Indian troops crossed the border and liberated the state with surprisingly little resistance. It became a Union Territory of India, but after splitting from Daman and Diu (Gujarat) in 1987, it was officially recognised as the 25th state of the Indian Union.

2008	May 2014	June 2014	5 December 2016
On 26 November a series of coordinated bombing and shooting attacks on landmark Mumbai sites begins; the terrorist attacks last three days and kill at least 163 people.	Narendra Modi, born into a Gujarati family, becomes prime minister after achieving a historic landslide victory for the Hindu-nationalist-oriented Bharatiya Janata Party (BJP), routing the Congress Party.	The northern part of Andhra Pradesh splits off to become India's 29th state, Telangana, following years of agitation and allegations of neglect and unfair treatment.	Tamil Nadu's adored former Chief Minister Jayalalithaa Jayaram – one of India's most popular and controversial politicians – passes away in Chennai, following several months of illness.

The Way of Life

Spirituality is the common thread in the richly diverse tapestry that is India. It, along with family, lies at the heart of society, and these two tenets intertwine in ceremonies to celebrate life's milestones. Despite the rising number of nuclear families – primarily in the more cosmopolitan cities such as Mumbai (Bombay), Bengaluru (Bangalore) and Delhi – the extended family remains a cornerstone in both urban and rural India, with males – usually the breadwinners – considered the head of the household.

Marriage, Birth & Death

South India's different religions practise different traditions, but for all communities, marriage, birth and death are important and marked with traditional ceremonies according to faith. Hindus are the 80% majority in India, while only 14.2% of the population is Muslim (though at 176 million, Indian Muslims roughly equal the population of Pakistan).

Marriage is an exceptionally auspicious event for Indians – for most Indians, the idea of being unmarried by their mid-30s is unpalatable. Although 'love marriages' have spiralled upward in recent times (mainly in urban hubs), most Indian marriages are still arranged, be the family Hindu, Muslim, Sikh or Buddhist. Discreet enquiries are made within the community. If a suitable match is not found, the help of professional matchmakers may be sought, or advertisements may be placed in newspapers and/or on the internet. In Hindu families, the horoscopes of both potential partners are checked and, if propitious, there's a meeting between the two families.

Dowries, although illegal since 1961, are still a key issue in many arranged marriages (mostly in conservative communities), with some families plunging into debt to raise the required cash and merchandise. Figures from the National Crime Records Bureau (NCRB) suggest that a woman is murdered roughly every hour over dowry demands; the majority are young, new brides. Health workers claim that India's high rate of abortion of female fetuses (sex identification medical tests are banned in India, but they still clandestinely occur) is predominantly due to the financial burden of providing a daughter's dowry. Muslim grooms have to pay what is called a *mehr* to the bride.

The Hindu wedding ceremony is officiated over by a priest and the marriage is formalised when the couple walk around a sacred fire seven times. Muslim ceremonies involve the reading of the Quran; traditionally the husband and wife view each other via mirrors. Despite the existence of nuclear families, it's still the norm for a wife to live with her husband's family once married and assume the household duties outlined by her mother-in-law.

Divorce and remarriage is becoming more common (primarily in bigger cities), but divorce is still not granted by courts as a matter of routine and is not looked upon favourably by society. Among the higher castes, in more traditional areas, widows are traditionally expected not to remarry and to wear white and live pious, celibate lives. It is still legal for Muslim males in India to obtain oral divorce according to sharia law (by uttering

Matchmaking is now, inevitably, online, with popular sites including www.shaadi.com, www.bharat matrimony.com and, in a sign of the times, www.secondshaadi.com – for those seeking a partner again.

the word *talaq* ('divorce') three times, though these days it's increasingly emailed or texted).

The birth of a child is another momentous occasion, with special ceremonies that take place at various auspicious times during the early years of childhood. For Hindus these include the casting of the child's first horoscope, name-giving, feeding the first solid food, and the first hair cutting.

Hindus cremate their dead, and funeral ceremonies are designed to purify and console both the living and the deceased. An important aspect of the proceedings is the *sharadda*, paying respect to one's ancestors by offering water and rice cakes, repeated at each anniversary of the death. After the cremation, the ashes are collected and, 13 days after the death (when blood relatives are deemed ritually pure), a member of the family scatters them in a holy river such as the Ganges or in the ocean. Sikhs similarly wash then cremate their dead. Muslims also prepare their dead carefully, but bury them. The minority Zoroastrian Parsi community place their dead in 'Towers of Silence' (stone towers) to be devoured by vultures.

The Wonder That was India by AL Basham proffers descriptions of Indian civilisations, major religions and social customs – a good thematic approach to weave the disparate strands together.

The Caste System

Although the Indian constitution does not recognise the caste system, caste still wields powerful influence, especially in rural India, where the caste you are born into largely determines your social standing and your vocational and marriage prospects. Castes are further divided into thousands of *jati*, groups of 'families' or social communities, which are sometimes but not always linked to occupation. Conservative Hindus will only marry someone of the same *jati*. In some traditional areas, young men and women who fall in love outside their caste have been murdered.

According to tradition, caste is the basic social structure of Hindu society. Living a righteous life and fulfilling your dharma (moral duty) raises your chances of being reborn into a higher caste. Hindus are born into one of four varnas (castes): Brahmin (priests and scholars), Kshatriya (soldiers and administrators), Vaishya (merchants) and Shudra (labourers). The Brahmins were said to have emerged from the mouth of Lord

INDIAN ATTIRE

Widely worn by Indian women, the beautiful, elegant sari comes in a single piece (between 5m and 9m long and 1m wide), ingeniously tucked and pleated into place without pins or buttons. Worn with the sari is the choli (tight-fitting blouse) and a drawstring petticoat. The *palloo* is the part of the sari draped over the shoulder. Also commonly worn is the *salwar kameez*, a traditional dresslike tunic and trouser combination for women, accompanied by a dupatta (long scarf).

Traditional attire for men includes the dhoti, and in the south the *lungi* and the *mundu*. The dhoti is a loose, long loincloth pulled up between the legs. The *lungi* is more like a sarong, with its end usually sewn up like a tube. The *mundu* is like a *lungi* but always white. A kurta is a long tunic or shirt worn mainly by men, usually with no collar. Kurta pyjama is a cotton shirt and trousers set worn for relaxing or sleeping. *Churidar* are close-fitting trousers often worn under a kurta. A *sherwani* is a long coatlike men's garment, which originated as a fusion of the *salwar kameez* with the British frock coat.

There are regional and religious variations in costume – for example, you may see Muslim women wearing the all-enveloping burka.

In South India's bigger cities, like Mumbai, and touristy areas such as Goa and Kerala, Western-style clothing is increasingly common, particularly among younger-generation Indians.

ADIVASIS

India's Adivasis (tribal communities; Adivasi translates to 'original inhabitant' in Sanskrit) have origins that precede the Vedic Aryans and the Dravidians of the south. These groups range from the Gondi of the central plains and the animist tribes of the Northeast States to Tamil Nadu's Todas. Today, they constitute less than 10% of the population and are comprised of more than 400 different tribal groups. Around 95% of India's Adivasis live in rural areas, mostly in mountain regions. The literacy rate for Adivasis is significantly below the national average.

Historically, contact between Adivasis and Hindu villagers on the plains rarely led to friction as there was little or no competition for resources and land. However, in recent decades an increasing number of Adivasis have been dispossessed of their ancestral land and turned into impoverished labourers. Although they still have political representation thanks to a parliamentary quota system, the dispossession and exploitation of Adivasis has reportedly sometimes been with the connivance of officialdom – an accusation the government denies. Unless more is done, the Adivasis' future is an uncertain one.

Read more about Adivasis in *Archaeology and History: Early Settlements in the Andaman Islands* by Zarine Cooper, *The Tribals of India* by Sunil Janah and *Tribes of India: The Struggle for Survival* by Christoph von Fürer-Haimendorf.

Brahma at the moment of creation, Kshatriyas from his arms, Vaishyas from his thighs and Shudras from his feet.

Beneath the four main castes are the Dalits (formerly Untouchables), who hold menial jobs such as sweepers and latrine cleaners. Many of India's complex codes of ritual purity were devised to prevent physical contact between people of higher castes and Dalits. A less rigid system exists in Islamic communities in India, with society divided into *ashraf* (high born), *ajlaf* (low born) and *arzal* (equivalent to the Dalits). The word 'pariah' is derived from the name of a Tamil Dalit group, the Paraiyars. Some Dalit leaders, such as the renowned Dr BR Ambedkar (1891–1956), sought to change their status by adopting another faith – in his case, Buddhism.

If you want to learn more about India's caste system, read *Interrogating Caste* by Dipankar Gupta and *Translating Caste* edited by Tapan Basu.

At the bottom of the social heap are the Denotified Tribes. They were known as the Criminal Tribes until 1952, when a reforming law officially recognised 198 tribes and castes. Many are nomadic or seminomadic tribes, forced to eke out a living on society's fringes.

To improve the Dalits' position, the government reserves a considerable number of public-sector jobs, parliamentary seats and university places for them. Today these quotas account for almost 25% of government jobs and university (student) positions. The situation varies regionally, as different political leaders chase caste vote-banks by promising to include them in reservations. The reservation system, while generally regarded in a favourable light, has also been criticised for unfairly blocking tertiary and employment opportunities for those who would have otherwise got positions on merit. On the other hand, there is still regular discrimination against Dalits in daily life.

Pilgrimage

Devout Hindus are expected to go on a *yatra* (pilgrimage) at least once a year. Pilgrimages are undertaken to implore the gods or goddesses to grant a wish, to take the ashes of a cremated relative to a holy river, or to gain spiritual merit. The elderly often make Varanasi their final one, as it's believed that dying in this sacred city releases a person from the cycle of rebirth. The pilgrimage to Sabarimala (p290) in Kerala is one of India's largest Hindu pilgrimages. Sufi shrines in India attract thousands of

Muslims to commemorate holy days, such as the birthday of a sufi saint; many Muslims also make the hajj to Mecca in Saudi Arabia.

Most festivals in India are spiritual occasions, rooted in religion (even those that have a carnivalesque sheen), and are thus a magnet for throngs of pilgrims. Remember to behave respectfully at festivals. Be aware that there are deaths at festivals every year because of stampedes.

Women in South India

According to the most recent census (2011), India's population includes 586 million women, with an estimated 68% of these working in the agricultural sector. Women in India are entitled to vote and own property. While the percentage of women in politics has risen over the past decade, they're still notably underrepresented in the national parliament, accounting for 11% of parliamentary members.

Although the professions are male dominated, women are steadily making inroads, especially in urban centres. Kerala was India's first state to break societal norms by recruiting female police officers (1938) and establishing an all-female police station (1973). For village women it's much more difficult to get ahead, but groups such as Gujarat's Self-Employed Women's Association (SEWA; www.sewa.org) have shown what's possible, organising socially disadvantaged women into unions and offering microfinance loans.

In low-income families especially, girls can be regarded as a serious financial liability because a marriage dowry must often be supplied. An estimated 300,000 to 600,000 female fetuses are illegally aborted each year as a result.

For the urban middle-class woman, life is much more comfortable, though pressures still exist. Broadly speaking, she is far more likely to receive a tertiary education, but once married is still usually expected to 'fit in' with her in-laws and be a homemaker. Like her village counterpart, if she fails to live up to expectations – even if it's just not being able to produce a grandson – the consequences can sometimes be dire, as demonstrated by the extreme practice of 'bride burning', wherein a wife is doused with flammable liquid and set alight, typically by her husband or mother-in-law. In 2013 the National Crime Records Bureau (NCRB) figures reported 8083 incidences, around one every hour; it's thought that actual numbers are even higher. Acid attacks by would-be suitors on women who have rejected them are also common.

Although the constitution allows for divorcees (and widows) to remarry, relatively few reportedly do so: divorcees are traditionally considered outcasts from society. Divorce rates in India are among the worlds' lowest, though rising. Most divorces happen in urban centres and are deemed less socially unacceptable among upper society.

In October 2006, following women's civil rights campaigns, the Indian parliament passed a landmark bill (on top of existing legislation) which gives women suffering domestic violence increased protection and rights. Prior to this legislation, although women could lodge police complaints against abusive spouses, they weren't automatically entitled to a share of the marital property or to ongoing financial support. Critics claim that many women, especially those outside India's larger cities, are still reluctant to seek legal protection because of the social stigma involved. Despite legal reforms, conviction rates remain low enough for perpetrators to feel a sense of impunity. A 2012 Unicef study revealed that almost 60% of Indian adolescent males believe it's justifiable to beat a wife.

India remains an extremely prudish and conservative society, and despite the highly sexualised images of women churned out by Bollywood,

The distressing, important BBC documentary *India's Daughter*, directed by Leslee Udwin, details the events of the much-publicised 2012 Delhi gang rape and murder of Jyoti Singh. The documentary was banned in India (after it emerged that the filmmakers had interviewed one of the jailed rapists), but widely circulated online.

As of 2016, Prime Minister Narendra Modi's Beti Bachao, Beti Padhao (Save the Daughter, Teach the Daughter) campaign – launched to fight gender inequality by discouraging female feticide – includes publicly screened antidowry 'adverts' in which Indian brides fight back against their dominating, dowry-demanding in-laws.

many traditionally minded people consider a woman wanton if she so much as goes out after dark.

According to India's NCRB, reported incidences of rape have gone up over 50% in the last 10 years (34,000 rape cases were reported in 2015), but most sexual assaults go unreported, due to family pressure and/or shame, especially if the perpetrator is known to the family (often the case). Women themselves continue to be blamed for rapes.

Following the highly publicised gang rape and murder of 23-year-old Indian physiotherapy student Jyoti Singh (Nirbhaya, 'Fearless One') in Delhi in December 2012, tens of thousands of people protested in the capital, and beyond, demanding swift government action to address the country's escalating gender-based violence. It took a further year before legal amendments were made to existing laws to address the problem of sexual violence, including stiffer punishments such as life imprisonment and the death penalty. There is still limited recognition of marital rape (a horrifically common phenomenon) and government permission is necessary before security forces can be prosecuted for criminal offences.

Despite the action taken, shocking cases are horrifyingly regular occurrences. The NCRB reported that in 2015, 327,394 gender-based crimes were committed against women. Of these, 34,651 were rape and 84,222 were 'other' sexual offences (sexual harassment, assault, stalking, kidnapping etc). The conviction rate for rape was just 27.1% in 2013, the same year that a 22-year-old photojournalist was gang raped in Mumbai (Bombay). In 2014 a Danish woman was gang raped in Delhi, and most recently, there has been international outcry over the 'mass molestation' of women by groups of men in Bengaluru (Bangalore) on New Year's Eve 2016 – just a few in a long line of recent sexual assaults on women in India. It's doubtless that sexual violence is a pervasive social problem in India and, despite government efforts, including Modi's Beti Bachao, Beti Padhao (Save the Daughter, Teach the Daughter) campaign and harsher sentences, remains rampant. Most female visitors' Indian travels progress safely, but it is important to be careful and alert (p492).

Sport

Cricket has long been engraved on the Indian nation's heart, with the first recorded match in 1721, and India's first test match victory in 1952 in Chennai (Madras) against England. It's not only a national sporting obsession, but a matter of enormous patriotism, especially evident whenever India plays against Pakistan. Matches between these South Asian neighbours – who have had rocky relations since Independence – put players under immense pressure to do their respective countries proud. The most celebrated Indian cricketer of recent years is Sachin Tendulkar (the 'Little Master'), who, in 2012, became the world's only player to score 100 international centuries, retiring on a high the following year. Cricket – especially the Twenty20 format (www.cricket20.com) – is big business in India, attracting lucrative sponsorship deals and celebrity status for its players. In 2016 India hosted the ICC World Twenty20, into its sixth edition. International games are played at various centres – see Indian newspapers or check online for details. Keep your finger on the cricketing pulse at www.espncricinfo.com (rated most highly by many cricket aficionados) and www.cricbuzz.com.

The 2013 launch of the Indian Super League (ISL; www.indiansuperleague.com) has achieved its aim of promoting football as a big-time, big-money sport. With huge crowds, celebrity funding and international players, such as legendary Juventus footballer Alessandro del Piero (who was signed for the Delhi Dynamos in 2014, then retired a year later) or Marco Materazzi (of World Cup headbutt fame) as trainer of Chennai,

---

Sati: A Study of Widow Burning in India by Sakuntala Narasimhan explores the history of *sati* (a widow's ritual suicide on her husband's funeral pyre; now banned) on the subcontinent.

Based on Rabindranath Tagore's novel, *Chokher Bali* (directed by Rituparno Ghosh) is a poignant film about a young widow living in early 20th-century Bengal who challenges the 'rules of widowhood' – something unthinkable in that era.

India has one of the world's largest diasporas – over 25 million people – with Indian banks holding an estimated US$70 billion in Non-Resident Indian (NRI) accounts.

HIJRAS

India's most visible nonheterosexual group is the *hijras*, a caste of transvestites and eunuchs who dress in women's clothing. Some are gay, some are hermaphrodites and some were unfortunate enough to be kidnapped and castrated. *Hijras* have been part of the subcontinent's culture for thousands of years. In 2014 the Indian Supreme Court officially recognised *hijras* as a third gender and as a class entitled to reservation in education and jobs. Conversely, in 2013, homosexuality was ruled to be unlawful (having been legal since 2009), though in 2016 the Supreme Court agreed to reconsider this decision.

Hijras work mainly as uninvited entertainers at weddings and celebrations of the birth of male children, and possibly as prostitutes. In 2014, Tamil Nadu's Padmini Prakash became India's first transgender daily television news show anchor, indicating a new level of acceptance.

Read more about *hijras* in *The Invisibles* by Zia Jaffrey and *Ardhanarishvara the Androgyne* by Dr Alka Pande.

the ISL has become an international talking point. The I-League is the longer-running, less popular domestic league.

India is also known for its historical links to horse polo, which intermittently thrived on the subcontinent (especially among nobility) until Independence, after which patronage steeply declined due to dwindling funds. Today there's a renewed interest in polo thanks to beefed-up sponsorship, and it's attracting attention from the country's burgeoning upper middle class. Believed to have its roots in Persia and China around 2000 years ago, polo is thought to have first been played on the subcontinent in Baltistan (in present-day Pakistan). Some say that Emperor Akbar (who reigned in India from 1556 to 1605) first introduced rules to the game, but that polo, as it's played today, was largely influenced by a British cavalry regiment stationed in India during the 1870s. The world's oldest surviving polo club, established in 1862, is Kolkata's Calcutta Polo Club (www.calcuttapolo.com). Polo takes place during the cooler winter months in major cities, including Delhi, Jaipur, Mumbai, Kolkata (Calcutta) and Hyderabad, and occasionally in Ladakh and Manipur.

Although officially the national sport, field hockey no longer enjoys the same fervent following it once did, though, as of 2016, India's national men's/women's hockey world rankings are 6/12 respectively. During its golden era, between 1928 and 1956, India won six consecutive Olympic gold medals in hockey; it later bagged two further Olympic gold medals, one in 1964 and the other in 1980. Tap into India's hockey scene at Hockey India (http://hockeyindia.org) and Indian Field Hockey (www.bharatiyahockey.org).

Kabaddi is another competitive sport popular across India and especially in Tamil Nadu. Two teams each occupy one side of a court. A raider runs into the opposing side, taking a breath and trying to tag one or more members of the opposite team. The raider chants 'kabaddi' repeatedly to show that they have not taken a breath, returning to the home half before exhaling.

Other sports which are gaining ground in India include tennis (the country's star performers are Sania Mirza, Leander Paes and Mahesh Bhupathi; delve deeper at www.aitatennis.com) and horse racing, which is reasonably popular in larger cities such as Mumbai, Delhi, Kolkata and Bengaluru (Bangalore), and in Ooty (Udhagamandalam).

At the 2016 Rio Olympics, India scored just two medals – both by women. PV Sindhu became the first Indian woman to win a silver medal (for badminton), while Sakshi Malik set a record as India's first female wrestler to win an Olympic medal (bronze).

Cricket lovers are likely to be bowled over by *The Illustrated History of Indian Cricket* by Boria Majumdar and *The States of Indian Cricket* by Ramachandra Guha.

Several of the Indian Super League teams are co-owned by Bollywood superstars, for example, Pune by Hrithik Roshan, Mumbai City by Ranbir Kapoor, and Chennai by Abhishek Bachchan.

Spiritual India

From elaborate city shrines to simple village temples, spirituality suffuses almost every facet of life in India. The nation's major faith, Hinduism, is practised by around 80% of the population and is one of the world's oldest extant religions, with roots extending beyond 1000 BC. Buddhism, Jainism and Zoroastrianism are also among the oldest religions, dating back to the 6th century BC.

Hinduism

Hinduism has no founder or central authority and it isn't a proselytising religion. Hindus believe in Brahman, who is eternal, uncreated and infinite. Everything that exists emanates from Brahman and will ultimately return to it. The multitude of gods and goddesses are merely manifestations – knowable aspects of this formless phenomenon.

Hindus believe that earthly life is cyclical: you are born again and again (a process known as 'samsara'), the quality of these rebirths depending upon your karma (conduct or action) in previous lives. Living a righteous life and fulfilling your dharma (moral code of behaviour; social duty) will enhance your chances of being born into a higher caste and better circumstances. Alternatively, if enough bad karma has accumulated, rebirth may take animal form. But it's only as a human that you can gain sufficient self-knowledge to escape the cycle of reincarnation and achieve moksha (liberation). Almost 80% of India's population is Hindu.

Gods & Godesses

All Hindu deities are regarded as manifestations of Brahman, who is often described as having three main representations, the Trimurti: Brahma, Vishnu and Shiva.

Brahman

The One; the ultimate reality. Brahman is formless, eternal and the source of all existence. Brahman is *nirguna* (without attributes), as opposed to all the other gods and goddesses, which are manifestations of Brahman and therefore *saguna* (with attributes).

The Hindu pantheon is said to have around 330 million deities; those worshipped are a matter of personal choice or local tradition.

Brahma

Only during the creation of the universe does Brahma play an active role. At other times he is in meditation. His consort is Saraswati, goddess of learning, and his vehicle is a swan. He is sometimes shown sitting on a lotus that rises from Vishnu's navel, symbolising the interdependence of the gods. Brahma is generally depicted with four (crowned and bearded) heads, and today is the least worshipped of the Trimurti gods.

Vishnu

The preserver or sustainer, Vishnu is associated with 'right action'. He protects and sustains all that is good in the world, and has 10 avatars. He is usually depicted with four arms, holding a lotus, a conch shell (it can be blown like a trumpet so symbolises the cosmic vibration from which existence emanates), a discus and a mace. His consort is Lakshmi, goddess of wealth, and his vehicle is Garuda, the man-bird creature. The Ganges is said to flow from his feet.

Shiva

Shiva is the destroyer without whom creation couldn't occur – he destroys to deliver salvation. Shiva's creative role is phallically symbolised by his representation as the frequently worshipped lingam. With 1008 names, Shiva takes many forms, including Nataraja, lord of the *tandava* (cosmic victory dance), who paces out the creation and destruction of the cosmos.

Sometimes Shiva has snakes draped around his neck and is shown holding a trident (representative of the Trimurti) as a weapon while riding Nandi, his bull. Nandi symbolises power and potency, justice and moral order. Shiva's consort, Parvati, takes many forms.

Ganesh

Elephant-headed Ganesh is the god of good fortune, remover of obstacles and patron of scribes (the broken tusk he holds was used to write sections of the Mahabharata). His animal vehicle is Mooshak (a ratlike creature). How Ganesh came to have an elephant's head is a story with several variations. One legend says that Ganesh was born to Parvati in the absence of his father Shiva. One day, as Ganesh stood guard while his mother bathed, Shiva returned and asked to be let into Parvati's presence. Ganesh, who didn't recognise Shiva, refused. Enraged, Shiva lopped off Ganesh's head, only to later discover that he had slaughtered his own son. He vowed to replace Ganesh's head with that of the first creature he came across: an elephant. The Ganesh Chaturthi (p45) festival is particularly popular in South India.

Krishna

Krishna is the eighth incarnation of Vishnu, sent to earth to fight for good and combat evil. His dalliances with the *gopis* (milkmaids) and his love for Radha (a favourite mistress when he lived as a cowherd) have inspired countless paintings and songs. Depicted with blue-hued skin, Krishna is often seen playing the flute.

Hanuman

Hanuman is the hero of the Ramayana and loyal ally of Rama (the seventh incarnation of Vishnu). He embodies the concept of bhakti (devotion). He is the king of the monkeys, but capable of taking on other forms.

Shakti & Female Goddesses

Among Shaivites (followers of Shiva), Shakti, the universe's divine feminine creative force, is worshipped in her own right. The concept of *shakti* is embodied in the ancient goddess Devi (divine mother), who is also manifested as Durga and Amman, and in a fiercer, evil-destroying incarnation, Kali. Other widely worshipped goddesses include Lakshmi, goddess of wealth, and Saraswati, goddess of learning.

Murugan

Murugan, one of Shiva's sons, is a popular deity in South India, especially in Tamil Nadu. He is sometimes identified with another of Shiva's sons, Skanda (also Kartikiya), who enjoys a strong following in North India. Murugan's main role is that of protector, and he is depicted as young and victorious.

Unravelling the basic tenets of Hinduism are two books both called *Hinduism: An Introduction* – one by Shakunthala Jagannathan, the other by Dharam Vir Singh.

Shiva is sometimes characterised as the lord of yoga – a Himalaya-dwelling, marijuana-smoking ascetic with matted hair, an ash-smeared body and a third eye symbolising wisdom.

Ayyappan

A son of Shiva who, like Murugan, is identified with the role of protector is Ayyappan, whose temple at Sabarimala (p290) in Kerala attracts 40 to 60 million pilgrims a year. It's said that he was born from the union of Shiva and Vishnu, both male. Vishnu is said to have assumed female form (Mohini) to give birth.

Sacred Texts

Hindu sacred texts fall into two categories: those believed to be the word of god (*shruti*, meaning 'heard') and those produced by people (*smriti*, meaning 'remembered'). The Vedas are regarded as *shruti* knowledge and considered the authoritative basis for Hinduism. The oldest and longest of the Vedic texts, the Rig-Veda, was compiled over 3000 years ago. Within its 1028 verses are prayers for prosperity and longevity, as well as an explanation of the universe's origins. The Upanishads, the last parts of the Vedas, reflect on the mystery of death and emphasise the oneness of the universe. The oldest of the Vedic texts were written in Vedic Sanskrit (related to Old Persian). Later texts were composed in classical Sanskrit, but many have been translated into the vernacular.

The *smriti* texts comprise a collection of literature spanning centuries and include expositions on the proper performance of domestic ceremonies, as well as the proper pursuit of government, economics and religious law. Among its well-known works are the Ramayana and Mahabharata, as well as the Puranas, which expand on the epics and promote the notion of the Trimurti. Unlike the Vedas, reading the Puranas is not restricted to initiated higher-caste males.

The Mahabharata

Thought to have been composed around 1000 BC, the Mahabharata focuses on the exploits of Krishna. By about 500 BC the Mahabharata had evolved into a far more complex creation with substantial additions, including the Bhagavad Gita (where Krishna proffers advice to Arjuna before a battle).

The story centres on conflict between the heroic gods (Pandavas) and the demons (Kauravas). Overseeing events is Krishna, in human form. Krishna acts as charioteer for the Pandava hero Arjuna, who eventually triumphs in a great battle against the Kauravas.

The Ramayana

Composed around the 3rd or 2nd century BC, the Ramayana is believed to be largely the work of the poet Valmiki. Like the Mahabharata, it centres on conflict between the gods and the demons.

The story goes that Dasharatha, the childless king of Ayodhya, called upon the gods to provide him with a son. His wife duly gave birth to a boy. But this child, named Rama, was in fact an incarnation of Vishnu, who had assumed human form to overthrow the demon king of (Sri) Lanka, Ravana.

As an adult, Rama, who won the hand of the princess Sita in a competition, was chosen by his father to inherit his kingdom. At the last minute Rama's stepmother intervened and demanded her son, Barathan, take Rama's place. Rama, Sita and Rama's brother, Lakshmana, were exiled and went off to the forests, where Rama and Lakshmana battled demons and dark forces. Ravana captured Sita and spirited her away to his palace in Lanka.

Rama, assisted by an army of monkeys led by the loyal monkey god Hanuman, eventually found the palace, killed Ravana and rescued Sita. All returned victorious to Ayodhya, where Rama was welcomed by Bara-

Did you know that blood-drinking Kali is another form of milk-giving Gauri? *Myth = Mithya: A Handbook of Hindu Mythology*, by Devdutt Pattanaik, sheds light on this and other fascinating Hindu folklore.

Two recommended publications containing English translations of holy Hindu texts are *The Bhagavad Gita* by S Radhakrishnan and *The Valmiki Ramayana* by Romesh Dutt.

> **OM**
> ....
> One of Hinduism's most venerated symbols is 'Om'. Pronounced 'aum', it's a highly propitious mantra (sacred word or syllable). The 'three' shape symbolises the creation, maintenance and destruction of the universe (and thus the holy Trimurti). The inverted *chandra* (crescent or half moon) represents the discursive mind and the *bindu* (dot) within it, Brahman. Buddhists believe that, if intoned often enough with complete concentration, it will lead to a state of blissful emptiness.

than and crowned king. It is this legend that is celebrated in Tamil Nadu at Rameswaram's Ramanathaswamy Temple (p386).

Naturally Sacred

Animals, particularly snakes and cows, have long been worshipped on the subcontinent. For Hindus, cows represent fertility and nurturing; snakes (especially cobras) are associated with fertility and welfare. Naga stones (snake stones) serve the dual purpose of protecting humans from snakes and appeasing snake gods.

Plants can also have sacred associations. Banyan trees represent the Trimurti, and mango trees are symbolic of love – Shiva married Parvati under one. Meanwhile, the lotus flower is said to have emerged from the primeval waters and is connected to the mythical centre of the earth through its stem. Often found in the most polluted of waters, the fragile yet resolute lotus has the remarkable ability to blossom above murky depths. The centre of the lotus corresponds to the centre of the universe, the navel of the earth: all is held together by the stem and the eternal waters. Embodying beauty and strength, the lotus is a reminder to Hindus of how their own lives should be. So revered has the lotus become that today it's India's national flower.

Worship

Worship and ritual play a paramount role in Hinduism. In most Hindu homes you'll find a dedicated worship area, where members of the family pray to the deities of their choice. Beyond the home, Hindus worship at temples. *Puja* is a focal point of worship, ranging from silent prayer to elaborate ceremonies. Devotees leave the temple with a handful of *prasad* (temple-blessed food), which is shared among others. Other forms of worship include *aarti* (auspicious lighting of lamps or candles) and the playing of bhajans (devotional songs).

Islam

Islam is India's largest minority religion, followed by approximately 14.2% of the population. It's believed that Islam was introduced to northern India by Muslim rulers (parts of the north first came under Muslim rule in the 12th century) and to the south by Arab traders.

Islam was founded in Arabia by the Prophet Mohammed in the 7th century AD. The Arabic term islam means 'to surrender', and believers (Muslims) undertake to surrender to the will of Allah (God), revealed in the scriptures, the Quran. In this monotheistic religion, God's word is conveyed through prophets (messengers), of whom Mohammed was the most recent.

Following Mohammed's death, a succession dispute split the movement; the legacy today is the Sunnis and the Shiites. The Sunnis emphasise the 'well-trodden' path or the orthodox way. Shiites believe that only imams (exemplary leaders) can reveal the Quran's true meaning. Most Indian Muslims are Sunnis.

All Muslims, however, share a belief in the Five Pillars of Islam: the shahada (declaration of faith: 'There is no God but Allah; Mohammed

Few parts of India worship the Hindu gods as passionately as Tamil Nadu, the state in which South India's splendid temple architecture reaches its peak. Tamil Nadu's most worshipped deity is Shiva, in widely varied forms including dancing Nataraja. Shiva's peacock-riding son Murugan is also immensely popular.

For an insight into the depth, breadth and quirks of Tamils' Hindu beliefs, as well as absorbing travel writing, read Michael Wood's *A South Indian Journey*.

is his prophet'); prayer (ideally five times a day); the zakat (tax), in the form of a charitable donation; fasting (during Ramadan) for all except the sick, young children, pregnant women, the elderly and those undertaking arduous journeys; and the hajj (pilgrimage) to Mecca, which every Muslim aspires to do at least once. Muslims form around a quarter of the population of Kerala; over 10% in Maharashtra and Karnataka; and around 6% in Tamil Nadu.

Sikhism

Sikhism, founded in Punjab by Guru Nanak in the 15th century, began as a reaction against the caste system and Brahmin domination of ritual. Sikhs believe in one god and, although they reject the worship of idols, some keep pictures of the 10 Sikh gurus as a focus point. The Sikhs' holy book, the Guru Granth Sahib, contains the teachings of the 10 gurus. Like Hindus and Buddhists, Sikhs believe in rebirth and karma. In Sikhism, there's no ascetic or monastic tradition ending the cycles of rebirth. Almost 2% of India's citizens are Sikhs; 75% of them live in Punjab.

Born in present-day Pakistan, Guru Nanak (1469–1539) was dissatisfied with both Muslim and Hindu religious practices. He believed in family life and the value of hard work: he married, had two sons and worked as a farmer when not travelling, preaching and singing self-composed *kirtan* (Sikh devotional songs) with his Muslim musician, Mardana. He is said to have performed miracles and he encouraged meditation on God's name as a prime path to enlightenment.

Nanak believed in equality centuries before it became socially fashionable and campaigned against the caste system. He was a practical guru, and appointed his most talented disciple to be his successor, not one of his sons.

His *kirtan* are still sung in gurdwaras (Sikh temples) today and his picture is kept in millions of homes on and beyond the subcontinent. Members of the Khalsa (Sikh brotherhood) adopt five symbols known as the Five Kakars (or Five Ks):

➡ *kesh* – uncut hair, covered with a *keski* (turban), which some regard as the *kakar* instead of the hair

➡ *kanga* – wooden comb

➡ *kaccha* or *kachhera* – cotton undershorts

➡ *kara* – steel bracelet

➡ *kirpan* – small sword

Buddhism

About 0.8% of India's population is Buddhist. Bodhgaya, in the state of Bihar, is one of Buddhism's most sacred sites, drawing pilgrims from across the world.

Buddhism arose in the 6th century BC as a reaction against the strictures of Brahminical Hinduism. The Buddha (Awakened One) is believed to have lived from about 563 to 483 BC. Formerly a prince (Siddhartha Gautama), the Buddha, at 29, embarked on a quest for emancipation from the world of suffering. He achieved nirvana (the state of full awareness) at Bodhgaya, aged 35. Critical of the caste system and the unthinking worship of gods, the Buddha urged his disciples to seek truth within their own experiences.

The Buddha taught that existence is based on Four Noble Truths: that life is rooted in suffering, that suffering is caused by craving, that one can find release from suffering by eliminating craving, and that the way to eliminate craving is by following the Noble Eightfold Path. This path consists of right understanding, right intention, right speech, right action,

In recent years, Indian women have begun fighting for their right to enter temples, mosques and other sacred sites from which discrimination bans them, either because of their sex or while they are menstruating. In 2015 gender-rights activist Nikita Azad's 'Happy to Bleed' social media campaign went viral.

A sadhu is someone who has surrendered all material possessions in pursuit of spirituality through meditation, the study of sacred texts, self-mortification and pilgrimage. Read more in *Sadhus: India's Mystic Holy Men* by Dolf Hartsuiker.

right livelihood, right effort, right awareness and right concentration. By successfully complying with these one can attain nirvana.

Buddhism was spread widely around India by the Mauryan emperor Ashoka in the 3rd century BC. Buddhist communities were quite influential in Andhra Pradesh between the 3rd century BC and 5th century AD; missionaries from Andhra helped establish monasteries and temples in countries such as Thailand. But Buddhism had ceased to play a major role in India by the 12th century AD. It saw a revival in the 1950s among intellectuals and Dalits, disillusioned with the caste system.

About three-quarters of Indian Buddhists today live in Maharashtra, making up 5.8% of the state's population. The number of Buddhists has been further increased with the influx of Tibetan refugees into India. Both the current Dalai Lama and the lama (monk) widely accepted as the 17th Karmapa reside in the northern state of Himachal Pradesh. There are several Tibetan refugee communities in South India, the biggest being Bylakuppe (p199) in Karnataka, a state in which Buddhists comprise 0.2% of the population.

To grasp the intricacies of Sikhism read *Volume One* *(1469–1839)* or *Volume Two* *(1839–2004)* of *A History of the Sikhs*, by Khushwant Singh.

SPIRITUAL INDIA JAINISM

Jainism

Jainism arose in the 6th century BC as a reaction against the caste restraints and rituals of Hinduism. It was popularised by Mahavira, a contemporary of the Buddha.

Jains believe that liberation is attained by achieving complete purity of the soul. Purity means shedding all *karman* (matter generated by one's actions that binds itself to the soul). By following various austerities (fasting, meditation) one can shed *karman* and purify the soul. Right conduct is essential, and fundamental to this is ahimsa (nonviolence) in thought and deed towards any living thing.

The religious disciplines of followers are less severe than those for monks (some Jain monks go naked). The slightly less ascetic maintain a bare minimum of possessions, including a broom to sweep the path before them to avoid stepping on any living creature, and a piece of cloth tied over their mouth to prevent accidental inhalation of insects.

Today, around 0.4% of India's population is Jain, the majority in Gujarat, Rajasthan, Maharashtra and Mumbai (Bombay). Notable Jain holy sites in South India include Sravanabelagola (p201) in Karnataka.

Set in Kerala against the backdrop of caste conflict and India's struggle for independence, *The House of Blue Mangoes*, by David Davidar, spans three generations of a Christian family.

Christianity

There are various theories circulating about Christ's link to the Indian subcontinent. Some, for instance, believe that Jesus spent his 'lost years' in India, while others say that Christianity came to South India with St Thomas the Apostle in AD 52. However, many scholars attest it's more likely Christianity is traced to around the 4th century with a Syrian merchant, Thomas Cana, who set out for Kerala with around 400 families. India's Christian community today stands at about 2.3% of the population, with the bulk residing in South India.

Catholicism established a strong presence in South India in the wake of Portuguese explorer Vasco da Gama's visit in 1498, and orders that have been active – not always welcomed – in the region include the Dominicans, Franciscans and Jesuits. Protestant missionaries are believed to have begun arriving – with a conversion agenda – from around the 18th century.

The Zoroastrian funerary ritual involves the 'Towers of Silence' (seen, for example, in Mumbai and Hyderabad), where the corpse is laid out and exposed to vultures that pick the bones clean.

Zoroastrianism

Zoroastrianism, founded by Zoroaster (Zarathustra), had its inception in Persia in the 6th century BC and is based on the concept of dualism, whereby good and evil are locked in a continuous battle. Zoroastrianism isn't quite monotheistic: good and evil entities coexist, although believers

RELIGIOUS ETIQUETTE

➡ When visiting a sacred site, dress and behave respectfully. Don't wear shorts or sleeveless tops (this applies to men and women), and refrain from smoking. Loud and intrusive behaviour isn't appreciated, and neither are public displays of affection.

➡ Before entering a holy place, remove your shoes (tip the shoe-minder a few rupees when retrieving them) and check if photography is allowed. You're permitted to wear socks in most places of worship – often necessary during warmer months, when floors can be uncomfortably hot.

➡ Religious etiquette advises against touching locals on the head, or directing the soles of your feet at a person, religious shrine or image of a deity. Protocol also advises against touching someone with your feet or touching a carving of a deity.

➡ Head cover (for women and sometimes men) is required at some places of worship – especially gurdwaras (Sikh temples) and mosques – so carry a scarf.

➡ There are some sites that don't admit women and some that deny entry to nonadherents of their faith; enquire in advance. Women may be required to sit apart from men and some sites ask that menstruating women not enter. Jain temples request the removal of leather items you may be wearing or carrying. Non-Hindus are often not allowed into the inner sanctums of Hindu temples.

➡ When walking around any Buddhist sacred site (chortens, stupas, temples, gompas) go clockwise. Don't touch them with your left hand. Turn prayer wheels clockwise, with your right hand.

➡ Taking photos inside a shrine, at a funeral, at a religious ceremony or of people taking a holy dip can be offensive – ask first. Flash photography may be prohibited in certain areas of a shrine, or may not be permitted at all.

are urged to honour only the good and a pleasant afterlife does depend on one's deeds, words and thoughts during earthly existence.

Zoroastrianism was eclipsed in Persia by the rise of Islam in the 7th century. Over the following centuries some followers emigrated to India, where they became known as Parsis. Historically, Parsis settled in Gujarat and became farmers; during British rule they moved into commerce, forming a prosperous community in Mumbai.

There are now believed to be only around 61,000 Parsis left in India, 40,000 to 45,000 of whom reside in Mumbai.

Tribal Religions

Tribal religions have merged with Hinduism and other mainstream religions so that very few are now clearly identifiable. It's believed that some basic tenets of Hinduism may have originated in ancient tribal culture.

Village and tribal people in South India have their own belief systems, which are much less accessible or obvious than the temples, rituals and other outward manifestations of the mainstream religions. The village deity may be represented by a stone pillar in a field, a platform under a tree or an iron spear stuck in the ground. Village deities are generally seen as less remote and more concerned with the community's immediate happiness and prosperity. There are also many beliefs about ancestral spirits, including those who died violently.

Delicious India

India's culinary terrain is a feast for all the senses. Its multifaceted vegetarian cuisine is especially impressive – and South India is particularly famous for it. You'll delight in everything from sensational street food to work-of-art thalis, from contemporary fusion masterpieces to 50-year-old family-run stalls serving up one speciality, all using fresh local ingredients. Regional variations add extra flair. There's plenty for carnivores and seafood-lovers too. Indeed, it's this sheer diversity that makes eating your way around South India so deliciously rewarding.

A Culinary Carnival

India's culinary story is an ancient one: the food you'll find in South India today reflects millenniums of regional and global influences, with distinct local variations.

Land of Spices

Christopher Columbus was actually searching for the black pepper of Kerala's Malabar Coast when he stumbled upon America. The region still grows the finest quality of the world's favourite spice, integral to most savoury Indian dishes.

Turmeric is the essence of the majority of Indian curries, but coriander seeds are the most widely used spice and lend flavour and body to just about every savoury dish. Indian 'wet' dishes ('curries' in the West) usually begin with the crackle of cumin seeds in hot oil. Tamarind is sometimes known as the 'Indian date' and is a popular souring agent in South India. The green cardamom of Kerala's Western Ghats is regarded as the world's best; you'll find it in savouries, desserts and warming chai (tea). Saffron, the dried stigmas of crocus flowers grown in Kashmir, is so light it takes more than 1500 hand-plucked flowers to yield just one gram.

Spotlighting rice, *Finest Rice Recipes*, by Sabina Sehgal Saikia, shows just how versatile this humble grain is, with sophisticated creations such as rice-crusted crab cakes.

Rice Paradise

Rice is a staple throughout India, and especially in South India. Long-grain white-rice varieties are most popular, served hot with every thali and just about any 'wet' cooked dish. From Assam's sticky rice in the far northeast to Kerala's red grains in the extreme south, you'll find countless regional varieties. The title of best rice in India is usually conceded to basmati, a fragrant long-grain variety grown in northern and central India and widely exported around the world. Rice is usually served after you have finished with the rotis (breads), and usually accompanied by enriching curd.

Pongal, the major harvest festival of the south, is closely associated with a dish of the same name, made with the season's first rice plus jaggery, nuts, raisins and spices.

Flippin' Fantastic Bread

Although rice is South India's mainstay, traditional breads are also eaten. Roti, the generic term for Indian-style bread, is a name used interchangeably with chapati to describe the most common variety, the irresistible unleavened round bread made with whole-wheat flour and cooked on a *tawa* (hotplate). It may be smothered with ghee (clarified

SOUTHERN BELLES

Savoury *dosas* (also spelt dosai) – large, crispy, papery, rice-flour crêpes, usually served with a bowl of hot *sambar* (soupy lentil dish) and another of cooling coconut *chatni* (chutney) – are a South Indian breakfast speciality that can be eaten at any time of day, all over India. Most popular is the *masala dosa* (stuffed with spiced potatoes), but other fantastic *dosa* varieties include the *rava dosa* (batter made with semolina), the Mysore *dosa* (like *masala dosa* but with more vegetables and chilli), and the *pessarettu dosa* (batter made with mung-bean dhal) from Telangana and Andhra Pradesh.

The humble *idli*, a traditional South Indian snack or breakfast, is a nutritious, low-calorie alternative to oil, spice and chilli. *Idlis* are spongy, round, white, fermented rice cakes that you dip in *sambar* and coconut and other *chatnis*. *Dahi idli* is an *idli* dunked in very lightly spiced yogurt (brilliant for tender tummies). Other super southern snacks include *vadas* (doughnut-shaped deep-fried lentil savouries), *uttapams* (thick, savoury rice pancakes with finely chopped onions, green chillies, coriander and coconut) and *iddiyappams* (rice-flour string hoppers) served with spicy curry or coconut milk and sugar.

butter) or oil. In some places, rotis are bigger and thicker than chapatis, and sometimes cooked in a tandoor. *Paratha* is a layered pan-fried flat bread that may also be stuffed and which makes a popular breakfast; South India's *parotta* is similar. Naan is a larger, thicker, tandoor-cooked bread, usually eaten with meaty sauces or kebabs. *Puri* is an unleavened bread that puffs up when deep-fried, served with accompaniments such as *bhajia* (vegetable fritters).

Dhal-icious!

In coastal areas, especially Goa and Kerala, it's hard to beat the beach shacks for fresh, inexpensive seafood, from fried mussels, prawns and calamari to steamed fish, crab and lobster.

The whole of India is united in its love for dhal (curried lentils or pulses). You may encounter up to 60 different pulses: the most common are *channa* (chickpeas); tiny yellow or green ovals called *moong* (mung beans); salmon-coloured *masoor* (red lentils); the ochre-coloured southern favourite *tuvar* (yellow lentils; also known as *arhar*); *rajma* (kidney beans); *urad* (black gram or lentils); and *lobhia* (black-eyed peas).

Meaty Matters

Although India probably has more vegetarians than the rest of the world combined, it still has an extensive repertoire of carnivorous fare. Chicken, lamb and mutton (sometimes actually goat) are the staples; religious taboos make beef forbidden to devout Hindus, and pork to Muslims.

Fish is a staple of nonvegetarian Maharashtrian food; Maharashtra's signature fish dish is *bombil* (Bombay Duck; a misnomer for this slimy, pikelike fish), which is eaten fresh, sun-dried or deep-fried.

In South India, meaty Chettinadu cuisine from Tamil Nadu is beautifully spiced without being too fiery. In some southern restaurants you'll find meat-dominated Mughlai cuisine, which includes rich curries, kebabs, koftas and biryanis – the last is a particular speciality of Hyderabad. This spicy cuisine traces its history back to the (Islamic) Mughal empire that once reigned supreme over much of India. Tandoori meat dishes are another North Indian favourite also found in the south. The name is derived from the clay oven, or tandoor, in which the marinated meat is cooked.

Deep-Sea Delights

India has around 7500km of coastline, so it's no surprise that seafood is a key South Indian ingredient, especially on the west coast, from Mumbai (Bombay) down to Kerala. Kerala is the biggest fishing state, while Goa boasts particularly succulent prawns and fiery fish curries; the fishing communities of the Konkan Coast – between Mumbai and

Goa – are renowned for their seafood. The far-flung Andaman Islands are a treat for seafood lovers, with fresh catch on all menus, while fresh seafood also abounds in coastal Tamil Nadu and Andhra Pradesh.

Dear Dairy

Milk and milk products make a staggering contribution to Indian cuisine. *Dahi* (curd/yoghurt) is commonly served with meals and is great for subduing heat; paneer (soft unfermented cheese) is a godsend for the vegetarian majority; lassi (yoghurt drink) is one of a host of sweet and savoury beverages; ghee is the traditional, pure cooking medium; and some of the finest mithai (Indian sweets) are made with milk.

The Fruits (& Vegetables) of Mother Nature

A visit to any South Indian market reveals a vast, vibrant assortment of fresh fruit and vegetables, overflowing from baskets or stacked in tidy pyramids. The South is especially well known for its abundance of tropical fruits such as pineapple, papaya and avocado (this last grown almost exclusively on southern hillsides). Mangoes abound during summer months (especially April and May); the pick of India's 500 luscious varieties is the sweet Maharashtrian Alphonso. You'll find fruit inventively fashioned into a *chatni* (chutney) or pickle, and flavouring lassi, *kulfi* (flavoured, firm-textured ice cream) and other sweet treats.

Naturally in a region with so many vegetarians, *sabzi* (vegetables) make up a predominant part of the diet. Vegetables can be cooked *sukhi* (dry) or *tari* (in a sauce), and within these two categories they can be fried, roasted, curried, baked, mashed and stuffed into *dosas* (large South Indian savoury crêpes), or dipped in chickpea-flour batter to make a deep-fried *pakora* (fritter). Potatoes are ubiquitous and popularly cooked with various masalas (spice mixes), with other vegetables, stuffed inside *masala dosas* (*dosas* stuffed with spiced potatoes) or mashed and fried for the street snack *aloo tikki* (mashed-potato patties).

Onions are fried with other vegetables, ground into a paste for cooking with meats or served raw as relishes. Heads of cauliflower are cooked dry on their own, with potatoes as *aloo gobi* (potato-and-cauliflower curry), or with other vegetables such as carrots and beans. Fresh green peas turn up stir-fried with other vegetables in pilaus and biryanis. *Baigan* (eggplant/aubergine) can be curried or sliced and deep-fried. Also popular is *saag* (leafy greens), which can include mustard, spinach and fenugreek. Something a little more unusual is the bumpy-skinned *karela* (bitter gourd), which, like the delectable *bhindi* (okra), is commonly prepared dry with spices. Tamil Nadu is known for growing the drumstick vegetable – a long, thin pod often used in *sambar* (a South Indian soupy lentil dish).

Ghee is made by melting butter and removing the water and milk solids: ghee is the clear butter fat that remains. It's better for high-heat cooking than butter, and keeps for longer.

Bulbul Sharma's *The Anger of Aubergines: Stories of Women and Food* is an amusing culinary analysis of social relationships interspersed with enticing recipes.

PAAN

Meals across India are often rounded off with *paan*, a fragrant mixture of betel nut (also called areca nut), lime paste, spices and condiments wrapped in an edible, silky *paan* leaf. Peddled by *paan*-wallahs, usually strategically positioned outside busy restaurants, *paan* is eaten as a digestive and mouth-freshener. The betel nut is mildly narcotic and some aficionados eat *paan* the same way heavy smokers consume cigarettes; over the years these people's teeth can become rotted red and black. Usually the gloopy red juice is spat out – not particularly sightly.

There are two basic types of *paan*: mitha (sweet) and saadha (with tobacco). A parcel of *mitha paan* is a splendid way to finish a meal. Pop the whole parcel in your mouth and chew slowly.

THE GREAT SOUTH INDIAN THALI

In South India, the thali is a favourite all-you-can-eat lunchtime meal, often called just a 'meal'. Inexpensive, satiating, wholesome and incredibly tasty, this is Indian food at its simple best. The name 'thali' refers to the stainless-steel plate on which the meal is served. In North India the plate usually has indentations for the various side dishes, but in South India a thali is traditionally served on a flat steel plate often covered with a fresh banana leaf, or on a banana leaf itself.

In a restaurant, when the steel plate is placed in front of you, you can follow local custom and pour some bottled or filtered water on the leaf then spread it around with your right hand. A waiter will pile rotis (breads) on to your plate, followed by servings of dhal, *sambar* (soupy lentils), *rasam* (dhal-based broth flavoured with tamarind), vegetable dishes, chutneys, pickles and *dahi* (curd/yoghurt). When you're done with the rotis, waiters will materialise with large pots of rice and top-ups of side dishes. Using the fingers of your right hand, mix the side dishes with the rice, kneading and scraping it into mouth-sized balls, then scoop it into your mouth using your thumb to push the food. It's considered poor form to stick your hand right into your mouth or to lick your fingers. Observing fellow diners will help you master your thali technique. If it's all getting a bit messy, there's usually a finger bowl of water available. Waiters will continue refilling your plate until you wave your hand over one or all of the offerings, or fold over your banana leaf, to indicate you have had enough.

Pickles, Chutneys & Relishes

Pickles, chutneys and relishes are accompaniments that add zing to meals and appear alongside almost every South Indian *idli* (fermented rice cake), *dosa* or *uttapam* (savoury rice pancake). A relish can be anything from a tiny pickled onion to a delicately crafted fusion of fruit, nuts and spices. One of the most popular side dishes is yoghurt-based *raita*, a tongue-cooling counter to spicy food. *Chatnis* come in all kinds of varieties (sweet or savoury) and can be made from many different vegetables, fruits, herbs and spices.

Technically speaking, there's no such thing as an Indian 'curry' – the word, an anglicised derivative of the Tamil word *kari* (sauce), was used by the British as a term for any spiced dish.

Sweet at Heart

India has a colourful kaleidoscope of often sticky and squishy *mithai* (Indian sweets), most of them sinfully sugary. The main categories are *barfi* (a fudgelike milk-based sweet), soft halwa (made with vegetables, cereals, lentils, nuts or fruit), *ladoos* (sweet balls made of gram flour and semolina) and sweet balls made from *chhana* (unpressed paneer) such as *rasgullas* (syrupy cream-cheese balls). There are also simpler – but equally scrumptious – offerings such as crunchy *jalebis* (orange-coloured coils of deep-fried batter dunked in sugar syrup; served hot) all over India.

Payasam (*kheer* in the north) is one of South India's most popular desserts. It's a creamy rice pudding with a light, delicate flavour, enhanced with cardamom, saffron, pistachios, flaked almonds, chopped cashews or slivered dried fruit. Other favourites include *gulab jamun* (deep-fried dough balls soaked in rose-flavoured syrup) and *kulfi*.

In Maharashtra's hill areas you'll find *chikki* (rock-hard, toffee-like confectionery for snacking). Madurai, in Tamil Nadu, is famous for its refreshing drink *jigarthanda* (boiled milk, almond essence, rose syrup and vanilla ice cream). Each year, an estimated 14 tonnes of pure silver is converted into the edible foil that decorates many Indian sweets, especially during Diwali.

The fiery cuisine of Karnatakan coastal city Mangaluru (Mangalore) is famed for its flavour-packed seafood dishes. Mangalorean cuisine is diverse, distinct, and characterised by its liberal use of chilli and fresh coconut.

Vegetarians & Vegans

South India is king when it comes to vegetarian food in India. There's little understanding of veganism ('pure vegetarian' means without eggs) and animal products such as milk, butter, ghee and curd are included in most Indian dishes. As a vegan, your first problem is likely to be getting the cook to understand your requirements, though big hotels and larger cities are getting better at catering to vegans.

For further information, check out Indian Vegan (www.indianvegan.com) and Happy Cow (www.happycow.net).

Dakshin: Vegetarian Cuisine from South India, by Chandra Padmanabhan, is an easy-to-read, beautifully illustrated book of southern recipes.

Where to Fill Up?

You can eat well everywhere in South India, from ramshackle *dhabas* (simple streetside eateries) and frenzied lunchtime 'messes' (canteens) to other-worldly five-star hotels. Most midrange restaurants serve a few basic genres: South Indian (which usually means the vegetarian food of Tamil Nadu and Karnataka) and North Indian (which largely comprises Punjabi/Mughlai fare), plus, often, Indian interpretations of Chinese dishes. You'll also encounter the cuisines of neighbouring regions and states. Indians frequently migrate for work and these restaurants cater to large communities seeking familiar home tastes.

Not to be confused with burger joints and pizzerias, restaurants in the south advertising 'fast food' are some of India's best. They serve the whole gamut of tiffin (snack) items and often have separate sweet counters. Many upmarket hotels have outstanding restaurants, some with pan-Indian menus so you can explore various regional cuisines, others deliciously specialised. Meanwhile, the independent restaurant-dining scene keeps mushrooming in India's larger cities, with every kind of cuisine available, from Mexican and Mediterranean to Japanese and Italian.

Dakshin Bhog, by Santhi Balaraman, offers a yummy jumble of southern stars, from iconic dosas and idlis to kootan choru (vegetable rice).

Dhabas are oases to millions of truck drivers, bus passengers and sundry travellers going anywhere by road. The original *dhabas* dot the North Indian landscape, but you'll find versions of them throughout the

---

STREET FOOD TIPS

Tucking into street eats is one of the joys of travelling in South India; here are some tips to help avoid tummy troubles.

➡ Give yourself a few days to adjust to the local cuisine, especially if you're not used to spicy food.

➡ If the locals are avoiding a particular vendor, you should too. Also take notice of the profile of the customers: any place popular with families will probably be your safest bet.

➡ Check how and where the vendor is cleaning the utensils, and how and where the food is covered. If the vendor is cooking in oil, have a peek to check it's clean. If the pots or surfaces are dirty, there are food scraps about or too many buzzing flies, don't be shy about making a hasty retreat.

➡ Don't be put off when you order some deep-fried snack and the cook throws it back into the wok. It's common practice to partly cook the snacks first and then finish them off once they've been ordered. Frying them again kills germs.

➡ Unless a place is reputable (and busy), it's best to avoid eating meat from the street.

➡ The hygiene standards at juice stalls vary, so exercise caution. Have the vendor press the juice in front of you and steer clear of anything stored in a jug or served in a glass (unless you're absolutely convinced of the washing standards).

➡ Don't be tempted by glistening presliced melon and other fruit, which keeps its luscious veneer with regular dousings of (often dubious) water.

FEASTING: INDIAN-STYLE

Most people in India eat with their right hand. In the south, they use as much of the hand as is necessary; elsewhere they use the tips of the fingers. The left hand is reserved for unsanitary actions such as removing shoes. You can use your left hand for holding drinks and serving yourself from a communal bowl, but it shouldn't be used for bringing food to your mouth. Before and after a meal, wash your hands.

Once your meal is served, mix the food with your fingers. If you are having dhal and *sabzi* (vegetables), only mix the dhal into your rice and have the *sabzi* in small scoops with each mouthful. If you are having fish or meat curry, mix the gravy into your rice. Scoop up lumps of the mix and, with your knuckles facing the dish, use your thumb to shovel the food into your mouth.

country. The rough-and-ready but satisfying food served in these happy-go-lucky shacks has become a genre of its own known as '*dhaba* food'.

Street Food

Got the munchies? Grab *Street Foods of India*, by Vimla and Deb Kumar Mukerji, which has recipes for much-loved Indian snacks.

Whatever the time of day, street-food vendors are frying, boiling, griddling, roasting, peeling, simmering, mixing, juicing or baking different types of food and drink to lure peckish passers-by. Small operations usually have one special that they serve all day; other vendors have different dishes for breakfast, lunch and dinner. The fare varies as you venture between neighbourhoods, towns and regions; it can be as simple as puffed rice or peanuts roasted in hot sand, or as complex as the riot of different flavours known as *chaat* (savoury snack). *Idli sambar* (rice patties served with lentil sauce and chutney) is a favourite in Chennai, along with *vadas* (doughnut-shaped deep-fried lentil savouries) and *uttapams*. Mumbai is famed for its *pav bhaji* (spiced veg and bread) and *bhelpuri* (fried rounds of dough with puffed rice, lentils, lemon juice, onion, herbs and chutney), while *misal pav* (spicy bean sprouts and pulses) is a Maharashtrian breakfast favourite. *Mirchi bhajji* (chilli fritters stuffed with tamarind, sesame and spices) are a Hyderabad delicacy. Samosas (deep-fried pastry triangles filled with spiced vegetables) and *golgappa/panipuri/gup chup* (puffed spheres of bread with spicy filling) are all over India.

The *Penguin Food Guide to India*, by Charmaine O'Brien, is engrossing and evocative.

Railway Snack Attack

One of the thrills of travelling by rail in India is the culinary circus that greets you at almost every station. Roving vendors accost arriving trains, yelling and scampering up and down carriages; fruit, *namkin* (savoury nibbles), omelettes, nuts and sweets are offered through the window grilles; and platform cooks try to lure you from the train with the sizzle of spicy goodies like fresh samosas. Frequent rail travellers know which station is famous for which food item: Maharashtra's Lonavla station is known for *chikki*, while Chennai Central is (predictably) famed for *idlis*, *vadas* and *dosas*.

Goan cuisine is a delicious blend of Portuguese and South Indian flavours, with lots of meats and fresh seafood. The famous, fiery vindaloo (curry in a marinade of vinegar and garlic) is a Goan favourite.

Daily Dining Habits

Three main meals a day is the norm in India. South Indians generally have a light, early breakfast, often *idlis* with *sambar*. Lunch can be substantial (perhaps a thali) or lighter, especially for time-strapped office workers. Many people also have several tiffin (between-meal snacks) throughout the day. Dinner is the main meal of the day: usually large serves of rice, rotis, vegetables, curd and spicy side dishes (maybe also meat), all served at once. Desserts are optional and most prevalent during festivals or other special occasions; fruit may wrap up a meal. In many Indian homes, dinner can be a late affair (post 9pm) depending on personal preference and the season (eg later dinners during warmer months). Restaurants usually spring to life after 9pm in big cities, but get busy earlier in small towns.

Spiritual Sustenance

For many Indians, food is considered just as critical for fine-tuning the spirit as it is for sustaining the body. Broadly speaking, Hindus traditionally avoid foods that are thought to inhibit physical and spiritual development, although there are few hard-and-fast rules. The taboo on eating beef (the cow is holy to Hindus) is the most rigid restriction. Jains avoid foods such as garlic, onions and potatoes, which, apart from harming insects on their extraction from the ground, are thought to heat the blood and arouse sexual desire. You may come across vegetarian restaurants that make it a point to advertise the absence of onion and garlic from their dishes for this reason. Devout Hindus may also avoid garlic and onions. These items are banned from many ashrams too.

Some foods, such as dairy products, are considered innately pure and are eaten to cleanse the body, mind and spirit. Ayurveda, the ancient science of life, health and longevity, also influences food customs.

Pork is taboo for Muslims, and stimulants such as alcohol are avoided by the most devout. Halal is the term for all permitted foods, and haram for those prohibited. Fasting is considered an opportunity to earn the approval of Allah, wipe the sin-slate clean and understand the suffering of the poor.

Buddhists and Jains subscribe to the philosophy of ahimsa (nonviolence) and are mostly vegetarian. Jainism's central tenet is ultravegetarianism, and rigid restrictions are in place to avoid injury to any living creature. India's Sikh, Christian and Parsi communities have few or no restrictions on what they can eat.

The Bangala Table: Flavors and Recipes from Chettinad, by Sumeet Nair, Meenakshi Meyyappan and Jill Donenfeld, is a gorgeous, photo-heavy recipe tome on southern Tamil Nadu's Chettinadu region.

Nimi Sunilkumar's award-winning Keralan cookbooks *Lip Smacking Dishes of Kerala* and *4 O'Clock Temptations of Kerala* offer a tantalising insight into local cuisine.

COOKING COURSES

You might find yourself so inspired by South Indian food that you want to take home a little Indian kitchen know-how. Recommended cooking courses are offered in Goa, Kerala, Tamil Nadu, Telangana and elsewhere. Some are professionally run, others informal. Most require a few days' notice.

Goa

Masala Kitchen, Palolem (p154) Well-established cooking courses.

Mukti Kitchen, Arpora (p137) Five-dish cooking classes (Goan, Indian, ayurvedic).

Rahul's Cooking Class, Palolem (p154) One of Palolem's original culinary schools.

Kerala

Bar-B-Que, Kumily (p291) Cooking and feasting.

Cook & Eat, Kochi (p302) Popular classes at Leelu Homestay.

Nimi's Lip Smacking Classes, Munnar (p295) Expert-led Keralan cooking.

Tamil Nadu

Chettinadu (p380) Heritage hotels give cooking demos and classes.

Sita, Puducherry (p362) Tamil, French and North Indian cuisine.

Storytrails, Chennai (p333) Food tours and in-house cooking courses.

Telangana

Detours, Hyderabad (p234) Outstanding food tours incorporating cooking lessons.

Drinks, Anyone?

Alcoholic Beverages

New 2013 legislation finally paved the way for microbreweries in Mumbai. Following the lead of pioneering brew-pub Barking Deer, the city is now exploding in hops.

Gujarat, Nagaland, Mizoram and Bihar, all in the north, are India's only dry states, but there are drinking laws in place all over the country. Each state may have regular dry days when the sale of alcohol from liquor shops is banned. Kerala, where alcohol consumption was twice the national average, removed liquor licences from some 700 bars in 2014; some have reopened as beer or wine parlours, while Indian-made foreign liquor (IMFL) is available from state-run shops or in five-star hotel bars; at the time of writing, Kerala's planned move towards full prohibition looked unlikely to go ahead. On Gandhi's birthday (2 October), you'll find it hard to get alcoholic drinks anywhere. In Goa, alcohol taxes are lower and the drinking culture is less restricted.

You'll find excellent watering holes in most big cities, all at their liveliest on weekends. Bengaluru (Bangalore) is India's craft-beer capital, but Mumbai (Bombay) and Pune are now racing up behind with their own lively brew-pub scenes. More upmarket bars serve an impressive selection of domestic and imported alcohol plus draught beers. Plenty of bars turn into heaving nightclubs anytime after 8pm. Many of South India's best bars are in flashy hotels. In smaller towns, the bar scene is usually a seedy, male-dominated affair – not the kind of places thirsty female travellers should venture into alone.

Containing handy tips, including how to best store spices, Monisha Bharadwaj's *The Indian Spice Kitchen* is a slick cookbook with more than 200 traditional recipes.

Despite India's domestic wine-producing industry still being relatively new, wine-drinking is steadily on the rise. The favourable climate and soil conditions in certain areas – especially parts of Maharashtra and Karnataka – have spawned commendable Indian wineries like Nasik's Grover Zampa (p86) and Sula Vineyards (p86); Fratelli Wines, southeast of Pune, is another top Indian winery.

Stringent licensing laws discourage drinking in some restaurants, though places that depend on the tourist rupee may covertly serve you beer in teapots and disguised glasses – but don't assume anything, at the risk of causing offence. Very few vegetarian restaurants serve alcohol.

Home-Grown Brews

An estimated three-quarters of India's drinking population quaffs 'country liquor', such as the south's notorious arak (liquor distilled from coconut-palm sap, potatoes or rice). This is widely known as the poor-man's drink; millions are addicted to the stuff. Each year, many people are blinded, paralysed or even killed by the methyl alcohol in illegal arak.

An interesting local drink is *mahua*, a clear spirit with a heady pungent flavour, distilled from the flower of the *mahua* tree. It's brewed in makeshift village stalls all over central India during March and April, when the trees bloom. *Mahua* is safe to drink as long as it comes from a trustworthy source, but there have been plenty of cases of people being blinded after drinking *mahua* adulterated with methyl alcohol.

Complete Indian Cooking, by Mridula Baljekar, Rafi Fernandez, Shehzad Husain and Manisha Kanani, contains a host of over 400 favourite southern recipes, from chicken with green mango to Goan prawn curry.

Toddy (sap from palm trees) is drunk in coastal areas, especially Kerala, while feni is the primo Indian spirit and the preserve of laid-back Goa. Coconut feni is light and unexceptional but the more popular cashew feni – made from cashew fruit – is worth a try.

Nonalcoholic Beverages

Chai, the much-loved drink of the masses, is made with copious amounts of milk and sugar. A glass of steaming, frothy chai is the perfect antidote to the vicissitudes of life on the Indian road; the disembodied voice droning '*garam* chai, *garam* chai' (hot tea, hot tea) is likely to become one of the most familiar and welcome sounds of your trip. Masala chai adds cardamom, ginger and other spices.

While chai is most of India's traditional choice, South Indians have long shared their loyalty with coffee. The popular South Indian filter coffee is a combination of boiled milk, sugar and a strong decoction made from freshly ground coffee beans, often with a dash of chicory. In bigger cities, you'll find countless branches of modern coffee-house chains (Café Coffee Day, Barista, even Starbucks), plus an ever-growing number of fashionable independent cafes, all serving standard international coffees.

> Food that is first offered to the gods at temples then shared among devotees is known as *prasad*.

Masala soda is the quintessential Indian soft drink: a freshly opened bottle of fizzy soda, pepped up with lime, spices, salt and sugar. You can also try a plain lime soda, with fresh lime, served sweet (with sugar) or salted. Also refreshing is *jal jeera*, made of lime juice, cumin, mint and rock salt. Sweet and savoury lassi, a yoghurt-based drink, is another wonderfully cooling beverage, popular nationwide. *Sol kadhi*, a pink-coloured, slightly sour drink made from coconut milk, is a staple of South India's Konkan Coast (between Mumbai and Goa).

Falooda is a rose-flavoured drink made with milk, cream, nuts and strands of vermicelli, while *badam* milk (hot or cold) is flavoured with almonds and saffron.

MENU DECODER

achar	pickle
aloo	potato; also *alu*
aloo gobi	potato-and-cauliflower curry
aloo tikki	mashed-potato patty
appam	South Indian rice pancake
arak	liquor distilled from coconut milk, potatoes or rice
baigan	eggplant/aubergine; also *brinjal*
barfi	fudgelike sweet made from milk
bebinca	Goan 16-layer cake
besan	chickpea flour
betel	nut of the betel tree; also areca nut
bhajia	vegetable fritters
bhang lassi	blend of lassi and bhang (a derivative of marijuana)
bhelpuri	thin, fried rounds of dough with rice, lentils, lemon juice, onion, herbs and chutney
bhindi	okra
biryani	fragrant, spiced steamed rice with meat or vegetables
bonda	mashed-potato patty
chaat	savoury snack, may be seasoned with *chaat masala*
chach	buttermilk beverage
chai	tea
channa	spiced chickpeas
chapati	round, unleavened Indian-style bread; also *roti*
chawal	rice
cheiku	small, sweet brown fruit
dahi	curd/yoghurt
dhal	spiced lentil dish
dhal makhani	black lentils and red kidney beans with cream and butter

dhansak	Parsi dish; meat, usually chicken or lamb, with curried lentils, pumpkin or gourd, and rice
dosa	large South Indian savoury crêpe
falooda	rose-flavoured drink made with milk, cream, nuts and vermicelli
faluda	long chickpea-flour noodles
feni	Goan liquor distilled from coconut milk or cashews
ghee	clarified butter
gobi	cauliflower
gulab jamun	deep-fried balls of dough soaked in rose-flavoured syrup
halwa	soft sweet made with vegetables, lentils, nuts or fruit
iddiyappam	rice-flour string hoppers
idli	South Indian spongy, round, fermented rice cake
imli	tamarind
jaggery	hard, brown, sugarlike sweetener made from palm sap
jalebi	orange-coloured coils of deep-fried batter dunked in sugar syrup; served hot
jigarthanda	drink made with boiled milk, almond essence, rose syrup and vanilla ice cream
karela	bitter gourd
keema	spiced minced meat
kheer	creamy rice pudding; *payasam* in South India
khichdi	blend of lightly spiced rice and lentils; also *khichri*
kofta	minced vegetables or meat; often ball-shaped
korma	currylike braised dish
kulcha	soft, leavened Indian-style bread
kulfi	flavoured (often with pistachio), firm-textured ice cream
ladoo	sweet ball made with gram flour and semolina; also *ladu*
lassi	yoghurt-and-iced-water drink
malai kofta	paneer cooked in a creamy sauce of cashews and tomato
masala dosa	large South Indian savoury crêpe (*dosa*) stuffed with spiced potatoes
mattar paneer	unfermented-cheese and pea curry
methi	fenugreek
mishti doi	Bengali sweet; curd sweetened with jaggery
mithai	Indian sweets
momo	savoury Tibetan dumpling
naan	tandoor-cooked flat bread
namak	salt
namkin	savoury nibbles
pakora	bite-sized vegetable pieces in batter
palak paneer	unfermented cheese chunks in a puréed spinach gravy
paneer	soft, unfermented cheese made from milk curd
pani	water
pappadam	thin, crispy lentil or chickpea-flour circle-shaped wafer; also *pappad*
paratha/parantha/ parotta	flaky flat bread (thicker than chapati); often stuffed
phulka	chapati that puffs up on an open flame
pilau	rice cooked in spiced stock; also *pulau, pilao* or *pilaf*
pudina	mint

puri	flat, savoury dough that puffs up when deep-fried; also *poori*
raita	mildly spiced yogurt, often containing shredded cucumber or diced pineapple
rasam	dhal-based broth flavoured with tamarind
rasgulla	cream-cheese balls flavoured with rose water
rogan josh	rich, spicy lamb curry
saag	leafy greens
sabzi	vegetables
sambar	South Indian soupy lentil dish with cubed vegetables
samosa	deep-fried pastry triangles filled with spiced vegetables
sol kadhi	pink-coloured, slightly sour drink made from coconut milk
sonf	aniseed; used as a digestive and mouth-freshener; also *saunf*
tandoor	clay oven
tawa	flat hotplate/iron griddle
thali	all-you-can-eat meal; stainless steel (sometimes silver) plate
thukpa	Tibetan noodle soup
tiffin	snack; also refers to meal container often made of stainless steel
tikka	spiced, often marinated, chunks of chicken, paneer etc
toddy	alcoholic drink, tapped from palm trees
upma	*rava* (semolina) cooked with onions, spices, chilli peppers and coconut
uttapam	thick, savoury South Indian rice pancake with finely chopped onions, green chillies, coriander and coconut
vada	South Indian doughnut-shaped, deep-fried lentil savoury
vindaloo	Goan dish; fiery curry in a marinade of vinegar and garlic

The Great Indian Bazaar

South India's bazaars and shops sell a staggering range of goodies: from woodwork to silks, chunky tribal jewellery to finely embroidered shawls, sparkling gemstones to rustic village handicrafts. The array of arts and handicrafts is vast, with every area – sometimes every village – maintaining its own traditions, some of them ancient. Be prepared to encounter (and bring home) spectacular items. Indeed, South India's shopping opportunities are as inspiring and multifarious as the region itself.

Bronze Figures, Pottery, Stone Carving & Terracotta

In southern India (and parts of the Himalaya), small bronze images of deities are created by the age-old lost-wax process. A wax figure is made, a mould is formed around it, then the wax is melted, poured out and replaced with molten metal; the mould is then broken open to reveal the figure inside. Figures of Shiva as dancing Nataraja (a tradition going back to medieval Chola times in Tamil Nadu) are the most popular, but you can also find images of numerous other Hindu deities, and images of the Buddha and Tantric deities. Don't confuse bronze (a copper tin alloy) with brass (a cheaper copper-zinc alloy).

In Mamallapuram (Mahabalipuram) in Tamil Nadu, craftspeople using local granite and soapstone have revived the ancient artistry of Pallava sculptors; souvenirs range from tiny stone elephants to enormous half-a-tonne deity statues. Tamil Nadu is also known for bronzeware from Thanjavur and Trichy (Tiruchirappalli).

A number of places produce attractive terracotta items, ranging from vases and decorative flowerpots to images of deities and children's toys. In Chettinadu (southern Tamil Nadu), enormous terracotta horses and other beasts are crafted as offerings to the popular pre-Hindu deity Ayyanar.

Outside temples across India you can buy small clay or plaster effigies of Hindu deities.

State-government handicraft emporiums usually have reasonable fixed prices and good local crafts. Try Tamil Nadu's Poompuhar (http://tnpoompuhar.org); Lepakshi (www.lepakshihandicrafts.gov.in) in Andhra Pradesh and Telangana; Kerala's SMSM Institute (www.keralahandicrafts.in); and Karnataka's Cauvery Handicrafts Emporium (www.cauveryhandicrafts.net).

Carpets, Carpets, Carpets!

Carpet-making is a living craft in India. Workshops throughout the country produce fine wool and silkwork, though most of the finest carpets are made in the north. Most Tibetan refugee settlements have cooperative carpet workshops (there are several Tibetan refugee communities in South India). 'Antique' carpets usually aren't antique, unless you buy from an internationally reputable dealer; stick to 'new' carpets.

Coarsely woven woollen *namdas* (*numdas*) from Kashmir and Rajasthan are much cheaper than knotted carpets. Various regions manufacture flat-weave *dhurries* (kilim-like cotton rugs); Warangal in Telangana is one of the south's main centres. Puducherry (Pondicherry) and Bengaluru (Bangalore) are other South India carpet producers.

Children have been employed as carpet weavers in the subcontinent for centuries. Child labour maintains a cycle of poverty, driving down adult wages, reducing adult work opportunities and depriving children of education. Carpets produced by Tibetan refugee cooperatives are almost always made by adults; government emporiums and charitable cooperatives are usually best for buying.

Costs & Shipping

The price of a carpet is determined by the number and the size of the hand-tied knots, the range of dyes and colours, the intricacy of the design and the material. Silk carpets cost more and look more luxurious, but wool carpets usually last longer. Expect to pay upward of US$200 for a 90cm by 1.8m traditional wool carpet, and around US$2000 for a similar-sized silk carpet.

Many places ship carpets home for you, although it may be safest to send things independently to avoid scams. Shipping for a 90cm by 1.8m carpet costs around ₹4000 to Europe and ₹4500 to the USA. You can also carry carpets as check-in baggage on a plane (allow 5kg to 10kg of your baggage allowance for a 90cm by 1.8m carpet; check your airline allows oversized baggage).

Jewellery

Virtually every Indian town has at least one bangle shop with an extraordinary range, from colourful plastic and glass bracelets to brass, silver and gold creations. In Telangana, Hyderabad is a centre for making and selling bangles made from lac (a resinous insect secretion), encrusted with colourful beads or stones.

Heavy folk-art silver jewellery can be bought in various parts of India, as can chunky Tibetan jewellery made from silver (or white metal) and semiprecious stones. Many Tibetan pieces feature Buddhist motifs and text in Tibetan script, including the famous mantra *Om Mani Padme Hum* (Hail to the Jewel in the Lotus). There's a huge industry in India, Nepal and China making artificially aged Tibetan souvenirs. Loose beads of agate, turquoise, carnelian and silver are also widely available. In South India's Western Ghats, you might find beautiful, rare tribal

Be cautious when buying items that include international delivery, and avoid being led to shops by smooth-talking touts, but don't worry about too much else – except your luggage allowance!

THE GREAT INDIAN BAZAAR JEWELLERY

THE ART OF HAGGLING

Government emporiums, fair-trade cooperatives, department stores and modern shopping centres almost always charge fixed prices. Almost anywhere else you need to bargain. Shopkeepers in tourist hubs are accustomed to travellers who have lots of money and little time to spend it, so you may be charged double or triple the going rate. Souvenir shops are the most notorious.

The first 'rule' of haggling is to never show too much interest in the item you've got your heart set upon. Second, resist purchasing the first thing that takes your fancy. Wander around several shops and price items, but don't make it too obvious: if you return to the first shop, the vendor will know it's because they are the cheapest (resulting in less haggling leeway).

Decide how much you would be happy paying, then express a casual interest in buying. If you have absolutely no idea of the going rate, a common approach is to start by slashing the price by half. The vendor will, most likely, look aghast, but you can now work up and down respectively in small increments until you reach a mutually agreeable price. Many shopkeepers lower their 'final price' if you head out of the shop saying you'll 'think about it'.

Haggling is a way of life in India and usually taken in good spirit. It should never turn ugly. Always keep in mind how much a rupee is worth in your home currency, and how much you'd pay for the item back home, to put things in perspective. If you're not sure of the 'right' price for an item, think about how much it is worth to you. If a vendor seems to be charging an unreasonably high price, look elsewhere.

jewellery crafted by local indigenous communities, such as the Todas near Ooty (Udhagamandalam).

Pearls are produced by most Indian seaside states, but they're a particular speciality of Hyderabad. You'll find them at most state emporiums across the country. Prices vary depending on colour and shape: you pay more for pure white pearls or rare colours such as black, and perfectly round pearls are more expensive than misshapen or elongated pearls. A single strand of seeded pearls can cost as little as ₹500, but better-quality pearls are upward of ₹1200.

Beware of scams involving buying jewels and reselling them overseas – jewels are often fake, or the buyer they were intended for never shows up.

Throughout South India you'll find finely crafted gold and silver rings, anklets, earrings, toe rings, necklaces and bangles; pieces can often be crafted to order.

Leatherwork

As cows are sacred in India, leatherwork is, in theory, made from the skin of buffaloes, camels, goats or other animals. Most large cities offer smart, modern leather footwear at very reasonable prices, some stitched with zillions of sparkly sequins. Jootis (traditional, often pointy-toed, slip-in shoes) from the northern states of Punjab and Rajasthan can be found in South India.

Chappals, those often curly-toed leather sandals, are sold throughout India, but the Maharashtrian cities of Kolhapur, Pune and Matheran are particularly famous for them. Tamil Nadu is a big leather producer, while Puducherry (Pondicherry) is known for its international-influenced leather creations.

Cow slaughter (for consumption, leatherwork or anything else) is illegal in most of India, and some states, such as Maharashtra, have also banned the killing of bulls and bullocks, but discerning travellers will want to be aware that India's leather industry is rife with reports of malpractice and involves complex, unsettling animal-welfare issues.

Metalware

You'll find copper and brassware throughout India. Candle holders, trays, bowls, tankards and ashtrays are popular buys.

In all Indian towns you can find *kadhai* (Indian woks, also known as balti) and other cookware for incredibly low prices. Beaten-brass pots are particularly attractive, while steel storage vessels, copper-bottomed cooking pans and steel thali trays are also popular souvenirs. Ask if you can have your name engraved on them (free of charge).

Many Tibetan religious objects are created by inlaying silver in copper: prayer wheels and traditional document cases are inexpensive purchases.

The people of Bastar in Chhattisgarh use an iron-smelting technique similar to one discovered 35,000 years ago to create abstract sculptures of spindly animal and human figures. These are often also made into functional items such as lamp stands and coat racks, and are found in tribal-crafts shops around India.

Bidri, a damascening method where silver wire is inlaid in gunmetal (a zinc alloy) and rubbed with a paste incorporating soil from Bidar (Karnataka), is used for jewellery, boxes and ornaments, particularly in Bidar itself and Hyderabad.

Top Musical Instrument Shops
....
BX Furtado & Sons (Mumbai)
....
Sri Sharada Grand Musical Works (Mysuru)

Musical Instruments

Quality Indian musical instruments are mostly available in larger cities; prices vary according to each instrument's quality and sound.

Decent tabla sets – a pair of hand drums comprising a wooden tabla (tuned treble drum) and a metal *dugi* or *bayan* (bass drum) – cost upward of ₹5000. Cheaper sets are generally heavier and often sound inferior.

Sitars range from ₹5000 to ₹25,000 (possibly even more). The sound of each sitar will vary with the wood used and the shape of the gourd, so try a few. Note that some cheaper sitars can warp in colder or hotter climates. On any sitar, make sure the strings ring clearly and check the gourd carefully for damage. Spare string sets, sitar plectrums and a screw-in 'amplifier' gourd are sensible additions.

Other popular instruments include the *shehnai* (Indian flute), the sarod (like an Indian lute), the harmonium and the *esraj* (similar to an upright violin). Conventional violins are great value, starting at ₹3500.

Paintings

India has a sizeable contemporary-art scene, and major cities such as Chennai (Madras), Bengaluru (Bangalore) and Hyderabad host many independent galleries and shops selling work by local artists.

Miniatures

Reproductions of Indian miniature paintings are widely available, but quality varies: the cheaper ones have less detail and are made with inferior materials. A bigger range of quality miniatures is generally found in northern India than in the south, but state-run craft emporiums and antique shops are always worth a browse.

In southern regions such as Kerala and Tamil Nadu, you'll come across miniature paintings on leaf skeletons that portray domestic life, rural scenes and deities.

Tanjore Paintings

Tamil Nadu's famous Thanjavur (Tanjore) paintings typically depict Hindu deities in bright colours with gold foil and glass beads, or occasionally gemstones. They may be done on canvas, wood or glass. Much of today's output is a somewhat kitschified version of a venerable tradition that goes back to the 17th century, but it's worth keeping an eye open for authentic old works in antique shops.

Folk Art & Kalamkari

Telangana's *cheriyal* paintings, in bright, primary colours, were originally made as scrolls for travelling storytellers. The ancient textile-painting art of *kalamkari* is practised in Andhra Pradesh, where Sri Kalahasti is the best place to see artists at work and buy their art, and at Chennai's Kalakshetra Foundation (p333), which offers *kalamkari* courses. It involves priming cotton cloth with resin and cow's milk, then drawing and

India's bazaars are the heart and soul of its commercial life. The name bazaar often refers to a street lined with shops and/or stalls, rather than a separate trading area.

THE GREAT INDIAN BAZAAR PAINTINGS

PUTTING YOUR MONEY WHERE IT COUNTS

Overall, a comparatively small proportion of the money brought to India by tourism reaches people in rural areas. Travellers can make a greater contribution by shopping at community cooperatives, set up to protect and promote traditional cottage industries, and to provide education, training and a sustainable livelihood at the grassroots level. Many of these projects focus on low-caste women, tribal people, refugees and others living on society's fringes.

The quality of products sold at cooperatives is high and prices are usually fixed, so you won't have to haggle. A share of the sales money is channelled directly into social projects such as schools, health care, training and other advocacy programs for socially disadvantaged groups. Shopping at the national network of Khadi & Village Industries Commission emporiums (www.kvic.org.in), or the shops of Tribes India (http://tribesindia.com), the profits of which help support tribal artisans, also contributes to rural communities.

Wherever you travel, keep your eyes peeled for fair-trade cooperatives.

painting deities or legendary or historic events with a pointed bamboo stick *(kalam)* dipped in fermented jaggery and water; dyes are made from cow dung, ground seeds, plants and flowers. *Kalamkari* from Machilipatnam, also in Andhra Pradesh, employs block-printing in combination with freehand drawing.

Thangkas

Tibetan craft shops often sell *thangkas* (rectangular Tibetan cloth paintings) depicting Tantric Buddhist deities and ceremonial mandalas. Some re-create the glory of murals in India's medieval gompas (Tibetan Buddhist monasteries); others are simpler. Prices vary, but expect to pay at least ₹5000 for a decent-quality A3-size *thangka*, and a lot more (up to around ₹50,000) for large intricate *thangkas*.

Textiles

Textile production is India's major industry. Around 40% takes place at village level, where the cloth produced is known as *khadi* (homespun cloth, usually cotton) – hence the government-backed *khadi* emporiums around the country. These inexpensive superstores sell all sorts of items made from *khadi*, including the popular Nehru jackets and kurta pyjamas (long shirt and loose-fitting trousers), with sales benefiting rural communities. *Khadi* has recently become increasingly chic, with India's designers referencing and incorporating the fabrics in their collections.

You'll find a truly amazing variety of weaving and embroidery techniques all over India. In tourist centres such as Goa, Kerala, Rajasthan and Himachal Pradesh, patterned textiles are made into shoulder bags, wall hangings, cushion covers, bedspreads, clothes and more. Items from Adivasi (tribal) peoples of Telangana, Gujarat and Rajasthan often have small pieces of mirrored glass eye-catchingly embroidered on to them.

Among the tribal communities of Tamil Nadu's Nilgiri Hills, the embroidery-skilled Todas make, wear and sell unique, beautiful black-and-red-embroidered shawls.

Shawls

Indian shawls are famously warm and lightweight. It's worth buying one to use as a blanket on cold night journeys. Shawls are made from all sorts of wool; many are embroidered with intricate designs. The best-known varieties all come from northern India but some make their way to outlets in the south, including Kashmiri *pashmina* shawls (made from the downy hair of the pashmina goat) and subtly embroidered and mirrored lambswool shawls from Gujarat's Kachchh (Kutch) region. Authentic *pashmina* shawls cost several thousand rupees, though many 'pashminas' are actually a *pashmina*-silk blend, which means they're cheaper (around ₹1200) but still beautiful.

GANDHI'S CLOTH

Almost 100 years ago Mohandas Gandhi urged Indians to support the freedom movement by ditching their foreign-made clothing and turning to *khadi* (homespun cloth). *Khadi* became a symbol of Indian independence, and the fabric is still closely associated with politics. The government-run, nonprofit group Khadi & Village Industries Commission (www.kvic.org.in) serves to promote *khadi*, which is usually cotton, but can also be silk or wool.

Khadi outlets are simple, no-nonsense places where you can pick up genuine Indian clothing such as kurta pyjamas, headscarves, saris and, at some branches, assorted handicrafts – you'll find them all over India. Prices are reasonable and often discounted in the period around Gandhi's birthday (2 October). A number of outlets also have tailoring services.

TAILORS

Many South Indian tailor's shops can run up new items for you the same day; if you just want a good copy of your favourite garment, they'll do that too. In Tamil Nadu, Madurai's Pudhu Mandapa (p383) is a 16th-century temple pavilion filled with finely sculpted stone pillars, along with dozens of tailors busy treadling away at sewing machines for just this purpose; a cotton top or shirt can cost ₹350.

Saris

Saris are a very popular souvenir, especially as they can be easily adapted to other purposes (from cushion covers to skirts). Real silk saris are the most expensive; the silk usually needs to be washed before it becomes soft. India's 'silk capital' is Kanchipuram in Tamil Nadu (Kanchipuram silk is also widely available in Chennai), but you can also find fine silk saris (and cheaper scarves) in other centres including Mysuru (Mysore). You'll pay upward of ₹3000 for a quality embroidered silk sari.

Aurangabad, in Maharashtra, is the traditional producer of Himroo shawls, sheets and saris, made from a blend of cotton, silk and metallic thread. Silk and gold-thread saris produced at Paithan (near Aurangabad) are some of India's finest; prices range from around ₹8000 to a mind-blowing ₹150,000. Madhya Pradesh is famous for its cotton Maheshwari saris (from Maheshwar) and silk Chanderi saris (from Chanderi), while Chettinadu (Tamil Nadu) is known for its handwoven silk-and-cotton Kandaangi saris.

Patan in Gujarat is the centre for the ancient, laborious craft of Patola-making: every thread in these splendid silk saris is individually hand-dyed before weaving, and patterned borders are woven with real gold.

Appliqué & Block Print

Appliqué, where decorative motifs are sewn on to a larger cloth, is an ancient art in India, with most states producing their own version, often featuring abstract or anthropomorphic patterns. Traditional lampshades and *pandals* (marquees) used in weddings and festivals are usually produced using this technique.

Block-printed and woven textiles are made, and sold by fabric shops, all over India: each region has its own speciality. Block-printing involves stamping the design on the fabric with carved wooden blocks – a laborious but highly skilled process that produces beautiful results. India-wide retail chain stores Fabindia (www.fabindia.com) and Anokhi (www.anokhi.com) strive to preserve traditional patterns and fabrics, transforming them into home-decor items and Indian- and Western-style fashions.

Woodcarving

Woodcarving is an ancient art form throughout India. Sandalwood carvings of Hindu deities are one of Karnataka's specialities, with high prices to match: a 10cm-high Ganesh costs around ₹3000 in sandalwood (which releases fragrance for years), compared to roughly ₹300 in kadamb wood. Beautiful deity figures and decorative inlaid boxes and furniture are carved from rosewood in Andhra Pradesh, Karnataka and Kerala.

Buddhist woodcarvings are a speciality of Tibetan refugee areas – including wall plaques of the eight lucky signs, carved dragons and reproductions of *chaam* masks used for ritual dances.

Indian Textiles (John Gillow and Nicholas Barnard) explores the cultural background of India's many beautiful textile techniques, including weaving, block-printing, painting, tie-dye and embroidery, and details products of different regions.

On the Papier Mâché Trail

Artisans in Jammu and Kashmir have been producing lacquered papier mâché for centuries, and papier mâché–ware is now sold across India, making inexpensive yet beautiful gifts. The basic shape is made in a mould from layers of paper (often recycled newsprint), then painted with fine brushes and lacquered for protection. Prices depend on design complexity and quality and the amount of gold leaf used. Many pieces feature patterns of animals and flowers, or hunting scenes from Mughal miniature paintings. You can find papier mâché bowls, boxes, coasters, trays, lamps, puppets and Christmas decorations. Colourful Rajasthani puppets are another Indian papier mâché speciality.

Other Great Finds

It's little surprise that Indian spices are snapped up by tourists. Virtually all towns have shops and bazaars selling locally made spices at great prices. Karnataka, Kerala, Uttar Pradesh, Rajasthan and Tamil Nadu produce most of the spices that go into garam masala (the 'hot mix' used to flavour Indian dishes), while the Northeast States and Sikkim are known for black cardamom and cinnamon bark. Note that some countries, such as Australia, have stringent rules regarding the import of animal and plant products.

Attar (essential oil, mostly made from flowers) can be found around the country. Mysuru (Mysore), in Karnataka, is famous for its sandalwood oil, while Mumbai (Bombay) is a major centre for the trade of traditional fragrances, including valuable *oud,* made from a rare mould that grows on the bark of the agarwood tree. In Tamil Nadu, Ooty and Kodai produce aromatic and medicinal oils from herbs, flowers and eucalyptus.

Indian incense is exported worldwide, with Karnataka's Bengaluru (Bangalore) and Mysuru being major producers. Incenses, as well as clothing, essential oils and perfumed candles, from Auroville in Tamil Nadu and Sri Aurobindo Ashram (p360) in Puducherry (Pondicherry) are also renowned and easy to find locally.

A Goan speciality is feni: a head-spinning spirit distilled from coconut milk or cashews that often comes in decorative bottles.

Quality Indian tea is sold in parts of South India, such as Munnar in Kerala and the Ooty area in Tamil Nadu's Western Ghats. There are also top tea retailers in urban hubs.

Thanjavur in Tamil Nadu is famed for its brightly painted bobble-head dolls, made from terracotta or wood.

Fine-quality handmade paper – often fashioned into cards, boxes and notebooks – is worth seeking out, especially in Puducherry and Mumbai.

Indian cities have some good bookshops, with books at competitive prices, including leather-bound titles. Higginbothams (p341) in Chennai, in business since 1844, is India's oldest bookshop and still going strong. Asian Educational Services publishes old (17th- to early-20th-century) and out-of-stock titles in original typeface.

Ever bigger, brighter and flashier, modern malls are an integral part of the South Indian city shopping scene. They're full of Indian and international fashion, with prices similar to those in the Western world.

The Arts

Over the millenniums India's many ethnic groups have spawned a rich artistic heritage, and today you'll experience art both lofty and humble around every corner: from intricately painted trucks on dusty roads to harmonic chanting emanating from ancient temples and booming Bollywood blockbusters. The wealth of creative expression is a highlight of travelling in South India, and today's artists fuse ancient and modern influences to create art, dance, music and literature that are as evocative as they are beautiful.

Dance

The ancient Indian art of dance is traditionally linked to mythology and classical literature.

Classical

Classical dance is based on well-defined traditional disciplines. Of India's eight schools of classical dance, these are the ones you're most likely to encounter in South India.

➡ *Bharatanatyam*, which originated in Tamil Nadu, has been embraced throughout India. Noted for its graceful movements, it was traditionally performed by solo women, but now often includes male dancers and/or group performances. Songs, poems, prayers and Carnatic (characteristic of South India) music are part of the performance.

➡ Kathakali, with its roots in Kerala (possibly around the 17th century), is a classical dance-drama with drum and vocal accompaniment, based on the Hindu epics.

➡ Kuchipudi is a 17th-century dance-drama that originated in the Andhra Pradesh village from which it takes its name. The story centres on the envious wife of Krishna.

➡ *Mohiniyattam,* the 'dance of the enchantress', is a graceful Keralan form performed by solo women.

Folk

Indian folk dance ranges from the theatrical dummy-horse dances of Karnataka and Tamil Nadu to Punjab's high-spirited bhangra dance. Northern Kerala's *theyyam* rituals feature wild drumming and frenzied dancing by participants embodying deities or heroes, with headdresses sometimes several metres high.

Pioneers of modern dance forms in India include Uday Shankar (older brother of the sitar master Ravi Shankar), who once partnered Russian ballerina Anna Pavlova. The dance you'll most commonly see, though, is in films, often combining traditional, folk, modern and contemporary choreography.

Music

Indian classical music traces its roots back to Vedic times, when religious poems chanted by priests were first collated in the Rig-Veda. Over the millenniums classical music has been shaped by many influences, and the legacy today is Carnatic and Hindustani (the classical style of North

Indian Classical Dance, by Leela Venkataraman and Avinash Pasricha, is a lavishly illustrated book covering various Indian dance forms, including *bharatanatyam,* Kuchipudi and Kathakali.

Most big South Indian cities have venues staging regular classical dance or music performances, but Chennai (Madras) and Mumbai (Bombay) have the most frequent performances (almost nightly). Kochi (Cochin) is the best place to catch Kathakali performances.

India) music. With common origins, they share a number of features. Composition and improvisation are both based on the raga (the melodic shape of the music) and the *tala* (the rhythmic meter characterised by the number of beats); *tintal,* for example, has a *tala* of 16 beats. The audience follows the *tala* by clapping at the appropriate beat, which in *tintal* is at beats one, five and 13. The ninth beat is the *khali* (empty section), indicated by a wave of the hand.

Both Carnatic and Hindustani music are performed by small ensembles, generally comprising three to six musicians, and both have many instruments in common. The most obvious difference is Carnatic's greater use of voice. Hindustani has been more heavily influenced by Persian musical conventions (a result of Mughal rule); Carnatic music, as it developed in South India, cleaves more closely to theory.

One of the best-known Indian instruments is the sitar (a large stringed instrument), with which the soloist plays the raga. Ravi Shankar, master of the sitar, is generally praised as the 20th century's most influential Hindustani classical musician, bringing sitar-playing to the international stage in the 1960s. Other stringed instruments include the sarod (which is plucked) and the *sarangi* (played with a bow). Also popular is the tabla (twin drums), which provides the *tala*. The drone, which runs on two basic notes, is provided by the oboe-like *shehnai* or the stringed *tampura* (also spelt tamboura). The hand-pumped keyboard harmonium is used as a secondary melody instrument for vocal music.

Indian regional folk music is widespread and varied. Wandering musicians, magicians, snake charmers and storytellers often use song to entertain their audiences; the storyteller usually sings the tales from the great epics.

You might also come across *qawwali* (Sufi devotional singing), performed in mosques or at musical concerts.

A completely different genre altogether, filmi (music from films) includes modern, slower-paced love serenades along with hyperactive dance songs, typically performed by lip-synching actors.

Painting

South India's earliest art was painted on cave walls and reached its supreme expression around 1500 years ago when artists covered the walls and ceilings of the Ajanta Caves (p165), in Maharashtra, with scenes from the Buddha's past lives. The figures are endowed with an unusual freedom and grace. Later, painters also decorated the walls of temples and palaces, though little of this mural art has survived from before the time of the Vijayanagar empire (14th to 16th centuries), which left fine frescos at Hampi's Virupaksha Temple (p210).

The Indo-Persian painting style, coupling geometric design with flowing form, developed in Islamic royal courts, with some indigenous influences. Persian influence blossomed when artisans fled to India following the 1507 Uzbek attack on Herat (in present-day Afghanistan), and with

Get arty with *Indian Art*, by Roy C Craven; *Contemporary Indian Art: Other Realities*, edited by Yashodhara Dalmia; and *Indian Miniature Painting*, by Dr Daljeet and Professor PC Jain.

Around 2000 feature films are produced annually in India. Apart from hundreds of millions of local Bolly , Tolly and Kollywood buffs, there are also millions of Non-Resident Indian (NRI) fans, who have played a significant role in catapulting Indian cinema on to the international stage.

MEHNDI

Mehndi is the traditional art of painting a woman's hands (and sometimes feet) with intricate henna designs for auspicious ceremonies, such as marriage. If quality henna is used, the orange-brown design can last up to one month.

In touristy areas, *mehndi*-wallahs are adept at applying henna tattoo 'bands' on the arms, hands, legs and lower back; allow at least a few hours for the design and drying time. It's wise to request that the artist do a test spot on your arm before proceeding: some dyes contain chemicals that can cause allergies. Avoid 'black henna', which is mixed with chemicals that may be harmful.

CLASSICAL DANCE & MUSIC FESTIVALS

Mumbai Sanskruti (p45) January

Thyagaraja Aradhana (p374) Thiruvaiyuru, Tamil Nadu; January

Mamallapuram Dance Festival (p350) Tamil Nadu; January/February

Natyanjali Dance Festival (p368) Chidambaram, Tamil Nadu; February/March

Elephanta Festival (p45) Mumbai; February/March

Ellora Ajanta Aurangabad Festival (p82) Aurangabad; October/November

Chennai Festival of Music & Dance (p333) December/January

trade and gift-swapping between Shiraz, a Persian centre for miniature production, and Indian provincial sultans. The most celebrated Indo-Persian art developed at the Mughal court in northern India from the mid-16th century, particularly under emperor Akbar (r 1556–1605). The Mughal style, often in colourful miniature form, largely depicts court life, architecture, battle and hunting scenes, as well as detailed portraits.

Miniature painting also flourished in the Deccan sultanates of the 16th and 17th centuries. The landscapes and floral backgrounds here reflect Persian influence, though Deccani in subject matter, while the elongated figures draw on Vijayanagar traditions. Colours are rich, with much use of gold and white.

Temple mural painting, on multifarious historical and mythological themes, continued to flourish in the south: there are fine Nayak-era frescos at Thanjavur, (p372) Kumbakonam (p369) and Chidambaram (p368) in Tamil Nadu. Superb Hindu-myth murals were painted at Kochi's Mattancherry Palace (p301) in the 16th century.

A unique local South Indian art known as Tanjore painting took root in Thanjavur from the 17th century, typically depicting Krishna and other Hindu deities in bright colours, against a background of thrones, curtains and arches which, along with the deities' clothing, are picked out in gold leaf studded with gemstones or glass beads. This tradition lives on today in a somewhat debased, kitsch form.

Kerala's Ravi Varma (1848–1906) popularised oil painting with colourful, European-style treatments of scenes from Indian mythology and literature, including depictions of Hindu goddesses modelled from South Indian women, and has had a huge influence on subsequent religious art and movie posters. Maharashtra's Maqbool Fida Husain, India's major post-Independence artist, was famed for his often controversial modified cubist works, among them representations of naked Hindu gods.

The Madras Movement, whose cooperative base you can visit at Cholamandal Artists' Village (p346) near Chennai, pioneered modern art in South India in the 1960s. In the 21st century, paintings by modern and contemporary Indian artists have been selling at record numbers (and prices) around the world. Delhi and Mumbai (Bombay) are India's contemporary-art centres, but most large cities have worthwhile galleries.

The top-earning Bollywood male actors, all raking in over US$20 million a year according to Forbes (www.forbes.com), are Shahrukh Khan, Salman Khan, Amitabh Bachchan and Akshay Kumar. The highest-earning female actor, at US$10 million, is Deepika Padukone.

Cinema

India's film industry was born in the late 19th century; the first major Indian-made motion picture, *Panorama of Calcutta*, was screened in 1899. India's first real feature film, *Raja Harishchandra*, was made during the silent era in 1913 and it's ultimately from this film that Indian cinema traces its vibrant lineage.

Today, India's film industry is the biggest in the world. Mumbai, the Hindi-language film capital, aka 'Bollywood', is the biggest name, but

Top Film Festivals

Mumbai Film Festival; October

International Film Festival of India Panaji, Goa; November

India's other major film-producing cities – Chennai (Kollywood), Hyderabad (Tollywood) and Bengaluru (Sandalwood) – also have a huge output. In recent years there has also been a surge in the number of films produced in Goa.

Broadly speaking, there are two categories of Indian films. Most prominent is the mainstream 'masala' movie, named for its 'spice mix' of elements for every member of the family: romance, action, slapstick humour and moral themes. Three hours and still running, these often tear-jerking blockbusters are packed with dramatic twists interspersed with song-and-dance performances. There's no explicit sex in Indian films; even kissing is rare. Instead, it's all about intense flirting and loaded innuendo; heroines are often seen in skimpy or body-hugging attire.

The second genre is art house, or parallel cinema, which adopts Indian 'reality' as its base and aims to be socially and politically relevant. Usually made on infinitely smaller budgets than their commercial cousins, these films are the ones that win kudos at global film festivals. The late Bengali director Satyajit Ray, most famous for his 1950s work, is the father of Indian art films.

Shot on shoestring budget by Dalit director Nagraj Manjule, anti-Bollywood *Sairat* (2016) tells the heart-wrenchingly realistic story of doomed inter-caste love between an uppercaste girl and a fisherman's son. To date, it is the highest-grossing film in Marathi cinema history.

Literature

India has a long tradition of Sanskrit literature, and works in the vernacular languages have also contributed to a particularly rich legacy. The Tamil poetic works known as the Sangams, written between the 3rd century BC and 3rd century AD, are the earliest known South Indian literature.

Bengal is traditionally credited with producing some of India's finest literature, and Rabindranath Tagore (1861–1941) was the first Indian writer to really propel India's cultural richness on to the world literary stage, through the fiction, plays and poetry he wrote in Bengali.

One of the earliest Indian authors to receive an international audience was RK Narayan, who wrote in English in the 1930s and whose deceptively simple writing about life in a fictional South Indian town called Malgudi is subtly hilarious. Keralan Kamala Das (Kamala Suraiyya) wrote poetry and memoirs in English; her frank approach to love and sexuality broke ground for women writers in the 1960s and '70s.

The prolific writer and artist Rabindranath Tagore won the Nobel Prize in Literature in 1913 for *Gitanjali*. For a taste of Tagore's work, read *Selected Short Stories*.

India has an ever-growing list of internationally acclaimed contemporary authors. Winners of the prestigious Man Booker Prize have included Chennai-bred Aravind Adiga (2008), for his debut novel *The White Tiger*, set between Bengaluru (Bangalore) and northern India, and Kiran Desai (2006) for *The Inheritance of Loss*. Desai's mother Anita Desai has thrice made the Booker shortlist, as has Rohinton Mistry, a Mumbai-bred Parsi, with three novels all set in Mumbai. Kolkata-born Amitav Ghosh's *Sea of Poppies* (the first in his *Ibis* trilogy) was shortlisted for the 2008 Booker. In 1997 Keralan Arundhati Roy won the Booker for *The God of Small Things*, set in a small Keralan town, while Mumbai-born Salman Rushdie took this coveted award in 1981 for *Midnight's Children*.

Architectural Splendour

From lofty temple gateways adorned with rainbows of delicately carved deities to whitewashed cube-like village houses, South India has a fascinatingly rich architectural heritage. Traditional buildings often have a superb sense of placement within the local environment, whether perched on a boulder-strewn hill or a lakefront. British bungalows with corrugated-iron roofs and wide verandahs linger in most hill stations, but most memorable are buildings that beautifully blend European and Indian architecture, such as breathtaking Mysuru Palace (p184).

Sacred Creations

Temples

Throughout India, most early large-scale architecture was not built but excavated. Buddhist, Hindu and Jain temples, shrines and monasteries were carved out of solid rock or developed from existing caves at various times between the 3rd century BC and 10th century AD. Outstanding rock-cut architecture in South India includes Maharashtra's awe-inspiring Ajanta (p165) and Ellora (p165) Caves, Mamallapuram (Maha-balipuram) in Tamil Nadu, Mumbai's (Bombay's) Elephanta Island cave temples (p57), Karnataka's Badami (p219) cave temples, and Andhra Pradesh's Buddhist complex Guntupalli (p247).

It was during the Gupta period in North India (4th to 6th century AD) that the first free-standing temples were built, to enshrine Hindu deities. The Badami Chalukyas of Karnataka took up the idea at Aihole and Pattadakal between the 4th and 8th centuries, as did the Pallavas of Tamil Nadu at Kanchipuram and Mamallapuram in the 8th century. Towers called *vimanas* on southern temples were equivalent to the *sikhara* towers of North Indian temples. The three great 11th- and 12th-century Chola temples at Thanjavur and outside Kumbakonam, with enormous *vimanas* rising above their central shrines, represent the apogee of early southern temple architecture. In many later southern temples, tall, sculpture-encrusted entrance towers called *gopurams* replaced *vimanas* as the main architectural feature. Madurai's Meenakshi Amman Temple (p381), in Tamil Nadu, with its 12 tall *gopurams*, is reckoned to be the peak of South Indian temple architecture. Also typical of what has become known as the Dravidian temple style is the *mandapa*, a pavilion of often richly carved columns that serves as a meeting hall or approach to the central shrine.

The Hoysala empire based in southern Karnataka in the 12th and 13th centuries developed a distinctive style of temples covered in elaborate, detailed carving, with relatively low *vimanas*, as seen at Belur, Halebid and Somnathpur. The 14th-to-16th-century Vijayanagar empire took the *gopuram* and *mandapa* to some of their finest levels not only at the capital, Karnataka's Hampi, but also at Vellore and Trichy's Sri Ranganathaswamy Temple (p375) in Tamil Nadu.

Discover more about India's diverse temple architecture (in addition to other temple-related information and recommendations) at insightful Temple Net (www.templenet.com).

Masterpieces of Traditional Indian Architecture, by Satish Grover, and *Introduction to Indian Architecture*, by Bindia Thapar, Surat Kumar Manto and Suparna Bhalla, offer interesting insights into temple and other architecture.

Holy Squares & Purifying Waters

For Hindus, the square is a perfect shape, and southern temples often take the form of several square (or rectangular) compounds of diminishing size nested one inside another. Complex rules govern the location, design and building of temples, based on numerology, astrology, astronomy and religious principles. Essentially, a temple represents a map of the universe. At the centre is the *garbhagriha* (inner sanctum), symbolic of the 'womb-cave' from which the universe is believed to have emerged. This provides a residence for the deity to which the temple is dedicated.

Commonly used for ritual bathing and religious ceremonies, as well as adding aesthetic appeal to places of worship, temple tanks have long been a focal point of temple activity. These often vast, angular, engineered reservoirs of water, sometimes fed by rain, sometimes fed by rivers (via complicated drainage systems), serve both sacred and secular purposes. The waters of some temple tanks are believed to have healing properties; others are said to wash away sins. Devotees (as well as travellers) may be required to wash their feet in a temple tank before entering a place of worship.

The basic elements of mosque layout are similar worldwide. A large hall is dedicated to communal prayer; within is the mihrab, a niche indicating the direction of Mecca. Outside is often a courtyard with a pool or fountain for ritual preprayer ablutions. The faithful are called to prayer from minarets.

Islamic Monuments

Muslim rule over much of northern India from the late 12th century, extending later to the Deccan, saw typical Islamic forms such as domes, arches and minaret towers dominate monumental architecture. Karnataka's 15th-century Bahmani Tombs (p224) at Bidar are among the earliest major Islamic monuments on the Deccan. They were followed by the great 16th- and 17th-century Qutb Shahi monuments of Hyderabad and Golconda – magnificent big-domed royal tombs (p233), a huge mosque (p228) and a unique mosque-landmark, the Charminar (p228) – and Vijapura's (Bijapur's) wonderful 17th-century mausoleum, the Golgumbaz (p221). The latter was completed in Karnataka just a few years after Mughal architecture in northern India achieved its peak of perfection in the Taj Mahal. In Maharashtra, Aurangabad's Bibi-qa-Maqbara (p87), or the poor man's Taj, also dates from the 17th century.

Southern Tamil Nadu's Chettinadu region contains 10,000 (maybe 30,000) magnificent mansions, some of them genuinely palatial, built by traders made rich in the 19th century. Many are now abandoned or decaying, but some are open to visitors. A few have been transformed into fascinating hotels, including Visalam (p380) and Saratha Vilas (p380).

Churches & Cathedrals

Most of India's estimated 27.8 million Christians reside in South India, and the extended presence of European colonialists here engendered many majestic churches. According to legend, Christianity was introduced to India through Kerala in AD 52 by St Thomas the Apostle, who was martyred at St Thomas Mount (p333), Chennai (Madras), and buried at what is now the city's 19th-century neo-Gothic San Thome Cathedral (p332). Chennai's Portuguese-built 1516 Luz Church (p333) is reputed to be one of India's most ancient churches.

Thanks to the Portuguese (who controlled Goa from the 16th century until 1961), it is Goa that famously takes South India's church architecture to its finest heights. Sporting sumptuous interiors, Goa's late-Renaissance- or baroque-inspired churches are typically made of whitewashed laterite. You'll find some of the best in Old Goa, including the celebrated 1605 Basilica of Bom Jesus (p128). Goa is also known for its Portuguese Manueline church architecture, exemplified by Old Goa's Church of Our Lady of the Rosary (p129).

In Kerala (controlled variously by the Portuguese, Dutch and British), Kochi's (Cochin's) impressive collection of centuries-old churches includes 16th-century St Francis Church (p301), India's oldest European-built church – and the original burial spot of Portuguese voyager Vasco da Gama (his remains were later moved to Lisbon).

Former French colony Puducherry (Pondicherry) hosts some of India's most magnificent churches, including 19th-century Notre Dame des Anges (p362) and Goa-like 1791 Our Lady of the Immaculate Conception Cathedral (p362). British-built churches tend to be neoclassical or neo-Gothic; Chennai's St Andrew's Church (p333) is an exquisite example of the former. Most of South India's hill stations have moody colonial-era British-style churches.

Forts & Palaces

The frequent wars between old Indian kingdoms and empires, as well as the later involvement of colonial powers, naturally led to the construction of some highly imposing fortresses. A typical South Indian fort sits on a hill or rocky outcrop, with a ring or rings of moated battlements protecting the inner citadel. It usually has a town nestled at its base. Gingee (p359) in Tamil Nadu is a particularly good example. Vellore Fort (p355), also in Tamil Nadu, is one of India's best-known moated forts, while Bidar (p223) and Vijapura (Bijapur) in Karnataka and Golconda (p231) in Hyderabad host great metropolitan forts.

Daulatabad (p91) in Maharashtra is another magnificent structure, with 5km of walls surrounding a hilltop fortress reached by passageways filled with ingenious defences like spike-studded doors and false tunnels. Maharashtra's many other impressive forts include several built or used by the 17th-century Maratha hero Shivaji, including Raigad (p102) and Pratapgad (p115) forts. The 16th-century Janjira fort (p101), off Maharashtra's Konkan Coast, was built by descendants of African slaves and will blow you away with its 12m walls rising straight from the sea, brooding gateway and mighty bastions. Like Goa's almost as impressively situated 17th-century Fort Aguada (p131), it was never conquered.

Few old palaces remain in South India: conquerors often targeted these for destruction. The remains of the Vijayanagar royal complex at Hampi indicate local engineers weren't averse to using the sound structural techniques and fashions (domes, arches) of their Muslim adversaries, the Bahmanis. In Tamil Nadu, the remarkable palace of the Travancore maharajas at Padmanabhapuram (p391) dates back to 1550 and is South India's finest example of traditional Keralan architecture. Other notable palaces include Mattancherry Palace (p301) in Kochi (Cochin), Kerala; Thanjavur (Tanjore) Royal Palace (p372), Tamil Nadu; Aga Khan Palace (p109) in Pune, Maharashtra, where Gandhi was once imprisoned; and Tipu Sultan's Summer Palace (p193) at Srirangapatnam.

Indo-Saracenic, a conflation of European, Islamic and Hindu architectural styles that blossomed all over India in the late 19th century, produced not only grandiose functional edifices, such as Mumbai's Victoria (Chhatrapati Shivaji) Terminus (p47) railway station and Chennai's Madras High Court (p330), but also numerous flamboyant Indian royal palaces. The opulent diamond of the south is marvellous Mysuru Palace (p184), its interior a kaleidoscope of stained glass, mirrors and mosaic floors.

You can get a good idea of the unbelievable wealth of Hyderabad's former rulers, the nizams, from their Chowmahalla and Falaknuma Palaces, the latter now a luxury hotel.

George Michell's *Southern India: A Guide to Monuments, Sites & Museums* shines a detailed light on the region's multifaceted architectural treasures, from Tamil Nadu's psychedelic temples to Goa's elegant churches.

ARCHITECTURAL SPLENDOUR FORTS & PALACES

Wildlife & Landscape

South India's wildlife is a fascinating melange of animals whose ancestors roamed Europe, Asia and the ancient southern supercontinent Gondwana, in a great mix of habitats from steamy mangrove forests and jungles to expansive plains. The South Asian subcontinent is an ancient block of earth crust that arrived with a wealth of unique plants and animals when it collided with the Eurasian Plate 40 million years ago, after a 100-million-year journey from Gondwana.

Wildlife

Signature Species

India's national animal is the tiger, its national bird is the peacock and its national flower is the lotus. The national emblem of India is a column topped by three Asiatic lions.

It's fortunate that Asian elephants – a thoroughly different species from the larger African elephant – are revered in Hindu custom and were able to be domesticated and put to work. Otherwise they may well have been hunted to extinction long ago, as in neighbouring China. Indian wild-elephant numbers were estimated to be around 30,000 in 2012, up from 27,700 in 2007, despite poaching and habitat destruction. These 3000kg animals migrate long distances in search of food and require huge parks, running into predictable conflict when herds attempt to follow ancestral paths now occupied by villages and farms. The purchase of ivory souvenirs supports the poaching of these magnificent creatures, and many countries have strict customs guidelines preventing ivory importation.

The tiger is fixed in the subcontinent's subconscious as the mythological mount of the powerful, demon-slaying goddess Durga, while prowling the West's image of India as Mowgli's jungle nemesis. This awesome, iconic animal is endangered, but its numbers in India seem to be on the rise, up from 1706 in 2010 to 2226 in 2014 according to India's official census (though there are some doubts about data accuracy). The tiger can be seen, if you're lucky, at India's tiger reserves.

Despite India's seemingly encouraging tiger numbers, a shocking 74 tigers were documented to have died in the first six months of 2016. At least 30 of them were poached; other causes include infighting, loss of prey and habitat, vehicle accidents and human-wildlife conflict.

India is also home to 15 other species of cat. Leopards are quite widespread in different types of forest and in several parks and sanctuaries in the south – but elusive, nevertheless. In recent decades some leopards have increasingly been found close to (and even within) some of India's ever-expanding towns and cities, where they prey on dogs, cats, pigs and rodents (with the occasional human fatality too).

Common Encounters

Easily the most abundant forms of wildlife you'll see in India are deer (nine species), antelope (six species), goats and sheep (10 species), and primates (15 species). The ones you're most likely to see in the parks and reserves of the south include the chital (spotted deer), sambar (a large deer), nilgai or bluebull (a large antelope), the elegant grey (Hanuman) langur with its characteristic black face and ears, and the bonnet macaque which often loiters around temples and tourist sites. Also fairly often spotted are the gaur (Indian bison) and wild boar; you can also hope to see the occasional sloth bear (with its long white snout), golden jackal or giant squirrel.

PROJECT TIGER

When naturalist Jim Corbett first raised the alarm in the 1930s, no one else believed that tigers would ever be threatened. At the time it was believed there were 40,000 tigers in India, although no one had ever counted them. Then came Independence, which put guns into the hands of villagers who pushed into formerly off-limits hunting reserves seeking highly profitable tiger skins. By the time an official census was conducted in 1972, there were only an estimated 1800 tigers left and international outcry prompted Indira Gandhi to set up Project Tiger. The project has since established 50 tiger reserves totalling 71,027 sq km (including buffer zones) that not only protect this top predator but all animals that live in the same habitats. After an initial round of successes, neglect, habitat loss, corruption and relentless poaching saw tiger numbers down to just 1411 in 2006, the first year a relatively reliable counting system based on camera traps was used. That year, Project Tiger was transformed into the National Tiger Conservation Authority (http://projecttiger.nic.in, www.tigernet.nic.in), a statutory body with a bigger budget, more on-the-ground staff, and more teeth to fight poaching and the trade in tiger parts. Tiger numbers rose to 1706 in the 2010 census and 2226 in the 2014 census – encouraging statistics, but tigers continue to be poached, their habitat outside tiger reserves is shrinking and there's still doubt over the reliability of collected data. India's tigers account for around 70% of the total world tiger population.

WILDLIFE & LANDSCAPE WILDLIFE

Endangered Species

Despite its amazing biodiversity, India faces an ever-growing challenge from its exploding human population. Wildlife is severely threatened by poaching, habitat loss and human-animal conflict. The 2016 Red List of the International Union for Conservation of Nature listed 1052 threatened species in India, including 387 plant species, 92 mammal species, 87 bird species, 54 reptile species, 75 amphibian species, 222 fish species and 128 invertebrate species. Of these, 75 are in the most at-risk category, 'critically endangered'; 205 are in the next most imperilled group, 'endangered'; and 385 are 'vulnerable'.

Even the massively resourced National Tiger Conservation Authority faces an uphill battle every day. The number of tiger reserves is growing, but the total amount of territory roamed by tigers is shrinking. And every encouraging tiger news story seems to be followed by another of poaching gangs or tiger or leopard attacks on villagers. The Wildlife Protection Society of India documented 1060 tigers and 4226 leopards killed by poachers between 1995 and 2015, but warns that total numbers may be far higher. 'Critically endangered' animals found in South India include the great Indian bustard, a large, heavy bird of which less than 250 survive in isolated pockets of South and North India; the Anamalai flying frog (living only in Tamil Nadu's Anamalai Tiger Reserve); the Malabar large-spotted civet (less than 250 in the Western Ghats, possibly even extinct); and four species of vulture (p486).

Species of South India on the 'endangered' list include the tiger; elephant; dhole (wild dog; around 2000 surviving); the lion-tailed macaque, with its splendid silvery-white mane (3000 to 3500 remaining, in the Western Ghats); and the Nilgiri tahr, a wild sheep of the Nilgiri Hills (around 1800 remaining).

Birds

With over 1250 highly varied species (925 of which breed here), India is a birdwatcher's dream. Wherever critical habitat has been preserved in the midst of dense human activity, you might see phenomenal numbers of birds in one location. Winter (November to February) is a particularly good time, as wetlands host northern migrants flocking to the subtropical warmth of the Indian peninsula.

Founded by celebrated tiger champion Belinda Wright, the Wildlife Protection Society of India (www.wpsi-india.org) is a premier wildlife conservation organisation campaigning for animal welfare via education, lobbying and legal action against poachers.

Spanning Karnataka, Kerala and Tamil Nadu, the contiguous Bandipur, Nagarhole, Wayanad, Sathyamangalam and Mudumalai protected areas in South India's Western Ghats are home to 570 tigers (according to the 2014 tiger census) – the world's single largest tiger population.

INDIA'S DISAPPEARING VULTURES

The story of India's vultures is perhaps the most devastating of all India's wildlife struggles – especially that of the white-rumped vulture, which in the 1980s numbered around 80 million. Today white-rumped vultures number no more than several thousand – a near-annihilation blamed on the veterinary chemical diclofenac, which causes kidney failure in birds that eat the carcasses of cattle that have been treated with it. The absence of vultures has led to a rise in the number of disease-spreading feral dogs, feeding on carcasses that would formerly have been picked clean by the birds.

Plants

India was once almost entirely covered in forest; now its total forest cover is around 20%. The 2016 Red List of the International Union for Conservation of Nature listed 77 'critically endangered' Indian plants, plus 172 'endangered'. But the country still boasts over 45,000 documented plant species, over 4000 of them endemic.

Nearly all of India's lowland forests are types of tropical forest, with native sal forests forming the mainstay of the timber industry. Some of these tropical forests are true rainforest, staying green year-round, such as in the Western Ghats, but most forests are deciduous, losing their canopies during hot, dry April and May.

High-value trees such as Indian rosewood, Malabar kino and teak have been virtually cleared from the Western Ghats, and sandalwood is endangered across India due to illegal logging for the incense and woodcarving industries. A bigger threat on forested lands is firewood harvesting.

Several Indian trees have significant religious value, including the huge silk-cotton tree, under which Pitamaha (Brahma), the creator of the world, sat after his labours. Two well-known figs, the banyan and peepal, grow to immense size by fusing branches into massive jungles of trunks and stems. It is said that the Buddha achieved enlightenment sitting under a peepal (also the Bodhi tree).

India harbours some of the world's richest biodiversity. There are around 400 mammal species, 1250 bird species, 500 reptile species, 340 amphibian species and 3000 fish species – nearly 7% of the earth's animal species on just 2.5% of its land, which is also inhabited by 18% of the planet's human population

Parks, Sanctuaries & Reserves

Before 1972 India had only five national parks. That year, the Wildlife Protection Act was introduced to set aside national parks and stem the abuse of wildlife. The act was followed by a string of similar pieces of legislation with bold ambitions but often too few teeth with which to enforce them.

India now has over 100 national parks and 500 wildlife sanctuaries, covering around 5% of its territory. There are also 50 tiger reserves and 18 biosphere reserves (designed to protect ecosystems and biodiversity while permitting human activities), often overlapping with other protected areas. Many contiguous parks, reserves and sanctuaries in the highly biodiverse Western Ghats provide valuable migration corridors for wildlife.

One consequence of creating protected areas has been that about 1.6 million Adivasis (tribal people) and other forest-dwellers have had to leave their traditional lands. Many were resettled into villages and forced to abandon their age-old ways of life. The Forest Rights Act of 2006 forbids the displacement of forest-dwellers from national parks (except in so-called 'critical wildlife habitat'), and should protect the four million or so people who still live in them.

Visiting Protected Areas

Many parks, sanctuaries and reserves encourage visitors, and your visit adds momentum to efforts to protect India's natural resources. The best parks and reserves take time to reach, but usually have a range of accommodation inside or just outside the park. In some parks, guided hikes and 4WD safaris are available; others may offer only cursory minibus

Top Parks for Birds

Kumarakom Bird Sanctuary, Kerala is a top spot for migratory waterbirds between November and February.

Thattekkad Bird Sanctuary, Kerala is home to 320 mainly forest species.

tours. Independent operators offer 4WD safaris or guided treks on some parks' fringes, which can be just as wildlife-rich as the parks themselves. Free hiking within parks is generally banned for safety reasons.

The monsoon months (June to August in most places) are usually least favourable for visits; during holiday periods parks and their accommodation overflow with visitors. A few parks close during the ultradry and hot couple of premonsoon months, though this can be the best time to view wildlife, as animals seek out scarce waterholes.

The Lie of the Land

The Himalaya, the world's highest mountains, form an almost-impregnable barrier separating India from its northern neighbours (India's highest peak, Khangchendzonga, reaches 8598m). The Himalaya were formed when the Indian subcontinent, after a 100-million-year northward drift from Gondwana, slammed slowly into the Eurasian continent, buckling the ancient sea floor upward.

South of the Himalaya, the floodplains of the Indus and Ganges Rivers form the fertile heartland of North India. To their south, the elevated Deccan plateau forms the core of India's triangular southern peninsula. The Deccan is bounded by the hills of the Western and Eastern Ghats. The Western Ghats, stretching from north of Mumbai (Bombay) almost to India's southern tip, drop sharply down to a narrow coastal lowland, forming a luxuriant slope of rainforest. Their highest peak is Anamudi (2695m) in Kerala. With many endemic species, they are one of the world's top biodiversity hot spots; 39 areas of the Western Ghats were inscribed on the World Heritage list in 2012 for their natural values. The lower Eastern Ghats stretch from West Bengal to south-central Tamil Nadu, and are cut by the four major rivers of peninsular India, flowing west-to-east across the Deccan: the Mahanadi, Godavari, Krishna and Cauvery.

Offshore are a series of island groups, politically part of India but geographically linked to the land masses of Southeast Asia and islands of the Indian Ocean. The 572 Andaman and Nicobar Islands, far east in the Andaman Sea, are the peaks of a submerged mountain range extending almost 1000km between Myanmar (Burma) and Sumatra. The coral atolls of Lakshadweep, 300km west of Kerala, are a northerly extension of the Maldives islands.

Environmental Issues

Given India's 2016 population of 1.3 billion (expected to reach 1.5 billion by 2030), ever-expanding industrial and urban centres, and growth in chemical-intensive farming, the country's environment is under tremendous pressure. An estimated 65% of the land is degraded. Many current problems are a direct result of the Green Revolution of the 1960s, when chemical fertilisers and pesticides enabled huge growth in agricultural output, at enormous cost to the environment.

Despite numerous environmental laws, corruption has exacerbated environmental degradation – exemplified by flagrant flouting of laws by companies involved in hydroelectricity and mining. Agricultural production has been reduced by soil degradation from overfarming, rising soil salinity, loss of tree cover and, increasingly, lack of water resources. The human cost is heart-rending, and India constantly grapples with the dilemma of how to develop economically without destroying what's left of its environment.

Prime Minister Narendra Modi, elected in 2014, continues to offer mixed signals about his priorities. On one hand, Modi has famously instigated plans to clean the appallingly polluted Ganges River by 2019; launched the much-publicised Swachh Bharat Mission to reduce trash pollution nationwide; supports large-scale solar-power generation; and,

WILDLIFE & LANDSCAPE THE LIE OF THE LAND

Top Parks for Wild Elephants

Nagarhole National Park, Karnataka

Wayanad Wildlife Sanctuary Kerala

Mudumalai Tiger Reserve, Tamil Nadu

Top Parks for Tigers

Tadoba-Andhari Tiger Reserve, Maharashtra and Madhya Pradesh's Pench Tiger Reserve in North India (easily accessed from Nagpur in Maharashtra) are among India's top spots for tiger sightings

Nagarhole and Bandipur National Parks, Karnataka and Periyar Wildlife Sanctuary, Kerala. Chances are slimmer, but not negligible

by ratifying the UN's Paris Agreement, has committed to producing 40% of India's electricity from non-fossil-fuel sources by 2030. But his government has also pledged to increase domestic coal mining and double coal use, adding significantly to India's greenhouse-gas emissions (which account for about 4.5% of global greenhouse-gas emissions).

As anywhere, tourists tread a fine line between providing an incentive for change and making the problem worse. Many of Goa's environmental problems, for example, are the direct result of irresponsible development for tourism.

Climate Change

Changing climate patterns, linked to global carbon emissions, have been creating dangerous weather extremes in India. While India's per capita carbon emissions still rank far behind those of the West and China, the sheer size of its population makes it the world's third-largest carbon-dioxide emitter.

It has been estimated that by 2030 India will see a 30% increase in the severity of its floods and droughts. Islands in the Lakshadweep group, as well as the low-lying Ganges delta, are being inundated by rising sea levels.

Evidenced by recent deadly heatwaves, cyclones, drinking-water shortages and other disasters, climate change is a major issue in the south. A 2015 heatwave is thought to have caused the death of at least 2500 people, with Telangana and Andhra Pradesh worst affected. Also in 2015, South India's heaviest floods in over a century killed at least 500 people, most in Tamil Nadu. Meanwhile, there is growing conflict over the south's water resources.

Deforestation

Since Independence, over 50,000 sq km of India's forests have been cleared for logging and farming, or destroyed by urban expansion, mining, industrialisation and river dams. The number of mangrove forests has halved since the early 1990s, reducing the nursery grounds for the fish that stock the Indian Ocean and Bay of Bengal.

India's first Five Year Plan in 1951 recognised the importance of forests for soil conservation, and various policies have been introduced to increase forest cover. Almost all have been flouted by officials or criminals and by ordinary people clearing forests for firewood and grazing.

Water Resources

Arguably the biggest threat to public health in India is inadequate access to clean drinking water and proper sanitation. With the population continuing to grow, agricultural, industrial and domestic water usage are all expected to spiral. Sewage-treatment facilities can handle only about a quarter of waste water produced. Many cities dump untreated sewage and partially cremated bodies directly into rivers. Open defecation is a simple fact of life, practised by over 50% of the rural population, though Modi's Swachh Bharat Mission is working to end open defecation by 2019.

Rivers are also affected by run-off, industrial pollution and sewage contamination. At least 70% of the freshwater sources in India are now polluted in some way.

In addition, there is South India's growing strife over shared water resources. In 2016 decades-old disputes over plans to send water from drought-stricken Karnataka to also-dry Tamil Nadu culminated in strikes, violence and a transport breakdown between the states.

Since 1947 an estimated 35 million Indians have been displaced by major dams, mostly built to provide hydroelectricity. Valleys across India are being sacrificed to create new power plants, and displaced people rarely receive adequate compensation.

Get the inside track on Indian environmental issues at Down to Earth (www.downtoearth.org.in), an online magazine that delves into stories overlooked by mainstream media.

Online Wildlife Resources

Wildlife, conservation and environmental awareness-raising at www.sanctuaryasia.com

Wildlife Trust of India news at www.wti.org.in

Top birdwatching information at www.birding.in

Survival Guide

Scams

India has an unfortunately deserved reputation for scams, both classic and newfangled. Of course, most can be avoided with some common sense and an appropriate amount of caution. They tend to be more of a problem in the big cities of arrival (such as Delhi or Mumbai), or very touristy spots (such as Rajasthan), though in Goa and Kerala they are relatively rare. Chat with fellow travellers to keep abreast of the latest cons. Look at the India branch of Lonely Planet's Thorn Tree Travel Forum (www.lonelyplanet.com/thorntree), where travellers often post timely warnings about problems they've encountered on the road. Be aware there have been several cases where scammers who can speak the language target Japanese tourists.

Contaminated Food & Drink

➡ The late 1990s saw a scam in North India where travellers died after consuming food laced with dangerous bacteria from restaurants linked to dodgy medical clinics; we've heard no recent reports but the scam could resurface. In unrelated incidents, some clinics have also given more treatment than necessary to procure larger payments from insurance companies.

➡ Most bottled water is legit, but ensure the seal is intact and the bottom of the bottle hasn't been tampered with. While in transit, try and carry packed food if possible. If you eat at bus or train stations, follow the crowd and buy food only from fast-moving places

Credit-Card Con

Be careful when paying for souvenirs with a credit card. While government shops are usually legitimate, private souvenir shops have been known to surreptitiously run off extra copies of the credit-card imprint slip and use them for phoney transactions later. Ask the trader to process the transaction in front of you. Memorising the CVV/CVC2 number and scratching it off the card is also a good idea, to avoid misuse. In some restaurants, waiters will ask you for your PIN with the intention of taking your credit card to the machine – never give your PIN to anyone, and ask to use the machine in person.

Druggings

Occasionally, tourists (especially those travelling solo) have been drugged and robbed or apparently attacked. A spiked drink is the most commonly used method for sending them off to sleep – chocolates, chai from a co-conspiring vendor, 'homemade' Indian food and even bottled water are also known to be used.

Gem Scams

Smooth-talking con artists who promise foolproof 'get rich quick' schemes can be incredibly convincing, so watch

KEEPING SAFE

➡ A good travel-insurance policy is essential.

➡ Email copies of your passport identity page, visa and airline tickets to yourself, and keep copies on you.

➡ Keep your money and passport in a concealed money belt or a secure place under your shirt.

➡ Store at least US$100 separately from your main stash.

➡ Don't publicly display large wads of cash when paying for services or checking into hotels.

➡ Consider using your own padlock at cheaper hotels.

➡ If you can't lock your hotel room securely from the inside, stay somewhere else.

out. In this scam, travellers are asked to carry or mail gems home and then sell them to the trader's (nonexistent) overseas representatives at a profit. Without exception, the goods – if they arrive at all – are worth a fraction of what you paid, and the 'representatives' never materialise.

Don't believe hard-luck stories about an inability to obtain an export licence, and don't believe the testimonials they show you from other travellers – they are all fake. Travellers have reported this con happening in Agra, Delhi, and Jaisalmer among other places, but it's particularly prevalent in Jaipur. Carpets, curios and *pashmina* woollens are other favourites for this con.

OTHER TOP SCAMS

➡ Gunk (dirt, paint, poo) suddenly appears on your shoes, only for a shoe cleaner to magically appear and offer to clean it off – for a price.

➡ Some shops are selling overpriced SIM cards and not activating them; it's best to buy your SIM from an official shop and check it works before leaving the area where you bought it (activation can take up to 24 hours).

➡ Shops, restaurants or tour guides 'borrow' the name of their more successful and popular competitor.

➡ Touts claim to be 'government-approved' guides or agents, and sting you for large sums of cash. Enquire at the local tourist office about licensed guides and ask to see identification from guides themselves.

➡ Artificial 'tourist offices' that are actually dodgy travel agencies whose aim is to sell you overpriced tours, tickets and tourist services.

Overpricing

Always agree on prices beforehand while availing services that don't have regulated tariffs. This particularly applies to friendly neighbourhood guides, snack bars at places of touristy interest, and autorickshaws and taxis without meters.

Photography

Use your instincts (better still, ask for permission) while photographing people. If you don't have permission, you may be asked to pay a fee.

Theft

➡ Theft is a risk in India, as anywhere else. Keep luggage locked and chained on buses and trains. Remember that snatchings often occur when a train is pulling out of the station, as it's too late for you to give chase.

➡ Take extra care in dormitories and never leave your valuables unattended.

➡ Remember to lock your door at night; it is not unknown for thieves to take things from hotel rooms while occupants are sleeping.

Touts & Commission Agents

➡ Cabbies and autorickshaw drivers will often try to coerce you to stay at a hotel of their choice, only to collect a commission (included within your room tariff) afterward.

➡ Wherever possible, pre-arrange hotel bookings (if only for the first night), and request a hotel pick-up. You'll often hear stories about hotels of your choice being 'full' or 'closed' – check things out yourself. Reconfirm and double-check your booking the day before you arrive.

➡ Be very sceptical of phrases like 'my brother's shop' and 'special deal at my friend's place'. Many fraudsters operate in collusion with souvenir stalls.

➡ Avoid friendly people and 'officials' in train and bus stations who offer unsolicited help, then guide you to a commission-paying travel agent. Look confident, and if anyone asks if this is your first trip to India, say you've been here several times. Telling touts that you have already prepaid your transfer/tour/onward journey may help dissuade them.

Transport Scams

➡ Upon arriving at train stations and airports, if you haven't prearranged a pick-up, call an Uber or go to the radio cab, prepaid taxi and airport shuttle bus counters. Never choose a loitering cabbie who offers you a cheap ride into town, especially at night.

➡ While booking multiday sightseeing tours, research your own itinerary, and be extremely wary of anyone in Delhi offering houseboat tours to Kashmir – we've received many complaints over the years about dodgy deals.

➡ When buying a bus, train or plane ticket anywhere other than the registered office of the transport company, make sure you're getting the ticket class you paid for. Use official online booking facilities where possible.

➡ Train station touts (even in uniform or with 'official' badges) may tell you that your intended train is cancelled/flooded/broken down or that your ticket is invalid or that you must pay to have your e-ticket validated on the platform. Do not respond to any approaches at train stations.

Women & Solo Travellers

Women Travellers

Although Bollywood might suggest otherwise, India remains a conservative society. Unfortunately, reports of sexual assaults against women are on the increase in India, despite tougher punishments being established following the 2012 gang rape and murder of a Delhi woman. There have been numerous instances of tourists being attacked over the last few years.

Female travellers should be aware that their behaviour and choice of attire are likely to be under constant scrutiny.

Unwanted Attention

Unwanted attention from men is a common problem.

➡ Be prepared to be stared at; you'll have to live with it, so don't let it get the better of you.

➡ Refrain from returning male stares; this can be considered encouragement.

➡ Dark glasses, phones, books, tablets and headphones are useful for averting unwanted conversations.

Clothing

More touristy regions (such as Goa) and bigger, cosmopolitan cities (like Mumbai) can be less conservative in terms of what to wear, especially in bars, hotels or restaurants popular with younger Indian women (who may well dress in fitted jeans and even minidresses here). But it depends on your destination; if in doubt, keep things conservative.

Elsewhere, women dress conservatively and traditionally; avoiding culturally inappropriate clothing will help avert undesirable attention.

➡ Generally speaking, dress modestly and avoid strappy tops, shorts, short skirts (ankle- or, at least, midi-length skirts are recommended) and anything else that's skimpy, see-through or tight-fitting.

➡ Wearing Indian-style clothes is viewed favourably.

➡ Draping a dupatta (long scarf) over T-shirts is shorthand for modesty; also handy for shrines that require covering your head.

➡ Wearing a *salwar kameez* (traditional dresslike tunic and trousers) will help you blend in; a smart alternative is a kurta (long shirt) over jeans or trousers.

➡ Avoid going out in public wearing a choli (sari blouse) or a sari petticoat (which some foreign women mistake for a skirt); it's like strutting around half-dressed.

➡ Aside from at pools, many Indian women wear long shorts and a T-shirt when swimming in public; wear a sarong from beach to hotel.

Health & Hygiene

Sanitary pads are widely available but tampons are usually restricted to pharmacies in big cities and tourist towns (even then, choice is limited). Carry additional stocks for travel off the beaten track.

Sexual Harassment

Many female travellers report some form of sexual harassment while in India, such as lewd comments, invasion of privacy, provocative gestures, getting 'accidentally' bumped into and even groping and being followed. Follow similar safety precautions as you would at home.

➡ Incidents are particularly common at crowded public events (such as the Holi festival) and busy transport hubs or markets. If a crowd is gathering, make yourself scarce or find a safer spot.

➡ Women travelling with a male partner will receive far less hassle, but this is not a guarantee of safety.

Staying Safe

➡ Always be aware of your surroundings. If it feels wrong, trust your instincts. Don't be scared, but don't be reckless either.

➡ When travelling after dark, use recommended, registered taxi services.

➡ Don't travel in such a way that you're hanging out in bus/train stations late at night. Arrive before dark.

➡ Keep conversations with unknown men short; getting involved in an inane conversation with someone you barely know can be misinterpreted as a sign of sexual interest.

➡ Some women wear a pseudo wedding ring, or announce early on in the conversation that they're married, perhaps meeting up with their husband shortly (regardless of the reality).

➡ If you feel that a guy is encroaching on your space, he probably is. A firm request to keep away usually does the trick, especially if your tone is loud and curt enough to draw the attention of passers-by. The silent treatment can also be very effective.

➡ Follow local women's cues and instead of shaking hands say *namaste* (the traditional, respectful Hindu greeting).

➡ Avoid wearing expensive-looking jewellery and flashy accessories.

➡ Some women have reported being molested by male therapists. Check the reputation of any teacher or therapist before a solo session (get recommendations from travellers), and request female therapists.

➡ Lone women may want to invest in good-quality hotels in better neighbourhoods.

➡ At hotels, keep your door locked, as staff (particularly at budget and midrange places) can knock and walk in without permission.

➡ Avoid wandering alone in isolated areas, even during daylight. Steer clear of *galis* (narrow lanes) and deserted roads.

➡ When taking rickshaws alone, call or text someone, or pretend to, to show someone knows where you are.

➡ Act confidently in public; to avoid looking lost (and thus vulnerable) consult maps at your hotel (or at a restaurant) rather than on the street.

➡ Never get into a taxi or autorickshaw containing anyone other than the driver.

➡ In larger towns, smartphone users can use maps to track where they are – this makes it easier to tell if a taxi or rickshaw is taking the wrong road.

Taxis & Public Transport

Women can usually queue-jump for buses and trains. On trains there are special ladies-only carriages; there are also women-only waiting rooms at some stations.

➡ Solo women should prearrange airport pickups with their hotel, especially if their flight arrives after dark.

➡ Some cities have licensed prepaid radio cab services; they're more expensive than regular prepaid taxis, but are promoted as safe, with drivers who have been vetted. The Uber and Ola Cabs taxi apps are similarly useful.

➡ If you do catch a regular prepaid taxi, write down the car registration and driver's name – in front of the driver – and give it to the airport police.

➡ Avoid taking taxis alone late at night and never agree to have more than one man (the driver) in the car; ignore claims that this is 'just my brother' etc.

➡ Solo women have reported less hassle when taking more expensive classes on trains.

➡ If you're travelling overnight in a two- or three-tier train carriage, the uppermost berth gives you more privacy (and distance from potential gropers).

➡ On public transport, don't hesitate to return any errant limbs, be vocal (attracting public attention, thus shaming the pest), or simply find a new spot.

➡ Sit next to other women on transport and, for long-distance buses, book seats towards the front.

Solo Travellers

One of the joys of travelling solo in India is that you're more likely to be 'adopted' by families, especially when commuting together on long rail journeys. Tourist hubs such as Goa and Kerala are popular places to link up with fellow travellers. You may also find travel companions on Lonely Planet's Thorn Tree Travel Forum (www.lonely planet.com/thorntree).

Cost

➡ Single-room accommodation rates are sometimes not much lower than double rates.

➡ Some midrange and top-end places don't even offer a single tariff.

➡ It's always worth trying to negotiate a lower rate for single occupancy.

Safety

Most solo travellers experience no major problems in India but, like anywhere else, it's wise to stay on your toes in unfamiliar surroundings.

➡ Some less honourable souls (locals and travellers alike) view lone tourists as easy targets for theft and sexual assault.

➡ Single men wandering around isolated areas have been mugged, even during the day.

Transport

➡ You'll save money if you find others to share taxis and autorickshaws, as well as when hiring cars for longer trips. The Uber and Ola Cabs taxi apps also offer shared services.

➡ Solo travellers may be able to grab the 'copilot' (near the driver) seat on buses, which not only has a good view but is also handy for big bags.

Directory A–Z

Accommodation

It's usually advisable to book ahead and essential during high seasons.

Categories

As a general rule, budget ($) covers everything from basic hostels, hotels and guesthouses in urban areas to traditional homestays in villages. Mid-range hotels ($$) tend to have larger, cleaner rooms, usually with air-conditioning, and are more likely to have restaurants. Top end places ($$$) vary from luxurious chain hotels to gorgeous, one-of-a-kind heritage palaces and resorts.

Costs

Costs vary widely: highest in large cities (especially Mumbai [Bombay]), lowest in small cities and rural areas. Costs are also highly seasonal; hotel prices can drop by 20% to 50% outside peak season. Most establishments raise tariffs annually, so prices may have risen since the time this destination was last researched.

Reservations

➡ It's a good idea to book ahead, online or by phone, especially for more popular destinations. Some hotels require a credit-card deposit for bookings.

➡ Some budget places won't take reservations as they don't know when people are going to check out; call ahead or just turn up around check-in time.

➡ Other places may want a deposit or full payment at check in; ask for a receipt and be wary of any request for you to sign a blank impression of your credit card. If the hotel insists, pay cash.

➡ Verify the check-out time when you check in – some hotels have a fixed check-out time (usually 10am or noon), while others offer 24-hour check out (you have the room for 24 hours from the time you check in). Sometimes you can request to check in early or check out late, and hotels will oblige if the room is empty.

Seasons

➡ High season usually coincides with the best weather for the area's sights and activities – normally spring in the hills (April to June), and the cooler months in the lowlands (around November to February).

➡ In areas popular with tourists, there's an additional peak period over Christmas and New Year; make reservations well in advance.

➡ At other times you may find significant discounts, if the hotel seems quiet, it's worth asking.

➡ Some hotels in places like Goa close during the monsoon period.

➡ Many temple towns have additional peak seasons around major festivals and pilgrimages; book ahead.

Taxes & Service Charges

➡ State governments slap a variety of taxes on hotel accommodation (except for the cheapest hotels); these are added to room costs.

➡ Taxes vary from state to state and rates increase with room price.

➡ Some upmarket hotels and restaurants also add a 'service charge' (around 10%).

➡ Hotels often quote rates excluding taxes; check first.

➡ Rates we quote include taxes unless noted.

➡ Note that India's new Goods & Services Tax (GST), due

SLEEPING PRICE RANGES

Here are sample accommodation costs, but these vary across South India so consult the sleeping price ranges given for each region. Lonely Planet price indicators refer to the cost of a double room with private bathroom, in high season, unless otherwise noted.

$ less than ₹1500

$$ ₹1500–6000

$$$ more than ₹6000

to come into force in 2017, may affect accommodation taxes and charges across the country.

Accommodation Types

BUDGET & MIDRANGE HOTELS

➡ Sometimes you'll find budget and midrange hotels in atmospheric old houses or heritage buildings, but most are modern-style concrete blocks with varying degrees of comfort. Some are charming, clean and good value; others less so.

➡ Room quality can vary considerably within a hotel, so inspect a few rooms first. Many places have a range of prices for rooms of different quality. Avoid carpeted rooms at cheaper hotels (which can smell mouldy).

➡ Shared bathrooms (often with squat toilets) are usually only found at the cheapest lodgings.

➡ Most rooms have ceiling fans and better rooms have mosquito-screened windows; cheaper rooms may lack windows altogether.

➡ If you're mostly staying in budget places, bring your own sheet or sleeping-bag liner (or even a sarong/shawl). Sheets at cheap hotels can be stained, worn and dirty. You may also have to provide a towel, toilet paper and soap.

➡ Insect repellent and a torch (flashlight) are recommended for budget hotels.

➡ Noise can be irksome (particularly in urban hubs); pack good-quality earplugs and request a room that doesn't face a busy road.

➡ Keep your door locked, as staff (especially in budget hotels) may knock and walk in without awaiting permission.

➡ Blackouts are common (especially during the monsoon), so double-check that the hotel has a backup generator if you're paying for electric 'extras' (air-conditioners, TVs, wi-fi).

➡ Some hotels lock their doors at night. Staff might sleep in the lobby, but waking them up can be a challenge. Let the hotel know in advance if you'll be arriving late at night or leaving early.

➡ Away from tourist areas, cheaper hotels may not have the required foreigner-registration forms, and so may be unable to accommodate foreigners.

CAMPING

➡ There are very few public campgrounds. The only places where you're likely to find yourself sleeping in a tent are a few coastal resort hotels or lodges in and around wildlife sanctuaries, where tents are usually permanently sited and often as large and comfortable as hotel rooms, with bathrooms too.

GOVERNMENT-RUN ACCOMMODATION

➡ The Indian and state governments maintain networks of guesthouses for travelling officials and public workers, known variously as rest houses, dak bungalows, circuit houses, PWD (Public Works Department) bungalows and forest rest houses. These may accept travellers if no government employees need the rooms, but permission is often required from local officials.

➡ Most state governments run chains of budget and midrange hotels aimed primarily at domestic tourists, including a few lovely heritage properties; most are functional but bland. State tourism offices normally provide details.

HOMESTAYS

➡ Available only in some areas, these family-run guesthouses will appeal to those seeking a small-scale, uncommercial, intimate setting, with home-cooked meals.

➡ Standards range from mud-and-stone village huts with hole-in-the-floor toilets to comfortable, middle-class city homes.

➡ Particular popular in Kerala, where Fort Cochin is the homestay capital of India, with Alappuzha (Alleppey) close behind.

➡ Local tourist offices often provide lists of participating families.

HOSTELS

➡ Goa and Kerala, as well as Karnataka, Tamil Nadu and Mumbai, have an expanding number of genuine backpacker hostels with clean dorms, free wi-fi, lockers, communal kitchens and shared lounges. Some are independent, others chain-run.

➡ Popular tourist spots with good hostels include Anjuna, Vagator, Palolem and elsewhere in Goa, and Fort Cochin and Alleppey in Kerala.

➡ **Vedanta Wake Up!** (www.vedantawakeup.com) and **Zostel** (www.zostel.com) operate several hostels (of varying quality) in Kerala, Goa, Karnataka and Tamil Nadu.

➡ The YWCA, YMCA and Salvation Army run a few hostels, sometimes called 'guesthouses', usually with clean, comfy rooms (some with AC) as well as (or instead of) dorms, at high-budget or low-midrange prices.

RAILWAY RETIRING ROOMS

➡ Most large train stations (listed at www.irctctourism.com) have basic rooms for travellers holding an ongoing train ticket or Indrail Pass. Some are grim; others are surprisingly pleasant, but can suffer from the noise of passengers and trains.

→ They're useful for early-morning train departures and there's usually a choice of dormitories or private rooms (24-hour check-out) depending on the class you're travelling in.

→ Some smaller stations only have waiting rooms, with different rooms for passengers in different classes and for men and women.

TEMPLES & PILGRIMS' REST HOUSES

→ Accommodation is available at some ashrams (spiritual communities), gurdwaras (Sikh temples) and dharamsalas (pilgrims' rest houses) for a donation or fee.

→ These have been established for genuine pilgrims so please exercise judgement about the appropriateness of your staying in one.

→ Always abide by any protocols. Smoking and drinking are complete no-nos; there's usually a curfew.

TOP-END & HERITAGE HOTELS

→ South India has a wealth of top-end properties, from contemporary high-end chain hotels to glorious palaces, luxury beach resorts and dreamy lodges in and around national parks and wildlife sanctuaries.

→ Heritage hotels give you the unique opportunity to stay in former (or sometimes still current) palaces, mansions and other abodes of Indian royalty and aristocracy.

Customs Regulations

→ Technically you're supposed to declare any amount of cash over US$5000, or total amount of currency over US$10,000 on arrival.

→ Indian rupees shouldn't be taken out of India; however, this is rarely policed.

→ Officials very occasionally ask tourists to enter expensive items such as video cameras and laptop computers on a 'Tourist Baggage Re-export' form to ensure they're taken out of India at the time of departure.

Electricity

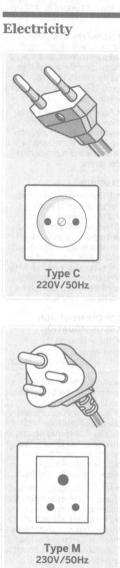

Type C
220V/50Hz

Type M
230V/50Hz

Type D
220V/50Hz

Embassies & Consulates

Most foreign diplomatic missions are based in Delhi, but several nations operate consulates in other Indian cities (see websites, where provided). Many missions have certain timings for visa applications, usually mornings; phone for details.

Australian Chennai (☑044-45921300; www.chennai.consulate.gov.au; 9th fl, Express Chambers, Express Avenue Estate, White's Rd, Royapettah; ⊘9am-5pm Mon-Fri); Delhi (☑011-41399900; www.india.highcommission.gov.au; 1/50G Shantipath, Chanakyapuri; Ⓜ Racecourse); Mumbai (☑022-67574900; www.mumbai.consulate.gov.au; 10th fl, A Wing, Crescenzo Bldg, G Block, Plot C 38-39, Bandra Kurla Complex)

Bangladeshi Delhi (☑011-24121394; www.bdhcdelhi.org; EP39 Dr Radakrishnan Marg, Chanakyapuri; Ⓜ Chanakyapuri); Kolkata (☑033-40127500; 9 Circus Ave; ⊘visas 9-11am Mon-Fri)

Bhutanese Delhi (☑011-26889230; www.bhutan.gov.bt; Chandragupta Marg, Chanakyapuri; Ⓜ Chanakyapuri);

Kolkata (Tivoli Court, Ballygunge Circular Rd; ⊙10am-4pm Mon-Fri)

Canadian Delhi (☑011-41782000; www.canadainternational.gc.ca/india-inde; 7/8 Shantipath, Chanakyapuri; ⊙consular services 9am-noon Mon-Fri); Mumbai (☑022-67494444; www.canadainternational.gc.ca; 21st fl, Tower 2, Indiabulls Finance Centre, Senapati Bapat Marg, Elphinstone Rd West)

Chinese Delhi (☑011-26112345; http://in.china-embassy.org; 50-D Shantipath, Chanakyapuri; Ⓜ Chanakyapuri)

Dutch Delhi (☑011-24197600; www.netherlandsworldwide.nl/countries/india; 6/50F Shantipath, Chanakyapuri; ⊙9am-5pm Mon-Fri); Mumbai (☑022-22194200; www.netherlandsworldwide.nl/countries/india; 1st fl, Forbes Bldg, Charanjit Rai Marg, Fort)

French Delhi (☑011-24196100; www.ambafrance-in.org; 2/50E Shantipath, Chanakyapuri; Ⓜ Chanakyapuri); Mumbai (☑022-66694000; www.ambafrance-in.org/-Consulate-in-Bombay-; Wockhardt Towers, East Wing, 5th fl, Bandra Kurla Complex, Bandra East); Puducherry (☑0413-2231000; www.ambafrance-in.org/-Consulate-in-Pondicherry; 2 Marine St; ⊙8am-5pm Mon-Fri)

German Chennai (☑044-24301600; www.india.diplo.de; 9 Boat Club Rd, RA Puram; ⊙7.30am-3.30pm Mon-Thu, to 1.30pm Fri); Delhi (☑011-44199199; www.new-delhi.diplo.de; 6/50G Shantipath, Chanakyapuri; Ⓜ Chanakyapuri); Kolkata (☑033-24791141; 1 Hastings Park Rd, Alipore); Mumbai (☑022-22832422; www.india.diplo.de; 10th fl, Hoechst House, Nariman Point)

Irish Delhi (☑011-24940 3200; www.dfa.ie/irish-embassy/india; C17 Malcha Marg, Chanakyapuri; Ⓜ Chanakyapuri)

Israeli Delhi (☑011-30414500; www.embassies.gov.il/delhi; 3 Dr APJ Abdul Kalam Rd; ⊙9.30am-1pm Mon-Fri); Mumbai (☑022-61600500; www.embassies.gov.il/mumbai;

Marathon Futurex, 1301, A Wing, NM Joshi Marg, Lower Parel)

Japanese Chennai (☑044-24323860; www.chennai.in.emb-japan.go.jp; 12/1 1st St, Cenotaph Rd, Teynampet; ⊙9am-5.45pm Mon-Fri); Delhi (☑011-26876581; www.in.emb-japan.go.jp; 50G Shantipath, Chanakyapuri; ⊙9am-1pm & 2-5.30pm Mon-Fri); Mumbai (☑022-23517101; www.mumbai.in.emb-japan.go.jp; 1 ML Dahanukar Marg, Cumballa Hill)

Malaysian Chennai (☑044-24334434; www.kln.gov.my; 7 1st St, Cenotaph Rd, Teynampet; ⊙9am-5pm Mon-Fri); Delhi (☑011-24159300; www.kln.gov.my/web/ind_new-delhi/home; 50M Satya Marg, Chanakyapuri; ⊙8.30am-4.30pm Mon-Fri); Mumbai (☑022-26455751; www.kln.gov.my/web/ind_mumbai/home; 5th fl, Notan Classic Bldg, off Turner Rd, Bandra West)

Maldivian Delhi (☑011-41435701; www.maldiveshighcom.in; B2 Anand Niketan)

Myanmar Delhi (☑011-24678822; www.myanmedelhi.com; 3/50F Nyaya Marg; ⊙9.30am-4.30pm Mon-Fri); Kolkata (☑033-24851658;

mcgkolcg@gmail.com; 57K Ballygunge Circular Rd; ⊙visas 9am-noon Mon-Fri)

Nepali Delhi (☑011-23476200; www.nepalembassy.in; Mandi House, Barakhamba Rd; ⊙9am-1pm & 2-5pm)

New Zealand Chennai (☑044-28112472; www.mfat.govt.nz; Rane Holdings Ltd, Maithri, 132 Cathedral Rd, Gopalapuram; ⊙9am-5.30pm Mon-Fri); Delhi (☑011-46883170; www.nzembassy.com/india; Sir Edmund Hillary Marg, Chanakyapuri; ⊙8.30am-5pm Mon-Fri); Mumbai (☑022-61316666; www.mfat.govt.nz/en/countries-and-regions/south-asia/india/new-zealand-high-commission/new-zealand-consulate-general-mumbai-india; Level 2, Maker Maxity, 3 North Ave, Bandra Kurla Complex)

Singaporean Chennai (☑044-28158207; www.mfa.gov.sg; 17A North Boag Rd, T Nagar; ⊙9am-5pm Mon-Fri); Delhi (☑011-46000915; www.mfa.gov.sg/newdelhi; E6 Chandragupta Marg, Chanakyapuri; ⊙9am-1pm & 1.30-5pm Mon-Fri); Mumbai (☑022-22043209; www.mfa.gov.sg/content/mfa/overseasmission/mumbai.html; Maker Chambers IV, 10th fl, 222

PRACTICALITIES

Magazines Incisive current-affairs magazines include *Frontline* (www.frontline.in), *India Today* (www.indiatoday.intoday.in), *The Week* (www.theweek.in), *Tehelka* (www.tehelka.com) and *Outlook* (www.outlookindia.com).

Newpapers Major English-language dailies include the *Hindustan Times* (www.hindustantimes.com), *Times of India* (www.timesofindia.indiatimes.com), *Indian Express* (www.indianexpress.com), *The Hindu* (www.thehindu.com), *Daily News & Analysis* (DNA; www.dnaindia.com) and *Economic Times* (www.economictimes.indiatimes.com).

Radio Government-controlled All India Radio (AIR; www.allindiaradio.gov.in) is India's national broadcaster with over 400 stations broadcasting local and international news. Also private FM channels broadcast music, current affairs, talkback and more.

TV The national (government) TV broadcaster is Doordarshan (www.ddindia.gov.in). More people watch satellite and cable TV.

Weights & measures Officially India is metric. Terms you're likely to hear are: lakh (one lakh = 100,000) and crore (one crore = 10 million).

DIRECTORY A-Z EMBASSIES & CONSULATES

Jamnalal Bajaj Rd, Nariman Point)

Sri Lankan Chennai (☏044-28241896; www.sldhcchennai.org; 56 Sterling Rd, Nungambakkam; ☺9am-5.15pm); Delhi (☏011-23010201; 27 Kautilya Marg, Chanakyapuri; ☺8.45am-5pm Mon-Fri); Mumbai (☏022-22045861; www.mumbai.mission.gov.lk; Mulla House, 34 Homi Modi St, Fort, Mumbai)

Thai Chennai (☏044-42300730; www.vfs-thailand.co.in; 3 1st Main Rd, Vidyodaya Colony, T Nagar; ☺8am-noon & 1-3pm Mon-Fri); Delhi (☏011-49774100; http://newdelhi.thaiembassy.org; D-1/3 Vasant Vihar; ☺9am-5pm Mon-Fri); Kolkata (☏033-24407836; 18B Mandeville Gardens, Ballygunge); Mumbai (☏022-22823535; www.thaiembassy.org/mumbai; 12th fl, Express Towers, Barrister Rajni Patel Marg, Nariman Point)

UK Chennai (☏044-42192151; www.gov.uk; 20 Anderson Rd, Nungambakkam; ☺8.30am-4.30pm Mon-Thu, to 1.30pm Fri); Delhi (☏011-24192100; Shantipath; Ⓜ Racecourse); Kolkata (☏033-22885172; 1A Ho Chi Minh Sarani); Mumbai (☏022-66502222; www.gov.uk/government/world/organisations/british-deputy-high-commission-mumbai; Naman Chambers, C/32 G Block Bandra Kurla Complex, Bandra East)

USA Chennai (☏044-28574000; http://in.usembassy.gov; 220 Anna Salai, Gemini Circle; ☺8.30am-5pm Mon-Fri); Delhi (☏011-24198000; http://newdelhi.usembassy.gov; Shantipath); Kolkata (☏033-39842400; https://kolkata.usconsulate.gov/; 5/1 Ho Chi Minh Sarani); Mumbai (☏022-26724000;

https://mumbai.usconsulate.gov; C49, G Block, Bandra Kurla Complex)

Food

See Delicious India (p459) for information about food in South India.

Insurance

➡ Comprehensive travel insurance to cover theft, loss and medical problems (as well as air evacuation) is strongly recommended.

➡ Some policies specifically exclude potentially dangerous activities such as scuba diving, motorcycling and even trekking: read the fine print.

➡ Some trekking agents may accept only customers who have cover for emergency helicopter evacuation.

➡ If you plan to hire a motorcycle in India, make sure the rental policy includes at least third-party insurance.

➡ Check in advance if your insurance policy will pay doctors and hospitals directly or reimburse you later for overseas health expenditures (keep all documentation for your claim).

➡ It's crucial to get a police report in India if you've had anything stolen; insurance companies may refuse to reimburse you without one.

➡ Worldwide travel insurance is available at www.lonelyplanet.com/travel-insurance. You can buy, extend and claim online any time – even if you're already on the road.

Internet Access

➡ Internet cafes are a dwindling breed. Where found, connections are usually reasonably fast, except in more remote areas.

➡ Wi-fi access is available in most places to stay, and at many cafes, bars and restaurants in larger cities. Access is most often free but not always – you'll still come across the occasional holdout.

➡ Wi-fi signals everywhere are subject to temporary outages because of power cuts and the vagaries of servers.

Language Courses

South India's choice of language courses is limited, but, if you're keen, the following places offer language courses, some requiring a minimum time commitment.

Mumbai Beginners' courses in Hindi, Marathi and Sanskrit at **Bharatiya Vidya Bhavan** (☏022-23631261; www.bhavans.info; 2nd fl, cnr KM Munshi Marg & Ramabai Rd, Girgaum; language per hr ₹500, music per month ₹900; ☺4-8pm).

Tamil Nadu Tamil courses at Chennai's **International Institute of Tamil Studies** (☏044-22542992, 9952448862; www.ulakaththamizh.org; CIT Campus, 2nd Main Rd, Tharamani; 3-/6-month course ₹5000/10,000).

Legal Matters

If you're in a sticky legal situation, contact your embassy as quickly as possible. However, be aware that all your embassy may be able to do is monitor your treatment in custody and arrange a lawyer. In the Indian justice system, the burden of proof can often be on the accused and stints in prison before trial are not unheard of.

Antisocial Behaviour

➡ Smoking in public places is illegal throughout India but this is very rarely enforced;

fines are ₹200, though there are proposals to raise this to ₹1000.

➡ People can smoke inside their homes and in most open spaces such as streets (heed any signs stating otherwise).

➡ Some Indian cities have banned spitting and littering, but this is also variably enforced.

Drugs

➡ Indian law does not distinguish between 'hard' and 'soft' drugs; possession of any illegal drug is regarded as a criminal offence, which will result in a custodial sentence.

➡ Sentences may be up to a year for possession of a small amount for personal use, to a minimum of 10 years if it's deemed the purpose was for sale or distribution. There's also usually a hefty fine on top of any sentence.

➡ Cases can take months, even several years, to appear before a court, while the accused may have to wait in prison.

➡ Be aware that travellers have been targeted in sting operations in Goa and other backpacker enclaves.

➡ Police are getting particularly tough on foreigners who use drugs, so you should take this risk very seriously.

➡ Marijuana grows wild in various parts of India, but consuming it is still an offence, except in towns where bhang is legally sold for religious rituals.

➡ Pharmaceutical drugs that are restricted in other countries may be available in India over the counter or via prescription. Be aware that taking these without professional guidance can be dangerous.

Police

➡ You should always carry your passport; police are entitled to ask you for identification at any time.

➡ If you're arrested for an alleged offence and asked for a bribe, note: it is illegal to pay

a bribe in India. Many people deal with an on-the-spot fine by just paying it to avoid trumped-up charges.

➡ Corruption is rife so the less you have to do with local police the better; try to avoid all potentially risky situations.

LGBTQ Travellers

➡ Homosexuality was made illegal in India in 2013, having only been decriminalised since 2009 (punishments are as severe as life imprisonment).

➡ Gay and lesbian visitors should be discreet in this conservative country. Public displays of affection are frowned upon for both homosexual and heterosexual couples.

➡ Despite the ban, there are gay scenes (and Gay Pride marches) in a number of cities including Mumbai, Chennai, Bengaluru (Banglaore) and Hyderabad, as well as a holiday gay scene in Goa.

Resources

Bombay Dost (www.bombaydost.co.in) A reputable Mumbai-based LGBTQ publication.

Gay Bombay (www.gaybombay.org) Lists gay events and offers support and advice.

Gaylaxy (www.gaylaxymag.com) Probably India's best gay e-zine, including news, blogs, articles, reviews and fashion.

Gaysi Zine (www.gaysifamily.com) A thoughtful monthly magazine and website featuring gay writing and issues.

Indian Dost (www.indiandost.com/gay.php) News and information including contact groups in India.

Indja Pink (www.indjapink.co.in) Travel agency and India's first 'gay travel boutique', founded by a well-known Indian fashion designer.

Orinam (www.orinam.net) This Chennai-based site offers advice and support, and lists gay events. Its Twitter @chennaipride is useful too.

Queer Azaadi Mumbai (www.queerazaadi.wordpress.com) Mumbai's queer pride blog, with news.

Queer Ink (www.queer-ink.com) Online bookshop specialising in gay- and lesbian-interest books from the subcontinent.

Maps

Maps available inside India are of variable quality. Most state-government tourist offices stock basic local maps. These are some of the better map series, which should be available at good bookshops:

PROHIBITED EXPORTS

To protect India's cultural heritage, the export of certain antiques is prohibited, especially those which are verifiably more than 100 years old. Reputable antique dealers know the laws and can make arrangements for an export-clearance certificate for old items that are OK to export. Detailed information on prohibited items can be found on the government webpage www.asi.nic.in/pdf_data/8.pdf. The rules may seem stringent, but the loss of ancient artworks and sculptures due to the international trade in antiques has been alarming. Look for quality reproductions instead.

The Indian Wildlife Protection Act bans any form of wildlife trade. Don't buy any product that endangers threatened species and habitats – doing so can result in heavy fines and even imprisonment. This includes ivory, shahtoosh shawls (made from the down of the rare chiru, the Tibetan antelope) and anything made from the fur, skin, horns or shell of any endangered species. Products made from certain rare plants are also banned.

Eicher (www.eicher.in)

Nelles (www.nelles-verlag.de)

Survey of India (www.surveyofindia.gov.in) Many maps are downloadable free from the website.

TTK (www.ttkmaps.com)

Money

The Indian rupee (₹) is divided into 100 paise, but only 50 paise coins are legal tender and these are rarely seen. Coins come in denominations of ₹1, ₹2, ₹5 and ₹10 (the ₹1s and ₹2s look almost identical); notes come in ₹5, ₹10, ₹20, ₹50, ₹100, and the newly introduced ₹500 and ₹2000 (this last is handy for paying large bills but can pose problems when getting change for small purchases). The Indian rupee is linked to a basket of currencies and has been subject to fluctuations in recent years.

See Need to Know (p14) for exchange rates and information on costs.

ATMs

➡ ATMs are found in most urban centres.

➡ Visa, MasterCard, Cirrus, Maestro and Plus are the most commonly accepted cards.

➡ ATMs at Axis Bank, Citibank, HDFC, HSBC, ICICI and State Bank of India recognise foreign cards. Other banks' ATMs may accept major cards (Visa, MasterCard etc).

➡ Most ATMs have a limit of ₹10,000 to ₹20,000 per withdrawal. Citibank ATMs generally allow you to withdraw even more in one transaction, reducing transaction charges, which are often in the ₹200 to ₹250 range.

➡ Before your trip, check whether your card can reliably access banking networks in India and ask for details of charges.

➡ Notify your bank that you'll be using your card in India to avoid having it blocked; take along your bank's phone number just in case.

➡ Away from major towns, always carry cash and possibly also travellers cheques as back up.

Bargaining

➡ Haggling is the norm in markets and in many tourist-oriented shops; the 'starting price' may be elevated by 50% or more.

➡ You will usually need to bargain for a fair fare in taxis and rickshaws, though the introduction of Uber and Ola taxi apps has eliminated this in many metropolitan areas.

➡ More upmarket shops charge fixed prices.

Black Market

➡ Black-market money changers exist, but legal money changers are so common there's no reason to use illegal services.

➡ If you're approached on the street with offers to change money, you're probably being set up for a scam.

Cash

➡ Major currencies such as US dollars, pounds sterling and euros are easy to change throughout India, although some bank branches insist on travellers cheques only.

➡ Some banks also accept other currencies such as Australian and Canadian dollars, and Swiss francs.

➡ Private money changers deal with a wider range of currencies than banks, but Pakistani, Nepali and Bangladeshi currency can be harder to change away from the border.

➡ When travelling off the beaten track, always carry an adequate stock of rupees.

➡ Whenever changing money, check every note. Don't accept any filthy, ripped or disintegrating notes, as these may be difficult to use.

➡ It can be tough getting change in India so keep a stock of smaller currency; ₹10, ₹20 and ₹50 notes are helpful.

➡ Officially you cannot take rupees out of India, but this is laxly enforced. You can change any leftover rupees back into foreign currency, most easily at the airport (some banks have a ₹1000 minimum). You may have to present encashment certificates or credit-card/ATM receipts, and show your passport and airline ticket.

Credit Cards

➡ Credit cards are accepted at many shops, better restaurants and midrange and top-end hotels, and they can usually be used to pay for flights and train tickets.

➡ Cash advances on major credit cards are possible at some banks.

➡ MasterCard and Visa are the most widely accepted cards.

➡ Always keep the emergency lost-and-stolen numbers for your credit cards in a safe place, separate from your cards, and report any loss or theft immediately.

Encashment Certificates

➡ Indian law states that all foreign currency must be changed at official money changers or banks.

→ For every (official) foreign-exchange transaction, you'll receive an encashment certificate (receipt), which will allow you to change rupees back into foreign currency when departing India.

→ Encashment certificates should cover the amount of rupees you intend to change back to foreign currency.

→ Printed receipts from ATMs are also accepted as evidence of an international transaction at most banks.

International Transfers

→ If you run out of money, someone back home can wire you cash via money changers affiliated with **Moneygram** (www.moneygram.com) or **Western Union** (www.westernunion.com). A fee is added to the transaction.

→ To collect cash, bring your passport and the name and reference number of the person who sent the funds.

Money Changers

→ Private money changers are usually open for longer hours than banks, and are found almost everywhere (many also double as internet cafes and travel agents).

→ Upmarket hotels may also change money, but their rates are usually not as competitive.

Taxes & Refunds

India's Value-Added Tax (VAT) is 15% and is in the stated price of goods. Note that India's new Goods & Services Tax (GST), due to come into force in 2017, may affect taxes and charges for restaurants and accommodation across the country.

Goa is currently the only place where tourists can reclaim VAT on luxury items bought in the region; make your claim, with supporting receipts, at the airport.

Tipping

Restaurants A service fee ranging from 4% to 10% is often added to your bill; tipping is optional.

Hotels Some hotels charge a service fee on top of a service tax; tip at your discretion.

Porters Train/airport porters appreciate anything around ₹50.

Taxis & Rickshaws Not normally tipped beyond rounding to nearest ₹10.

Hired Cars Around 10% is recommended for good service.

Travellers Cheques

→ American Express (Amex) and Thomas Cook are the most widely accepted brands.

→ Euros, pounds sterling and US dollars are the safest currencies, especially in smaller towns.

→ Keep a record of the cheques' serial numbers separate from your cheques, along with the proof-of-purchase slips, encashment vouchers and photocopied passport details.

→ If you lose your cheques, contact the Amex or Thomas Cook office in Delhi. To replace lost travellers cheques, you need the proof-of-purchase slip and the numbers of the missing cheques, and possibly a photocopy of the police report and a passport photo.

Opening Hours

For information on typical opening hours see Need to Know (p15).

Photography

For useful tips and techniques, read Lonely Planet's guide to *Travel Photography*.

→ Memory cards are available from photographic shops in most large cities and towns. Quality is variable – some don't carry the advertised amount of data. Expect to pay upward of ₹700 to ₹1500 for a 32GB card.

→ To be safe, regularly backup your memory cards. If your camera isn't wi-fi-enabled, take a memory card reader with you. Alternatively some internet cafes will write your pictures to CD.

Restrictions

→ India is touchy about anyone taking photographs of military installations – this can include train stations, bridges, airports, military sites and sensitive border regions.

→ Photography from the air is mostly OK, unless you're taking off from (or landing in) airports actively shared by defence forces.

→ Many places of worship – such as monasteries, temples and mosques – prohibit photography. Taking photos inside shrines or at funerals or religious ceremonies, or of people publicly bathing (including in rivers) can be offensive – ask first.

→ Flash photography may be prohibited in certain areas with shrines or historical monuments.

→ Exercise sensitivity when photographing people, especially women – some may find it offensive, so obtain permission first.

→ It is not uncommon for people in tourist areas to demand a posing fee in return for being photographed. Exercise your discretion in these situations. In any case, ask first to avoid misunderstandings later.

Post

India Post (www.indiapost.gov.in) runs the most widely distributed postal service on earth, with nearly 155,000 post offices. Mail and poste-restante services are generally good, although the speed of delivery will depend on the efficiency of any given office. Airmail is faster and more reliable than sea mail, although it's best to use courier services (such as DHL and TNT) to send and receive items of value – expect to pay around ₹3000 per kilogram for a carry-on size box to Europe, Australia or the USA. Smaller private couriers are often cheaper, but goods may be repacked into large packages to cut costs and things sometimes go missing.

Receiving Mail

➜ India still has a poste-restante system by which you can have mail sent to you at post offices.

➜ Ask senders to address letters to you with your surname in capital letters and underlined, followed by Poste Restante, GPO (main post office), and the city or town in question.

➜ To claim mail you'll need to show your passport.

➜ Letters sent via poste restante are generally held for around one to two months before being returned.

➜ Many 'lost' letters are simply misfiled under given/first names, so check under both your names and ask senders to provide a return address.

➜ It's best to have any parcels sent to you by registered post.

Sending Letters

➜ Posting airmail letters to anywhere overseas costs ₹20 (aerogrammes cost ₹15).

➜ International postcards cost around ₹12.

➜ For postcards, stick on the stamps before writing on them, as post offices can give you as many as four stamps per card.

➜ Sending a letter overseas by registered post costs an extra ₹70.

Sending Parcels

➜ Posting parcels can be either relatively straightforward or involve multiple counters and lots of queuing; get to the post office in the morning.

➜ All parcels sent through the government postal service must be packed up in white linen and the seams sealed with wax – agents near post offices usually offer this service for a small fee.

➜ An unregistered airmail package up to 250g in weight costs around ₹350 to ₹875 to any country, plus ₹45 to ₹130 per additional 250g (up to a maximum of 2kg; different charges apply for higher weights).

➜ Parcel post has a maximum of 20kg to 30kg depending on the destination.

➜ Airmail takes one to three weeks, sea mail two to four months, and Surface Air-Lifted (SAL) – a curious hybrid where parcels travel by both air and sea – around one month.

➜ Express mail service (EMS; delivery within three days) costs around 30% more than the normal airmail price.

➜ Customs declaration forms, available from the post office, must be stitched or pasted to the parcel. No duty is payable by the recipient for gifts under the value of ₹1000.

➜ Carry a permanent marker to write on the parcel any information requested by the desk.

➜ You can send printed matter via surface mail 'Bulk Bag' for ₹350 (maximum 5kg, plus ₹100 for each additional kilogram). The parcel has to be packed with an opening so it can be checked by customs – tailors can do this in such a way that nothing falls out.

➜ **India Post** (www.indiapost.gov.in) has an online calculator for domestic and international postal tariffs.

Public Holidays

There are three official national public holidays – Republic and Independence Days and Gandhi's birthday (Gandhi Jayanti) – plus a dizzying array of other holidays celebrated nationally or locally, many of them marking important days in various religions and falling on variable dates. The most important are the 18 'gazetted holidays' (listed) which are observed by central-government offices throughout India. On these days most businesses (offices, shops etc), banks and tourist sites close, but transport is usually unaffected. It's wise to make transport and hotel reservations well in advance if you intend visiting during major festivals.

Republic Day 26 January

Holi February/March

Ramanavami March/April

Mahavir Jayanti March/April

Good Friday March/April

Dr BR Ambedkar's Birthday 14 April

Buddha Jayanti May

Eid al-Fitr June/July

Independence Day 15 August

Janmastami August/September

Eid al-Adha August/September

Dussehra September/October

Gandhi Jayanti 2 October

Muharram September/October

Diwali October/November

Guru Nanak Jayanti November

Eid-Milad-un-Nabi November/December

Christmas Day 25 December

Safe Travel

➜ Travellers to South India's major cities may fall prey to petty and opportunistic crime, but most problems can be avoided with a bit of common sense and an appropriate amount of caution.

➜ Have a look at the India branch of Lonely Planet's Thorn Tree travel forum (www.lonelyplanet.com/thorntree/forums/asia-indian-subcontinent), where travellers often post timely warnings about problems they've encountered on the road.

➜ Women should take extra precautions (p492).

➜ Schemes and frauds (p490) change as often as the bedsheets.

➜ Always check your government's travel advisory warnings.

Political Violence

India has a number of (sometimes armed) dissident groups fighting on behalf of various causes, which have employed the same tried and tested techniques of rebel groups everywhere: assassinations and bomb attacks on government infrastructure, public transport, religious centres, tourist sites and markets. Certain areas, mostly in the north of the country, are prone to insurgent violence: read the latest government travel advisories for recent reports on where is considered unsafe.

International terrorism is as much of a risk in Europe or the USA, so this is no reason not to go to India, but it makes sense to check the local security situation carefully before travelling (especially in high-risk areas).

Strikes and political protests can sometimes close the roads (as well as banks, shops, etc) for days on end in any region.

Telephone
Calling Booths

➡ There are few payphones in South India (apart from in airports), but private STD/ISD/PCO call booths do the same job, offering inexpensive local, interstate and international calls at lower prices than calls made from hotel rooms.

➡ A digital meter displays how much the call is costing and usually provides a printed receipt when the call is finished.

➡ Costs vary depending on the operator and destination but can be from ₹1 per minute for local calls and between ₹6 (Hungary) and ₹100 (Cook Islands, Cuba, East Timor) for international calls.

➡ Some booths also offer a 'call-back' service – you ring home, provide the phone number of the booth and wait for people at home to call you back, for a fee of around ₹20 on top of the cost of the preliminary call.

Directory Information

Useful online resources include the **Yellow Pages** (www.yellowpages.co.in) and **Justdial** (www.justdial.com).

Mobile Phones
GETTING CONNECTED

➡ Indian mobile numbers usually have 10 digits, mostly beginning with 9 (but sometimes 7 or 8), and operate on the GSM network at 900MHz, the world's most common, so mobile phones from most countries will work on the subcontinent.

➡ Mobiles bought in some countries may be locked to a particular network; you'll have to get the phone unlocked, or buy a local phone (available from as little as ₹500) to use an Indian SIM card.

➡ Getting connected is inexpensive but requires a bit more hoop-jumping than in many other parts of the world. It's easiest to obtain a local SIM card in large cities and tourist centres.

➡ Foreigners must supply between one and five passport photos, and photocopies of their passport identity and visa pages. Often mobile shops can arrange all this for you, or you can ask your hotel to help you.

➡ You must also supply a residential address, which can be the address of your hotel, as well as a local reference (hotel is usually fine for this, too). Usually the phone company will call your hotel (warn the hotel a call will come through) any time up to 24 hours after your application to verify that you are staying there.

➡ It's a good idea to obtain the SIM card in a place that you're staying for a day or two so that you can return to the vendor if there's any problem. To avoid scams, only obtain your SIM card from a reputable branded phone shop.

➡ SIMs are sold as regular size from some vendors, but most places have machines to cut them down to the required size if necessary; official stores usually have multifit SIMs.

➡ Another option is to get a friendly local to obtain a connection in their name.

➡ Prepaid mobile-phone packages are readily available for short-term visitors. SIMs can cost anywhere from nothing to ₹500, which includes a small allotment of talk time; then you can sign on for a data package. **Airtel** (www.airtel.in), for example, offers anywhere from 5GB (₹700) to 50GB (₹5000). **Vodafone** (www.vodafone.in) examples include 16GB (₹247) to 40GB (₹3999). It pays to shop around. Most large data packages are good for 28 days.

➡ You can then purchase more credit, sold as direct credit. You pay the vendor and the credit is deposited straight into your account, minus

---

GOVERNMENT TRAVEL ADVICE

The following government websites offer travel advice and information on current hot spots.

Australian Department of Foreign Affairs (www.smarttraveller.gov.au)

British Foreign Office (www.gov.uk/fco)

Canadian Department of Foreign Affairs (www.voyage.gc.ca)

German Foreign Office (www.auswaeriges-amt.de)

Japan Ministry of Foreign Affairs (www.mofa.go.jp)

Netherlands Ministry of Foreign Affairs (www.government.nl)

New Zealand Ministry of Foreign Affairs & Trade (www.safetravel.govt.nz)

US State Department (www.travel.state.gov)

some taxes and a service charge.

CHARGES & COVERAGE

➡ There's roaming coverage for international GSM phones in most cities and large towns.

➡ The Telecom Regulatory Authority of India (Trai) imposed stiff ceilings on roaming charges in 2015, with rates being slashed by as much as 75%. Most major mobile companies now offer very cheap roaming packages. International charges range between ₹8 and ₹100 per minute.

➡ SMS messaging is even cheaper. International outgoing messages cost ₹5. Incoming calls and messages are less than ₹1 and free, respectively.

➡ Unreliable signals and problems with international texting (messages or replies not coming through or being delayed) are not uncommon.

➡ The leading service providers are Airtel, Vodafone, Reliance, Idea and BSNL. Coverage varies from region to region – Airtel has among the widest coverage.

➡ As the mobile-phone industry continues to develop, rates, coverage and suppliers are all likely to evolve.

Phone Codes

➡ Calling India from abroad, dial your country's international access code, then ✆91 (India's country code), then the area code (without the initial zero), then the local number. For mobile

phones, the area code and initial zero are not required.

➡ Calling internationally from India, dial ✆00 (the international access code), then the country code of the country you're calling, then the area code (without the initial zero) and the local number.

➡ Indian landline phone numbers have an area code followed by up to eight digits.

➡ Toll-free numbers begin with 1800.

➡ To make interstate calls to a mobile phone, add 0 before the 10-digit number.

➡ To call a landline phone from a mobile phone, you always have to add the area code (with the initial zero).

➡ To access an international operator, dial ✆000 127. The operator can place a call to anywhere in the world and allow you to make collect calls.

➡ Home Country Direct service, which gives you access to the international operator in your home country, exists for the US (✆000 117) and the UK (✆000 4417).

GET TO KNOW YOUR BATHROOM

Most of South India's midrange hotels and all top-end ones have sit-down toilets with toilet paper and soap. Bathrooms in this category are generally improving and increasingly modern; the best have amenities like rainhead showers and a range of toiletries.

In ultracheap hotels, bus/train stations and places off the tourist trail, squat toilets are the norm and toilet paper is often not provided. Squat toilets are described as 'Indian-style', 'Indian' or 'floor' toilets; the sit-down variety may be called 'Western' or 'commode' toilets. In a few places, you'll find the curious 'hybrid toilet'; a sit-down version with footrests on the edge of the bowl.

'Attached bath', 'private bath' or 'with bath' means that the room has its own en suite bathroom. 'Common bath', 'no bathroom' or 'shared bath' means communal bathroom facilities.

Not all rooms have hot water. 'Running' or '24-hour' water means that hot water is available round-the-clock (not always the case in reality). 'Bucket' hot water is only available in buckets (sometimes for a small charge).

Many places use wall-mounted electric geysers (water heaters) that need to be switched on up to an hour before use. The geyser's main switch is often outside the bathroom.

Hotels that advertise 'room with shower' may be misleading; sometimes the shower is just a pipe sticking out of the wall. Meanwhile, some hotels surreptitiously disconnect showers to cut costs, and showers at other places render a mere trickle of water. Glassed-in showers are rare in lower price brackets.

Where possible, we recommend hotel rooms that have their own private bathroom.

Time

➡ India uses the 12-hour clock.

➡ The local standard time is known as Indian Standard Time (IST).

➡ IST is 5½ hours ahead of GMT/UTC.

➡ The floating half-hour was added to maximise daylight hours over such a vast country.

Toilets

➡ Public toilets are most easily found in major cities and tourist sites; the cleanest are usually at modern restaurants, shopping complexes and cinemas.

➡ Beyond urban centres, toilets are often of the squat variety and locals may use the 'hand-and-water' technique, which involves performing ablutions with a small jug of water and the left hand. It's always a good idea to carry toilet paper/baby wipes and hand sanitiser, just in case.

Tourist Information

In addition to Government of India tourist offices (also known as 'Indiatourism'), each state maintains its own network of tourist offices. These vary in their efficiency and usefulness – some are run by enthusiastic souls who go out of their way to help, others are little more than a means of drumming up business for State Tourism Development Corporation tours.

The first stop for information should be the Government of India tourism website, **Incredible India** (www.incredibleindia.org); for details of Indiatourism's regional offices around the country, click on the 'Essential' tab at the top of the homepage, followed by 'India Tourism Offices'. The government has also introduced a toll-free tourist helpline: ☑1800-111363. Official state tourism websites often also contain helpful information.

Handy Government of India tourism offices in South India include the following:

Bengaluru (GITO; ☑080-25585417; indtourblr@dataone.in; 2nd level, 48 Church St; ☺9.30am-6pm Mon-Fri, 9.30am-1pm Sat; Ⓜ MG Rd)

Chennai (☑044-28460285, 044-28461459; http://incredibleindia.org; 154 Anna Salai; ☺9.15am-5.45pm Mon-Fri)

Mumbai (Government of India Tourist Office; ☑022-22074333; www.incredibleindia.com; Western Railways Reservation Complex, 123 Maharshi Karve Rd; ☺8.30am-6pm Mon-Fri, to 2pm Sat)

Travellers with Disabilities

India's crowded public transport, crush of humanity and variable infrastructure can test even the hardiest able-bodied traveller. If you have a physical disability or are vision-impaired, these can pose even more of a challenge. If your mobility is considerably restricted, you may like to ease the stress by travelling with an able-bodied companion.

Accommodation Wheelchair-friendly hotels are almost exclusively top-end. Make pretrip enquiries and book ground-floor rooms at hotels that lack adequate facilities.

Accessibility Some restaurants and offices have ramps but most tend to have at least one step. Staircases are often steep; lifts frequently stop at mezzanines between floors.

Footpaths Where pavements exist, they can be riddled with holes, littered with debris and packed with pedestrians. If using crutches, bring along spare rubber caps.

Transport Hiring a car with driver will make moving around a lot easier; if you use a wheelchair, make sure the car-hire company can provide an appropriate vehicle to carry it.

For further advice pertaining to your specific requirements, consult your doctor before heading to India.

Download Lonely Planet's free Accessible Travel guide from http://lptravel.to/AccessibleTravel.

The following organisations may be able to provide further information:

Access-Able Travel Source (www.access-able.com)

Accessible Journeys (www.disabilitytravel.com)

Global Access News (www.globalaccessnews.com)

Mobility International USA (MIUSA; www.miusa.org)

Visas

E-Tourist Visa Scheme

➧ Citizens of around 150 countries, including Argentina, Australia, Brazil, Canada, Chile, China, Colombia, Israel, Japan, Mexico, New Zealand, Republic of Korea, Singapore, Taiwan, Thailand and the USA, in addition to most European countries, must apply for an e-tourist visa (eTV) at www.indianvisaonline.gov.in a minimum of four days and maximum 30 days before they are due to travel.

➧ The nonrefundable fee ranges between US$48 and US$60 for most countries plus a 2.5% bank transaction charge.

➧ You have to upload a photograph as well as a copy of your passport.

➧ The single-entry eTV is valid for entry through 16 designated airports including Bengaluru (Bangalore), Chennai (Madras), Kochi (Cochin), Delhi, Goa, Jaipur, Kolkata (Calcutta), Mumbai (Bombay), Trichy (Tiruchirappalli), Thiruvananthapuram (Trivandrum) and Varanasi.

➧ The eTV is valid from the date of arrival; your passport must be valid for at least six months from the date of arrival.

➧ There is talk of further simplification of India's visa scheme and a name change to 'e-visa scheme' (see how much easier that is?). Check online for updates.

Other Visas

If you want to stay longer than 30 days, or are not covered by the eTV scheme, you must get a visa before arriving in India (apart from Nepali or Bhutanese citizens, who do not need visas). Visas are available from Indian missions worldwide, though in many countries, applications are processed by a separate private company. In some countries or where biometrics are required, you must apply in person at the designated office as well as filing an application online.

➧ Your passport must be valid for at least six months from the date of your visa application (or from the date of issue of your visa or its date of expiry, depending on which arm of Indian bureaucracy is dealing with it), with at least two blank pages.

➧ Most people are issued with a standard six-month

tourist visa, which for most nationalities permits multiple entry.

➡ Tourist visas are valid from the date of issue, not the date you arrive in India.

➡ Student and business visas have strict conditions: journalist, missionary and research visas, among others, require biometric enrolment as of 2016. Consult the Indian embassy for details.

➡ Five- and 10-year tourist visas are available to US citizens under a bilateral arrangement, and five-year visas are available to some European and Latin American nationalities applying in Australia; however, you can still only stay in India for up to 180 days continuously.

➡ Currently visa applicants are required to submit two passport photographs with their application; these must be in colour and must be 5.08cm by 5.08cm (2in by 2in; larger than regular passport photos).

➡ An onward travel ticket is a requirement for some visas, but this isn't always enforced (check in advance).

➡ Additional restrictions apply to travellers from Bangladesh and Pakistan, as well as certain Eastern European, African and Central Asian countries. Check any special conditions for your nationality with the Indian embassy in your country.

➡ Visas are priced in the local currency and may have an added service fee.

➡ Extended visas are possible for people of Indian origin (excluding those in Pakistan and Bangladesh) who hold a non-Indian passport and live abroad.

➡ For visas lasting more than six months, you're supposed to register at the **Foreigners' Regional Registration Office** (FRRO; ☎011-26711443; frrodil@nic.in; Level 2, East Block 8, Sector 1, Rama Krishna Puram; ⊗9.30am-3pm Mon-Fri; Ⓜ Green Park) in Delhi within 14 days of arriving in India; enquire about these special conditions when you apply for your visa.

Re-entry Requirements

Most tourists are permitted to transit freely between India and its neighbouring countries. However, citizens of China, Pakistan, Iraq, Iran, Afghanistan, Bangladesh and Sudan (and foreigners of Pakistani or Bangladeshi origin) are barred from re-entry into India within two months of their last exit.

Travel Permits

Even with a visa, you're not permitted to travel everywhere in South India. Some national parks and forest reserves call for a permit. A special permit is required to visit the Andaman Islands or Lakshad-

weep, and for trekking in the Wayanad region of Kerala.

Visa Extensions

➡ India has traditionally been very stringent with visa extensions. At the time of research, the government was granting extensions only in circumstances such as medical emergencies or theft of passport just before the expiry of an applicant's visa.

➡ If you do need to extend your visa due to any such exigency, you should contact the Foreigners' Regional Registration Office (FRRO) in Delhi. This is also the place to come for a replacement visa, and if you need your lost/stolen passport replaced (required before you can leave the country). Regional FRROs are even less likely to grant an extension.

➡ Assuming you meet the stringent criteria, the FRRO is permitted to issue an extension of 14 days (free for nationals of most countries). You must bring your confirmed air ticket, one passport photo (take two, just in case), and a photocopy of your passport identity and visa pages. Note that this system is designed to get you out of the country promptly with the correct official stamps, not to give you two extra weeks of travel and leisure.

Transport

GETTING THERE & AWAY

Entering the Region

South India is most easily accessed via its major international airports at Bengaluru (Bangalore), Chennai (Madras) and Mumbai (Bombay). Some countries also offer charter flights to Goa. The South is also well served by India's extensive rail network as well as inexpensive (and often adventurous) buses from elsewhere in India. Flights, cars and tours can be booked online at lonelyplanet.com/bookings.

Passports

To enter India you need a valid passport and an onward/return ticket, and a visa. Note that your passport needs to be valid for at least six months beyond your intended stay in India, with at least two blank pages. If your passport is lost or stolen, immediately contact your country's representative. Keep photocopies of your airline ticket and the identity and visa pages of your passport in case of emergency. Better yet, scan and email copies to yourself.

Air

India is a big country so it makes sense to fly into the airport that's nearest to the area you'll be visiting. South India has three main gateways for international flights: Bengaluru (www.bengaluru-airport.com), Chennai (www.aai.aero/chennai) and Mumbai (www.csia.in); however, there are a number of other cities servicing international carriers. Direct charter flights from the UK, Russia and certain parts of Europe land at Goa's Dabolim Airport and, while you can get some cheap deals, you must also return via a charter flight.

India's national carrier is **Air India** (www.airindia.com), which has had a relatively decent air-safety record in recent years.

Land

It's possible, of course, to get to South India overland via the long haul through North India. The classic hippy route from Europe to Goa involves travelling via Turkey, Iran and Pakistan. Other popular overland options are via Bangladesh or Nepal. If you enter India by bus or train you'll be required to disembark at the border for standard immigration and customs checks.

You *must* acquire a valid Indian visa in advance, as no visas are available at the border.

For detailed information about crossing into India from neighbouring countries, consult Lonely Planet's *India*.

CLIMATE CHANGE & TRAVEL

Every form of transport that relies on carbon-based fuel generates CO_2, the main cause of human-induced climate change. Modern travel is dependent on aeroplanes, which might use less fuel per kilometre per person than most cars but travel much greater distances. The altitude at which aircraft emit gases (including CO_2) and particles also contributes to their climate change impact. Many websites offer 'carbon calculators' that allow people to estimate the carbon emissions generated by their journey and, for those who wish to do so, to offset the impact of the greenhouse gases emitted with contributions to portfolios of climate-friendly initiatives throughout the world. Lonely Planet offsets the carbon footprint of all staff and author travel.

Car & Motorcycle

Drivers of cars and motorbikes will need the vehicle's registration papers, liability insurance and an international driving permit in addition to their domestic licence. You'll also need a *Carnet de passage en douane*, which acts as a temporary waiver of import duty.

To find out the latest requirements for the paperwork and other important driving information, contact your local automobile association.

Sea

There are several sea routes between India and surrounding islands but none leave Indian sovereign territory. There has long been talk of a passenger ferry service between southern India and Colombo in Sri Lanka but this has yet to materialise. Enquire locally to see if there has been any progress.

Tours

Many international companies offer tours to India, from straightforward sightseeing trips to adventure-based holidays.

Cox & Kings (www.coxandkings. com) Long-standing operator offering tours across South India, including houseboat options.

Dragoman (www.dragoman. com) One of several reputable overland tour companies.

Exodus (www.exodus.co.uk) A wide array of specialist trips, including tours with a trekking focus.

India Wildlife Tours (www. india-wildlife-tours.com) All sorts of wildlife tours, plus jeep/horse safaris and birdwatching.

Indian Panorama (www.indianpanorama.in) Tamil Nadu–based agency whose itineraries include temples, wildlife and food.

Intrepid Travel (www.intrepidtravel.com) Endless possibilities, from wildlife tours to sacred rambles.

Kerala Connections (www.keralaconnections.co.uk) Tailor-made trips.

KOKOindia (www.kokoindia. com) UK- and Goa-based company for bespoke tours, retreats and safaris.

Shanti Travel (www.shantitravel. com) A range of tours from a Franco-Indian team.

Village Ways (www.villageways. com) Walking- and village-based itineraries involving local communities.

World Expeditions (www. worldexpeditions.com) Options include trekking and cycling tours.

GETTING AROUND

Air

India has a very competitive domestic airline industry. Air India and Jet Airways are the established international carriers. There are also a host of budget airlines offering discounted fares on a variety of domestic sectors. Airline seats can be booked directly by telephone, through travel agencies or cheaply over the internet.

At the time of writing, the following airlines were the major players operating across various destinations in South India. Keep in mind, however, that fares fluctuate dramatically. Holidays, festivals and seasons also have a serious affect on ticket prices; check the latest fares online.

Security at airports is generally stringent. You must present your passport and a valid ticket/boarding pass (print or digital) to enter airline terminals. All hold baggage must be X-rayed prior to check-in and every item of cabin baggage needs a label, which must be stamped as part of the security check (don't forget to collect tags at the check-in counter).

The recommended check-in time for domestic flights is one hour before departure. The usual luggage allowance is 20kg (10kg for smaller aircraft) in economy class and 30kg in business.

Air India (www.airindia.in; ☑1800 1801407)

GoAir (www.goair.in; ☑092-23222111)

IndiGo (www.goindigo.in; ☑9212783838)

Jet Airways (www.jetairways. com; ☑1800 225522)

SpiceJet (www.spicejet.com; ☑9871803333)

Vistara (www.airvistara.com; ☑9289228888)

Bicycle

South India offers loads of variety for the cyclist, from pretty coastal routes to winding roads passing fragrant spice plantations and breezy coconut groves.

There are no restrictions on bringing a bicycle into the country. However, bicycles sent by sea can take a few weeks to clear customs, so it's better to fly bikes in. It may actually be cheaper – and less hassle – to hire or buy a bicycle in India.

Read up on bicycle touring before you travel – Rob Van Der Plas' *Bicycle Touring Manual* and Stephen Lord's *Adventure Cycle-Touring Handbook* are good places to start. Consult local cycling magazines and cycling clubs for useful information and advice. The **Cycling Federation of India** (☑011-23753529; www.cyclingfederationofindia.org; 12 Pandit Pant Marg; ⊘10am-6pm Mon-Fri; Ⓜ Patel Chowk) in New Delhi can provide local information.

Hire

➡ Tourist centres and traveller hang-outs are the easiest spots to find bicycles for hire – simply enquire locally.

➡ Prices vary; places charge anywhere between ₹75 and ₹100 per day for a roadworthy, Indian-made bicycle. Mountain bikes, where available, can run between ₹200 to ₹600 per day (try www.rentomo.com).

➡ Hire places may require a cash security deposit (avoid leaving your airline ticket or passport).

Practicalities

➡ Mountain bikes with off-road tyres give the best protection against India's puncture-prone roads.

➡ Roadside cycle mechanics abound but you should still bring spare tyres and brake cables, lubricating oil and a chain repair kit, plus plenty of puncture repair patches.

➡ Bikes can often be carried for free, or for a small luggage fee, on the roof of public buses – handy for uphill stretches.

➡ Contact your airline for information about transporting your bike and customs formalities in your home country.

Purchase

➡ Mountain bikes from reputable brands, including **Hero** (www.herocycles.com) and **Atlas** (www.atlascycles.co.in), generally start at around ₹3500.

➡ Reselling is usually fairly easy – ask at local cycle or hire shops or put up an advert on travel noticeboards.

➡ If you purchased a new bike and it's still in reasonably good condition, you should be able to get back around 50% of what you originally paid.

Road Rules

➡ Vehicles drive on the left in India but otherwise road rules are virtually nonexistent. Cities and national highways can be hazardous places to cycle so, where possible, stick to back roads.

➡ Be conservative about the distances you expect to cover – an experienced

cyclist can manage around 60km to 100km a day on the plains, 40km to 60km on sealed mountain roads and 40km or less on dirt roads.

Boat

➡ Ships travel to the Andaman Islands from Kolkata (Calcutta), Chennai and Visakhapatnam, leaving several times per week.

➡ Between October and May, there are boat services from Kochi (Cochin; Kerala) to the Lakshadweep Islands.

➡ There are numerous shorter ferry services across rivers, from chain pontoons to coracles, and various boat cruises.

Bus

➡ Buses go almost everywhere in South India and tend to be the cheapest way to travel. Services are fast and frequent.

➡ Buses are the only way to get around many mountainous areas.

➡ Roads in curvaceous terrain can be especially perilous: buses are often driven with wilful abandon and accidents are always a risk.

➡ Avoid night buses unless there's no alternative. Driving conditions are more

hazardous and drivers may also be suffering from lack of sleep.

➡ All buses make snack and toilet stops (some more frequently than others), providing a break but possibly adding hours to journey times.

➡ Shared jeeps complement the bus service in many mountain areas.

Classes

➡ There are state-owned and private bus companies and both offer 'ordinary' buses and more expensive 'deluxe' buses. Many state tourist offices run their own reliable deluxe bus services.

➡ 'Ordinary' buses tend to be ageing rattletraps while 'deluxe' buses range from less decrepit versions of ordinary buses to flashy Volvo buses with AC and reclining two-by-two seating.

➡ Buses run by the state government are usually the more reliable option (if there's a breakdown, another bus will be sent to pick up passengers), and seats can usually be booked up to a month in advance.

➡ Private buses are either more expensive (and more comfortable), or cheaper, with kamikaze drivers and conductors who try and cram on as many passengers as possible to maximise profits.

RIDING THE RAILS WITH YOUR BIKE

For long hauls, transporting your bike by train can be a convenient option. Buy a standard train ticket for the journey, then take your bike to the station parcel office a day prior with your passport, registration papers, driving licence and insurance documents. Packing-wallahs will wrap your bike in protective sacking for around ₹50 to ₹250 and you must fill out various forms and pay the shipping fee. Charges, based on distance and weight, are quite reasonable (₹34.83 for an average 13kg mountain bike going 500km, for example) – plus an insurance fee of 1% of the declared value of the bike. Bring the same paperwork to collect your bike from the goods office at the other end. If the bike is left waiting at the destination for more than six hours, you'll pay a storage fee of ₹10 per hour.

➡ Travel agencies in many tourist towns offer relatively expensive private two-by-two buses, which tend to leave and terminate at conveniently central stops.

➡ Be warned that some agencies have been known to book people on to ordinary buses at superdeluxe prices – if possible, book directly with the bus company.

➡ Timetables and destinations may be displayed on signs or billboards at travel agencies and tourist offices.

➡ Earplugs are a boon on all long-distance buses to muffle the often deafening music. On any bus, try to sit between the axles to minimise the bumpy effect of potholes.

Costs

➡ The cheapest buses are 'ordinary' government buses, but prices vary from state to state.

➡ Add around 50% to the ordinary fare for deluxe services, double the fare for AC, and triple or quadruple the fare for a two-by-two service.

Luggage

➡ Luggage is carried either in compartments underneath the bus (sometimes for a small fee) or on the roof.

➡ Arrive at least an hour ahead of the departure time – some buses cover the roof-stored bags with a large sheet of canvas, making last-minute additions inconvenient or impossible.

➡ If your bags go on the roof, make sure they're securely locked and tied to the metal baggage rack – some unlucky travellers have seen their belongings go bouncing off the roof on bumpy roads!

➡ Theft is a minor risk so keep an eye on your bags at snack and toilet stops and *never* leave your daypack or valuables unattended inside the bus.

Reservations

➡ Most deluxe buses can be booked in advance – usually up to a month in advance for government buses – at the bus station or local travel agencies. **Red Bus** (www.redbus.in) is India's best and most comprehensive booking site/app.

➡ Reservations are rarely possible on 'ordinary' buses and travellers often get left behind in the mad rush for a seat.

➡ To maximise your chances of securing a seat, either send a travelling companion ahead to grab some space, or pass a book or article of clothing through an open window and place it on an empty seat. This 'reservation' method rarely fails.

➡ If you board a bus midway through its journey, you'll often have to stand until a seat becomes free.

➡ Many buses only depart when full – you may find your bus suddenly empties to join another bus that's ready to leave before yours.

➡ At many bus stations there's a separate women's queue, although this isn't always obvious because signs are often not in English and men frequently join the melee. Women have an unspoken right to elbow their way to the front of any bus queue in India.

Car

Self-drive car hire is possible in South India's larger cities, but given the hair-raising driving conditions most travellers opt for a car with driver. Hiring a car with driver is wonderfully affordable, particularly if several people share the cost. Seat belts are either nonexistent or tucked so deep into the backseat they require a bulldozer to dig out. International rental companies with representatives in India include **Budget** (www.budgetinternational.com) and **Hertz** (www.hertz.com).

Hiring a Car & Driver

➡ Most towns have taxi stands or car-hire companies where you can arrange short or long tours.

➡ Not all hire cars are licensed to travel beyond their home state. Even those vehicles that are licensed to enter different states have to pay extra (often hefty) state taxes, which will add to the rental charge.

➡ Ask for a driver who speaks some English and knows the region you intend to visit, and try to see the car and meet the driver before paying any money.

➡ Hindustan Ambassador cars look great (and are sadly disappearing – production of these Indian classics ended in 2014), but they can be rather slow and uncomfortable when travelling long distances; if you can find one, keep it for touring cities.

➡ For multiday trips, the charge should cover the driver's meals and accommodation. Drivers should make their own sleeping and eating arrangements.

➡ It is *essential* to set the ground rules from day one; politely but firmly let the driver know that you're boss in order to avoid anguish later.

Costs

➡ The price depends on the distance and the terrain (driving on mountain roads uses more petrol, hence the higher cost).

➡ One-way trips usually cost the same as return ones (to cover the petrol and driver charges for getting back).

➡ Hire charges vary from state to state. Some taxi unions set a time limit or a maximum kilometre distance for day trips – if you go over, you'll have to pay extra.

➡ To avoid potential misunderstandings, ensure you get *in writing* what you've been promised (quotes should include petrol, sightseeing stops, all your chosen destinations, and meals and accommodation for the driver). If a driver asks you for money to pay for petrol en route because they are short of cash, get receipts so you can be reimbursed later.

➼ For sightseeing day trips within a single city, expect to pay anywhere upward of ₹850/1200 for a non-AC/AC car with an eight-hour, 80km limit per day (extra charges apply beyond this). For out of town journeys, charges hover around ₹2400 to ₹2700 for an AC car plus tolls, parking and sometimes a driver's meal, with 250km to 300km per day. Extra kilometres are around ₹10 per kilometre.

➼ A tip is customary at the end of your journey; ₹150 to ₹175 per day is fair (more if you're really pleased with the driver's service).

Hitching

Hitching is not much of an option in South India; considering the inexpensive public transport options available, the concept of a 'free ride' is relatively unknown. Be aware that truck drivers have a reputation for driving under the influence of alcohol.

Hitching is never entirely safe, and we don't recommend it. Travellers who hitch should understand that they're taking a small but potentially serious risk. As anywhere, women are strongly advised against hitching alone or even as a pair. Always use your instincts.

Local Transport

➼ Buses, cycle-rickshaws, autorickshaws, taxis, boats and urban trains provide transport around South India's cities. Costs for public transport vary from town to town.

➼ On any form of transport without a fixed fare, agree on the price *before* you start your journey and make sure that it covers your luggage and every passenger.

➼ Even where local transport is metered, drivers may refuse to use the meter, demanding an elevated 'fixed' fare. If this happens, insist on the meter – if that fails, find another vehicle.

➼ Fares usually increase at night (by up to 100%) and some drivers charge a few rupees extra for luggage.

➼ Carry plenty of small bills for taxi and rickshaw fares as drivers rarely have change.

➼ Some taxi/autorickshaw drivers are involved in the commission racket (p491), wherein they may pressure you to switch to a hotel of their choice. Stand your ground and walk if necessary.

Autorickshaw, Tempo & Vikram

➼ The Indian autorickshaw is basically a three-wheeled motorised contraption with a tin or canvas roof and sides, providing room for two passengers (although you'll often see many more bodies squeezed in) and limited luggage. They are also referred to as autos, scooters, riks or tuk-tuks.

➼ They are mostly cheaper than taxis and are usually metered, although getting the driver to turn on the meter can be a challenge.

➼ Travelling by auto is great fun but, thanks to the open windows, can be smelly, noisy and hot!

➼ Tempos and *vikrams* (large tempos) are outsize autorickshaws with room for more passengers, running on fixed routes for a fixed fare.

➼ In country areas, you may also see the fearsome-looking 'three-wheeler' – a crude, tractorlike tempo with a front wheel on an articulated arm.

Boat

Various kinds of local boats offer transport across and down rivers in South India, from big car ferries to wooden canoes and wicker coracles. Most of the larger boats carry bicycles and motorcycles for a fee. Kerala is especially renowned for its breathtaking backwater boat cruises.

Bus

Urban buses, particularly in the big cities, are fume-belching, human-stuffed mechanical monsters that travel at breakneck speed (except during morning and evening rush hours, when they can be endlessly stuck in traffic). It's usually far more convenient and comfortable to opt for an autorickshaw or taxi.

Cycle-Rickshaw

➼ A cycle-rickshaw is a pedal cycle with two rear wheels, supporting a bench seat for passengers. Most have a canopy that can be raised in wet weather, or lowered to provide extra space for luggage.

➼ Many of the big cities have phased out (or reduced the number of) cycle-rickshaws, but they are still a major means of local transport in many smaller towns.

➼ Fares must be agreed upon in advance – speak to locals to get an idea of what is a fair price for the distance you intend travelling. Tips are always appreciated, given the slog involved.

Taxi

Most towns have taxis with meters; however, getting drivers to use them can be a major hassle. To avoid fare-setting shenanigans, use prepaid taxis or taxi apps (p512).

➼ Most Indian airports and many train stations have a prepaid-taxi booth, normally just outside the terminal building. Here, you can book a taxi for a fixed price (which will include baggage) and thus avoid commission scams. Hold on to the payment coupon until you reach your chosen destination.

➡ Smaller airports and train stations may have prepaid autorickshaw booths instead.

➡ Taxi meters are almost always outdated, so fares are calculated using a combination of the meter reading and a complicated 'fare adjustment card'. Predictably, this system is open to abuse. If you spend a few days in any town, you'll soon get a feel for the difference between a reasonable fare and a blatant rip-off. When in doubt, seek advice from locals, or stick with taxi apps.

Motorcycle

In terms of motorcycles as public transport, Goa is the only place in South India where they are a licensed form of conveyance. They take one person on the back and are a quick, inexpensive way to cover short distances.

Despite the traffic challenges, South India is an amazing region for long-distance motorcycle touring. However, motorcycle touring can be quite an undertaking; there are some popular mo-

torcycle tours for those who don't want the rigmarole of going it alone.

Weather is an important factor to consider – a monsoon-sprayed motorcycle tour is probably not on your to-do list.

To cross from neighbouring countries, check the latest regulations and paperwork requirements from the relevant diplomatic mission.

Driving Licence

To hire a motorcycle in India, technically you're required to have a valid international drivers' permit in addition to your domestic licence. In tourist areas, some places may rent out a motorcycle without asking for a driving permit/licence, but without a permit you won't be covered by insurance in the event of an accident, and may also face a fine.

Hire

➡ The classic way to motorcycle around India is on an Enfield Bullet, still built to the original 1940s specifications. As well as making a satisfying chugging sound, these bikes are fully manual, making them easy to repair (parts can be found almost everywhere in India). However, Enfields are often less reliable than many of the newer, Japanese-designed bikes; and, at time of writing,

production wasn't keeping up with demand, creating a scarcity in the market and higher prices.

➡ Plenty of places rent out motorcycles for local trips and longer tours. Japanese- and Indian-made bikes in the 100cc to 220cc range are cheaper than the big 350cc to 500cc Enfields.

➡ For three weeks' hire, a 500cc Enfield costs between ₹25,000 to ₹30,000. The price includes excellent advice and an invaluable crash course in Enfield mechanics and repairs.

➡ As a deposit, you'll need to leave a large cash lump sum (ensure you get a receipt that also stipulates the refundable amount), your passport or your air ticket. It's strongly advisable to avoid leaving your air ticket or passport, the latter of which you'll need to check in at hotels, and the police can demand to see at any time.

Purchase

➡ If you're planning a longer tour, renting is the way to go, but purchasing a motorcycle is not impossible. Though nonresident foreigners cannot officially purchase a bike, loopholes vary by state and secondhand bikes are widely available (the paperwork is a lot easier for these than for a new machine). Finding a secondhand motorcycle is a matter of asking around. Check travellers noticeboards and approach local motorcycle mechanics and other bikers.

➡ A well-looked-after secondhand 350cc Enfield will cost anywhere from ₹50,000 to ₹100,000. The 500cc model costs anywhere from ₹75,000 to ₹100,000. You will also have to pay for insurance.

➡ It's advisable to get any secondhand bike serviced before you set off.

➡ When reselling your bike, expect to get between half

TAXI APPS

➡ Taxi apps like **Uber** (www.uber.com) and **Ola Cabs** (www.olacabs.com) have completely changed the game on intra-city travel for foreigners in India – no more arguments, no more rip-offs, no more discussions whatsoever. At time of writing, Uber was operating in 29 Indian cities; Ola is usually available in smaller cities where Uber is not (over 100) and includes an autorickshaw option.

➡ Ola introduced Ola Outstation in 2016 – one-way fares for long-distance trips, meaning you will no longer have to pay for the return kilometres of your driver. At time of writing, it was available in the South Indian cities of Kolkata (Calcutta), Mumbai (Bombay), Bengaluru (Bangalore), Chennai (Madras) and Pune.

and two-thirds of the price you paid, if the bike is still in reasonable condition.

➡ Shipping an Indian bike overseas is complicated and expensive – ask the shop you bought the bike from to explain the process.

➡ Helmets are available for ₹500 to ₹5,000 and extras like panniers, luggage racks, protection bars, rear-view mirrors, lockable fuel caps, petrol filters and extra tools are easy to come by. One useful extra is a customised fuel tank, which will increase the range you can cover between fuel stops. An Enfield 500cc gives about 25km/L; the 350cc model gives slightly more.

➡ A useful website for Enfield models is www.royalenfield. com.

➡ Ask around for dealer recommendations. A Mumbai institution is **Allibhai Premji Tyrewalla** (✆022-23099417, 022-23099313; www.premjis.com; 205/20 Dr D Bhadkamkar (Lamington) Rd; ⏰10am-7pm Mon-Sat).

OWNERSHIP PAPERS

➡ There's plenty of complicated paperwork associated with owning a motorcycle; seek advice from the company selling the bike and allow two weeks to tackle the paperwork.

➡ Foreign nationals cannot change the name on the registration. Instead, you must carry blank transfer documents that are required to be changed within 30 days of purchase (the loophole here is that they will not carry a date). If you are involved in an accident, you are on the hook for any damages (and legal repercussions). If you have a residence permit and buy a new bike, the company selling it must register the machine for you, adding to the cost.

➡ For any bike, the registration must be renewed every 15 years (for around ₹5000) – you must make absolutely sure that it states the 'fitness' of the vehicle, and that there are no outstanding debts or criminal proceedings associated with the bike.

Fuel, Spare Parts & Extras

➡ Petrol and engine oil are widely available in the plains, but petrol stations are widely spaced in the mountains. If you intend to travel to remote regions, ensure you carry enough extra fuel (seek local advice about fuel availability before setting off). At the time of research, petrol cost around ₹70 per litre.

➡ If you're going to remote regions it's also important to carry basic spares (valves, fuel lines, piston rings etc). Spare parts for Indian and Japanese machines are widely available in cities and larger towns.

➡ For all machines (particularly older ones), make sure you regularly check and tighten all nuts and bolts, as Indian roads and engine vibration tend to work things loose quite quickly.

➡ Check the engine and gearbox oil level regularly (at least every 500km) and clean the oil filter every few thousand kilometres.

➡ Given the road conditions, chances are you'll make at least a couple of visits to a puncture-wallah – start your trip with new tyres and carry spanners to remove your own wheels.

➡ It's a good idea to bring your own protective equipment (jackets etc).

Insurance

➡ Only hire a bike with third-party insurance – if you hit someone without insurance, the consequences can be very costly. Reputable companies will include third-party cover in their policies; those that don't probably aren't trustworthy.

➡ You must also arrange insurance if you buy a motorcycle (usually you can organise this through the person selling the bike, though not if you are on a tourist visa).

➡ The minimum level of cover is third-party insurance – available for around ₹700 per year. This will cover repair and medical costs for any other vehicles, people or property you might hit, but no cover for your own machine. Comprehensive insurance (recommended) costs upward of ₹1400 to ₹1500 per year.

Organised Motorcycle Tours

Dozens of companies offer organised motorcycle tours around India with a support vehicle, mechanic and guide. Below are some reputable outfits (see websites for contact details, itineraries and prices):

Enfield Riders (www.enfield riders.com)

Indiabikes (www.indiabikes.com)

Peter's Classic Bike Adventure Tours (www.classic-bike-india. com)

Vintage Rides (www.vintage rides.travel)

Road Conditions

Given the varied road conditions, India can be challenging for novice riders. Hazards range from cows and chickens crossing the carriageway to broken-down trucks, pedestrians on the road, perpetual potholes and unmarked speed humps. Rural roads sometimes have grain crops strewn across them to be threshed by passing vehicles – a serious sliding hazard for bikers.

Try not to cover too much territory in one day and avoid travelling after dark – many vehicles drive without lights, and dynamo-powered motorcycle headlamps are useless at low revs while negotiating potholes.

On busy national highways expect to average 40km/h to 50km/h without stops; on winding back roads and dirt tracks this can drop to 10km/h.

Shared Jeeps

➡ In mountain areas, such as those around Aurangabad and Nasik in Maharashtra, shared jeeps supplement the bus service, charging similar fixed fares.

➡ Although nominally designed for five to six passengers, most shared jeeps squeeze in many more people. The seats beside and immediately behind the driver are more expensive than the cramped bench seats at the rear.

➡ Four-wheel drives leave only when full, and it is not uncommon for everyone to bail out of a half-full jeep and pile into a fuller vehicle that is ready to depart. Drivers will leave immediately if you pay for all the empty seats in the vehicle.

➡ Four-wheel drives run from jeep stands and 'passenger stations' at the junctions of major roads; ask locals to point you in the right direction.

➡ In some states, jeeps are known as 'sumos' after the Tata Sumo, a popular jeep.

➡ Be warned that some people can suffer from travel sickness, particularly on winding mountain roads; be prepared to give up your window seat to queasy fellow passengers.

Tours

Tours are available all over South India, run by tourist offices, local transport companies and travel agencies. Organised tours can be an inexpensive way to see several places on one trip, although they're often fast-paced. Tailor-made tours give you more freedom about where you go and how long you stay.

Drivers may double as guides or you can hire qualified local guides for a fee. In tourist towns, be wary of touts claiming to be professional guides.

Walking, cycling and food-focused tours are becoming increasingly popular across South India.

Train

Travelling by train is a quintessential Indian experience. Trains offer a smoother ride than buses and are especially recommended for long journeys that include overnight travel. India's rail network is one of the largest and busiest in the world and Indian Railways is the largest utility employer on earth, with roughly 1.5 million workers. There are around 6900 train stations scattered across the country.

There are hundreds of useful services. The best way of sourcing updated railway information is to use relevant internet sites such as **Indian Railways** (www.indianrailways.gov.in) and the useful **Seat 61** (www.seat61.com/India). There's also *Trains at a Glance*

(₹45), available at many train station bookstands as well as online at www.indianrailways.gov.in/railwayboard (under 'Important Information'), but it's published annually so it's not as up to date as websites. Nevertheless, it offers comprehensive timetables covering all the main lines.

Booking Tickets in India

You can either book tickets online, through a travel agency or hotel (for a commission), or in person at the train station. Big stations often have English-speaking staff who can help with choosing the best train. At smaller stations, midlevel officials, such as the deputy station master, usually speak English. It's also worth approaching tourist office staff if you need advice about booking tickets, deciding on a train class etc. The nationwide railways enquiries number is 📞139.

AT THE STATION

➡ Get a reservation slip from the information window, fill in the name of the departure station, the destination station, the class you want to travel and the name and number of the train. Join the long queue at the ticket window where your ticket will be printed. Women should avail themselves of the separate women's queue – if there isn't one, go to the front of the regular queue.

➡ Indian Railways began installing some 10,000 point-of-sale terminals within its nationwide network in late 2016, allowing for cashless machine ticket buying.

TOURIST RESERVATION BUREAU

Chennai, Kolkata and Mumbai have an International Tourist Bureau, which allows you to book tickets in relative peace – check www.indianrail.gov.in/international_Tourist.html for additional info.

FARE FINDER

To find out which trains travel between any two destinations, go to www.trainenquiry.com and click on 'Find Your Train' – type in the name of the two destinations (you may be prompted to choose from a list of stations) and you'll get a list of every train (with the name, number and arrival/departure times). Find the fare for your chosen train at www.indianrail.gov.in; click on 'Fare Enquiry'.

Costs

➜ Fares are calculated by distance and class of travel; Rajdhani and Shatabdi trains are slightly more expensive, but the price includes meals. Most air-conditioned carriages have a catering service (meals are brought to your seat). In unreserved classes it's a good idea to carry portable snacks.

➜ Seniors (those over 60) get 30% off all fares in all classes on all types of train. Children below the age of five travel free; those aged between five and 12 are charged half price.

➜ Indian Rail introduced surge pricing on Rajdhani, Shatabdi and Duronto express trains in 2016. Fares increase 10% with every 10% of berths sold subject to a prescribed ceiling limit.

Reservations

➜ Bookings open 90 days before departure and you must make a reservation for all chair-car, sleeper, and 1AC, 2AC and 3AC carriages. No reservations are required for general (2nd-class) compartments. Trains are always busy in India so it's wise to book as far in advance as possible; advance booking for overnight trains is strongly recommended. Train services to certain destinations are often increased during major festivals but it's still worth booking well in advance.

➜ Reserved tickets show your seat/berth number and the carriage number. When the train pulls in, keep an eye out for your carriage number, written on the side of the train (station staff and porters can also point you in the right direction). A list of names and berths is also posted on the side of each reserved carriage.

➜ Refunds are available on any ticket, even after departure, with a penalty – the rules are complicated so check when you book.

➜ Be aware that train trips can be delayed at any point in the journey so, to avoid stress, factor some leeway into your travel plans.

If the train you want to travel on is sold out, make sure to enquire about the following possibilities:

➜ **Reservation Against Cancellation (RAC)** Even when a train is fully booked, Indian Railways sells a handful of RAC seats in each class. This means that if you have an RAC ticket and someone cancels before the departure date, you will get that seat (or berth). You'll have to check the reservation list at the station on the day of travel to see where you've been allocated to sit. Even if no one cancels, as an RAC ticket holder you can still board the train, and even if you don't get a seat you can still travel.

➜ **Taktal Tickets** Indian Railways holds back a limited number of tickets on key trains and releases them at 10am (AC) and 11am (non-AC) one day before the train is due to depart. A charge of ₹90 to ₹500 is added to each ticket price depending on distance. 1AC and Executive Chair tickets are excluded from the scheme.

➜ **Tourist Quota** A special (albeit small) tourist quota is set aside for foreign tourists travelling between popular stations. These seats can only be booked at dedicated reservation offices in major cities, and you need to show your passport and visa as ID. Tickets can be paid for in rupees (some offices may ask to see foreign exchange certificates – ATM receipts will suffice).

➜ **Waitlist (WL)** Trains are frequently overbooked, but many passengers cancel and there are regular no-shows. So if you buy a ticket on the waiting list you're quite likely to get a seat, even if there are a number of people ahead of you on the list. Check your booking status at www.indianrail.co.in/pnr_Enq.html by entering your ticket's PNR number. A refund is available if you fail to get a seat – ask the ticket office about your chances.

Safety

➜ In all classes, a padlock and a length of chain are useful for securing your luggage to baggage racks.

➜ Be mindful of potential passenger drugging and theft.

EXPRESS TRAIN FARES (₹)

Distance (km)	1AC*	2AC*	3AC*	Chair Car (CC)**	Sleeper**	2nd (II)**
100	1,203	706	498	205	77	47
200	1,203	706	498	278	120	72
300	1,203	706	498	370	177	101
400	1,648	959	676	458	217	126
500	1,969	1,146	801	545	261	150
1000	3,306	1,928	1,333	916	439	253
1500	4,269	2,476	1,700	1,176	566	330
2000	5,255	3,013	2,033	1,433	692	410

* Rajdhani/Duronto Trains

** Mail/Express Trains

Health

There is huge geographical variation in India, so in different areas, heat, cold and altitude can cause health problems. Hygiene is poor in most regions so food and water-borne illnesses are common. A number of insect-borne diseases are present, particularly in tropical areas. Medical care is basic in various areas (especially beyond the larger cities) so it's essential to be well prepared.

Pre-existing medical conditions and accidental injury (especially traffic accidents) account for most life threatening problems. Becoming ill in some way, however, is common. Fortunately, most travellers' illnesses can be prevented with some common-sense behaviour or treated with a well-stocked travellers' medical kit – however, never hesitate to consult a doctor while on the road, as self-diagnosis can be hazardous.

Before You Go

You can buy many medications over the counter in India without a doctor's prescription, but it can be difficult to find some of the newer drugs, particularly the latest antidepressant drugs, blood-pressure medications and contraceptive pills. Be circumspect about self-medicating, as travellers mixing the wrong drugs or overdosing has on occasion ended in tragedy. Bring the following:

➡ medications in their original, labelled containers

➡ a signed, dated letter from your physician describing your medical conditions and medications, including generic names

➡ a physician's letter documenting the medical necessity of any syringes you bring

➡ if you have a heart condition, a copy of your ECG taken just prior to travelling

➡ any regular medication (double your ordinary needs).

Insurance

Don't travel without health insurance. Emergency evacuation is expensive. There are various factors to consider when choosing insurance. Read the small print.

➡ You may require extra cover for adventure activities such as rock climbing and scuba diving.

➡ In India, doctors usually require immediate payment in cash. Your insurance plan may make payments directly to providers or it will reimburse you later for overseas health expenditures. If you do have to claim later, make sure you keep all relevant documentation.

➡ Some policies ask that you telephone back (reverse charges) to a centre in your home country where an immediate assessment of your problem will be made.

Vaccinations

Specialised travel-medicine clinics are your best source of up-to-date information; they stock all available vaccines and can give specific recommendations for your trip. Most vaccines don't give immunity until *at least* two weeks after they're given, so visit a doctor well before departure. Ask your doctor for an International Certificate of Vaccination (sometimes known as the 'yellow booklet'), which will list all the vaccinations you've received.

Medical Checklist

Recommended items for a personal medical kit:

➡ Antifungal cream, eg clotrimazole

➡ Antibacterial cream, eg mupirocin

➡ Antibiotic for skin infections, eg amoxicillin/clavulanate or cephalexin

➡ Antihistamine – there are many options, eg cetrizine for daytime and promethazine for night

➡ Antiseptic, eg Betadine

➡ Antispasmodic for stomach cramps, eg Buscopam

➡ Contraceptive

➡ Decongestant, eg pseudoephedrine

➡ DEET-based insect repellent

➡ Diarrhoea medication – consider an oral rehydration solution (eg Gastrolyte), diarrhoea 'stopper' (eg loperamide) and antinausea medication (eg prochlorperazine). Antibiotics for diarrhoea include ciprofloxacin; for bacterial diarrhoea azithromycin; for giardia or amoebic dysentery tinidazole

➡ First-aid items such as scissors, elastoplasts, bandages, gauze, thermometer (but not mercury), sterile needles and syringes, safety pins and tweezers

➡ Ibuprofen or another anti-inflammatory

➡ Iodine tablets (unless you are pregnant or have a thyroid problem) to purify water

➡ Migraine medication if you suffer from migraines

➡ Paracetamol

➡ Pyrethrin to impregnate clothing and mosquito nets

➡ Steroid cream for allergic or itchy rashes, eg 1% to 2% hydrocortisone

➡ High-factor sunscreen

➡ Throat lozenges

➡ Thrush (vaginal yeast infection) treatment, eg clotrimazole pessaries or Diflucan tablet

➡ Ural or equivalent if prone to urine infections

Websites

There is a wealth of travel-health advice on the internet; www.lonelyplanet.com is a good place to start. Some other suggestions:

Centers for Disease Control and Prevention (CDC; www.cdc.gov) Good general information.

MD Travel Health (www.mdtravelhealth.com) Provides complete travel-health recommendations for every country; updated daily.

World Health Organization (WHO; www.who.int/ith) Its superb book *International Travel & Health* is revised annually and is available online.

Further Reading

Recommended references include *Travellers' Health* by Dr Richard Dawood and *Travelling Well* by Dr Deborah Mills, which is now also available as an app; check out the website (www.travellingwell.com.au) too.

In India

Availability & Cost of Health Care

Medical care is hugely variable in India. Some cities now have clinics catering specifically to travellers and expatriates; these clinics are usually more expensive than local medical facilities, and offer a higher standard of care. Additionally, they know the local system, including reputable local hospitals and specialists. They may also liaise with insurance companies should you require evacuation. It is usually difficult to find reliable medical care in rural areas.

Self-treatment may be appropriate if your problem is minor (eg traveller's diarrhoea), you are carrying the relevant medication, and you cannot attend a recommended clinic. If you suspect a serious disease, especially malaria, travel to the nearest quality facility.

Before buying medication over the counter, check the use-by date, and ensure the packet is sealed and properly stored (eg not exposed to the sun).

Infectious Diseases

MALARIA

This is a serious and potentially deadly disease. Before you travel, seek expert advice according to your itinerary (rural areas are especially risky) and on medication and side effects.

Malaria is caused by a parasite transmitted by the bite of an infected mosquito. The most important symptom of malaria is fever, but general symptoms, such as headache, diarrhoea, cough or chills, may also occur. Diagnosis can only be properly made by taking a blood sample.

Two strategies should be combined to prevent malaria: mosquito avoidance and antimalarial medications. Most people who catch malaria are taking inadequate or no anti-malarial medication.

Travellers are advised to prevent mosquito bites by taking these steps:

➡ Use a DEET-based insect repellent on exposed skin. Wash this off at night – as long as you are sleeping under a mosquito net. Natural repellents such as citronella can be effective, but must be applied more frequently than products containing DEET.

➡ Sleep under a mosquito net impregnated with pyrethrin.

➡ Choose accommodation with proper screens and fans (if not air-conditioned).

➡ Impregnate clothing with pyrethrin in high-risk areas.

➡ Wear long sleeves and trousers in light colours.

➡ Use mosquito coils.

➡ Spray your room with insect repellent before going out for your evening meal.

There are a variety of medications available:

Chloroquine & Paludrine combination Limited effectiveness in many parts of South Asia. Common side effects include nausea (40% of people) and mouth ulcers.

Doxycycline (daily tablet) A broad-spectrum antibiotic that helps prevent a variety of tropical

HEALTH ADVISORIES

It's a good idea to consult your government's travel-health website before departure, if one is available:

Australia (www.smartraveller.gov.au)

Canada (www.travelhealth.gc.ca)

New Zealand (safetravel.govt.nz/health-and-travel)

UK (www.fco.gov.uk/en/travelling-and-living-overseas)

US (www.cdc.gov/travel)

REQUIRED & RECOMMENDED VACCINATIONS

The only vaccine required by international regulations is **yellow fever**. Proof of vaccination will only be required if you have visited a country in the yellow-fever zone within the six days prior to entering India. If you are travelling to India from Africa or South America, you should check to see if you require proof of vaccination.

The World Health Organization (WHO) recommends the following vaccinations for travellers going to India (as well as being up to date with measles, mumps and rubella vaccinations):

Adult diphtheria & tetanus Single booster recommended if none in the previous 10 years. Side effects include sore arm and fever.

Hepatitis A Provides almost 100% protection for up to a year; a booster after 12 months provides at least another 20 years' protection. Mild side effects such as headache and sore arm occur in 5% to 10% of people.

Hepatitis B Now considered routine for most travellers. Given as three shots over six months. A rapid schedule is also available, as is a combined vaccination with hepatitis A. Side effects are mild and uncommon, usually headache and a sore arm. In 95% of people lifetime protection results.

Polio Only one booster is required as an adult for lifetime protection. Inactivated polio vaccine is safe during pregnancy.

Typhoid Recommended for all travellers to India, even those only visiting urban areas. The vaccine offers around 70% protection, lasts for two to three years and comes as a single shot. Tablets are also available, but the injection is usually recommended as it has fewer side effects. Sore arm and fever may occur.

Varicella If you haven't had chickenpox, discuss this vaccination with your doctor.

These immunisations are recommended for long-term travellers (more than one month) or those at special risk (seek further advice from your doctor):

Japanese B encephalitis Three injections in all. Booster recommended after two years. Sore arm and headache are the most common side effects. In rare cases, an allergic reaction comprising hives and swelling can occur up to 10 days after any of the three doses.

Meningitis Single injection. There are two types of vaccination: the quadravalent vaccine gives two to three years' protection; meningitis group C vaccine gives around 10 years' protection. Recommended for long-term backpackers aged under 25.

Rabies Three injections in all. A booster after one year will then provide 10 years' protection. Side effects are rare – occasionally headache and sore arm.

Tuberculosis (TB) A complex issue. Adult long-term travellers are usually recommended to have a TB skin test before and after travel, rather than vaccination. Only one vaccine given in a lifetime.

diseases, including leptospirosis, tick-borne disease and typhus. Potential side effects include photosensitivity (a tendency to sunburn), thrush (in women), indigestion, heartburn, nausea and interference with the contraceptive pill. More serious side effects include ulceration of the oesophagus – take your tablet with a meal and a large glass of water, and never lie down within half an hour of taking it. It must be taken for four weeks after leaving the risk area.

Lariam (mefloquine) This weekly tablet suits many people. Serious side effects are rare but include depression, anxiety, psychosis and seizures. Anyone with a history of depression, anxiety, other psychological disorders or epilepsy should not take Lariam. It is considered safe in the second and third trimesters of pregnancy. Tablets must be taken for four weeks after leaving the risk area.

Malarone A combination of atovaquone and proguanil. Side effects are uncommon and mild, most commonly nausea and headache. It is the best tablet for scuba divers and for those on short trips to high-risk areas. It must be taken for one week after leaving the risk area.

OTHER DISEASES

Avian flu 'Bird flu' or Influenza A (H5N1) is a subtype of the type A influenza virus. Contact with dead or sick birds is the principal source of infection and bird-to-human transmission does not easily occur. Symptoms include high fever and flu-like symptoms with rapid deterioration, leading to respiratory failure and death in many cases. Immediate medical care should be sought if bird flu is suspected. Check www.who.int/en/or www.avianinfluenza.com.au.

Cholera There are occasional outbreaks of cholera in India. This acute gastrointestinal infection is transmitted through contaminated water and food, including raw or undercooked fish and shellfish. Cases are rare among travellers, but those who are travelling to an area of active transmission should consult with their healthcare practitioner regarding vaccination.

Dengue fever This mosquito-borne disease is becomingly increasingly problematic, especially in the cities. As there is no vaccine available it can only be prevented by avoiding mosquito bites at all times. Symptoms include high fever, severe headache and body ache and sometimes a rash and diarrhoea. Treatment is rest and paracetamol – do not take aspirin or ibuprofen as it increases the likelihood of haemorrhaging. Make sure you see a doctor to be diagnosed and monitored.

Hepatitis A This food- and water-borne virus infects the liver, causing jaundice (yellow skin and eyes), nausea and lethargy. There is no specific treatment for hepatitis A, you just need to allow time for the liver to heal. All travellers to India should be vaccinated against hepatitis A.

Hepatitis B This sexually transmitted disease is spread by body fluids and can be prevented by vaccination. The long-term consequences can include liver cancer and cirrhosis.

Hepatitis E Transmitted through contaminated food and water, hepatitis E has similar symptoms to hepatitis A, but is far less common. It is a severe problem in pregnant women and can result in the death of both mother and baby. There is no commercially available vaccine, and prevention is by following safe eating and drinking guidelines.

HIV Spread via contaminated body fluids. Avoid unsafe sex, unsterile needles (including in medical facilities) and procedures such as tattoos. The growth rate of HIV in India is one of the highest in the world.

Influenza Present year-round in the tropics, influenza (flu) symptoms include fever, muscle aches, a runny nose, cough and sore throat. It can be severe in people over the age of 65 or in those with medical conditions such as heart disease or diabetes – vaccination is recommended for these individuals. There is no specific treatment, just rest and paracetamol.

Japanese B encephalitis This viral disease is transmitted by mosquitoes and is rare in travellers. Most cases occur in rural areas and vaccination is recommended for travellers spending more than one month outside of cities. There is no treatment, and

DRINKING WATER

⇒ Never drink tap water.

⇒ Bottled water is generally safe – check the seal is intact at purchase.

⇒ Avoid ice unless you know it has been made hygienically.

⇒ Be careful of fresh juices served at street stalls in particular – they may have been watered down or may be served in unhygienic jugs/glasses.

⇒ Boiling water is usually the most efficient method of purifying it.

⇒ The best chemical purifier is iodine. It should not be used by pregnant women or those with thyroid problems.

⇒ Water filters should also filter out most viruses. Ensure your filter has a chemical barrier such as iodine and a small pore size (less than four microns).

it may result in permanent brain damage or death. Ask your doctor for further details.

Rabies This fatal disease is spread by the bite or possibly even the lick of an infected animal – most commonly a dog or monkey. You should seek medical advice immediately after any animal bite and commence postexposure treatment. Having pretravel vaccination means the postbite treatment is greatly simplified. If an animal bites you, gently wash the wound with soap and water, and apply iodine-based antiseptic. If you are not prevaccinated you will need to receive rabies immunoglobulin as soon as possible, and this is very difficult to obtain in much of India.

Tuberculosis While TB is rare in travellers, those who have significant contact with the local population (such as medical and aid workers and long-term travellers) should take precautions. Vaccination is usually only given to children under the age of five, but adults at risk are recommended to have pre- and post-travel TB testing. The main symptoms are fever, cough, weight loss, night sweats and fatigue.

Typhoid This serious bacterial infection is also spread via food and water. It gives a high and slowly progressive fever and headache, and may be accompanied by a dry cough and stomach pain. It is diagnosed by blood tests and treated with antibiotics. Vaccination is recommended for all travellers who are spending more

than a week in India. Be aware that vaccination is not 100% effective, so you must still be careful with what you eat and drink.

TRAVELLER'S DIARRHOEA

This is by far the most common problem affecting travellers in India – between 30% and 70% of people will suffer from it within two weeks of starting their trip. It's usually caused by a bacteria, and thus responds promptly to treatment with antibiotics.

Traveller's diarrhoea is defined as the passage of more than three watery bowel actions within 24 hours, plus at least one other symptom, such as fever, cramps, nausea, vomiting or feeling generally unwell.

Treatment consists of staying well hydrated; rehydration solutions like Gastrolyte are the best for this. Antibiotics such as ciprofloxacin or azithromycin should kill the bacteria quickly. Seek medical attention quickly if you do not respond to an appropriate antibiotic.

Loperamide is just a 'stopper' and doesn't get to the cause of the problem. It can be helpful, though (eg if you have to go on a long bus ride). Don't take loperamide if you have a fever or blood in your stools.

Amoebic dysentery Amoebic dysentery is very rare in travellers but is quite often misdiagnosed

HEALTH IN INDIA

CARBON-MONOXIDE POISONING

Some mountain areas rely on charcoal burners for warmth, but these should be avoided due to the risk of fatal carbon-monoxide poisoning. The thick, mattress-like blankets used in many mountain areas are amazingly warm once you get beneath the covers. If you're still cold, improvise a hot-water bottle by filling your drinking-water bottle with boiled water and covering it with a sock.

by poor-quality labs. Symptoms are similar to bacterial diarrhoea: fever, bloody diarrhoea and generally feeling unwell. You should always seek reliable medical care if you have blood in your diarrhoea. Treatment involves two drugs: tinidazole or metronidazole to kill the parasite in your gut and then a second drug to kill the cysts. If left untreated complications such as liver or gut abscesses can occur.

Giardiasis Giardia is a parasite that is relatively common in travellers. Symptoms include nausea, bloating, excess gas, fatigue and intermittent diarrhoea. The parasite will eventually go away if left untreated but this can take months; the best advice is to seek medical treatment. The treatment of choice is tinidazole, with metronidazole being a second-line option.

Environmental Hazards

AIR POLLUTION
Air pollution, particularly vehicle pollution, is an increasing problem in most of India's urban hubs. If you have severe respiratory problems, speak with your doctor before travelling to India. All travellers are advised to listen to advisories on pollution levels from the press or government officials (if the Air Quality Index measures 100 or above in any of its eight pollutant categories, this is poor). It's worth taking a disposable face mask if you are affected by air quality.

DIVING & SURFING
Divers and surfers should seek specialised advice before they travel to ensure their medical kit contains treatment for coral cuts and tropical ear infections. Divers should ensure their insurance covers them for decompression illness –

get specialised dive insurance through an organisation such as Divers Alert Network (www. danasiapacific.org). Certain medical conditions are incompatible with diving; check with your doctor.

FOOD
Dining out brings with it the possibility of contracting diarrhoea. Ways to help avoid food-related illness:

➡ eat only freshly cooked food

➡ avoid shellfish and buffets

➡ peel fruit

➡ cook vegetables

➡ soak salads in iodine water for at least 20 minutes

➡ eat in busy restaurants with a high turnover of customers.

HEAT
Many parts of India, especially down south, are hot and humid throughout the year. For most visitors it takes around two weeks to comfortably adapt to the hot climate. Swelling of the feet and ankles is common, as are muscle cramps caused by excessive sweating. Prevent these by avoiding dehydration and excessive activity in the heat. Don't eat salt tablets (they aggravate the gut); drinking rehydration solution or eating salty food helps. Treat cramps by resting, rehydrating with double-strength rehydration solution and gently stretching.

Dehydration is the main contributor to heat exhaustion. Recovery is usually rapid and it is common to feel weak for some days afterwards. Symptoms include:

➡ feeling weak

➡ headache

➡ irritability

➡ nausea or vomiting

➡ sweaty skin

➡ a fast, weak pulse

➡ normal or slightly elevated body temperature.
Treatment:

➡ get out of the heat

➡ fan the sufferer

➡ apply cool, wet cloths to the skin

➡ lay the sufferer flat with their legs raised

➡ rehydrate with water containing one-quarter teaspoon of salt per litre.

Heatstroke is a serious medical emergency. Symptoms include:

➡ weakness

➡ nausea

➡ a hot, dry body

➡ temperature of over 41°C

➡ dizziness

➡ confusion

➡ loss of coordination

➡ seizures

➡ eventual collapse.
Treatment:

➡ get out of the heat

➡ fan the sufferer

➡ apply cool, wet cloths to the skin or ice to the body, especially to the groin and armpits.

Prickly heat is a common skin rash in the tropics, caused by sweat trapped under the skin. Treat it by moving out of the heat for a few hours and by having cool showers. Creams and ointments clog the skin so they should be avoided. Locally bought prickly-heat powder can be helpful.

ALTITUDE SICKNESS
If you are going to altitudes above 3000m, acute mountain sickness (AMS) is an issue. The biggest risk factor is going too high too quickly – follow a conservative acclimatisation schedule found in good trekking guides, and *never* go to a higher altitude when you have any symptoms that could be altitude related. There is no way to predict who will get altitude sickness and it is quite often the younger,

fitter members of a group who succumb.

Symptoms usually develop during the first 24 hours at altitude but may be delayed up to three weeks. Mild symptoms include:

➡ headache

➡ lethargy

➡ dizziness

➡ difficulty sleeping

➡ loss of appetite.

AMS may become more severe without warning and can be fatal. Severe symptoms include:

➡ breathlessness

➡ a dry, irritative cough (which may progress to the production of pink, frothy sputum)

➡ severe headache

➡ lack of coordination and balance

➡ confusion

➡ irrational behaviour

➡ vomiting

➡ drowsiness

➡ unconsciousness.

Treat mild symptoms by resting at the same altitude until recovery, which usually takes a day or two. Paracetamol or aspirin can be taken for headaches. If symptoms persist or become worse, immediate descent is necessary; even 500m can help. Drug treatments should never be used to avoid descent or to enable further ascent.

The drugs acetazolamide and dexamethasone are recommended by some doctors for the prevention of AMS; however, their use is controversial. They can reduce the symptoms, but they may also mask warning signs; severe and fatal AMS has occurred in people taking these drugs.

To prevent AMS:

➡ ascend slowly – have frequent rest days, spending two to three nights at each rise of 1000m

➡ sleep at a lower altitude than the greatest height reached during the day, if possible. Above 3000m, don't increase sleeping altitude by more than 300m daily

➡ drink extra fluids

➡ eat light, high-carbohydrate meals

➡ avoid alcohol and sedatives.

INSECT BITES & STINGS

Bedbugs Don't carry disease but their bites can be itchy. You can treat the itch with an antihistamine.

Lice Most commonly appear on the head and pubic areas. You may need numerous applications of an antilice shampoo such as pyrethrin.

Ticks Contracted walking in rural areas. Ticks are commonly found behind the ears, on the belly and in armpits. If you have had a tick bite and have a rash at the site of the bite or elsewhere, fever or muscle aches, see a doctor. Doxycycline prevents tick-borne diseases.

Leeches Found in humid rainforest areas. They do not transmit any disease but their bites are often itchy for weeks and can easily become infected. Apply an iodine-based antiseptic to any leech bite to help prevent infection.

Bee and wasp stings Anyone with a serious bee or wasp allergy should carry an injection of adrenalin (eg an Epipen).

SKIN PROBLEMS

Fungal rashes There are two common fungal rashes that affect travellers. The first occurs in moist areas, such as the groin, armpits and between the toes. It starts as a red patch that slowly spreads and is usually itchy. Treatment involves keeping the skin dry, avoiding chafing and using an antifungal cream such as clotrimazole or Lamisil. The second, *Tinea versicolor*, causes light-coloured patches, most commonly on the back, chest and shoulders. Consult a doctor.

Cuts and scratches These become easily infected in humid climates. Immediately wash all wounds in clean water and apply antiseptic. If you develop signs of infection (increasing pain and redness), see a doctor.

SUNBURN

Even on a cloudy day sunburn can occur rapidly.

➡ Use a strong sunscreen (factor 30) and reapply after a swim.

➡ Wear a wide-brimmed hat and sunglasses.

➡ Avoid lying in the sun during the hottest part of the day (10am to 2pm).

➡ Be vigilant above 3000m – you can get burnt very easily at altitude.

If you become sunburnt, stay out of the sun until you have recovered, apply cool compresses and, if necessary, take painkillers for the discomfort. One per cent hydrocortisone cream applied twice daily is also helpful.

Women's Health

For gynaecological health issues, seek out a female doctor.

Birth control Bring adequate supplies of your own form of contraception.

Sanitary products Pads, but rarely tampons, are readily available.

Thrush Heat, humidity and antibiotics can all contribute to thrush. Treatment is with antifungal creams and pessaries such as clotrimazole. A practical alternative is a single tablet of fluconazole (Diflucan).

Urinary-tract infections These can be precipitated by dehydration or long bus journeys without toilet stops; bring suitable antibiotics.

Language

The number of languages spoken in India helps explain why English is still widely spoken here, and why it's still in official use. Another 22 languages are recognised in the constitution, and more than 1600 other languages are spoken throughout the country.

While Hindi is the predominant language in the north, it bears little relation to the Dravidian languages of India's south and few people in the south speak Hindi. The native languages of the southern regions covered in this book (and in this chapter) are Tamil, Kannada, Konkani, Malayalam, Marathi and Telugu. Most of them belong to the Dravidian language family, although they have been influenced to varying degrees by Hindi and Sanskrit. As the predominant languages in specific geographic areas, they have in effect been used to determine the regional boundaries for the southern states.

Many educated Indians speak English as virtually their first language and for a large number of Indians it's often their second tongue, so you'll also find it very easy to get by in South India with English.

Pronunciation

The pronunciation systems of all languages covered in this chapter include a number of 'retroflex' consonants (pronounced with the tongue bent backwards), and all languages except for Tamil also have 'aspirated' consonants (pronounced with a puff of air). Our simplified pronunciation guides don't dis-

tinguish the retroflex consonants from their nonretroflex counterparts. The aspirated sounds are indicated with an apostrophe (') after the consonant. If you read our coloured pronunciation guides as if they were English, you'll be understood. The stressed syllables are indicated with italics for languages that have noticeable word stress; for others, all syllables should be equally stressed.

TAMIL

Tamil is the official language in the South Indian state of Tamil Nadu (as well as a national language in Sri Lanka, Malaysia and Singapore). It is one of the major Dravidian languages of South India, with records of its existence going back more than 2000 years. Tamil has about 62 million speakers in India.

A pronunciation tip: aw is pronounced as in 'law' and ow as in 'how'.

Basics

Hello.	வணக்கம்.	va·*nak*·kam
Goodbye.	போய்.	*po*·i
	வருகிறேன்.	va·*ru*·ki·reyn
Yes./No.	ஆமாம்./இல்லை.	aa·maam/il·lai
Excuse me.	தயவு செய்து.	ta·ya·vu sei·du
Sorry.	மன்னிக்கவும.	man·nik·ka·vum
Please.	தயவு செய்து.	ta·ya·vu chey·tu
Thank you.	நன்றி.	nan·dri

How are you?
நீங்கள் நலமா? neeng·kal na·la·maa

Fine, thanks. And you?
நலம், நன்றி. na·lam nan·dri
நீங்கள்? neeng·kal

What's your name?
உங்கள் பெயர் என்ன? ung·kal pe·yar en·na

My name is ...
என் பெயர் ... en pe·yar ...

WANT MORE?

For in-depth language information and handy phrases, check out Lonely Planet's *India Phrasebook*. You'll find it at **shop.lonelyplanet.com**, or you can buy Lonely Planet's iPhone phrasebooks at the Apple App Store.

Do you speak English?
நீங்கள் ஆங்கிலம் *neeng·kal aang·ki·lam*
பேசுவீர்களா? *pey·chu·veer·ka·la*

I don't understand.
எனக்கு *e·nak·ku*
விளங்கவில்லை. *vi·lang·ka·vil·lai*

Accommodation

Where's a அருகே ஒரு ... *a·ru·ke o·ru ...*
... nearby? எங்கே உள்ளது? *eng·ke ul·la·tu*

guesthouse விருந்தினர் *vi·run·ti·nar*
இல்லம *il·lam*

hotel ஹோட்டல *hot·tal*

Do you have உங்களிடம் *ung·ka·li·tam*
a ... room? ஓர் ... அறை *awr ... a·rai*
உள்ளதா? *ul·la·taa*

single தன *ta·ni*

double இரட்டை *i·rat·tai*

How much is ஓர் ... *awr ...*
it per ...? என்னவிலை? *en·na·vi·lai*

night இரவுக்கு *i·ra·vuk·ku*

person ஒருவருக்கு *o·ru·va·ruk·ku*

bathroom குளியலறை *ku·li·ya·la·rai*
bed படுக்கை *pa·tuk·kai*
window சன்னல *chan·nal*

Directions

Where's the ...?
... எங்கே இருக்கிறது? *... eng·key i·ruk·ki·ra·tu*

What's the address?
வீலாசம் என்ன? *vi·laa·cham en·na*

Can you show me (on the map)?
எனக்கு (வரைபடத்தில்) *e·nak·ku (va·rai·pa·tat·til)*
காட்ட முடியுமா? *kaat·ta mu·ti·yu·maa*

How far is it?
எவ்வளவு தூரத்தில் *ev·va·la·vu too·rat·til*
இருக்கிறது? *i·ruk·ki·ra·tu*

It's ... அது *a·tu*
இருப்பது ... *i·rup·pa·tu ...*

behind ... ... க்குப் *... kup*
பின்னால *pin·naal*

in front of ... ... க்கு *... ku*
முன்னால *mun·naal*

near (to ...) (... க்கு) *(... ku)*
அருகே *a·ru·key*

on the ஓரத்தில *aw·rat·til*
corner

straight நேரடியாக *ney·ra·di·yaa·ha*
ahead முன்புறம் *mun·pu·ram*

Turn ... ... புறத்தில் *pu·rat·til*
திரும்புக. *ti·rum·pu·ka*

left இடது *i·ta·tu*
right வலது *va·la·tu*

Eating & Drinking

Can you நீங்கள் ஒரு ... *neeng·kal o·ru ...*
recommend பரிந்துரைக்க *pa·rin·tu·raik·ka*
a ...? முடியுமா? *mu·ti·yu·maa*

bar பார் *paar*
dish உணவு வகை *u·na·vu va·kai*
place to eat உணவகம் *u·na·va·ham*

I'd like எனக்கு தயவு *e·nak·ku ta·ya·vu*
(a/the) ..., செய்து ... *chey·tu ...*
please. கொடுங்கள். *ko·tung·kal*

bill வீலைச்சீட்டு *vi·laich·cheet·tu*
menu உணவுப்– *u·na·vup·*
பட்டியல் *pat·ti·yal*
that dish அந்த உணவு *an·ta u·na·vu*
வகை *va·hai*

(cup of) (கப்) காப்பி/ *(kap) kaap·pi/*
coffee/tea ... தேனீர் ... *tey·neer ...*

with milk பாலுடன் *paa·lu·tan*
without சர்க்கரை– *chark·ka·rai·*
sugar இல்லாமல *il·laa·mal*

a bottle/ ஒரு பாட்டில்/ *o·ru paat·til/*
glass of கிளாஸ ... *ki·laas ...*
... wine வைன் *vain*

red சீவப்பு *chi·vap·pu*
white வெள்ளை *vel·lai*

Do you have vegetarian food?
உங்களிடம சைவ *ung·ka·li·tam chai·va*
உணவு உள்ளதா? *u·na·vu ul·la·taa*

I'm allergic to (nuts).
எனக்கு (பருப்பு *e·nak·ku (pa·rup·pu*
வகை) உணவு *va·kai) u·na·vu*
சேராது. *chey·raa·tu*

beer பீர் *peer*
breakfast காலை உணவு *kaa·lai u·na·vu*
dinner இரவு உணவு *i·ra·vu u·na·vu*
drink பானம் *paa·nam*
fish மீன் *meen*
food உணவு *u·na·vu*
fruit பழம் *pa·zam*
juice சாறு *chaa·ru*
lunch மதிய உணவு *ma·ti·ya u·na·vu*
meat இறைச்சி *i·raich·chi*

milk	பால்	paal
soft drink	குளிர் பானம்	ku·lir paa·nam
vegetable	காய்கறி	kai·ka·ri
water	தண்ணீர்	tan·neyr

Emergencies

Help! உதவ! u·ta·vi

Go away! போய் வீடு! pow·i vi·tu

Call a doctor!
ஐ அழைக்கவும் i a·zai·ka·vum
ஒரு மருத்துவர்! o·ru ma·rut·tu·var

Call the police!
ஐ அழைக்கவும் i a·zai·ka·vum
போலீஸ்! pow·lees

I'm lost.
நான் வழி தவறி naan va·zi ta·va·ri
போய்விட்டேன். pow·i·vit·teyn

I have to use the phone.
நான் தொலைபேசியை naan to·lai·pey·chi·yai
பயன்படுத்த வேண்டும். pa·yan·pa·tut·ta veyn·tum

Where are the toilets?
கழிவறைகள் எங்கே? ka·zi·va·rai·kal eng·key

Shopping & Services

Where's the market?
எங்கே சந்தை eng·key chan·tai
இருக்கிறது? i·ruk·ki·ra·tu

Can I look at it?
நான் இதைப் naan i·taip
பார்க்கலாமா? paark·ka·laa·maa

How much is it?
இது என்ன வலை? i·tu en·na vi·lai

That's too expensive.
அது அதிக வலையாக a·tu a·ti·ka vi·lai·yaa·ka
இருக்கிறது. i·ruk·ki·ra·tu

There's a mistake in the bill.
இந்த விலைச்சீட்டில் in·ta vi·laich·cheet·til
ஒரு தவறு இருக்கிறது. o·ru ta·va·ru i·ruk·ki·ra·tu

bank	வங்கி	vang·ki
internet	இணையம்	i·nai·yam
post office	தபால்	ta·paal
	நிலையம்	ni·lai·yam
tourist office	சுற்றுப்பயண	chut·rup·pa·ya·na
	அலுவலகம்	a·lu·va·la·kam

Numbers

1	ஒன்று	on·dru
2	இரண்டு	i·ran·tu
3	மூன்று	moon·dru
4	நான்கு	naan·ku
5	ஐந்து	ain·tu
6	ஆறு	aa·ru
7	ஏழு	ey·zu
8	எட்டு	et·tu
9	ஒன்பது	on·pa·tu
10	பத்து	pat·tu
20	இருபது	i·ru·pa·tu
30	முப்பது	mup·pa·tu
40	நாற்பது	naar·pa·tu
50	ஐம்பது	aim·pa·tu
60	அறுபது	a·ru·pa·tu
70	எழுபது	e·zu·pa·tu
80	எண்பது	en·pa·tu
90	தொன்னூறு	ton·noo·ru
100	நூறு	noo·ru
1000	ஓராயிரம்	aw·raa·yi·ram

Time & Dates

What time is it?
மணி என்ன? ma·ni en·na

It's (two) o'clock.
மணி (இரண்டு). ma·ni (i·ran·tu)

Half past (two).
(இரண்டு) முப்பது. (i·ran·tu) mup·pa·tu

morning	காலை	kaa·lai
evening	மாலை	maa·lai
yesterday	நேற்று	neyt·tru
today	இன்று	in·dru
tomorrow	நாளை	naa·lai
Monday	திங்கள்	ting·kal
Tuesday	செவ்வாய்	chev·vai
Wednesday	புதன்	pu·tan
Thursday	வியாழன்	vi·yaa·zan
Friday	வெள்ளி	vel·li
Saturday	சனி	cha·ni
Sunday	ஞாயிறு	nyaa·yi·ru

Transport

Is this the ... to (New Delhi)?
இது தானா i·tu taa·naa
(புது– (pu·tu
டில்லிக்குப்) til·lik·kup)
புறப்படும் ...? pu·rap·pa·tum ...

bus	பஸ்	pas
plane	விமானம்	vi·maa·nam
train	இரயில்	i·ra·yil

One ... ticket (to Madurai), please.	(மதுரைக்கு) தயவு செய்து ... டிக்கட் கொடுங்கள்.	(ma·tu·raik·ku) ta·ya·vu chey·tu ... tik·kat ko·tung·kal
one-way	ஒரு வழிப்பயண	o·ru va·zip·pa·ya·na
return	இரு வழிப்பயண	i·ru va·zip·pa·ya·na

What time's the first/last bus?
எத்தனை மணிக்கு முதல்/இறுதி பஸ் வரும்? — et·ta·nai ma·nik·ku mu·tal/i·ru·ti pas va·rum

How long does the trip take?
பயணம் எவ்வளவு நேரம் எடுக்கும்? — pa·ya·nam ev·va·la·vu ney·ram e·tuk·kum

How long will it be delayed?
எவ்வளவு நேரம் அது தாமதப்படும்? — ev·va·la·vu ney·ram a·tu taa·ma·tap·pa·tum

Please tell me when we get to (Ooty).
(ஊட்டிக்குப்) போனவுடன் தயவு செய்து எனக்குக கூறுங்கள். — (oot·tik·kup) paw·na·vu·tan ta·ya·vu chey·tu e·nak·kuk koo·rung·kal

Please take me to (this address).
தயவு செய்து என்னை இந்த (விலாசத்துக்குக) கொண்டு செல்லுங்கள். — ta·ya·vu chey·tu en·nai in·ta (vi·laa·chat·tuk·kuk) kon·tu chel·lung·kal

Please stop/wait here.
தயவு செய்து இங்கே நிறுத்துங்கள்/ காத்திருங்கள். — ta·ya·vu chey·tu ing·key ni·rut·tung·kal/ kaat·ti·rung·kal

I'd like to hire a car (with a driver).
நான் ஒரு மோட்டார் வண்டி. (ஓர் ஓட்டுநருடன்) வாடகைக்கு எடுக்க விரும்புகிறேன். — naan o·ru mowt·taar van·ti (awr aw·tu·na·ru·tan) vaa·ta·haik·ku e·tuk·ka vi·rum·pu·ki·reyn

Is this the road to (Mamallapuram)?
இது தான் (மாமல்லபுரத்துக்கு) செல்லும் சாலையா? — i·tu taan (maa·mal·la·pu·rat·tuk·ku) chel·lum chaa·lai·yaa

airport	விமான நிலையம்	vi·maa·na ni·lai·yam
bicycle	சைக்கிள்	chaik·kil
boat	படகு	pa·ta·ku
bus stop	பஸ் நிறுத்தம்	pas ni·rut·tum
economy class	சிக்கன வகுப்பு	chik·ka·na va·kup·pu
first class	முதல் வகுப்பு	mu·tal va·kup·pu
motorcycle	மோட்டார் சைக்கிள்	mowt·taar chaik·kil
train station	நிலையம்	ni·lai·yam

KANNADA

Kannada is the official language of the state of Karnataka. It has 38 million speakers.

The symbol oh is pronounced as the 'o' in 'note' and ow as in 'how'.

Basics

Hello.	ನಮಸ್ಕಾರ.	na·mas·kaa·ra
Goodbye.	ಹಿಗೋಣ.	si·goh·na
Yes./No.	ಹೌದು./ಇಲ್ಲ.	how·du/il·la
Please.	ದಯವಿಟ್ಟು.	da·ya·vit·tu
Thank you.	ಥ್ಯಾಂಕ್ಯೂ.	t'ank·yoo
Excuse me.	ಸ್ವಲ್ಪ ದಾರಿ ಬಿಡಿ.	sval·pa daa·ri bi·di
Sorry.	ಕ್ಷಮಿಸಿ.	ksha·mi·si

What's your name?
ನಿಮ್ಮ ಹೆಸರೇನು? — nim·ma he·sa·rey·nu

My name is ...
ನನ್ನ ಹೆಸರು ... — nan·na he·sa·ru ...

Do you speak English?
ನೀವು ಇಂಗ್ಲೀಷ್ ಮಾತಾಡುತ್ತೀರಾ? — nee·vu ing·lee·shu maa·taa·dut·tee·ra

I don't understand.
ನನಗೆ ಅರ್ಥವಾಗುವುದಿಲ್ಲ. — na·na·ge ar·t'a·aa·gu·vu·dil·la

How much is it?
ಎಷ್ಟು ಇದು? — esh·tu i·du

Where are the toilets?
ಟಾಯ್ಲೆಟ್ಟುಗಳು ಎಲ್ಲಿ? — taay·let·tu·ga·lu el·li

Emergencies

Help!	ಸಹಾಯ ಮಾಡಿ!	sa·haa·ya maa·di
Go away!	ದೂರ ಹೋಗಿ!	doo·ra hoh·gi
Call ...!	... ಕಾಲ್ ಮಾಡಿ!	... kaal maa·di
a doctor	ಡಾಕ್ಟರಿಗೆ	daak·ta·ri·ge
the police	ಪೋಲೀಸಿಗೆ	poh·lee·si·ge

I have to use the phone.
ನಾನು ಫೋನು ಬಳಸಬೇಕು. — naa·nu foh·nu ba·la·sa·bey·ku

I'm lost.
ನಾನು ಕಳೆದುಹೋಗಿರುವೆ. — naa·nu ka·le·du·hoh·gi·ru·ve

Numbers

1	ಒಂದು	on·du
2	ಎರಡು	e·ra·du
3	ಮೂರು	moo·ru
4	ನಾಲ್ಕು	naa·ku
5	ಐದು	ai·du
6	ಆರು	aa·ru

7	ಏಳು	ey·lu
8	ಎಂಟು	en·tu
9	ಒಂಬತ್ತು	om·bat·tu
10	ಹತ್ತು	hat·tu
20	ಇಪ್ಪತ್ತು	ip·pat·tu
30	ಮೂವತ್ತು	moo·vat·tu
40	ನಲವತ್ತು	na·la·vat·tu
50	ಐವತ್ತು	ai·vat·tu
60	ಆರವತ್ತು	a·ra·vat·tu
70	ಎಪ್ಪತ್ತು	ep·pat·tu
80	ಎಂಬತ್ತು	em·bat·tu
90	ತೊಂಬತ್ತು	tom·bat·tu
100	ನೂರು	noo·ru
1000	ಸಾವಿರ	saa·vi·ra

KONKANI

Konkani is the official language of the state of Goa. It has 2.5 million speakers. The Devanagari script (also used to write Hindi and Marathi) is the official writing system for Konkani in Goa. However, many Konkani speakers in Karnataka use the Kannada script, as given in this section.

Pronounce eu as the 'u' in 'nurse', oh as the 'o' in 'note' and ts as in 'hats'.

Basics

Hello.	ಹಲ್ಲೋ.	hal·lo
Goodbye.	ಮೆಳ್ಯಾಂ.	mel·yaang
Yes./No.	ವ್ಯೆಯ್./ನಾಂ.	weu·i/naang
Please.	ಉಪ್ಕಾರ್ ಕರ್ನ್.	up·kaar keurn
Thank you.	ದೇವ್ ಬರೆಂ ಕರುಂ.	day·u bo·reng ko·roong
Excuse me.	ಉಪ್ಕಾರ್ ಕರ್ನ್.	up·kaar keurn
Sorry.	ಚೂಕ್ ಜಾಲಿ, ಮಾಫ್ ಕರ್.	ts'ook zaa·li, maaf keur

What's your name?
ತುಜೆಂ ನಾಂವ್ ಕಿತೆಂ? — tu·jeng naang·ung ki·teng

My name is ...
ಮ್ಹೆಜೆಂ ನಾಂವ್ ... — m'eu·jeng naang·ung ...

Do you speak English?
ಇಂಗ್ಲಿಶ್ ಉಲೆಯ್ತಾಯ್ಗೀ? — ing·leesh u·leuy·taay·gee

Do you understand?
ಸಮ್ಜಾಲೆಂಗೀ? — som·zaa·leng·gee

I understand.
ಸಮ್ಜಾಲೆಂ. — som·zaa·leng

I don't understand.
ನಾಂ, ಸಮ್ಜೊಂಕ್–ನಾಂ. — naang som·zonk·naang

How much is it?
ತಾಕಾ ಕಿತ್ಲೆ ಪೈಶೆ? — taa·kaa kit·le peuy·she

Where are the toilets?
ಟೊಯ್ಲೆಟ್ ಕ್ಯೆಂಚರ್ ಆಸಾತ್? — toy·let k'eu·ing·ts'eur aa·saat

Emergencies

Help!	ಮ್ಹಾಕಾ ಕುಮಕ್ ಕರ್!	m'aa·kaa ku·meuk keur
Go away!	ವಚ್!	weuts'
Call ...!	... ಆಪೈ!	... aa·pai
a doctor	ದಾಕ್ತೆರಾಕ್	daak·te·raak
the police	ಪೊಲಿಸಾಂಕ್	po·li·saank

I have to use the phone.
ಮ್ಹಾಕಾ ಫೋನಾಚಿ ಗರ್ಜ್ ಆಸಾ. — m'aa·kaa fo·na·chi g'eurz aa·saa

I'm lost.
ಮ್ಹೆಜೀ ವಾಟ್ ಚುಕ್ಲ್ಯಾ. — m'eu·ji waat ts'uk·lyaa

Could you help me, please?
ಮ್ಹಾಕಾ ಇಲ್ಲೊಚೊ ಉಪ್ಕಾರ್ ಕರಿಶೀಗೀ? — m'aa·kaa il·lo·ts'o up·kaar keur·shi·gee

Numbers

1	ಏಕ್	ayk
2	ದೋನ್	dohn
3	ತೀನ್	teen
4	ಚಾರ್	chaar
5	ಪಾಂಚ್	paants'
6	ಸೊ	so
7	ಸಾತ್	saat
8	ಆಟ್	aat'
9	ನೋವ್	nohw
10	ಧಾ	d'aa
20	ವೀಸ್	wees
30	ತೀಸ್	tees
40	ಚಾಳೀಸ್	ts'aa·lees
50	ಪನ್ನಾಸ್	pon·naas
60	ಸಾಟ್	saat'
70	ಸತ್ತರ್	seut·teur
80	ಐಂಶಿಂ	euyng·shing
90	ನೊವೋದ್	no·wod
100	ಶೆಂಭರ್	shem·bor
1000	ಹಜ್ಜಾರ್	ha·zaar

MALAYALAM

Malayalam is the official language of the state of Kerala. It has around 33 million speakers.

Note that zh is pronounced as the 's' in 'measure'.

Basics

Hello.	ഹലോ.	ha·lo
Goodbye.	ഗുഡ് ബൈ.	good bai
Yes.	അതെ.	a·t'e
No.	അല്ല.	al·la
Please.	ദയവായി.	da·ya·va·yi
Thank you.	നന്ദി.	nan·n'i
Excuse me.	ക്ഷമിക്കണം.	ksha·mi·ka·nam
Sorry.	ക്ഷമിക്കുക.	ksha·mi·ku·ka

Do you speak English?
നിങ്ങൾ ഇംഗ്ലീഷ് സംസാരിക്കുമോ? — ning·al in·glish sam·saa·ri·ku·mo

I don't understand.
എനിക്ക് മനസ്സിലാകില്ല. — e·ni·ku ma·na·si·la·ki·la

What's your name?
താങ്കളുടെ പേര് എന്താണ്? — t'ang·a·lu·te pey·ru en·t'aa·nu

My name is ...
എന്റെ പേര് ... — en·te pey·ru ...

How much is it?
എത്രയാണ് ഇതിന്? — et'·ra·yaa·nu i·t'i·nu

Where are the toilets?
എവിടെയാണ് കക്കൂസ്? — e·vi·de·yaa·nu ka·koo·su

Emergencies

| Help! | സഹായിക്കൂ | sa·ha·yi·koo |
| Go away! | ഇവിടുന്ന് പോകൂ! | i·vi·du·nu po·koo |

Call ...!	... വിളിക്കൂ!	... vi·li·koo
a doctor	ഒരു ഡോക്ടറെ	o·ru dok·ta·re
the police	പൊലീസിനെ	po·li·si·ne

I have to use the phone.
എനിക്ക് ഈ ഫോൺ ഒന്നു വേണമായിരുന്നു. — e·ni·ku ee fon o·nu vey·na·maa·yi·ru·nu

I'm lost.
എനിക്ക് വഴി അറിഞ്ഞുകൂട. — e·ni·ku va·zhi a·ri·nyu·koo·da

Numbers

1	ഒന്ന്	on·na
2	രണ്ട്	ran·d'a
3	മൂന്ന്	moo·na
4	നാല്	naa·la
5	അഞ്ച്	an·ja
6	ആറ്	aa·ra
7	ഏഴ്	e·zha

8	എട്ട്	e·t'a
9	ഒമ്പത്	on·pa·t'a
10	പത്ത്	pa·t'a
20	ഇരുപത്	i·ru·pa·t'a
30	മുപ്പത്	mu·p'a·t'a
40	നാൽപത്	naal·pa·t'a
50	അമ്പത്	an·ba·t'a
60	അറുപത്	a·ru·pa·t'a
70	എഴുപത്	e·zhu·pa·t'a
80	എൺപത്	en·pa·t'a
90	തൊണ്ണൂറ്	t'on·noo·ra
100	നൂറ്	n'oo·ra
1000	ആയിരം	aa·ye·ram

MARATHI

Marathi is the official language of the state of Maharashtra. It is spoken by an estimated 71 million people. Marathi is written in the Devanagari script (also used for Hindi).

Keep in mind that oh is pronounced as the 'o' in 'note'.

Basics

Hello.	नमस्कार.	na·mas·kaar
Goodbye.	बाय.	bai
Yes.	होय.	hoy
No.	नाही.	naa·hee
Please.	कृपया.	kri·pa·yaa
Thank you.	धन्यवाद.	d'an·ya·vaad
Excuse me.	क्षमस्व.	ksha·mas·va
Sorry.	खेद आहे.	k'ed aa·he

What's your name?
आपले नाव ? — aa·pa·le naa·nav

My name is ...
माझे नाव ... — maa·j'e naa·nav ...

Do you speak English?
आपण इंग्रजी बोलता का ? — aa·pan ing·re·jee bol·taa kaa

I don't understand.
मला समजत नाही. — ma·laa sam·jat naa·hee

How much is it?
याची काय किंमत आहे ? — yaa·chee kaay ki·mat aa·he

Where are the toilets?
शौचालय कुठे आहे ? — shoh·chaa·lai ku·t'e aa·he

Emergencies

| Help! | मदत ! | ma·dat |
| Go away! | दूर जा! | door jaa |

Call ...!	कॉल करा ... !	kaal ka·*raa* ...
a doctor	डॉक्टरांना	dok·ta·raan·*naa*
the police	पोलिसांना	po·li·saa·*naa*

I have to use the phone.
मला फोन वापरायचा आहे. — ma·*laa* fon vaa·pa·raa·ya·*chaa* aa·*he*

I'm lost.
मी हरवले आहे — mee ha·ra·va·*le* aa·*he*

Numbers

1	एक	ek
2	दोन	don
3	तीन	teen
4	चार	chaar
5	पाच	paach
6	सहा	sa·*haa*
7	सात	saat
8	आठ	aat'
9	नऊ	na·*oo*
10	दहा	da·*haa*
20	वीस	vees
30	तीस	tees
40	चाळीस	chaa·*lees*
50	पन्नास	pan·*naas*
60	साठ	saat'
70	सत्तर	sat·*tar*
80	ऐंशी	ain·*shee*
90	नव्वद	nav·*vad*
100	शंभर	sham·*b'ar*
1000	एक हजार	ek ha·*jaar*

TELUGU

Telugu is the official language of the states of Telangana and Andhra Pradesh. It has 70 million speakers.

Remember to pronounce oh as the 'o' in 'note'.

Basics

Hello.	నమస్కారం.	na·mas·*kaa*·ram
Goodbye.	వెళ్ళొస్తాను.	vel·loh·*staa*·nu
Yes./No.	అవును./కాదు.	a·vu·nu/*kaa*·du
Please.	దయచేసి.	da·ya·*chay*·si
Thank you.	ధన్యవాదాలు.	d'an·ya·vaa·*daa*·lu
Excuse me.	ఏమండి.	*ay*·an·di
Sorry.	క్షమించండి.	ksha·min·*chan*·di

What's your name?
మీ పేరేంటి? — mee pay·*rayn*·ti

My name is ...
నా పేరు ... — naa pay·ru ...

Do you speak English?
మీరు ఇంగ్లీషు మాట్లాడుతారా? — mee·ru ing·*lee*·shu maat·laa·du·*taa*·raa

I don't understand.
అర్థం కాదు. — ar·t'am *kaa*·du

How much is it?
అది ఎంత? — a·di *en*·ta

Where are the toilets?
బాత్రూములు ఎక్కడ ఉన్నాయి? — baat·room·lu ek·ka·da un·*naa*·yi

Emergencies

| Help! | సహాయం కావాలి! | sa·*haa*·yam kaa·vaa·li |
| Go away! | వెళ్ళిపో! | vel·li·poh |

Call ...!	... పిలవండి!	... pi·la·van·di
a doctor	డాక్టర్ని	daak·*tar*·ni
the police	పోలీసుల్ని	poh·lee·sul·ni

I have to use the phone.
నేను ఫోను వాడుకోవాలి. — nay·nu p'oh·nu vaa·du·koh·vaa·li

I'm lost.
నేను దారి తప్పి పోయాను. — nay·nu daa·ri tap·pi poh·*yaa*·nu

Numbers

1	ఒకటి	oh·ka·ti
2	రెండు	ren·du
3	మూడు	moo·du
4	నాలుగు	naa·lu·gu
5	ఐదు	ai·du
6	ఆరు	aa·ru
7	ఏడు	ay·du
8	ఎనిమిది	e·ni·mi·di
9	తొమ్మిది	tohm·mi·di
10	పది	pa·di
20	ఇరవై	i·ra·vai
30	ముప్పై	mup·p'ai
40	నలభై	na·la·b'ai
50	యాభై	yaa·b'ai
60	అరవై	a·ra·vai
70	డెబ్బై	deb·b'ai
80	ఎనభై	e·na·b'ai
90	తొంభై	tohm·b'ai
100	వంద	van·da
1000	వెయ్యి	vey·yi

GLOSSARY

Adivasi – tribal person

Agni – major deity in the *Vedas*; mediator between men and the gods; also fire

ahimsa – discipline of non-violence

air-cooler – noisy water-filled cooling fan

Ananta – serpent on whose coils *Vishnu* reclined

apsara – heavenly nymph

Arjuna – Mahabharata hero and military commander who married Subhadra

Aryan – Sanskrit for 'noble'; those who migrated from Persia and settled in northern India

Ashoka – ruler in the 3rd century BC; responsible for spreading Buddhism throughout South India

ashram – spiritual community or retreat

autorickshaw – noisy, three-wheeled, motorised contraption for transporting passengers, livestock etc for short distances; found throughout the country, they are cheaper than taxis

avatar – incarnation, usually of a deity

ayurveda – ancient and complex science of Indian herbal medicine and healing

azad – free (Urdu), as in Azad Jammu & Kashmir

baba – religious master or father; term of respect

bagh – garden

baksheesh – tip, donation (alms) or bribe

banyan – Indian fig tree; spiritual to many Indians

Bhagavad Gita – Hindu Song of the Divine One; *Krishna*'s lessons to *Arjuna*, the main thrust of which was to emphasise the philosophy of *bhakti*; it's part of the *Mahabharata*

bhajan – devotional song

bhakti – surrendering to the gods; faith

bhang – dried leaves and flowering shoots of the marijuana plant

bhavan – house, building; also spelt *bhawan*

BJP – Bharatiya Janata Party; political party

bodhisattva – literally 'one whose essence is perfected wisdom'; in Early Buddhism, bodhisattva refers only to *Buddha* during the period between his conceiving the intention to strive for Buddhahood and the moment he attained it; in *Mahayana* Buddhism, it is one who renounces nirvana in order to help others attain it

Bollywood – India's answer to Hollywood; the film industry of Mumbai (Bombay)

Brahma – Hindu god; worshipped as the creator in the *Trimurti*

Brahmin – member of the priest/scholar caste, the highest Hindu *caste*

Buddha – Awakened One; the originator of Buddhism; also regarded by Hindus as the ninth incarnation of *Vishnu*

cantonment – administrative and military area of a Raj-era town

Carnatic music – classical music of South India

caste – a Hindu's hereditary station (social standing) in life; there are four castes: the *Brahmins*, the *Kshatriyas*, the *Vaishyas* and the *Shudras*; the Brahmins occupy the top spot

chaitya – Sanskrit form of 'cetiya', meaning shrine or object of worship; has come to mean temple, and more specifically, a hall divided into a central nave and two side aisles by a line of columns, with a votive *stupa* at the end

chappals – sandals or leather thonglike footwear; flip-flops

charas – resin of the marijuana plant; also referred to as 'hashish'

chital – spotted deer

choli – sari blouse

chowk – town square, intersection or marketplace

dagoba – see *stupa*

Dalit – preferred term for India's *Untouchable* caste

dargah – shrine or place of burial of a Muslim saint

darshan – offering or audience with someone; auspicious viewing of a deity

Deccan – meaning 'South', this refers to the central South Indian plateau

Devi – *Shiva*'s wife; goddess

dhaba – basic restaurant or snack bar; especially popular with truck drivers

dharamsala – pilgrims' rest house

dharma – for Hindus, the moral code of behaviour or social duty; for Buddhists, following the law of nature, or path, as taught by *Buddha*

dhobi – person who washes clothes; commonly referred to as *dhobi-wallah*

dhobi ghat – place where clothes are washed by the *dhobi*

dhoti – like a *lungi*, but the ankle-length cloth is then pulled up between the legs; worn by men

dhurrie – rug

dowry – money and/or goods given by a bride's parents to their son-in-law's family; it's illegal but still exists in many arranged marriages

Dravidian – general term for the cultures and languages of the deep south of India, including Tamil, Malayalam, Telugu and Kannada

dupatta – long scarf for women often worn with the *salwar kameez*

durbar – royal court; also a government

Durga – the Inaccessible; a form of *Shiva*'s wife, *Devi*, a beautiful, fierce goddess riding a tiger/lion

filmi – slang term describing anything to do with Indian movies

Ganesh – Hindu god of good fortune and remover of obstacles; popular elephant-headed son of *Shiva* and *Parvati*, he is also known as Ganpati; his vehicle is a ratlike creature

Ganga – Hindu goddess representing the sacred Ganges River; said to flow from *Vishnu*'s toe

Garuda – man-bird vehicle of *Vishnu*

gaur – Indian bison

ghat – steps or landing on a river, range of hills, or road up hills

giri – hill

gopuram – soaring pyramidal gateway tower of *Dravidian* temples

gurdwara – Sikh temple

guru – holy teacher; in Sanskrit literally *goe* (darkness) and *roe* (to dispel)

Hanuman – Hindu monkey god, prominent in the *Ramayana*, and a follower of *Rama*

Indo-Saracenic – style of colonial architecture that integrated Western designs with Islamic, Hindu and Jain influences

Indra – significant and prestigious Vedic god; god of rain, thunder, lightning and war

Jagannath – Lord of the Universe; a form of *Krishna*

ji – honorific that can be added to the end of almost anything as a form of respect; thus 'Babaji', 'Gandhiji'

Kailasa – sacred Himalayan mountain; home of *Shiva*

kalamkari – designs painted on cloth using vegetable dyes

Kali – the ominous-looking evil-destroying form of *Devi*; commonly depicted with dark skin, dripping with blood, and wearing a necklace of skulls

kameez – woman's shirtlike tunic

Kannada – state language of Karnataka

karma – Hindu, Buddhist and Sikh principle of retributive justice for past deeds

khadi – homespun cloth; Mahatma Gandhi encouraged people to spin this rather than buy English cloth

Khan – Muslim honorific title

kolam – elaborate chalk, rice-paste or coloured powder design; also known as *rangoli*

Konkani – state language of Goa

Krishna – *Vishnu*'s eighth incarnation, often coloured blue; he revealed the *Bhagavad Gita* to *Arjuna*

Kshatriya – Hindu *caste* of soldiers or administrators; second in the caste hierarchy

kurta – long shirt with either short collar or no collar

lakh – 100,000

Lakshmana – half-brother and aide of *Rama* in the *Ramayana*

Lakshmi – *Vishnu*'s consort, Hindu goddess of wealth; she sprang forth from the ocean holding a lotus

lama – Tibetan Buddhist priest or monk

lingam – phallic symbol; auspicious symbol of *Shiva*; plural 'linga'

lungi – worn by men, this loose, coloured garment (similar to a sarong) is pleated at the waist to fit the wearer

maha – prefix meaning 'great'

Mahabharata – Great Hindu Vedic epic poem of the Bharata dynasty; containing approximately 10,000 verses describing the battle between the Pandavas and the Kauravas

mahal – house or palace

maharaja – literally 'great king'; princely ruler

mahatma – literally 'great soul'

Mahavir – greater-vehicle of Buddhism

Mahayana – last *tirthankar*

mahout – elephant rider or master

maidan – open (often grassed) area; parade ground

Malayalam – state language of Kerala

mandapa – pillared pavilion; a temple forechamber

mandir – temple

Maratha – central Indian people who controlled much of India at various times and fought the *Mughals* and *Rajputs*

marg – road

masjid – mosque

mehndi – henna; ornate henna designs on women's hands (and often feet), traditionally for certain festivals or ceremonies (eg marriage)

mela – fair or festival

moksha – liberation from samsara

mudra – ritual hand movements used in Hindu religious dancing; gesture of *Buddha* figure

Mughal – Muslim dynasty of subcontinental emperors from Babur to Aurangzeb

Naga – mythical serpentlike beings capable of changing into human form

namaste – traditional Hindu greeting (hello or goodbye), often accompanied by a respectful small bow with the hands together at the chest or head level

Nandi – bull, vehicle of *Shiva*

Narasimha – man-lion incarnation of *Vishnu*

Narayan – incarnation of *Vishnu* the creator

Nataraja – *Shiva* as the cosmic dancer

nizam – hereditary title of the rulers of Hyderabad

NRI – Non-Resident Indian

Om – sacred invocation representing the essence of the divine principle; for Buddhists, if repeated often enough with complete concentration, it leads to a state of emptiness

Parsi – adherent of the Zoro-astrian faith

Partition – formal division of British India in 1947 into two separate countries, India and Pakistan

Parvati – a form of *Devi*

PCO – Public Call Office from where to make local, interstate and international phone calls

Pongal – Tamil harvest festival

pradesh – state

prasad – temple-blessed food offering

puja – literally 'respect'; offering or prayers

Puranas – set of 18 encyclopaedic Sanskrit stories, written in verse, relating to the three gods, dating from the 5th century AD

Radha – favourite mistress of *Krishna* when he lived as a cowherd

raga – any of several conventional patterns of melody and rhythm that form the basis for freely interpreted compositions

raj – rule or sovereignty; British Raj (sometimes just Raj) refers to British rule

raja – king; sometimes *rana*

Rajput – Hindu warrior caste, former rulers of northwestern India

Rama – seventh incarnation of *Vishnu*

Ramadan – the Islamic holy month of sunrise-to-sunset fasting (no eating, drinking or smoking); also referred to as Ramazan

Ramayana – the story of *Rama* and *Sita* and their conflict with *Ravana* is one of India's best-known epics

rana – king; sometimes *raja*

rangoli – see *kolam*

rani – female ruler or wife of a king

rathas – rock-cut *Dravidian* temples

Ravana – demon king of Lanka (modern-day Sri Lanka)

rickshaw – small, two- or three-wheeled passenger vehicle

sadhu – ascetic, holy person; one who is trying to achieve enlightenment; often addressed as *swamiji* or *babaji*

sagar – lake, reservoir

sahib – respectful title applied to a gentleman

salwar – trousers usually worn with a *kameez*

salwar kameez – traditional dresslike tunic and trouser combination for women

sambar – deer

Saraswati – wife of *Brahma*; goddess of learning; sits on a white swan

Sati – wife of *Shiva;* became a *sati* ('honourable woman') by immolating herself; although banned more than a century ago, the act of *sati* is still (very) occasionally performed

satyagraha – nonviolent protest involving a hunger strike, popularised by Mahatma Gandhi; from Sanskrit, literally meaning 'insistence on truth'

Scheduled Castes – official term used for the *Untouchables* or *Dalits*

shahadah – Muslim declaration of faith ('There is no God but Allah; Mohammed is his prophet')

Shaivite – follower of *Shiva*

Shakti – creative energies perceived as female deities; devotees follow Shaktism

Shiv Sena – Hindu nationalist political party

Shiva – the Destroyer; also the Creator, in which form he is worshipped as a *lingam*

Shivaji – great Maratha leader of the 17th century

shola – virgin forest

Shudra – *caste* of labourers

sikhara – Hindu temple-spire or temple

Sita – the Hindu goddess of agriculture; more commonly associated with the *Ramayana*

sitar – Indian stringed instrument

Sivaganga – water tank in temple dedicated to *Shiva*

stupa – Buddhist religious monument composed of a solid hemisphere topped by a spire, containing relics of *Buddha*; also known as a *dagoba* or pagoda

Sufi – Muslim mystic

Surya – the sun; a major deity in the *Vedas*

swami – title of respect meaning 'lord of the self'; given to initiated Hindu monks

tabla – twin drums

Tamil – language of Tamil Nadu; people of *Dravidian* origin

tandava – *Shiva*'s cosmic victory dance

tank – reservoir; pool or large receptacle of holy water found at some temples

tempo – noisy three-wheeler public-transport vehicle; bigger than an *autorickshaw*

Theravada – orthodox form of Buddhism practised in Sri Lanka and Southeast Asia that is char-

acterised by its adherence to the Pali canon; literally 'dwelling'

tilak – auspicious forehead mark of devout Hindu men

tirthankars – the 24 great Jain teachers

Trimurti – triple form; the Hindu triad of *Brahma, Shiva* and *Vishnu*

Untouchable – lowest *caste* or 'casteless', for whom the most menial tasks are reserved; the name derives from the belief that higher castes risk defilement if they touch one; now known as *Dalit*

Vaishya – member of the Hindu caste of merchants

Vedas – Hindu sacred books; collection of hymns composed in preclassical Sanskrit during the second millennium BC and divided into four books: Rig-Veda, Yajur-Veda, Sama-Veda and Atharva-Veda

vihara – Buddhist monastery, generally with central court or hall off which open residential cells, usually with a *Buddha* shrine at one end

vikram – *tempo* or a larger version of the standard *tempo*

vimana – principal part of Hindu temple; a tower over the sanctum

vipassana – insight meditation technique of *Theravada* Buddhism in which mind and body are closely examined as changing phenomena

Vishnu – part of the *Trimurti*; Vishnu is the Preserver and Restorer who so far has nine *avatars*: the fish Matsya, the tortoise Kurma, the wild boar Naraha, *Narasimha*, Vamana, Parasurama, *Rama, Krishna* and *Buddha*

wallah – man; added onto almost anything, eg *dhobi*-wallah, chai-wallah, taxi-wallah

yali – mythical lion creature

yatra – pilgrimage

zenana – area of a home where women are secluded; women's quarters

Behind the Scenes

SEND US YOUR FEEDBACK

We love to hear from travellers – your comments keep us on our toes and help make our books better. Our well-travelled team reads every word on what you loved or loathed about this book. Although we cannot reply individually to your submissions, we always guarantee that your feedback goes straight to the appropriate authors, in time for the next edition. Each person who sends us information is thanked in the next edition – the most useful submissions are rewarded with a selection of digital PDF chapters.

Visit **lonelyplanet.com/contact** to submit your updates and suggestions or to ask for help. Our award-winning website also features inspirational travel stories, news and discussions.

Note: We may edit, reproduce and incorporate your comments in Lonely Planet products such as guidebooks, websites and digital products, so let us know if you don't want your comments reproduced or your name acknowledged. For a copy of our privacy policy visit lonelyplanet.com/privacy.

OUR READERS

Many thanks to the travellers who used the last edition and wrote to us with helpful hints, useful advice and interesting anecdotes:

Daniel Morris, Della Matheson, Jacob Joseph, Julia Butterworth, Lauren McAlee, Linda Mlynski, Malcolm Beck, Michael Fairbairn, Patricia Keith, Paul Thompson, Rafael Zamora Riesco, Ramavtar Garhwal, Stine Porsbjerg, Uwe Düffert, Will Pitcher.

WRITER THANKS

Isabella Noble

Thanks to everyone in Tamil Nadu, Ashish and Rucha Gupta and Shoshana Treichel in Chennai, Bernard Dragon and Michel Adment in Chettinadu, Raja Balasubramanian in Trichy, Junaid Sait and team in Ooty, Vijay Kumar in Kodai, and Mr Krishnamurthi on the Kanyakumari–Puducherry Express. In Madhya Pradesh, huge thanks to Belinda Wright and Saptarishi Saigal. Thanks to the dream India co-author team, especially John Noble for laughs, tips and tiger safaris. At home, extra-special thanks to Jack, Andrew and Sarah.

Kevin Raub

Thanks to my wife, Adriana Schmidt Raub, Joe Bindloss, Sarina Singh, John Noble, Izzy Noble, Paul Harding and all my partners-in-crime at Lonely Planet. On the road, Anil Wadwa, Amit Arora, Dhanya Pilo, Sarita Hedge Roy, Tanvi Maidkaker, Roshnee Desai,

Greg Kroitzsh, Rishupreet Oberoi, Bindu Panicker, Aditya Dhanwatay, Ashok T Kadam, Abha Lambah, Karina Aggarwal and Pankil Shah.

Paul Harding

Thanks to all my dear friends in Goa and Kerala who helped out with company, advice and friendship – you all know who you are. Thanks also to new people, travellers and locals, I met on this trip. The biggest thanks goes to Hannah and my worldly young daughter Layla for accompanying me at least part of the way and putting up with my absences at other times.

Sarina Singh

Thank you to everyone who worked on this edition, with special thanks to Joe for being such a fab destination editor. Gratitude, also, to the many readers who took the time to send in their feedback and travel experiences – much appreciated indeed. Finally, warm thanks to my wise and wonderful parents who have always encouraged me to walk my own path.

Iain Stewart

Thanks to Trent Holden and John Noble for tips and contacts, and Joe Bindloss and the Lonely Planet team in London and Melbourne. On the road I was helped by Jonty in Hyderabad, Poornima Dasharathi in Bengaluru, the teams at Golden Mist in Kodagu and Uramma in Hampi, Prakash in Vijapura, Oliver the yogi in Gokarna and Vijay in Vizag.

ACKNOWLEDGMENTS

Climate map data adapted from Peel MC, Finlayson BL & McMahon TA (2007) 'Updated World Map of the Köppen-Geiger Climate Classification', Hydrology and Earth System Sciences, 11, 1633–44.

Illustration pp186–187 by Michael Weldon.

Cover photograph: Fishing harbour near Kovalam, Kerala; Tuul & Bruno Morandi / SIME / 4Corners

THIS BOOK

This 9th edition of Lonely Planet's *South India & Kerala* guidebook was curated by Isabella Noble and researched and written by Isabella Noble, Kevin Raub, Paul Harding, Sarina Singh and Iain Stewart. The previous edition was written by John Noble, Abigail Blasi, Paul Harding, Trent Holden, Isabella Noble and Iain Stewart. This guidebook was produced by the following:

Destination Editor
Joe Bindloss

Product Editors Rachel Rawling, Catherine Naghten

Cartographers
Lonely Planet Cartography

Book Designer
Katherine Marsh

Assisting Editors Imogen Bannister, Bruce Evans, Victoria Harrison, Charlotte Orr, Gabrielle Stefanos

Cover Researcher
Naomi Parker

Thanks to Daniel Fahey, Gemma Graham, Indra Kilfoyle, Kate Mathews, Claire Naylor, Karyn Noble, Martine Power, Kathryn Rowan, Tom Stainer

Index

Map Legend

Sights
- 🏖 Beach
- 🐦 Bird Sanctuary
- 🔱 Buddhist
- 🏰 Castle/Palace
- ✝ Christian
- ☯ Confucian
- 🕉 Hindu
- ☪ Islamic
- Jain
- ✡ Jewish
- ❗ Monument
- 🏛 Museum/Gallery/Historic Building
- ⊗ Ruin
- ⛩ Shinto
- Sikh
- Taoist
- 🍷 Winery/Vineyard
- Zoo/Wildlife Sanctuary
- ⊙ Other Sight

Activities, Courses & Tours
- Bodysurfing
- Diving
- Canoeing/Kayaking
- Course/Tour
- Sento Hot Baths/Onsen
- Skiing
- Snorkelling
- Surfing
- Swimming/Pool
- Walking
- Windsurfing
- Other Activity

Sleeping
- Sleeping
- Camping

Eating
- Eating

Drinking & Nightlife
- Drinking & Nightlife
- Cafe

Entertainment
- Entertainment

Shopping
- Shopping

Information
- $ Bank
- Embassy/Consulate
- ✚ Hospital/Medical
- @ Internet
- Police
- ✉ Post Office
- Telephone
- Toilet
- ℹ Tourist Information
- • Other Information

Geographic
- Beach
- ⊷ Gate
- Hut/Shelter
- Lighthouse
- Lookout
- ▲ Mountain/Volcano
- Oasis
- Park
-)(Pass
- Picnic Area
- Waterfall

Population
- Capital (National)
- Capital (State/Province)
- City/Large Town
- Town/Village

Transport
- Airport
- Border crossing
- Bus
- Cable car/Funicular
- Cycling
- Ferry
- Ⓜ Metro station
- Monorail
- P Parking
- Petrol station
- S Subway station
- Taxi
- Train station/Railway
- Tram
- Underground station
- • Other Transport

Note: Not all symbols displayed above appear on the maps in this book

Routes
- Tollway
- Freeway
- Primary
- Secondary
- Tertiary
- Lane
- Unsealed road
- Road under construction
- Plaza/Mall
- Steps
- Tunnel
- Pedestrian overpass
- Walking Tour
- Walking Tour detour
- Path/Walking Trail

Boundaries
- International
- State/Province
- Disputed
- Regional/Suburb
- Marine Park
- Cliff
- Wall

Hydrography
- River, Creek
- Intermittent River
- Canal
- Water
- Dry/Salt/Intermittent Lake
- Reef

Areas
- Airport/Runway
- Beach/Desert
- Cemetery (Christian)
- Cemetery (Other)
- Glacier
- Mudflat
- Park/Forest
- Sight (Building)
- Sportsground
- Swamp/Mangrove

Iain Stewart
Karnataka & Bengaluru, Telangana & Andhra Pradesh Iain trained as a journalist and worked as a reporter and restaurant critic in London in the 1990s. He started writing guidebooks in 1997 and has penned more than 60 titles for destinations as diverse as Ibiza and Cambodia. For Lonely Planet, Iain's worked on books including *Mexico*, *Indonesia*, *Croatia*, *Vietnam*, *India*, *Sri Lanka* and *Central America*. Other passions include tennis, scuba and freediving. He'll consider working anywhere there's a palm tree or two and a beach of a generally sandy persuasion. Home is Brighton, UK, within firing range of the city's south-facing horizon. He tweets at @iaintravel.

OUR STORY

A beat-up old car, a few dollars in the pocket and a sense of adventure. In 1972 that's all Tony and Maureen Wheeler needed for the trip of a lifetime – across Europe and Asia overland to Australia. It took several months, and at the end – broke but inspired – they sat at their kitchen table writing and stapling together their first travel guide, *Across Asia on the Cheap*. Within a week they'd sold 1500 copies. Lonely Planet was born.

Today, Lonely Planet has offices in Franklin, London, Melbourne, Oakland, Dublin, Beijing and Delhi, with more than 600 staff and writers. We share Tony's belief that 'a great guidebook should do three things: inform, educate and amuse'.

OUR WRITERS

Isabella Noble

Tamil Nadu & Chennai English-Australian on paper but Spanish at heart, Isabella has been wandering the globe since her first round-the-world trip as a one-year-old. Having grown up in a whitewashed Andalucian village, she is a Spain specialist travel journalist, but also writes extensively about India, Thailand, the UK and beyond for Lonely Planet, the *Daily Telegraph* and others. Isabella has co-written Lonely Planet guides to Spain and Andalucía, and is a *Daily Telegraph* Spain expert. She has also contributed to Lonely Planet *India*, *South India*, *Thailand*, *Thailand's Islands & Beaches*, *Southeast Asia on a Shoestring* and *Great Britain*, and authored *Pocket Phuket*. Find Isabella on Twitter and Instagram (@isabellamnoble).

Kevin Raub

Mumbai (Bombay), Maharashtra Atlanta native Kevin Raub started his career as a music journalist in New York, working for *Men's Journal* and *Rolling Stone* magazines. He ditched the rock 'n' roll lifestyle for travel writing and has written more than 40 Lonely Planet guides, focused mainly on Brazil, Chile, Colombia, USA, India, the Caribbean and Portugal. Raub also contributes to a variety of travel magazines in both the USA and UK. Along the way, the self-confessed hophead is in constant search of wildly high IBUs in local beers. Follow him on Twitter and Instagram (@RaubOnTheRoad).

Paul Harding

Goa, Kerala As a writer and photographer, Paul has been travelling the globe for the best part of two decades, with an interest in remote and offbeat places and cultures. He's an author and contributor to more than 50 Lonely Planet guides to countries and regions as diverse as India, Iceland, Belize, Vanuatu, Iran, Indonesia, New Zealand, Finland and – his home patch – Australia.

Sarina Singh

Andaman Islands After finishing a business degree in her hometown of Melbourne, Sarina went to India to pursue a corporate traineeship before working as a journalist. After five years she returned to Australia and completed postgraduate journalism qualifications before authoring Lonely Planet's first edition of *Rajasthan*. Apart from numerous Lonely Planet books, she has written for a raft of other publications and has been a scriptwriter and expert commentator. Sarina is also the author of *Polo in India* as well as *India: Essential Encounters*. Her award-nominated documentary premiered at the prestigious Melbourne International Film Festival before screening internationally.

OVER MORE
PAGE WRITERS

Published by Lonely Planet Global Limited
CRN 554153
9th edition – October 2017
ISBN 978 1 78657 148 9
© Lonely Planet 2017 Photographs © as indicated 2017
10 9 8 7 6 5 4 3 2 1
Printed in Singapore

Although the authors and Lonely Planet have taken all reasonable care in preparing this book, we make no warranty about the accuracy or completeness of its content and, to the maximum extent permitted, disclaim all liability arising from its use.